D1432100

Historical Dictionaries of Asia, Oceania, and the Middle East
Edited by Jon Woronoff

Asia
1. *Vietnam*, by William J. Duiker. 1989. *Out of print. See No. 27.*
2. *Bangladesh*, 2nd ed., by Craig Baxter and Syedur Rahman. 1996. *Out of print. See No. 48.*
3. *Pakistan*, by Shahid Javed Burki. 1991. *Out of print. See No. 33.*
4. *Jordan*, by Peter Gubser. 1991.
5. *Afghanistan*, by Ludwig W. Adamec. 1991. *Out of print. See No. 47.*
6. *Laos*, by Martin Stuart-Fox and Mary Kooyman. 1992. *Out of print. See No. 35.*
7. *Singapore*, by K. Mulliner and Lian The-Mulliner. 1991.
8. *Israel*, by Bernard Reich. 1992
9. *Indonesia*, by Robert Cribb. 1992. *Out of print. See No. 51.*
10. *Hong Kong and Macau*, by Elfed Vaughan Roberts, Sum Ngai Ling, and Peter Bradshaw. 1992
11. *Korea*, by Andrew C. Nahm. 1993. *Out of print. See No. 52.*
12. *Taiwan*, by John F. Copper. 1993. *Out of print. See No. 34.*
13. *Malaysia*, by Amarjit Kaur. 1993. *Out of print. See No. 36.*
14. *Saudi Arabia*, by J. E. Peterson. 1993. *Out of print. See No. 45.*
15. *Myanmar*, by Jan Becka. 1995
16. *Iran*, by John H. Lorentz. 1995
17. *Yemen*, by Robert D. Burrowes. 1995
18. *Thailand*, by May Kyi Win and Harold Smith. 1995. *Out of print. See No. 55.*
19. *Mongolia*, by Alan J. K. Sanders. 1996. *Out of print. See No. 42.*
20. *India*, by Surjit Mansingh. 1996. *Out of print. See No. 58.*
21. *Gulf Arab States*, by Malcolm C. Peck. 1996
22. *Syria*, by David Commins. 1996. *Out of print. See No. 50.*
23. *Palestine*, by Nafez Y. Nazzal and Laila A. Nazzal. 1997
24. *Philippines*, by Artemio R. Guillermo and May Kyi Win. 1997. *Out of print. See No. 54.*

Oceania
1. *Australia*, by James C. Docherty. 1992. *Out of print. See No. 32.*
2. *Polynesia*, by Robert D. Craig. 1993. *Out of print. See No. 39.*

47. *Afghanistan*, 3rd ed., by Ludwig W. Adamec. 2003
48. *Bangladesh*, 3rd ed., by Craig Baxter and Syedur Rahman. 2003
49. *Kyrgyzstan*, by Rafis Abazov. 2004
50. *Syria*, 2nd ed., by David Commins. 2004
51. *Indonesia*, 2nd ed., by Robert Cribb and Audrey Kahin. 2004
52. *Republic of Korea*, 2nd ed., by Andrew C. Nahm and James E. Hoare. 2004
53. *Turkmenistan*, by Rafis Abazov. 2005
54. *Philippines*, 2nd ed., by Artemio Guillermo. 2005
55. *Thailand,* 2nd ed., by Harold E. Smith, Gayla S. Nieminen, and May Kyi Win. 2005.
56. *New Zealand,* 2nd ed., by Keith Jackson and Alan McRobie. 2005.
57. *Vietnam, 3rd ed.,* by Bruce Lockhart and William J. Duiker, 2006.
58. *India, 2nd ed.,* by Surjit Mansingh, 2006.

Historical Dictionary of India

Second Edition

Surjit Mansingh

Historical Dictionaries of Asia, Oceania, and the Middle East, No. 58

The Scarecrow Press, Inc.
Lanham, Maryland • Toronto • Oxford
2006

SCARECROW PRESS, INC.

Published in the United States of America
by Scarecrow Press, Inc.
A wholly owned subsidiary of
The Rowman & Littlefield Publishing Group, Inc.
4501 Forbes Boulevard, Suite 200
Lanham, Maryland 20706
www.scarecrowpress.com

PO Box 317
Oxford
OX2 9RU, UK

Copyright © 2006 by Surjit Mansingh

All rights reserved. No part of this publication may be reproduced, stored
in a retrieval system, or transmitted in any form or by any means, electronic,
mechanical, photocopying, recording, or otherwise, without the prior permission
of the publisher.

British Library Cataloguing in Publication Information Available

Library of Congress Cataloging-in-Publication Data
Mansingh, Surjit, 1937–
  Historical dictionary of India / Surjit Mansingh.—2nd ed.
    p. cm.—(Historical dictionaries of Asia, Oceania, and the Middle East ;
no. 58)
  Includes bibliographical references.
  ISBN-10: 0-8108-4770-1 (hardcover : alk. paper)
  ISBN-13: 978-0-8108-4770-5 (hardcover : alk. paper)
  1. India–History–Dictionaries. I. Title. II. Series: Historical dictionaries of
Asia, Oceania, and the Middle East ; 58.
DS405.M27 2006
954.003—dc22   2005030343

First edition by Surjit Mansingh, Asian/Oceanian Historical Dictionaries,
No. 20, Scarecrow Press, Lanham, MD, 1996   ISBN 0-8108-3078-7

∞™ The paper used in this publication meets the minimum requirements of
American National Standard for Information Sciences—Permanence of Paper
for Printed Library Materials, ANSI/NISO Z39.48-1992.
Manufactured in the United States of America.

For my sons, Arjun and Kabir

Contents

Editor's Foreword

Few countries are as vast and as varied as India. Few possess as large a population and as strategic a location. And few can boast as impressive a past as well as a promising future. As many observers have realized, India is a special place and one that is extremely difficult to sum up within a single book. Nonetheless, this *Historical Dictionary of India* is an excellent introduction to the country, touching on its size and variety, its population and position, its past history, present situation, and future prospects. This is done with considerable insight and almost palpable affection.

Obviously, one volume—however large—cannot cover all of the relevant aspects. But this second edition does include an amazingly broad range of entries on significant persons, places, and events, government institutions and political parties, and important facets of the economy, society, culture, and religion. There are more than a hundred new entries in the dictionary, and many others have been expanded and updated. The same was done for other sections. There is also a useful glossary, comprising key vernacular terms that will be encountered here and elsewhere. A broad chronology and an extensive introduction pave the way. For those who want to read more, a comprehensive if selective bibliography suggests many other works of interest.

Although it is possible to know India well from having lived there and examined it from within, it is certainly easier to present it to others after having viewed it from a distance as well. Surjit Mansingh, until recently a professor at the School of International Studies of Jawaharlal Nehru University in New Delhi, has done just that. She studied history at Delhi University and international relations at American University and taught at universities in India and abroad. Dr. Mansingh has lectured widely and authored or coauthored several books. Based on her knowledge and experience, she has prepared this highly readable, interesting, and informative passage to India.

Jon Woronoff
Series Editor

Acknowledgments

This second edition of the *Historical Dictionary of India* is an introduction to Indian history and civilization, as was the first edition. The invaluable help in their preparation that has been provided by the Nehru Memorial Museum and Library and the India International Centre Library in New Delhi and the Library of Congress in Washington, D.C., is gratefully acknowledged. Many friends, relatives, and colleagues have shared their experiences and insights, to illuminate many of the entries. Errors in fact or interpretation are mine alone. New maps 1, 2, 3, and diagram 8 are from *Geographical Dictionary of India* and are used with permission of its publisher, Vision Books. Oxford University Press kindly renewed permission to again use maps 4, 5, 6, and 7 from Collin Davies' *Historical Atlas of the Indian Peninsula*.

Abbreviations and Acronyms

AEC	Atomic Energy Commission
AIADMK	All India Anna Dravida Munnetra Kazhagam
AICC	All India Congress Committee
AITUC	All India Trade Union Congress
APHC	All Party Hurriyat Conference
ASEAN	Association of South East Asian Nations
BARC	Bhabha Atomic Research Centre
BIMSTEC	Bangladesh, India, Myanmar, Sri Lanka, Thailand Economic Cooperation
BJP	Bharatiya Janata Party
BMAC	Babri Masjid Action Committee
BSF	Border Security Force
BSP	Bahugana Samaj Party
CBMs	Confidence Building Measures
CDS	Chief of Defense Services
CII	Confederation of Indian Industry
CPGB	Communist Party of Great Britain
CPI	Communist Party of India
CPI(M)	Communist Party of India (Marxist)
CPI(M-L)	Communist Party of India (Marxist Leninist)
CRPF	Central Reserve Police Force
CSE	Centre for Science and Environment
CTBT	Comprehensive Test Ban Treaty
CWC	Congress Working Committee
DMK	Dravida Munnetra Kazhagam
EC	Election Commission
EIC	East India Company
FDI	Foreign Direct Investment

FICCI	Federation of Indian Chambers of Commerce and Industry
GNP	Gross National Product
GSLV	Geosynchronous Satellite Launch Vehicle
HIV/AIDS	Human Immune-deficiency Virus/ Acquired Immune Deficiency Syndrome
IAEA	International Atomic Energy Agency
IAS	Indian Administrative Service
IB	Intelligence Bureau
ICS	Indian Civil Service
IMF	International Monetary Fund
INC	Indian National Congress
INSAT	Indian National Satellite System
INTUC	Indian National Trade Union Congress
IPCC	Inter Governmental Panel on Climate Change
IPKF	Indian Peace Keeping Force
IPS	Indian Police Service
IRMA	Institute of Rural Management
IRSS	Indian Remote Sensing Satellite
ISI	Inter Services Intelligence (Pakistan)
ISPRO	Indian Space Program Research Organization
IT	Information Technology
J&K	Jammu and Kashmir
JCC	Jharkhand Coordination Committee
JD	Janata Dal
JKLF	Jammu and Kashmir Liberation Front
LAC	Line of Actual Control
LKD	Lok Dal
LOC	Line of Control
NAM	Nonaligned Movement
NARI	National AIDS Research Institute
NCP	National Congress Party
NDA	National Democratic Alliance
NEFA	North East Frontier Agency
NGO	Non Governmental Organization
NHRC	National Human Rights Commission
NPT	Nuclear Non-Proliferation Treaty
NSG	National Security Guards

NSSP	Next Steps in Strategic Partnership
NWFP	North West Frontier Province
OBCs	Other Backward Castes
ONGC	Oil and Natural Gas Corporation
PNE	Peaceful Nuclear Explosion
POTA	Prevention of Terrorism Act
PSLV	Polar Satellite Launch Vehicle
PSP	Praja Socialist Party
PUCL	People's Union for Civil Liberties
PUCLDR	People's Union for Civil Liberties and Democratic Rights
PUDR	People's Union for Democratic Rights
PWG	Peoples' War Group
R&AW	Research and Analysis Wing
RSS	Rashtriya Swayamsevak Sangh
SAARC	South Asian Association for Regional Cooperation
SAFTA	South Asian Free Trade Area
SC	Scheduled Castes
SEWA	Self Employed Women's Association
SGPC	Shiromani Gurdwara Prabhandhak Committee
SIMI	Students Islamic Movement India
SNDP	Sri Narayana Dharma Paripalana Yogam
SP	Samajwadi Party
SRC	States Reorganization Commission
SSP	Samyukta Socialist Party
ST	Scheduled Tribes
TADA	Terrorist and Disruptive Activities (Prevention) Act
TDP	Telugu Desham Party
TERI	Tata Energy Research Institute
TRS	Telengana Rashtra Samiti
UKFA	United Liberation Front of Asom
UN	United Nations
UNESCO	United Nations Educational, Scientific, and Cultural Organization
UNSC	United Nations Security Council
UP	Uttar Pradesh (earlier United Provinces)
UPA	United Progressive Alliance
VHP	Vishwa Hindu Parishad

VOC	Vereinigde Oostindische Compagnie
WTO	World Trade Organization
WWI	World War I
WWII	World War II

Map 1. States and Union Territories (Yanam, Karaikal, and Mahe are part of Pondicherry)

Map 2.   Languages

Legend:
- Indo · Aryan languages
- Dravidian languages
- Tibeto · Burman languages
- Austric languages

Area within which Hindi is the
language of education, etc.

Modified after S.K. Chatterji and R. Tirtha

0   200   400   600 km

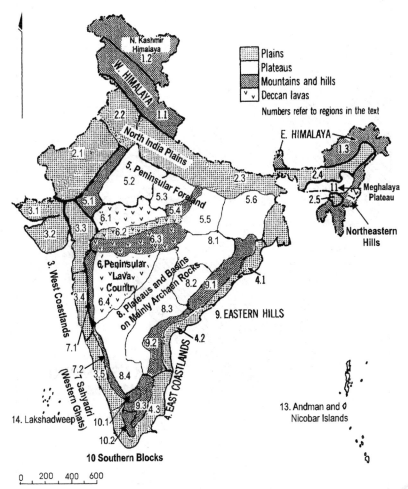

Map 3.   **Physiographic Regions**

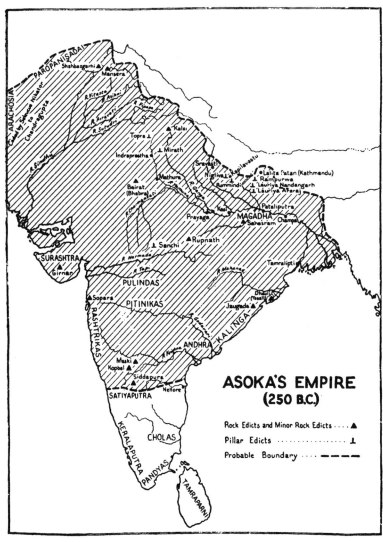

Map 4.   Asoka's Empire in 250 B.C.

Map 5.   India in 1030

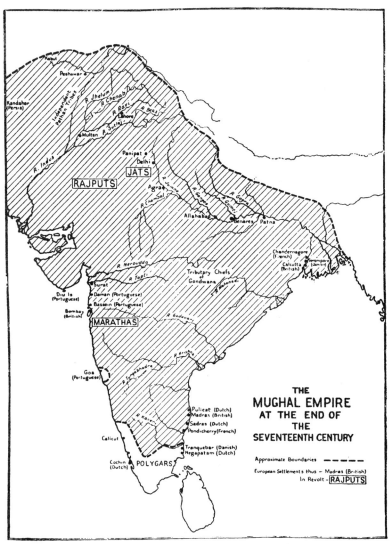

Map 6. The Mughal empire at the end of the seventeenth century

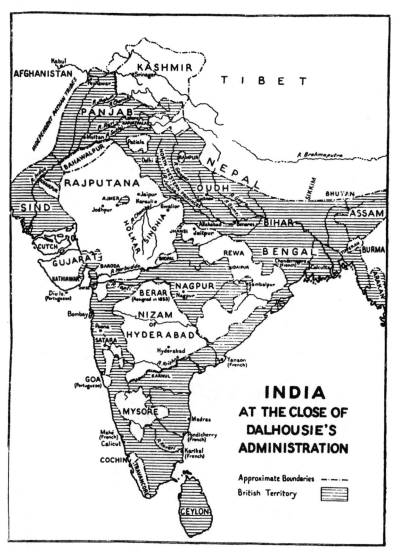

Map 7. India at the close of Dalhousie's administration in 1856

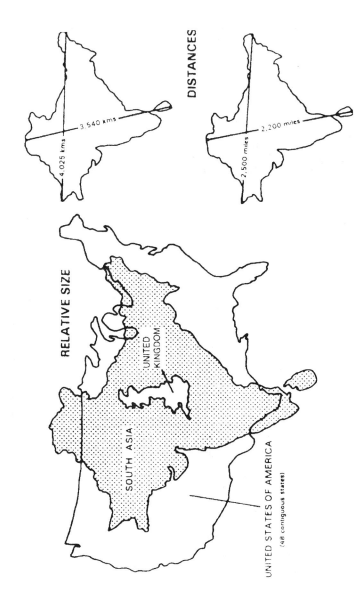

Map 8. Size and Location

RELATIVE SIZE

SOUTH ASIA

UNITED KINGDOM

UNITED STATES OF AMERICA
(48 contiguous states)

DISTANCES

4,025 kms

3,540 kms

2,500 miles

2,200 miles

Chronology

Before the Common Era (BCE)

c. 400,000–200,000 Interglacial period, early human activity with stone implements and cave paintings.

c. 40,000–3,000 Scattered sites of the middle stone age. Evidence of domesticated plants and animals, wheel-turned pottery, copper, and bronze.

3,102 Beginning of the Kali Yuga, an astronomical era,

The Antecedents

c. 3,000–1,500 Urban civilization in the Indus valley at Harappa and other locations east and south. Commerce with West Asia.

c. 1,500–500 Age of the Vedas. Probable migrations of Indo-Aryan speaking groups into India. Spread of iron usage. Neolithic and chalcolithic cultures in various locations.

c. 800–400 Age of painted grey ware pottery in north India. Urbanization in the Ganges valley.

Formation of States and Emergence of Empire

c. 700–500 Period of 16 *mahajanapadas,* kingdoms and republics; rise of Magadha.

c. 560–467 Life of Mahavira, Jain Thirthankara.

c. 556–468 Life of Siddharatha Gautama, the Buddha.

513–485 Reign of Bimbisara in Magadha.

362–321 Nanda dynasty rules in Ganges valley.

327–325 Alexander of Macedon in northwestern India.

321 Accession of Chandragupta, founder of Mauryan dynasty with capital at Pataliputra.

268–231 Reign of Ashoka. Spread of Buddhism in south, central, and southeastern Asia.

c. 250 Third Buddhist Council held at Pataliputra.

2003 Termination of Mauryan dynasty and accession of a Shunga king.

c. 200 BCE to c. 150 C.E. Saka (Indo-Greek) rule in northwest. Satavahana power in Deccan. Sangam period in Tamil culture. Emergence of Mahayana school of Buddhism. Jain cleavage into Digambaras and Shvetambaras. Rise of mercantile communities. Extensive trade with China, Egypt, Rome, Southeast Asia. Gandhara school of art flourishes.

58 Beginning of Vikrama era in Hindu calendar.

Common Era (C. E.)

First century Buddhist missionaries go to China. Mission of St. Thomas to southern India by tradition. Pandya, Chera, and Chola kingdoms in south India. Probable composition of the Bhagvata Gita.

78 Accession of Kanishka as Kushan emperor. Founding of the Saka era in Hindu calendar.

150 Rudradaman, Saka king, ruling in western India.

Emergence of the "Classical" Pattern

c. 200 Decline of Kushan, Satavahana, and Saka power.

c. 300–500 Rise and consolidation of Gupta power. Flowering of Sanskrit literature, arts, mathematics, sciences.

319/20–335 Reign of Chandra Gupta I, founder of Gupta dynasty.

335–375   Reign of Samudra Gupta.

375–415   Reign of Chandra Gupta II Vikramaditya.

405–411   Travels of Faxian, Chinese pilgrim, in India.

c. 470–600   Huna invasions in northwest. Rise of Chalukya power in Deccan from Badami. Rise of Pallava power in south from Kanchi.

606–647   Reign of Harshavardhana of Kanauj.

609–642   Reign of Pulakeshin II, Chalukya king, who successfully attacks Kanauj in 620. Beginning of Chalukya-Pallava rivalry.

622   Beginning of Hijra era in Muslim calendar.

630–644   Travels of Xuanzang, Chinese chronicler.

680–720   Reign of Narasimhavarman II of Pallava dynasty. Shore temples built at Mahabalipuram.

c. 700   Padmasambhava spreads Buddhism in Tibet.

Formation of Regional States

711   Arab invasion of Sindh.

735   First settlement of Persian Zoroastrians in western India.

736   Founding of the first identifiable city of Delhi.

754–973   Rashtrakuta dynasty established in Deccan; expands in all directions as "imperial" power.

c. 770   Pala dynasty established in eastern India.

c.780–826   Life of Shankara, expounder of Vedanta.

c. 840–890   Rise of Gujara-Pratihara power around Kanauj.

855–1182   Utpala dynasty rules in Kashmir.

c. 890–1182   Chandela dynasty rules in central India.

c. 899–1279   Establishment, consolidation, and expansion of Chola power in south India. Mercantile and naval dominance.

1001–1026   Mahmud of Ghazni raids temples in northwestern India.

1017–1030 Travels of Al Biruni (Alberuni) in north India.

1110–1326 Hoysala Dynasty in Karnataka.

1175–1186 Muhammad Ghori captures Punjab and Sindh.

1192 Prithvi Raj Chauhan of Delhi defeated by Muhammad Ghori at battle of Tarain.

Realignment of Kingdoms in Pre-Mughal India

1206–1212 Establishment of Turkish Sultanate around Delhi.

1288, 1293 Marco Polo visits south Indian port of Kayal.

1290–1316 Expansion of Delhi Sultanate by Khalji dynasty.

1320–1388 Tughlaq dynasty in Delhi Sultanate.

1336–1565 Vijayanagar Empire in peninsular India.

1347 Bahmani Sultanate established in Deccan.

1398 Timur the Mongol sacks Delhi.

1420 Nicolo Conti visits Vijayanagar.

1440–1515 Life of Kabir.

1469–1539 Life of Nanak.

1498 Vasco da Gama reaches Calicut port in southwest.

1510 Portuguese capture Goa.

1526 Battle of Panipat, defeat of Ibrahim Lodi of Delhi by Babur who establishes Mughal dynasty.

1542–1545 Sher Shah Sur master of north India.

Mughal India

1556–1605 Reign of Akbar; expansion of Mughal Empire by conquest and matrimonial alliances.

1565 Vijayanagar defeated by Bahmani Sultanate at Battle of Talikota.

1579 Abolition of *jiziya* tax on Hindus by Akbar.

1580 First Jesuit mission at Mughal court.

1597 Death of Rana Pratap of Mewar.

1600 English East India Company chartered.

1602 Dutch East India Company (VOC) chartered.

1605–1627 Reign of Jahangir and Nur Jahan.

1615–1619 Sir Thomas Roe at Mughal court obtains permission for East India Company to trade in India.

1628–1657 Reign of Shah Jahan. Construction of magnificent buildings, including Taj Mahal.

1630–1680 Life of Shivaji, Maratha leader.

1657–1658 War of succession among sons of Shah Jahan.

1658–1707 Reign of Aurangzeb.

1664 French East India Company founded.

1666–1708 Life of Gobind Singh, tenth Sikh Guru.

1668–1669 Rebellions against Mughals in northern India.

1670 Shivaji sacks port of Surat.

1674 Francois Martin founds Pondicherry. Shivaji assumes royal title.

1681 Aurangzeb moves to Deccan for war against Marathas.

1690 Calcutta founded.

1707–1712 Reign of Bahadur Shah II followed by virtual independence of several Mughal provinces.

1739 Nadir Shah of Persia sacks Delhi.

1740–1760 Power struggles in Bengal and south India among princes and European trading companies.

1757 Battle of Plassey. Robert Clive defeats Nawab of Bengal.

1761 Third battle of Panipat. Ahmad Shah Abdali defeats Marathas.

Rise and Consolidation of British Power in India

1764–1765 Battle of Baxar. East India Company awarded *dewani* (right to collect land revenue) in Bengal, Bihar, and Orissa by Mughal Emperor Shah Alam II.

1767–1799 Four Anglo-Mysore Wars; East India Company expands control in southern and eastern India.

1769–1799 Haidar Ali and Tipu Sultan expand power in Mysore.

1772–1833 Life of Raja Ram Mohun Roy.

1773–1774 Regulating Act passed by British Parliament; Warren Hastings appointed Governor General of India.

1775–1782 First Anglo-Maratha war.

1793 Lord Cornwallis introduces "permanent settlement" of land revenue in huge Bengal province.

1799–1839 Reign of Ranjit Singh in Sikh Empire of northwest.

1803–1805 Second Anglo-Maratha war.

1817–1818 Final Anglo-Maratha war.

1828–1833 Governor Generalship of Lord William Bentinck.

1829 Prohibition of sati.

1835 English declared official language of administration.

1838–1842 First Anglo-Afghan war.

1845–1849 Two Anglo-Sikh wars. Lord Dalhousie annexes several princely states.

1853 First railway and telegraph lines opened.

1856 Law permitting remarriage of Hindu widows.

1857–1858 Uprising against British, also known as Sepoy Mutiny. Mughal Emperor exiled, East India Company abolished.

India under the British Crown: Freedom Movement

1817–1898 Life of Syed Ahmad Khan.

1824–1883 Life of Dayananda Saraswati.

1858–1887 Universities established at Calcutta, Bombay, Madras, Lahore, and Allahabad.

1861 Codification of civil and penal laws.

1863–1902 Life of Swami Vivekananda.

1865–1876 Widespread famines.

1869 Suez Canal opened.

1877 Queen Victoria proclaimed Empress of India.

1878–1880 Second Anglo-Afghan war.

1880–1884 Viceroyalty of Lord Ripon.

1883 Ilbert Bill controversy.

1885 Indian National Congress founded.

1892 Indian Councils Act provides for more Indians in provincial legislative councils.

1897 Ramakrishna Mission founded.

1899–1905 Viceroyalty of Lord Curzon.

1905 Partition of Bengal arouses intense opposition.

1906 Congress declaration on Swaraj. Formation of All-India Muslim League.

1909 Morley-Minto reforms. Muslim separate electorates.

1911 Delhi Durbar of King George V. Partition of Bengal reversed. Capital moved from Calcutta to Delhi.

1914–1918   World War I.

1916   Lucknow Pact between Congress and Muslim League.

1917   Montagu declaration promising "responsible government" in India.

1919   Rowlatt Acts arouse opposition. Jallianwala Bagh massacre. Third Anglo-Afghan war. India member of the League of Nations.

1920–1922   Noncooperation movement. Khilafet movement. M. K. Gandhi emerges as Congress leader.

1921   Montagu-Chelmsford reforms introduce dyarchy in the provinces.

1928   Simon Commission in India. All-parties meeting on constitutional reform results in Nehru Report. Congress resolves *purna swaraj* (full independence).

1930   Gandhi leads Salt March and nonviolent civil disobedience movement.

1930–1932   The Great Depression.

1931   Gandhi-Irwin Pact.

1932   Indian Military Academy founded in Dehra Dun.

1933   Royal Indian Air Force formed.

1935   Government of India Act introduces provincial autonomy and widens franchise.

1937   Congress wins elections in eight out of eleven provinces.

1939–1945   World War II.

1940   Muslim League adopts Pakistan resolution.

1942   Quit India movement, mass arrests. Cripps mission fails. Japanese victories in Southeast Asia. Indian National Army formed in Malaya.

1942–1944   Bengal famine.

1944   Gandhi-Jinnah talks break down.

1945 British Labour Government announces intention of granting early independence to India.

1946 Mutiny in Royal Indian Navy. British Cabinet Mission in India. Elections to Constituent Assembly. Muslim League campaigns for Pakistan. Communal riots. Interim government; Jawaharlal Nehru vice-president.

1947 Lord Mountbatten appointed viceroy. Announces plan to partition India. Widespread communal riots.

Independent India

1947 August 15 and 14: India and Pakistan independent. Raiders from Pakistan attack Jammu and Kashmir; state accedes to India. **October 27**: military operations.

1947–1949 Integration of Princely States to Indian Union.

1948 January 30: Mahatma Gandhi assassinated.

1950 January 26: Republic of India adopts Constitution.

1951–1956 First Five-Year Plan; public investment in infrastructure.

1952 First general election; adult franchise. Congress wins in center and states.

1953 Mount Everest summit climbed. City of Chandigarh inaugurated. India mediates in Korean War.

1954 French territories incorporated. India and China enunciate five principles of peaceful coexistence. Tata Institute of Fundamental Research founded. Bhakra-Nangal canal inaugurated.

1955 Conference of Asian and African nations, Bandung. Hindu Reform Bills debated and passed.

1956 Reorganization of states along linguistic lines.

1956–1957 Second Five-Year Plan. Public investment in heavy industry.

1957 Second general election; Communist Party victory in Kerala. First atomic reactor in Bombay. Decimal coinage introduced.

1959 Dalai Lama receives asylum in India.

1960 Indus Waters Treaty signed between India, Pakistan, and the World Bank. Bombay state divided between Gujarat and Maharashtra.

1961 First summit conference of Nonaligned States at Belgrade. Liberation of Goa from Portugal.

1962 Third general election; Congress victory. Border war with China.

1963 India signs Partial Test Ban Treaty. Nagaland becomes 16th state.

1964 **May 22:** Nehru dies. Lal Bahadur Shastri elected prime minister.

1965 Anti-Hindi riots in Madras state. Official language conference adopts Three-language formula. **September:** Pakistan-India military conflict.

1966 Tashkent Agreement in January restores status quo. Shastri dies. Indira Gandhi elected prime minister.

1967 Fourth general election reduces Congress majority at center and defeat in some states. Naxalite movement in Bengal.

1969 Indira Gandhi splits Congress, nationalizes banks.

1971 Fifth general election gives Indira Gandhi solid victory. Civil war in Pakistan; 10 million refugees enter India. India assists in the liberation of Bangladesh, formerly East Pakistan. Indo-Soviet Treaty signed.

1972 Simla Agreement between India and Pakistan, June.

1973 Oil price hike. Economic stringencies.

1974 Mass demonstrations in Bihar and Gujarat. Railway workers' strike. India conducts underground nuclear test. Sikkim merged with India.

1975 Protest movement led by J. P. Narayan. Emergency proclaimed June.

1977   Janata Party coalition formed from opposition parties. Emergency lifted. Congress defeated in sixth general elections. Morarji Desai becomes prime minister.

1978   Forty-fourth Constitutional Amendment annuls some amendments made in 1970s and during Emergency.

1979   Janata government splits. Desai resigns. Charan Singh forms caretaker government. Mother Teresa of Calcutta awarded Nobel Peace Prize.

1980   Seventh general election returns Indira Gandhi to power.

1982   Indian Scientific Expedition to Antarctica. Asian Games held in New Delhi. Sheikh Abdullah dies.

1983   Nonaligned Summit in New Delhi. Agitation in Punjab. Nellie massacre in Assam. Sarkaria Commission reviews center-state relations.

1984   Rakesh Sharma first Indian in space. Punjab declared "dangerously disturbed." **June**: Security forces enter Golden Temple, Amritsar, in Operation Blue Star. **October 31**: Indira Gandhi assassinated. Rajiv Gandhi appointed prime minister. Anti-Sikh riots in Delhi and elsewhere. Poisonous gas from Union Carbide plant in Bhopal kills thousands. **December**: General election gives Congress (I) massive victory.

1985   Union budget signals economic liberalization. **June**: Air India trans-Atlantic flight of "Kanishka" blown up. Punjab Accord; Assam Accord. First summit meeting of South Asian Association of Regional Cooperation (SAARC) at Dhaka, Bangladesh.

1986   Controversy over Shah Banu case. Pope John Paul II visits. Union territories of Mizoram and Arunachal Pradesh in northeast become states.

1987   Bofors scandal on defense commissions. Communal riots. Indo-Sri Lanka Accord, Indian Peace Keeping Force sent to Sri Lanka to help resolve ethnic conflict there.

1988   Rajiv Gandhi visits China, signs agreements.

1989   "Agni" intermediate range ballistic missile test launched. Ninth general election results in heavy Congress (I) losses. Rajiv Gandhi resigns. V. P. Singh forms National Front coalition government.

1990   Violence erupts in Kashmir valley. Crisis in relations with Pakistan. Indian Peace Keeping Force withdrawn from Sri Lanka by March. V. P. Singh announces implementation of Mandal Commission recommendations on reservations for "other backward castes" (OBCs); agitation in northern India. Dispute over sacred site at Ayodhya escalates. **November 9:** V. P. Singh resigns. Chandra Shekhar heads caretaker government.

1991   Gulf War. Indian contingent with United Nations Observer Mission. **May 21:** Rajiv Gandhi assassinated. Tenth general election gives no party a majority. P. V. Narasimba Rao elected leader of Congress and prime minister. Balance of payments crisis. Union budget presented by Dr. Manmohan Singh announces major economic reforms. India formally recognizes Russian Federation and 11 other states after break up of the Soviet Union.

1992   First Indian built submarine, INS Shalki, commissioned. Indian designed and fabricated communications satellite, INSAT-2A, placed in orbit. First Indo-US joint naval exercise. Harshad Mehta scandal involving massive fraud in banks, stock exchange, and securities market. Babri Masjid in Ayodhya destroyed December 6 by Hindu militants. Communal violence follows. Temples in Bangladesh, Britain, and Pakistan vandalized. BJP leaders indicted for incitement of communal hatred; BJP governments in four north Indian states dismissed and president's rule imposed. Rao wins vote of confidence in Lok Sabha.

1993   Russian President Boris Yeltsin visits India. Constitutional amendment enabling devolution of power. **March 12:** Bomb blast on destroys Bombay stock exchange temporarily; underworld figures assisted by Pakistan accused of conspiracy. India and China sign agreement on maintaining "peace and tranquility" along the Line of Actual Control. Ambassadors exchanged for first time with Israel. Full diplomatic relations established with post-apartheid South Africa. National Human Rights Commission headed by former Chief Justice commences work. Earthquake in Maharashtra kills thousands. Conflict continues in Jammu and Kashmir; crisis over Hazratbal shrine overcome without violence. Elections in four north Indian states result in BJP defeat in three.

1994   Non-violent protests led by social activists and environmentalists against large dams succeed in halting some constructions on the

Narmada river (Maharashtra and Gujarat) and at Tehri (UP). Women commissioned as officers in air force and navy as well as army. Economic indicators continue upward. Attempts made to open dialogue with various groups and individuals in Jammu and Kashmir so as to restore normalcy; simultaneous efforts made by security forces to combat militants and capture infiltrators; in the diplomatic arena India permits foreign visitors to Jammu and Kashmir but rejects idea of third party mediation in disputes with Pakistan.

1995: Indian television begins telecasts to 50 Southeast and West Asian countries. First exclusive Indian Communications Satellite launched. L. K. Advani elected President of BJP. Eighth SAARC Summit, agreements to create preferential trade area for South Asia leading to free trade region. Jawaharlal Nehru Award for International Understanding conferred on Aung San Suu Kyi of Burma.

1996: Fodder scam in Bihar. President's rule in Gujarat. Cyclone hits Andhra Pradesh. Congress Party elections return P. V .N. Rao as parliamentary leaders, Sitaram Kesri as party president. Charges against Rao and seven others for bribery. **May:** Eleventh general election gives no single party a majority. A. B.Vajpayee forms BJP government for 12 days. H. D. Deve Gowda forms a United Front coalition government of five parties. Elections in state of Jammu and Kashmir bring 57% voter turn out and National Conference wins 57 out of 87 seats in Assembly.

1997: Food and milk production continue to rise. Congress withdraws outside support to government; I. K. Gujral replaces Deve Gowda as prime minister in May. Enunciates "Gujral 'Doctrine" of benevolence in relations with neighbors. K. R. Narayanan elected president.

1998 Twelfth general election in 543 Lok Sabha constituencies. BJP led 13-party alliance issues common National Agenda for Governance; A. B. Vajpayee elected prime minister in March. **May 11 and 13:** Series of underground nuclear tests at Pokharan; United States imposes sanctions but engages in dialogue. Amartya Sen receives Nobel Prize for economics and Bharat Ratna. India and Pakistan agree to initiate a bus service between Delhi and Lahore.

1999 **February:** Vajpayee takes bus to Lahore for meetings with Pakistan Prime Minister Nawaz Sharif; they issue Lahore Declaration on process of normalizing relations and achieving nuclear safety. **May:**

Pakistan regular and irregular troops attack across Line of Control near Kargil; "war-like situation" develops; defused only when Pakistan withdraws in July under pressure of defeat and US persuasion. **August:** India issues draft nuclear doctrine based on minimum credible deterrent and no first use. **October:** Military coup in Pakistan. **December:** Indian Airlines airplane from Kathmandu hijacked to Kandahar via Lahore; release of passengers negotiated with UN team and Taliban. Pope John Paul II visits India again. Thirteenth general election returns BJP-led coalition to office. Bus service between Kolkata and Dhaka initiated. Economic reforms further liberalization of economy. ICICI Bank and Infosys Company list shares on the New York Stock Exchange for the first time. Sange Sherpa and Kushang Dorjee are first mountaineers to climb Everest from all three sides of the peak in the same season. India and US form joint working group to counter terrorism; India estimates over 25,000 persons killed in terrorist attacks over 10 years.

2000   India informs China of the arrival of Orgyen Trinley Dorji, 17th Karmapa of Tibet, in Dharamsala; no diplomatic crisis, expulsion, or formal application for asylum. Constitution Review Committee formed amid debate on appropriate form of government. Central Vigilance Commission recommends criminal proceedings again top civil servants for corruption and publishes 91 names on its web site. **March:** US President Bill Clinton visits India for five days amidst public acclaim; several bilateral agreements signed. Tensions rise over application of Hindutva ideology in educational and research institutions; Vajpayee warns VHP and RSS leaders not "to push too far" in propagating views. Violence against Christians in Bihar, Gujarat, Orissa, UP on conversion and property issues; NHRC takes up cases. Six domestic airports upgraded to international status. Three new states of Chhatisgarh, Jharkhand, and Uttaranchal formed.

2001   January–February: Maha Kumbh Mela held and 25 million people bathe at junction of three rivers near Allahabad. Pro-business budget passes parliament pledging privatization of some public sector enterprises and removal of many import restrictions. Decennial Census completed in March show total population figure of 1,027,000,000 and overall slowing of rate of population growth. **March:** Tehelka World Wide Web site launches undercover sting operation and publicizes corruption in arms deals. Securities and Exchange Board of India (SEBI) promulgates ethics code. Dispute between Maharashtra and Enron company on Dahbol Power Company worsens; Enron declared bankrupt in United States in December. **July:** Agra Summit between Vajpayee and General Musharraf fails. **September 11:** Terrorist attacks in US; India and US cooperate in war against terrorism, also in rebuilding of Afghanistan after defeat of Taliban. Terrorist attack on Parliament on December 13 results in tense relations with Pakistan.

2002: India demands extradition of 20 terrorists from Pakistan, which refuses. **January 12:** General Musharraf makes speech promising a crackdown on terrorism from Pakistan. Indo-Pakistan tensions increase over continued cross-border terrorist attacks in Jammu and Kashmir resulting in massive troop deployments on both sides of border. **February:** BJP loses elections in states of Manipur, Punjab, Uttaranchal, and Uttar Pradesh. Free and fair elections in Jammu and Kashmir result in defeat of the National Conference; Farooq Abdullah replaced by Sayeed Mufti as chief minister; talks take place between Indian government and various militant groups; Hurriyat refuses to participate in talks in March over objections of civil liberties organizations and opposition parties. **April:** Attack on train at Godhra, Gujarat, opens a wave of sectarian violence in Gujarat that leaves many dead and 120,000 Muslims in refugee camps. Impartial observers allege a deliberate "pogrom." Gujarat State Assembly dissolved; fresh elections held in December and result reelection of BJP government led by Narender Modi. Indian government approves genetically modified cotton for planting, despite continued controversy. **May:** BSP leader Mayawati elected chief minister of Uttar, Pradesh, but World Bank warns UP to improve its chaotic administration in order to qualify for continued loans. India signs cooperative defense agreements with Russia and the US for military supplies and engages in joint exercises with United States military and naval forces.

2003: Defense minister George Fernandes visits Moscow and leases long-range bombers and nuclear submarines. Mass immunization campaign against polio conducted throughout the country. **February:** Elections in states of Himachal Pradesh, Meghalaya, Nagaland, and Tripura indicate moderate revival of Congress Party. Peace Accord reached with Bodo Liberation Tigers Force in Assam. **June:** Visit to China by Vajapayee results in signing of several important agreements, including accelerated attention to the border problem and economic cooperation.

Controversy on Ayodhya issue continues through the year, with contradictory reports from the Archaeological Survey of India and sporadic sectarian violence. BJP leaders urge restraint on VHP and Bajrang Dal.

Disinvestment and privatization program continues as part of economic liberalization. Foreign direct investment increases. **August:** The BJP-BSP coalition in UP collapses, and Mulayam Singh Yadav replaces Mayawati as chief minister. **September:** Israel's Prime Minister Ariel Sharon visits India for the first time. Canada eventually brings to trial suspects in the 1985 bombing of Air India passenger aircraft Kanishka.

Orissa court sentences Dara Singh to death and 12 others to life imprisonment for murder of Graham Staines and two sons in 1999. **November:** India and Pakistan agree to a cease-fire along the LOC **December:** BJP wins handsomely in elections to state legislative assemblies and replaces Congress governments in Madhya Pradesh and Rajasthan.

2004   February: Prime Minister calls for early general elections; Lok Sabha dissolved. India announces 8.2% economic growth rate for the previous year. BJP adopts "India Shining" as election slogan. Vajpayee attends SAARC summit meeting at Islamabad and issues joint statement with Musharraf to resume India-Pakistan composite dialogue. SAARC Summit approves introduction of regional free trade in 2006. **March:** Indian cricket team tours Pakistan after a lapse of 16 years and wins both the test series and the one-day match series. **April and May:** General elections held in with electoral machine voting in all 543 constituencies for the first time. BJP wins only 138 seats in Lok Sabha compared to 182 in 1999 and key allied parties in the coalition also lose badly. Vajpayee resigns. Congress wins 145 seats, compared to 114 in 1999. **May 22:** Sonia Gandhi elected Leader of the Congress Parliamentary Party. Manmohan Singh sworn in as prime minister of United Progressive Alliance (UPA) coalition government. Indian government continues talks with dissident groups in Kashmir. India-Pakistan composite dialogue proceeds on schedule in cordiality but without dramatic breakthrough. **July:** New budget pledges to reduce federal deficit, increase spending on defense and rural infrastructure, and continue with economic liberalization by lifting caps on foreign direct investment in important sectors and reducing protection of small-scale industries. India, Brazil, China, and South Africa cooperate in meetings of World Trade Organization. **September:** Manmohan Singh meets US President

Bush and "next steps in strategic partnership' (NSSP) are discussed. US lifts long-standing ban on export of certain high technology items for use in India's commercial space program and nuclear power plants. India, Brazil, Germany, and Japan act together claiming permanent seats on the United Nations Security Council and promising to work for "meaningful reform" of the organization. India announces an unmanned lunar exploration mission scheduled for 2006–2007. First ASEAN-India summit meeting signifying "full partnership" held in Laos. **December 26:** Massive tsunami or tidal waves triggered by an Indian Ocean earthquake of 9 on the Richter scale devastate the Andaman and Nicobar Islands as coast of Tamil Nadu in India as well as Sri Lanka, Maldives, and parts of Sumatra. India part of the "core group" organizing and delivering relief and supplies.

Introduction

India is attracting international attention as a rising power in this first decade of the 21st century. Established powers, including the United States, seek strategic partnership with it. India has one of the fastest growing economies in the world, with a strong knowledge base in the sciences and a comparative advantage in information technology. India is self-sufficient in food grains and exports processed agricultural products. The World Bank ranks India as the 10th largest economy in terms of Gross Domestic Product in 2005, and many expect it to be the third largest in the world within a few decades. The achievements of individual Indian citizens, or persons of Indian origin who have settled around the world in varied fields, elicit the admiration of others and an interest in the family and cultural backgrounds of those who excel—and interest in Indian civilization, complex and ancient as it is. As importantly, and perhaps surprisingly to some, India today is a unified, vibrant, and mature democracy despite glaring variegations of human development among its heterogeneous population of over one billion.

When India in the mid-20th century commenced its historically unique effort of promoting economic development and social change in a democratic polity with universal adult franchise in a largely poor and illiterate population, when it began to build a federal unity out of diverse administrative, ethnic, linguistic, religious, and political entities in an area the size of Europe, not many expected it to succeed. Fifty-five years later there are numerous domestic and foreign critics of India's many shortcomings—economic, political, and social—but there are few doomsayers. Among countries that gained their independence after World War II, India stands out amid many authoritarian or failing states for its peaceful transition of power through regular elections, for its cohesion in the face of separatist movements and terrorist attacks, and for its democracy. Given the human scale involved and such innovations as *panchayati raj* (local government) by elected village councils with one third of the members mandatorily women, the theory and practice of Indian democracy is as exciting, and likely to be as influential on a worldwide trend toward democracy, as those initiated by the American and French revolutions.

In the parlance of today, India possesses elements of both "soft" and "hard" power. The figure of Mahatma Gandhi is an icon for all those who seek non-violent resolution of conflict. In the decade following independence, Jawaharlal Nehru won for India some influence in world councils. Indian films, music, dance, and cuisine have audiences in the far corners of the globe, and not merely among the diaspora of ethnic Indians. The outstanding reputation of Indian doctors, engineers, and scientists as well as some Indian institutions lead other countries to send officials to India for training in specialized functions, and their citizens to seek admission to Indian educational and medical facilities. Some Indian companies are now internationally competitive. Indian entrepreneurial and engineering talent, especially in information technology and services, has already had an impact on global market places.

In 1998, India conducted underground nuclear tests and declared itself a nuclear weapons state ready to accept all the responsibilities of recognized nuclear powers. While there are divergent opinions on the necessity or efficacy of that step for Indian national security, as on its implications for nuclear non-proliferation regimes, the *fact* of India as a responsible nuclear power is being gradually accepted by world powers. India's military capabilities are not insignificant, and the Indian army commands respect for its proven capabilities, for its solid contributions to United Nations peacekeeping operations over decades, and for its non-political and scrupulous obedience to civilian control. In geo-strategic terms well-recognized by the British, though by relatively few Indians, India's location at the head of the Indian Ocean is a commanding one and connects it with the entire littoral east and west both historically and in contemporary times. A vital interest for India and other powers today is the flow of petroleum from producer countries in West Asia to consumer countries in South and East Asia; the Indian Navy plays a recognized role in the protection of sea lines of communication, as it did in rescue and aid operations following the tsunami of December 2004.

Historical India occupies a natural subcontinent between the Arabian Sea and the Bay of Bengal, stretching from the high mountain ranges of the north, known as Himalaya, to the Indian Ocean in the south. The region is now termed South Asia, of which the Republic of India constitutes almost 80% of the area, population, resources, wealth, and skills. Some dictionary entries refer to places not within the boundaries of the Republic of India but which are part of historical India. The river Sindhu, or Indus, long ago gave its name to the land, the cultures, and the people of India, who became known to others such as Greeks, Persians, and Arabs, as Hindu or Hindavi—inhabitants of the land of the Indus. Only in modern times did the term Hindu come to be used for the religious faiths and social customs of that part of the population (the majority) not identified more precisely as Buddhist, Christian, Muslim, or Sikh. And only in recent decades have attempts been made to designate India more in terms of its Hindu, rather than its composite, identity.

One of the oldest civilizations in the world emerged in India more than 5,000 years ago and is certainly not "changeless" or "timeless," although some have depicted it so. At the same time, India's people are conscious of a cultural continuity that is comparable in its temporal and spatial dimensions only to that of China. Indian culture influenced wide areas beyond the subcontinent and is itself the product of diverse indigenous and exogenous peoples. The land has endured many migrations and invasions as well as the formation, expansion, and disintegration of political entities that controlled parts or sometimes all of the subcontinent. People of India evolved distinctive philosophical beliefs—such as non-dualism, reincarnation, and *karma*—and social features—such as hierarchic and endogamous castes—that persist in one form or another to the present day, irrespective of religious identity. Politically speaking, different states were prominent in different eras, although the strategic importance of such places as Delhi was constant, as were the opposing centripetal and centrifugal pulls in every large empire established on the subcontinent. For various reasons, and unlike China, India did not construct a narrative of one unified state dominant in history but has stressed underlying cultural commonality across the subcontinent. The most recent phase of Indian history began in 1947 when a uniquely non-violent national movement led by Mahatma Gandhi (1869–1948) won independence from Britain, which had gradually assumed control of India and its environs in the 18th and 19th centuries.

India's population of slightly more than one billion encompasses thousands of ethnic, linguistic, social, and religious communities that retain many distinctive features of custom, diet, dress, modes of worship, occupation, and physiognomy and so present a bewildering kaleidoscope to observers from less heterogeneous societies. The many faces of India are further multiplied by the physical juxtaposition of contrasts: space age technologies launching satellites and Neolithic implements polishing rock or cashew nuts; crass consumerism and sublime spirituality; modern cities and primitive villages or nomadic camps; nuclear power plants and women foraging for water or fuel—the list of opposites in apposition is long. Impressive achievements are matched with persistent problems. Travelers from the earliest times to the present have commented on the colorful variety that they experienced in India. It is not surprising, therefore, that Indian attitudes of mind typically reconcile contradictions in non-dualism, or that the proverbial tale of six blind men describing an elephant in ways that are mutually incomprehensible is one of Indian origin. The discovery of India—by Indians as much as by foreigners—is apt to be intensely personal, influenced both by experience and perceptions, as well as by varying ideas about what it means to be Indian.

Scholars have explored ideas and perceptions of India and the ways in which image influences reality. Suffice it to say here that the "Orientalist discourse" defining modern Britain and Europe in masculine, Christian, rational, and civilizing terms depicted India (specifically the Hindu—the "Other") in derogatory colors as "feminine," "heathen," "conquerable," "emotional," "lacking in history," and "needing despotic control." One such influential text was James Mill's 10-volume *History of British India* published in 1818. As David Rubin illustrates, derogatory images were perpetuated in English-language fiction set in India and continue to influence, perhaps subconsciously, journalists and policy-makers in the West because perceptions are slow to change. Many Indians under British rule internalized these insulting images and then sought to refute them by reforming their own communities along more aggressive, masculine, lines. Results of these efforts seen in the 20th century were decidedly mixed and are analyzed by social anthropologists, such as Asish Nandy and by political scientists. Two contrasting images of India also stand out from the record: a land of fabulous wealth and spirituality that enticed adventurers, entrepreneurs, invaders, and seekers of truth over the millennia; and a land stricken with disease, famine, and poverty holding out a begging bowl in the 20th century. The reality of India is much more multifaceted, compelling, and scintillating than any single image. India today is an important member of the contemporary international community and is worthy of study; its rich civilization and long history provide ample reward for study.

LAND AND PEOPLE

The Indian subcontinent of more than one and a half million square miles was called "an intelligible isolate" by one geographer who saw it marked off from the rest of Asia by more than tectonic plates. The giant ramparts of the Himalaya and related ranges insulate the land from the climate of Central Asia, giving it a monsoon system of its own, and peninsular India forms the keystone of an arch bordering the Indian Ocean. Within this girdle of mountains and seas, considerably influenced by the lay of the land as well as by soils and climates, the historical civilizations of India developed. But "isolate" is a relative term. Mountain passes allowed a steady two-way flow of traders, pilgrims, and ideas between Central and South Asia, on occasions preserved in collective memory. Military adventurers and their loot-hungry followers swept in through the same passes. Surrounding oceans with their predictable seasonal winds connected India with lands to the west—Mesopotamia, Egypt, the Persian Gulf, eastern Africa—and to the east—maritime and mainland Southeast Asia, China, Japan—since earliest times through trade in goods and ideas. The spread of Buddhism outward from India about 2,000 years ago was along well-known trading routes by land and sea. More recently, Britain's naval dominance in the Indian Ocean after the Anglo–French wars of the 18th century enabled it to rule India as the brightest jewel in its empire for more than a century. But the colonial experience divided Asia according to rival European overlords and disrupted the historical links among Asian peoples and countries; efforts to reestablish links marked the 20th century and are gaining momentum at the present time.

South Asia lies in the northern hemisphere, between 6 and 36 degrees north, and 60 and 95 degrees east. It contains the Republic of India, Pakistan in the west, Nepal and Bhutan in the north, Bangladesh in the east, and the island Republic of Sri Lanka at the southern tip. Two groups of islands belong to India: the Laccadive, Minicoy, and Amandivi islands in the Arabian Sea, and the Andaman and Nicobar Islands in the Bay of Bengal. Political boundaries are not the same as geographical demarcations in South Asia as sketched here (see Maps 1 and 2). The Indian subcontinent falls into three contrasting macro-regions: the broad mountain wall of the north, the expansive Indo-Gangetic plains south of it, and the triangular block of the peninsula. These are intimately related with one another, and each of them contains several distinct geographical divisions that are not always clearly marked off in their gradual transitions. The resulting variety of topography and climate that is typical of India has helped to produce and preserve the diversity of its regional cultures and languages.

The peninsula is wholly within India. As befits part of antediluvian Gondwanaland, the peninsula is geologically stable and is formed mainly of old rock, which also juts north into the Aravali range and the Malwa and Chhota Nagpur plateaus. The peninsula contains the Deccan plateau that tilts from the thickly forested Western Ghats close to the sea down toward the lower Eastern Ghats and a broad coastal plain. Major rivers that intersect the peninsula are named Krishna, Godaveri, Tungabhadra, and Kaveri; they are rain-fed and run from west to east into the Bay of Bengal. The peninsula is set off from the northern plains by the Vindhya and Satpura ranges that are drained by the Tapti and Narmada Rivers that run east to west into the Gulf of Cambay of the Arabian Sea. Lying entirely within the tropics, peninsular India is generally hot, except in the hills. The northwestern part of the peninsula and the southwestern coastal plain receive most of their annual rainfall during the summer months of the southwest monsoon, but the southeastern portions fall in the "rain shadow" area and are chronically short of water; they receive limited rainfall during the northeast monsoon of the winter months.

North of the central Indian forests and ranges lie the Indo-Gangetic plains produced by deposits of alluvium borne by the Himalayan river systems. The plains extend about 3,000 kilometers in a great crescent from the Indus delta in the west to the Ganges delta and Assam in the east, varying between approximately 160 and 650 kilometers wide. Average rainfall and humidity increase from west to east; dryness typifies the northwest, whereas some places in the east record up to 1,000 centimeters of rainfall annually. The plains can be divided into five sub-regions: the Indus Valley in Pakistan, the Punjab (land of five rivers) shared between India and Pakistan, the Yamuna-Ganga or middle-Ganges in India and southern Nepal, the lower Ganges shared between India and Bangladesh, and the middle Brahmaputra Valley in India. Historically, the strategic heart of northern India has been the node of Delhi, lying on the divide between the Indus and the Ganges river systems, which is also the passage between the geologically oldest range of the Aravali, and the youngest range of the Himalaya.

The Himalaya is the youngest and highest mountain system in the world. It is geologically unstable and is still rising; it extends for more than 3,000 kilometers along the northern frontiers of India, Pakistan, Nepal, and Bhutan. The Himalaya actually comprises a series of mountain ranges, which, along with the Karakoram, Kun Lun, and Hindu Kush ranges, fan out from the Pamir knot just north of the subcontinent. As many as 92 peaks in the Himalaya and Karakoram are more than 7,300 meters high, and among those above 8,000 meters the three highest are Mt. Everest on the Nepal–Tibet border, K-2 in northern Kashmir, and Kanchenjunga on the India-Nepal border. The perennially snow-fed rivers watering the Indo-Gangetic plains arise in the Himalaya or the high plateau of Tibet that lies beyond. Between the various ranges are plateaus, gorges, and fertile valleys, such as those of Kulu and Kashmir, where the flora, fauna, and natural beauty excite scientists and poets alike. It is impossible to overestimate the tangible importance of the Himalaya to India or to ignore the high place it occupies in Indian mythology and culture.

According to the 2001 census, India's population was estimated at 1,027, 015, nearly three times what it was at the time of independence in 1947 and five times what it was estimated to be in the 18th century. Demographic change was dramatic in the 20th century; birth and death rates were virtually equal at more than 4% before 1920, and gradually diverged by the early 1980s to a 3.3% birth rate and a 1.2% death rate. Improved health and control of epidemics made a huge difference, which is reflected in average life expectancy estimated at 32 years in 1941 but rising to 65 years in 2004. The independent Indian government was aware early of the likely problems posed by a large population; it introduced a modest and voluntary family planning scheme in the 1950s, along with plans for economic development. However, these had little effect on birthrates. By the 1960s, it was evident that unanticipated population growth was forestalling the expected higher rates of economic growth. A brief experiment with allegedly coercive sterilization in the mid-1970s proved to be a major setback to the family planning program in the 1980s. It was made more appealing to the public and was sensibly integrated with better health care for women in the 1990s, without losing its voluntary character. Fertility and birth rates have declined significantly in some Indian states, especially those experiencing economic growth and urbanization, but remain high in the poorer and more populous states of Bihar and Uttar Pradesh. Moreover, India's immediate neighbors, Bangladesh and Nepal, have higher rates of population growth and lower rates of economic growth. Significant numbers of their citizens regularly cross the borders into India and usually remain there.

India's average population growth rate has declined from over 2% a year in the 1970s and 1980s to less than 2% in the decade 1991–2001. Demographic experts, such as Tim Dyson, project a stabilization of population growth within two decades, with a steady decrease in the proportion of children (0–14) and the elderly to people of working age, and a total of about 1.5 billion by the middle of the 21st century. The ratio of male to female is skewed and varies from state to state, but the chronic shortage of females causes concern. (See Appendix F.) The scale and patterns of demographic growth in India have had and will have major implications for every aspect of public and private life, especially in rapidly growing cities that even today lack adequate infrastructure or security. There were only five Indian cities in 1951 that had more than 1 million inhabitants; in 2001 there were 35 such cities, and three of them—Delhi, Kolkata and Mumbai—had populations of more than 10 million. Population density is high in rural areas, too, and the problems of underemployment or unemployment are acute.

Some see the promise of rapid economic growth in the expected bulge of working age population; others visualize severe sociopolitical strains unless increased employment can match that bulge. Faster deterioration of the natural environment under pressure of so many more consumers is almost inevitable. One of the most profound and least quantifiable impacts of population growth is on ways of thinking, because the favorable ratio of land to occupation that has molded traditional attitudes of mind and social customs among Indians no longer exists. India today accounts for more than 16% of the world's population inhabiting less than 2.5% of the earth's surface. Coping with this imbalance presents challenges for India as well as for the international community as a whole.

Diversity is an even more striking feature of India's population than numbers. Indeed, India's ethnic heterogeneity dates back to earliest times, as archaeological excavations reveal and as are tabulated in Sanskrit and Persian chronicles as well as in British ethnographic surveys. Diversity was reinforced by geography and history and was maintained by traditional social customs frowning on intermarriage. Notwithstanding processes of interaction and integration, especially in modern times, the multiplicity of identifiable groups in India today is unparalleled in any other single country. The Anthropological Survey of India in 1985 named 6,748 communities defined by culture, ecology, ethnicity, history, and language and made detailed studies of nearly 5,000 of them. In terms of faith, India is home to every world religion, each one with many branches and sects, as well as numerous other more localized religions. Appendix G shows the numerical breakdown of religious affiliation among Indians according to the 2001 census. There is no one Indian "race" comparable to the Han who constitute more than 90% of the Chinese people. Most Indians come from one or another branch of the Indo-Aryan or Caucasoid racial group, but there are substantial numbers, especially those listed in the Constitution as Scheduled Tribes, who belong to either Mongoloid or proto-Australoid racial groups. Social identity was traditionally derived from caste, which is not a simple construct and is not correlated with racial origin.

Language more accurately reflects both India's diversity as well as the consolidating effects of modern communication. (See Map 2.) A British survey of 1923 identified 179 languages and 544 dialects found in India; the 1981 census reported 112 "mother tongues"; the Anthropological Survey of India listed only 75 "major languages" within a total of 325 in use during the 1990s. These languages fall into four broad families: the Indo-Aryan or Indo-European group is the largest, comprising the classical languages of Sanskrit and Persian and their modern derivatives used by about 80% of the population; the Dravidian group is the next largest, comprising the classical language of Tamil and others used predominantly in south India; Tibeto–Burman languages predominate in the sparsely populated Himalayan region; and many tribal peoples use languages belonging to the Austro–Asiatic group, such as Munda.

Since language is the main instrument of cultural transmission and social identity, it has been a source of strife from time to time. The Indian Constitution (as amended) lists 18 official languages, each with its own script, for educational and public use as well as English, thus finessing the contentious issue of choosing a "national language." Adoption of a "three language formula" in 1965, whereby publicly supported schools taught the regional language, Hindi, and English, defused serious tensions between south and north. Many feared that the administrative reorganization of India in the late 1950s on the basis of linguistic states would endanger unity of the country, but economic integration and social mobility have proven to be as strong forces as regionalism, and almost all Indians are familiar with two or more languages.

The many deep divisions, vertical and horizontal, among Indian citizens bewilder those who define nation-states in 19th-century European terms of one people, one language, one God. Some deny that there is, or ever could be, a single political entity called India. But the founders of modern India and Indians today are comfortable with their multiple identities. They take pride in a national culture that not only tolerates diversity but nurtures and celebrates it.

HISTORICAL BACKGROUND

Antecedents

Traces of human activity in the form of cave paintings and stone implements found in India go back to the second interglacial period, between 400,000 and 200,000 BCE. Evidence of settled agriculture, wheel-turned pottery, and permanent settlements dating from the fourth millennium BCE has been found as well. Accidental archeological discoveries made in 1921 and subsequently dated and correlated to other discoveries reveal remains of a remarkably sophisticated and far-flung urban culture flourishing from about 2,700 to 1,500 BCE and engaged in commercial relations with contemporary Mesopotamia and Egypt. The two major cities of this period were located in the Indus Valley and were named Mohenjo-Daro and Harappa, but many other smaller related sites have been discovered well to the south and the east. Bones interred on the sites indicate the presence of more than one ethnic strain, and the artifacts recovered lead many historians to infer social and religious practices that reappeared at a later period. Though many examples of a written pictographic script were recovered, it has not been definitively deciphered as yet; debates center on whether the script is a prototype of a north Indian pre-classical language, Brahmi, a prototype of the classical Dravidian language of the south, or an early example of Munda.

As more knowledge of the Harappan civilization (see Dictionary) is garnered, the origins of Indian culture are seen to be older, more broadly based, and less dramatic than the once popular myth of an "Aryan invasion" forcefully supplanting all that came in its way. It now seems likely that cities gradually declined for ecological reasons and that migrations from Central Asia across the mountain ranges occurred during the second millennium BCE, as they were to recur later. These early migrants are known as Arya, or Aryan, from their language, which was close to that of the Avesta in Iran as well as early Greek and Latin; that is, belonging to the Indo–European group. Their literary legacy consists of four compendiums of hymns, prayers, and liturgy known as the Vedas; commentaries on them are known as the Brahmanas and Upanishads, and traditional histories or Puranas, which include two lengthy epics called the *Mahabharata* and the *Ramayana*.

An unbroken oral tradition, maintained with singular purity despite some interpolations and overlays at various times and in different places, makes this early body of scripture and literature part of the living tradition of India. Despite difficulties in dating, historians use it as source material to estimate the wanderings of a pastoral, pantheistic, tribal people through the forests and fields of the subcontinent because the archeological record for the period 1500–600 BCE is still sparse. During the Vedic and Epic periods, groups following hereditary chieftains waged wars among themselves and with others, often prevailing because their knowledge of astronomy and mathematics, their horse-drawn chariots, and their familiarity with iron ware and superior weapons gave them an advantage. But they also absorbed the knowledge and the practices of those they met. They gradually became a settled, agricultural people with consolidated territories and specialized occupations.

Interaction among peoples in the Indo-Gangetic plain as well as the peninsula produced multidimensional cultural diffusion, although some indigenous tribal groups took refuge from change in less accessible forests and hills. The civilization that had emerged in India by the time for which written, epigraphical, and archeological records are extant, namely around 600 BCE, came to be called Hindu—from the Indus or Sindhu River—or Brahmanic, from the social system it created. This was characterized by the organization of life and society around the principles of *varna-ashrama-dharma*. These terms are almost impossible to translate adequately in English but are central to an understanding of Indian culture.

Briefly, *varna* refers to color, actually class, as determined by occupation and ritual purity, and thereby to status, in a fourfold division. Highest in rank was the brahman priest or intellectual; next was the kshatriya ruler and warrior; below was the often wealthy and sometimes heterodox vaishya or merchant, skilled artisan, or cattle breeder; lower still was the sudra cultivator and laborer. The composition and functions of the four *varnas* were more fluid in practice than in written theory. In later times, proliferating *jati* (kinship groups), or endogamous and occupation-specific castes with varying social rank, were somehow fitted into the categories of the four stable classes, especially those of kshatriya and vaishya. This practice facilitated the accommodation of many pre-existing and new groups—often endogamous and occupation-specific as well—into an increasingly sophisticated and complex system. But many groups regarded as outcaste, polluting, and therefore "untouchable," were excluded in that process, thereby creating a major moral and social problem that has troubled all Indian reformers in historical times.

Ashrama refers to stage of life. The model for the individual man idealized in Hindu classics was a progression from the stage of celibate student to that of responsible householder, to retirement and relinquishment of worldly attachments in late middle age, to a final stage of renunciation, asceticism, and preparation for spiritual emancipation. *Dharma* means a general norm of conduct or righteousness derived from divine will or natural law applicable to all. But *dharma* was also regarded as being specific to the individual, whose appropriate rights, duties, and obligations were determined by gender, station, and stage of life. Hindu classical literature and mythology extol social stability and harmony by equating the "golden age" with maintenance of the *varna–ashrama–dharma*. In Hindu cosmogony, confusion, strife, cruelty, and disharmony characterize the *Kali-yuga,* or final aeon before dissolution of the universe. This *Kali-yuga* is said to have commenced at the time of the *Mahabharata* war recounted in the epics and manifestly continues today.

Early Empires and New Religions

By the sixth century BCE, 16 kingdoms and tribal republics had come into being in northern India, and these kingdoms jostled for more territory, larger revenues, and higher status. Forests had given way to plowed fields. Many towns were centers of commerce, industry, luxurious living, and intellectual vivacity. Rulers were usually confirmed in their titles—gained by conquest no less than by birth—through elaborate Vedic rituals and sacrifices mediated by brahman priests. The *Ashvamedha* or horse sacrifice, in particular, spectacularly legitimized conquests and established dependencies for rulers of distinction. Brahman and kshatriya worked as partners, although there were also non-kshatriya (even sudra) ruling dynasties, and found ways of increasing their appropriation of revenue, sometimes by greater efficiency of administration. Intellectual and social ferment in that period produced two major reform movements led, respectively, by Mahavira (the Great Hero) and Siddharatha Gautama (better known as the Buddha). Both men were well rooted in Hindu philosophic soil and retained belief in a cycle of life and death caused by karma, or spiritual merit and demerit, from which the individual being sought liberation. Both were opposed to the dominating hold of *varna*, to the proliferation of rituals, and to animal sacrifice. Each offered the common man paths to spiritual liberation based on an ethical life embodying ahimsa or non-violence rather than on Brahmanic prescriptions. From their heterodox teachings grew two great religions— Jainism and Buddhism.

Jain and Buddhist texts illuminate the political and economic scene in India in the sixth, fifth, and fourth centuries BCE, as do Greek and Persian accounts of that period. Links between Indic, Greek, and Persian cultures were strengthened by Alexander the Great of Macedon, who raided northwestern India in 326 BCE, and by the establishment of Hellenistic kingdoms in Bactria and Sogdiana. Coins and sculpture, philosophy, mathematics, and art all testify to the fruitfulness of those links, epitomized in Gandhara art and in the history of the Silk Road.

Meanwhile, the kingdom of Magadha, situated in the middle Ganges region, expanded into a vast empire covering three quarters of India—from present-day Kashmir to Mysore, from Afghanistan to Bangladesh—through the military skill and administrative acumen of successive emperors of the Maurya Dynasty. The efficient and all-encompassing Mauryan State was to become a model for future empires, but it had, itself, disintegrated by about 200 BCE.

Among the many kingdoms and dynasties that rose and fell between 200 BCE and 300 CE, several are particularly noteworthy. Among them were the Kushan-controlled sectors of the Silk Road that was the artery of lucrative trade between the Indian, Persian, Chinese, and Roman Empires as well as the highway for the outward spread of Buddhism. The Chola, Chera, and Pandya Dynasties established themselves in the southern part of the peninsula, and their kingdoms evolved a blend of Brahmanic and Dravidian practices that were discernibly different from those of the Indo-Gangetic plain. For example, matrilineal property rights were institutionalized in the southwest; the sudra were much more numerous, economically important, and theoretically classified than in the north; and caste ranking for *jatis* was not the same. Administrative and economic decentralization was more commonplace in the south than in the north, perhaps because agriculture depended on locally controlled small-scale tank irrigation, or because of topography or the effects of steady maritime activity. A great flowering of art and Tamil literature took place during these centuries, referred to as the Sangam period.

The Classical Age

Historians call the period 300–700 CE the classical age of Hindu or Brahmanic civilization. The Gupta Dynasty rose in Magadha and expanded its sway over the Indo-Gangetic plain, Kashmir, and the Deccan. Archaeological excavations and contemporary literature, as well as travelers' accounts, especially by Chinese Buddhist pilgrims, testify to the peace and prosperity of the population as a whole, the smoothness of administration, the rarity of serious crime, and the humanity of the judicial code during this period.

Sanskrit literature throws light on newly emerging social practices. Class differences were becoming more pronounced, expressed not only in varying behavior and speech patterns but in actual language: Sanskrit for educated males and Prakrit for others; Prakrit became the root of modern languages in northern India. Guilds of different kinds of craftsmen and merchants were well organized and powerful, providing supportive networks for members who traveled as well as disciplinary checks on those who strayed. The joint family was considered the unit of society. Typically, it had several generations of fathers and sons (and their wives) living in one household under the authority of the eldest male, with immovable property passing to all the sons equally. Women of the classical age were less free by law and custom than they had been in early Vedic times. However, alternate modes of life were available; a classic text of mutual sexual pleasure and fulfillment, the *Kamasutra,* dates from this period; "renouncers" and ascetics were beyond social convention.

In northern India the political ascendancy of the Guptas was shattered by a series of Huna invasions from Central Asia in the fifth and sixth centuries, to be revived briefly by Harsha-Vardhana of Kanauj in the seventh century. But the various kingdoms that emerged from the breakup of empire sustained earlier established patterns of social practice, culture, and administration. Recent scholarship has illuminated these developments so that the later-Gupta and post-Gupta periods are no longer regarded as the "dark ages." Different schools of philosophy flourished, with the non-dualism of Vedanta reaching a majestic maturation in the teachings of Sankara. Moreover, connecting links between north and south were strengthened, and progress and prosperity reached new heights throughout peninsular India, as is evident in the architectural monuments of the period. Maritime commercial relations took the influence of Indian languages, religions, and art to Southeast Asia, as is still evident in present-day Burma, Thailand, Cambodia, Malaysia, and Indonesia.

The Coming of Islam and the Mughal Era

Well before the end of the first millennium an all-India cultural synthesis, especially among the elites, had come to underlie political fragmentation. The coming of Islam to India introduced radically different elements into the existing mixture with varying results visible in succeeding centuries.

Islam is a revealed religion propagated by the Prophet Muhammad in early-seventh-century Arabia. The teachings of Muhammad were first spread in India by Muslim holy men who, in turn, transmitted elements of Vedanta into the mystic, or Sufi, tradition of Islam. Islam gave the Arab tribes unity and zeal in a burst of commercial and military expansion in the seventh and eighth centuries, which reached Sindh but had only a slight effect on the rest of India through Arab traders on the west coast. The political-military thrust of Islam in India came from the nomadic, Turkic peoples of Central Asia who had been newly converted to Islam and were adapting to Persian culture. Eager for gold, Sultan Mahmud (979–1030) of Ghazni (Afghanistan) launched a series of devastating attacks on the richest and holiest of north Indian temples, such as Somnath. These raids form the basis of folk memories reconstructed in 20th-century Hindu nationalist histories as a continuous chronicle of "predatory" Muslims committing atrocities against Hindu temples and Hindu women. Ghazni established a foothold in the Punjab, and 200 years later the followers of Muhammed Ghori established the Delhi Sultanate. Successive Turko-Afghan dynasties based in Delhi battled other contenders for power in northern India and the Deccan, until they were eclipsed by the Mughals in the sixteenth century.

Twentieth-century historians often look back on this turbulent period in the light of events in our own time and see the roots of some negative trends today in the features of early medieval Indian polity, economy, and society. In particular, they note the following: the Hindu ruling classes lacked comprehension of the outside world and were complacent to a fault; they failed to perceive the strategic significance of expanding Islam or the military superiority of new tactics and weapons used by the Turks, with disastrous consequences to their own power. Hindu society, for the most part, reacted to the iconoclastic depredations of the invaders by increasing conservatism of religious practices and decreasing social capacity to assimilate new groups, proclaimed as "unclean" and ineligible for marriage or even inter-dining. Nor were these newest arrivals—unlike their predecessors—willing to be assimilated into Hindu society, which their divines or *Ulema* denounced as idolatrous and infidel, although they made India their home in a way that later Europeans never did. Ideologues in the cities pronounced the contrariety of Hindu and Muslim beliefs, and while practices in the countryside bridged gulfs, the peasantry of any faith was powerless at the time. The invaders were few and maintained a large army, for which they extracted as much tax as possible from merchants and agriculturalists, often with ruinous results. The brutal realities of constant warfare and ruthless methods of tax extortion created a gulf in India between Turko-Afghan military rulers and their predominantly Hindu subjects. Conversions to Islam sometimes were made by force; some caste or kinship groups converted for economic or social reasons but retained their identities; perhaps most conversion took place through the popular appeal of Sufi saints. None of these were mass conversions as had occurred elsewhere in the Islamic world; a 1976 study based on historical evidence of the 17th century estimated the number of Muslims in India at no more than 10% of the population in 1600, nearly 400 years after establishment of the Delhi Sultanate.

Not all features of the period were malignant. For 200 years the new Muslim rulers of Delhi guarded the northwestern marches and staved off Mongol attacks from Central Asia, which had such devastating effects on China, Persia, Russia, and Eastern Europe at this time. Though there was no single Indian political entity and the subcontinent formed a checkerboard of kingdoms, they came to resemble each other in their military, administrative, technological, and financial structures and practices. Moreover, their fluctuating alliances and conflicts were shaped by many factors, only one of which (and not necessarily dominant) was the religious identity of the ruler. Within most of these kingdoms there was a resurgence of international trade and urban culture; mobility of artisans, literati, merchants, peasants, pilgrims, soldiers, and workers was high, and frontiers were fluid. Distinctive styles of art and artifacts, courtesy and cuisine, and language and music evolved in these centuries and often were syncretic. Most importantly, reformists of religious belief and social practices appeared in different parts of the country from the eighth to the fifteenth century and exerted enormous appeal at the popular level; their efforts are collectively known as the Bhakti movement. All this reflected the creative interaction of Hindu and Muslim cultures in a rich synthesis comprising both conflict and cooperation, which reached an acme during the Mughal era.

The Mughal Empire was established by Babur in 1526 and formally brought to an end by the British in 1857. It is often compared to the contemporaneous Safavid Empire in Iran, the Ottoman Empire in Turkey, and the Qing Empire in China because of similarities in the vastness of their territories, the detail of their administrative and other records, their great levels of wealth, trade, production, and technologies, and their inner weaknesses that led ultimately to European domination in one form or another.

Each of the first six Mughal rulers—the "Great Mughals" Babur, Humayun, Akbar, Jehangir, Shah Jahan, and Aurangzeb—is renowned in history for different contributions to the expansion, consolidation, and embellishment of the empire. At its height under Akbar and Shah Jahan, the Mughal Empire—in which the (Hindu) Rajput princes were honored partners—included much of present-day Afghanistan and all of the Indian subcontinent except for its southern tip and northeastern corner. Before Aurangzeb fell prey to Islamic fanaticism, the Mughals generally practiced religious tolerance and social pluralism. European travelers of the time described the wealth and splendors of Mughal India—some of which, such as the Taj Mahal, remain visible today despite repeated depredations—and their accounts lured more adventurers and fortune hunters to India.

But the glitter could not entirely conceal the weaknesses of the Mughal Empire. It, too, relied on a large army and an administrative system that was constructed around military commanders, or *mansabdars*, who were given rights to collect taxes (but not ownership) over areas that became fiefdoms. Many *mansabdars* lacked long-term stakes in the land and became extortionate, so that cultivation suffered, peasants departed, village handicrafts began to collapse, and famines became endemic. Insurrections, such as that of the Marathas led by Shivaji, increased in frequency and ferocity; the power of the emperor declined at the center; large fiefdoms became virtually independent. Even though India remained at the hub of thriving maritime commerce it did not develop a capitalist class, and the eyes of Mughal rulers did not turn seaward; shipbuilding declined and there was no imperial navy. Simultaneously, Europeans were gaining control over all sea-borne trade worldwide and were establishing their presence in port cities and principalities on the Indian Ocean littoral.

The 18th century saw a de facto disintegration of the empire under the nominal sovereignty of the Mughal enthroned in Delhi. While commercial activity continued apace and many towns demonstrated a remarkable talent for self-regulation and the provision of essential services, new political entities contended for power in the twilight of the

Mughal Empire. The Marathas expanded far beyond their Deccan base and warred against independent Hyderabad and Mysore as well as against Mughal viceroys in Bengal; the Marathas became the protectors, not the vassals, of the emperor in Delhi. The Afghans reasserted themselves in the northwest and prevailed against the Marathas at Panipat, near Delhi, in 1761. In the Punjab a new group of warrior saints—the Sikh Khalsa—established dominion over a large area controlling the Indus and the northwest. In the 17th century, European trading posts became part of the local scene in major ports, gradually enlarging their functions beyond the collection and transshipment of Indian goods to building fortifications and providing mercenaries, drill masters, and artillery to contending Indian princes as the Mughal Empire disintegrated. The English East India Company proved to be the most effective in protecting its establishments, lining its coffers, winning local military-political sweepstakes—often in competition with the French—and acquiring political and territorial rights of its own from the Mughal figurehead. He, too, became a pensioner of the East India Company, whose forces finally defeated the Marathas in 1818.

Company Rule and the British Raj

British rule in India is commonly held to have begun with the decisive Battle of Plassey in 1757 that gave the East India Company control of Bengal. Expansion, mainly by military means, continued through succeeding decades with a blurring of distinction between commercial, administrative, and military tasks and increasing supervision from London. It was in these first one hundred years that Britain extended its military might in India the most, indulged in economic rapacity that extended into China through the opium trade, and had profound cultural impacts on Indians through deliberate efforts to "civilize" them by English law and language. One unintended result was the Great Uprising or Mutiny of 1857–1858 that replaced Company administration with the direct rule of the British Crown. The opulent splendor of the British Raj, so evident in the late 19th and early 20th centuries, is fully documented, and representations of it continue to appeal to popular imagination in many parts of the world. Perhaps ironically, establishment of a seemingly permanent empire was accompanied by the birth and growth of an Indian national movement that ultimately replaced the British Raj.

British territorial expansion reached inward from the seaports of Madras, Calcutta, and Bombay in waves that successively engulfed southern India, the lower Ganges valley, central and northeastern India, western India, the lower Indus and upper Ganges valleys, and finally the Punjab. This was a reversal of historical patterns of northwest-to-southeast spread of empire on the subcontinent. British methods of expansion also enlarged on traditional ones of military conquest or slow diffusion. These methods included indirect penetration as traders and revenue collectors on behalf of the Mughal Emperor and the signing of unequal or "subsidiary" treaties with Indian princes who accepted ceremony and protection against internal revolt in exchange for tribute, territory, and subordination to the British paramount power.

British motivations for expansion were often debated between Company directors and members of Parliament, generating an impressive body of discursive and analytic literature on the nature of imperialism itself. Three sets of motivation stand out: economic gain, cultural mission, and considerations of military-political security. The latter included perceptions of threat not only from various Indian powers but also from Burma and Nepal, from France, from Tsarist Russia, and from the Kaiser's Germany. These threat perceptions spurred the British to establish direct or indirect control over land and sea routes to India as well as the strategic outposts of the subcontinent where the "Great Game" was played. The British Indian Army was constantly engaged along the northwest frontier. The Royal Navy, combined with money and men from India, helped maintain the Pax Britannica throughout the Indian Ocean and beyond.

In the economic and cultural domains, initial British thrust was encouraged—and sometimes invited—by particular Indian groups, which anticipated improvements for themselves thereby. For example, the expectation, extension, and diversification of trade which drove the East India Company was matched by the eagerness of certain Indian groups, especially Hindu bankers and merchants, to enlarge their own profits and areas of activity through the linkages of town and country, subcontinent and world, provided by the Company. A sense of cultural mission inspired British utilitarians to attempt social engineering in India based on ideas of the European Enlightenment in the early 19th century. They found some Indians eager to spread the English language, codify Indian law in the light of British legal principles, and thereby reform oppressive Indian socio-religious customs with British help.

There were negative aspects to Company rule as well. The rapacity and greed of Company servants in the late 18th century and the damaging effects on agriculture of the Bengal permanent revenue settlement became legendary even in British accounts of the period. As Britain became the industrial heart of the world, Indian craftsmen lost their employment and their markets, and India's relatively self-sufficient economy was reduced to a raw materials producing famine-prone dependency. The first cross-cultural contacts had stimulated Europeans to pursue profound scholarship in Indian civilization and had given birth to an Orientalist movement in European arts, letters, and philosophy. In contrast, the Victorian age was marked by a self-satisfied belief in the superiority and "civilizing mission" of Englishmen, a denigration of Indian culture and literature, and the rationalization of aggressiveness by a theme of "carrying the White Man's Burden."

Outright annexation of territory was one cause of the uprisings of 1857 that marked a watershed in British Indian history. Once these uprisings were quelled, the Mughal Empire was formally terminated and the last emperor, Bahadur Shah, was banished to Burma. As the historian David Ludden demonstrated, modern sedentary territorialism became an accepted norm, and the mobility of peoples typical of earlier centuries was frowned upon as deviant. Indeed, as the decennial census was institutionalized, many nomadic, itinerant, or vagrant groups were listed as "criminal castes and tribes." Political boundaries within India were frozen, leaving intact (but dependent) some 562 Princely States of varying size and status interspersed among the provinces of British India, which now comprised three-fifths of the Indian subcontinent (see Map 7). In 1877, Queen Victoria was proclaimed Empress of India.

At the apex of government in India stood the viceroy or governor general, answerable only to the British cabinet in London, but assisted by an Executive and Legislative Council in India. Provinces were headed by governors and divided into districts, the basic units for administration and revenue collection. The district officer was the powerful, paternal, lynchpin of the system. The reports written by these district officers remain important sources of knowledge today. The district officer's efficiency and impartiality often is cited as a role model for his present-day successors. District officers usually were drawn from the prestigious Indian Civil Service (ICS), which held the entire edifice together, set a high standard of personal integrity and dedicated service, attracted the best products of British schools and universities, and manned the higher ranks of the British-Indian government. Only reluctantly, and narrowly, did the ICS open its doors to Indians.

The uprisings of 1857–1858 built a wall of racial distrust between the white-skinned rulers and their darker-skinned subjects, which was embodied in a physical separation of European residences and social life from those who were now disparagingly labeled "natives." Racial criteria were also used in a dramatic overhaul of the British Indian Army to exclude Indian officers and accelerate recruitment of troops from the specific ethnic groups that had assisted the British in 1857 and came to be dubbed "martial races." Race relations form the subject of many literary works from and about the Raj. Race relations also proved a potent fillip to political nationalism. Denied social equality, educated Indians soon demanded political equality.

Although the British Raj after 1858 was socially, politically, and economically conservative, it became the instrument of profound change in India in all three areas. For example, many of the customary caste restrictions and social practices among Hindus were eroded in the face of a unified legal system, an easy means of rail and road communication throughout the country, and the necessity of study in England for entry to the ICS or success in the higher professions. Indians seeking upward mobility, both Hindu and Muslim, were prepared to modify their behavior without abandoning their cultural traditions or religious beliefs and sought creative synthesis. The impact of Christian missionaries was strong, if double-edged. They stimulated reform through the schools and hospitals they operated as much as from their individual examples of ethical living. On the other hand, their proselytizing zeal provoked reactions among Hindus, Muslims, and Sikhs, especially in northern India, and led directly to the reification of these religions as well as to their 20th century political assertiveness in a phenomenon known as "communalism."

Economic policies of the Raj produced great change, both positive and negative. New lands were brought under cultivation through canal irrigation, and new employment at all but the highest levels was opened up for Indians in government services, coal mines, plantations, public works departments, professions, and in many other parts of the British Empire. Thus, many Indians benefited from the Raj and were loyal to it, not least because it provided stability, law, and order. But the transfer of resources from Indian to British hands was substantial and gave rise to the "drain of wealth" theory held by nationalists. Pauperization was greater and more evident than before, and economic discontent was widespread among peasants, the landless, and tribal groups. Rebellions, riots, and no-rent movements, were, however, localized and were swiftly suppressed by official force or intimidation. In the early 20th century, British power in India appeared to be unchallenged. Two world wars that sapped British power and the emergence of a mass-based national movement in India finally destroyed that illusion of permanence.

From Empire to Independence

Britain's contributions to India undoubtedly include the maintenance of external and internal peace and stability for the most part, and the construction of administrative machinery as well as networks of communications that tangibly unified India. Greater contributions, readily admitted by Indians today, flowed from Britain's introduction of ideas, institutions, and language conducive to the evolution of a liberal democracy in an independent modern state. Three separate processes were interlinked in the unsteady and far from smooth passage from the British Empire in India to the sovereign independent Republic of India and are briefly noted.

One process unfolded within Britain itself as the Liberal, Conservative, and (later) Labour Parties debated the most suitable forms of government in changing socioeconomic circumstances and so generated concepts of "good government," institutions of "representative government," and "democracy" first within Britain and then echoed in dependencies such as India. Another process was set in motion in India by the specific institutions, laws, and declarations made by the British in order to ease their task of ruling India by associating more Indians with it. Major landmarks were the creation of elective municipal councils in the late 19th century, the reforms of 1909 and 1919, and the Government of India Act of 1935, each of which furthered representative, partially democratic institutions, though more slowly and less completely than many Indians wished, along with crippling caveats of communal electorates and reserved powers. The varied reactions of politically conscious Indians to these two separate developments constitute a third process, the Indian national movement.

A broad account of the Indian national movement, for most practical purposes, is a history of the Indian National Congress, though the contributions of many individuals and groups that did not belong to it should not be underestimated. The Indian National Congress was founded in December 1885 and grew in stages from a relatively small association of urban, middle-class, Western-educated men to become the preeminent vehicle of organized nationalist sentiment on an all-India, multi-class scale.

For the first two decades of its history, Congress was led by those who trusted British promises, were pacific in their language as they strove to educate Indian and British public opinion, and were moderate in their petitions for Britain to lighten the financial burdens of administration and defense and to associate more Indians with them. A different stream of revolutionary rejection of British rule, sometimes accompanied by violence, was provoked by Lord Curzon's decision to partition Bengal in 1905. All-India movements for *swadeshi* and *swaraj* were born and were soon taken up by "extremist" Congress leaders such as Bal Gangadhar Tilak; his passionate cry: "Swaraj is my birthright and I will have it," reverberated across the subcontinent long after he had been arrested and exiled in 1908.

A Liberal Government in Britain passed the Indian Councils Act of 1909, which introduced the qualified elective principle to the selection of nonofficial members of legislative councils but simultaneously gave separate electorates to Muslims. In 1911, King George V and Queen Mary visited India, held formal audience in a *durbar*, and announced reversal of the partition of Bengal as well as transfer of the capital from Calcutta to Delhi—strategic heart of India.

World War I began with a remarkable outpouring of loyalty, financial contribution, and manpower from India to defend the British Empire against the Kaiser's Germany. But disillusionment came to many with the squalid conditions of a brutal European war squandering lives, along with influenza, high taxes, rising prices, and disrupted trade in India. Revolutionary and anti-British activity by Indians were further stimulated by the Bolshevik Revolution in Russia. In India, the constitutional reforms of 1919 fell far short of expectations raised by Britain's

1917 promise of "responsible government" and were implemented only in 1921. By then, repressive legislation of the immediate postwar years and the massacre at Jallianwallah Bagh, Amritsar, had sparked mass opposition to British rule among all communities.

Congress leadership at this time passed into the hands of Mohandas Karamchand Gandhi (known as the Mahatma or "great soul"), who transformed it into a disciplined mass organization infused with a moral commitment that went beyond mere political independence for India to social uplift and courageous self-reliance in every sense of the term. Gandhi forged an instrument called Satyagraha, defining it as "the force which is born of truth and love and nonviolence." He launched the first nationwide Satyagraha campaign in 1919 to protest repressive laws. He led other civil disobedience and non-cooperation movements over the next 25 years, with varying degrees of success in tangible terms but with an incalculable moral effect in building courage, discipline, and solidarity among his followers. They may not always have agreed with him, but they accepted his powerful influence until the early 1940s; thereafter, the men squabbling over the nuts and bolts of transferring power and partitioning India largely ignored Gandhi.

During the 1920s and 1930s, more Indians became politicized. They were not unified in their objectives or in the methods used to advance them in the short term, although many of them envisaged independence from Britain. Some Indians gladly participated in the institutions created by the 1921 and 1935 constitutional reforms; others shunned them in "non-cooperation." Many joined governmental and armed services as they opened to Indians, and they later became the professionals of independent India. The Communist Party of India was formed in 1925 with a revolutionary credo but weak organization. As the All-India Muslim League founded in 1906 and claiming to speak for all Muslims appeared to receive official favor, other communities also demanded separate electorates and special attention. The All-India Hindu Mahasabha was established in 1906 and became very active after formation of the Rashtriya Swayamsewak Sangh (RSS) in 1925. Both were militant and socially revivalist organizations composed of mainly high caste Hindus working for realization of a Hindu nation, but the organizations were deemed politically "moderate" by the British. At the same time, a powerful anti-brahman movement in south India found political expression in the Justice Party.

The Indian National Congress expanded its activities in rural areas and to a lesser extent in some of the Princely States; it engaged in constructive community work and created an organizational structure parallel to that of the government. As an umbrella organization, Congress evolved a pluralistic ethos and was multi-religious, multi-linguistic, and pan-Indian in composition. Congress claimed to represent all of India and all shades of opinion in opposition to imperialism. Though Britain and some Indians did not accept that claim, the cause of Indian independence was brought to international attention through the figure of Gandhi, leader of Congress.

Britain and its allies used India as a base of supply and operations during World War II. The Army was expanded to more than two million, the navy and air force were modernized, and Indian officers were commissioned in all three services; Indian industry was encouraged to expand although there were strict controls on the economy. Congress, however, was not prepared to cooperate in the war effort only on the basis of deferred promises, demanding instead the formation of a "national government" during the war and Indian freedom after it. The British countered with a proposal for postwar dominion status, an invitation to join the existing council of the viceroy, and a refusal to yield on any issue of substance or prestige. Congress governments in the provinces resigned, and a nationwide civil disobedience campaign was launched—the "Quit India" movement. This "Quit India Movement" of 1942 was the most serious rebellion against British rule since 1857.

Meanwhile, Mohammed Ali Jinnah reorganized the Muslim League into a mass movement with Islamist ideology, courted support in the Punjab and Bengal, cooperated with the British throughout the war, and propagated the idea that Muslims be considered a distinct "nation" in India. The League resolved in 1940 that Muslim majority areas should be grouped to constitute separate autonomous provinces; confederation was envisaged but partition was predicted. This Pakistan issue, introduced by the League and opposed by Congress, came to dominate negotiations on the transfer of power in India throughout the 1940s, with the British treating the League on a par with Congress. Attempts made by Sir Stafford Cripps in 1942 and the Cabinet Mission of 1946 to reconcile three different positions failed, as did gestures by League and Congress leaders to work together in an interim government in 1946. The British Labour Government of 1945 decided to grant Indian independence sooner rather than later and to partition the country if necessary; Lord Louis Mountbatten was appointed viceroy in 1947 with instructions to implement these decisions speedily. The Dominion of India was inaugurated on August 15, 1947, amidst the violent tragedy of partition.

Independent India

The new government of India, headed by Prime Minister Jawaharlal Nehru, faced three immediate tasks: to formulate a new democratic constitution; to stem the tide of communal violence and ease the plight of some six million refugees; and to complete negotiations with Princely States on their accession to India. All three were addressed within three years with very substantial success, although marred by the assassination of Mahatma Gandhi by a Hindu fanatic in January 1948 and by Pakistan's military attack on Kashmir and its refusal to accept as legal the accession of the Princely State of Jammu and Kashmir to India in October 1947. The immediately ensuing conflict and subsequent ones were symptomatic of a hostility between Pakistan and India that created chronic insecurity in India's external environment—insecurity that was further deepened by the international politics of the Cold War, during which the United States embraced Pakistan as a military ally and the Soviet Union courted India with assistance in heavy industry and defense materials.

The detailed Constitution adopted by the Republic of India in January 1950 combines the idealism of the national movement in its provisions for justiciable fundamental rights and the emphasis on social reform and social welfare with practical concerns for national unity, public order, and coherent administration. The framers of the Constitution drew on the Government of India Act of 1935 and also borrowed from other constitutions such as the United States constitution. In its Objectives Resolution of December 1946, the framers explicitly revived commitments by the Congress to secure for all the people of India justice, equality, and freedom, with adequate safeguards for minorities and depressed classes. Three strands were woven through the Constitution: protecting national unity and integrity, establishing the institutions and spirit of democracy based on universal adult suffrage, and fostering a social revolution to improve conditions for the masses. Each strand was inextricably intertwined with and dependent on the others. Although the Constitution has been amended many times under the pressure of changing needs and battles over how the country should live up to its ideals, its basic character remains intact. An independent Supreme Court protects it.

The 1950s were dominated by the figure of Nehru, whose passionate commitment to parliamentary democracy, modernization, peace, pluralism or secularism, inculcating a scientific spirit, and building social equity molded the institutional infrastructure laid in that decade. Defense expenditures were kept to a minimum. Impressive public investments were made in agriculture, communications, education, health, industry, irrigation, transport, and technology through Five Year Plans intended to create a "self-reliant" "mixed economy" and a non-ideological "socialistic pattern of society." Moderate measures of land reform and social reform were introduced through legislation and consensus, not coercion. Minority communities, low-caste groups, and women were given some relief from abuse and the hope of wider horizons in the future. Nevertheless, implementation of land reforms varied widely from state to state, as is evident in present day disparities between Bihar, which did not enact them and Haryana or Punjab, which did. Provisions of the Hindu Code Bill ameliorating the status and rights of women were fiercely contested, and no similar reforms of Muslim personal law were attempted then, or subsequently. Economic and political demands by low-caste and other marginal groups were somewhat muted in the first decades after independence but became strident in the last decades of the 20th century.

Political strains—and there were many—during the years of Nehru's dominance were mostly resolved within the umbrella-like "Congress system" of intra-party accommodation and compromise facilitated by having Congress governments in states as well as at the center and having political leaders who had worked together and were accustomed to compromise. Vallabhbhai Patel, before his death in December 1950, had secured the accession of the Princely States to the Indian Union and the full cooperation of the civil services. Administration was generally clean, tried to be compassionate, and attracted the best and brightest of educated Indians. Nehru enunciated a foreign policy of nonalignment in the Cold War, actively promoted Asian and African solidarity, decolonization, nuclear disarmament, and peace through the United Nations; India's prestige exceeded its tangible power.

Economic underdevelopment and the poverty of its people were the main constraints on India's power. India adopted a developmental strategy to accelerate the economic growth rate—so as to provide both employment and revenue that would help alleviate poverty—through a planning framework and enhanced public investment. India inherited low agricultural output, high inflation, and strict government controls from the war, and also some industry and an active entrepreneurial class of nationalist businessmen who drafted the Bombay Plan of industrialization with government assistance in 1948. The First Five-Year Plan (1951–1956) emphasized agriculture, development with stability, and infrastructural investment. It was an indicative plan without strict controls or targeted allocations with respect to new industries. The First Five-Year Plan was reasonably successful and generated considerable optimism and inducements to invest within India as well as abroad.

The Second Five-Year Plan (1957–1962) was based on a compromise Industrial Policy Resolution of 1956 that envisaged a mixed economy. The Plan assigned important roles to the private sector and to private foreign capital, subject to state regulation. Included were the development of village and cottage industries, and an expanded scope for the public sector, especially at the "commanding heights" of basic, defense, and heavy industries. The Plan adopted what economist Jagdish Bhagwati termed "a radical 'pull-up' strategy" of poverty eradication that differed from the "trickle down" approach, leading to a vaguely defined "socialistic pattern of society." There was no ideological or coercive attempt to redistribute wealth or to impose social equality as had been the case in revolutionary China. Neither was there a significant constituency for free market enterprise among the vocal and influential sections of the Indian middle class—academics, civil servants, economists, and political leaders. As I. G. Patel has shown, their attitudes toward capitalism and direct foreign investment were ambivalent, or suspicious, and they looked on government direction as benignly paternal. Indian industrialists and business houses, although fiercely acquisitive and competitive in behavior, were willing to accept special provisions for small-scale and village industries as well as various controls on their own expansion in return for almost complete protection against foreign competition and generous financial assistance from the state. Indian industry preferred to produce import substitutes for a growing domestic market and a wide variety but small quantity of exports rather than engage in international competition. This remained true until very recently.

A balance of payments crisis in 1958 and a food grain crisis in the mid-1960s precipitated exchange controls, an increasing dependence on foreign aid for capital-intensive industrial development, and the failure to implement either the third or fourth five-year plans. More controls were introduced over the years, in an ad hoc fashion, to limit the concentration of economic power in private hands. Many concessions were offered to attract industry to backward areas or to satisfy the demands of special interest groups and the populist "*garibi hatao*" (remove poverty) rhetoric of Prime Minister Indira Gandhi and other political leaders. The result has been aptly termed a "license-permit-quota-subsidy raj" stifling market forces and healthy economic growth. Journalist Prem Shankar Jha described the 1960s and 1970s in terms of a "political economy of stagnation" based on a nexus among corrupt politicians, corrupt bureaucrats, and corrupt business houses. The underground or "black" economy flourished. The absence of competition diluted efficiency and eroded the work ethic in both the public and private sectors. Inattention to the infrastructure, especially in terms of electric power, transportation, and health and education of the work force, reduced returns on investment and made India an unattractive destination for foreign or domestic capital. India ignored the example of certain East Asian states that invested in agriculture, foreign trade, foreign investment, literacy, and technology. These countries turned outward and came to be known as the Asian Tigers, while inward turned India looked like a crippled giant limping along at a 3.5% "Hindu rate of growth."

Some liberalization was effected during the 1980s with immediate results in an acceleration of average rates of economic growth to 5%. But foreign capital was no longer available on concessionary terms, and borrowing from foreign commercial banks brought on a financial crisis of near bankruptcy in 1990–1991 that New Delhi's prudent fiscal and monetary policies had hitherto averted. That crisis, however, enabled Narasimha Rao's Congress government to introduce economic reforms the need for which had been recognized for some time. Reformers had to hasten slowly, however, partly because the chasm was too wide to be crossed in one leap, and partly because during the 1990s different political parties came to power in varying combinations at the Union level as well as in states with no power or authority to carry out large-scale reform. More importantly, tangible and visible benefits were necessary in order to build popular support for liberalization to counter vested interests against it. Appendix I summarizes the economic reforms introduced between 1991 and 2004. The rate of economic growth rose to averages of 6% or 8%, and exports, services, manufacturing, and industry grew at rates testifying to the efficacy of liberalization. The proportion of the population living at or below the poverty line fell from about one third to about one fourth. Literacy drives showed results, as did the establishment of telecommunication links throughout the country. The optimism of the present generation of Indians stands in contrast to the pessimism of the previous one.

Not all Indian states or sections of society benefited equally from market reforms. The urban middle classes appear to be thriving, whereas peasants in some parts of the country are taking to banditry or committing suicide because they face acute deprivation. There are glaring disparities between the economically dynamic states in western and southern India that bear comparison with the Asian Tigers, and the huge Gangetic states of Bihar and Uttar Pradesh that are pulling down national statistics. In this respect, India's experience with the varying impacts of globalization is not unique. Differences of opinion are expressed on almost every aspect of India's economic development since independence, notably on the role of the state; but the release of creative energies among the Indian people is undeniable, as are the greatly enlarged opportunities and skills that exist as rewards for that creativity.

Politics has had a direct impact on Indian economic policies and performance, as on every other aspect of life in India. And to a large extent politics is the story of political parties. (See Appendix H) As already mentioned, the Congress Party inherited the ethos and organizational capacity of the Indian National Congress so that a system of one-party dominance within multiparty competition prevailed into the 1960s. That decade encompassed the deaths of two prime ministers, two wars, and three years of drought. The 1967 general elections showed a sharp drop in support for Congress, which was perceived as complacent and corrupt, both in important states and in Parliament.

Despite winning impressive electoral victories in 1971, 1979, 1984, and 1991, Congress's strength continued to decline for many reasons. Indira Gandhi was Congress leader from 1966 to her assassination in 1984, but she caused a split in the party twice in that period. Her personalized and centralized style of leadership weakened intra-party democracy and precluded the emergence of a second rung of party leaders with independent bases of political support. Her strong identification of herself with India and the choice of her son, Rajiv, to succeed her as party leader and prime minister, moreover, created an image of the Congress as a fiefdom of the Nehru-Gandhi dynasty that remained unchallenged during the tenure of P. V. Narasimha Rao as prime minister (1991–1996) and by the appointment of Dr. Manmohan Singh to that position in 2004.

Much of the political strength of Congress derived from its strong ethos of pluralism, or secularism, and the inclusion of all communities and classes in its organization and mass base. When Congress itself tried to play communal politics by building "vote banks"—as it allegedly did among Muslims and Scheduled Castes—or undermining an opposition party by supporting an extremist religious faction—as against the Akali Party in the Punjab during the late 1970s—it lost the moral high ground, compromised its ideology and therefore its appeal, and also created serious national security problems on occasion, as in 1984. At present, efforts to revitalize Congress are still being made.

Other political parties of different hues drew voters away from Congress in the late 20th century. Some built their appeal on regional or ethnic solidarity, or on "sons of the soil" sentiments, and concentrated their efforts on just one or less than four states. Their strength in large states such as Andhra Pradesh, Assam, Maharashtra, and Tamil Nadu ensured their inclusion in coalition governments formed in New Delhi and thus bolstered the federal character of the Indian polity. Some parties, often including the term *Janata* in their names, were breakaways from Congress, stood at center-left on the ideological arc, and drew support from what Christopher Jaffrelot termed India's "silent revolution"—the rise and politicization of the backward castes. Coalitions of these parties formed governments in New Delhi twice during the 1990s. The short-lived National Front government of V. P. Singh is remembered chiefly for trying to implement recommendations of the Mandal Commission to reserve government jobs for backward castes. Two United Front governments in the mid-1990s attempted to build a secular "third force" but fell to factional disputes.

The most dramatic political phenomenon of the 1980s and 1990s was the rise of the Bharatiya Janata Party (BJP). Owing nothing to Congress and explicitly avowing a Hindutva platform roughly translated as Hindu Nationalism, the BJP possessed disciplined cadres of workers and the support of a vigorous social movement of Hindu revitalization launched in the 1920s—the Rashtriya Swayamsevak Sangh (RSS). BJP leaders tried to mobilize mass support by emphasizing a common identity among Hindus, who form the majority of India's population, and by launching a grand campaign to build a Ram *mandir,* or temple, at the site of a derelict 16th-century mosque in Ayodhya. *Mandir* versus Mandal was *the* political conflict of the early 1990s, resulting in much loss of blood. Led by Atal Behari Vajpayee, the BJP also learned to build coalitions with regional parties and broadened its electoral appeal by espousing moderation in a common minimum program that did not include the more strident demands of Hindutva. Vajpayee led a coalition government in New Delhi from 1998 to 2004 and took far-reaching steps in foreign relations, such as authorizing nuclear tests, opening the path for closer relations with the United States, improving ties with the Peoples Republic of China, and initiating a composite peace dialogue with Pakistan. Although weakened by tensions between the RSS and political moderates, the BJP remains the main national opposition to Congress.

Politics at the national, state, and local levels generate intense public interest and ever-widening and ever-deepening participation, but polls show that politicians as a group command little or no respect and usually are blamed for most of the ills that beset the country. All political parties share responsibility for activities that lead, in the words of critic Arun Shourie, to "a state hollowed out by termites." Such activities include putting private gain above public good; failing to discipline members who cause grievous harm—as in the case of anti-Sikh riots around Delhi in 1984 and Gujarat's anti-Muslim pogrom in 2002; allowing avarice of electoral finance to overcome scruples against contact with or even appointment to office of known criminals; undermining the civil services by preferring sycophancy or "commitment" over honest performance of duty; neglecting primary education and contributing to the erosion of the work ethic and standards of excellence in universities;

neglecting recommendations of numerous commissions on improving the police forces to the extent that law and order has disappeared from parts of the country and allowing enemies of the state, including local and foreign-supported terrorists, to entrench themselves; gross misuse of public funds, leaving planned projects unfulfilled and leading, inevitably, to alienation of populations and even insurgency, as in the northeast and Kashmir; and failing to devise and implement consistent or effective policies toward neighboring countries and so permitting their severe internal problems to spill over into India.

Such blanket condemnation of the political class should not obscure India's most remarkable achievement since independence: practicing and institutionalizing representative democracy so that it has taken deep root and is a stable system, even when governments change frequently. Nor can the remarkable activities of the voluntary sector in fields ranging from social welfare to ensuring transparency of government be hidden or underestimated, although they cannot substitute for a functioning state. People at the lower rungs of the socioeconomic ladder, especially women, display capabilities for self-help and collective action that are showing visible results, in Kerala, for example. Many will consider these to be mere drops in the bucket, but as Mahatma Gandhi was fond of saying, the ocean itself is composed of individual drops. And the number of outstanding individual Indians in every field of activity from art to science may well amount to a critical mass bringing the goals set forth in Vision 2020 documents within grasp. However, India faces many challenges arising from the various paradoxes of its economic, historical, political, and social developments, as well as from its location in a highly unstable and militarized neighborhood of hostile or fragile states and a rapidly changing international environment. It remains to be seen how India will meet these challenges in the 21st century. The resilience of Indian civilization and the inner strength of Indian society are evident in history, ancient and modern. Those who read history as cycles of civilization may well share the author's view that Indian civilization, most fluorescent when pluralism and law prevail, is once again in an ascending phase.

The Dictionary

– A –

ABASTANOI. Abastanoi is the Greek name for the people who lived along the Chenab River and probably were encountered by **Alexander of Macedon**. Described as a fighting race, the Abastanoi are mentioned in various annals of ancient times, including the *Mahabharata*, under the **Sanskrit** name of Ambastha.

ABDAL. This is an ancient and endogamous community found in **Bengal**, **Bihar**, **Gujarat**, **Himachal Pradesh**, and **Uttar Pradesh**. Members of the Abdal community have functioned as bards and musicians for chieftains of hill regions, and they fill distinct roles in Muslim society by their veterinary and leatherwork. The social organization of the Abdal varies by region, but at the present time the members are generally poor.

ABDALI, AHMAD SHAH (1722–1773). Born in the Abdali clan of western Afghanistan, Ahmad Shah was a young soldier in the army of the Persian **Nadir Shah** when he sacked **Delhi** in 1739. After Nadir Shah's assassination in 1747, Abdali established himself as ruler of Afghanistan and led marauding expeditions into India. In 1757, he obtained the **Punjab**, **Kashmir**, and Sind from the feeble **Mughal** emperor of the time. He was unable to hold dominion in the Punjab for long against constant attack by the **Sikhs**. He also clashed with the **Marathas**, who were then advancing their control northward as the de facto protectors of their Mughal overlord. Abdali defeated the Maratha army at the third battle of **Panipat** in January 1761 and reinstalled Shah Alam II on the throne of Delhi. This decisive battle accelerated the process of disintegration of the Mughal

Empire but checked the expansion of Maratha dominion as a possible replacement. Indirectly, it contributed to the rise of Sikh power in the northwest and the spread of British territorial control in the rest of the subcontinent.

ABDULLAH, SHEIKH MUHAMMAD (1905–1982). Called the Lion of Kashmir, he identified closely with the people of **Kashmir** and had a charismatic appeal for them.

Born near **Srinagar** into a family of shawl merchants, Abdullah was educated in Lahore and at Aligarh Muslim University where he took a master's degree in science in 1930. As a high school teacher in Srinagar he organized Kashmiri Muslims to campaign for better representation in the Dogra Maharaja's (see Glossary) government but was subsequently dismissed. At this formative time of his life he was influenced by the ideas of **Muhammad Iqbal**, but he was not attracted to **Mohammed Ali Jinnah**. Abdullah's long political career began with a protest against police firing in 1931 and continued through the remainder of his life, through intermittent periods of imprisonment and house arrest (totaling more than 15 years, mostly after independence) as well as during his tenures as prime minister/chief minister of the state of **Jammu and Kashmir** (1948–1953, 1975–1982). He was a close friend of **Jawaharlal Nehru**, and the mutual affection between the two men remained despite their political differences after 1953.

Abdullah was the molder and near-lifetime president of the National Conference, a **political party** formed in 1939 as representative of the Kashmiri people. He mobilized popular resistance in Kashmir, first against the maharajah and then against the tribal invaders from **Pakistan** in 1947. He supported accession of the state to India, and his leadership was an important factor in the decisions made by Nehru at the time regarding Kashmir, including his offer of a plebiscite made in good faith and with confidence that a popular vote would favor accession to India. Sheikh Abdullah was also a member of the **Constituent Assembly** of India. He won the first elections based on adult franchise in Jammu and Kashmir in 1952, and the newly elected legislature led by him confirmed accession to India while retaining a special status under Article 370 of the **Indian Constitution.**

In August 1953, following communal and political problems in Jammu and Kashmir and difficulties with New Delhi, Abdullah was dismissed and arrested on charges (never proven) of plotting with foreign powers for Kashmiri independence. He was released in April 1964 and briefly assumed the role of negotiator between Nehru and President Ayub Khan of Pakistan before the former's death ended that effort. Abdullah's strong pronouncements on Kashmiri identity, Islamic unity, India, democracy, culture, and secularism often sounded inconsistent and created confusion among his followers and mistrust in New Delhi, but his commanding personality could never be ignored. Prime Minister **Indira Gandhi** reached accord with him in 1975 when he was once again elected chief minister and remained so to the time of his death. His son, Farouq Abdullah, then assumed leadership of the National Conference, with its varying fortunes and declining influence, in the last decade of the 20th century.

ABU'L FAZL (1551–1602). He was the second of six sons born to the learned Shaikh Mubarak Abu'l Fazl. He showed an early aptitude for scholarship and joined his elder brother, the poet Faizi, at the court of **Mughal Emperor Akbar** in 1574. The two brothers were closely associated with Akbar's policy of religious tolerance and his promulgation in 1582 of a new court faith, **Din-I-Ilahi**, which was criticized as heretical by orthodox Muslim chroniclers of the times, such as Badaoni.

Abu'l Fazl was given high rank and military command by the emperor but is best known for his monumental history, the *Akbar Nama*. Written in ornate Persian, this multivolume work is much more than a chronicle of Akbar's reign or even a treatise on the theme of a just ruler. It is a well-researched and detailed reference guide to events and persons and to all imperial regulations in force at the time. Its final section constitutes the *Ain-i-Akbari,* which relates details on the imperial household, court, army, administration, and accounts. These volumes are primary source material for modern economic and historical analyses of 16th-century India.

ADIVASI. This term means "original inhabitant" in **Sanskrit**. The **Constitution of India** designates the descendants of these indigenous peoples as "Scheduled Tribes" who are entitled to special assistance. Numbering nearly 68 million or approximately 8% of the total population according to the 1991 census, and belonging to 250 major tribes as well as many minor ones, Adivasis are heterogeneous in language, culture, physical features, and economic pursuits. For the most part, high percentages of Adivasis live in the forested tracts of the Himalayas especially in the northeastern states, in the hills and forests of central and southern India, and on India's island territories.

The tribes forming a majority of the population in the northeastern states of **Arunachal Pradesh**, **Mizoram**, and **Nagaland** were relatively free of outside influences and control until recent times, and many of their customs and institutions remain intact. Those inhabiting the Andaman and Nicobar Islands have been the most isolated from developments on the Indian mainland. Elsewhere, and throughout historical times, there has been a process of cultural and economic adaptation between the Adivasis, organized along tribal lines and engaged in hunting and gathering or swidden cultivation, and the rest of the population organized along *jati* or **caste** lines pursuing a variety of occupations. Less than 100 groups are currently defined as pre-agricultural and pre-literate. **Christian** missionaries and **Hindu** social reformers were active among tribal peoples in the 19th and 20th centuries with varying impact on the Adavisi religious beliefs, dietary habits, social customs, and sense of identity.

Adivasis inhabited the broad central belt of India, from **Gujarat** in the west to **Bengal** in the east, experienced the most radical and disruptive changes to their traditional ways of life in the modern period as forests and common lands were overtaken by increased population, cultivation, towns, and new industry. Even the largest groups, such as the **Bhils**, **Mundas**, and **Santals**, suffered deprivation and exploitation at the hands of men who could best manipulate new financial and legal procedures. Discontent with British rule triggered a serious Santal rebellion in east central India from 1855 to 1857, which was overcome by police and troops only with difficulty. Continued grievances combined with identity politics in independent India to fuel movements for separate states within the Indian Union where the Adivasis would form a numerical majority. In eventual response to these demands, and having reached consensus with other political parties on the subject, the coalition government in New Delhi, led by the **Bharatiya Janata Party**, created the states of **Chhatisgarh** and **Jharkhand** in the year 2000.

Article 46 of the Indian Constitution directs the State to "promote with special care the educational and economic interests" of the Scheduled Tribes and "protect them from social injustice and all forms of exploitation." In furtherance of this directive, seats are reserved for them in parliament, in some state legislatures, in government service, and in educational institutions. Special grants, scholarships, and preferments are made available to them. Various "Integrated Tribal Development Projects" channel public investment to raise their living standards above the poverty line without destroying their sociocultural identity. **Non-governmental organizations** are also active in the field. While some progress has been made, problems remain, and Adivasi politicization continues to increase.

ADVANI, LAL KRISHNA (1927–). Advani became Deputy Prime Minister of India in July 2002 and was perceived as the likely successor to Prime Minister **Atal Behari Vajpayee**. Advani was born in Karachi, Sindh, and was schooled there before taking a law degree in **Bombay**. He joined the **Rashtriya Swayamsevak Sangh (RSS)** in 1942, became secretary of its Karachi branch within five years, and has remained a loyal volunteer since. After **Partition** he moved to **Rajasthan** where he joined the **Jana Sangha** in 1951. He was an active party worker and moved up the hierarchy, from secretary of the Delhi Office 1958–1963, to vice president 1965–1967, to president of the party 1973–1977. In 1970 he became joint editor of the *Organiser*, the principal journal of the Jana Sangha, and also a member of the **Rajya Sabha**. Advani became general secretary of the **Janata Party** when it was formed in 1977, and later was Minister of Information and Broadcasting in that government from 1977–1979. The **Bharatiya Janata Party (BJP)** was formed in 1980 with Advani as secretary until 1986; he later became president of the BJP in 1989–1990 and again in 1993–1994 and as such was Leader of the Opposition in the **Lok Sabha** from 1990 to 1996. He has held the important portfolios of Home Affairs and **Kashmir** Affairs in Vajapyee's cabinets since the BJP-led coalition government came to power in 1998. In this capacity he appointed a government interlocutor to engage dissident groups from the Kashmir Valley in talks to resolve outstanding issues.

Advani has a reputation as a political hardliner and advocate of **Hindutva** ideology. In 1990 he mounted a *rath yatra*, or countrywide procession led by a chariot-like vehicle, to mobilize support for building a **Ram** temple at **Ayodhya**. The accompanying crowds and belligerent slogans sparked communal riots, and Advani was prevented from entering **Uttar Pradesh (UP)** in the interests of law and order. However, on December 6, 1992, he was present at the site when the Babri Masjid was demolished, which neither the BJP government of UP nor the **Congress** government in New Delhi acted to prevent. Advani has expressed his regret for that destructive incident more than once since then. More importantly, his 2003 south-to-north *rath yatra* was part of a pre-election campaign that took as its theme the broad achievements of the BJP-led government; this time the slogan was a non-religious one of *Uday Bharat* or India Shining. Advani has sent other signals, too, that he regards Hindutva more as an inclusive civilizational concept for India as a whole rather than an exclusive sectarian one that minority communities have reason to fear. He has joined Vajpayee in trying to broaden membership of the BJP beyond its middle class, urban, caste **Hindu** core.

The general elections of 2004 resulted in a defeat of the BJP led coalition and its replacement by a Congress-led coalition government. However, Advani had been reelected to his seat in the **Lok Sabha** and became Leader of the Opposition.

AGA KHAN. This is the title of the hereditary Imam, or spiritual leader, of the Khoja Ismaili community who are spread throughout western and southern Asia and Africa. Many Khojas immigrated to India from Iran during the 19th century and prospered. Sultan Muhammad Shah (1877–1957), referred to here as the Aga Khan, was the third in line of these Imams. After his death a magnificent mausoleum was erected in **Bhopal** along with educational and medical facilities for his followers. The title passed to his grandson, and the Aga Khan Foundation funds much useful work in South Asia and elsewhere.

Immensely wealthy, the Aga Khan played an active role in pre-independence Indian politics. He was cofounder of the **All-India Muslim League** in 1906 and served as its president from 1906 to 1913. Concerned about the socioeconomic welfare of his community, the Aga Khan supported modern education for Indian Muslims, including that offered by Aligarh Muslim University. He successfully pressed for separate electorates and for reserved seats in legislatures for Muslims. He also subscribed to the "two nation theory" which led to **Partition** in 1947.

The Aga Khan remained steadfastly loyal to the British all his life. He was knighted for his help during World War I and was considered for conferment of a princely title and estate. His diplomatic talents were used at the League of Nations and for missions to Turkey and Egypt in the 1920s. He led the Indian delegation, entirely selected by **Lord Irwin**, to the first **Round Table Conference** in 1930; there he pressed for minority safeguards, communal representation, and reserved powers in any new constitutional framework. The Aga Khan did not pretend to be a democrat. His approval of **Mahatma Gandhi** was combined with disapproval of mass mobilization and political participation. Gandhi was incarcerated in the Aga Khan's palace in **Poona** from 1942 to 1945.

AGARWAL, ANIL (1947–2002). Argarwal was one of the most prominent and respected environmental activists in India. Trained as an engineer and working as a journalist, Agarwal was inspired by the **Chipko Movement** in the 1970s to investigate matters of environmental conservation and destruction. He established a Centre for Science and Environment (CSE) in New Delhi in 1980, which published the *Citizens Report on the Environment,* and also launched a journal, *Down to Earth,* that addressed issues of development and environment. Anil Agarwal wrote extensively and spoke publicly against ongoing pollution of air and water all over India. The alternative he, and others, propagated is the concept and practice of "sustainable development." His pioneering and innovative work in environmental conservation was recognized in India and abroad through various awards, and in 1987 the United Nations Environmental Program elected Anil Agarwal to the Global 500 Honor Role. Despite his untimely death, the CSE remains a leading **Non Governmental Organization** specializing in environmental issues.

AGRA. A city on the **Yamuna** river in **Uttar Pradesh**, Agra flourishes as a center of commerce, education, handicrafts, transport, and tourism.

Probably founded by **Rajputs** a millennium ago, Agra was rebuilt as the capital of the **Delhi Sultanate** by Sikander Lodi in 1505 and became one of the most important cities of the **Mughal Empire**. Along with **Delhi** and occasionally Lahore, Agra served as the Mughal administrative capital and residence of the imperial court. Splendid buildings were erected in and around Agra during the 16th and 17th centuries, notably the Red Fort and the **Taj Mahal**.

AHMED, FAKHRUDDIN ALI (1905–1977). Fakhruddin Ahmed was born and educated in **Delhi** and studied law in Cambridge, England. He qualified for the Bar from the Inner Temple, London, and returned to India where he established his legal career in **Assam**. He joined the **Indian National Congress** in 1931, was imprisoned for his political activities from 1940 to 1944, and became a member of the Congress Working Committee in 1946. He was a keen sportsman and actively encouraged sports in independent India. He held various portfolios in Assam governments before being asked to join **Indira Gandhi**'s government in New Delhi in 1966.

Fakhruddin Ali Ahmed was elected president of India in August 1974. He supported Prime Minister Indira Gandhi's decision to declare a state of **Emergency Rule** in June 1975 and issued the necessary promulgation. Before it was lifted, the president died suddenly of a heart attack in February 1977.

AHMEDABAD. The capital of **Gujarat**, Ahmedabad is a major industrial city on the west coast of India. The present city was founded by Sultan Ahmad Shah, ruler of Gujarat in the early 15th century, close to the site of a much older city, and generated a strong tradition of textiles, manufacturing, and powerful guilds. Ahmedabad prospered further as a center of administration and commerce after Gujarat was absorbed into the **Mughal Empire** in the mid-16th century. International trade in cotton and silk textiles, gold, and other commodities brought great wealth to the city even after it was taken over by the **Marathas** in 1758 and later came under British rule. The various noblemen and rich merchants who lived there constructed many fine buildings over the centuries, including mosques, **Hindu** and **Jain** temples, and mausoleums, all of which testified to the rich pluralism of the city.

As India began to industrialize in the latter half of the 19th century, cotton mills and textile factories were established in Ahmedabad, the site of one of **Mahatma Gandhi**'s early **Satyagrahas**. The city was a base for some prominent leaders in the freedom struggle, such as **Vallabhai Patel**. It continued to prosper after independence, retaining its entrepreneurial character and pro-business outlook. The city attracted workers from different parts of the country as well as investment from the far-flung Gujarati **diaspora**. In the late 1980s and early 1990s, however, economic and social tensions erupted in violent sectarian disturbances. Political manipulation of such tensions in early 2002 led to even greater violence, especially against Muslim communities, but the city's long mercantile tradition and the pragmatism of its citizens enabled it to recover stability and to reject candidates representing militant **Hindutva** in the general elections of 2004.

AIBAK, QUTBUDDIN (d. 1210). He was the true founder of the **Delhi Sultanate**. An Ilbari Turk slave officer serving the ruler of Ghor in present-day Afghanistan, he proved to be a victorious general in the second battle of Tarain (1192) between Muhammad Ghor and **Prithviraj Chauhan** that gave the Turks command of **Delhi**. Aibak ruled in Delhi as a viceroy from 1206 until his death. He ordered the many of temples around Delhi dismantled, and on one prime site ordered the construction of the Quwatul Islam mosque and a victory tower, named Qutb Minar after him. These structures are now major tourist attractions. Aibak was succeeded by another Turkish slave officer, **Iltutmish** who ruled in his own name and established the first dynasty of the Delhi Sultanate.

AJANTA. Site of a remarkable and world famous series of manmade cave temples and monasteries on the **Deccan** in **Maharashtra**, the structure contains sculptures and wall paintings executed by Buddhist religious communities between the second century BCE and the seventh century CE. Iconoclastic Islamic raids and subsequent wars resulted in some damage to the caves, and their abandonment at an unknown date.

Twenty-nine of these secluded caves were accidentally discovered in the early 19th century and were subsequently explored, photographed, and opened to visitors. The caves themselves, as well as the sculptures within them, had been carved in solid rock from the top down, thus eliminating the need for scaffolding. The rock walls were then plastered with a mixture of clay, cow dung, and rice husks to a thickness of one half inch. A thin lime coating was then applied before painting scenes and figures in vibrant colors produced locally — still incomparable in their richness. The walls were polished to a high luster, which remains more or less visible despite being eroded by exposure and dimmed by the shellac mistakenly applied as a preservative in the 19th century. UNESCO and the Government of India sponsored a preservation project in the 1950s, naming Ajanta as a treasure house of world art.

Ajanta's frescoes and sculptures depict episodes from the life of the **Buddha** and also illustrate the popular Jataka stories about the Buddha's previous lives. In the process, they illuminate the life, people, costumes, and manners of the unsigned artists' contemporary civilization. Although the style is predominantly exuberant and sensuous, slight changes in technique as well as subject matter enable scholars to estimate that the caves were created and inhabited over many hundreds of years. During that time **Buddhism** evolved, and its religious art flourished in India.

AJMER. A salubrious town in **Rajasthan**, Ajmer is located in the foothills with command over the major north-south trading route across the desert. The present town was founded by a **Rajput** ruler of the Chauhan clan in 1100 CE. Khwaja Muinuddin Chishti (c.1141–1236), a **Sufi** saint of the **Chisti** order, settled in Ajmer, sired a family there, and identified himself with the poor and hungry people of the town.

Ajmer passed under Muslim rule soon after the defeat of **Prithviraj Chanhan** by Mohammed of Ghor in 1192. A royal palace was constructed in 1556 for the **Mughal Emperor Akbar**, who went to pay his respects to the spiritual descendant of Muinuddin Chisti and to ask for an heir. The subsequent heir was named Salim after him and later became the Emperor Jehangir, who liked to stay at Ajmer, where he eventually received **Sir Thomas Roe** as the first British Ambassador from the Court of St. James. It was close to strategically important Ajmer that **Aurangzeb** won the final battle against his brothers, rivals for the peacock throne of the Mughal Empire.

Ajmer's relative obscurity during the period of British rule in India was never total, and it draws many visitors from near and far in the present day. Nearby lakes are the setting for the colorful Pushkar Fair at which livestock and local wares are exhibited and traded annually. The tomb of Khwaja Muinuddin Chishti has long been regarded as a holy place, a shrine of pilgrimage for Muslim and **Hindu** alike.

AKALI DAL. Initially organized in 1920 as a semi-military band of volunteers active in the **Sikh** community to gain management of all Sikh shrines, the Akali Dal contested Punjab elections in 1937 as a **political party**. In the 1920s and 1930s Akalis played an important role in politicizing the Sikh peasantry in the **Punjab** and neighboring **Princely States**. They tried but failed to obtain some kind of "Sikh homeland" in the pre-independence and pre-partition negotiations of the 1940s. After 1947 the Akalis led a campaign for a "Punjabi Subah," or state in which Punjabi would be the official language. This goal was achieved in 1966.

The Akali Dal also stood for greater decentralization of power within the Indian Union and passed the Anandpur Resolution in 1973, demanding effective autonomy for the Punjab from central control. Some in New Delhi interpreted this as a bid for secession or independence, as was made subsequently by the Khalistan movement. Terrorism and counter-terrorism disrupted normal life in the Punjab during the 1980s. Since then, the highly factionalized Akali Party, commanding allegiance mainly among Sikh agriculturalists. has competed with the **Congress Party** for power in the Punjab while remaining in general alignment with the **Bharatiya Janata Party** in parliament.

AKBAR (1542–1605). Grandson of the first **Mughal** Emperor, **Babur**, Akbar was born in the deserts of **Rajasthan** when his father, Humayun, was being driven out of India by **Sher Shah Suri**. Humayun had begun to recover territories and reclaim the throne at **Delhi** when he died in 1556. Akbar, at the age of 13, was proclaimed successor. Over the next two years he substantiated his inherited title with military prowess. His victory at **Panipat** in 1558 established Mughal supremacy over areas around Delhi and in northwestern India. Over the following 10 years he extended his domain from **Gujarat** to **Bengal** to the **Deccan**. More importantly, Akbar consolidated and legitimized his power, and consequently the authority of the Mughal Empire was beyond serious challenge for more than a hundred years after his death and remained titular until 1858.

Akbar's qualities surfaced early and lasted throughout his lifetime. As a military leader he was noted for personal bravery and stamina and for his lightning marches, often in the guise of hunting expeditions. He had a rarer quality, too, of establishing dominion through peaceful means. Akbar chose not to carry on an endless war of attrition against **Rajput** strongholds. Instead, beginning with his marriage to the daughter of the Raja of Amber in 1562, he contracted matrimonial alliances with all of the important Rajput rulers except for the Sisodia Rana of Mewar who remained opposed to Mughal paramountcy. Rajput (**Hindu**) princesses became mothers to future viceroys or emperors without converting to **Islam**. Rajput princes became generals leading Mughal armies to victory in a steady extension of empire. They enjoyed privileges protecting their customs and beliefs but joined the aristocracy of Persian, Turk, and Afghan Muslims in Mughal service. In short, Akbar created a partnership with the Rajputs that enriched the Mughal era in every way.

Akbar fit the mold of a classical Indian emperor, paternal toward all his subjects, distributing patronage among all sacred places, and recognizing the fact of diverse faiths among a heterogeneous population with a vast Hindu majority. In 1564 he lifted bans on temple building and the pilgrimage tax imposed by some former Muslim rulers. In 1579 he abolished the *jiziya* (see Glossary), a tax levied on non-Muslims, and won acclaim from those most affected, the Hindu cultivators. Faced with criticism from the *ulema* (see Glossary) or orthodox Muslim divines, Akbar declared himself, as unquestioned head of the state, to be the final arbiter on any disputes of law derived from the *Shari'a* (see Glossary). Akbar delighted in intellectual interchanges. He encouraged debate, theological argument, and philosophic discussion around him among scholars and priests of different faiths—Muslim, Hindu, **Zoroastrian**, and **Christian**. In 1580 he initiated a syncretic court religion called the **Din-i-Ilahi**. In theory, the new cult demanded no more than loyalty to the emperor; in practice, it offended orthodox Muslims at the court for appearing to deify the emperor.

Akbar was both statesman and brilliant administrator. He had a rare capacity of spotting talent, inspiring dedication, and coordinating different aspects of effort toward a grand imperial idea. Among his notable achievements was the creation of imperial service based on merit and graded according to military rank. Officers were called *mansabdars*; they held their appointments directly from the emperor and drew their salaries in cash rather than in inheritable land grants. Despite drawbacks in the **mansabdari system**, which surfaced later, it attracted men of exceptional ability and formed the backbone of the **Mughal Empire**. Akbar also ensured a revenue flow to the imperial treasury without having to resort to further military conquests because **Todar Mal** drew up schemes of agricultural revenue assessment and collection that were accepted by the people as reflections of inherited custom in India. When properly implemented, these levies did not impoverish the cultivators. The relative stability of Akbar's reign over half a century also permitted enlarging the areas under cultivation and increasing levels of trade and communication.

On the death of Akbar, India was more prosperous than it had been under the **Delhi Sultanate** or would be in the next 200 years. Akbar's reign (1556–1605) was chronicled in laudatory but meticulous detail by the court historian **Abu'l Fazl**, whose compendium of data remains a major source of information on Mughal administration. A brilliant critique of Akbar's policies was written by another contemporary historian, Badauni, and was more representative of orthodox Muslim opinion in the aristocracy. In 20th-century assessments, Akbar ranks with the **Mauryan Emperor Ashoka** as one of the greatest rulers known to the Indian subcontinent. *See also* MUGHAL EMPIRE.

AKSAI CHIN. Considered a part of **Ladakh**, the Aksai Chin is an isolated, inhospitable, and largely uninhabitable plain on the northern tip of the Indian subcontinent where the Pamir knot joins together the Hindu Kush and Karakoram mountain ranges. The Aksai Chin is geographically an extension of the Tibetan plateau, traversed by valleys and enclosed by the Karakorum to the west and south, and the Kuen Lun range to the north and east. The Chinese call it White Stone Desert and regard it as a strategically vital link between Sinkiang and **Tibet**.

The Aksai Chin is disputed territory between India and China and has figured in discussions on the boundary question between officials since 1960. Various proposals concerning the legal disposition of the Aksai Chin, taking into account Chinese de facto control, were made before and after the 1962 border war between China and India. *See also* MCMAHON LINE.

AL BIRUNI or ALBERUNI (c. 970–1039). Al Biruni was born in Khwarizm, then a flourishing town in Central Asia near present-day Khiva. He was well known as an astronomer, author, mathematician, and philosopher when **Mahmud of Ghazni** captured Khwarizm in 1017. Al Biruni joined Mahmud's court, accompanied him on raids in India, and traveled there. He engaged in learned discussions with other scholars, studied Indian languages and civilization, and translated some **Sanskrit** texts on astronomy into Arabic. His penetrating work on India, *Alberuni's India* (an English translation was published in 1888) covered a wide range of topics. He paid particular attention to astronomy and religion, drew comparisons between Greek and Indian ideas, described the social system prevailing in areas he visited, and quoted extensively from Indian sources. No other Islamic scholar for several hundreds of years produced an equally learned or objective analysis of India. Al Biruni's study remains an incisive and valuable literary source for the history of that period.

ALBUQUERQUE, DOM ALPHONSO D' (1459–1515). Albuquerque laid the foundations of Portugal's command of trade routes across the Indian Ocean during the 16th century. A strategist of imperial rather than commercial vision, he was less concerned with cultivating the support of local rulers than in gaining control of their ports. He captured **Goa** on the west coast of India in 1510 and later Diu; he also secured Melaka (Malacca) on the Malay peninsula in 1511 and Hormuz at the entrance to the Persian Gulf in 1515. As Portuguese viceroy in India, Albuquerque advocated a policy of fortified sea bases, military assertiveness, and permanent settlement of Portuguese colonists on the land. He advocated mixed marriages and conversion of the native population to the Roman Catholic Church, sometimes by force. *See also* PORTUGUESE.

ALEXANDER OF MACEDON (356–323 BCE). Alexander was, of course, a key figure in European civilization, but he also played a role in Indian history. He continued marching east after defeating the armies of the Achaemenid Empire in Anatolia and Persia and adopting features of Persian imperial administrative style. Alexander and his forces crossed the Hindukush mountains on the northwestern borders of the Indian subcontinent in 327 BCE and campaigned near modern Kabul and Peshawar before crossing the **Indus** river and entering **Taxila** the following year. He defeated the gallant king Porus (Paurava) on the banks of the Jhelum river but restored to him his kingdom and continued battling with other chieftains to the south and east. Forced to turn back by his weary men, Alexander sailed downstream on the **Indus** and west along the coast on to Babylon; there he died without consolidating his spectacular conquests. The successors of the satraps he left behind, however, presided over a rich blend of Indic and Hellenistic cultures that flowered over the next few centuries in what came to be known as **Gandhara** art.

Greco-Roman sources suggest that Alexander was drawn to India not only by his legendary determination to conquer the world but by the renowned wealth of India, especially the **Ganges** valley where the kingdom of **Magadha** was expanding. The young Sandracottus, who met Alexander, has been identified as **Chandragupta Maurya**, who subsequently built a great empire with its capital at Magadha.

ALI BROTHERS, SHAUKAT ALI (1873–1938) and **MOHAMMED ALI (1878–1931).** Both of the Ali brothers were graduates of Aligarh Muslim University and were deeply committed to Muslim welfare in India and pan-Islamism. They led the **Khilafet Movement** after **World War I** in collaboration with **Mahatma Gandhi** and participated in the **Non-Cooperation Movement** of 1920–1922. Maulana Ali served as president of the **Indian National Congress** in 1923.

The Ali brothers broke with Congress in 1928. They attended the **Round Table Conference** in London and urged special consideration for Indian Muslims in any proposed constitutional reforms.

ALIGARH MOVEMENT. This movement takes its name from the Muslim Anglo-Oriental (MAO) College founded at Aligarh by

Sayyid Ahmad Khan in 1875 and reconstituted as Aligarh Muslim University in 1920. The Aligarh movement represented one type of response to the challenges posed by British hegemony in India to a Muslim aristocracy that felt itself to be dispossessed, discredited, and isolated after the **Uprising of 1857** had been crushed and the last **Mughal** emperor banished. The Aligarh movement was based on faith in British tutelage and British education as a means of reinvigoration and upward mobility for sons of the Muslim landed gentry. It was rooted in and intended to reinforce a strong sense of cultural, ethnic, and religious identity among Indian Muslims but not in opposition to the British.

The MAO College, under its first principal, Theodore Beck, aspired to be another Cambridge, carrying forward Western liberal values in education, literature, and social life without neglecting the religious content of **Islam**, and attracting students from all over India and countries beyond. If Beck's hopes were not entirely fulfilled, Aligarh's student body or influence was not limited to its immediate environs but spread through northern India and to **Hyderabad**. Many of its graduates joined secular professions in education, government service, law, and public life. They contrasted in many ways with the products of the **Deoband** movement, which represented a more traditional or revivalist response among Indian Muslims to their changed circumstances under British rule. The Deoband school was led by learned *ulema* (see Glossary) who expanded *madrassah* (see Glossary) education and application of the *Shar'ia* (see Glossary), promoted Urdu publications, and reached into less affluent classes.

Parallels can be drawn between the Aligarh movement of the late 19th century and the **Hindu** social reform movement of the early 19th century. Both were led by men from the upper levels of society who were reformers rather than revolutionaries. Both movements drew on the English language and on Western science and the humanities to revitalize their own cultural traditions; both movements produced men who were loyal to the British Raj and who saw themselves as playing important and fulfilling roles in it. Although both movements were initially non-political, their inculcation of nationalist sentiment, in the sense of patriotism and drive for political self-expression, make politicization appear to be inevitable.

Political expression in early-20th-century India took various forms, depending on the particular circumstances of time, place, and individual. Broadly speaking, however, men identified with the Aligarh movement distanced themselves from the ideas of representative democracy and independence as espoused by the **Indian National Congress**, partly because of birth but largely because Sir Sayyid Ahmad Khan himself instructed them to do so. Inevitably, therefore, historians differ in assessments of the Aligarh movement made in the context of **Partition** and the creation of **Pakistan** in 1947.

ALL-INDIA MUSLIM LEAGUE. *See* MUSLIM LEAGUE.

ALLAHABAD. *See* PRAYAG.

AMARAVATI. Located in present-day **Andhra Pradesh**, Amaravati was the political, commercial, and cultural center of the **Satavahana** dynasty that ruled the **Deccan** at the turn of the millennium BCE and CE. Amaravati is most famous for the art, architecture, and sculpture that flourished there, giving full and naturalistic expression to the profound impact of **Buddhism** on the people. The Amaravati style is presently judged to be indigenous and distinct, without Hellenistic influence, and predating both the **Gandhara** and the Mathura schools.

AMBANI, DHIRUBHAI H. (1932–2002). Became known as Mr. Reliance, Ambani was a man who built a giant, multifaceted, global enterprise with little more than bold ambition and skill. He was born to a schoolmaster in a tiny village of southwest **Gujarat** and left home at the age of 16 for a clerking job with a trading firm in the British Crown Colony of Aden, then administered from **Bombay**. In 1958, he moved to Bombay and formed Reliance Commercial Corporation to trade in cashews, pepper, and synthetic fibers. He took advantage of government export promotion schemes to multiply exports of rayon fabrics woven from imported nylon yarn and established his own textile factory in 1966 to produce high unit value polyester and art silk for export. His sales climbed exponentially, and when Reliance Textile went public in 1977 its share values appreciated dramatically. Ambani expanded his projects, always investing in the best equipment and technology for superior products; he established a plant for production of polyester yarn at Patalganga outside Bombay in collaboration with the American corporate giant Du Pont in 1981 and also took over the "sick" Sidhpur Mills for modernization. Subsequently, he entered the telecommunications field as well and succeeded spectacularly. Along the way Ambani obtained substantial government loans for new machinery and thereby gained an edge over his competitors.

Success brought controversy, and allegations in the press and in parliament of Ambani manipulating stock prices, regulations on foreign investment, taxes, and government contacts at the highest level to his own advantage. The crash of Reliance share prices caused a crisis on the Bombay Stock Exchange in 1982, but by the mid-1980s Ambani had recovered. He also moved into the petrochemical sector and increased his corporate worth to match that of **Tata** and **Birla**, India's top two industrial families. Ambani's rise and impact owed much to aggressive marketing and a hands-on managerial style, passed on to his sons and nephews who now manage his industrial empire. But many evaluate Ambani's contribution not only in terms of creating wealth but also in terms of distributing it through easy availability of equity. The weekly news magazine *Outlook* estimated in 2002 that one out of four Indian investors was a Reliance shareholder with a stake in the company's success.

Dhirubhai's sons, Mukesh and Anil, disputed ownership and management of the many companies constituting the industrial empire they had inherited. Their disputes became public in 2004 and threatened the share prices and stability of Reliance Industries. Dhirubhai's widow, Kokilaben, intervened and a family conclave in December 2004 reached the decision to legally split assets. Over the following months ICICI Bank Managing Director K. V. Kamath mediated a solution based on the principles of proper valuation of assets, fair division of the companies, direct communication between the two brothers, avoidance of legal complications, and full protection of the interests of some three million shareholders. Minister of Finance **P. Chidambaram** expressed satisfaction with the settlement reached by the Ambani family. It is likely that the Securities and Exchange Board of India (SEBI) as well as the public will continue to be interested in the future of all Reliance companies.

AMBEDKAR, BHIMRAO RAMJI (1891–1956). The fourteenth child of Mahar (**Untouchable**) parents, Bhimrao first experienced as a child the humiliations that flowed from the irrational but intense prejudice prevalent against his **caste** in Indian society and he never forgot them. Bhim's father retired from the army and enrolled his five-year-old son in school, where his brilliance and hard work—despite discrimination by his classmates—attracted the favorable attention of his high-caste teachers; one of them gave the boy his own name, Ambedkar. Bhimrao was educated at Elphinstone High School and College in **Bombay** before receiving a scholarship from the Maharaja of **Baroda** in 1913 that enabled him to study at Columbia University in New York. There he received M. A. and Ph.D. degrees in Economics. He returned to a civil service position in Baroda and once again confronted social discrimination of the worst kind. He left for **Bombay** and three years later went to the London School of Economics where he obtained a doctorate and also qualified as a Barrister at Law from Gray's Inn.

There is little doubt that Ambedkar was profoundly influenced by his early experiences of untouchability, as well as by his firsthand encounter with individual liberty and intellectual enrichment in the United States and Britain. He became a major spokesman in India for protection of minority rights and rejection of caste as an organizing principle of society. He was the acknowledged leader of his community and a key architect of the **Constitution** adopted by the Republic of India in 1950, which provided for political democracy and justiciable Fundamental Rights for all citizens.

In 1924, Ambedkar started legal practice in Bombay and founded the Depressed Classes Institute (Bahishkrit Hitkarnini Sabha) to provide accommodation, education, and libraries. He also founded and wrote for journals advocating social equality, established boarding houses for Untouchables, and he actively propagated inter-dining and intermarriage between castes. As a member of the Bombay Legislative Council (1926–1934), he sponsored several welfare bills. In 1927 he led a **Satyagraha** to establish the right of Untouchables to draw water from a public tank and won a lawsuit on the subject before the Bombay High Court in 1937. He also led a Satyagraha to establish the right of Untouchables to enter the famous Kala Ram Temple at Nasik (1930–1934).

As a delegate to the **Round Table Conferences** in London, Ambedkar demanded separate electorates for Untouchables similar to those granted to **Muslims**. This led to a standoff between Ambedkar and **Mahatma Gandhi**, who vehemently opposed the **Communal Award** as divisive of **Hindu** society and declared a "fast unto death" against it. Ambedkar agreed to a compromise of reserved seats for Untouchables in the general category embodied in the Poona Pact of 1932 so as not to endanger Gandhi's life. But the two men differed fundamentally on the issue of caste, although both advocated social reform and equal treatment of those whom Gandhi termed "Harijans," or "People of God." Ambedkar rejected the very concept of caste as divisive and demoralizing to Hindu society, destructive of individual achievement or liberty, and an obstruction to the growth of democracy. He also dismissed arguments for the racial or economic basis of caste distinctions as being empirically weak and attributed caste and untouchability to social and religious developments within **Hinduism** alone. During the 1930s, Ambedkar almost despaired of Hindu capacity for self-reform and began exploring the desirability of Untouchables converting en masse to another religion, such as **Christianity**, **Islam**, or **Sikhism**. He finally made the break in October 1956, when he was disillusioned with the lack of progress in land reform and social equality promised at independence. He and several hundred thousand of his followers embraced **Buddhism**.

Ambedkar was critical of the **Indian National Congress** as unlikely to grant social equality to his community. He clearly saw the linkage between political power and social status and founded the Independent Labour Party in 1936, the Scheduled Castes Federation in 1942, and the Republican Party in 1956 as instruments of progress for his community. He also made lasting contributions in the field of Law. As chairman of the Drafting Committee in the **Constituent Assembly** 1946–1949 and as Law Minister in **Jawaharlal Nehru**'s first cabinet, Ambedkar drafted constitutional provisions and piloted legislation promising economic development, social equality, and justice without discrimination on grounds of caste, creed, or sex for all of India's people. In the continuing struggle to effectively implement these laws and to realize the full potential of a democratic polity, Ambedkar remains an inspirational and ideologically important figure of contemporary India. *See also* DALIT.

AMRITSAR. The site of the Golden Temple, Amritsar is a major city of the **Punjab** and one that is especially sacred to the **Sikhs**. The **Mughal Emperor Akbar** bestowed the site on the fourth Sikh guru, Ram Das, in 1577. The foundations of what was to become the Golden Temple and surrounding pool were dug by his **Hindu** and Muslim followers working together. The fifth guru, Arjun Dev, compiled the holy book of the Sikhs—the Adi Granth—at Amritsar; it was installed in the Golden Temple that Maharajah **Ranjit Singh** enlarged and embellished in the 18th century.

Amritsar was the site of the **Jallianwala Bagh** massacre of 1919 that galvanized the Indian national movement. After **Partition** in 1947, Amritsar became the home of many Sikh and Hindu refugees from districts in west Punjab, which were incorporated into **Pakistan**. Their enterprise and hard work brought wealth and industry to the city. During the 1980s Amritsar suffered because of infiltration from across the border and from socioeconomic unrest and the militant activities of **Sant Bhindranwale** and his followers who camped within the temple premises. Prime Minister **Indira Gandhi** ordered an armed onslaught on the complex in June 1984, named Operation Bluestar, which profoundly alienated the local population, especially Sikhs, from her government. Normal commercial life and order were largely restored in Amritsar by the early 1990s.

AMTE, MURLIDHAR DEVIDAS (1914–). Popularly known as Baba Amte, he was born near Wardha and educated at Nagpur. Amte studied at the School of Tropical Medicine in **Calcutta**, taking special training in the treatment of leprosy. He joined **Mahatma Gandhi** for the **Quit India Movement** in 1942 and was among those who were imprisoned. After independence, Amte established the Maharogi Seva Samiti for the treatment, training, and rehabilitation of leprosy patients at Warora. The institution has become famous over the decades and attracts many volunteers to work with the patients.

Baba Amte has become a living legend widely known for his non-violent action. He has participated in peace marches and protests in the cause of civil rights and the environment. For example, he was part of a peace mission to the **Punjab** in 1985, undertook a bicycle march from Kanya Kumari in the extreme south to **Kashmir** in the north for *Bharat Jodo* (knit India together), and took leading roles in non-violent protests against high dam projects on the **Narmada** river. He has published numerous poems and books and has received many national and international awards. He is not an uncontroversial man.

ANDAMAN AND NICOBAR ISLANDS. A group of 572 islands, only 36 of which are inhabited, the Andaman and Nicobar Islands constitute a Union Territory situated in the Bay of Bengal with the capital at Port Blair. Roughly equidistant from **Chennai (Madras)** and **Kolkata (Calcutta)**, Port Blair is connected to both groups of islands by air and by sea and maintains regular inter-island ferry services. Tourism is becoming important as the beaches, underwater corals and marine life, dense forests with rare flora and fauna, and places of historical interest attract a growing number of people to the islands. The indigenous peoples belonging to Negrito and Mongolian tribes continue, for the most part, to live in the forests by hunting and fishing and are shy of strangers.

The **East India Company** tried to establish a post on the Andamans in 1789 but soon abandoned it. After the **Uprising of 1857**, however, the British Government of India used the Andamans, also known as *Kalapani* or Black Water, as a penal colony to which they deported freedom fighters from mainland India, many of them renowned figures such as **Veer Savarkar**. Japanese forces occupied the Andaman and Nicobar Islands in 1942 because of their proximity to **Burma (Myanmar)** and surrendered them in 1945. British-Indian and then Indian administration has continued since, and the dank former prison is now a tourist attraction. The island forests contain a variety of valuable timber species. Coconut, arecanut, rice, pulses, fruits, and spices are cultivated for cash and consumption. Fisheries and small scale handicraft industries provide other occupation for the small population. The islands were badly hit by the tsunami of December 2004.

ANDHRA PRADESH. With an area of 275,068 square kilometers and a population estimated at more than 76 million, Andhra Pradesh is the largest state in southern India. The long and rich history of the Andhra people, first mentioned in the rock inscriptions of **Ashoka**, spans many dynasties and kingdoms, including those of the **Satavahanas**, the **Chalukyas**, **Vijayanagar**, and more recently, the **Princely State** of **Hyderabad**, although their territorial jurisdictions varied. The modern state of Andhra Pradesh in the Indian Union was created in 1953 after agitation (including the fast and death of **Sriramulu Potti**) led to the separation of the Telegu-speaking coastal region around Rayalseema from **Madras** and its amalgamation with the **Telengana** region. The creation of Andhra was a major step in the direction of reorganizing the administrative divisions of India along linguistic lines. With the passage of the **States Reorganization Act** in 1956, areas around the predominantly Urdu-speaking city of Hyderabad were added and that city is the capital of Andhra Pradesh.

Agriculture is the main occupation of the people, accounting for more than 50% and 90%, respectively, of India's castor and Virginia tobacco production. Much of the state is arid, despite major irrigation works such as those constructed by the Tungabahdra and Nagararjunasagar projects and various canals. Farmers themselves are involved in the management of irrigation, and numerous **Non Governmental Organizations** are active in Andhra. Nevertheless, farmers over a large swathe of land, especially in the inland Telengana region, are impoverished and disaffected. Their votes in the 2004 elections contributed in no small measure to the defeat of the **Telugu Desham Party (TDP)** and the change of government in New Delhi to a coalition led by the **Congress Party**. Parts of rural and forested Andhra suffer from low intensity but prolonged insurgencies led by the **Naxalite Peoples' War** Group (PWP) as well as the **Telengana Movement**. State governments have attempted negotiations with the PWG from time to time without success. The Telengana movement spawned a political party, the Telengana Rashtra Samiti (TRS), that demands a separate state. However, although the TRS allied with Congress in the 2004 elections it seems unlikely that its chief demand for a separate state will be met soon; **Dr. Manmohan Singh**'s government in New Delhi has offered Andhra Pradesh a special package of development measures.

Several defense training and management institutions as well as major industries are located in and around Hyderabad. TDP leader Chandra Babu Naidu, who was chief minister of the state from 1994 to 2004, made successful efforts to attract domestic and foreign investment to Hyderabad and to build a high-technology center there to rival **Bangalore** in **Karnataka**. The other major city of Andhra is Visakhapatnam, also a major ship-building and ship repair port and the center of India's Eastern Naval Command. Industry, mining, and tourism, are all important sources of employment and revenue, and Andhra has made significant progress in social indicators including literacy. Telugu and Urdu are the principal languages of the state.

ANDREWS, REVEREND CHARLES FREER (1871–1940). Andrews was educated at Cambridge and ordained in the Church of England in 1896. His introduction to India was made as a teacher at St. Stephen's College, **Delhi**, from 1904–1912. There he insisted on the appointment of an Indian as principal in 1907 and met several Indians active in the national movement. He knew and admired **Rabindranath Tagore**. He became a close friend of **Mahatma Gandhi**, whom he visited in South Africa in 1914 and whose ideals of *ahimsa* (see Glossary) and **Satyagraha** he shared.

Andrews was critical of British imperial rule, and after **World War I** he publicly advocated Indian independence. Through his lectures and writings he served as an interpreter between India and Britain. He acted as a liaison between Gandhi and members of the British government, especially in the early 1930s. His concern for the poor was constant throughout his life, leading him first to early social work in the north of England and then to investigating and combating the system of indentured labor practiced in many British colonies. He helped improve working conditions for Indian labor in various industries, and participated in the struggle against untouchability. His life and his writings are testimony to his profoundly Christian faith.

ANGLO-AFGHAN WARS (1838–1842, 1878–1880, 1919). The proximate causes of three wars waged in Afghanistan by the British from India were different in each case, but the underlying factors of Anglo-Russian rivalry were the same. Conflicts of interest between the expanding empires of Britain and Russia extended beyond Europe to the Ottoman Empire, Persia, and Afghanistan, with Whitehall and St. Petersburg seeking to bring pressure on each other at distant and vulnerable spots and so raising alarms. Secondly, as the British consolidated their dominion in India and as the Russians spread over the khanates of Central Asia in the 19th century, both wanted Persia and Afghanistan to form a buffer zone between them; but each tried to gain influence or dominance there at the expense of the other and so precipitated conflict. Competing contenders for the Afghan throne seeking external aid to win their bids, and fluctuations in control of the eastern and western frontiers of Afghanistan, further prompted British military intervention in that country.

Governor General Lord Auckland's decision in 1838 to forcibly replace the independent-minded Dost Muhammad with a compliant Shah Shuja in Kabul led to complicated negotiations with the **Sikh** emperor **Ranjit Singh** and the breaking of earlier treaties with the Amirs of Sind. The consequent war in Afghanistan cost British India 15 million pounds sterling and 20,000 lives in four years of military disasters. In the end, Dost Muhammad recovered his throne. His death in 1863 was followed by a five-year war of succession, from which Sher Ali emerged victorious and obtained both British and Russian recognition. Subsequently, a Conservative government in Britain and their appointee as viceroy of India, Lord Lytton, reversed the then-prevailing policy of non-interference, or "masterly inactivity," toward the tribesmen and areas west of the **Indus** river. Sher Ali was asked to sever connections with Russia and accept a British Resident in Kabul; he refused. Three British-Indian columns advanced on Kabul from Peshawar, and a fourth proceeded to Kandahar. The Treaty of Gandamak of 1879 appeared to secure British objectives, but Afghan revolts and passion for independence made it impossible for the British to hold Afghanistan as a forward bastion.

The emergence of Abdur Rahman as effective ruler in Kabul, Russian reluctance to risk another war, and a change to Liberal Party government in Britain produced an uneasy Afghan settlement. In 1887 agreement was reached on a boundary between the North West Frontier of India and Afghan territories along the famous "Durand Line," but the area remained heavily garrisoned. Although what **Rudyard Kipling** termed the "Great Game" continued to be played out in the high frontiers of India and the plateaus of Central Asia, respective spheres of imperial influence were recognized in the Anglo-Russian Agreement of 1907.

The third war of 1919 was precipitated by Afghan nationalism, personified by King Amanullah (1890–1939). British reluctance to relinquish control in Kabul, especially in the context of rising unrest in India after the end of **World War I**, led to hostilities between British and Afghan forces in the area of the Khyber Pass. They were soon concluded by the Treaty of Rawalpindi, which confirmed the Durand Line as frontier, discontinued the British subsidy to Kabul, and recognized Afghanistan as an independent sovereign state free to conduct its own foreign relations.

ANGLO-INDIAN. A term used in the 18th and 19th centuries for British people working and living in India, Anglo-Indian subsequently became synonymous with persons of mixed blood: Eurasian. Under conditions of British rule in India, Anglo-Indians manifested some features typical of Indian **caste**, such as marrying within the group and following paternal occupations. In particular, they acquired an occupational niche in the railroad, postal, and customs services of British India and identified, or were assumed to identify, with the British, who remained socially and professionally superior. The community was given reserved seats for representation in provincial legislatures under the **Government of India Act of 1935**.

Predominantly urban and **Christian**, Anglo-Indians were listed as a minority community in the **Indian Constitution** of 1950 and were guaranteed freedom of worship, autonomous educational institutions, and equal treatment with other Indian citizens in employment and in all aspects of public life. Some Anglo-Indian families migrated to Australia, Britain, and elsewhere after 1947, but many individuals, such as **Frank Anthony** and others, have had outstanding careers in India.

ANSARI, DR. MUKTHAR AHMAD (1880–1936). Dr. Ansari was educated in Ghazipur, **Allahabad**, and **Hyderabad** before studying medicine at **Madras**. Ansari earned his higher medical degrees in England. After working as a surgeon in London hospitals, he returned to India in 1910 and set up practice in **Delhi**. He continued his professional career until his death and always maintained a scientific world view.

Dr. Ansari was drawn beyond medicine toward involvement in national issues. He joined the two major organizations of the time, the **Indian National Congress** and the **All-India Muslim League**, and played an important role in reconciling their respective positions in the **Lucknow Pact** of 1916. He held responsible positions in both political organizations, serving as president of the League in 1920 and president of Congress in 1927. He also chaired the All-Parties Conference of 1928 that was convened to draft a constitution acceptable to Indians. The resulting draft came to be known as the **Nehru Report**, named after the chairman of the special committee, **Motilal Nehru**. The report was rejected by the Muslim League.

Ansari was well aware of the need for independent institutions of higher education in India, and he helped establish the Kashi Vidyapith at **Banaras** and the Jamia Millia Islamia at Delhi. He was appointed vice chancellor (president) of the latter in 1928 and continued to so serve until his death in 1936.

ANTHONY, FRANK (1908–1993). Frank Anthony was the leader of the **Anglo-Indian** community from 1942, when he succeeded Sir Henry Gidney as its nominated representative in the Central Legislative Assembly, to the time of his death 50 years later. Anthony was vocally critical of the British Raj in India for its racial discrimination in matters of pay and allowances, and for failing to acknowledge the sterling military and civil contributions made by Anglo-Indians to the Raj. Anthony vociferously opposed **Partition** and fought for the best interests of his community as Indians, not Britishers. He was a member of the **Constituent Assembly** and also of the Language Commission formed in 1955, where he argued ably for the retention of English as an official language of India and resisted what he and many others, especially in South India, termed "hindi imperialism." Frank Anthony's greatest contribution to his community and to the civil society of his country was surely the network of Frank Anthony Schools built over the years, which imparted an excellent education to all its pupils without communal discrimination.

ANTHROPOLOGICAL SURVEY OF INDIA. This body was established in December 1945 with eight regional centers to pursue biocultural research among different population groups. Its objectives were redefined in October 1985 when the ASI launched a project on the People of India to generate a brief, descriptive, anthropological profile of all the communities in India, the impact on them of economic and social change, and the links that bring them together. In short, the ASI set out to fill gaps in knowledge about the human face of India.

The identification and listing of communities began at an early period in Indian history and are found in **Sanskrit** and in Persian regional chronicles as well as in ethnographic surveys conducted by British administrators, especially the **Census of India** from 1881 to 1941. The People of India project drew on these earlier sources, the lists of Scheduled Castes and Tribes prepared by the Government of India, and the lists of Backward Classes included in the **Mandal Commission** Report. Initially, 6,748 communities were identified at the start of the project and 4,693 were finally studied and summarized in a series of volumes that have been published by the Anthropological Survey of India since 1991. The data was also computerized. Research by 500 scholars was conducted between 1985 and 1992 in 3,581 villages and 1,011 towns situated throughout Indian territory.

This exhaustive survey covers 96 eco-cultural zones defined by ecology, language, culture, history, and administration. It includes information on diet, education, family patterns, life-cycle ceremonies, marriage customs, occupations, property holdings, religion, social hierarchy, and status of **women**. The survey reveals linkages across communities and regions, showing how traditional and modern processes of integration and interaction continue to bring people together in many economic, political and social activities despite the existence of contradictions and conflicts among them. This pathbreaking survey directed and edited by K. R Singh has laid the groundwork for a comprehensive ethnography of the diverse people of India.

ARJAN SINGH (1919–). Arjan Singh was designated the first Marshal of the Indian Air Force (equivalent to the army's Field Marshal) in 2002 in recognition of his services and leadership in building a modern, highly professional, armed service. As a boy, Arjan Singh had been fascinated with flying, and he joined the Royal Air Force College at Cranwell, England. He was commissioned a pilot in the Royal Air Force in 1939 and won the Distinguished Flying Cross (DFC) in 1943—rarely bestowed on Indians—for leading his squadron against the Japanese in the Burma Campaign of **World War II.** He continued to excel after India's independence and was appointed Air Chief Marshal to head the Indian Air Force in 1964. He introduced some structural reforms to heighten capability, and during the 1965 and 1971 wars with **Pakistan**, the IAF played a key, though only supportive, role in India's victories. Arjan Singh held two ambassadorial posts after his retirement from the IAF in 1969, and also was lieutenant governor of **Delhi** for the period 1989–1990. An inspiring yet kindly man, he enjoys wide respect.

ARTHASASTRA. This treatise on statecraft is attributed to **Chanakya/ Kautilya**, chief adviser to **Chandragupta Maurya** who ruled **Magadha** in the fourth century BCE. Though the present form of the book probably dates from a later period, it is of exceptional interest as a primary source on the theory and practice of political economy in ancient India, especially of the **Mauryan Empire**. The *Arthasastra* deals with the arts of acquiring, maintaining, and extending political power while ensuring a full exchequer and the economic prosperity of the kingdom. The author clearly had administrative and military experience and wrote a practical handbook for rulers rather than a purely theoretical treatise.

The *Arthasastra* exalts royal power and a centralized bureaucracy within the state. It advocates balance of power politics in relations with other states, postulating wily ways of undermining adversaries and acquiring allies that find echoes in Machiavelli's *The Prince* written in 16th-century Italy. The tone of the *Arthasastra* is pragmatic and worldly wise throughout. It counteracts both the social exclusiveness of the **brahmans** and the renunciatory tendencies of the early **Buddhists**, which find expression in much of the extant literature of ancient India. Though ancient in origin, the *Arthasastra* can be applied to modern times as well, dealing as it does with eternal problems of statecraft. Renewed interest in its teachings, and hence new translations of the **Sanskrit** text, surfaced in 20th-century India.

ARUNACHAL PRADESH. Located among the forested mountains of the northeast, and inhabited by a variety of tribal peoples speaking languages belonging to the Tibeto-Burman group, Arunachal Pradesh became a state of the Indian Union at the end of 1986. It covers an area of 83,743 square kilometers, and its population is estimated at more than one million according to the 2001 census. No archaeological remains have been discovered in Arunachal, and there are few historical references to it in the pre-modern period. The traditional ways of life have been but little disturbed in what was called the North East Frontier Agency in British India. Administration of the area for the first few decades after Indian independence was strongly influenced by the advice of anthropologist **Verrier Elwin**.

Conditions changed to some extent with the construction of roads commencing in 1960 in the context of the Sino-Indian border problem and the military hostilities of 1962. Indian awareness of Arunachal's strategic importance remains high; the more so as China advances territorial claims in the area from time to time. Outsiders from the rest of India or abroad were not encouraged to visit Arunachal until the 1990s.

Ecological conditions in the northeast sector of India favor horticulture, but the infrastructure of marketing and a monetary economy remain undeveloped. **Non governmental organizations** are active in some areas, and handicraft centers and technical training institutes have been established in towns, including Itanagar, the capital. Some private and governmental enterprises look to eco-friendly adventure tourism as one way of promoting sustainable development in the state. Arunachal Pradesh retains rich timber resources, and environmentalists seek protection of this forest cover from the predatory demands of the Indian market and further depredations of road building. Possible threats to the rich biodiversity of the state also cause concern.

ARYANS. These are presumed to have been tribal peoples speaking Aryan (Indo-European) languages who probably originated somewhere in Central Asia and settled in Iran and in India during the third or second millennium BCE. Knowledge of their religious beliefs, pastoral life, political organization, and social customs is deduced from an oral tradition later written down in old Persian and in **Sanskrit**. While some in Europe, India, and elsewhere refer to an "Aryan race," the term refers to language rather than to ethnicity.

The Vedas, prose commentaries on the Vedas, and the great epics *Ramayana* and *Mahabharata* are the major sources used by historians to sketch the spread of Aryan civilization in India. Sanskrit texts and legal codes refer to the Indo-Gangetic plains as Aryavarta, or country of the Aryans, and to their first King as Bharata, after whom

India is called Bharat. Some today postulate India as the original home of the Aryans and theorize a subsequent northwestward migration. Much remains in the realm of speculation until such time as archeological discoveries can be matched with literary evidence.

The term *Aryan* is replete with sociopolitical connotations in India and elsewhere. For example, it was used for long time as a justification for **brahman** domination of other **castes**; however, a 20th-century **Dravidian** movement directly challenged that claim. European Orientalists "discovered" the Aryan link, and Indians used it to assert claims to equality with European (also Aryan) civilization, which imperialism did not admit. Scientific historians such as **Romila Thapar** restrict the definition of Aryan to a group of Indo-European languages with a common root and resist cultural polemics.

ARYA SAMAJ. Founded by **Dayananda Saraswati** in 1875, the Arya Samaj became the most powerful movement for **Hindu** social reform and revival of Vedic values in northern India in the late 19th and early 20th centuries. It exerted greater attraction than the older **Brahmo Samaj**, probably because it proudly asserted an ancient faith free of alien influences and did not require its adherents to break with Hindu society, and because it combated conversion of Hindus to **Christianity**, **Islam**, and **Sikhism** through *shuddhi* (see Glossary) or reconversion. As the Arya Samaj moved from a defensive to an offensive position in the latter activity, it provoked similar processes of reification among Muslims and Sikhs and so contributed to the growth of belligerent communalism in the 20th century, especially in the **Punjab**.

Notwithstanding its call "back to the **Vedas**," the Arya Samaj was distinctly modern in its approach to communication, education, and organization. Under a general controlling authority, local bodies were left free to determine their own rules; social purposes were elevated over other aims; most impressively, a network of Dayanand Anglo-Vedic (DAV) schools and colleges was established throughout northern India for both girls and boys. The Arya Samaj continues to play an important role in contemporary India.

ASAF ALI, ARUNA (1909–1995). Aruna was born to an orthodox **brahman** family of **Calcutta** and was schooled in convents. Against the wishes of her parents and social convention, she went to college and married Asaf Ali, a prominent Muslim lawyer more than 20 years her senior. The marriage was a happy one, and Aruna's cultural, political, and social horizons were enlarged. Her life was transformed through contact with **Mahatma Gandhi** and other leaders of the **Indian National Congress**. Aruna joined the **Civil Disobedience** movement of 1930 and was imprisoned for a year in Lahore. Thereafter she became a radical nationalist and joined the Congress Socialist Party, of which **Jawaharlal Nehru**, **J. P. Narayan**, **Ram Manohar Lohia**, and **Achyut Patwardhan** were also members. Aruna offered individual **Satyagraha** in 1941 and became a fiery heroine of the **Quit India** movement when she went underground. She and her associates bitterly opposed **Partition** as well as the retention of many features of the British Indian system after independence.

Aruna Asaf Ali was elected president of the Delhi Pradesh Congress Committee in 1947 and became the first mayor of **Delhi** in 1958. She left Congress for the Socialist Party and then for the **Communist Party of India** and abjured membership of any political party in 1958. However, she rejoined Congress in 1964. She ran Link House which published the leftist journal, *Patriot,* and devoted her considerable energies to adult literacy in slums, education and employment of women, and the National Federation of Indian Women. Regarded as "the grand old lady of the independence movement," Aruna believed passionately in the transformation of Indian society through the democratic process. She received the Nehru Award for International Understanding in 1992.

ASHOKA (r. 269–232 BCE). Ashoka was the third and most enlightened ruler in the **Mauryan Dynasty**. He is most often cited in contemporary India as a worthy model ruler.

Ashoka added to his already vast domains by conquering Kalinga in the southeast, approximating present-day **Orissa**. He renounced war after witnessing the destruction of Kalinga. From the location and texts of his inscriptions, historians deduce that he controlled a centralized empire that extended from the Hindu Kush mountains in the northwest through the **Indus** valley, **Kashmir**, **Nepal**, the entire **Ganges** valley, and the **Deccan** as far south as **Mysore**. He had close relations with, if not jurisdiction over, Khotan in Central Asia and the three **Tamil** states of southernmost India. He sent missions to neighboring kingdoms in southeast and west Asia, including **Burma** and **Sri Lanka**, which adopted **Buddhism** in consequence.

High levels of artistic, commercial, cultural, and economic activity were attained during Ashoka's reign, which knit together the entire Indian subcontinent and maintained peace. Agriculture, crafts, and trade expanded considerably. Taxes financed a large army, an elaborate administrative structure, and extensive building of roads, irrigation works, and shrines. The Ashokan pillars of highly polished stone capped with exquisitely carved animal capitals evoke admiration to this day. The four-lion capital of the Sarnath pillar was adopted by the Republic of India as its state emblem in 1950.

Ashoka's outstanding contribution to Indian civilization was his introduction of **dharma** (see Glossary) (or *dhamma*) as the binding factor in a vast and heterogeneous empire. Ashoka's policy of dharma, with its emphasis on social responsibility, toleration, and nonviolence, was derived partly from his personal faith in Buddhism and partly from his grasp of administrative requirements in ruling diverse groups of people. A special cadre of officers was appointed to implement the policy of dharma to ensure efficient, centralized administration of the state and provide social welfare for the subjects. The social, economic, and sectarian tensions generated by increased contacts among groups at a time of rapid change were softened by the toleration of different groups, beliefs, and ideas enjoined on all officials and non-officials by Ashoka. He promoted nonviolence toward all living beings, not just humans, urging restraint in hunting animals, birds, and fish and forbidding animal sacrifice. The principles of dharma were defined in broad terms acceptable to any religious sect; superfluous rituals and socio-religious hierarchy were reduced; all alike were declared to be "children" of a paternal emperor who made himself available for public business at all times and toured his domains regularly.

The primary archaeological sources on Ashoka's reign are his own stone inscriptions displayed in prominent places close to religious, trading, or urban centers and on roadways. They consist of 14 major and several minor rock edicts found at 22 locations, seven pillar edicts, and other widely spread inscriptions. Local scripts were used: Greek and Aramaic in the far west, Kharoshthi in the region near

Peshawar, and Brahmi elsewhere in India. A few edicts deal specifically with Ashoka's interest in Buddhism; most are expositions on his achievements, intentions, and instructions. Their full importance was gauged only after the Brahmi script was deciphered in 1837. Ashoka was identified by name with his titles Devanampiya Piyodassi, as late as 1915. The same titles appear elsewhere in inscriptions and literature, and a general picture of Ashoka's reign began to take shape. Less is known about his successors; it is presumed that they probably were unable to maintain the extent, integrity and power of the empire for very long.

Another important source of information on Ashoka is Buddhist literature, especially the Ceylon chronicles. These depict Ashoka as a passionate convert to Buddhism who had 84,000 **stupas** (reliquary mounds) built, who sent his son and daughter out as Buddhist missionaries to Ceylon, who sent other missionaries east, north, and west, and who called a meeting of the Third Buddhist Council at **Pataliputra** in c. 250 BCE. Greek writings of the time and the **Arthasastra** are good secular literary sources on that period, and recent archeological and numismatic discoveries add to the still growing body of knowledge on early India and one of its greatest rulers.

ASHVAMEDHA. Also known as the horse sacrifice, the ashvamedha was a Vedic ritual by which a great king asserted his power and authority over lesser chieftains. A consecrated horse was set free to wander at will for one year under the guardianship of young armed warriors or **kshatriyas** who were prepared to overcome any resistance. The king who was performing the ashvamedha claimed all the lands through which his horse passed. At the end of the year, the horse was sacrificed amid lengthy and elaborate ceremonies involving the chief queen, music, narration of heroic tales about earlier royal feats, the feeding of **brahmans**, and other spectacular rites on a vast scale.

In principle, the ashvamedha could only be performed by powerful kings or emperors who could fulfill grand ambitions. In early medieval practice, some lesser kings in both north and south India also claimed to have performed the ritual. After the vast empires ruled by the **Gupta** and **Chalukya** dynasties had passed from India's political-military scene, the practice of the horse sacrifice diminished markedly.

ASIATIC SOCIETY. Founded by **William Jones** in **Calcutta** in 1784, the Asiatic Society of **Bengal** was modeled on the Royal Society in England to set high standards for research in the then new field of Oriental Studies. Its journal and other publications reflected serious scholarship and stimulated British and European interest in Indology. The Asiatic Society encouraged the collection of manuscripts, coins, and antiquities and sponsored their exhibition in an excellent museum in Calcutta. Indians were first admitted as members of the Asiatic Society only in 1829. Members of the society still continue scholarly inquiries into the antiquities, humanities, and sciences of India.

ASSAM. The state of Assam has an area of 78,438 square kilometers and an estimated population of 26,638,407 according to the 2001 Census. **Partition** isolated Assam and the northeast from the rest of India by leaving only a narrow connecting corridor, or "chicken's neck," north of **Bangladesh**. Assam includes part of the **Brahmaputra** valley in the north, the Cachar hills, and the Barali plains in the south. It corresponds in part to the ancient kingdom of Kamarupa, referred to in the Indian epic, *Mahabharata*, and is described in the chronicles of the seventh-century Chinese pilgrim **Xuanzang** as ruled by Bhaskaravarman, an ally of **Harsha-vardhana**.

The Ahom people entering Assam from upper **Burma** in the 13th century overran and consolidated their power over a fragmented polity consisting of **Hindu** principalities and tribal associations. The Ahoms absorbed local languages and religions into their own. The resulting amalgam was predominantly **Tantric**, reformed to some extent by a popular Vaishnava movement of the 16th century but surviving to the present day. The Ahom kingdom reached its apogee under Rudra Singh (r. 1696–1714) when it came into conflict with **Mughal** might. It subsequently suffered from Burmese incursions and war. In 1817, Assam was annexed by the **East India Company** and was added to the **Bengal** Presidency.

The economy and demography of Assam were transformed under British rule. Plantations of tea, rubber, chinchona (for production of quinine), hemp, and jute were established, and contract labor was brought in, mainly from Bengal. Bengali was made the official language. Considerable migration of Nepali dairymen, **Marwari** money lenders, and **Sikh** traders also took place. After independence and Partition in 1947, and again after the independence of Bangladesh in 1971, further migrations of Bengalis—Hindu and Muslim—occurred in large numbers. Ethnic identity became the major factor in Assam politics. Ethnic issues have been subjects of controversy between state and central governments and have frequently been the occasion for agitation, violence, and acts of terrorism since the 1980s. In addition to Assamese/Ahom resentment against "foreigners," the **Bodos**, claiming to be indigenous peoples, have agitated against the Assamese since 1992. Assam's boundaries have been altered from time to time as new states were formed to accommodate the aspirations of some tribal groups.

Assam is a potentially wealthy state. Tea cultivation remains dominant, accounting for more than 15% of the world's supply of tea. Oil and natural gas production continues to grow in importance but is vulnerable to sabotage. Recent initiatives to link the economies of northeastern India with those of Southeast Asia and Southwest China offer promise.

AURANGZEB or ALAMGIR (1618–1707). He was the third of four sons of **Shah Jahan** and the last of the "Great **Mughals**"—that proud title fit none of the 11 emperors who followed him. Aurangzeb's outstanding military and administrative abilities were honed as a prince who was kept away from the court in the outposts of empire—the **Deccan**, **Gujarat**, Kandahar. He prevailed over his brothers in a war of succession (1657–1658), dispatched them and their sons to death by one means or another, and imprisoned his father. At its zenith, his rule extended over almost the entire subcontinent, from Kabul to Chittagong, from **Kashmir** to the **Kaveri** river. (See map 3.)

Aurangzeb spent the last decades of his reign attempting to suppress rebellion—with nominal success but with substantial depletion of resources, prestige, and morale. These many rebellions usually had more than one cause—personal, economic, political, or religious. Aurangzeb, therefore, fought the **Rajputs** in the west, the Afghans in the north, the Ahoms in the east, the **Jats** and Satnamis close to **Delhi**, the **Sikhs** in the **Punjab**, and, most debilitating of all, the **Marathas** in the Deccan. His move south in 1681 proved to be a watershed. Although he overcame the rebellious Shi'a sultanates of **Bijapur** and

Golconda, he was unable to gain a decisive victory over the guerilla tactics of the Marathas and was, in effect, defeated. Meanwhile, Hindustan languished in the absence of the emperor and his court.

The decline of the **Mughal Empire** after Aurangzeb was the consequence of institutional and economic weaknesses as well as external factors, but the personal qualities of the emperor at any given time were always decisive. Aurangzeb possessed only half the number of qualities needed to be a successful ruler of India. He inspired awe but lacked both the warmth of personality to attract outstanding lieutenants and the trust to delegate authority. He was an orthodox Sunni Muslim whose personal piety and austerity commanded respect and won him the support of the *Ulema* (see Glossary) and much of the aristocracy. His puritanical zeal in enforcing the letter of the Koranic law to correct what he considered to be earlier excesses of heterodoxy cost him the sympathy of vital partners in the empire—the Rajputs—and provoked the antagonism of others. He abolished music at court, was not a great patron of the arts, and left only a few buildings—including two exquisite mosques—in memoriam. He forbade the building of new temples and permitted the destruction of old ones. In 1679, he reimposed the *jiziya* (see Glossary) tax on non-Muslim males of arms-bearing age that had been abolished by **Akbar** a hundred years earlier, with predictable results of resentment among the majority of his subjects.

Some modern historians ascribe to Aurangzeb the intention of ruling India as an Islamic country and depict the Maratha rebellion led by **Shivaji** as an early stage of **Hindu** nationalism. Some go further in tracing the seeds of **Partition** in 1947 to him. Farfetched though such judgments may be, it is certain that Aurangzeb died, in his own words, "forlorn and destitute," and soon after that his empire disintegrated.

AUROBINDO (SRI AUROBINDO GHOSE) (1872–1950). Born in an educated, Anglicized, middle class family of **Bengal**, Aurobindo was sent to study in England at the age of seven. He excelled in languages, took a first in the Classical Tripos at Cambridge, and passed the entrance examination to the **Indian Civil Service** (ICS). Instead of joining the ICS, however, he served as civil servant and educator in the **Princely State of Baroda** between 1892 and 1906, where he studied **Sanskrit** and Indian philosophy and became politically active.

Aurobindo was disappointed in the moderate platform and elitist membership of the **Indian National Congress** at that time and advocated an alternate strategy, one that envisaged the boycott of British goods, schools, and legal and governmental institutions, and the adoption of *swadeshi* or indigenous production and initiative. He became a natural ally of **Bal Gangadhar Tilak** in the 1906 and 1907 sessions of Congress, when their efforts to lead it in a more radical direction promoted a split of the Extremists from the "moderate" leadership of **Gopal Krishna Gokhale**. In 1906, Aurobindo went to **Calcutta** as principal of a new college (now Jadavpur University), started the Bengali daily *Yugantar*, and published in **Bipin Chandra Pal**'s English daily, *Bande Mataram*. The British authorities considered Aurobindo one of the more dangerous leaders of the revolutionary agitation against the partition of Bengal and arrested him in 1908; he was defended by **C. R. Das** and was acquitted and released after one year in prison.

In 1910, Aurobindo moved to the French enclave of **Pondicherry** where he devoted himself to **yoga**, study, and writing. In his numerous publications he advocated spiritual and moral regeneration as a prelude and accompaniment to political advancement, spoke of a world society, and propounded theories of education that catered to Indian needs. He was assisted by a French couple, Paul and Mira Richard, and was joined by his family and by an ever increasing circle of friends and disciples in what became an *ashram* (see Glossary). He declined invitations to return to active politics but continued to comment on issues of the day. In 1926, Aurobindo went into seclusion and remained so until his death in December 1950, leaving the administration of the growing and international ashram and its many educational and social activities to Mira Richard, who was known as the Mother.

Aurobindo is a major figure in modern Indian political thought, remembered for his contributions to a radical ideology for the Indian national movement. He emphasized the concepts of spiritual nationalism and the divinity of the motherland, the goal of complete freedom from foreign rule, the theories of boycott and passive resistance as well as the use of force, and the vision of a broader Indian role in an international society. At the same time, Aurobindo failed to address the communal problem and alienated most Muslims. He probably will be best remembered for his sense of spiritual power and the *ashram* he founded at Pondicherry, next to which a new center, Auroville, has been named after him.

AVITABILE, PAOLO DI BARTOLOMEW (1791–1850). Avitabile was a French soldier of fortune. He had a career in Naples and Persia and eventually found employment in the **Punjab** under **Ranjit Singh.** A ruthless military commander, Avitabile was appointed governor of Peshawar in 1834. He assisted British troops retreating from Kabul after the first Afghan War (in 1842) and left India a year later.

AWADH or OUDH. A fertile region around **Ayodhya** in the middle **Ganges** valley west of **Banaras** and south of the **Himalaya,** Awadh was known as Kosali in early India. Awadh was an administrative unit of the **Mughal Empire** and was ruled autonomously by a dynasty of **Nawabs** (see Glossary) in the 18th century. Lucknow, the chief city, became well known for its refined way of life and eclectic architecture; administration was lax. Awadh soon came under pressure from an expansionist **East India Company** in the 1760s, signed a **subsidiary alliance** with it in 1801, and was finally annexed by **Lord Dalhousie** in 1856. The latter event precipitated the **Uprising of 1857.**

AYODHYA. This small town in Faizabad district of eastern **Uttar Pradesh (UP)** was the capital of the **Kosala** kingdom in the sixth century BCE and is famous in epic literature as the birthplace (*Ram janam bhoomi*) and capital of Ram, god-hero of the **Ramayana.** Ayodhya was an important trading center during the rule of the **Gupta Dynasty,** and as a pilgrimage site replete with temples its continued prosperity was ensured in the following centuries of political oblivion.

Ayodhya became notorious in the 20th century as a focus of communal passion and violent competition for political power in UP. A bitter **Hindu-Muslim** dispute arose in the 1930s over the site of the 16th-century mosque (*Babri Masjid*) which was constructed, it was alleged, over a prior temple on the birthplace of Ram; the building was closed to the public by government order. In 1949, statues of Hindu deities mysteriously appeared within the mosque, and it was locked without incident. During the 1980s, extremist Hindu organizations, such as the **Vishwa Hindu Parishad (VHP)**, agitated for the demolition or transposition of the mosque and the construction of a temple to Ram. Some Muslims formed a Babri Masjid Action Committee (BMAC) to protect the mosque as well as the civil rights of Indian Muslim citizens. In 1986, a local official opened the closed site to worship by Hindus, and a well-financed campaign to construct a Ram temple in Ayodhya gathered momentum through northern India and among Hindu communities abroad. This campaign, which also included a cross-state and violence ridden procession led by L. K. Advani and some damage to the mosque in 1990, became part of a bid for political power at the state and Union level then being made by the **Bharatiya Janata Party (BJP)**. A BJP government came to power in UP in 1991, acquired land around the mosque, and did nothing to restore calm or order. Passions were kept at a high point by both the VHP and the BMAC.

Rational or scholarly discussion on factual matters such as when the mosque was built or what archaeological evidence existed for an earlier temple or who held legal title to the land on which the edifice stood was overwhelmed in the overheated political and intellectual atmosphere of the early 1990s. The dispute came to a head on December 6, 1992, when bands of young men using sledgehammers, crowbars, and bare hands demolished the *Babri Masjid*. Security forces were present but were not ordered to intervene. Some BJP leaders were arrested but were subsequently released on grounds of insufficient evidence of their direct involvement in the arson. (In March 2004 the Justice Liberhan Commission of Inquiry indicted three BJP leaders for conspiracy in the demolition.) In December 1992, waves of communal violence unprecedented since **Partition** engulfed many cities in India, and temples were destroyed in **Bangladesh** and **Pakistan**. Normalcy was only gradually restored in the UP and the rest of India.

The dispute moved into the **Supreme Court**, which made the government "statutory receiver" of undisputed land around the site and ruled in 1993, in 1994, and again in 2002 that the status quo (i.e., no new construction) must be upheld until titles to land ownership were proven in the lower courts. Agitation for construction of a Ram temple continued even while local and national bodies of Hindus and Muslims, which included highly respected religious figures as well as secular notables, attempted to cool passions and reach a mutually agreed upon solution through negotiation. Although the BJP listed building a Ram temple in its election manifesto of 1998, it dropped that item from the manifesto of the winning National Democratic Alliance out of deference to its coalition partners and agreed to abide by judicial decisions on Ayodhya. At the same time, the VHP continued agitation and set a March 15, 2002, deadline for commencing construction of a temple. Troops were deployed to prevent such action, and Prime Minister **Atal Behari Vajpayee** appealed to his supporters on the Hindu Right not to disrupt order. He was much criticized by them, especially when the BJP unexpectedly lost the general elections of 2004. Later in the year Ayodhya was resurrected as a vote mobilizer for the BJP, although its efficacy among a population apparently sickened by communal violence cannot be predicted.

AZAD, MAULANA ABUL KALAM (1888–1958). Abul Kalam was born in Mecca to an eminent scholar and an Arab mother. He was educated at home in **Calcutta** along traditional Islamic lines, but at an early age he questioned conventional wisdom and secretly studied English. He traveled in Egypt, Iraq, Syria, and Turkey as a young man and was exposed to the nationalist and revolutionary ideas circulating there at the time. On his return to Calcutta he founded a weekly Urdu paper, *Al-Hilal*, in which he challenged the loyalist attitude toward Britain espoused by the **Aligarh Movement** among Indian Muslims. Later, he formed a Nationalist Muslim Party within the **Indian National Congress**, disputed the **All-India Muslim League**'s claim to represent all Muslims, and headed various efforts to resolve communal problems. Along with other Congress leaders, he was imprisoned several times.

Azad was president of Congress in 1923 and again from 1940 to 1946, during which time he conducted negotiations for independence with **Sir Stafford Cripps** in 1942 and with **Lord Wavell** and the **Cabinet Mission** in 1946. He was passionately opposed to **Partition**, and in his autobiography, *India Wins Freedom*, blames Congress leaders for it as much as **Mohammed Ali Jinnah**. After independence, Azad was Minister of Education in **Jawaharlal Nehru**'s cabinet and fostered scientific laboratories and other institutions of higher learning. Lacking the attributes of a mass mobilizer, Azad was renowned for his integrity, piety, rationality, and moderation.

AZARIAH, VADANAYAKAM SAMUEL (1874–1945). The son of a village pastor in **Madras**, Azariah became secretary of that city's Young Men's Christian Association (YMCA) in 1895. He rose by his own efforts and against considerable opposition from British as well as Indian members of the Anglican Church to become the first Indian bishop and was appointed to head the diocese of Dornakal in 1912. He helped found the Indian Missionary Society in 1902. Throughout his life he campaigned for indigenous leadership and for equal treatment of Indian and expatriate Christian missionaries, addressing the subject at a World Missionary Conference held at Edinburgh in 1912. Azariah was ecumenical and took a leading role in promoting church union, resulting in the establishment of the United Church of India soon after independence.

AZMI, SHABANA (1950–). This icon of India's New Indian Cinema, she is the daughter of film lyricist Kaifi Azmi and the actress Shaukat. She graduated from the Film and Television Institute of India in 1972, acted on the stage and in some Western films, and became a regular presence in films directed by **Shyam Benegal**. Shabana Azmi is equally well known as a courageous political activist working with various **Non Governmental Organizations** to fight for the causes of Mumbai's slum and pavement dwellers, freedom of expression, and communal harmony. The latter took on special urgency in Mumbai in the aftermath of terrorist bombings and communal violence in 1993 and 2002.

– B –

BABUR (1483–1530). The founder of the **Mughal Empire** in India. Babur was born in Farghana (present-day Uzbekistan) of a lineage that included both **Timur** and Chengiz Khan the Mongol. From the age of 11, he was one of several Timurid princes competing for various thrones in Central Asia while Uzbeg power steadily expanded. Babur eventually abandoned his ambition to hold Samarkand and consolidated his kingdom of Kabul. He then turned his attention to the north Indian plains where the ruling **Lodi** dynasty was in trouble.

Using newly acquired guns from Turkey, Babur defeated Sultan Ibrahim Lodi at the battle of **Panipat** in April 1526 and proceeded to capture **Delhi** and Agra. Preparing to face a formidable **Rajput** confederacy led by Rana Sangha of Mewar in 1527, Babur used dramatic gestures such as destroying his drinking cups and invoking **Islam** to raise the morale of his flagging followers. He prevailed in a close-fought battle at Khanua, and two years later fought and won in the east over Afghan chiefs. He was now Emperor of Hindustan in both fact and name. Although his own early death and the military-administrative weakness of his son, Humayun, prevented an immediate consolidation of Babur's victories in India, the Mughal Dynasty that he founded ruled most of the Indian subcontinent into the 18th century and nominally in Delhi until 1857.

Babur emerges from the pages of his journal, the *Baburnama*, and other contemporary accounts as a man of outstanding ability, valor, grace, and refinement. His belief in conciliating rather than antagonizing or victimizing defeated enemies and in winning over local populations for the sake of effective rule resurfaced in the policies of his grandson **Akbar**. Babur's warm personality also generated loyalty. He recorded his observations of events, people, flora, and fauna with a naturalist's eye and a poet's pen. Wherever he lived he created gardens, and his patronage of the arts was continued by his successors. His yearning for the formal gardens and cooler climate of his ancestral lands was expressed in his desire to be buried in Kabul. The first of his dynasty to rule in India, Babur was in many ways the most appealing.

BACHCHAN, AMITABH (1942–). His name has been a household word in India since the 1970s when he was the biggest star of Hindi cinema, and more recently, when he hosted a popular **television** quiz program. Amitabh Bachchan was born in **Allahabad** to the noted poet Harivanshrai Bachchan, friend of **Jawaharlal Nehru** and his family. The friendship continued through subsequent generations and

Amitabh, as a member of the **Congress Party** then headed by **Rajiv Gandhi**, was elected to Parliament in 1984 for one term.

Amitabh Bachchan portrayed angry, brooding, tough, outlaw heroes in his early starring roles, but he also acted in films that had political undertones or historical themes, such as **Satyajit Ray**'s *Shatranj ke Khiladi* (1977). In 1995, Bachchan founded a corporation to market entertainment products, including his own charismatic presence and mellifluous voice. In 2003 he was chosen to be the worldwide Ambassador for the United Nations Children's Emergency Fund.

BAHADUR SHAH II (1775–1862). The last **Mughal** Emperor, 19th in the line of **Babur,** Bahadur Shah occupied the throne at **Delhi** from 1837–1858 but in name only. In fact, he was a pensioner of the British and his domain scarcely extended beyond the compounds of his palaces. Nevertheless, he was a patron of the arts and literature and had innumerable dependents. The brilliant but melancholic atmosphere of his court is conveyed in the poetry of **Ghalib** and Zauq.

Bahadur Shah, without taking the initiative himself, became the symbolic head of the great Mutiny or **Uprising of 1857**. The British sacked the Mughal forts and tombs when they recaptured Delhi, and they imprisoned the emperor and exiled him to Rangoon, **Burma**. His health rapidly deteriorated in that humid climate until he died and was buried there. His chief claim to fame is not as a political figure but as a poet. He wrote in Persian and in Urdu, using the pseudonym Zafar.

BAHMANI DYNASTY. In 1347, dissident nobles under the **Tughlaq Dynasty** of the **Delhi Sultanate** established an independent kingdom in the **Deccan** under Ala ud-din Bahman Shah. He and his successors more or less replicated the military habits and harsh revenue-collecting institutions of their counterparts in the north and were engaged in continual hostilities with their southern neighbor, the **Vijayanagar Empire**. They also attracted many foreigners to their court. An eclectic culture emerged that expressed itself in vigorous schools of Deccani architecture, literature, and painting.

After 1482 the Bahmani sultanate broke into five parts: Ahmadnagar, Berar, Bidar, Bijapur, and Golconda, each with its own independent dynasties. These were subsequently overcome by the Mughals.

BAHUJAN SAMAJ PARTY (BSP). In 1984, Kanshi Ram formed the BSP to voice the demands of the poor and dispossessed. A former civil servant, Kanshi Ram entered politics as a result of working among the Dalits and other disadvantaged groups in Indian society. Although he lost the first election he contested from **Allahabad** in 1988, he made his party's name familiar throughout the country within a short time. The BSP claims allegiance to the memory of Dr. **Ambedkar** and his struggle to raise the status of the outcastes. Members of the party gained much media attention by their denigration of **Mahatma Gandhi**'s ways of approaching the same cause.

The BSP platform is justice for the dispossessed, and it draws its membership and support from the Dalits and, more recently, from the Muslims. In the 1989 general elections to the **Lok Sabha** the BSP won 2 of the 75 seats it contested, with 9.9% of the vote, in the state of **Uttar Pradesh (UP)**. It also won a few seats in the state legislative assemblies of **Andhra Pradesh** and **Madhya Pradesh** in state elections of 1990. Kanshi Ram and the BSP continued activities among the Dalits, an increasing number of whom were now literate and doubly dissatisfied, as a confrontationalist atmosphere between **caste**, class, and religious groups intensified in UP during the early 1990s. The **Bharatiya Janata Party (BJP)** state government did not prevent **Hindu** militants from destroying the 16th-century mosque at **Ayodhya** in December 1992, and it was dismissed by New Delhi soon after and was defeated in the fresh state elections 1993. A coalition government composed of the **Samajvadi Party** and the BSP, which won 60 seats, took office in Lucknow under the chief ministership of Mulayam Singh Yadav. The BSP subsequently formed coalition governments in the UP with the BJP, led by Kanshi Ram's successor **Mayawati**.

The taste of political power in the heavily populated and politically key state of UP galvanized Dalits all over India. The BSP is recognized as a national **political party** and won eight seats to the Lok Sabha in the general elections of 1996, 20 seats in 1998, 26 in 1999, and 36 in the recently concluded general elections of 2004.

BAJAJ, RAHUL (1940–). Bajaj is the grandson of Jamnalal Bajaj (1889–1942), founder of the Bajaj industrial group, who was a friend and supporter of **M. K. Gandhi** from 1920 until the latter's death in

1948. Rahul's father, Kamalnarayan Bajaj, enlarged and diversified his inheritance by entering into joint ventures or technical collaborations with leading European companies, including Italy's Piaggio and Company for the manufacture of scooters by Bajaj Auto Limited. Rahul took over management of the company in 1968, after studying economics and law in university, taking an MBA degree from Harvard University in 1964, and serving a rigorous apprenticeship. Between 1960 and the early 1980s Bajaj Autos enjoyed a virtual monopoly of scooter sales in India's protected market and made a successful export thrust in the 1970s that provoked Piaggio to retaliate by linking with competitive Indian companies. Bajaj Autos continued to lead the field, producing a range of two-wheeled vehicles that were rugged, reliable, economical and long lived enough to be used by the **Indian Army** on the **Siachin Glacier** as well as by millions of middle-class Indians even today. Production expanded from 3,995 in the year 1961 to 4,400 a day in 1998, making Bajaj the world's largest scooter producer and fourth largest two-wheeler producer after three Japanese companies.

Rahul Bajaj maintains his family's Gandhian style of simple, modest living, often at the factory itself, maintaining a spotless manufacturing complex outside **Pune** and following a determined work ethic in cooperation with workers and technical managers. He invested seriously in research and development only in the late 1990s. He is a spokesman for industry in India and has become celebrated for his forthright and blunt opinions on various aspects of public life.

BAJI RAO I (1698–1740). Baji Rao succeeded his father Balaji Vishvanath as **Peshwa** in 1720 and formulated a bold plan of **Maratha** expansion. In the twilight of the **Mughal Empire** he suggested, "let us strike at the trunk of the withering tree. The branches will fall of themselves. Thus would the Maratha flag fly from the Krishna to the Indus." (R. V. Nadkarni, *The Rise and Fall of the Maratha Empire,* 176.)

Baji Rao concentrated on winning influence in north India and obtained permission from the Mughal Emperor to extend Maratha sovereignty over substantial parts of Malwa and **Gujarat** in 1731. He secured the friendship of important **Rajput** princes, reached a compromise agreement with the Nizam of **Hyderabad**—a hereditary enemy—and captured territory on the west coast from the **Por-**

tuguese. As a result, he expanded the area over which the Marathas held supremacy by collecting levies of *chauth* (one quarter of estimated products) and *sardeshmukhi* (acknowledgment of revenue ownership). He also projected the goal of a **Hindu** empire and figures as heroic in the sociocultural agenda of **Hindutva**.

One of the effects of enhanced power and prestige was loss of cohesion in the Maratha empire and armies. Able chiefs who extended Maratha dominion, but not necessarily on behalf of the Peshwa, created rival principalities. Baji Rao was succeeded by his son, Balaji Baji Rao, who employed non-Maratha mercenaries in the army, gave up the ideal of a united Hindu empire, and resorted to predatory warfare, which alienated Hindu and Muslim alike. Baji Rao was not able to organize united resistance to the invasion of **Nadir Shah** from Persia in 1736. Worse still, Maratha successors were defeated by the Afghan **Ahmad Shah Abdali** at **Panipat** in 1761. In short, Baji Rao's achievements, though impressive, proved ephemeral because the Marathas failed to step into the shoes of the Mughals.

BAJRANG DAL. This youth wing of the **Vishva Hindu Parishad** (VHP) was formed in 1984 under the leadership of Vinay Katiyar of the **Rashtriya Swayamsevak Sangh** (RSS). More than a hundred thousand young men were recruited from the poorly educated, upper caste but lower middle class, urban unemployed. They were trained in camps to "be bold." They were not issued uniforms or provided with the discipline of daily classes and doctrinal rigor as in the RSS, but their frustrations were channeled into fighting Muslims (of whom they held negative stereotyped images) and advancing the cause of building a Ram temple at **Ayodhya**. Members of the growing Bajrang Dal, with their saffron headbands, have been prominent in violent communal riots since the mid-1980s, in agitation against implementation of the **Mandal Commission** Report in 1990, and above all in the demolition of the Babri Masjid on December 6, 1992. The Government of India banned the organization for its likely use of criminal violence against other religious communities; but because the courts refused to confirm notification of the ban, it was lifted in June 1993. The Bajrang Dal is similar in sociology and psychology to the **Shiv Sena**, but is more widely spread through northern Indian states. It is the ugly face of the **Hindutva** movement and is an embarrassment to the **Bharatiya Janata Party** as leader of a governing coalition for the period 1998–2004.

BALBAN, GHIYAS UD-DIN (r. 1266–1285). Balban was one of the "famous forty" Turkish (Central Asian) slaves of **Iltutmish**, the real founder of the **Delhi Sultanate**. After these men were brought to Delhi in 1232, Balban's abilities as a military commander won him high rank at court. He joined other nobles in opposing the brief rule of Raziyah, daughter and heiress of Iltutmish, and succeeded in deposing her in favor of her brother. Balban became his close adviser, father-in-law, and then successor on the throne at a time of turbulence. He tried to enhance the majesty of the Delhi Sultanate by introducing elaborate court rituals and enforcing strict justice. He reorganized the army and stamped out rebellions. More importantly, Balban guarded the western marches of India against Mongol attacks with vigilance and substantial success.

BANARAS. *See* VARANASI.

BANDA (SINGH) BAHADUR (1670–1716). He was an ascetic who chose to bind himself (*banda*) to **Gobind Singh**, tenth guru of the **Sikhs**. The guru baptized him into the Khalsa (see Glossary) and commissioned him to lead its struggle for survival against an increasingly oppressive and intolerant **Mughal** state. Banda and his men spread through the hills and valleys between the Sutlej and the **Yamuna** rivers to lead an agrarian revolt against large landowners and to prevail over the forces of the Mughal Viceroy Wazir Khan.

Banda sustained Sikh rule in areas in and around the **Punjab** outside the framework of the Mughal state from 1710 to 1715. He attributed his victory to God formally in the coins he struck and the seal he used. Thereafter, the phrase "the Khalsa shall rule" (*raj karega khalsa)* was incorporated in the daily prayer of the Sikhs. In 1715, the army of Mughal Emperor Farukh Siyar defeated Banda and his followers. They were tortured and executed by methods designed to deter future revolts, which had the opposite effect. Banda and his Sikh followers refused to renounce their faith and became martyrs immortalized in daily recitation of prayers.

BANDE MATARAM. A patriotic song using Mother (Goddess) as a metaphor for India, "Bande Mataram" was written by **Bankim Chandra Chatterji** and first published in 1875. It became popular in **Bengal** after **Rabindranath Tagore** composed new music for it in 1882, but it was raised to the level of a nationalist slogan by protesters against the 1905 **partition of Bengal**. The song's immortality was assured when the British government proscribed it, and police bore down heavily on its singers at the Calcutta session of the **Indian National Congress** in 1906. "Bande Mataram" was the opening song of all Congress gatherings until the 1930s, when some Muslims objected to what they considered idolatrous imagery and some non-Bengalis declared it excessively parochial. For these reasons, the Congress Working Committee decided in 1937 that only the first two stanzas would be sung as invocation. The great majority of the **Constituent** Assembly, selecting a national anthem on the eve of Indian independence, preferred another Tagore song, "Jana Gana Mana." "Bande Mataram" gradually faded from the official national scene even though the **Bharatiya Janata Party**–led coalition government in New Delhi (1998–2004) attempted to revive it.

BANDUNG CONFERENCE. This gathering of the heads of government of 29 Asian and African states in April 1955 was hosted by Indonesia with the full cooperation of India. The main subjects of the conference were economic and cultural cooperation, human rights and self-determination, problems of dependent peoples, promotion of world peace, and nuclear disarmament. Its members condemned colonialism "in all its manifestations."

Indian Prime Minister **Jawaharlal Nehru** recommended that newly independent states in Asia and Africa approach world problems in a spirit of mutual friendship and cooperation, peaceful coexistence among different systems, and nonalignment from military alliances. The Bandung Conference reflected and advanced a sense of self-respect among participating countries and a desire to be heard in world councils. The deliberately imprecise final communiqué accommodated different points of view. The Bandung Conference has come to be regarded as the beginning of a reform movement within the international system led by the nonaligned Afro-Asian and Latin

American countries—also known as the "Third World" and the "South"—to bring about a more equitable distribution of political and economic power in the world.

BANERJEA, SURENDRANATH (1848–1925). Banerjea belonged to a Bengali *bhadralok* (see Glossary) or gentry family. He was educated in **Calcutta** and in England. He appeared for the competitive examinations for the **Indian Civil Service** in 1869 and excelled, gaining second place. (Two other Indians, Romesh Chandar Dutt and Behari Lal Gupta, were also successful that year.) But Banerjea was disqualified on grounds of misrepresenting his age, Indian reckoning of age being different from the English reckoning. He sued the British government, won his case, and was reinstated. Soon after, however, the District Collector under whom he served had him dismissed for a minor infringement of rules. Though Banerjea often spoke in praise of individual Englishmen, he was critical of the bureaucratic system that they had established to rule India. He found the government impervious to public opinion and was struck by the "helpless impotency of our people." He was a skilled orator and found himself a popular hero when he made a lecture tour of northern India in 1877 and 1878.

Surendranath Banerjea took over the *Bengalee,* a daily newspaper critical of the government, in 1876 and also became a college teacher of English. He helped found Ripon College in Calcutta in 1882. He also founded the Indian Association, one of several voluntary groups that sprang up throughout British India in the late 19th century, pressing for representative institutions and higher participation of Indians in administration. He was part of a delegation that went to London in 1890 to plead this case. He served on Calcutta's Municipal Council and participated in the All-India National Conference, a precursor of the **Indian National Congress**.

As one of the first generation of modern Indian nationalists, Banerjea attended every session of Congress during his lifetime and was president in 1895 and again in 1902. He was a moderate who believed in constitutional reform as the path to self-government. He drafted petitions and organized public meetings, press conferences, and deputations to present the Indian case and to appeal to the British conscience. He redoubled his efforts after the unpopular **partition of**

Bengal in 1905 and left the Calcutta Municipal Corporation along with 28 other Indians.

Although Banerjea, **Gopal Krishna Gokhale**, and other "moderates" appeared to prevail when Congress split in 1907, **Bal Gangadhar Tilak** and the "extremists" seemed to have greater popular appeal in the gathering momentum of the national movement. Banerjea lost public acclaim and elections in 1912; his 1915 schemes for constitutional reform did not bear fruit. He had no sympathy for **Mahatma Gandhi** or his methods, despite Gandhi's leading role in Congress. Banerjea retained his English friends even to the close of his life. One was Lord Ronaldshay, Governor of Bengal, who appointed Banergjea as the first Indian Minister when the new constitutional scheme of **"dyarchy"** was implemented in 1921.

BANGALORE. The capital city of the state of **Karnataka**, Bangalore was once a quiet and green administrative center for the **Princely State** of **Mysore** with a salubrious climate and some fine institutions, including the Indian Institute of Science, founded in 1933. Prime Minister **Jawaharlal Nehru** named Bangalore a "city of the future" and encouraged the growth and spread of scientific enterprise there in the 1950s. By the 1980s, Bangalore had 3 universities, 14 engineering colleges, 47 polytechnic schools, a variety of research institutes, and hosted high-tech public sector companies such as Hindustan Aeronautics, Bharat Electronics, Hindustan Machine Tools, and part of the Indian Space Research Organization. A software technology park was established outside Bangalore in the early 1990s as an economic free trade zone with fewer of the regulatory constraints that hampered business in other parts of India. An effort was also made to provide Bangalore with world-class infrastructure facilities in terms of roads, fiber-optic telecommunication lines, health and recreational facilities, housing loans, and more industrial parks. **Narayana Murthy**, who founded Infosys, and companies such as **Wipro Infotech**, established campuses employing thousands of software experts and engineers. Some of the largest and most successful companies in the world, such as Microsoft, Motorola, and Texas Instruments among others, were attracted to locate major facilities in the city. Bangalore became a major center for providing "outsourced" services to advanced countries. By the end of the 20th century, Karnataka or Bangalore accounted for one third of India's total software exports, which had already reached impressive levels. Leading international figures, such as America's President Bill Clinton, made a point of visiting Bangalore.

Bangalore's very success and expanded population, from half a million to over five million in less than 20 years, has produced inevitable problems. Notable among these are traffic congestion, high property prices, an influx of rural immigrants, and breakdowns in power supply and telephone connections that disrupt operations. Other cities strove to attract high-tech and information technology companies with some success, especially **Hyderabad**, **Chennai**, **Pune**, **Delhi**, and, more recently, **Kolkata**. Nevertheless, Bangalore is likely to remain one of the most successful IT centers in Asia, rivaling Silicon Valley in California.

BANGLADESH. Formerly East Pakistan, Bangladesh is an independent country of 142,776 square kilometers located in the eastern part of the Indian subcontinent astride the deltaic region of the **Ganges** and **Brahmaputra** rivers. It has a typical monsoon climate but is subject to cyclones. From 1947 to 1971 it was East Pakistan, and before that it shared the history and culture of **Bengal**; the national language is Bengali.

The Peoples Republic of Bangladesh is one of the most densely populated areas in the world and one of the poorest. Natural disasters and endemic diseases take a heavy toll, and there is great dependence on foreign aid. As in the rest of the subcontinent, many ethnic groups make up its population, but the religious affiliation is predominately **Islam** (80%, with **Hindus** amounting to about 10% and the rest made up of **Buddhists**, **Christians**, and tribal religions. Although literacy rates are low, Bangladesh has a strong tradition of political consciousness and a vibrant civil society. **Non governmental organizations** have carried out several innovative development schemes including the world renowned micro credit program of the Grameen Bank. Since independence in 1971 democratic government has been interrupted by periods of authoritarian, military administration, but there are two main political parties contesting for political power.

Relations between India and Bangladesh are complicated by many factors including those originating in the period before the **partition** of India in 1947, India's crucial role in Bangladesh's liberation war against

Pakistan in 1971, the pressures perceived in Bangladesh of being a smaller country effectively surrounded by India, and intra-Islamic politics and tensions. Since the early 1980s, Bangladesh has been a keen advocate of regional cooperation and is a member of the **South Asian Association for Regional Cooperation**. Trade and investment between India and Bangladesh has increased steadily since the mid-1990s, with India offering some non-reciprocal concessions. Various programs have also been initiated, calling for greater economic integration among the geographically contiguous entities in the eastern part of the Indian subcontinent and those of Southeast Asia and southwest China.

BARANI, ZIA UD-DIN. He came from Baran (present-day Bulandsher) and lived in **Delhi** at the courts of Mohammad and Firoze Shah **Tughlaq**. His contemporary account, *Ta'rikh-i-Firuz Shahi*, is ranked among the most important literary sources for history of the **Delhi Sultanate** in the 13th and 14th centuries and is full of vivid detail.

BARODA. Baroda was originally the capital city of a leading **Maratha** state formed by the Gaekwar in the 18th century. As Maratha power declined, the Gaekwar signed a **Subsidiary Alliance** with the **East India Company** in 1805 and accepted British **paramountcy**. The efforts of a far-sighted ruler in the early 20th century gave Baroda a higher rate of literacy and a better school system, railway, and administration than most other parts of India, whether under British or Princely rule. After Indian independence, Baroda was administratively integrated with **Bombay** and later with **Gujarat** state. The city of Baroda hosts a fine university and many industries.

BASSEIN, TREATY OF. This treaty signed between **Peshwa** Baji Rao II and the Marquis of **Wellesley** in 1802 gave the British effective control of the **Maratha** homeland and supremacy over the **Deccan** and western India.

The Peshwa solicited an alliance with the **East India Company** in an effort to reestablish his authority in the wake of conflicts that were tearing apart the Maratha confederacy. In return for British recognition of his claims in **Poona** and a British subsidiary force stationed in his dominions, he relinquished all rights to **Surat**, signed over the revenues of several districts, accepted British arrangements with the

Nizam of **Hyderabad** and the Gaekwar of **Baroda**, and promised to abstain from war or relations with foreign powers without prior British approval. The following year he surrendered further territories in Bundelkhand.

Other Maratha leaders did not initially accept the Peshwa's surrender of independence in this treaty. But superior British forces prevailed in the two Maratha wars that followed, and in 1818 took Bassein itself, a coastal fortress.

BASU, JYOTI (1914–). As Chief Minister of West **Bengal** from 1977 to 2000, Basu held the position of elected chief executive in a state of the Indian Union longer than anyone else.

Basu was born in **Calcutta** and was educated in the manner typical for the Bengali elite of his generation: at St. Xavier's School and Presidency College, Calcutta, followed by legal studies at the Middle Temple, London. He joined the Calcutta Bar in 1940 and the **Communist Party of India (CPI)** shortly after. He was elected to the Bengal Legislative Assembly in 1947 and was active in opposition to the **Congress** government of the state, serving as leader of the opposition from 1957 to 1971.

When the CPI split in 1964, Jyoti Basu became a prominent figure in the breakaway **CPI-Marxist** party. He has been a leading member of the Politburo and National Secretariat since that time, concentrating on West Bengal. Basu's CPI(M) government initially had to strive to restore order in a state racked by violence, industrial and land disputes, and various forms of sponsored protection rackets through the late 1960s and early 1970s. During the 1980s, rural development and rural education programs were put into operation with considerable success. Jyoti Basu also provided incentives to domestic and foreign industrialists for reinvestment in what was once an important industrial belt in India but made only small public investments in modernizing the city of Calcutta. His personal credibility carried weight— despite continuous feuds with Congress governments in New Delhi—and in the mid-1990s his name was put forward as a possible consensus prime minister of a coalition government. Basu declined.

BATUTA, IBN (1304–1378). A traveler and scholar, Batuta journeyed from his home in North Africa to Mecca, where he spent three years, and then to India, where he spent eight years. He was an elder contemporary of Ibn Khaldun, the great Arab historian and philosopher.

The full text of Ibn Batuta's travelogue was rediscovered in the 19th century and is an important literary source for the political history of the **Khalji** and **Tughlaq** dynasties of the **Delhi Sultanate** as well as for socioeconomic conditions in mid-14th century India. Ibn Batuta differs from another contemporary historian, **Zia ud-din Barani**, in praising the administration of **Alauddin Khalji** and criticizing Muhammad bin Tughlaq's move of his capital from **Delhi** to the **Deccan** in 1327. Ibn Batuta was close to Tughlaq and served as his ambassador to **China**, then ruled by the Yuan or Mongol dynasty. Batuta lived in China for a few years before returning to India by sea through Southeast Asia. His glowing descriptions of India recall those of Chinese travelers in earlier times.

BAXAR or BUXAR, BATTLE OF. This battle was fought on October 22, 1764, between two rival claimants for power in eastern India: Nawab Mir Kasim, nominally head of **Bengal** under the **Mughal** Emperor Shah Alam on the one hand, and on the other the **East India Company**, de facto holders of power in Bengal since their victory at **Plassey** in 1757.

Mir Kasim was engaged in a contest with the British for supremacy and formed an alliance with the Nawab of **Awadh** and the legal suzerain, Shah Alam, to recover power. Mir Kasim's poorly led cavalry and infantry were outmaneuvered and defeated in a series of military engagements through the summer of 1764 culminating at Baxar, 120 kilometers west of **Patna**. The victorious forces of the East India Company at Baxar consisted of artillery, 5,297 Sepoys (see Glossary), and 857 European troops under the command of Hector Munro. Mir Kasim fled; he died in obscurity in 1777.

Shah Alam joined the English camp and became a British pensioner. Still emperor in name, he conferred the title *Bahadur* and rights of *dewani* (see Glossary) or revenue collection on the East India Company. By these actions he legitimized and confirmed British rights of conquest in the huge *subah* (see Glossary) of Bengal. Therein lies the significance of Baxar, on a par with the more frequently remembered Plassey.

BEDI, KIRAN (1949–). Kiran Bedi was the first woman officer in the Indian Police Service, commissioned in 1972. She had a happy and secure childhood but was always ambitious and controversial, defying the conventional assumptions of male superiority. Her police career, too, was marked by achievement and controversy. Kiran Bedi is best known for her contributions to prison reform through the introduction of **yoga** and meditation, and to treatment for drug and alcohol abuse. In 1987 she founded the Navjyoti Organization that provided free community-based therapeutic treatment for addicts. In 1994 she received the Magsaysay Award for government service and established the India Vision Foundation that provided schools for children of prisoners and funding projects for the rural disabled.

BENEGAL, SHYAM (1934–). Born in **Andhra Pradesh**, filmmaker Benegal works in both Telegu and Hindi languages. He studied at Osmania University, where he founded the Hyderabad Film Society. He worked in **Mumbai** with advertising agencies from 1959 to 1973 and made many documentary films before going to the United Kingdom and the United States on a **Homi Bhabha** scholarship to gain experience in television production. On his return to India, he used a quasi-realist style in his film *Ankur,* and went on to direct many political and documentary movies as well as commercial films in a new sector called "middle cinema." He is an influential figure in national organizations formulating policy on the **film industry**.

BENGAL. The present-day Indian state of West Bengal is part of the much larger region known as Bengal in history, which more or less comprised the lower **Ganges** and **Brahmaputra** valleys, their common deltaic area, and hilly terrain to the southeast, north, and east. The principal language of West Bengal, Bengali, is also the language of **Tripura** and Cooch Bihar in India as well as of the independent state of **Bangladesh**.

Archaeology has uncovered the existence of pre-**Aryan** urban sites in Bengal, which was probably outside the Vedic zone and on the edge of Aryavarta. By the fourth century BCE the region was part of the north Indian political-cultural landscape and included in the **Mauryan** and **Gupta** empires. Bengal was commercially important, connected as it was by maritime trade and travel to the Indianized kingdoms of **Burma** and Southeast Asia and to **China**, as well as to **Ceylon**. The Romans knew Bengal, which is mentioned in *The Periplus of the Erythrean Sea* of the first century CE and in Ptolemy's *Geography* of the following century. Chinese **Buddhist** pilgrims such as **Faxian** and **Xuanzang** also visited Bengal. It became the chief center of Mahayana Buddhism and **Tantra**, which then spread to **Nepal** and **Tibet**.

Bengal attained wealth and power in the 8th and 9th centuries under the **Pala Dynasty**, which revived the ancient city of Pataliputra as its capital and encouraged literary endeavor in the evolving vernacular **language**. The Palas were in military competition with the **Cholas** of the south and the **Chandellas** of central India. The succeeding Sena Dynasty extended control over Kalinga (**Orissa**) and Kamarupa (**Assam**) but fell to the Turks in the 13th century. Bengal figures prominently in the history of the **Delhi Sultanate**, which could not exercise the continuous or tight control over eastern India that it wanted. During these centuries **Sufi** *pitrs* (see Glossary) spread a popular syncretic **Islam**, especially in the north and east. The local mosque and tomb architecture of the period expresses a similar eclecticism. This continued during the **Mughal** era when Bengal was firmly incorporated into the empire and was prized for its high revenues from cultivated land and export of textiles. For the same reasons, Bengal attracted European trading companies, which set up their factories and competed for influence at a court that was virtually independent of Delhi in the 18th century.

The **East India Company** established mastery over Bengal through intrigue, trade, and military victories at **Plassey** and **Baxar**. The maladministration, extortion, and corruption practiced by the company was aptly termed "shaking the pagoda tree" by one English historian. Regulation by London followed in the 1770s and 1780s. The Bengal Presidency became not only the vanguard of the British Empire in India but the arena for its early attempts at social engineering, including the **Permanent Settlement** of 1793 and the abolition of **sati** in 1829. Promoting English as the medium of education after 1835 had immense and far-reaching effects. Men from high caste Bengali **Hindu** families who were educated in English—such as **Ram Mohun Roy** and members of the **Tagore** family—took leading roles in what is often called the Indian Renaissance of the 19th century; social reform was high on their agenda. A similar process of adapting to British rule through modernization took place among Muslims late in the 19th century.

A drive for political participation followed naturally, and many Bengalis were in leading and influential positions in the nationalist movement. **Lord Curzon's partition of Bengal** in 1905 galvanized political activity of all kinds, as did subsequent decisions on the part of the British government or the **Indian National Congress**. Relations between politicized Hindus and Muslims in Bengal fluctuated during the first half of the 20th century: communal conflicts on the streets were not uncommon. Coalitions in the legislature were formed by **C. R. Das** of the **Swaraj Party** in the 1920s and by **Abul Fazl** Haq of the Krishak Praja Party after 1937. Only after 1945 did the **All-India Muslim League** led by **Mohammed Ali Jinnah** win support in Bengal. His Direct Action Day of August 16, 1946, unleashed a communal frenzy of violence that led the way to **Partition** and the creation of **Pakistan**. A proposal for a united independent Bengal did not carry weight in the pre-independence negotiations. In August 1947, Muslim majority districts in the east and north were formed into East Pakistan, which became Bangladesh in 1971.

West Bengal has an area of 88,752 square kilometers and a population of 80,221,171 according to the 2001 census. Agriculture accounts for about 50% of the state's income and provides 55% of its employment. Industry is of major importance, with steel, chemicals, electronics, ordnance, locomotive, and shipbuilding prominent in the public sector of the post-independence period; coal, tea, jute, and textiles dominate in the traditional and private sector. Substantial progress made in rural electrification, employment, and education has somewhat relieved the population pressure on the chief city, **Calcutta/Kolkata**, if not to visible effect.

BENGAL, PARTITION OF (1905). Lord Curzon's proposal of 1903 to divide the largest province of British India in two was approved by London as a solution to **Calcutta**'s longstanding administrative problems and an expedient method of thwarting the influence of nationalists in **Bengal** over the rest of India. Partition was carried out over protests in 1905 by transferring Bengal's seven eastern districts and its four hill tracts to **Assam**, thus creating a new province of East

Bengal under its own Lieutenant Governor. It proved to be a "grand folly" with far-reaching consequences.

Most immediately, the partition of Bengal provoked an unprecedented reaction of hostility to vivisection of a cultural and linguistic unit and to the perceived British intent of pitting Muslims against **Hindus** by creating a separate Muslim-majority province. A movement of intense nationalism sprang up, especially among Bengali Hindus such as **Aurobindo Ghose**. It spread throughout India under the slogan "**Bande Mataram**" and the triple leadership of "Lal, Bal, and Pal" that is, **Lala Lajpat Rai**, **Bal Gangadhar Tilak**, and **Bipin Chandra Pal**. The movement used a variety of tactics, including bomb throwing and assassination, which were met sternly by the authorities and came to be called "extremist" or "terrorist." Other tactics included the boycott of British goods, work strikes, and **Swadeshi**, by which Indians tangibly demonstrated their rejection of British dominance and also stimulated domestic industrial and handicraft production. These latter tactics were used later to greater effect under the leadership of **Mahatma Gandhi**.

The second consequence of the partition of Bengal was the clash within the **Indian National Congress** between the "extremists" led by Tilak and the constitutionalists, or "moderates," led by **Gopal Krishna Gokhale**, which surfaced at the **Surat** session in 1907. The growing influence of Congress was inevitably reduced and did not revive until after **World War I**.

The indirect consequences of the partition were seen in British reactions to the Indian opposition it sparked. Repressive administration, prosecution of extremists, and Tilak's arrest, conviction, and exile were followed by small measures of constitutional reform passed by a Liberal Government as the India Councils Act in 1909. This introduced the principle of direct election to the legislative councils while simultaneously creating separate communal constituencies and representation for Muslims. Two years later, King George V announced the reunification of Bengal, albeit without Orissa and **Bihar**, at his grand coronation durbar (see Glossary). This was held at **Delhi** in 1911, not in Calcutta, which now lost its status as capital of British India.

BENTINCK, LORD WILLIAM (1774–1839) was a follower of the British Utilitarian political philosopher Jeremy Bentham, who carried out financial, judicial, revenue, and social reforms during his tenure as governor general of the **East India Company**'s dominions in India from 1828 to 1835. Bentinck was backed in London by the Company directors who saw the need for peace and economy to reverse a deficit budget, by the Whig Government, which was also responsible for parliamentary reform in England and the abolition of slavery in the British Empire, and by a climate of British opinion conducive to Evangelicals, free traders, and social engineers.

Bentinck introduced extensive economies in expenditure, including cutting back military allowances, and did not undertake wars of expansion. He launched a new semi-permanent revenue settlement in the northwest territories of the upper **Ganges** valley, signing 30-year agreements confirming existing rights according to local custom. He raised revenue and left a surplus budget. In the judicial sphere, he simplified the court system, replaced Persian as the court language with English in the higher and the local language in the lower courts, and increased the powers and salaries of Indian judges. He started a process that led to the codification of Indian civil and criminal law. Bentinck's administration, combined with the end of the Company's monopoly over trade in 1833, opened India to the economic revolution of 19th-century industrial capitalism, which created first dependence and then the impetus to independence. He abolished transit duties, encouraged steam transport and road and canal building, and permitted the beginnings of iron and coal extraction and the plantation of tea and coffee.

Bentinck is best remembered for his social reform measures that were to prove as decisive as economic changes in shaping the course of events. The abolition of **sati** in 1829 raised a storm of controversy among Indians for and against legislation by an alien power to change an intimate social custom. Bentinck's campaign against child sacrifice, infanticide, and **thagi** (ritual murder and robbery in the name of the goddess Kali) was based, as in the case of abolishing sati, on the superiority of a "universal moral law" over debased local practices. Although no frontal attack on **Hindu** or Muslim faiths or places of worship followed, a law of 1833 removed change of religion as a bar to inheritance and was perceived in India as a measure favoring Christian missionaries. Backed by **Thomas Babington Macaulay**, the Law member on his council, Bentinck declared in 1835 that the content of higher education financed by the Company would be Western, not Eastern, learning, and that the language of instruction would be English, not **Sanskrit** or Persian. English was substituted for Persian as the official language of government business.

Although the reformist impetus that was personified by Bentinck did not last long as a motivation of British policies, a new class of Indians educated in English took the Whig promise of imperial government "in trust" for the interests of the natives seriously. They were Bentinck's true legatees.

BESANT, ANNIE (1847–1933). Annie Besant was a half-Irish woman of boundless energy, wide interests, and powerful oratory. Separated from her husband in 1873, Mrs. Besant began social reform work in London and joined first the Fabian Society and then the **Theosophical Society** in 1889. She was elected president of the latter body in 1907 and held that position until her death.

Her life in India began in 1893 with lecture tours and soon extended to other fields of activity. She became interested in the cause of Indian political advance and expressed her views through a weekly newspaper, *New India*. She founded the **Home Rule League** in 1916 and campaigned in London for constitutional reform. Annie Besant was elected president of the **Indian National Congress** in 1917 but later withdrew from that body in opposition to **Mahatma Gandhi**'s leadership.

Annie Besant continued her organizational and educational work in India for the rest of her life. She founded the Indian Boy Scouts Association, the Women's Indian Association, and the Society for the Promotion of National Education. She also established a National University at her hometown of Adiyar, near **Madras**.

BETEILLE, ANDRE (1934–). Beteille was born in Chandernagore to a French father and an Indian mother whose Bengali family was fervently nationalist. Beteille went to **Calcutta** in 1946 and studied first science and then anthropology with Nirmal Kumar Bose, who encouraged him to do unusual fieldwork among slum dwellers and clerical employees of the Calcutta Municipal Corporation. Beteille moved to the Delhi School of Economics in 1959 and worked with **M. N. Srinivas** in a newly established wing of sociology. Both men are internationally recognized as eminent leaders in the fields of sociology and anthropology for their theoretical daring, rigorous methodology, and intensive fieldwork. Beteille's doctoral thesis resulted in the publication of *Caste, Class and Power: Changing Patterns of Social Stratification in a Tanjore Village* in 1965. It stressed the multiple identities and affiliation of individuals, the play of individuality and social cohesion, and the complexity and fluidity of social arrangements and political processes in democratic India. He found single cause explanations of social structure—whether caste, tribe, or class—inadequate and rejected alike the views of Marxists and Western anthropologists such as Louis Dumont and Robert Redfield as being too narrow. Beteille went on to explore systematically the dispersion of power in society and the diversity of causes for social stratification in contemporary India.

Beteille did not attempt to build a formal "school" of his disciples, but he exercises considerable intellectual influence through his pedagogic example and his writings. These include books entitled *Six Essays in Comparative Sociology* (1976), *Inequality Among Men* (1977), *The Idea of Natural Inequality and other Essays* (1983), and *Society and Politics in India* (1991).

BHABHA, HOMI JEHANGIR (1909–1965). Bhabha was a brilliant physicist from a **Parsi** family who took his doctorate from Cambridge in 1934 and became a Fellow of the Royal Society in 1941. He was Professor at the **Tata** Institute of Fundamental Research when Prime Minister **Jawaharlal Nehru** appointed him Director of India's newly formed Department of Atomic Energy in 1947.

Bhabha projected a three-stage program for developing commercially viable nuclear power in energy-short India and recruited an impressive group of scientists and engineers to implement it. He was awarded the Padma Bhushan in 1954 and received many academic honors in Britain, France, and the United States. His career and life were cut short by an unexplained air crash in 1965. He is regarded as the founder of India's nuclear and space programs. *See also* NUCLEAR POWER PROGRAM.

BHAGAT SINGH (1907–1931). Bhagat Singh was born in a **Sikh** family of peasant proprietors in the Lyallpur district of western **Pun-**

jab and educated at the D.A.V. High School and College run by the **Arya Samaj** at Lahore. From an early age he participated in agitation against British rule. He also wrote for and edited Urdu and Punjabi newspapers in **Amritsar**. He justified the use of revolutionary force in the cause of national freedom and popularized the slogan, *Inquilab Zindabad* (Long live revolution). In 1928, he and an associate shot and killed a police officer; in 1929, they threw a bomb into the Central Legislative Assembly at **Delhi** and afterward gave themselves up for arrest. Bhagat Singh was executed by hanging in 1931. He remains a hero to revolutionary youth.

BHAGAVATA GITA/BHAGVADGITA/GITA. Literally translated as the "Lord's Song," the Gita occupies the sixth part of the epic *Mahabharata* and consists of 700 verses in 18 chapters. It is written in the form of a dialogue between Arjuna, the warrior, and **Krishna**, his charioteer, just before the great battle of Kurukshetra. Arjuna's initial request for guidance on righteous action springs from despondency and confusion at the thought of killing his kinsmen and former teachers on the opposing side. The gist of Krishna's response is that as a **kshatriya** or warrior, Arjuna must do his duty and fight with courage, and not be troubled by the consequences. More generally, Krishna stresses the importance of performing one's prescribed duty as selfless work without attachment to or undue concern with the fruits of such action. This teaching of the Gita was frequently reiterated by **Mahatma Gandhi**, and it inspires others who seek spiritual salvation in a life of action.

Many different philosophies and paths to salvation are discussed in the *Bhagavata Gita*. These include the classical schools of **Hindu** thought and the prescribed paths of meditation, **yoga**, knowledge, sacrifice through priests, and righteous conduct, as well as devotional faith in God. Not surprisingly, therefore, learned commentaries on the Gita—and there have been many since that of **Shankara**—seldom agree on its central message. Some see it as the forerunner of the **Bhakti** movement because it explicitly acknowledges Krishna as an *avatar*, or incarnation of God, revealing himself to Arjuna at one point in the discourse and promising to return to the world in times of need.

Opinions vary on the date of composition, but the *Bhagavata Gita* is generally regarded as a later interpolation in the *Mahabharata* but with a longer oral history than the written record. It is not included in traditional lists of *sruti* or canonical texts but is recognized as a *smriti* text or commentary with the status of an **Upanishad**. The **Sanskrit** of the Gita is not excessively difficult, and many translations in English and other modern languages are extant. Large numbers of people today use the Gita as Gandhi did, as a source of inspiration and guidance and also as a prayer book.

BHAKTI. A **Sanskrit** noun derived from a verb meaning "to share," bhakti is used in a religious sense of passionate love or devotion to God; thus bhakta means "devotee" or "lover of God" and, often, "saint." A central concept in the **Hindu** tradition, bhakti is one of three recognized paths to spiritual salvation, as are *gnana*, or knowledge of the Absolute, and *karma*, or righteous action. The worship of a personal God as manifestation of the Supreme Being is at the core of bhakti.

Many devotional schools gave form to a personal God (*saguna*). Three principal deities—**Shiva**, Shakti, and **Vishnu**—were worshipped under various aspects, with Shiva predominating in the south and Kashmir, Shakti in the east, and Vishnu in the north through the two most popular incarnations, **Ram** and **Krishna**. The most important literary sources for these were the two epics, the *Ramayana* and the *Mahabharata*, and the **Puranas**, especially the later Bhagavata Purana. The devotional compositions of **Tamil** poet-saints in the south and, among others, of Tulsidas, Surdas, and Mira in the north, added immeasurably to Indian culture and remain current. Other devotional schools focused on a formless God (*nirguna*) but were no less influential, as the large and extant followings of Ravidas, **Kabir**, and **Nanak** testify.

Bhakti is historically important as a continuous movement from the 6th to the 16th centuries, arising in the south of India and spreading through the subcontinent in several parallel streams. Various dynasties offered support and patronage to particular bhakti groups; some rulers attempted to suppress them as subversive of the traditional social order.

Certain common features among the several streams gave bhakti the force of a populist sociocultural movement molding the history of India, comparable to the Protestant Reformation in Europe.

The bhakti movement within **Hinduism** was separate from and often antagonistic to the brahmanical tradition. Bhakti saints were usually critical of brahmanical ritualism, formalism, and exclusiveness. Priestly intercession was unnecessary among the devotional congregations typical of the movement. All people without restriction by **caste** or sex were regarded as equal in worship, and human dignity was related to actions rather than birth; new caste-less communities were sometimes formed with institutions of their own. Vernacular languages replaced **Sanskrit** in devotional hymns. Further, bhakti saints such as Kabir and Nanak consciously transcended sectarian differences and blended elements of **Islam** and Hinduism in their teachings. All preached the fundamental equality of human beings and the unity of purpose in religions—devotion to the supreme One.

BHARATENDU, HARISH CHANDRA (1850–1885). Harish Chandra of **Varanasi** was a prolific writer of prose and poetry. He made a pioneering contribution to modern Hindi literature, translated old works, also wrote in **Sanskrit** and Urdu, and was familiar with other north Indian languages. Many of his writings portray the agonies and aspirations of middle-class Indians in transition from tradition to modernity under British rule. He was influenced by the social reformer **Ishwar Chandra Vidyasagar** and himself promoted ideas of social reform through his speeches, writings, and the chain of literary journals that he started. His admirers designated Harish Chandra "Bharatendu" in 1880. He is known by that name in Hindi literature.

BHARATIYA JANATA PARTY (BJP). The BJP was leader of the 23-member National Democratic Alliance (NDA) coalition government in power from 1999 to 2004. The BJP came into existence as a political party as a result of a split in the **Janata Party** in April 1980 on the issue of dual membership with the **Rashtriya Swayamsevak Sangh (RSS)**. The Janata Party executive committee having decided against dual membership, members of the erstwhile **Jana Sangha** led by **Atal Behari Vajpayee** formed a new party, the BJP. Its ties with the RSS and various Hindu right-wing organizations collectively known as the Sangh Parivar (or RSS family) remain very strong; men of RSS background dominate in the BJP leadership and much mobilization of support for the BJP during the 1990s came through the efforts of the RSS, **Vishva Hindu Parishad (VHP)**, and **Bajrang Dal**. At the same time, tensions surface from time to time between the BJP as a political party seeking or exercising governmental power, and what some have called a radical social movement for **Hindutva** or Hindu nationalism spearheaded by the Sangh Parivar. These tensions over cultural and economic policy were deliberately dampened, though not eliminated, when the BJP was in power; they became obvious when the BJP lost the general elections of April 2004 and members argued over reasons for their unexpected defeat.

From its inception, the BJP has functioned as a tightly knit, disciplined, ideologically committed political party with nationally prominent leaders and a mass membership. Its representation in Parliament grew rapidly in the decade 1989–1999 (See Appendix H). The BJP won only two seats in the **Lok Sabha** and eight seats in the **Rajya Sabha** in the general elections of December 1984, but it became the most vigorous critic of the **Congress (I)** government led by **Rajiv Gandhi** on grounds of corruption, inefficiency, and what it called "pseudo secularism" or "pandering to Muslims." The BJP supported the **Janata Dal** against Congress and gained 86 Lok Sabha seats in the December 1989 general elections. Further, in the February 1990 Legislative Assembly elections, the BJP came to power in the states of **Himachal Pradesh**, **Madhya Pradesh**, and **Rajasthan** and was part of the ruling coalition in **Gujarat**. But the BJP broke with the Janata Dal government of **V. P. Singh** when he announced his decision to implement recommendations of the **Mandal Commission** report on affirmative action for other backward castes (OBCs). BJP leader **L. K. Advani** led a jubilant 10,000 kilometer procession from Somnath Temple in Gujarat to **Ayodhya** in **Uttar Pradesh (UP)** in 1990 to rally mass support for building a **Ram** temple. Despite the communal violence that accompanied the procession and Advani's arrest in October, the BJP was elected to power in UP in 1991 and won 117 Lok Sabha seats in the general elections of May 1991. The violent demolition of the *Babri Masjid* in Ayodhya on December 6, 1992, however, resulted in New Delhi's dismissal of BJP state governments, embarrassment for the BJP leadership, and subsequent criminal prosecution of some of the party members. The BJP hoped to reap electoral rewards from its militant Ayodhya campaign to create the biggest mass movement in independent India around the issue of Hindu identity excluding Muslims. But public opinion polls showed that most of the population disapproved. In the November 1993 Legislative Assembly elections the BJP lost in Madhya Pradesh and UP, although it comfortably came to power in Gujarat and with a slim majority in alliance with the **Shiv Sena** in **Maharashtra**.

Without abandoning its Hindutva platform or losing its high **caste** urban male image, the BJP strove to enlarge its social base by highlighting economic (*roti*) as well as cultural (*mandir*) issues, capturing some traditional Congress backing and courting the OBC and even the Scheduled Caste vote, often by utilizing the rabble-rousing, hate-inciting, oratory of women leaders Uma Bharati and Sadhvi Rithambara. The BJP also tried to expand beyond the Hindi heartland into southern, eastern, and northeastern India where the issue of a Ram temple did not resonate. In order to do so, it projected itself as a responsible centrist party after 1993 while benefiting from the generous funding for the temple that poured in from the **Diaspora**. The president of India invited the BJP to form a government in 1996 since it was the largest single party in the Lok Sabha. The government lasted only 13 days and gave way to the United Front coalition led by **Deve Gowda**. The BJP campaigned for the 1998 general elections on a platform containing its core demands: building a temple at Ayodhya, abrogating Article 370 of the **Constitution** providing a special status for **Jammu and Kashmir**, introducing a uniform civil code for all communities (offensive to Muslims), abolishing the Minorities Commission, banning cow slaughter, and making India's nuclear capability overt. Obliged to form a coalition before being able to form a government, the BJP subscribed to a national agenda that dropped the issues of the temple, common civil code, and Article 370.

Prime Minister Vajpayee ordered the nuclear tests of May 1998 and committed his government to proceeding rapidly with economic liberalization—despite the *swadeshi* or self-reliant preference of the Sangh Parivar. He moved quickly to normalize relations with the United States and other important powers to raise India's international profile. He promised a strong state and an effective government at home to prove that the BJP was the "natural party of governance." More controversial were his government's determined efforts to rewrite school history textbooks and administer various intellectual and cultural institutions in a Hindutva (or "saffron") mode. Pressure from coalition partners compelled the BJP to soften its rhetoric, and the election platform of the NDA in 1999 made no mention of the three core issues pushed by the RSS. Many commentators praised Vajpayee's statesmanship in foreign affairs and the apparently centrist and "modernizing" trend of the BJP led NDA government, especially because economic growth rates manifestly improved. But an ugly nativist streak remained evident, not only in periodic attacks against Muslims as being "anti-Indian" and "pro-Pakistan" but in personalized detraction of Congress President **Sonia Gandhi** as being foreign-born and Roman Catholic. Having completed almost a full term in office, the NDA called for early elections and campaigned in 2004 on a Vision Document promising to make India a major global power very soon, and on a platform of "India Shining." It lost.

Recriminations from the Sangh Parivar for the BJP abandoning its Hindutva agenda were inevitably shrill, as were its calls to renew militancy and once again embrace the social movement. Observers pointed out that the BJP leadership's failure to dismiss or even censure Gujarat Chief Minister Narendra Modi for the shameful anti-Muslim pogrom let loose in that state in 2002 was not forgotten by India's multi-religious electorate that resents outbursts of communal hatred and their violent aftermath. The BJP lost in both **Ayodhya** and **Kashi**, both temple towns and religious centers for Hindus. Other reasons given for the BJP defeat in national as well as important state elections in 2004 are that it had lost its "clean" and disciplined image when in power, that it was let down by its allies in **Andhra Pradesh** and **Tamil Nadu**, and that the majority of rural voters rejected the urban middle class bias of globalization. But the BJP was also decisively defeated in the cities of **Chennai**, **Delhi**, **Hyderabad**, and **Mumbai**. It is possible that the majority of Indians who still have to eke out a living laughed at the BJP claim of "India shining" and opted for parties that promised economic reforms "with a human face"; that the innate gentility of ordinary Indians was offended by the language used against Sonia Gandhi who was campaigning vigorously for the Congress; and that all yearned for social stability free of communal violence.

No post-election analysis suggests that the BJP has ceased to be a political force of considerable strength and many advantages competing for power in the major states of India and at the national level.

BHATT, ELA R. (1933–). Ela Blatt was born to a nationalist **brahman** family in **Ahmedabad**. Her mother and maternal grandfather had joined **Mahatma Gandhi** on the **Dandi March** of 1930, and her father and brother were lawyers. Ela grew up in **Surat** and as a college student helped conduct field research in city slums for the first **Census** of independent India. She married Ramesh Bhatt of the Youth Congress, took a law degree, joined the Textile Labour Association (TLA), and subsequently started a women's wing of that powerful trade union. From 1960 to 1968 she was an employment officer for the state government of **Gujarat** but continued to maintain a very simple lifestyle.

Ela Bhatt discovered what is best described as her "vocation" when two large textile mills in Ahmedabad closed down in 1968 and men were laid off; their wives supported the families but their labor went unrecognized. Then, in 1969, a major communal riot victimized women. Ela Bhatt set about organizing the miserably paid, hardworking women who were engaged in vegetable vending, stitching, head loading, and other "informal" tasks of the city. She founded the **Self Employed Women's Association (SEWA)** in 1972 and affiliated it with the TLA. Recognizing women's need for the credit and savings facilities that the established banks refused to extend, Ela Bhatt established the Mahila Sewa Sarkari Bank Limited in 1974 and went on to organize women in rural areas with the help of the National Dairy Development Board and the National Institute of Design in Ahmedabad. She also openly espoused the cause of **Dalits**.

Ela Bhatt received a Magsaysay Award for community leadership in 1977, and has subsequently received many other national and international awards. She has been a member of the **Planning Commission** as of the **Rajya Sabha** and practices Gandhi's precept that wealth and talent are to be held as a public trust.

BHAVE, VINOBA (1895–1982). Bhave was a saintly public figure who preached and practiced *ahimsa* (see Glossary) in the spirit of

Mahatma Gandhi. Along with **Jayaprakash Narayan**, Bhave founded the Sarvodaya movement of self-help and attention to basic human needs. He campaigned long and strenuously for *bhoodan*, or land-gift. He and his followers covered 72,000 kilometers throughout India on foot, persuading landowners to donate their surplus property to the landless. Bhave's success was limited but brought him much praise. He took a vow of silence in the mid-1970s.

BHIL. The name is that given to nomadic tribes of central India famous for their skills in tracking, hunting, and archery. The Bhils are located mainly in the Vindhya ranges of **Madhya Pradesh** and Chhatisgarh. Numbering several million, they speak several related dialects of the **Munda** group of languages. Many have taken to sheep rearing and cultivation and have adopted some beliefs and practices of popular **Hinduism**. Their traditional occupation of hunting is threatened as forests diminish. *See also* ADIVASI.

BHINDRANWALE, JARNAIL SINGH (1947–1984). Jarnail Singh was born to a **Sikh** farming family of the **Punjab** and was trained in religious studies at the Damdami Taksal. He became its chief preacher in 1971 and assumed the surname Bhindranwale. He also became increasingly fanatical, or fundamentalist, as he witnessed the rising affluence but declining faith of semi-educated Sikh youth who belonged to the agricultural or **Jat** caste. He campaigned vigorously, often violently, against those whom he termed "heretics."

Bhindranwale was encouraged by some members of **Indira Gandhi**'s **Congress** government to counter the electoral popularity of the **Akali Dal** among Punjabi agriculturalists during the early 1980s. As Bhindranwale's ambitions grew unchecked and he voiced demands for a separate Sikh state, or Khalistan, so did the level of violence and lawlessness in the Punjab. He and his followers fortified the Golden Temple at **Amritsar** and lost their lives when it was stormed by the Indian army in Operation Blue Star of June 1984.

BHOPAL. Today the capital city of **Madhya Pradesh**, Bhopal was founded by Raja Bhoj in the 11th century CE. It was renovated in the 18th century by a dynasty created by an Afghan adventurer in the twilight of the **Mughals**. A successor signed a **Subsidiary Alliance** with the **East India Company** in 1817. Three able women, Begums, ruled Bhopal between 1844 and 1926 and beautified the city. Bhopal was the principal Muslim state of Malwa in central India.

Bhopal's ruler, Nawab Hamidullah Khan, played a prominent role in the **Chamber of Princes** and was its Chancellor in 1931–1932 and 1946–1947. During the pre-independence negotiations he initially opposed joining either India or **Pakistan**, wishing to remain independent and neutral. He was persuaded by **Vallabhbhai Patel** to sign the Instrument of Accession with India in July 1947. In 1949 Bhopal was merged with surrounding territories to form the new state of Madhya Bharat, which, after some constitutional changes, became Madhya Pradesh in 1956.

The modern city of Bhopal was the scene of rapid development and planned expansion. In 1984 it was hit by one of the worst industrial disasters in history when the Union Carbide chemical plant exploded, killing and maiming hundreds of thousands of people.

BHUBANESWAR. The capital city of **Orissa** today, it was the capital of Kalinga in the 4th and 3rd centuries BCE. An ancient place of worship, Bhubaneswar presents a panorama of art history, especially the development of temple architecture between the 8th and 13th centuries CE in the "Nagara" style of northern India. This style reached its zenith in the 10th and 11th centuries, from which time date some 500 of an original 7,000 intricately sculpted temples surrounding a lake. The Great Lingaraj temple to **Shiva**, built around 1000 CE, is acclaimed as one of the finest in India.

BHUTAN. Bhutan is a small **Himalayan** kingdom of approximately 52,000 square kilometers lying between **Assam** on the south and **Tibet** on the north, with **Arunachal Pradesh** on the east and **Sikkim** on the west. The early history of Bhutan is linked with that of its neighbors and with the spread of **Buddhism**. Close relations with Tibet were formed well before the 18th century. In the 19th century, as British interests expanded, there were several clashes of arms and annexations of traditionally Bhutanese territory by the **East India Company**. Treaties signed in 1864 and 1910 reduced Bhutan to a "protected" state of the British Crown.

Ugyen Wangchuk was recognized by Britain as the hereditary ruler of Bhutan in 1907, and during the reign of his son Bhutan's separate identity from both British India and the **Princely States** was secured in the **Government of India Act** of 1935. A close and cooperative relationship was embodied in the Indo-Bhutan Treaty of 1949, signed after Indian independence. King (Druk Gyalpo) Jigme Dorji Wangchuk (r. 1952–1972) formed a very friendly relationship with Indian Prime Minister **Jawaharlal Nehru**. A carefully paced introduction of modern political and economic institutions, with protection of traditional Bhutanese culture in mind, received the substantial assistance of India. In 1971, Bhutan became a member of the United Nations with Indian support and has gradually widened its participation in the international community. By choice, it remains relatively isolated, although it is an active member of the **South Asian Association for Regional Cooperation (SAARC)**. The present occupant of the throne is Jigme Singye Dorji Wangchuk, born in 1955.

BIHAR. Bihar is a state situated in the middle **Ganges** valley with a population of 82,878,796 according to the 2001 census. Before parts of its territory were incorporated in the new state of **Jharkhand** in 2000, Bihar accounted for about 40% of India's mineral production and hosted industries based on minerals, notably steel and heavy engineering. Agriculture, however, is the principal source of employment. In terms of literacy rates and other indices of socioeconomic development, Bihar falls below the national average. Today, Bihar is regarded as one of the poorest and most backward states of the Indian Union, in contrast to its ancient heritage.

Bihar is composed of three regions: Videha, Vaishali, and Magadha. Each of these was immensely important in the cultural, economic, religious, and political evolution of ancient Indian civilization. Archaeological discoveries made in 2003 uncovered sites that are more than 3,000 years old as well as rock structures and coins of the **Kushan** period. Vaishali was the capital of the large republican state of the **Lichchavis** for several hundred years. Videha or Mithila was visited frequently by **Mahavira** and became a center of **Jainism**. **Magadha** was the heart of early empires, especially that created by the **Maurya** dynasty in the fourth century BCE, and was the cradle of **Buddhism**. Magadha's ancient capital of Pataliputra is the site of **Patna**, the present-day capital of Bihar. **Brahmanical** religion and learning continued to flourish throughout, and the Pala dynasty revived centralized administration in the 8th and 9th centuries.

Bihar received its name from the Turkish invaders of the 12th and 13th centuries who were struck by the profusion of Buddhist Viharas (monasteries) they found—and destroyed—in the middle Ganges region. Most famous among these was **Nalanda**, a seat of learning for some 1,500 years. Subsequently, **Sufi** saints preached a popular **Islam**, which was the religion of the dynasties ruling from **Delhi**. The Afghan **Sher Shah Sur** was from Sasaram in Bihar, and **Mughal Emperor Akbar** made Bihar a *subah*, or viceregal province, of his empire in 1582. Its production of textiles, indigo, and saltpeter was commercially important to the Mughals and later to European traders.

The history of Bihar became entwined with that of **Bengal** with the advent of British rule in the mid-18th century, and the province experienced consolidation, exploitation, uprising, and neglect before being administratively separated in 1911. **Mahatma Gandhi** led an early **satyagraha** in behalf of the peasants of Champaran in 1917. Bihar was an important recruiting ground for the **Indian National Congress** and was the home state of such national figures as **Rajendra Prasad**, **Jayaprakash Narayan**, and **Ram Manohar Lohia**. A bronze memorial to the 1942 **Quit India Movement** stands at Patna. The principal language of the state is Hindi. Some economists attribute Bihar's poverty to the iniquities of the **permanent settlement** and the absence of land reform after Indian independence. Other analysts point to the deep divisions among **castes** and social classes and to the venality—even criminality—of politicians. Social and political discontent is manifest, and Bihar has a reputation for poor governance and low investment.

BIJAPUR. Located in the western **Deccan**, Bijapur was once a provincial capital of the **Chalukya** dynasty. The territory that it controlled fell to the **Delhi Sultanate** and then formed part of the **Bahmani** kingdom in the 14th century. In 1489, Bijapur declared its independence under Yusuf Adil Khan, whose dynasty ruled until 1686 when the country was annexed by **Mughal Emperor Aurangzeb**. Bijapur interacted with other powers in southern and western India, including the **Portuguese**. The architecture, language, music, and painting of Bijapur reflect a rich Deccani culture, blending strands from north and south and from **Hindu** and **Islamic** traditions.

BIKANER. A city in the desert of northwestern **Rajasthan**, Bikaner was founded in 1465 by a **Rajput** chief of the Rathor clan that controlled Jodhpur. In 1570, the Mughal emperor **Akbar** brought Bikaner into alliance, and thereafter its rulers ranked high among Mughal commanders. After suffering at the hands of the **Marathas**, Bikaner signed an alliance with the British in 1818. Maharajah Ganga Singh (r. 1898–1942) played a prominent role at the League of Nations and in the **Chamber of Princes**. At the **Round Table Conferences** of 1930–1932 he supported the goal of Indian federation and **Dominion status**. Bikaner acceded to the Indian Union in 1947 and became part of greater Rajasthan in 1949.

BIMBISARA (r. c. 544–493 BCE) was the ruler of the prosperous kingdom of **Magadha**. He expanded his domain by annexing the neighboring kingdom of Anga to the east and entering into matrimonial alliances with the rulers of **Kosala** and Vaishali to the west and north. He built the city of Rajagriha, famous in **Buddhist** chronicles. Bimbisara was patron to the most enlightened men of his age, including **Mahavira** and Gautama **Buddha**.

BIRBAL (1528–1586). Birbal was a **brahman** wit and courtier who became friend and confidant of the Mughal emperor **Akbar**. Birbal was given the title of Kavi Priya, or poet laureate. His poetry became as famous as the many amusing stories about him at Akbar's court. Birbal joined the **Din-illahi** and occupied an elegant house in Fatehpur Sikri. He was killed in battle on the northwest frontier.

BIRLA, GHANASHYAMDAS (1894–1983). G. D. Birla was born in a **Marwari** family that owned jute, cotton, and paper mills in **Calcutta**. He supported the **Indian National Congress**. He played host to **Mahatma Gandhi** on many occasions and contributed financially to his cause. It was at Birla House, New Delhi, that Gandhi met his assassin on his way to an afternoon prayer meeting.

G. D. Birla was a philanthropist who built many temples, schools, and research institutions. More importantly, he built one of the largest and most prosperous industrial and commercial empires in independent India. Its operations reach out to other countries as well, and Birla Group is listed among the Fortune 500.

BODO or BORO. The more than one million strong Bodo tribal community is regarded as among the aboriginal groups of the **Assam** plains. They may have introduced rice cultivation and silk weaving, along with domesticated cattle into the Assam valley. The Bodos are of Tibeto-Burman stock and are dispersed throughout India's northeast and in **Bangladesh** and **Bhutan**. Since the 1980s, the Bodos have come into conflict with Assamese speakers of the **Brahmaputra** valley in cycles of increasingly strident rhetoric and violence, including the Nellie massacre of 1983 that claimed more than 1,000 lives, and attacks on tea plantations and oil pipe lines in the 1990s. The National Democratic Front of Bodoland, backed by the Bodoland Tiger Force and other armed groups, demand a separate state of Bodoland with wide borders (within the Indian Union), and the use of Hindi in the devanagari script and English as official languages rather than Assamese. Those who have studied the area and the problem most closely say that ethnicity and language are tools in the development of political identity that underscores the deep fear among local people of land alienation by undocumented immigrants and other non-tribals. The constant struggle for land among subsistence agriculturalists led to armed clashes between Bodos and **Santhals** in 1996. The rage of the dispossessed is more difficult to assuage than demands for constitutional autonomy, of which there are many examples in the northeastern states of India.

BOMBAY/MUMBAI. The capital of the state of **Maharashtra**, it was the capital of Bombay state from 1947 to 1960 and before that of Bombay province. It is the largest port on India's west coast and is a principal center of banking, commerce, finance, industry, and shipbuilding. Consisting of seven islands joined with the mainland by land reclamation, the city of Greater Bombay is densely populated. People from near and far have long been drawn to this cosmopolitan and polyglot city and come from all religious communities, including the **Parsis**, whose largest single concentration is in Bombay.

Probably inhabited since prehistoric times, Bombay has early **Buddhist** and **Shiva** temples. Its magnificent bay (Bom Bahia or Mumbai or Mumbadevi) attracted the **Portuguese**, who obtained it from the Sultan of **Gujarat** in 1534 and gave it in dowry with Catherine of Braganza when she married Charles II of England in 1661. Charles II passed it on to the **East India Company**, which found it an increasingly useful base as **Maratha** power expanded in the 18th century. Bombay Presidency was the home ground of many able British administrators and generals, and they ultimately prevailed over the Marathas. British interests in the Persian Gulf and the administration of Aden also came to be centered in Bombay. For the British sailing to India, Bombay was truly the "Gateway of India" long before the monumental arch of that name was constructed.

Bombay's 19th century prosperity, so often portrayed in Indo-British writings and sketches, is reflected in the many public buildings of the Victorian era. By the end of the century Bombay had become the center not only of India's new textile industry and **trade union** activity but also of new representative institutions and of the nationalist movement. The first meeting of the **Indian National Congress** was held in Bombay in 1885, and many of its leading members had their homes in the city or cut their political teeth in its Municipal Council.

Bombay's prosperity and cosmopolitanism continued after Indian independence, augmented by the burgeoning **film industry** and by extensive ties with Iran and the Arab world, the location of advanced research and ship maintenance facilities there, and by the discovery of oil offshore. People from all parts of India were drawn into Bombay's workforce; migrants from the rural hinterland in Maharashtra flowed to the pavements. For the most part, the administrative machinery coped well with the problems of growth but was unable (or unwilling) to control the spread of an underground network of exploitation, crime, and political chicanery. Urban economic inequalities were expressed in contrasts of lifestyle. The aspirations of the poor and the lower middle class often translated into disappointment, anger, and heightened political activity. Fear, chauvinism, communalism, parochialism, and violence against Muslims and non-Marathi speakers increased, frequently fanned by the **Shiv Sena** led by Bal Thackery. As a direct consequence, parts of Bombay were literally and metaphorically burned in December 1992 and early 1993, with the **terrorist** bombing of the Bombay Stock Exchange in March dealing a serious blow to the city's financial prominence. It recovered rapidly.

During the 1990s Bombay, renamed Mumbai, lost some of the cosmopolitanism and commercial dynamism that had characterized it earlier. Several inter-community citizens groups and **non governmental organizations** worked with individuals in the police and administration to counteract negative trends, with some local success. **Economic liberalization** policies undercut some of the criminal fraternities but by no means all of them. The thriving film industry, or Bollywood, continues to spawn dreams and unanticipated consequences. Congested slums are veritable beehives of multiple activities. In short, Mumbai is as bewildering and exciting a city as any other world metropolis with a population that exceeds 10 million.

BONNERJEE, WOMESH CHANDRA (1844–1906). Bonnerjee presided over the first session of the **Indian National Congress** in 1885 and again in 1892. He belonged to the Bengali *bhadralok* (see Glossary)—high-caste, English-educated, and wealthy families—who maintained pressure on the British to permit basic English freedoms in their Indian empire. In many respects, Womesh Chandra was typical of his class. He studied law and qualified for the Bar at Middle Temple, London. He was the first Indian to be appointed standing counsel to government and gained fame in his spirited defense of **Surendranath Banerjea**. He maintained a lavish lifestyle, and his wife was converted to Christianity. He refused offers to become a judge, opting instead to continue his legal practice. He became president of the Law Faculty at **Calcutta** University in 1886.

Bonnerjee had great faith in the British sense of justice and in constitutional reform as the path to self-government in India. He pressed for representative institutions in India and for much greater administrative responsibility in the hands of Indians. He believed that personal relationships could transcend artificial barriers of race and creed, as demonstrated in his own life. He did not take an active interest in issues of social reform, but he supported the **Indian**

National Congress as an institution of "dignity and respectability" that could command British respect.

In 1902 Bonnerjee moved to England where he argued cases before the highest court in the British Empire, the Privy Council. He also advised the Parliamentary Standing Committee on India and financed a journal, *India*.

BOSE, RASHBEHARI (1880–1945). Rashbehari was frustrated as a young man in his desire to join the army in British India and became an anti-British conspirator and would-be revolutionary instead. While working with his father at the Government Press, **Simla**, he and his friends were suspected of attempting to assassinate the viceroy. Rashbehari fled Simla and traveled around India before departing for Japan in 1915. There he met other Indians who were opposed to British rule and founded the Indian Independence League in 1924. He married a Japanese woman and took Japanese citizenship without losing his commitment to India's freedom. Rashbehari Bose was a strong influence on Indian students and visitors in Japan, impressing them with his calm, austere, and cosmopolitan personality. After the outbreak of **World War II** he joined with Captain Mohan Singh and Sardar Pritam Singh to mobilize an **Indian National Army (INA)**. He had moved to Singapore when that British colony—and many Indian prisoners of war—fell under Japanese control. There, Rashbehari Bose handed over command of the INA to **Subhas Chandra Bose** in 1943. The two were not related by blood.

BOSE, SATYENDRANATH (1894–1974). An outstanding scientist who studied physics at Presidency College, **Calcutta** under Jagdishchandra Bose, Satyendranath Bose gained international fame in 1926 when he published a paper verifying Albert Einstein's quantum theory with mathematical equations and reconciling the theory with Planck's law. Bose conducted a long distance collaborative correspondence with Einstein and saw his own contribution honored when a set of subatomic particles of finite mass were named "bosons," even as "fermions" honored Enrico Fermi who addressed the qualities of electromagnetic radiation taking a different approach from Bose and Einstein.

Bose was the son of an accountant who founded the East India Chemical and Pharmaceutical Works. He was born in Calcutta where he became lecturer in physics before moving to the University of Dacca. From 1945 to 1956 Bose was professor of physics at the University of California before becoming vice chancellor of Vishva Bharati University, founded by **Rabindranath Tagore**, and National Professor in India. He helped found the Science Association of Bengal and was made a Fellow of the Royal Society in 1958.

BOSE, SARAT CHANDRA (1889–1950). Sarat Chandra was the second son of Janaki Nath Bose, a high **caste** Bengali school teacher and lawyer who settled in Cuttack. Sarat studied at the Protestant European School in Cuttack, the Ravenshaw Collegiate School, and Presidency College, **Calcutta**. He became a fine orator in English, and as a student he was witness to the politics of resistance to the 1905 **partition of Bengal** and the **Swadeshi movement**. He was enrolled at Lincoln's Inn, London from 1912 to 1914 to qualify for the bar and became a firm believer in the rule of law and individual freedom as he observed them practiced in England. Throughout his career he argued for their application and against preventive detention in India whether by the British or, later, the independent government of India.

Sarat Chandra Bose practiced civil and criminal law in Calcutta and was actively involved in politics from the 1920s on. He joined the **Indian National Congress**, was a member of the **Swaraj Party**, and made his home a meeting place as well as a communication and nurturing center for those resisting British rule, especially for his charismatic younger brother **Subhas Chandra Bose**. Sarat reached the peak of his own political career between 1937 and 1946 as an elected member of the Bengal Legislative Assembly, the leader of the Congress Parliamentary Party in **Bengal**, a member of the Congress Working Committee, and a member of the Interim Government in 1946, before his resignation in November of that year. His role, both as lawyer and as politician, was essentially one of mediation among communities as well as classes, seeking to reconcile differences in the larger public interest.

The thrust of Sarat Chandra's work was for civil and political liberty and against the increasing communalization of Bengal politics after 1937. He opposed **Fazlul Huq**'s **Muslim League** government in Bengal as well as the activities of the **Hindu Mahasabha** and bitterly opposed **Partition**. Along with Husain Suhrawardy, he proposed a united, socialist Bengal in a loose federation of autonomous states and denounced Congress' acceptance of Partition as the "result of a defeatist mentality" that risked increased "armed communal conflicts" and a retreat to medievalism.

Sarat Chandra Bose left Congress in 1946 and formed a new Socialist Republican Party. He started an English-language newspaper, *Nation*, in 1948. He was critical of the new **Indian Constitution** as being insufficiently protective of "basic freedoms." His role in a parliamentary opposition was cut short by his death.

BOSE, SUBHAS CHANDRA (1897–1945). Commonly known as Netaji, he was a charismatic figure of the Indian national movement around whose colorful career a body of myths (including denial of his death) has grown, especially in **Bengal**. Subhas Chandra was the fifth son of Janaki Nath Bose and his orthodox wife, Prabhavati, from whom the boy gained access to the mythology and religion of the Mother Goddess, Durga or Kali. Early in his life, Subhas displayed a competitive and rebellious spirit, an ability to match his brothers whom he followed through school, and a passionate commitment to the goal of freedom and revival of his Motherland, India. As a student, Subhas was deeply influenced by the examples of **Ramakrishna Paramhansa**, **Swami Vivekananda**, and **Aurobindo** and was inspired by **Bankim Chander Chatterji**'s nationalist novel *Ananda Math*. He sought discipline of the senses and for a time inclined toward the life of a *sannyasin* (see Glossary) or asceticism.

In 1919, Subhas was sent to England where he took a degree from Cambridge and passed the entrance examinations for the **Indian Civil Service (ICS)**. He refused to join on the grounds that his nationalist and spiritual aspirations were incompatible with obedience to its oath of covenant. He returned to India in 1921 and went to see **Mahatma Gandhi**, but he was disappointed in not receiving answers to his eager questions on a militant strategy to achieve independence. Subhas joined **C. R. Das** in **Calcutta**, and during the **Non-Cooperation Movement** of 1921–1922 he worked as a captain in the National Volunteer Corps, a teacher, a principal of an alternate Bengal National

College, and with a Bengali weekly, *Banglar Katha*. He became a member of the **Indian National Congress** and helped organize a boycott of the Prince of Wales' visit to Calcutta. He was interned for eight months along with Das, and was critical when Gandhi called off Non-Cooperation in 1922.

Subhas Chandra subsequently worked with the **Swaraj Party** and became an Alderman on the Calcutta Municipal Corporation in 1924 and later mayor of Calcutta in 1930. He outlined ambitious plans for the city in the areas of health, education, housing, and employment. As president of the Bengal Provincial Congress Committee and president of the All-India Trade Union Congress, he gained responsibility and experience in organizing workers and youth. He was subjected to two long periods of detention as a political dissident, from 1924 to 1927 and 1932 to 1935, much of the time in **Burma**. His religion sustained his spirits, but his health suffered badly. Upon his release, he traveled extensively in Europe.

Subhas Chandra Bose was unanimously elected Congress president at its Haripura session in 1938. He stood for a vigorous effort toward full independence, without spurning assistance from Britain's main adversaries in Europe—the Soviet Union and Nazi Germany—and without necessarily abjuring violence in the process of struggling toward a desired goal. Among the tangible measures he advocated were economic planning and Hindustani written in the Roman script as a national language. The predominantly conservative Congress Working Committee (CWC) did not favor Bose, and **Jawaharlal Nehru** advised him not to contest again. When Bose was reelected Congress president at the Tripuri session of 1939 over Gandhi's nominee, the CWC interpreted this as a defeat for Gandhi and resigned. Bose received no overt support and was compelled to step down. He formed a Forward Bloc within Congress, drawing on younger, radical elements. They demanded a provisional national government in 1940 after the outbreak of **World War II** and the resignation of Congress ministries in the provinces, but without effect.

Expecting to be rearrested, Bose disappeared from Calcutta and surfaced first in Kabul and then in Berlin, where he met Hitler as well as Indian students in his efforts to supplement the freedom struggle at home, and from where he made regular radio broadcasts in 1942. Disappointed, no doubt, by the lack of commitment to his cause on the part of the Nazi leadership who wished to use him for their own purposes, Bose proceeded by submarine to Singapore, then in Japanese hands. There, he met **Rashbehari Bose** and took over command of the **Indian National Army (INA)** formed from among Indian prisoners of war. Netaji Subhas Chandra Bose proclaimed an Azad Hind (Free India) government from Singapore in October 1943. The INA marched alongside Japanese forces through Burma into northeastern India where they were overwhelmed. The Japanese government announced the death of Netaji in an air crash over Taiwan in 1945.

Many Indians, especially in Bengal and **Maharashtra**, refused to believe that announcement, perhaps because of the uncertainty surrounding the exact time and place of Bose's death, perhaps because they yearned for a martial "savior" from the violence and confusion before and after independence in 1947. Perhaps, also, they had a deep-seated need to believe in an immortal hero, a saintly warrior king, even a Kalki or future incarnation of Vishu, who would return to the nation when needed. The Indian government instituted two inquiry commissions, by the Shah Nawaz committee in 1956 and by Justice G. D. Khosla from 1970 to 1974, both of which confirmed Bose's death but without markedly influencing rumors of sightings. Another popular myth—that of Bose's celibacy—was also not diminished by his family's acceptance of the Austrian Emilie Schenkl as his wife; their daughter Anita, born in 1942, receives a warm public welcome on her visits to India. In short, the Bose cult has not died, despite his lack of a broad political base or solid political achievement when he was alive. He was posthumously awarded India's highest civilian honor, the Bharat Ratna, in 1991.

BOUNDARY COMMISSION (1947). This body was appointed in July 1947 a month before Indian independence and **Partition**, scheduled for August 15 by Governor General **Lord Mountbatten**. The task of the Boundary Commission was to draw lines of division in **Bengal** and **Punjab** between India and **Pakistan** on the basis of ascertaining contiguous areas of majority Muslim and non-Muslim population. The Boundary Commission consisted of eight Indian high court judges, four from Bengal and four from Punjab, under the chairmanship of Sir Cyril Radcliffe. The **Indian National Congress** nominated half the number of judges and the **All-India Muslim**

League nominated the other half. In the absence of agreement among them and the approaching deadline of August 15, Radcliffe made all the final decisions.

In Bengal, Congress claimed 46% of the population and 59% of the area as having a **Hindu** majority, but India received only 36% of the area and 35% of the population; 42% of the population of east Bengal assigned to Pakistan was non-Muslim. There was equal controversy over the division in the Punjab where the **Sikhs** put forward their special claims for territory, which were overruled. India received control over the three eastern rivers of the Punjab approximating only 38% of the area and 45% of the population.

Communal violence and forced migration of peoples occurred before and after the Radcliffe Award was announced on August 17. Neither India nor Pakistan was satisfied. No major changes of boundary have been effected by force, and rationalizations at specific points have been made by mutual agreement between the two countries.

BRAHMAN. This term of neuter gender is used in the *Rig Veda* to mean the magic of the sacred word. It is discussed at length in the *Upanishads* as the One entity filling all space and time, from which the whole universe has emerged, which is also the human soul.

In lower case, the term brahman or brahmin was originally used for one possessed of magical power; it came to be applied to an entire category of persons, the priestly or intellectual class. In early Indo-Aryan society, and subsequently in *Smriti* (scriptural) law, a brahman belonged to the highest ranking *varna* or class, whose function was to study and teach, to perform sacrifice and other priestly duties, and to give and receive gifts. Brahmans claimed many privileges in law but were always expected to follow higher and stricter standards of conduct than lower ranking *varnas*; the brahman was frequently mocked in satirical literature. Some occupations, such as trade in certain commodities, were forbidden brahmans, and agricultural pursuits were generally discouraged, though some brahman families came to own land. Many served rulers in varying capacities, but especially as scribes and advisers, throughout the ages. According to **Hindu** tradition, the spiritual and intellectual power of the brahman was strictly separate from the temporal power of the **kshatriya** or ruler and warrior class; the two were usually in alliance. Various religious treatises raise the question of who is a brahman and answer it by emphasizing character and spiritual bent rather than birth; traditionally ascriptive Indian society, however, valued birth.

Within the brahman *varna* there were historic divisions by *gotra*, or legendary sage, and *pravara*, or ancestry, that restricted matrimonial choice and dictated rituals, so that by the medieval period the brahman *varna* was composed of many castes linked by endogamy and common practices. In the 19th and 20th centuries, reforms among brahmans sought to reduce ritualism and rationalize secular conduct. Despite the unifying influence of the **Sanskrit** texts used by brahmans, regional differences among them were considerable, especially in the sphere of inter-caste behavior.

Throughout India brahmans enjoyed high status and access to learning which gave them power. Sometimes power was abused and often it begat arrogance. Not surprisingly, every movement of religious reform in India, including **Buddhism** and **Bhakti**, opposed brahmanical power if it was used to deny others equal access to the spiritual path. Anti-brahmanical movements in the modern period, especially in south India, took on economic and political dimensions and restrictions on their access to educational institutions and government employment that they had formerly dominated. Nevertheless, brahmans continue to demonstrate great ability and success inside and outside India.

BRAHMAPUTRA RIVER. The literal translation of Brahmaputra is "son of Brahma the creator," and the adjective "mighty" is a common prefix to the name of a 2,900-kilometer-long river that has its origins close to Lake Manasarovar in **Tibet**. Known as the Tsang Po in Tibet, the river flows almost due east before cutting gorges northeast and then abruptly turning south to pass through the eastern **Himalaya** and the forests of **Arunachal** before descending to the **Assam** plains. The Brahmaputra joins the **Ganges** river in the delta region of **Bangladesh**. The river is navigable for most of its course, except through the mountains, and an abundance of varied forests, other vegetation, and animal life is watered by it. The upper reaches of the Brahmaputra were explored only late in the 19th century.

Though the Brahmaputra deposits rich silts in the plains, it is better known for its changes of course and for the disastrous floods that occur from time to time. Few bridges can be erected across this mighty stream, and it poses major problems in hydrology. Far-reaching plans to harness the potential of the Brahmaputra for power and for irrigation, and for augmenting the waters of the eastern Ganges are currently under study in India and Bangladesh.

BRAHMO SAMAJ. Founded in 1828 by **Ram Mohun Roy** as a society of monotheistic faith combining the philosophy of the *upanishads* with the ethics of **Christianity**, the Brahmo Samaj was in the vanguard of 19th-century **Hindu** social reform and the **Bengal** Renaissance. Its initial appeal was limited to the educated, high caste, middle class in Bengal, but the dynamic leadership of **Keshub Chandra Sen** made it an all-India movement in the 1860s. Although membership was never large, individual members, including those of the **Tagore** family, often exercised great influence over their contemporaries.

The Brahmo Samaj can be credited with setting the major objective of all modern Indian social reform movements: social freedom and cultural advancement of Indian **women**. Supporting the abolition of **sati** in 1829, the Brahmo Samaj further advocated widow remarriage, raising the minimum age of marriage or consent, and even inter-caste marriage. Enabling legislation was passed in 1856 and 1872 despite vocal opposition from high-caste Hindus who opposed "interference" in personal law by an alien government. Members of the Brahmo Samaj also worked for the education of females and the working class, and for temperance, charity, and the end of *purdah* (see Glossary), idolatry, illiteracy, and **caste** restrictions. In other words, they were modernizers and remained so even after the initial strength of the social reform movement diminished.

BRAHUI. The term refers to a tribal people living in the Brahui hills of Baluchistan and speaking a **Dravidian** language. Their presence in the northwestern portion of the subcontinent, more or less in isolation, has puzzled many and is sometimes used to suggest that the people who created the **Harappan culture** were Dravidian.

BRANDIS, DIETRICH. German-born Dietrich Brandis was the first Inspector General of Forests in India, 1864–1883. Brandis was born in Bonn and educated in Copenhagen and Gottingen but joined the newly established Indian Forest Service in 1856. He spent five years as superintendent of forests in **Burma**, the southern half of which had been annexed by the **East India Company** after a war in 1852. His great achievement in India was founding the Forest Research Institute in Dehra Dun, where valuable research continues to be conducted. Brandis published *Forest Flora of Northwest and Central India* in 1871 and *Indian Trees* in 1906. After retirement he formulated a system of forest management in Madras Presidency and a practical course for use in both India and Europe.

BROWN, WILLIAM NORMAN (1892–1975). He was born in Baltimore, Maryland, and accompanied his parents to India in 1900. His father was principal of a mission high school in the then Central Provinces. Norman Brown's early exposure to Indian scripts and his father's knowledge of **Sanskrit** and Arabic spurred a lifelong study of Indian literature and comparative philology. He became the foremost American scholar of Indology in his day. He occupied the chair of Indology at the University of Pennsylvania in Philadelphia from 1926 to 1966, and established a department for Indian studies there in 1948. That department remains a center of excellence. As scholarly author, editor of the *Journal of the American Oriental Society*, and consultant to major museums and art galleries, Norman Brown actively propagated the study of contemporary South Asia in the United States. He was president of the Association of Asian Studies from 1960 to 1961 and helped to found the American Institute of Indian Studies, which he headed from 1961 to 1971. His eminence as a scholar was widely recognized, as was his promotion of better understanding between the United States and India. Brown's *The United States and India and Pakistan* was first published in 1953; several editions of this work have been subsequently published and it remains a standard work in the field.

BUDDHA, SIDDHARATHA GAUTAMA (c. 550–468 BCE). The son of a Sakya chief of Kapilavastu, a dependency of **Kosala** in the Terai area of what is now **Nepal**, Siddharatha Gautama is known as the Buddha, the Enlightened or Awakened one, from having attained knowledge of the Absolute.

A multitude of beautiful myths surround the central story of the historical Buddha—his birth to Queen Maya at Lumbini, his marriage to Yasodhara who shared his birth date, his great renunciation of family, home, and princely power, his years of severe asceticism, and his realization in meditation that the path to spiritual salvation was the "Middle Way," which he first preached at Sarnath, near **Varanasi**. These events, and also accounts of the Buddha's previous lives as told in the *Jatakas*, have been immortalized in art, literature, and sculpture inside and outside India.

After his first sermon at Sarnath, the Buddha continued to wander and to preach for another 45 years. He founded an order of monks and later an order of nuns, and received many gifts from kings, merchants, and citizens. He passed away peacefully in the presence of his followers during the reign of Ajatsatru of **Magadha**.

The Buddha's teachings form the basis of one of the world's great religions, **Buddhism**. His teachings were ethical rather than metaphysical, psychological rather than philosophical. Their essence lay in the Four Noble Truths: life is sorrowful, sorrow is caused by craving, release from sorrow comes from cessation of craving, and craving is overcome by following the Noble Eightfold Path of Right Views, Right Aspirations, Right Speech, Right Conduct, Right Livelihood, Right Effort, Right Mindfulness, and Right Contemplation. *See also* BUDDHISM.

BUDDHISM. One of the oldest and greatest of world religions grew out of the example and teachings of the **Buddha**. His first sermon, called *Turning the Wheel of Law*, was the nucleus of his teachings. Briefly, it incorporated the Four Noble Truths that the world is full of suffering, that suffering is caused by craving, that suffering can be ended by cessation of craving, and that craving can be overcome by following the Eight Fold Path of Righteousness. This consisted of a balanced, moderate life based on right views, resolves, speech, conduct, livelihood, effort, mindfulness, and meditation. The Buddha opened the way to salvation, defined as *nirvana* (see Glossary) or liberation from the cycle of rebirth, to all, irrespective of birth. Although the doctrine of *karma* (see Glossary) was part of the Buddha's teachings, he did not use it to explain the social institution of **caste**, and he postulated nirvana as attainable by any person with an understanding of reality and moral preparation. He called his way "the Middle Path" and told his followers to avoid the extremes of attachment to the pleasure of the senses and the attachment to self-mortification. This was later expanded to mean the middle way between materialism and rationalism, between faith and skepticism, between belief in the existence and the non-existence of the soul. The Buddha focused on the concrete problem of alleviating suffering and avoided metaphysical controversy. Buddhism was a non-theistic religion because no god was postulated; it gave no privileged position to a priestly caste.

During the 45 years of his public ministry, the Buddha traveled constantly and sent out his disciples to preach to the laity. He founded the *sangha* or monastic order, consisting initially of 1,250 monks; he established an order of 500 nuns a few years later. Historians frequently equate the history of Buddhism with the history of the *sangha*. No ascriptive qualifications were necessary to join the monastic order, but more than 70% of the early monks and nuns came from cities; many belonged to the upper classes, including **brahmans**. The Buddha himself showed his concern for the spiritual welfare of members of the emerging urban civilization in the **Ganges** valley in the sixth century BCE, and it was they, in turn, notably the merchants and itinerant traders, who responded in largest numbers to the new religion. The laity was an integral part of Buddhism, supporting the *sangha*; a Buddhist was one who took "refuge" in the "three jewels" of the Buddha, the *dharma* or teachings, and the *sangha*.

Buddhism spread along the major trade routes of the next thousand years, first throughout the Indian subcontinent and then beyond to **Ceylon** and Southeast Asia in the south, to Central Asia in the north, and east to China and beyond. It received the protection and patronage of many kings and flourished among peasants as well. Many changes of form and doctrine evolved over time and space, and though Buddhism always carried traces of its Indian origin in its view of Reality and its art, it was essentially independent of culture and capable of coexisting with other religious systems that were not exclusive. Buddhism's contributions to the art, architecture, and general literacy of the areas to which it spread are immense and are increasingly well documented. By the 14th century CE, **Islam** had destroyed the monasteries and extinguished Buddhism in Central Asia and northern India, but it was well rooted elsewhere. Buddhism reached America and Europe in the 20th century and was being revived in India as a refuge for the lower castes by **Bhimrao Ramji Ambedkar** and his followers.

Comprehensive histories of Buddhism are rare because the material is so vast and in so many different languages. Summaries are sometimes over simplistic in specifying four major phases: the earliest and purely Indian, or Hinayana (Little Vehicle) Buddhism (known as "Theravada" or "pure" in Sri Lanka and Southeast Asia) focusing on individual salvation; the growth of the Mahayana (Great Vehicle) school with its concept of the "Boddhisattva" or "savior" and its spread to central and eastern Asia; the rise of **Tantra** in eastern India, **Nepal**, and **Tibet** and development of the Ch'an and Zen schools in China and Japan; and the post-11th century and contemporary era. A slightly amplified chronology of important developments would run as follows:

Sixth to third century BCE: Life of the Buddha; first and second councils of the *sangha* to codify his teachings and establish rules for wanderers, mendicant monks, and *viharas* or monasteries; art and sculpture use symbols rather than the human face or form in depicting the Buddha.

Third to first century BCE: The Emperor **Ashoka** convenes the third council of the *sangha* and addresses two rock edicts specifically to it; Ashoka sends his son and daughter as missionaries to Ceylon and his edicts charge all emissaries and administrators within his Empire to abide by the nonviolent code of the *dharma*; other missions sent to central and western Asia; several thousand *stupas* constructed through the Buddhist world, many of them artistically embellished.

First to third century CE: The transnational spread of Buddhism, with the **Kushan** Empire at its core, becomes more pronounced; **Kanishka** convenes the fourth council of the *sangha*; **Gandhara** art flowers and Buddhist sculptures of the human form proliferate in stone and metal; the concept of the Boddhisattva develops in the Mahayana school and gains increasing popularity.

Fourth to seventh century: Buddhism in India flourishes alongside other **Hindu** faiths and goes through a phase of intense intellectualism and synthesis; **Xuanzang** makes an informal census of monasteries and estimates a total of 115,000 Hinayana and 120,000

Mahayana monks; Buddhist art reaches an apogee in **Ajanta**; Buddhism is "domesticated" in China, and hundreds of Chinese pilgrims and traders visit India.

Seventh to eleventh century: Buddhism takes root in Japan and Tibet; flourishes throughout central and southeast Asia; Tantra grows and influences Buddhism, especially in eastern India, Nepal, and Tibet; **Shankara** challenges Buddhist and other heterodox religions in India and stimulates a brahmanical revival.

Eleventh to fifteenth century: Destruction of the Buddhist monasteries including those at **Taxila** and **Nalanda**, effectively extinguishes its visible presence in India in Central Asia; vigor shown in Burma, Tibet, and east Asia.

Fifteenth to nineteenth century: Buddhism falls victim to inertia and isolationism in the face of assertive missionary efforts of Islam and **Christianity**.

Twentieth century: Buddhism is revived in India (see Appendix G), especially among **Dalits**, and finds followers in the West.

Various explanations are offered for the decline of Buddhism in India and is attributed variously to the Muslim invasions, withdrawal of royal patronage, brahmanical persecution, and internal decay. However, contrasts with the survival of another contemporary heterodox faith, **Jainism**, suggest alternate or additional explanations. It is likely that the growth of the Mahayana school, permitting deification of the Boddhisattva, rendered Buddhism more vulnerable to assimilation, a dominant characteristic of **Hinduism**, as Buddhist and Hindu deities became virtually indistinguishable in popular devotional cults. Tantra has similar integrative and assimilationist tendencies. Further, it seems as if the later *sangha* in India neglected its earlier role in the education and cultivation of the laity and thereby lost support to the *bhakti* cults, which did so. It is also possible that by maintaining silence on key metaphysical questions central to Indian culture and by failing to supply an alternative social order to the hierarchical caste system it criticized, Buddhism gradually lost its saliency in India. Be that as it may, the vibrant contributions of Buddhism to India for more than a thousand years—as well as to the rest of the world—remain unquestionably great.

BURMA/MYANMAR. Adjacent to India on the east, Burma's political history has been separate, except for the brief period (1886–1935) when it was administered from India. Trade and cultural contracts, however, existed from early times, with evidence of a **Buddhist** mission sent by **Ashoka** in the third century BCE and Indian settlements in the first century CE. Although the form of Buddhism adopted by Burma came from **Ceylon**, the art and architecture of Pagan, capital of a larger and unified Burmese kingdom of the 9th, 10th, and 11th centuries, show marked Indian influences. Tribal migrations between upper Burma and northeastern India were probably frequent and continued into the modern period.

British control of **Bengal** and expansion into northeastern India and Southeast Asia led to three Anglo-Burmese Wars in 1824–1826, 1852, and 1885–1886. The first was expensive and indecisive. The second resulted in annexation of lower Burma and the Arakan coast. The third led to annexation of upper Burma and establishment of the capital at Mandalay. Indians settled in Burma as workers on rice fields, as merchants and professionals, and as government officials under British administration. The **Government of India Act** of 1935 separated Burma from India. The independence movements of the two countries took different forms, partly because Burma was under Japanese occupation during **World War II.**

The independent governments of Burma and India established close and friendly relations at first, cooperating within the Commonwealth and the Nonaligned Movement (NAM) as well as in their attempts to control insurgents. Soon after the military coup of General Ne Win in 1962, however, the relationship began to change. By the mid-1960s about half a million of the Indian **diaspora** had left Burma, or were forced to leave, deprived of their property. Approximately 200,00 remained as rice farmers at the subsistence level. Burma remained more or less in international isolation for many years, quitting the NAM and declining an early invitation to join the **South Asian Association for Regional Cooperation (SAARC).** The long common border was dangerously porous, and India and Burma signed a border agreement in 1966 to check illicit traffic in persons and drugs. A maritime border agreement was signed in 1986.

Initially, India did not attempt to revive close relations with Burma or seek to counteract the growing and worrisome influence of China on Myanmar's military rulers. Indian support for the democratic movement within Burma in the late 1980s and early 1990s took a moral or declaratory form, with no more material content than giving asylum to thousands who fled. Indian sympathy for democratic leader Aung San Suu Kyi was strong, however, and she was honored with the award of the Nehru Prize for International Understanding, even as she received the Nobel Peace Prize in 1991. Shortly thereafter, the governments of India and Myanmar established regular contact, reaching cooperative agreement on management of the border and opening land trade over roads built by India on request. These arrangements were facilitated by Myanmar's membership in the Association of South East Asian Nations (ASEAN) and India's full partnership with that organization.

BUSSY, MARQUIS DE (1718–1785). Charles Pattisiar, or the Marquis de Bussy, joined the **French East India Company** in 1737 and, along with **Joseph Dupleix**, was chiefly responsible for establishing French influence in the **Deccan** in the latter half of the 18th century. Bussy trained the troops of the Nizam of **Hyderabad** in Western methods of warfare and undertook several military expeditions for the Nizam against the **Marathas**, refractory vassals, and coastal settlements of the **English East India Company**. In return, he obtained territory, prestige, and trading concessions for the French.

Bussy and Dupleix were skilled at playing the politics of Indian states against their chief adversary, the English East India Company. They did not, however, receive sufficient backing from Paris or the full support of other French commanders in the field. Bussy was recalled at the zenith of his influence in 1759. He died at **Pondicherry**, the French coastal enclave south of **Madras**.

BUTLER, SIR HARCOURT (1869–1938). Butler chaired a three-member committee appointed by His Majesty's Government in Britain in 1927 to inquire into the relationship between the Indian **Princely States** and the British Government of India or Paramount Power in response to a controversy between the Nizam of **Hyderabad** and the Government of India on the interpretation of an earlier treaty. Other Indian Princes were concerned and demanded an impartial inquiry.

The British group, consisting of Sir Harcourt, Professor W. S. Holdsworth, and S. C. Peel, was called the Indian States Committee. They visited 16 **Princely States**. The rulers forcefully presented views on the responsibilities of the British Crown to which, they claimed, they owed sole allegiance. In opposition to these views, the **States Peoples Conference**—closely linked to the **Indian National Congress**—submitted a written statement to the Butler Committee declaring their objective to be representative and responsible government in the Indian princely states, as in British India.

Butler and his colleagues visited India at a time of intensive agitation, negotiation, and politicking on the subject of constitutional reform and eventual independence in India. They submitted their report in February 1929. It was strong on historical analysis but weak on political recommendation. It found the concept of **paramountcy** beyond definition and subject to the "shifting necessities of the time." The report noted the apprehensions of the princes regarding possible transfer of relationship to control by an elected Indian legislature. The **Simon Commission** endorsed these findings. To assuage the princes' anxiety, the **Government of India Act** of 1935 separated the functions of the viceroy in dealing with the princes from his functions as governor general heading the Government of India.

– C –

CABINET MISSION (March–June 1946). A team consisting of Lord Pethick-Lawrence, Secretary of State for India, **Sir Stafford Cripps**, President of the Board of Trade, and Lord A. V. Alexander, First Lord of the Admiralty, was appointed by British Prime Minister Clement Atlee in the spring of 1946. His postwar Labour Government wanted to resolve the many constitutional and political problems that impeded the promised early grant of independence to India. The principal impediment was disagreement between the **Indian National Congress** and the **All-India Muslim League** on the form and content of the new constitution and their respective roles in independent India. Both parties felt strengthened by the results of the elections that had been held in the winter of 1945–1946 and were unwilling to compromise on their basic positions formulated earlier. Another impediment was the confusion inherent in the concept of **"paramountcy"** over the relationship between the Indian princes and the future government of independent India.

Beginning in March 1946, the Cabinet Mission conducted intensive discussions in India and took into account a wide range of opinion. It tried but failed to mediate differences between Congress and the League during a conference at Simla and finally published a plan of its own on May 16. The Cabinet Mission Plan proposed a union of British India and the Indian **Princely States** to deal with foreign affairs, defense, and communications, having a central government vested with all "necessary" financial powers to do so. All other subjects and residual powers were to be vested in the Princely States and the provinces themselves. The Union Government would consist of an executive and a legislature, with the former responsible to the latter. Any question of major interest to either community was to be decided only by a majority of the representatives of each community and in each legislative house. Provinces were to be free to form—or to leave—three sub-federal groups: A, comprising **Hindu** majority provinces, or most of British India; B, comprising Muslim majority provinces of **Punjab**, **North West Frontier Province**, Baluchistan, and Sind; and C, comprising **Assam** and **Bengal**. The **Constituent Assembly** was to consist of 292 members to be elected by provincial assemblies on the basis of communal representation and 93 members to be appointed by the Princely States. Minorities and tribal peoples were to receive special attention by an advisory committee in drafting the rights of citizens. Pending a new constitution, administration was to be carried out by an interim government.

The Cabinet Mission Plan was a remarkable and complex scheme that conceded many demands made by the Muslim League but it rejected partition; it did not concede Congress demands for direct, noncommunal representation in the legislature or a strong central government. Many have praised the Cabinet Mission Plan as the last chance for a united India; it has been equally criticized as an impractical falling between two stools. The grouping scheme may well have proved unworkable had it been tried, and weak federal unions instituted in other parts of the British Empire about the same time did not last long. But the Cabinet Mission Plan was not implemented. **Jawaharlal Nehru** refused to bind Congress or the Constituent Assembly in advance to details of the plan; **Mohammed Ali Jinnah** abandoned constitutional methods and called for direct action by Muslims in favor of **Pakistan** on August 16, 1946. After the widespread communal violence unleashed by that call, the road ran downhill to **Partition**.

CALCUTTA/KOLKATA. Calcutta is among the largest cities in India, with a population exceeding 10 million. Before 1947 it was the second largest city in the British Empire. It was founded as a trading center of the **East India Company** in 1690 on the highest point of the river Hughly, navigable from the sea, and taking its name from an Anglicization of Kali Ghat, a temple to the goddess Kali that was located on the site.

Calcutta was central to the expansion of British power through commerce to administration and military conquest. Descriptions of life in Calcutta feature prominently in the writings and drawings of Company officials in the late 18th and 19th centuries. It naturally became the capital of the **Bengal** presidency and was the seat of the British Government of India for five cool months of the year until 1911, when the capital was shifted north to **Delhi**. Calcutta's wealth, university, elegance, and lively social, cultural, and intellectual life made it a meeting place of Indian and British cultures. The Bengali *bhadralok* (see Glossary) or gentry were an integral part of this symbiosis and were central to the Indian renaissance of the 19th and early 20th centuries. Not surprisingly, Calcutta was also an important center of the Indian struggle for freedom from British rule and was the site of a high level of political participation throughout the 20th century.

Calcutta's commerce and industry were badly hit by **Partition** in 1947; the eastern portions of its hinterland were incorporated as East **Pakistan**, and the northeastern portions were rendered almost inaccessible. Moreover, there was a heavy and steady influx of destitute refugees from East Bengal for many years, not only immediately after 1947 but also in huge numbers before and after the liberation of **Bangladesh** in December 1971 that further strained the city's infrastructure. **Mother Teresa's** humanitarian work there attracted international attention.

After 1977, the **Communist Party of India (Marxist)** government of West Bengal deliberately paid more attention to rural districts instead of Calcutta. Much private industry fled the city, to be lured back in the 1990s and after. Notwithstanding its severe socioeconomic and political problems, Calcutta, renamed Kolkata, remains one of the most vibrant cities in India.

CAMA, BHIKAJI (1861–1936). Bhikaji Cama was born in Bombay to a prosperous **Parsi** family named Patel and married the scion of an equally prosperous family in 1885. She had differences of opinion with her scholastic husband, Rustomji Cama, on the new nationalism led by the **Indian National Congress.** As a result, she moved to Europe where she met **Dadabhai Naoroji** in London in 1902 and assisted with his election to the British House of Commons. She came to know several Indian revolutionaries such as **Bipin Chander Pal, Hardayal,** and **Veer Savarkar** in the first decade of the 20th century and regularly addressed audiences in Hyde Park, London, herself.

Madame Bhikaji Cama moved to Paris in 1909 and made her home a headquarters for Indian rebels against British rule. She arranged for the smuggling of explosives and proscribed literature to British India through **Pondicherry** and engaged in various other "revolutionary activities" which brought her three terms of imprisonment in France and a ban on her return to India. However, she did eventually return to India in 1935 and died the following year.

CAREY, WILLIAM (1761–1835). Carey was an English shoemaker turned Baptist missionary who arrived in **Calcutta** in 1793 to propagate the faith. He was without money or friends and worked for some time in an indigo factory. Functionaries of the **East India Company** at the time did not look with favor at evangelical activities that might interrupt commerce, and Carey was forced to join the Danish settlement at nearby Serampore. Carey and his colleagues translated the Bible into Bengali and other Indian languages, compiled dictionaries and grammars, and used the printing press at Serampore to publish books and two Bengali journals. They also founded a college with a Western curriculum.

Lord Wellesley recognized Carey's remarkable linguistic skills and appointed him professor of **Sanskrit** and Bengali in 1801 at the

Fort William college, which had been set up for the Company's new British employees. Carey advocated social reform and education in Western science and English literature and probably influenced thinking along similar lines on the part of **Raja Ram Mohun Roy** and **Lord William Bentinck**. Later, the Serampore printing press (and settlement) came under British control and censorship.

CARIAPPA, KODENDRA MADAPPA, FIELD MARSHAL (1899–1993). Cariappa was born in the hills of **Coorg** to an educated and well-respected family. He attended Presidency College in **Madras** and was selected during **World War I** to train for the army. He was among the first Indian officers to receive a King's Commission in the **Indian Army**. Many other recognitions as "first Indian to . . ." ornamented his military career, notably his appointment as deputy chief of general staff just before independence, and as commander-in-chief with the rank of a four star general in January 1949.

After Cariappa's retirement from the army in 1953 he served as India's envoy to Australia and New Zealand and then continued to be active in public life though in a private capacity. He paid special attention to education, sports, the needs of ex-servicemen, and tribal peoples. He was awarded the honorary rank of field marshal in 1979.

CASTE. Indians and non-Indians alike commonly believe that the institution of caste characterizes **Hindu** society. Caste is conventionally defined as a system of social stratification of corporate groups formed through descent and perpetuated through endogamous marriage and traditional hereditary occupations. But there are considerable differences in scholarly opinion on explanations for caste: its ideological or material basis, and its rigidity, flexibility, or adaptability in the past, as well as its contemporary economic, political, or social relevance. In short, caste is a Pandora's box of open questions to which every answer has some qualifications.

The word caste is derived from *castas*, used by Portuguese traders of the 16th century to describe various "species" of men they encountered on the west coast of India. British administrators of the 19th century saw caste as a concrete, measurable entity that enabled them to impose a mental order on an otherwise bewildering confusion of India's living mosaic of peoples. But the one term caste was used for two quite different Indian concepts, those of *varna* (see Glossary) and *jati* (see Glossary). The former, *varna*, referred to function, occupation, and so, broadly speaking, to class, in a fourfold classification of a harmonious society; that is, **brahman** or priests and intellectuals, **kshatriya** or warriors and rulers, **vaishya** or a broad spectrum of "middle class" occupations, and **sudra** or peasants and workers. *Jati*, referred to a distinct community defined sometimes by occupation or religion and more frequently by tribe or kinship group.

Much of the difficulty in proposing a theory of caste or understanding its operation arises from trying to find a correspondence between *varna* and *jati* which may or may not exist. In short, while the presence of groups with known membership and boundaries since the time of the **Vedas** is undeniable, the exact nature of these boundaries and the hierarchies of rank are less certain, and vary with time and place. For example, particular *jatis* might be slotted into different *varnas* in different places or in the same place at different times; although both brahman and kshatriya were recognized as the "twice born" or high caste, their ranking with respect to each other was variable; the *avarna* or "outcaste" and **"untouchable"**—whose plight at the bottom of the socioeconomic heap has evinced compassion from reformers throughout the ages—also ranked themselves according to *jati*. Moreover, heterodox religious groups such as **Buddhism** and those established by the **Bhakti** saints denied the relevance of both *varna* and *jati* to spiritual salvation, but they usually retained caste identification for social purposes of marriage and commensality. The same was true even in such ideologically egalitarian communities as **Christianity**, **Islam**, and **Sikhism** on the Indian subcontinent.

Favorable land-population ratios until the 18th century contributed to social mobility and variety in inter-caste relationships. Stable and non-competitive relationships of mutual interdependence were a feature of India's agrarian economy. It is almost certain that scriptural injunctions against any "confusion" of caste duties and privileges—and there are many such brahmanical writings—originated in times of major political and social upheaval such as that which occurred after the Huna and the Turkic invasions. Caste rigidity, as portrayed in modern literature, was a product of the 19th century when British administration and the beginning of social anthropology affected local practices. Eight volumes of *The People of India* published between 1868 and 1875 depicted caste and tribal groups photographically with annotated and stereotypical labels attached. The 1871 census recorded, described, and ranked castes in a hierarchy that was based on contemporary brahmanical pronouncements and on ancient documents but was not necessarily accurate. The ranking brought many protests from newly formed caste associations. Listings on caste identity were omitted from the 1931 census and from subsequent census reports.

Recent scholarly inquiry has produced some explanations of caste, including Louis Dumont's *Homo Hierarchicus* (revised English edition, Chicago, 1980) that contrasts traditional, holistic society with modern, individualistic society. Dumont's theory was elegant but left much Indian practice unexplained, perhaps because he was addressing questions more salient to modern European societies rather than to traditional Indian societies. Others, critical of Dumont and seeing elements of caste beyond India, have related caste to Asian concepts of kingship, to the social structure of complex agrarian societies, to the self-preservation of pluralistic, decentralized societies in the face of political-military insecurity, and to priestly legitimization of force in political power as well as socioeconomic exploitation of an underclass. The empirical studies of contemporary Indian socio-anthropologists, especially **M. N. Srinivas** and **Andre Beteille**, illuminate important subjects, including the tactics of upward social mobility—such as Sanskritization—used by some caste groups, the relationship between power and status, the relative inclusiveness of the kshatriya *varna* in historic practice, the utility of caste identity, and the roots of inequality in Indian society. And key figures in India's social and political reform, such as **Jotiba Govind Phule** and **Bhimrao Ramji Ambedkar**, have challenged the very concept of graded inequality that underpins caste.

The **Indian Constitution** made the practice of untouchability a criminal offense and outlawed discrimination on grounds of caste, sex, or creed. At the same time, the Constitution provided for protective discrimination for the Scheduled Castes and Tribes through reservations for them in educational institutions and public services. There is little or no correspondence between *varna*, *jati*, and occupation in the modern sector of the Indian economy; nevertheless, caste remains relevant in social relationships, such as marriage, in both rural and urban India. Moreover, in the less developed areas of the country there is a correlation between high caste, high education, and relative wealth and power, on the one hand, and low caste, low skills, little or no education, low status, and low income, on the other. Not surprisingly, therefore, caste has assumed a new role as the basis of political protest, political identity, and possible voting blocs in India's democratic politics. It is so used by all **political parties**, some more openly than others. In this respect, the **Dalit** movement and implementation of the **Mandal Commission** Report were only the beginnings of a development with far-reaching and possibly revolutionary consequences.

CENSUS OF INDIA. The census of India was established in 1871 to conduct the first numerical survey of British India, identifying individuals by **caste**, and, after 1901, ranking castes according to local opinion on social precedence. Volunteers, rather than professionals, collected census data, and recording caste often became a matter of negotiating status. The Census Commissioner received petitions to change the names of some castes to those of higher status as well as complaints about bias or the forms of questioning. The decennial census became a source of controversy and intense politicking as political mobilization around social divisions of caste, language, and religion intensified in the 1920s and 1930s and community perceptions of advantage in larger relative numbers became important. Caste data was collected in 1941 but was not published, and the 1951 Census collected caste data only from those belonging to the Scheduled Castes and Tribes for use by the First Backward Classes Commission. The **Mandal Commission** on Other Backward Castes of 1978 conducted countrywide surveys based on enumerations made in 1931 and 1941.

In 1948, the independent Government of India established a single organization under a Registrar General to collect and check vital statistics of the entire population with the objective of determining size, disability, distribution, fertility, growth, language, literacy, marital age and status, migration, occupation, sex ratio, transport, and urbanization. Census questions were published in advance, and for the first time in 1951 persons were allowed to read the forms before signing them. Information on religious affiliation was not demanded, although the six major religions that were practiced in India were assigned code numbers and others were spelled out (See Appendix G).

The 14th census conducted in February and March 2001 was the most comprehensive in the world. Two million enumerators counted 1,027 million persons (220 million households) in 28 states (including **Jammu and Kashmir**, which had been omitted in 1991, and three newly created states) and seven Union Territories, covering 593 districts, 640,000 villages, and 5,161 towns or cities. Instruction manuals were prepared in 18 languages, and training was imparted to enumerators over two years. This gigantic administrative exercise was carried out expeditiously, and a provisional demographic profile of India was published by the end of March 2001. Innovations facilitating future comparative study included data on occupation, houses, household amenities and assets such as drinking water and latrines, and on identifying slum blocks in towns of over 50,000 inhabitants and assigning a unique eight-digit Permanent Location Code Number to each village and urban ward. Maps depicting information such as population density, literacy rates, and sex ratio by district have proved to be as useful as the more conventional tables on male and female population categorized as main, marginal, and nonworkers.

Some of the highlights of the 2001 Census published to date are:

- A total population of 1,025,251,059 compared to 846 million in 1991, showing an overall decline in the population growth rate to 1.93%, with variation between the highest of 2.84 in Bihar to the lowest of 0.94 in Kerala and the sharpest decline to 1.39 seen in Andhra Pradesh. An overall improvement in the sex ratio from 927 females to 1,000 males in 1991 to 933 females to 1,000 males in 2001 with variation between the highest of 1058 in Kerala to 861 in Haryana.
- Literacy rates improved over those of 1991 to 75.9% for males and 54.2% for females with an absolute decline of illiterate persons by 32 million.
- A total urban population of 284,999,688 compared with a total rural population of 740,255,371.

- A total working population of 402,512,190 consisting of 275,463,736 males and 127,048,454 females, and 313,173,394 categorized as main workers. Cultivators are numbered as 127,628,287, agricultural labor as 107,447,725, household industry workers as 16,395,870, and "other" as 151,040,308.

CEYLON. *See* SRI LANKA.

CHAITANYA (1485–1533). A **Bhakti** saint and worshipper of **Krishna**, Chaitanya was born into a **brahman** family and was educated along traditional lines. He took *sanyas* (see Glossary), or renounced the world, when only in his twenties. He was a mystic who drew crowds and exercised great influence through his devotional hymns. He preached his message of bhakti, or loving surrender to God, in **Orissa**, **Bengal**, the eastern **Deccan**, and the **Ganges** valley, gathering many followers. He led them in devotional song and dance, often in an ecstatic mode. Chaitanya is believed by some to be an incarnation of Radha and Krishna together, in divine union.

CHALUKYA DYNASTY. The early Chalukyas rose to power in northern **Karnataka** in the sixth century CE under Pulakesin I of Vatapi. He performed the **ashvamedha** or horse sacrifice, which entitled him to proclaim dominion over considerable territory. His successors further expanded the kingdom in all four directions, with Pulakesin II (r. 609–642) engaging **Harsha vardhana** of **Kanauj** on battlefields north of the Vindhya mountains as well. This was an unusual enterprise, seldom repeated before the northward expansion of **Maratha** power in the 18th century.

The Chalukya Dynasty patronized various religious denominations and all of the arts. Some exquisite examples of early Chalukyan temples and sculpture remain at Badami, Aiholi, and Pattadkal in western Karnataka. Later Chalukya dynasties—and more than one family appears to have taken that name—played their parts in the shifting fortunes of southern and Deccani kingdoms from the 10th to 13th century before the advent of the **Bahmani** and **Vijayanagar** kingdoms.

CHAMBER OF PRINCES. Established by Royal Proclamation in 1921 as part of the **Montagu-Chelmsford Reforms**, the Chamber of

Princes was a deliberative, consultative, and advisory body consisting of 120 rulers of **Princely States**. The viceroy—another designation for the head of the British Government of India, or governor general— presided permanently over the Chamber of Princes. A chancellor and vice chancellor were elected annually from among the members, 108 of whom sat in their own right and other rulers of lesser status elected the remaining 12.

The Chamber of Princes accomplished one of its objectives, which was to end the isolation of individual Princely States, whose scattered territories were interspersed in British India. But the Chamber was unable to fulfill its larger purposes, that is, evolving a common set of political principles for the princes to follow and bridging the gaps between princely and British India. There were many reasons for this failure. The Chamber was neither an executive body nor was it empowered to discuss the crucial questions of earlier treaties, current administration, or future relationships. Important states such as **Hyderabad** and **Mysore** stayed aloof; there was mutual mistrust between most princes and the prime vehicle of Indian nationalism, the **Indian National Congress**; and although the British were dominant, they were confused about their own obligations under **paramountcy** and vacillated in their advice to the princes.

Institutions take time to mature, even in favorable circumstances, and the Chamber did not carry weight in the 1940s. Although individual rulers played prominent roles as diplomats and negotiators in the pre-independence period and later in the public life of India, the Chamber of Princes became legally defunct in 1947.

CHANAKYA. *See* KAUTILYA.

CHANDELLA DYNASTY. This dynasty surfaced among competing powers of the ninth century CE and established itself in Bundelkhand of central India. The Chandellas were patrons of literature and the arts. Their capital was at Khajuraho, where a distinctive local style of the early medieval period was expressed in vibrant sculpture and numerous temples. Having survived early raids from the **Delhi Sultanate**, the Chandellas disappeared from the political scene in the 14th century.

CHANDIGARH. A planned city, designed and built by the famous French architect Le Corbusier at the request of **Jawaharlal Nehru**, it was the capital of **Punjab**, since **Partition** had removed the traditional capital, Lahore, from India. The city was meant to make a modern, national statement and have an international impact, which it did. At the same time, many criticized Corbusier's design as unsuitable for the local climate and landscape. Chandigarh is situated in a salubrious climate in the foothills of the **Himalaya** and is an agreeable living environment.

Since the further administrative division of Punjab in 1966, Chandigrah has served as the joint capital of **Haryana** and **Punjab** with the status of Union Territory.

CHANDRA GUPTA I (Fourth Century CE). See **GUPTA EMPIRE**.

CHANDRA GUPTA II VIKRAMADITYA. (r. c. 380–413 CE). Grandson of **Chandra Gupta I**. See GUPTA EMPIRE and VIKRAMADITYA.

CHANDRAGUPTA MAURYA (r. c. 324–298 BCE). Chandragupta was probably the young man who met **Alexander of Macedon** in 326 BCE and is named Sandrocottus by Greek historians. He also figures in the **Jain** tradition, **Buddhist** chronicles, and the **Puranas** as the king who overthrew the Greek prefects who ruled east and west of the **Indus** River. He then effected a revolution in **Pataliputra** on the **Ganges**, exterminated the Nanda Dynasty that ruled there, and took control of their rich and powerful kingdom, **Magadha**. Chandragupta expanded its territories and is known as the first historical Emperor of India. Toward the end of his reign he concluded a marriage treaty with Alexander's General Seleukos Nikator ruling in Babylon and obtained from him the satrapies of Kabul, Kandahar, and Herat in present-day Afghanistan.

Chandragupta's exact lineage is not known, although his mother probably belonged to the Moriya clan of eastern India. He was greatly assisted in all his exploits by a **brahman** adviser, **Kautilya**, whose *Arthasastra* is read as a commentary on political-administrative practices in Magadha. According to the Jain tradition, Chandragupta renounced princely life in middle age and died as an ascetic in southern

India. His son Bindusara succeeded him. *See also* ASHOKA and MAURYA DYNASTY.

CHARTER ACTS. Royal charters governed the functions and administration of the English **East India Company**. The first charter granted by Queen Elizabeth I in December 1600 gave the Company the exclusive right to trade with India. Subsequent charters confirmed its trading monopoly and recognized its expanding functions at trading posts in India. The innovative **Regulating Act** of 1773 established parliamentary control over the Company, largely because its immense financial transactions as well as its growing political power in India excited many questions of propriety in England. The governor of Bengal was elevated to the rank of governor-general at this time.

Periodic parliamentary probes into the finances and wars waged by the Company inevitably brought about greater regulation, in line with the changing climate of opinion in Britain. The Charter Act of 1813 ended the East India Company's monopoly of trade with India, proclaimed British sovereignty over territories captured in India, permitted Christian missionaries to settle there, and allocated a grant for educational purposes. The even more comprehensive Act of 1833 abolished all commercial transactions by Company officials, removed restrictions on British immigration to India, and empowered the governor-general in an enlarged council to legislate for all persons residing in British India. Parliamentary control was further widened in 1853. Once the Mutiny or **Uprising of 1857** had been suppressed, all of the dominions and functions of the East India Company were taken over by the British Crown in 1858.

CHATTERJI (CHATTOPADHYAYA), BANKIM CHANDRA (1838–1894). Bankim Chandra was born into an old **brahman** family of **Bengal**. He was educated in English and in Bengali, studied Law, and was the first graduate of Calcutta University. He was in government service and was both appreciative and critical of British administration in India. His fame and very considerable influence derived from his literary career as essayist and novelist.

Bankim Chandra explored serious historical, philosophical, and social questions through his writings. He was among the first to clearly enunciate sentiments of nationalism—a concept that gathered momentum in succeeding decades. His novel *Anandamath* (1882), which incorporated the nationalist hymn "**Bande Mataram**," stimulated the spread of revolutionary fervor in Bengal at the turn of the century. Bankim Chandra is remembered as one of the heroes of the Indian freedom struggle.

CHATTOPADHYAYA, KAMALADEVI (1903–1988). Kamaladevi is indelibly associated with the remarkable revival and development of handicrafts in India after independence, inspired by the concept of **swadeshi**. The traditional crafts of basket makers, cane workers, potters, vegetable dyers of textiles, and other crafts had languished under colonial rule, and Kamaladevi implemented a new nationwide infrastructure for their rejuvenation. The All-India Handicrafts Board, which she chaired from 1952 to 1967, provided a means for designing and marketing handicrafts, and other institutions such as the Crafts Museum and various awards brought recognition and acclaim to master craftsmen. Handloom textiles received special fillip from the All-India Handlooms Board and the Cottage Industries Emporium, in which Pupul Jayakar and Jasleen Dhamija played crucial roles. Kamaladevi took up the cause of traditional performing arts and theatre during the last two decades of her life, setting up institutions to encourage young performers, and widening the cultural scope of the India International Centre of which she was vice president.

Kamaldevi had begun her work at the grassroots early. She joined the **Civil Disobedience** Movement in 1930 by breaching the Salt Laws, leading and addressing protest marches, and raising funds through the auction of homemade salt. She was arrested in May 1930 and was placed in solitary confinement during her third prison term 1933–1934. She became a founding member of the Congress Socialist Party and its president in 1936. She was also an outspoken leader of the Congress Women's Seva Dal and president of the All India Women's Conference. Probably because she divorced her husband and openly advocated contraception in the early 1930s, Kamaldevi incurred the displeasure of **Gandhi**, but she remained a loyal participant in the **Quit India Movement**. Kamaladevi was a reserved, sometimes intimidating, woman who was both an artist and a social activist but never a politician.

CHAUHAN or **CHAHAMANA.** These are the names of a clan of **Rajputs** who claim descendance from an ancient sacrificial fire and who took political power in northern India during the early medieval period. A Chauhan Dynasty ruled part of **Rajasthan** with **Ajmer** as its capital for many centuries and controlled **Delhi** in the 12th century. Prithviraj, or Rai Pithora, was the most famous ruler of that dynasty. A great soldier, he defeated the **Chandella** king, and his deeds of valor and of love—especially his elopement with the daughter of a rival Rajput ruler, Raja Jaychandra of Kanauj, in 1175—continue to be recited by bards to the present day.

The Rajputs were on the fighting front of an expanding Turk-Islamic frontier along the northwest of the Indian subcontinent for centuries, and Prithviraj's victory against Muhammad Ghor at the first battle of Tarain was much celebrated. Unfortunately, he did not alter his military tactics or form alliances to meet renewed attacks. He was defeated and killed by Muhammad Ghor at the second battle of Tarain in 1192.

CHENNAI. *See* MADRAS.

CHETTIAR. A *jati* of the **vaisya** *varna* or class specializing in finance and found mainly in **Tamil Nadu**, the Chettiars played important socioeconomic roles throughout southern India, **Sri Lanka**, and the Indian Ocean region from the time of the **Chola** Empire to the present day. From the 16th century onward they concentrated on banking and money lending. The Chettiars did not lose either their social cohesion or their financial abilities during the rule of the **East India Company**. They expanded their activities to other parts of the British Empire, especially Africa, **Burma**, and Malaya, and remain active among the Indian **diaspora** of the present day.

Operating through far-reaching familial networks, the Chettiars and other well-known trading **castes** extended credit, accepted deposits, and fulfilled many financial functions in an informally organized system whose origins and evolution belong to India's unrecorded past.

The system survived British efforts to centralize and regulate it and was estimated at 90% of total internal trade by the Central Banking Inquiry Committee of 1929.

CHHATISGARH. A new state of 135,100 square kilometers in the Indian Union, it was created at the end of 2000 from 16 neighboring districts in **Madhya Pradesh** and **Andhra Pradesh** located in the Mahanadi basin and on the Dandakaranya Plateau. Its estimated population of 17,610,000 is composed mostly of Gond and other **Adivasi** tribes. Geologically, it is part of ancient Gondwana and is rich in coal, copper, iron ore, and other valuable minerals. Chhatisgarh enjoys a monsoon climate and is richly forested with abundant wildlife; it contains the Bastar Wildlife Sanctuary and sites of Project Tiger protecting India's magnificent carnivores. Population density is relatively low with only five cities in the state, including the state capital Raipur, and the ratio of females to males is higher than the national average.

CHIDAMBARAM, PALANIAPPA (1945–). Chidambaram was born in **Tamil Nadu** and took an active part in state politics as a member of the **Congress Party**. He was minister of commerce in the government of **P. V. Narasimha Rao** for the period 1991–1996 and was closely in tune with the minister of finance, **Dr. Manmohan Singh**. Factional strife within Congress left Chidambaram out of favor with the new Congress leadership of **Sonia Gandhi**. At the same time, the rift enabled him to join the National Front governments of **H. D. Deve Gowda** and **I. K. Gujral** as minister of finance, 1996–1998. Chidambram proceeded steadily to implement further economic reforms, such as cutting taxes and lowering tariffs, loosening price controls on agricultural products, and encouraging private enterprise in new industrial ventures such as telecommunications. He is credited with some of the success resulting from India's economic liberalization. He was general secretary of the Congress Jnananayaka Party, a splinter group in Tamil Nadu. He won a seat to the **Lok Sabha** in the general elections of 2004 and was appointed minister of finance in the Congress-led coalition government of Dr. Manmohan Singh.

CHILD, SIR JOSIAH (1630–1699). Child was familiar with the operations of the **East India Company** from his father Joseph Child and went on to direct them from the Company's London headquarters at Leadenhall Street. He was chairman of the Board of Directors from 1674 to 1689, but for more than 20 years he treated it as if it were his private business, getting his way by whatever means he found necessary, including drama. His ambition, well ahead of his time, was to establish civil and military power in India and "secure such a large revenue as may be the foundation of a large, well-grounded, sure English Dominion in India for all time to come." (Keay, *The Honourable Company*, 174.)

Neither the Company nor Britain was in a position to realize such an ambition in the late 17th century. For example, although Child persuaded King James II to mount an expensive naval expedition to seize **Bengal's** port of Chittagong, in 1685, the expedition was easily defeated by **Mughal** forces that also expelled English traders from that province. In the following century and a half, however, the Company's fortunes in Bengal, **Bombay**, and **Madras** progressed in the direction envisaged by the much-quoted Sir Josiah Child.

CHIPKO MOVEMENT. It takes its name from *chipko* or "hugging" of trees by women in the forested hills of **Uttar Pradesh** to prevent their being felled for commercial purposes. The movement is internationally acclaimed as one of the most effective environmentalist efforts launched at the grassroots level in India during the 1970s and continuing to the present day.

The philosophic roots of the Chipko movement are ancient and holistic. The deprivation that villagers face from deforestation provides the economic imperative. The examples of **Mahatma Gandhi** and **Vinoba Bhave** in the practice of non-violent action lend further inspiration. The Chipko movement has gradually spread to other parts of India and has won some significant victories against mindless exploitation of forest resources.

CHISTI or CHISTIYYA. One of the most influential of the **Sufi** or Islamic mystic orders established in India, the order took its name from the place in Syria where its founder lived. It first became popular in India through the lives of Khwaja Muinuddin Chisti of **Ajmer** and his spiritual descendants, including **Farid** and Nizamuddin Auliya.

The cardinal principles of spiritual life imparted by the Chisti sages hinged on the Unity of Being as man's focus and motive force. Further, they practiced nonviolent conduct, eschewing revenge for the sake of a healthy social order, and looked on private property as a negation of faith in God. What set the Chistiyya apart from other well-established Sufi orders, such as the Suhrawardy, was their refusal to have any relationship with the state or to accept any stipend from a ruler, and their indifference as to whether initiates were formally converted to **Islam** or not. Chisti practices were similar to those of other mystics, including recitations, meditation, breathing control, and periodic confinement for prayer and contemplation. The great Chisti sages were renowned not only for their piety and wit, but for their identification of devotion to God with service to the weak, the poor, and the suffering. They were fearless in criticizing oppressive rulers of the **Khalji** and **Tughlaq** dynasties.

The history of the Chisti order in India includes four broad phases. The years 1200–1356 were the era of the great sheikhs who lived in rural areas of present-day **Rajasthan, Punjab**, and **Uttar Pradesh**, and who formulated the basic rules of the order, avoided identification with the newly established Muslim state of the **Delhi Sultanate**, and chose their successors on the basis of spiritual learning and devotion alone. The Chisti centralized structure suffered when the Delhi Sultanate itself disintegrated. The 14th and 15th centuries saw the establishment of several provincial Chisti centers where sheikhs were willing to accept state endowments from newly independent rulers. A third phase of revivalism followed, with the original Chisti teachings being spread in eastern India, the **Deccan**, and **Gujarat** in the 16th and 17th centuries. Efforts were made to recentralize the order and revive its influence in the northwestern areas of the subcontinent during the 18th century.

The Chistiyya profoundly influenced the popular religious culture of India and were venerated by the common people as well as by emperors such as **Akbar**. A substantial literature exists, consisting of recorded conversations with Chisti sheikhs, letters, works on doctrine and practice, biographical accounts, and mystic poetry, including compositions by **Amir Khusru**.

CHITOR. A walled fortress in southern **Rajasthan** of about 12 kilometers in circumference, Chitor was built on the precipitous edge of a tableland in the seventh century and dominated the surrounding land for close to 900 years. It was the capital of the Sisodia clan of **Rajputs** who ruled Mewar and constructed temples and victory towers to celebrate their exploits, which are also the subject of heroic folk tales.

Chitor was sacked three times in its history: by Alauddin Khalji of **Delhi** in 1303, by Bahadur Shah of **Gujarat** in 1534, and by the **Mughal Emperor Akbar** in 1568, after which it was abandoned. On each occasion, when defeat appeared certain, the Rajput women immolated themselves inside the fortress while the men fought to the death outside the walls. Chitor became a symbol of the Rajput code of honor.

CHOLA DYNASTY. The **Tamil** country in the far south of the subcontinent saw much dynastic struggle over the centuries, with the Cholas, Cheras, **Pandyas**, and **Pallavas** all competing in a seesaw of power in peninsular India. The Cholas were based in the **Kaveri** valley and along the Coromandel coast. They were known in **Mauryan** times and surfaced militarily in the second century BCE. Their earliest historical king was named Karikal. By about 100 CE, the Cholas were prominent but became most famous after defeating the Pallavas at the close of the ninth century.

Through a combination of military raids, sophisticated administration, and efficient revenue collection, the Cholas rapidly established themselves as the recognized overlords of most of peninsular India and remained so until the last quarter of the 13th century. The Cholas also sponsored maritime expansion into **Ceylon**, the **Laccadive** and **Maldive** island groups, and eastward to the Malay peninsula and Sumatra. The Cholas were motivated more by an interest in overseas trade than acquisition of territory. Although backed by a powerful navy, Chola expansion overseas was cultural rather than colonial, and of relatively short duration.

The Chola kings worshiped **Shiva** but were tolerant of other sects and religions. Tamil culture blossomed under the Cholas. This culture can be appreciated even today through Tamil literature, especially the *Kural* of Tiruvallur, through the uncommonly graceful bronze sculptures of the period, especially that representing Shiva Nataraj or the Dancing Shiva, and from the many temples of the period constructed in a distinctive style. This **Dravidian** style of temple architecture was characterized by a profusion of sculpture, many pillared halls and colonnades, a series of receding terraces called shikhara over the shrine, and large gateway towers or *gopuram* also covered with sculptures. Grand concepts were executed with the delicacy of jewelry, as can be seen at the Shiva temple at **Tanjore.**

Chola rulers Rajaraja I (985–1016) and Rajendra I (1016–1035) provided a pattern for kingship followed by others, weaving ancient local societies into a common social, cultural, and administrative system in which many **Sanskritic** elements were merged with the Tamil base. Loyalty to the central authority in the person of the king was assured, but actual administration was not highly centralized. For example, elected local assemblies having jurisdiction over village groupings known as *kottam* managed those subjects of vital concern to an agrarian economy such as irrigation, water control, and even revenue collection (amounting to one-sixth to one-third of produce and paid in either cash or kind). *Kottams*, in turn, were grouped in a district or *nadu*, several of which composed a province or *mandala*. There were six provinces in the Chola Empire at its height, each corresponding to an older kingdom or administrative area, whose ruling families survived in positions of responsibility.

Under Chola rule, **brahmans**, and landowners, were the principal beneficiaries of the agricultural surplus generated by cultivators. At the same time, urbanization and the growth of new temple complexes bespoke increased trade and influential roles for merchants and artisans in society. Inscriptions on 13th-century temples reflect cooperative relationships among different groups of people sharing economic and political dominance in the Chola Empire. The tradition was not seriously affected until Malik Kafur, in the service of the Muslim **Delhi Sultanate**, overran the **Hindu** kingdoms of the **Deccan**, made a lightning strike at the chief Chola city, Tanjore, in 1310, and upset the existing order. By the end of the 14th century, the whole of peninsular India had passed under the sway of two opposing and equally militarized states, the **Bahmani** Sultanate of the Deccan and **Vijayanagar** in the south, whose rulers sometimes claimed succession to the great Cholas.

CHRISTIANITY. According to the 2001 Census of India, Christians numbered about 24 million, or over 2% of the total population. They form a majority in the northeastern states of **Meghalaya**, **Mizsoram**, and **Nagaland**, and a prominent minority in **Goa**, **Kerala**, and **Pondicherry**. Generally speaking, they enjoy higher literacy rates than others in equivalent income or kinship groups.

According to popular tradition, the Apostle Thomas came to southern India in the first century CE and founded the Syrian Christian Church. Its followers form a respected and influential community in Kerala. **Saint Francis Xavier** came to Goa in 1542; and his embalmed body which was enshrined there subsequently became a destination for pilgrims. The **Portuguese** brought **Jesuits** with them in the 16th century and undertook mass conversion to the Roman Catholic Church in their colonies on the west coast. Later, Protestant missionaries used different tactics. The social and ethnic origin of Christian converts varied; many came from the outer fringes of **Hindu** society among **Adivasis** and **untouchables**; some came from influential upper-caste families.

Protestant missionaries of various denominations were permitted to work in India following the **Charter Act** of 1833, and their numbers steadily increased through the 19th century. They provided educational, social, and medical services as accompaniments to their evangelical work and were active in collecting real information about the people they were trying to convert. British and American missionaries formed strong bonds with each other, as representatives of what they called an "Anglo-Saxon Empire," although they were kept outside the official circles of the British Empire in India. Missionaries generally depicted Indian men as weak, emotional, excessive, feminine, and needing a strong injection of "masculine values." Missionaries also deplored the status and treatment of **women**. These images frequently were internalized by students and affected their adult behavior. It is clear that Christian missionaries had a strong impact on the reification of religion among all communities in the late 19th and early 20th centuries, and hence can be said to have influenced events far beyond the number of actual conversions.

After Indian independence, the various Protestant denominations formed a United Church of India and lessened their dependence on foreign missionaries. The Roman Catholic Church in India also became increasingly Indianized, with two cardinals and numerous bishops leading it since the 1980s and the Pope making two visits. Indian clerics also held many positions in the Vatican, while **Mother Teresa** and the nuns of her order became internationally renowned.

Militant advocates of **Hindutva** targeted Christians as "foreigners," and they suffered some casualties, especially in **Gujarat** and **Orissa** in the 1990s and after. But the general elections of 2004 showed that the political attempt to defame **Sonia Gandhi**—and by implication, all Christians—had failed.

CIVIL DISOBEDIENCE. This is an expression of dissent from the government in power and a denial of its legitimacy to rule. Persons engaged in civil disobedience may contravene specific laws and/or refuse to pay taxes. The phenomenon is not confined to one country or to one era, but civil disobedience took on a particular aura of moral power in India under the leadership of **Mahatma Gandhi** in the first half of the 20th century.

Movements of mass civil disobedience, in addition to but distinct from individual assertions, became a formidable and non-violent instrument of the Indian national movement under Gandhi's leadership in the 1920s and 1930s. Mass civil disobedience movements contested the justice of particular laws such as the **Rowlatt Acts** and the tax on salt (1930), and in a wider sense challenged the legitimacy of the British government of India itself. For example, high levels of self-discipline, mobilization, and organization were prerequisites for mass civil disobedience, helping to shatter the alleged Indian psychology of dependence. Further, the ability of unarmed men and women in their thousands to withstand the onslaughts of police batons and other state instruments of organized force, to accept fines, harsh punishments, and uncertain terms of imprisonment, and to sustain struggle for the sake of principle, had a tremendous impact on public opinion inside and outside India. At the very least, these demonstrations refuted Britain's claim to rule India by consent, revealing the armed might at its core.

Gandhi used civil disobedience or **Satyagraha** as a method of self-purification and striving after truth and also as a method to influence, unite, and strengthen the **Indian National Congress** as the spearhead of Indian nationalism. These objectives were visible in the **Non-Cooperation Movement** of 1921–1922 and were much further advanced in the Civil Disobedience Movement of 1930–1931. Gandhi's famous **Dandi March** protesting a new tax on salt heralded the latter. The first phase of the civil disobedience movement was most intense, especially in **Bombay**, **Gujarat**, **Bihar**, the cities of the United Provinces (present day **Uttar Pradesh**), **Orissa**, and the coastal areas of **Madras** and Malabar. Large numbers of women and teenagers participated for the first time, adding to perceptions of national mobilization. With the arrest and imprisonment of Congress leaders, a second wave of regional leaders and local issues surfaced in the countryside and forest belts, drawing in the peasantry and tribals, including those of **Maharashtra** and central India. By late 1931, the movement was simultaneously flexible, radicalized, and in decline. It was relatively weak in **Assam**, **Bengal**, **Punjab**, and Sindh. More importantly, this movement was not backed by organized labor or by the leader of the Mahars, **Dr. Ambedkar**, and left most Muslims unaffected, except in the North West Frontier Province where **Abdul Ghaffar Khan** had emerged as a Pakthun leader in the Gandhian mode.

Notwithstanding lacunae, links among a wide spectrum of Indians of different groups were reinforced wherever local campaigns on specific issues dovetailed with the all-India protest. Official records of the period show that civil disobedience threatened a breakdown of administration in certain provinces and that Congress was establishing parallel organizations. Thus, Congress's claims to represent India and provide an alternative to British administration gained credence, giving it corresponding leverage. The 1930–1931 civil disobedience movement undoubtedly spurred **Lord Irwin** to reach a compromise pact with Gandhi in March 1931 and call for reconvening the **Round Table Conference**. *See also* NON-COOPERATION MOVEMENT, QUIT INDIA MOVEMENT, and SATYAGRAHA.

CLIVE, ROBERT (1725–1774). Clive served the **East India Company** first as a lowly clerk or writer—but one with unexpected military talents—in **Madras**, from 1744–1753, then as a trader and a commanding officer of troops in **Bengal**, from 1755–1760, and finally as Lord Clive, Governor of Bengal, from 1765–1767. Described by his contemporaries as sturdy, violent, self-centered, emotional, generous, courageous, and brilliant in adversity, Clive was one of those men who laid the foundations of British rule in India.

As a young man, Robert Clive established British military superiority over the French in south India by his audacious march to Arcot, capital of the Carnatic, in 1751. He went on to Bengal and defeated the numerically superior forces of Nawab Siraj ud-Daula at **Plassey** in 1757. He presided over a lucrative and exploitative system in which the British received the revenue, deference, and commercial perquisites of power in Bengal, without having to discharge the administrative responsibility or expenditures that beleaguered the Indian ruler who was formally in authority.

Clive acquired enough wealth in India to fulfill his ambition of obtaining a seat in the British House of Commons as well as an Irish peerage at home. The Company Directors sent him back to Bengal in 1765 to restore their high profits and reform the blatant corruption there. Meanwhile, a British victory over **Mughal** forces at **Baxar** in 1764 resulted in an increase of the Company's administrative functions because the Mughal Emperor in **Delhi** gave the Company Bahadur the status of dewan (see Glossary) with the right to collect revenues in **Bengal, Bihar**, and **Orissa**. Clive attempted to reform the worst abuses in **Calcutta**. He tried to regulate private trade by British officials and abolished the custom of their receiving private presents and drawing double military allowances in addition to their normal salaries. He raised their salaries and tried to enforce financial and moral discipline, but met with small success.

The climate of opinion was changing in London, and tolerance was declining for freebooters and conquistadors who enriched themselves in the process of acquiring an empire for their country. Clive's critics — and there were many — instigated a parliamentary inquiry against him. Eminent Liberals cried out against the servants of the Company in the House of Commons. Although Clive was acquitted honorably in 1773, he took his own life the following year. At about the same time, the British Parliament passed the famous **Regulating Act** to guide future activities of the East India Company.

COCHIN/KOCHI. One of the largest Indian ports, Cochin, or Kochi, is located on the southwestern coast of **Kerala**. Cochin has long been a prosperous center of trade in spices and other commodities, of the coir, cashew, fishing, and food processing industries, and is currently an important naval base. The capital city of the erstwhile **Princely**

State of the same name, Cochin's rich and varied past is reflected in its architecture. A **Jewish** synagogue, Syrian Christian and Portuguese churches, Dutch and English mansions, old and new mosques, and many temples are to be seen there, along with Chinese fishing nets on inland waterways and the seafront. All testify to historic trading and cultural links between India and other parts of the world.

Cochin was a natural object of European colonial competition in the 16th and 17th centuries but remained under the rule of a dynasty claiming descent from Cheraman Perumal of ancient times. In 1791, the ruler signed an alliance with the **East India Company** for protection against the depredations of **Tipu Sultan** of **Mysore**. Cochin and its southern neighbor Travancore were similar in that their ruling families and a majority of the population followed a matrilineal pattern of inheritance, and were known for their progressive administration and outstanding encouragement of education for both females and males. Cochin had an elected legislative council as early as the 1920s and sent elected members to the **Constituent Assembly** in 1946. Cochin was among the first of the Princely States to accede to the Indian Union in 1947. It was joined with Travancore and the Mallayali speaking Malabar district of **Madras** to form the state of Kerala in 1956.

COMMUNAL AWARD (1932). British Prime Minister Ramsay MacDonald announced the communal award as a voting scheme to be discussed in the **Round Table Conferences**. It was subsequently incorporated (with minor amendments) in the **Government of India Act** of 1935. The Communal Award provided for separate electorates, weighted representation, and reserved seats in legislatures for certain communities—**Anglo-Indians**, Christians, Europeans, Muslims, and **Sikhs**. All other voters were categorized as a "general" constituency. In 1934, provisions of the Communal Award were extended to government services as well, with certain percentages reserved for Muslims and other minority communities.

The Communal Award initially made similar provisions of separate electorates and seat reservations for **Untouchables**, but **Mahatma Gandhi** launched a fast unto death in protest against giving them a political identity separate from that of other **Hindus**. He reached an agreement with their leader **Dr. Ambedkar** that modified the original proposals by increasing the number of reserved seats for Harijans (Gandhi's name for Untouchables) in return for joint electorates in the general category.

The Communal Award was cautiously accepted by the **All-India Muslim League** as a safeguard of minority rights, but was opposed by the **Indian National Congress** as a "barrier . . . to the development of Indian unity."

COMMUNIST PARTY OF INDIA (CPI). The CPI was founded as a national party representing the working class, peasantry, and toilers of India in December 1925 but was given legal recognition only in 1942. The CPI brought together a number of volunteer groups with Marxist and revolutionary leanings that had sprung up clandestinely in India after the Russian Revolution of October 1917. Individually and collectively, functioning inside and outside the **Indian National Congress**, the communists demanded complete independence from British rule, were active in the **trade union** movement, and initiated *kisan* or peasant movements in some areas. They were subject to even stricter surveillance by the British authorities than other nationalists and suffered a reversal when almost their entire leadership, including 31 trade union officials, were arrested in the Meerut Conspiracy case of 1929.

The CPI grew apart from the mainstream of the Indian national movement in the 1930s and 1940s, partly because it did not share **Mahatma Gandhi**'s philosophy of non-violent action, partly because socialist ideas and programs were espoused by radical members of Congress itself, and also because it opposed the **Quit India** movement and instead collaborated with the British authorities during **World War II** on Moscow's instructions. The independent government of India did not abrogate provisions such as preventive detention designed for dealing strictly with communists. There was considerable ideological debate at three Communist Party congresses held in 1943, 1948, and 1953 when various strategies and tactics for future action were discussed, including the armed revolution unsuccessfully used in the **Tebhaga** and **Telengana** movements. There emerged a fairly moderate position of participating in the parliamentary processes of independent India, supporting the anti-imperialist foreign policy of **Jawaharlal Nehru**, while opposing his "capitalist" domestic economic policies, and aiming for a united front instead of blindly following the Russian or Chinese examples. The CPI explicitly accepted the possibility of a peaceful transition to socialism at its fifth congress of 1958.

The CPI won enough seats in the **Lok Sabha** in the general elections of 1952, 1957, and 1962 to give it the status of principal opposition party. (See Appendix H.) In 1964, however, the CPI split in the wake of India's border war with China and the Sino-Soviet split, and an important segment of the membership left to form the **Communist Party India (Marxist) [CPI(M)]**. Partly because of public perceptions of its identification with Moscow, and also because it lacked an active cadre working in the grassroots, the CPI did not fare well in the elections of 1967, 1971, 1977, or 1980 and its general secretary, **S. A. Dange**, resigned in 1981, giving way to C. Rajeshwara Rao. Despite new programs, the CPI won only six seats in the Lok Sabha in 1984 and twelve in 1989. It supported the National Front government of **V. P. Singh** although it was not a member of his **Janata Dal** coalition. CPI confidence and fortunes suffered badly from the collapse of the Soviet Union.

Since the early 1990s the CPI has attempted to rally what are known as "progressive" or "secular forces" against the communalization of Indian politics. It was equally critical of the **Bharatiya Janata Party (BJP)** and the Congress Party, especially when **P. V. Narasimha Rao**'s government passed major measures of economic liberalization, and held on to its modest number of parliamentary seats. Along with other leftist parties, the CPI, led by General Secretary A.B. Bardhan, agreed in 2004 to support the Congress-led United Progressive Alliance coalition government of **Dr. Manmohan Singh** from the outside in the hope of gaining more influence and perhaps slowing the process of **economic liberalization** and globalization in India.

COMMUNIST PARTY OF INDIA (MARXIST) [CPI (M)]. The CPI (M) emerged as a separate entity as the result of a split within the **Communist Party of India** in 1964. Ideological disputes within the party had become acute after Indian independence, especially on the question of whether or to what extent the CPI should cooperate with the "progressive" **Congress** government of **Jawaharlal Nehru**. Conflict between the two groups came into the open with the Chinese invasion of October 1962, when the group opposing links with Congress was labeled "pro-China" and "anti-national." Developments in the international communist movement during the late 1950s and early 1960s, notably the revelations of the 20th Congress of the Communist Party of the Soviet Union and the rupture, both ideological and political, between China and the Soviet Union, sharpened the inner-party conflict in India. A climax was reached at the seventh party congress held at **Calcutta** in November 1964 when 32 members of the CPI National Committee left to form a new party.

The CPI(M) is recognized by the **Election Commission** as a national party since it operates in most states of the Indian Union and has 19 state committees. The CPI(M) claims to embody the legitimate continuation of the communist movement; its program is anti-imperialist, anti-communalist, anti-authoritarian, and genuinely secular and nationalist. Its greatest strength is in **Kerala**, **West Bengal**, and **Tripura** where it has formed governments, sometimes in coalition, implemented necessary land reforms to some extent, and helped ameliorate rural conditions. The CPI(M) has enjoyed power in West Bengal under the leadership of **Jyoti Basu** and his successor, Buddhadeb Bhattacharya, since the mid-1970s and recently has won acclaim from prospective foreign investors for its efficiency. The CPI (M) won 19 seats in the **Lok Sabha** as compared to the CPI's 23 in the 1967 general elections and has done significantly better since as the leading leftist party. (See Appendix H.) Led first by **E. M. S. Namboodiripad**, and after 1991 by Harkishen Singh Surjeet, the CPI(M) vigorously opposed both the Congress and the **Bharatiya Janata Party** through the 1980s and 1990s and actively sponsored agricultural and industrial labor groups as well as students unions. The CPI(M) won 43 Lok Sabha seats in the general elections of 2004 and, along with other leftist parties, agreed to support **Dr. Manmohan Singh**'s United Progressive Alliance coalition government from the outside. CPI(M) General Secretary Harkishan Singh Surjeet and other Central Committee members are regularly consulted by the government. They urge foreign policy review, support dialogue with **Pakistan** and improvement of relations with China and Russia, and demand a stop to disinvestment or privatization of large profit making public sector units.

COMMUNIST PARTY OF INDIA (MARXIST-LENINIST) [CPI (M-L)]. This group was so named as a new "truly revolutionary party" in April 1969 by Kanu Sanyal, **Charu Mazumdar**, and other leaders of the **Naxalite** movement who had been expelled by the **Communist Party of India (Marxist)**. The CPI (M-L) was shunned by other Indian communists not only because it eschewed parliamentary methods and favored violence, but because it was officially supported for some years by the Chinese Communist Party. In turn, the CPI(M-L) supported various tribal and peasant armed struggles within India with the declared intention of creating "innumerable points of guerrilla struggle throughout the countryside" and building a People's Liberation Army on the Chinese model to lead a revolution.

The CPI (M-L) is better known as the Naxalites, and unlike the **CPI** and the CPI (M), it is not recognized by the **Election Commission** as a political party in any state of India. Over the years the CPI (M-L) suffered attrition from ideological and personal differences within its leadership as well as from governmental efforts to control its activities. It was banned under **Emergency Rule** in July 1975, but the ban was lifted in April 1977 when the party's general secretary gave assurances of renouncing terrorism. During the 1980s and early 1990s, however, the Naxalites intensified their guerilla activities, sometimes in behalf of oppressed peoples and sometimes in alliance with criminal groups, in several states of eastern and peninsular India where they are also known as the People's War Group. *See also* NAXALITE.

CONFEDERATION OF INDIAN INDUSTRY (CII). This is the most visible business association in India. It was formed in 1992 in direct response to the policy of **economic liberalization** introduced by Finance Minister **Manmohan Singh** the previous year. The CII traces its ancestry to1895 when five British engineering firms in **Bengal** formed an association, and to 1942 when the Association of Indian Engineering Industry was formed during **World War II**. The two associations joined in 1974 when Indian engineering firms were expanding despite a highly regulated economic framework. The CII now has a direct membership of about 5,000 companies, private and public, small and large, with a high representation of engineering companies specializing in machinery and equipment, consulting and technical services, metal products, and computer services. Institutional partnerships and indirect membership further enlarge CII's scope of action.

The CII is not a government agency, nor a profit making organization. It is led and managed by industry, and its aim is to take a proactive role in the economic development of India, especially by improving the internal investment climate, exploring markets abroad, and strengthening Indian industry. The CII works in cooperation with both government and industry through advisory and consultative processes and acts as a catalyst for thought, plan, and action toward the goal of better integration into the world economy. At present, the CII has 41 offices within India and has an ambitious program of creating databases, raising public awareness, building consensus and networks, and projecting a positive image of Indian business. The CII also sends high-level delegations abroad, has 216 institutional partnerships in 94 countries, and has 15 overseas offices in Asia, Africa, Australia, Europe, the United Kingdom, and the United States. The CII, led by its Director General Tarun Das, emphasizes improving the efficiency and competitiveness of Indian business and has taken a leading role in forging new and mutually beneficial relations based on enhanced trade and investment with both the United States and China.

CONGRESS PARTY (INDIAN NATIONAL CONGRESS). (Also referred to as Congress (I) from 1977 to 1992.) The Congress Party currently leads a 10-party coalition, United Progressive Alliance (UPA), government in **New Delhi**. The UPA defeated the previous National Democratic Alliance (NDA) coalition government led by the **Bharatiya Janata Party (BJP)** in the 14th general elections held in 2004. On May 15, 2004, **Dr. Manmohan Singh** was sworn in as prime minister, along with 28 cabinet ministers including 18 Congress Party members and nine members from the southern Indian states of **Tamil Nadu** and **Andhra Pradesh**.

Congress leader **Sonia Gandhi**, who had campaigned vigorously and enabled the Congress to form a pre-election coalition with other parties at the national level for the first time in its long history, remained president of the Congress Parliamentary Party in the **Lok**

Sabha and acknowledged leader of the party. She declined the office of prime minister, probably because her foreign birth had become politically contentious. It remains to be seen whether she and other Congress leaders, old and young, can revitalize a party that had lost so much of its strength and popularity over the decades.

The Congress Party had a solid majority in the **Constituent Assembly** elected on a limited suffrage in 1946. It formed the interim and then the first government of independent India under the leadership of Prime Minister **Jawaharlal Nehru** and Deputy Prime Minister **Vallabhbhai Patel** and also took power in the provinces under men who had participated in the freedom struggle and had a solid base of popular support. During this first phase, 1946–1951, there were tussles for authority between the party organization and the government as well as some differences of opinion on matters of policy between Nehru and Patel and between the prime minister and state chief ministers, but habits of self-restraint and resolution of differences through compromise that had been formed during the freedom struggle prevailed. Nehru emerged as an arbiter within the party and a supremely popular national leader through the 1950s. The Congress Working Committee (CWC) functioned as a coordinator between the party and government as well as between the center and states, restraining the pugnacity of local party bosses. The unchallenged legitimacy of Congress, inherited from the national movement, as well as its democratic structure and functioning, its powers of mobilization and patronage that enabled it to co-opt diverse groups and social forces to itself, and its loose reformist and secular ideology gave it a favorable image that lasted long. Political scientist Rajni Kothari sympathetically analyzed the "Congress system" in terms of "one party dominance" providing a "framework for national consensus." (Kothari, *Politics in India*, 1970.)

Congress suffered many defeats in the 1967 general and state elections, was badly factionalized, and suffered a split in 1969. One section—Congress R (for Requisitioned, and then for Ruling)—came under the domination of **Indira Gandhi**, and the other section gradually lost political weight. For many reasons having to do with her personality, the demise of older leaders, and the diminished caliber of younger party bosses, as well as increasing complexity and strains in the Indian economy and polity, Congress lost much of its earlier capacity to contain and reconcile the play of emerging interests. The party became personalized and centralized, so that a change of name to Congress I (for Indira) after another split on the issue of **Emergency Rule** merely formalized a well-known fact: the preponderant role played by Mrs. Gandhi and her younger son Sanjay in a party that eschewed internal elections after 1972. After Sanjay's death in an air crash in the summer of 1980, Mrs. Gandhi prevailed on her reluctant elder son, **Rajiv Gandhi**, to take his place. When Indira Gandhi was assassinated in October 1984, Congress elected Rajiv to succeed her as party president and, in consequence of winning the December 1984 general elections by a landslide, prime minister of India.

He addressed the Congress Party meeting to celebrate the centenary of its founding with initial praise and lengthy castigation. Congress, he said, had become a party of low standards, vested interests, pettiness, and patronage; it was blighted with the parochialism of **caste**, **language**, and religion and was emptied of the spirit of service, sacrifice, and courage that had characterized it in the past. Congress organization, he added, had shrunk away from the grassroots and become prey to "brokers of power" to "convert a mass movement into a feudal oligarchy." It was already evident that though Indira Gandhi's personal appeal to the Indian people had been great and her populist platform of "*garibi hatao*" or "end poverty" gained votes, Congress had lacked an army of grassroots workers dedicated to the kind of socioeconomic transformations that might in fact have alleviated poverty. Instead, Congress had become vulnerable to pressure groups with the money to finance electoral campaigns and, along with other parties, utilized methods of voter mobilization—including appeals to narrow caste and communal considerations—that not only lowered the timbre of public life but led to major crises in India's multi-ethnic, multi-religious society in the 1980s.

Rajiv Gandhi was unable to change the culture of his party; personalization and centralization continued and was now identified with what came to be called "the Dynasty" or "the Family" (that is, descendants of Jawaharlal Nehru). Congress was no longer able to maintain a balance between center and state through internal adjustments, as it had during the 1950s, and state Congress leaders had become dependent on New Delhi's favor. Congress never dominated state legislatures as it had dominated the Lok Sabha, and after 1967 there was a stronger trend toward coalitions and defections in state governments. Moreover, since the late 1970s until the present day there had been a definite rise in the popularity of regional parties outside the Congress. Thus, Congress's hold in **Andhra, Kerala**, the Northeastern states, **Orissa, Punjab, Tamil Nadu**, and **West Bengal** was weak. The 1989 elections (and subsequent ones) demonstrated Congress' equally weak hold in the northern Indian Hindi-speaking heartland where it lost out both to the cadre-based and ideologically coherent Bharatiya Janata Party (BJP) and the explicit appeal to "backward" classes and minorities (formerly Congress supporters) made by the **Janata Dal** and other parties. *See* POLITICAL PARTIES.

The low-profile leadership of **P. V. Narasimha Rao** after Rajiv Gandhi's assassination in May 1991 encouraged some supporters while others remained critical, and factional competition for leadership combined with sycophancy toward a retiring Sonia Gandhi reduced the prestige of the party. Elections to the All India Congress Committee and the CWC were re-instituted in 1992, and Congress was able to roughly maintain its voter share and parliamentary strength for some time and remain at the core of the system. India's electoral system of single member constituencies and majority vote enabled Congress to avoid defeat except when non-Congress parties combined to contest seats. They did so in the general elections of 1977, 1989, 1996, and most successfully in 1998 and 1999, when Congress won only 141 and 114, seats, respectively, in the Lok Sabha and its share of votes dropped to 26% and 28% in the two elections compared to earlier averages above 35%. Although some aspiring leaders such as **Sharad Pawar** broke away, Congress was the main opposition party for eight years and learned that the Indian political system itself had changed; "one party dominance" had turned into what some called "catch-all coalitions." Having eschewed pre-election coalition building in 1998 and 1999, before the 2004 elections the Congress Party, now led indisputably by Sonia Gandhi, conducted a veritable storm of alliances with parties opposed to the BJP or its coalition partners and helped draft a common "minimum program." Congress also released a Vision Document highlighting economic development as its electoral platform and emphasized secularism and tolerance as the heart of Indian civilization and the primary need of the time. Congress had controlled several states even during its years in opposition in Delhi, including large states such as **Karnataka**, **Madhya Pradesh** and **Rajasthan**, regained power in others to a total of 12, and is trying to rebuild a mass base of support in **Uttar Pradesh**. It is a party of consequence in most states as well as at the national level. (See Appendix H for Congress' share of seats in the Lok Sabha 1952–2004.)

CONSTITUENT ASSEMBLY. This was an elected body charged with drafting a constitution for independent India. Its members were indirectly elected in 1946 from the provinces of British India as well as from the **Princely States**. The **Indian National Congress** had a huge majority in the Constituent Assembly, but its ideological embrace was so wide as to include virtually all informed opinion in India. All communities (including Muslims) were represented in the Constituent Assembly although the **All-India Muslim League** refused to participate after the failure of the **Cabinet Mission**.

The Constituent Assembly doubled as India's first parliament. Its committee chairmen also held responsible offices in government. Thus, its members had an immediate awareness of the practical issues of governance and were infused with a pan-Indian rather than a parochial consciousness. Equally significant was the caliber of its 20 most influential members. All were university graduates. Four— **Jawaharlal Nehru**, **Vallabhbhai Patel**, **Abul Kalam Azad**, and **Rajendra Prasad**—were veteran heroes of the national movement. Some, such as **B. R. Ambedkhar**, had never been members of Congress at all. Another, B. N. Rau, was an eminent jurist and not a politician at all; he played a critical role as Constitutional Advisor. In addition to their intellectual ability and political power, these men were accustomed to working within democratic procedures, held high moral standards, and carried considerable prestige and authority in the country. After careful research and exhaustive debate, the Assembly passed a detailed **Constitution** for the new Republic of India that came into force on January 26, 1950.

CONSTITUTION OF INDIA. The Constitution of the Republic of India came into effect on January 26, 1950; this date was the 20th anniversary of a resolution passed by the **Indian National Congress** demanding *purna swaraj* or full independence from British rule. The Constitution was drafted by a **Constituent Assembly** convened in December 1946. Its provisions show three powerful influences.

One influence was the Indian national movement with its drive for social reform, economic development, and political independence. Aspirations for a freely chosen representative and responsible government that derived its authority from the Indian people and secured for all of them justice, equality, and freedom in a unified country were expressed in an "Objectives Resolution" setting out the aims of the constitution makers. These aims denoted nothing less than bringing about a social revolution in a civilization as firmly traditional and hierarchical as India's. Key constitutional provisions were designed to further these objectives. Most important, universal adult franchise was introduced without separate communal electorates; the age of voting was lowered from 21 to 18 by an amendment of 1988. Democracy and voluntarism are the base and the instrument for change in India. Equally important, Part III of the Constitution listed Fundamental Rights, including prohibition of any discrimination on grounds of "religion, race, caste, sex, or place of birth," equality before the law and equal protection of the law, freedom of speech and expression, peaceful assembly and association, occupation, movement, and other classic liberties and made them justiciable. Freedom to acquire, hold, and dispose of property as a fundamental right was much disputed in Parliament and before the **Supreme Court** over the years in the light of legislation designed to further economic and equity aims, but it remains a constitutional right. Some of the philosophy and specific objectives of the national movement were embodied in the Directive Principles of State Policy contained in Part IV. These were not made justiciable but permitted the state to ameliorate conditions for traditionally backward **castes** and tribes, which were listed in attached Schedules, to ensure equitable distribution of material resources, to protect women and children, and to provide education and health services for all.

A second strong influence on the Indian constitution makers was the British legacy. This included the administrative structure of British India and the semi-representative **Government of India Act** of 1935. Much of the latter was incorporated with only minor alterations into constitutional provisions setting up the bicameral legislative structure at the center and the states and the powers of governors. The Emergency Powers of the President (of the central government, in effect) and Part XI, dividing powers between the central or union and state governments according to subjects of their jurisdiction, with 97 on the union list, 66 on the state list, and 47 listed as concurrent, also owed much to the 1935 Act. The federal structure of the Indian union was thus tilted in a centralized and bureaucratic direction by the Constitution itself. An equally important aspect of the British legacy, however, must not be underestimated. It consists of the liberal assumptions and procedural conventions of the Westminster model of parliamentary democracy. These can be seen to have taken sufficiently strong root among Indians to enable them to overcome aberrations such as the mid-1970s **Emergency Rule**, to maintain national unity in the face of many strains while adjusting to local conditions, and to hold regular free and fair elections on an enormous scale for an electorate of over 600 million. Indeed, being the world's largest democracy is India's most frequent vaunt after more than half a century of working within the Constitution.

The third powerful influence on the constitution makers was their own direct experience of politics and administration gained as the Constituent Assembly simultaneously functioned as the (provisional) national parliament and grappled with the problems caused by **Partition** and the integration of over 550 **Princely States** with the Indian Union. The constitution makers tackled the problems of protecting and fostering national unity and integrity while simultaneously preserving the rich diversity of Indian culture and governance. Among the constitutional provisions that addressed these subjects were those providing for single citizenship (of India) and ruling out secession of states, recognizing 15 (later 18) major Indian languages and also English as official languages, allowing for gradual integration of areas with different administrative structures by setting up separate categories, and ensuring state neutrality or secularism in matters of religion and personal law. An amendment of 1976 added the words "socialist" and "secular" to the Preamble's definition of "India that is Bharat" as a "Sovereign, Democratic Republic." The belief of the constitution makers that Indian unity, democracy, and secularism were three mutually reinforcing and inextricable strands was proven over the decades to follow.

The Indian Constitution is a lengthy document, containing a pre-amble, 370 articles, and 10 Schedules. Textual changes can be effected by a simple majority vote in both houses of Parliament. Substantive amendments require a two-thirds majority in both houses and, in some cases, a further process of ratification by the legislatures of a majority of the states. Eighty-five amendments have been passed in more than 50 years of rapid change, but less than a third of that number are substantive. The 44th amendment, passed in 1977, was notable for repealing earlier amendments adopted during **Emergency Rule**. The **Supreme Court**, at the apex of an independent judicial system, enjoys powers of advice and review similar but not identical to those of the United States Supreme Court. In 1973, the Supreme Court of India ruled that no amendments to the Constitution should damage its "basic structure," and that ruling has been respected. Political developments during the 1990s resulted in some demands for review of the Constitution, including its key institutions and procedures. Accordingly, a committee for **Constitutional Review** was formed in 2000. Its recommendations were made in 2002 but were not revolutionary.

CONSTITUTIONAL REVIEW. The 1950 **Constitution** of the Republic of India was designed to respond to the changing needs of a dynamic and newly independent country and so laid out amendment procedures that were not as arduous as in some other written constitutions. By the end of the 20th century, 85 constitutional amendments had been enacted. Sweeping and controversial amendments passed during **Emergency Rule** had been altered or repealed and the **Supreme Court**'s ruling that no law or amendment should alter the "basic structure" of the Constitution was respected. During the 1990s when governments were weak and frequently changed and socioeconomic issues were politically charged, public debates surfaced on whether or not the Constitution and the main institutions of government in India's parliamentary democracy were functioning well or needed to be changed. A National Commission to Review the Working of the Constitution was established in February 2000 on the authorization of both Houses of Parliament called after the 13th general elections.

Former Chief Justice M. N. Venkatachaliah chaired this Commission consisting of him and 10 other distinguished jurists, attorneys, and intellectuals. They submitted their report and recommendations in March 2002 after conducting exhaustive consultations with various expert bodies, academic institutions, advisory panels, and public opinion informed by debates on periodically released working papers. (See *Report of the National Commission to Review the Working of the Constitution Volume 1*. New Delhi: Universal Law Publishing Company, 2002.) The Commission drew up an objective balance sheet of achievements—especially the deep rooting and stabilization of India's democratic base and federal polity—and many failures—especially low public confidence, misuse of institutions, financial instability, and social neglect. The Commission made a long list of areas of concern growing out of a loss of public faith in the ability of governments to serve their needs, to safeguard their social or national security, to anticipate crises, or to remain financially viable. It was particularly critical of a pervasive misuse of the electoral process: opportunistic, unprincipled, politics, the decay of the criminal justice system, and the disturbing state of the social infrastructure.

The Commission made 249 recommendations, only 58 of which required constitutional amendment, with legislative or executive action sufficient for the others. The recommendations concerned fundamental rights and directive principles, electoral processes and political parties, legislatures, public administration, the judiciary, Union-State relations, decentralization and devolution, and socioeconomic development. Some of the recommendations are precise and detailed, as in respect of electoral processes, the judiciary, and decentralization. Many recommendations are broad, and all are couched in non-provocative phraseology. The Commission avoided tackling politically controversial issues, such as the rights of foreign-born citizens, and did not advocate radical overhaul of any institution, not even the "first past the gate" electoral system, much less that of prime minister or president. Some of its recommendations relating to elections and political parties were implemented before the 14th general elections. It remains to be seen if others will come into effect or if the Commission's report will be shelved and ignored. In any case, what seemed in the 1990s to be compelling demands for constitutional review have given place to a sense that the federal, parliamentary, democratic and secular polity of India was the best framework within which elected governments must strive to do better in order to serve the people—and so remain in power.

COOMARASWAMY, ANANDA KENTISH (1877–1947). Coomaraswamy was a scholar whose interpretations of Indian art and culture became internationally famous. He was born in **Ceylon** but spent much of his working life in the United States, where he influenced educated opinion on India through teaching and writing. Coomaraswamy was the author of some 200 titles—including *The Dance of Shiva*, in which he explored the aesthetic, historical, metaphysical, and symbolic content of traditional Indian civilization.

COOPERATIVES. Modern cooperatives as organizations owned by and operated for the benefit of those using their services probably first began in the industrial areas of mid-19th century Britain and became popular in Germany and Scandinavia later in the century. Cooperative societies were formed in India as well and were institutionalized by the Cooperative Credit Societies Act of 1904. Cooperatives were assigned a central role in the development strategy adopted by the government of independent India, mainly as instruments of extending rural credit to enhance the productivity of agriculture.

A belief that the formation of rural cooperatives would facilitate land reform and would benefit the actual cultivators of the land, and not merely landowners, prompted the **Congress Party** led by **Jawaharlal Nehru** to pass a resolution in favor of what was called "cooperative joint farming" in 1959. It proposed that land would be pooled for joint cultivation, with farmers getting a share of produce in proportion to their land and cultivators getting a share in proportion to their work. Those who saw it as a copy of the Soviet-Chinese model of collective farming heralding the end of property rights voiced fierce opposition to the proposal in Parliament and within the Congress Party. No legislation was passed on the subject; nor did the Indian state have the persuasive or coercive capacity to implement such putative legislation. At the same time, voluntary cooperatives proved to be pivotal for the supply of critical inputs to agriculture and contributed to the **Green Revolution**. Dairy cooperatives, such as those inspired by **Dr. V. Kurien**, brought about increases in milk supply that came to be known as the White Revolution. Many **non-governmental organizations** helped the formation and proliferation of cooperatives in the unorganized or informal sectors of the economy to help disadvantaged groups, such as **women**. Cooperative societies continue to be popular sources of credit. According to the **Planning Commission**, there are more than 500,000 cooperative societies of various kinds operating in India at present, with a membership of more than 200 million persons, and almost every village has its own multi-purpose cooperative society.

Not all cooperatives are efficient, or as transparent and democratically operated as is intended. Nor can many of them compete with other entities, including multinational corporations, in India's new market economy integrating with a globalized world economy. The Ministry of Agriculture and other branches of the Indian government have initiated programs of financial education and management training to promote professionalism and democratization in the operation of cooperatives. No one should underestimate the importance of good leadership and good governance to the success of cooperatives; and no one can underestimate the continuing importance of cooperatives to India's economic and social development.

COORG/KODAGU. This district is west of **Mysore** in the state of **Karnataka** lying along the crest and on the eastward slopes of the Western Ghats. Its rugged terrain, thick forests, and hardy people—of distinctive ethnic origin and distinguished physique—gave Coorg rough autonomy, or even independence, in the fluctuating fortunes of peninsular India over the millennia.

Coorg was annexed to British India in 1834. Its climate appealed to the British, and its soil proved suitable for coffee plantation. Many Coorgi men, including Field Marshal **Cariappa** and General **Thimayya**, had illustrious careers in the armed forces before and after Indian independence. The languages spoken in Coorg are Coorgi and Kanarese. The main town is Mercara. It is the source of the **Kaveri River**.

CORBETT, JIM (1875–1955). Born in Nainital, a hill station in the Kumaon district of present day **Uttaranchal** state, Jim Corbett became one the most famous hunters of his time, beloved by the villagers for ridding them of about 50 man-eating tigers and leopards. In his later years, he turned to wildlife photography and became an ardent conservationist, establishing a forest reserve in the foothills of the middle **Himalaya** in 1936. The reserve has been greatly enlarged to 1,318 square kilometers since Indian independence and is named the Corbett National Park. Jim Corbett published eight books, including *Maneaters of Kumaon*, which remains popular. Although Corbett left India for Kenya in 1947, his house in Nainital is consecrated to his memory.

CORNWALLIS, LORD CHARLES (1738–1805). Lord Cornwallis already had a distinguished military career and a reputation for integrity when he was appointed governor general of India in 1786. He was sent to India by the British Directors of the **East India Company** in London with instructions to cleanse the administration in **Calcutta** of corruption, to reform the judicial system, and to settle the matter of collection of revenue. Cornwallis removed private trade from the hands of Company officials and separated collection of revenue from their judicial functions. He raised the salaries of British officials and excluded Indians from covenanted, or executive, positions. He set up four provincial courts of appeal consisting of three English judges, each assisted by Indian advisers on **Hindu** and **Islamic** Law. He systematized the collection of land revenue according to a **Permanent Settlement** decreed in 1793, in the hopes of creating a responsible class of landowners in the English sense; instead, it had disastrous long-term effects on the land and its cultivators.

Cornwallis's tenure marked a change from the old free-booting style of the East India Company to a stable administrative system concerned with law and order as well as commerce. He laid the foundations of an **Indian Civil Service (ICS)** known for its honesty and of a new landowning class known for its loyalty. But Cornwallis's tenure was also a watershed between the rough equality and similar styles of living among British and Indian men in the 18th century, and the cultural, economic, and racial divide between them that transpired in the 19th century. Cornwallis was reappointed governor-general for a second term in 1805 but died within three months of his arrival in India.

CORREA, CHARLES M. (1930–). Charles Correa, born in **Goa**, is one of the best-known contemporary architects in India, having received the Padma Shri award in 1972. Correa took his higher education at the University of Michigan and the Massachusetts Institute of Technology in the United States and has been in private practice in **Mumbai** since 1958. He designed low-cost housing projects in many cities, specializing in the use of locally available materials and timeless technology, and in constructing buildings attuned to the climate and open to the sky. Correa also designed larger, more visible, projects such as the State Assembly buildings and Arts Centre in **Bhopal**, and the British Council headquarters in **Delhi**. He argued in favor of simple (indigenous and inexpensive) solutions to the problem of recycling urban land in Mumbai as well as other issues. Many of these solutions were considered when he served on the National Commission on Urbanization appointed by **Rajiv Gandhi** to report on linking urban and rural development in different parts of India.

CRIPPS, SIR STAFFORD RICHARD (1889–1952). Cripps was a distinguished lawyer, parliamentarian, and socialist whose career in England included appointments as Lord Privy Seal, leader of the House of Commons, and cabinet minister during **World War II**. Cripps was a personal friend of **Jawaharlal Nehru** and, as one of the leaders of the Labour Party, was committed to the idea of constitutional reform toward Indian independence. In that capacity Cripps went to India during 1942 on a mission to resolve an impasse between the British government and Indian nationalist leaders; he was also a key member of the three man **Cabinet Mission** of 1946.

The Cripps Mission of March 1942 took place after leaders of the **Indian National Congress** had withdrawn their cooperation from the British-Indian war effort (committed without consulting them), and after Japan's capture of Singapore and Rangoon had adversely affected the Allied position in Asia. Under pressure from United States President Franklin D. Roosevelt and Labour Party leader Clement Atlee, Prime Minister Winston Churchill agreed to let Cripps try and win Congress' collaboration without jeopardizing the flow of Muslim recruits to the army.

Cripps offered Congress **Dominion Status** for India after the war, a constituent assembly elected by proportional representation, and less than adult franchise to draft a new constitution for a federation, which no province would be compelled to join and from which any could secede. He suggested additional seats for Indians on the Viceroy's Executive Council during the war, in return for *full cooperation* in the Allied war effort. Cripps formally called on **Muslim League** leader **Mohammed Ali Jinnah** and also suggested "special consideration" for the **Sikhs** in the **Punjab**. None of these steps was palatable to Nehru or to Congress. Some of the contemporary controversy surrounding the Cripps Mission has since been illuminated by the publication of salient papers. They show that his brief was not clarified in London before he left, that the War Cabinet was divided on the issue, with Churchill adamantly opposed to any gesture of conciliating Congress, and that the viceroy, Lord **Linlithgow**, did not give Cripps a free hand.

The Cripps Mission was a deep disappointment to Congress. **Mahatma Gandhi** referred to his offer as "a post-dated check on a failing bank." Congress launched a massive **Quit India** movement of civil disobedience in August 1942. Congress leaders disliked the significant concessions made by Cripps to Jinnah's 1940 demands for **Pakistan**. The Muslim League was the only Indian political party to welcome the proposals. **C. Rajagopalachari** suggested a different path from non-cooperation to deal with this new contingency, but to no effect; he left Congress. The British continued to administer India during the war, but in the opinion of many, the Cripps offer could not be withdrawn, making Indian independence after the war inevitable and **Partition** a strong possibility. The Cripps offer became the starting point of negotiations among three distinct entities—the British, Congress, and the Muslim League—that reopened in 1946.

CURZON, LORD GEORGE NATHANIEL (1859–1925). Lord Curzon was governor general and viceroy of India from 1899 to 1905. He was an ideological imperialist with a passion for India as the pivot of British dominance east of Suez. He prepared himself for his position in India by years of study, travel, and writing, and he ruled as a benevolent despot with the maxim of efficiency and justice in administration. He was the apogee of an era, epitomized in the pomp and circumstance of the *durbar* (see Glossary) that was staged for King Edward VII, Emperor of India, in 1903. Ironically, his insensitivity to the opinion of educated Indians and his **partition of Bengal** in 1905 energized nationalist forces that ultimately brought about the end of the British empire.

Curzon tried to reform the vast British-Indian bureaucratic machine that he inherited. The Indian Police Service was overhauled, upgraded, and centralized. The Indian **Railways** were placed under their own board and over 9,500 kilometers of new track were laid. Curzon created a Department for Commerce and Industry and welcomed **Tata**'s first steel mill. Land revenue was a controversial subject at a time when the population was declining because of recurrent famines and impoverishment, and the government wanted money. Curzon's land measures included protecting cultivators from eviction for debt and establishing agricultural credit societies. He also pushed forward irrigation works, established experimental farms, and founded an agricultural research institute at Pusa, near **Delhi**, which continued high-quality work after independence.

Curzon's love of Indian art and architecture led to laws protecting historical monuments and the appointment of Sir John Marshall as Director General of Archaeology—resulting later in the discovery of the ancient sites Mohenjo-Daro and **Harappa**. Curzon's attempts to reform the educational system by centralizing control of the universities and affiliated colleges, and putting more stress on primary education, were admirable in themselves but aroused suspicion and opposition among middle-class Indians. To an even greater extent, his partition of Bengal in 1905 for good administrative reasons was suspect because it was perceived as part of a design to separate Muslim from **Hindu**. Sustained protest movements nationwide led to its annulment in 1911.

Curzon was Russophobic and followed an assertive foreign policy. He aimed to bring the Persian Gulf, Persia, **Afghanistan**, and **Tibet** within the British sphere of influence from India. He personally visited the Persian Gulf with a naval flotilla in 1903 and dispatched **Francis Younghusband** on an expedition to obtain special privileges for British India in Tibet. Curzon moved more cautiously in the northwest, leaving routine control of the Afghan border in the hands of local tribal levies and separating the administration of a new North West Frontier Province from that of neighboring **Punjab**.

Governor-General Curzon clashed with an equally imperious **Lord Kitchener**, commander-in-chief of the **Indian Army**. Curzon resigned at the start of his second term in 1905 when London failed to back him. He became a cabinet minister during **World War I**, but was unable to fulfill his ambition of becoming prime minister of Great Britain.

– D –

DALAI LAMA. The Dalai Lama is the spiritual head of the largest, Gelupa, sect of Tibetan Buddhism (Vajrayana or Thunderbolt Vehicle). He also was the temporal head of **Tibet** until 1959. The position was not hereditary. The search and choice of each Dalai Lama has been conducted according to rituals based on belief in successive reincarnation of the Boddhisatva embodied in him.

A politically active 13th Dalai Lama (1876–1933) had entered into diplomatic exchanges with Russia, incurred the displeasure of **Lord Curzon**, and asserted an independent status for Tibet when the overthrow of the Qing dynasty in China ended the traditional Choyon, or priest-patron, relationship between the Dalai Lama and the Chinese Emperor. He introduced administrative changes within Tibet and granted special concessions to British India. His emissary signed a treaty in 1914 defining Tibet's borders, including the **McMahon Line**. Tenzin Gyatso, the fourteenth Dalai Lama (1935–), was forced out of Tibet in 1959 after unsuccessful attempts to reach a negotiated settlement on Tibet's autonomy with the People's Republic of China led to a military occupation of his country. The Dalai Lama and some 100,000 followers were given sanctuary in India, where their distinct cultural and social identities have been preserved and a government in exile established; however, political activity that might offend China is discouraged. The outstanding leadership of the Dalai Lama as religious and secular head of the Tibetan refugee community worldwide, and as a prime spokesman for non-violent resolution of conflict, was acknowledged when he was awarded the Nobel Peace Prize in 1989. The Dalai Lama is deeply revered in India and receives the humanitarian protection of successive Indian governments.

DALHOUSIE, MARQUESS OF (1812–1860). Dalhousie was born to Scots parents and was named James Andrew Ramsay. He served as a Member of Parliament for 10 years before being appointed governor general of India in 1848. He retired from that position in 1856.

Dalhousie is best known for pushing ahead an aggressive policy of conquest, annexation, and absorption of territory ruled by Indian Princes with the declared aim of "rationalizing" the irregular map of **East India Company** domains. Hence, the second Anglo-Sikh War of 1848 resulted in the annexation of the **Punjab**, a brief war with **Sikkim** brought more than 4,000 square kilometers of real estate under direct British rule in 1850, and all of lower **Burma** was taken over after the Second Burmese War of 1852. In this respect, Dalhousie conformed to the established pattern of British imperial expansion in India.

In addition, Dalhousie applied a novel and non-Indian idea called "Doctrine of Lapse," which had been used sparingly by his predecessors. He assumed the imperial prerogative of refusing to recognize adopted heirs of allied princes. In the absence of a natural male heir, he said, sovereignty would lapse to the paramount power—by now, the East India Company in effect rather than the titular **Mughal Emperor**—and the territory of that state would be brought under direct British rule. In pursuit of this doctrine, Dalhousie annexed Satara in 1848, Baghat, Jaitpur, and Sambalpur in 1850, Udaipur in 1852, Jhansi in 1853, Nagpur in 1854, and Karauli in 1855. Further, he swept away titles and pensions of several rulers or their heirs, as in the cases of the Nawab of Carnatic, the Raja of Tanjore, and the **Maratha Peshwa**.

Dalhousie also attempted to apply a maxim of trusteeship, or "good of the governed," to the **Princely States** of India. Some rulers undoubtedly neglected both administration and the welfare of their subjects with impunity, being protected from external enemies or internal revolt by the **Subsidiary Alliances** they had signed earlier. But Dalhousie used accusations of misgovernment to force the Nizam of **Hyderabad** to cede territory, and to annex entirely the rich lands of the ever-loyal Nawab of **Awadh** in 1856. A frisson of fear passed through all of the Indian princes. Many of them joined in the Mutiny or great **Uprising of 1857**, which followed soon after the departure of Lord Dalhousie from India and was, in some measure, caused by him.

DALIT. This is a Marathi word for those who have been broken—who have been deliberately ground down and exploited. The term was adopted almost as a title in the late 1960s by groups of Scheduled Castes in **Maharashtra**, who saw no significant alleviation of their traditional oppression by upper **castes** since Indian independence despite the anti-discriminatory provisions of the **Constitution**. Dalit is a term redolent of anger and resistance, carrying a different connotation from **Mahatma Gandhi**'s euphemism "Harijan," and the Dalit Panthers admired the militancy of the American Black Panthers.

Dalit movements and literature are inspired by the theoretical and practical work of **Dr. B. R. Ambedkar**, who rejected the very concept of hereditary caste as a socioeconomic category and associated it with the **Hindu** religion. The Ambedkar Centre for Justice and Peace, established in 1990, works hard for the Dalit cause inside and outside India. Many educated Dalits became Marxist or **Naxalite**. Older habits of emulating higher castes through "Sanskritization" also continue. But all Dalits see injustice in the fact that despite the legal abolition of untouchability and special reservations for them in educational institutions and government services, their numbers in higher echelon positions remain low, and traditional prohibitions on use of village wells and temple entry persist in some places. Successful individuals and families are thus decried as a "creamy layer" co-opted by the upper caste establishment. There is now a considerable body of Dalit literature.

Dalit politicization was inevitable, given their large numbers and the efforts made by **political parties**, including the **Congress Party**, to secure their votes. The formation and development of the **Bahujan Samaj Party (BSP)** marked a more vigorous stage of political mobilization, as did the implementation of the **Mandal Commission** recommendations for Other Backward Castes often pitted against the Scheduled Castes. Another inevitable development toward the end of the 20th century, given rapid communications and a large Indian **Diaspora**, was the interaction of the Indian and international discourses on human rights of both individuals and groups. Although the Indian Government and most scholars argue that caste is not the same as race, an umbrella organization named the National Campaign for Dalit Human Rights (NCDH) tried hard to air grievances before United Nations conferences and commissions that were concerned with eradicating racial discrimination, or with rights of indigenous peoples, or with the rights of minorities. The UN World Conference against Racism (WCAR) held at Durban, South Africa, in late 2001 did indeed address the issue of caste-based discrimination in South Asia. And within India, the **National Human Rights Commission** receives innumerable requests to examine and redress many cases relating to Dalits. The struggle for dignity and equality continues, even though the legal and probably material conditions of living have greatly improved for Dalits in India since independence.

DANDI MARCH/SALT MARCH 1930. In protest against new taxes on salt levied by the British Government of India, which enjoyed a complete monopoly of supply, **Mahatma Gandhi** and a band of volunteers marched from Sabartmati Ashram near **Ahmedabad** to Dandi on the coast from March 30 to April 5, 1930.

Gandhi led the march personally, beginning it with solemn prayers and after three days of fasting and silence. He and his followers proceeded on foot at the rate of about 25 kilometers a day. On reaching Dandi, they picked up the salt formed from the evaporation of sea water from the sand. This simple act of non-violent **civil disobedience** was symbolic of large issues. Salt is a necessity of life for all people, and popular resentment ran high against new taxes in a time of economic depression. The salt march epitomized India's will to freedom as expressed by the common man, non-violently.

Governor General **Lord Irwin** initially ignored Gandhi's Dandi March. But its dramatic impact on the press inside and outside India, combined with widespread civil disturbances, provoked Irwin to order a crackdown on all "illegal" collections of sea salt. People were arrested in masses, and there was no delicacy of treatment of women or men. One year later, Irwin met Gandhi and the two reached agreement on some of the major issues of the day. *See also* CIVIL DISOBEDIENCE, GANDHI-IRWIN PACT.

DANGE, SHRIPAD AMRIT (1899–1994). The longtime leader of the **Communist Party of India (CPI)**, Dange was drawn to socialism in the 1920s when he became disillusioned with the **Non-Cooperation Movement** led by **Mohandas Gandhi**. Dange became an active member of the **trade union** movement in **Bombay**, was imprisoned from 1929 to 1935 and from 1939 to 1943, and was elected president of the All-India Trade Union Congress in 1945. He followed Moscow's leadership, first supporting and then repudiating the revolutionary line of B. T. Ranadive in the late 1940s. He followed a constitutional path thereafter. Dange became a skilled parliamentarian in the 1950s. He retained his leadership of the Moscow-inclined part of the CPI after its split in 1964 but retired from that position in 1981.

DARA SHIKOH (1614–1659). The eldest and favorite son of **Mughal Emperor Shah Jahan** and Mumtaz Mahal, Dara Shikoh was a man of eclectic views, liberal disposition, and scholarly instincts. He commissioned Persian translations of **Sanskrit** texts and encouraged discourse at court among men of different faiths. Dara Shikoh lacked the administrative experience and military-political acumen of his brother Alamgir (**Aurangzeb**), by whom he was defeated in the fratricidal war of succession of 1657–1658. Dara Shikoh was hunted from place to place by Aurangzeb's troops and was captured, humiliated, and brutally executed in **Delhi**.

DAS, CHITTA RANJAN (1870–1925). C. R. Das was also called Deshbandhu or "friend of the country." He was, in many ways, typical of the Bengali *bhadralok* (see Glossary), being educated in English and in the law and belonging to the **Brahmo Samaj**. He was a man of letters and public service, commanding high fees as a barrister but not afraid of renouncing his legal practice when he joined the **Non-Cooperation Movement** of 1920–1921.

C. R. Das first gained prominence through his successful defense of **Aurobindo Ghose** in 1908. He became an active member of the **Indian National Congress** in 1917, soon after its **Lucknow Pact** with the **All-India Muslim League**. Das opposed the postwar **Montagu-Chelmsford Reforms** as an inadequate advance toward the promise made of "responsible government" for India within the British Empire. Although he joined the Non-Cooperation Movement as a matter of conviction, he had many differences with the new Congress leader, **Mohandas Gandhi**. Das, along with **Motilal Nehru** and other liberals, formed the **Swaraj Party**, which swept the polls in **Bengal** during the 1923 elections and tried to work the reforms.

C. R. Das was an impressive leader who pioneered in taking the nationalist platform to all classes of **Hindus** and Muslims in Bengal. He made an electoral pact with leaders of the Muslim community at the provincial level and discouraged communalism. As the elected mayor of the Calcutta Municipal Corporation in 1924 and 1925, he trained members, including the young **Subhas Chandra Bose**. Most importantly, C. R. Das demonstrated that committed leadership and good administration could maintain inter-class and inter-communal harmony in a big city.

DAS, TARAKNATH (1884–1958). Taraknath was a youthful revolutionary in **Calcutta**, agitating against the **partition of Bengal** in 1905 before he left for Japan to escape arrest. He went on to San Francisco, where he established the Indian Independence League with other Indian expatriates and helped **Lala Hardayal** organize the **Ghadr Party**. He became a graduate student in Washington, D.C., in 1910 an American citizen in 1914, and he married an American widow in 1924.

As professor of political science at Columbia University, New York, Taraknath Das promoted educational and cultural relations between the United States and India, setting up a foundation for this purpose and evoking sympathy for the Indian national movement. He toured extensively in Europe and Asia, lecturing and writing about Indian independence, and sometimes was implicated in conspiracies against British rule. He vehemently opposed the **Partition** of 1947 and visited India only once, in 1952, after that event and independence.

DAYANANDA SARASWATI (1824–1883). Dayananda was born Mul Shankar to a well-to-do **brahman** family in the **Princely State** of Kathiawar. He began to question the worship of images and other traditional **Hindu** rituals at an early age. At the age of 21 he renounced marriage and life as a householder and became a wandering *sannyasin* (see Glossary) for the next 15 years. In 1860, he became the disciple of a blind guru, Virjananda, who bridged for him the gap between the nobility of the **Vedas** and the degraded popular **Hinduism** of the times.

In 1868, Dayananda began his active career of religious and social reform, using the classical language **Sanskrit** for his discourses and scorning raiment. In 1869, he engaged the leading brahmans of **Banaras** in a *shastrath*, or debate on the scriptures, challenging them to prove that the Vedas sanctioned idol worship. His denunciation of child marriage, female subordination, **caste** hierarchy, and other social customs having to do with caste, food, marriage, and travel were equally iconoclastic. He attributed India's degradation to their enforcement by hypocritical and self-serving priests. Like **Vivekananda** after him, Dayananda attempted to re-inject contemporary Hindu culture with the vigor, self-assertion, and physical courage that he read into its past. That was the message of his social reform campaign.

Dayananda published his religious beliefs in the *Satyarth Prakash* (Light of Truth) in 1874, the most important of his many works written in Hindi. Central to his thought were his beliefs in a dualistic universe, of mind and matter, and in the separation of God and the human soul; both ran counter to the dominant philosophy of *advaita* (see Glossary) or non-dualistic Vedanta. The only traditional doctrines that he accepted were transmigration and *karma* (see Glossary). Dayananda was unusual for his time in adopting a tone of belligerent criticism toward **Christianity** and **Islam**, holding up the Vedas as timeless revealed truth superior to the Bible and the Koran. His preachings were echoed by 20th-century advocates of **Hindutva**. Dayananda did not claim to be a mystic, much less an *avatar* or divine incarnation, and adopted a rational, practical approach to religion.

Dayananda met the leaders of the **Brahmo Samaj, Keshub Chandra Sen** and **Vidyasagar** in 1873. They persuaded him to wear a reasonable amount of clothing in public and to speak in Hindi rather than in Sanskrit in order to gain a wider audience. They probably imparted organizational instruction as well, and in 1875 Dayananda founded the **Arya Samaj** to propagate what he considered to be the "only true and universal faith." He left the world of temples, ashrams, and pilgrimages in which he had formerly preached and functioned as a modern social reformer, although he was not a product of Western education as were many other social reformers at the time. He engaged in enterprises aimed at the amelioration of the physical, spiritual, and social conditions of northern India and used modern methods of communication and organization in order to do so. Dayananda did not visit southern India, and **Bombay** found him too radical to accept, but his influence in the **Punjab** and upper **Ganges** valley was immense. It is carried forward to the present time through the **Arya Samaj.**

DECCAN. Deccan, a word derived from the **Sanskrit** *dakshina* or south, is the plateau land of peninsular India that was part of the ancient Gondwanaland. The Deccan is set off from the northern plains by the Vindhya and Satpura mountain ranges and tilts from west to east. Dry, difficult to cultivate, and prone to famine, the Deccan breeds hardy people. It is mentioned in the **Puranas** and has a rich mythology and checkered history. A distinctive culture evolved in the interactions of the **Bahmani** kingdoms with their northern and southern neighbors. The **Marathas** dominate the history of the Deccan in the modern age.

DELHI/NEW DELHI. The traditional and present-day capital of India, Delhi stands in a triangle formed by the **Yamuna** River on the east and spurs from the Aravalli range on the west and south. It is a strategic point in northern India and has been a coveted prize for all empire builders and conquerors, especially those who came over the Hindu Kush mountains in the northwest to the **Ganges** valley in the east. Thus, many capital cities have occupied the site of Delhi; some of their remains are still visible today.

Tradition places Indraprastha (c. 1450 BCE) of *Mahabharata* fame at or near Delhi. One of two inscriptions on an ancient iron pillar is attributed to **Chandra Gupta II Vikramaditya** (c. 375 CE). The history of Delhi can be reconstructed more accurately after 800 CE, since when eight cities have been constructed in the same triangular area. **Prithviraj Chauhan** was one of the last **Rajput** rulers at Delhi, also known as Dilli, or Dhillika. In the early 13th century, the city passed into the hands of five successive Turkish and Afghan dynasties of the **Delhi Sultanate.** Their walled cities and numerous monuments showed a unique blend of mosque and temple, Central Asian and Indian, in their style, craftsmanship, and decorative motifs. The city built by **Sher Shah Sur** early in the 16th century was taken over by **Babur**, and though his immediate successors in the **Mughal** dynasty established another capital further east at **Agra**, Shah Jahan built the seventh city of Delhi, Shahjahanabad, containing the famous Red Fort and Jama Masjid. For six centuries Delhi was a vibrant cultural center where dance, music, and poetry flourished. Much of this city and its cultural life were badly damaged by the British during the Mutiny or great **Uprising of 1857**.

The capital city of British India was initially **Calcutta** but was moved to Delhi in 1911. Another city, New Delhi, was constructed south of Shahjahanabad according to the majestic plans of Edwin Lutyens. This also serves as the capital of the Republic of India. Since 1947, the city has expanded to cover an immense area housing a vast heterogeneous population of about 12 million and more motor vehicles than any other Indian city.

DELHI SULTANATE/SULTANATE OF DELHI. Established by **Qutbuddin Aibak** in 1206 and overthrown by **Babur** in 1526, it was the first **Muslim** state in the heartland of India, although Arab rule in 8th-century Sind and **Mahmud of Ghazni**'s incorporation of northwestern areas in his kingdom in the 11th century served as backdrops. The Delhi Sultanate was ruled successively by five dynasties: the Slave Dynasty of Turki military men in service, 1206–1290; the Khalji Dynasty dominated by the figure of **Alauddin Khalji**, 1290–1320; the **Tughlaq Dynasty**, 1320–1388; the undistinguished Sayyid Dynasty, 1414–1450; and the **Lodi** Dynasty of Afghan antecedents, 1450–1526.

Each of these dynasties had sultans or rulers whose abilities varied but whose claim to power rested essentially on military prowess and personal despotism. Most of them maintained formal and ceremonial allegiance to the Khalifa or Caliph as temporal head of the Islamic world, but all of them exercised — or attempted to exercise — absolute power within the territories they controlled. Islamic law or the *Shari'a* (see Glossary) offered some legal check on autocracy, and the *ulema* (see Glossary), or Muslim divines, advised the sultan to uphold **Islam** and be merciless with unbelievers. Such advice went against interests of the majority of the sultan's subjects, who were **Hindu**, and also against the interests of the ruler who needed a class of producers (again, Hindu) that he could tax. In practice, therefore, there was no institutional or legal limitation on the sultan's despotism; fear of rebellion from the nobles and the absence of a clear tradition of succession under Islam only served to tighten the hold of a powerful ruler and prevent peaceful transitions from one strong man to another.

The territorial extent of the Sultanate fluctuated with conquests, rebellions, and invasions; **Delhi**'s sway was widest under Muhammad Tughlaq but sometimes shrunk to its own immediate environs; the Sultanate's hold on the rich but distant provinces of **Bengal**, the **Deccan**, or **Gujarat** was never more than tenuous. Perhaps the greatest service to India provided by the Sultanate was to guard the western marches against the Mongol invasions that devastated large parts of Eurasia in the 13th and 14th centuries but only once managed to penetrate India as far as Delhi in 1398. Delhi at that time stood almost as a unique city in the region, with a walled circumference of 65 kilometers, mosques, colleges, hospitals, and palaces made of dressed and ornamented stone, a rich cultural life and thriving trading marts. Food suppliers and merchants were important to the city, as were the large numbers of artisans and workers who lived inside the city and produced luxury goods for export and use by the nobility. Able rulers devised policies to keep these artisans and workers settled as lucrative sources of tax. Control of Hindustan was envied around the world as "the source of wealth and the fountain of blessedness."

Considerable controversy exists on the socioeconomic impact of the Sultanate on the majority of its subjects, who were Hindu agriculturalists and traders. Constant warfare, rapacious taxation, deliberate humiliation, and occasional persecution of *brahmans* and *banias* (see Glossary), the wholesale destruction of temples and the sometimes vitriolic writings of contemporary Muslim chroniclers all convey a grim picture of Muslim ruler versus Hindu ruled. On the other hand, wise sultans had to keep in mind the interests of Hindu cultivators if they were to feed their increasingly demanding urban proletariat of Muslim soldiery and citizenry; for the most part, rural India continued under the control of traditional (Hindu) *rais* and *rajas* (see Glossary). Islam spread only to a limited extent, and more through the influence of **Sufis** or the imperative of employment than through state-sponsored conversion. Moreover, religious affiliation was not necessarily of prime importance in the frequent wars of the period; booty and territory were as important as loyalty, and Hindu soldiers of the sultan would fight for him as valiantly as Muslim soldiers of a Hindu Raja. Most important of all, the social and cultural life of urban centers in the Sultanate was vibrant, mobile, and syncretic. New art and architectural styles, new literature and languages, notably Hindavi or Dehlavi (that developed into Hindi and Urdu), new styles of music, and new religious movements collectively known as the **Bhakti** movement sprang up as testimony to the absorptive and synthesizing capacity of Indian civilization.

DEOBAND. A place of great antiquity and sanctity in **Uttar Pradesh**, Deoband is the site of an ancient Devi or Goddess temple and many Muslim monuments dating from the periods of the **Delhi Sultanate** and the **Mughal Empire**. Deoband is best known for its great school of Islamic learning, the Dar al-'Ulum, where students from all over India and beyond are enrolled. The Dar al-'Ulum or Deoband seminary was founded by Muhammad Abid Hussayn in 1867. He combined the traditions of **Delhi** on law and jurisprudence, of Lucknow on prayer and meditation, and of Khairabad on philosophy in the program of teaching offered at Deoband. The influence of Shah Wali Allah Dihlawi and the Indian Wahhabis was strong, as also the feeling of resistance to domination by Britain and Western culture. Attempts to combine secular and religious learning did not succeed, and Deoband aimed at the revival and purification of classical **Islam**. Its scholasticism was always profound, and its library and manuscript collection on Islam was the largest in (undivided) India. Deoband gained prestige throughout the entire Muslim world and ranked second only to the al-Azhar University of Cairo in the 20th century.

Deoband's influence over Indian Muslims in the late 19th and the 20th century was considerable, since it was the training center for most of the orthodox Muslim divines in town and village mosques. While socially conservative, Deoband was politically progressive. Some of its members joined the **Ghadr** revolutionaries in 1915; institutionally, it supported the freedom movement and the **Indian National Congress**; Principal Mahmud al-Hasan lavished praise on the young **Abul Kalam Azad** as a religious thinker. After **Partition** and Indian independence, Deoband has remained outside politics while broadly supportive of the Indian government; it continues to focus on scholastic Islam, which some modernizers regard with suspicion.

DEORAS, MADHUKAR DATTATRAYA (BALASAHEB) (1916–1996).

Deoras was named the successor chief executive or *Sarsanghchalak* of the **Rashtriya Swayamsevak Sangh (RSS)** in 1973 by Madhava Sadashiv Golwalkar, then on his deathbed. Deoras's name is associated with a highly activist phase of the RSS in independent India. As a young man in 1949, he had been part of successful negotiations with Home Minster **Vallabhbhai Patel** to lift the government ban on the organization placed after the assassination of **Mahatma Gandhi**. As RSS General Secretary, 1965–1973, Deoras improved coordination between the RSS and its affiliates, especially with labor and student groups, and with the **Vishva Hindu Parishad (VHP)**. He encouraged the latter's missionary work overseas and among **Adivasi** and scheduled **caste** groups at home, and supported increased assertiveness and agitation by all parts of the *Sangh parivar* or Hindu right-wing "family."

Deoras was a self-confident man who envisaged the RSS playing a larger role than building the bodies and character of young **Hindu** men. He supported **Jai Prakash Narayan**'s call for "total revolution" in 1974, and the RSS was especially active underground during the nearly two years of **Emergency Rule** 1975–1977 when it was once again banned. When the issue of "dual membership" with the RSS and a political party became controversial in the new **Janata** government 1977–1979, Deoras and the RSS stayed aloof from elections and did not suggest merging with any political party. But he worked closely with the leadership of the **Bharatiya Janata Party** after it was formed in April 1980. Meanwhile, he had opened the door of RSS membership to non-Hindus—whose response was unsurprisingly lukewarm—and, more significantly, tried to define *Hindu rashtra* in non-theocratic and secular or plural terms.

Deoras's terms in high office saw a surge in RSS membership, especially in the four South Indian states. When Deoras stepped down as *sarsanghchalak* due to ill health, he nominated Rajju Baiyya as his successor.

DEROZIO, HENRY LOUIS VIVIAN (1809–1831).

Derozio was born to a **Portuguese** man and his Indian wife in the city of **Calcutta** and became a famous poet at the age of 18. He taught English and history at the newly opened Hindu College in Calcutta, and during his brief life he stimulated his students to unorthodox thought and practice. He wrote for several journals. Many of his students were in the forefront of what is often called the Indian Renaissance of the early 19th century.

DESAI, BHULABHAI (1877–1946). Bhulabhai was born into a family of poor cultivators. He walked to the village school as a boy but then went on to university in **Bombay**, studied law, and launched a professional career. His presentations in court on behalf of the agriculturalists of Bardoli who were engaged in a "no tax" **Satyagraha** campaign protesting higher assessments of land revenue in 1922 helped to bring substantial remissions there. And Desai came to know **Vallabhbhai Patel**, who organized **civil disobedience** in Bardoli at the time.

Bhulabhai Desai formally joined the **Indian National Congress** in 1930 and proved to be an able party leader in the provincial legislative assembly. Though loyal to **Mahatma Gandhi**, and a practitioner of Satyagraha himself, Desai was skeptical about the benefit of applying Gandhi's economic and political theories in modern India. He was also critical of the 1942 **Quit India** resolution by Congress. In an attempt to resolve the impasse between Congress and the **Muslim League** in the mid-1940s, Desai entered into a pact with **Liaqat Ali Khan**, leader of the League in the Central Legislative Assembly, on forming a two-party coalition to run the interim government in New Delhi before independence. Both the Muslim League and Congress repudiated the pact.

Desai was not a Congress candidate for the elections to the **Constituent Assembly** held in winter 1945–1946. His last act of public service was performed as a defense lawyer for members of the **Indian National Army** who were standing trial for "treason" in 1945.

DESAI, MORARJI (1896–1995). Morarji was born in the **Surat** district of **Gujarat**. He graduated from college in **Bombay** and joined the provincial civil service. He left it in 1930, responding to **Mahatma Gandhi**'s call for **civil disobedience** and remained an ardent Gandhian ever after. He served as cabinet minister with **Jawaharlal Nehru**, **Lal Bahadur Shastri**, and **Indira Gandhi** but split with the latter in 1969 and went into opposition. Desai's personal rectitude and fastidiousness on matters of diet and health are famous as contributing to his longevity. He was prime minister in the **Janata Party** government from 1977 to 1979.

DEVE GOWDA, H. D. (1933–). Deve Gowda was born to a farming family of intermediate **caste** in **Karnataka** and was trained as a civil engineer. He joined politics as a young man and first won a seat in the **Lok Sabha** as an independent in 1962. When the **Congress Party** split later in the decade, he stood with the faction that opposed Prime Minister **Indira Gandhi**. He was imprisoned during the **Emergency**, and became important to the **Janata Party** in the late 1970s and 1980s.

Deve Gowda was a shrewd and pragmatic politician who projected the image of an unsophisticated and phlegmatic farmer. This image was reinforced by his lack of facility in either Hindi or English, but he did indeed uphold farmers' interests when he became chief minister of Karnataka in 1994 and implemented some of the measures that were successful in neighboring **Maharashtra**. He cleverly defused possible tensions arising from implementation of the **Mandal Commission** recommendations in Karnataka, and he was also a strong advocate of states rights, castigating New Delhi for errors and neglect.

The 1996 general elections resulted in a parliament where no single **political party** enjoyed a majority. Deve Gowda was elected prime minister of a coalition United Front government. Because the United Front included numerous regional parties, especially from southern India, states enjoyed a more than customary say in policymaking and gained the power to approve such schemes as modernization in the power sector, without New Delhi's prior concurrence. Although Deve Gowda had been a vociferous opponent of the **economic liberalization** policies initiated by the previous Congress government, he injected new life into the reform process as prime minister. In particular, he restructured the Foreign Investment Promotion Board and speeded up approval of new proposals. Deve Gowda lost his position when Congress withdrew its support in 1997 and a new United Front government was constituted under the prime ministership of **I. K. Gujral**.

DHAKA. The city was founded in 1610 as a garrison town for the lower **Ganges** delta area after **Bengal** became a *subah* (see Glossary) of the **Mughal Empire**. Dhaka was renowned for the fine silk and cotton textiles produced and traded there and was adorned with many gardens and monuments that were constructed in a distinctive style of architecture. Dhaka is the capital of the present-day Republic of **Bangladesh**.

DHARMA. Derived from the **Sanskrit** root *dhr*, "to sustain," dharma is an all-encompassing concept at the core of Indian culture. It defies literal translation. The broad meanings of righteousness, duty, and virtue convey only part of its flavor.

The concept of dharma comprises precepts aimed at securing the material and spiritual sustenance of the individual, society, and the universe; without dharma, they would collapse. Precepts of moral law are found in the *Smriti* literature of law books and epics, of later date than the **Vedas**, and probably composed between c. 500 BCE and c. 500 CE. These *Dharma shastras*, of which the *Manu-smriti* may be the most famous, are the earliest sources of **Hindu** law. Later precepts taught by the **Buddha** as *dhamma* (dharma) were collected as guides for his followers and were subsequently adopted by the **Emperor Ashoka** as the moral code of his reign. The **Jain** teachers also gave special connotations to the familiar term, dharma.

A notable feature of dharma is that it was never static. Its content changed according to the context of time, place, and social environment; what was appropriate conduct for one person was not for the other, provided all alike were bound by a commonly understood sacred law or dharmic code. Important aspects of such a dharmic code expounded in *Smriti* literature included the organization of society through four *varnas* or classes and the progression of an individual through four *ashramas* or stages of life. The duty of a just ruler was to protect this *varna- ashrama-dharma* or social order, into which all other regulations and relationships were fitted. It must be remembered that the *Dharma-shastras* were written by **brahman** men, who were given a special status in them, and may not always have reflected actual practice.

Dharma provided an integrated philosophy of life and social organization in ancient times, which incorporated in large measure the heterodox beliefs and practices found on the Indian subcontinent and so withstood the influx and rule of foreigners from time to time. This remarkable resilience was, in part, the result of a continual synthesis between Vedic religion and other faiths, which came to be known as **Hinduism**. This is illustrated by modern usage of the term "Sanatana Dharma" (the Eternal Dharma) for Hinduism itself. The concept of dharma is not confined to Hinduism or to the past. It carries forward to the present day and, with some changes in content, remains central to Indian civilization and to Indians of all religions.

DIASPORA. The term literally means a dispersion of peoples beyond their homeland, either forced or voluntary, who retain an awareness of their identity that varies in intensity and level of contact with place of origin according to circumstances and personal predilections. The Indian diaspora was conservatively estimated at the end of the 20th century to be more than 20 million people settled in 136 countries. These include Overseas Indians or Non Resident Indians (NRI), that is Indian nationals working and living outside India for extended periods of time, and Persons of Indian Origin (PIO), that is foreign national descendants of Indians who left India in the last few decades or centuries. Although ancient trading links between India and other countries probably led to some overseas settlement at that time, present day discussions of the diaspora conventionally focus on 19th- and 20th-century migrations.

The first wave of migration was to other parts of the British Empire where the abolition of slavery in 1833 was followed by a system of indentured labor under which large numbers of economically deprived Indians, especially from **Madras** province and the **Ganges** valley, went to work in sugar and rice plantations in the Caribbean, South Africa, Fiji, and Mauritius. The **Indian National Congress** protested against abuses of the indentured labor system which resulted in its termination after **World War I**. In the late 19th and early 20th century, the demand for Indian labor to work in rubber, rice, and tea plantations was high in Malaya, **Burma**, and **Ceylon**, and to build roads and railway lines in East Africa. Wherever Indian labor settled, traders—especially from **Gujarat**, others from all parts of India offering services, professionals, and civil servants followed; they were beneficiaries of and participants in British imperial expansion. A few hundred agriculturalists from the **Punjab** migrated to western Canada and United States in the first decade of the 20th century, but legal bars to immigration and racial discrimination kept more Indians out of North America at that time.

A second wave of Indian emigration followed the end of **World War II** and the **Partition** of India. Some soldiers remained in the Middle East to engage in construction and business. Many displaced people from the **Punjab** of all religious communities went to Britain and also participated in the reconstruction of Western Europe. Other Indians seeking higher education or an escape from poverty at home followed them. The United Kingdom now has several Members of Parliament and 11 peers of Indian origin. What might be termed a third wave of Indian emigration has taken place since the early 1970s and has gone to different destinations. Approximately three million Indians, about half from **Kerala**, work in the oil-rich kingdoms of Saudi Arabia and the Persian Gulf in occupations that range from semi-skilled to professional. They are denied rights of citizenship and sometimes suffer human rights abuses, but they make significantly large annual remittances home and have made a visual impact on the landscape of Kerala. Some hundreds of thousands of Indians have settled in Canada and Australia, with a few individuals in the former taking political office. Changes in United States immigration law in 1965 enabled large numbers of talented and highly educated Indians, now close to two million, to make their contribution to American creativity and productivity. Indian-Americans as a community rank in the highest income, highest educated, most law abiding, brackets and are beginning to exert influence in both political parties.

Most Indians working abroad in the late 19th and early 20th centuries faced appalling living conditions, racial abuse, and harsh treatment from white settlers in power, and hostility from indigenous populations that colonial governments sometimes instigated, as in Fiji and East Africa. In contrast, communal harmony prevailed in the Indian Ocean French colonies of Mauritius and Reunion, with PIOs forming a majority government in the former since independence. South Africa's discriminatory laws provided the laboratory for **M. K. Gandhi**'s groundbreaking work of instilling courage and unity into cowed peoples, and developing the concept of **satyagraha** into a practical movement toward just ends. Subsequently, independent India led the United Nations campaign against apartheid in South Africa and forged close links with post-apartheid South Africa in the 1990s.

During the 1950s and 1960s, the presence of large numbers of Indians in newly independent countries posed dilemmas for New Delhi, which wanted to cement good relations with these countries and also ensure equal treatment for Indian minorities everywhere. The Indian government adopted somewhat ambiguous positions of urging overseas Indians to identify fully with the countries of their residence but maintain cultural and kinship ties with India, of disclaiming responsibility for them but expressing concern for their welfare. India entered into protracted negotiations with Ceylon on citizenship rights and repatriation of tea plantation workers. It did not retaliate when Ne Win's Burma expelled most Indians without compensation in 1964, or when Idi Amin's Uganda did so in 1968–1972. Cultural contacts with the Diaspora were encouraged from India, but officials refrained from interfering in the complex ethnic politics of countries such as Guyana, Malaya, and Trinidad where Indians formed large minorities or even majorities. However, the unseating of two ethnic Indian governments in Fiji by questionable means in the 1980s and 1990 did arouse resentment in Indian public opinion. Indian consular officials in the Persian Gulf and Saudi Arabia devoted considerable time to the problems of Indian workers there. The Diaspora was becoming more important for India, both negatively and positively.

Within India, attitudes toward the Diaspora changed, for several reasons. Cultural diplomacy, the popularity of Festivals of India abroad, sister-city arrangements, the presence of PIO and NRI students in Indian educational institutions, and increased facility of all kinds of communication helped the process. Transcontinental marriages became more common. Hub and spoke relationships were supplemented by relationships around the rim of an imaginary wheel. The "brain drain" of those who had been educated in India spending their talents outside India began to appear as a possible "brain bank" of health care, and cultural, scientific, and technical exchange, charitable contributions, and national prestige. On the negative side, political activism by dissident Indians settled in the West created diplomatic and security problems for India, especially over the issues of Khalistan and **Kashmir**. By the same token, political activism could—and did—ease problems between India and its Western interlocutors.

Economic prosperity and ethnic awareness within the Diaspora itself led to the forging of a global organization of people of Indian origin. Initially weak and self-serving, it had the potential for building mutual cooperation and acting as a catalyst for economic change in India. China's rapid economic growth was obviously spurred by investment from the Chinese Diaspora that was larger and wealthier than India's but invited comparison. India's **economic liberalization** policies after 1991 cried out for direct foreign investment even more than remittances, and because the Diaspora was seen as one promising source of investment New Delhi paid attention to its expressed grievances over bureaucratic harassment. It took incremental steps to reduce impediments to travel and financial flows so as to make NRIs and PIOs feel welcome in India. In 1999, PIO cards were issued to qualified persons on payment, giving them visa-free access to India for 10 years. The Indian government next formed a High Level Committee on the Indian Diaspora, with a mandate to compile reliable information on numbers and characteristics of the Diaspora all over the world and inquire into four broad areas: how and where it could play a progressive role in cementing good bilateral relations between host countries and India; in what ways it could make a positive contribution to Indian's development; what were its expectations from India; and how could India best fulfill its obligation to safeguard the welfare of its far flung Diaspora. The committee published its report in 2002, recommending a flexible policy framework as also the possibility of offering dual citizenship to PIOs in selected countries with reciprocal arrangements. Meanwhile, the Diaspora showed heightened awareness of developments in India; according to Reserve Bank of India reports, Indians abroad contributed $18 billion in remittances during 2003, making India the largest recipient of private transfers globally. It is likely that beneficial interactions between India and its Diaspora will continue to increase in importance.

DIN-I-ILAHI. This was the name given to a syncretic cult proclaimed by the **Mughal Emperor Akbar** for his court in 1582. It propounded a simple monotheism, exhorted the moral virtues of wisdom, courage, chastity, and justice, and enjoined its members to devote life, property, honor, and belief to the emperor. It borrowed ceremonies from other faiths—**Hinduism**, **Islam**, **Zoroastrianism**, and **Christianity**—in a kind of royal theosophy.

The Din-I-Ilahi provided a focus of loyalty to officials above the two great religions of the people, Islam and Hinduism, and so gave the imperial throne itself a kind of divine sanctity. The motive and effect of proclaiming such a cult were political rather than religious, legitimizing the emperor's supreme authority in the state. This naturally outraged the *ulema* (see Glossary) or Muslim theologians, who accused Akbar of being an apostate to Islam. Though the Din-i-Ilahi had a small membership of courtiers and was not continued by Akbar's son and successor Jahangir, the nimbus around the Mughal Emperor long persisted in art as in popular belief.

DOMINION STATUS. The **Indian National Congress** first demanded dominion status within the British Empire in 1908 with an eye to the virtual self-government in internal affairs enjoyed by Canada. No precise definition of dominion status was given until 1926 when an Imperial Conference held in London defined Dominions as "autonomous communities within the British Empire, equal in status . . . united by a common allegiance to the Crown." This definition, explicitly granting sovereignty in internal affairs and full autonomy in external affairs with the right to sign treaties, was recognition of post-**World War I** realities and was subsequently embodied in the Statute of Westminster, 1931. Because Indians were proud of their own civilization and contributions to the Allied war effort, because India, too, was a member of the League of Nations, and because India's nationalist movement was also a struggle against racism in the British Empire, educated Indians wanted their country to have the same legal status after the war as the "white" dominions: Australia, Canada, New Zealand, and South Africa.

Britain did not concede dominion status as a goal of its policies in India until late 1929, when Governor General **Lord Irwin** announced that it was the "natural aim" of constitutional reform and had been implied in the famous **Montagu Declaration** of 1917 promising "responsible government" in India. Irwin's announcement did not preempt the Congress resolution of 1930 demanding *purna swaraj* or full independence, in which dominion status was criticized as inadequate. Similarly, Congress declined the offer made by **Sir Stafford**

Cripps (in 1942) for dominion status after the end of **World War II**. British withdrawal from India, concretized in the Independence of India Act of 1947, was accompanied by **Partition** of the subcontinent and grant of dominion status to both India and **Pakistan**. India rapidly became a republic, owing no allegiance to the British Crown other than as "head of the Commonwealth of Nations."

DRAVIDA MUNNETRA KAZHAGAM (DMK). The DMK, a major **political party** in **Tamil Nadu**, was the outgrowth of a populist **Dravidian** movement led by **E. V. R. Naicker** early in the 20th century. The DMK platform was social-reformist and anti-establishment. It opposed traditional **brahman** dominance, as well as the perceived post-independence imposition of Hindi, a north Indian language, over the Tamil-speaking south. The DMK's demand for greater state autonomy and use of the regional language appeared to be strident and secessionist when first made in the early 1960s. Its position softened after New Delhi accepted a three-**language** compromise, and after the 1967 general elections brought the DMK rather than the **Congress Party** to power in Tamil Nadu.

The DMK soon split due to rivalry between leaders and personality clashes, rather than policy differences, and the All India Anna Dravida Munnetra Kazhagam (AIADMK) came into being. Although each is willing to ally with national parties if expedient to do so, the DMK and AIADMK are essentially regional parties that dominate politics in Tamil Nadu in a fairly stable two-party system. The AIADMK led by **Jayalalitha** supported the **Bharatiya Janata Party** led coalition and was similarly defeated in the general elections of 2004. The DMK led by Karunanidhi was in alliance with the Congress and won 16 seats to the **Lok Sabha**. Subsequently, party members secured several positions in the new cabinet of **Dr. Manmohan Singh**, and Tamil was recognized as a classical language.

DRAVIDIAN. The name given to peoples who probably originated in the eastern Mediterranean region and Iranian plateau, and entered the Indian subcontinent long before the **Aryan** peoples, the Dravidians may well have been the originators of the **Indus Valley Civilization** or **Harappan Culture**, although the linguistic and archaeological evidence on this subject is not yet conclusive. It is likely that they were pressed southward as a consequence of Aryan settlements in the Indo-Gangetic plains. In historical times the Dravidian peoples have predominated in south India in the area corresponding to the present states of **Andhra**, **Karnataka**, **Kerala**, and **Tamil Nadu**. The Dravidians, therefore, constitute one of the major ethnic-linguistic families in India. **Tamil** is the senior language of a group that includes Kannada, Malayallum, and Telegu. Written alphabetically, they are characterized by retroflexed consonants.

The racial, cultural, and religious intermixing of Dravidian and Aryan components is a fruitful field of research for those probing the foundations and evolution of Indian civilization with its distinctive social system and popular religion of **Hinduism**. Dravidian social organization was class-based but did not adopt the *varna* (see Glossary) and *jati* features of the **caste** system as practiced in northern India. The dominant position of **brahmans** in early Tamil kingdoms was associated with a process of Sanskritization and the introduction of Vedic rites for rulers who were sometimes integrated into the brahman community or accorded **kshatriya** status. Most of the population, however, remained outside the caste hierarchy. With the advent of Muslim rule in northern India and the **Deccan** in the 13th and 14th centuries, the southern kingdoms became bastions of orthodox Hinduism. The brahmans combined religious authority as custodians of rituals with economic power derived from land ownership. They tended to separate themselves socially and physically from the lower castes and increased their political control over them. The non-brahmanical folk culture probably transmitted a high content of Dravidian lore.

The brahmans of the south were the first to respond to Western influences in the colonial period and added command of English and administrative service to their inherited advantages. Similarly, they were the first to participate in All-India movements of social reform and political nationalism, though **Jyotiba Phule** of **Maharashtra** and later the **Theosophists** also preached the virtues of social service and education for the lower castes. By the late 19th century, a wide gap between brahman and non-brahman was conspicuous in the Madras Presidency; the Dravidian movement was a reaction to this. A counter elite with a Dravidian thrust began to emerge from the well educated and politically articulate non-brahman urban classes. Dr. C. Natesa Mudaliar founded the Dravidian Home as a student hostel in 1914 and the Dravidian Association for social uplift in 1916. The South Indian Peoples Association issued a manifesto pointing out that brahmans constituted less than 5% of the population but virtually monopolized positions in educational and governmental bodies in Madras Presidency; it voiced alarm at the agitation for "Home Rule" and asserted devotion and loyalty to British rule. From 1917 to the 1930s the **Justice Party** first rose and then declined on the rope of British support.

The Dravidian movement gathered momentum after 1939 behind the leadership of **E. V. Ramaswamy Naicker** on a platform of a separate independent Dravidasthan aiming for an egalitarian, casteless society and presupposing a Dravidian racial stock, culture, and language distinct from that of north India. In 1945, Naicker's party, the Dravida Kazhagam, adopted a black flag with a red center symbolizing a subjected people with their hope. Images of Hindu deities were destroyed, **Sanskrit** epics such as the *Ramayana* debunked, and the Tamil language "purified" of Sanskrit accretions as part of a Dravidian renaissance campaign glorifying the Tamil past.

Opposition to alleged northern domination was combined with opposition to the **Congress** government of **C. Rajagopalachari** in an appeal to Tamil/Dravidian solidarity and separatism in the 1950s. However, the movement did not spread to the other southern states. Within Madras, soon renamed Tamil Nadu, the Dravida Kazhagam was replaced in prominence by the **Dravida Munnetra Kazhagam (DMK)** and the All India Dravida Munnetra Kazhagam (AIDMK) **political parties**; non-brahman Tamil sentiment was also mobilized for Congress by **Kamaraj**, himself of humble Nadar caste. The trilanguage formula adopted by India in 1965 which indefinitely postponed making Hindi the national language defused much of the Tamil agitation, and caste considerations in politics proved to be more complicated than merely non-brahman versus brahman. Dravidian pride and cultural-linguistic assertiveness remained lively but was conducted within the political boundaries of the Indian Union and the competitiveness of a multi-party parliamentary system.

DUFFERIN, LORD FREDERICK TEMPLE HAMILTON (1826–1902). Viceroy and governor general of India from 1884–1888,

Dufferin was appointed by the British Liberal Prime Minister William Gladstone to succeed **Lord Ripon** and to continue his policies. Dufferin chose instead to put his weight on imperial interests. Therefore, his administration was actively engaged in Afghanistan and **Tibet** and was responsible for the annexation of upper **Burma** to India, supposedly to counter Russian advances in Central Asia and the French presence in Indochina. Within India, too, Dufferin favored the landowning class, safeguarding its interests in various tenancy laws, and he cultivated the Indian Princes, even restoring Gwalior fort to **Sindhia**.

Dufferin recognized the growing importance of the educated middle class in India. The University of **Allahabad** was established during his administration, and constitutional reform of the provincial legislative councils was undertaken; both actions benefited this class. Dufferin did not pretend to like the men who belonged to this class, however, describing them as "unrepresentative," and himself as the "benevolent protector" of the "Indian masses." Moreover, Dufferin posited a conflict between Muslim and Hindu interests in India and discouraged Muslim membership in the **Indian National Congress**, which was formed by leaders of the educated middle class, with the active encouragement of some British officials such as **Allan Octavian Hume** in 1885. Dufferin interdicted official support for or representation in Congress, perhaps unintentionally encouraging Congress criticism of his viceroyalty as "reactionary" and "expensive." Indeed, Dufferin raised direct and indirect taxes to meet additional expenditures, including the construction in wood of a castle-like Viceregal Lodge in Simla and the lavish entertainments and elaborate ceremony preferred by Lord and Lady Dufferin.

DUPLEIX, JOSEPH FRANCOIS (1697–1764). Dupleix began his career in commercial service with the **French East India Company** and rose to be governor of **Pondicherry** in 1742 and director general of all the French factories in India. Brilliant and patient, he aimed at establishing French supremacy in southern India by defending amenable Indian princes against their adversaries as well as against the British. He was among the first to translate the technical superiority of European artillery and drilling of infantry to political-diplomatic advantage in the fractious skirmishes of post-**Mughal** India. His rival, the Englishman **Robert Clive**, was another.

Dupleix's successes—in capturing **Madras** in 1746, in gaining support, titles, and territory from the Nizam of **Hyderabad**, and in other battles of the Carnatic wars—were diluted by lack of support from Paris. The establishment of English naval supremacy in the 18th century and the absence of easy wealth in the Carnatic, as compared to **Bengal**, further tipped the scales away from realization of Dupleix's strategic vision. He was ordered home in 1754, was subjected to indignities, and died 10 years later in penury.

DURAND LINE. The Durand Line was named after Sir Mortimer Durand (1850–1924) who joined the **Indian Civil Service** in 1870 and served in the Foreign and Political Service. Much of his career was spent in dealing with the consequences of the **Anglo-Afghan wars**. Durand negotiated an agreement between the Afghan Amir Abdur Rahman and the Government of India in 1893, dividing their respective spheres of influence through the tribal belt on the northwest frontier of the Indian subcontinent. All of the important passes, including the Khyber, fell within British-Indian jurisdiction and were constantly manned against possible attacks. The Pakhtun tribesmen of the area were not consulted while this 2,250 kilometer dividing line from Gilgit in the north to Baluchistan in the southwest was demarcated between 1894 and 1896. The Durand Line was frequently challenged in the 20th century as an international border. After the independence and **Partition** of India in 1947, the problem was inherited by **Pakistan**.

DUTCH EAST INDIA COMPANY (VEREENIGDE OOSTINDISCHE COMPAGNIE, VOC). The VOC was chartered in 1602 with an initial capital investment 10 times greater than its contemporary, the **English East India Company**. Within three years the VOC sent 38 ships into the Indian Ocean, defeating the **Portuguese** off Johore and taking a fortress at Ambiona. More important, secret Portuguese maps and oceanic charts were captured and were published as a "sailing guide" to the eastern seas. In the religious and trade wars that marked 17th-century Europe, the Protestant Dutch and English aimed at breaking the hold of Catholic Spain and Portugal over the spice trade formerly dominated by the Muslim Arabs. Maps permitted Dutch and English ships to run the blockade successfully and earn enormous profits in the process.

The VOC used traditional Asian and Arab trading routes, making Pulicat on the Coromandel Coast of India their main base. They led the way in a triangular trade of Indian goods sold in the East Indies for spices sold in Europe. The Dutch fastened a jealous grip on the East Indies (present-day Indonesia) and forced the English to focus on trading in India.

DUTT, RAJANI PALME (1896–1974). R. Palme Dutt, as he signed himself, was born to an Indian doctor and his Swedish wife in Cambridge, England. Rajani was a brilliant student both in school and at university at Oxford and developed a lifelong commitment to Marxism during **World War I**. He was a founding member of the Communist Party of Great Britain (CPGB) and served on its executive committee from 1922 to 1965. Together with Philip Spratt, he set up a Colonial Bureau in the CPGB and corresponded with or met a large number of more or less leftist-inclined nationalists throughout the British Empire. Dutt was a prolific writer, and his books include *Modern India* (1926) and *India Today* (1956). He also edited *Labour Monthly* and *Workers Weekly*.

Rajani Dutt naturally exerted considerable influence during his life on Indian Marxists and on the **Communist Party of India (CPI)**, although not always directly. Some read his articles as veiled directives to the CPI to support the foreign and perhaps domestic policies followed by Prime Minister **Jawaharlal Nehru** in the mid-1950s.

DUTT, ROMESH CHUNDER (1848–1909). Romesh belonged to a well-placed Western-educated family of **Calcutta**, which included the female poet, Toru Dutt. Romesh was selected for the **Indian Civil Service** in 1871 and served in it for 26 years. Suspecting that racial prejudice would obstruct his promotion to the highest positions, he retired to literary and political pursuits.

Dutt's analysis of the economic devastation caused by **Cornwallis's Permanent Settlement** was the first of its kind. His two-volume *Economic History of British India 1757–1837*, published in 1902, was a well documented exposition of the "economic drain" theory of colonial rule elaborated later by others. Dutt was elected president of the **Indian National Congress** in 1899 and was a friend and colleague of other early leaders, **Dadabhai Naoroji** and **W. C. Bonnerjee**. They were not opposed to British rule in India as such, but wanted it improved through the application of basic English freedoms and representative democratic processes of government in India, and the inclusion of a larger number of Indians in the higher echelons of the administration. They tried to educate British public opinion along those lines.

DYARCHY. One feature of the Government of India Act 1919 or **Montagu-Chelmsford Reforms** was to introduce a dual form of government, or dyarchy as it came to be called, in the eight governors provinces of **Assam**, **Bengal**, **Bihar**, **Bombay**, Central Provinces, **Orissa**, **Punjab**, and United Provinces. Certain matters, such as agriculture, education, local government, and public health, were "transferred" to the administrative control of Indian ministers chosen from and answerable to the provincial legislative assembly, which now had an elected majority. Other matters, including finance, irrigation, law, land revenue, labor, and police, were "reserved" to the governor and his nominated Executive Council, composed of an equal number of officials and non-officials and responsible only to Whitehall. There was an expectation that the two halves of government would be kept separate and yet would cooperate; governors were to decide cases of disagreement on expenditure.

Some of the governors raised objections of practicability to the scheme when it was announced. The **Indian National Congress** denounced the reforms as a travesty of the 1917 **Montagu Declaration** promising "responsible government" and adopted a stance of **Non-Cooperation** toward them. Not surprisingly, despite the efforts of the **Swaraj Party** and some governors, dyarchy proved extreme in practice. The absence of mutual trust and consensus on governmental programs and expenditure between Indian ministers and British officials ensured its failure. Nevertheless, the **Government of India Act 1935** introduced dyarchy as a feature of the central government.

DYER, BRIGADIER REGINALD EDWARD HARRY (1864–1927). Dyer became notorious for ordering continued firing on unarmed celebrants of a religious festival at **Jallianwala Bagh** in **Amritsar** on April 13, 1919. Indian opinion throughout the subcontinent was outraged by the massacre; the nationalist movement gained momentum. Dyer attempted to justify the firings, as well as his orders for the crawling and flogging of Indians, on grounds of necessity for stern action to quell possible rebellion. A British parliamentary committee heard him but concluded that he was motivated by racial revenge and may also have been suffering from mental illness. He was relieved of his command and returned to England where he received some accolades and a purse of 26,000 pounds sterling from his admirers.

– E –

EAST INDIA COMPANY. It was established in London by Royal Charter in 1600 as a trading company and became a territorial power in India after 1757. It was replaced by the British Crown as the Government of India in 1858 and was formally dissolved by Act of Parliament in 1874. Changing its aims and character over time in response to new circumstances in Europe and in Asia, the East India Company was both a manifestation and the chief instrument of Britain's expansion in Asia. With its long history, colorful cast of characters, haphazard growth from a limited joint stock Company to a state within a state, and its carefully preserved records, the East India Company has inspired an enormous body of literature.

In order to extend English trade in the 17th century, the Company made strenuous and ultimately successful efforts to obtain permission of the **Mughal** emperors, provincial governors, and local authorities to establish and operate trading posts, or "factories," on Indian shores. **Surat** in **Gujarat**, chief port of the Mughal Empire, was the first to be established in 1619, followed by Masulipatam and **Madras** on the Coromandel Coast in 1640, and Hughli in **Bengal** in 1658. **Bombay** on the west coast came to the Company from the **Portuguese** via King Charles II, who promoted the Company's growth by giving it virtually self-governing powers overseas in competition with the **Dutch East India Company**. Early Dutch exclusion of the English from the East Indies—source of the lucrative spices which lured European merchants and adventurers to Asia—combined with

London's reluctance to export precious metals, the only European commodity for which there was an Indian demand, pushed the Company into the "triangular trade" of investing gold in Indian products, especially textiles, and selling them in the East Indies for the spices which brought astronomical profits in London. Competition from and amalgamation with other English trading companies produced a stronger, more modern body in the early 18th century.

A pattern of Anglo-Indian partnership was established at this time, which drew the British deeper into India and was challenged only much later when Indians found that they had become victims. For example, in the course of pursuing a triangular trade, English ships sometimes served Mughal interests at sea; Company servants formed mutually beneficial relationships with Indian merchants and producers, adapting to Indian customs, languages, and lifestyles; legal and other institutions introduced in the "factories" run by the English, known as the John Company, did not disturb the influence of local notables and came to provide security for all their inhabitants in troubled times. In the first half of the 18th century troubles were not infrequent along the fringes of the Mughal Empire, especially as it gradually lost power to the **Marathas** and provincial rulers. The John Company began to play a triple role of trader, banker, and local administrator, securing fiscal privileges from the Mughals equivalent to those enjoyed by Indians in similar positions.

The Company's prosperity waxed, as did the influence and patronage of its directors in the City of London. This combination of autonomous action in India and support from London proved to be an important factor in mid- and late-18th-century conflicts, when the English and the French (*see* FRENCH EAST INDIA COMPANY) companies with their drilled troops and artillery backed rival Indian contenders for power in the Carnatic, Bengal, and elsewhere. **Robert Clive**'s victory at **Plassey** led to the acquisition of territorial power in eastern India for the Company—along with venality and military expenses. The ability of the English to act in concert with each other despite individual jealousies was as important in the long run as sea power and military technique in giving them superiority over their Indian and European rivals on the subcontinent.

In the latter half of the 18th century the personal wealth of Company servants or "nabobs" (see Glossary) returning to England, and the professed inability of the Company to pay its annual taxes provoked inquiry into its affairs by the British Parliament and led to efforts at reform. The **Regulating Act** of 1773 and Pitt's India Act of 1784 altered the administrative structure of the Company and gave the British government financial, military, and political control over its possessions in India. The **Charter Acts** made specific changes. Although there were occasional spirited debates on the proper aims and functions of the Company, its steady military expansion was the result, in part, of subcontinental conflict with other powers, notably the **Marathas** and **Mysore**, and of worldwide conflict between England and France. Britain's loss of its American colonies in 1783 also spurred interest in finding a replacement in India. Periodic financial brakes exerted from London on military action allowed time for consolidation of British possessions in India.

During the half century 1780 to 1835, there was a rough balance on the Company's board of directors between the interests of London and **Calcutta**, and the Company exercised direct influence in Parliament through about 100 members. This balance altered in London's favor as the Company lost its trading monopoly in 1813 and the British electoral and representative system was reformed in 1832. The predominance of British interests became an established fact in the first half of the 19th century, leading to many anomalies. For example, the Company's power of taxation in India made salt the most important source of revenue; it was drawn from the impoverished peasants whom the British claimed to protect. British regulation of the production and sale of opium in India made it the main—if illegal—export to China, where Britain fought its first war in 1839. Confining the company to administrative rather than commercial duties led to a situation in which a private corporation acquired vast territories through treaties and wars in the 1840s and 1850s that ultimately sparked the Mutiny or **Uprising of 1857**. This was quelled only with the arrival of British troops sailing from Europe. Company Raj was over.

ECONOMIC LIBERALIZATION. India adopted a strategy of planned economic development after independence that emphasized rapid industrialization by the state as the best means to eradicate poverty. Businessmen, trade union leaders, economists, and political leaders had favored this approach since the 1940s, partly because the Soviet transformation of agrarian Russia into an industrial power evoked respect, partly because of the acute shortage of private capital within India, and partly because an objective of economic growth with social equity embraced by the **Indian National Congress** logically led to its 1955 espousal of a "socialistic" system of "mixed economy." Agriculture remained the largest employer and in the private sector, but the state dominated new and heavy industry, encouraged import substitution, and controlled all foreign exchange transactions. With a more or less autarchic economy, India's share of world trade fell from about 2% in 1950 to less than 0.50% in 1980, consumer choice was limited, and market forces were distorted by political compulsions. Macroeconomic management by the state, no matter how well intentioned and financially conservative, led to a proliferation of controls, known colloquially as "the license permit *raj*" that spawned rent seekers and what one columnist called "the political economy of stagnation." Attempts to liberalize the economy were made in the mid-1980s (and twice earlier), but half-heartedly; there was no significant political support for reform or sense of crisis despite the evident limitations of India's development strategy, especially in contrast to the "Asian Tigers" of Southeast and East Asia.

A serious macroeconomic and balance of payments crisis in 1991 forced a rethinking of development strategy and the initiation of a series of economic reforms enumerated in Appendix I. The immediate objective of these reforms was to stabilize the economy and overcome the balance of payments crisis brought about by the surge in oil prices, by lax fiscal policies in the late 1980s and an increase in foreign debt, by borrowing at commercial rates from foreign banks, and by the withdrawal of volatile non-resident deposits from Indian banks. Foreign exchange reserves fell to US $1.2 billion in June 1991, and in November India signed a two-year arrangement with the International Monetary Fund (IMF) for a US $2.3 billion loan. Finance Minister **Dr. Manmohan Singh** in the **Narasimha Rao** government quickly stabilized the situation through devaluation of the rupee, reduction of the central fiscal deficit, abolition of most industrial licenses, other restrictions, and price controls on private sector industry, invitations to foreign investors, and some liberalization of the foreign trade and foreign exchange sectors. By 1993–1994, the economic growth rate had accelerated, exports were increasing, and the external payments position had improved so that India did not need to apply to the IMF for another loan.

The next stage of reform had the longer-term objective of achieving a pattern of higher economic growth for India similar to that of market-oriented East Asian economies and necessitated drastic overhaul of the tariff structure, among other changes. A serious impediment to the reform process was vocal opposition, often in the name of poverty alleviation and from within the ruling party itself, to reform proposals going beyond liberalization of the industrial sector, which did have broad-based support. The Rao government was weak and was succeeded in New Delhi by two left-of-center United Front coalition governments in 1996–1997 and then by a National Democratic Alliance (NDA) coalition government led by the **Bharatiya Janata Party (BJP)** that had a strong *swadeshi* (see Glossary) component in 1998 and again in 1999. Thus, economic reforms in India, unlike those in China after 1980, were introduced gradually, in stops and starts, and in a democratic political environment of constant criticism and amendment. Even before the NDA government was replaced by a **Congress**-led coalition government in 2004, however, it was evident that all major political parties had accepted economic liberalization as necessary, so that the question was no longer if, but when and how, particular reforms—such as in the finance and banking sector—were put into effect. Meanwhile, India's economic growth rate accelerated to over 6% and then over 8%, the poverty ratio of the population declined from around 50% in the 1970s to 33% in 1993 to 26% in 2000, exports increased significantly, especially exports of information technology goods and services. The Asian financial crisis of 1997 did not affect India, and foreign direct investment (FDI) rose from US $77 million in 1992 to close to US $4 billion in 2001–2002. India's performance by every economic and social indicator was improving but fell far below that of China; total factor productivity clearly needed to be boosted in India. The Tenth Five-Year Plan (2002–2007) drafted by the **Planning Commission** targeted higher annual growth rates that would simultaneously raise per capita income and reduce poverty, and explicitly dealt with the issues of generating more employment, providing good governance, and vitalizing the physical and social infrastructure as essential elements of economic growth.

The current generation of economic reforms is likely to carry liberalization into the agricultural sector by postulating reduction or abolition of subsidies on electricity, fertilizer, and water, further reduce the role of government in banking, industrial and trading sectors, and encourage massive public, private, and even foreign investment into key elements of the infrastructure. Prime Minister Manmohan Singh also has called on Indians to "think globally" and integrate competitively with the world economy. *See also* CHIDAMBARAM, PLANNING COMMISSION, MANMOHAN SINGH, and Appendixes I and J).

ELECTION COMMISSION. This is an independent constitutional authority that was established under Article 324 of the **Constitution** to superintend, direct, and prepare electoral rolls and to conduct elections to Parliament, state legislatures, and the offices of president and vice president. The Chief Election Commissioner functioned alone from 1950 to 1989, when two more persons were appointed as Election Commissioners with equal powers and emoluments. The three commissioners enjoy the same salary and status as justices of the **Supreme Court**, they serve for six years or to the age of 65, and they cannot be removed from office without a difficult and untried procedure. The Election Commission has demonstrated its efficiency, experience, impartiality, and independence repeatedly in state and national elections.

Elections in India, ever since the first general elections to the **Lok Sabha** in 1952, are phenomenal undertakings, given the fact that electoral rolls are prepared on the basis of a house-to-house canvas, that distances are enormous, and that the total size of the Indian electorate was 619 million in 1999 and more than 671 million in 2004 with a high voter participation rate of approximately 60%. National polls conducted by the Centre for the Study of Developing Societies in the late 1990s show higher respect for the Election Commission in the public than for any other state institution. Voter identity cards and technological advances in polling methods have helped to check abuses; electronic voting machines that are simple to operate and tamper proof were used in ALL of the 687,407 polling stations in the 543 parliamentary constituencies for the general elections of 2004. This election was conducted in four stages, from March 23 to May

10, and four million people were employed by the Election Commission to ensure proper procedures with backing from police and security forces who were appropriately deployed.

The Election Commission has become more active and assertive in recent decades as the frequency of parliamentary and state legislature elections increases, and as **political parties** proliferate, split, and have proved to be ill disciplined. The Election Commission alone can assign a symbol to a political party and list it as a national or state party—in short, confer legitimacy—before elections. The Election Commission also has tried to check blatant abuses of the electoral process through such mechanisms as "booth capturing," fraudulent voters lists, spending by candidates far in excess of legal limits, and the involvement of "strong men" or violence to capture political power. The Election Commission conducts another poll in places where it judges an initial poll to be rendered invalid by abuses of process. Political parties have agreed to comply with a seven-section code of conduct for electioneering, which includes a ban on using vehicles with loudspeakers and combining official visits of personnel with campaigning. But political parties have resisted efforts by the Election Commission to make them internally democratic, to purge criminals from their rosters, and to ban appeals based on caste or communal feeling. Recent Chief Election Commissioners (see Appendix E) have not hesitated to speak their minds openly but have faced an uphill task in keeping India's elections free and fair to all. Success in doing so has been internationally recognized in the form of requests for Indian observers, training, and assistance, in conducting elections elsewhere.

ELLORA. A unique city of carved cave temples was created in the **Deccan** between the 7th and 11th centuries CE. The city was damaged and left uninhabited after the Muslim **Bahmani Dynasty** took over the area. The cave temples were accidentally rediscovered in the 19th century and are presently a tourist attraction. Ellora illustrates the flowering and passing of **Buddhist**, **Hindu**, and **Jain** artistry under royal patronage in the early medieval period.

One group of 12 cave temples and monasteries are Buddhist, recalling the equally marvelous wall paintings in nearby **Ajanta**.

Among the 17 cave temples dedicated to various Hindu deities, the huge freestanding Kailasa Temple to **Shiva**, enriched with endless sculpted ornament, is the acme of early art and technology. It was carved out of a single rock by carvers, working from the top downward, in the reign of Krishna I of the **Chalukya** Dynasty. Another group of cave temples is Jain, testifying to the mutual tolerance that was the Indian norm at the time.

ELPHINSTONE, MOUNTSTUART (1778–1859). Elphinstone was born in Scotland and joined the **East India Company** as a writer in 1796. He studied Persian and **Sanskrit**, read Latin and Greek, became versed in Marathi and Gujarati, and published several important works in the course of his life, including a treatise on Afghanistan and a *History of India*. He embodied the qualities of the all around soldier-scholar-diplomat-administrator so highly valued at the time.

Elphinstone's career in India spanned a time of enormous increase in British power on the subcontinent and an evolution in British opinion on how to administer these newly acquired territories. Three broad tendencies emerged. Some men, known as the Orientalists, respected Indian traditions and institutions, saw the danger of hasty innovations, and held their primary duty to be maintenance and restoration of order until such time as Indian society had recovered, so to speak, from its evident torpor. Another group of men, including **William Bentinck** and **Thomas Macaulay**, were radicals with a belief in reason and in progress, advocating bold innovation to redeem a moribund Eastern society through Western wisdom. Elphinstone belonged to a third group, liberal-conservative in attitude, which saw the desirability of introducing some Western ideas while remaining convinced of the strength and value of traditional Indian institutions, and they looked to an eventual integration of the two. Along with Elphinstone, **John Malcolm**, **Charles Metcalfe**, and Thomas Munro belonged to this pragmatic (and prophetic) school and are generally regarded as the best administrators of the period.

When Elphinstone served as resident or advisor to the **Peshwa** at **Poona** from 1810 to 1819, he found that the Maratha system of civil administration and criminal justice worked well under men of integrity.

He introduced some simple rules of procedure and expected the district collectors to exercise their powers with flexibility, humanity, and a personal touch. As governor of **Bombay** from 1819 to 1829, Elphinstone used similar principles and added the education of Indians to his goals. He was ahead of his time in granting public funds to voluntary societies for schools and books and in encouraging education in the vernacular languages as well as in English so that more Indians could fill governmental positions. Among other achievements, he encouraged codification of laws and removal of excessive restrictions on the press. Together, Elphinstone's measures gave Bombay a head start over other parts of British India in the social and political reform movements that gathered momentum in the 19th century.

Elphinstone declined offers of a baronetcy as well as the governor generalship, choosing instead to retire in 1829 to friends and scholarship.

ELWIN, VERRIER (1902–1964). Elwin came to India in 1927 after a brilliant academic record in literature and theology at Oxford. He adopted India as his own country and made significant contributions to the national movement, to the anthropology of tribal communities, and to administrative policy toward tribals. Elwin's work in India into three phases. He first joined a small sect in **Poona** attempting to "indigenize" **Christianity**. He was attracted to **Mahatma Gandhi** and the **Indian National Congress** and wrote a series of books and articles aimed at drawing the Indian Christians into the national movement and presenting the nationalist case before the British public. Elwin also conducted two inquiries on behalf of Congress regarding state repression in **Gujarat** and the **North West Frontier Province**.

In January 1932 Verrier Elwin moved to a tribal village in present day **Madhya Pradesh** with the intention of bringing health care and education to the **Adivasi** communities there. He gradually moved from social work to anthropological study and toured widely through central India during the following two decades. *The Baiga* (1939) *The Muria and The Ghotul* (1947) are among the authoritative monographs that he wrote on different tribal groups, in addition to compiling collections of their folklore. His deep concern about the cultural and economic impoverishment of the adivasis and the urgent need for both colonial administrators and nationalist leaders to take remedial action was best expressed in *The Aboriginals* (1943).

By now an Indian citizen, Elwin was offered the position of Adviser on Tribal Affairs in the North East Frontier Agency—NEFA, present day **Arunachal Pradesh**—in 1954. He worked there with a group of dedicated Indian officials in trying to integrate isolated tribal communities into a newly independent nation without sacrificing their autonomy or distinctive cultures. Elwin's *A Philosophy for NEFA* (2nd ed., 1968) influenced New Delhi's policy and its implementation. Elwin also served on several high level committees on tribal development, delivered lectures on All India Radio, and enjoyed a close relationship with Prime Minister **Jawaharlal Nehru**. He was honored with the Padma Bhushan in 1961. His moving autobiography, *The Tribal World of Verrier Elwin*, was published soon after his sudden death.

EMERGENCY RULE. The aberrant and controversial period of incipient authoritarianism in India to which this applies lasted 20 months from June 1975 to March 1977.

On June 26, 1975, Indian President **Fakhruddin Ahmed**, advised by prime minister **Indira Gandhi** to exercise powers conferred on him by Article 352 of the **Constitution**, proclaimed, "that a grave emergency exists, whereby the security of India is threatened by internal disturbances." The Government of India immediately assumed extraordinary powers, arresting more than 600 opposition leaders under earlier security legislation, imposing rigid press censorship, banning 26 organizations deemed to be "extremist," and suspending judicial protection of the Fundamental Rights granted by the Constitution.

Parliament—with a massive **Congress (I)** majority—formally approved imposition of the Emergency by a vote of 336 to 59 and subsequently confirmed various presidential ordinances. Parliament also initiated sweeping constitutional amendments designed to diminish the powers of the judiciary relative to that of the legislature and to further enhance executive power. Indira Gandhi and her supporters sought to justify the Emergency by the disorders that had preceded it, which included mass agitations and a nationwide railway strike. Her critics accused her of using the Emergency to remain in power despite a ruling against the validity of her election in 1971 by the Allahabad High Court on June 12, 1975, and state election results adverse to Congress.

The prime minister called for national order, discipline, and implementation of a 20-point program of economic development, which temporarily found favor in some quarters including state governments. Her son, Sanjay Gandhi, played a prominent if unconstitutional role, as for example in slum clearance and compulsory sterilization programs, throughout the period of Emergency rule. Administration became more centralized and personalized; it was deprived of normal democratic feedback; it assumed Indira Gandhi's popularity and underestimated popular discontent with the suspension of customary freedoms.

On January 18, 1977, Indira Gandhi announced relaxation of Emergency rules in preparation for general elections to be held in March. Congress lost those elections to the **Janata Party**, campaigning on a promise to "revive Democracy." Emergency was lifted before the new government took office. It appointed a commission in 1978 to inquire into the Emergency and rescinded most of the legislation and constitutional amendments passed under it. No further attempt has been made so far to repeat that episode.

EZHAVA (ILAVA). A community of **Kerala** formerly ranked as *avarna* or **untouchable**. The Ezhavas were in the forefront of social reform movements in Kerala during the late 19th and early 20th centuries.

Dr. Palpu, Sri Narayana Guru, and the poet Kumaran Asan guided their Ezhava community with a skill perhaps unsurpassed by any other **caste** association of the time. The Ezhavas educated their children, gave up practices associated with "lower" castes, such as the eating of meat, animal sacrifice, and polygamy, and "Sanskritized" their religious rites. Further, they used all forms of public education effectively and united their efforts in an association, the Sri Narayana Dharma Paripalana (SNDP) Yogam. This group was able to exert economic, political, and social pressure on the authorities of the time.

An issue of vital interest to the Ezhavas was inter-caste relations in Kerala, where **Hindu** customs with respect to pollution kept temples out of bounds to low castes. The SNDP Yogam launched a crusade against public discrimination based on caste. It staged mass **Satyagraha** in 1924 to open access to the Vaikom temple, and another in 1931–1932 to open access to the Guruvayoor temple. **Mahatma Gandhi** supported these movements of **civil disobedience** and included Kerala in his nationwide campaign against untouchability. Pressure from public opinion mounted; the Princely ruler of Travancore (presently part of Kerala) issued a proclamation in November 1936 abolishing caste restrictions on temple entrance. Upward mobility of the Ezhavas through voluntary and non-violent efforts continued.

– F –

FARID (1175–1265). Farid was a highly venerated **Sufi** who was born in western **Punjab** to an Afghan family that had settled there in the time of **Mahmud of Ghazni**. He was nurtured by his mother on an absolute love of God and was given a traditional education at the *madrassa* (school) attached to a mosque. Later, he became the disciple first of Sheikh Kutbuddin Bhakhtiyar Kaki and then of Khwaja Muinuddin Chisti, renowned Sufi masters. Farid's interpretation of the rules and rituals of the **Chisti** order transformed it into a powerful movement in popular religious culture that attracted many to **Islam**.

Farid traveled widely and stayed close to the people. He used the vernacular languages for his hymns and teachings that were written in the earliest forms of Urdu, Hindi, and Punjabi. Many of Farid's verses in praise of God were later incorporated in the sacred *Granth* of the **Sikhs**. His influence transcended sects; his name was given to a town, and his tomb—endowed by many kings—became a center of pilgrimage for **Hindus**, Muslims, and Sikhs alike.

FAXIAN (also spelled FA-HSIEN) (d. c. 420 CE). He was one of the most famous early Chinese pilgrims to India engaged in locating, copying, and translating authentic **Buddhist** texts. Faxian's special interest was in the *Vinaya-pitaka* on monastic discipline. He left an account of his travels overland from China through Central Asia and throughout large parts of India, which included descriptions of cities and social life.

Faxian spent many years in the **Ganges** and **Yamuna** plains, center of the **Gupta** Empire, during the reign of **Chandra Gupta II Vikramaditya**. His comments on daily life, social customs, and local administration portray the land and people as peaceful, prosperous, and well governed. His chronicle is a principal literary source for the history of the Gupta period.

FERISHTA, MOHAMMAD QASIM. The author of *Gulshan-i-Ibrahimi*, better known as *Tarikh-i-Ferishta*, he wrote in Persian during the early 17th century. The book was translated in the mid-19th century and was published in English as *History of the Rise of the Mahomedan Power In India, Till the Year A.D. 1612*.

Ferishta used diverse sources for his accounts of the **Delhi Sultanate** and other parts of India from the 13th to the 16th centuries. He provides detailed histories of the **Bahmani** kingdoms and of **Vijayanagar** based on documentary and oral sources as well as his firsthand experience in the service of sultans of Ahmednagar and **Bijapur**. He also writes about the early **Mughal** emperors, having traveled in northern India during the reign of Jahangir. Ferishta's statements are generally regarded as accurate and are authenticated by other contemporary evidence. His accounts are especially valuable because many of the documentary sources he was able to tap are no longer available.

FERNANDES, GEORGE (1930–). Born in Mangalore, by the age of 19 Fernandes had launched a political career by joining the Socialist Party in his locality. He moved to **Bombay** and soon became active at a national level. However, he became dissatisfied with the lack of achievement in behalf of industrial workers and to further that aim he formed the *Hind Mazdoor Panchayat* (Indian workers panchayat) in 1958 and the Bombay Labour Cooperative Bank in 1968. Fernandes was elected to the Bombay Municipal Corporation in 1961, and to the **Lok Sabha** 1967–1971, 1977–1979, 1980–1984, and regularly since 1989. He became president of the All-India Railwaymen's Federation in 1973 and called for a nationwide strike in May 1974. The Government of India declared the strike of workers in an essential service illegal, and detained Fernandes and many other union leaders. The threatened railway strike, among other economic, political, and personal crises besetting Prime Minister **Indira Gandhi** at the time, probably strengthened her resolve to declare a national **Emergency** in June 1975 and to incarcerate opposition leaders. Fernandes escaped arrest by going underground. He was implacably opposed to Mrs. Gandhi and to any dialogue with her on restoring normal political life. This was eventually done, in 1977 when the **Congress** was soundly defeated in the general elections. Individualist Fernandes, as Minister of Commerce and Industry, and his tiny Samyukta Socialist Party, were part of the coalition **Janata Party** that formed a short-lived government 1977–1979.

George Fernandes was only briefly married; he lives and dresses simply, and is a nominal **Christian**. He was an advocate for various human rights causes, including those of **Burma** and **Tibet**, while in opposition. Many were surprised, therefore, when he joined the National Democratic Alliance coalition led by the right-wing **Bharatiya Janata Party (BJP)** in 1998 and accepted a cabinet post of Minister of Defence. He continued to serve in that position until May 2004, when the BJP-led coalition government lost the general elections.

FILM INDUSTRY. India is the largest producer of films with mass appeal in the world, and next to the United States has the most influential and independent film industry. Cinema replaced theatre as popular entertainment in the late 1930s and has not been supplanted by television. There are approximately 250 film societies all over India. About 1,000 feature films are produced in a year in all **languages**, especially in Hindi/Urdu, **Tamil**, and Telugu. Styles and content of films vary greatly, reflecting the immense diversity of history, culture, economic and social concerns encompassed in India at any given time as well as over the past decades.

Bollywood, as the center of the film industry is called, churns out many lengthy features that are escapist in intent and content, full of melodrama, song and dance routines, and social stereotypes such as the angry young man and the victimized woman. Bollywood movies reach mass urban and rural audiences and have a wide export market including Africa, Asia, China, the Central Asian Republics, the Middle East, Russia, and throughout the Indian **Diaspora**. Film stars—such as **Raj Kapoor** and **Nargis** in the 1950s, **Amitabh Bachchan** in the 1970s, and Shah Rukh Khan in the 1990s—became familiar figures around the world, as did Indian **music** and dance. Entertaining blockbusters are not the only product of Bollywood. Some films, such as *Salaam Bombay* (1989) or *Lagaan* (2001) have been nominated for an Academy Award and have gained critical international recognition.

The first Indian full-length silent film (subtitled in Hindi), *Raja Harishchandra*, was released in 1899, the first talkie, *Alam Ara* in 1931, and the first color film in 1937. Many remarkable films on social issues were produced in the 1930s and 1940s, including *Mother India* (1938). **Satyajit Ray**'s *Pather Panchali* (1953) heralded the arrival of "new" serious cinema that now has many talented directors who direct public attention to social and political problems, including **Shyam Benegal**, Adoor Gopalkrishnan, Mira Nair, **Anand Patwardhan**, Mrinal Sen, and others. The Film and Television Institute of India in **Pune** offers training and grants that support nonconformist approaches. The film industry in India has also produced prominent political leaders who first gained popularity because of the godlike or heroic roles they played on screen. These include former chief ministers of **Andhra Pradesh** and **Tamil Nadu**. Serious study of Indian films is now part of many academic programs devoted to the study of Indian society.

FOREIGN POLICY/FOREIGN RELATIONS. Jawaharlal Nehru, India's first prime minister, is credited with being the philosopher, architect, engineer, and chief spokesman of independent India's foreign policy. He said his policies flowed naturally from India's geo-strategic location, its history, culture, and unique national movement. He projected a role for India in the world that would appeal to the widest possible strata of Indian opinion and would transcend the many vertical and horizontal divisions within the country. He did not reject the British legacy, explicitly retaining India's membership in the Commonwealth as a Republic, but he was opposed to imperialism. Nehru tried to reconcile a natural tension between national security goals and international systemic goals by pursuing both simultaneously through India's contributions to international law, participation in the United Nations (UN), and efforts to ensure world peace.

Appallingly low socioeconomic indicators in 1940s India—such as average life expectancy: 32 years; literacy rate: 11%; infant mortality rate: 190 per thousand; negligible per capita income or savings—set the domestic determinants of policy. Measuring these against its aspirations of being a democratic, economically dynamic, modern, secular state, India's most urgent need was for peace and economic development. But peace and international attention to alleviating poverty appeared to be evanescent while the Cold War and the national interests of the super powers set the external determinants of policy in the post-**World War II** nuclear age.

Nehru was an internationalist figure in the **Indian National Congress** and formulated his worldview during the inter-war period. He laid out the basic tenets of Indian foreign policy in his first broadcast to the nation as head of the interim government on September 7, 1946, and rephrased them many times thereafter, both before Parliament and the public, as follows.

- India would participate fully and cooperatively in international affairs as an independent nation, not as a satellite of another country.
- India would, "as far as possible," "keep away from the power politics of groups, aligned against one another," that had caused wars before and might do worse in future.
- India believed that peace and freedom were indivisible, was interested in the emancipation of colonial and dependent countries and people, and utterly repudiated racism in any form.
- India offered friendship to the two great modern nations bearing especially heavy responsibilities in shaping world events, the United States and the Soviet Union.
- India stood at the pivot of Asia and looked forward to renewing its friendly contacts with the peoples of Asia, in particular with neighboring China.

The above principles were rooted in national self-interest but were articulated in high-sounding, normative, and idealistic phrases that washed Indian diplomacy in moralistic pomposity at times. The manner in which Nehru's government avoided entangling alliances and steered the ship of state through the shoals of demands and insults from both Cold War rivals earned India's foreign policies the sobriquet of **nonalignment** that was never repudiated by Nehru's successors even when they amended its substance to meet the needs of the moment. Allied to Nehru's personal prestige, nonalignment brought

India international standing, significant economic assistance from both capitalist and socialist developed economies, and apparent influence in world councils during the 1950s that exceeded its tangible power. But India's calls for universal nuclear disarmament were not heeded, and New Delhi chose not to sign the Nuclear Non Proliferation Treaty (NPT) of 1968 on grounds that it was "discriminatory" and did not place equal obligations of restraint on existing and potential nuclear states.

Nonalignment was not salient either to security threats that India faced from Pakistan and from China that preoccupied New Delhi after the border conflict of 1962, or to often-troubled relations with smaller neighbors in South Asia conducted on pragmatic considerations. Nonalignment did appeal, however, to other newly independent states, and a Nonaligned Movement (NAM) was formed in the 1960s. It urged a reformulation of international structures and norms, especially economic ones, so as to benefit weak and developing countries, including India. NAM acted within the United Nations like a trade union. Boosted by high revenues of oil exporting members, NAM took many radical stances during the 1970s that could not be sustained during the "new cold war" and the market emphasis of the 1980s. NAM contributed little more than rhetorical affinity to India's dealings with other Asian and African states, but nonalignment had become a *mantra* that could not be discarded.

The United States found what it called India's "neutralism" (nonalignment) morally repugnant and sought to contain communism through a network of military alliances, which included strategically located **Pakistan**. Thus, relations between the two largest democracies in the world, the United States and India, were what one author called "estranged" throughout the Cold War, despite many mutually beneficial interactions among individuals and in UN Peacekeeping Operations. The Soviet Union initially condemned nonaligned India as a "lackey of imperialism," but after the death of Josef Stalin in 1952, and especially after its rift with China in the late 1950s, Moscow found it advantageous to develop economic, military, and political ties with India. In July 1971, the United States and China established direct and increasingly close links with each other. Both then supported a military government of Pakistan ferociously facing a rebellion in East Pakistan that forced an exodus of 10 million refugees and precipitated a brief winter war won by India and soon to be independent **Bangladesh**. Meanwhile, in August 1971, India and the Soviet Union signed a Treaty of Peace, Friendship, and Cooperation, and the Soviet Union became the main external source of advanced equipment for the **Indian Armed Forces**. In June 1972, India and Pakistan signed the Simla Agreement that promised peaceful and bilateral resolution of all disputes (including **Kashmir**). Official Indo-US relations reached their nadir and remained cool even while the flow of Indian students and highly qualified emigrants to the United States increased over succeeding decades.

The **Janata** government of the late 1970s, and **Indira Gandhi**, after her return to power in 1980, attempted to restore diplomatic balance and improve relations with the West, but they were handicapped by problems at home and by India's uninspiring economic performance under semi-autarchic policies. **Rajiv Gandhi**'s foreign policy initiatives included launching an international campaign for nuclear disarmament that soon lost momentum, sending a peace keeping force to **Sri Lanka** in 1987 that was withdrawn in 1990, and sharply rebuffing the King of **Nepal** for suspending democracy and flirting with China. Also, Rajiv Gandhi undertook an ice-breaking visit to China in 1988 that laid the basis of subsequent improved relations between the neighboring Asian giants. While the end of the Cold War was widely welcomed, India was challenged in 1991 by an acute financial crisis and by the collapse of its steady supporter, the Soviet Union. India appeared to be isolated and boxed into South Asia, with its natural predominance in the region ever challenged by Pakistan.

The shocks of 1991 provided Prime Minister **Narasimha Rao** and his successors from different **political parties** with opportunities for taking policy initiatives that led to the far reaching changes in India's foreign relations that are visible today. These may be summarized as follows:

- **Economic liberalization** and accompanying reforms (see Appendix I) led to expanding trade relations, especially with the European Union, (See Appendix J) and increased attention from capital surplus nations interested in India's emerging large market, including the United States.

- Rao's "Look East" injunction led India to become first a sectoral and then a full dialogue partner with the Association of South East Asian nations (ASEAN) and a member of its Asian Regional Forum that also included China, Japan, and the United States. India became a participant in multilateral discussions of issues of common interest, including Asian security, at various levels of official and non-official interaction.

- In 1992 India awarded the Nehru Prize for International Understanding to Aung San Suu Kyi, the imprisoned leader of **Burma**'s democracy movement. New Delhi also opened talks with the military government of that country on trade and on the security of their common land border, with a view to diluting the preponderant Chinese presence in Myanmar.

- In early1993, India raised its diplomatic recognition of Israel to the ambassadorial level. The two countries shared intelligence on **terrorism**, cooperated in development of arid wastelands, and entered agreement on Israel's supply of certain high-technology defense equipment to India. To the surprise of some, India's multifaceted relations with Islamic countries were not adversely affected. Indian professionals and labor remained important in the Persian Gulf and in Saudi Arabia and interest in laying pipelines to convey oil and gas with an emphasis on energy security strengthened ties between India and Iran.

- The end of apartheid in South Africa in the early 1990s was a triumph for India, and Africa was depicted as a neighbor with which economic and trade relations could expand. (See Appendix J.)

- Security concerns and the desire to articulate India's interests along a wider horizon than the subcontinent led to new cooperative exercises between the Indian navy and other navies, including that of the United States, and a rising Indian profile throughout the Indian Ocean.

- From the mid-1990s, India attempted to bolster the **South Asian Association of Regional Cooperation (SAARC)**, offered special economic and trading incentives to its smaller neighbors, and entered into cooperative arrangements linking the eastern part of the subcontinent with Southeast Asia and Southwest China.

- The nuclear issue loomed large in the 1990s. By the late 1980s, probably, New Delhi had decided that Pakistan's declared possession of (untested) nuclear weapons and the discriminatory nature of the international non-proliferation regime demanded weaponization of India's nuclear option, kept deliberately ambiguous since the Peaceful Nuclear Explosion (PNE) of 1974. The decision on when to test was influenced by the need for absolute secrecy as well as by calculating economic costs of likely international sanctions, but India vigorously resisted foreclosure of its options by indefinite extension of the NPT in 1995 and refused to become a signatory of the 1996 Comprehensive Test Ban Treaty (CTBT) that it had initially co-sponsored. Prime Minister **Atal Behari Vajpayee** ordered India's nuclear tests of May 1998. These, followed by those of Pakistan, had the expected diplomatic fallout of censure by the UN Security Council, Japan, and Australia, but the sanctions imposed were neither universal nor costly.
- Beginning in June 1998, and for more than a year, US Deputy Secretary of State Strobe Talbott engaged in regular dialogue with Indian Special Envoy **Jaswant Singh** that began a transformation of the Indo-US relationship. Washington's better understanding of India's security concerns led it to put unusual pressure on Pakistan in 1999 to withdraw from Kargil and to restore the sanctity of the Line of Control (LOC) in **Jammu and Kashmir**. India's appreciation was expressed in the rapturous welcome given to President Clinton throughout his five-day visit to India in March 2000. Soon after President George W Bush took office, US sanctions on India were quietly dropped, India's **nuclear doctrine** was tacitly accepted, and discussions began on various aspects of bilateral cooperation, including defense. Washington made efforts to look at India as an emerging world power and without hyphenating it with Pakistan, with partial success. For its part, India was the only major country to welcome Bush's proposals for missile defense, and after the terrorist attacks in New York on September 11, 2001, India made an unprecedented offer of its land and airspace for use by the United States in its "war against terror." India assisted in and welcomed overthrow of the Taliban regime in Afghanistan and is an important supporter of

the Karzai government in that country, renewing both ancient and modern ties. Vajapayee referred to democratic India and the United States as "natural allies," and the government of his successor, **Dr. Manmohan Singh**, is currently implementing an agreement on Next Steps in Strategic Partnership together with the administration of re-elected George W. Bush.

- Because the Cold War is now part of history, India's improved relations with the United States had no impact on its relations with Russia. Once Russia had recovered, in part, from the internal problems following the collapse of the Soviet system, it was eager to resume as much of its partnership with India as possible. President Boris Yeltsin's 1993 visit to New Delhi was followed by suggestions of a Russia-China-India strategic partnership, implicitly to balance the hyper power of the United States. Vladimir Putin's visit to India in October 2000 resulted in important defense supply agreements. But private enterprise in both countries has been slow to explore possible markets, and the volume of trade shows a marked decline. (See Appendix J.)
- Pakistan remains a complicating factor in Indo-US relations as well as a constant threat to India through its support of terrorism and low intensity conflict. Traditional Indian diplomacy and intermittent peace overtures have proved to be unequal to the task of either containing or forging a non-hostile relationship with Pakistan. An attempt at coercive diplomacy made in 2002 after terrorist attacks on the Indian Parliament and elsewhere raised international fears of a nuclear conflagration on the subcontinent but also resulted in some Anglo-American pressure on Pakistan President General Musharraf to curtail terrorist activity. Another effort at crafting peace commenced in early 2004 with graduated engagement by Indian and Pakistani officials on different subjects, including trade, water, **Siachin**, and Kashmir, in a "composite dialogue." Popular enthusiasm for peace in both countries is manifest, especially during the playing of cricket test matches that recommenced after 16 years, for which tens of thousands of visas were issued by both governments, Some people believe that Pakistan business is attracted to India's growing economy and that internal political fragility combined with external pres-

sure from allies will persuade the General to settle with India. Others see little evidence of Pakistan's accepting the LOC as the international border and so resolving the Kashmir dispute on realistic grounds, or of the Pakistan Army abandoning its entrenched hostility to India, much less its dominant place in the state of Pakistan. It is thus difficult to predict the future course of India-Pakistan relations.

• Enmity with China, however, has abated and has been replaced by denial of threat from either side and an increasing volume of trade and economic cooperation. Were India to become a full member of the Shanghai Cooperation Organization, there would be many more opportunities for working together to meet their growing energy needs from Central Asia. Exchanges of high level visits between India and China from 1988 to the present have expanded the number of subjects discussed and the areas of possible cooperation. Specific agreements on maintaining peace along the Line of Actual Control (LAC) and confidence-building measures reached in the 1990s diminish the importance of the 1962 border conflict in popular perceptions, and regular meetings of experts hold out the hope of eventual agreement on the long common border. While commercial competition and, perhaps, diplomatic rivalry between India and China may grow, the likelihood of conflict between them is likely to be less.

• India articulated its right to be treated with respect more clearly in the 1990s than at any time since the 1950s. It has formally laid claim to a seat as Permanent Member of the UN Security Council and has won explicit support for it from a number of important governments. India will canvass for more support even though the outcome is entangled in the complications of UN reform. This claim is in keeping with India's widening horizons and emergent power.

It is evident even from the above brief summary that Indian foreign policy today is different from what it was a half-century ago and that Indian foreign relations have expanded to reach countries and subjects, such as inviting private investment and buying equity in oil fields, that were not then feasible. The external environment is at once less hostile to independent India and more complex and variable than during the Cold War. India's socioeconomic indicators certainly have improved over the last 57 years, but the sociopolitical divisions against which Nehru warned remain deep and dangerous. The persistence of old attitudes, even prejudices, can inhibit Indian diplomacy, and old problems continue to burden South Asia. Yet, for all its caution, which is probably wise, India shows a growing sense of self-confidence in dealing with the rest of the world.

FRENCH EAST INDIA COMPANY (COMPAGNIE DES INDES ORIENTALES). It was floated as a joint stock company in Paris with a capital of 15 million pounds sterling in August 1664. The French East India Company was authorized by a royal declaration; its coat of arms carried the royal emblem of the fleur-de-lis; its first shareholders meeting was held in the Louvre Palace and was presided over by King Louis XIV himself. Comptroller General Colbert was elected the first director and was the moving force behind it from the start. Thus, though inspired in large measure by the commercial successes of the **Dutch** and **English East India companies**, the French Company was unlike them in projecting an official rather than a mercantile image.

Trade was not the primary motivation for the French interest in India. Rather, adventurers, explorers, missionaries, men of letters, and soldiers of fortune went to India on varied searches in the 17th century, often from maritime Brittany. Some of them, notably Jean Baptiste Tavernier and Francois Bernier, wrote accounts of their travels through and beyond **Mughal** domains that sparked French interest and did much to mold European images at the time of India's great wealth and exotic social customs.

A French Ambassador won the favor of Princess Jahanara, daughter of the Mughal Emperor **Shah Jahan**, and obtained permission to establish a trading post at **Surat** in 1666. The Sultan of Golconda granted the right to a trading post on the Coromandel Coast at Masulipatam in 1669 and followed that a year later with a gift of land for settlement at **Pondicherry**. Within two decades the French Company had obtained a trading concession in **Bengal** at Chandernagore, and by 1721 it had established a post at Mahe on the Malabar coast of southwest India.

Notwithstanding these gains, the Company did not prosper. Its disabilities were largely self-created: capital was diverted from trade to fortifying trading posts and acquiring lands for colonization on Madagascar; the small group of monopolistic shareholders was unwilling to float loans or expand its base of financial support in ways used by the Dutch and English; French industry and the customs bureaucracy were antagonistic to imports of superior Indian textiles and levied prohibitory tariffs to keep them out; constant wars against the English in India were costly. Fortunes improved in the mid-18th century when French taxes were reduced, demand increased, and the Company's traffic between India and France rose to 11 ships a year as compared with one ship in two years. The French reached their zenith at Pondicherry. Mughal Emperor Muhammad Shah rewarded **Joseph Dupleix**'s military victories against the English in the Carnatic Wars of the 1740s with high rank and title, *jagirs* (see Glossary) or land holdings, and the right to mint coins.

For more than 50 years France and Britain were more or less constantly at war on land and sea, in Europe, America, and India, where they backed rival Princes, engaged directly in hostilities, and handed territories back and forth. Pondicherry, Chandernagore, and Mahe remained French possessions through the period of British rule in India; their reintegration with India was negotiated after independence. Frenchmen continued to travel and work in India through the 18th and early 19th centuries. Some of them contributed their skills to the military prowess of Indian Princes, including the Nizam of **Hyderabad**, **Mahadji Sindhia**, **Haidar Ali**, and **Maharaja Ranjit Singh**. Some made fortunes; some, such as Abbe Jean-Antoine Dubois, made notable contributions to European scholarship on India. Indian fables, epics, and the images of India garnered by men of the French East India Company and its offshoots passed into French literature and also nourished attitudes that came to be known as Orientalism.

– G –

GAMA, VASCO DA (1460–1524). Da Gama sailed around the Cape of Good Hope after a half-century of **Portuguese** navigational effort to reach India. He arrived in command of the *San Gabriel* at Calicut, a thriving port and small independent principality on the Malabar Coast in southwest India, in May 1498. He returned in 1500 to establish a trading post or "factory" and again in 1502 to blast the port and capture or plunder Arab vessels.

Vasco da Gama opened the era of European expansion in the Indian Ocean and was a man typical of his role. A devout Roman Catholic who kept a nightlong vigil in a Lisbon chapel before his historic voyage, he was ruthless in his treatment of non-Christians. Vasco da Gama was appointed governor of all Portuguese possessions in India shortly before he died in **Cochin**. *See also* PORTUGUESE.

GANDHARA. An area in the upper **Indus** valley on the northwest of the subcontinent, now within the borders of **Pakistan** and Afghanistan, Gandhara features prominently in early Indian history and epic literature. Further, an interplay of Indian, Persian, and Hellenistic influences there produced a unique school of Gandhara art and aesthetic appreciation.

Gandhara sculpture and art were intimately associated with the evolution of Mahayana **Buddhism** in the last centuries BCE and its spread along trade routes through Central Asia. Freestanding and bas relief images of the **Buddha** in various stylized postures were sculpted and stories from his life and teachings rendered in stone with fluid vitality. Western observers recall Greek naturalism.

Gandhara artists evidently enjoyed the patronage of the **Kushan** rulers as well as wealthy merchants. Equally important, there was a strong demand for their products from pilgrims, traders, and travelers in a wide region of many countries. Excavations along the **Silk Road** and around **Taxila** continue to uncover exquisite examples of Gandhara art, though much has been destroyed in recent wars and fundamentalist waves of **Islam** in the region.

GANDHI, INDIRA (1917–1984). Indira Gandhi was the elected prime minister of India from January 1966 to March 1977 and again from January 1980 to October 1984. Indira Priyadarshani (Nehru) Gandhi was the only child of **Jawaharlal Nehru** and his wife, Kamala. **Motilal Nehru** quelled family disappointment that his first grandchild was not a boy by retorting, "This daughter of Jawahar, for all we know, may prove better than a thousand sons" (Inder Malhotra, *Indira Gandhi*: 26). The remark is often quoted.

Indira described her childhood as "lonely" and "insecure." Not only did she lack companionship of her own age and feel that her frail mother was insufficiently appreciated in the Nehru household, she grew up at a time when the whole family and their friends, including **Mahatma Gandhi**, were intensely engaged in the national movement. She had a peripatetic and unsystematic education, too young to fully understand the letters her father wrote from prison in the early 1930s (later published as Nehru's *Glimpses of World History*) and fully enjoying only a year at the college in Shantiniketan founded by **Rabindranath Tagore**, and one year at Somerville College, Oxford, shortly after her mother died in Lausanne in 1936. The outside world, represented by the British Government of India, struck hard and repeatedly at the liberty, property, and connubial life of her family. To some analysts of her political record, it seemed as if Indira never lost her sense of solitariness in a hostile world, always sought security in ways that made her intolerant of criticism, and identified herself so completely with India that she made little distinction between her person, her family, her government, and her country.

On her return to India in early 1941, Indira defied social custom and cautionary advice by marrying a young **Parsi**, Feroze Gandhi, (who had courted her in Europe) the following year. The couple was imprisoned (separately) in the wake of the **Quit India movement** and then set up house in Lucknow where their sons Rajiv and Sanjay were born in 1944 and 1946. Indira was also attentive to her father's needs after his release from prison and his appointment as interim prime minister in 1946. She moved into Nehru's house in **New Delhi** and kept it running through the agonies of **Partition** and the establishment of independent India's first government. Feroze Gandhi became a member of Parliament and made a name for himself as an outspoken critic of Nehru's government. Long before being widowed in 1960, Indira had become her father's closest confidante and counselor, while maintaining a quiet and modest demeanor.

Indira Gandhi was elected to the Congress Working Committee in 1955 and president of the **Congress Party** in 1959. She was responsible for two difficult decisions that year: to separate **Gujarat** and **Maharashtra** on the linguistic basis recommended by the **States**

Reorganization Commission; and to dismiss the elected government of **Kerala** formed by the **Communist Party of India** and impose president's rule there preparatory to new elections. She did not seek office in the last years of Nehru's life but was appointed Minister of Information and Broadcasting by Prime Minister **Lal Bahadur Shastri** in 1964. Mrs. Gandhi demonstrated the same kind of charisma, personal rapport with the Indian masses, and vote-getting ability that Nehru had possessed. After Shastri's unexpected death in 1966 the collective leadership of Congress, known as "the Syndicate," backed her candidacy as successor, reportedly because they mistakenly considered her to be pliable, a *"ghungi guriya"* or "dumb doll." Subsequently challenged by **Morarji Desai** in the Congress Parliamentary Party, Indira won an election against him by a vote of 355 to 169.

Mrs. Gandhi's inheritance in office was harsh, with India reeling from two and a half wars in four years, two changes of top leadership forced by death, an insurgency in the northeast, and successive monsoon failures threatening food grain production. She was handicapped by her own administrative inexperience and awkwardness in parliament as well as the lack of national or party consensus on how to deal with these problems. Her decision to devalue the rupee in 1966, without adequate preparation at home or financial assistance from abroad, for example, had disastrous political consequences. Congress won only 283 seats in the 520-seat **Lok Sabha** and lost power in eight states in the general elections of 1967. However, Indira herself won the sobriquet "Mother India" as she appealed to the people over the heads of party bosses and promised to "look after the weaker members of my family." Her penchant for populism deepened as her dislike grew for the pressures put on her by the Syndicate. There was a struggle over the choice of candidate to succeed President **Zakir Husain** who died in May 1969. Vice President **V. V. Giri** won with Mrs. Gandhi's active support, but the Congress Party split in two; the majority went with Indira and the rump was called Congress (O).

Indira Gandhi effectively established dominance over party, parliament, and country. She reshuffled her cabinet, created a new external intelligence agency, and initiated several populist ("leftist") measures including the nationalization of banks, introduction of a commission to regulate future expansion of industry and trade, abolition of the old managing agency system, and abolition of the princes' privy purses. The **Supreme Court** of India invalidated the latter measure but was subsequently unable to prevent its passage into law. General elections were announced for early 1971, and Mrs. Gandhi conducted her election campaign with ferocious energy on the platform of "*Garibi Hatao*" or "Remove Poverty." Congress won a sensational victory with 352 seats in the Lok Sabha. Parliament nationalized insurance and took for itself the right to amend any part of the **Constitution**, including the chapter on Fundamental Rights. In a close (7:6) judgment of February 1973, a full bench of the Supreme Court allowed Parliament that right, provided that the "essential features" of the Constitution were kept intact. Mrs. Gandhi retaliated by bypassing senior judges in choosing a Chief Justice. She called for "committed" civil servants and judges to serve the country.

Through 1971, Indira Gandhi and her government grappled with the immense problems of 10 million refugees thrown on India by the genocidal actions of the **Pakistan** army in East Bengal. She also undertook an extensive diplomatic campaign with other governments; she was largely successful, except with American President Richard Nixon who supported Pakistan as part of his opening to China. Mrs. Gandhi's government signed a Treaty of Peace, Cooperation, and Friendship with the Soviet Union in August 1971 and prepared for an apparently inevitable war. A rapid and complete Indian victory brought about the liberation of **Bangladesh** in December, followed speedily by a withdrawal of the Indian army and fresh agreements with an elected government of the new nation. In a further act of statesmanship, Mrs. Gandhi signed the Simla Agreement with Prime Minister Zulfiqar Ali Bhutto of Pakistan in June 1972 to peacefully resolve all conflicts bilaterally. Relations with the United States improved after 1973 but did not become close.

Although Indira Gandhi lacked the wide vision and idealistic stance her father had, she too took an active role on the world stage, not only in the **Nonaligned Movement** which elected her chairman in 1983, but also interacting with other chief executives in Europe and Asia. She was impatient with "moral influence" and wanted India to build tangible power. To that end, she encouraged scientists in India's **nuclear power program** to proceed with an underground "peaceful nuclear explosion" in May 1974. She did not follow this with a weapons program, however, but accepted the enhanced prestige (and penalties) for India of "nuclear capability."

The year 1973 brought a precipitate slide downwards in the economic and political conditions of India, with concomitant factionalism in Congress. Party elections were cancelled in 1972 and were not held for twenty years; party funds were collected in ways that invited charges of corruption. Governmental controls on the economy were collectively derided as the "license permit *raj*" and stunted legitimate growth but stimulated a parallel economy in "black money." Both party and government became over-centralized and over-personalized, with New Delhi intervening openly in state level political struggles. A rash of strikes and protests against anti-inflationary measures reached a crescendo in the railway strike of May 1974 led by **George Fernandes**; it was crushed brutally. A near-revolutionary "J. P. Movement" swept **Gujarat** and **Bihar** behind the saintly figure of **J. P. Narayan**. Mrs. Gandhi perceived a "grave threat" to the country "in peril from internal and external enemies" with "no one else" but herself to "save" it. When the Allahabad High Court ruled against her on June 12, 1975, for relatively minor infractions of election laws in 1971 she appealed to the Supreme Court. Obtaining only a conditional stay order on June 24 and confronted by J. P.'s mass rally in Delhi, Mrs. Gandhi advised the president to issue a proclamation of Emergency under Article 352 of the Constitution. Her government arrested several hundreds of persons secretly that night.

The imposition of **Emergency Rule** proved to be a catastrophic mistake for Indira. She withdrew into her shell. Her son Sanjay became prominent, and the excesses committed in his name, particularly in furtherance of family planning through vasectomies, swelled by word of mouth in the absence of an unfettered press. Mrs. Gandhi announced new elections in January 1977 and lifted the Emergency in March. She and Congress as a whole were abandoned by the minorities and were soundly defeated by the **Janata** coalition party. The new government appointed Supreme Court Justice J. C. Shah to investigate Mrs. Gandhi's excesses. Justice Shah publicly vilified her, and she was arrested and briefly imprisoned in December 1978. Ironically, that episode helped to rehabilitate Indira's public image, and when the Janata government fell apart in 1979 she was poised for a return to power.

Mrs. Gandhi's reliance on her son Sanjay was very obvious after her reelection as prime minister in January 1980. She did not conceal her expectation that he would succeed her. His death in an air crash that summer was a crushing personal blow that she bore with outward courage and calm and by an introduction of her elder son, **Rajiv Gandhi**, to the party and to politics. But Indira was not able to handle the many economic, political, and security problems then besetting India with equal good sense. Nor did she have experienced and wise counsel. In pursuit of electoral gains and an assumed "Hindu Vote," she stooped to petty and communal politics that only exacerbated sectarian tensions. For example, her mishandling of problems in the **Punjab** prevented normalization and permitted the growth of **terrorism** and a strengthening of **Sikh** militants. Her order to the Indian army to crush the latter through Operation Blue Star on June 6, 1984, led directly to her assassination, at the hands of two of her Sikh security guards, on the morning of October 31, 1984.

GANDHI, MOHANDAS KARAMCHAND (also known as **MAHATMA GANDHI**) **(1869–1948).** Gandhi's life is a testimony to the impact that one individual can have on history. Mohandas entered adulthood as an ordinary, diffident, middle **caste** (*vaisya*) man. He became the leader of the Indian national movement, mobilizing millions of people, but he never lost touch with the common man and woman. They called him Bapu, or father, and he communicated with them in a moral yet practical language to which they responded with confidence. In their service he discovered wells of courage in himself and inspired people to overcome fear and perform extraordinary feats, no less heroic for being non-violent. The result was a peaceful transfer of power from British to Indian hands in 1947.

Gandhi's life was singularly transparent. In the course of his unceasing search for truth, which he equated with God, Gandhi shared his thoughts on every matter from the most intimate to the most public with others, through his journals *Indian Opinion, Young India,* and *Harijan,* several thought-provoking books, including *Hind Swaraj* (1909), *Ethical Religion* (1922), and a two-volume autobiography, *Story of My Experiments with Truth* (1922, 1927), and through countless letters giving attention, affection, and advice as necessary. His collected writings fill 90 large volumes. The literature about him is equally voluminous.

Mohandas was born in a small **Princely State** of present-day **Gujarat** where his father was dewan (see Glossary). He was the fourth child and was married to Kasturbai at the age of 13, shortly before his father died. He was an indifferent student, self-conscious of his failings but willing to experiment with forbidden pastimes. He kept a promise to his pious mother that he would abstain from alcohol, meat, and sex when studying in England from 1888 to 1891. On returning to India, he was unable to make a living in **Bombay** as a practicing lawyer. A job offer from an Indian merchant in South Africa involved in a civil suit took Gandhi there in May 1893. He stayed for 20 years of crucial experience. Gandhi found himself among a timid Indian community that was drawn from diverse backgrounds and faced with harsh racial discrimination in law and daily life. Gandhi taught himself the political skills of organization, negotiation, and publicity through practice. From unpromising beginnings he rose to lead a heterogeneous group—of men and women, followers of **Hinduism** and **Islam**, rich and poor, businessmen and laborers, people from different parts of India—in unified protest. This **Satyagraha**, that included agitation, protest marches, non-violent resistance to unjust laws, and intermittent imprisonment, lasted over a period of years. This unprecedented movement in South Africa won some concessions for Indians from General Jan Smuts in 1908 and 1914. That the concessions were minimal in nature does not detract from the importance of what Gandhi discovered and put into practice then, and later in India.

Through experience as well as readings in Christian, Hindu, Muslim, and other religious texts, Gandhi was convinced that all persons have an innate spark of truth or the divine, which can be heard in the inner voice of conscience by those who prepare themselves by austerities to be receptive, and which can be appealed to in others by those whose struggle is self-disciplined and truthful. For him, individual freedom and the individual conscience were of the highest importance. He could consider no system of government that violated these legitimate. Searching for non-exclusive, non-sectarian criteria of truth, and for means appropriate to noble ends, Gandhi was satisfied only with *ahimsa* (see Glossary), or non-violence, that is, abstention from doing harm in thought, word and deed, and action suffused with love without attachment to personal gain. He expounded on this theme frequently throughout his life, ruling out any equation of non-violence with passivity or lack of courage. His belief in the spiritual nature of man made him passionately dedicated to religious tolerance; his public prayer meetings and the daily routine in the ashrams (see Glossary) that he established included hymns and recitations from many religious traditions. He enjoyed close relations with persons, such as **C. F. Andrews**, of different faith than his own.

Gandhi's personal life in South Africa also underwent radical and permanent change toward simplicity, looking after his needs by his own labor and casting off possessions. He withdrew his children from school and set up a small community farm at Phoenix near Durban in 1904, where he tried out the theories of John Ruskin, Henry Thoreau, and Leo Tolstoy. (He entered into correspondence with the latter.) Gandhi took a formal vow of celibacy in 1906. He redoubled his emphasis on the value of physical labor in India; the symbol of this commitment was the spinning wheel at which he spent time daily and enjoined on his followers as well. Gandhi further reduced his diet to the minimum and his garments to the sandals, loincloth, and cotton shawl of a typical peasant. He fasted regularly as a means of spiritual discipline, often in self-imposed mortification over actions that he opposed. He formulated his ideas on the future of India along the same ethical principles. These ideas were spelled out in *Hind Swaraj*, a biting castigation of the materialism, hedonism, exploitation, and mechanistic tyranny of Western industrial civilization as he observed it. He exhorted Indians to base national life on village self-sufficiency rather than dependence on foreign goods, on inter-dependence and harmony rather than on competition and exploitation. On the eve of independence in the 1940s, Gandhi repeated his conviction that India would not gain true *swaraj* (independence) until its economy was self-sustaining and village-based. Gandhi's economic ideas found faint echo in the non-justiciable directive principles of the **Indian Constitution** but were not adopted by the independent Government of India. They have been put into practice by various individuals and **non-governmental organizations** in scattered pockets of India and ironically find some resonance in the post-industrial West of today.

Gandhi returned permanently to India in January 1915 where he received a hero's reputation. In deference to a suggestion made by his mentor, **Gopal Krishna Gokhale**, Gandhi abstained from political comment and stayed aloof from **Annie Besant** and the **Home Rule Movement**. Instead, he set up Sabarmati ashram near **Ahmedabad**, went to Shantiniketan to spend time with **Rabindranath Tagore**, and traveled around the country. He was appalled by the poverty to which most Indians had been reduced under British rule. He wanted to lead a religious life but found he could not do so unless he identified himself with mankind. He felt bound to respond with maternal (the quality to which he aspired) solicitude to injustice or grievance calling for help; this led him inexorably into politics, as he did not find it possible to divide economic, political, social, and religious work into watertight compartments.

The first calls came from the peasants of Champaran in **Bihar**, squeezed by the rack rents of indigo planters, and the textile mill workers in Ahmedabad who were working on a pittance wage. Gandhi used the methods of Satyagraha—meticulous collection of data, definition of the principle at stake, setting of minimum demands, patient negotiation, timely publicity, non-violent resistance to pressure—in both cases, with success. Able young educated volunteers, including **Jawaharlal Nehru**, **Vallabhbhai Patel**, and **Rajendra Prasad**, soon joined him in his work and were inspired. Gandhi imparted the non-violent values of Satyagraha to those who agitated against the **Rowlatt Acts** and the massacre at **Jallianwala Bagh** in 1919 and explained them to his British inquisitors too, as he was to do throughout his life when leading movements of **civil disobedience**. He formed networks of loyalty among those who had personal links with him or who commanded local support. Gandhi was convinced that Hindus and Muslims could and should work together for the cause of Indian independence. He championed the cause of the interned **Ali brothers**, **Mohammed and Shaukat**, and embraced the **Khilafet movement** as his own in 1919. In the course of 1920 he persuaded the rank and file of the **Indian National Congress**, over the heads of its established leadership, to join him in a non-violent **Non-Cooperation Movement** as the shortest road toward attaining *swaraj* from the British. A formal resolution to this effect was passed at the Nagpur session of Congress in December 1920. Gandhi called off the movement in 1922 after incidents of violence but did not lose faith in its efficacy.

For the next 25 years, Gandhi was the accepted leader of Congress, although seldom in a formal position. Members of the Congress Working Committee deferred to him even when they differed with his views, tactics, or choice of persons to lead, as they frequently did. Gandhi's dramatic rise to power within Congress as an outsider is the subject of many studies. Contributing factors were, briefly, as follows: The old leadership of Congress had passed away, and neither moderate nor revolutionary methods espoused by them were effective after **World War I**; Gandhi offered new approaches to national regeneration that caught the imagination of many, many Indians. Mahatma Gandhi's charismatic name had the power to move millions of village dwellers, especially after the success of early Satyagrahas, to identify Gandhi with their own local causes and swell the ranks of nationalists. Indian politicians, who seldom were converted wholly to his ideal of non-violence, calculated that their local and provincial interests would be better served by alliance with him than by opposition, and so joined in the all-India national struggle. Thus, new groups in Bihar, Gujarat, **Madras**, **Punjab**, and present-day **Uttar Pradesh** joined with older groups from **Bengal** and **Bombay** in Congress. Moreover, when Congress dues were reduced to four annas (one quarter rupee) on Gandhi's suggestion, masses of new members were enrolled in the 1920s and after. Students and women were inspired by him to participate in civil disobedience and public life as never before, imparting mass urban support for the national struggle. Congress under Gandhi's leadership truly became an all-India umbrella-like representative organization.

Mahatma Gandhi's personal prestige waxed in India as he willingly accepted suffering, through fasting and imprisonment, rather than disregard his conscience. Gandhi's fame spread through the world, too, because the British made a martyr of him and also negotiated directly with him, as in the **Gandhi-Irwin Pact** and the **Round Table Conference** of the early 1930s, and he attracted attention from the international press. Mahatma Gandhi seemed to fit the ancient Indian image of a renouncer active in the world and became a model of the saintly idiom in Indian politics.

Despite his political activity, Gandhi himself placed more emphasis on his constructive work, that is the reconstruction of village life, imparting dignity to physical labor and ameliorating conditions for the **Untouchables**, whom he called Harijan or Children of God, by bringing about a change of heart among higher-caste Hindus. He supported legislation as well as civil disobedience to secure temple entry for Harijans—such as the **Ezhavas** of **Kerala**—collected funds for them, and often lived among them. Gandhi spent years in constructive work between periods of imprisonment and peaks in his political career, marked by the Non-Cooperation Movements of 1920–1922, 1930–1934, and 1940–1942. It was his wish that once independence was achieved, Congress should abjure office and devote itself to constructive work among the people. But Gandhi's hold on Congress had weakened by the mid-1940s, and his wish remained unfulfilled. Gandhi's inner search for truth and purity continued, causing several British officials to wonder aloud whether he was saint, politician, or social reformer. Gandhi was more like a revolutionary in his drive to transform society and human psychology, but he was a revolutionary in a mask of tradition because of his use of religious symbols and his refusal to countenance forceful methods of change. He has been both compared and contrasted with China's Mao Zedong.

Gandhi was a controversial figure who continues to provoke criticism from different ideological sources for the limitations and failures of his leadership. The main criticisms are, briefly: Gandhi's ethical standards of personal and public conduct were set too high for the common man or average politician, contributing to hypocrisy in Congress. It was difficult to synchronize means and ends. In contrast, the sinews of Satyagraha, including fasting, were easily corrupted in his absence to pressure tactics exerted for parochial interests. Gandhi's non-violence may have been unrealistic and unworkable on an all-India scale. By calling off the all-India Non-Cooperation Movements when he did, in 1922 and 1932 and by allowing the **Quit India** movement to proceed in 1942 without adequate training or preparation, he is accused of having retarded independence, not advanced it. Some see Gandhi's attitude toward Untouchables as patronizing, also the term Harijan; in calling for conversion, not compulsion, of the higher castes, he failed to recognize or tackle the economic and political basis of oppression in Hindu society. Some **Dalits** accuse Gandhi of helping perpetuate their misery by successfully opposing **Dr. B. R. Ambedkar**'s bid to win separate electorates for Untouchables under the **Government of India Act of 1935**. Marxists typically criticize Gandhi's economic theories and his acceptance of financial support from wealthy Indian businessmen as being reactionary; they do not recognize him as a revolutionary.

Further, say other critics, Gandhi's use of prayer and tradition in mobilizing the masses, Hindu and Muslim, propelled a process of mixing religion with politics with baleful effects in India. It first alienated and was later emulated by the secular elitist **Mohammed Ali Jinnah** to mobilize Indian Muslims. The flood of religious passion got out of hand, leading to exacerbated communal conflict and eventually the **Partition** that Gandhi so bitterly opposed but was powerless to prevent. Gandhi's immense personal courage in quenching the flames of communal conflict and succoring its (Muslim) victims at **Calcutta** and Noakhali in 1946 is undeniable. But it antagonized many orthodox Hindus who were already offended by Gandhi's championing of Muslims and Untouchables and his adoption of some Christian maxims and practices. One such offended **brahman** member of the **Rashtriya Swayamsevak Sangh (RSS)**, **Nathuram Godse**, shot Mahatma Gandhi dead on his way to an afternoon prayer meeting in **New Delhi** on January 30, 1948.

GANDHI, RAJIV (1944–1991). Rajiv was the elder of two sons born to Feroze and **Indira Gandhi**. He was educated at the Doon School, Dehra Dun, and at Cambridge University, England. He married an Italian Catholic, Sonia Maino, in 1968 and fathered two children. He became a pilot with Indian Airlines and, despite his family background, shunned politics for most of his life.

Prime Minister Indira Gandhi persuaded Rajiv to become her close advisor in place of his brother, Sanjay, who died in an air crash in 1980. Rajiv was elected to the **Lok Sabha** from his brother's constituency in **Uttar Pradesh** and was elevated to the position of general secretary of the **Congress (1) Party** in 1983. The dignity and forbearance that he displayed at the time of his mother's assassination on October 31, 1984, earned him plaudits, and almost immediately he was sworn in as prime minister by President **Zail Singh**. He led the Congress (I) to a record victory in the general elections of December 1984.

Prime Minister Rajiv Gandhi's charm, youthful energy, and modern outlook on science and technology won him initial popularity at home and abroad. So did his introduction of reforms toward **economic liberalization**, his attempts to cleanse and rejuvenate the Congress (I), and the accords he signed with rebel leaders in **Assam** and the **Punjab** in order to heal conflicts. However, he lacked the political skill to sustain gains or resolve the serious problems facing the government. His assertive foreign policy, which included sending Indian troops to assist **Sri Lanka** to quell insurgency, proved costly in men, money, and damaged prestige, and his government was tainted with allegations of deep corruption. The Congress (I) was defeated in the 10th general elections of December 1989.

After the successive collapse of two minority governments, led respectively by **V. P. Singh** and **Chandra Shekhar**, forced India to the polls again, Rajiv Gandhi led a vigorous campaign for reelection in the early summer of 1991. He was assassinated by a suicide bomber belonging to the Liberation Tigers of Tamil Eelam, a Sri Lankan terrorist organization, while addressing a campaign meeting in **Madras** on May 21, 1991.

GANDHI, SONIA (1946–). Born Sonia Maino to a working-class family in the Italian village of Ovassanjo near Turin, she met **Rajiv Gandhi** in England while he was a student at Cambridge in 1965 and married him three years later in the residence of his mother, Prime Minister **Indira Gandhi**, who became very fond and solicitous of her elder daughter-in-law. Sonia was a shy woman, strongly opposed to her husband leaving his job as an airline pilot and entering politics at the behest of his mother in 1980. She complied, however, renouncing her Italian citizenship in 1983 in order to become an Indian national and model spouse of a public figure. Sonia's fears were exacerbated when Rajiv Gandhi was assassinated in May 1991 during an election campaign. She retired with their two children into a large and tightly secured residence provided by the Indian government in central New Delhi and refused to assume leadership of the **Congress Party** that was offered to her. Nevertheless, she continued to receive formal visits from Congress Prime Minister **P. V. Narasimha Rao**, foreign dignitaries, other public figures, and various supplicants. She also inherited charge of trusts and funds of the **Nehru** family and soon became head of the newly established Rajiv Gandhi Foundation.

The Congress fared poorly in the general elections of 1996, securing only 120 seats in the **Lok Sabha** (See Appendix H), and turned again to Sonia Gandhi for leadership. This time she did not decline. She embarked on a hurricane election campaign in 1998, trying to emulate the style of her mother-in-law, delivering carefully prepared speeches in Hindi, and making emotional appeals on the basis of her (husband's) family's contribution to the nation. She succeeded in her own constituency, and since Congress won 141 seats in the Lok Sabha, Sonia Gandhi was invited to be Leader of the Opposition. She made a bid to form a minority government with outside support when **Atal Behari Vajpayee**'s government lost a vote of confidence in April 1999 but failed. She refused to try and build a coalition government with other **political parties** and also scorned the idea of forming coalitions in the states, saying that Congress would contest all elections alone. Congress appeared to be held together only by loyalty to what was called "the dynasty." The party was humiliated in the 1999 elections, reduced to only 114 seats in the Lok Sabha; Congress also lost control of **Madhya Pradesh** and **Rajasthan** in their December 2003 elections to state legislative assemblies. Though Sonia Gandhi remained leader of the faction-ridden Congress, she had alienated many able members of her party, some of whom left to form factional parties of their own, such as **Sharad Pawar** with the Congress National Party.

In preparation for the 2004 general elections, Sonia Gandhi made overtures to leaders of splinter groups and other political parties opposed to the **Bharatiya Janata Party (BJP)**-led coalition in power, without much initial success. Sonia conducted a vigorous election campaign throughout the country, as did her son and daughter, for the fourteenth general election and won a surprise victory. BJP attacks on her foreign origin and **Christian** religion failed. She and her son won seats to the **Lok Sabha** from **Uttar Pradesh**, and Sonia Gandhi was elected Leader of the Congress Parliamentary Party. Although this position entitled her to become prime minister, and many urged her to do so, she graciously and wisely declined in May 2004, in favor of **Dr. Manmohan Singh**.

GANDHI-IRWIN PACT (1931). The **Civil Disobedience** movement initiated by the **Dandi March** of 1930 generated worldwide publicity, rallied massive new support for the **Indian National Congress**, and paralyzed the functioning of the British Government of India for months. **M. K. Gandhi** and other Congress leaders were imprisoned. Governor General **Lord Irwin** considered how best to resolve the stalemated situation. He tried, but failed, to persuade Congress to participate in the first **Round Table Conference** on constitutional reform scheduled to meet in London later that year. Gandhi knew that the Congress Working Committee had refused to halt civil disobedience or to consider any cooperation with the government, without having its essential conditions of a promise of *purna swaraj* (independence) met, but he was concerned by the effects of a breakdown of discipline, police brutality, and economic hardships on common people.

"Moderates" M. R. Jayakar and **Tej Bahadur Sapru** prepared the ground for direct talks between Gandhi and Irwin. Probably recollecting how his meetings with J. C. Smuts in 1908 and 1911 had somewhat improved the conditions of Indians in South Africa, Gandhi wrote a personal letter (from prison) to Irwin asking for an interview. The governor general responded favorably, hoping to establish personal rapport with the Mahatma. The two men met several times in late February and early March 1931, not so much as political opponents but as two spiritually sensitive human beings; they convinced each other of their personal sincerity. They deferred constitutional issues to future discussions in London and tackled the practical problems arising from the Indian boycott of British goods, police conduct with those engaged in **Satyagraha**, government forfeiture of lands, and the salt monopoly.

What came to be known as the Gandhi-Irwin Pact was agreement on a limited list of items announced on March 5, 1931. Congress agreed to halt civil disobedience; the government agreed to withdraw the special powers and punitive police detailed for it but ruled out inquiry into police misconduct. The government agreed to release all prisoners taken during the civil disobedience movement, restore forfeited lands if not sold, treat village officials applying for their old posts with liberality, and not prosecute persons collecting salt for home consumption. The government monopoly on salt remained. Congress did not modify its demand for responsible government and *purna swaral,* but it agreed to participate in the ongoing London discussions on constitutional reform and proposed federation between **Princely States** and British India.

GANGES or GANGA RIVER. This river flows from its sources in the Indian **Himalaya** in northwest **Uttaranchal** state more than 2,500 kilometers southeast to the Bay of Bengal. The plains on either side are among the most fertile and densely populated regions of the world and form the heartland of what is known as Hindustan, cradle of traditional Indian civilization. Well over 300 million people inhabit these cultivated plains at the present time, although evidence has been found of dense forests standing as late as the 16th and 17th centuries. The Ganga is formed from the joining of the Alakananda and Bhagirathi mountain rivers, after which it emerges at Rishikesh and descends to the plains at **Hardwar**. Running as a broad, golden, and slow moving stream, it receives several major tributaries including the **Yamuna**, the Gomati and, from the south, the Son. The waters are perennial, fed by melting snows and monsoon rains, and have filled irrigation canals in the Doab or land between the rivers since the fourth century BCE; many more canals were constructed in the 12th and the 19th centuries.

Many famous cities, ancient and modern, stand on the banks of the Ganges, including **Allahabad**, **Varanasi**, and **Pataliputra**. The Ganges is navigable for most of its course and was an important bearer of trade before railways were constructed in the 19th century. The river turns south near Farakka, below which its large delta commences. **Calcutta** is situated on a western distributary and, in order to flush out its badly silted port, a barrage was constructed at Farakka. The mighty **Brahmaputra** joins the Ganga and augments the eastern distributaries in present-day **Bangladesh**.

The Ganges is the most sacred river in India and is personified as a goddess whose various names indicate her qualities: "swift-goer," "milky way," "flowing from heaven," and "from Vishnu's left foot." The myth of origin is that **Vishnu** yielded to the austerities of a great sage and sent the goddess Ganga to earth; Shiva caught the waters in his matted hair so that the sage and those whose salvation he sought could bathe in them. Most **Hindus** believe in the high spiritual merit of drinking and bathing in Ganga waters as well as submersing the earthly remains of their bodies in it. Centers of pilgrimage abound along the river, with the **Kumbha Mela** held at confluences attracting millions. Though the Ganga is mentioned but twice in the Rig **Veda** it obviously gained importance in post Vedic times. The epic *Mahabharata* features the goddess Ganga prominently, as wife of King Santanu and mother of Bhishma. Pollution of the river became a major issue in the late 20th century, with various schemes put forward but indifferent success.

GHADR (GADAR) PARTY. Founded in San Francisco by **Lala Hardayal** in 1913, this was a revolutionary group dedicated to the goal of freeing India from British rule. It published the journal *Ghadr* in several languages for circulation among the Indian **diaspora**. Most members of the Ghadr Party were Punjabi agriculturalists, including **Sikhs**, who had emigrated to Canada and California in the first decade of the 20th century but faced strong prejudice and racial discrimination there.

Ghadr leadership at the start of **World War I** was drawn from among young radical intellectuals who were well funded (partly from Germany), well organized, and ardent in their chosen task of infiltrating India in groups. They were foiled by British and Indian police forces sometimes supplied with intelligence reports from the United States. Of the some 1,000 Ghadr Party followers who found their way back to the **Punjab**, 145 were killed or hanged and 306 were sentenced to transportation. They had more of an impact on the minds of future revolutionaries than on the ground. The movement had collapsed by 1917, and subsequent attempts to revive it failed.

GHAFFAR KHAN, KHAN ABDUL (also known as BADSHAH KHAN) (1890–1988). Born to a Pathan or Pakthun village headman in Peshawer district of the **North West Frontier Province** (NWFP), now in **Pakistan**, Abdul Ghaffar Khan came to be known as "the Frontier Gandhi." He was a social reformer who actively encouraged and established schools for girls as well as for boys in the NWFP. He was a nationalist who joined the **Indian National Congress** in 1920, organized the **Khilafet Movement** in the NWFP, and was a close friend of **Mahatma Gandhi** and **Jawaharlal Nehru**. Like them, Ghaffar Khan was arrested on several occasions and was imprisoned for many years. He was a member of the Congress Working Committee between 1930 and 1946 and was elected to the **Constituent Assembly**.

Badshah Khan stands out in contemporary history as an inspiring leader who transformed Pakthun society in considerable measure by turning traditional preoccupations with feuds, revenge, and violence toward essential teachings of **Islam**, non-violence, and solidarity. This remarkable achievement was no easy task. To accomplish it, he founded the Khudai Khidmatgar (Servants of God), which was dedicated to the service of country and people, in 1929. Its members, already imbued with a high sense of honor, further disciplined themselves to a code of ethical and non-violent conduct that held firm even under police beatings. Under Badshah Khan's leadership, the Khudai Khidmatgar refuted many stereotyped images of the tribal Pakthuns and grew in size and appeal despite attempts by the British authorities to intimidate or ban it. As a political as well as a social organization, it won a majority of seats in the NWFP provincial legislature during the elections of 1937 and 1946. Equally important, its principles survived among its adherents despite the implicit betrayal of **Partition** in 1947 and the explicit policy of suppression subsequently followed by Pakistan.

Badshah Khan opposed the **All India Muslim League** led by **Mohammed Ali Jinnah**, especially its separatist platform after 1940. He was bitterly disappointed when Congress accepted the **Mountbatten** plan for the partition of India in 1947 and was justifiably critical of the "injustice" so done to the Pathans of the NWFP. He and his supporters boycotted the referendum held in the NWFP in July 1947. In any case, geographical imperatives and the emotional appeal of religious commonality used by the Muslim League made the incorporation of the NWFP in Pakistan virtually inevitable.

Badshah Khan moved his residence to Afghanistan from whence he campaigned for an independent Pakhtunistan, without success. He eschewed office and wealth all his life. He remained a man of independence and integrity, fearless in his criticism of the decline of moral values and public probity in post-independence India, which he visited from time to time. Khan Abdul Ghaffar Khan was awarded the Bharat Ratna, India's highest civilian decoration, and was given a state funeral in **Delhi** when he died at the age of nearly one hundred.

GHALIB, MIRZA ASADULLAH KHAN (1797–1869). Court poet to the last Mughal, **Bahadur Shah Zafar**, Ghalib expanded the scope and horizon of Urdu literature in the 19th century far beyond its traditional romantic focus. His artistic sensibility distilled for an enduring audience his experiences as a man of fluctuating fortunes witnessing the stagnation of his own society and suffering the conquering onslaught of the British in **Delhi** in 1857. He was buried in Delhi.

Ghalib wrote in both Urdu and Persian, but his fame rests more on a self-selected collection of 2,000 Urdu couplets than on the 11,000 Persian couplets and other prose works that also survive. Ghalib's poetry remains alive in contemporary India and **Pakistan**; an institute named for him in New Delhi facilitates further study of his life and works.

GIRI, V. V. (1894–1980). V. V. Giri was the fourth president of the Republic of India, 1969–1974. He was born to a **brahman** lawyer of **Madras** province who was active in the nationalist movement and **Swaraj Party**. Giri went to university in Dublin, Ireland, where he was associated with and influenced by the Sinn Fein movement of militant nationalism. When he returned to India he focused on organizing labor and bringing **trade unions** into the nationalist movement. He was elected president of the Trade Union Congress in 1926 and again in1942 and held the labor portfolio in the Congress governments of Madras in 1937–1940 and 1946.

Soon after independence, Giri was invited to join **Jawaharlal Nehru**'s cabinet as Minister of Labour (1952–1954). Thereafter, Giri filled various gubernatorial positions in different states before being elected vice president in 1967. He succeeded President **Zakir Hussain**, who died suddenly in 1969.

GOA. A small state of the Indian Union situated on the Konkan coast and encompassing many islands, Goa's natural harbors were the outlets for the various kingdoms that included Konkan in their territories over the centuries. Thus, the **Satavahana**, **Chalukya**, Kadamba, Yadava, and **Rashtrakuta** dynasties contributed to Goa's rich historical heritage.

The **Portuguese** sailor-general Alphonse **D'Albuquerque** captured Goa in 1510, and it remained under Portuguese rule until 1961.

Much of the population was converted to **Christianity**, and some magnificent cathedrals were constructed. The Jesuit, Saint **Francis Xavier**, preached in Goa from 1542 to 1547, and his undecayed body was placed there after his death in China and draws thousands of pilgrims every year. As Portuguese power declined in Europe, Goa became a colonial backwater. It remained untouched by the expanding British domain in western India in the early 19th century because of close Anglo-Portuguese ties.

After 1947, the independent government of India attempted to negotiate a peaceful transfer of power with Portugal, without success. A popular movement for integration with India sprang up in Goa and in nearby **Bombay**, but Lisbon remained unmoved. Ultimately, New Delhi sent in the Indian army, which entered Goa in December 1961 and encountered minimal resistance. Goa was administered from New Delhi as a Union Territory before becoming a state in May 1987. Goa's wide and unspoiled beaches make it a popular tourist resort in the present day. *See also* PORTUGUESE.

GOBIND SINGH (1666–1708). The tenth and last guru of the **Sikhs** and founder of the Khalsa (see Glossary) was born Gobind Rai in **Patna**. He was only nine when he had to perform cremation rites for the severed head of his martyred father, Guru Teg Bahadur, who had been executed with the tacit approval of **Mughal** Emperor **Aurangzeb**. For more than a decade the young guru lived in the foothills of western **Uttar Pradesh**, studying Persian and **Sanskrit**, hunting, writing devotional hymns, and ministering to the growing community of disciples left in his charge. His teachings were in direct continuation of **Nanak** and drew many converts, especially among the **Jat** peasantry of the region. The **Rajput** rulers of hill states grew jealous and attacked; the Sikhs prevailed.

Gobind Singh returned to his ancestral home in the **Punjab** foothills, known today as Anandpur Sahib, and began the transformation of the Sikhs into a warrior community. He built an army around a nucleus of 500 Muslim Pathan soldiers and accepted offerings of arms and horses. He had his center fortified and a chain of fortresses built between the rivers Sutlej and **Yamuna**. He gave his followers military training, and at the same time he engaged in scholarly activity, received poets and scholars, and sent men to **Banaras** to study Sanskrit and the **Vedas** in order to better interpret the teachings of the earlier Gurus.

Guru Gobind dealt with chronic problems of factionalism and succession struggles by striking at their roots. He abolished the *masands* or intermediaries who controlled access to the guru. He then took the revolutionary step of abolishing the institution of the human guru itself, declaring the *Granth* or Scripture to be the inviolable and permanent guru of the Sikhs because it contained the teachings of all 10 gurus. He invested secular authority in the *Panth*, or community of Sikhs, in emulation of the time honored Indian *panchayat* (see Glossary) tradition. He abolished all symbols of **caste** distinction in name or ornamentation; all Sikh males were given the surname Singh (lion), and all Sikh females took the surname Kaur (lioness or princess). Men and women alike wore steel bracelets, double-edged steel daggers, short pants next to the skin, unshorn hair, and combs. These dramatic steps were taken at the spring festival of Baisakh, April 13, 1699, amidst a huge congregation from whom the guru demanded "sacrifice." The first five men to offer themselves were baptized by him, and they in turn baptized him. According to the report of a news writer from the Mughal court who was present on the occasion, 20,000 men stood up to take the vows of the Khalsa that day.

More baptisms followed on a grand scale as the peasantry responded to the soldier-saints who were ready to "train the sparrow to hunt the hawk and one man to fight a legion" as popular folklore put it. The assertiveness of the lower classes in the form of bearded, beturbaned, fully armed crusaders prompted the hill chieftains to appeal for help from their overlord, Wazir Khan, the Mughal governor of Sirhind and Lahore. The major battles of Sirsa and Chamkaur in 1705 resulted in thousands of deaths, including those of Gobind Singh's four sons. Two Pathans saved the guru's life, and he spent the following year raising a new army and making more converts. He penned a famously critical letter to Aurangzeb, the *Zafarnama*, explaining his decision to take up arms when all other means of redressing wrongs were exhausted. He compiled a definitive edition of the *Adi Granth* and collected his own works in the *Dasam Granth*.

In 1707, Gobind Singh sent a detachment of troops to help Aurangzeb's successor, Bahadur Shah and then accompanied the new emperor on a tour of **Rajasthan** and the **Deccan**. The guru was murderously assaulted, probably by Wazir Khan's hirelings, while encamped on the river Godaveri in September 1708. Guru Gobind Singh is the subject of innumerable legends and pictorial depictions among Sikhs worldwide as hero, martyr, and saint.

GODHRA. This small town in **Gujarat** was the scene of a tragedy on February 27, 2002. A railway coach carrying **Hindu** *karsewaks* (volunteers) back from **Ayodhya** was set on fire when the train made its scheduled stop at Godhra station; 58 people were reported killed. The media accorded the event tremendous publicity; every aspect of it became contentious, including the cause and location of the fire, the identity of those who set it, and the identity of the victims. A wave of communal riots swept through the state of Gujarat, with **Muslims** being targeted in particular. Estimates of the numbers killed varied, less or more than 2,000 perhaps, but many more thousands were rendered homeless and were deprived of their means of livelihood. Indian and international human rights organizations took up their cause. Open allegations were made that the **Rashtriya Swayamseval Sangh** and its affiliates in the Sangh Parivar were perpetuating atrocities against Muslims with the complicity of the **Bharatiya Janata Party (BJP)** state government headed by Chief Minister Narender Modi. An investigation by retired Justice V. R. Krishna Iyer was carried out and made a caustic report, although the report was not given official recognition.

In 2003, 80 Muslim men were arrested in Gujarat under the Prevention of Terrorism Act (POTA) in connection with the Godhra fire. Other cases were lodged against Hindus, arising out of the rapes, looting, and killing that had followed that episode, including the Best Bakery Case, which remains *sub judice*. The **Supreme Court** of India ruled that the trial of all such cases should take place *outside* Gujarat so as to ensure judicial impartiality. The **National Human Rights Commission** ordered the government of Gujarat to supply more complete information in a range of inquiries. The BJP leadership in New Delhi did not publicly censure or dismiss the Modi government, but fresh elections to the state legislature were ordered for December 2002. The BJP won.

Godhra has become a synonym for the worst communal riots (amounting to a pogrom in the opinion of some) to take place in independent India. It is an indelible blot despite the fact that not a single other state or district in India permitted an imitation or replication of the sequence to occur in their jurisdiction either at that time or later.

GODSE, NATHURAM VINAYAK (1911–1949). Nathuram, the assassin of Mahatma **Gandhi**, belonged to a **brahman** family of **Poona**, was intensely proud of **Hindu** culture, and looked on **Veer Savarkar** as his hero. He joined the **Rashtriya Swayamsevak Sangh (RSS)** and the **Hindu Mahasabha**. He founded a paramilitary organization within the RSS during **World War II** and was the editor of two Mahasabha journals, *Agrani* and *Hindu Rashtra*. Nathuram was a militant activist, bitterly critical of both Gandhi and the **Indian National Congress** for what he interpreted as the "emasculation of the Hindu community" by advocating *ahimsa*, or non-violence, and their "pro-Muslim bias." He saw **Partition** in 1947 and Gandhi's January 1948 resolve to fast to the death for the sake of Hindu-Muslim unity within India as insulting and harmful to the "Hindu Nation."

Nathuram Godse shot Mahatma Gandhi dead after bowing to him at his daily prayer meeting in **New Delhi** on the evening of January 30, 1948. Godse neither ran away, nor killed himself and was immediately apprehended. He argued his own case with conspicuous ability at the trial, which was conducted by a special court, denying involvement in a conspiracy with the others accused of an earlier explosion on January 20 and giving vent to his thoughts on defending the Hindu community and ridding it of Mahatma Gandhi. The court found Godse and his associate Narayan Apte guilty and sentenced them to death on February 10, 1949. Of the other eight accused, **Veer Savarkar** was acquitted, one was given a pardon, and six were transported for life. Godse and his associate, Apte, were executed by hanging on November 15, 1949.

GOENKA. The lineal descendants of an enterprising **Marwari** trader Ramdutt Goenka, who moved to **Calcutta** at the start of the 19th century, own and manage a large number of manufacturing companies in contemporary India and carry his name. Ramdutt was a broker and selling agent for several early British firms venturing into the Indian market. His sons and grandsons expanded the business, and by the

20th century the Goenkas were prominent in the jute and tea trades as well as in the commercial, social, and emerging political scenes of Calcutta. Badridas Goenka (born 1893) was knighted by the British, clashed with the more nationalist **G. D. Birla** over representation of the Marwari Association in the central legislature, and became the first Indian chairman of the Imperial Bank of India. He was later the founder and director of the Reserve Bank of India and President of the Federation of Indian Chambers of Commerce and Industry. His sons Keshav Prasad (KP) and Lukhi Prasad also showed entrepreneurial talent. They expanded into the automobile ancillary industry and also took over companies dealing with cotton textiles and electric cables.

K. P. and his three sons not only survived the disastrous decade of the 1950s in the tea industry and the depredations caused by rupee devaluation in 1966, but acquired substantial interests in many other industries, including tobacco. The Goenkas were one of the fastest growing industrial groups in India during the 1970s and moved their base to **Bombay**. They were vocally critical of the government's economic policies, and Ramnath Goenka (1904–1991) from another branch of the family became renowned for his audacity in fighting **Emergency Rule** through his newspaper *The Indian Express*, which actively embraced investigative journalism. In 1979, K. P. Goenka divided his industrial empire between his three sons, who each continued to expand holdings and create new enterprises. The combined list of Goenka-owned companies manufacture a very wide range of products, from power transmission towers to heavy organic chemicals to cotton and jute articles. Management techniques evolved from tight family control to professionals with initiative. Goenka companies also entered into joint ventures with the Indian public sector as well as with foreign private enterprise. Not surprisingly, the fifth generation of Goenka executives is as prominent in business and industrial associations as their forbears were, and probably have greater political influence.

GOKHALE, GOPAL KRISHNA (1866–1915). Gokhale was born to a relatively poor Chitpavan **brahman** family of **Maharashtra** and was schooled in Kolhapur and at Elphinstone College, **Bombay**. He became a teacher first at the New English High School and then at

Fergusson College in **Poona** at a time when the latter institution and Poona itself were hives of intellectual vibrancy, social reform, and political activity. Gopal Krishna contributed articles to the *Mahratta*, run by **Bal Gangadhar Tilak** and to Gopal Ganesh Agarkar's *Sudharkar*; he edited *Quarterly* from 1887 to 1895. Gokhale became an assistant to **Mahadev Govind Ranade** in 1887 and always acknowledged the deep influence of the older man on his life and thinking. Both men espoused the cause of social reform, especially with respect to education of all persons and the emancipation of women, despite opposition from the orthodox and militant **Hindu** revivalists, such as Tilak. In addition, Gokhale drew up plans for rural credit and rural cooperative societies to ameliorate economic conditions in the countryside.

Although Gokhale saw the economic consequences of British rule as nothing short of disastrous for India, he had a passion for English literature and an unshakable faith in British liberal thought and constitutional methods. He devoted his life to bringing about political change in India toward self-government using constitutional methods of political mobilization and organization, the education of public opinion in India and in Britain, participation in elective bodies, and a willingness to cooperate with — and be critical of — the British government. For these reasons, Gokhale came to be known as a "moderate" as contrasted with the "extremists" who advocated the more radical means typified by Tilak.

Gokhale joined the **Indian National Congress** in 1889 but remained a backbencher for some years, not afraid to criticize his compatriots. He served on a Royal Commission on Indian Expenditure in 1897 and in the Bombay Legislative Council (1899–1901) where he proved to be a powerful speaker. In 1902, he was elected to the Imperial Legislative Council in **Calcutta** where he is remembered for his speeches on the budget and finance. Gokhale made frequent trips to England where he became friends with **Dadabhai Naoroji** and the Liberal Lord Morley. The latter invited him to London in 1906 to help shape the constitutional changes that were introduced in India as the **Morley-Minto Reforms** in 1909.

Gokhale, Ranade, and other social reformers clashed with Tilak and other revivalists in the prolonged debate through the 1880s over the Age of Consent Bill, eventually passed in 1891 to prohibit consummation of marriage below the age of twelve, that is, presumed puberty. The social reformers sought legislation by an alien authority to curb a domestic social evil; Tilak argued that marriage was a religious matter that Indians alone should manage, that the first priority was to rid the country of the British after which social questions could be examined. The clash between Gokhale and Tilak over goals and methods reached a climax in 1905 when Gokhale was President of Congress. Meanwhile, a revolutionary wing called the New Party had been formed to fight the **partition of Bengal** in particular and British rule in general. Gokhale, fully backed by **Pherozeshah Mehta**, refused to endorse nomination of Tilak, one of the revolutionary leaders, as President of the next session at **Surat** in 1906. Congress split between "Moderates" and "Extremists" and was relatively ineffective for the next ten years. Though Gokhale and Tilak were and are frequently contrasted, in historical perspective they can be seen to have been both competitive and complementary.

In 1905, Gokhale launched the Servants of India Society in which he invested his high ideals, his ethical conduct, and his transparent sincerity to public service and well-rounded education for all. He was supportive of **Mohandas K. Gandhi**'s groundbreaking work in South Africa; he kept in touch with the younger man and introduced him to Congress leaders and to political life on his return to India. Gandhi called Gokhale "Rajaguru" or "prince of teachers" and always credited him with making lasting contributions to modern India.

GOPALAN, A. K. (1902–1977). Gopalan was born to a **Nair** family of northern Malabar. His father was a forward-looking man who edited two weekly journals and founded an English-language middle school. The young Gopalan became a teacher but soon became involved in politics, working full time in movements led by **Mahatma Gandhi** for spreading *khadi* (see Glossary) and in adult education. Gopalan participated in the Salt **Satyagraha** of 1930 and the Temple Entry Satyagraha of 1932. He joined the Congress Socialist Party in 1934 and worked with **E. M. S. Namboodiripad** and others to build up a *kisan* or peasant movement in Malabar. He was a good orator and agitator, precipitating mass action in **Madras** and Travancore.

Gopalan joined the **Communist Party of India (CPI)** in 1940 and was arrested in 1941. He escaped from prison and worked underground.

He was again arrested after independence in December 1947 but moved a habeas corpus petition in the Madras High Court; which secured not only his release but the legal recognition of the CPI. He was elected to the **Lok Sabha** in 1952 and repeatedly after that. He became the leader of the CPI Parliamentary Group and, after the CPI split in 1964, was leader of the **CPI (Marxist)** party. The headquarters of the latter is named after him.

GOUBERT, EDOUARD (1894–1979). A Franco-Indian born in **Pondicherry**, Goubert was educated in French Indochina and in France. He became active in politics at the time of Indian independence. He tried to negotiate a special status for the French enclaves in India that would give them autonomy from both France and India. Neither **New Delhi** nor Paris was responsive to this idea. By 1954, Goubert had changed his mind and was leading a popular movement for the merger of the French enclaves with India.

France transferred sovereignty by treaties with India signed in 1951 and in 1956 and ratified in 1962. At the same time, former French enclaves were permitted to retain many institutional links with France, especially in the fields of culture and science. As leader of the **Congress Party** in Pondicherry, Goubert became the first chief minister of the new state, leading the government between 1955 and 1965.

GOVERNMENT OF INDIA ACT (1919). *See* MONTAGU-CHELMSFORD REFORMS.

GOVERNMENT OF INDIA ACT (1935). This was the product of five years of weary wrangling between the **Indian National Congress** and the British Government of India, three **Round Table Conferences**, a White Paper published by His Majesty's Government in London, and an intense debate in the British Parliament. The Bill was criticized by Conservatives such as Winston Churchill for giving too much power to the Indians and by members of the Labour Party, such as Clement Attlee, for giving too little. None of the Indian participants in the preceding negotiations were satisfied with this attempt to buttress rather than dissolve the British Empire in India, but they had no mutually acceptable alternative to offer. The 1935 Act was the last

British-made constitution implemented (incompletely) in India, and some of its administrative provisions were incorporated in the **1950 Constitution** of the Republic of India.

The 1935 Act aimed to create an All-India Federation composed of 11 provinces—including three new provinces of **Orissa**, Sind, and the **North West Frontier Province (NWFP)**—of British India that were enjoying responsible government, several hundred **Princely States** under various forms of accession and association, and a few centrally administered areas. This particular federation never came into existence; none of the concerned parties evinced sufficient enthusiasm for it, not even the princes whose weight in the proposed central government would have been considerable. The outbreak of **World War II** in 1939 rendered the protracted negotiations on the subject irrelevant.

The most important principle of the 1935 Act was "provincial autonomy," inaugurated in April 1937 after elections were held in the provinces. The very restricted franchise was expanded to cover about 35 million persons, including 6 million women and 10 million **Untouchables**. Because of the many reserved seats for special interests and separate electorates for minority communities as listed in the **Communal Award**, less than half of the nearly 1,600 provincial legislative seats contested were open to the general electorate; Congress candidates won them all, and 59 more from the separate electorates. **The Muslim League** won only 109 seats, considerably less than half of the seats reserved for Muslims.

Congress had a distinct sense of victory in 1937 and agreed to form governments in the provinces. The **"dyarchy"** at provincial level, enjoined by the **Montagu-Chelmsford Reforms**, was replaced in 1935 by executive responsibility to the legislature in all departments, with the governors retaining extensive "reserve" and discretionary powers to safeguard special and minority interests and/or the public peace. The focus of Indian politics moved to the provinces, where power and patronage now lay mainly in Indian hands. This fact had a profound impact on political styles and bargaining, on party linkages and leadership, and on increasing familiarity among Indians with the institutions and procedures of parliamentary democracy. The two and a half years in which provincial autonomy was implemented, 1937–1939, were of crucial importance in the development of Congress and the League, and to the deteriorating relations between the two.

The 1935 Act separated **Burma** from India and gave the Viceroy/Governor General of India greater freedom from Whitehall control. The Imperial Legislative Council in **New Delhi** was enlarged in both size and function, and dyarchy was introduced in the central government. The 1935 Act also envisaged an accelerated pace of Indianization in government services, both civil and military, although its framers certainly did not anticipate complete Indian independence a decade later. Despite the fact that several cracks had developed in the constitutional edifice by late 1939, a longer implementation of the 1935 Act might have permitted the peaceful evolution of political solutions to political problems had not World War II transformed the entire canvas.

GREEN REVOLUTION. This is an internationally accepted term used to describe the process by which India's production of wheat, rice, maize, and some millets rose dramatically in the late 1960s and 1970s. India's claim to self-sufficiency in food grains replaced its earlier reliance on food aid. A threefold increase in wheat production and 16% rise in rice production was brought about mainly as a result of new agricultural technologies using high-yielding hybrid varieties of seed, applications of chemical fertilizers and pesticides, and timely and regulated water supply.

Key factors contributing to the success of the new technologies were: prior public investment in irrigation, institutions of rural credit and agricultural research, and the high quality of the cultivator with secure tenurial rights in the land. These factors were all present in the **Punjab**, which tripled its output of food grains within 10 years and sustained high output. **Haryana** and the western districts of **Uttar Pradesh** also demonstrated success. However, the new technologies were less applicable to lands that were subject to flooding or waterlogging, or to prolonged dry spells (typical of areas where rice or millets were cultivated) and did not succeed in the eastern **Ganges** valley state of **Bihar** where land reforms had not been carried out and where cultivators lacked secure tenure.

Critics of the Green Revolution pointed out that the new strategies were adopted only after India had suffered three consecutive years of drought in the mid-1960s, became heavily dependent on imports of food grains from the United States, and was subjected to political pressure from Washington. Critics further stressed the fact that benefits of the Green Revolution have been regionally and sectorally differentiated, widening inequalities of income between wealthy landowners, sometimes called "bullock capitalists," and landless labor, thus indirectly fueling sociopolitical tensions. Some saw the major problems facing independent India—how to achieve equity with growth—reduced to a technological debate as a consequence of the Green Revolution, with no easy solutions in sight. The Green Revolution is no longer a controversial topic and is regarded as a qualified success story.

GUHA, RANAJIT (1923–). Guha is a leading figure among the Subalternist Group of historians. They have reset the parameters of historiography by looking at the politics of people at the lower strata of society as an autonomous domain in the colonial and post-colonial periods. Although Guha maintains links with the tradition of cultural history writing in his native **Bengal**, he has rejected what he sees as complicity between colonial and Indian historians in focusing only on elites. Guha tried to analyze subaltern consciousness in his voluminous *Elementary Aspects of Peasant Insurgency in Colonial India,* which detailed 110 peasant revolts in 117 years of British occupation. He thus challenged the myth of British rule by consent.

Ranajit Guha edited the first six volumes of *Subaltern Studies*, published between 1982 and 1989. His own "Prose of Counter Insurgency" (1982) is regarded as a classic statement of the Subaltern School. He delivered several influential lectures in **Calcutta** in 1987, arguing for an "autonomous" history of India as an alternative to British and British-inspired histories of the colonial period.

GUJARAT. One of the largest and most prosperous states of the Indian Union, Gujarat covers more than 196,000 square kilometers and has a population of more than 50 million. It is located on the west of the subcontinent just south of **Pakistan** and has a long coastline with 40 ports, large and small. Kandla is presently the most important port, but **Surat** has the longest continuous history as a major trading center for all of northern India, and the excavated site of Lothal gives evidence of seaborne trade dating back to the third or second millennium BCE when **Harappan culture** probably spread through Gujarat. Epic literature designates Dwarka—meaning gateway—in Gujarat as the final worldly destination of **Krishna**.

Many kingdoms flourished in Gujarat, and Somnath was the site of wealthy temples, frequently sacked (as by **Mahmud of Ghazni** in 1025) for their gold, jewels, and precious carvings, and as frequently rebuilt. Gujarat's general prosperity was more or less constant, whether its rulers were independent or subordinate to an imperial center, or whether they were **Hindu** or **Muslim**. It attracted settlers from abroad, such as the **Parsis**, and also sent out many emigrants, especially in the 19th and 20th centuries. Gujaratis are usually prominent among the Indian **Diaspora**. Gujarat was an important *subah* (see Glossary) of the **Mughal Empire**; one where **Todar Mal**'s new revenue system was first implemented and where European trading companies sought and gained access to the busy port of Surat. With the disintegration of the Mughal Empire and the rise and fall of **Maratha** power, large parts of present-day Gujarat fell under British rule while other parts remained as **Princely States**. **Mahatma Gandhi** was born in one such state.

Gujarat featured prominently in the history of the **Indian National Congress** and the struggle for Indian independence, providing a solid base of support for such leaders as Gandhi and **Vallabhbhai Patel** from among agriculturalists as well as businessmen and industrialists. The present-day boundaries of Gujarat were drawn in 1960 when Gujarati-speaking districts and the erstwhile Princely States of Saurashtra were separated from the huge bilingual state of **Bombay**. Agriculture employs the largest number of people, with cash crops such as cotton, groundnuts, and tobacco supplementing the cultivation of food grains and oil seeds. Large-scale and small-scale irrigation projects have added to the area under cultivation and the Sardar Sarovar Project on the **Narmada River** has augmented the supply of electric power to the state, including its major city of **Ahmedabad**.

Gujarat had a long tradition of hand-woven textiles and became the first site of modern textile factories, many of which were concentrated in Ahmedabad. Newer industries such as petrochemicals, diamond processing, engineering, electronics, fertilizers, machine tools, and pharmaceuticals also thrive in Gujarat's pro-business environment that houses one of India's finest institutes of management. Some large industrial estates with good infrastructure facilities have been established to attract direct foreign investment, with some success. However, large scale communal rioting following the **Godhra** episode in 2002, and Chief Minister Narender Modi's seeming intention of making the state a laboratory for **Hindutva**, adversely affected Gujarat's image in the rest of India and abroad, despite its continuing upward graph of economic growth.

GUJRAL, INDER KUMAR (1919–). Gujral was prime minister of a coalition United Front government from April 1997 to the following year. He had previously been foreign minister in the coalition governments of **Deve Gowda** (1996–1997) and **Vishwa Pratap Singh** (1989–1990). Gujral began his political career as a member of the **Congress Party**. He was Minister of Information and then ambassador to the Soviet Union in **Indira Gandhi**'s government during the 1970s. Disillusioned with her, he joined the **Janata Party** in 1977.

I. K. Gujral was born in Jhelum, in present-day **Pakistan**, joined the **Communist Party of India** as a student in Lahore, and became a refugee from the **Partition** massacres of 1947. His artist and architect brother, Satish Gujral, vividly depicted the agony of those days. Inder Gujral, whether in or out of office during the 1990s, placed a very high priority on trying to achieve normal relations with Pakistan, partly through cultivating warm personal relationships in civil society and by widening contacts between the two countries at many levels. As foreign minister and prime minister, he strengthened the **South Asian Association for Regional Cooperation** as a multilateral organization. He also enunciated a "Gujral Doctrine" of dealing with India's smaller neighbors in a spirit of generosity, without demanding strict reciprocity in matters of trade concessions, for example.

GUPTA DYNASTY/GUPTA EMPIRE (c. 320–547 CE). The discovery in the 19th and 20th centuries of many inscriptions and coins dating from the first few centuries CE enabled scholars to reconstruct the history of the Gupta era with a fair degree of accuracy. The main sources for that period are large numbers of distinctive and standardized coins, stone and iron pillars, inscriptions on stone pedestals and slabs, records of donations to temples, copper plate land grants, and quantities of seals. These supplement traditional literary sources such as the **Puranas**, the texts of **Kalidasa** in **Sanskrit**, and accounts by foreign travellers, notably the contemporary **Faxian**, although **Xuanzang** and **Al Biruni** also made valuable retrospective comments on the Guptas.

Evidence of a flourishing culture and economy led most nationalist historians to depict the Gupta epoch as a "golden age" during which classical Indian civilization reached its apogee. Sanskrit was the court language; the sciences of astronomy, mathematics, and medicine thrived; treatises on art, dance, music, and sculpture were produced, and the artistic achievements of the period to be seen, for example, at **Ajanta**, were high indeed. The great epics *Mahabharata* and *Ramayana*, as well as major texts in the **brahmanical** or **Hindu** tradition were written down, probably in forms close to those used today. Religious tolerance was the norm, permitting orthodox Hinduism and heterodox faiths such as **Buddhism** and **Jainism** to coexist and debate to be lively. Some scholars have questioned the "golden age" depiction by focusing on the social and religious institutions of the Guptas and seeing evidence of discrimination against **women**, **sudras**, and **Untouchables**. Opinions also differ on identifying the original home and precise **caste** of the Gupta emperors, the political condition of India before their rise to imperial dominance, the degree of centralization or decentralization that characterized their administration, and the causes for its eventual collapse. But the main features of the Gupta Empire are now clear.

The decline of **Kushan** and **Satavahana** power in northern and peninsular India, respectively, resulted in the emergence of many independent republics and kingdoms in the third century CE. Sri Gupta and then his son Ghatotkacha ruled one such kingdom in the mid-**Ganges** valley. Chandra Gupta I assumed the title Maharajadhiraj, symbolic of suzerain power, shortly after marriage to the **Lichchavi** princess Kumaradevi. The two issued gold coins in their joined names, probably united their territories, which included **Awadh**, **Prayag**, and **Bihar**, and appear to have been full partners in the new empire. Their son, Samudragupta (r. 330–375) engaged in a series of conquests in the north, the west, the **Deccan**, and the hilly regions of central and eastern India. These are enumerated in a eulogy inscribed on **Ashoka**'s pillar at Allahabad and in striking contrast to it in tone and substance. Samudragupta broke the power of the chiefdoms and republics of the northwest that had served as buffers to the Gangetic plains. He also established feudatory or diplomatic relations with outlying republics and kingdoms on the subcontinent and in southeast Asian islands. He issued gold coins to celebrate his conquests, patronized the arts, and performed the **ashvamedha** or horse sacrifice as the overlord of kings, which may have been in abeyance for some time.

Samudragupta was briefly succeeded by his son Ramagupta, whose humiliation by the **Sakas** led to his being ousted by his brother **Chandragupta II Vikramaditya**, who ruled to 412 CE. Chandragupta, too, was a great warrior who extended the frontiers of his empire across the **Indus** into present-day Afghanistan, and consolidated his power through all of northern India and part of the Deccan. He made a series of matrimonial alliances—as with the **Vakataka dynasty**—that further extended his influence, but he did not attempt to establish tight central control over far-flung territories. He issued copious gold coinage. He is the subject of a fine Sanskrit inscription on an iron pillar near **Delhi**. Chandragupta II is usually identified with the legendary Vikramaditya (sun of prowess) praised by Kalidasa for his humane administration, his personal wisdom, and the intellectual brilliance of his court. Chandragupta II was briefly succeeded by his elder son Govindagupta and then by his second son Kumaragupta I (r. 415–455). The Gupta Empire reached the zenith of its glory in those 40 years. All the material evidence testifies to a time of peace and plenty during which art, music, literature, and foreign trade flourished from the **Himalaya** in the north to the **Narmada** river in the south, from **Bengal** in the east to **Gujarat** in the west.

The immediate succession to Kumaragupta is controversial, but his son Skandagupta ascended the throne in 455 CE and ruled to 467 or perhaps later. He had to contend with court rivalries, the breaking away of feudatories, and repeated incursions from the northwest by the Hepthalites from central Asia known as the **Hunas**. Skandagupta is usually depicted as a heroic figure repulsing the Hunas, reestablishing imperial Gupta authority, reorganizing his administration around civilian provincial governors, and paying attention to general welfare schemes such as irrigation. But a fiscal crisis is suggested by the debasement of high value coins issued in this period, and the central authority of the Guptas evidently declined rapidly after his reign. He upheld the social and moral order known as *varna-ashrama-dharma*, as did his successors, but the last known ruler of the imperial Gupta line was Vishnugupta (d. 550).

Repeated Huna invasions from outside (similar to but perhaps weaker than those that assailed the Roman Empire) and assertive feudatories and/or governors from inside brought about the breakdown of a more than 200-year-old empire into many small kingdoms. Defense was now conceived in terms of temporary combinations for local needs, and many aspects of north Indian life were disrupted. In particular, Buddhist monks and monasteries had suffered greatly, although the agrarian economy, the practice of religious tolerance, and brahmanical social institutions continued much longer and absorbed the many migrants from central Asia that came in the wake of the Hunas. The cultural achievements in smaller successor states or under kings depicted as the "later Guptas" were significant, although a decline in creativity is noticeable in Sanskrit literature after the seventh century. **Harshavardhana** too is sometimes classified with the Guptas, not because of his lineage but because of his benevolence and the prosperity of his people.

GUPTA, MAITHILI SARAN (1886–1964). One of the most important poets of modern Hindi literature, he was born near Jhansi to a wealthy landowning family of **Ram** devotees and received a traditional education at home in **Sanskrit**, but subsequently learned Urdu and English. A senior writer, Mahavir Prasad Dwivedi, inspired him to use the spoken vernacular language known as *khari boli* for his writings.

The British authorities banned Gupta's nationalist poem *Bharat Bharati* (Indian India) in 1912. His considerable output was varied, including devotional, epic, and patriotic poetry, many translations, and prose works contributing to a revival of interest in creative **Buddhist** and **Hindu** thought. **Mahatma Gandhi** referred to him as "Rashtriya Kavi" or "National Poet" in 1936. After India's independence, Gupta was honored with the Padma Vibhushan and was a member of the **Rajya Sabha** from 1952 to 1964.

– H –

HAIDAR ALI (1721–1782). Haidar was an able adventurer who became the de facto ruler of **Mysore** in 1761. His efficient administration and military exploits in the south enlarged the kingdom but excited the jealousy of ambitious neighbors: the **Marathas**, the Nizam of **Hyderabad**, and the **East India Company**. They combined forces against Haidar Ali in two wars of 1767–1769 and 1780–1784 but lost more territory to Mysore. By this time, the Anglo-French rivalry added to the existing complex of intrigue and conflict in peninsular India; Haidar Ali preferred the French to the British and employed French soldiers of fortune to train his army and gunners. His son, **Tipu Sultan**, succeeded him and continued intermittent war against the English but was eventually defeated in 1799.

HAILEYBURY COLLEGE, ENGLAND. This school was established in 1806 to train young British "writers" and "clerks" for covenanted service with the **East India Company** in India. By that time, the Company Bahadur, as it was called, was engaged in the administration of justice, collection of revenue, diplomacy, and sundry other tasks of an expanding domain. Haileybury's two-year course in Western classics and general subjects replaced the former three-year training in Indic studies imparted at a college in Fort William, **Calcutta** established by **Lord Wellesley**. Haileybury College thus embodied 19th-century British convictions of their own superiority over other civilizations, the ability of "gentlemen" with a general education to perform better than specialists, and the maxim that they were "bound to govern India for the natives and for India itself."

The collective life and course of studies at Haileybury was something between an English public school and a college at Oxford or Cambridge. Young men in their early 20s were exposed to some outstanding thinkers and lecturers. More importantly, they came to know each other well and in an atmosphere that fostered a team spirit without discouraging individual endeavor. Underlying the official maxims accepted by Haileybury, men could be found with an independent outlook, a readiness to state a critical opinion of the administration, and a confidence in the integrity and judgment of the man on the spot that did much to augment British power and prestige in India. Some of the great empire builders, innovative administrators, and successful diplomats of the 19th century were products of Haileybury, but so were some of the dullest of the period.

The principle of competition rather than patronage had been introduced to the recruitment of the covenanted service in 1833 and was reaffirmed in 1853. When British India passed to the Crown in 1858, Haileybury College ceased to be the training ground for the **Indian Civil Service**.

HARAPPA. One of the first large urban centers on the Indian subcontinent, Harappa was accidentally discovered in 1921, as was Mohenjo-Daro, a twin city in the lower **Indus** valley (both are presently located in **Pakistan**). The sites were excavated at the time by D. R. Sahni of the Indian Archeological Department headed by Sir John Marshall, and subsequent carbon dating of the remains found there places them in the third millennium BCE.

Harappa was a geometrically planned brick city built on the banks of the Ravi river. Granaries, grain pounding platforms, and what appear to be workmen's quarters were located near the river, while a walled citadel containing a large tank dominated higher ground. The culture of the earliest known civilization of India, the **Indus Valley Civilization**, takes its name from Harappa, and its motifs reappear in later times. *See also* HARAPPAN CULTURE.

HARAPPAN CULTURE/INDUS VALLEY CIVILIZATION (c. 2700–1500 BCE). This was essentially an urban culture sustained by surplus agricultural produce and extensive commerce. It flourished in the **Indus** valley in the third and second millennia BCE and was the most extensive of the ancient riverine civilizations of the time. As the earliest known civilization of India, the Harappan culture has generated considerable interest and archaeological endeavor.

Two major cities belonging to the Indus Valley civilization were accidentally discovered and then excavated in the early part of the 20th century. These two, **Mohenjo-Daro** and **Harappa** (both in present-day **Pakistan**) were constructed on almost identical plans of streets laid out in a grid pattern, elaborate drainage systems, public baths, residential areas of flat-roofed brick houses, granaries, large platforms, and fortified administrative centers. The constructions imply a large deployment of organized labor with an effective system of recruiting, paying, and managing labor. The absence of recognizable temples of religious buildings and elaborate tombs is in striking contrast to the cities of other ancient civilizations. Palaces are hard to discern, and few weapons or evidence of warfare have been discovered. About 70 smaller sites with similar features have been subsequently discovered: further east in the Indus basin as at Rupar, in **Rajasthan**, and in the upper part of the **Ganges** valley; further south as at the presumed ports of Lothal and Surkotada in **Gujarat** and upper **Maharashtra**; and as far north as Shortughai in the Pamir Mountains. Thus, modern scholars safely postulate a much wider spread of the civilization than suspected in the first half of the 20th century. They also deduce regular sea trade between western India and the Persian Gulf and Tigris-Euphrates delta that has been continuous since then, and land trade with Afghanistan and Iran over mountain passes in the northwest. The possibility of trade and settlement in Indian Ocean islands, such as the **Maldives**, also exists.

Harappan artifacts and town designs have been found over an extensive area. Among the common characteristics of the sites discovered: weights and measures were standardized and sophisticated; cotton was spun, woven, and dyed for clothing and trade; wheat, barley, rice, and millet were cultivated and a variety of animals domesticated; water conduits and small canals indicate controlled irrigation; engraved stamp seals were in use, perhaps to identify property; pottery carried distinctive designs in black painted on red; and crafted products such as beads show a high degree of skill and organization in assembling raw materials from distant places. The similarities found in far-flung centers of Harrapan Culture has led some historians to assume centralized administration with twin capitals, if uncertain whether authority lay with a priestly or a commercial oligarchy; a warrior-king was deemed to be unlikely. Other historians read more complex and varied authority systems into the range of sites discovered and the very long period of time spanned by the Indus Valley Civilization; they postulate an interface of local cultures with a wider, perhaps commanding, one that has characterized Indian cultural history throughout.

Knowledge of Harappan culture is deduced from bones, pottery, and other artifacts discovered by archaeologists. Among the most exciting, yet frustrating, artifacts are large numbers of small, exquisite steatite seals engraved with realistic portraits of animals and, less often, men or gods. Some motifs, such as the *pipal* leaf and tree, persist to the present day. The horse is not depicted. Philologists from all parts of the world have subjected the short inscriptions in a unique pictographic script on these seals to intense study, but the script has not been definitively deciphered as yet. Debates usually center on whether it is proto-**Dravidian** or proto-**Sanskrit**, although the script appears to be read from right to left. Resolution of that debate could shed light on the originators of Indian civilization, because it is now generally admitted that the Harappan culture was indigenous to and widespread throughout the Indian subcontinent.

Analyses of the bones interred at Mohenjo-Daro and Harappa indicate that the people who inhabited these cities in the third and second millennium BCE came from more than one ethnic stock, setting a pattern of ethnic diversity that lasts to the present day on the Indian subcontinent. An early theory of a racial dichotomy and violent encounter between the Harappan people and **Aryan** displacers has been discredited. A more likely sequence of continuous migrations into the Indus valley and beyond from central Asia is postulated. The abandonment of Mohenjo-Daro and Harappa is currently explained by urban decline, caused perhaps by ecological changes such as flooding, soil salinity, and desertification. Archaeological evidence is lacking for the type of invasion and war extrapolated from later mythic or literary sources. The coexistence of different peoples and cultures, gradual migrations, changes, and urban decline recurs throughout Indian history and is not unlikely for the early phase, too.

Although the next recrudescence of urban culture in India took place some 1,000 years later, and in the middle-Ganges valley, the initial image drawn by historians of a sharp break between Harappan cities and succeeding pastoral Indo-Aryan cultures seems overdrawn. The exact links in a presumed chain of continuity are yet to be definitively established, but some indications are seen in the following facts. Vedic Sanskrit is alone among Indo-European languages to contain retroflexed sounds, typical of Dravidian languages, which may have predominated in the Harappan culture. Religious and social practices that are inferred from Harappan artifacts recur in the later **brahmanical** culture of India, for example, ritual bathing, phallus worship, ascetic practices, and differentiated residence according to social class. It is possible, too, that matri-focal societies, still extant in parts of India, flourished in Harappan times. Clearly, the answers to many questions await further archaeological discoveries, scholarly interpretations, and deciphering of the Indus valley script. *See also* HARAPPA.

HARDAYAL, LALA (1884–1939). Hardayal played a brief role in the Indian nationalist movement from San Francisco and was therefore unusual. He was born in **Delhi** and educated at elite institutions, including Oxford, England. He and his friends were attracted by ideas of **Hindu** revivalism and Indian freedom from British rule. Hardayal returned to India and organized groups of ascetic youths as revolutionaries. These activities brought him under police surveillance and forced him to leave the country in 1911.

While a lecturer in **Sanskrit** at the University of California, Berkeley, Hardayal helped to organize the **Ghadr Party**, which tried but failed to ignite revolution in the **Punjab** during **World War I**. He fled from arrest to Germany and later lived in Sweden and in Britain. The latter half of his life was devoted to writing and lecturing. He continued to inspire other Indian revolutionaries who would meet him in Europe.

HARDWAR. This word means literally, doorway to Hari, another name for the **Hindu** deity **Vishnu**. Built on the banks of the **Ganga**, where the young river leaves the mountains for the plains, the town of Hardwar arose around one of the most ancient and most sacred places of Hindu pilgrimage in India. It was known by the name Mayapuri in classical times and was visited by the Chinese pilgrim **Xuanzang** in the seventh century. As is the case with **Varanasi**, Hardwar is replete with ascetics, bathing ghats, mendicants, and temples with astrological, mythological, and strong religious associations. It is located in the present day state of **Uttaranchal**.

HARIJAN. *See* UNTOUCHABLE.

HARSHA-VARDHANA or HARSHA (r. 606–647). Four kingdoms effectively controlled north India after the **Gupta Empire** declined. One of them had as its capital Thanesar, north of **Delhi**, and was ruled by Harsha for 41 years. His reign was unusually well documented in the biographical *Harishcharita* authored by the learned Banbhatta and in detailed accounts penned by the Chinese pilgrim **Xuanzang** who spent many years in the kingdom.

Harsha had ambitions of reviving the imperial reach of the Guptas and formed a matrimonial alliance with a powerful family ruling in the western **Ganges** valley. He took the title of *Maharajadhiraj* and moved his capital east to **Kanauj**, which was situated in rich agricultural land and commanded important trade routes. Through incessant warfare as well as alliances, Harsha spread his domain over much of northern India and included among his feudatories the kings of **Punjab**, **Kashmir**, **Nepal**, and **Gujarat**. He also received an embassy from the T'ang Emperor of China at his court. But his attempt to venture south failed when he suffered a major military defeat at the hands of Pulakeshin II, the **Chalukya** ruler of the **Deccan**, in c. 641.

Harsha was an energetic ruler who toured extensively and maintained a large army. He made himself accessible to his subjects, distributed charitable donations, supervised tax collections, and inspected the general working of administration in a loosely connected empire. The locally powerful institutions of the Gupta imperial system, including village chieftains, land grants to individual functionaries as well as temples and monasteries, and trade and crafts guilds, continued to function more or less as they had before. The socioeconomic features of Gupta rule continued too, especially the far flung entrepreneurial and trading enterprises of Indians in central and southeast Asia and the Indian Ocean region. Both **Buddhism** and **Hinduism** flourished in Harsha's kingdom, with monks and **brahmans** benefiting equally from royal patronage. Chroniclers of his reign remarked on Harsha's liberality, his literary and scholastic pursuits, and most of all, his just and mild rule. His successors, however, were not equally able, and locally powerful potentates soon asserted their independence of Kanauj.

HARYANA. A small state of the Indian Union contiguous with **Delhi** that shares **Chandigarh** as capital with the **Punjab**. Haryana has an area of approximately 44,000 square kilometers and an estimated population of 21 million. Haryana came into being as a consequence of dividing the Punjab along linguistic lines in 1966; Hindi is its principal language. Haryana is well developed, with high agricultural production, thriving industries, a lively tourist trade, and complete rural electrification. Its literacy rate is at the national average, lower than in the Punjab but higher than in neighboring **Uttar Pradesh**. Sex ratio is low, with only 9,755,331 women to 11,327,658 men according to the 2001 **census**.

The rich historical legacy of Haryana dates from the epic *Mahabharata*, which describes a great battle at Kurukshetra. Nearby **Panipat** was the site of several decisive battles in history. Epigraphical, archaeological, and literary evidence all place Haryana at the heart of successive empires in northern India, as it occupies the strategic watershed area between the **Indus** and **Ganges** river systems.

HASTINGS, WARREN (1732–1818). Hastings first went to India as a writer or clerk for the **East India Company** in 1750 and rose to occupy its highest ranks. He was appointed governor of **Bengal** in 1772, and two years later the **Regulating Act** named him first governor general with ultimate authority over the British Presidencies of **Madras** and **Bombay**. Hastings retired to England in 1785 and was impeached the following year by the House of Commons for "high crimes and misdemeanors" committed during his tenure in India. The House of Lords acquitted him of all charges.

Much of the controversy surrounding Warren Hastings in his lifetime was the consequence of changing circumstances in India and changing standards in Britain. On arrival in Bengal he said he found "a confused heap of undigested materials." He himself knew Persian, respected Indians and their culture, and encouraged the Orientalists, in part by founding the **Asiatic Society**. He wanted to expand British power at minimum expense by extending indirect rule through a series of **Subsidiary Alliances** with Indian princes, such as the ruler of **Oudh** (or Awadh), while keeping a strong base in Bengal. He believed that revenue collection and local administration should be left to Indians and that Englishmen should be kept in **Calcutta**. He did not favor outright war with Indian rulers such as the **Marathas**, as advocated by other Englishmen in India at the time, because of its cost, He thought English power in India would be short-lived, and his style of functioning was more in keeping with that of a past **Mughal** feudatory than of a future British proconsul. Hastings was not above extorting money from his Indian allies and dependents, such as Raja Chait Singh of Banaras and the Begums of Oudh, over whose cases there was some scandal, but he was not unusual in that respect.

Circumstances changed with the British assumption of *dewani*, or rights to collect revenue, in 1765 and the passage of the Regulating Act. The system of a trading company acting in the name of the Mughal emperor with which Hastings was familiar could no longer work, partly because the British Parliament was now supervising the activities of the East India Company. The Regulating Act created a new council, and intrigue and opposition within it, especially from Philip Francis, thwarted Hasting's authority and undermined the support of East India Company Directors in London, essential to any success in India. Further, the Governors of Bombay and Madras were embroiled in wars with the Marathas and **Mysore** and were resistant to direction or control from Calcutta. English opinion at the time was offended by Hastings's financial indiscretions and his summary execution of an offender such as Nand Kumar. In short, Warren Hastings's actions were judged by standards different from his own and were found wanting by his English contemporaries.

Hastings's reputation did not, however, suffer for long. When he was asked to testify in 1813 on the subject of Company administration, he received a standing ovation in Parliament. By then he was recognized as one of the founders of British dominion in India, and his compatriots welcomed the vast territorial expansion he had initiated.

HEDGEWAR, KESHAVRAO BALIRAM (1889–1940). He was the founder of the **Rashtriya Swayamsevak Sangh (RSS)** in 1925. Hedgewar was born in Nagpur to an orthodox **brahman** family loyal to the memory of the old **Maratha** rulers of central India, especially the Bhonsle family and the 17th-century warrior-king, **Shivaji**.

Hedgewar took a medical degree but did not practice medicine. Nor did he marry. Instead, in 1905 he traveled to **Bengal** and the **Punjab** to join the ardent revolutionaries attempting to undo the recent **partition of Bengal**. He witnessed there the heady atmosphere created by these young men and their lack of both unity and discipline. He himself had a sense of history and resolved to inspire the young and recreate a glorious past for India. He was the head and the preceptor of the tightly organized RSS, and he rallied the loyalty of young men to a *Bhagawan Dhwaja* or sacred saffron flag, standing for **Hindu** revivalism. Hedgewar and his organization were banned from legal political activity in the 1930s because of their contribution to communal violence and public disorder.

HIMACHAL PRADESH. A small, hilly, beautiful northern state of the Indian Union composed predominantly of former **Princely States**. Historically, these hill principalities enjoyed relative autonomy from the rulers of the northern plains toward whom their loyalties fluctuated. Distinctive schools of art, such as Pahari and Kangra, flourished in these states during the 18th and 19th centuries. Himachal Pradesh is the least urbanized state in the Indian Union. It has an area of 55,673 square kilometers and an estimated population of six million. The principal languages are Hindi and Pahari, a hill language. **Simla**, former summer capital of the British Raj, is its capital. Another flourishing town, Dharamsala, is the principal residence of the **Dalai Lama**. Fruit growing and processing, tourism, and small industries have supplemented subsistence agriculture to good effect.

HIMALAYA. This is a **Sanskrit** term meaning "abode of the snows" and refers to the mountainous belt separating the Indo-Gangetic plains from the central Asian plateaus. The highest mountain range in the world, with 12 peaks rising above 8,000 meters, the Himalaya are also among the youngest. Formed only some 45 million years ago, they are composed of relatively light material and remain geologically active.

Three major rivers, the **Brahmaputra**, **Ganges**, and **Indus**, and hundreds of smaller ones have their sources in the Himalaya, or just across it, and are perennially fed by its melting snows. The Himalaya protect the Indian subcontinent from Siberian blasts and cause the southwest monsoon clouds to drop their rain. It is impossible to underestimate the importance of the Himalaya to Indian climate, agriculture, and culture. But the climate of the Himalayan region itself—some 800 kilometers wide and more than 3,000 kilometers long, with alternating ranges of hills and mountains and valleys, with deep gorges, high passes, frequent earthquakes, and violently erosive rivers—is unpredictable and not uniform. Historically, the Himalaya have functioned as the northern rampart of India, inhibiting military expansion in either direction, though not trade or pilgrimage, and protecting the autonomy of hill kingdoms and their uniquely hybrid cultures.

The Himalaya are prominent in Indian mythology as the abode of the gods and are the destination of those who seek spiritual liberation in their peaks. They are dotted with **Hindu** and **Buddhist** temples, monasteries, and places of pilgrimage as well as countless shrines to local deities. But modern developments, with attendant road building, affluent tourists, and rapid population growth, have devastated the rich forests and violated the pristine sanctuary of the snows. The fragile ecology of the Himalaya is under threat today with only tentative regional efforts to protect it for tomorrow.

HINDU. The word originally had a geographical meaning, not a religious one. It is derived from *Sindhu*, the Indo-Aryan word for river, and *Hindavi*, the term used by Arabs, Persians, and Turkic speaking peoples after the eighth century CE to refer to all of the people, irrespective of religious identity, living beyond the **Indus River**. People of the Indian subcontinent generally identified themselves by **caste** or *jati,* and by sect within the broader parameters of Saiva (worshippers of **Shiva**), Vaishnava (worshippers of **Vishnu**), **Buddhist**, **Jain**, and others. Nor were there monolithic communities known as Hindu or Muslim, since sect, language, and place of origin distinguished the followers of **Islam** as well. The **Sanskrit** word *mlechcha* was applied to those who were culturally and racially alien and outside caste society, but without derogatory connotations.

Indians now known as Hindu probably did not use the term for themselves before the 14th or 15th century. In the 17th century, **Shivaji** used the term Hindu to distinguish his followers from the **Mughals** they were fighting. In 18th- and early 19th-century British writings, the word "Hindoo" applied to any native of India, but as British administration was extended over the Indian subcontinent, differentiations were made between Hindu and Muslim, and codifications of "Hindu law" were also attempted. In modern times, therefore, Hindu has come to mean followers of certain norms of conduct and social practices known as **Hinduism**, another composite term for the many non-Semitic, non-exclusive religions of India.

Hindu self-consciousness came in response to British rule and found some articulation in the writings of **Ram Mohun Roy** and subsequent leaders of the social reform movement in the 19th century. Self-definition became even more urgent in the Indian nationalist movement of the 20th century when separate communal electorates for Muslims, **Christians**, and **Sikhs** accompanied constitutional reform and the categorization of **Untouchables** as Hindu was controversial. Hindu nationalism as a social and political phenomenon was a product of the first half of the 20th century. It reasserted itself in the 1980s and 1990s, when socioeconomic strains seemed to have undermined the secular administrative and political structure established by the **Indian Constitution**.

The Constitution guarantees "freedom of conscience and the right freely to profess, practice and propagate religion." Its references to Hindus are only in the context of carrying forward social reform objectives, including the erosion of caste barriers, access to public religious institutions, and amendments to personal law permitting improvement in the status (and inheritance rights) of **women**. An explanatory clause for Article 25 (permitting the state to pass laws on these subjects) says that for such purposes "the reference to Hindus shall be construed as . . . persons professing the Sikh, Jain or Buddhist religion." In other words, the term Hindu has mainly geographical and social connotations and, as such, refers to the majority of the people of India.

HINDU MAHASABHA, ALL INDIA. The Hindu Mahasabha was founded in 1915 as a **political party** by **Punjabi Hindus** who resented the extra weight given to Muslims in the province by the system of separate electorates that was introduced in 1909. Later, led by its president **Madan Moham Malaviya**, the Hindu Mahasabha overhauled its organization and declared its larger goal to be "the maintenance, protection and promotion of the Hindu race, Hindu culture and Hindu civilization for the advancement of the Hindu Rashtra [nation]." To that end, it projected India as a Holy Land, adopted Hindi as its language, advocated cow protection as state policy, and encouraged an active program of *shuddhi*, or purification, and "reconversion" of **Christians, Muslims**, and **Sikhs** to the Hindu fold.

The Hindu Mahasabha could not compete effectively with the **Indian National Congress** in the political arena nor could it build a separate national organization, although joint membership was permitted. The Mahasabha party was soundly defeated in the provincial elections of 1937. Under the leadership of **V. D. Savarkar** and B. S. Munje in the 1940s, the Mahasabha gained financial and moral support from some Hindu princes, landowners, and industrialists, and it cooperated with the British authorities. The party criticized the secular democratic platform of Congress and opposed all attempts to reach a negotiated settlement with the **Muslim League**. The Mahasabha was routed again in the 1946 elections. Banned temporarily after the assassination of **Mahatma Gandhi** in 1948, it soon ceased to operate as a political party, although many of its objectives and members found a home in the **Jana Sangha** founded in 1951 and the **Bharatiya Janata Party** embraced its **Hindutva** program.

HINDUISM. The term has come to be used to refer to the religious beliefs and social observances of the majority of the people of India. (See Appendix G.) Hinduism cannot be defined in precise terms because it has no common credo, dogmas, doctrines, or universally acceptable canon. It has no church or clerics or hierarchy of ecclesiastical authority. It has no uniformity of worship and does not necessarily entail belief in God. Indeed, the use of Hinduism in the singular is apt to be misleading because the term encompasses a multitude of faiths, philosophies, and social observances that have been born or have evolved in the Indian subcontinent from before the beginning of historical time. Some commentators see Hinduism as characterized by orthopraxis—customary observances relating to **caste**, diet, pollution, and rites of passage—rather than by orthodoxy or conformity of belief. Acceptance of the doctrine of karma (see Glossary) and the cycle of rebirth is common throughout India.

For the above reasons, perhaps the most conspicuous characteristics of Hinduism are its pluralism and absorptive capacity that often translate into tolerance of differences and what in the present day is termed "secularism" or the absence of an established state religion. Over the millennia, old and new influences were melded in thought while aboriginal and new immigrant groups were accommodated in society, resulting in linkages among various theistic pantheons as well as discrete developments in different parts of the subcontinent or different times. In very broad historical terms and without in any way implying linear development, a chronological tabulation of Hinduism could read as follows:

1. Pre-**Dravidian** faiths and practices that probably included animism and totemism.
2. Pre-Vedic faiths and practices that almost certainly included meditative techniques, **yoga**, lingam or phallic worship, and perhaps non-theistic faiths that found full expression later.
3. Vedic religion based on the **Vedas** and associated with the Indo-Aryan speaking peoples, their sacrificial rites, and worship of a pantheon of deities.
4. **Brahmanism**, stressing the authority of the Vedas and associated with a systematization of *varna-ashrama-dharma* as a way of life and a hierarchical organization of settled society by caste. Metaphysical theories and the philosophy of advaita (see Glossary) or nondualism were fully developed. At a time of intense intellectual, social, and spiritual inquiry the **Buddhist** and **Jain** belief systems were developed and expanded.
5. Puranic Hinduism as distinguished from Vedic Brahmanism because it absorbed some Buddhist influences and because the **Puranas**, composed in the early centuries of the Common Era, provided the basis for the worship of specific deities in the form of a personal God. Various sects developed, notably the Vaishnava or worshippers of **Vishnu**, the Shaiva or worshippers of **Shiva**, and the Shakta or worshippers of manifestations of Shakti the Goddess. Many differentiations existed within each.
6. **Bhakti** movements after the eighth century gave rise to devotional sects worshipping an incarnate God, especially **Krishna** or **Ram**, as well as a non-incarnate One. Bhakti showed the influence of strong mystic traditions originating within India as well as in **Sufic Islam**.
7. Reformist or revivalist Hinduism of the 19th century was born under the impact of evangelical **Christianity** and rigorous self-criticism among the Hindu elite. The **Brahmo Samaj**, the **Arya**

Samaj, and the **Ramakrishna Mission** epitomized various aspects of this phase.

8. Nationalistic Hinduism of the 20th century shares many characteristics with other religious traditions, including Christianity and **Islam**, undergoing reification under the stress of modernization. Efforts are made to introduce or enforce conformity and discipline and introduce a political and social agenda.

HINDUTVA. This 20th-century ideology was first elaborated by **Veer Savarkar** in a book by that name which was published in 1923. Savarkar distinguished between **Hinduism** as a religion, which he called Sanatan Dharma, and Hindutva, which he defined in cultural, historical, linguistic, racial, and religious terms as the unifying cement of the Indian (Hindu) people who loved and worshipped their fatherland. This definition explicitly excluded those Indians whose language and faith originated outside India, such as Christians and Muslims, irrespective of their allegiance to and citizenship of the other nation, their parentage, their numbers, or the long history of their faith being practiced in India. They were designated "foreigners." Savarkar further asserted the superiority of Hinduism, which according to him included religions born and developed in India, such as **Buddhism, Jainism**, and **Sikhism**, over all other faiths and called on Hindus to unite and fight their enemies. Hindutva developed through the century as a socio-religious movement as well as a political initiative that gathered momentum during the 1990s.

Hindutva is centrally concerned with goals of social solidarity, focusing on questions of identity and symbols and practices that link members of a national community. It is equally concerned with matters of prestige, exhorting its adherents to take pride in being Hindu through the slogan: "*garv se kaho hum hindu hain*" ("say with pride, we are Hindu") and demanding an elevated status for India in the international community. Many people today translate Hindutva as Hindu Nationalism or Nationalist Hinduism. These phrases underline both the self-assertiveness of the ideology and the problems that it creates for minority communities in multi-religious, secular, India.

Hindutva as a socio-religious movement grew out of 19th-century efforts at reform and revivalism that took many forms. Some perceived "Hindu weakness" to be both cause and effect of successive subjugation by Muslim Turks and Christian Europeans and tried to purge weaknesses and develop strengths among Hindus along British standards of the day. One revivalist stream, expressed subsequently as Hindutva, strove to create a more cohesive, coherent, masculine indeed muscular, Hinduism than its pluralistic tradition and practice. Toward this goal, the **Rashtriya Swayamsevak Sangh (RSS)** was organized in 1925. The RSS undertook vigorous training first of young high caste Hindu males in western India and later in a widening circle of communities, with a separate and vigorous cadre of women. Its social and humanitarian work at the grassroots level in many states has had a cumulative and favorable impact sometimes exceeding that of other movements. Hindutva projects the aspiration of recreating a "golden age" in India, epitomized in the phrase *Ram Rajya* (Rama's reign of righteousness). A vigorous cultural program glorifies India's pre-Islamic, pre-British, past and toward that end it advocates the rewriting of school textbooks and the introduction of new (in fact, ancient and sometimes esoteric) subjects of instruction at university level. Scientific historians and other modernists in academia contest these efforts in acrimonious debate. Hindutva forces seek to reclaim many Hindu temples that were allegedly destroyed or were buried under mosques that were constructed during the **Delhi Sultanate** and **Mughal** periods. The most eloquent and violence-ridden emblem of this aim is the decades-long controversy over building a temple to Ram on the disputed land of **Ayodhya**.

Hindutva as a political movement first found expression in the **Hindu Mahasabha** created as a political party in 1914–1915 and then in the **Jana Sangha** founded in 1951. Both were opposed to the inclusive policy of secular nation building that was a major plank of the **Indian National Congress**. The **Bharatiya Janata Party (BJP)** was formed in 1980 as a successor to the Jana Sangha and with its leadership drawn from RSS cadres, but it functions as one among many national **political parties**. The **Vishva Hindu Parishad (VHP)** or World Hindu Council formed in 1984 is more vociferous and single minded in pursuing the aim of welding heterogeneous Hindu groups together into a dominant majority in India, often with material help from the Indian **diaspora**.

The dramatic rise of the BJP from a small party with only two **Lok Sabha** seats in 1984 to a confident party that won 182 seats in the

1998 and 1999 elections and leading the governing coalition in power until its defeat in the 2004 general elections has led some to ascribe its political success to the appeal of Hindutva ideology. As illustration they point to Hindutva's hardliner Narendra Modi's sweeping electoral victory in the **Gujarat** elections of December 2002, even after he conducted a virulently communal campaign and allegedly used state institutions against Muslims. Others point out that the BJP failed to gain a majority in many other state elections on a Hindutva platform, especially those held in 1993 after demolition of the Babri Masjid, and in 2004 lost resoundingly in Gujarat and the temple towns of Ayodhya, Mathura, and Varanasi. Significantly, the BJP was able to lead a governing coalition of 23 political parties only by modifying its stance and appealing to what it called "genuine secularism." In 1998, the BJP signed a National Democratic Alliance common electoral platform from which key items of the Hindutva agenda were omitted; that is, building a Ram temple at Ayodhya, repealing the special constitutional status of **Jammu and Kashmir**, and legislating a common civil code for all communities in India, including Muslims. Moreover, there is little doubt that the success of the BJP in 1998 and 1999 owed much to the numerical strength of regional political parties that were willing to ally with it in the Lok Sabha as well as to the decline of **Congress** after 1989. Meanwhile, **Dalits** and rural Other Backward Castes have become increasingly empowered, while the traditional appeal of Hindutva was to the urban upper castes. The relative weight of ideology, **caste** identity, class interests, and other influences on voter behavior is variable. In short, despite its powerful rhetoric, high visibility, and sociocultural thrust, Hindutva is only one among several factors operating in Indian politics today.

HIV/AIDS. The disease known as acquired immune deficiency syndrome (AIDS) caused by the human immunodeficiency virus (HIV) has reached epidemic levels in some parts of India. It is attracting national and international attention because the absolute number of people involved is large even though the percentage of total population affected is still small, especially in comparison with some African countries. The Indian government in 2003 estimated 4.58 million persons, or about 1% of the adult population, to be infected with the HIV virus; the total number of AIDS cases registered in 2002 was estimated at 600,000. Unofficial estimates tend to be higher, with the head of the National Aids Control Organization (NACO) projecting figures of 10 to 14 million infected persons by 2010.

The states of **Andhra Pradesh**, **Karnataka**, **Maharashtra**, and **Tamil Nadu** in the south, and **Manipur** and **Nagaland** in the northeast are regarded as high-risk and high-prevalence states. In addition, there are pockets of high prevalence in the states of **Gujarat**, **Goa**, and **Pondicherry** and the likelihood of high prevalence pockets in all cities, including **Delhi** and **Kolkata**, as well as in the highly populated but least developed states of **Bihar** and **Uttar Pradesh**. HIV transmission in India is predominantly through heterosexual sex, with concentrations among sex workers and subsequent spread to the general population by truckers and migrant workers. The second most frequent route of transmission is through intravenous drug use and the sharing of syringes, especially in the northeast and in cities like Delhi. Because condom use is very low in India, the epidemic can spread quickly, and data compiled in Andhra Pradesh show little variation between urban and rural districts in terms of HIV prevalence. The generally low status of **women**, their poverty and lack of power, make them and their children especially vulnerable to HIV/AIDS, the more so because many cases are undiagnosed and untreated. India's thin spread and underfinanced public health facilities compound the risks of the epidemic reaching crisis proportions in the coming decade unless prophylactic measures prove effective.

The topic of HIV/AIDS was generally taboo in India until recently, largely because very conservative attitudes toward sex made it hard to discuss sexually transmitted diseases or to disseminate information on preventive or curative measures. Other inhibitions are the heavy social stigma attached to HIV/AIDS, ostracism of infected persons, and widespread belief that only marginal populations were threatened while most Indians are somehow "culturally protected." Awareness is spreading beyond the circle of public health officials and **non-governmental organizations (NGOs)** most concerned, however, because political leaders, including the prime minister, health minister, and chief ministers of some states, have put the issue of HIV/AIDS squarely on the map in the past year or two. And also because measures taken by foreign donor agencies including the World Bank, the Global Fund to Fight AIDS, Tuberculosis and Malaria, the Bill and Melinda Gates

Foundation, and the Clinton Foundation, HIV/AIDS initiatives have been well publicized. Many NGOs are actively involved in the prevention and treatment of HIV/AIDS as well as in rehabilitation of patients; others attempt to mobilize public personalities from various walks of life to communicate on the subject and to motivate local administrators and politicians to act.

India's wealth of human skills in health, medicine, pharmaceuticals, social development, and science could check a pandemic. The National AIDS Research Institute (NARI) and NACO were established in the early 1990s, from part of the international network against HIV/AIDS, and have established decentralized frameworks nationally. For example, NACO led a vigorous and pioneering television campaign on HIV/AIDS directed at young people, for which it won a Commonwealth award in 2003. NGOs vary by size and location; their specific efforts are usually well rewarded by results, although the long-term goal of ending gender discrimination demands more effort. Leading Indian pharmaceutical companies, such as Cipla and **Ranbaxy Laboratories Ltd.**, already manufacture generic drugs used for HIV/AIDS at competitive prices and supply them to other badly infected countries. The health ministry in India and state governments expect the Indian pharmaceutical industry to play a leading role in combating AIDS by making antiretroviral (ARV) medications available at affordable prices in government hospitals in a program that commenced in 2004. Other suggestions on how best to control the spread of HIV/AIDS surface often, and it is likely that patterns of response will vary greatly, even as levels of alarm vary from place to place and from group to group. Perhaps the only valid generalization is a statement that the coming decade will be a decisive one for HIV/AIDS in India.

HOME RULE LEAGUE. Bal Gangadhar Tilak and **Annie Besant** established two organizations in 1916 with the same name as the Irish Home Rule League and had similar objectives of advancing India toward self-government. Tilak's efforts were focused mainly in western India, while Annie Besant was more active in the rest of the country; many followers joined both.

The Home Rule movement was essentially moderate—educating public opinion, organizing peaceful agitations, and basing its claims on India's contributions to **World War I** and to Britain's sense of justice. Governmental reaction, however, was typically heavy-handed until the **Montagu Declaration** of August 1917 promised "responsible government." Evaluations of the Home Rule League vary. Neither organization was strong; neither appeared to achieve much; yet both served to sustain momentum in the national movement and the **Indian National Congress** between the pre-war era and the very different post-war period of **Mahatma Gandhi**'s leadership and mass mobilization.

HOYSALA DYNASTY (1047–1327). The dynasty ruled **Mysore** for more than 300 years before being overthrown by a general of the **Tughlaq** Dynasty in **Delhi**. At first subordinate to the **Chalukya** Dynasty, the Hoysala kings gained their independence and extended their territories until theirs became the most powerful kingdom of the **Deccan** in the 12th century. Originally a **Jain**, King Vishnuvardhana converted to the worship of **Vishnu** because of the sage **Ramanuja**. The Hoysalas built several star-shaped temples covered by extraordinarily beautiful and complicated sculpture, sometimes in great sheets of bas-relief. The temples at Belur and Halebid are the best known and are the chief source of Hoysala fame today.

HUME, ALLAN OCTAVIAN (1829–1912). Hume was of Scottish descent and went to India as a member of the **Indian Civil Service (ICS)** in 1849. He had already taken some scientific and medical training, which was unusual for ICS recruits. Hume's work as a district officer in **Bengal** was infused by his desire to improve Indian agriculture, education, and health. He became critical of British indifference to the welfare of their Indian subjects, especially during the viceroyalty of Lord Lytton (1876–1880) when imperial interests were markedly in ascendance. Hume voluntarily retired from the ICS in 1882 but remained in India.

Hume started an organization of educated Indians drawn from the cities of **Bombay**, **Calcutta**, and **Madras** in 1883. The purposes of this organization were to encourage personal acquaintanceship and the habit of discussing political issues of moment among a network of similarly inclined Indians and, perhaps, to influence the British Government of India by reasoned debate. Hume tried, but failed, to obtain official support and participation by approaching **Lord Dufferin**. Initially named the Indian National Union, the organization founded by Hume was renamed the **Indian National Congress** at its Bombay meeting of 72 delegates in 1885. Hume was its secretary and used his organizational talents, first in India until 1893, and then in London where **Dadabhai Naoroji** and **William Wedderburn** had earlier formed the British Committee of Congress, to educate British public opinion on India.

At its annual session in 1912, Congress formally recorded its gratitude to Hume, naming him "father and founder" of the pan-Indian organization in the vanguard of the national movement which ultimately won independence in 1947.

HUNAS or HUNS. This is a generic term used for a variety of nomadic tribes from central Asia that assailed India at the end of the fifth and through the sixth century CE. Among other acts of destruction, they razed the city and great **Buddhist** monasteries of **Taxila**. They were related to the Hun tribes that had invaded Europe and Persia somewhat earlier, and to the Epthalites or White Huns who had established themselves in the Oxus valley and Afghanistan at about the same time. Constant pressure from the Hunas absorbed the energies of Kumara Gupta and his successors of the **Gupta Dynasty**. Defense of the northwestern marches absorbed resources that could have been used to consolidate the empire.

The Hunas were the catalyst for disintegration of an imperial system into a number of small kingdoms and diminished the potential of recreating a northern Indian empire. Besides the physical destruction they wreaked, the Hunas caused a displacement of peoples and added new ethnic elements to the north and west of the subcontinent. Some of those who subsequently became politically and socially important there, such as the **Rajputs** and the **Jats**, might have been descended from the Hunas. In the opinion of some historians, the absorption of the Hunas into the existing socio-religious culture of India left the ruling elite of northern India psychologically unprepared for the next set of invasions from central Asia in the 10th century and after by people whose Islamic faith made them resistant to assimilation into **brahmanical** society.

HUQ/HAQ, ABUL KASIM FAZLUL (1873–1962). The son of a lawyer, Fazlul Huq was educated in Arabic and Persian and then joined Presidency College in **Calcutta**, where he took a science degree in 1894 before studying law. He was successively teacher, journalist, and editor before entering politics. He did not belong to the landowning class or even to the intelligentsia, and he put himself forward as a champion of the poor. As a Muslim from East Bengal, Huq supported **Lord Curzon**'s 1905 **partition of Bengal** and worked behind the scenes in behalf of the Nawab of Dacca for the formation of the **All-India Muslim League** in 1906. Huq was president of the League from 1916 to 1921, while also serving as a joint secretary in the **Indian National Congress**. He was a member of the committee set up to investigate the **Jallianwala Bagh** massacre of 1919.

Huq entered the Bengal Legislative Council in 1913 and remained a member of it until 1947, except for the time he was in the Central Legislative Assembly from 1934 to 1936. He became a minister under the system of provincial **dyarchy**, amended the Calcutta Municipal Act to give more representation to Muslims, supported institutions of higher education, and gained administrative experience as well as the power of patronage. In 1929, he formed the Krishak Praja Party to represent Bengal's peasantry, attacking the **Permanent Settlement** and its beneficiaries, the Hindu *bhadralok*, or gentry, in the process. Although the Krishak Praja Party did not long remain united, it gave Huq and his Bengali followers political bargaining power within the Muslim League, where they clashed with **Mohammed Ali Jinnah** who was striving for recognition as sole spokesman of the Indian Muslims.

No party won a majority in Bengal in the 1937 elections that were held in the numerically expanded but communally separated electorate specified by the **Government of India Act** of 1935. Congress, the largest single party, was slow to accept office, and Huq headed a coalition ministry, which came to lean on League support before breaking again with Jinnah. In 1941, Huq was invited first to join the Viceroy's Defence Council and then to form a new ministry in Bengal. He headed the latter and included some Congress followers of **Sarat Chandra Bose** as well as the right-wing Hindu Shyama Prasad Mookerji. Huq did not win the full support of other Muslim leaders in Bengal and was unable to pose an effective challenge to Jinnah in the 1940s. After **Partition**, Huq was an active politician in East Pakistan and was chief minister in 1954–1955 before the martial state became firmly established in that country.

HURRIYAT. The All Party Hurriyat Conference (APHC) is an umbrella alliance of about 30 religious, political, and social groups (the estimated number varies between 26 and 34) furthering the cause of **Kashmir**'s secession from the Indian Union. Although headed by a seven-member Executive Council the Hurriyat is faction ridden, and constituent groups often disagree on both objectives and tactics. The Hurriyat was formed in March 1993 when the 1989 insurgency and ensuing **terrorist** violence in **Jammu and Kashmir** seemed to be subsiding in the face of counter-insurgency operations launched by the Indian security forces and peaceful ending of a siege at the famous Hazrat Bal mosque in **Srinagar**.

Pakistan welcomed and sponsored the Hurriyat as part of its continuing campaign to gain control over all of Kashmir. Pakistan's Inter Service Intelligence (ISI) organization, which had honed its proxy war skills in Afghanistan against the Soviet Union, sought to marginalize moderate elements of the indigenous Jammu and Kashmir Liberation Front (JKLF) who were pleading for independence or autonomy and to replace them by militant Islamist groups preaching *jihad* (holy war) against India. Some of these pro-Pakistan groups were linked to the *Jamaat-I-Islami*, others to the *Hizbul Mujaheddin*, and their chief spokesman was Sayyid Ali Shah Gilani, calling for "liberation." Unlike some other Hurriyat leaders, notably Maulvi Abbas Ansari and the late Abdur Ghani Lome, Gilani refused to enter into talks with the Indian government and pressed for trilateral talks seating Pakistan.

Although initially popular in Kashmir and given prominence by Pakistan's leaders and diplomats, the Hurriyat has gradually lost support among the Kashmiri people. Revulsion caused by atrocities committed by an estimated 3,000 "foreign" militants—Afghan, Arab, and Pakistani—sent across the Line of Control by the ISI is probably one reason for its diminished appeal. Another reason is factionalism with the Hurriyat, a merger of Kashmir with Pakistan is only a minority view; most favoring independence or at least greater autonomy within the Indian Union. The 2002 free and fair elections in Jammu and Kashmir and India's open attempts since then to placate and win over public opinion in Kashmir may also have made a difference.

Successive governments in **New Delhi** and **Srinagar** have vacillated in their dealings with the Hurriyat between total opposition, to willingness to talk at high levels, to ensuring through stupidity that Hurriyat members boycott elections, to offering unilateral concessions such as travel permits to its leaders. The future role of the Hurriyat is obviously entwined with the prospects of crafting peace in Kashmir.

HUSAIN, MAQBOOL FIDA (1915–). Hussain is one of the best-known and most popular artists of contemporary India. He began his career as a 20-year-old, painting posters for Bombay's burgeoning **film industry**, and from the 1950s to the present day he has held one-man exhibitions of his paintings all over the world. He was awarded the Padma Shri in 1966 and the Padma Bhushan in 1973, and was nominated to the **Rajya Sabha** in 1986. He is eclectic in his choice of subject matter, and is refreshingly individualistic and down to earth in his manner and style of life. From time to time, he and his work have been vandalized by rowdy elements of the **Bajrang Dal** or **Shiv Sena**, but he does not appear to carry a grievance. Husain is generous to aspiring artists and is willing to collaborate with film-makers. One film about himself made in 1967 is *Through the Eyes of a Painter*. His paintings are found in many private and public collections.

HYDERABAD. The capital city of **Andhra Pradesh**, Hyderabad was formerly the capital of a large **Princely State** of the same name situated in the **Deccan**. Its schools of painting, architecture, and Urdu literature expressed a distinctive culture combining elements from its long line of Muslim rulers and its predominantly **Hindu** population, from northern India as well as from the Deccan.

The territory of Hyderabad had been ruled under various names by many different dynasties over the millennia but became part of the **Bahmani Sultanate** in the 15th century CE and then the kingdom of Golconda, conquered by the **Mughal Emperor Aurangzeb** in 1687. As a Mughal province, Hyderabad was ably governed by Nizam ul-Mulk Asaf Jah, who made himself virtually independent of **Delhi** after the death of Aurangzeb; Asaf Jah and his successors took the title of Nizam. They commanded the main trading and military routes across the Deccan, owned almost legendary wealth based on Hyderabad's gold and diamond mines, and played a prominent role in the fluctuating alliances and conflicts of peninsular India among the **Marathas**, **Mysore**, the **English East India Company**, and the French, through the latter half of the 18th century.

By the end of the century the Nizam of Hyderabad had been forced to cede much of his territory to the British, with whom he signed a **Subsidiary Alliance** in 1798. Owing to its large size (equivalent to France) and immense wealth, Hyderabad enjoyed a considerable degree of autonomy in internal affairs, subject to overall supervision of the British Resident. But its rulers were never entirely comfortable with permanent loss of a territory such as Berar and sometimes questioned British interpretations of earlier treaties, leading on one occasion to an inquiry by **Sir Harcourt Butler** and his disquisition on **paramountcy**.

Hyderabad state was connected by road, railway, and postal services with surrounding territories of British India but kept largely insulated from the currents of nationalist opinion flowing there. Despite some able administrators, such as **Salar Jang**, the Nizam's government remained autocratic and seemed to become more so during the decade 1937–1947 when constitutional provisions for the future of India were under discussion. The last Nizam entertained illusions of independence after the departure of the British. After some altercation and a limited "police action" ordered by New Delhi, Hyderabad was joined to the Indian Union in 1948. Territorial changes were brought about by the reorganization of Indian states on the basis of **language** after 1958, and the (largest) portion inhabited by Telegu speakers was incorporated into Andhra Pradesh. Since the mid-1990s, the city of Hyderabad has been a hub of information and other high technology under the leadership of Chandrababu Naidu of the governing **Telegu Desham Party**.

– I –

ILBERT BILL (1883–1884). This is the popular name for the Criminal Procedure Amendment Code Bill introduced in the Central Legislative Council by law member Sir Courteney Ilbert during the administration of **Lord Ripon** (1880–1884). The Bill had been prepared with the concurrence of governors in the presidencies as well as the Secretary of State for India in William Gladstone's liberal government in Britain. It proposed to give jurisdiction in trying British or European as well as Indian offenders to those members of the **Indian Civil Service (ICS)** serving as district magistrates and sessions judges, irrespective of color, **caste**, or creed.

The proposed legislation aroused a storm of protest from the British and European community in India that launched an unprecedented agitation against it, amounting almost to a "white mutiny." Ripon refused to withdraw the bill but agreed to a compromise by which British and European offenders could demand trial by a jury in which half the numbers would be European. The racist basis of the agitation, as well as the compromise, widened the existing gulf between British rulers and Indian subjects, notwithstanding the popularity of Lord Ripon among the latter for attempting to narrow it.

One unintended consequence of the Ilbert Bill controversy was to accelerate moves among educated Indians to organize themselves into all-India associations, or pressure groups, for political purposes. It was no coincidence that the first meeting of the **Indian National Congress** was held in 1885.

ILTUTMISH, SHAMS UD-DIN (r. 1211–1236). Iltutmish belonged to the Ilbari tribe of Turkestan. He was in the service of **Qutbud din Aibak** who occupied **Delhi** after his master, Muhammad Ghori, defeated **Prithviraj Chauhan** in 1192. Iltutmish consolidated Aibak's conquests in northern India by successively defeating the **Rajput** chiefs of Ranthambhor, Mandawar, Gwalior, Malwa, and **Ujjain**. He also subdued opposition from other Turkish generals either by force or by making grants of land revenue (*iqta*) to them. He legitimized his authority among fellow Muslims by obtaining a patent of investiture from the reigning caliph of Baghdad and striking silver coins in the Caliph's name. His other important achievement was in blocking the advance of Mongol raids led by Chengiz Khan into the Indian subcontinent.

Iltutmish was the real founder of the **Delhi Sultanate**, which was ruled by five dynasties of Turkish or Afghan descent before the **Mughal Empire**. He set the pattern that they followed of mixing Indian traditions of local civil administration with Turkish military rule and Koranic law. He confirmed the *dhimmi* (see Glossary) status of non-Muslims, assuring them of the protection of the state as long as they paid the extra taxes required of them, and permitted most **Hindu** Rajas to retain control of their domains. At the same time, he rewarded his own Muslim generals, reorganized the army, and made it the mainstay of his throne at Delhi. Finding his sons incompetent to rule after him, Iltutmish named his highly able daughter, Raziya, his successor.

INDIAN ADMINISTRATIVE SERVICE (IAS). Commonly regarded as the successor to the **Indian Civil Service (ICS)** in prestige, power, and presumption of high motivation toward public service, the IAS has performed a wider spectrum of duties than its predecessor of the British Raj under the vastly changed circumstances of an independent parliamentary democracy launching planned economic development. Numbering less than 5,000 out of several million government employees, the IAS is an elite cadre, and its members occupy the highest echelons of bureaucracy in the central and state governments. In the course of their careers, the men and women of the IAS administer remote rural districts as well as modern public sector industries. They serve much of their time in the state to which they are allocated at the start of their careers and go to the central government on deputation, for shorter or longer periods, in rotation. They may also serve in foreign missions or with international organizations. The ICS preference for generalists has been carried into the IAS despite considerable pressure for specialization.

The basic conditions for the recruitment and terms of the all-India civil services—the Indian Administrative Service, the Indian Police Service, and the Indian Foreign Service, with an Indian Forest Service established in 1966—were set out in the **Indian Constitution** of 1950 and the All-India Services Act of 1951. The Union Public Service Commission, an independent advisory body appointed by the president and with its own secretariat, is responsible for all matters relating to recruitment and discipline of the all-India services. Recruitment is from college graduates aged 21 to 28, or 31 for members of the Scheduled Castes and Tribes, who must qualify in a series of written examinations and interviews. Competition is stiff, with approximately 100 being taken to the IAS in a year from among applicants numbering nearly 100,000. Although most recruits in the first decades after independence were English-speaking high-caste males from famous universities, the social composition of the IAS has been widened considerably by the entrance of fairly large numbers of women (approximately 20%), provisions for taking examinations in regional languages after 1978, constitutional reservations for Scheduled Castes and Tribes as well as 'Other Backward' Classes who see government service as the prime ladder for upward mobility, and regular promotion to the IAS from state civil services. The service is no longer socially homogeneous, but strong personal and professional bonds often are forged among its members.

IAS recruits receive training at a foundation course in Mussoorie for one year before field training in the states to which they are assigned. Approximately 50% of a state's cadre is drawn from outside that state, but considerable tension between union and state governments has been generated on the subject of IAS appointments. Having successfully completed probation and passed language and other examinations, IAS members are promoted and transferred according to seniority and merit; they enjoy security of tenure with pension and other benefits. IAS pay scales, however, are low in comparison to what its members could command in the private sector. Some of the unfortunate consequences of this discrepancy are: a gradual decline in the caliber of young people choosing public service as their first career option, a leakage of competent mid- and senior level administrators who leave the service early, and suspicion in the perception of others that the IAS is not immune to corruption and abuse of its very considerable powers.

There are other reasons why the IAS in particular and officialdom in general command less respect in India 50 or more years after independence than they did before. One reason is the frequently uncomfortable relationship between the political leadership, especially in the states, and civil servants. IAS members swear to uphold the Constitution and the laws of the country, may not join political parties while in service, are required to give honest, frank, and politically neutral advice, and yet are obliged to implement the decisions of politicians whose criteria of judgment may be different from their own and whose connections with legitimate or criminal sources of funds may be strong. Mutual trust and confidence under circumstances of constant political interference is difficult to achieve and has often given way either to mutual accommodation and complaisance, or to subservience or recalcitrance in the bureaucracy, all at the expense of honesty and efficiency in administration.

Another reason for the loss of prestige was the greatly expanded role of government in socioeconomic developmental activities after independence, which demanded qualities of expertise and character sometimes beyond those possessed by traditional civil servants; it also opened them to undesirable influences and temptations. More than 20 committees and commissions have been set up since 1947 and have recommended administrative reforms conducive to responsiveness and accountability necessary in a democracy, without noticeable effect. Economic reforms reducing governmental control—and opportunities for corruption of officials—may incidentally help to curtail the power but restore public confidence in the IAS.

INDIAN ARMED FORCES. The Republic of India has 1,325,000 men and women, all volunteers, on active duty in the armed forces with reserves of 500,000 and a volunteer Territorial Army of 40,000. Supreme command is constitutionally vested in the President of India, which means that the prime minister, along with the defense minister and the Political Affairs Committee of the cabinet, are responsible for political control of the armed forces. Civilian supremacy over the military is firmly entrenched in India, with defense policy and procurements also in civilian hands for the most part. The three service chiefs are responsible for the functioning of their respective services, army, navy and air force, often competing for lean budgetary allocations. Some steps were taken in the 1990s to increase defense policy input from the military; articulate retired senior officers were appointed to the National Security Advisory Board, and several new security related journals and academic programs catered to active and retired service personnel. A decision to appoint a Chief of Defense Services (CDS) and CDS staff intended to promote greater coordination and cooperation among the three services was announced, but the actual appointment of a CDS is yet to take place. At a slightly lower level, however, a joint three-service command was established in the **Andaman and Nicobar Islands** in 2000. India's emergence as a nuclear weapons state in 1998, its enunciation of a draft **nuclear doctrine** in 1999, and its claims to a clear command and control system necessitated establishing a Strategic Forces Command to take charge of all nuclear operations, if and when necessary. Although all three services are equipped with missiles, there is no public information on whether or where nuclear warheads might be deployed.

The Indian Army is the oldest of the three services and over one million strong. It is organized in five regional commands, 12 corps, three armored divisions, four RAPID divisions, 18 infantry divisions, 10 mountain divisions, two artillery divisions, 16 independent brigades, and four engineering brigades. In late 2004, the army published a new doctrine stressing greater reliance on special forces capable of acting rapidly and over long distances, greater coordination with air and sea forces, and increased reliance on surveillance systems.

Much of the equipment of the Indian army is produced within India, and trials of indigenous main battle tanks and missiles are conducted. Moderately sophisticated artillery, armor, and missiles are imported from more than one source. There was heavy reliance on Soviet supplies in the 1970s and 1980s, and Russia remains an important and reliable supplier, especially of T-72 and new T-90 S battle tanks to be assembled in India under a technology transfer agreement signed in 2001. After 1992, India established ambassadorial and cooperative relations with Israel that included intelligence sharing to counter **terrorism** and purchases of high technology specialized items of defense equipment. New Delhi also envisages high technology defense purchases from the United States as the New Steps in Strategic Partnership (NSSP) agreed to in 2003–2004 is implemented.

The Indian Army is deployed defensively, mainly along the perimeters of continental India: close to the western border with **Pakistan**, in the north on the Line of Control (LOC) in **Jammu and Kashmir** and in **Ladakh**, in the northeast close to the mountainous **Line of Actual Control** (LAC) with China, and in the east on the border with **Myanmar**. After a terrorist attack on Parliament in December 2001, ascribed to Pakistan's agents, the army was mobilized and deployed in Operation *Parikrama* for several months in 2002; there were no open hostilities. An Indian Peace Keeping Force (IPKF) of about 50,000 was sent to **Sri Lanka** on the basis of an accord between President Jayawardene and Prime Minister **Rajiv**

Gandhi in 1987 but was withdrawn in 1990. Indian forces have served with distinction under the flag of the United Nations as international peacekeepers or military observers in Korea, the Middle East, the Congo, Cyprus, the Iran-Iraq border, Ethiopia, Somalia, and Sierra Leone. India declined a request by the United States to send a division of troops to fight in Iraq in 2003 because that operation was not under United Nations auspices.

The Indian army has a long and impressive heritage of non-political, dedicated service to the state. Its present form, esprit de corps, ethics, and traditions owe something to the long indigenous military history of the subcontinent but descend directly from the British Indian Army. This was initially raised by the **East India Company** in the 18th century and was radically altered after the great **Uprising of 1857** to exclude Indians from technical arms and officer status. Further reforms were introduced in the first half of the 20th century, first by **Lord Kitchener**, and then after **World War I** when equipment was improved and the principle of appointing Indians as officers was gradually accepted under nationalist prodding. The Indian Military Academy was established in 1936. During **World War II**, the Indian Army grew to 2,500,000 men and served in North Africa, the Middle East, Europe, and Southeast Asia, operating the most complex mechanical equipment and winning awards for gallantry. The Indian Army was divided at **Partition**; Pakistan refused to accept any non-Muslims, but the Indian armed forces include members of all religious and ethnic communities.

A conscious choice was made in independent India *not* to jettison British Indian military traditions, especially those of civilian authority, in favor of nationalist or revolutionary models that were surfacing elsewhere. But in contrast to British India, there was continuous neglect of the armed forces by the political leadership and very low defense budgets of about 1.5% of GNP between 1947 and 1962. India's debacle in a border war with China in 1962 led to some budget increases for augmentation of numbers and equipment. Throughout the 1980s and 1990s, defense budgets fell in real terms while outlays on pensions and salaries rose and procedures for procurement of new equipment became more complex and opaque. The national budget projected for 2005 was expected to raise the defense budget to about 4% of GNP. Bruised in 1962, the Indian army recovered its self-esteem in wars with Pakistan in 1965 and in 1971 as well as in the "war like situation at Kargil" in 1999, and it is confident of maintaining peace and tranquility along the LAC. For decades, the army has assumed the difficult and dirty task of controlling insurgencies in the northeastern states, in the Punjab, and in **Kashmir** with some success and a remarkably high level of discipline, but it has not been immune to charges of human rights abuses. The army would prefer not to be used routinely for maintenance of internal security at the cost of training and rest for the troops, although it is constitutionally obliged to act as aid to civilian authority and in disaster relief, when necessary,

The Indian navy numbers 55,000 and includes a small naval air wing and 1,200 marines. It consists of three commands, with bases at Visakhapatnam, **Kolkata**, and Port Blair for the eastern fleet, **Mumbai**, **Goa**, **Lakshadweep**, and Karwar for the western fleet, and Kochi (**Cochin**) for the southern fleet. Because investment in ships requires perspective planning and high capital expenditure, the navy is far below the strength required for a country with India's geographic location, strategic interests, increasing foreign trade, long coastline, offshore oil extraction, and extensive economic zone. In 2003, the Indian Navy had only 19 submarines, eight destroyers, 16 frigates, four Corvettes, 18 minesweepers, seven amphibious vessels, and two aircraft carriers with a third under construction at Mazagaon Docks in Mumbai. Three "stealth" frigates are also under construction to be commissioned as front line ships in 2007. The Indian navy was part of the British Royal Navy before independence and was commanded by senior British officers until the mid-1950s. Its development as a blue water navy was slow, but it is an important instrument in asserting India's strategic interests in the Indian Ocean and in expanding India's diplomatic cooperation with other powers. Since 1992, the Indian navy has participated in small but significant bilateral exercises with the navies of the United States, Singapore, and China, and it is recognized as crucial to keeping open the vital sea lanes of communication between the Straits of Hormuz and the Straits of Malacca. The coast guard, with 52 patrol craft, also performs important functions but is separate from the Indian navy.

The Indian air force is the youngest of the three armed services, with 170,000 personnel; it began accepting women recruits for pilot training in the early 1990s. It is deployed in five regional air commands, and in 2003 the air force consisted of 740 combat aircraft and 40 armed helicopters. Many of these aircraft are old and have been overused in harsh conditions, so that despite high performance standards there have been too many casualties in the last decade. Replacements became imperative, despite their high cost. An indigenously designed and manufactured light combat aircraft was produced in 2004 with some foreign collaboration and after long delay. In 2004, the first Indian built long range fighter aircraft, the Russian designed Sukhoi 30, was put into service. This will probably replace the sturdy MIG 29 as the mainstay of the Indian air force. In late 2003, India signed an agreement with British Aerospace for the supply of 66 Hawk advanced jet trainers and is negotiating with the United States for purchases of surveillance aircraft.

Various paramilitary forces have been raised in India since the 1960s to supplement the three services of the armed forces for specific purposes. They include the Assam Rifles, the Border Security Force, the Central Industrial Security Force and Central Reserve Police Force, the Home Guard, Indo-Tibetan Border Police, the Ladakh Scouts, the National Security Guards, the Provincial Armed Constabulary, the Rashtriya Rifles, the Railway Protection Forces, and the Special Protection Group. Lightly armed and with widely differing standards of training and performance, the total number in paramilitary forces is now estimated at more than one million.

As a nonaligned state, India has no foreign bases or military advisers on its territory.

INDIAN CIVIL SERVICE (ICS). The ICS was the "steel frame" holding together the British Indian Empire. It came into being formally in 1858 when the British Crown assumed sovereignty over the Indian domains of the **East India Company**. The ICS reached the apogee of its power and privilege in the last quarter of the 19th century and the first decade of the 20th, although its members retained their prestige as Plato-inspired "guardians" for far longer. Their diverse achievements have inspired a considerable body of biographical and fictional literature. Some political scientists describe the ICS as approaching the Weberian model of bureaucracy: a politically neutral, impersonal, legal body of salaried professional men with high standards of personal integrity, organized hierarchically into departments. Others emphasize the tension between bureaucratic despotism, epitomized by the ICS, and political activity, generated by the national movement, in modern Indian history.

The beginnings of the ICS were in the turbulent days of the late 18th century, when the East India Company expanded its role from trading to those of collecting revenue and administering justice, and when **Lord Cornwallis** instituted a well-paid "covenanted" service for the Company as one means of reducing graft and corruption. During the 19th century, this service came to reflect deepening British convictions of their own superiority over "natives" in administering the infinite variety of India's peoples, as well as the equally entrenched belief in the ability of "gentlemen" with general education to perform whatever tasks became necessary. The **Charter Act** of 1833 introduced open competition, rather than patronage, as a method of recruitment, and this was confirmed by the Queen's Proclamation of 1858; however, emphasis on gentlemanly character, generalist background, and social compatibility remained constant features of the ICS.

Competitive examinations supervised by special commissioners were held in London. The first Indian to pass was Satyendranath Tagore in 1864. In 1876, the qualifying age was lowered from 23 to 19. With examinations confined to European classical subjects, the base of recruitment was effectively narrowed to British upper middle class males educated at public (i.e., private) schools. Although not excluded in law, when an Indian of the intelligence and wealth of a **Surendranath Banerjea** excelled in the examinations and joined the ICS, the fine print of minor rules was invoked to expel him from what had by then become a "club," whose members literally held the power of life and death over the rural millions they ruled, often with affection, as district collectors, but who seldom had fondness or respect for the educated, urban, high caste Indian. Not surprisingly, it was the latter who aspired toward the ICS for their sons, and the annual resolutions passed by the **Indian National Congress** from the time of its inception in 1885 regularly demanded raising the age limit to 21 and holding simultaneous examinations in India and England for recruitment to the ICS. These demands were long ignored by the British authorities—who preferred to appoint

Indians of the landowning aristocracy to positions of limited responsibility—but were finally met in 1922.

At the time of **World War I**, Indians filled only 5% of all available positions in the ICS and the closely linked Indian Police Service (IPS). In 1923, the Lee Commission was asked to make recommendations on the Indianization of public services, and a Public Service Commission for India was appointed in 1926. British recruitment to the ICS ceased only with the outbreak of **World War II** in 1939. By 1942, there were 597 Indian members of the ICS and 588 British members. (The corresponding numbers for the IPS were 186 and 422.) Only a handful of British officials stayed on in India after its independence in 1947; the **Indian Administrative Service (IAS)**, established soon after, is often regarded as a successor to the ICS.

INDIAN NATIONAL ARMY (INA). Rashbehari Bose and Mohan Singh formed the INA in September 1942, recruiting from among the 60,000 Indian soldiers who had been taken prisoner by the Japanese in Malaya and Singapore during **World War II**. The INA included men of all religious communities and also had a section of women soldiers.

An impending rift between Indians and Japanese on terms of cooperation and command was averted in the summer of 1943 when **Subhas Chandra Bose** arrived from Germany, took command, and reorganized the INA. He proclaimed a Provisional Government of Azad Hind (Free India) and led one division of troops across **Burma** with the battle cry *Chalo Dilli* or "Onward to Delhi." They entered **Assam** and took the towns of Kohima and Imphal in May 1944. However, they could not contact Indian nationalist leaders (then mostly in prison) or liberate India by force of arms. Instead, the INA was turned back by the superior force of the British Indian Army and subsequently surrendered to Allied forces in Rangoon in May 1945. Bose escaped.

INA officers were put on trial for "treason" in **Delhi** that winter, and the issue of conflicted loyalty raised by their cases caused serious concern within the army. But in the court of public opinion they were elevated to the status of "patriot" and "national hero" by the eloquence of their defense lawyers, who included **Bhulabhai Desai** and **Jawaharlal Nehru**, and the strength of Indian opposition to continued British rule. Mutiny of the Royal Indian Navy in **Bombay** harbor and a threatened mutiny by the Royal Indian Air Force in **Calcutta** in 1946 undoubtedly hastened British recognition of their tenuous hold on the Indian armed forces and the need to transfer power quickly to an independent Indian government.

INDIAN NATIONAL CONGRESS (CONGRESS or INC). The history of the Indian National Congress, one of the oldest, most effective, and unique political bodies in Asia, is also in large measure the history of the Indian national movement. Congress is the subject of an immense body of literature, and varying interpretations have been applied to every phase of its development and every leader of note, both by contemporary comment and in retrospect. But it is undeniable that from a relatively small gathering of Anglicized Indian men aspiring to the larger benefits of British rule, Congress grew to be a mass movement, first challenging the legitimacy of the British presence in India and then replacing it in power. For purposes of convenience, the name Indian National Congress is used here for the body in 62 years before independence. A **political party** of the same name held power in New Delhi from 1947 to 1977, from 1980 to 1989, from 1991 to 1996, and in May 2004 returned as leader of a coalition government; it is referred to as the **Congress Party**.

Founded in December 1885 as a political organization, the Indian National Congress passed through many changes in membership, concerns, organization, and styles of leadership, reflecting the widening circle of persons mediating between the imperial and all-India domain on the one hand and the common people of India concerned mainly with local issues on the other. **World War I** was, for many reasons, the great divide, ushering in an age of mass-based politics dominated by the saintly and shrewd figure of **Mahatma Gandhi**. The decades before and after were not static either, with phases of vitality and ascendancy oscillating with periods of transition and apparent decline. Five main stages, with some overlap, can be distinguished as follows.

The first phase, 1885–1905, was a period of "moderates." Congress was founded by **Allan Octavian Hume** and 72 English-educated, socially and materially secure Indian men practicing the learned professions, especially law, mainly in the presidency cities of

Bombay, **Calcutta**, **and Madras**, and already familiar with forming civic associations. In 1888, 1,249 delegates attended the fourth session, including **Badruddin Tyabji** and other Muslims. At their first meeting in December 1885, presided over by **W. C. Bonnerjee**, members of the INC proclaimed their loyalty to the British Crown and manifested their liberal faith in rational, gradualist constitutional progress as well as their secular and all-India mental outlook. Their demands were modest—inclusion of more Indians in the higher administrative offices, broadening the base of representative bodies, reducing taxes and military expenditure, and assisting Indian industry—and were couched in respectful terms. Nevertheless, even the early Congress was aware of its historic mission toward "regeneration of the Indian people" and formulated a critique of imperialism summed up in the phrase "the un-Britishness of British rule in India." Specifically, Congress criticized British racial arrogance and exclusiveness, as well as military and economic policies that led to what **Dadabhai Naoroji** documented as the "drain of wealth" from India to Britain. Congress tried to make a good impression on British public opinion, maintaining an office in London for the purpose, but British officialdom in India was generally mistrustful of Congress and actively discouraged its allies in the old aristocracy, both **Hindu** and Muslim, from joining or financially supporting the new organization.

The early Congress suffered from the lack of a permanent fund, weak organization entirely dependent between sessions on General Secretary Hume, and the absence of a program to mobilize large numbers of Indians. **Syed Ahmed Khan** attacked its political purpose and kept the north Indian Muslim gentry out of Congress. The percentage of Muslim membership fell from 13.% to 7.% by the turn of the century. A deliberate decision not to discuss divisive issues created a gulf between the first generation of Congress leaders, who favored Hindu social reform, and stalwarts of Hindu revivalism such as **Bal Gangadhar Tilak** in **Maharashtra**, **Aurobindo Ghose**, the followers of **Vivekananda** and **Bipin Chandra Pal** in **Bengal**, and members of the **Arya Samaj**, such as **Lala Lajpat Rai** in northern India. Moreover, Congress' commitment to constitutional procedures evoked no positive response from youthful idealists, not always from the same social class, who gravitated more eagerly toward revolutionary ideologies and methods.

The second phase, 1905–1920, opened with a bitter factional struggle between the "moderates" led by **Gopal Krishna Gokhale** and **Pherozeshah Mehta** on the one hand and on the other those whom the British called "extremists," exemplified by Tilak. Unseemly squabbles in the **Banaras** session of 1905 and the Calcutta session of 1906 culminated in an open split at the **Surat** session of 1907 when Tilak and his followers were expelled. There were jealousies, too, between the Bengal and Bombay delegations and a failure in Congress to agree on how best to oppose the **partition of Bengal** that was announced by **Lord Curzon** in 1905. An underground revolutionary movement emerged in Bengal outside the Congress framework, although some of the tactics used, notably boycott and **swadeshi**, and the cause of reunification itself, became permanently associated with Congress. Stimulated by external as well as internal events, feelings of militant nationalism intensified in the first two decades of the 20th century in India, as elsewhere. These found expression in many spontaneous but scattered anti-British moves, but although Congress was an all-India body calling for "home rule," it lacked the leadership and organizational capacity to harness grassroots support in a national cause.

Congress developed that capacity during the third phase, 1919–1934, behind the leadership of Mahatma Gandhi. By deepening and widening its appeal, Congress came to represent every major social group and geographical region of India and created a permanent organization paralleling that of the government. The great transformation was made at the 35th session at Nagpur in 1920, attended by 14,582 delegates, who acclaimed Gandhi's call for **Non-Cooperation** with the government. Congress's objective was defined as "the attainment of Swaraj by peaceful and legitimate means." Congress was organized into 213 district committees (comparing well with the 220 districts of official administration), grouped in provincial committees, sending funds and representatives to the All India Congress Committee (AICC), which itself was steered by an apex body of 15 members, the Congress Working Committee (CWC). Funding, too, was put on a permanent basis of (cheap) membership fees reinforced by the Tilak

Swaraj Fund of Rs10 million and the **Khilafet** Fund of Rs 2 million raised in 1921 and used to pay full-time workers and to promote *khadi* (see Glossary). Funds needed constant replenishment, especially as Congress premises and assets were periodically seized by the police, spurring recruitment drives such the one in 1929 that brought in 500,000 members, and through special appeals to which the Federation of Indian Chambers of Commerce and Industry (FICCI) responded favorably in 1930 and after.

Gandhi's contribution to the deepened social base of Congress cannot be underestimated. His selfless work among the peasants of **Bihar** and **Gujarat** and the textile workers of **Ahmedabad** even before 1919 spread what later official reports called "the power of his name" to practically every village and town in India by word of mouth. His compassion for the oppressed brought on thousands of local struggles throughout the subcontinent under the Congress umbrella, including those taking place in the peninsular, tribal areas and the **North West Frontier Province**. Gandhi's high ethical standards and personal courage appealed to idealistic youths and women as nothing else could; his **Satyagraha** offered, in the words of **Jawaharlal Nehru**, "a way out of the tangle, a method of action that was straight and open and possibly effective." Gandhi's embrace of the Khilafet cause allied large numbers of Indian Muslims with Congress in the early 1920s, although that did not last long. Gandhi's work for the uplifting of **Harijans** or **Untouchables**, although criticized as inadequate by **Dr. Ambedkar** and Marxist critics, brought this enormous underclass within the fold of Congress. Young radicals carried forward mass contact programs with peasants, workers, Harijans, and Muslims during the 1930s on socialist principles.

Gandhi's leadership of Congress was informal rather than formal — he was president only once, in 1924 — and was most evident during the Non-Cooperation Movement (1920–1922) and the **Civil Disobedience** Movement (1930–1931). Thus, it can be said that the British iron fist shown after World War I in the **Rowlatt Acts** and the **Jallianwala Bagh** massacre, and British racial arrogance in the form of the 1927 **Simon Commission** assisted mightily in the transformation of Congress into a vehicle of Indian nationalism. Congress found it more difficult to handle the velvet glove of constitutional reform. For example, implementation of the **Montagu-Chelmsford Reforms** generated a controversy within Congress between those who advocated joining the provincial legislative councils (now open to election), such as **C. R. Das** and **Motilal Nehru**, and those who called for continued non-cooperation. This could have led to a split as serious as the one of 1907; instead, in a Gandhian spirit of compromise, members of the newly formed **Swaraj Party** operated in the councils without resigning from Congress or binding the "no-changers." Although the Swarajists walked out of the councils in 1926, their experience was undeniably useful in drafting the 1928 **Nehru Report**, a constitutional blueprint for India.

Congress did not participate in the first **Round Table Conference**, and Gandhi was its sole representative at the second. The **Government of India Act of 1935** that grew out of those deliberations scarcely met the Congress goal of *purna swaraj* or "full independence" declared at the Madras session in 1929. Moreover, while in 1930 a high ranking member of the **Indian Civil Service** could report that "their numbers, their discipline, their organization . . . produce a vivid impression of the power and the success of the Congress movement," the inability to hold regular meetings because of government repression took a heavy toll. By 1934, Gandhi wanted to resign from Congress and devote himself entirely to what he called "constructive work." He was not permitted to do so by his colleagues, not all of whom were equally sincere in the theory and practice of non-violent action; yet all regarded Gandhi as indispensable to the national movement against the British.

The fourth phase, 1934–1940, was a decisive and controversial one. It was marked by a debate within Congress on the efficacy of Gandhian methods and by severe factional disputes over the reelection and rejection of **Subhas Chandra Bose** as president in 1939. Another debate focused on the desirability of contesting elections and taking office under terms of the 1935 Act. Congress's electoral victories brought it to office in 8 out of 11 provinces to experience first hand the frustrations of circumscribed power, the temptations of patronage, and the problems of guiding and controlling a mass party in a communally charged atmosphere. Congress was no longer the relatively homogenous body of its early phase but was now an umbrella under which many locally strong and ideologically distinct groups flourished. And despite (or because of) its mass contact program with Muslims, Congress failed to gain the cooperation or endorsement of the **Muslim League**, which had fared badly in the elections and had set about creating a mass base for itself on the themes first of "**Islam** in danger" and then of "two nations." A controversy also arose over Congress's relationship with agitations for popular government in the **Princely States** whose federation with British India, envisaged in the 1935 Act, was not implemented. Finally, the outbreak of **World War II** and **Lord Linlithgow**'s tactless refusal to consult Congress on India's participation in the war effort precipitated another debate within Congress on whether or not to continue in office. All eight Congress governments had resigned by early 1940.

The fifth and final pre-independence phase, 1940–1947, was an eventful one with a mixed impact on the development of Congress. As the **Quit India movement** demonstrated, Congress was able to mobilize larger numbers of people behind it than any other national movement of the time, including the Chinese, and to generate a large number of leaders and organizers whose strength lay in grassroots support and decentralized decision making. But with its policy of non-cooperation and its leaders in prison for much of the period, Congress was at a disadvantage throughout the war in negotiations with both the Muslim League and the British government, headed by Winston Churchill who was adamantly opposed to making any concessions to Indian nationalist sentiment. Thus, mediatory initiatives taken by American President Franklin Roosevelt, Labour Minister **Sir Stafford Cripps**, and Chinese leader Chiang Kai-shek all failed, as did the 1944 meeting between **Gandhi** and **Mohammed Ali Jinnah**. Although the end of the war brought hopes of an early transfer of power from British to Indian hands, negotiations at **Simla** and with the **Cabinet Mission** failed to resolve difficult issues to the satisfaction of all parties. The writings of eminent Congress leaders—Asaf Ali, **Abul Kalam Azad**, **Jawaharlal Nehru**, **Gobind B**. **Pant**, **Vallabhbhai Patel**, **Rajendra Prasad**, Pattabhai Sittaramayya, and Gandhi himself—reveal some of the physical and mental strain under which these men in their late middle age labored. As they moved toward what Nehru called India's "tryst with destiny" or independence, they saw some of the finest fruits of their efforts destroyed in the communal violence of **Partition**.

Gandhi's suggestion that Congress renounce politics and devote itself to rebuilding the Indian nation was not taken seriously. On the other hand, Congress's contribution to the drafting of the Indian **Constitution** and the first decade of governing an immense subcontinent, demonstrated its vitality and commitment to the vision of a democratic polity fostering the social and economic progress of the Indian people. *See also* CONGRESS PARTY.

INDIGO RIOTS (1859–1860). Also known as the "Blue Mutiny" to distinguish it from the Sepoy Mutiny or **Uprising of 1857**, riots in 1859 began as a labor strike in the indigo growing districts of **Bengal**. This grew into a revolt against the cruelty and exploitation suffered by cultivators and indentured labor at the hands of European planters and their middlemen. It was the first of a series of peasant rebellions in the late 19th century.

Indigo became a profitable export for the **East India Company** in the late 18th century. Bengal provided 67% of the total indigo supply to London in the year 1795–1796 and even more by 1809. An influx of British planters and a mid-century slump in the world price of indigo weakened the industry. The planters passed the costs of this on to the cultivators by forcing them to continue growing indigo at one-third to one-half the market price, rather than producing food grains for their own consumption, on pain of beatings, eviction, or worse. The cultivators were denied access to justice because Europeans were not subject to the district law courts at this time. The plight of the indigo cultivator gained the attention of a few individuals, but only the riots of 1859—in which planters were assaulted, indigo crops destroyed, and factories burned—brought about appointment of an Indigo Inquiry Commission, after suppression of the uprising in Bengal. Ten years later, a similar scenario was played out in **Bihar**, but the conditions of the indigo cultivators were still appalling in 1917 when **Mahatma Gandhi**'s Satyagraha at Champaran on their behalf brought some relief.

INDUS RIVER. Sindhu, the early **Sanskrit** word for river, is mentioned in the Rig **Veda** and in the earliest chronicles of the Indo-Aryan speaking peoples in India who called their country Bharat or Bharatavarsha. In the form of Indos (Greek), Sindh or Sindhavi

(Arabic), and Hind or Hindavi (Persian), the river Indus gave its name to the Indian subcontinent and later to the faiths (**Hindu**) followed by most of its people.

The Indus runs 2,900 kilometers from its **Himalayan** source in southwest **Tibet** to its outlet on the Arabian Sea. Initially, it flows northwest through the high plateau of **Ladakh** and is fed by mighty glaciers in the Karakoram Range. Crossing west in the northern tip of **Kashmir**, the river takes a sharp turn southwest, and the rest of its course lies through present-day **Pakistan**. The use of its waters and those of its five major tributaries—Chenab, Jhelum, Ravi, Beas, and Sutlej—were divided between India and Pakistan in the Indus Waters Treaty of 1960.

There is considerable physiographic and historical evidence to prove that the Indus river has been shifting its course westward for 5,000 years, at least since the Indus Valley civilization reached its heights at **Harappa** and Mohenjo-Daro. Some historians attribute the precipitate decline of the latter city in the lower Indus valley to such shifts by the river and consequent environmental changes. And only 200 years ago the Indus flowed into the Rann of Kutch southeast of its present delta.

The Indus is navigable for much of its course, and major historical events have been enacted on it. For example, **Alexander of Macedon** and his men sailed down the Indus in the third century BCE after his brief triumph in northwestern India; Arabs sailed up the Indus after conquering Sindh in the eighth century CE but were turned back by the formidable deserts of its middle reaches; the British used the Indus to check the southward expansion of **Ranjit Singh**'s power and make their own ill-fated assault on Afghanistan in the mid-19th century. In the present day, the upper streams of the Indus in Ladakh are used for white water rafting by young adventurers

INDUS VALLEY CIVILIZATION. *See* HARAPPAN CULTURE.

INFOSYS TECHNOLOGIES LIMITED. *See* NARAYANA MURTHY.

IQBAL, MUHAMMAD (1877–1938). Iqbal was born in the **Punjab** and educated in philosophy in Lahore and Cambridge, England. He was attracted to pan-Islamic ideas current at the time and gave, in his own words, "the best part of my life to a careful study of **Islam**." From that study, he evolved his *falsafa i khudi* or philosophy of the Self, the kernel of which was expressed in his lengthy poem *Asrar-i-Khudi*, or Secrets of the Self, published in 1915. In it, he exhorted Muslims to mobilize their inner resources of spiritual energy and so exert themselves in the world.

Iqbal had a law degree and became involved in politics after being knighted in 1922 and elected to the Punjab Legislative Council in 1926. He presided over the annual session of the **All-India Muslim League** in 1930. There, he put forward a proposal that the provinces of **Punjab**, **North West Frontier Province**, Sindh, and Baluchistan be consolidated into a single self-governing state within the British-Indian Empire as "the final destiny of the Muslims" of northwestern India. Ten years later this became the nucleus of the **Pakistan** resolution of the League. Iqbal argued for separate communal electorates at the **Round Table Conferences** and persuaded **Mohammed Ali Jinnah** to return to India and contest the provincial elections of 1937.

Iqbal is honored in Pakistan as one of its founders. Urdu speakers throughout the Indian subcontinent venerate Iqbal as a poet and philosopher.

IRWIN, LORD EDWIN F. L. (1881–1959). The Honorable Edward Fredrick Lindley Wood was created Baron Irwin in 1925 and bore that name throughout his tenure as Viceroy and Governor General of India from 1926 to 1931. He inherited the title of Viscount Halifax in 1934 and was created Earl in 1944. As Lord Halifax, he served as British Ambassador to the United States through **World War II** and received many honors in his life.

Irwin was appointed to India by a Conservative Party government but served there through the tenure of a Labour Party government from 1929–1931 as well. The vagaries of British party politics affected Irwin's ability to address a difficult situation in India imaginatively. His assets were an impressive record of public service, a fine presence, and a reputation as a practicing Christian and a man of integrity and of earnestness. On arrival in India, he found a rising tide of communal violence spurred by the growth of sectarian organizations among both **Hindus** and **Muslims** that did not heed calls for communal harmony issued either by him or by leaders of the **Indian National Congress**. Feelings of frustration among politically conscious Indians were also noticeable. This frustration derived from many causes, including diminution of fervor for the **Non-Cooperation Movement**, **Mahatma Gandhi**'s withdrawal to his ashram (see Glossary), the discovery by the **Swaraj Party** of the very modest nature of the 1919 **Montagu-Chelmsford Reforms** that were then being implemented, and British refusal to recognize Congress as the major political force in the country. Irwin attempted to break the impasse by suggesting a review of the 1919 reforms earlier than required by the law. A parliamentary commission headed by Sir John Simon went to India for that purpose.

The all-British composition of the **Simon Commission** aroused the ire of Indians to a degree that Irwin had not anticipated. Congress boycotted its meetings, demonstrated against it, and passed a resolution demanding complete independence at its session of December 1927. The **Nehru Report** prepared a draft constitution for a self-governing **Dominion** of India in 1928. The same year, Gandhi and **Vallabhbhai Patel** organized a mass peasant upheaval in Bardoli, **Gujarat**, which grew into a movement of civil disobedience and nonpayment of taxes. Initially, the government met this with unhesitating coercion.

Irwin wisely embarked on a healing course of compromise. Bardoli was granted a considerable reduction in land revenue rates. Irwin went to London for consultations and after his return issued a declaration on October 31, 1929, stating "the natural issue of India's constitutional progress, as the [**Montagu Declaration** of 1917] contemplated, is the attainment of dominion status." (Percival Spear, 1975, *India: A Modern History*: 375). At the same time he suggested a **Round Table Conference** at which British and Indian representatives could discuss constitutional changes. He also maintained personal contacts with leading members of Congress such as Gandhi and **Motilal Nehru** through **Vithaldas Patel**; they congratulated him for escaping an assassination attempt in December 1929.

Irwin lost support in England by this approach, and in India the cycle soon turned back to mistrust and Congress non-cooperation after the execution of **Bhagat Singh**, various brutal police actions, and another rise in communal rioting. Gandhi's **Dandi** or **Salt March** of

1930 spearheaded a **civil disobedience** movement that was qualitatively different from earlier ones. He and some 100,000 others were arrested, and Congress boycotted the first Round Table Conference. Judging that conference to be a success, and intending to break the deadlock in India, Irwin ordered Gandhi's release in January 1931 and initiated a series of meetings with him from February 17 to March 5. Irwin and Gandhi were able to communicate with each other on the basis of moral sincerity. Gandhi later said that he had succumbed not so much to Lord Irwin as to the honesty in him. They announced agreement on what came to be known as the **Gandhi-Irwin Pact**, ratified at the next meeting of Congress.

Irwin drove a hard bargain, refusing to entertain Gandhi's demand for an inquiry into police brutality or to make concessions on matters of substance. At the same time, he agreed to release most of the detainees, remit fines, and permit peaceful picketing. What Gandhi and Congress gained was prestige. The public, including an angry Winston Churchill, saw Gandhi as a plenipotentiary negotiating on terms of equality with the viceroy himself. Irwin and his home government had finally begun, regretfully and incompletely no doubt, to recognize Congress as the intermediary between the British Government of India and the Indian people.

ISLAM IN INDIA (MUSLIMS). According to the 2001 **Census of India**, Islam was the religion of 11.7% of the population of India, totaling more than 138 million people. Muslims in India presently constitute the third largest Muslim population in the world, after Indonesia and Pakistan, and the second largest religious community in India after **Hindus**. (See Appendix G.) Muslims constitute a majority in the Indian state of **Jammu and Kashmir** and in the Union Territory of **Lakshadweep**; they form a significant minority in the states of **Andhra Pradesh, Assam, Bihar, Karnataka, Kerala, Maharshtra, Uttar Pradesh**, and **West Bengal**, and are visibly present in every other state. More than 70% of Muslims live in rural areas alongside other communities, but a slightly higher percentage than the national average are urban dwellers engaged in commerce, crafts, and labor.

Although many Muslims occupy positions of prominence and trust, from president of India, Dr. Abul Kalam, to the middle and upper strata of artistic, commercial, governmental, industrial, professional, political, and sporting life in contemporary India, the Muslim middle class is relatively small. The former class of large landholders was diminished by migration to **Pakistan** in 1947 or later and by the impact of land reforms in India. Most Indian Muslims are at the lowest rung of the socioeconomic ladder in terms of civic amenities, consumption patterns, education, income, and job opportunities. Their needs, as those of other Indians on the bottom rungs, have not been fully addressed by any political party, although articulated often by the **Congress Party** whose leader **Jawaharlal Nehru** was recognized as their most ardent protector. After Nehru's death in 1964, Muslims were somewhat marginalized or taken for granted as "vote banks" for Congress until sectarian violence in the 1980s shocked the politically aware into reexamination of secularism as well as political participation in India. Attempts have been made since the early 1990s to form political alliances on the basis of class between Muslims and other deprived groups, such as "backward" and Scheduled **Castes**, especially in Bihar and Uttar Pradesh. And in 2004 the issue of possible reservations or affirmative action for Muslims in Andhra Pradesh became contentious.

Islam in India is a confluence of diverse Indian groups and four major extra-subcontinental ethno-cultural streams: the Arab, Turkish, Persian, and Afghan. The Arab stream had the most impact on the trading communities of the west coast and southern India; the Persian influence was seen in elite culture, art, and **language**; the Turkic and Afghan streams entered largely by lure of adventure or force of arms through the northwest, forming a ruling class over most of northern India and the **Deccan** from the 13th to the 18th century. The Muslim majority provinces in pre-**Partition** India that make up present-day Pakistan and **Bangladesh** were those that had been longest under Muslim rule before the British established their dominion, and many conversions to Islam probably occurred under duress or for the sake of convenience. But it was the **Sufis** who were among the most formative of Islamic influences, and even today India is the largest center of Sufism in the world. The four major Sufi *silsile* or orders—the **Chisti**, Qadriya, Naqshbandiya, and Suhrawardiya—trace their lineage back to the 12th–15th centuries.

Islam encountered an ancient civilization in India that it could not wholly convert and into which it could not be absorbed entirely. Less than 25% of the total population of the Indian subcontinent was Muslim at any time. But most Muslim rulers followed the Hanafi school of Islamic jurisprudence that implicitly accorded the status of *dhimmi* (protected People of the Book) to Hindus, and India was not regarded as *Dar ul Harb* or state of war. Islam became part of the Indian mosaic, in which the different parts had multifaceted relationships with each other in varying tones of harmony or dissonance over time and space. A composite Hindu-Muslim culture was evolving over the centuries of interaction that remains visible today in the arts, crafts, and **music** of the subcontinent. But with the passing of the **Mughals**, there was little or no social cohesion between Muslim and Hindu communities; their responses to the British cultural, economic, and political impact on India were not the same, or similar responses occurred at different times. For example, movements for social reform, Western education, and political participation arose earlier and more intensely among Hindus than among Muslims in the 19th century, not overlooking the pioneering work of **Syed Ahmad Khan**. Constitutional reforms in the first half of the 20th century paid attention to Muslims as a minority community entitled to separate electorates and reserved representation, reducing the incentive for building inter communal political bridges. Muslim community identity tended to be posited in distinction to the Hindu majority and was often equated with orthodox Sunni interpretation of the Shari'a or Islamic law. **Mohammed Ali Jinnah**'s efforts to forge a single Muslim identity behind his leadership out of a congery of groups divided by sect, **caste**, and geography, was one of the factors that contributed to the 1940 resolution of the **All-India Muslim League** demanding a separate "homeland" for the Muslims. But the creation of Pakistan in 1947 did not solve the felt problems of the millions of Muslims who chose to remain in India. On the contrary, divided families and suspicion of divided loyalties created additional difficulties for them, as epitomized in the epithet *"Mian Musharaff"* ("Mister Musharaff") flung at many Muslims subjected to persecution in **Gujarat** in 2002.

India's secular, democratic **Constitution** guarantees non-discrimination on grounds of religion, freedom of worship to all, and protects the right of minorities to conserve their personal law and maintain educational institutions such as Aligarh Muslim University. The Congress Party for the most part took pains to reassure

Muslims of their safety and equal status as Indian citizens, both as a matter of principle and with an eye to their vote. The **Communist Parties** and other Leftists stood by secular constitutional principles in practice. But advocates of **Hindutva** such as Hindu militant groups, the **Shiv Sena**, the **Bharatiya Janata Party**, and some intellectuals labeled such efforts "pseudo-secularism," "appeasement of minorities," and "neglect of majority interests." Some tried to demonize Islam and present the Muslim as a feared "Other" to the Hindu. Internal economic and political factors conducive to the power of criminal and smuggling groups in **Mumbai** and elsewhere and the phenomenon of fundamentalist or militant Islam externally in Iran and Afghanistan aggravated communal relations in India in the 1980s and 1990s.

Foreign funding has spawned the building of numerous mosques and attached *madrassahs* (religious schools) around the country in the last two decades, especially along sensitive borders with Bangladesh and Nepal, and in Gujarat and **Rajasthan** close to the border with Pakistan. Illegal immigration of millions of people from Bangladesh compounds the problem by altering the demographic profile of districts in Assam, **Tripura**, and West Bengal. Reports by Indian task forces on border management and on internal security remark on efforts to Arabize or Talibanize students in *madrassahs* and point to the hand of Pakistan's Inter Service Intelligence (ISI) in sowing dissidence and encouraging operations associated with **terrorism**. State governments in India have been unable—or unwilling because of electoral considerations—to take on the problem of mosque and *madrassah* proliferation. The Student's Islamic Movement of India (SIMI) was founded in 1977, severed ties with the conservative *Jama'at- i-Islami (Hind)* in 1982, and conducted an active mass-contact program on a radical pan-Islamic ideology. New Delhi banned the SIMI in 2001 for alleged ties to terrorists. Serious inter-communal violence has erupted in certain cities from time to time, often organized, and usually taking the heaviest toll on women and other innocent people of both communities. A campaign to build a **Ram Temple** on the site of the 16th-century Babri Masjid mosque at **Ayodhya** stimulated some Muslims to form a Babri Masjid Action Committee (BMAC); it could not prevent destruction of the mosque by Hindu militants in December 1992 or orchestrate an appropriate response. The dispute over ownership of the site was referred to the courts that have yet to pass judgment, and now it appears as if most Indian Muslims are indifferent to the outcome.

Scholarly research and intensive discussions have taken place among thinking Indians, including Muslims, on questions such as the place of Islam in India, the role of reason in Islam, the causes of inter-communal violence, and Muslim responses to problems within India as well as to the post-September 2001 international environment in which Islam itself can appear to be under siege. Hindu-Muslim riots are found to be more of an urban than a rural phenomenon in India, related to electoral politics as well as to the demographic profile of the location, and less likely to occur where there are strong inter-communal associational networks of civic engagement and economic interdependence, as in Lucknow, than where they are weak or absent, as in **Hyderabad**. Local inter-communal peace committees, sometimes formed by **women** and working with sympathetic police and other officials, have proven to be effective in preventing or soothing the after effects of violence, as in **Mumbai** since 1993. Inter-faith dialogue as practiced by Ashgar Ali Engineer and others is a continuing process to erode popular perceptions that Islam is incompatible with modernity or with contemporary India.

Some Indian Muslims sometimes resent being labeled "minority" and no longer feel obliged to change their names to achieve stardom in the **film industry** (as **Dilip Kumar** did) or on the cricket field, or in any other sphere of activity. Muslim political figures are now found in almost every political party and the *Jama'at I- Islami (Hind)* has moved away from its former apolitical cultural stance to one of advocating participation in electoral politics. With the exception of militant dissidents in **Kashmir** and *jihadi* products of *madrassahs*, Indian Muslims show no interest in violent opposition to the state or in joining international networks such as Al Qaeda. And journalists from Pakistan touring India have been struck by the convictions expressed by Indian Muslims that Kashmir should remain *within* the Indian Union and that their own interests are best served in a democratic secular polity. Reform of Muslim personal law to bring it in conformity with Indian civil law has been a political football for militates against reform. Muslim women took heart from a recommendation of the All-India Muslim Personal Law Board made in 2004 that the "triple *Talaq*" (divorce merely by a man reciting the words three times) should *not* be used, the obligations of the marriage contract should be fulfilled, and marital discord should be settled by counseling advice.

In short, Muslims are a vital part of the Indian population and share similar aspirations and problems with other Indians of comparable socioeconomic standing. Islam cannot and should not be displaced from the history and contemporary life of India.

ISMAIL, MIRZA MUHAMMAD (1883–1959). Mirza Ismail was born in **Bangalore** to a Shi'a **Muslim** family of Persian descent and was educated in that city. He entered the service of **Mysore** state in 1905 and became its dewan, or prime minister, in 1926. With the friendship and support of the maharajah or ruler he brought impressive economic, educational, and industrial development to the state; for example, the first scheme of rural electrification in India was implemented in Mysore. In many other respects as well, notably civic order and respect, Mysore was a model state and Bangalore a beautiful and efficiently run city.

Mirza Ismail was knighted in 1930 as an outstanding administrator. He was nominated by **Lord Irwin** to participate in the **Round Table Conferences** at London to discuss constitutional reforms in India. He supported the idea of an all-India federation in which the **Princely States** would join the provinces of British India in a **Dominion**.

On retirement from Mysore in 1941, Sir Mirza was appointed Dewan of **Jaipur**, where he initiated constitutional reforms, town planning, and the founding of Rajasthan University. He was on friendly terms with **Mahatma Gandhi** and other leaders of the **Indian National Congress** as well as with British officials. He was firmly committed to the concept of a united India and did not lend his support to the **Muslim League**'s demand for a separate Muslim nation.

Sir Mirza was in the service of the Nizam of **Hyderabad** as dewan for a relatively short period of time in the 1940s. He did not approve of the various types of agitations instigated in that state, especially those of the Razakars or Muslim fanatics demanding independence or accession to **Pakistan**. Retiring to Bangalore, Mirza Ismail did not remain in public service after Indian independence but continued to command respect.

IYENGAR, KASTURI RANGA (1859–1923). Iyengar was born to a middleclass Vaishnavite **brahman** family in the **Tanjore** district of **Madras**. He became a lawyer but found greater satisfaction in politics and in journalism. He was a member of the **Indian National Congress** in its earlier years, backing **Bal Gangadhar Tilak** and his "extremist" group at the Congress split in 1907. He later became a supporter of **Mahatma Gandhi**.

From 1905 to the time of his death, Iyengar's major preoccupation was building up a fledgling weekly that he had acquired, *The Hindu*, to an effective daily newspaper. His nephew, A. Rangaswami Iyengar (1877–1934), and his son, K. Srinivasan Iyengar (1887–1959) helped him and were successive editors of the paper. Between them, they made *The Hindu* one of the best-produced and most influential newspapers in contemporary India to the present day.

IYER, C. P. RAMASWAMI (1879–1966). Iyer was born into an educated **brahman** family and was educated in **Madras**. He became a lawyer and was attracted to the idea of "home rule" as propounded by **Annie Besant**. Drawn to political life, Iyer joined the **Indian National Congress**. He was elected to the Madras Corporation Council in 1912 and to the Madras Legislative Council in 1919. He resigned from Congress over the issue of **Non-Cooperation** in 1920, preferring to try and work the system of **dyarchy** introduced by the **Montagu-Chelmsford Reforms**. His brilliance as a lawyer came to the attention of the British Government of India in **New Delhi**, which then used his services and subsequently had him knighted.

Sir C. P. Ramaswami Iyer served as dewan, or prime minister, of the **Princely State** of Travancore from 1936 to 1947. He enjoyed the confidence of the enlightened ruling family as well as of the British Resident, and his administration was known for its efficiency. Economic, educational, industrial, and social progress was fostered, especially after the maharajah's historic proclamation opening all temples to **Ezhavas** in 1936. At the same time, Sir C. P.—as he was known by then—vigorously battled the Congress-sponsored **States Peoples Conference** as well as the **Communist Party of India**, which were each seeking footholds in the densely populated and highly literate maritime states of Travancore and **Cochin**.

Sir C. P. gained some notoriety in 1947 for a bid to make Travancore independent after **Lord Mountbatten** announced his plan for **partition**, transfer of power, and lapse of **paramountcy**. However, **V. P. Menon** and pressure from New Delhi persuaded the maharajah to sign the instrument of accession to India by the end of July. Travancore and Cochin were subsequently joined to form the state of **Kerala**.

After Indian independence, Iyer bent his considerable talents to the enrichment of cultural life and higher education in southern India. He was benefactor and vice chancellor, in turn, of universities at Travancore and **Banaras** and was one of the founders of Annamalai University in **Tamil Nadu**.

– J –

JAIN. This is a community with ancient antecedents whose name is derived from *Jina*, meaning "conqueror" or "great hero" in reference to **Mahavira** of the sixth century BCE. Mahavira gave shape to preexisting Jain ideas and spread them through his teaching. Oral traditions were later collated and recorded and a non-theistic, ascetic system of moral and spiritual discipline enjoined on the community of his followers, Jains. The core of their discipline lies in the "Three Jewels" of right faith, right knowledge, and right conduct, which entail vows of *ahimsa*, or non-violence, truth, chastity, charity, and non-attachment. Jain teachings postulate no creator but eternal law, according to which the universe continually passes through cycles of progress and decline; all things are composed of matter and jiva, or soul; the purpose of living is to purify the soul and release it from matter so that it may reside in bliss. The descending curve of each cosmic cycle is marked by progressive evil and suffering alleviated by Great Souls or Thirthankaras. Mahavira is considered to be the last of 24 Thirthankaras.

Non-violence or *ahimsa* is so heavily stressed in Jain teaching that agricultural pursuits—which inevitably endanger lives of insects and others—are considered impure. Probably for that reason, Jains are usually to be found among the commercial, mercantile, and trading professions. Indeed, from the time of the **Mauryas** in the fourth century BCE to the present day, the Jain faith came to be associated with urban culture, financial transactions, maritime commerce, and wealth. At the same time, the strict discipline of spiritual purity as taught by Mahavira could best, or perhaps only, be practiced by monks, and several monastic orders were founded. Early in their history, these monastic orders split into two schools: the Digambaras or "sky clad" wore no clothes; the Shvetambaras or "white clad" wore only white. Jain monks were supported by the lay community and received royal patronage from several dynasties over the millennia, especially in **Karnataka, Gujarat**, and **Rajasthan**, where many Jain temples, ancient and modern, are to be found.

Jain influence on Indian culture has been as profound as that of **Buddhism** and probably precedes Brahmanic **Hinduism** in chronology. Jain teachings have remained relatively unchanged over more than 2,000 years. The doctrine of *ahimsa* was spread largely by Jains throughout that period and undoubtedly contributed to the ecological preservation of India to modern times. The revival of *ahimsa* as a political doctrine by **Mahatma Gandhi** can be traced to Jain influence in his hometown and early life. Jain monks were encouraged to study, teach, and write on secular as well as philosophical themes. They contributed greatly to indigenous medical knowledge, including treatment of birds and animals, as well as to mathematics, astronomy, linguistics, and literature in the vernacular languages of the medieval period. They maintained libraries where they preserved ancient **Sanskrit** texts and executed a profusion of illuminated manuscripts. The magnificent statue of Mahavira erected at Sravana Belgola in Karnataka during the 10th century and the elaborate temple cities of Girnar, Shatrunjaya, and Abu in Rajasthan are living monuments of Jain art.

Although the Jain community presently accounts for less than 0.05% of India's population (see Appendix G), its generally high standard of personal morality and social ethics, as well as its relative wealth, gain it national respect. According to the **Indian Constitution** of 1950, Jains and Buddhists are considered to be Hindus for purposes of personal law.

JAIPUR. The present-day capital of the state of **Rajasthan**, Jaipur takes its name from the famous astronomer prince, Maharaja Jai Singh, who founded the city when he moved his capital from the rock-girt fortress of Amber to the adjoining valley in 1727. The city was laid out in a rectangular grid surrounded by a crenellated wall, in a form symbolic of the sacred cosmic order, with the palace at the center. Jaipur was planned to accommodate ten times more than its then 25,000 inhabitants but has been overtaken by the vast population increases and rural-urban migrations of the post-independence period.

The erstwhile ruling dynasty of the **Princely State** of Jaipur belong to the Kachwaha clan of **Rajputs** who carved out a principality of their own in the 12th century. Necessarily attentive to the paramount power in nearby **Delhi**, Jaipur was the first Rajput ruling family to sign a matrimonial alliance with the **Mughal Emperor Akbar**; a princess of Jaipur was the mother of his successor Jehangir. Raja Sawai Man Singh of Jaipur was one of the most famous and successful generals of the Mughal army, and the tradition of cooperation continued. At a later date, Jaipur did not make common cause with the **Marathas** against the Mughals or the British and signed an alliance with the victorious **East India Company** in 1818.

The **States Peoples Conference** was active in Jaipur during the 1930s and 1940s, propagating nationalist ideas, and the state sent representatives to the **Constituent Assembly** in April 1947. The dewan (see Glossary) of Jaipur participated in pre-independence negotiations on arrangements to replace **paramountcy**, and the ruler was one of the first to accede to the Indian Union. His family has taken an active part in post-independence diplomacy and politics.

JALLIANWALA BAGH MASSACRE. This event was a landmark in the history of modern India. Jallianwala Bagh is a walled garden in the city of **Amritsar** where unarmed people gathered to celebrate the **Sikh** festival of Baisakh on April 13, 1919. They were continuously fired upon by troops on orders of Brigadier General **R. E. H. Dyer**. According to official estimates, 379 persons were killed and 1,200 were wounded, including women and children.

The Jallianwala Bagh massacre took place against a background of rising Indian discontent after **World War I** and increasing British nervousness about insurrection. Both were evident in the **Punjab** where the **Ghadr** party had been active, where thousands of veterans were unemployed or were dying of influenza, where a remarkable harmony among **Hindus,** Muslims, and Sikhs prevailed at the time, and where the governor rigorously applied the repressive **Rowlatt Acts** passed in March 1919. In protest, **Mahatma Gandhi** called for a nationwide *hartal*, or suspension of work, on April 8. On April 10, a mob killed five Englishmen in Amritsar. Brutal and humiliating punishments were inflicted on all Indian inhabitants of the city, and public meetings were banned. Those gathering at Jallianwala Bagh were massacred, and martial law was imposed in the Punjab. During succeeding months, official brutality resulted in 1,200 deaths, 3,600 wounded, 258 public floggings, and numerous other punishments.

Dyer, who had the prior backing of the governor, subsequently defended his action as one required to "produce the necessary moral and widespread effect . . . throughout the Punjab." (Sir Penderal Moon, *The British Conquest and Dominion of India*: 944.) The moral effect of the massacre was indeed widespread. It caused revulsion in the minds of all sensitive Indians—for example, **Rabindranath Tagore** renounced his knighthood. It politicized people throughout the country and so accelerated the national movement. The Jallianwala Bagh massacre was the beginning of the end of British rule in India.

JAMMU AND KASHMIR. The former **Princely State** of Jammu and Kashmir at the northern apex of the Indian subcontinent acceded to the Indian Union in October 1947 after military incursions from **Pakistan.** After an inconclusive war with India, Pakistan occupied more than one-third of the state's 222,236 square kilometers and subsequently annexed the mountainous northern areas. The area under Indian administration has three main geocultural zones: the submontane plain and hills of Jammu north of **Punjab** and connected by rail to the rest of India; the valley of Kashmir and surrounding mountains in the center; and the high plateau of **Ladakh** in the northeast. Many **languages** are in use, principally Kashmiri, Ladakhi, Punjabi, and Urdu. Many religions are practiced, including Shi'a, Sunni, and Sufic **Islam** (the majority), Tibetan **Buddhism, Sikhism,** and various sects of **Hinduism.** Tribal groups, such as Gujars, are significant parts of the population. A pluralistic and tolerant culture of *Kashmiriyat* flourished over the centuries before recent efforts by militant Islamists to forcibly overlay diversity.

Archaeological discoveries of **Gupta**, **Harappan**, **Kushan**, and **Mauryan** artifacts testify to Jammu's ancient lineage as an urban site. It is also mentioned in the *Mahabharata*. Jammu is currently the winter capital of the state, **Srinagar** being the summer capital. The early history of the state is chronicled in the 12th century *Rajtarangini*. The total population of Jammu and Kashmir exceeds 10 million, according to the 2001 **census**. The principal means of livelihood are from agriculture, handicrafts, horticulture, pilgrimages, and tourism. *See also* KASHMIR.

JANA SANGHA. Dr. Shyama Prasad Mookerji formed this **political party** in 1951. He was a sharp critic of Prime Minister **Jawaharlal Nehru** and resigned the presidency of the moribund **Hindu Mahasabha** for the purpose of building a rightist parliamentary opposition to the ruling **Congress Party**.

The declared objective of the Jana Sangha was to rebuild India, preferably termed Bharat, in accordance with **Hindu** religious precepts and four fundamentals: one country, one nation, one culture, and the rule of law. The party was the political arm of the older and well organized but technically non-political **Rashtriya Swayamsevak Sangh (RSS)** from the start. They aimed at "nationalizing all non-Hindus by inculcating in them the ideal of Bharatiya Culture." The Jana Sangha advocated a unitary state with Hindi as the national language and cow protection as a national policy. Although membership in the party was theoretically open to all, the flavor of its ideology was Hindu chauvinist. The Jana Sangha considered secularism as practiced by the Congress governments to be merely an appeasement of "minorities"—a euphemism for Muslims. Its foreign policy statements were sharply anti-Pakistan and anti-China, and called for stronger defense in India.

The Jana Sangha made substantial gains at the 1967 general elections in the Hindi belt of northern India and enjoyed considerable support from small traders and lower level government servants in north Indian cities including **Delhi**; its popularity declined in 1971 and 1972 when **Indira Gandhi** swept the polls. In 1977, the Jana Sangha joined the **Janata** coalition to form a new government, with its leader, **Atal Behari Vajpayee**, as minister for external affairs. The party was disbanded on the issue of its relationship with the RSS but subsequently reemerged in the slightly different form of the **Bharitiya Janata Party (BJP)**.

JANATA DAL PARTY. *See* SINGH, VISHWANATH PRATAP.

JANATA PARTY. Originally called Janata Morcha or Peoples Movement, the Janata Party was formed in 1977 as a coalition in opposition to Prime Minister **Indira Gandhi** and her **Emergency Rule**. The four **political parties** in the coalition were the breakaway **Congress (O)** led by **Morarji Desai**, the Bharatiya Lok Dal led by **Charan Singh**, the **Jana Sangh** led by **Atal Behari Vajpayee**, and the Socialists led by **George Fernandes**; they were joined by a splinter group from Congress led by **Jagjivan Ram**.

The Janata launched a spirited campaign for restoration of democracy and basic rights during the elections of March 1977. It won a massive victory, carrying 43% of the vote and 55% of the seats in the **Lok Sabha**. Although broadly based, it drew its main support from the urban middle class and landed agriculturalists of the Hindi-speaking belt in northern India. Subsequent elections to state legislative assemblies confirmed Janata's victory nation wide.

The Janata formed a government with Morarji Desai as prime minister and a 20-member cabinet reflecting the relative strength of the different parties. One of its first acts was to restore press freedom and civil and judicial rights by repealing laws of internal emergency and concomitant constitutional amendments. Vajpayee initiated improvement in India's relations with China and Pakistan through visits to those countries. The Janata government also initiated an economic strategy based on labor-intensive private industry, some liberalization of investment, and cooperation between governmental and voluntary groups in rural areas. But the implementation of policy was feeble, and there was a rising tide of strikes, communal violence, and frustration in the late 1970s. The Janata coalition was plagued throughout by pursuits that were trivialized or criticized by the press, such as attempting to arrest and prosecute Indira Gandhi, as well as by ego clashes among its leaders and factional disputes. The Janata coalition government collapsed early, in July 1979, and was replaced by a caretaker government, headed by Charan Singh, and a call for general elections by the end of the year, which restored congress.

JASWANT SINGH (1938–). Born into a **Rajput** land-owning family in the **Princely State** of Jodhpur, Jaswant Singh was educated at the elite Mayo College and joined a cavalry regiment in the Indian army, where he rose to the rank of major before resigning his commission in 1966 and taking to public affairs. As a member of the **Lok Sabha**, he established a reputation for expertise in foreign policy, international affairs, and national security. He served on several important parliamentary committees and authored serious work on those topics, including *Defending India* (Macmillan, 1999). Jaswant Singh joined the **Bharatiya Janata Party (BJP)** in the early 1980s and enjoyed the friendship and trust of **Atal Behari Vajpayee**, though not of the **Rashtriya Swayamsevak Sangh (RSS)** and militant members of the Sangh Parivar. Jaswant Singh was appointed deputy chairman of the **Planning Commission** after the BJP-led coalition government took power in 1998 and also acted as the prime minister's special envoy in the special and extra-sensitive international arena after India's detonation of five **nuclear** tests at Pokharan in May 1998.

Jaswant Singh was engaged in a "dialogue" with United States Deputy Secretary of State Strobe Talbott that lasted through 14 meetings in seven different countries between June 1998 and September 2000. To some extent, Washington came to appreciate India's security concerns, perhaps for the first time in more than 50 years of diplomatic relations between the two countries. US President Clinton's visit to India in March 2000 formed the basis for a substantially improved bilateral relationship that continued into the administration of George W. Bush and led to the lifting of US sanctions against India in September 2001. Jaswant Singh became Minister of External Affairs formally in 1999 and continued to press for international recognition of India as a "responsible" nuclear weapons state entitled to the same trading rights as "established" nuclear-weapons states. He had a variety of other difficult problems to handle as well, especially those ensuing from the hijacking of an Indian Airlines passenger aircraft to Kandahar, Afghanistan, by Pakistan-based terrorists in December 1999. Jaswant Singh exchanged positions with Finance Minister Yashwant Sinha in the summer of 2002 and pushed **economic liberalization** in his budget. He became leader of the opposition in the **Rajya Sabha** after the defeat of the BJP led government in May 2004.

JAT. An identifiable community that displays characteristics of **caste**, tribe, and ethnic group, Jats are probably descended from people entering the subcontinent with the **Hunas** in the fifth and sixth centuries CE who settled in parts of present-day **Pakistan** and the present-day Indian states of **Haryana, Punjab**, western **Uttar Pradesh**, northern **Rajasthan**, and **Madhya Pradesh**. Jats in all of these areas share many similar social customs and usually follow agricultural or military pursuits although by religious identity they may be **Hindu, Muslim,** or **Sikh**.

Jats gained some political prominence in the 17th century and after. In the reign of **Mughal Emperor Aurangzeb** they staged rebellions around **Delhi** that were not easily quelled. In the 18th century, Jat rule was established in the state of Bharatpur (near Delhi) under Suraj Mal. Many Jats in the Punjab plains became followers of the Sikh Guru, **Gobind Singh**; consequently, a large proportion of present-day Sikhs are Jat. Jat solidarity as an agricultural interest group is a factor that all **political parties** recognize, and it resulted in Jat support for the **Akali Dal** in the Punjab and the **Lok Dal** in Harayana and in western UP for some decades.

JAYALALITHA, C. JAYARAM (1948–). Jayalalitha was born in **Mysore** to a **brahmin** family and began appearing in **Tamil** films at a very young age. She played in over 100 films and was a close associate of the film star M. G. Ramachandran who went on to become chief minister of **Tamil Nadu**. She joined his political party, the All-India Anna Dravida Munnetra Kazhagam, in 1982 as propaganda secretary and became deputy leader of the party two years later. On Ramachandran's death, Jayalalitha successfully wrested control of the party from other contenders. She has been elected as chief minister of Tamil Nadu three times, in 1991, 1999, and 2001.

Although much was accomplished in raising the social and economic indicators of the state during Jayalalitha's tenures in office, she acquired the reputation of being autocratic, intolerant, and disrespectful of civil servants, a populist, and exceedingly corrupt. She was tried and convicted of corruption in 2000, and the sentence obliged her to resign and barred her from standing for elections for six years. However, the Madras High Court stayed the order, and she won a handsome majority at the polls in 2001. Jayalalitha's relations with the leaders of the **Bharatiya Janata Party** as well as with **Sonia Gandhi** leading the **Congress Party** fluctuated with her temperament and her perception of what tactics would best secure **New Delhi**'s favor for Tamil Nadu, especially in the matter of its dispute with **Karnataka** on distribution of waters of the **Kaveri River**.

In short, Jayalalitha is one of the more colorful characters on the Indian political scene.

JESUITS. Ignatius of Loyola founded the Society of Jesus in 1540. One year later, **Francis Xavier** arrived in **Goa**. He and his fellow Jesuits sought audience and influence in India, as in China, at the courts of princes, with the hope of converting them and their people to the Roman Catholic faith. The Jesuits Rodolfo Aquaviva and Antonio Monserrate engaged in learned discourse at the court of the **Mughal Emperor Akbar**, but his successors did not show interest. Jesuits also approached various rulers in southern India in the 16th and 17th centuries, without notable success. Moreover, forced conversions and the repressive role of the Inquisition in **Portuguese** Goa did not enhance the popularity of Jesuits at the time. However, their letters to Lisbon and Rome, carefully preserved, are valuable source materials for that period of Indian history.

By the 18th century, Jesuits had more or less abandoned their earlier tactics and had become Indianized in their methods of spreading their faith. They frequently adopted the dress and mores of **brahmans** in order to gain more respect in southern India. And, as in Europe, they focused on education. By the late 19th century the Jesuits had established a very high reputation for the quality of education they offered in India, and they sustained that appeal through the last phase of British rule and beyond. Laws passed after independence in 1947 restricted visas to foreigners pursuing purely evangelical work, and the Society of Jesus as well as the Roman Catholic Church in general took steps to Indianize its personnel. By the 1990s, 90% of Jesuits in India were Indian. They operated 88 schools, 21 colleges, two theological seminaries, and one social service institute, all of high quality.

JEWS. Jews have a long history—probably more than 2,000 years—in India. They were able to settle, retain their religious and cultural identity, and participate fully in economic life without suffering either persecution or pressure for "assimilation" at any time. The first groups of Jews went to the west coast of India, in the Konkan and Malabar districts, perhaps during the first diaspora after destruction of the Temple at Jerusalem. According to oral tradition, other groups followed after **Islam** spread in Arabia, North Africa, and Spain in the 7th and 8th centuries. In the 10th century, the ruler of **Cochin** made a land grant in perpetuity to the Jewish community there; it is preserved on copper plate in a synagogue built in the 16th century. The Inquisition drove out Jews from Spain and Portugal in the 15th and 16th centuries, and some came to India.

The number of Jewish settlers in India was never very large. According to estimates made in 1951, the Marathi-speaking Jewish community of the Konkan numbered about 20,000. The community of Cochin Jews was smaller and suffered from the effects of inbreeding. Both communities spoke the local Indian languages and came to be known as the "Bene Israel." Many migrated to Israel after its creation in 1948, with varying experiences; some have returned to India since the 1990s. A third group of a few thousand Jewish merchants and their families from Baghdad and Central Europe settled in the bustling ports of British India, notably **Bombay** and **Calcutta**, during the 19th century. Many of these identified more with Europeans than with Indians and emigrated after Indian independence in 1947. Recent estimates number the Jewish community at less than 20,000. They are included in the "other" category of religious affiliation listed by the Indian **census**. Many outstanding Jewish individuals have contributed in no small measure to Indian culture and contemporary achievements.

JHARKHAND. This is a new state of 79,714 square kilometers in the Indian Union created in November 2000 after prolonged agitation by the Jharkhand Mukti Morcha. After much negotiation among all **political parties**, consensus was reached, and the area covered by the 1995 Jharkhand Area Autonomous Council was elevated into a full fledged state. It comprises 18 districts of **Bihar**, mainly forest tracks of the Chhotanagpur plateau and **Santhal** district, bordering on West **Bengal** on the east, **Orissa** on the south, and **Chhatisgarh** and **Uttar Pradesh** on the west.

Jharkhand's estimated population of 21,840,000 includes numerous tribal, **Christian**, **Hindu**, and **Muslim** communities who speak a variety of **languages** and dialects but have a distinct cultural tradition dating back to ancient times and setting them apart from mainstream, **caste**-based society. Jharkhand contains some large cities, such as Bokaro, Dhanbad, Jamshedpur, and the capital Ranchi, the two largest steel mills in the country including the first established by **Tata** early in the 20th century, three universities, and several scientific research institutions. Overall socioeconomic development, however, has been long retarded and characterized by exploitation of tribal and **Dalit** populations, widespread deforestation, and forced migrations. Literacy and the sex ratio is low, although gender equality is high, and agriculture is poorly rewarding.

The area now comprising Jharkhand is rich in coal and other minerals so that mining is very important to the economy, as are heavy engineering, fertilizer, and large steel plants. It remains to be seen whether state governments will adopt alternate developmental strategies. Major road and rail lines connecting **Kolkata** to **Delhi** and **Mumbai** pass through Jharkhand, but much of the state is inaccessible and forested.

JINNAH, MOHAMMED ALI (1876–1948). Jinnah was born in Karachi to a Khoja family, followers of the **Agha Khan**. At no time was he a devout Muslim, although he recognized early the political potency of **Islam**. In 1892 Jinnah was sent to England where he qualified for the bar, became an Anglophile in manner and dress, and was excited by the election of **Dadabhai Naoroji** to the British House of Commons as a Liberal. Within a decade of his return to India he had established a lucrative legal practice in **Bombay** and was taking an active interest in politics. Law and politics dominated his life, for he had few friends and only a brief, unhappy marriage.

The first phase of Jinnah's public life, from 1906 to 1920, was in every way successful. In 1906 he joined the **Indian National Congress**, whose liberal moderate leaders, **Gopal Krishna Gokhale** and **Pherozeshah Mehta**, liked and trusted him. He was elected to the Imperial Legislative Council for the first time in 1910 and subsequently in 1915, 1923, 1926, and 1934. In 1913 he joined the **All-India Muslim League**, soon became president, and persuaded it to hold its annual sessions at the same time and place as Congress. Gokhale called him an "ambassador of Hindu Muslim unity," and

Congress President Bal **Gangadhar Tilak** signed the **Lucknow Pact** with him in 1916. This spelled out a compromise agreement according to which the League joined Congress in demanding self-government and a parliamentary system in India, and Congress conceded the League's demand for separate Muslim electorates and weighted representation in the central and some provincial legislatures.

The second phase of Jinnah's career was more turbulent. It began in 1920 when he resigned from the Legislative Council in protest against the repressive **Rowlatt Acts**. He opposed the **Khilafet Movement** for mixing religion with politics. He left Congress because he disapproved of **non-cooperation** and of **Mahatma Gandhi**'s leadership. Jinnah disliked Gandhi's program and methods, seeing in them the danger of "complete disorganization and chaos." When Jinnah returned to the Legislative Council he continued to argue for constitutional advance and Indianization of the civil and military services. He also tried to build a rapprochement between League and Congress, with both parties boycotting the **Simon Commission** and participating in the parallel All-Parties Conference of 1927. to draw up a draft constitution for India. Jinnah submitted 14 points for inclusion, dealing with provincial autonomy, federalism, separate electorates, and other safeguards for Muslims. In the end, however, these points were excluded from the **Nehru Report** of 1928.

Jinnah left India to take up his legal practice in London, adopting a constructive but unobtrusive posture at the **Round Table Conferences**. While in London, Jinnah was persuaded by **Muhammad Iqbal** to return to India and revive the Muslim League, even though in the prevailing atmosphere of communalism he was often taunted as not being a true representative of (generally devout) Indian Muslims. Jinnah took over leadership of the League in 1935, resolving to rebuild it as a mass-based foil to Congress and a prop for his own claim to be regarded as the sole spokesman for Muslims in India. He pursued these goals within the constraints of the **Government of India Act of 1935** by playing on emotional themes of communal differences, in contrast to his earlier stand on communal cooperation. He did not succeed. The League won only 5% of the Muslim vote in the 1937 elections; the governments in Muslim majority **Bengal** and **Punjab** were coalitions in which the League had no standing. A jubilant and victorious Congress turned down Jinnah's suggestion of a coalition government in the United Provinces (present-day **Uttar Pradesh**).

Thereafter, in the penultimate stage of his career, Jinnah accused Congress of abusing Muslim rights and formulated a "two nation theory," postulating that the **Hindus** and Muslims of India constituted separate nations that must be equally accommodated. He drafted a deliberately ambiguous paragraph passed by the League in its 1940 session, the famous **Pakistan** resolution demanding an autonomous homeland for the Indian Muslims. After the outbreak of **World War II**, Congress resigned its provincial ministries, and British interest in keeping Muslim support—and increasing Muslim recruitment to the army—was high. The fortunes of the Muslim League improved, and Jinnah's skill as a politician won him dividends. In 1944, he exchanged letters and met with Gandhi on a status of equality; however, there was no meeting of minds. British viceroys all found Jinnah difficult to deal with but were obliged to do so.

Jinnah's strenuous activity in the 1940s succeeded in directing a substantial majority of the Muslim vote to the League, and the results showed in the elections of 1946. He nearly succeeded in attaining his goal of parity between the Muslim League and Congress in the interim Central Government at New Delhi. He was suspicious of the plan offered by the **Cabinet Mission** that would have kept India united and was even more mistrustful of a possible Congress government at the center. He issued a call to Muslims for "Direct Action" in favor of Pakistan on August 16, 1946; the resulting communal carnage undoubtedly hastened **Partition**. For these reasons, his name has been reviled in India, as it has been honored in Pakistan as founder of the state and its first supreme leader, the *Quaid-i-Azam*.

JONES, WILLIAM. Jones studied Arabic and Persian at Oxford and went to **Calcutta** in 1783 as an established linguist and orientalist scholar employed by the **East India Company**. He had the support of Governor General **Warren Hastings** in encouraging research in Indian subjects. Jones was the founding President of the **Asiatic Society** of **Bengal**; its publications enhanced his scholarly reputation and contributed to Orientalism and the new but growing field of Indology in Europe.

During his 10 years in India, Jones studied **Sanskrit** with Indian scholars, collected rare manuscripts, and translated **Kalidasa**'s play, *Shakuntala*, as well as an ancient collection of tales, *Hitopadesa* into

English. He introduced standard principles for the transliteration of Sanskrit into English and helped establish the dates of **Chandragupta Maurya** through Greek writings of the fourth century BCE. He was knighted for his contributions to knowledge. Jones was engaged in compiling a manual of Indian law based on Sanskrit, Arabic, and Persian sources at the time of his death in Calcutta.

JOSHI, SHARAD (1935–). Joshi was born to a high-caste, educated, family in Satara, **Maharashtra**, and studied in Bombay and Switzerland before joining government service in 1957. He emerged as an agriculturalist and peasant leader during the 1980s when he led mass agitations in many states demanding remunerative prices on agricultural products, low tariffs on electricity, and liquidation of rural debts. He founded a peasant's organization in Maharashtra called *Shetkari Sanghatana* and a Kisan (peasant) Coordination Committee at the national level. He also founded the *Shetkari Mahila Aghadi*, an organization of rural women that rapidly grew in size and is celebrated for its work on property rights for women and its program of conferring legal land titles on rural women.

Joshi did not extol village life as simple or spiritual in a manner reminiscent of **M. K. Gandhi**, or seek to pit tenants and share-croppers against landowners. Instead, he argued that there was an essential conflict between rural and urban interests, with government policies of taxation and negative subsidies deliberately skewed to extract surplus at the expense of the agricultural sector. He coined the catchy slogan of "Bharat (rural) versus India (urban)." More seriously, Joshi put forward a convincing case that giving market incentives to agriculture would increase production and demand for labor, raise rural income and wages, and thereby lead to higher rates of industrial and overall economic growth in India. His books and articles in Marathi were translated into other Indian languages and widely published. In addition, he is a columnist for some English language newspapers.

As the most articulate spokesman of a modern, secular, non-violent peasants' movement not tied to any political party, Sharad Joshi caught the attention of **Rajiv Gandhi**, who appointed him an adviser to the Ministry of Food and Agriculture in 1987. Successive prime ministers continued to value his advice and made significant changes in taxation and other policies benefiting rural India. Joshi is chairman of more than one company established by farmers processing and marketing agricultural products or developing industrial estates, as well as the South Asia chapter of the World Agricultural Forum. He continues to advocate minimal government and non-intervention by the state in commodity markets and the economy generally.

JUSTICE PARTY. The Justice Party was formally known as the South Indian Liberation Federation whose official publication was *Justice*. The **political party** was founded in 1916–1917 by C. N. Mudaliar, T. M. Nair, and P. Thyagaraja Chetti on behalf of the intermediate **caste** groups jealous of high-caste, that is **brahman**, predominance in the educational institutions, governmental services, and politics of the **Madras** Presidency. The Justice Party issued "The Non-Brahman Manifesto," listing its grievances, and tried to widen opportunities for non-brahmans through caste quotas. It began a movement for **Dravidian** self-assertion, subsequently led by **Ramaswami Naicker**.

On political issues, the Justice Party voiced alarm at the growing agitation for self-government led by the brahmans and expressed loyalty to the British who, it said, "are able to hold the scales even between creed and class." Naturally, British officials and commercial interests in Madras cultivated this emergent political party as a tool with which to undercut the public appeal of the **Indian National Congress** and its demand for more and higher positions for Indians in the Civil Services. Further constitutional reforms made similar provisions of separate representation through reserved seats in the Madras Legislative Council for non-brahmans as for **Anglo-Indians**, Europeans, Indian Christians, and Muslims.

The Justice Party did well at the polls in the 1920s and cooperated with the Madras government in working the 1919 Reforms. It declined in the 1930s and was defeated by Congress in the 1937 elections.

– K –

KABIR (c. 1398–1448). Kabir was one of the most famous **Bhakti** saints of the *nirguna* or "without attributes" school. His was a stringent, passionate, and confident voice expressing in verses sung to the present day his profound conviction that God cannot be seen, named, described, or bound. Kabir ridiculed prescribed forms of ritualistic worship in both **Hinduism** and **Islam**. His absolute faith in a formless God of boundless love transcended all conventional religions with their doctrinal differences and their institutional hierarchies.

Little of historical certainty is known about the life of Kabir, as later commentaries typically contain much hagiography. His name is from the Koran, and he was born in **Banaras**. It is generally believed that his family belonged to a low status weaver **caste** and had recently converted to Islam, and that he was thoroughly familiar with Hindu thought and practice. Popular accounts abound of his outlandish behavior toward all authority. He died in Magahar, some kilometers to the north, where his followers quarreled over funeral rites for the body: Hindu-style cremation or Muslim-style burial?

Kabir's salty, skeptical poems, poking fun at Pundits (**brahmans**) and Qazis (Muslim divines) alike but singing always of God, have been on the lips of the common people of northern India for over 500 years. Many are included in the holy book of the **Sikhs**. Kabir's followers, known as Kabir Panthis, have codified his nonsectarian teachings and have raised his memory to an object of worship.

KALAM, AVIL PAKIR JALALUDDIN ABDUL (1931–). Dr. Kalam was born at Rameswaran in **Tamil Nadu** near the southern tip of India to a humble Muslim family. He showed a scientific flair early in life and took an advanced degree at the Madras Institute of Technology in 1958. He worked with the Defence Research and Development Organization (DRDO) for five years before joining the Indian Space Research Organization (ISRO) with whom he remained for nearly 20 years. Dr. Kalam returned to DRDO in 1982 and left it in 1992 to become scientific adviser to the Ministry of Defence, and secretary of the Department of Research and Development until 1999. He enjoyed cabinet rank as principal scientific adviser to the Government of India 1999–2001.

Dr. Kalam was primarily a nuclear scientist who is credited with the launching of India's first satellite in 1980 and with masterminding the indigenous development of India's integrated guided missiles, the Prithvi, the Trishul, and the Agni, and also the testing of nuclear weapons at Pokhatan in May 1998. He was honored for his work with the Padma Vibhushan in 1990 and the Bharat Ratna in 1997. At the same time, he had a life long passion for Tamil poetry and the Indian classics, as well as a deep affinity with children. After formal retirement in 1999, he undertook tours around the country to meet children and inspire in them, especially those of high school age, a passion for science. He also opened a website to inculcate a scientific bent of mind and drafted a millennium Vision Science policy paper.

In July 2002, Abdul Kalam was elected president of India by an overwhelming majority and with the backing of all of the major political parties. A few questions were raised in the press at the time about the level of his knowledge of the **Constitution**, as well as about the possibly political motivation or "tokenism" of the **Bharatiya Janata Party (BJP)** supporting a Muslim candidate for the highest position in the land so soon after a communal carnage took place in **Gujarat** under the aegis of a BJP chief minister, but there was no real controversy. President Kalam graces his office and continues to reach out to children and ordinary people in every part of India.

KALELKAR, DATTATRAYA BALKRISHNA. Kalelkar was born to a Saraswat **brahman** family at Satara, **Maharashtra**, did his undergraduate studies at Fergusson College, **Poona**, and became a school teacher and headmaster. He was drawn both to the activist political arena of the freedom struggle and to a reclusive spiritual quest; he wandered indecisively for some years. His meeting with **Mahatma Gandhi** in February 1915 resolved his inner dilemmas, and he became an ardent follower of Gandhi for the rest of his life.

Kalelkar made his principal contributions to Gandhi's constructive work for Indian revitalization in the field of education. He was the head of Sabarmati School where the scheme of Basic Education was evolved; he was professor and then vice chancellor of the National University of **Gujarat**. He also undertook the task of popularizing Hindi (rather, Hindustani or everyday spoken Hindi) as the national language, reforming the Nagari script in which Hindi was written and selecting suitable systems of Hindi shorthand and keyboards for Hindi typewriters. He worked in this field for 30 years, both before and after Indian independence.

Kakasaheb Kalelkar, as he was known, advocated social and religious reform toward equality and freedom in the spirit of his teacher, Gandhi. He wrote many books in English, Gujarati, Hindi, and

Marathi advancing Gandhi's ideas, including that of a self-sufficient, labor-intensive rural economy. He dedicated his life to social service but also traveled extensively, usually to study the problems of overseas Indian communities and to develop cultural relations with them. He was a member of the **Constituent Assembly** and a member of Parliament from 1952 to 1964. He was honored with the Padma Vibhushan in 1965. He gradually withdrew after that to an increasingly simple and ascetic life.

KALIDASA (c. 375–455 CE). Kalidasa is generally accepted as the greatest poet and dramatist in the **Sanskrit language**. His life is traditionally placed in or about the reigns of **Chandra Gupta Vikramaditya** and Kumara Gupta of the **Gupta Dynasty**, and the internal evidence of his works tends to confirm such an estimate. Kalidasa probably belonged to Mandasore, close to the Gupta capital at **Ujjain**. He saw classical Indian courtly culture at its height and participated in the active commercial and intellectual life of the age. Although there is no reliable information about his life, his works show him to have been a well-educated and well-traveled man, with an understanding of the world.

Kalidasa's surviving works include four long poems, *Kumarasambhava*, or "The Birth of the War-God," *Raghuvamsa,* or "Dynasty of Raghu," *Ritusamhara*, or "Garland of Seasons," and *Meghaduta* or "Cloud Messenger." The latter vividly depicts Indian topography as well as the anguish of separated lovers. Three plays of Kalidasa have survived, complete with detailed stage instructions, *Malvika and Agnimitra*, a comedy of harem intrigue, *Urvasi Won by Valor*, and, most famous of all, *The Recognition of Sakuntala* which has been translated often, in many world languages.

In addition to being literary masterpieces in Sanskrit, leading to a comparison of Kalidasa with Shakespeare in English, Kalidasa's works provide a picture of the social manners, dress, behavior, and beliefs prevalent in the Gupta era.

KALPAVRIKSH. A non-governmental organization (NGO) founded in 1979, it deals with environmental conservation through a variety of methods including public education, research and publications, campaigns to raise awareness, cooperation with other groups, and direct action. The nucleus of the organization was originally formed by students at Delhi University who wanted to save the precious forest-cum-wilderness on the last remaining ridge of the ancient Aravalli Range located next to their campus from further depredations of urban development. Kalpavriksh has subsequently grown into a well-known NGO based in both **Delhi** and **Pune** and working on local, national, and global issues. It operates on a limited budget and is financed by grants without strings from other NGOs and government.

Members of Kalpavriksh have trekked through parts of the **Himalaya** in solidarity with the **Chipko Movement**, have made detailed studies of the impact of high dams on the **Narmada River**, and have conducted nature walks. The NGO has lobbied for wildlife protection in newly threatened areas such as the **Andaman and Nicobar Islands** and has undertaken a general campaign for conservation of India's biodiversity. As is the case for many other NGOs and environmentalists, Kalpavriksh often has been in confrontation with the instruments of state, including police forces. At the same time, the aims and objectives of this voluntary group on a number of environment and development issues can be, and are, advanced best through cooperation with other elements of civil society supporting elements of the state. Thus, Kalpavriksh attempts to build bridges of mutual understanding between representatives of communities, especially tribal communities whose livelihood and culture is dependent on preservation of forests and biodiversity, governmental officials, and corporate advocates of modern development. One of the best examples of such collaboration is the National Biodiversity Strategy and Action Plan (NB-SAP) drafted in 2000 and funded through the United Nations Development Program. This process indicates alternative paths to sustainable development; it also points towards patterns of governance that have moved away from an over-centralized alienating colonial model to more decentralized and participatory forms and reality.

KAMARAJ, KUMARASWAMI (1903–1975). Kamaraj was president of the **Congress Party** from 1963 to 1966, managing two smooth transitions of executive power after the successive deaths of Prime Ministers **Jawaharlal Nehru** in May1964 and **Lal Bahadur Shastri** in 1966. He authored the Kamaraj Plan to revitalize Congress.

Kamaraj was born in the extreme south of India to an undistinguished family belonging to the Nadar **caste**. Although his father kept a coconut shop, the Nadars were hereditary toddy-tappers ranked barely above **Untouchables**, and yet they were upwardly mobile in the early 20th century and claimed the previously denied right to enter temples as well as higher status. The Nadars established self-help societies and free schools in the three southern districts where they were concentrated. From the age of five, Kumaraswami was educated in these schools; 50 years later, as chief minister of **Madras** state (later **Tamil Nadu**), he promoted the cause of universal education statewide through improving old schools, building new ones, and providing free school meals for children.

Kamaraj joined the **Indian National Congress** and became a follower of **Mahatma Gandhi** after the **Jallianwala Bagh Massacre** of 1919. He devoted himself to the national movement and did not marry. He was not vociferously anti-**brahman** as were **Ramaswami Naicker** and members of the **Justice Party**, nor was he close to **C. Rajagopalachari**, all prominent in Madras politics of the 1930s. Kamaraj was elected to the Madras legislature in 1937, became Congress president there in 1940, supported the **Quit India movement**, and was imprisoned from 1942 to 1944.

After independence, Kamaraj was actively involved in state politics, gaining a reputation as a "king maker," and was elected chief minister in 1954. His nine-year tenure is generally regarded as an outstanding success for laying the infrastructure of economic development, for accessible, firm, and impartial administration, and for striking at caste hierarchy without undue confrontation or rhetoric. Nevertheless, the populist movement led by the **Dravida Munnetra Kazhagam** gathered momentum in Tamil Nadu, at the expense of Congress. Kamaraj gave up his position in 1963 in order to work for the revitalization of Congress from **New Delhi**. He was one of the "Syndicate" or collective leadership that managed party affairs until **Indira Gandhi** broke from them in 1969. Although Kamaraj was elected to the **Lok Sabha** in 1969, he was no longer a prominent player on the national stage or even in his home state.

KANAUJ. An ancient city on the east bank of the **Ganges** river, Kanauj first finds mention in the **Mahabharata** and is referred to in the works of **Patanjali** and **Faxian** as a center of brahmanical learning. The city gained its greatest prominence as the imperial capital of **Harsha-Vardhana** when it had a teeming population and numerous **Hindu** temples and **Buddhist** monasteries. **Xuanzang** stayed in and around Kanauj for seven years and lavished praise on the city.

Control over Kananj was contested by competing successor dynasties. As capital of the **Pratiharas**, it was raided by **Mahmud of Ghazni** in 1018. Its ruler, Jaichand Rathore, was defeated by Mohammed Ghor in 1194. The city was virtually destroyed during the war between Humayun and **Sher Shah Sur** in 1540 and was never rebuilt to anything resembling its former glory.

KANISHKA. The greatest ruler of the **Kushan** dynasty, Kanishka's exact dates are uncertain, although he probably lived in the first or second century CE. Tradition ascribes his accession to the throne to 78 CE, the beginning of the Saka era, a system of dating widespread in India to the present time.

Kanishka's capital was Purushapura or Peshawer in the northwest of the Indian subcontinent. From there, he waged a series of successful wars and accomplished the extremely difficult task of subduing the trans-Pamir kings of Khotan, Yarkand, and Kashgar in Chinese Turkestan. He ruled an empire stretching from the Oxus river in the north to the lower part of the **Indus** river in the south, that included **Kashmir** and much of the **Ganges** valley. Modern archaeological research deduces the extent of his dominions and other particulars of his reign from coins, inscriptions, and other discoveries. A remarkable headless statue of Kanishka, clad in long coat and boots, stands at Mathura.

Kanishka appears to have honored many religious sects in his dominions, including **Buddhism**. He followed the example of **Mauryan Emperor Ashoka** in convening a Buddhist Council to settle theological disputes on doctrine and practice. Buddhism at this time was undergoing a great transformation and an enormous expansion in appeal. This was furthered under Kanishka's patronage. His realm was a hub of trade among three major centers of civilization, India, China, and the Roman Empire connected by the **Silk Road**. Kanishka and the Kushan dynasty are closely associated with the flowering of the **Gandhara** school of art and sculpture.

KAO, RAMJIN. A pandit from **Kashmir**, Kao is best known for founding and heading India's external intelligence service, the Research and Analysis Wing (R&AW) in 1968. Kao joined the Imperial Police Service (IPS) in British India and moved to the Intelligence Bureau (IB) immediately after independence. He was charged with the personal security of the prime minister and other high dignitaries. **Jawaharlal Nehru** was impressed by Kao's austerity, honesty, professionalism, and tact, and deputed him on a series of sensitive assignments. Indira Gandhi too held him in regard, and as prime minister she came to rely on his thoroughly professional and non-partisan counsel, especially with respect to national security matters and situations within neighboring countries. She also heeded the advice, reportedly given by Kao, to put an end to the **Emergency** and called general elections in 1977, which she lost. Although Kao retired from official service in 1977, he was appointed security adviser to the government in 1980 and, among other tasks, undertook discreet missions to Washington and Beijing to pave the way for improved relations between India and the United States and China.

KAPOOR, RAJ was born in Peshawer to the famous actor, Prithviraj Kapoor, and began acting as a child. He became the megastar of the Hindi **film industry** in the 1940s and was immensely popular throughout India, China, the Middle East, and the Soviet Union. Later in life he became an audacious maker of films as well.

KARNATAKA. The present-day state of Karnataka was formed in 1960 after a reorganization of state boundaries on the basis of **language**. Kannada-speaking districts of **Bombay**, **Maharashtra**, and **Hyderabad** were added to the former **princely state** of **Mysore**. Karnataka has an area of 191,791 square kilometers and an estimated population of 52,733,958 according to the 2001 **census** report.

Karnataka has a rich historical heritage from ancient times that includes the achievements of the **Chalukya** and **Hoysala** dynasties as well as the **Vijayanagar** Empire and **Marathas**. **Jain** scholars flourished in Karnataka and the early manifestations of the **Bhakti** movement were centered there. Thus, Karnataka abounds in temples and other monuments of architectural and archaeological importance and has a rich literary and intellectual tradition. About 20% of its area is under forest, renowned for sandal, teak, and rose wood. The state is famous for its silk and other handicrafts and is also rich in mineral resources, including iron ore in the west and gold, mined at Kolar. Mangalore is its chief port. The **Kaveri River** has its source in **Coorg** district and allocation of its waters is the subject of a long-standing dispute with **Tamil Nadu.**

Karnataka's capital city of **Bangalore** attracts international attention as the home of high technology industry, especially electronics and information technology. Substantial foreign direct investment has come to Bangalore after India's **economic liberalization** in the 1990s. *See also* MYSORE.

KASHMIR. Kashmir is a high-altitude region of lakes and valleys surrounded by mountains in the northernmost section of the Indian subcontinent. It is renowned for the beauty of its landscape and its inhabitants. Kashmir was known to the composers of the **Vedas** and formed part of the territories ruled by the **Maurya** and **Kushan** dynasties before the Common Era. Kashmir was an abode of **Sanskrit** learning and played an important role in the spread of **Buddhism** to adjoining **Tibet** and Chinese Turkestan. Many pilgrimage sites, including the ice-lingam cave at Amarnath sacred to **Shiva**, are located in Kashmir, and the Martand temple dedicated to the Sun god in the 12th century is famous. Kashmir's early history is detailed in the *Rajatarangini*, written by Kalhan in the 12th century. Ruling dynasties and **brahman** pundits appear to have prospered together without much concern for the common people. The majority of the people in the Kashmir valley were converted to **Islam**—Sunni, Shi'a and Sufi—after a Muslim adventurer from Swat seized the throne in the mid-14th century. Subsequently, Kashmir developed a composite culture known as *Kashmiriyat* that remained characteristic until recent efforts by militant Islamists to "purify" it. Works from Sanskrit, Arabic, and Persian were translated, and the Kashmiri **language** with its branches was written in both Nagari and Persian scripts. **Mughal Emperor Akbar** annexed Kashmir in 1587 and it was a favorite pleasure resort for his successors. Mughal gardens and monuments are permanent tourist attractions in Kashmir.

Kashmir suffered Afghan raids in the 18th century and then was annexed to the Sikh empire of **Ranjit Singh**. The British sold Kashmir to the Dogra chief Gulab Singh when the former defeated the Sikh army in 1846, and his dynasty ruled Kashmir, Jammu, and **Ladakh** under the paramount power of the British—who remained watchful of Russian intentions—until 1947. Kashmir was not immune to the political currents flowing in the rest of India in the 20th century. The **States Peoples Conference** supported the emergence of a movement for democracy led by **Sheikh Abdullah** called the National Conference; the **All-India Muslim League** tried winning Kashmir, the majority of whose inhabitants were Muslim, to the cause of **Pakistan**. On British announcement of impending independence, partition, and lapse of **paramountcy** in 1947, the ruler of Jammu and Kashmir hesitated in making a decision to join either **Dominion**. His hand was forced when armed Pathan tribals backed by Pakistan invaded the Kashmir valley. The maharajah turned to India for protection and signed the Instrument of Accession to the Indian Union on October 27. An elected state Assembly led by Abdullah subsequently confirmed the accession and special provisions of autonomy. Military conflict in the state between India and Pakistan in 1947–1948 was ended by a United Nations ceasefire, but neither negotiations nor another Pakistani attack and ensuing war in 1965 brought about resolution of a dispute over the status of Jammu and Kashmir.

The Simla Agreement of 1972 between India and Pakistan rationalized a de facto partition along a Line of Control (LOC), with Pakistan in control of the northern territories and a western slice of Kashmir, India in control of about two-thirds of the Kashmir Valley, Jammu and Ladakh, and China in control of strategic areas around the Karakoram Pass. Dissidence against India grew among the majority Sunni population of the Kashmir Valley largely because of gross mismanagement of administration and corruption of National Conference governments supported by **New Delhi**, blatant rigging of elections in the 1980s, and gradual erosion of autonomy. An insurrection broke out in 1989, with the Jammu and Kashmir Liberation Front (JKLF) demanding *azadi* or independence. Since the early 1990s, Pakistan has been a financier, sponsor, supplier, and organizer of various militant groups preaching *jihad* (holy war) against India and a merger of Muslim majority Kashmir with Pakistan. Indian security forces have been engaged in counter-insurgency operations against these cross border **terrorists**. International attention has been drawn to the danger of war breaking out and escalating to nuclear exchanges.

In February 1999, Prime Minister **Atal Behari Vajpayee** went to Lahore and took a major step toward negotiating agreement with Pakistan on a peace process and composite dialogue, but Pakistan's (failed) attempt to militarily alter the LOC by attacking in Kargil derailed it. India-Pakistan talks on a range of disputes, including Kashmir, resumed in 2004 without remarkable success—or failure. Meanwhile, New Delhi entered into talks with Kashmiri dissidents, offering the state many economic inducements, and ensuring free and fair elections in 2002, which resulted in the replacement of the National Conference by a more popular government and a resumption of some semblance of normality. Many possible "solutions" to the Kashmir problem have been published in India and abroad, but by late 2004 the military government of Pakistan had refused to accept variants of the status quo and the Indian government had refused to consider any changes of the map. The Kashmiri people themselves have tired of insurgency and counter insurgency and are now taking a part in cross border peace efforts. *See also* JAMMU AND KASHMIR and HURRIYAT.

KAUTILYA (also known as CHANAKYA and VISHNUGUPTA) (c. Latter half of fourth century BCE). The exact dates of Kautilya's life are not known, but he authored the *Arthasastra* and was a close adviser to **Chandragupta Maurya** whose reign has been dated from Greek sources. Evidence suggests that he initially served the Nanda Dynasty of **Magadh** and helped Chandragupta overthrow the last Nanda King, who may have been of low caste and unorthodox faith.

Kautilya was educated at **Taxila** and certainly had a firm grasp of both the theory and practice of administration and politics. His *Arthasastra* elevates the state to a position where service to it entails imperatives unknown to morality. Although the work contains some normative admonitions to the "just king," it is regarded as a compendium of previous political treatises and an accurate account of the polity, administration, and economy of the **Mauryan Empire**. Later writers refer back to Kautilya as a "wise and revered teacher" as well as a wily **brahman** minister. Present-day commentators sometimes compare Machiavelli of 16th-century Italy to Kautilya, 2,000 years earlier.

KAVERI RIVER. It rises in **Coorg** and flows east across peninsular India to empty in the Bay of Bengal. It is known as Dakshina Ganga or the **Ganges** of the south, and numerous centers of pilgrimage are found along its banks, notably at Seringapatam, Sivasamudram, and Seringam. Though not navigable, the Kaveri has always been an important source of water for irrigation and a barrage dating to the second century is still in use. The river has also been harnessed for hydroelectric power in recent times. Proportionate use of its waters is long and hotly disputed between the riparian states **Karnataka** and **Tamil Nadu**, both within the Indian Union, and efforts made by water tribunals, judicial bodies, and Union government mediation have not yet resolved the dispute.

The large Kaveri delta is one of the most fertile rice-growing areas of the Indian subcontinent. The heartland of **Tamil** country and **Chola** culture, it features many historic towns, such as **Tanjore**, and an abundance of temples and learned persons.

KERALA. One of India's smaller states, Kerala encompasses 38,863 square kilometers in area with an estimated population of close to 32 million. A microcosm of multi-religious India, Kerala's population is 59% Hindu, 21% Christian, and 20% Muslim; each community has important subdivisions and **caste** rankings. The state has the highest literacy rate in the country, more females than males, enjoys many social services, and has prospered economically from its export of goods as well as migration of its people to different parts of the world. The present boundaries of Kerala were formed after independence on a linguistic basis by joining Malabar to the southern **Princely States** of Travancore and **Cochin**. The city of Trivandrum is its capital and Malayalam its principal **language**.

Located in the southwest between the Western Ghats and the Arabian Sea, and with a fine natural harbor at Cochin, Kerala has an ancient maritime tradition. An early Chera or Keralaputra King of the second century BCE is reputed as a conqueror on land and sea. The existence of fairly constant trading links with Rome, Arabia, China, and island kingdoms in Southeast Asia are deduced from archaeological and literary sources. The Keralaputras were mentioned by the Greek envoy **Megasthenes** and in an inscription of **Mauryan Emperor Ashoka** of the third century BCE as one of the southern kingdoms with which the Mauryas had friendly relations. The rulers of Kerala were alternately partners and rivals in an early southern confederacy of the **Chola**, Chera, and **Pandya** dynasties.

The great Vedanta philosopher **Shankara** was born in Kerala in the eighth century. **Shiva** worship was widespread and the Syrian Christian Church was founded early; the society was predominantly matrilineal. An extremely elaborate **caste** structure emerged over time in which the intellectual and religious power of the Namboodiri **brahmans** was balanced to some extent at the top by the economic and military dominance of the **Nairs**, and intricate rules of pollution governed social distances between these higher and other lower, or avarna (untouchable), castes. Throughout the medieval and early modern periods, Kerala's coastal principalities were less affected by political events in north India or the **Deccan** than by power rivalries in the Indian Ocean. By the 18th century, two independent states of Travancore and Cochin had been formed in the south; they remained substantially autonomous and well administered, in alliance with the British.

In the late 19th and early 20th centuries, far-reaching social changes were initiated in Travancore and Cochin through the efforts of social reformers and enlightened rulers in response to economic imperatives and vigorous intellectual questioning of custom. Specifically, educated men of the Namboodiri, Nair, and **Ezhava** communities spearheaded reform of matrilineal Marumakkathayam law so as to permit partition of *tarwads*, or extended family estates, monogamous marriage, and inheritance from father to son. Removal of onerous caste restrictions, including those on female wearing apparel and access to Hindu temples, was another major target of social reformers. (Issues such as child marriage, **sati**, and widow remarriage, which were high on the social reform agenda in north India, were not of importance in Travancore and Cochin where women were relatively free and educated.) A rich Mallayallum literature portrays the individual courage and social conflicts of the period. In Malabar, peasant mobilization, labor unrest, and political volatility was expressed in the **Moplah revolts** of 1921–1922 and led also to the organization there of a strong branch of the **Communist Party of India (CPI)**.

The CPI was voted to power in Kerala in the 1957 elections, becoming the first communist government in the world formed and working within a parliamentary system. Despite its removal in 1959, a party split in 1964, and strenuous efforts by the **Congress Party** to counteract it, the **CPI(M)** remains a potent force and occasional government in Kerala. The migration of men from Kerala to other parts of India and to the Persian Gulf area transformed the economy and the physical features of the state in the latter part of the 20th century.

KHALJI, ALAUDDIN (r. 1296–1316). This able and ruthless ruler considerably expanded the domains of the **Delhi Sultanate** in a blood-soaked reign. He came to power by murdering his aged father-in-law, Jalaludin Khalji—who had been elected Sultan by the Delhi nobles after the death of **Balban**—and embarked on conquest. Alauddin had raided Malwa and Devagiri for treasure before taking the throne and plundered **Gujarat** after. He defeated the **Rajputs** of Ranthambhor and **Chitor**—whose beautiful Queen Padmini he was reputed to covet—and then turned to the four wealthy kingdoms of the **Deccan** south of the Vindhya mountains. His military prowess also kept the Mongols at bay in the northwest.

Although Alauddin Khalji gained vast treasure by his conquests, it was not sufficient to maintain the large standing army he felt obliged to maintain. He initiated a series of revenue and administrative measures designed to strengthen his own position and fill his treasury. For example, he discontinued the practice of seeking investiture from the caliph in Baghdad and declared himself supreme judicial authority in the Delhi Sultanate, thus ridding himself of the **Islamic** theologians usually at the ruler's side. He took the bold step of revoking all *iqtas*, or land grants, made as gifts, pensions, religious endowments, or salaries by earlier Sultans. He assumed all land as property of the state, and increased assessment of revenue from the customary one-fifth or one-third to one-half of produce. He levied taxes on all sales and consumption of goods, issued price controls, forbade convivial meetings amongst nobles, and enlarged his espionage and police service to enforce these regulations. He also used the discretionary *jiziyah* (see Glossary), or protection tax, for non-Muslims, as a regular source of revenue.

The burden of Alauddin Khalji's administration fell heaviest on cultivators and tradesmen who were predominantly **Hindu**. The contemporary Muslim historian Barani wrote, "no Hindu could hold up his head." He also noted that all "people were so absorbed in obtaining the means of livelihood that the very name of rebellion was hardly mentioned." (Ziauddin Barni, "Tarikh-i Feroz Shahi," in Elliott & Dowson, *The History of India by Her Own Historians*: 183 and 179.) While Alauddin dreamed of building an empire that would extend over the entire subcontinent, he overreached himself. His protégé, Malik Kafur, raided **Madurai**, farther south than any earlier raid from Delhi, but Kafur offended nobles at court and created his own domain. Gujarat, Chitor, and Devagiri reestablished independence. Four years after Alauddin's death, his line was replaced by another general in revolt, Ghiyasuddin **Tughlaq**.

KHAN, ALI AKBAR (1922–). Ali Akbar Khan was born in East **Bengal** to Allauddin Khan, the legendary maestro who trained many of the finest 20th-century exponents of Indian classical **music**, including Ravi Shankar. Ali Akbar's chosen instrument was the *sarod* and he made his debut in 1936. His world tours commenced in 1956 and have continued since. His musical collaboration with Yehudi Menuhin and Ravi Shankar brought prominence to Indian classical music in the West, as did his many joint performances with jazz groups such as Duke Ellington's. Ali Akbar Khan founded colleges of music named for him in **Calcutta** in 1956, in San Rafael, California, in 1968, and in Basel, Switzerland, in 1982. He was the musical director for many films made in Hollywood and **Bombay**, and has composed new *ragas as* well as concerti and ballet suites for *Kathak* classical dance. His frequent radio broadcasts and public appearances have made him a familiar figure to music lovers around the world. He received numerous awards, including the Padma Vibhushan for outstanding achievement in 1989.

KHAN, VILAYAT (1928–2004). One of the premier exponents of classical instrumental music on the *sitar*, Vilayat Khan was born in eastern **Bengal** to the noted maestro Inayet Khan. He made his first recording in 1936, and after the death of his father in 1938 he moved to **Delhi**. Vilayat Khan developed a distinctive style, marked by energy, fluidity, inventiveness, and great sweetness. He is credited with an innovative vocal technique in sitar playing known as *gayaki ang* and created new tunings, both supple and versatile. He soon attained an international reputation but always defended the purity and continuity of multiple local traditions within the classical Indian music tradition, which also allows for experimentation. Vilayat Khan was fiercely independent. He declined state functions and awards, but music lovers bestowed on him the title of *aftaab-e-sitar* (radiant star of the sitar).

KHILAFET MOVEMENT. This movement arose among Indian Muslims after **World War I** in protest against Allied treatment of the defeated Ottoman Empire of Turkey, dismantled by the Treaty of Sevres. The movement took its name from the Ottoman caliph or khalifa, formally regarded as the temporal head of **Islam**. Its central demand was that the khalifa retain control of places sacred to Islam and be left with sufficient territory to enable him to defend the Islamic faith and its holy places. The Khilafet movement grew into a potent, if short-lived, voice of Indian nationalism.

The Khilafet movement contained two different elements. Prosperous **Bombay** merchants provided the moderate, constitutional element. A larger, radical strand was drawn from the urban lower middle class intelligentsia and *ulama* (see Glossary) influential in India's small towns and villages, and led by the **Ali brothers**, Mohammed and Shaukat. They pressed for a countrywide *hartal* (see Glossary) against the British Indian government and were eager to win the cooperation of **Hindus** to make the protest effective. **Mahatma Gandhi**, rising leader of the **Indian National Congress** at the time, had influence with both Khilafet groups and was eager to demonstrate Hindu–Muslim unity in the cause of Indian nationalism. The **All-India Muslim League** was also supportive of the protest and passed a resolution to that effect.

In June 1920, a Central Khilafet Committee announced a program of non-cooperation including nonpayment of taxes, and in September Gandhi persuaded Congress to adopt a similar plan around the three issues of Punjab, Khilafet, and *swaraj*, or independence. A populist groundswell around the country and much peasant and labor unrest made the **Non-Cooperation Movement** of 1920–1922 a general revolt against British authority at the all-India level, with many regional and local variations among Hindus and Muslims. Some 20,000 Muslims in the northwest left for Afghanistan in *hijrat*, or exodus, away from a government that was dishonoring the khalifa. The boycott of government-run educational institutions led to the founding of the Jamia Millia for the higher education of Muslims. The economic boycott against British goods was even more successful and led to an increased indigenous production. The Muslim Mappilla or **Moplahs** of Malabar revolted in 1921 and set up a number of "Khilafet Republics." The Gandhian program of village reconstruction focused on issues that unified Hindus and Muslims and cut across class lines—self-help, temperance, and taxes.

The Khilafet Movement collapsed in 1922. It lost its focus for the Muslim world when Kemal Ataturk took power in Turkey and abolished the office of the khalifa altogether. Within India, the movement was deprived of leadership when the Ali brothers were imprisoned. When Gandhi suddenly called off the Non-Cooperation Movement in 1922, both Hindu and Muslim followers were left bewildered and bereft.

KHORANA, HAR GOVIND (1922–). A Nobel Prize winner in 1968 for his work in medicine and physiology, Khorana was born in Raipur and took his initial science degrees in Lahore, **Punjab** before going to Liverpool in 1945. Khorana earned his doctorate in organic chemistry from Cambridge University, England, and then pursued an academic career in the United States. While at the University of Wisconsin he became the first person to artificially synthesize a gene, thereby elucidating the genetic code. Khorana moved to the Massachusetts Institute of Technology (MIT) as professor of biology and chemistry and was also visiting professor at Delhi University in 1997–1998. He is currently professor emeritus at MIT.

KHUSHWANT SINGH (1915–). Columnist, editor, historian, journalist, and short-story **Sikh** writer with an international reputation, he was born in the **Punjab** and educated at Government College, Lahore, Kings College, and Inner Temple, London. Khushwant Singh practiced law at the High Court of Lahore from 1940–1947. His father, Sir Sobha Singh, was a well-known builder both in the Punjab and in **New Delhi** after **Partition**. The human tragedies associated with that event are evoked in Khushwant Singh's widely read *Train to Pakistan* (1961). He served for some years as press attaché in India's missions in Britain and Canada and on the communications staff of the **Planning Commission** before turning to writing as a full-time occupation. His two volume *History of the Sikhs* (1963, 1966) filled a lacuna, and he has made numerous other contributions to explaining the spiritual and historical legacy of his community in particular and India in general in articles, books, and broadcasts, as well as in lectures while he was a visiting faculty member at various American and British universities.

Khushwant shaped important journals as editor in the past but is best known more recently for his witty and malicious newspaper columns and his encouragement of youthful talent. His love of nature and of his home city, Delhi, has translated into urging civic action to preserve the parks and historical monuments that abound there.

KHUSRU/KHUSRAV, AMIR ABUL HASAN YAMINUDDIN (1253–1325). Born in **Delhi** as the younger son of a Turkish migrant to India, Amir Khusru grew up to be a prolific writer and the most famous Indian poet of his era. Nearly 100 prose works on various subjects are credited to him as well as about half a million verses of historical, mystic, and romantic import. As court poet and librarian, he enjoyed the patronage of six rulers of the **Khalji** and **Tughlaq** dynasties. His writings, including letters, poems, and other documents, are treated by historians as primary source material on the military, political, and social conditions prevailing in the **Delhi Sultanate**. Writing mainly in Persian, he also contributed to the newly developing literature of Urdu and Hindi, spoken languages of northern India on which the influences of both Persian and **Sanskrit** were obvious. He was an intimate of the Muslim nobility and also a disciple of the revered **Sufi**, Nizamuddin Auliya; Khusru's poetry is infused with mysticism and humanism.

Amir Khusru was also a musician. He is credited with the invention of new musical instruments and ragas in the classical tradition of Indian **music**. Amir Khusru exemplified the best of cultural synthesis between Hindu and Muslim, Indian and Turk or Persian that was beginning in his lifetime.

KIDWAI, RAFI AHMAD (1894–1954). Kidwai was born to a landowning Muslim family; he studied first at a village school, then at home with a tutor, and later at the Muslim Anglo-Oriental College in

Aligarh. As a youth, he met the famous **Ali brothers**, **Motilal Nehru**, and **Mahatma Gandhi** who deeply attracted him. Rafi Ahmad joined the **Non-Cooperation Movement** in 1921; he was subsequently imprisoned and upon release became private secretary to Motilal Nehru. Kidwai was elected to the Central Legislative Assembly as a member of the **Swaraj Party** in 1926 and later organized members of the **Indian National Congress** in the legislature.

Kidwai's political bent was more radical than conservative. He was unorthodox, progressive, and non-acquisitive in his personal, religious, and social attitudes. During the early 1930s, he spearheaded the Congress agrarian movement in the United Provinces—present-day **Uttar Pradesh** (UP)—and a no-rent campaign to protect the peasantry against the ravages of the world depression. He became a minister in the Congress government of the UP formed under the **Government of India Act of 1935** and put through legislative measures preparatory to the abolition of *zamindari* (see Glossary) in that state. A prominent Muslim, he remained in India after **Partition** and joined the Cabinet of **Jawaharlal Nehru** who found in him a friend, supporter, and honest critic. As minister of Posts and Communications, Kidwai introduced some innovations and later won applause as Minister of Food and Agriculture for his efforts to raise agricultural production and ensure equitable distribution of food-grains.

KIPLING, RUDYARD (1865–1936). Kipling was born in **Bombay**, where he spent a happy childhood before being sent back to England for education, as was the British colonial custom of the time. He returned to India and worked as a prolific journalist for seven years in Lahore and **Allahabad**. Subsequently, he traveled and devoted himself to writing. He was awarded the Nobel Prize for Literature in 1907.

Kipling's books, including *Departmental Ditties* (1888), *Plain Tales from the Hills* (1889), *The Jungle Book* (1894–1895), and *Kim* (1901), convey the landscape and folklore of British India at the end of the 19th century probably better than any other **Anglo-Indian** literature. Later, Kipling's name became controversial among Indian nationalist circles because he wrote as "the bard of Empire" and his characters frequently express racist sentiments, albeit appropriate to them at the time. Dispassionate readers see that the works mentioned above, as well as others written later in the United States or at "Batemans," his home in Sussex, England, are infused with Kipling's love for India, the land of his childhood, and something of its philosophy as well.

KIRLOSKAR, LAXMAN KASHINATH (1869–1956). Kirloskar was one of five children born in a poor Maharasthrian **brahman** family. He showed a marked mechanical and artistic bent of mind early in life and persuaded his father and elder brother to send him to **Bombay** at age 16. He took up mechanical drawing and joined the Victoria Jubilee Technical Institute where he worked as an assistant teacher and learned how to repair and install machines. He was ambitious to start his own business and in partnership with his brother started a small bicycle shop in the small town of Belgaum at the turn of the century, later expanding it to produce iron plows and other agricultural implements.

Kirloskar admired **Mahatma Gandhi** but did not share his disdain for modern technology. On the contrary, Kirloskar believed that industrialization would further the goals of Indian nationalism and was compatible with the simple, austere life he himself led.

Early tribulations were eased when the progressive young ruler of Aundh, in southern **Maharashtra**, gave the Kirloskar brothers land for a factory in 1910. It became a thriving industrial township in which illiterate peasants were trained to manufacture goods of precision and high quality, and where social reforms, such as abolition of untouchability, were put into practice. **World War I** ushered in a production boom in the 1920s that nearly collapsed during the Great Depression of the 1930s. Meanwhile, Laxmanrao's son Shantanu and his cousin studied mechanical and electrical engineering at the Massachusetts Institute of Technology (MIT) and Boston University respectively, and another son went to Cornell University to study agriculture and animal husbandry. These men of the younger generation benefited from their exposure to American technology and business practices and returned to India in the 1930s to open a machine tools factory in **Mysore**. The demand for indigenously produced products during **World War II** greatly expanded their works into the manufacture of trucks, diesel engines, alternators, pumps, and other electrical equipment.

Kirloskar companies became one of the largest and most diversified industrial empires in India and in the 1970s went international by establishing joint ventures in Malaysia and Kenya. They also collaborated with firms in Britain, Germany, and the United States. The Kirloskar corporate culture remained rooted in the needs of India's huge agricultural sector, and their after-sales services had much to do with their success.

KISAN SABHA, ALL INDIA. This body was formed in 1936 under the aegis of the **Indian National Congress**. It was an amalgam of existing kisan or peasant associations, including that of the Andhra region led by N. G. Ranga, a South Indian Federation of Peasants and Labour led by **E. M. S. Namboodiripad**, and was initially chaired by Sahajanand Saraswati of **Bihar**. The Congress Socialist Party and other radicals such as **Jawaharlal Nehru** supported the idea of a Kisan Sabha movement but did not succeed in persuading the established organization of Congress leadership to back their program in more than name.

The Kisan Sabha focused on the grievances of peasant cultivators owning some land vis a vis zamindars (see Glossary), moneylenders, traders, and the government. Though it did suggest transferring uncultivated land to the landless, establishing **cooperatives**, and abolishing zamindari, the Kisan Sabha did not explore problems of class differences among peasants or take up the cause of landless labor. Its early activities were mainly in support of local struggles against zamindars and government, especially in **Bengal**, Bihar, and **Uttar Pradesh** where some political leaders emerged from the Kisan Sabhas. Equally important, spontaneous peasant outbreaks in the more feudal and oppressive **Princely States** drew the support of the Kisan Sabha and the newly formed **States Peoples Conference**. Congress at this time began to take a more systematic interest in a possible future federation of Princely and British India having a democratic thrust.

KITCHENER, GENERAL LORD HORATIO HUBERT (1850–1916). Kitchener was commander-in-chief of the Indian army from 1902 to 1907. He had already established his reputation as a fine soldier in Egypt, the Sudan campaigns of 1896–1899, and the Boer War in South Africa 1900–1902. He was appointed C-in-C, India in order to effect needed administrative reforms in the Indian army. He reorganized the distribution of troops, raised more Indian troops, and ensured that certain divisions were always ready to move into action. He regarded India's northwest frontier as vulnerable to raids from Afghanistan and possibly Russia. Kitchener and Governor General **Lord Curzon** shared apprehensions of Russia's intentions and expansion in Central Asia and shaped the foreign and defense policies of British India accordingly.

Kitchener clashed with Curzon on an issue that two less masterful men might have easily resolved, that is, whether the traditional practice of seating an army officer (invariably junior to the C-in-C) as Military Member on the Governor General's Executive Council should be continued or whether the C-in-C should be the sole channel of communication between the army and the civilian authority. Kitchener attacked the idea of divided control, and Curzon did not want his own absolute authority diluted. The controversy, symbolized by their equally palatial residences at opposite ends of **Simla**, became serious in 1904. Both men had friends, supporters, and detractors in Whitehall, and British Prime Minister Balfour offered a solution that was not acceptable to Curzon. He resigned in 1905. Kitchener returned to England in 1907, was put in charge of the War Office on the outbreak of **World War I** in 1914, and killed soon after.

KOH-I-NUR. Perhaps the most brilliant diamond known in the world, the Koh-i-Nur or "Mountain of Light" had a colorful history embedded in legend and superstition before it was moved to London. The diamond was originally acquired by the **Mughal Emperor Shah Jahan** from the Golconda mines in the **Deccan** and formed a prominent part of his treasure. When the Persian adventurer, **Nadir Shah**, plundered **Delhi** in 1739, he took the Koh-i-Nur for himself along with the equally famous Peacock Throne and other valuables from the Mughal court. Nadir Shah was assassinated in 1747, and the new ruler of his domain, **Ahmad Shah Abdali**, obtained the Koh-i-Nur. Abdali's grandson Shah Shuja and his wife Wafa Begum had it in their possession when forced out of Kabul much later; they gave it to the **Sikh** ruler **Ranjit Singh** in 1813 when seeking sanctuary in his domain.

The British defeated the Sikh armies after Ranjit Singh's death, deposed his young son, and annexed the **Punjab** in 1849. They took the Koh-i-Nur from Lahore and presented it to Queen Victoria. Since that time it has been the principal jewel in the crown of the British queen.

KOLKATA is the capital city of West **Bengal**. *See* CALCUTTA.

KOSALA. This was the ancient name of a region in the central-eastern **Ganges** valley that played a crucial role in the development of early Indian culture and political practice. The **Puranas** describe Kosala as a kingdom ruled by the Ikshvaku or solar dynasty to which kings Dasaratha and Rama of the epic *Ramayana* belonged; their capital was **Ayodhya**. It was in this kingdom and region that concepts of hereditary and divine kingship, sanctified by sacrifices performed by **brahmans**, evolved over time. By the sixth century BCE, Kosala was an established kingdom that included within its purview certain tribal republican territories. One such was Kapilavastu, where the **Buddha** was born.

Kosala is listed in **Buddhist** and **Jain** chronicles as one of 16 large states in northern India. Kosala, along with Kashi, **Magadha**, and the Vriji confederacy, competed for control of the lucrative trade passing through the Ganges valley. These states interacted with each other in a mixed relationship of conflict, rivalry, and matrimonial alliance. For example, during the lifetime of the Buddha, the sister of Kosala's King Prasenjit married King **Bimbisara** of Magadha. Their son Ajatsatru combined the two kingdoms in the first stage of Magadha's imperial expansion that molded history for several centuries. Although no longer a separate political entity of importance, Kosala remained at the heart of northern India's evolving culture in succeeding eras.

KOSAMBI, DAMODAR DHARYANAND (1907–1966). Kosambi was born into a family with a long tradition of learning. His father was a scholar of **Buddhist** scriptures who taught at Harvard University and encouraged Damodar in eclectic studies of classical and modern languages, law, mathematics, and science. Kosambi did not study Indology in a classroom at Harvard or elsewhere but gained command over **Sanskrit** and translated or edited several texts. He was an admirer of **M. K. Gandhi** and came into contact with people involved in the Indian National Movement when he taught mathematics at Banaras Hindu University (1929–1931), Aligarh Muslim University (1931–1932), and at Fergusson College (1933–1947) and started exploring ancient sites and monuments before undertaking extensive archaeological fieldwork in the **Deccan**. He was a prolific writer on a variety of topics and published several books and numerous articles, sometimes in obscure journals. Many have been collected and introduced by Brajadulal Chattopadhyaya in a book published by Oxford University Press in 2002.

Kosambi—the scientist and linguist attracted by Marxist analysis but never by economic determinism—became a historian because he asked profound questions about the India in which he lived, molded by its past, and was not satisfied by the answers offered in conventional accounts written by European and European-trained historians. He delved for answers with more meaning in contemporary reality, and thereby made a lasting impact on the writing of Indian history. He decisively shifted its methodology, paradigms, periodization, source materials, and subject matter away from what was officially fashionable to more scientific lines. Very briefly, Kosambi's combined methodology rested on supplementing the study of texts and inscriptions with the intelligent use of archaeology, anthropology, sociology, and a great deal of honest and competent fieldwork, set within a suitable historical perspective, and questions about how and why people lived as they did. He dismissed dynastic tables and epigraphs of conquests as being of less interest than modes of production, forms of social organization, and unifying ideology in a land of as much diversity as India. He discarded the over-precise and misleading periodization of Indian history under the heads of "ancient" (Hindu), "medieval" (Muslim) and "modern" (British) in favor of a chronological order without sharp barriers of successive changes in the means and relations of production. He identified major transitions as being: the urban culture of the **Indus Valley Civilization**, the **Aryan** society based on using horse, iron, plough and social hierarchy to create village and state, the clearing and settling of forested plains of the **Ganges** and other rivers and enabling empires, systems of land-grants that developed over many centuries into different forms of feudalism in different parts of the country, and most recently, modern capitalism. Above all, Kosambi redefined and expanded the scope of historical inquiry from the military and political exploits of rulers and elites to the entirety of culture and society. His social concerns were as diverse as his intellectual engagements, though all were focused on the reality of life as it was lived by Indians and how that might be improved.

KRIPALANI, J. B. (1888–1982). Kripalani was a distinguished parliamentarian of independent India and the author of several books on the philosophy of **Mahatma Gandhi**. He was the sixth child born to an upper class Vaishnava family, and most of his siblings, like himself, were high-strung individualists with bright eyes, sharp tongues, and an aversion to established authorities.

J. B. Kripalani was educated in **Bombay** and **Poona** and became a teacher of English and history. From 1920 to 1927, he was Principal of a school founded by Gandhi, after which he was addressed as "Acharya." He married Sucheta Mazumdar in 1926, and their unusually close personal partnership lasted for more than four decades, even though each belonged to an opposing political party after 1951.

J.B. was a General Secretary of the **Indian National Congress** from 1935 to 1945 and briefly President before resigning in 1947 after a disagreement with **Jawaharlal Nehru** on the respective roles of the organizational and parliamentary wings of the party. Kirpalani was a founder member of the **Praja Socialist Party** but resigned from it in 1954. As an Independent repeatedly elected to the **Lok Sabha**, he remained a stringent critic of the government to the time of his retirement from politics in 1971.

KRISHNAMURTI, JIDU (1895–1986). Born in a small town west of **Madras** to a poor **brahman** family, Krishnamurti's father was a minor government official; his mother died when he was 10. The boy Jidu was seen by Charles Webster Leadbeater of the **Theosophical Society** as the "vehicle" for the world teacher, or Lord Maitreya, whose arrival was then awaited by the Theosophists; **Annie Besant** endorsed Leadbeater's choice and more or less adopted Jidu and his younger brother. An Order of the Star of the East was created in 1911, and Jidu Krishnamurti was named as its head. He and his brother were educated in England from 1912 to 1921. Thereafter, they traveled first to Australia and then to California where they were given an estate in the Ojai valley. The younger brother died there of consumption.

After several years of lecturing and teaching, Jidu Krishnamurti was presented by Annie Besant to the international press as the "World Teacher" in April 1927. Two years later he dissolved the Order of the Star, telling its 43,000 registered members "I do not want you to follow me." Having broken with the Theosophists, he developed his own unique philosophy, drawing on his intense spiritual experience of August 1922 and starting from what he termed "the vacant mind." He claimed no authority, no religion, no ideology, and no program of social reform and postulated nothing less than a total transformation of the individual self as a cure for conflict and suffering in the world.

Many famous people, including **Indira Gandhi**, sought advice and solace from Jidu Krishnamurti. His public lectures drew many to his teachings, though he did not accept followers and enjoined his audiences to think for themselves, to feel passionately, to shed the burdens of past or future, and to free their minds of fear.

Beginning with the Rishi Valley School founded in the hills of southern India in 1928, several coeducational residential schools have been established across India on the basis of Krishnamurti's exhortations on individuality, creativity, and free thinking.

KSHATRIYA. This term means warrior, ruler, or aristocrat; one belonging to a high, "twice born," *varna*, or social order, among the Indo–Aryans. The mythical origin of the kshatriya, according to a hymn in the Rig **Veda**, was from the arms of the first sacrificial Man. The duty of the kshatriya was to protect all beings and the social order in his realm.

In early Indian writings and practice, kshatriyas and **brahmans** were partners: brahmans alone could perform sacrifice and legitimize power, but they needed protection; kshatriyas had wealth and power but needed priests-cum-intellectuals to govern well. Both *varnas* had high status with brahmanical writings ranking brahmans first, while **Jain** and **Buddhist** writings ranked kshatriyas first. **Mahavira** and the **Buddha** were both born kshatriya.

Not all **Hindu** rulers were kshatriya. Many dynasties were from the lowest *varna* of **sudra**, or were from foreign stock. But if they were sufficiently powerful, they could be, and usually were, given kshatriya status by the brahmans and accepted as such by society. The **Rajputs**, for example, were of uncertain origin and yet were most insistent on their royal lineage and kshatriya status. This mutual adjustment between temporal and spiritual power was one of the mechanisms by which Hindu society was able to successfully accommodate rising indigenous and foreign communities. Several upwardly mobile mercantile and agricultural jati, or **castes**, for example, claimed kshatriya status from time to time, with varying success. Few kshatriya castes are found in south India.

KUKA RAM SINGH (1826–1885). The son of a carpenter, Kuka founded the Sant Khalsa based on the austere discipline of **Guru Gobind Singh**. Ram Singh had served in **Ranjit Singh**'s army and reacted against the idol worship, **caste** distinctions, and female infanticide that he saw creeping into the **Sikh** community after incorporation of the **Punjab** into British India in 1849. Ram Singh's fundamentalist sect came to be known as the Namdhari or Kuka movement, with its members noted for their uniform white clothes and straight turbans. They raided butcher shops, slaughterhouses, and liquor stores in their efforts to cleanse the faith. The British authorities became alarmed and placed Ram Singh under surveillance. The Kukas were subsequently outlawed as anti-British rebels, and in 1872 several were arrested and executed at Malerkotla. The sect also encountered severe difficulties in the 1980s when other militant fundamentalists attempted to homogenize the Sikh community.

KUMAR, DILIP (1922–). Kumar was born in Peshawar as one of 12 children in a Muslim Pathan family that moved after **Partition** to **Mumbai**, where they sold fruit and worked in army canteens. The young boy attracted the attention of a director in the **film industry** who renamed him and introduced him to the screen. He attained stardom in *Jugnu*, often played opposite **Nargis**, and was a megastar of the 1950s and 1960s. In such movies as *Deedar* and *Devdas*, Dilip Kumar explored the complex psychological terrain of conflicting social pressures. After many years of public neglect, he was awarded prestigious honors in 2003.

KUMBHA MELA. According to the Guinness Book of World Records, the largest gathering of people in the world engaged in a single pursuit takes place at the Kumbha Mela held every 12 years at **Allahabad/Prayag**, where the rivers **Ganges**, **Yamuna**, and concealed Saraswati conjoin. The estimated number who performed this exceptionally auspicious pilgrimage for **Hindus** in early 2001 was more than 15 million.

The literal meaning of kumbha is pot or container, mythologically associated with mother goddesses. A possible origin of the Kumbha Mela is prehistoric fertility rites in which pots of grain were immersed in rivers. Another possible origin is the myth of the churning of the universal ocean by gods and demons to extract the nectar of immortality; a pot of nectar was stolen by the demons and, in their flight, they spilled some of its contents in rivers at Prayag, **Hardwar**, **Ujjain**, and Nasik on the Godaveri River. Pilgrimages to all these sites are called Kumbha Mela and considered auspicious.

Seventh century CE accounts of the Emperor **Harsha-Vardhana** describe him distributing alms to ascetics of all faiths gathered for the Kumbha Mela. Later, **Shankara** systematized the rites, and pilgrimages on a large scale became the norm. As theologians, philosophers, sages, ascetics, and adherents of various faiths and sects gathered at the Kumbha Mela, animated and rigorous debates took place spontaneously or were organized. Records from the 13th century to the present day show the occasion, lasting approximately a month, to be a veritable parliament of **Hinduism**.

KUNZRU, HRIDAY NATH (1887–1978). Born to an upper class Kashmiri **brahman** family settled in the United Provinces, now **Uttar Pradesh**, Kunzru was educated in **Agra** and at the London School of Economics. He was a member of the UP Legislative Council from 1921 to 1923 and the Indian Legislative Assembly from 1927 to 1930. In both legislative bodies he showed an active interest in the Indianization of civil and military services and the treatment of Indians settled in other parts of the British Empire. Kunzru joined the

Servants of India Society as a young man while its founder, **Gopal Krishna Gokhale** was alive, and was elected its life President in 1936. Kunzru was a member of the Council of States from 1937 to 1946 and also of the **Constituent Assembly** from 1946 to 1949.

As a well-traveled and cosmopolitan lawyer and educationist, Kunzru fostered the study of international affairs in independent India. He was the founder/chairman of the Indian Council of World Affairs. As a member of the **States Reorganization Commission** that redrew the state boundaries of India on the basis of **language**, Kunzru stressed the importance of safeguarding the rights of linguistic minorities. He also wrote a penetrating study of public services in India.

KURIEN, VERGHESE (1921–). Sometimes called India's *doodhwallah* or milkman, he spearheaded what came to be called the "white revolution." In 1949, Kurien, with an excellent education in science and engineering acquired in **Madras** University, at the **Tata** Steel Technical Institute, and Michigan State University in the United States, was posted as an engineer to a government dairy at Anand, southern **Gujarat**. He chose instead to help an infant **cooperative** dairy run by a milk producers union and sparked a grassroots transformation in the production, collection, and distribution of milk that also had profound socioeconomic effects. This "white revolution" was based on regular collection of milk from individual rural families with some cattle (not necessarily many) in refrigerated trucks, its pasteurization and further processing at a the dairy, now long famous as AMUL, and the marketing of these dairy products through a growing network of cooperative owned groceries.

Because **women** traditionally take care of animals and milk cattle in rural India, and because the Amul truck drivers operated strictly on a 'first come first served' basis in milk collection and immediate payment for it, girls and women without wealth or feminist rhetoric began to feel empowered all along the milk routes. And because Amul's success led to Dr. V. Kurien becoming the founder chairman of the National Dairy Development Board, India's enormous modern dairy industry was forged in Operation Flood, launched in the 1970s on the earlier pattern of cooperatives. Similar procedures for edible oils were used in Operation Golden Flow of the 1980s.

Kurien has a talent for building and managing institutions, and he prefers those that benefit people at the lower end of the socioeconomic scale. Among the most famous of the institutions he chairs is the Institute of Rural Management (IRMA) founded in 1979 at Anand. It trains hundreds of men and women, many with urban or privileged backgrounds, to work usefully in village India, often in **non-governmental organizations (NGOs)** and with a dedication and absence of arrogance exemplified in the personality of Kurien himself.

Kurien's outstanding work has been recognized inside and outside India, and he has received numerous national and international honors and awards, including the Magsaysay Award (1963), the World Food Prize (1989), the French *Ordre du Merite Agricole* (1997), and the Padma Vibhushan (1999).

KUSHAN DYNASTY. This dynasty reached its height in fame and fortune during the rule of **Kanishka**, probably in the first century CE. The Kushans belonged to a branch of the central Asian nomadic Yuezhi (Yueh-chi) tribe that displaced the **Sakas** in the Oxus valley, Bactria, and Sogdiana by the second century BCE.

Under the leadership of Kadphises I, the Kushans created a large trans-Oxus state that extended south of the Hindu Kush mountains into **Gandhara** and the **Indus** region where the Saka King Gondophernes was ruling. Kadphises II extended his rule east to the **Ganges** valley and south to the **Narmada** river but was defeated north of the Pamir mountains by a Chinese force. Although Kanishka does not appear to have been related to Kadphises II and may not have succeeded him immediately, he followed the same traditions and further extended his domains in Central Asia as well as on the Indian subcontinent, keeping his capital at Peshawer. Mathura on the **Yamuna** river functioned as a second capital, perhaps under the viceroyalty of his son Huvishka, whose inscriptions overlapped with his for 30 years. Huvishka retained possession of these extensive territories, continued a liberal religious policy, and issued a varied series of coins, some depicting the **Buddha** and different deities. He is associated with setting up a **Buddhist** monastery in **Kashmir** in addition to those that flourished at **Taxila**.

The Kushan Dynasty presided over a significant phase in India's cultural history. Kushan coins in gold, silver, and copper are known for their standardized weights and exquisite designs. Sculpture of the Gandhara school was most prolific, but other notable art centers were Mathura, Sarnath near **Banaras**, and Amaravati in **Andhra**. The economic base of the state was strong, and trade along the **Silk Road** connecting China, India, Persia, and Rome furthered prosperity and intellectual stimulation. Kushan notions of kingship showed an amalgam of influences as did its art. It was in the Kushan period, too, that **Buddhism** developed the Mahayana or Greater Vehicle doctrines, which spread to Iran, central Asia, and China. Yet, from the name Vasudeva attributed to a Kushan ruler, the dynasty is assumed to have been Hindu, with both **Vishnu** and **Shiva** worshipped within its territory.

The exact details of Kushan decline are not known, but it appears to have been a gradual process, taking place in the third and fourth centuries CE. It is likely that the western provinces were absorbed by the rising Sassanian power in Persia, the southern and eastern provinces were taken over by the expanding **Gupta** Empire and the dynasty continuing in Kabul was swept away in the **Huna** invasions a century or more later.

– L –

LACCADIVE ISLANDS. *See* LAKSHADWEEP.

LADAKH. Known also as "Little Tibet," Ladakh or Land of the High Passes, is the northeastern district of the state of **Jammu and Kashmir**. Ladakh is one of the highest inhabited plateaus in the world, with an area of about 50,000 square kilometers; its principal town, Leh, is over 3,350 meters above sea level. Ladakh's high, dry, mountainous landscape is dominated by the Karakorum and western **Himalaya** ranges and is traversed by the upper reaches of the river **Indus**. Important sections of the ancient **Silk Road** lie in Ladakh and were in use through the first half of the 20th century for trade between India and central Asia. Ladakh today attracts many adventure tourists and trekkers.

The people of Ladakh, for the most part, are similar in religion and ethnic origin to the people of western **Tibet**. Great monasteries of Vajrayana **Buddhism** and the palaces of former semi-independent rulers remain in use today or are being restored. Ladakh was conquered by Zorawer Singh in 1820 and, along with Jammu and Kashmir, was annexed to the empire of Maharajah **Ranjit Singh** and turned over to a Dogra ruler by the British in 1846 after the second **Sikh** war. Skardu, formerly part of Ladakh, fell under **Pakistan** occupation in 1947 and was subsequently annexed. The uninhabited extreme northeast section of Ladakh, the **Aksai Chin**, passed under de-facto Chinese control around 1956. Ladakh is strategically vital for India, and formations of the Indian army and air force are regularly stationed there. Ladakh's salience was increased by armed conflict near the **Siachin Glacier** in the 1980s and by the Kargil conflict in the summer of 1999.

Tensions within Kashmir and attempts by militants to impose their version of **Islam** in the whole state had inevitable effects on Ladakh. The mainly Buddhist, non-Urdu speaking people of Ladakh demanded autonomy from **Srinagar**, and obtained their own Autonomous Council in 1993. Significant numbers of **Hindu** and Muslim refugees from violence-ridden areas in other parts of Jammu and Kashmir have settled in Ladakh, with incalculable results. Development projects undertaken by the army as well as by **non-governmental organizations (NGOs)** have increased food supply and income, but these projects have also affected the ecology and, perhaps, climate, of Ladakh. Adventure tourism remains an important source of revenue.

LAKSHADWEEP. A small, lightly populated, Union Territory, Lakshadweep consists of 36 coral islands, many of which are uninhabited, set in the Indian Ocean southwest of **Kerala**. Their early history is still unknown, but they lie along the trading routes across the Arabian Sea and were certainly used as outposts by Arab traders after the eighth century CE and probably by other traders before that. Archaeological discoveries of sixth- or seventh-century **Buddhist** settlements support that supposition. Conversions to **Islam** are usually dated to the 14th century.

The islands sought and gained the protection of the Raja of Cannanore, in present-day Kerala, against possible **Portuguese** attacks in the 16th century. **Tipu Sultan** annexed the islands when he overran coastal kingdoms at the end of the 18th century. After his defeat by British forces, the Laccadive Islands became part of British India. They were governed directly from New Delhi after independence as a Union Territory and were not affected by the reorganization of states on the basis of **language** in 1958. They were renamed in 1973.

Coconut is the main crop, and making its by-products the main occupation besides fishing. Tourism generates income; the beautiful atolls, beaches, and reefs of Lakshadweep draw many vacationers from the mainland of India as well as abroad.

LAKSHMI BAI, RANI OF JHANSI (c. 1835–1858). Lakshmi Bai features as a heroine in the popular, patriotic history of contemporary India. She was orphaned as a child in **Maharashtra** and was brought up in the household of the **Peshwa**, Baji Rao II. She was married as a child to the seemingly eligible ruler of Jhansi and continued to study and play at the martial arts with male relatives of about her own age. Lakshmi Bai was widowed without child in 1853. She was named Regent of Jhansi, ruling in behalf of her husband's adopted son, aged five years. Governor General **Lord Dalhousie**, however, annexed Jhansi. He invoked a hitherto little used "doctrine of lapse" by which the British assumed the right to take over a **Princely State** in alliance with the **East India Company** if its line of succession were not clear.

Rani Lakshmi Bai appealed the decision, but to no avail. She, like **Nana Saheb**, her old companion in the Peshwa's household, and other Indian rulers similarly affected by Dalhousie's policies of territorial expansion, joined the great **Uprising**, which followed the **Mutiny** of Indian sepoys or soldiers against the British in May 1857. The Rani of Jhansi was the most colorful character of the 1857–1858 conflict. She mobilized her state and her forces for resistance and rode to Gwalior to establish the Peshwa's authority there. Innumerable ballads, paintings, and films have immortalized her spirited fight on horseback against attacking British forces, led by Sir Hugh Rose, and her death in battle on June 16, 1858.

LANGUAGE. (See Map 2.) The multiplicity of languages and scripts in use across the vast subcontinent of India is expressive of the huge diversity among peoples who inhabit it, as well as of their intimate contact with other peoples over the millennia. Estimates of the number of languages, "mother tongues," and dialects vary from over 1,000 to less than 100. An authoritative British survey of 1923 identified 179 languages and 544 dialects; the 1981 **Census** of India reported 112 "mother tongues," and subsequent censuses did not tabulate language separately; the **Anthropological Survey of India** identified 75 'major languages' within a total of 325 languages in use during the early 1990s.

The **Constitution** of India in its Eighth Schedule (amended in 1992) lists 18 "official" languages for educational and public use. These are: Assamese, Bengali, Gujarati, Hindi, Kannada, Kashmiri, Konkani, Malayalam, Manipuri, Marathi, Nepali, Oriya, Punjabi, Sanskrit, Sindhi, Tamil, Telugu, and Urdu. They fall into four broad linguistic families or groups, of which the Indo-Aryan or Indo-European group is the largest, comprising the classical languages of former elites—**Sanskrit** and Persian—and their modern derivatives used by approximately 80% of the population. The next largest family is **Dravidian**, of which **Tamil** is the oldest. Dravidian languages are used by approximately18% of the population, mostly in southern India with small pockets elsewhere. Tibeto-Burman languages are in use throughout the **Himalaya**, where population density is less than in the plains. About 1% or less of the population, mainly **Munda** or other tribal people living in central and eastern India, speak languages belonging to the Austro-Asiatic group. Languages within the same linguistic family often are mutually understood in their spoken and written forms, even as each spawns a variety of dialects, and the number of Indians familiar with more than one language keeps increasing as education expands and mobility increases. English, although not indigenous to India, is well established and is recognized as 'an official' language by law. It is widely preferred as the language of upward social mobility at home and abroad. Indian writers in English have gained international renown.

Language is a badge of individual and social identity as well as the chief instrument of cultural transmission. Language has been the subject of political conflict in 20th-century India on more than one occasion. Communal polarization between Hindu and Muslim intelligentsia in late 19th- and early-20th-century United Provinces was expressed in a fierce rivalry between Hindi and Urdu; in fact, these were one language of multiple roots written in two different scripts derived from Sanskrit and Persian, respectively. That conflict eventually submerged Hindustani, the *lingua franca* of the common people in northern India and **M. K. Gandhi**'s preference for a national language; refined Urdu became the national language of **Pakistan**, and Hindi chauvinists in India attempted to purge the language of non-Sanskritic influences. The **Constituent Assembly** debated the question of a "national language," or a "link" language, at length and with acrimony. Advocates of Hindi as a national language to replace English projected the need for a common language used by more than 40% of the population to promote the independence and unity of India. They clashed with those who stressed the practicality of retaining English in public life as well as with those who asserted the rival claims of other rich Indian languages such as Bengali and Tamil over Hindi. More than symbols were at stake in a polyglot country, including relative advantage or disadvantage of linguistic groups in education and future employment, and the treatment of linguistic minorities. A compromise was reached: Article 343 of the Constitution stipulated that the 'official' language of the Indian Union would be Hindi in the Devanagari script with international numerals, but English would be retained for 15 years or until Parliament legislated otherwise (as it did in 1965). At the same time, major regional languages too were listed as "official"in the Eighth Schedule, and state governments were permitted to choose the language in which to conduct their own affairs.

The **Indian National Congress** before independence had put forward the idea of linguistic provinces as natural cultural units. Soon after independence, language became the basis for demands to redemarcate state boundaries; in 1953 a **States Reorganization Commission** was appointed to explore the feasibility of doing so. The process of creating new states and adjusting administrative boundaries to conform to the mother tongues of most inhabitants was accompanied by some agitations and violence but was more or less completed by the mid-1960s. New Delhi's effort to make Hindi the official and link language in 1965 led to violent protest in southern India and secessionist threats in **Tamil Nadu**. Conflict was averted through adoption of a "three-language formula," whereby all schools in the country would compulsorily teach in the regional language and in Hindi and English.

Many, including **Jawaharlal Nehru**, feared that linguistic chauvinism would reinforce regionalism and centrifugal tendencies to pull India apart, and New Delhi financed several governmental schemes to spread Hindi and enhance national unity. Such fears seem exaggerated at the dawn of the 21st century. Instead, it appears that the economic and political integration of India is taking place alongside—and not instead of—strong regionalism. Further, public and privately financed enterprises—such as *Katha*—to reward literary works of merit and translate them into other Indian languages as well as English enable more people to appreciate and celebrate India's rich cultural and linguistic diversity.

LATA MANGESHKAR (1929–). Known as the "nightingale of India," Lata Mangeshkar was the most popular playback singer in the Hindi **film industry** for several decades after her initial successes with *Andaaz* in 1947 and *Mahal* in 1949. Lata was born in Indore, one of five children of a traveling classical singer and had no formal education. She started acting in Marathi films at the age of 12 and attracted the attention of a leading music director in **Bombay**, who recognized the range (over three octaves) and sweetness of her voice. The Royal Albert Hall in London recorded a computer graph of her voice as "most perfect," and in 1974 the *Guinness Book of World Records* listed her for having recorded the maximum number of songs in the world. The number exceeded 30,000 by 2001 when she was awarded the Bharat Ratna, India's highest civilian award. Lata Mangeshkar draws huge crowds wherever she goes, but she retains the modest demeanor and humble faith that have characterized her since childhood. She has endowed a medical research center and hospital in **Pune**.

LAWRENCE, HENRY MONTGOMERY (1806–1857). Henry Lawrence was an energetic, hardworking, generous, and unconventional Englishman whose tempestuous temperament, multifaceted life, and heroic death have stimulated a number of serious and fictional biographies. Lawrence was born in **Ceylon**, educated in England, and served in the first Anglo–Burmese War with the Bengal Artillery, which he had joined in 1823. He later returned to civilian life and began to serve in a semi-diplomatic capacity in the **Punjab**

in 1840. He came to love and admire the people and did not approve of **Lord Dalhousie**'s assertive policies that led to the Anglo–Sikh Wars of 1846 and 1849 and the annexation of the Punjab. Nevertheless, he, along with his brother **John Lawrence** and Charles Mansel, administered the Punjab to 1853 in a manner that did much to reconcile the **Sikhs** to British rule.

Henry Lawrence was appointed Agent in **Awadh** in 1857 and was invested with military command on the outbreak of the great **Uprising** in May of that year. His Residency at Lucknow was besieged on June 30. He died of bullet wounds four days later received in defense of the people gathered under his protection. His epitaph reads, "Here lies Henry Lawrence who tried to do his duty." He continues to be remembered in India, especially at the Lawrence School of Sanawar. Originally established with his financial assistance for the children of British soldiers serving in India, it is one of the best coeducational boarding schools in the country. **Rudyard Kipling** sent his famous fictional character, Kim, to the Lawrence School.

LAWRENCE, SIR JOHN (1811–1879). John Lawrence joined the covenanted service of the **East India Company** in 1830. After the second Anglo–Sikh war and the annexation of the **Punjab** in 1849, he was appointed to administer the Punjab, first as one of a three-member board and then as chief commissioner in sole command. John Lawrence administered the Punjab with a vigorous paternalism. He became known for his hard work, quick decisions, physical courage, ruthlessness in action, direct personal dealings with peasants, suspicion of intermediaries or local notables, attentiveness to the construction of public works rather than the repair of complex human relations, and confidence in the British mission to rule.

John Lawrence snuffed out revolt among his sepoys (soldiers) during the **1857 Uprising** and sent troops reinforced with new **Sikh** recruits to the relief of the British garrison at **Delhi**. Lawrence personally supervised that metropolis when the Uprising was crushed. Lawrence was governor general from 1864 to 1869 and tried to apply the principles he had used in the Punjab to all of British India. Roads were built, extended, or repaired, the most famous of these being the Grand Trunk Road from **Calcutta** to Peshawer. Great works of canal irrigation were commenced. Railways were developed. Public loans were raised for these purposes. He adopted a policy of "masterly inactivity" rather than war toward Afghanistan and the tribal areas of the northwest. He sought to enhance revenue through efficient collection of land revenue and minimal expenditures on famine relief or welfare but left the exchequer in deficit.

LIAQAT ALI KHAN (1895–1951). Born into an aristocratic landowning, Muslim family, Liaqat Ali was educated at the Muslim Anglo–Oriental College at Aligarh and at Oxford, and qualified for the bar from London. Returning to India to make a political career, he joined the **All-India Muslim League** and was its general secretary in 1936 before becoming deputy leader in 1940. He was the close lieutenant of **Mohammad Ali Jinnah**. Liaqat became a member of the United Provinces—now **Uttar Pradesh**—Legislative Council in 1926 and a member of the Central Legislative Assembly in 1940. He gained the reputation of being a good lawyer with a quiet manner and a cool temperament.

Liaquat Ali was one of the Indian political leaders with whom **Sir Stafford Cripps** held talks in 1942 and with whom **Bhulabhai Desai** of the **Indian National Congress** subsequently discussed possible arrangements that would satisfy the League's demand for a Muslim homeland in a united and independent India. The latter talks did not bear fruit. Liaqat was the League's nominee to the Viceroy's Executive Council in 1946 and served as finance member. After **Partition** he migrated to **Pakistan** where he became prime minister after Jinnah's death in 1948.

Liaqat Ali Khan came to be known in Pakistan as *Quaid-e-Millat* or "leader of the nation." He signed a multifaceted agreement with Indian Prime Minister **Jawaharlal Nehru** in 1950, providing for humanitarian resolution of several problems arising from Partition. Liaquat was assassinated by a Muslim fanatic at Rawalpindi on October 16, 1951.

LICHCHAVI. This is the name of a tribe or a clan of north **Bihar** that played a prominent part in ancient Indian history for over a thousand years. An assembly of notables with an elected chief governed the

Lichchavis. Their republican form contrasted with that of hereditary and sanctified kingship adopted by many neighboring peoples in the **Ganges** valley by the sixth century BCE.

The Lichchavis included, or had as feudatories, the Sakya clan to which the **Buddha** belonged. In the early **Buddhist** period the Lichchavis were in matrimonial alliance with the King of **Magadha**. Several centuries later, another matrimonial alliance between the Lichchavis and the rulers of Magadha formed the nucleus for the extensive **Gupta Empire**. The Lichchavis also supplied a line of rulers in **Nepal** up to the seventh century CE and are believed to have had many ties of kinship with **Tibet**.

The Lichchavi capital was at Vaishali, well known to archaeologists as an example of early urbanization. It lies due north of the Ganges in a direct line from **Pataliputra**, some 50 kilometers distant.

LINGAYAT. This is the name of sect that emerged in **Karnataka** during the 12th century under the leadership of Basavaraja and the patronage of the reigning **Chalukya** king. The Lingayats were so named for their devotional worship of **Shiva** in the lingam, or phallic form. **Buddhist**, **Islamic**, and **Jain** tenets probably influenced the Lingayat sect, which also had characteristics of a reform movement in the **Bhakti** tradition. One effect of the spread of the Lingayat faith was the ousting of Jainism from Karnataka.

The Lingayats went beyond attacking religious hypocrisy and supremacy of **brahmans**. They questioned the authority of the **Vedas** and the doctrine of rebirth. They encouraged late post-puberty marriage and remarriage of widows. Their liberal social attitudes pitted them against the brahmans and brought them adherents from lower **caste** groups. Both features remained visible in the 20th century.

LINLITHGOW, MARQUESS OF (1887–1952). Linlithgow was viceroy and governor general of India from 1936 to 1943. His first important task was to implement the **Government of India Act of 1935**. A large, hardworking, firm man, he lacked the spark to inspire others, the human warmth to make friends among Indians, and the imagination to grasp the timely moment for bold decisions. Thus, his tedious efforts to bring the princes into the proposed federation failed and precluded a major portion of the constitutional reform envisaged in the 1935 Act. Linlithgow did proceed with enlarging the Indian membership of his Executive Council, held elections in 1937, and permitted elective governments responsible to the legislatures to be formed in the provinces of British India. But he showed no understanding for leaders of the largest **political party** of the day, the **Indian National Congress**, and his declaration of war against Germany on India's behalf made in September 1939, without first consulting them, was politically inept while legally correct. Congress resigned its ministries and turned away from cooperation with the war effort.

Linlithgow then turned to the **All-India Muslim League** to form provincial governments and helped to build the prestige of its leader, **Mohammed Ali Jinnah**, at the expense of other Muslim leaders. With Jinnah's advocacy of a separate state of **Pakistan** after 1940, the gulf between Congress and the League widened. Linlithgow seemed to ignore the dangerous implications of this rift and assumed that British rule in India was indispensable and permanent. His view found resonance with British Prime Minister Winston Churchill, and no constitutional progress was made in India during the course of **World War II**.

Linlithgow's achievement lay in organizing a massive Indian contribution to the Allied war effort. More than two million men were mobilized. Existing industry was expanded, and new industries were permitted to develop. The **Quit India Movement** of 1942 was ruthlessly suppressed. India was made the principal supplier of various commodities, including manufactured items and food-grains, to the Middle Eastern and Southeast Asian sectors of the war effort. One tragic consequence of these efforts was the great **Bengal** famine of 1943; Linlithgow's successor, **Lord Wavell**, had to organize relief efforts.

LODI. The **Lodi** was an Afghan tribe that provided the last three rulers of the **Delhi Sultanate**. After **Timur** had devastated **Delhi** in 1398, anarchy and ruin prevailed for some decades. Eventually Buhlul Lodi seized Delhi in 1451, was declared Sultan, and asserted his authority over neighboring areas. He also recovered Jaunpur, a wealthy district in the **Ganges** valley, which had severed allegiance. Buhlul was succeeded by his second son, Sikander, in 1489.

Contemporary Muslim historians praised Sikander for his adherence to **Islamic** law, his suppression of **Hindu** chiefs, and his annexation of more territory. Accounts of the time remark on the exceptionally low prices of food and other goods in Delhi. Modern historians gather from such accounts that city people benefited at the expense of the countryside in Lodi times. Sikander built a new town at **Agra** as his capital in order to keep closer control over the eastern provinces. He died there in 1517 and was succeeded by his eldest son, Ibrahim.

Ibrahim Lodi was not able to control the Afghan and Turki nobles at his court, and he also alienated the semi-independent governor in the **Punjab**, Daulat Khan Lodi. The latter invited **Babur**, then ruling in Kabul, to intervene in their quarrel. Babur defeated Ibrahim Lodi at **Panipat** in 1526 and stayed on to establish the **Mughal Empire** in India. The Lodis failed to combine military prowess with administrative skill and were unable to build either political unity or social solidarity in their kingdom. They are remembered today chiefly for their beautifully constructed architectural monuments.

LOHIA, RAM MANOHAR (1910–1967). Lohia was born near **Ayodhya** to a business family. He was brought up by his grandparents and was schooled close to home. He then attended Bombay University, Banaras Hindu University, and Vidyasagar College, Calcutta. He obtained his doctorate from the University of Berlin in 1932, writing his thesis on "Salt and Civil Disobedience." His father had a textile business in Bombay and was an active member of the **Indian National Congress**.

Ram Manohar joined the Congress Socialist Party in 1934, edited its weekly journal *Congress Socialist*, and became secretary of its foreign department. He voiced opposition to British exploitation of Indian manpower and resources during **World War II** and was arrested in 1939 and again in 1940. He supported the **Quit India** movement of 1942 and went underground to work with **Jaya Prakash Narayan**. Lohia was caught and imprisoned from 1944 to 1946.

Lohia had sharp differences of opinion with Prime Minister **Jawaharlal Nehru** after Indian independence on several issues, including foreign policy, reform of **Hindu** personal law, and combining political and governmental functions. Lohia and other Socialists broke with Congress in 1948 and formed the **Praja Socialist Party** in 1952. But he resigned from this party as well and became the first Chairman of the Socialist Party in 1956. He edited its journal, *Mankind*, advocating Hindi as a national **language**, attention to the rights of **Untouchables** (and other oppressed peoples), and greater protection of civil liberties in India. As an elected member of the **Lok Sabha**, Lohia was an articulate critic of the government as well as of orthodox Hindu society and customs. He was fluent in several languages and participated in various international meetings of the socialist movement. He insisted on his own personal interpretation of socialist ideas oriented toward specifically Indian conditions.

Ram Manohar Lohia did not marry. He was a prolific writer and a ceaseless worker. He evolved concepts such as "new socialism," "permanent civil disobedience," and "functional federalism" that were intensely patriotic and inspiring to younger men and women but seemed impractical within the new constitutional framework of independent India.

LOK DAL. Charan Singh formed a **political party** in 1974 under the formal name Bharatiya Lok Dal, or People's Party of India. In 1984 it merged with various disaffected splinters of other parties to become the Dalit Mazdoor Kizan Party but changed its name back to Lok Dal in 1986. It drew strong support from the middle peasantry, often **Jat**, in western **Uttar Pradesh**, parts of **Rajasthan**, and the states of **Bihar** and **Haryana**.

Headed by Devi Lal, the Lok Dal won the state elections in Haryana and formed a government there in 1986. It was also an important ingredient of **V. P. Singh**'s government in New Delhi in 1989–1990. Factional splits within the party and the rise of other political parties appealing to the same constituency have deprived it of much influence recently.

LOK SABHA. The House of the People is the lower but more powerful chamber of a bicameral Indian Parliament and is largely modeled on the British House of Commons. A government is formed from the **political party**, or coalition, that has a majority of seats in the Lok Sabha, and its leader becomes prime minister. The prime minister by convention must be an elected member of the House and is responsible to it.

A government may fall if it loses the confidence of the House and is defeated in a vote taken on an important issue. Examples of this convention working are to be seen in the resignations of the **V. P. Singh** government in November 1990, the **Deve Gowda** government in April 1997, and the **Atal Behari Vajpayee**-led government in April 1999. In each case, a caretaker government was installed, and general elections were held soon after.

The Lok Sabha consists of 544 members directly elected on the basis of adult franchise from territorial constituencies roughly equal in population and represented by a single member winning the largest number of votes. Proposals to introduce proportional representation similar to practices in continental Europe are made from time to time but have been rejected. Proposals to reserve one third of the seats for **women** have not yet fructified either, although all political parties pay lip service to the concept. One reform passed into law in 1985 made impermissible a formerly frequent occurrence of "defection"—that is, members switching from one political party to another—unless one third of the legislative party "split" from the rest. And a party must have 50 members in the Lok Sabha to qualify for the designation of official opposition party. The Lok Sabha has a term of five years, but the Indian president, acting on the advice of the prime minister, may dissolve the House before that time and call fresh elections—as was done in mid-1991 and early 2004. According to the **Indian Constitution**, the life of a given parliament can be extended for one year at a time under a proclamation of emergency. During **Emergency Rule** of 1975–1977 the Lok Sabha was more or less reduced to a rubber stamp of the executive, but it subsequently recovered its consequence.

The Lok Sabha must meet twice a year and usually holds three sessions in a calendar year, with the first session devoted to the budget. Routine business is conducted through 18 standing committees, including three finance committees drawn from both ruling and opposition parties. These standing committees do not have their own separate research or secretarial staffs, as do congressional committees in the United States, but the services of the Lok Sabha Secretariat and the excellent Parliamentary Library are available to all members. The first hour of the parliamentary day is devoted to oral or written questions addressed to the government, usually by members of opposition parties or independents, and are intended to elicit information, reveal inefficiency or scandal, or otherwise embarrass the government. Most business is conducted in Hindi or English, but members may speak in any of 22 official **languages** of India if they wish.

The Lok Sabha is presided over by a Speaker elected from among its members. Required by the Constitution to act above party affiliation, the Speaker can exert considerable influence, so that much political bargaining among political parties precedes any appointment. The Speaker is responsible for maintaining order and correct procedure in the House, a job that has become increasingly difficult since the 1980s because of declining standards of decorum and a tendency among many members to resort to physical disruption of proceedings rather than debate. The high intellectual standards of Lok Sabha debates that were established soon after independence have also fallen, even though the formal education of members is higher than before, and parliamentary proceedings are extensively reported in the daily press and so command the attention of government and the public.

The Lok Sabha developed healthy conventions during the 1950s. When the government, that is the ruling party, has not commanded an absolute majority—as it did not from 1967 to 1971 and from 1989 to 1992—parliamentary maneuvering among parties was intricate and often unseemly. Yet, the huge majority enjoyed by the **Congress (I)** in 1972 and from 1985 to 1989 also reduced the importance of the legislative body. Nevertheless, the democratic power of the Lok Sabha should not be underestimated. Elections are keenly contested, voter participation is high, and incumbents are frequently unseated at the next election. Members of Parliament today show a greater variety of family background, **caste**, and profession than in the first decade after independence. Broadly speaking, the number of urban lawyers and other professionals has dropped and the number of rural agriculturalists has risen significantly, although the number of women is only slightly higher. This shift among representatives and therefore of legislative power reflects the ever widening and deepening spiral of Indian democracy. (See Appendix H for Lok Sabha composition by political party 1952–2004.)

LUCKNOW PACT (1916). The **Indian National Congress** headed by **Bal Gangadhar Tilak** and the **All-India Muslim League** led by **Mohammed Ali Jinnah** jointly presented a draft of constitutional reform toward self-government at the Lucknow sessions of their parties in December 1916. This Congress-League Pact was an event of historic importance, but unfortunately not the first of many.

Both parties had put forward demands for self-government during their concurrent sessions at **Bombay** in 1915 and had set up committees to draft concrete proposals. Congress leaders sought unity, without which they could hardly advance their goals of getting the British to leave India as soon as possible. Tilak was sufficiently pragmatic by then to accommodate demands by the Muslim League for the sake of the larger cause. Jinnah, too, was anxious to bring the fledgling Muslim League and the more experienced Congress together. Accordingly, the League pledged full support for Congress's aims of self-government and a parliamentary system for India—which meant executive responsibility to an elected legislature—while Congress accepted the League's demand for weighted representation and separate electorates for Muslims.

The Congress-League Scheme of Reforms, as the Lucknow Pact was formally known, specified proportions of Muslim representation in several provinces as well as the center along lines subsequently institutionalized by the British under the **Montagu-Chelmsford Reforms**. The Lucknow Pact also included other nationalist demands made annually by Congress, such as shifting imperial war expenses from the Indian to the British exchequer, racial equality throughout the British Empire, and the opening of commissioned ranks in the armed forces to Indians, that received a less sympathetic response from the British.

There were many reasons why the spirit of Hindu–Muslim unity encapsulated in the Lucknow Pact disintegrated over the following decades and could not be revived, despite efforts to do so. Not least among these reasons, probably, was the post-**World War I** phenomenon of mass mobilization in Indian politics that undercut the authority of older leaders.

– M –

MACAULAY, THOMAS BABINGTON (1800–1859). Thomas Babington was the son of Zachary Macaulay, a stalwart of the anti-

slavery movement in Britain in the early 19th century. He grew up as a reformer, a follower of Jeremy Bentham and James Mill of the Utilitarian school of political thought. These men sought to legislate "happiness" in the "best interests" of the largest number. They saw a challenging opportunity for social engineering in those parts of India that were controlled by Britain and administered through the **East India Company**, especially when Lord **William Bentinck** was appointed governor general in 1829.

The **Charter Act** of 1833 opened India to unrestricted entry of British mercantile and missionary enterprise and gave additional powers to the governor general. Macaulay accepted a lucrative appointment as the first law member on Bentinck's new council and moved to **Calcutta** in 1835. His two-year review of the judicial procedures then in force and his draft of a new penal code found eventual expression in the Codes of Civil and Criminal Procedure enacted for India in 1860 and 1861. His arguments for transferring jurisdiction over Europeans to Indian courts and for ending press censorship, liberal as they were, took much longer to be implemented in British India.

Macaulay is frequently associated with his famous "Minute on Education." This was his contribution to a debate on the most useful method of allocating modest funds for education in 1835. Some council members argued in favor of the prevailing mode of teaching in Indian **languages**; others wondered aloud if they should instead be teaching English to the Indians who were themselves demanding Western learning in Calcutta at the time. Macaulay spoke with wit and is still quoted. He denigrated *all* Eastern learning—including the classics of **Sanskrit**, Persian, and Arabic literature—as unequal to that of an average English schoolboy. More seriously, he advocated a type of education for Indians that would produce reliable clerical servants for the British: as he put it, "a class of persons, Indian in blood and colour, but English in taste, in opinion, in morals, and in intellect." Macaulay's view prevailed. Only in the 20th century did later generations come to ridicule this class as *babus*, "brown sahibs," "Macaulay's children," or, simply, as misfits without authentic roots anywhere.

Macaulay returned to England and became a cabinet minister under Lord Melbourne in 1839. His popular and elegant essays both reflected and shaped middle-class Victorian opinion. His monumental five-volume *History of England* occupied most of his time before he was elevated to the peerage in 1857.

MADHAVAN, T. K. (1886–1930). Madhavan was born in the state of Travancore to a landowning **Ezhava** family. He was influenced by his maternal uncle Kunju Pillai, who represented the Ezhava community in the Travancore legislative assembly and followed him there as a member. Madhavan became a social reformer early and dedicated his life to uplifting **Untouchables**, among whom the Ezhavas were then numbered. Madhavan organized and led a **Satyagraha** to gain them right of access to **Hindu** temples, which was still denied in 1924. This Satyagraha was staged at the famous Vaikom temple, lasted 20 months, and was joined by **Mahatma Gandhi** in 1925. They won the right to use roads adjoining the temple; only in 1936 were all Hindu temples in Travancore opened to them by order of the maharajah. Madhavan also led an active campaign for temperance and prohibition of alcohol as part of his social reform program.

Madhavan was editor and publisher of a major daily newspaper in the Malayalam **language**. He took a political role and was a member of the Working Committee of the **Indian National Congress** in the 1920s.

MADHYA PRADESH. A state formed in 1956 and situated in the central part of the subcontinent, Madhya Pradesh is replete with names and places originating in antiquity—such as **Ujjain** and the paleolithic cave paintings of Betak—and rich in places of archaeological, architectural, and historical interest—such as Sanchi, Mandu, and Gwalior. Madhya Pradesh is well forested and home to a number of wildlife sanctuaries and National Parks. In November 2000, its eastern districts were reconstituted into the state of **Chhatisgarh**.

Madhya Pradesh consisted of regions such as Malwa, Bundelkhand, and Chhattisgarh that were historically difficult to control. Much fought over by expanding empires based in **Delhi** or elsewhere, kingdoms and principalities easily reverted to semi-independence or lawlessness when administration slackened. Parts of present-day Madhya Pradesh came under direct British rule in the 19th century, but much of it was composed of **Princely States** that acceded to the

Indian Union in 1947. Almost one quarter of its approximately 60 million population is **Adivasi**. Gond queens and other female rulers won important places in history.

Tourism is an important industry in Madhya Pradesh, though some automobile and high technology industries have been introduced recently. Traditional handicrafts enjoy a wide market. Rich deposits of bauxite, coal, and iron ore make mining important. But the general level of economic and social development remains relatively low. The 1984 tragedy at the Union Carbide chemical plant in **Bhopal** and controversy over damming the river **Narmada** has given a special prominence to the work of social activists and conservationists in **non-governmental organizations (NGOs)** in present-day Madhya Pradesh. The principal **language** is Hindi.

MADRAS/CHENNAI. The capital city of **Tamil Nadu**, Madras reverted to its name of Chennai in the 1990s. A local chieftain granted the site for Madras, on the Coromandel coast of southeastern India, to the **East India Company** in 1640. Fort St. George was constructed there and became a prosperous trading center and the principal British settlement in peninsular India. The British gradually established autonomy in Madras with a municipal administration and court of justice, while maintaining good relations with local elites and neighboring rulers.

During the Anglo–French and Carnatic Wars of the mid-18th century, Madras changed hands between the British and French twice and then became the base for expanding British power in southern India. Although the British Parliament placed Madras under the authority of the governor general in **Calcutta** by the **Regulating Act** of 1773 and Pitt's India Act 10 years later, they did not curb war against **Mysore** or the French. From Madras, the British expanded their territorial control along the coast, in the **Deccan**, and in **Karnataka**.

Madras Presidency came to include most of peninsular India; the city of Madras was its capital, and a university was established there in 1857. Madras city continued to prosper, and its educated men and women played important roles in **Hindu** social reform and growth of the Indian national movement. Several distinguished political leaders of the post-independence period were nurtured in Madras, including **C. Rajagopalachari**, **S. Radhakrishnan**, and **K. Kamaraj**, and large numbers of people from Madras/Tamil Nadu are conspicuous in the civil and defense services throughout India. Although the extent of Madras's administrative and political jurisdiction shrank to Tamil-speaking districts in the late 1950s with the reorganization of Indian states on the basis of **language**, the commerce, cultural life, trade, and production of this port city remained vibrant and its influence widespread. Chennai's population is estimated at 4,216,268 according to the 2001 **census**.

MADURAI. The site of many magnificent temples, Madurai is an ancient city located south of **Chennai**. The double temple to Sundareshvara and the goddess Meenakshi built in the **Dravidian** style with four high, elaborately sculptured *gopuram*, or gate towers, draws hundreds of thousands of worshippers to the present day.

Kautilya mentions Madurai in his *Arthasastra* of the fourth century BCE as a source of fine textiles and pearls. It was the capital city of the **Pandya** kingdom at the turn of the millennium. More than a thousand years later, its great wealth attracted the plundering raids of **Alauddin Khalji** and other raiders. Madurai formed part of the **Vijayanagar** Empire in which foreign trade and commerce flourished. On its collapse after 1565, Madurai became the capital of a successor Nayak kingdom. Its textile and other craft products continue to be famous and lucrative.

MAFATLAL, GAGALBHAI (1873–1944). The son of a master weaver and petty merchant of **Ahmedabad**, Mafatlal began his working life as a small boy peddling home woven fabric and gold lace from house to house; he ended it as head of the third largest industrial empire in India producing mill-made cotton textiles, jute products, petrochemicals, caustic soda, dyes, and a variety of building materials. Mafatlal was an intensely ambitious entrepreneur whose natural talent compensated for his lack of formal education. Also, he was able to benefit from changes that were taking place in India and in the world during in his lifetime.

Some important developments were the following. The **swadeshi movement** protesting the **partition of Bengal** in 1905 increased the demand for domestic textiles, and Mafatlal's newly acquired mills prospered. **World War I** stimulated India's infant industries, and

Mafatlal formed a limited company bearing his own name in 1920. There was a demand for venture capital, and Mafatlal was able to partially finance new enterprises or take over mills ruined by the economic depression of the early 1930s; thus, he entered the lucrative management agency business that was still dominated by British firms. The **Indian National Congress** urged production and consumption of domestic goods, and as the momentum of nationalism accelerated through the 1920s and 1930s Mafatlal diversified into jute, sugar, and also a shipping venture in cooperation with other Indian merchants. Finally, **World War II** decisively stimulated Indian industrial production while the gradual disinvestment of English and European groups helped Mafatlal acquire their assets. He left his sons a very substantial heritage.

MAGADHA. A region in the mid-southern portion of present-day **Bihar** was named Magadha. One of the earliest organized states in India, it competed for power with the kingdoms of Kashi and **Kosala** and the Vriji confederacy of the **Lichchavis** in the seventh century BCE. Magadha rose to unquestioned preeminence in the fourth century BCE, and for nearly a thousand years the history of Magadha was virtually the history of northern India. It was well placed for such a role, situated on the trade-bearing river **Ganges** and endowed with abundant natural resources in rich, easily cultivable land, forests yielding timber for building and elephants for warfare, and iron for superior weapons and tools.

The concept of a state ruled by a hereditary monarch with a centralized administration, systematic collection of revenues, and a standing army evolved early in Magadha's history. The Saisunaga Dynasty founded a capital at Rajagriha, which subsequently became the more famous **Pataliputra**, near present-day **Patna**. **Bimbisara** and his son Ajatsatru were contemporaries of the **Buddha** and extended their domain to include the Ganges delta, thus controlling coastal and sea trade as well. They laid down roads and claimed most cultivated land for the crown. Rice was grown. New military technologies were introduced to break fortress walls with catapults and mow down enemy troops from horse-drawn chariots. The Nanda Dynasty is sometimes described as the first empire builder of India and raised a huge army. It was overthrown by **Chandragutpa Maurya** in

321 BCE, and his dynasty gave full expression to the imperial idea in India.

Modern historians have commented on the extraordinary precision and efficiency of the Mauryan governmental machine, as much as on the excellence of their stone workers who erected the **Ashoka** pillars and built the **stupa** at Sanchi. The intellectual ferment and commercial wealth of Magadha are amply reflected in **Jain** and **Buddhist** writings, for the teachings of **Mahavira** and the Buddha were first heard in Magadha and then spread outwards through the subcontinent. **Nalanda** near Pataliputra served as a center of Buddhist learning for over a thousand years.

Magadha was once again the core of the **Gupta Empire** in which the classical tradition of India developed in the first few centuries CE. The later Guptas continued to rule in Magadha after their empire had disintegrated and **Kanauj** had replaced Pataliputra in importance. The three Hindi dialects of modern Bihar—Bhojpuri, Maithili, and Magadhi—developed from the **Prakrit** spoken at the time of the later Guptas. Magadha then came under the sway of the **Pala Dynasty of Bengal** and eventually fell into oblivion under the Turks of the **Delhi Sultanate** in the 13th century.

MAHABALIPURAM. Presently a fishing village located on the Coromandel coast close to **Chennai**, Mahabalipuram was once the principal port of the **Pallava** kingdom. A brisk trade was maintained with Southeast Asia from this port and some migrations also may have taken place between the 6th and 9th centuries CE. Mahabalipuram is the site of groups of highly carved monolithic stone monuments and temples constructed in Pallava times. Because the sea has encroached on the shore, only a few examples remain standing. Bas-relief sculptures of exquisite naturalism testify to the skill and devotion of the artisans.

MAHABHARATA. Historical reconstruction of post-Vedic Indo–Aryan institutions and social mores is based in large part on the great epic, *Mahabharata.* Ascribed to the poet Vyasa, the *Mahabharata* is probably a compendium of compositions by different persons at different times weaving diverse but important episodes into the central story. This concerns a feud over land between two groups of cousins, the

5 Pandavas and the 100 Kauravas, in which all the kings and peoples of the Indian subcontinent came to be ranged on one side or the other when the climax of their dispute was finally reached in a bloody 18-day battle at Kurukshetra, north of **Delhi**. The epic remains a living part of Indian culture as also in parts of Southeast Asia today and every enactment or depiction of the epic includes episodes and characters of local interest. As Peter Brook, an English producer adapting the drama for contemporary Western audiences, said, the *Mahabharata* is "the story of mankind."

The *Mahabharata* as presently known as the longest poem in the world, consisting of more than 100,000 verses arranged in 18 chapters. Written in **Sanskrit**, probably in the first few centuries CE, the *Mahabharata* refers to events of a much earlier period, perhaps between c. 1000 and 700 BCE. However, the traditional **Hindu** date for the great war at Kurukshetra is 3102 BCE. Archaeological excavations in Delhi and near Mirat are sometimes said to reveal cities built around 900 BCE and could have been the Indraprastha of the Pandavas and the Hastinapur of the Kauravas, respectively. But reconstructing the political history of early India from the *Mahabharata* may be as futile a task as reconstructing the early history of Britain from Tennyson's *Idylls of the King*.

The epic is a rich source for current research on evolving social practices, morality, amusements, statecraft, and religious thought in India. For example, Draupadi, the crucial female character in the drama, becomes the common wife of the five Pandava brothers; this polyandrous marriage (common among certain hill peoples to the present day) is justified to Draupadi's father as a custom of "earlier times." The plot hinges on a great gambling tournament in which the eldest Pandava loses his kingdom to his Kaurava cousin; details of the dice game as well as discourses on rights of property, rules of slavery, and the conscience of a king surround the episode. The account of the great war itself is prefaced by a treatise on statesmanship and abounds in lessons on fair and unfair tactics in battle or the rules of war.

At the heart of the feud lies the question of succession; should succession be determined by primogeniture, by ability, by law, or by force? The Pandavas became heirs to the throne because Dhiratrashtra, father of the Kauravas, was blind and therefore was not eligible to rule. He divided the kingdom between the cousins, but his sons upset that arrangement in a gambling match and sent the Pandavas into exile for 13 years. At the end of that period the Pandavas claimed their kingdom, were denied it, declared war, and won. Their victory was attributed to their righteousness as much as to their valor; this was symbolized in the participation of divine **Krishna** on their side as charioteer to the warrior Arjuna.

The greatest interpolation in the *Mahabharata* is the sixth book, the **Bhagavata Gita**, in which Krishna as the Supreme Deity expounds on the nature of **dharma** and the paths to spiritual emancipation. Clearly, by the time an orally transmitted warrior epic was written down in a form accessible to the present day, Hindu brahmanic culture and religious thought were in full flower.

MAHARASHTRA. With its prosperous and teeming capital of **Mumbai**, a population of more than 99 million, an area of 307,690 square kilometers, and an economic growth rate well above the national average, Maharashtra is obviously a very important state of the Indian Union. Its present boundaries were drawn in 1960 when states were reorganized on the basis of **language** and Marathi-speaking areas— themselves an amalgamation of erstwhile British India and **Princely States**—and the city of **Bombay** were separated from Gujarati-speaking areas of the huge bilingual state of Bombay. It is located in western India and includes coastal areas, the forested mountains of part of the Western Ghats, as well as the upper **Deccan**.

Maharashtra's long historical heritage encompasses contributions by the **Satvahana**, **Chalukya**, and Yadava dynasties before the **Khalji** and **Tughlaq** conquests from **Delhi** in the 13th and 14th centuries. Thereafter, a composite culture flourished in the **Bahmani** kingdom and its successor sultanates. Many sites of artistic and architectural splendor, such as **Ajanta** and **Ellora**, of religious significance or natural beauty attract tourists to Maharashtra.

Modern political consciousness in Maharashtra draws sustenance from the emergence of **Shivaji** as a hero in wars against the **Mughal Emperor Aurangzeb** in the 17th century and the subsequent rise of **Maratha** power to an almost dominant position in the subcontinent before succumbing to British expansion in the 19th century. British administrators in Maharashtra, such as **Mountstuart Elphinstone**, refrained from wholesale destruction of existing institutions but added new ones, notably schools, colleges, and Bombay University. Training centers for the **Indian armed forces** established by the British have been augmented after independence. In the latter half of the 19th century, **Poona** contributed stalwarts to the cause of **Hindu** social reform as well as becoming a center for Hindu revivalism and nationalism; **Mahadev Ranade, Bal Gangadhar Tilak,** and **Gopal Krishna Gokhale** were all prominent citizens of Pune. At the same time, the port of Bombay thrived as a center of commerce and new industry and a training ground for a generation of Indian leaders.

Agriculture is the main source of employment in Maharashtra, with dry land subsistence farming supplemented by cash crops, especially cotton and sugar. Farmers' movements, such as those led by **Sharad Joshi,** and **cooperatives** as in milk production, are conspicuous. Many modern industries, including chemicals, electrical machinery, electronics, petrochemicals, pharmaceuticals, ship building, and other transport equipment are well established in the greater Mumbai metropolis as well as other parts of Maharashtra. The social and political health of Maharashtra has been compromised in recent decades by the growth of chauvinist organizations with a dependence on brute force and violent rhetoric, as well as the operations of smugglers and criminal gangs in slums and at the border of **political parties** and the underworld. The blowing up of the Bombay Stock Exchange buildings in March 1993 presaged too the increase of **terrorism** all over India.

MAHAVIRA, VARDHAMANA (c. sixth century BCE d. 527 or 467 BCE).

A scion of the Jnatrika and **Lichchavi** clans of Vaishali in north **Bihar,** Mahavira left his home at age 30, joined an existing ascetic order for 12 years, gained enlightenment, and became a religious teacher. He preached in **Magadha** under the patronage of Kings **Bimbisara** and Ajatashatru and throughout the **Ganges** valley for about 30 years. He was an older contemporary of the **Buddha,** and he is mentioned in Buddhist texts as Nigantha Nataputta, "the naked ascetic of the Jnatrikas."

Mahavira founded a disciplined order of naked monks supported by lay folk, based on or allied to existing groups of ascetics looking back to an earlier teacher Parshva. Mahavira was known as *kevalin* or "completed soul," and *jina* or "conqueror"; his followers came to be known as **Jain**, a derivative of the latter title. They believed him to be the twenty-fourth Tirthankara or "fordmaker" in the present cycle of cosmic decline. The existence of God was irrelevant to Mahavira's teachings, which stressed purity of the soul, rather than knowledge, ritual, or worship, as the path to spiritual salvation.

Mahavira taught that the whole world is alive and that every piece of matter contains a living soul capable of suffering. Therefore, he laid tremendous emphasis on *ahimsa,* or non-violence. This concept may already have been in circulation, but it subsequently became an essential part of normative Indian culture through the influence of the Jains. *See also* JAIN.

MAHMUD, SULTAN OF GHAZNI (968–1030). Mahmud was a key figure in the history of Muslim expansion into India. In the seventh century CE, when the Arabs embraced **Islam**, the Indian (**Hindu–Buddhist**) cultural and political frontier extended into the Afghan–Iran plateau. Five hundred years of Arab–Turk attacks over stubborn resistance pushed that frontier east and south in stages: the battle for Sindh from 636 to 713; the battle for Afghanistan from 643 to 870; the struggle for **Punjab** from 870 to 1030; the advance through the Indo–Gangetic plain from 1175 to 1206.

Mahmud, warrior leader of a principality in eastern Afghanistan, hammered at a loose **Rajput** confederacy by attacking Peshawer in 1001, Punjab in 1004, and then executing a series of brilliant raids on temple cities: Kangra in 1009, Lahore in 1015, Mathura in 1018, **Kanauj** in 1019, Gwalior in 1022, and most daringly of all, Somnath in 1025. Mahmud's motive was plunder of the legendary wealth of India so as to finance his politico–military ambitions in Central Asia; he carried away Indian craftsmen to beautify his home city of Ghazni. A secondary but more highlighted motive was iconoclastic zeal in destroying "infidels" and their places of worship so that Mahmud could claim the title of "al-ghazi," or God's warrior.

Mahmud's success had profound results. The Punjab was annexed to Ghazni and became the base of sustained Muslim–Turk expansion in India. According to **Al Biruni**, many **brahmans** and Rajputs retreated to hill kingdoms. Mahmud of Ghazni epitomized images of

Muslim rapine and brutality against Hindus that nourished communal conflict in 20th-century India.

MAJITHIA, SUNDER SINGH (1872–1941). Sunder Singh was born in the **Punjab** to a landowning **Sikh** family, which had been in the service of Maharaja **Ranjit Singh** and had matrimonial connections with some ruling princes. Majithia became a sugar magnate and received many honors in his life, including a knighthood in 1926.

From 1902 to 1921 Majithia was Secretary of the Chief Khalsa Diwan. This was an organization formed in 1902 to direct the Singh Sabha movement of Sikh revivalism, to safeguard Sikh rights to representation in the armed forces and other government services, and to "cultivate loyalty to the Crown." Majithia himself was an ardent supporter of the British Raj, condemning the **Ghadr** revolutionary movement, praising the **Montagu–Chelmsford Reforms**, and serving on various bodies appointed by the Viceroy. With the introduction of autonomous provincial governments in 1937, Majithia became minister for revenue in the **Unionist** government of the Punjab and encouraged agrarian improvements.

Majithia was identified with Singh Sabha efforts to counteract the proselytizing activities of the **Arya Samaj** and **Christian** missionaries. Perhaps the most important achievements of the Singh Sabha movement were literary and educational, such as the Sikh National Educational Fund founded by Majithia, which built many Khalsa schools and colleges with Sikh scriptures and the Gurmukhi language as part of the curriculum and high academic and athletic standards.

MALABARI, BEHRAMJI (1853–1912). Malabari was born in Baroda to a **Parsi** family and educated in **Surat** at missionary schools. The Scottish Presbyterian Vice Chancellor of Bombay University, Dr. J. Wilson, influenced Malabari in expanding his own vision and work far beyond his own community.

The Parsi community was in the process of carrying out religious reforms and social welfare schemes for itself in the mid-19th century, along lines advocated in **Dadabhai Naoroji**'s newspaper *Rast Goftar*, and culminating in the Parsi Marriage and Divorce Act of 1865. Malabari, who was a brilliant writer in English and knew what public opinion could accomplish in England and in India, turned his journalistic talents to crusading for social reform legislation for the majority of Indians, who were **Hindu**. From 1884 to 1891 he led a campaign against child marriage and for widow remarriage and female education in the vociferous controversy surrounding the Age of Consent Bill.

Controversy raged not so much on the need to raise the age of marriage for Hindu girls—all educated Indians were agreed on that social issue—but on whether or not an alien power should legislate on so intimate a subject as the age of sexual intercourse between marriage partners. Malabari's newspaper, *The Indian Spectator*, and his "Notes" on "Infant Marriage" and "Enforced Widowhood"—4,000 copies of which were sent to leading opinion makers in England and India—amplified his voice on the subject with vivid descriptions of the hardships to which young widows and younger wives could be subjected in India. His position was that of an individualist sensitive to the nation's ills and a nationalist convinced that social reform must precede political advancement. He was supported by the leading members of the Parsi community and by eminent Hindu social reformers including **Mahadev Govind Ranade**, **Ishwar Chandra Vidyasagar**, and T. M. Iyer. They were vehemently opposed by orthodox Hindus and by **Bal Gangadhar Tilak**, the radical nationalist demanding self-rule before self-reform.

Though the Age of Consent Bill was eventually passed in 1891, the attention of the new Indian elite had shifted from social issues to political reform of the British Raj. Malabari retired from public life and devoted himself to the educational, medical, and material assistance of women of all communities in western India, especially widows. He helped found the organization Seva Sadan for that purpose.

MALAVIYA, MADAN MOHAN (1861–1946). Malaviya was born in **Allahabad** to a learned **brahman** family, educated in **Sanskrit** at an early age, and sent to school where he studied English. He practiced Law for some years but preferred public service. Between 1907 and 1921 he founded several daily and weekly journals in Hindi so as to educate the public and give voice to their opinions on national and local issues.

Malaviya joined the **Indian National Congress** in 1886 and was elected president of that body in 1909, 1918, 1932, and 1933. He was considered a 'moderate' because he welcomed the **Montagu– Chelmsford Reforms** of 1919 and was generally cooperative with the British government even though he joined the **Civil Disobedience** Movement in 1930. He was a good friend of **Motilal Nehru** and other Congress leaders.

Malaviya was a conservative and a devout **Hindu** who believed in a social system ordered along lines of the *varna-ashrama-dharma* (see Glossary) described in Sanskrit texts. He was a co-founder of the All India Hindu Mahasabha and was popular among his coreligionists. His most enduring achievement was the Banaras Hindu University founded in 1916 and opened in 1921 with substantial private donations as well as government support; he was vice chancellor from 1919 to 1938. Pandit Madan Mohan Malaviya was closely associated with the intellectual and cultural awakening among Hindus in the first part of the 20th century, both in his private capacity and through the institutions he helped build.

MALCOLM, JOHN (1769–1833). John Malcolm was one of 17 children born to a Scots small farmer. He joined the **East India Company** at the age of 13 and served in India to the date of his retirement in 1830 in a variety of capacities: soldier, administrator, diplomat, and governor. Malcolm's career spans a period of British territorial expansion in India, and he contributed much to establishing a reputation for the new rulers of honesty, hard work, versatility, and humanity toward the Indian peasant.

The young Malcolm fought in wars against **Tipu Sultan** and the **Marathas**. He was also sent by **Lord Wellesley** on delicate missions to negotiate **Subsidiary Alliances** with the Maratha chiefs Scindhia and Holkar, as well as to Persia where he obtained permission for a British Resident at Muscat and facilities on Oman. He was closely identified with Wellesley, and along with **Mountstuart Elphinstone** and Thomas Munro tamed the Maratha country in central India and the northern **Deccan**. Put in charge of the administration of central India, Malcolm brought the **Pindari** raiders under control.

John Malcolm was a keen observer of the Indian peoples and their customs. He authored several books on the political history of India, on the **Sikhs,** and on central India. He was knighted and was awarded an honorary doctorate from Oxford. He succeeded Elphinstone as governor of **Bombay** in 1827 and furthered the modernization of that bustling commercial city. After his retirement he became a member of Parliament in the British House of Commons.

MALDIVES, REPUBLIC OF. The Maldives consist of a group of tropical islands in the Indian Ocean, not all of which are inhabited, extending over 800 kilometers from the Minicoy islands in the north to the Adders in the south. The captial is at Male. The Republic of the Maldives is a member of the **South Asian Association for Regional Cooperation** and has been culturally and ethnically connected with India and **Sri Lanka** since prehistoric times. Archaeological excavations lead some scholars to postulate evidence of **Harappan** culture in the Maldives. More obvious signs of **Buddhism** remain, although a 12th-century ruler and then his people converted to **Islam.**

The Maldives inevitably featured in the oceanic and trading rivalries of the Arabs, **Portuguese,** Dutch, British, and French from the 15th to the 19th century; many economic transactions were handled by merchants from **Gujarat** in western India. A British Protectorate was established in 1897. The Maldives became a Republic in 1953 and fully independent of Britain in 1965, although it joined the Commonwealth in 1982. Close ties with India and Sri Lanka were cultivated, and a tourist industry developed as part of a drive for modernization. An attempted coup d'etat against President Maumun Abdul Gayum was quickly extinguished with the help of Indian marines and paratroops in 1989; there have been no such further episodes.

MANDAL COMMISSION. Formally known as the Backward Classes Commission, it was appointed by Prime Minister **Morarji Desai** of the **Janata** government in December 1978. The five-member Commission, chaired by B. P. Mandal, was asked to "determine the criteria for defining the socially and educationally backward classes," to "recommend steps to be taken for the advancement of . . . citizens so identified," to "examine the desirability" of making reservations in their favor, and to report to the President of India. These tasks were in keeping with directive principles in the **Indian Constitution** to ameliorate conditions for historically disadvantaged **castes**.

The Mandal Commission conducted countrywide surveys using 11 indicators of backwardness and computerized data. It submitted its two-volume, 14-chapter report with 21 appendixes on December 31, 1980. Despite the fact that no caste enumerations had been made in **census** reports after 1931, the commission found a close linkage between caste ranking and social, educational, and economic status. In its report, it remarked on a permanent stratification of society in most areas, with discrimination against lower castes and vested interests of higher castes impeding changes introduced at varying rates in different states. It also discovered that though the ritual importance of caste had decreased, its political importance had increased because caste identity was an easy means of electoral mobilization under conditions of adult franchise.

The criteria for "backward class" formulated by the Mandal Commission were low social position in the **Hindu** caste hierarchy, lack of general educational proficiency, inadequate representation in government services, and inadequate representation in trade, commerce, and industry, or in modern sectors of the economy. It premised its recommendations on the belief that equality of opportunity and treatment militates against the backward classes, who need special protection and privileges in compensation. It was explicitly aware of the implicit conflict between chapters two and three of the Indian Constitution of 1950, which directed the government to alleviate the backward, on the one hand, and prohibited discrimination on grounds of caste, creed, or gender, on the other. It advocated using "affirmative action" to overcome discrimination.

The Mandal Commission prepared lists of Other Backward Castes (OBCs) for each state, amounting to 52% of India's total population. This was in addition to the Schedules of Castes and Tribes included in the Constitution for whom 22.5% reservations were legally required. The Mandal Commission recommended a further reservation of 27% for OBCs in all central and state government services and in technical and professional institutions; special educational facilities for upgrading the cultural environment and competitive ability of the OBCs; special programs to upgrade the skills of artisans; special networks of financial and technical institutions; land reform to alter the structural relationships of economic dominance and bondage between the higher and backward castes; and central government assistance to state governments to carry out these recommendations.

The president of India formally accepted the Mandal Commission Report, but the **Congress** governments in power through the 1980s did nothing to implement it. **Political parties** in opposition also ignored it. On August 7, 1990, Prime Minister **V. P. Singh**, heading a minority National Front government, announced to both houses of Parliament that the recommendations of the Mandal Commission would be implemented forthwith, calling it a "momentous decision of social justice." His orders for direct recruitment of OBCs to government services, the higher professions, and educational institutions were met with a storm of complaints that soon gathered momentum in public protests, student agitations, and a few highly publicized self-immolations by young high-caste men. Resistance to the Mandal premises and recommendations from virtually all "forward" caste groups and modern sectors threatened to plunge India into a vicious caste war. At the same time, there was mounting agitation from groups not mentioned in the Mandal Report, notably non-Hindus and poor forward caste Hindus, that they were as or more disadvantaged than OBCs and deserved similar protection.

V. P. Singh was criticized for tarnishing his "clean" image by resorting to political expediency in a factional rift with Deputy Prime Minister Devi Lal, and, more seriously, for having failed to build a national consensus or to even consult his civil servants and political colleagues before taking a unilateral action of such magnitude. After some ineffective compromises, Singh staked his government on the issue. He lost the vote of confidence in Parliament and resigned in November 1990. The Mandal Commission Report gradually lost its political potency, although New Delhi and state governments have unobtrusively implemented its main recommendations since then, and groups scramble to be listed as OBCs.

MANEKSHAW, FIELD MARSHAL SAM HORMUZJI FRAMJI JAMSHEDJII (1914–). Manekshaw was born to a **Parsi** family in **Amritsar** and educated at Sherwood College, Nainital, and the Indian Military Academy, Dehra Dun. He was commissioned as an officer in the Indian Army in 1934 and saw active service during **World War II** in **Burma**; he was awarded the Military Cross for gallantry.

Manekshaw was promoted to major general in 1957 and served as chief of army staff from 1969 to 1972. He was in overall command of India's military operations during the two-week war with **Pakistan** that resulted in the liberation of **Bangladesh** in 1971. He was honored with the Padma Vibhushan award. After his retirement from the army, he received the honorary rank of field marshal, as did the first Indian commander-in-chief, **K. M. Cariappa.**

MANIPUR. A small, beautiful, and well-forested state in the Indian Union bordering on **Burma**, the kingdom of Manipur, sometimes ruled by females such as Rani Gaidinliu, had a picturesque if little recorded history of well over a thousand years before the **East India Company** spread its activities into neighboring **Assam** in the 18th century. Manipur became an ally of the British but managed to retain its autonomy, its unique cultural identity, and most of its territory even during the Anglo–Burmese wars of the early 19th century.

Manipur was the scene of action at Imphal during **World War II**. The ruler of Manipur acceded to India at the time of independence in 1947. The territory was administered directly from New Delhi until it gained full statehood in 1972. The population of Manipur is a little more than two million, engaged mostly in agriculture. The forests are the home of some unique plants, including varieties of orchids and lilies. Improvements in agricultural production and the introduction of processing and electronic industries have followed recent irrigation and power generation schemes. Manipur's capital is Imphal.

MANMOHAN SINGH (1932–). India's 13th prime minister was sworn into office by President **Abdul Kalam** on May 22, 2004. Manmohan Singh had been minister of finance in the **Congress** government of **Narasimha Rao** from 1991 to 1996, and leader of the opposition in the **Rajya Sabha** (the upper house of parliament) from 2001 to 2004. In the former position, he formulated and implemented the first stage of India's new policy of **economic liberalization** and integration with global markets. He was able to extricate the country from its foreign exchange crisis of 1991 and to negotiate substantial credits from the International Monetary Fund. Although his policies lacked the active support of his cabinet colleagues other than the prime minister at the time, Manmohan Singh was well known as an economist and a man of integrity, and enjoyed respect in international circles. He displayed considerable parliamentary skills both as finance minister and as Rajya Sabha member, and won the Outstanding Parliamentarian Award for 2002. He has shown the same respect for institutional discipline and personal decorum as India's chief executive.

Dr. Manmohan Singh was educated at the University of Punjab, at Nuffield College, Oxford, and St. John's College, Cambridge. He returned to teach first at the University of Punjab in **Chandigarh** and then at the Delhi School of Economics. His career spanned academics and government. He was a consultant at the World Bank and other international trade and financial institutions. He was governor of the Reserve Bank of India from 1980 to 1985 and deputy chairman of the **Planning Commission** from 1985 to 1987. As a distinguished but secular **Sikh**, and known as a technocrat, he had no political base of his own and apparently no political ambitions. He stood for election to the **Lok Sabha** from a South **Delhi** constituency in 1999 and lost. He remained loyal to **Sonia Gandhi**, by then leader of the **Congress Party**. With the unexpected victory of a Congress-led coalition during the general elections of 2004, and Sonia Gandhi's rejection of the prime ministerial office open to her as leader of the Congress Parliamentary Party, the president asked Manmohan Singh to form a government, which he speedily and efficiently did.

MANORAMA, RUTH (1952–). Manorama was born in a suburb of **Madras** to a Christian mother and a father with the Post and Telegraphs Service who kept an open house and educated their children. Manorama took a science degree at Women's Christian College and then a master's degree in social work. She worked with a **nongovernmental organization (NGO)** among the slums of South India and started the journal *Women's Voice* to articulate needs of the urban poor. She also formed the Domestic Workers Union and became a social activist in behalf of **Dalits** and women workers in the informal sector. Manorama became the national convener of the National Federation of Dalit Women and president of the National Alliance of Women. The latter was formed after Manorama attended the Fourth United Nations World Conference on Women held in Beijing in 1995. She saw there both the similarities and the differences in the situations of women in different cultures and environments and wanted to correct the image of the women's movement in India as an urban, upper class/caste phenomenon. She continues to battle for human rights, freedom, and social justice.

MANSABDARI SYSTEM. The backbone of the **Mughal Empire**, the mansabdari system was created by **Akbar** in the mid-16th century as a graded imperial service whose higher members were appointed by him and called mansabdars. They were remunerated in cash, not in *iqtas* or land grants, as was the case for high officials in the **Delhi Sultanate** and earlier empires. Mansabdars were obliged to serve in whatever place and capacity the emperor ordered them, and to provide and maintain cavalry and foot soldiers in numbers graduated by multiples of ten according to their rank. Amirs, or nobles, commanded one thousand horses or more. By giving officials high status and high salaries but no heritable land, Akbar was able to recruit men of exceptional ability to the service of empire without giving them the wherewithal to revolt against his authority.

The Mughal nobility of high ranking mansabdars or Amirs always included Indian-born Muslims and others from Afghanistan, Iran, and Turkistan, as well as **Hindus**, especially **Rajputs**, who were generally confirmed in their hereditary chieftainships. Mansabdars acted as military commanders, administrators, and financial officials as need, ability, and the emperor decreed. Their levels of efficiency and compassion inevitably varied with their perceptions of the emperor's wishes.

The mansabdari system suffered from certain institutional disabilities, some of which were common to all bureaucratic organizations and many of which were unique to itself. These surfaced in the mid-17th century—when the Mughal Empire was at its height—and contributed to its administrative and economic decline over the following hundred years. The main drawbacks of the mansabdari system were the following. The personal focus of loyalty was to the emperor or a possible successor rather than the state as in a modern bureaucracy. There was a lack of objective or uniform standards of recruitment and performance. A gap appeared and widened between paper rank, remuneration, and actual number of troops maintained for service, which led to corruption and military decline. There was a gradual substitution of cash salaries by grants of jagirs (see Glossary) or grants of revenue from lands which led to clashes between a natural tendency among the nobility to pass on these lands to their heirs, and the emperor's legal right to resume the title and property of a deceased official and make a fresh appointment.

The effects of these institutional disabilities were limited as long as the empire was expanding and the emperors themselves were men of exceptional ability capable of holding the system together. But mansabdars were always factionalized and liable to support rival contenders to the throne, notably in the fratricidal war of succession in 1657–1658. The nobility did not act as a unifying force in the court wrangles of the 18th century. More importantly, they did not develop as a true aristocratic class identifying with the land and the people they controlled. Instead of acting as long term nurturers and investors, mansabdars, by the very conditions of their service, tended to behave as short-term extractors of revenue notable for their conspicuous expenditure. They became an additional burden on the cultivator as well as on the imperial exchequer.

Thus, while the mansabdari system represented an advance over preceding military rapacity, it did not produce the administrative ethos or capability appropriate to a modern state. *See also* MUGHAL EMPIRE.

MANU is the name of the First Man in **Hindu** mythology. Manu is also the name of a mythical god-king in the early concept of kingship evolved in **Ganges** valley kingdoms such as **Magadha**. According to legend, Manu was nominated by the deities and elected by men to a position of divine authority in order to end anarchy at the turn of a cosmic cycle.

An historic Manu is regarded as the author of the *Manava Dharmashastra* or *Manusmriti*, a codification of brahmanic law made in the first or second century CE. Later commentaries, such as those of the 12th century, elevated the *Manusmriti* over other legal treatises of the same period, and in the 19th century it was quoted as the main authority on social laws among Hindus. It elaborates on the *varna-ashrama-dharma* (see Glossary), or social order based on a **caste** hierarchy, in which the **brahman** was superior in status and held to higher standards of personal conduct than others, in which **Untouchable** castes were ranked by occupation and status, and in which the duties and rights of kingship—including the administration of justice through *danda*, or punishment—were clearly prescribed.

The *Manusmriti* considered a patriarchal joint family to be the basic unit of society. It treated marriage as indissoluble and made harsh prescriptions on the duties and treatment of **women**. Not surprisingly, social reformers of the 19th and 20th centuries have been openly critical of the *Manusmriti*.

MARATHA. All **Hindu** inhabitants of **Maharashtra** came to be called Maratha in the 17th century. From an inchoate mass of **brahmans** and **sudras** they were welded into a superbly mobile fighting force by **Shivaji** and his successors. They also fought under the saffron flag of religion against Muslim rulers.

The Marathas first broke **Mughal Emperor Aurangzeb**'s power in the **Deccan**, by guerilla warfare. They subsequently established control in the southern and western parts of India, and extended over lordship as far east as **Orissa** and as far north as **Delhi** in the 18th century. The Marathas were, for a time, chief contenders for the mantle of the Mughal Emperor as paramount power in India, but fell prey to disputes among their chieftains and military defeat at the hands of **Ahmad Shah Abdali** in 1761. In the early 19th century, the Marathas fought, but finally succumbed to, the rising power of the **East India Company**. Pride in Maratha achievements and ideas of reviving a Hindu empire remained alive, however, variously inspiring participants in the **Uprising of 1857**, social reform and revivalism in the late 19th century, and nationalist Hinduism or **hindutva** in the 20th century.

The rise of Maratha power is associated with the name of Shivaji, who assumed the royal title of *Chatrapati* at an elaborate coronation ceremony in 1674. His death in 1680 and the full force of Aurangzeb's counterattack did not interrupt Maratha expansion. The large but cumbersome Mughal armies were harassed by lightly equipped Maratha guerilla forces operating from hill forts, living off the land, and avoiding pitched battle. Aurangzeb's successor confirmed Maratha overlordship of the Deccan in return for token acknowledgment of Mughal sovereignty in Delhi. Shivaji's grandson Shahu appointed the able brahman Balaji Vishvanath as **Peshwa**, an office that became virtually that of chief executive. Maratha dominion expanded under the leadership of Peshwas **Baji Rao I**, Balaji Rao, and Madhava Rao, to the point where they were invited to act as protectors of the Mughal Emperors in the internal and external affairs of the north. A Maratha empire in both south and north India seemed a possibility, until defeat at the battle of **Panipat** in 1761 and the death of Madhava Rao in 1772 put an end to those ambitions. Thereafter, a loose Maratha confederacy was formed among the Peshwa Nana Phadnavis of **Pune**, Mahadji Scindia of Gwalior, Tukoji Holkar of Indore, the Bhonsle Raja of Berar, and the Gaekwar of Baroda. Together and separately, these Maratha chieftains and their respective successors operated as contenders for territory, revenue, and power in a fluid situation also involving the Nizam of **Hyderabad**, the rulers of **Mysore**, and the East India Company based in **Madras**, **Bombay**, and **Calcutta**. With the **Treaty of Bassein** signed in 1802, the Peshwa became a pensioner, or **subsidiary ally** of the British; Sindhia and Holkar succumbed soon after. A third Anglo-Maratha War spelled the end of Maratha independence and the abolition of the Peshwaship in 1818.

Notwithstanding impressive Maratha achievements in the military, political, literary, commercial, and artistic life of 18th-century India, evident from the extensive written records of the period, historians have focused on the causes of Maratha downfall. First, the incapacity of later Maratha chieftains to institutionalize cooperation and to win over the **Rajput** Chiefs to their cause was a major source of debilitation. Second, their lightning strikes and heavy taxes—named *chauth* (one fourth) and *sardeshmakhi* (one tenth)—gave the Marathas the appearance of predators rather than protectors in the conquered lands outside Maharashtra, alienating local peoples. Third, the Marathas neglected science and education in civilian life and did not infuse their military forces with the training and artillery used, for example, by forces of the East India Company; strategically, therefore, they were at a disadvantage. And finally, they espoused religion and ritual at the expense of modernization, looking backward rather than forward. Thus, the Marathas failed to reach their goal of erecting a Hindu empire in the ashes of Mughal disintegration, which they had helped to hasten. In that struggle for power, the British, standing in the wings, emerged as the ultimate victors.

MARWARI. This term is used for a **Hindu** commercial and industrial community originally from Marwar in **Rajasthan** and belonging to one or another of a cluster of *bania* or **vaisya** **castes**. Marwaris are sometimes compared to the Memons, a Muslim trading community of western India and **Pakistan**, and to trading communities from **Gujarat**. They share characteristics such as familial solidarity, work ethic, distant migrations, and a high level of material success.

The Marwar area, with Jodhpur as a center, encompasses ancient trade routes across northern India. British rule impoverished traditional trading centers in **Princely States** but opened new opportunities elsewhere. Marwari emigration to central, eastern, and southern India as well as to **Burma** and other parts of the British Empire dates to the 19th century. Many began as moneylenders and traders before entering the fields of banking and manufacturing, opening jute and textile mills and adapting to modern managerial techniques in the cities of **Bombay** and **Calcutta**. As members of a socially conservative and generally non-litigious community, the Marwaris had their own caste associations and social reformers. Many were personally attracted to **Mahatma Gandhi** and became strong supporters of the **Indian National Congress** in the vanguard of the Indian independence movement, donating liberally to its cause. For example, the Marwari donation to the Tilak Memorial Fund established by Congress in 1921 was Rs. 100 million, sufficient to finance the **States Peoples Conference** launched soon after. **G. D. Birla** met all of Gandhi's expenses, and Jamnalal Bajaj followed suit.

Marwari industrialists, in turn, benefited from the patronage of Congress provincial governments after 1937 and took advantage of new avenues to wealth opened by **World War II**. After independence they were quick to buy European managing agencies in India and participate in the drive for industrial self-reliance that characterized the 1950s and 1960s. Marwaris were estimated to control about 60% of India's total industry in the 1960s, when a scholarly investigation was made, and the proportion is unlikely to have changed very much since then. The names of Bajaj, Birla, Dalmia, **Goenka**, and Poddar rank high among those of well-known Marwari family houses.

MAURYA DYNASTY (c. 322–180 BCE). The Mauryas ruled over the first centralized Indian empire, encompassing almost the entire subcontinent. (See Map 3.) Written accounts by **Megasthenes** and **Kautilya**, as well as epigraphic, numismatic, and archaeological evidence, illuminate the historical picture.

The founder of the Dynasty, **Chandragupta Maurya**, may have taken the name of his maternal tribe with the *mor* or peacock as its emblem when supplanting the Nanda rulers in **Magadha**. He extended his domain far into present-day Afghanistan and consolidated his rule in the entire Indo–Gangetic plain before abdicating in favor of his son Bindusara in 297 BCE. Bindusara conquered "the land between the two seas," probably the **Deccan**, and continued in his father's tradition of tight government for another quarter century. He was succeeded by his son **Ashoka**, who conquered Kalinga (present-day **Orissa**), and introduced a novel **Buddhist** principle of dhamma or **dharma**, meaning righteousness based on compassion and nonviolence, in his administration. Ashoka was succeeded directly by two grandsons ruling in eastern and western provinces, who were credited with the construction of numerous **Jain** temples. The *Puranas* record the names of other successors but little is known for certain about them. The rule of the Indo–Greeks in the northwest and the Sunga Kings in Magadha indicate some break up of the Mauryan Empire on or before 180 BCE.

The Mauryas enjoyed friendly contacts with **Alexander the Great**'s successors, the Seleucids, in central and western Asia, exchanging envoys and gifts with them and with China, Khotan, **Kashmir**, **Nepal**, **Ceylon**, and the **Tamil** kingdoms of the extreme south. These contacts, along with the long period of relative peace and security and state encouragement of manufacturing and road building, certainly stimulated internal and external trade. The **vaisyas**, or mercantile communities, prospered; large and complex craft guilds were formed, provisions for usury point to an informal banking system, and heterodox Jain and Buddhist doctrines conducive to commercial activity spread during the Mauryan era.

A government of paternal despotism and centralized bureaucracy is described in Kautilya's *Arthasastra*. The emperor had a council of ministers to advise him, **brahmans** to remind him of sacred duties, well-armed female bodyguards to protect him, and a regular schedule of tours to keep him in touch with his subjects. The empire was divided into four provinces under viceroys; smaller units were under governors. Districts were the building blocks of administration; each village had its headman, accountant, tax collector, and other officials. The emperor urged extension of cultivation by assigning **sudras** to work the land (owned by him) and construct tanks, canals, and dams for irrigation. Urban administration was a separate department. Megasthenes describes the capital city of **Pataliputra** as having 4 wards and 30 officials dealing with matters including law and order, cleanliness, registration of births and deaths, tax collection, fire protection, retail trade and price controls, care of foreigners, and public works.

Underpinning this detailed administration was an espionage system described by Kautilya and corroborated by Greek writers. The emperor maintained a large secret service responsible for intelligence work as well as for encouraging political loyalty. A stern code of justice enforced social and fiscal regulations and protected property. Crimes were severely punished. Torture and the death penalty were used. The Mauryan army was formidably large, composed of corps of fighting elephants, chariots, cavalry, and foot soldiers, under a war office. Tamil literary sources portray the Mauryan army in action; the *Arthasastra* details its organization. The severity of Chandragupta's rule was apparently softened by Ashoka, who held diverse peoples together with the principles of social responsibility and mutual tolerance.

Modern historians point to three main causes for the political decline of the Mauryan Empire. Heavy expenditures on salaries and public works led to high taxation—up to 25% of agricultural produce—which may have created economic pressures; coins were debased by the end of the period. Although administration was centralized in the person of the emperor, he became dependent on local notables to carry out his instructions; the Mauryas did not introduce an objective system of recruitment to imperial service analogous to the examination base of the Chinese imperial bureaucracy. Finally, the idea of the state implicit in Kautilya's theory of kingship was replaced at some stage by the idea of the Social Order—the *varna-ashrama-dharma*—(see Glossary), which it was the king's duty to maintain. Thus, though the imperial vision, administrative grid, and revenue system organized by the Mauryas had modern features and inspired future empires to emulate them, it was the **caste** society dominated by brahmans that endured from one period to the next.

MAYAWATI (1956–). Mayawati succeeded Kanshi Ram as president of the **Bahujan Samaj Party (BSP)** in September 2003. She has been chief minister of **Uttar Pradesh (UP)** three times, albeit briefly: June to October 1995, March to September 1997, and May 2002 to August 2003. As the only **Dalit** woman to have attained such exalted status, Mayawati is a source of pride for other Dalits and an inspiration toward their further political organization, largely in support of the BSP. Her exercise of power, too, resulted in concrete and symbolic benefits for them. For example: a village scheme for socioeconomic development under India's Integrated Rural Development Program was directed toward building roads, houses, and water pumps in Dalit neighborhoods; grants for Dalit children to attend primary school were doubled; schemes for rehabilitating sweepers were announced; hundreds of Dalits were recruited as police-clerks; and various colleges, parks, stadiums, and roads were renamed after **Dr. Bhimrao Ambedkar**.

Mayawati was born in a Chamar family in Ghaziabad district but was unusually well educated. She has a law degree and worked as a teacher for several years before entering politics in 1984. Her fiery oratory made her an effective crowd puller and vote gatherer for the BSP. She was elected to the **Lok Sabha** in 1989 and to the **Rajya Sabha** in 1994 and championed the cause of Dalit welfare while in parliament before returning full time to UP. Each time she held power as chief minister, Mayawati antagonized many people in the civil services and outside by her wholesale transfer of officers and appointment of personal supporters to key administrative positions. Her autocratic style and lack of intellectual or ideological depth may have alienated potential supporters of the BSP from communities other than its original and fairly narrow base. Her willingness to form expedient alliances with **political parties** at apparently opposite poles, such as with the **Bharatiya Janata Party (BJP)**, in order to win power is questioned by some. But there is no doubt about the fact of Mayawati's popularity among the Dalits of UP.

MAZUMDAR, CHARU (1918–1972). Mazumdar was born to a landowning family of **Bengal** but joined the **Communist Party of India (CPI)** in 1938. He took a leading part in the **Tebhaga** movement of the 1940s and then tried to organize tea plantation labor in

Assam. When the CPI split in 1962, Mazumdar went with the **CPI (Marxist)**, was arrested, and wrote a series of nine essays from prison which established him as the chief ideologue of a "New Democratic Revolution" in India based on armed struggle by the poor and landless peasantry.

Charu Mazumdar participated in the industrial labor agitations in **Calcutta** that brought down the United Front government in 1967 and 1968. More importantly, he provided the inspirational leadership of the **Naxalite** movement in northern Bengal during the late 1960s; he interpreted the latter as a bid for state power, not merely for land, on the part of the peasantry. Mazumdar published penetrating analyses on the nature of the Indian state, asking the question: "Why is it that the Indian revolution has not succeeded as yet?" He answered in terms of a failure of leadership and technique and lauded China's prevailing Cultural Revolution as an "exploding moral atom bomb." Mazumdar broke away from the CPI(M) because of ideological and tactical differences and along with Kanu Sanyal formed the **CPI (Marxist-Leninist)** in April 1969. Several independent groups and some middle-class students from Calcutta joined them in propagating revolution and conducting guerilla activities that the government termed "terrorist." They wanted to join hands with the communist revolutionaries of East Pakistan, formerly East Bengal, but lacked party support and were sidelined by events culminating in the **Bangladesh** liberation war of December 1971. The CPI(M-L) was concentrated in and focused on Calcutta where the **Congress Party** led West Bengal government made a determined effort to crush it in 1972. Charu Mazumdar was arrested on July 16, 1972, and died in hospital shortly after.

MCMAHON LINE. Named after Sir Henry McMahon (1862–1949), it is approximately 1,500 kilometers along the northeastern frontier of India. The McMahon line is often used as a synonym for the highest crest of the eastern **Himalaya**, that is, the natural geographical divide between **Tibet** and areas traditionally within the jurisdiction of Indian states. McMahon sketched the line on a small-scale map when he was the British plenipotentiary at a tripartite Simla conference held with representatives of Tibet and China in 1913 and 1914. This was a time when the British-Indian government was extending its administration over tribal territories in the eastern Himalaya, and when it aimed for a buffer zone in Tibet because it was gravely concerned about Russian and Chinese moves in that country. The main British purpose at the tripartite conference was to divide areas of Chinese jurisdiction—"inner Tibet"—from autonomous "outer Tibet." The line dividing Tibet from India had already been the subject of discussion and notes between the British–Indian and Tibetan representatives who declared McMahon's line binding on themselves. The Chinese representative initialed McMahon's map, but neither the Republican government of the day nor its successors ratified the Simla Convention. This line was intended to confirm India's sovereignty over the tribal belt in the northeast. It has been shown on maps of the **Survey of India** as a firm border since the 1930s.

The McMahon line became a subject of controversy between India and the People's Republic of China after 1959 when the Chinese military occupation of Tibet, suppression of a rebellion there, and the flight of the **Dalai Lama** and his followers to India led to strained relations. In the course of official talks on the border in 1960 and thereafter, China disparagingly referred to the "so-called" or "illegal" McMahon line and laid claim to large tracts of territory south of it. During the Sino-Indian border conflict of 1962, much of this area was overrun by Chinese forces, which then withdrew. Indian administration was subsequently reestablished in the area of present-day **Arunachal Pradesh**, and India's claims to the "natural, historic, and traditional border" were reasserted. But the nomenclature "McMahon line" has not been emphasized since India and China normalized their relations in the late 1980s. Instead of theoretical discussion or historical review, officials of both countries meet regularly to determine the line of actual control along the ground. The agreement signed by Prime Minister **P. V. Narasimha Rao** and his Chinese counterpart, Li Peng, in September 1993 to "maintain peace and tranquility" along "the line of actual control" has been reaffirmed subsequently and reinforced with confidence building measures, direct military to military contacts, rapidly increasing economic exchanges and regular talks at very high level to resolve the border problem.

MEGASTHENES was the long-time ambassador of Seleukos Nikator of Babylon to the court of **Chandragupta Maurya** at **Pataliputra**

from c. 302 BCE. Megasthenes compiled an account of the geography, products, institutions, and customs of India as he observed them in the capital city of the **Mauryan Empire** and in the course of his travels. Although his record has not survived in its entirety, later Greek and Latin authors quoted from it frequently. It was the first authentic, detailed, and connected description of India by a foreign traveler and is therefore regarded as a major literary source of information on the ancient period in general and the Mauryan era in particular.

MEGHALAYA. This is a small, landlocked, hilly state of the Indian Union situated in the northeast. It was part of **Assam**, though administered more or less autonomously, before gaining statehood in 1972. Tribal peoples, including the Garos, Jaintias, and Khasis, are the inhabitants of Meghalaya. Their distinctive ethnic origins, **languages**, and customs set them apart from people of the plains. A majority of the people converted to **Christianity** as a result of missionary activity in the 19th and 20th centuries.

Shillong is the capital of Meghalaya. Created as a favored hill station by the British, Shillong is the site of excellent schools and colleges as well as various coordinating offices for the administration and defense of all the northeastern states.

MEHTA, PHEROZESHAH (1845–1915). Mehta was born in Bombay to a **Parsi** family of merchants and educated there before qualifying for the bar at Lincoln's Inn, London. He returned to India in 1868 and had a fruitful career in law and public life.

In England, Mehta became friends with **Dadabhai Naoroji**, **Badruddin Tyabji**, and other Indian liberals who became founder members and early leaders of the **Indian National Congress**. Mehta was president of the 1890 session of Congress and in charge of its funding and organization for 20 years. He was, like **G. K. Gokhale**, a typical "moderate," putting his trust in public education and constitutional reform and condemning mass agitation. He was instrumental in expelling the "extremists" led by **B. G. Tilak** after the Surat session of 1907.

Pherozeshah Mehta was one of the molders of the Bombay Municipal Corporation, which he chaired in 1884, 1885, and 1905, setting a high standard of financial and administrative probity. He was instrumental in having the elective principle introduced in the Municipal Act of 1888. His concern for preventing financial waste and mismanagement was also evident in his criticisms of the British–Indian government while serving on the Bombay Legislative Council and on the Imperial Legislative Council. He supported development of industry within India and was among the first to invest in textile mills and soap manufacture. Although critical of governmental domination of universities, he regarded English language education in India as "the greatest gift of British rule."

MENON, V. K. KRISHNA (1896–1974). Krishna Menon was born to a large and wealthy **Nair** family. He studied at **Madras** and was influenced by **Annie Besant** and her **Home Rule League**. He proceeded to London in 1924 where he studied at the London School of Economics and qualified for the bar at the Middle Temple. He launched the India League in 1929 to influence British public opinion in favor of Indian independence. In London he formed a lifelong friendship with **Jawaharlal Nehru** and worked with the Fabian Socialists and the Labour Party. He was an agnostic, a nationalist, and a voracious reader all his life.

Krishna Menon returned to serve independent India in 1947. He was India's high commissioner in London and ambassador to the Republic of Ireland from 1947 to 1952 and leader of India's delegation to the United Nations for the following 10 years. He also performed many other diplomatic tasks for India, notably in negotiations to end the Korean War, in disarmament talks, and in efforts to bring about an Indo–China settlement at Geneva in 1954. He was intellectually and emotionally very close to Nehru, who used him as a radical articulator of his own thinking.

Brilliant, unmarried, sharp-tongued, and acerbic in manner, Krishna Menon made many enemies both inside and outside the **Congress Party** and India. He was widely criticized because the Indian Army was ill prepared to cope with the heightened tensions and border conflict with China, which coincided with his tenure as Defense Minister from 1957 to 1962. Menon resigned. Although he remained a member of the **Lok Sabha** until 1974, he ceased to play an important political role after Nehru's death in 1964.

MENON, VAPAL PANGUNNI (1894–1966). V. P. Menon played a crucial role in negotiating the accession of many **Princely States** to the Indian Union as secretary to **Lord Mountbatten** and adviser to the Ministry of States and Home from 1946 to 1949. His account of these events was published in *Story of the Integration of Indian States* (1955) and *The Transfer of Power in India* (1957).

Menon had had a modest education and joined government service as a clerk in 1914. He rose through hard work and an acute intelligence to the positions he held. **Sardar Vallabhbhai Patel** found him an invaluable aide in the Home Ministry after independence, and for some time in 1951 Menon was officiating Governor of **Orissa**.

METCALFE, CHARLES THEOPHILUS (1785–1846). Metcalfe was the youngest, and in the opinion of some the greatest, of a quartet of men who expanded the territorial domains of the **East India Company** in India in the early 19th century. They used military and diplomatic methods but administered these territories with efficiency, humanity, and justice. The other three linked with Metcalfe are **Mountstuart Elphinstone**, **Thomas Munro**, and **John Malcolm**.

Metcalfe was born in **Calcutta** to an English family; his father was in the service of the Company and later a director of it in London. The young Charles was educated at Eton before joining the Fort William training college for members of the covenanted service of the Company in 1801. He was a complex and introspective man who nevertheless made friends easily. In 1808 (when the Napoleonic wars had broken out again in Europe), the young Metcalfe was sent on a special mission to the court of Maharajah **Ranjit Singh** at Lahore with instructions to obtain an alliance against France and to give as little as possible. He remained in Lahore for two years and may have married and had sons there. Ranjit Singh did not enter into an alliance with the British but did agree not to expand his power east of the Sutlej River; he and Metcalfe signed the Treaty of Amritsar to this effect in 1809.

Charles Metcalfe served as British resident at **Delhi** from 1811 to 1819. The **Mughal** Emperor was nominally sovereign but was little more than a British pensioner by this time. Metcalfe's achievements lay in establishing an enlightened administration ahead of its time in

Europe or India. There were no executions or floggings, prisoners were trained in a trade, and settlement of land revenue was made directly with the cultivators. Metcalfe was later honored by the independent Government of India, which made Metcalfe House in Delhi the training school for the new generation of Indian civil servants.

Metcalfe went to the court of the Nizam of **Hyderabad** as British resident in 1820, but his attempts to reform a corrupt administration indebted to a British trading house were frustrated. He served as Governor of **Agra** and was a member of the Governor General's Council from 1827 to 1834. As acting governor general 1835–1836 he abolished restriction on the **press** in India, thereby antagonizing the Company's directors in London. Although they appointed him lieutenant governor of the then North West Provinces — present-day **Uttar Pradesh** — in 1836, two years later they overruled recommendations from Calcutta that Charles Metcalfe become the governor general on grounds that he did not belong to the peerage. Metcalfe resigned and went to live in Canada and Jamaica. Long a baronet, he was made a baron in 1845.

MITRA, RAJENDRALAL (1822–1891). A pioneer in the study of Indology, Mitra was born to a cultivated family in **Calcutta** and received a sound general education. He was appointed Assistant Secretary and Librarian of the **Asiatic Society** in 1846 where he learned the practicalities of antiquarian research and nurtured his scholastic leanings. He was the director of a school from 1856 to 1880 but remained active with the Asiatic Society, becoming president in 1885.

Mitra's scholarly output was large and included descriptive catalogues of manuscripts and antiquities, annotated texts from the **Vedas** and **Upanishads** with his learned commentaries on them, as well as renderings of **Buddhist** texts and the Yoga Sutras of **Patanjali**. Mitra made outstanding contributions to the study of early Indian architecture, a subject still in its infancy during the 19th century. He also wrote books and articles in Bengali and edited a monthly journal for public education.

MIZORAM. A small hill state of the Indian Union, Mizoram occupies about 21,000 square kilometers and is inhabited by less than one million people belonging to various highland tribes, especially the Mizo and the Lushai. Their **languages** do not have a written script, but 81% of the people are literate in English. **Christian** missionaries have been active among them for several decades.

Mizoram is strategically situated in the northeast frontier zone bordering **Bangladesh** and **Burma**. Heavily forested and lightly administered as part of **Assam** until 1972 and then as a Union Territory, it was subject to insurrections of one sort or another until it was granted statehood in 1987. The town of Aizawl is the state capital. Hydroelectric power, tea growing, and fruit processing have been introduced to the state recently to supplement tourism as a source of revenue.

MOHENJO-DARO. *See* HARAPPAN CULTURE.

MONTAGU DECLARATION (1917). During **World War I**, the British War Cabinet discussed postwar constitutional changes in India in the light of India's significant contribution to the war effort as well as pressure from the **Home Rule League** and Indian nationalists to make a political gesture. The Secretary of State for India, Edwin Samuel Montagu, made an announcement in the House of Commons on August 20, 1917, that was taken as seriously by Indians as the Balfour Declaration of about the same time was taken by European Jews. Montagu said, in part:

The policy of His Majesty's Government, with which the Government of India are in complete accord, is that of the increasing association of Indians in every branch of the administration and the gradual development of self-governing institutions, with a view to the progressive realization of responsible government in India as an integral part of the British Empire.

The Montagu declaration was a skillfully worded statement, replacing the term "self-government" in Montagu's first draft with "responsible government," and leaving decisions on appropriate "successive stages" for "progressive realisation" entirely in British hands. Nevertheless, by the second decade of the 20th century the term "responsible government" was considered in British constitutional practice to mean accountability of the executive branch of government to the representatives of the people seated in the legislature. Well versed in law as they were, leaders of the **Indian National Congress** welcomed the

Montagu Declaration and looked forward to postwar fulfillment of its implicit promise. They were to be disappointed.

MONTAGU–CHELMSFORD REFORMS (often contracted to MONTFORD). Officially the Government of India Act 1919, cosponsored by Secretary of State for India, Edwin Montagu, and the Viceroy, Lord Chelmsford, constitutional reforms were enacted in partial fulfillment of the **Montagu Declaration** of 1917 and were put into effect in 1921.

The Montford reforms were only a halfway house to "responsible government," and were hard to implement. Their distinctive feature was "**dyarchy**" in provincial government. Certain subjects such as local government, agriculture, and education were "transferred" to Indian ministers who were answerable to provincial legislatures, but more important subjects such as revenue, police, and famine relief were "reserved" for the governor's discretion. Governors retained enormous discretionary powers and could overrule ministers, especially on allocation of funds. Governors were enjoined to keep in mind "training" Indians for self-government, in tutelage. . . . Members were added to provincial legislative councils, but they were to be elected on the basis of community and special interests, not from territorial constituencies of uniform size and population. Religious minorities were given weighted representation. The franchise was extended to women, but property and other qualifications were limited to the total electorate, to less than 3% of the total adult population of British India.

Equally important provisions of the Montford reforms addressed the relationship between His Majesty's Government in Whitehall and the Government of India in **New Delhi**. The viceroy-cum-governor general of India remained answerable to the British Crown in Parliament and retained his extensive powers over his own and provincial governments. Although the viceroy was not responsible to the Imperial Legislative Council in New Delhi, this body was enlarged in size and function. There was some devolution of authority from Whitehall, with India getting fiscal autonomy and representation in the League of Nations. In short, some changes were initiated, but they were not profound ones. A review inquiry was scheduled for 1929.

Indian reaction to the Montford reforms was mixed and often confused. The nationalist mainstream led by **Mahatma Gandhi** and the

Indian National Congress was bitterly disappointed and launched a **Non-Cooperation Movement** against implementation. Many Indians active in public life, however, welcomed the reforms as an initial step to be mastered and used. Opinions differ too on the experience of 15 years of attempting to work "dyarchy." Many consider dyarchy to have diverted Indian political development along a mistaken path; some think the experiment was useful, others say that it worked badly and served to exclude potentially able leaders. And some consider the Montford Reforms to have been a deliberate stepping back by the British from their declared intent.

Certainly, had "responsible government"—with a popularly elected Indian legislature controlling the executive—been introduced in 1921 as a decisive step toward self-government, the subsequent history of India could have been rather different. *See also* MONTAGU DECLARATION.

MOOKERJI, ASUTOSH (1864–1924). A great educator and jurist of simple living and advanced thinking, Mookerji was born to a middle class **brahman** family in **Calcutta** and showed academic brilliance as a student. As an academic on the faculty of the University of Calcutta from 1889 to 1924 and its vice chancellor on two occasions, 1906–1914 and 1921–1923, Asutosh Mookerji helped give that institution its high reputation for intellectual purpose and national character. He transformed it from an examining body to a teaching university and introduced modern Indian **languages** to the curriculum for the first time in 1922. Although he preferred to stay out of politics, he resisted efforts by the British authorities to curb the autonomy of the university and resigned in 1923 with a famous speech on "freedom first, freedom second, freedom always."

Asutosh Mookerji was also a judge on the Calcutta High Court from 1899 to 1924. He received many honors in his life, including a knighthood in 1911.

MOPLAH or MAPPILLA REVOLTS. The Moplahs are a Muslim community of Malabar composed of descendants of Arab settlers and early converts to **Islam** among Malayali-speaking people. In the early 20th century most of them were engaged in small agriculture, as petty traders, or as landless laborers influenced by local religious leaders. Religion had served to crystallize anti-landlord and anti-foreign feelings of the Moplahs since the time of **Portuguese** attempts to force their conversion to **Christianity** in the 15th century. British rule in Malabar after 1792 fortified the power of high caste **Hindu** landlords (*jenmis*) and moneylenders, creating agrarian discontent among Muslims and Hindus and provoking a series of small Moplah revolts in the 19th century—nearly 30 between 1836 and 1896.

The most serious Moplah revolt occurred in 1921. A tenants' rights agitation begun in 1916 was taken up by the **Khilafet Movement** and was further stimulated by the **Non-Cooperation Movement** initiated by the **Indian National Congress** in 1920. The arrest of Congress and Khilafet leaders left the field open for radicals preaching an egalitarian or millenarian ideology. A police raid on a mosque in August 1921 sparked a major rebellion in southern Malabar which acquired communal overtones when about 600 Hindus were killed and rumors spread of forced conversions to Islam.

The British authorities used police, army, and artillery to regain control by the end of the year, killing 2,337 and taking 45,404 prisoner. Famine was widespread in the following year. Tenancy reform providing some relief to the Moplahs began only in the 1930s.

MORLEY–MINTO REFORMS (1909). The Government of India Act of 1909, sponsored by Secretary of State for India John Morley and Governor General Gilbert Elliot, fourth Earl of Minto, is popularly known by the term Morley Minto Reforms. Its chief provisions were as follows. Legislative councils in the provinces of British India were enlarged with the addition of non-official members, but officials remained in a majority on the Governor General's Council. The number of elected relative to nominated members was increased, but the franchise was extremely limited and separate electorates were created for landlords, chambers of commerce, and Muslims. Legislative councils were permitted for the first time to discuss financial matters although no resolutions passed by them were binding on the governments, and important subjects such as defense, foreign affairs, and **Princely States** remained on the prohibited list. Indians were appointed to executive councils for the first time, one to the Governor General's Council and two to the Council of the Secretary of State for India in London.

The reforms were the product of a reformist Liberal Party in Britain and received the support of **Gopal Krishna Gokhale**, then leader of the **Indian National Congress**. The reforms did not widen representation; they contained no hint of "responsible government" in the parliamentary sense of that term much less of future self-government; and they introduced what proved to be the controversial and divisive measure of separate communal electorates. Moreover, the administration of Lord Minto used draconian measures to suppress the growing tide of Indian nationalist activity. Nevertheless, the Morley–Minto Reforms are regarded as a constitutional landmark heralding more substantial advances in the decades to come.

MOUNTBATTEN, LORD LOUIS (1900–1979). A great-grandson of Queen Victoria and the first Earl Mountbatten of Burma, Mountbatten's first visit to India was in 1921 when he accompanied the Prince of Wales on a tour. He had a distinguished career in the Royal Navy before and after his 15-month term of office in India in 1947–1948.

Mountbatten succeeded **Lord Wavell** as viceroy in March 1947 with enhanced powers to implement decisions taken in London by the Labour Party government. The British were no longer able or willing to expend the degree of force required to hold India against the will of its people. It was Mountbatten's task to transfer power to Indian hands, by partition if necessary, salvaging as much as possible for British interests and prestige in future relations with the new Dominion. He performed his duties with a skill and charm that won him and his wife Edwina friends and admirers in India. Not the least of these was **Jawaharlal Nehru**, who invited Mountbatten to stay on as the first governor general of independent India, handing over to **C. Rajagopalachari** in June 1948. (No corresponding invitation was forthcoming from **Mohammed Ali Jinnah**, to Mountbatten's often-expressed regret.)

Fulsome praise of Mountbatten in popular and historical literature has been accompanied by controversy before and after his assassination by members of the Irish Republican Army in 1979. In particular, he is criticized for pushing the "Mountbatten Plan" of June 3, 1947. This called for British withdrawal from India at a pace that shipped British troops home at the very time when the **Punjab** and **Bengal** were aflame with riot and massacre. Mountbatten's plan also called for **Partition** of British India and delayed announcing new boundary lines between **Pakistan** and India until the day *after* independence. Moreover, Mountbatten was equivocal on the subject of **Princely States** and left the status of **Kashmir** and **Hyderabad** unresolved.

MUGHAL EMPIRE (1526–1858, rapid decline after 1739). Babur founded the Mughal Empire by supplanting the **Lodi** dynasty in **Delhi** and defeating a powerful **Rajput** confederacy led by Rana Sangha. Except for a brief interregnum under **Sher Shah Sur**, Babur's lineal descendants ruled in India for 300 years. The area they ruled initially expanded—eastwards from Kabul in present-day Afghanistan through the Indo–Gangetic plains to **Assam** and **Bengal** and southwards from **Kashmir** to first the Godaveri and then the **Kaveri** rivers—and later contracted under the onslaught of invasions, independent governors, and advances made by the **Marathas**, the **Sikhs**, and the **East India Company**. Only Delhi was left to **Bahadur Shah II** before the British deposed and exiled him in 1858.

The achievements of the Mughal dynasty are credited to the first six emperors—Babur, Humayun, **Akbar**, Jehangir, **Shah Jahan**, and **Aurangzeb**—who shared two traits in very six different personalities. One was the charm to attract able men to their service, and the other was determination to stamp out rebellion. These six are known as the Great Mughals; they made the very word mughal/mogor/moghol synonymous with splendor. The later emperors were less gifted and became dependent on others, never wholly reliable, in the face of mounting challenges from within and without the empire

The Mughal Empire is comparable to contemporary empires in Persia under the Safavids, in Turkey under the Ottomans, and in China under the Ming and Qing Dynasties. The political unification of the Indian subcontinent and the preservation of relative peace for more than a hundred years certainly stimulated commerce as well as agriculture and horticulture. Indian textiles and high value manufactured items flowed into world trade. An impressive variety of foodgrain and cash crops was grown in every district, and a diversity of fruits, especially mangos, were cultivated or introduced in Mughal times. Stable Mughal rule succeeding the more turbulent **Delhi Sultanate** produced a composite culture in which Indian and Persian,

Hindu and **Islamic** elements mixed and flowered in art and architecture, dance and **music**, literature and philosophy, cuisine, dress, court manners, customs, **language**, and popular religion. One legacy of that culture was the Urdu language, forged in the multi-ethnic, polyglot, mobile imperial camp and known from the 18th century to the present day as a language of poetry and refinement in northern India and the **Deccan**.

Primary written sources for the Mughal period are more plentiful than for any earlier period in Indian history. They include detailed court chronicles and administrative records, such as those maintained by **Abu'l Fazl** during the reign of Akbar, records kept at the courts of allied Rajput Princes, account books maintained by wealthy merchants and shipwrights, frequently Hindu or **Parsi**, and the journals of many European ambassadors, traders, adventurers, and travelers such as the Frenchman Francois Bernier. A fairly complete picture can be drawn from these accounts. Akbar established a highly centralized system of administration over an empire divided into *subas* or provinces, further divided into *sarkars* and *parganas* or districts, which his successors retained. He established a **mansabdari system** of administration by which official functions in each unit were divided and non-hereditary; all higher officials were appointed by the emperor and paid directly by the imperial treasury in cash or by *jagir* (see Glossary) or transferable revenue assignments, according to their mansab or rank. A high (probably 70) percentage of the highest ranks were filled by men who had come into India in the 16th century or later and also by Indian Muslims, Rajputs, and a few other Hindus such as **Todar Mal**. The system encouraged individual prowess but also personal rivalries, conspicuous consumption and hoarding, rather than teamwork, saving, and investment.

Land revenue was the main source of imperial income, and various methods of assessment and collection were employed, depending on the quality of the land, the amount of rainfall, local customs, and the willingness of the peasants to cultivate. Abandonment of arable land was a serious problem of the times. Despite injunctions to officials to safeguard the welfare of the cultivator, and recorded expenditures on irrigation canals and wells, written accounts suggest that share demands made on agricultural produce by several levels of intermediaries left most peasants living at subsistence level, with little or no investment made to enhance productivity of the land. Crafts and industries flourished in the Mughal period with imperial *karkhanas*, or factories, taking a lead in production and many nobles, male and female, engaged in commerce. The skill of the Indian artisan was legendary, and his output in the form of architectural masterpieces such as the **Taj Mahal** or fine woolen shawls or jewelry or paintings remain unequalled in beauty. But the tools of craftsmen remained rudimentary and their remuneration low. In the many cities of 17th century India, as in the countryside, there were striking disparities between rich and poor. The substantial number of people with incomes in the middle range usually chose to conceal that fact. Present-day studies of Mughal agriculture, commerce, industry, technology, and trade raise crucial questions of Indian political economy in the early modern period. What factors inhibited technological progress? What suppressed incipient capitalist development? Several scholastic treatises attempt to answer these questions by looking at Mughal institutions and practice.

Another topic of lively interest in the present day—when the liberal, secular principles of the **Indian Constitution** are under pressure from religious militants of various sects—is the religious policy followed by the Mughals. They constructed a semi-divine monarchy to rule over subjects of different faiths but were inconsistent in their treatment of different faiths. Akbar's policy of visible tolerance of non-Muslims (the vast majority) and his encouragement of theological debate established a tradition that was carried forward by some, such as Prince Dara Shikoh, but was disputed by others, especially orthodox Sunni (see Glossary) Muslim clerics and nobles. Their point of view found expression in Aurangzeb. He demolished the Visveswara temple at **Banaras** and the Keshava temple at Mathura and replaced them with mosques; the **Vishva Hindu Parishad** Hindu right wing pledged to reverse those and similar actions in the 1990s. In 1679, Aurangzeb also re-imposed the *jiziya* (see Glossary) tax that had been abolished by Akbar. Thereafter, it is claimed, the alienation and rebellion of certain Rajput Princes, as well as the revolts of **Jats**, Satnamis, **Sikhs**, and **Marathas**, took on a religious flavor. By the end of the 17th century, the Mughal state was financially and militarily crippled as a consequence of waging war for decades in the Deccan against Maratha guerilla techniques and stamping out rebellions in the north as well. It was not able to repel the looting raids of **Nadir Shah** in 1739 or **Ahmad Shah Abdali** in 1761 from the northwest and sank into a crepuscule of faded elegance.

MUNDA. The name has been given to a group of Austro–Asiatic **languages** spoken by more than six million people spread through central India and the Chota Nagpur plateau area of eastern India. Three numbers (singular, dual, and plural), two gender classes (animate and inanimate) for nouns, and the use of either suffixes or auxiliaries for indicating verb tenses and forms characterize the Munda languages. Lacking as they do a known script, connections between Munda languages and **Harappan**, **Sanskritic**, or **Dravidian** languages are conjectural.

The origin and history of the Munda people is not documented. It is possible that they were both indigenous to the Indian subcontinent and widespread over it. The areas they inhabit at present are relatively inaccessible and are peripheral to the centers of classical Indian civilization. No marked physical differences distinguish them from neighboring groups of people in the highly heterogeneous population of India. Although the Munda are usually classified as **Adivasi** and many groups have preserved distinctive tribal customs, values, and sense of identity, their interactions with neighboring **Hindu** groups— classified by **caste**—are often intimate and very long standing.

Among the Munda peoples, the **Santal** rank high in number and importance. The British authorities ruthlessly suppressed the Santal uprisings of 1855 and 1856 against systematic economic exploitation by traders, moneylenders, and agents of the **East India Company**. A hundred years later, similar resentments against economic exploitation grew into a demand for a state of their own, which was ultimately won in 2000. *See also* **CHHATISGARH** and **JHARKAND**.

MURTHY, NARAYANA (1948–). Murthy is the founder chairman and was for long the chief executive officer of **Infosys Technologies Limited**. Established in 1981 with a capital investment of US $250, this software engineering firm became the first Indian company to list its shares on the New York Stock Exchange (1998) and is presently valued at $24 billion with an unprecedented, and perhaps unexpected, global reach of services.

Narayana Murthy is a brilliant and far-sighted man who lives very modestly by a code of ethics, transparency, and hard work that could be called "traditional" to his native **Karnataka**. But he is also seen as an intensely "modern" role model throughout Indian industry. He built a company of highly qualified people and gave them a full share in the fortunes of the firm. The informal, egalitarian, and well-tended campus-like atmosphere of Infosys headquarters at **Bangalore** is conducive to debate and exchange of ideas. This is combined with a very conservative financial structure and personal investment in upgrading human capital, so that outstanding persons have been attracted to Infosys and have stayed there despite lucrative offers from multinational competitors, and all have genuine affection for Naryana Murthy. His brainchild was born of his perception of the enormous price differential between the salaries of software engineers in India and those in the United States and Europe. He offered a skilled workforce in the area of software development technology and software services, created an Offshore Software Development Centre at Bangalore, opened offices abroad, built up an infrastructure of skills, and followed an aggressive marketing strategy. The ISO 9001 marking, the Carnegie Mellon University Software Engineering Institute Capability Maturity Model Level 4, and other benchmarks provide global recognition for the high standards of his company in business ethics and the quality of services provided.

Naryana Murthy faces the challenges of going global, including intense competition in a time of rising costs, overcoming stereotyped Western images of Indian products being low cost and sub-standard, as well as protectionist measures against outsourcing. He is trying to create an international brand name of high standard as an employer and as a supplier of knowledge-based services. His personal values of honesty, courtesy, and fairness infuse his company and are expressed also in his admiration for **J. R. D. Tata**. It is possible that Naryana Murthy and Infosys will be to India of the 21st century what Tatas was in the 20th.

MUSIC. The Indian musical tradition encompasses the history of the subcontinent. Artifacts from the **Indus Valley Civilization** depict wind, string, and percussion instruments. The chants of the **Vedas** were set to rhythmic melodies, collectively known as *samagana*, believed to be the fount of all Indian classical music. Central to it is the concept of *Nada-Brahma*, or Sound is God. Music is a recognized path of self-realization and approach to God.

Music is an important element in sacred ritual, individual devotion, drama, rites of passage, festivals, and popular religion, as well as nonsectarian entertainment in India. It draws on written texts as sources, especially the *Naradishiksha* and *Natyashastra* of the first two centuries CE, and on *deshi*, or country, folk, and tribal sources, including those recorded by Matanga in the fifth century. In the 12th and 13th centuries the central musical tradition of India divided into two major streams, the Karnatic School of south India and the Hindustani school of north India. The former (Karnatic) drew on **Tamil** and Telugu literary and **Hindu** devotional traditions; it was developed in *sampradayas*, or schools, along regular, organized, and precise lines. The latter (Hindustani) drew additionally on Persian influences, the innovations of **Amir Khusru**, the demands of **Mughal** and other courts, and the requirements of **Hindu**, **Sikh**, and **Sufi** devotional traditions. Both Muslim and Hindu artists enriched the Hindustani tradition, and different *gharanas* or lineages cultivated particular repertoires and performance styles. The Hindustani tradition extends to present-day **Bangladesh** and **Pakistan** and musical meets are important events in people-to-people contacts.

Master musicians of the Karnatic and Hindustani schools in the 20th century are learning from each other as they again explore their common heritage. Classical training frequently underpins popular music and dance throughout the subcontinent, including that used in India's large **film industry**.

Indian classical music uses melody and rhythm but has no system comparable to the Western tradition of harmony and counterpoint. The Indian scale consists of seven notes, but in addition to the 12 semitones used in the Western classical tradition, 22 microtones may be sung, played, and notated, producing the characteristic quality of Indian music. The heart of musical theory and practice is the *Raga*, a definite yet subtle melodic arrangement established by tradition or by a master artist such as Tan Sen of the 16th century or an occasional *ustad* or master in the 20th century. The *Raga* in performance becomes the aesthetic projection of an artist's inner spirit through his/her dwelling on, expanding, elaborating, and embellishing its particular mood. There are 72 primary or parent *Ragas* in the Karnatic tradition and 10 in the Hindustani tradition. Each one is associated with one of nine basic moods or sentiments: *shringara* or romantic, *hasya* or comic, *karuna* or longing, *raudra* or anger, *veera* or heroism, *bhayanaka* or fright, *vibhatsa* or disgust, *adhbhuta* or wonderment, and *shanta* or peace and tranquility. Association of specific *Ragas* with particular seasons of the year or times of the day or night naturally follow, as does the anthropomorphic depiction of *Ragas* and *Raginis* (the feminine form) in painting or sculpture.

Tala is the essential element of rhythm and time and denotes an organized rhythmic cycle composed of various units. One rhythmic cycle may be composed of three beats up to 108 beats, though 15 to 20 beats are used most frequently. There are three main speeds but many more combinations. *Talas*, like *Ragas*, have their own particularities. In short, Indian music has developed an extremely complex system of rhythm and a variety of drum instruments to supply it, both in the Karnatic and the Hindustani traditions. Drums may be played in accompaniment to voice or other instruments, as well as in solo performance; drums are an important element in dance and dance drama.

Indian classical music was traditionally taught in a *guru-shishya*, or teacher–disciple, system stressing thorough grounding, years of discipline and a spiritual attitude of humility and devotion. It remains the preferred pedagogic method and is used by Indian masters such as **Ali Akbar Khan** and **Ravi Shankar** even in the West. Larger, less personalized music and dance schools are also appearing in present-day India. Prime place was given to the human voice, although many kinds of wind, string, and percussion instruments were developed over the centuries. India's cultural revival in modern times has also reinvigorated its tradition of music and dance.

MUSLIMS. See Islam.

MUSLIM LEAGUE, ALL INDIA. The **Aga Khan** and Nawab Viqar-ul-Mulk, with British encouragement, formed the Muslim League as a **political party** specifically for Muslims on December 31, 1906. Its three objectives were listed as promoting loyalty to the British government, protecting and advancing the political interests of Indian Muslims, and preventing feelings of hostility among them toward other communities.

Formation of the Muslim League was a natural step in a process that had started in late-19th-century **Bengal** among some Muslims who attempted to reverse a sharp downward trend toward decadence and oblivion in India by forming associations and educating their sons in the English language. A similar process had begun more than half a century earlier among certain classes of **Hindus** and had met with success in many fields. In another sense, the launching of a political organization was a step away from the direction laid down by the premier Muslim modernizer, **Sir Syed Ahmed Khan**, that Indian Muslims should abjure politics and shun the **Indian National Congress** as inherently "seditious." The fact that a small but significant number of educated Muslims, including the brilliant lawyer **Mohammed Ali Jinnah**, had already joined Congress, and 50 Muslims participated in the annual Congress session of 1905, provided an immediate incentive for creating a separate Muslim League. Another incentive for politically aware Muslims was their fear of being numerically swamped and politically outmaneuvered by Hindus in any representative institutions introduced by long-awaited and projected constitutional reforms, especially in the politically active and key provinces of **Bombay** and United Provinces (present-day **Uttar Pradesh**), where Muslims were in a minority.

Thus, a deputation of Muslims led by the Aga Khan petitioned the viceroy, Lord Minto, in October 1906 that in any future constitutional arrangements Muslims should receive representation commensurate with their historical and political importance rather than their numbers, and that Muslims should be elected by Muslims alone. Such a denial of individual enfranchisement and acceptance of communal representation was written into the **Morley–Minto Reforms** for many reasons, including British imperial interests in the Middle East and Minto's wish to keep ambitious Muslims out of what he called "the ranks of seditious opposition" at a time when protests against the **partition of Bengal** were mounting. The issue of communal electorates was to become a major obstacle to political cooperation among different groups of Indians, especially the Muslim League and Congress, in the decades that followed.

The Muslim League was financed for some years mainly by annual grants from the Raja of Mahmudabad, and landed aristocrats from the **Ganges** valley provided much of its membership. Muslims of the professional classes who joined were often members of Congress as well, and committees of the two organizations together framed a scheme of constitutional reforms toward self-government in the **Lucknow Pact** of 1916. The Muslim League remained languid for the following decade with a total membership of 1,330 in 1927. It participated in the All-Parties Conference held from 1927 to 1928 to review the working of the **Montagu-Chelmsford Reforms** and was prepared to give up separate electorates in return for Congress concessions on other subjects; but it received no satisfaction in the final version of the **Nehru Report** that was issued after the review in 1928. By then, the Muslim League was articulating Muslim political interests in terms of a continued British presence, provincial autonomy, and a weak central government, while Congress pressed for a strong center with powers progressively transferred from the British to Indians. This basic difference of approach to the future constitutional structure of an independent India was another major obstacle to Congress–League cooperation in the following decades.

In December 1930, **Muhammad Iqbal**, as president of the Muslim League, called for the creation of a "Muslim India . . . within the body politic of India" in the northwestern provinces of the subcontinent. Iqbal also urged Jinnah to return from England and take over leadership of the League. Jinnah revived the lethargic body by vigorous opposition to the federal scheme posited in the **Government of India Act** of 1935, and thereafter the fortunes of the League were fused with his ambitions and career. According to Ayesha Jalal, a reputed scholar from **Pakistan**, Jinnah aimed to make the Muslim League—and himself—the "sole spokesman" for all the Muslims of India but found himself initially unwelcome in provinces with the largest concentration of Muslims: Bengal, **North West Frontier Province**, and **Punjab**. The Muslim League fared badly in the 1937 elections held on the basis of an enlarged franchise; contesting only Muslim seats, it won one out of 86 in Punjab, three out of 33 in Sind, 39 out of 117 in Bombay, 20 out of 29 in Bengal, 27 out of 64 in the UP, ten out of 28 in **Madras**, and nine out of 34 in **Assam**. Congress did much better than expected, claimed to represent all Indians, initiated a "mass contact" program to increase Muslim membership, and declined to include the League as partner in the provincial government of the UP.

Jinnah set out to rebuild the Muslim League as a mass party. Membership was thrown open with low fees and appeals issued saying, "if you are a Muslim, come join the Muslim League." The Congress was portrayed as a "Hindu" party and was accused of committing atrocities against Muslims in provinces with Congress governments. The League Council was enlarged, its powers were concentrated, and attention was focused on winning support from the Muslim members of Unionist governments in Bengal and Punjab. The British found in Jinnah the best guarantee against a united political opposition in India and turned to the Muslim League for cooperation when the Congress ministries resigned in protest against **Lord Linlithgow**'s declaration of war against Germany without consulting them. At its Lahore session of March 1940, the Muslim League passed a somewhat ambiguously worded resolution referring to the Muslims as a "nation" and demanding that "areas in which Muslims are numerically in a majority . . . shall be autonomous and sovereign." Newspapers promptly dubbed this the "Pakistan Resolution," and it is so considered today by historians who admit, however, that it may have been a bargaining counter to gain the League parity with Congress in the central government of a united India.

Whatever Jinnah's motives might have been, he gained in status by being treated on a par with **Mahatma Gandhi** in negotiations between 1942 and 1947 on the transfer of power from British to Indian hands. The Muslim League reaped success from his vigorous campaign in the elections of 1945 and 1946 by winning all of the Muslim seats in the central Legislative Assembly, 75 out of 175 in Punjab,126 out of 250 in Bengal, and 75% of the total Muslim vote as compared to the mere 4.4% gained in 1937. The Muslim League accepted the **Cabinet Mission** proposals for a three-tier grouping of provinces with a weak center on June 6, 1946, but went a step further in July by reiterating its goal of a separate state and resolving "Direct Action" unless it was given parity with Congress. Direct Action Day on August 16, 1946, unleashed uncontrolled forces of communal violence in **Calcutta**, which resulted in 4,000 dead and 15,000 injured.

The Muslim League joined the newly formed interim government in **New Delhi** in October 1946, although it did not get the portfolios it wanted, but it stayed out of the **Constituent Assembly** convened in February 1947. Having once loosed the slogan of "**Islam** in danger" (from Hindu domination after Indian independence), the Muslim League found no way of turning back from **Partition**, even had it wished to do so. It ceased to exist as a national political party in India after independence and did not last long as a ruling party in Pakistan. The Muslim League is recognized as a state party in **Kerala** where it has occasionally participated in coalition governments.

MUTINY OF 1857. *See* UPRISING OF 1857.

MYANMAR. See BURMA.

MYSORE. At present a district and city in the state of **Karnataka**, Mysore was formerly a **Princely State** of premier rank and importance in southern India. Founded by a feudatory of **Vijayanagar** at the end of the 14th century, Mysore was ruled throughout by the same Wadiyar family to the time of its accession to the Indian Union in August 1947, except for the periods 1765–1799 and 1831–1881.

As the Vijayanagar Empire declined and collapsed, Mysore became one of the successor states and engaged in intermittent conflict with its neighbors Bijapur and **Madurai** over territory. Raja Wadiyar established his capital as Seringapatnam on the **Kaveri** River in 1617. His tolerant and financially effective administration was conducive to prosperity, the arts, and literature. Raja Chikkadevaraja Wadiyar enhanced his treasury, acquired **Bangalore**, standardized weights and measures, and sent an embassy to the court of the **Mughal Emperor Aurangzeb** in 1700. Subsequent **Maratha** invasions and frequent warfare fed the power and ambition of a commanding general, **Haidar Ali**, who usurped the throne in 1757. He and his son **Tipu Sultan** enlarged Mysore's territorial domains but had to face the separate and then combined hostility of the Nizam of **Hyderabad**, the Marathas, and the **East India Company**. Tipu Sultan was killed in the third Anglo–Mysore War in 1799, and Mysore passed under British rule.

The British initially appointed five commissioners to administer Mysore. They conciliated the Nizam and the Marathas with some territory in the north, annexed some lands in the south to **Madras** Presidency, restored the young Krishna Raja Wadiyar III to the throne, and stationed a military force in Mysore at his expense. The British took over direct administration in 1831, partly for financial reasons, but left most institutions and administrators in place. Agitation for the restoration of the Wadiyars mounted after Queen Victoria's Proclamation of 1858 offering friendship to the Indian princes, and there was an important debate on the subject in the British Parliament in 1866 and 1867. The adopted heir, Chamarajendra Wadiyar, was installed with a regent in 1868 and was given full ceremonial powers at the age of 18 in 1881; in all substantive matters Mysore was subordinate to the viceroy, and administration was in the hands of a Dewan (see Glossary).

Mysore gained the reputation of being one of the best-administered princely states. Its educational system was progressive and effective. Dewan **Visvesvaraya** (1912–1918) introduced hydroelectric power, new industries, and banks; Dewan **Mirza Ismail** (1926–1941) brought the steel, paper, cement, glass, and aircraft industries to Mysore, expanded educational institutions, and further beautified Bangalore. He also encouraged village handicrafts and local self-government. Mysore was the first princely state to establish a representative assembly, allow the **Indian National Congress** to function in its domain, and send representatives to the **Constituent Assembly**.

Although there was some talk in 1947 that the then Dewan was advising the maharajah to hold out for independence after the lapse of **paramountcy**, Mysore's accession to the Indian Union was smoothly executed in August of that year. Mysore became an eponymous state with the same territory in 1949. When states were reorganized on the basis of **language** in the late 1950s, however, territorial and administrative changes made Mysore part of, but not coterminous with, Karnataka.

– N –

NADIR SHAH (d. 1747). Born to an obscure family in Khorasan, eastern Iran, Nadir Shah supported a restoration of Safavid rule in Iran but then deposed the ruler he had helped and declared himself Shah in 1736. He stormed through Kandahar and Ghazni in Afghanistan, defeated the **Mughal** governor of Kabul in 1738, and turned toward the legendary wealth of the Indo-Gangetic plain in India.

The Mughal governor of the **Punjab** purchased his own life from Nadir Shah who proceeded to **Delhi**, defeating the imperial army at

Karnal. The incompetent Mughal Emperor Muhammad Shah attempted to buy peace with courteous meetings, a joint ceremonial entrance into Delhi, and treasure, all of which Nadir Shah accepted. His occupation turned into a slaughter of the inhabitants of Delhi and an orgy of plunder and rape in the spring of 1739, luridly described in contemporary accounts. Nadir Shah and his men returned home laden with treasure—including the famous Peacock Throne and **Koh-i-Nur** diamond. They in turn were harassed by bands of armed **Sikhs** who relieved them of some of the booty. Nadir Shah continued his military campaigns in central Asia until Muhammad Khan Qajar assassinated him in 1747 and went on to rule Iran.

Nadir Shah's five-month stay in India disrupted the administration of the Punjab, depleted the imperial treasury, and impoverished the inhabitants of Delhi and surrounding areas. Sikh bands became "protectors" in the Punjab; **Marathas** became overlords in much of the subcontinent. The already reduced Mughal Empire was left bleeding, prostrate, and vulnerable to external aggression and internal collapse.

NAGALAND. A state of 16,579 square kilometers with a population of less than two million in northeast India, bordering on **Burma**, Nagaland was created in 1963 from territory in **Assam** inhabited by the Naga tribes. The Naga tribes of India and Burma had a distinctive culture and way of life that did not lend themselves easily to definite state boundaries, bureaucratic administration, or a monetary economy. Indirect administration of the area by the British had left their tribal traditions more or less intact, despite conversion of many to **Christianity** by Baptist missionaries.

Efforts by independent India to control its border areas met with hostility from some Nagas led by A. E. Phizo, apparently supported by missionary networks in Britain and America. A Naga National Council was formed to appeal to the United Nations, organize a parallel administration, and set up a government-in-exile in London. Indian military forces were deployed in 1956 to put down a serious rebellion, which they did with time and effort. Meanwhile, a political solution within the Indian Union was sought by the Naga leadership represented in the Naga People's Convention as well as by distinguished individuals including **J. P. Narayan** and **Venrier Elwin**. The most satisfactory solution was found in administrative separation from Assam and Naga statehood. Insurgency erupted from time to time but in controllable forms and probably due to the economic backwardness of the state. Meanwhile, many Nagas entered the mainstream of Indian life.

Agriculture is the principal occupation in Nagaland, with sericulture and handicrafts as cottage industries. Some modern industries have been introduced recently, along with small-scale power and irrigation projects. New efforts are being made to develop the northeastern states, helped by the normalization of relations between India and Myanmar since the mid-1990s. Kohima is the capital of Nagaland and is the site of a large cemetery for casualties of the city in **World War II**.

NAICKER, E. V. RAMASWAMI (1879–1973). Also known as Periyar or "Great Sage," Naicker was born to an artisan family of pious disposition and comfortable means in Erode, South India. He married young but became a religious mendicant soon after. His faith as a **Hindu** was shaken by what he witnessed of popular religion in his travels through India. He returned home a virtual iconoclast, a vigorous critic of **brahman** domination, image worship, **caste** hierarchy, and suppression of **women**; he openly advocated widow remarriage, prohibition of alcohol, and eradication of **untouchability**.

Naicker joined the **Indian National Congress** and nearly became President of the Madras Congress Committee in 1922. In 1925, he organized a "Self-Respect Movement" for **Dravidian** upliftment, ridiculing Hindu laws—especially those of **Manu**—rituals, and institutions, as "inhuman" instruments of brahmanic, male, and "**Aryan**" exploitation in an unjust social system. He propagated his views through **Tamil** journals that he founded. In 1937, when **C. Rajagopalachari**'s Congress government made the Hindi **language** a compulsory subject in schools, Naicker led a vigorous black flag protest against the "insult" to Tamil culture and had the regulation changed. Meanwhile, he had visited the Soviet Union, joined the **Justice Party**, and formulated a 14-point program of mass revolution. In 1939 he began demanding a separate state for the Tamil, Telegu, Kannada, and Malayalam-speaking peoples of South India, that is, for an independent caste-less federation of Dravidasthan; he supported the **Muslim League**'s demand for **Pakistan** but received no reciprocal support from **Mohammad Ali Jinnah**.

In 1944, Naicker reorganized the fading Justice Party as the Dravida Kazhagam; as a movement of social change and cultural revivification it exerted mass appeal among Tamils. But Naicker's disrespect for the flag and **Constitution** of independent India, his marriage at age 72 to a girl of 28, and his authoritarian style of party leadership diluted his popularity. His ablest followers left him to form the **Dravida Munnetra Kazhagam** in 1949, which gained most of his objectives within the Indian Union. Naicker continued his campaign against religious superstition, social inequality, and political domination for the rest of his life, offending those who were in power. He is generally considered one of the most dynamic and colorful political leaders of modern India.

NAIDU, CHANDRA BABU. *See* TELUGU DESHAM PARTY.

NAIDU, SAROJINI (1879–1949). Sarojini was born to remarkable **brahman** parents in **Hyderabad** where her father had helped establish the Nizam's College and pioneered education in English for **women** and men. She had a brilliant academic career at home, in London, and at Cambridge and was widely acclaimed for the poetry she published between 1905 and 1917. During those years she also met the personalities who influenced her most and were leading figures in Indian public life, including **G. K. Gokhale**, **M. A. Jinnah**, **Rabindranath Tagore**, and **Mohandas K. Gandhi**.

Sarojini worked for women's rights, youth welfare, labor, Hindu-Muslim unity, and Indian nationalism from 1906 to the end of her life. She participated in all of the major movements of the time led by Gandhi, including the **Non-Cooperation Movement**, the Champaran and salt **Satyagrahas**, and the **Civil Disobedience Movement**. She also espoused Indian' rights when she was in South Africa in the 1920s and had a triumphant lecture tour of the United States in 1928. She played a notable role in the **Round Table Conference** in London in 1930 and 1931.

Sarojini married a non-brahman, Dr. Govindarajulu Naidu, in 1898 and had four children by him; their daughter Padmaja was later governor of West Bengal. Sarojini was elected president of the **Indian National Congress** in 1925 and was always active in the organization. She was imprisoned after the **Quit India** movement in 1942, and during her imprisonment she comforted and inspired fellow prisoners with her courage and wit. She became the first woman governor of a state in independent India and died in office.

NAIPAUL, VIDYADHAR SURAJPRASAD (1932–). Naipaul was born in Trinidad, then a British colony, to the descendants of Indian indentured laborers brought over in the 19th century. They had recreated an Indian village in Chaguanas where Vidya spent his childhood. His father was a journalist who turned to writing fiction, was attracted to the reformist **Arya Samaj**, and lived in Port of Spain with his wife's wealthy extended family. They are immortalized in V. S. Naipaul's *A House for Mr. Biswas* (London, 1961). Vidya won a full government scholarship in 1948 to study English literature at University College, Oxford, from where he went to London, working with the British Broadcasting Corporation and writing regularly for the *New Statesman*. He gained literary success with his early novels set in the West Indies as well as recognition from the then prime minister of Trinidad and Tobago, but he could no longer feel at home there.

V. S. Naipaul fulfilled a deep longing to visit the land of his ancestors but was bitterly disappointed by his first experiences in India, an account of which he entitled *An Area of Darkness* (London, 1964). The fascination with India remained, however, as did his **Hindu** faith and the pain of confronting the source of his identity in the throes of transition. Not surprisingly, Naipaul's ambitious and psychoanalytical *India: A Wounded Civilization* (New York, 1977) infuriated many Indians, even as his *Among the Believers: An Islamic Journey* (New York, 1982) angered many Muslims, and his non-fiction accounts of the Caribbean aroused hostile responses from many West Indians. Part of the explanation may lie in the fact that Naipaul chose to make his home in Britain. His literary fame continued to grow, as did his understanding, expressed in autobiographical books as well as *India: A Million Mutinies Now* (New York, 1990). He became an acclaimed figure of the Indian **diaspora** and was welcomed with honor in India on his occasional visits, the more so when he was awarded the Nobel Prize for literature in 2001.

NAIR, K. MADHAVAN (1882–1933). He was born to a middle-class Nair family in Malabar and was educated in schools and college in

Cochin and Travancore. A product of the matrilineal system prevailing among Nairs, Madhavan campaigned along with other social reformers for abolition of customs that led to the thraldom of Nair women to Namboodiri men and gave the eldest maternal brother rather than the father authority over the extended family and its property among Nairs. He also participated in the temple-entry **Satyagrahas** of 1924 and 1931–1932 led by the **Ezhavas**.

Madhavan Nair joined the **Indian National Congress** in 1916 and was a member of the Madras Legislative Council in the 1920s. In 1923 he commenced publication of the *Mathribhumi* (Motherland) daily newspaper in the Malayali **language**, which has one of the largest circulations in India.

NALANDA. A Buddhist monastery near **Patna**, **Bihar**, Nalanda was founded in the first few centuries of the Common Era and grew to be the most famous Buddhist university city of the following era. It was supported by the income from perhaps one hundred villages and provided free education and residence to students for 10 years or more. Although most students were probably Buddhist monks, Nalanda accepted students of other faiths and instructed all of them in the **Vedas**, Philosophy, Grammar, Rhetoric, Composition, Mathematics, and Medicine, in addition to Buddhist doctrines. Nalanda attracted students from different parts of India, China, and central and southeast Asia.

Xuanzang, the Chinese pilgrim, described in detail Nalanda's vigorous intellectual life in the seventh century when he stayed there among 1,000 students. In the eighth century Nalanda was protected by the **Pala** dynasty of eastern India, received endowments from the King of Sumatra, and sent the monk Padmasambhava to preach **Buddhism** in Bhutan and Tibet. Ties with Buddhist communities outside India proved useful in the early 13th century when Turko-Afghan raids down the **Ganges** valley destroyed the library and monastery of Nalanda; the monks found sanctuary elsewhere.

Archaeological excavations at Nalanda in the 20th century have revealed examples of Buddhist art and architecture and have corroborated literary accounts of the university city.

NAMBOODIRIPAD, E. M. S. (1909–1998). Born to an orthodox, landowning, **brahman** family of Malabar district of northern **Kerala**,

Namboodiripad retired from public life in the late 1980s as the general secretary of the **CPI(M)**. His life encapsulates the socioeconomic-political transformations of 20th-century India, and he recounts it as such in his autobiography, *Reminiscences of an Indian Communist* (1987).

As the highest **caste** in Kerala, the Namboodiri community was the last to be touched by the social reform movement of the late 19th century. Young radicals advocating monogamy, modern education, and nuclear families formed the Namboodiri Yogakshema Sabha in 1908. The young E. M. S., hitherto educated at home in **Sanskrit**, joined the school founded by this society as a teenager, worked for its young men's association, and edited its weekly journal *Unni Namboodiri*. He was attracted to the mass movement led by **Mahatma Gandhi** and participated in **civil disobedience** in 1932. After his imprisonment, he refused to perform the *prayaschitta* rituals prescribed for "purification" after contact with polluting persons or objects; as he put it, "my generation of 'highest caste' patriots had to defy a backward looking community to defy the alien political authority."

E. M. S. gravitated to the socialist wing of the **Indian National Congress**, but joined the **Communist Party of India (CPI)** in 1936, became a member of its Central Committee in 1941, and was elected to its Politburo in 1951. He participated in intra-party debates on doctrine and tactics. He made detailed studies of the agrarian problem in Kerala and wrote at length about it. More importantly, as chief minister in the first communist government in the world to be elected to power in a free and fair election (Kerala in 1957), he put land reforms into effect, initiated private industrial investment, and introduced curbs on powerful private schools. Fear that the "communist infection" would spread to other states, along with vociferous pressure from landlords, Christian churches which owned many schools, Nairs, and the Kerala Congress Party, led New Delhi to dismiss his government in 1959 and impose President's Rule on the state. It was a controversial act.

The CPI was plagued with intra-party disputes related to the rift between China and the Soviet Union in the late 1950s and early 1960s. In 1963 Namboodiripad resigned his position and the following year joined 32 others in leaving the CPI and forming the CPI(M). It was as leader of the latter party that he once again became chief minister in Kerala, 1967–1969. A moderate and practical man, he continued to enjoy influence as an elder statesman.

NANA SAHEB (c. 1800–1859). Govind Dhondu Pant, adopted as son and heir by the last **Maratha Peshwa** Baji Rao II in 1827, was popularly known as Nana Saheb. He succeeded to the Peshwa's title and residence at Kanpur (Cawnpore) in 1851 but was refused the annual pension of Rs 800,000 pledged by the **East India Company** in return for the Peshwa renouncing claim to Maratha sovereignty in 1818. In this refusal, as in his dealings with other princes, Governor General **Lord Dalhousie** seeded resentment that found expression in the great **Uprising of 1857**, or **Sepoy Mutiny**.

British writings in 1857 depicted Nana Saheb as a fiend, embodying all that they hated and feared in the land they fought to hold. He was reported to have toured the country in the early months of 1857, inciting rebellion. He was said to be chosen leader by "rebel" Indian troops en route to Delhi in May and to have raised the saffron flag of the Marathas as a symbol of national uprising against foreign domination. His men did lay siege to an English settlement in Kanpur in June, but whether he was personally responsible for ordering their evacuation and safe conduct or their ambush and massacre is a matter of allegation and speculation. What is certain is that the British inflicted cruel and brutal punishment on all those associated with Nana Saheb once the uprising was quelled.

Henry Havelock defeated Nana Saheb in July, but Saheb joined the forces of **Awadh**, or Oudh, led by the wife of the deposed ruler, and gave succor to **Lakshmi Bai** of Jhansi in 1858. Although British reinforcements put down the uprisings, Nana Saheb was never captured. He escaped to **Nepal** and was later presumed dead.

NANAK (1469–1539). A poet saint of the **Bhakti** movement, Nanak is almost always referred to as guru, that is, teacher or preceptor. His followers came to be known as **Sikhs** from *sishya*, or pupil, and form a distinctive religious community.

Nanak was born in the **Punjab** to a literate family of *khatri* (merchant) **caste**. He later described that time as "like a knife. Kings are butchers. Modesty and religion have disappeared because falsehood reigns supreme." (Hawley & Juergensmeyer, *Songs of the Saints of*

India: 65). Throughout his early life as a student, family man, trades-
man, and accountant, Nanak showed a preference for philosophical
discussion and congregational hymn singing over conventional pastimes. After his mystic experience, he became an itinerant teacher,
traveling not only through the subcontinent but west to Mecca, Med-
ina, and Baghdad and north to Afghanistan, **Kashmir**, and **Tibet**, thus
touching the most holy places of pilgrimage for **Hindus**, **Buddhists**,
and followers of **Islam**. He finally settled on the banks of the Ravi
river, institutionalizing his teachings in a practical way that no other
Bhakti saint attempted. In particular, he initiated the *Guru ka langar*
or "kitchen of the Lord," where everyone, irrespective of birth, ate together from a common vessel, thus effectively striking at the core of
caste restrictions and **brahman** domination.

Guru Nanak is reported to have emerged from *samadhi* (see Glossary) with two pronouncements: "There is One God. He is the
Supreme Truth." "There is no Hindu, there is no Muslim." (Hawley
& Juergensmeyer: 69). These became the keynotes of his ministry.
Around them he erected a more systematic theology than any of his
contemporaries; it is transmitted through the *Adi Granth*, the sacred
book of the Sikhs, in which the hymns of Nanak, his spiritual predecessors, and early successors are collected. The first words in the *Adi
Granth* are attributed to Nanak, *ek Omkar* or God is One. Nanak
preached the overarching truth of God, beyond all time, space, or human description. Contemplation of God through listening, remem-
brance, and repetition of the Word is his first prescription for a spiritual life. According to Nanak, spiritual salvation does not require
rigorous austerities or withdrawal from the world; rather, purity is to
be sought in daily life through the Word.

Nanak's uncompromising monotheism, his religious vocabulary
drawn from both the Arabic and **Sanskrit** traditions, his two closest
companions, one Muslim one Hindu, his relations with other religious teachers—Hindu Yogis and Muslim **Sufis**, his garments which
marked him as a holy man in either tradition, as well as his teachings
and practice, interpose him between Hinduism and Islam not as a
broker but as one who clarifies how the rituals of each fall short of
the Truth. He offers a path of salvation that encompasses and transcends both. Central to this path is the role of the guru, both as the inner voice of God in man and as the external teacher pointing the way

to Truth. Nanak also stressed the importance of the congregation, which was drawn from both Hindus and Muslims in the Punjab. Traditional accounts of a dispute over the disposal of his mortal remains—Hindu disciples suggesting cremation, Muslim disciples, burial—are similar to those about **Kabir** and reaffirm Nanak's bridging of the two major faiths on the Indian subcontinent.

NANDA, GULZARI LAL (1898–1995). Nanda was born at Sialkot and was educated at Lahore, before going to Allahabad University for higher studies. He joined the **Indian National Congress** and the **Non-Cooperation Movement** and participated in later movements of **civil disobedience** as well, for which he was jailed in 1932 and 1942. He made his career as a lawyer and an organizer of labor in **Bombay** and **Ahmedabad**, where he was secretary of the Textile Labour Association. He was a member of the Bombay Legislative Assembly from 1937 to 1939 and held positions in the Bombay government after independence.

Nanda was elected to the **Lok Sabha** and joined **Jawaharlal Nehru**'s Cabinet in the early 1950s. He held various portfolios until 1966. Regarded as a dependable member of the old guard in Congress, Nanda was twice asked to fill the post of prime minister at moments of transition: for a month after the death of Nehru in May 1964, before the election of **Lal Bahadur Shastri**, and for a month after the death of Shastri in January 1966, before the election of **Indira Gandhi**.

NAOROJI, DADABHAI (1825–1917). A **Parsi** educated in **Bombay**, Naoroji became the first Indian professor at Elphinstone College before taking charge of the London office of a business firm in 1855. Thereafter, he commuted regularly between England and India and provided a personal link among Englishmen interested in India and Indians active in public life. Naoroji acted on his conviction that reform of British rule in India necessitated education of British public and legislative opinion on the subject. He formed the East India Association in 1866 in London, which became the India Lobby in 1871 with branches in **Calcutta**, **Madras**, and Bombay. In 1883 he launched a newspaper, *Voice of India*, for the same purpose. He was active in British politics as a member of the Liberal Party and stood for Parliament. Although he was defeated in 1886, in 1892 he became the first Indian to be elected to the British House of Commons from an English constituency. He saw himself as a representative of India (and was so perceived by the Indian public) with a duty to promote political reform. He provided a home away from home to Indian students in London, including **Mohandas K. Gandhi**.

Naoroji made a significant contribution to economic theory and history in his paper, "Poverty in India," enlarged to a book, *Poverty and Un-British Rule in India*, published in 1901. On the basis of detailed comparisons of national and per capita incomes in 15 countries, estimates of agricultural and nonagricultural produce, foreign trade figures, domestic prices, and taxation, he concluded that British rule produced a "drain of wealth" or unilateral transfer of capital from India to Britain without concomitant measures of economic development taking place in India. He explained India's poverty as a consequence of continuous exploitation "for the exclusive advantage of a privileged minority, and existing to the great dishonour of the British name." (From Naoroji's Presidential Address to the Indian National Congress in 1893. In Zaidi, *Congress Presidential Addresses*: Volume One: 148–187). The "drain of wealth" theory became the credo of the **Indian National Congress** thereafter.

Dadabhai Naoroji became dewan of the **Princely State** of **Baroda** in 1873. He initiated reforms to benefit the people, and his administrative talent demonstrated the benefits that could accrue from Indian government. He made similar contributions as an elected member of the Bombay Municipal Corporation in the 1880s. He worked in his individual capacity to spread education among the poor and **women**, endowing schools and forming literary societies, for which he was honored in Bombay.

Naoroji played an important role in Congress along with other leaders who wanted improvement, not elimination, of British rule through Indianization of government services and reduction of military expenditure. He was President of the Congress sessions in 1886 and 1893. Naoroji stayed above internal quarrels in Congress at the turn of the century and acted as peacemaker when a split between "moderates" led by **G. K. Gokhale** and "extremists" led by **B. G. Tilak** threatened in 1905; both men were his friends. Naoroji was asked to be president again, so as to preserve the unity of the movement.

Though he was sometimes criticized as being too Anglicized, he was fondly known as "the Grand Old Man" of the Indian national movement and is so remembered.

NARAYAN, JAYAPRAKASH (1902–1979). Affectionately known as J. P., he was born in **Bihar** to a middle-class Kayastha (see Glossary) family and educated in **Patna** and **Banaras**. He then studied in the United States and was influenced by Marxist ideas and the writings of **M. N. Roy**. Soon after returning to India in 1929 he joined the **Civil Disobedience** movement of 1930 led by **Mahatma Gandhi**. J. P.'s arrest and imprisonment reinforced his criticism of British rule. Contact with fellow prisoners **Achyut Patwardhan**, Ashok Mehta, and Minoo Masani strengthened J. P.'s socialist leanings. In 1935 and 1936, they organized the All-India Socialist Congress Party, which was connected with the **Kisan Sabha**. They acted as a left-inclined ginger group within the **Indian National Congress**. J. P. himself was intensely involved in the formidable mass rebellion against British rule following Gandhi's **"Quit India"** call of August 1942.

Narayan renounced party politics soon after independence and joined **Vinoba Bhave**, seeing in his *bhoodan* movement "the germ of a total agrarian revolution." J. P. sought a Gandhian alternative to the problems of modernization in the concept of Sarvodaya, which he called "people's socialism." By following the path of self-sacrifice and service, and speaking out frankly on social, economic, and political ills, J. P. fitted the Indian idiom of "saintly politics" and commanded public respect. The Indian government sometimes used his services as a mediator in restoring peace to troubled areas, as with the Nagas (see **Nagaland**) in the northeast during the 1950s.

J. P. openly criticized **Indira Gandhi** in 1974 as India's internal situation deteriorated. He soon became the symbol of an oppositional, if not exactly revolutionary, movement. In Bihar and **Gujarat** he led the opposition against corrupt state governments run by the **Congress Party**. J. P. called for student boycott of classes, nonpayment of taxes by cultivators, and resignation of legislators; he collected two million signatures appealing for dissolution of the Bihar legislature. On the national stage as well, J. P. publicly reminded all serving officers, civil and military, of Mahatma Gandhi's stress on individual conscience — rather than obedience to orders—as the criteria of legitimate action. He called on the prime minister to resign. She did not do so, and J. P. was among the first to be arrested in anticipation of the **Emergency** proclamation of June 25, 1975. He was released five months later because of his poor health and failing kidneys.

Although the patriarch and spiritual guide of the **Janata Party** coalition that came to power after the general elections of March 1977, Jayaprakash Narayan refrained from taking up any position of formal leadership. By the time of his death he appeared to be as disillusioned with the prospects of "total revolution" as he was with factionalism within the Janata government.

NARAYAN, R. K. (Rasipuram Krishnaswami) (1906–2001). Born in **Madras** to an educated middle-class **brahman** family, Narayan was brought up largely by his grandmother. From childhood days he was fascinated by the seemingly endless stream of stories that flowed from **Tamil** mythology as well as from the lives of diverse visitors to his grandmother. He graduated from Maharaja College in **Mysore** and soon took the then unusual step of writing full time; he later explained that he did so mainly because it was the only career that guaranteed him the freedom he craved.

R. K. Narayan's first novel, *Swami and Friends*, was published in England in 1935 and was set in a fictional small town of Malgudi, which he populated with believable if often eccentric individuals through whom he presented village and small town India. Narayan returned to Malgudi in many of his novels and short stories so that it became a real place to his readers all over the world. The characters in *The English Teacher*, *The Guide*, *The Financial Expert*, *The Vendor of Sweets*, and others deal with real issues of the human condition, painful or otherwise, and the author wins sympathy and understanding for them and for the rich diversity of Indian culture without ever being didactic. Graham Greene once likened Narayan's sense of beauty and sadness to that of the Russian playwright Anton Chekhov.

R. K. Narayan was one of the first Indians writing in the English **language** to win international acclaim—a generation before the current group. He was arguably the most prolific of them in his creation of stories, essays, newspaper articles, and memoirs, in addition to 34 novels. His works have been translated into dozens of languages. His brother, R. K. Laxman, is one of the best and most prolific cartoonists in India. Narayan received many awards in his life, including the Sahitya Akademi national prize in 1958, and the American English Speaking Union prize in 1975; he was honored with the Padma Bhushan and nomination to the **Rajya Sabha** in 1985. He was also a member of the American Academy of Arts and Letters, and his papers and manuscripts were given to the University of Texas at Austin and to Boston University.

NARAYANAN, KOCHARIL RAMAN (1920–2005). Narayanan was president of India from 1997 to 2002. He was born to a family listed among the Scheduled Castes in the progressive **Princely State** of Travancore (**Kerala**) and demonstrated acute intelligence early in life. He was educated in Travancore before proceeding to the London School of Economics. On his return to India he worked as a journalist with English **language** newspapers, *The Hindu* and *The Times of India*, and as a college lecturer, before joining the newly created Indian Foreign Service after independence. Narayanan served in **Burma** (where he married Usha Ma Tint Tint), Japan, Australia, Vietnam, and at IFS headquarters before being appointed ambassador to Thailand and then to Turkey. He went to Beijing in 1976 when India restored ambassadorial relations with **China** after a lapse of 16 years; subsequently he served as ambassador to the **United States** 1980–1983.

K. R. Narayanan was elected to the **Lok Sabha** in 1984 after retirement from the diplomatic service and occupied junior minister positions in **Congress** governments before being elected vice president in 1992 and president in 1997. He proved to be a more than usually active president during a term marked by a fragmentation and reorientation of **political parties**, several changes of government in states and at the center, uncertain parliamentary majorities, and shifting coalitions. He added luster to the office by the depth of his knowledge, his defense of the **Constitution**, and his adherence to correct procedures and the rule of law. For example, in October 1997 he took the unprecedented step of returning for reconsideration a cabinet recommendation for imposition of President's Rule in **Uttar Pradesh** when the government in that state lost its majority. It is unlikely that he endeared himself with politicians.

Narayanan maintained his interest in philosophy and literature throughout his career and associated himself with Delhi University after leaving office.

NARGIS (1929–1981). She was the female megastar of the **film industry** in the late 1940s and 1950s. Nargis was born in **Allahabad** and was introduced to films at the age of five by her mother Jaddanbai, who was an actress, film-maker, and singer. Nargis played the romantic lead opposite **Raj Kapoor** in many films, including blockbusters such as *Awara*, *Shri 420*, and *Andaaz*, and gained international renown. Typically, Nargis was presented as a beautiful woman doomed to destruction by fate, working through a feudal patriarchy and/or capitalism. She took the lead role in *Mother India* (1958), an epic depiction of the historic, psychoanalytic, and technological symbols of Indian nationalist fervor. Nargis retired from the screen after her marriage to Sunil Dutt and lived long enough to see their son, Sanjay, make his debut in films.

NARMADA or NARBADA RIVER. This river flows through central India. It rises in the Maikala Ranges of **Madhya Pradesh** and follows a tortuous route to the spectacular marble rock gorge almost at the exact center of the Indian subcontinent where it enters a natural trough between the Vindhya and Satpura ranges. The river then flows westward and across part of **Gujarat** before emptying into the Gulf of Cambay on the Arabian Sea through a wide estuary. Unlike the rivers of the northern plains, it is not a perennially snow-fed river but is prey to fluctuations in levels dependent on rainfall. Its valley includes heavily forested areas as well as those that are short of water and sparsely cultivated.

The Narmada created an important trade route connecting the **Ganges** valley to western ports in ancient times and is mentioned by the Roman geographer Ptolemy. It is also a sacred river and traditional pilgrimage route lined with various temples from ancient and medieval eras. In the present day, it is better known as the scene of confrontation between two conflicting views of economic development. The Indian government in cooperation with the World Bank planned a large and multi-purpose Sardar Sarovar Project, which included construction of a massive dam on the Narmada. Developmental objectives included irrigating potential **Green Revolution** agricultural districts in western **Maharashtra** and meeting the water needs of parched districts in southern Gujarat. Work on the project was commenced after 1978. In 1985, however, opposition surfaced under the name of *Narmada Bachao Andolan* or Movement to Save the Narmada. Opposition focused on the fact that the dam and its reservoir would result in the submergence of 248 villages over more than 35,000 hectares in the forested areas of Madhya Pradesh 300 kilometers upstream from the areas targeted for development. The people most adversely affected were mainly tribals and subsistence cultivators facing "resettlement" elsewhere, despite their resistance. A nonviolent movement gathered momentum spontaneously under the leadership of social activists including Medha Phatkar, who undertook voluntary fasts. Indian and foreign environmentalists also commented unfavorably on the impact of the project as planned. Construction of the dam was brought to a virtual halt for some years and the World Bank withdrew its support. There was a public debate on developmental strategies and court cases filed against Medha Phatkar who sustained the opposition despite a ruling from the **Supreme Court** to resume construction of the dam. Some provisions for compensation and resettlement of adversely affected people in Madhya Pradesh were made at the same time. Meanwhile, the Narmada flows on, as does tourist and pilgrim traffic to its shores.

NATIONAL HUMAN RIGHTS COMMISSION. The NHRC is an autonomous institution created under the Protection of Human Rights Act of 1993. It is chaired by a former chief justice of the **Supreme Court** and has four other members, two from the Supreme Court or High Courts, and two from among those with particular knowledge and practical experience in matters relating to human rights. Chairpersons of three other national commissions—for Minorities, Scheduled Castes and Tribes, and Women—are *ex officio* members. The NHRC has its own administrative, investigative, scientific, and technical staff and can draw on the services of the Union or State governments as well as **Non-Governmental Organizations** (NGOs) when necessary.

The primary function of the NHRC is to inquire into violations of human rights in India, or the abetment or negligence of a public servant in preventing such violations, either on its own initiative (*suo moto*) or on the basis of petitions made to it, and make appropriate recommendations. In furtherance of this function the NHRC may visit any prison, place of detention, or institution where people are lodged to survey conditions and recommend improvements. It may review factors, including acts of terrorism, that inhibit human rights and can call for reports from branches of government. It may intervene in court proceedings. The NHRC is empowered to summon and examine witnesses on oath, call for the discovery and production of any document, receive evidence, requisition public records, and take any other necessary measure. It is deemed to be a civil court. The NHRC also undertakes and promotes research on various aspects of human rights including child labor, treatment of disabled or mentally ill persons, training of police forces, and socioeconomic conditions in disturbed areas such as the northeastern states and **Jammu and Kashmir**. It promotes awareness of human rights and their safeguards among the general public and security forces and is easily accessible to petitions made in person, in writing, through state reporters, or electronically through an active NHRC website.

The impact of the NHRC in its 10 years of existence has been far greater than, perhaps, the government and Parliament anticipated when creating it. The number of cases it examines and takes action on has multiplied exponentially, as is evident from its annual reports, and a great many people have benefited from the compassion, fearlessness, and independence of the NHRC. It is more effective, naturally, when Union or state governments and their functionaries accept NHRC recommendations and implement them, and less effective when deep-rooted socioeconomic malaise produces such chronic violations of human rights as child labor. The case of systematic violence against Muslims in the state of **Gujarat** in 2002 (with a related court case in 2003) belonged in a separate category, and the NHRC took it up *suo moto*. It sent repeated strong notes to the Government of Gujarat warning against permitting religious processions that could reignite communal passions and calling attention to the unambiguous duty of the police and magistracy to uphold the law of the land and maintain public peace. It communicated the essential principle of human rights jurisprudence—that the state is responsible for acts of its own agents, those of non-state players, as well as for any inaction that may cause or facilitate the violation of human rights. Although the NHRC cannot, by itself, enforce action against a recalcitrant state government, its public iteration of basic principles of the rule of law adds to the rest of its work in tangibly improving the protection of human rights in India.

NAXALITE. The name derives from Naxalbari, a hilly area in northern **Bengal** where peasants forcibly occupied lands in an anti-landlord movement of 1967. The move was lauded by China as a step to create a "liberated base" from which to launch armed revolution in India. Thereafter, the term "Naxalite" was applied to the radical Indian communists led by **Charu Mazumdar**, who called for a protracted armed struggle by peasants and an encirclement of the cities, on the model of China's communist revolution led by Mao Zedong.

The government of West **Bengal** stamped out the rebellion over a period of years but not before the Naxalites had succeeded in terrorizing parts of **Calcutta** and establishing organizational networks in the states of **Bihar** and **Andhra Pradesh**. In 1969, the Naxalites broke away from both halves of the **Communist Party of India** to form a third communist party (CPI-Marxist-Leninist) dedicated to revolution. This party was banned during **Emergency Rule**, and its leaders were arrested; they were eventually released in 1979. Charu Mazumdar died in 1972.

As a non-parliamentary and factionalized party, the full strength of the Naxalites is unknown. But sporadic land-grab movements in the 1970s and an upsurge of agrarian unrest in the 1980s and 1990s indicate their continued activity and possibly expanding influence, especially among rural populations that are highly politicized and polarized. For example, in Andhra Pradesh Naxalites operate under the name of the Peoples' War Group and the Maoist rebels in **Nepal** in the new century may well have contacts with Indian Naxalites in Bihar.

NEHRU, JAWAHARLAL (1889–1964). The first prime minister of independent India, Nehru has been the subject of many biographical studies, numerous interviews, and much commentary, both appreciative and critical. He exerted a profound influence on his compatriots both through what he did and what he did not do, and he won for India a status in world councils far above that accorded other newly independent poor countries. One biographer has described him living in "crowded loneliness" alleviated by writing. He was a prolific writer in English, and his autobiography, *Towards Freedom* (1936), ran nine editions in the first year alone. Emotional sensitivity and intellectual passion infused his writings, many of which first took form as letters or speeches, and give them unusual appeal and topicality even today.

Jawaharlal was the first-born child and only son of **Motilal Nehru** and the orthodox Swarup Rani. He grew up without companions of his own age in a luxurious and anglicized home, tutored by F. T. Brooks who introduced him to literature, theosophy, and science. From age 15 to 23 Jawaharlal studied in England at Harrow, Cambridge, and the Inner Temple, returning to India in 1912 with a Tripos in the natural sciences, qualifications at the Bar, and the tastes of a cultivated English gentleman. He resumed life as his father's son at **Allahabad** with an arranged marriage in 1916, but he manifested a sharp agnosticism and a vague discontent with comfort. Through his work among the distressed peasants of **Awadh** in 1918–1919, his tour of the **Punjab** after the **Jallianwala Bagh** massacre of 1919, and his whole-hearted participation in the **Non-Cooperation Movement** 1920–1922, he found a cause to absorb him all his life—the independence and uplift of India. He began to grow into a man. At the same time, Jawaharlal the incipient intellectual became a disciple of **Mohandas Gandhi** the saintly activist; he so acquired another father to whose austere ways he converted his biological father. The relationships between these three men and the different qualities that each embodied illuminate the history of the **Indian National Congress** in that period.

The public career of Jawaharlal Nehru between the age of 30 and his death at age 75 falls into two parts, before and after Indian independence in 1947. Between 1920 and 1945, Nehru spent a total of 11 years in prison at different times. Outside prison, he was numbered among the "young radicals" of Congress, pressing for *purna swaraj*, or full independence, and a leftist platform. He was elected president of Congress in 1930, 1936, and 1937 and proved to be an excellent election campaigner when provincial autonomy was introduced under the **Government of India Act of 1935**. On occasion he traveled in Europe. He was a delegate to the International Congress Against

Colonial Oppression and Imperialism held in Brussels in 1927, visited the Soviet Union in 1928, and reinforced his strong negative reactions to Fascism while attending the deathbed of his wife in Switzerland in 1935 and 1936. In 1942, Gandhi formally designated Nehru as his successor. Nehru participated in the abortive independence negotiations with Sir **Stafford Cripps** in 1942 and the **Cabinet Mission** in 1946 and was vice president of the Interim Government, 1946–1947.

Nehru's contributions in the pre-independence period were considerable. He gave an economic dimension to nationalism, forming a planning board within Congress, pushing forward work among workers and peasants, and preventing the total domination of the national movement by the Indian bourgeoisie. He acted as a bridge between the scientific socialism of the Left, to which he was intellectually inclined, and the semi-religious mass appeal of Gandhi. Mild and timid, perhaps, in his reluctance to break with Gandhi on important issues where they differed, Nehru shielded Congress from an ideological split in the 1930s and helped make it representative of the total spectrum of India. In the same vein, he advocated more vigorous recruitment by Congress among followers of **Islam** and the peoples of the **Princely States**. Further, Nehru put India's national movement in its international context as part of a worldwide struggle against imperialism, a spearhead in the cause of suffering humanity. He felt passionately engaged in the war against Fascism but was precluded from committing Congress to active participation in the fight by the British refusal to offer even a verbal assurance of honorable status to India during or after **World War II**.

Against these contributions stand severe criticisms. Nehru's leftist radicalism was more verbal than substantial; he was better at drafting resolutions than at implementing programs to benefit peasants and workers. Nehru developed a mutually stimulating rapport with crowds but was less successful in bonding his colleagues into a loyal group. Other bright young leaders, including **Subhas Chandra Bose** and **Jayaprakash Narayan**, left Congress, and older leaders opposed him. Nor did he grasp the organizational levers of domestic power, as did **Vallabhbhai Patel**, being more interested in international affairs. His leadership of Congress, in the opinion of some, owed more to Gandhi's choice than to his own achievements. Most serious of all, Nehru is blamed for Congress's refusal to form coalition governments with **Fazlul Huq** in **Bengal** and the **All-India Muslim League** in the United Provinces, now **Uttar Pradesh (UP)** after its electoral victories in 1937, and also for publicly envisaging future amendment of the **Cabinet Mission** proposals in 1946 once Congress came to power in an independent India. These proved to be strategic blunders that alienated the Muslim League led by **Mohammed Ali Jinnah** and so contributed to **Partition**.

Nehru's main contributions to the evolution of independent India can be seen most clearly in the strength of its democratic institutions in the parliamentary tradition with regular elections based on adult franchise, several parties in and out of government, a free press, and an independent judiciary. For Nehru, it was self-evident that India's diversity could best be held together through democracy and secularism, by which he meant freedom of religious thought and practice and separation of private faith from public affairs. He fought the forces of right-wing **Hindu** chauvinism to keep the **Constitution** and the government secular and kind to minorities. It was equally evident to Nehru that political democracy needed to be clothed with economic and social equity, which he encapsulated in the vague phrase "socialistic society." He established legal equality between men and women and among all **castes** through the Constitution and the Hindu Code legislation of the mid-1950s in the face of powerful vested interests in a hierarchical Hindu tradition. Nehru also introduced economic planning, heavy industry, and a mixed economy of a strong state sector and a wide private sector. Impressive growth took place through 1965 before what came to be known as the "license permit raj" began to stifle initiative. As a modernist with a scientific bent, Nehru encouraged the development of scientific and technical institutions that became India's pride. India's remarkable economic and technical advances since the 1990s owe much to the infrastructure laid by Nehru. And, with his lifelong interest in international affairs, Nehru gave to India and the world the concept of **nonalignment**. He led India along the path of an independent foreign policy without entanglement in the military alliances of the Cold War but committed it to the cause of peace and international cooperation.

Many have criticized Nehru's record as prime minister, mainly along the following (sometimes contradictory) lines. He did not push hard enough for land reforms or other institutions of social and economic equity. He imposed socialism. He could not prevent the resurgence of communal politics, although he tried hard to inculcate secular values among his political colleagues. He pandered to "minorities." He did not deliver the promised goal of universal primary education; he invested too much in universities. He failed to anticipate the crippling effects of population growth; he relied too heavily on voluntarism. Nehru's blueprint of a planned mixed economy evoked equal criticism from left and right, of falling between two stools, of neglecting agriculture, and of pampering organized labor. In his chosen field of foreign affairs, Nehru was unable to win peace with **Pakistan**. He neglected defense and was devastated when his faith in friendship with China proved humiliatingly illusory in the border war of 1962. He failed to anticipate or overcome the hostility of the United States to India's nonalignment. And many find it ironic that Nehru the democrat should have, in effect, founded a dynasty that ruled India through 1989 (with two interruptions, 1964 to 1966 and 1977 to 1979), that papered over a factionalized **Congress Party** in the years of its decline, and that brought it back to power in 2004.

Behind the inevitable controversy surrounding his name and his policies, Nehru's character shines out as Gandhi once described it. "He is pure as crystal, he is truthful beyond suspicion. He is a knight *sans peur, sans reproche*. The nation is safe in his hands." (Tendulkar, *Mahatma: Life of Mohandas Karamchand Gandhi*, Volume II: 490.) Jawaharlal Nehru was a man who first "discovered" India as an adult, who wrote *Discovery of India* (1946) and then found, as he spelled out in his will, that "the affection of all classes of the Indian people has come to me in such abundant measure that I have been overwhelmed by it." He said that he hoped for nothing more than that "I shall not be unworthy of my people and their affection." (Norman, *Nehru: The First Sixty Years*: 593). It is not surprising that Nehru's life, his vision of a new India and a new world—and the seeming frustration of that vision at the end of the 20th century—should have inspired many scholars and commentators to explore sources again and publish their own assessments of this gentle yet influential man.

NEHRU, MOTILAL (1861–1931). Motilal was born in a **brahman** family that had moved from **Kashmir** to **Delhi** in the early 18th century. He grew up as a high-spirited lad in the household of his elder brother and acquired a liking for English culture in the course of his education. After he established a lucrative legal practice at the Allahabad High Court in the 1890s, Motilal maintained an anglicized standard of life complete with trips to Europe, English tutors and governesses for his three children, and an education at Harrow and Cambridge for his only son **Jawaharlal**.

Motilal Nehru was a moderate in the **Indian National Congress** and was relatively inactive in politics until he was jolted into awareness by **World War I**, the **Jallianwala Bagh** massacre in 1919, the ineffable appeal of **Mohandas Karamchand Gandhi**, and the radical views of his son. In 1920, Motilal was elected president of the Congress and gave his support to Gandhi's **Non-Cooperation** resolution. He switched his household to *swadeshi* (see Glossary) and abjured foreign goods. Along with another moderate, **C. R. Das**, he gave up his legal practice in protest against British courts. He participated in the nationwide boycott of the Prince of Wales' visit in 1921 and was arrested. In 1922, after Gandhi was criticized for suddenly calling off the Non-Cooperation Movement, Motilal and a Congress committee made an inquiry and concluded that although the movement had succeeded in many respects, it could not have been long sustained at the time.

Congress in 1922 debated the question of Council entry; that is, whether to cooperate with the government in working the **Montagu-Chelmsford Reforms**. Motilal and Das opposed Gandhi and those who advocated non-cooperation. Instead, they formed a new **Swaraj Party** to contest elections and enter legislatures where they said they would demand the right to frame a constitution for India and, if denied, would obstruct government. Later they were re-acknowledged as members of Congress. Under Motilal's leadership in the Central Legislative Assembly, the Swaraj Party raised many important demands on budgetary matters, Indianization of services, financial autonomy, industrial protection, and constitutional reform. Although the British Indian government did not concede these demands, it made some concessions toward them.

Motilal Nehru chaired a committee of the All-Parties Conference of 1928 charged with drawing up a constitution for India, published as the **Nehru Report**. Although rising communalism, radicalism, and particularism in India saddened Motilal toward the end of his life and isolated him to some extent, his personal influence was undeniable. A man of hearty appetites, abundant affection, and many friends, both Indian and European, his opinion was widely sought. His home in **Allahabad** served as an unofficial Congress headquarters on numerous occasions. His son Jawaharlal, with whom he had an affectionate, if difficult, relationship, went on to become Gandhi's chosen successor as leader of the Indian National Congress and of independent India.

NEHRU REPORT (1928). This report was named after **Motilal Nehru** of the **Indian National Congress**. He was chairman of a committee established by the All-Parties Conference attended by representatives of 29 political organizations in February 1928 and charged with drafting the principles of a constitution for independent India. This move augured well for the unity of India and was, in some respects, intended as a riposte to the all-British **Simon Commission**, which was inquiring into the question of constitutional reform at the same time.

Although not formally a draft constitution, the Nehru Report comprised seven chapters, two schedules, three appendixes, and a list of recommendations amounting to a constitutional framework. The main features were: **Dominion Status** for India; freedom of conscience, profession, and practice of religion; lower houses of legislatures in provinces and at the center to be elected on the basis of adult franchise and joint (mixed) electorates; reservation of seats for followers of **Islam**, that is Muslims, at the center and in provinces where they formed a substantial minority; reservation of seats for **Hindus** in the **North West Frontier Provinces** where they were in a minority; enumeration of different subjects for central and provincial authority; and a unitary rather than a federal structure.

Some of these recommendations were introduced under pressure from the **Hindu Mahasabha**, which obtained rejection of **Mohammed Ali Jinnah**'s 14-point demands in behalf of the **All-India Muslim League** by the All-Parties Conference. The key issue in 1928 was delineation of electorates, with the League demanding separate communal electorates and the Nehru Report recommending joint mixed electorates. Jinnah later described the episode as a "parting of the ways" between the League and Congress. In this respect, the Nehru Report contrasted with the **Lucknow Pact**, in which Congress and the League agreed to join their ways by making mutual concessions.

Although the Nehru Report was immediately overtaken by events, it was a substantial step toward the democratic **Constitution** adopted by the Republic of India in 1950.

NEPAL. A landlocked **Hindu** kingdom of 147,181 square kilometers in the central **Himalaya**, Nepal shares a 1,593-kilometer-long border with India on its south, east, and west and a shorter border to the north with **Tibet**, China. The main Himalayan range, containing many of the world's highest peaks, occupies the northern third of the country. The capital, Khatmandu, and other towns are located in central valleys. A southern sub-montane belt, or Terai, merges with the Indian Terai in the states of **Uttar Pradesh** and **Bihar**. Nepal's main rivers drain into India and feature several multipurpose or hydroelectric projects that are heavily assisted by India. India has been a major donor of economic assistance to Nepal, along with international lending agencies, the United States, and China.

More than 80% of Nepal's estimated 20 million people, including its hereditary rulers and aristocratic class, are closely linked to those of northern India by historical origin, linguistic similarity, educational background, and religious affiliation. The Indo-Nepal border is open, Nepalis enjoy the legal right of working and living in India on the same basis as Indian citizens, and estimates of the number of Nepalis in India range around 10 million. Repeated talk since the 1990s of proposed efforts to regulate this movement of people by the introduction of multipurpose identity cards and crackdowns on trafficking in women and children has not yet fructified into meaningful action in either country. Nor does it seem feasible to close the long land border, although India did suspend trade for some months in 1989 after a crisis in the relationship. Gurkha soldiers from Nepal have long been an important component of the Indian army and also serve with the British and Malaysian armies.

Official relations between India and Nepal are based on a Treaty of Peace and Friendship signed in 1950 and a periodically renewed and amended Trade and Transit Treaty. Occasional crises, often originating in Nepal's domestic politics of clashes between the palace and parliament, or India's apprehension of excessive Chinese influence in Khatmandu, have occurred, but within the framework of a normally close and amicable relationship. India has increased its military and other assistance to the government of Nepal in coping with a spreading and lethal Maoist insurgency, while urging a restoration of democracy in the country and a negotiated settlement.

Nepal is a founder member of the **South Asian Association for Regional Cooperation**, and Khatmandu is the headquarters of its permanent Secretariat.

NILGIRIS. Literally translated as "blue mountains," Nilgiris is the name given to a hilly tableland in western **Tamil Nadu** with an area of 12,549 square kilometers and a height ranging between 900 and 2,100 meters. It rises abruptly from the surrounding plains and forms a distinct ecological region in terms of soil, flora, fauna, and climate. The biodiversity of the Nilgiris is the subject of intensive study.

Most of the population in the Nilgiris is drawn from four **Adivasi** groups speaking **Dravidian languages**: Toda, Kota, Kurumba, and Badaga. During the 19th century, British officials and missionaries were attracted to the cool climate and beautiful scenery of the Nilgiris. Ootacamund was designated the summer administrative headquarters of Madras Presidency and became the favorite resort of Europeans in southern India. Good schools and tea and coffee plantations were established in the hills and continue to prosper today. Descendants of workers on these plantations, as well as many other Indians retired from their professions, have settled in the Nilgiris. The Staff College of the **Indian Armed Forces** is located at Wellington in the Nilgiris.

NIMBARAK (c. 1130–1200). Nimbarak was a Telugu **brahman** who was an astronomer and became a mystic saint. He held the view that Brahman or God has an independent and infinite reality as Creator, while individual souls and the inanimate world are created and finite, sustained by and dependent on Brahman but distinct. He did not consider that *moksha* or spiritual salvation was possible in the physical body. He stressed **bhakti** more than learning or meditation as a spiritual path, highlighting united Radha and **Krishna** as the object of worship. Nimbarak was a friend of Jayadeva, who composed the often-recited *Gita Govinda* in praise of Radha and Krishna.

Nimbarak's school of thought is known as *dvaita-advaita* or dualistic non-dualism. His followers formed a separate sect known as Nimandi that flourished at Mathura and produced a considerable literature.

NIVEDITA, SISTER (1867–1911). Born Margaret Elizabeth Noble in Northern Ireland and brought up in the Wesleyan and Congregational Christian Churches there, she started a school in 1892 in Wimbledon and then became acquainted with the teachings of **Swami Vivekananda**. Margaret Noble went to **Calcutta** in 1898, where she was initiated into the newly formed **Ramakrishna Mission** and renamed Nivedita by Vivekananda. She opened a girls' school in Calcutta, engaged in relief work during a plague epidemic, and helped to raise funds abroad.

From 1902 to the time of her death, Sister Nivedita wrote and lectured about India, raising consciousness in the West as well as among Indians. She was critical of British policy and supportive of national education for Indians and the **Swadeshi movement**. She encouraged Indian artists and was friendly with leaders of various persuasions in the emerging national movement. With her striking good looks, her intense spirituality, her self-effacing austere life serving others, and her strong views, Sister Nivedita made a forceful impression on English and Indians alike.

NIZAM-UL-MULK, ASAF JAH (1671–1748). Born Chin Qulich Khan to a favorite officer of the **Mughal Emperor Aurangzeb**, he was given the title of Nizam-ul-Mulk and appointed viceroy of the **Deccan** in 1713. He played a balancing role in the factional rivalries among the Mughal nobility with some distinction and became wazir, or chief minister, of the new emperor in 1722 and attempted to reach a stable understanding with the **Marathas** and restore authority and order to Mughal administration. But by the 1720s the empire was fast disintegrating.

Nizam-ul-Mulk acquired complete control over the Mughal Deccan and was affirmed in this with the title of Asaf Jah in 1725. The

Nizam, as he was addressed, was virtually independent of **Delhi** and was more interested in consolidating his rule in the Deccan. He was defeated in battle by the Marathas led by **Peshwa Baji Rao** in 1731 and reached an understanding by which he would not interfere with Maratha expansion in north India and they would not impede him in the southeast. After his death, however, his successors were entangled in a complex web of conflict and alliance with the Marathas, **Mysore**, the French, and the English **East India Company**. Asaf Jah founded the state of **Hyderabad** and the dynasty that ruled it until 1948.

NONALIGNMENT. This is the term used to broadly describe the foreign policy of independent India as framed by **Jawaharlal Nehru**, continued by successive prime ministers until the late 1990s, and supported by national consensus. The underlying philosophy and assumptions of nonalignment were implicit in India's national movement itself and were made explicit by Nehru in various speeches even before the fact of independence. These were as follows: Colonialism, imperialism, and racism were to be opposed worldwide. India's national security was conceptualized in terms of internal economic, political, and social development rather than military confrontation with an external enemy. India could not be precommitted to any military alliance and/or war arising from great power rivalries. New Delhi would maintain a predilection for taking moral stances and psychological approaches rather than openly pursuing tangible interests through *realpolitik*. India's leaders were convinced that India's civilization and geopolitical position must give it an audible "voice" in world councils, especially on issues bearing on Asia. Nehru and his followers identified India's vital national interests with world peace, nuclear disarmament, and international cooperation.

The circumstances of the Cold War sharpened Nehru's emphasis on India's independence and autonomy of action and the imperative of world peace. His diplomacy during the Korean War demonstrated to both Moscow and Washington first, that India could not be categorized as part of the Western bloc as they had previously assumed, and second, that India played a useful mediatory and buffer role between them inside and outside the United Nations. During the 1950s, each superpower, for its own reasons, was willing to pay more attention to Nehru than had appeared likely in the 1940s. They were also willing to assist India's plans for economic development without extracting ideological conformity. Nonalignment in foreign affairs aptly reflected India's mixed economy and infinite diversity in domestic politics.

Though Nonalignment was often misunderstood in the United States and denigrated there as "immoral," "neutralism," or even as alignment with the Soviet Union, it appealed to other newly independent countries, which also wished to maximize their autonomy, minimize the risks of global war, and redress injustices in the international economic system. Thus, the heads of 25 governments met at Belgrade in 1961 at the first Nonaligned Summit meeting, chaired by President Josip Broz-Tito of Yugoslavia. When Indian Prime Minister **Indira Gandhi** chaired the Nonaligned Summit meeting at New Delhi in 1983, more than a hundred governments participated.

Nonalignment was not free of cost for India. It had no salience for the security challenges posed by Pakistan and China, which demanded from India more tangible responses than moral postures. Nor was nonalignment an adequate framework for dealing with smaller neighboring countries. The group dynamics of the Nonaligned Movement itself placed certain constraints on Indian foreign policy. Nonaligned India received less economic or military assistance per capita from abroad than did countries allied to the United States, but such assistance as it did receive in times of urgent need, such as from the Western powers in the aftermath of China's invasion of 1962, from the United States at a time of economic crisis in 1966 and 1967, and from the Soviet Union in 1971, made Indians and others uncomfortable. They knew that assertions of nonalignment must be accompanied by economic and military self-reliance to be credible.

Notwithstanding difficulties and differences of interpretation, Nonalignment commanded national consensus within India and is seen as an important contribution to the theory and practice of international affairs in the 20th century. *See also* FOREIGN POLICY.

NON-COOPERATION MOVEMENT. This movement in 1920–1922 was the first mass campaign against British rule led by the **Indian National Congress** that enjoyed support from all social classes, communities, and provinces in India. It constituted a formidable, if disorganized, revolt. The British Government of India responded with repression as well as offers to negotiate constitutional reform. The Non-Cooperation Movement brought **Mohandas Karamchand Gandhi** to the forefront of national leadership. His pursuit of truth, of which *ahimsa*, or non-violence, and *swadeshi*, or self-reliance, were essential elements, fundamentally altered the conceptual and practical framework of political action for decades to come.

The immediate stimuli for the Non-Cooperation Movement were provided by the **Khilafet** issue and post-**World War I** repression in the **Punjab**. Underlying these was widespread discontent with British rule because of economic, political, and psychological reasons, which varied among classes, communities, and localities but found points of linkage with the larger nationalist cause. The Non-Cooperation Movement went through successive phases. First, the Khilafet Committee that was mobilizing Muslim protest against British treatment of Turkey asked for Congress cooperation and received Gandhi's endorsement. He saw *swaraj*, or self-government, as rooted in Hindu-Muslim unity and the Khilafet issue as an occasion to express it; he also realized Congress's need for institutional and tactical advancement at the time. Next, Gandhi wrote to the viceroy when returning his war medals because of the "insufferable wrong" committed in the Punjab and called for fasting, prayer, and a day of *hartal* (see Glossary) as marks of protest in August. After that, a special session of Congress in September attended by Khilafet members went further, calling for redress of wrongs, a boycott of titles, councils, courts, educational institutions, and foreign goods, and defiance of state-made law. Only **Motilal Nehru** among the older leaders supported this resolution, but it was ratified at the regular December session of Congress which added the objectives of achieving *swaraj*, raising funds, encouraging *swadeshi* (see Glossary), and prohibiting liquor. Gandhi called the resulting movement "a state of peaceful rebellion" and promised *swaraj* within a year.

Response to the non-cooperation call was spectacular through 1921. With eminent lawyers boycotting the courts and students boycotting secondary schools and colleges, a host of volunteers was freed to raise funds, enroll members in Congress, distribute *charkhas*, or spinning wheels, for domestic production of cloth, organize public bonfires of foreign cloth, mobilize the masses, and staff alternate institutions of education and justice. Fiscal stringency and the short term interests of Indian businessmen made the economic boycott of British goods more effective than in the years 1905–1908, and cloth imports were halved. Although Gandhi did not subscribe to labor unrest or class conflict, 396 strikes in industry and strong non-cooperation movements among workers on tea gardens and jute plantations in **Assam** and **Bengal** that year added to the pressure on British commercial interests. The temperance movement, especially in the south, cut into state excise revenues. Although few titles were renounced and the boycott of legislative councils proved only temporary, these were symbolic actions bonding upper, middle, and lower classes.

Through 1921, Congress reorganized itself into a series of committees from the village level, through districts, divisions, and linguistically defined provinces to a 350-member national committee at the helm. Gandhi's "constructive program" with respect to eradicating **untouchability** and promoting *swadeshi* began. The Khilafet committee called on Muslims to leave the army. Local movements from the **Akali** struggle in the Punjab to the **Moplah** rebellion in Malabar, from the no land-revenue campaign in Bardoli district of **Gujarat** to coolie agitation for higher wages in **Assam**, were linked to the larger causes of Khilafet and Non-Cooperation through intricate organizational work and the awakening of national consciousness.

The most sensational point in the movement was reached with the boycott of the Prince of Wales's visit in November 1921. The boycott provoked the government to retaliate with mass arrests and police brutality against demonstrators. There was no shortage of volunteers for pickets, and upper-class **women**, led by the wife of **C. R. Das**, entered the fray for the first time in **Calcutta**. By December, 40,000 persons were in prison. Using moderate Indian intermediaries, the viceroy offered to negotiate reform through the mechanism of a round table conference. Gandhi refused to halt non-cooperation without an end to what he called "lawless repression." Das and others were bitterly critical. But on February 6, 1922, a violent encounter between police and demonstrators took place at Chauri Chaura in the United Provinces [now **Uttar Pradesh (UP)**], and 22 policemen were burned to death. There had been other incidents of violence and rioting, with overtones of class or communal strife, especially in **Bombay** and Malabar. On February 7, Gandhi unilaterally suspended the Non-Cooperation Movement to the consternation of other congressmen.

Gandhi admitted that his decision to suspend noncooperation may have been "politically unsound and unwise" but said it was "religiously sound." His passionate commitment to *ahimsa* did not permit any compromise with violence in the name of noncooperation. He sought to unite classes and communities, not divide them, and was more interested in raising the level of moral courage, self-reliance, and self-discipline among Indians than in the ethnic composition of their government. He did not claim to lead a revolution in the conventional sense of that term and may well have worried that radical and unruly elements would take over control if he continued the movement to the point of dislodging the existing British government.

Gandhi was arrested on March 10 and was imprisoned for six months. The Non-Cooperation Movement collapsed without achieving "swaraj within one year" or, indeed, much more than a raising of mass political consciousness. Congress did not throw up a revolutionary alternative to Gandhi but was divided and preoccupied by the question of entering or boycotting legislatures in the 1920s. The Khilafet movement had already been sapped by the arrest of the **Ali brothers**, and the 1920s were marked by communal riots rather than by Hindu-Muslim unity. Nevertheless, events in 1921 and 1922 had a deep impact on the people of India, as is evident not only from the official and non-official reports made at the time but in contemporary novels and biographies written in various Indian **languages**.

NON-GOVERNMENTAL ORGANIZATIONS (NGOs), also **VOL-UNTARY SECTOR.** India has a long tradition of voluntary action, especially in the domains of charity, disaster relief, education, health, social reform, and social welfare. Voluntary groups of different kinds sprung up in the course of the freedom movement, many of them inspired by the life and exhortations of **Mahatma Gandhi**, and their number increased after independence. Non-governmental organizations, that is, voluntary groups formed for specific and non-profit making purposes, proliferated worldwide as well and became important channels of public foreign aid, especially from Europe, by the 1990s. In India, successive Five-Year Plans allocated funds and technical assistance for voluntary organizations in recognition of their contributions to social and economic development and to encourage their initiative and cooperation in geographical and functional areas less accessible to governments—such as income generation for **women** or drinking water and sanitation schemes in rural areas.

No single or constant pattern of relationship between governments and NGOs can be discerned. The Central Social Welfare Board (1953), the People's Action for Development India (1973), and the Council for Advancement of People's Action of Rural Technology (1986) are examples of institutions that facilitate partnership between governments and nongovernmental organizations, as in **Kerala**. Provisions of the Foreign Contribution Regulation Act (1975), replaced by the Foreign Exchange Management Act, can be justly interpreted as attempts at governmental control of NGOs. The emergence of action and advocacy NGOs in different parts of the country since the 1970s, especially those working for human rights, freedom of information, emancipation of women, and redistribution of wealth and power toward the oppressed, provide many examples of confrontation, even conflict, between NGOs and different levels of government. Patterns of relationship vary, too, between state and state, district and district, and between one NGO and another so that the only uncontested generalization to be made would be that the number, functions, and visibility of NGOs in independent India has increased exponentially.

NGOs can be categorized by their functions. These range widely, from provision of basic services for the needy, through a forestation of degraded hillsides, rehabilitation of destitute children, literacy and skill generation for women, improved watershed management, environmental conservation, encouragement of traditional arts and crafts, and many others, to protection of human rights, and use of information technology and freedom of information legislation to bring about greater accountability and transparency at different levels of government. Many of the most effective NGOs, such as Tilonia in Rajasthan, are multipurpose and expand their functions as their capabilities increase and in response to local necessities. NGOs also vary by size, rural or urban location, duration, the degree of professionalism among the volunteers who may well be salaried, and success or failure in generating participation, meeting goals, and gaining credibility. One of the most successful and respected NGOs is **Self-Employed Women's Association (SEWA)**.

The strengths of NGOs in comparison to governments lie in the creativity, dedication, economy of resources, flexibility, and the participation and personal interaction that they can mobilize among volunteers and target groups alike, so that they are sometimes seen as substitutes for government in social and developmental work. This image, and the acronym GONGO (Governmental Nongovernmental Organization) used, is not always complimentary. Neither generically nor individually are NGOs free of problems. Most experience difficulties in defining their objectives and in advancing them in credible and participatory ways. Many are built around a single personality and cannot survive without him or her and end in internal conflict over succession. Some are authoritarian and resist accountability and transparency themselves while demanding them from governments. Hundreds of NGOs have been charged with fraud or misappropriation of funds. Some become dependent on foreign funding and distance themselves from the needs and realities of grassroots in India. The acronym DONGO (Donor Nongovernmental Organization) is apt to convey derision.

There are now about one million NGOs operating throughout the country, though not evenly distributed among states and regions. Despite variations in performance and intention, no critical or comparative survey of NGOs would deny their immense contribution to the growth and vitality of civil society in India.

NORTH WEST FRONTIER PROVINCE (NWFP). The NWFP was formed by **Lord Curzon** in 1901 out of six districts of the **Punjab** west of the river **Indus**, five adjoining political agencies, and some loosely controlled tracts along a Durand Line of 1893 demarcating British and Afghan spheres of authority among the Pakhtun or Pathan tribes. One reason Curzon formed a new province was to calm a region long troubled by Pathan resentment on the one hand and British vacillation on the other. The area at the beginning of the 20th century could be compared to an inflamed sore used as a live training ground for British forces.

Curzon withdrew regular British troops from the tribal tracts and concentrated them in bases, such as Peshawer, Kohat, and Quetta, that were accessible by roads and railways. He pursued an active diplomacy in the Persian Gulf to counter the assumed Russian threat to India, and he hoped to tame the Pathans by giving them a focal point of self-esteem and a measure of self-regulation. Curzon had only limited success. **Khan Abdul Ghaffar Khan**'s leadership and affiliation with the **Indian National Congress** brought political awakening and nationalism to the Pathans. They were not attracted to the **All-India Muslim League** and boycotted the referendum on **partition** held in July 1947. Nevertheless, the NWFP was joined to the new dominion of **Pakistan**, which inherited its problems.

NUCLEAR DOCTRINE. On May 11 and May 13, 1998, India successfully conducted two series of underground nuclear tests in the **Rajasthan** desert (Pokharan II) and declared itself a "responsible nuclear weapons state." Subsequently, the government announced a voluntary moratorium on further tests and on May 27 placed a paper on the evolution of India's nuclear policy before Parliament. This paper stressed India's leading role since the 1950s in calling for an end to nuclear testing and for global disarmament, its opposition to discriminatory international regimes on proliferation and willingness to join global arrangements, its self-reliance in scientific and technological advances demonstrated in 1974 (Pokharan I) and deliberate restraint thereafter, and the serious worsening in India's security environment that had led to finally exercising the nuclear option. Statements in various forums made by Prime Minister **Atal Behari Vajpayee** and others, as well as the paper itself, reiterated India's lack of aggressive intent, its commitment to peace, stability, and confidence building, and its willingness to discuss "no-first-use" agreements bilateral or multilateral. In short, nuclear weapons were only for self-defense and to ensure that India was not subjected to nuclear threats or coercion from any quarter.

American and domestic interlocutors pressed New Delhi to spell out details of nuclear policy, weaponization, force posture, command and control, and related topics. On August 17, 1999, the "*Draft Report of the National Security Advisory Board on Indian Nuclear Doctrine*" was officially released. It was an unendorsed, somewhat ambiguous, draft that aroused criticism from hawks and doves alike as well as detailed analysis in the public discussion that followed its release. Officially adopted in January 2003, the NSAB draft contains the key tenets of India's nuclear doctrine and emerging force posture, which are emphatically *not* analogous to those of the Cold War rivals. These tenets can be summarized as follows.

- India would not be the first to use nuclear weapons and would not use nuclear weapons against non-nuclear states.
- Nuclear weapons for India are, above all, political instruments of pure deterrence and not military implements of war fighting.
- India would build a minimum but credible deterrent sufficient to convince a potential aggressor that "any nuclear attack on India and its forces shall result in punitive retaliation with nuclear weapons to inflict damage unacceptable to the aggressor." (Draft Report, p. 2.)
- The likely timing or dimensions of punitive retaliation are not publicly spelled out.
- No specific targeting strategy is mentioned, although leading strategic analysts such as **K. Subrahmanyam** published recommendations for a "countervalue plus" and omni-directional strategy.
- India's nuclear posture was no longer one of "recessed deterrent" as prior to Pokharan II but nor was it a ready arsenal on the alert.
- India's nuclear forces would be based on land, sea, and in the air but no specifications or numbers of weapons were made public.

The Draft Nuclear Doctrine was more of a starting point than a summation of India's evolving policies and force postures. Much will depend on budgets, technological advances, new governments, and the security environment. Since 1999, India has successfully tested intermediate range surface to air missiles capable of carrying nuclear warheads and made capital investments in modernizing all three of its **armed forces**. While absolute civilian control of the military is a prominent feature of the Indian polity, welcome steps have been taken to bring the highest levels of the military into the national security decision-making process and institutionalize command and control structures. Attempts to hold nuclear confidence building meetings with **Pakistan**, the most likely adversary, have not entirely failed, and India's relations with both China and the United States have improved considerably. Nuclear doctrine and force posture will continue to evolve, probably in the same defensive and minimum direction as before. *See also* NUCLEAR POWER PROGRAM.

NUCLEAR POWER PROGRAM. India began an ambitious nuclear power program in 1946 under the direction of **Dr. Homi Bhabha**, who was a close friend of **Jawaharlal Nehru**. An Atomic Energy Commission was soon established and was upgraded to the Department of Atomic Energy in 1954 to stimulate scientific research, the generation of power in an energy-poor country, and the utilization of India's uranium and vast thorium resources. India is one of the founding members of the International Atomic Energy Agency (IAEA) and is on its Board of Governors.

The premier center for research is the Bhabha Atomic Research Centre, Trombay (near **Mumbai**), which built India's first indigenous research reactor APSARA in 1956 and cooperates with other facilities in the peaceful uses of nuclear energy in agriculture and industry and the Radiation Medicine Centre at Bombay. The Indira Gandhi Centre for Atomic Research at Kalpakkam (near **Chennai**) was established in 1971 for research in fast breeder development of nuclear fuel, metallurgy, radiochemistry, and fuel reprocessing. The Centre for Advanced Technology, opened at Indore in 1984, specializes in the technologies of lasers and accelerators. Advanced research is also carried out at **Kolkata** in the Variable Energy Cyclotron Centre and the Saha Institute of Nuclear Physics. The Tata Institute of Fundamental Research has facilities in Mumbai, **Hyderabad**, and Ootacamund, while the Tata Memorial Centre in Mumbai is the leading Indian institution for the treatment of cancer.

Bhabha envisaged a phased program of nuclear power generation using his foreign contacts, young Indian scientists, and Indian rare minerals found in **Bihar**, **Kerala**, and **Orissa**. A Cirus reactor was built in 1960 with Canadian help. India and the United States signed an agreement in 1963 to build the Tarapur Atomic Power Station near Bombay with two boiling water reactors of 210 mw capacities on a turnkey basis; it was commissioned in 1969. Two prototype Rajasthan Atomic Power Stations using commercially obtained heavy water came on line in 1972 and 1981. The Kalpakkam power station, which began commercial operations in 1986, was indigenously designed and constructed in entirety, as was the plant at Narora in **Uttar Pradesh** commissioned in 1989. Similar plants were commissioned in **Gujarat** in the 1990s. By 2003 there were 14 nuclear power reactors functioning in India with an installed capacity of 2720 Mwe, and two new reactors were under construction in **Tamil Nadu** under agreement with the Russian Federation. The third stage of the nuclear power program utilizing thorium for power generation has also begun. India has demonstrated comprehensive capability over all aspects of the nuclear fuel cycle that supports the nuclear power program, including mineral exploration and mining, processing of ores, fuel fabrication and production of heavy water, reprocessing and management of nuclear waste.

India's nuclear program did not proceed without setbacks, first caused by Bhabha's death in a mysterious air crash in 1965 and later by disputes with the United States on fuel supplies for Tarapur and with other suppliers after what India called a "peaceful explosion" conducted in the **Rajasthan** desert in May 1974 (Pokharan I). Creation of nuclear suppliers groups and the erection of barriers to the transfer of equipment, fuel or technology to non-signatories to the Nuclear Non Proliferation Treaty (NPT) of 1968, such as India, made smooth functioning difficult. Additional sanctions were imposed by the United States on India after its overt testing of nuclear weapons in 1998 (Pokharan II) and were lifted only in 2002. India's generation of nuclear power is still low, especially in comparison to Japan or France, amounting to less than 3% of the country's total electric consumption. This is likely to increase in the future because of its cost-effectiveness compared to fossil fuels, the good safety standards hitherto maintained, the availability of indigenously produced fuel and heavy water from a fast breeder reactor commissioned in 1985 and seven heavy water plants, and a recently concluded agreement with the United States on transfers of nuclear technology and equipment for peaceful uses.

India has been an articulate advocate of universal nuclear disarmament since the 1950s. It was one of the first signatories of the Partial Test Ban Treaty of 1963 and has been a constant supporter of a Comprehensive Test Ban Treaty and worldwide cessation of production of fissile materials. India did not, however, sign the Nuclear Non-Proliferation Treaty (NPT) of 1968 which it considers to be discriminatory in its application of obligations on non-nuclear weapons states without corresponding controls on the five acknowledged nuclear weapons states, or the Comprehensive Test Ban Treaty of 1996, for the same reasons. Notwithstanding perceived threats to its security from China's acquisition of nuclear weapons in 1964 and subsequent deployment of a substantial nuclear arsenal, India did not shift its focus from the development of nuclear power to the development of nuclear weapons, although its technical capability to do so was demonstrated at Pokharan I in 1974. The decision to exercise the nuclear option in 1998 seems to have resulted from several separate developments: Pakistan's public vaunt of possessing nuclear weapons made in 1987; proof of active Chinese assistance to Pakistan's militarily controlled nuclear weapons program; explicit or implicit threats of nuclear coercion to influence Indian defense policy; hardening of international proliferation regimes into what Foreign Minister Jaswant Singh called "nuclear apartheid" freezing the divide in status and power between nuclear have and have-not nations; the coming to power in New Delhi of the **Bharatiya Janata Party** that committed to nuclear testing in its election platform. Nevertheless, India's civilian controlled nuclear program is primarily devoted to the generation of electric power in an energy starved yet fast growing economy. *See also* NUCLEAR DOCTRINE.

NUR JAHAN (1575–1645). Nur Jahan was the daughter of a high-ranking Persian in the service of the **Mughal Emperor Akbar** and was named Mihr-un-Nissa. She was the widow of another nobleman at the time Jahangir fell in love with her and made her his queen in 1611, renaming her first Nur Mahal and then Nur Jahan (Light of the World).

Nur Jahan was a woman of great beauty, energy, and talent who was the effective ruler of the empire until Jahangir's death in late 1627. Her name and portrait were joined with his on the coins of the realm. She signed *firmans*, or royal orders: for example, an offer of terms of reconciliation to Prince Khurram for ending his revolt in 1625. Nur Jahan's daughter by her first husband was married to Jahangir's third son, Prince Shahriyar, an unsuccessful contender for the throne. Her brother, Asaf Khan, succeeded their father as chief minister to the emperor and was father-in-law to the able Prince Khurram, who subsequently became the **Emperor Shah Jahan** in 1628. Nur Jahan's mother invented the perfume "attar of roses," and both women controlled large businesses in the indigo and cotton trade of the time. Although she kept *purdah*, or female exclusion from male view, Nur Jahan was a superb hunter and an active participant in the public decisions of Jahangir's reign. Her family connections and her personal power reinforced each other, maintaining the administrative system of Akbar and propping up the charming but frequently inebriated Jahangir through the revolts of his two eldest sons and his General Mahabat Khan.

Nur Jahan had a tomb built for her father Itmat-u-daula at **Agra**, which is compared to an exquisite casket of white marble, jeweled with mosaic and pietra dura work. She also ordered Jahangir's magnificent tomb in Lahore and imparted designs for the fabulous textiles of Mughal India. Jahangir did more than any other person to foster Mughal painting and maintained a day-to-day diary, which surpasses that of **Babur** in its wealth of naturalistic detail and personal frankness. The splendor of the Mughal court, to which Nur Jahan added so much in the early 17th century, was amply described in contemporary accounts of travelers.

NYAYA. One of six schools of classical Indian philosophy that developed in the early centuries of the Common Era, Nyaya concentrated on logic and epistemology. Its main exponent, Akshapada Gautama, contended that clear thinking and logical argument were essential means to remove ignorance or erroneous knowledge and thereby achieve spiritual liberation. His followers were theists, pluralists, and realists. They accepted God as architect of the universe and used teleological arguments to prove the existence of God. They specialized in the methodology of thought and reasoning, typically using five- or seven-step syllogisms in their logic, and analyzing by definition, inference, and example.

Nyaya was coupled with the Visheshika school of philosophy that propounded a view of the physical universe as being constituted of analyzable units or atoms, each one being surrounded by its own *vishesha*, or ultimate unique quality. All six schools of classical Indian philosophy accepted the authority of the **Vedas** and are therefore known as "orthodox" **Hindu** philosophies in contrast to the "heterodox" **Buddhist** and **Jain** schools that repudiated the Vedas as scriptural authority and did not postulate the existence of God. Proponents of Nyaya defended the doctrine of God's existence against the Buddhists and Jains but also criticized the monistic concept of Advaita or nondualism that came to dominate Hindu thought.

– O –

OBEROI, MOHAN SINGH (1900–2002). India's foremost hotelier, owning 30 five-star hotels within India and abroad, Oberoi was born in the **Punjab** and lost his father at the age of six months. His mother ensured that he got a good education at **Arya Samaj** schools. In 1922, Oberoi went to work as a clerk at the Cecil Hotel in **Simla**, where he studied the ways of the wealthy and powerful as well as the detailed business of running a luxury hotel. By the mid-1930s, he had a wife and five children, the proprietorship of Clarkes Hotel, also in Simla, and ambitions of moving into a business traditionally operated by the British and Swiss. Just before the outbreak of **World War II** he took over the Grand Hotel in **Calcutta** and soon negotiated a contract with the Army command to provide board and lodging for 2,000 troops at a reasonable charge. By the end of the war he owned 10 hotels in different cities, and when four were lost to **Pakistan** he built a new hotel in **Orissa**, which proved to be a great success, and also went into the travel business. He opened the first five-star hotel in **Delhi** in 1965 and established a reputation for excellence of service that was maintained even as Oberoi's spread internationally, to countries in the Middle East and Southeast Asia, and Australia.

Oberoi overcame many obstacles and reverses in his long life, but he did not lose his equanimity. He and his family lived without ostentation, although he received many honors and was a member of Parliament in the 1960s. Oberoi was also a visionary and established a training school within India for all aspects of hotel management. His was also one of the earliest Indian companies to welcome **women** employees in better than menial positions and to advance their careers in management. He received valuable assistance from his son-in-law, children, and grandchildren, who now manage the business empire he left them.

OCHTERLONY, DAVID (1758–1825). Joining the Bengal Army of the **East India Company** as a cadet in 1777, David Ochterlony became a legendary figure in India, where he spent the rest of his life. In the course of his career, he participated in many wars against the **Marathas** and proved himself to be a cautious, methodical commander. His was the single successful campaign in an otherwise disastrous war against

Nepal in 1815, and he is credited with first bringing Gurkha soldiers into the Indian Army. Ochterlony succeeded **Charles Metcalfe** as British resident in **Delhi** in 1819 and subsequently became agent general in Rajputana.

As was not infrequent among Company officers at the time, Ochterlony lived in the style of an Indian *nawab* (see Glossary), with a full harem and a large retinue, spending his very considerable annual income freely. The British living in **Calcutta** erected an elegant pillar to his memory in 1841 that still stands.

OIL AND NATURAL GAS CORPORATION (ONGC). A Fortune 500 company valued at US $2 billion, the ONGC is one of the largest in terms of market capitalization, most profitable, and best managed Indian corporations. It is responsible for 77% of India's crude oil and 81% of India's natural gas production. ONGC headquarters are in Dehra Dun, capital of **Uttaranchal** state. At first wholly state-owned, ONGC sold 10% of its equity in early 2004, (mainly to enthusiastic foreign institutional investors) partly to raise funds for more explorations, and partly to further the privatization agenda of **economic liberalization** pushed by the National Democratic Alliance coalition government of the day. In late 2004, however, Prime Minister **Manmohan Singh** leading the successor United Progressive Alliance coalition government announced that there would be no further equity sales from ONGC.

The ONGC and Oil India Limited were founded in 1956, when the Second Five-Year Plan launched India on the path of becoming a self-reliant industrial power with the state controlling the "commanding heights" of the economy. At that time, Western oil companies, notably Burmah Shell, Standard Vacuum, and Caltex, had received concessionary terms for the refining and distribution of petroleum products in India but declined to diversify imports beyond the Persian Gulf or prospect for crude oil within India; disputes with New Delhi also arose over pricing. With Soviet and Rumanian assistance, the Indian public sector entered the field as a competitor and began refining cheaper crude oil imports from the Soviet Union in the 1960s. Oil fields in **Assam** were exploited and when off-shore petroleum deposits were discovered in Indian territorial waters in the Arabian Sea (Bombay High) ONGC became even more active and profitable.

ONGC was incorporated in 1993. Its attempts to attract foreign oil companies to invest in exploration and production of deep sea and shallow water oil deposits in Bombay High were not notably successful, and by the end of the century India's major oil fields were in decline. Those in Assam and **Tripura** were affected by insurgency and **terrorism**, too.

In 2001, ONGC took a major step toward acquiring equity in foreign oil fields by entering a consortium along with American, Japanese, and Russian companies for the Sakhalin field in eastern Russia; ONGC has a 20% interest. It also has a 45% participating interest in a Vietnamese gas project and is pursuing a 25% interest in a productive Sudan oil field. In partnership with Cairn Energy, ONGC is also prospecting in the Bay of Bengal and in the Arabian Sea. Petroleum products remain vital for a modern economy, and India's hunger for oil and gas (like China's) has become a feature of international market news. ONGC probably will continue to expand its activities at home and abroad.

ORISSA. This state has an area of 155,797 square kilometers and an estimated population of close to 37 million, of whom about 25% belong to the **Adivasi** or scheduled tribes. Oriya is the predominant **language**, and Bhubaneswar is the capital city. Much of the land is forested, and mineral extraction and industry, such as steel and aluminum, are important supplements to the predominantly agricultural economy of Orissa.

In ancient times, Orissa was known as the kingdom of Kalinga. Rulers of this vast domain controlled trade routes to the southern peninsula and pioneered maritime trade with Southeast Asia. The Mauryan Emperor **Ashoka** conquered it at a very high cost in lives, was overcome with remorse, as he stated in his edicts, and turned to non-violence. Kalinga or Orissa formed part of the **Gupta** and **Harsha** empires in classical times and waxed prosperous under its own Ganga and Sena Dynasties (with their sprinkling of female rulers) from the 8th to the 13th centuries CE. The great temples at Bhubaneswar, Konarak, and Puri were built in this period. Orissa was coveted by successive Turko-Afghan Muslim rulers in **Delhi** and **Bengal** but more or less maintained its independence—as did another **Hindu** kingdom of **Vijayanagar**—until absorbed in the **Mughal Empire** in 1568.

Located on the southeast coast of India, Orissa attracted the **Marathas** and European trading companies. The Marathas carried out raids and levied taxes on the population; the Dutch created modern links between Orissa and the Indonesian archipelago; the British annexed the area to Bengal in 1813. Orissa was made a separate province in 1936 and is a state in the Indian Union. Though its social indexes and per capita income are lower than the average in India, Orissa is the scene of activity for many **non-governmental organizations** and has spectacular tourist attractions, both cultural and natural. Because of its location and less than efficient government services, Orissa is subject to periodic disaster from typhoons that take a toll on the population. Efforts are being made to modernize road, railway, and air transportation and to develop the port of Paradeep.

– P –

PACHAURI, RAJENDRA KUMAR (1940–). Pachauri was born in Nainital, **Uttaranchal**, and took degrees from the Institution of Mechanical Engineers and Institution of Production Engineers in London. He worked at the Diesel Locomotive Works, **Varanasi**, before taking a double doctorate in industrial engineering and economics in the United States. He became director of the Tata Energy Research Institute (TERI) in 1981 and developed it into a leading research institute. He has received many awards in recognition of his work.

Pachauri's special interests as an environmentalist are in energy conservation, promoting the use of renewable energy sources, and in the sustainable management of natural resources; all of which are of crucial importance to the future of India and of the world. He has served with various international bodies promoting similar aims, and in 2002 he was elected chairman of the Inter Governmental Panel on Climate Change (IPCC). Having the sensitivity of an inhabitant of a developing country, Pachauri underlines the socioeconomic impact of climate change and encourages the participation of youth in research and environmental conservation.

PAINTING. The earliest surviving paintings in India are found in the prehistoric caves of Betak in **Madhya Pradesh** and on decorated pottery from the time of **Harappa**. Descriptions of paintings on wood, palm leaf, and cloth are found in the literature of ensuing periods when the polite arts were cultivated and patronized by the gentry, but the ravages of climate, insects, and war have destroyed all such paintings that were executed before c. 1000 CE. The paintings in the **Ajanta** caves, dated from the second century BCE to the fifth century CE, testify to the artistic achievements of that period in their complex compositions, spatial depth, rich colors, detailed depictions of people and natural and urban life, and in their mature style and sophisticated technique of tempera on plaster. Even in their present damaged condition, the Ajanta paintings are ranked among the glories of world art. Their influence spread south to **Sri Lanka** and northwards to central Asia and China, as recent excavations and openings of ancient **Buddhist** centers reveal.

Miniature painting has a history of at least 2,000 years in India, especially as illustrations to sacred texts or literary manuscripts in the possession of rulers, monasteries, and wealthy merchants. Examples from the 11th century onward survive. **Jain** and Buddhist patronage was particularly important for the evolution of a native manuscript illustration style in the earlier centuries, which was carried over into **Hindu** devotional paintings on cloth scrolls or palm leaf of the 14th and 15th centuries.

Although much Indian art was destroyed in the war-torn 13th century of Muslim-Turkic invasions, the new Persian influence that began to be felt in the 15th century and grew strong after the establishment of **Mughal** dominion revitalized Indian miniature painting. Several distinct styles developed from the 16th century onward. The Mughal school itself combined Persian elegance and technique with Indian vitality and representation of nature; themes based on history, Persian and **Sanskrit** literature, and portrayals of court life and royal hunts were the most recurrent. The paintings of the **Deccan** courts were similarly syncretic and dynamic but had recognizable styles of their own. The Mughal influence was also strong on the painting schools of the Hindu kingdoms in **Rajasthan**, central India, and the **Punjab** hills. But artists there found new themes in musical, romantic, and devotional literature and broke through the confines of both Jain and Persian traditional manuscript painting in the 17th and 18th centuries. Distinctive styles developed within the Rajasthani school, as at Bikanir, Bundi, Jaipur, Kotah, and Kishangarh. Within the Pahari school of the Punjab hill states too, unique styles emerged, as for example in Kangra and Baisohli. And throughout India, folk art in the form of wall paintings and cotton hangings depict folk or epic heroes and domestic scenes. These styles and crafts have been revived in independent India.

All of the traditional schools of art declined sharply as British power expanded—with the consequent loss of patronage—in the 19th century. As in China and Japan, most Indian painters of the late 19th and early 20th centuries showed the influence of Western art but not its mastery; Ravi Varma and Abanindranath Tagore were exceptions. Beginning with Amrita Sher Gill in the 1930s, however, Indian artists increasingly demonstrated enough originality, vigor, and artistic excellence to win recognition at home and abroad. The establishment of art schools and art galleries clearly helped encourage talent and technique. The market for contemporary Indian art has grown exponentially in recent decades with the expansion of a middle class with a growing disposable income, and with the interest shown by public and private bodies in sponsoring and acquiring paintings by Indian artists.

PAKISTAN, ISLAMIC REPUBLIC OF. This country covers nearly 800,000 square kilometers in the northwestern portion of the Indian subcontinent. Its capital is Islamabad. Most of its approximately 151 million population inhabit the Indus valley and more than half speak Punjabi; the official languages are Urdu and Pakhtun. Pakistan reinforces its Islamic identity by maintaining close ties with members of the Islamic Conference but faces internal problems from increased activity by radical Islamists or *jihadis*, who received official support during the 1980s because of the covert war against the Soviet Union in Afghanistan and in the 1990s because of the covert war against India. Pakistan became an ally of the United States during the Cold War and then again after September 2001 in the "war against terror" and is regarded by the United States as a strategic ally that should not be allowed to become a failed state. Since the early 1960s, Pakistan and China have cultivated a close "all-weather" friendship that has included military and nuclear transfers. Because of its geographical location and historical background, Pakistan is a natural founder member of the **South Asian Association for Regional Cooperation (SAARC)**, but it shows less enthusiasm than other members for regional trade and economic cooperation.

The independent state of Pakistan was created by the **Partition** of India in 1947 and the transfer of power from the British Crown to two independent **Dominions**. The name "Pakistan" first appeared in a pamphlet authored at Cambridge, England, in 1933 to stand for **Punjab**, Afghanistan or the **North West Frontier Province**, **Kashmir**, and Sind, or alternatively, "the land of the pure." The philosopher-poet **Muhammad Iqbal** developed the idea of an autonomous Muslim union in the northwestern part of India, but it was **Mohammed Ali Jinnah**, leader of the **All-India Muslim League**, who launched a demand for Pakistan (with ambiguous definition and motive) in 1940. The British conceded the demand in principle under the exigencies of **World War II**, and when the war ended they were unable to prevent or control the communal violence that accompanied Partition. Relations between Pakistan and India since then have been almost consistently strained or adversarial at the official level and often emotional—whether affectionate or hostile—at the personal level. The line between domestic and foreign politics has been soft and the establishment of normal or cordial relations between the two neighbors elusive.

Pakistan was initially composed of two wings separated by more than 1,600 kilometers of Indian territory: western Punjab, North West Frontier Province, Baluchistan, and Sind in the west and East Bengal with Sylhet district of **Assam** in the east. Early attempts to establish a parliamentary system of democracy failed. Military governments after 1956 alienated the politically lively people of East Bengal and refused to honor the results of a 1970 election giving the Awami League of East Bengal a majority. Revolt, repression, an exodus of 10 million refugees, and a civil war followed in 1971, culminating in military intervention by India and the proclamation of an independent **Bangladesh** in the former eastern wing. Indian Prime Minister **Indira Gandhi** and Pakistan President Z. A. Bhutto met at **Simla** in June 1972 and signed an agreement to resolve all disputes bilaterally by peaceful means.

Disputes and conflicts continued, however, for various reasons, including competing claims to Kashmir. Pakistan failed to obtain the accession of the **Princely State** of **Jammu and Kashmir** in 1947 and sent in forces that were halted by Indian troops along an uneven "ceasefire line," leaving large areas in the north and west under Pakistan's occupation and annexation. That line was rationalized in 1972 and incorporated into the Simla Agreement as the "line of control" (LOC) that could now, perhaps, form the basis of a permanent settlement. Pakistan's second attempt to take Kashmir by stealth or force in 1965 also failed. A 1989 insurgency in Kashmir was subsequently supported by Pakistan and resulted in prolonged "low intensity conflict" there and Indian charges of "cross border **terrorism**." Pakistan's unsuccessful efforts to detach Kashmir from India or change the territorial status quo included a daring military adventure at Kargil in 1999 that almost resulted in full-scale war. This carried the risk of nuclear escalation as well, since both Pakistan and India had openly tested nuclear weapons in May 1998. Democratic elements in both countries, as well as their friends and allies, deplore the effects of recurring conflict, and there is widespread support for the bilateral "composite dialogue" of 2004 intended to settle all disputes, reduce nuclear risks, and facilitate economic and people to people exchanges. Talks are deliberately paced and, to date, have neither succeeded nor failed.

Pakistan had civilian governments from 1972 to 1977 and from 1988 to 1998, but the army always has been politically—and now economically—dominant. Overtly so when Generals Ayub Khan, Zia ul Huq, and Pervez Musharraf occupied positions of head of government and head of state in 1958–1969, 1977–1988, and 1999 to the present, respectively. The army's enmity toward India is axiomatic, but it also faces challenges in Baluchistan and in the tribal territories of NWFP, and some officers may be inclined toward realistic reassessments of its capabilities and the need for peace with India. Pakistan's demographic trends of rapid population growth combined with a weak economy, an extremely poor educational system, the erosion of civil institutions, an apparent absence of democratic alternatives to military rule, centrifugal pulls, and the potentially disruptive impact of radical Islam prompt some scholars to make gloomy predictions. At the same time, Pakistan's internal collapse is clearly not in the interests of major powers, its neighbors or, above all, the people of Pakistan. *See also* ISLAM, PARTITION, SOUTH

ASIAN ASSOCIATION FOR REGIONAL COOPERATION, TERRORISM.

PAL, BACHENDIRI (1954–). Bachendiri Pal was the first Indian woman to reach the summit of Mount Everest, in 1984. Since then she has led many expeditions, including an India-Nepal women's expedition to Everest in 1993 that set seven world records, a rafting voyage down the **Ganga River** in 1994, and a trans-Himalayan trek from **Arunachal Pradesh** to the Karakoram Pass in 1997. Her feats have been recorded in world books and she has won many awards.

Bachendiri Pal was born into a poor family in Garhwal district of **Uttaranchal** state and used her household tasks of collecting water, firewood, and fodder from hillsides to hone her mountaineering skills. After obtaining a master's degree in education, she took a job with **Tata Steel**. She first came to the attention of a director of the National Adventure Foundation when he was selecting women for scholarships and has amply justified his faith in her.

PAL, BIPIN CHANDRA (1858–1932). Pal was born in a prosperous Kayastha (see Glossary) family of Sylhet in eastern **Bengal**. He joined the **Brahmo Samaj** at an early age and demonstrated his commitment to social reform by opposing **caste** restrictions, advocating education for **women**, supporting legislative action to raise the age of marriage, and by twice marrying **brahman** widows.

Pal had an erratic career but was noted for his rousing oratory and his nationalist essays in Bengali. He started the newspaper, *Bande Mataram*, edited by **Aurobindo** in 1906, and the monthly *Hindu Review* in 1911. He wrote for various journals and edited the *Independent*, founded by **Motilal Nehru**. Pal championed the cause of plantation and other workers and supported their right to strike; workers became involved in the larger nationalist movement at this time.

When Pal joined the **Indian National Congress** in 1886, he accepted the leadership of the "moderates" but later sided with the "extremists" led by **Bal Gangadhar Tilak**. In the immediate aftermath of **Lord Curzon's partition of Bengal** in 1905, Pal switched to revolutionary activity. Along with Tilak and **Lala Lajpat Rai** he formed the "New Party," which agitated for boycott of British goods, independence, and *swadeshi* (see Glossary). Bipin Chandra Pal became a national hero in the fierce repression that followed. Pal's public lectures in Bengal and **Madras** from 1905 to 1908 led the British authorities to label him "arch seditionist." He was arrested and deported. Upon returning to India he joined the **Home Rule League** led by **Annie Besant**. Pal did not like the turn to mass politics after **World War I** and did not support **Mohandas Gandhi** or the **Non-Cooperation Movement** in 1920. Pal left Congress, retired from active politics, and turned to the study of **Vedanta**, but he continued writing on public affairs.

PALA DYNASTY. The origin of the Pala Kings—whose names all ended with the word pala—is obscure, but they brought order to **Bengal** and eastern **Bihar** in the confused age following the death of **HarshaVardhana** and the decline of imperial **Kanauj**. The Palas ruled in eastern India from c. 750 CE to c. 1185 when the Sena Dynasty supplanted them.

With a military aristocracy to back them, the first two Kings, Dharamapala and his son Devapala, ruled for nearly 100 years and consolidated a large kingdom. They extended their power over **Assam** and **Orissa**, intervened in the succession at Kanauj, and came into conflict with the Gurjara-**Pratiharas** in the west and the **Dravidians** in the south. The Pala kings were in contact with the Srivijaya Kings of present-day Indonesia. The ninth king of the dynasty, Mahipala (c. 978–1030), dispatched a mission to **Tibet**, inscribed a building at Sarnath, and was attacked from the south by the army of Rajendra **Chola**.

Notwithstanding their military exploits, the Pala dynasty presided over an age of peace, prosperity, and artistic brilliance in eastern India. They restored the ancient city of **Pataliputra** and built or repaired irrigation tanks of earlier times. They established new universities and monasteries at Vikramsila and Paharpur and made endowments to the great university of **Nalanda**. **Buddhists** themselves, they employed **brahman** ministers and gave royal patronage to various **Shiva** and **Vishnu** cults of medieval **Hinduism**. The **Tantric** tradition probably emerged within both Mahayana Buddhism and **Hinduism** during the Pala period.

PALLAVA DYNASTY. This dynasty based in Kanchipuram ruled the **Tamil** country from the middle of the sixth to the end of the ninth century CE and was the dominant power in peninsular India for much of that time. It had faded from memory until the mid-19th century when its newly discovered inscriptions began to be examined by historians.

The literal meaning of Pallava, "young twig," may denote a forest or even foreign origin elevated to high **caste** by the performance of **Vedic** sacrifices such as the **Ashvamedha**, described in one of their early inscriptions. Whatever their origins, and the name features in second-century records, the Pallavas represent the culmination of a gradual process of assimilation by the Tamil upper class of **Aryan** or Vedic ideas and institutions as well as a reassertion of Tamil personality among the non-brahman classes. For example, their early inscriptions were in **Sanskrit** and **Prakrit**, then Tamil was introduced, and finally both Sanskrit and Tamil were used. Further, the high status and extensive land grants accorded **brahmans** reflected a supplanting of **Jains** and **Buddhists** by brahmans in ministerial positions and educational institutions. Royal patronage to Jain and Buddhist monasteries continued however, and the upsurge of popular devotional cults around **Shiva** or **Vishnu** combined elements of Sanskrit and Tamil culture.

The Pallava Dynasty was the first of consequence to rule the rich plains of the peninsula on the eastern coast. Geographically and dynastically it was engaged in a struggle with the **Chalukya** Dynasty ruling the plateau of the western **Deccan** for control over peninsular rivers. The province of Vengi, lying between the deltas of the Krishna and Godaveri rivers in present-day **Andhra Pradesh**, was a recurring bone of contention. Pulakeshin II Chalukya's conquest of that area was avenged by Narasimha-varman Pallava (c. 625–645) who conquered the Chalukya home base in Vatapi. A seesaw of conflict continued between the two evenly matched dynasties with others, such as the Pandyas of **Madurai** in the far south, occasionally attacking the Pallavas while the Cheras of the southwest coast maintained close contacts with them. The **Rashtrakutas** replaced the Chalukyas in the ninth century and the **Cholas** replaced the Pallavas, but similar points of conflict remained.

The terrain of peninsular India favored localized kingdoms in roughly even balance rather than the continental empires of north India. Similarly, power and administrative authority within the Pallava kingdom tended to be decentralized, although high-sounding titles of divine origin were attached to the king in conformity with Sanskritic practice. The ministerial council was an important institution, and a hierarchy of officials worked through and with village headmen. Village assemblies and committees met frequently at several levels, dealing with matters such as the census, crime and punishment, and endowments in processes reinforcing local autonomy. Inscriptions with respect to land grants and taxes on copper plates of the eighth century and the records maintained by certain brahman villages provide information on donations of land for the construction and maintenance of irrigation tanks by the community as a whole. The Pallavas encouraged the clearing and cultivation of land, probably presiding over a transition from a pastoral to an agricultural economy. But land revenue was limited in comparison to that of northern empires and was supplemented by other taxes. Maritime trade with Kamboja (Cambodia), Champa (Annam), and Srivijaya (Sumatra) in Southeast Asia became sufficiently important to necessitate shipyards at **Mahabalipuram** and Negapattinam and a naval fleet, subsequently expanded by the Cholas. Southeast Asian kingdoms imported the Tamil script, Pallava architecture, and brahmanical rituals as well as goods.

The temple was a nodal point of community life and culture. *Mathas* were attached to temples and served as rest houses and centers of learning, literary activity, and debate. Sanskrit was the language of courts and the literati, but Tamil became the vehicle for new compositions of the lyric, epic, and devotional variety. Temples were usually freestanding but Pallava architecture was much influenced by the Buddhist rock caves of the Deccan. The most famous Pallava monuments are the seven monolithic stone temples with their remarkable relief sculptures of scenes from the *Mahabharata* constructed by Narasimhavarman at **Mahabalipuram**. Kanchipuram also boasts numerous fine temples from the eighth century. **Music** and dancing were included in temple ritual and gave rise to the classical forms of Karnatic music and Bharata Natyam dance. The great philosopher **Shankara** preached in Pallava domains and from them sprang the beginnings of the **Bhakti movement**, which spread throughout India.

PANCHASHEEL or PANCH SHILA. The five principles of peaceful coexistence, which came to be known as panchasheel, were first set out by India and China in the preamble of an agreement on trade with **Tibet** that was signed on April 29, 1954. The five principles were: (1) mutual respect for each other's sovereignty and territorial integrity; (2) mutual non-aggression; (3) mutual noninterference in each other's internal affairs; (4) equality of standing and equal benefits; and (5) peaceful coexistence.

Prime Minister **Jawaharlal Nehru** proclaimed panchasheel as proof of India's own non-aggressive intentions in its neighborhood, as a psychological check on and obvious test of Chinese intentions soon after its revolution, and most of all, as conducive to the "climate of peace" he was most anxious to create in India's environs. In the latter sense, panchasheel was a cornerstone of Indian foreign policy, enabling cooperation with states of different ideological and political systems—such as the Soviet Union—without sacrifice of independence. When Nehru's policy of friendship with China failed, as it did after 1960, his critics also denounced panchasheel without, however, suggesting an adequate alternative short of armed confrontation. The Five Principles of Peaceful Coexistence have also been used to good effect by China in relations with its neighbors and other facets of its foreign policy. Not surprisingly, the principles of panchasheel have been reiterated often as India and China worked toward normalizing their relations since the 1980s.

PANCHAYATI RAJ. The literal meaning of the term is, rule by panchayat (see Glossary) or autonomous village councils, whose important role in administrative, civic, judicial, and social affairs has been traced back to the **Vedic**, **Mauryan**, **Gupta**, and even **Mughal** eras. Panchayats languished under bureaucratic and centralized British administration in India but were sometimes romanticized during the freedom struggle as examples of indigenous grassroots democracy. **Mohandas Gandhi's** *Hind Swaraj* (1908) postulated a self-governing India of autonomous village communities. One of the Directive Principles of the **Indian Constitution** of 1950 was to revive panchayats "to enable them to function as units of self-government," and their institutionalization was a major innovation of independent India.

Some states, including **Uttar Pradesh** and **Rajasthan**, passed legislation in the 1950s and 1960s creating panchayat raj institutions, and some gave these village councils roles in the implementation of community development and agricultural extension projects that were financed and controlled by state governments. But their effectiveness was mixed: most panchayats lacked financial resources, trained personnel, smooth dealings with officials, or even popular interest and support. Some panchayats enforced controls over behavior for traditional or even reactionary ends and discouraged social change. Other panchayats proved to be training grounds for the exercise of individual franchise and majority decisions. Some, as in the state of **Karnataka** from 1987 to 1991, were well-rounded and strong, acting to alert relevant authorities of impending rural crises as well as serving as instruments of ensuring official and political accountability to the grassroots. The centralization, personalization, and politicization of institutions that characterized India for some decades inevitably weakened panchayats. But all panchayats helped to raise awareness among traditionally powerless groups—such as **women** and the lower **castes**—of voting rights and party politics.

A committee headed by Ashoka Mehta and appointed by the **Janata Party** government in 1978 reported that strong panchayat raj institutions were "imperative" for democratic control over administration at the district level and should be encouraged. The **Sarkaria Commission**, although primarily concerned with center-state relations in a federal system, also recommended devolution of authority from state governments to districts, from districts to villages. In May 1989 the **Congress Party** government of **Rajiv Gandhi** introduced the 73rd constitutional amendment in parliament making panchayat raj institution obligatory in all states. The amendment failed to win the required two-thirds majority in the **Rajya Sabha** at the time but was passed in the first half of 1993. The Constitutional amendment specified that panchayats at the village and intermediate levels must be directly elected for five year terms and endowed with necessary powers and authority to enable them to function as units of self-government. Further, one third of panchayat seats were reserved for women. The National Front government of **V. P. Singh** and others kept alive the enthusiasm for panchayats. Villagers themselves welcomed the prospect of being able to transact business at places within easy walking distance instead of far away at district or state headquarters, and of controlling development monies allocated to their neighborhoods. By the end of 1990, nearly 580,000 villages in India, inhabited by close to 600 million people, elected about three million persons to over 270,000 panchayats and 300 Zilla Parishads (at the district level) to deal with local matters. Many **non-governmental organizations**, Indian and international, instituted training programs for panchayats, often emphasizing the training of women newly placed in managerial positions. The results have been extremely effective in raising the self-confidence, ability, and acceptability of rural women in positions of authority, such as *sarpanch* or village headman, and in grounding at the grassroots level democratic concepts of accountable and responsible government that can be changed by voters. Panchayati raj is widening and deepening democracy in India, as demonstrated in recent elections.

PANDIT, VIJAYLAKSHMI (1900–1991). Vijaylakshmi was born in **Allahabad** to **Motilal Nehru** and his wife 11 years after their son **Jawaharlal**. She was given a cosmopolitan upbringing at home and then married to Ranjit Pandit, a promising lawyer of the same Kashmiri **brahman** community as her own. Their participation in the **Civil Disobedience Movement** of 1930 and consequent imprisonment brought a different kind of privilege: association with **Mahatma Gandhi** and the leaders of India's freedom struggle. Vijaylakshmi entered elective politics in Allahabad, won a seat to the United Provinces—present-day **Uttar Pradesh**—legislative assembly in 1937, and became the first woman minister in **Govind Vallabh Pant**'s government 1937–1939.

Vijaylakshmi was known for many other firsts as well. In her individual capacity, she led an "unofficial" delegation to the San Francisco conference where the Charter of the United Nations was drafted in 1945 and proved more appealing than the official British-Indian delegation. Two years later she was elected the first woman president of the UN General Assembly. She was also India's first ambassador to the Soviet Union and the first woman Ambassador to the United States and to the United Kingdom. Her charm, her good looks, her hospitality, and her close links with her brother, the prime minister, were exceptional assets for a diplomat. Mrs. Pandit did not take an active part in Indian politics after 1969.

PANDYA. The Pandya Kingdom is associated with the southernmost portion of the Indian peninsula since the earliest historical times to the 14th century CE. The origins of this **Tamil** dynasty are unknown, but it was functioning in the fourth century BCE. Although very little information has come to light about the administrative and social arrangements of the early Pandyas, **Shiva** worship seems to have been prevalent. The Pandya Kingdom was known to **Megasthenes** and **Kautilya** at the **Mauryan** court and featured in **Ashoka**'s rock edicts. It was mentioned in the *Periplus of the Erythean Sea* and was known to Pliny and Ptolemy of the first century CE. Roman coins discovered in the area testify to trade between the Pandya kingdom and the Roman Empire.

The Pandyas were constant rivals of their neighbors, the **Pallavas** to the north and the Cheras of **Kerala** to the west, and in frequent conflict with rulers on the southern island of **Ceylon**. The northern boundary of the Pandya kingdom varied from time to time, but its capital at **Madurai** was constant, as also its inclusion of Kanya Kumari or Cape Comorin at the tip. Two brothers competing for the throne allowed the kingdom to be overrun by a general who was deputing for **Alauddin Khalji** in 1310. A Muslim Sultan of Madurai replaced the Pandyas, and soon declared independence from **Delhi**. **Hindu** rulers of **Vijayanagar** overthrew his successors in 1378.

Extant administrative records, epigraphic sources, and palm leaf revenue documents show the later Pandyas of the 13th century to have been harsh and extortionate rulers. But they made a major contribution to the arts and culture of the Vijayanagar Empire and to the temple architecture of southern India from **Chola** simplicity to Vijayanagar ornamentation. The full development of the *gopuram*, or gateway tower style, can be seen in the four towering *gopuram* with elaborate sculptures of the Meenakshi temple in Madurai, attributed to the Pandyas.

PANINI (c. between seventh and fourth century BCE). Panini was a poet and grammarian of **Sanskrit**. He wrote the *Ashtadhyayi*, the earliest standard Sanskrit grammar and authority still in use today, as well as eight other works containing rules in the form of *sutras* (see Glossary) totaling about 4,000. Panini's work was continued and critiqued by others, including **Patanjali**, making it almost a history of the Sanskrit language.

Little is known about Panini's background other than the name of his grandfather, Devala, a notable legislator, and that he is also known by his metronymic, Daksheya (son of Dakshi). It is likely that Panini was born at Attock in the **Gandhara** region of the northwest.

PANIPAT. An ancient and extant town named Panipat is located 85 kilometers northwest of **Delhi** on the river **Yamuna**. Panipat commands a low ridge separating the plains of the **Indus** from those of the **Ganges** and is therefore supremely important to armies moving from northwest to southeast. It is close to the field of Kurukshetra, on which the great mythological war described in the *Mahabharata* took place. The strategic importance of Panipat's location in ages before motorized transport and mechanized war is additionally testified to by three historically decisive battles in 1526, 1556, and 1761.

The first battle of Panipat, on April 20, 1526, pitted 12,000 men following **Babur**, the Timurid prince of Kabul, against the forces of Ibrahim Lodi, defending his weakening hold over the **Sultanate of Delhi**. Babur's easy victory on this occasion dates the beginning of the **Mughal Empire** in India. The second battle of Panipat, on November 5, 1556, was won by the young **Akbar**, grandson of Babur, against a possible contender for power in Delhi, Hemu. Only after this event did expansion and consolidation of the Mughal Empire become possible.

The third battle of Panipat, on January 6, 1761, culminated two months of skirmishes, sieges, and maneuvers between the forces of two uneasy alliances. One was between **Ahmad Shah Abdali**, disaffected Mughal feudatories, the **Rohillas**, and the Nawab of **Awadh**. Against that stood **Maratha** forces led by five equally powerful chiefs: the **Peshwa** of **Poona**, Bhonsle Raja of Berar, the Gaekwad of Baroda, Holkar of Indore, and Scindia of Gwalior. The Marathas were defending their own conquests in northern India as well as the now powerless Mughal Emperor. The initial advantage lay with them, but a series of reverses caused the Marathas to leave the field. Abdali did not linger in India after his men had plundered, and the defeated Mughal court remained somnolent. However, if an indecisive power vacuum appeared to be the immediate consequence in India of the third battle of Panipat, the ultimate result was to allow that vacuum to be filled by the **East India Company**, only in the wings of political ambition in 1761 but, less than a century later, masters in Delhi and the subcontinent.

PANT, GOVIND BALLABH (1887–1961). Born near Almora in the Kumaon region of the central **Himalaya** to a pious and well-placed **brahman** family, Pant was educated at home and a local school before going to college in **Allahabad** on scholarship. He studied law, qualified for the bar, and set up his own legal practice in 1910. He was drawn into local politics soon after when he started a weekly journal *Shakti*, campaigned vigorously against the prevailing custom of *kuli begar*, or forced labor, and served for two years on the Kashipur Municipal Board. By this time he was a supporter of the nationalist cause, an admirer of Pandit **Madan Mohan Malaviya**, and a member of the **Indian National Congress**.

Pant was one of those who persuaded the British authorities that Kumaon deserved to be taken off the list of "backward areas" and given elective representation under the **Montagu-Chelmsford Reforms**. He was elected to the Legislative Council of the United Provinces—present-day **Uttar Pradesh (UP)**—from Nainital district in 1923 and served there to 1930 as leader of the **Swaraj Party**; the official policy of Congress was to remain outside the councils. Pant demonstrated against the **Simon Commission** in 1928 and was badly injured as a result of police *lathi* (see Glossary) charges. He participated in the **Civil Disobedience Movement** of 1930, served his time in prison, gave up his law practice, and took up the constructive work adjured by **Mahatma Gandhi** in village uplift and hand spinning. Pant's character, his intellect, his honesty, and his eloquence won him high respect and affection from his colleagues in Congress, including **Jawaharlal Nehru**. When Congress won the 1937 elections in the UP and formed a ministry, Pant headed it. He was once again elected chief minister of the UP in 1946 after six years spent in non-cooperation and prison and led that state through the first post-independence years to 1954.

Pant was asked by Nehru to join his cabinet in New Delhi in January 1955 and served as Union Home Minister to his death in 1961. He and **Maulana Abul Kalam Azad** could give Nehru the kind of loyal but independent comradeship that the prime minister was denied from others of lesser stature. Many watching Pant at work recalled **Sardar Vallabhbhai Patel**, independent India's first home minister. Pant was not an ideological radical, but he supported the Congress commitment to social and economic reform. He was awarded the Bharat Ratna—India's highest civilian honor—in 1957.

PARAMOUNTCY. Paramountcy was a nebulous term used to describe the relationship between the British Crown acting through the Secretary of State for India and the governor general, on the one hand, and the Indian princes, on the other. The term had no precise legal or constitutional definition because the relationship was the outcome of a lengthy process of change in which treaties, engagements, and *sanads* (see Glossary) were supplemented by usage, sufferance, and decisions made as the British established their military and political supremacy and economic and social dominance in India. In that process, some princes waged war and others signed **Subsidiary Alliances** with the **East India Company**, but all lost the substance of their independence, even though their titles were derived from rights earlier than British grants.

By the time paramountcy was first enunciated as a concept by **Charles Metcalfe** in 1820, it implied the duty of the British to act as "supreme guardians of general tranquility, law and right to maintain the legal succession" in the **Princely States**. This was accomplished through the presence of a British Resident and sometimes of troops, enabling a limited enjoyment of power by the princely rulers but depriving them of their former international status. **Lord Dalhousie** also deprived many of them of their territory and title as he ruled on issues of succession. The great **Uprising of 1857** put an end to that aggressive policy. Queen Victoria's Proclamation of 1858 promised to "respect the Rights, Dignity and Honor of Native Princes as our own." This signaled British intentions to reward those princes who had stood as breakwaters in the recent storm and to bolster the feudal order as a conservative force in India. The fusion of British and princely interests appeared to be complete in the latter half of the 19th century and the word "paramountcy" did not appear in any of the legislation for constitutional reform in British India during the first half of the 20th century.

Two processes brought about an anomalous situation in which redefinition of paramountcy became necessary. One process was the spread of nationalist aspirations for popular representation and independence to the people of the princely states. This occurred both spontaneously and under the leadership of the **Indian National Congress**. Depending on personality and circumstance, princes reacted by reforming their own administrations and/or by expressing reliance on the paramount power, the British Crown, to protect their position against popular unrest. Another process was rationalization of the patchwork quilt of boundaries within India for administrative reasons, especially in the course of drafting and implementing the **Government of India Act of 1935**. For the first time, a Federation of India was envisaged to bring together British and Princely India, hitherto treated differently. The princes were urged by the viceroy to sign instruments of accession, but prolonged and excessive bargaining over terms prevented consummation of that federation. Schemes for the absorption of smaller principalities into larger contiguous states or for cooperative groupings of small states to facilitate attachment with British India were drawn up on paper but were not implemented. Again, respective rights and duties under paramountcy were left unclear.

By the end of **World War II**, the issue of how and when Princely India would be joined with the soon-to-be-independent British India had been raised but not resolved. By this time British attention had shifted to the fate of India as a whole. The Labour government was not as sympathetic to the princes as others were; paramountcy was a controversial term. The **Cabinet Mission** assumed that the princes would find a place in the new constitutional structure of India that was about to be drafted, and invited them to enter discussions on the subject. Congress leaders, especially **Jawaharlal Nehru**, assumed that the princely states were an integral part of India, just as the provinces were, and made it clear that while the friendship of the princes was desirable, in his opinion the ultimate authority lay with the people through their elected representatives. The Cabinet Mission issued statements on May 16 and May 22, 1946 saying that paramountcy was neither transferable to the future Government of India nor retainable by His Majesty's Government; it would lapse. To fill the void that this created, princely states were expected to cooperate in the new India, but the details of their political or federal arrangements were not spelled out.

Many princes were bewildered and troubled by the prospect of losing their British protectors on the eve of independence in 1947. A very few, such as the Nizam of **Hyderabad** backed by a British lawyer, interpreted "lapse of paramountcy" to imply resumption of independence; most princes found that impractical. They also were dismayed by the thought that under the Independence of India Act 1947 all but the barest minimum of connections between 562 scattered territories ruled by princes and the rest of the country would be snapped. The Political Department of the Interim Government, under the jurisdiction of Home Member **Vallabhbhai Patel**, busied itself in smoothing out the anomalies by inviting the princes to sign instruments of accession to India. **V. P. Menon** went from state to state negotiating terms. The viceroy, **Lord Mountbatten**, personally lent his considerable powers of persuasion and charm to the task of completing the process. He also addressed the **Chamber of Princes** on July 25, 1947, urging them to join India (or Pakistan), paying due regard to geographic contiguity and the wishes of their people, before August 15. The integration of the princely states with the rest of India followed speedily after the new **Constitution** was adopted on January 26, 1950, and owed nothing to the defunct doctrine of paramountcy.

PARSIS. A small ethno-religious community of **Zoroastrians** is named Parsi because members are descended from those who fled Persia after the seventh century invasion of Arabs spreading **Islam** and took sanctuary in India to save their religion. The *Avesta* plays a central role as the holy book of the Parsis and Firdausi's (934–1029) *Shah Namah* preserves an ancient Iranian tradition feeding Parsi ethnic consciousness. The *Kissah-I-Sanjan* (c. 1600) chronicles their exodus from Iran to Hormuz and settlement in India on the coast of **Gujarat** between the eighth and tenth centuries. They adopted the local dress and **language**, gave allegiance to the ruler, were allowed to preserve their religion, and consecrated an *atash bahram*, or holy fire, at Nausari early in the 16th century. They maintained their status when Gujarat was conquered by the **Mughal Emperor Akbar** in 1573; he invited the Parsi priest Meherji Rana to represent Zoroastrianism in the religious-philosophic discussions held at his court.

The Parsis were the preferred and skilled brokers and agents for European companies trading in the port city of **Surat** in the 16th,

17th, and early 18th centuries. For this reason they were encouraged to settle in **Bombay** by the British and granted land to establish their first **Dakhma**, or Tower of Silence for the dead, there. More than half of the Parsi population was concentrated in Bombay by the mid-19th century, and 90% of these filled occupations of trade, banking, book-keeping, secretarial, and watch-making. Some families, such as the Jeejeebhoys, made fortunes in the opium trade with China. With the opening of Bombay University, Parsis moved into the higher educational and technical professions. Unlike some **Hindus** or Muslims at the time, Parsis saw no incompatibility between their religion and modern education for men and **women** alike. With the beginning of industrialization in India, they rapidly established themselves in ship-building and the manufacture of cotton textiles. For example, the management of the Bombay shipyard was commissioned to the Wadia family from 1735 to 1885; the first modern cotton mills were founded by the Davar and Petit families; and the steel industry in India was started by the **Tata** family in the early 20th century. In short, the Parsis was the first Indian community to produce modern entrepreneurs and gain high status both with the British and within their own community.

That the Parsis not only survived but prospered as a small minority community from the time of their arrival in India to the present day can be explained largely by their collective behavior. They were strictly loyal to the ruling authority, kept apart from other group tensions and conflicts, and did not present a threat to any state. Nor did they invite state intervention in the economic, religious, or social affairs of their own community. A Parsi Panchayat, or council, formed in 1642 and enlarged or altered according to felt need, was virtually the self-governing body of the Parsis until 1836 when its authority was challenged by reform-minded men of the middle class. At about the same time, the Panchayat was transformed by private donations into a vast charitable trust which provided a comprehensive public welfare system for Parsis unequalled by other less compact and socially conscious communities; there are no Parsi beggars on record. The trust also built a network of schools and colleges in the late 19th century, but these did not keep pace with the best governmental or private institutions.

Until 1947, Parsis demonstrated complete loyalty to the British Raj and a strong Anglophilia at the social level, remaining aloof, for the most part, from Indian society and politics. Their self-identification with the British is reflected in the fact that 63 Parsis were knighted, three of the four Indian hereditary barons before 1908 were Parsis, and all three Indians elected to the British Parliament from English constituencies before 1930 were Parsis. However, their exceedingly small numbers precluded their being given a separate communal electorate, although substantial property and high educational qualifications always assured them more than proportionate representation among the Bombay justices of the peace and the Municipal Council in British times. Some Parsis, like some **Anglo-Indians**, emigrated to other British colonies at the time of Indian independence.

On the other hand, from the mid-19th century onward, some prominent middle-class members of the Parsi community not only identified completely with India, but provided leadership to the **Indian National Congress** for several decades after its founding and supported its goal of political independence. **Dadabhai Naoroji** and **Pherozeshah Mehta** were among such men. Moderate or conservative for the most part, the Parsis also produced the labor leader and communist party member S. D. Saklatvala in the 1920s. Though Parsis were not active in Congress during the decades of **Mohandas Gandhi**'s leadership, and may have frowned on the "socialistic" economic policies of **Jawaharlal Nehru**'s governments in the 1950s, they quickly discovered an honorable place for themselves in the life of independent India.

Parsi religion, customs, and personal law were guaranteed under the **Constitution**. Their individual capabilities achieved full recognition in all professions including science, industry, and the **armed forces**, such as those of Field Marshal **Manekshaw** and former Attorney General of India Soli Sorabjee. The Parsi community was not subjected to pressure from the majority Hindu community to conform, much less convert; even the **Shiv Sena** in Bombay did not target Parsis as objects of hate, though some incidents of vandalism have taken place. In short, the Parsis experience no external threat in independent India. But serious internal problems have surfaced in the community, chiefly because orthodox high priests vested with authority refuse to countenance inevitable social change, such as inter-community marriage, which is legal in India. As a result, well-educated Paris women who marry outside the community are expelled, and their children are excluded from all Zoroastrian religious rites. Combined with a steady emigration of Parsi men and low birth rates among Parsi couples, this means that numbers are declining. The high ratio of older Parsis to young working people poses a serious problem of care for the elderly and an increase of incidents of indigence among them. The National Minorities Commission recently estimated that 36% of Parsis lived below the poverty line in India, an astonishing fact in light of popular perceptions of Parsi prosperity. The brilliant novelist, Robinton Mistry, has movingly portrayed life in a Parsi community in post-independence India. While individual Parsis debate social reform and adapt to the demands of modernity, the personal laws governing the community remain those dictated by orthodox high priests. *See also* ZOROSTRIAN.

PARTITION. India's independence from British rule on August 15, 1947, was accompanied by Partition, or a division of British India, and the creation of **Pakistan** as another independent state on the subcontinent. Cyril Radcliffe of the **Boundary Commission** drew the line of division on a map in a **Delhi** office, but it was announced only on August 17, 1947. Partition was a traumatic act that not only separated provinces of the northwest where the majority of the population followed **Islam** from the **Hindu** majority provinces in the rest of India, but vivisected the composite provinces of **Bengal** and **Punjab** at an agonizing cost to all of the people who lived there.

Partition resulted in the deaths of about one million people and the displacement of approximately 10 million people from their ancestral homes as communal violence forced them to migrate across the new border. In the west, an unanticipated exchange of 4.3 million Hindus and **Sikhs** from west Punjab with 4.2 million Muslims from east Punjab and the United Provinces [present-day **Uttar Pradesh (UP)**] was more or less complete by the end of 1947. Rehabilitation of the Punjab refugees in India was reasonably speedy and successful because of heroic efforts made by the refugees themselves as well as by the government. In the east, the situation was different. 12 million Hindus—42% of the total Hindu population of undivided Bengal—remained in the new East Pakistan and very few Muslims of the approximately 40 million who stayed on in India migrated there. But conditions soon changed. In 1947, 344,000 Hindu refugees from East Pakistan flowed into **Calcutta**; more than twice that number came in 1948, more than one and a half million in 1950, and further batches were forced out later as Pakistan became increasingly Islamist and then broke up into two states in 1971.

Partition is probably the most controversial event in modern Indian, or British imperial, history. Publication of 12 thick volumes of British archives edited by Nicholas Mansergh relating to the transfer of power 1942–1947, as well as many volumes of factual data, literary expressions of experience, personal memoirs, and scholarly analysis has not diminished the controversy or the emotion evoked by Partition. Enough material exists in the public domain to support, or to contradict, any one of three main explanations offered about the causes of Partition.

One theory, popular among "anti-imperialists" in India, portrays Partition as the culmination of British imperial tactics to "divide and rule." The British pitted Muslim against Hindu at each stage of constitutional reform and delayed the introduction of responsible or majority government. "Divide and rule" led tragically to what senior British civil servant Penderell Moon called *Divide and Quit*. After **World War II** Britain was too weak to hold on to empire, yet it could not tolerate the idea of a strong and independent India. This theory ignores the contrary evidence contained in archives researched by Anita Inder Singh and others that with the onset of the Cold War so soon after the end of World War II, Britain was eager to keep the Indian subcontinent united for the sake of Western security but was unable to do so at that stage.

Another theory, popular in Pakistan but with currency in the West as well as in some circles in India, portrays Partition as an inevitable consequence of "two nations"—Hindu and Muslim—incompatible in one state. Tracing conflict to primordial ethnic or religious difference may be academically fashionable at times, but the "two nation theory" does not account for many facts about the Indian subcontinent in the 20th century. These facts include the differentiated behavior of Indian Muslims before and after Partition, the history of the **All India Muslim League** itself, and **Mohammed Ali Jinnah**'s distinguished record of pressing for constitutional reform and Hindu-Muslim unity before his 1940 bid for a separate "homeland" for Indian Muslims in Pakistan. Above all, if religious identity was the defining feature of nationalism, Pakistan should have remained one and India would not today be home to the second largest Muslim population in the world.

A third explanation offered by some historians stresses the role of contingent or accidental factors in the decade before Partition when the world was shaken by momentous events, especially World War II. Such historians examine the exigencies of wartime politics, the decline of **Mahatma Gandhi**'s influence, the post-war and post-imprisonment exhaustion of men called upon to negotiate and make final decisions, the not always harmonious relationships between British Prime Ministers Churchill and Attlee in London and Viceroys **Wavell** and **Mountbatten**, and the human frailties among the main characters of the final drama—such as Jinnah's vanity, **Jawaharlal Nehru**'s obstinacy, and Mountbatten's ambition—to explain what happened in 1947. Such an explanation does not hark back over centuries or decades but focuses on the sequence of main events immediately preceding Partition, summarized as follows.

Indian National Congress provincial ministries resigned office in December 1939; the **Quit India** movement was launched in 1942; most Congress leaders were in prison and out of all official decision making during World War II. The Muslim League adopted a resolution on March 23, 1940, calling for the formation of a separate Muslim majority state, and Jinnah undertook an intensive campaign to win support in the provinces that eventually formed that state. **Sir Stafford Cripps** undertook a mediatory mission to India in 1942, accepted the Pakistan demand in principle, and failed to convey British willingness to negotiate steps to self-government, a key Congress demand. Talks between Gandhi and Jinnah in September 1944 did not resolve their differences; various other unofficial attempts to bridge Congress and League positions also failed. The political atmosphere became virulently communal before the 1946 elections, and Wavell invited Indian leaders to meet at **Simla** in June 1946. Wavell noted in his diary that he found Congress cooperative but Jinnah "utterly intransigent." The new Labour Government in Britain sent a **Cabinet Mission** to India in 1946 that prepared a complex plan retaining the form of a united India but one with a weak central government and the option to secede open to provinces that were "grouped" on a communal basis. Nehru was publicly critical. Jinnah declared August 16,

1946, Direct Action Day; the resulting communal carnage awakened widespread fears of anarchy, and Gandhi stood almost alone. Congress and League leaders were included in an interim government that was formed in late 1946, but they clashed on important issues. The **Constituent Assembly** commenced its meetings in December without participation of the League.

In February 1947, the British government announced its decision to transfer power in India to one or more entities before June 1948; Wavell was replaced by Mountbatten, who rapidly came to the conclusion that the Cabinet Mission Plan would not work. By a combination of charm and pressure, Mountbatten obtained agreement on the principle of Partition from the League as well as Congress and announced that fact, along with his intention to partition Bengal and Punjab, on June 3. Thereafter, he moved with breakneck speed and secrecy toward a self-declared deadline of August 15 while communal violence mounted, uncertainty about the line of division prevailed, and British forces were shipped home without attempting to secure order.

Partition is a permanent blot on the record of British rule in India. It did not solve communal problems on the Indian subcontinent. It created new security and psychological burdens for the successor states of India, Pakistan, and Bangladesh that are yet to be alleviated despite the formation of a **South Asian Association for Regional Cooperation (SAARC)** in 1985.

PATALIPUTRA. The ancient capital of **Magadha**, located close to **Patna**, capital of the present-day state of **Bihar**, was named Pataliputra. Its historical origin was a fortress constructed for Ajatasatru, ruler of Magadha at the time of the **Buddha** in the sixth century BCE. Situated at the confluence of the rivers **Ganges** and Son, Pataliputra was originally a place of pilgrimage. The city was the capital of the **Mauryan Empire**. It was described by the Greek envoy **Megasthenes** as being built of timber and brick, fortified with walls 14 kilometers long, punctuated by 64 gates and 520 towers, and surrounded by a deep and wide moat. Megasthenes described the royal palace as being many pillared, richly carved and ornamented, and built of stone and teak wood. Modern archaeologists see Persian influences in the city's architecture and construction, with hints of Persepolis evident.

The famous Mauryan Emperor **Ashoka** was crowned at Pataliputra and convened the Third Buddhist Council there.

After the decline of the Mauryan Empire, Pataliputra became the capital of the **Lichchavi** state but had lost its importance, perhaps because the river Son changed its course. The Chinese pilgrim **Faxian**, who visited India in the fourth century CE, described it as virtually abandoned.

PATANJALI (c. second century BCE). Patanjali is the name of a noted **Sanskrit** grammarian who commented on **Panini**'s work, added to it, and was a contemporary of Pushyamitra, King in the Sunga Dynasty.

Patanjali is also the name of the celebrated author of the earliest treatise on **yoga**, the *Yoga-sutra*. He did not claim invention but systematized earlier doctrines, traditions, and techniques current among Indian ascetics; he came to be regarded as source and authority. The *Yoga-sutra* is of great antiquity, though there is no agreement on the exact date of its composition.

Because of the paucity of personal information, it is not clear whether Patanjali was one author of two notable sets of work or the name of two different men living at different times.

PATEL, VALLABHBHAI (1875–1950). Patel was born to a family of peasant proprietors in a small town near **Surat**. He took the unusual step in that family of studying law and going to England from 1910 to 1913; he was called to the bar from the Middle Temple, London. He returned to **Ahmedabad** in **Gujarat** where he soon became prominent and was elected to the Municipal Council in 1917. He served as its Chairman from 1924 to 1928 and worked hard to improve the civic and health amenities of the city. By this time he had joined the **Indian National Congress** where his organizational skills were at a premium.

Patel organized a **Satyagraha** of peasants in 1918 to obtain an exemption of land tax from the government in years when the crop failed. This attracted the notice of **Mohandas Gandhi**. By 1922 Patel's political and constructive work in the Grandhian sense had supplanted his legal practice in importance. He led a mass movement known as the Bardoli Satyagraha of 1928 against raising assessments of land revenue; thereafter, he was known as the Sardar and was addressed as such by Gandhi and others. Patel was a key player in the **Civil Disobedience Movement** launched by Gandhi in 1930 and served as President of the Indian National Congress in 1931. He was arrested in January 1932 and was incarcerated along with Gandhi in Yervada prison until May 1932 and again from 1942 to 1945.

Sardar Patel was not known as an orator, but he provided the main organizational drive of the Congress Parliamentary Board after 1935, especially for the Congress governments operating in eight provinces from 1937 to 1939. Alongside Gandhi, he planned the **Quit India** civil disobedience movement launched in 1942. He served as Home Member in the Interim Government formed in 1946 and, along with **Jawaharlal Nehru**, was one of the principal negotiators with the **Cabinet Mission** and the **Muslim League** in the transition to independence. As an unemotional and practical man identified as a conservative **Hindu**, Patel may have accepted the idea and fact of Partition as the price of independence with less anguish than some other Congress leaders, such as **Abul Kalam Azad** or Nehru, both of whom vehemently rejected the two-nation theory.

Patel is often contrasted with Nehru, especially in the context of possible rivalry between them before Gandhi named the latter as his "successor." Some suggest that Patel might have made a more decisive and practical prime minister than the idealistic Nehru. In fact, the two men had complementary qualities, with Patel making invaluable contributions as loyal home minister and deputy prime minister; his death left a void at the decision-making level. Their differences of opinion, for example, on India's choices in **Kashmir** in 1947 or the consequences of China's military action in **Tibet** in 1950, were not allowed to disrupt a close working relationship within the same government. Patel's assessments of both opportunity and challenge in these cases were more "realistic" or hardnosed than Nehru's.

Patel controlled the Congress Party machine better than anyone else before or since his time. He also won the admiration and loyalty of the civil services as he ensured a smooth transition of administration from the **Indian Civil Service (ICS)** to the **Indian Administrative Service (IAS)** and allied central services of the newly independent Union. His unequivocal objective of building a strong and united India and the example he set of administering it with courage, justice, correctness, and practicality continue to be recalled at the present time. Patel's cool courage averted the danger of possible breakdown in civil order at the time of Mahatma Gandhi's assassination in January 1948.

Undoubtedly, one of Patel's greatest achievements was bringing into the Indian Union 562 **Princely States** with a variety of administrative systems and 80 million people scattered around the subcontinent. (See Map 7.) With only three exceptions, this integration process was completed smoothly, through the exercise of shrewd and practical diplomacy. These cases of Junagarh, **Hyderabad** and **Jammu and Kashmir** were complicated by the conduct of the rulers and the enticements offered or interventions made by Pakistan. Patel ordered a referendum in Junagarh and a police action in Hyderabad, which resulted in the full integration of those two states. Patel reluctantly acquiesced when the Indian government submitted the issue of Kashmir to the United Nations; his method of dealing with the quandary posed by Pakistan's military action in 1947–1948 remains a matter of speculation.

PATEL, VITHALDAS JAVERI (1873–1933). The brother of **Vallabhbhai Patel**, Vithaldas also became a lawyer and joined the movement for Indian independence. He led an agitation in **Gujarat** against the repressive **Rowlett Acts** and participated in the **Non-Cooperation Movement** 1921–1922. As a member of the **Swaraj Party**, he was elected to the Indian Legislative Assembly several times. He served as its first elected non-official president but resigned in 1930 to take part in the **Civil Disobedience Movement**. The resulting imprisonment damaged his health, and he went to Vienna for treatment but did not recover.

PATIALA. The name of a city where the Punjabi University is located, Patiala was a **Princely State** founded by a chief of the Phulkian *misl* (see Glossary) in 1763. Although the ruler and most of his subjects were **Sikh**, he resisted **Ranjit Singh**'s plan of extending his Sikh Empire east of the Sutlej River. Instead, Patiala signed a **subsidiary alliance** with the British in 1809. Maharaja Bhupinder Singh (1891–1938) of Patiala took a prominent role in the **Chamber of Princes** in the first part of the 20th century and was one of India's representatives at the League of Nations. His son became the governor of a new state named PEPSU (Patiala and East Punjab States Union) that was formed after Patiala acceded to the Indian Union in 1947 and was merged with eight other princely states, all of which are now part of **Punjab**. Bhupinder Singh's grandson, Amarinder Singh, is currently the **Congress Party** chief minister of Punjab.

PATNA. The capital of the present-day state of **Bihar**, Patna has been in existence continuously for 27 centuries and has figured prominently in Indian history from time to time under different names. It was best known in ancient times as **Pataliputra**, capital of **Magadha**, and often described in glowing terms by foreign visitors such as **Megasthenes**. By the seventh century CE, however, Pataliputra seems to have suffered from the general de-urbanization associated with the later **Gupta Dynasty**, as well as from such natural disasters as flood and fire, and did not impress **Xuanzang** as more than a large village. **Buddhist** monasteries (*vihara*) flourished in the vicinity, however, and gave the name Bihar to the region.

The commercial and strategic importance of Patna's site—between the **Ganges** and Sona rivers—was early acknowledged by the **Pala** rulers of **Bengal**, and fully recognized by **Sher Shah Sur** in the 16th century. He ordered the construction of a new fortified city along the southern bank of the Ganges in 1541, as described in contemporary writings. **Mughal Emperor Akbar** captured this city of Patna in 1574 when he personally commanded a campaign to take control of the wealthy middle and lower Gangetic valley. For the next 200 years, Patna was the administrative seat of the Mughal *subahdar* (governor) of the region and grew as a commercial, cultural, educational, and political center. Numerous notable buildings were constructed during this period; some have survived. The birthplace of **Gobind Singh** in the city was subsequently embellished and enlarged. Patna's population was estimated at 200,000 in the mid-17th century.

Patna had a rich hinterland and was well connected by waterways and roads to other Mughal cities and international trade routes. European trading companies established their "factories" or trading houses there and found the provincial headquarters a useful listening post for court politics in **Delhi**. English, French, and Italian travelers of the times testified to the beauty and importance of Patna. The city was renamed Azimabad by Prince Azim, favorite grandson of Aurangzeb, when he was *subahdar* in the early 17th century. Patna continued to thrive during the twilight of the Mughals but was eclipsed by **Calcutta** when Bihar, like Bengal, passed under British control.

A new class educated in the English **language** grew up after the founding of Patna College in 1863 and the growth of a Law College and a Medical College in Patna University. **Jadunath Sarkar** was among the luminaries of the History faculty. Detailed accounts from the late 19th century on testify to the number of communities—Hindu, Muslim, Sikh, and Christian—living side by side in amicability despite the communal agitations of the **Hindu Mahasabha** and the **Muslim League** in the first half of the 20th century. Bihar was administratively separated from Bengal in 1912, and Patna once again became the capital of a province, one where Hindi journalism flourished and leaders of the **Indian National Congress** such as **Rajendra Prasad** were nurtured. Patna responded with tremendous enthusiasm to the **Quit India** movement of 1942 and with equal fervor to **Jayaprakash Narayan**'s call for "Total Revolution" more than 30 years later, in different circumstances. Patna remains a highly politicized city. It was badly damaged by the great Bihar earthquake of 1934, and physical amenities of a modern type are minimal. Because present day habitation covers much the same ground as earlier sites, complete archaeological excavations of ancient Pataliputra, known for its elaborate sewage system and general cleanliness—in contrast to present day Patna—have been inhibited.

PATWARDAN, ACHYUT SITARAM (1905–1971). Achyut was the son of a lawyer in Ahmednagar who belonged to a high **caste** English-educated family of **Maharashtra**. He studied Economics, attended the Theosophist College, and joined the **Civil Disobedience Movement** of 1930. He became one of the founding members of the Congress Socialist Party, served on its working committee, and ran educational camps for young people after 1935. During the **Quit India** movement of 1942, Patwardhan helped establish a parallel government to British administration in western India; officials denounced his activities as "terrorist." He retired from active politics in 1950 but continued college teaching and publishing until 1966.

PATWARDHAN, ANAND (1950–). Generally recognized as a master of the documentary form of **film**, Anand Patwardhan was born in **Bombay** and showed an early sensitivity to socio-political issues. While in his 20s, he worked on a rural development project in **Madhya Pradesh** run by a **Non-Governmental Organization (NGO)** and made a film about treatment of tuberculosis. In 1974, he also joined the popular JP Movement (named after **Jayaprakash Narayan**) in Bihar and filmed it before making a clandestine documentary during the months of **Emergency Rule**, which he titled *Prisoners of Conscience*.

Patwardhan went to McGill University in Montreal for graduate studies and produced *Guerilla Cinema: Underground and in Exile* for his thesis in sociology before returning to **Mumbai**. He formed a mobile cinema team to take films on sociopolitical problems to villages and towns and so stimulate social action. The films he makes are free of jargon or pedantry. They show the complexity of Indian social situations and the multiple **languages** used in daily conversation. They have addressed communal issues of sectarian violence, and *Jang aur Aman* released in 2002 tackles the question of war or peace on the Indian subcontinent.

PAWAR, SHARADCHANDRA GOVINDRAO (1940–). Pawar is president of the National Congress Party that he formed with P. A. Sangma and Tariq Ali when they were expelled from the **Congress Party** in 1999 for challenging **Sonia Gandhi**'s leadership on grounds of her foreign birth. The two parties allied after electoral gains in the 2004 general elections, however, and Pawar chose the Agriculture portfolio in the Congress-led United Progressive Alliance coalition government headed by **Dr. Manmohan Singh**. Pawar had previously served as minister of defence in the Congress government of **P. V. Narasimha Rao** in the early 1990s before becoming chief minister of **Maharashtra**. He negotiated the original and ill-fated agreement with Enron Corporation of the United States for construction and operation of a large power project in that state.

Sharad Pawar was first elected to the Legislative Assembly of Maharashtra in 1967 from his birthplace of Baramati. As a landowner and sugar producer himself, he did much to improve the water management and agricultural production of Maharasthra. He gained the reputation of being the ablest and most ambitious **Maratha** on the political scene, a "sugar baron" and a "strong man," but one with changing and unpredictable allegiances or alliances. Pawar did not join the National Democratic Alliance coalition government led by the **Bharatiya Janata Party (BJP)** as some had expected after his break with Congress; he has criticized the BJP on the subject of **Ayodhya**, and he has a strong and institutionalized rivalry with the **Shiv Sena**, which also enjoys support in Maharashtra. Pawar led his Nationalist Congress Party to victory in the October 2004 elections to the Maharashtra state legislature in a seat-sharing alliance with the Congress Party and eventually conceded the position of chief minister to the latter. He seems to be reconciled to the fact of Sonia Gandhi's leadership of Congress and the unlikelihood of himself gaining India's highest executive position in opposition to her.

PEOPLE'S UNION FOR CIVIL LIBERTIES AND DEMOCRATIC RIGHTS (PUCLDR). This body was formed in 1975 and 1976 by public figures and voluntary organizations opposing the **Emergency** proclaimed by **Indira Gandhi**'s government in June 1975. With the support of **Jayaprakash Narayan**, the **Janata**, and the **Communist Party of India (Marxist)**, it brought together the People's Union for Civil Liberties (PUCL), a continuation of a pre-independence movement for civil rights running parallel to the freedom movement, with a new Delhi-based organization, the People's Union for Democratic Rights (PUDR), aiming to restore the fundamental rights guaranteed by the **Indian Constitution** of 1950.

The PUCL and PUDR maintained their separate organizations and followed different rhythms of activity after the end of the Emergency. The record since 1980 shows that both act independently of government, political parties, and foreign organizations. They work through the law courts, investigative reporting, public opinion campaigns, and public interest litigation. They have been especially active in investigating and obtaining redress for the victims of communal riots, abuses of minorities, **women**, children, and bonded labor. Their members have opposed draconian counter-terrorist laws. Their reports are factual and enjoy public credibility, as for example, their reports on the anti-**Sikh** riots in 1984 and the **Gujarat** riots of 2002.

Both organizations are run entirely by their voluntary membership, consisting of educated persons drawn largely from the academic, legal, and journalist communities. Many recognize the need for improved networking and increased mass awareness to preserve and enhance civil liberties and democratic rights in India.

PERMANENT SETTLEMENT. A term applied to the form of revenue settlement introduced by the British Governor General **Lord Cornwallis** in 1793 to areas controlled by the **East India Company** in **Bengal**, **Bihar**, and **Orissa**. One objective of the new settlement was to end the rapacious system of annual reassessments and contracts to tax collectors that was introduced when the East India Company took over the rights of *dewani* (see Glossary) in 1765. Another declared objective of Lord Cornwallis was to create in Bengal a body of hereditary landlords who might extend cultivation, maximize production, and generally function with a sense of public purpose espoused by the 18th-century enlightened aristocracy in England.

The distinguishing feature of the Permanent Settlement, therefore, was that agents collecting taxes were confirmed in their positions for perpetuity in return for a fixed annual payment of dues to the government. They were forbidden to evict tenants or dispossess the actual cultivators of the soil.

The consequences of the Permanent Settlement were not as salutary as Cornwallis intended. While taxes or dues to the government remained constant, actual rents rose, increasing the burden on the cultivator without adding to the revenues of the government. Moreover, revenue collection was harsh and was unmitigated even in bad seasons. Third, members of the new class of *zamindar* (see Glossary) did not fit the ideal portrait painted by Cornwallis, who failed to understand the Indian reality. It is noteworthy that the Bombay and Madras Presidencies in British India did not emulate this system in their various revenue settlements, and that the Bengal Rent Act of 1859 modified the 1793 law by giving occupancy rights to tenants of 12 years' standing. The shortcomings of the Permanent Settlement surfaced soon.

Many 20th-century historians and economists of many nationalities regard the Permanent Settlement as an important contributing factor to the social tensions of eastern India in the 19th century and to the continuing social backwardness and agricultural impoverishment of the areas covered by it.

PESHWA. Peshwa was initially the title given to the chief of eight ministers in the court of **Shivaji** and his successors. The Peshwa was entrusted with the widest range of duties in the general public interest. During the reign of Shahu (1708–1748) the office gained tremendously in power and prestige because of the ability and achievements of successive incumbents, Balaji Visvanath, his son **Baji Rao I** and his grandson Balaji Baji Rao. So much so, that the Peshwa's office became hereditary and recognized as the supreme executive of the **Marathas** in 1749, after the death of Shahu. At the same time, the Maratha capital was moved from Satara to **Poona**.

The office of the Peshwa was abolished after the Third Maratha War (1817–1819) when Baji Rao II lost to the forces of the **East India Company**, although he himself was maintained on a British pension until 1853. His adopted son **Nana Saheb** was refused a pension despite many petitions and took a leading role in the **Uprising of 1857**. *See also* MARATHA.

PHADKE, WASUDEO BALWANT (1845–1883). A grandson of the **Peshwa**'s military commander in the last **Maratha** war with the **East India Company** in 1818, Phadke became a clerk in the railways and financial department of the Bombay Presidency but was temperamentally unsuited to serving the British, especially in the aftermath of the **Uprising of 1857**. Instead, he toured areas suffering from drought, famine, disease, inflation, and increased pressures of land tax and gave public lectures against exploitation by the British and their lackeys, such as moneylenders, *banias*, or merchants, and **Marwaris**. He organized an armed revolt among tribal people and called for the establishment of a republic. Phadke was eventually captured in July 1879, put on trial with 14 companions, and transported for life. He died in Aden.

PHADNIS, NANA (1742–1800). Born Balaji Janardhan, he occupied the post of phadnis, or accountant to the **Maratha** state on the death of his father in 1756. He was dismissed in 1761 but reinstated in 1768. Nana Phadnis controlled the public purse, combined the duties of administrator and spymaster, and came to be de facto chief minister after the Peshwaship was briefly usurped by Raghoba, brother of the deceased **Peshwa** Balaji Baji Rao, and then occupied by a minor. Nana Phadnis gradually supplanted members of a regency council of "twelve brothers" established in 1774 and concentrated power in his own hands.

During the next 20 years the Marathas maintained their power and territory through a partnership between the brilliant military commander Mahadji Sindhia, who operated in the north, and Nana Phadnis, who shrewdly maneuvered through the conflicts between **Hyderabad**, **Mysore**, and the **East India Company** in the south. Raghoba enlisted British assistance for his claims, and this precipitated the first Anglo-Maratha War, it was concluded with the British restoring Maratha territories and abandoning Raghoba at the Treaty of Salbai, in 1782. However, Nana Phadnis did not share Mahadji Sindhia's appreciation of the extent of the British threat and the need to train a modern Maratha army; their partnership was marred by friction and mistrust between unlike temperaments.

Nana Phadnis was loyal to the young Peshwa but did not recognize the limits to his own power. When death removed his caution and sagacity from Maratha councils, the confederacy fell open to dissension and defeat by the British.

PHULE, JOTIBA GOVIND (1827–1890). Phule was born in **Poona** to a family of gardeners that supplied flowers to the **Peshwa**'s household. He grew to be one of the leading social reformers of the 19th century and an inspiration to reformers in the 20th century, such as **Dr. Ambedkar**. Phule's practical efforts matched his convictions. His schooling was an interrupted one, but he took inspiration from the lives and writings of Indian and American leaders and became a prolific writer in Marathi and English. His most famous work was *Gulamgiri* (Slavery) published in 1872.

Phule took up the cause of the middle and lower **castes** against **brahman** domination, and in behalf of all **women** against crippling social customs. In 1848 he opened a school for non-brahman girls taught by his wife and subsequently set up three more schools and a library for low caste children as well as an orphanage for the children of brahman widows. In 1878 he opened another orphanage where

2,000 children were fed twice a day. Phule was a part-time teacher in the Scottish Mission school, raised funds from **Christians**, and blessed British rule for providing the means of liberation to those oppressed by the **Hindu** caste hierarchy. He demanded free education for all up to the age of 12, advocated technical and vocational training, and called for reform of Hindu marriage customs so as to dispense with priests. He formed a society for human rights and social justice in 1873 and used the press as a platform to propagate his views; they naturally provoked considerable opposition.

Phule received public recognition for his work within his lifetime and inspired later reform movements among lower castes, such as the Mahars.

PINDARI or PINDARA. The name is derived from Baidara or Bedar of **Karnataka** and applied to freebooters of the late 18th and early 19th centuries. The Pindaris were a kind of irregular and roving light cavalry armed with swords and spears, operating in groups under their own chiefs but attached to **Maratha** armies in a loose, non-salaried alliance. The origins of the groups are obscure, as their members did not share either ethnic or religious identity and followed leaders who were **Hindu**, Muslim, and Pathan. Their main source of livelihood was plunder.

As Maratha central authority declined, Pindaris became more active in central India, parts of **Rajasthan**, and certain districts of **Deccan**. The British encountered them in the process of expanding their own dominion over India, and Governor General Marquess Hastings mustered a strong force of over 100,000 men against them in 1817. **John Malcolm** and Thomas Hislop were among the British officers who broke up the Pindari bands and helped to resettle them, sometimes by allowing the chiefs to keep their lands.

PITRODA, SATYANARAYAN GANGARAM (SAM) (1942–). Pitroda was born in a remote village of **Orissa** to parents who were deeply influenced by **Mahatma Gandhi** and were innocent of modern technology. They sent their son back to their home state of **Gujarat** to be educated, and he took a masters degree in physics before proceeding to the United States to study electrical engineering in 1964. He worked with GTE Automatic Electric for some years and then became vice president of Wescom Telephone, Rockwell International. His special aptitude and inventive mind soon showed in the number of patents in telecommunications filed under his name; both in the United States and internationally; there were more than 50 by 2003. Pitroda conceived, designed, developed, produced, and marketed a family of nearly 600 digital switching systems worldwide. These are at the core of telecommunications. He is chairman of WorldTel, a company that he founded in 1995 to develop and support privately funded telecommunications in developing countries, including those of South Asia.

Sam Pitroda's technological brilliance is equaled by his social vision. He sees information technology (IT) as a means to modernize whole systems, from familial communications to administration, from employment to sanitation, from accountability to improvement of rural life. He was chief technology advisor to **Rajiv Gandhi** and helped to transform the then undeveloped telecommunications sector in India. Among the most visible manifestations of his contribution are the small, bright yellow booths in towns and villages providing easy public access to local, national, and international telephone connections, and the spreading network of rural exchanges throughout India that are using new technology. These are having profound effects within the country that equal, or exceed, in importance the improvement in India's foreign exchange earnings brought about by its well-known exports of IT services internationally.

PLANNING COMMISSION. In 1950, Prime Minister **Jawaharlal Nehru** won approval from the **Congress Party** and his Cabinet to launch a national program of planned economic and social development. A Planning Commission chaired by the prime minister and including the finance minister and a full-time deputy chairman was created to direct public investment; it quickly published the First Five Year Plan in 1951, encompassing many projects already under way and giving most development funds to agriculture, irrigation, and power generation. The Second Five-Year Plan, designed largely by Professor P. C. Mahalanobis, was much more ambitious. It was formulated on the basis of a 1956 consensus resolution on industrial policy that envisioned a mixed economy with ample room for the private sector and foreign capital but gave the Indian state the major role in basic and heavy industries, especially steel. The Third Plan followed similar lines of trying to blend socialistic goals and persuasive, as opposed to coercive, methods industry and agriculture, economic development and social transformation. Inner contradictions were elided. The Planning Commission was strengthened with an elaborate secretariat, a full complement of statistical and research staff on every aspect of the economy, and access to expert reports and recommendations. The decade 1956 to 1966 produced a massive industrial boom accompanied by generous foreign economic assistance that boosted optimism about India reaching the critical "take-off" stage of self-generating growth.

Planned development was then buffeted by unforeseen circumstances that also affected the output of the Planning Commission. Growth targets could not be met because of successive monsoon failures in the mid-1960s and early 1970s, the effects of wars with China and **Pakistan**, and the oil price hike of 1973. Western donors and the World Bank attacked the Indian development strategy for excessive dirigisme and foreign exchange was in very short supply. A "Plan holiday" was admitted in the late 1960s. The fourth, fifth, and sixth plans were adjusted to reflect new circumstances and to introduce concepts such as "minimum needs" into the economic lexicon, and the growth strategy of import substitution was questioned but not abandoned. Meanwhile, New Delhi had proliferated a system of permits, regulations, and licenses in pursuit of planned goals that alienated the business community and stifled growth; calls for **economic liberalization** multiplied in the late 1970s and the 1980s. Further, as a virtual adjunct of the central government, the Planning Commission had seemingly replaced the Finance Commission in power of allocating funds to states for local development projects; the system became overly centralized and provoked demands for decentralization and greater state autonomy. One result of the economic reforms introduced by **Dr. Manmohan Singh** in 1991 and carried forward through that decade, as well as of political changes that gave regional parties decisive roles in forming a government in New Delhi, is the more genuinely federal political and economic system visible in India since the 1990s.

The Planning Commission inevitably reevaluated its former role of macro-economic management in the era of liberalization, and the eighth and ninth plans reflected its first efforts to indicate priorities of investment in a market economy. The tenth plan highlights the importance of agriculture, infrastructure, knowledge, and good governance to India's economic development. The expertise of the Planning Commission is available to those bodies, public and private, that can use it, and at no time has planning in India been as wooden as its image. The Deputy Chairman of the Planning Commission is always very close to the prime minister of the day and undertakes tasks that go beyond those implied by the title.

PLASSEY, BATTLE OF. This was a historically decisive battle fought near a mango grove on the banks of the Bhagirathi river in **Bengal** between forces of the **East India Company** led by **Robert Clive** and those of Suraj-ul-Daula (b. 1733), then the inexperienced Nawab (see Glossary) of Bengal, a semi-independent province of the **Mughal Empire**. The battle lasted less than a day on June 23, 1757, and there were few casualties.

Clive led a force consisting of 700 European troops, 1,400 *sepoys* (see Glossary), and 171 pieces of artillery. Suraj-ul-Daula's much larger army of horsemen and foot soldiers, but only 50 cannon, was defeated in an engagement that demonstrated the military superiority of European drilling, discipline, and mortar over traditional Indian armies. Moreover, Suraj-ul-Daula's key general, Mir Jafar, switched sides during the course of the day. He supplanted Suraj-ul-Daula as Nawab and proceeded to deplete the treasury for the personal enrichment of himself and his masters in the East India Company before being replaced himself. Plassey is often represented in nationalist literature as a prime example of perfidy.

Victory at Plassey gave the East India Company control over a large part of the rich lower **Ganges** valley and so contributed significantly to British power and victories in the Carnatic wars of southern India. For this reason, the year 1757 is commonly regarded as the start of British rule in India. Some plotters of the great **Uprising of 1857** intended it to begin on the 100th anniversary of the battle of Plassey and be seen to avenge that event.

POLITICAL PARTIES. There have been many changes in the function, number, and type of political party operating in India since

independence, as more and more people belonging to different socioeconomic groups have gravitated toward electoral politics and
have demanded better representation. Democracy has taken firm
root, with active participation in civil society and in politics
widening and deepening in each decade, and the percentage of the
electorate voting in general elections increasing from less than
50% in the 1950s to more than 60% in the 1990s. The scale of such
elections involving hundreds of millions of voters with a diversity
of economic, ethnic, linguistic, regional, and religious background
unequaled, and perhaps unimaginable, in any other country distinguishes the Indian experience of building a democratic political
community and necessarily molds political parties. Political scientists use different terms to describe India's "party system" at one
period or another and identify fairly distinct phases in the past
half-century.

The **Congress Party** shaped the first phase of 20 years into what
Rajni Kothari and Morris Jones called "the Congress system" of one-
party dominance in a competitive multiparty environment. Carrying
the prestigious legacy of the **Indian National Congress**'s lead in the
freedom struggle and its immense organizational strength, Congress
enjoyed dominance in Parliament as well as in state legislatures, with
smaller political parties acting like pressure groups openly allied to
factions within Congress. Congress since pre-independence days was
a coalition of many ideologies and interests, a broad-based party of
consensus, able to prevent or reduce polarization and to neutralize
disaffection by respecting minorities, co-opting potential competition, and reducing center-state tensions by bargaining within the
party. **Jawaharlal Nehru** made the party subsidiary to government,
especially in terms of knitting together state and society, and the immense prestige of his name was a campaign asset for the party even
after his death.

The loss of Congress dominance became obvious in the **Lok
Sabha** elections of 1967 and the unseating of Congress in the governments of six large states. A fluid, market-style polity emerged,
with defectors moving from party to party as expedient. Disciplined,
cadre based parties on the right and the left had narrow social bases
and kept low profiles. New parties, new coalitions, and new political
leaders emerged in state politics, eroding Congress's organizational

strength. At the national level, **Indira Gandhi** took a confrontational stance toward all opposition, split her own Congress Party in 1969, and won decisively in the elections of 1971 and 1972. Her centralized, personalized style of decisionmaking and her abolition of intra-party elections, however, resulted in a pyramid-like party structure that was unable to cope creatively with new demands and socioeconomic conflicts or to effectively compete for power in major states, such as **Tamil Nadu**, where regional parties were strong. The reduced political capacity of Congress was intensified during **Emergency Rule** from June 1975 to March 1977, and a broad spectrum of opposition parties joined in the **Janata Party** coalition to defeat Mrs. Gandhi and form a government. But the Janata Party fell prey to factional struggles in 1979 and could not replace Congress as the defining pole of Indian politics.

Abrasive conflict was conspicuous during the 1980s with more people competing for limited resources, awakening to their citizenship rights, and demanding recognition of their demands. Notwithstanding its massive victory in the general elections of 1984, Congress found it difficult to cater to organized interests and so did other political parties and state institutions. "Self-determination" movements in **Assam, Jammu and Kashmir (J&K), Punjab,** and the northeast found expression in insurgency, and elections everywhere showed an anti-incumbent tendency that expressed voter disappointment in and disapproval of their representatives. Social groups tended to become parochial, chauvinistic, and prone to conflict with other social groups. Lines between many political parties and their social bases were blurred and the logic of politics at the state and national levels diverged. Regional or single-state parties emerged, such as the Akali Dal, the Biju Janata Dal, and the Shiv Sena, and state splinters of national parties such as the Trinamool Congress often went their own way. By 2004 there were 24 political parties recognized by the **Election Commission** that operated in fewer than four states. (See Appendix H.) The party system was highly competitive but was fluid and unstable. National unity was preserved but ties between national and state levels were loosening under centrifugal pulls on the Indian federation.

The party system was reformulated in the course of the 1990s under the influence of two opposing sociopolitical forces that were unleashed almost simultaneously—**caste** and religion. Caste-based political identity (or Mandalization) was one consequence of implementing the **Mandal Commission** Report after 1990. Caste based political parties such as the **Bahujan Samaj Party (BSP)** and the Rashtriya Janata Dal led by **Laloo Prasad Yadav** gained strength in the heartland states of **Bihar** and **Uttar Pradesh**. At the same time, the **Bharatiya Janata Party (BJP)** moved from the periphery to the center of politics nationwide by appealing to **Hindu** religious and majoritarian sentiments in a campaign to build a **Ram** temple at **Ayodhya** and redefine contemporary India in terms of **Hindutva** rather than secularism or multiculturalism. In addition, **economic liberalization** initiated by **Narasimha Rao**'s government in 1991 and slowly carried forward by subsequent governments of different political parties had varying sociopolitical effects on the electorate everywhere. And political devolution brought in through **Panchayati Raj** contributed to the proliferation of small parties constructed around a particular leader or a single issue. Political "entrepreneurship" by persons embracing political careers as a path to material prosperity became common; such middle level leaders, generally contemptuous of rules, institutionalization, or the "common good," were the main mobilizers of support in all political parties.

By the end of a decade in which five general elections were held—in 1989, 1991, 1996, 1998, and 1999—some general characteristics had become clear:

- No single political party could command a majority in the Lok Sabha and form a government that could be reasonably expected to last a full term.
- Coalition Union Governments were necessarily formed in New Delhi as they had been necessary in many states earlier.
- The BJP and the Congress emerged as the two parties around which other parties had to group; the Janata and its variants was not able to forge a strong third pole.
- Alliance building between national and regional parties was the key to success at the polls, as the BJP-led 25 party National Democratic Alliance demonstrated in 1998 and 1999 when Congress insisted on standing alone and failed to win confidence, and as the Congress-led 10 party United Progressive Alliance proved in 2004.

In both cases, the pre-election alliances drew up a common minimum program modifying the platform of the leading party.

- Regional and single-state parties were able to consolidate their constituencies as the polity and economy became more decentralized. Fairly stable two-party systems emerged in some states including **Andhra Pradesh**, **Delhi**, **Gujarat**, **Himachal Pradesh**, **Karnataka**, **Madhya Pradesh**, **Maharashtra**, **Punjab**, **Rajasthan**, and Tamil Nadu.
- **Dalits** and "backward castes" accelerated their participation in electoral politics, contributing to the strength of the BSP, the RJD, the Samaj Party, and the Samajvadi Party in northern India and compelling parties that were identified with high-caste support, such as the BJP or Congress, to become more inclusive.
- Social turmoil, economic backwardness, corruption, and factionalism characterized the two large states of Bihar and Uttar Pradesh, where multi-party competition continues.
- The Election Commission's ruling in 1998 that only parties that held regular internal elections would be eligible to field candidates was one example of numerous efforts being made in India to strengthen institutions and ensure political and fiscal accountability.
- Frequent anti-incumbency votes add to anecdotal evidence of increasing sophistication among voters. They demand material improvement in their living conditions. It is likely that governments at both the center and state levels will come to stand or fall by their performance in alleviating poverty rather than by the charisma of their leaders or the appeal of their ideologies.

Since the introduction of universal suffrage in 1950, the party system and political parties in India have changed. Further alterations in response to new circumstances are inevitable but cannot be anticipated here. *See also* Appendix H. BHARATIYA JANATA PARTY, BAHUJAN SAMAJ PARTY, COMMUNIST PARTY OF INDIA, COMMUNIST PARTY OF INDIA (MARXIST), CONGRESS PARTY, DRAVIDA MUNNETRA KAZHAGAM, JANATA DAL, SHIV SENA, and TELEGU DESAM PARTY.

PONDICHERRY. The small Union Territory of Pondicherry comprises the former French possessions of Karaikal, Mahe, and Yanam scattered in South India as well as the capital city of Pondicherry on the Coromandel coast of southeastern India. Known as Puducheira in the 16th century, the city was developed as a port and administrative center by the **French East India Company** after 1674. It was taken by the Dutch in 1693 and by the British several times in the course of 18th century wars with the French, but it was returned in 1816. It remained the main French settlement in India until its gradual merger with independent India after 1953. The principal **languages** are French and **Tamil**.

Although most of the population is engaged in agriculture and light industry, Pondicherry is a popular tourist attraction close to **Chennai**. It is a lively and cosmopolitan enclave of French culture in India and boasts charming architecture. Moreover, the *ashram* (see Glossary) founded by **Sri Aurobindo** and the new city of Auroville named after him draw many visitors and residents from various parts of India and the world.

POONA or PUNE. This is a city located at the confluence of the Mula and Mutha rivers on the **Deccan** in **Maharashtra**. Early mention of it is found in a copper plate inscription of the **Rashtrakuta** King Krishna I in 758 CE. It fell within the jurisdiction of the **Bahmani** Sultanate and one of its successor states, **Bijapur**, in the 14th and 15th centuries when it was lightly fortified.

Pune is famous as the place where **Maratha** leader **Shivaji** spent his childhood and rebuilt after his coronation in 1674. The city soon became a center of culture, learning, and power under the **Peshwas** who made it their capital in the 18th century. **Brahmanic** influence was strong in Pune and continued after the British captured it in 1818. Poona then became the summer capital of the Bombay Presidency and a center of English-language education as well as **Hindu** reform and revivalism in the 19th century. Leading figures of social reform and Indian nationalism, including **Mahadev Govind Ranade**, **Bal Gangadhar Tilak**, and **Gopal Krishna Gokhale** spent most of their lives in Pune.

Poona is an important industrial center and is the site of important training institutions of the **Indian Armed Forces** as well as the headquarters of Southern Command in the southern sector. The city has a lively cultural and civic life, though it gained some notoriety in the late 1970s as the headquarters of the Rajneesh Ashram, now called Osha. Pune city and district has a current population estimated at over seven million.

PORTUGUESE. The Portuguese were the first Europeans to establish a territorial foothold in India, in 1510, and the last to leave, in 1961. Their influence varied according to time and place, waned rapidly in the 17th century, and did not entail the socioeconomic transformations that were spurred by industrial capitalism as in the case of the British influence. The Portuguese impact on India was minor, but their excellent and well-preserved records enable present-day scholars to explore a larger canvas of modern Indian history than merely past encounters between two countries.

Portugal's maritime prowess and experimentation in the 15th century led to an outward thrust, with Bartolomeu Diaz rounding the southern tip of Africa in 1488 and **Vasco da Gama** arriving at the south Indian port of Calicut in 1498. The trading situation in the Indian Ocean at that time was complex, with different groups of Arabs and Indians dominating particular routes and commodities, and the major land powers were relatively uninvolved in commerce. According to the European Treaty of Tordesillas of 1494, the Pope awarded Portugal the eastern half of the "undiscovered world" and Spain the western half, triggering the race to the east from Europe.

Portugal's aims in the early 16th century were to win a monopoly of the immensely profitable spice trade from Asia to Europe, to establish a monopoly of trade between specific local ports and so control and tax all other traders on those routes, to carry out private trade, and to make converts to Roman Catholic **Christianity**. **Alphonso d' Albuquerque** followed a strategy of capturing ports in the Persian Gulf, along the west coast of India, and beyond: **Goa** in 1510, Malacca in 1511, Hormuz in 1515, Bassein in 1534, Daman and Diu in 1535, and Colombo in 1597. He met with no united opposition from coastal kingdoms and encountered no rival at sea armed to counter the artillery carried on his ships. Portugal's undertaking was a very large one, with a round trip between Lisbon and Goa taking one and a half years. Portugal needed a permanent fleet in the Indian Ocean in order to sustain a monopoly and could not long survive the entry of Dutch and English ships in the 16th century, especially with local potentates, not entirely powerless, playing one off against the other in order to evade Portuguese levies.

A Portuguese governor was appointed at Goa in 1515 with a separate department of religious affairs. Consistently anti-**Islam**, the Portuguese were initially curious rather than intolerant of **Hindus**. However, the onset of the Counter-Reformation in Europe and the arrival of the **Jesuits** in Goa resulted in all temples there being destroyed in the 1540s; large-scale construction of churches, seminaries, and monasteries were encouraged by the Pope, as were attempts at mass conversion. The Jesuits established the first printing press in Asia at Goa in 1556 to produce religious tracts. Some 175,000 converts had been baptized by 1600, mostly from the lower **castes**, but the numbers did not increase significantly later. The Church found it difficult to deal with the small but old established community of Thomas Christians (presently known as Syrian Christians), and the Inquisition tried more than 16,000 cases in the years that it operated, 1560–1774, which did not increase its popularity.

Portugal's power in India diminished in the 17th century for several reasons. Portugal was united to Spain for several decades and less active. The Dutch and the English proved themselves to be militarily and politically superior in the Indian Ocean. Brazil and Africa, and the slave trade were more profitable to Portugal than India. And first the **Marathas** and then the British kept the Portuguese confined to their small coastal enclaves. There was little social or economic change there. The bulk of the population retained its own language, customs, and social organization. Portuguese society was equally stratified, with military and civil officials at the top, followed by soldiers, settled men, clerics, mestico, or people of mixed blood, Hindus, and slaves. During the 19th and early 20th centuries there was a steady emigration of Goans to British India in search of better opportunities. Portugal itself was closely allied to Britain and was therefore tolerated in India; Portuguese neutrality in **World War II** made little difference to British attitudes.

Attempts by the government of independent India after 1947 to negotiate a transfer of Portuguese enclaves to the Indian Union in a peaceable manner similar to the process adopted with the French enclaves met with resistance from Lisbon. A legal dispute on rights of passage was referred by India to the International Court of Justice in the 1950s. The political stalemate came to an end when the Indian army, meeting minimal resistance, took over Goa in December 1961. Relations between India and Portugal were ruptured, but they improved rapidly after a change of regime in Lisbon was consolidated in the 1970s. Warmth of relationship in the 1990s were expressed not only in high-level exchanges of visits but in Portugal, which held the presidency of the European Union (EU) at the time, sponsoring regular EU-India summit meetings similar to those the EU held with Asean. The Indian **Diaspora** settled in Portugal and originating for the most part in former Portuguese territories, is also active, prosperous, and respected, with representation in parliament. *See also* GOA.

POTTI, SRIRAMULU (1901–1952). Sriramulu is best remembered for the final chapter of his life, beginning on October 19, 1952, with a 58-day fast to the death. This was undertaken in the cause of separating a Telugu-speaking state from **Madras**. The boundaries of Indian states were reorganized on the basis of **language** within the decade.

Potti Sriramulu had a respectable but undistinguished birth and early career in Madras until he met **Mahatma Gandhi**. He joined Gandhi's Sabarmati *ashram* (see Glossary) and became an ardent social worker, especially for prohibition of liquor, propagation of *khadi* (see Glossary) and other handicrafts, and, most of all, for the uplift of Harijans (see Glossary), or **untouchables**. He believed in Gandhi's concept of **Satyagraha** and practiced it, fasting in order that the Harijans in his home district of Nellore be given the right to enter and worship in **Hindu** temples. His memory is naturally venerated in **Andhra Pradesh** for the heroic contribution he made to its formation.

PRAJA SOCIALIST PARTY (PSP). This **political party** was formed after the general elections of 1952 with the merger of the Congress Socialist Party, the Socialist Party, and the Kisan Mazdoor Praja Party (Peasants, Workers and Peoples Party), which together polled the second largest number of votes after the **Congress Party**. The antecedents of the PSP can be traced to the socialist movement within the **Indian National Congress** during the 1930s. **Acharya Kripalani**, **Jayaprakash Narayan**, and **Ram Manohar Lohia** were prominent leaders of the new party. They offered a secular platform to surmount the easily visible communal, feudal, or parochial loyalties of the Indian electorate and provide a clear choice to a Congress government, depicted by them as increasingly conservative.

The PSP convention at **Allahabad** in 1953 adopted a platform emphasizing "Indianized socialism." Differences developed within the party soon after, not only on ideological issues, but on the correct relationships to be maintained with the Congress on the one hand, and the **Communist Party of India (CPI)** on the other. Concrete situations, such as those that developed in **Andhra Pradesh** and **Kerala** in the 1950s, were at either end of the ideological spectrum and evoked different responses from PSP leaders. Lohia left the party and, after Congress adopted a "socialistic pattern" of society and a mixed economy as its own goals by the time of the 1957 general elections, the PSP began to lose its distinctive identity. It faded from the national political scene in the 1960s.

PRAKRIT. This was the popular or spoken form of **Sanskrit** in towns and villages of northern India in the sixth century BCE and later. Prakrit, like Pali, was used for literary purposes in **Buddhist** and **Jain** texts during the ensuing period and therefore developed a grammar and syntax modeled on **Panini**'s rules and was written in the same script as Sanskrit. The spread of Prakrit to southern India and its use in some inscriptions of the **Satavahana** rulers of the **Deccan** is seen as part of the Aryanization or Sanskritization process in the Indian subcontinent.

Literature of the classical period, notably the dramas of **Kalidasa** written in the **Gupta** era depicts men of high social status speaking Sanskrit while all women and men of lower social standing converse in Prakrit. This probably reflected the relative social standing of the two related **languages**, but by the sixth and seventh centuries CE poetry and plays were being composed in Prakrit.

Prakrit was squeezed between Sanskrit as the court and literary language above and many new regional spoken languages below. Regional variations of Prakrit in Apabhramsha ("falling down") dialects subsequently developed into languages, notably Marathi and Gujarati, current in the present day.

PRASAD, RAJENDRA (1884–1963). Prasad was the first president of the Republic of India, and the only one to hold that elected office for two six-year terms, 1950–1962. He was born to a landowning, traditional *kayastha* (see Glossary) family in a village of north **Bihar** and never lost his simple piety or his roots in agriculture and village community. He studied Hindi and Persian at home and the arts and law at the University of Calcutta, where he excelled both academically and in popularity. He formed the Bihari Students Conference in 1908 and organized protests against the partition of **Bengal**. He set up legal practice in 1911 and moved to **Patna** in 1916 when a High Court was established there. He attracted favorable attention for his intellect and knowledge, as well as for what was recognized as an innate integrity and purity of character.

Rajendra Prasad first met **M. K. Gandhi** in 1915 and was closely associated with him at Champaran in 1916 and the trial that followed Gandhi's championship of peasants oppressed by indigo plantation owners. Thereafter, Prasad was an integral part and twice president of the **Indian National Congress**. He participated in the **Non-Cooperation Movement** of 1920–1922 and the **Civil Disobedience** movement after 1930, suffering imprisonment and confiscation of property as a result. He took a leading role in the constructive program and advocacy of *khadi* to rebuild rural communities and took the Food and Agriculture portfolio in the Interim Government of 1946, securing decontrol of food grains and sponsoring a "Grow More Food" campaign before relinquishing charge. He chaired the **Constituent Assembly** with firmness, grace, and skill, and was elevated to president of the new republic unopposed. He differed with Prime Minister **Jawaharlal Nehru** on many important issues, notably the relative stress to be placed on agriculture and industry in economic policies, and the relative powers of president and prime minister in the practical interpretation of the **Constitution**, but their personal and public relations remained those of mutual respect born of long association with each other and with Gandhi.

PRATAP, RANA (1540–1597). Rana Pratap was the son of Uday Singh, the **Rajput** ruler of Mewar belonging to the Sisodia clan, and succeeded him in 1572. Rana Pratap sustained a long, hard, and lonely struggle to maintain his independence and his honor against **Mughal Emperor Akbar**'s expanding domain. Mewar's almost impregnable capital, **Chitor**, had fallen to Akbar in 1567; Uday Singh had died while on the run from Mughal forces; every other Rajput ruler of consequence had been won over by Akbar into matrimonial and political alliance; but Rana Pratap struggled on.

He was defeated by an overwhelming Rajput-Mughal force at the Battle of Haldighati in 1576 and took to the hills. In 25 years of guerilla warfare before his death, Rana Pratap managed to recapture some of Mewar's desert strongholds, but his followers were attenuated. His son and successor submitted to Akbar's successor Jahangir and was permitted to build a new capital at Udaipur. Meanwhile, Rana Pratap's name had become synonymous with legendary Rajput valor, and praises are sung of his deeds to the present day.

PRATIHARA or GURJARA-PRATIHARA. This dynasty flourished in northern India between c. 750 and 1050 CE. It ruled first from Avanti in Malwa before moving its capital to the more famous and ancient city of **Kanauj**. Two great kings, Bhoja (r. 836–885 CE) and Mahendrapala (r. 885–914 CE), extended their domain from the **Himalaya** in the north to the Vindhya range in the south with outlets on the eastern and western seas, but made no lasting contributions to existing administrative tradition.

Neither of the Gurjara-Pratiharas were able to dislodge Arab rule from Sindh nor could they resist the invasions of **Mahmud of Ghazni** in the northwest. Moreover, they succumbed in their heartland to the **Rashtrakuta** expansion from the southwest. The Gurjara-Pratiharas were the last **Hindu** empire builders of northern India before the **Islamic** bid for pan-Indian imperial dominance.

PRAYAG. Also called Pratishthana and Triveni in early times, this is the modern city of **Allahabad**. Since ancient times it has been an important and holy place because of its site at the *sangam* (see Glossary) of three rivers: the **Ganges**, the **Yamuna**, and the invisible Saraswati, believed to run deep underground.

The Chinese pilgrim **Xuanzang** describes Prayag and mentions an undying banyan tree and temple court that might have marked a hermitage from **Vedic** times, as well as a stone pillar raised and inscribed by the **Mauryan Emperor Ashoka**.

Mughal Emperor Akbar recognized the sacred as well as the commercial and political importance of Prayag and renamed it Ilahabad. Its importance increased as a district headquarters in British India, with both the High Court and the University there enjoying great prestige. Many prominent figures in the Indian national movement, including **Motilal** and **Jawaharlal Nehru**, were born or educated in Allahabad. Prayag, or Allahabad, remains important in the present day. The **kumbha mela** held every 12 years at the *sangam* draws more than ten million pilgrims to bathe at the confluence of rivers there.

PREMCHAND (1880–1936). This was the pseudonym after 1910 of Dhanpat Rai, the writer. He was born in a village near **Banaras** and had access to a good education in Persian and Urdu. He lost his mother at a young age and left the home of his father shortly after the latter's remarriage. Premchand suffered from poor health all his life and ultimately succumbed to a gastric ulcer. He tried his hand at school teaching, publishing, screen writing, and journalism but truly flowered as a creative writer.

Premchand was extraordinarily prolific. His 12 published novels, more than 300 short stories, several plays, and many essays, letters, and editorials establish him as a major figure in modern Indian literature. He was a pioneer in Indian fiction writing, raising the level of the serious short story and novel to one comparable with European fiction of the time. His works reflect his inner growth as he moved from romanticism and fashionable patriotic themes to those of social justice. His portrayals of **women**, married life, and poverty continue to move readers today with their compassion, humor, sincerity, and understanding of the villager. The range of his narratives expanded beyond the village as he matured, but he never lost touch with the real world of human and social problems.

Premchand wrote both in Urdu and in Hindi, transcending the communal controversy over the two scripts (for the spoken **languages** shared grammar, syntax, and vocabulary) that raged during his lifetime. His early stories were written in Urdu, and while he gradually moved to Hindi, he continued to use the vernacular language of his surroundings and abjured the **Sanskrit** larding favored by newer Hindi writers. Premchand shared **Mahatma Gandhi**'s belief in a national language and a national literature that reconciled and blended traits of the major Indian languages. Toward that end he launched a journal, *Hans*, in 1930, which was later edited by **Kaka Saheb Kalelkar**. Premchand also helped to create an all-India association of writers, with the support of Gandhi and the Hindi Sahitya Sammelan, which became a forum for vigorous debate of national issues at the time.

Premchand's last and most famous novel, *Godan*, translated in English as *The Gift of a Cow*, was written in **Bombay** in the early 1930s and is regarded as a classic on the life of the north Indian peasant. His critique of capitalism and his call for a new code of social conduct not based on disparities of wealth are found in his last essays and in an incomplete, probably autobiographical, novel he wrote on his sickbed shortly before his death.

PRESS IN INDIA. In 2004, there were an estimated 51,960 news-related daily, weekly, and other publications, with a total circulation of 118,257,597 in India. Some of these journals are new; 45 were founded more than 100 years ago, such as the Gujarati paper, *Bombay Samachar*, started in 1830 and the *Times of India* in English, which was established in **Bombay** in1838. The Hindi-**language** press holds the first position in terms of number of publications as well as circulation, followed by the English-language press with 190 daily newspapers and more than 500 weeklies. Since the early 1990s, new technologies and styles in design and journalism, specialized or topical interests among the public, cross-media ownership, competition from electronic media, and the forces of **economic liberalization** and globalization have helped to make the Indian Press even more vigorous, activist, and pluralistic. At the same time, it operates under certain constraints, such as provisions in the **Constitution** Article 19(1) on freedom of expression, governmental control of newsprint, labor conditions and **trade union** demands, occasional tussles between editors and owners over editorial freedom, and the need for advertising income.

India's first modern newspapers catering to the **East India Company** were published from **Calcutta** in 1780 (*Bengal Gazette*) and

Bombay (*Saubad Kaumudi*) in 1789. **William Carey** and his fellow missionaries produced the first Bengali newspaper from Serampore in 1818. All of the newspapers struggled against harassment and censorship by government; acting Governor General **Charles Metcalfe** relaxed the rules somewhat in 1835. Some 33 new newspapers sprouted across British India between 1835 and 1857, mostly promoting social reform, but only six survived the stringent laws of penalty for "exciting dissatisfaction" enacted after the great **Uprising or Mutiny of 1857**. The Press and Regulation of Books Act of 1867 prescribed procedures for obtaining a government license to print books or newspapers, and some of these still remain in place. Newspaper publication was stimulated by the speeding of communications through an all-India postal and telegraphic service initiated in 1870 as well as the opening of the Suez Canal and domestic manufacture of paper. Two press agencies, Reuters and Associated Press of India, were opened in the late 19th century, the Press Trust of India in 1905, the United News of India in 1961 and the multi-language Samachar Bharati, and the Nonaligned News Agency Pool in 1976.

The Vernacular Press Act of 1878 stipulated that publishers and printers of journals in Indian languages must execute a bond and give a security deposit, undertaking not to excite disaffection with the government or instigate disturbance of the peace. Widespread agitation against this measure and its accompanying pre-censorship led **Lord Ripon** to repeal it in 1881, and no further direct legislation to control the press was enacted before the Indian Press Act of 1910. The first half of the 20th century saw the appearance of a spate of newspapers, mainly nationalistic in character and supportive of the freedom struggle. Many national leaders including **M. K. Gandhi** regularly wrote for newspapers. The British authorities in India issued ordinances or passed laws to keep the press under control, especially during the years of **civil disobedience** and war in the 1930s and 1940s. Despite harsh penalties, an underground nationalist press continued to function, and the most restrictive laws were repealed very soon after India's independence. Above ground, an All-India Newspaper Editors Conference was formed in 1940 to get restrictions withdrawn and maintain a channel of communication between press and government as well as to encourage a high level of journalistic professionalism and assertiveness.

The print media in independent India is free, vocal, and diversified in its range of political opinion. It was subjected to pre-censorship only during **Emergency Rule** 1975–1977. Although individual journals have complained at times of government harassment over specific reportage or editorial policy and Indian laws of libel are strict, investigative journalism and press criticism of government have become stronger over the decades of independence, not weaker. The Press Council of India provides some services to the profession without seeking to control it. The tradition of a free press as a safeguard of democracy has taken firm root in India, and the press has shown more vigorous and healthy growth as an institution than have many other institutions in contemporary India. See Bibliography for a list of daily newspapers with the largest circulation.

PRINCELY STATES. At the time of India's independence from Britain in 1947, between 562 and 600 (depending on definition) Princely States were scattered over two-fifths of the subcontinent. They ranged in size from petty principalities of a few hundred acres to domains as large as France. Their rulers were of similarly diverse lineage, traced back to mythological times as in the case of Mewar, to Afghan incursions as in the case of **Bhopal**, to the **Maratha** confederacy in the case of many west and central Indian states, to the **Sikh** chieftains in **Punjab**, or to assertive vassals of the **Mughal Emperor** as in the case of **Hyderabad**. Serious scholars have turned their attention to the internal and external dynamics of these Princely States only recently, although the deeds, misdeeds, and lifestyles of princes have been for long the material of pulp literature.

Princely States were survivors of traditional Indian polity in which four different levels of control might operate on the land and its produce: a local chieftain with a title befitting his power; a Raja (see Glossary) who would command allegiance and revenue from several little kingdoms; a higher functionary with an appropriate title such as Maharaja or Nawab (see Glossary), entitled to collect revenue from a large area and connect it directly with the imperial or paramount power; and the imperial power itself, which was the Mughal Emperor in the 18th century. The decline of Mughal power was accompanied by assertiveness and conflict at all the other levels. The **East India**

Company, seeking commercial gain, also engaged itself in military and political competition. It signed treaties, subsequently known as **Subsidiary Alliances**, with some ruling princes against others; it annexed many territories; it emerged as the de facto paramount power in the early 19th century; and it suppressed the **Uprising of 1857**, during which Indian princes fought both for and against the British.

In 1858, the British Crown assumed sovereignty over an Indian Empire and removed the princes' fears of expropriation. Their status was fixed by the number of guns fired in salute; 83 princes were entitled to 11 guns and over, 24 to 17 and over, and only five—**Baroda**, Gwalior, Hyderabad, **Jammu and Kashmir**, and **Mysore**—to 21-gun salutes. The British looked on the Indian princes as props of a conservative empire; they interacted with them in asymmetric personal transactions resembling patronage, appointing residents, dewans (see Glossary), and English tutors for purposes of "modernization" but remaining wary of active or ambitious princes. Although railway lines and posts and telegraphs ran through the Princely States as they connected different parts of British India, and though Indian familial and cultural ties surmounted political borders, there was little or no contact between the princes and the emerging, politically conscious, middle class of British India that founded the **Indian National Congress** in 1885.

By 1900, some Princely States such as Baroda, **Cochin**, Mysore, and Travancore had good administrative systems. The primary education schemes financed by the rulers of Tranvancore, Cochin, and Baroda were certainly better than any in British India. But the stereotyped image of Princely States was of feudal, backward despotisms. Indian princes provided the viceroy with pomp and pageantry, especially at the *durbar* (see Glossary) of King George V in Delhi in 1911. As military allies (in theory) of the King-Emperor, they rallied their troops for service in **World War I** but were disappointed with the meager recognition they received from the British. A few princes entered the all-India political arena in the first quarter of the 20th century, notably Maharajah Ganga Singh of Bikaner, Maharajah Bhupinder Singh of **Patiala**, Maharajah Scindia Madho Rao of Gwalior, and Nawab Hamidullah of Bhopal. Some of them represented India at the League of Nations; others were courted for their name and financial support by newly formed groups in British India.

A **Chamber of Princes** was established as a deliberative assembly with limited powers of advice in 1921, at the same time as the **Montagu-Chelmsford Reforms** were introduced in British India. Rulers of the more important states sat in their individual capacity, smaller states elected representatives from among themselves for the Chamber of Princes. There was an active membership of about 40 princes with a core of about 15 from different parts and different communities of India. World War I accelerated the pace of change in India, and the **Non-Cooperation Movement** demonstrated the need to readjust group relationships. But through the 1920s the princes remained clients of the imperial power, aloof from the national movement and seeking constant reassurance from the British for their own status and security in subsequent constitutional changes. The princes, for the most part, responded well to a suggestion made by **Sir Tej Bahadur Sapru** at the first **Round Table Conference** in 1930 for a federation between Princely India and British India. The federal scheme incorporated in the **Government of India Act** of 1935 however, became mired in the marshes of British ambivalence, princely intransigence, and Congress opposition before **World War II.** Mutual mistrust between most of the princes and Congress leaders was fueled, too, by the agitations led by the **States Peoples Conference** in the late 1930s for democratization in the Princely States.

The princes played no direct role in negotiations for the transfer of power during the 1940s. A very few, such as Bhopal, Hyderabad, and Travancore, entertained fantasies of independence when **Lord Louis Mountbatten**, last viceroy of India, announced on June 3, 1947, that **"paramountcy"** would lapse on August 15. Most of the princes recognized the imminent reality of a new paramount power in independent India and were willing to come to terms with it, as they had in the past with Mughals and British. Through the efforts of Mountbatten, **Vallabhbhai Patel**, and their troubleshooter **V. P. Menon**, 584 ruling princes signed Instruments of Accession to India by August 15,1947. The administrative harmonization of their domains with contiguous areas was completed by the mid-1950s. The varying cases of Hyderabad and Junagadh were resolved by 1948; the ruler of Jammu and Kashmir acceded to India in October 1947 but some of his territory was occupied by Pakistani military forces and remains disputed today.

At the time of accession, 284 of the princes were qualified to receive privy purses. These were abolished after the Derecognition of Indian princes proclamation introduced by **Indira Gandhi**'s government in 1971, later passed into law. Most princes and their families actively participate in the commercial, military, professional, political, and service streams of contemporary Indian life and many of their estates and former palaces are current tourist attractions.

PRITAM, AMRITA (1919–). Amrita Pritam is known as a poet and writer who has received the highest literary and national awards. No award, perhaps, is more precious than the knowledge that her essays, novels, and short stories in Hindi and Punjabi have been translated into 30 languages and that her epic, passionate poem on **Partition**, entitled *Waris Shah*, continues to be widely recited—and wept over—far and wide. Born and raised in a **Sikh** family of Lahore, Amrita Pritam worked with All India Radio first in Lahore, and in **Delhi** after Partition. The intensity of her feelings about love and death, knowledge, humanity, and valor, are expressed in her writings as well as in her life. Self-deprecating, Amrita Pritam has published two autobiographical novels, *Raside Ticket* (Revenue Stamp) 1970 and *Akshron ke Saaye* (Shadows of Works) 1997. She was nominated to the **Rajya Sabha** in 1984 and lives quietly in Delhi.

PUNE. See POONA.

PUNJAB. The present state of Punjab in the northwestern corner of the Indian Union has an area of little more than 50,000 square kilometers and a population of over 20 million. It is composed of the eastern 40% of pre-Partition united Punjab in British India, plus Patiala and seven other former **Princely States** merged with the Punjab in 1956, and minus the Hindi-speaking districts in the northeast and southeast joined with **Himachal Pradesh** and **Haryana** respectively in 1966. The principal **language** is Punjabi, and the capital of the state is **Chandigarh**. More than 80% of the area is cultivated to produce surpluses of food-grains as well as cash crops such as sugar cane and oil seeds. The **Green Revolution** flowered first in Punjab, with positive and negative consequences clearly visible today.

Punjab takes its name from the "five rivers" of the **Indus**, and the larger western portion, now in **Pakistan**, is also called Punjab. It was home to India's first known civilization with a major center at **Harappa**. The people of Punjab have cultural and ethnic affinities with people of the Iran-Afghan plateau. Punjab's geo-strategic location made it the natural crossroads for people entering or leaving the subcontinent from or to central Asia from earliest times. Punjabis are reputed to be readily adaptable to new ideas and ways of life in consequence. Ancient empires straddling present-day political boundaries, such as the **Mauryan**, Bactrian, **Kushan**, and **Saka**, found both prosperity and battlefields in the fertile plains of Punjab. Much later, from the 7th to 11th centuries CE, the Punjab was the borderline between **Hindu-Buddhist** and **Islamic** culture or between **Rajput** and Turk warriors. **Mahmud of Ghazni**'s frequent raids of plunder in India led him to annex western Punjab in 1021. This subsequently became a base for Mohammed Ghor who defeated **Prithvi Raj Chauhan** at Thanesar in 1192. The **Delhi Sultanate** used garrisons in Punjab to ward off Mongol invasions, but Punjab was substantially independent in the time of the **Lodis**. The establishment and consolidation of the **Mughal Empire** in the 16th century linked Punjab closely with present-day Afghanistan and Iran to the west as well as to **Kashmir** and the rest of India. It was in the Mughal period that the **Sikh** religion spread through Punjab and during the twilight of the Mughals that the first Sikh *misls* (see Glossary) and then **Ranjit Singh** established power.

The British annexed Punjab in 1849. The **Lawrence** brothers and members of the **Indian Civil Service (ICS)** set high standards of administration. The province has been a prime recruiting ground for the **Indian Armed Forces** since the latter half of the 19th century. Extensive schemes of canal irrigation and resettlement carried out in central Punjab led to demographic changes and a measure of prosperity, though the incidence of famine was not halted altogether. Social changes and the activities of **Christian** missionaries helped stimulate reform movements such as led by the **Arya Samaj** and **Akalis** among Hindus and Sikhs respectively. Resistance to British rule also grew in the early 20th century, with **Lala Lajpat Rai** and the **Ghadr** revolutionaries playing prominent roles; the **Jallianwala Bagh** massacre intensified sentiments of resistance.

A notable feature of Punjab was its composite culture or *Punjabiyet* and the feeling of a shared identity among members of all three communities, Hindu, Muslim, and Sikh. This found political expression in the strength of the **Unionist Party** in the 1930s and 1940s and the difficulty **Mohammed Ali Jinnah** experienced in winning the allegiance of the Punjab contingent of the **All-India Muslim League** before 1946. Leading Punjabis found the idea of **Partition** unthinkable even in the spring of 1947; the common people were caught unprepared for the violence and forced migrations of about eight million people in both directions.

Punjab benefited from Indian investments in irrigation and power during the first Five-Year Plan, as well as from a settlement with Pakistan on sharing of the Indus waters made in 1960. During the late 1970s, however, relations soured between Chandigarh and New Delhi, between different sects of Sikhs, and between Sikhs and Hindus. Most of the problems were economic, such as supplies of water and power, sharing of river waters, fragmentation of landholdings, and absence of industrial investment. Some were political, such as the distribution of powers between center and state, and the competition for state power between the **Congress** and Akali **political parties**. But a Sikh fundamentalist surge led by **Sant Bhindranwale**, combined with material and moral support from Pakistan, traffic in arms and narcotics, and gross mismanagement from New Delhi to produce a militant **terrorist** movement and counter-terrorist reaction that disrupted civic and political life in the state for the decade of the 1980s. Normalcy seemed to have been restored by the time of state elections in 1993, and since then Akali and Congress governments have roughly alternated in power, although both parties are severely factionalized.

PURANAS. These are collections of ancient lore expounding theogony, cosmogony, genealogies of kings and rishis (see Glossary), rites of worship, religious beliefs, social and political practices, and other miscellaneous matters pertaining to early Indian civilization. Much of the information is in the form of dialogue, with a sage responding to the questions of a disciple. Fables, stories, legends, and songs illustrate the dialogues. The expositions, therefore, are in a popular style, in contrast to the highly literate style of the **Vedas**. Some suggest that the

Puranas were originally composed in **Prakrit** or the vernacular and were only later transcribed into **Sanskrit**.

Puranic literature comprises two groups of 18 works each. They are ascribed to the great sage Vyasa, as is the epic *Mahabharata*. Their exact age is a subject of controversy, with some dating them to the fifth century BCE, while extant recensions are probably no earlier than the fourth century CE and some are likely to have taken a written form later still. The contents refer to a distant past, however, and the Puranas are almost the sole source of information—other than archaeology—about the early post-Vedic period; they are valued accordingly, though not accepted as formal history by purists.

As a historical source, the *itihasa purana* is linked to the bardic tradition and contains material in the form of eulogies, chronicles of heroic deeds, and genealogies of ruling families. Modern historians look on the myths embedded in the puranas as ways of explaining the origins and distinguishing features of clans and other social groups, as well as the processes integrating diverse groups with each other. For example, the relative opportunity of non-**kshatriya** men to gain membership of a warrior-ruler class can be gauged from the systematic dynastic genealogies provided in the Puranas. Although couched in the future tense rather than in the past, the Puranas show an integrated view of the past as seen from the dates when they were written down, probably in the middle of the first millennium CE. Two time markers used in the Puranas are a great flood occurring many thousands of years ago, and a great war dated according to a planetary configuration calculated to refer to 3102 BCE and frequently conflated with the great war depicted in the *Mahabharata* and the beginning of the *Kaliyuga* or present era. Puranic accounts of the first king Manu, the interventions of gods in the rise and fall of kingdoms, and the conflicts between good and evil, amount to a bible of popular and heterodox **Hinduism** and are so viewed by many. In particular, the *Bhagvata Purana* inspired sects that grew into the **Bhakti** movement.

PURVA-MIMAMSA. This is the name of one of the six schools of early Indian philosophy. It expounded the nature of **dharma** in the form of meritorious acts. It set up a system of exegetical principles to be employed when interpreting the **Vedas**. These principles were used in the sphere of civil law as well as religious ritual. With Mimamsa referring to the **brahmanic** philosophy based on the Vedas, the Purva-Mimamsa school is the earlier exposition, and the *uttara* or later school is the **Vedanta**.

– Q –

QUIT INDIA MOVEMENT. This was the widest and most bitter mass upsurge against British rule in India. The viceroy at the time, **Lord Linlithgow**, described it as "the most serious rebellion since 1857, the gravity and extent of which we have so far concealed from the world for reasons of military security." (Chopra, *Quit India Movement: The British Secret Report*: 1). The movement was crushed with the largest number of arrests and casualties from police beatings and army actions that had been experienced in British India. Unofficial estimates are much higher than the official admissions of more than 1,000 civilians killed and more than 3,000 injured between August and November 1942.

The genesis of this particular **Civil Disobedience** movement led by **Mahatma Gandhi** lay in **Indian National Congress** frustration with the obdurate refusal of Britain's Prime Minister Winston Churchill to consider any meaningful transfer of power in India and with the consequential failure of the **Cripps Mission** in March 1942. Congress had declined to cooperate with the British war effort since 1940, arguing that India in bondage could not effectively counter the Nazi-Fascist threat, and that India in subjection deprived the Allies of the moral superiority embodied in the Atlantic Charter of freedom. Japanese victories in Singapore, Rangoon, and the **Andamans** by early 1942 also raised questions about the appropriate response to a possible Japanese overland invasion of India. On April 26, 1942, Gandhi published an article in *Harijan* calling for "an orderly and timely British withdrawal from India" so as to permit the emergence of a self-reliant and dignified India. The Congress Working Committee meeting of July 14 appealed to the British to withdraw in goodwill or face massive civil disobedience; the All-India Congress Committee (AICC) subsequently passed a resolution along the same lines.

The British Government of India charged Congress with preparing for "unlawful, dangerous and violent activities," and on the night of August 8 they simultaneously arrested Gandhi, all members of the AICC, and Congress workers down to the town level. There was a burst of blind anger across the country, especially among students, with the Forward Bloc and other non-Communist nationalists in the forefront of violence against railways, post offices, and police stations. Government reprisals were similar to those following the **Uprising of 1857**. A massive government propaganda campaign was launched, especially in the United States where President Franklin D. Roosevelt had urged British concessions to Indian sensibilities, portraying nationalists as pro-Japanese and seditious. A report prepared by Justice T. Wickenden in 1943 on the disturbances was more objective but was not released to the public. Gandhi was released in 1944 for health reasons. By that time the movement had collapsed, the **Communist Party of India (CPI)** and the **All-India Muslim League** were cooperating with the British at the expense of Congress, and the dangers of a Japanese invasion had receded.

Assessments of the "success" or "failure" of the Quit India struggle in the context of the national movement vary. Mass participation increased, no doubt, but so did violence. Some scholars date the decline of Gandhi's preeminence in Congress to these events.

– R –

RADHAKRISHNAN, SARVEPALLI (1888–1975). President of India from 1962 to 1967, he was a noted philosopher of the Advaita (see Glossary) or non-dualistic school of **Vedanta**. He promoted a cultural synthesis between East and West, idealism and reason, for the development of a world civilization in the contemporary era, especially through his books, including *Hindu View of Life*, translation of the *Bhagvata Gita*, and *Eastern Religion and Western Thought*.

Radhakrishnan was born into a **brahman** family of **Madras** and was educated in Christian missionary schools and college where he majored in philosophy. He published *Idealist View of Life* in 1932 and was Spaulding Professor of Eastern Religion and Ethics at Oxford from 1935 to 1952. Between 1946 and 1950 he was India's representative at UNESCO, filled various educational positions, and was appointed India's ambassador to the Soviet Union in 1949. He was elected vice president of India in 1952 and president of India in 1962. He played an important and non-controversial role as head of state presiding over governmental changes following the deaths of Prime Ministers **Jawaharlal Nehru** in 1964 and **Lal Bahadur Shastri** in 1966.

RADHASOAMI SATSANG. This is a 20th-century socio-religious movement in northern India, with large residential centers at **Agra** and on the Beas river in **Punjab**. Swami Shiv Dayal Singh (1818–1878) was the founder and is revered as a teacher. The movement is squarely in the **Bhakti** *nirguna* tradition, which means that while emphasizing devotional faith, it does not incorporate anthropomorphic concepts of God, nor does it have a priesthood.

The appeal of the Radhasoami Satsang transcends class, **caste**, gender, religious affiliation, and nationality. There are presently well over one million adherents who run a complex of institutions for social welfare in India.

RAI, LALA LAJPAT (1865–1928). Lajpat Rai was born in **Punjab** to a **Hindu** family of a trading **caste** and was educated in Ludhiana and Lahore. He came under the influence of **Dayananda Saraswati** as a student and was an ardent worker for the **Arya Samaj** throughout his life.

Lajpat Rai joined the **Indian National Congress** in 1888 but considered its moderate constitutional verbiage ineffective. He shared the views of **Bal Gangadhar Tilak** and **Bipan Chandra Pal** about the need to fight for *swaraj*, or independence through mass agitation, boycott, and *swadeshi* (see Glossary). He was one of the leaders of the "extremists" who split from the "moderates" led by **Gopal Krishna Gokhale** in the Congress session of 1907. Lajpat Rai made forceful speeches at large meetings throughout the Punjab and wrote about the economic exploitation of India by the British. He was arrested in 1907 for organizing an agrarian revolt and was deported to **Burma**. The experience only deepened his radicalism, and he was associated with Lala Hardayal's **Ghadr Party** when abroad during **World War I**.

On his return to India in 1920, Lajpat Rai was shocked by the repression that followed the **Jallianwala Bagh** massacre. He was not inspired by the non-violent vision of **Mahatma Gandhi** but joined the **Non-Cooperation Movement** 1920–1922 and thereafter the **Swaraj Party** and then the **Hindu Mahasabha**. Lala Lajpat Rai led a procession in Lahore against the **Simon Commission** in 1928 and died from injuries inflicted by the police assault on the procession. He was known as *Sher-e-Punjab*.

RAILWAYS. These are the principal mode of transportation in India, carrying more than 300 million passengers and more than 350 million tons of freight by the end of the 20th century. From their first modest introduction over a 34-kilometer line from **Bombay** in 1853, the Indian railways have grown into one of the largest networks in the world, with about 7,000 stations spread over a total track of more than 100,000 kilometers. The network is divided in nine geographical zones further divided in divisions, with Users' Consultative Committees assisting the basic operating units. About 34% of the total track is electrified. By 2001, the rolling stock comprised 54 steam, 4,702 diesel, and 2,810 electric locomotives, with new fuel-efficient locomotives being introduced along with modern signaling, centralized traffic control, and high-speed coaches as they become available. The Indian Railways have made impressive progress in the indigenous production of rolling stock to the point of near-self-sufficiency.

Railways were tentatively introduced in India in 1853 after they had proved successful in Britain. The need for strategic communications to overcome the **Uprising of 1857** hastened the process of British railway construction in India. In a controversial move, the government underwrote private financing and guaranteed a 5% return. After 1869, the government itself purchased lines and financed construction and also tried to attract private capital. By the late 19th century, more than 6,000 kilometers of railway track, mostly in broad gauge, were in use. Railways proved to be immensely popular with Indians—so frequently engaged in familial or religious peregrinations—and were unintended facilitators of social reform, incipient nationalism, and national integration since independence. Indians did not reap the capital or technological benefits of the great railway bazaar as long as Britain maintained its monopoly on design and production. Since 1950, however, there has been impressive progress in the indigenous production of rolling stock, including locomotives, coaches, and other railway equipment, some of which is exported. The Research, Design and Standards organization at Lucknow is the research and development consultant to the railways.

Railways are one of the most vital planks of India's economic infrastructure, the Railway Budget is almost as important an event in the parliamentary calendar as the national budget itself, and the railway portfolio—currently held by **Laloo Prasad Yadav**—is one of the most important in the Union Cabinet. While railway administration in India has been conservative and efficient for the most part, the pressure of freight and passenger travel on the railways has increased as economic growth rates accelerate, and maintenance of track and equipment has not kept pace with heavy usage. Accidents inevitably take a heavy toll of life and attract media attention. Safety has suffered further from conditions of insurgency or breakdowns of law in order in certain states from time to time. Nevertheless, more than 100 new passenger trains have been introduced in the past five years, and the frequency of train-runs on established routes has increased. Revenue from freight traffic is substantial.

RAJAGOPALACHARI, CHAKRAVARTI (1879–1972). He was the last governor general of India, and the first Indian to fill that position, from 1948 when **Lord Mountbatten** left to 1950 when India became a republic. Rajagopalachari remained in political life, serving first as minister of home affairs in New Delhi and then as chief minister of the state of **Madras** from 1952 to 1954. His disagreement with some of **Jawaharlal Nehru**'s policies led him to become a founding member of the **Swatantra Party** in the mid-1950s.

C. Rajagopalachari was the youngest of three sons born to an orthodox **brahman** family of **Mysore** and educated at Bangalore and Presidency College, Madras. After meeting **Mahatma Gandhi**, he joined the **Indian National Congress**, was elected to the Congress Working Committee (CWC) in 1921, and became a leader of the **Civil Disobedience** movement in south India. He argued for full implementation of constitutional reforms, such as those passed in 1919 and 1935, and was active in the pre-independence politics of Madras where he headed a Congress government of 1937–1939. In that capacity, he was able to put into effect part of the Congress platform on land tenancy, abolition of **untouchability**, and prohibition of liquor.

Rajagopalachari was fully committed to the principles and practice of non-violence and self-discipline but differed with both Gandhi and Nehru on some of the key decisions taken by the Congress leadership after 1939. For example, he favored full participation in **World War II** and resigned from the CWC before the **Quit India** movement. He proposed formulas for a working agreement with **Mohammed Ali Jinnah** of the **Muslim League** in an Indian confederation much looser than the framework demanded by Congress, but Jinnah rejected the idea. After independence, Rajaji opposed nationalization of key industries, centralization of the political system, and the adoption of Hindi (rather than spoken Hindustani or English) as the national **language**.

Rajaji, as he was popularly known, was a man of reason and moderation rather than of ideology or populism. He was a powerful orator and writer in both **Tamil** and English, and among his lasting legacies are his translations of the *Ramayana* and *Mahabharata*.

RAJASTHAN. The state of Rajasthan formally came into being in 1958 as the culmination of a process of bringing together the former **Princely States** of Rajputana (home of the **Rajputs**) with geographically contiguous districts in the western part of the Indian Union. Bharatpur, **Bikaner**, **Jaipur**, Jaisalmer, Jodhpur, Kota, and Udaipur were among the historically important Princely States included in the second largest state in India with an estimated population of 56 million and an area of 342,239 square kilometers. Rajasthan has always been strategically important to rulers in nearby **Delhi**; it is even more so today since its entire western flank adjoins **Pakistan** and has been the site of armed clashes and incursions.

The checkered and often heroic history of Rajasthan goes back beyond the time of **Harappa** before rivers dried and the Thar Desert spread to its present expanse. Vital trade routes between other parts of India and ports in **Gujarat** as well as to Iran and lands further west traversed Rajasthan and may partially account for the commercial success of the **Marwari** community in modern times as well. And Rajputs dominated most of northern India and **Nepal** from about the seventh century CE onward, founding imperial systems of their own, as by the **Chauhans** battling the Turks, or being accommodated by the **Mughal Empire** after **Akbar**, and then in **Subsidiary Alliance** by the British. Fortresses such as **Chitor**, numerous palaces, a variety of nomadic pastoral communities, colorful festivals, and unusual social customs that are the legacy of the past combine with spectacular landscapes to make Rajasthan a favored destination for domestic and foreign tourists alike. Tourism is a well-developed source of livelihood in the state.

Rajasthan is rich in minerals, precious and semi-precious stones, salt, marble, and other valuable stone used in monumental buildings of the past and present. As a result, the geologically most ancient Aravali Range bifurcating Rajasthan has been ruthlessly mined and excavated, especially in modern times. Some industry is being developed, especially around the Export Promotion Industrial Park established in the capital, Jaipur.

The agricultural potential of Rajasthan has been enhanced in recent decades by the construction of irrigation canals from rivers in the **Punjab**, through the introduction of new technologies in arid land cultivation, sometimes with Israeli assistance, and by the revival of ancient methods of water conservation that have, for example, brought back flows to rivers in Alwar district. Different kinds of **Non-Governmental Organizations** and **Cooperatives** are very active in Rajasthan. They have helped mobilize rural communities, raised production and nutritional levels, founded income generating activities, sought to empower women through education and employment, and created effective mechanisms for demanding accountability from local governments, although they frequently face opposition from entrenched, patriarchal elites. Partly as a result of NGO as well as official efforts, social indicators such as literacy rates for males and females have shown marked improvement—from an admittedly low base—in recent decades. The two major political parties more or less alternating power in Rajasthan are the **Congress Party** and the **Bharatiya Janata Party**.

RAJNEESH (1939–1989). Rajneesh is also known as Bhagwan and Osho. He gained many followers in the West and in some sections of Indian society for his bold and unorthodox interpretations of ancient Indian teachings contained in the **Upanishads, Tantra,** and **Buddhist**

texts. He published a large body of writings on meditation and various cultural, philosophical, political, religious, sexual, and social issues and upheld the superiority of the traditional Indian approach to the contemporary Western approach to them. He taught that only those who had freed their minds of connotations of the word God could undertake fruitful inquiry into the nature of God. The Osho *ashrams* in India and in the United States attracted many visitors, but they also became controversial and were occasionally subject to official inquiries into their activities.

RAJPUT. This is a term derived from the **Sanskrit** *rajaputra* (son of a king) and refers to a **caste** traditionally associated with rulership and warriorhood. The origins of the Rajputs have been much debated and are variously ascribed as dating back to the **Vedas**, to the progeny of **Manu** the first Man according to mythology, to a sacrificial fire, to the **Hunas** or other Central Asian tribes entering India in the fourth and fifth century CE, or to groups outside caste society absorbed into it as *kshatriyas*. Literary and epigraphic sources suggest that Rajput origins were both indigenous and exogenous but that a self-conscious sense of their special identity arose in the seventh and eighth centuries as they established territorial domains and suitable lineage.

Bardic tradition holds that there were 36 founding clans of Rajputs born of a sacrificial fire from which sprang the solar, lunar, and fire lineages. There were many branch lines claiming the same ancestry and establishing dynasties in new settlements and territories in western, central, and northern India. Many of these myths, traditions, and accounts of heroic deeds were collected by a Colonel James Todd as he traversed **Rajasthan** in the 1820s and were subsequently published as the *Annals and Antiquities of Rajasthan*.

The Rajputs upheld an exceedingly strict code of martial honor based on the prescribed conduct for a *kshatriya* and similar in some respects to the Bushido of feudal Japan. In many centuries of warfare against Muslims during which the frontiers of Rajput control were pushed back, the most conspicuous expression of this code was collective ritual suicide, as at **Chitor** and Jaisalmer in the 14th century. Against overwhelming odds of battle, male Rajputs charged into attack and certain death (*jouhar*) while female Rajputs burned themselves within their fortresses as **sati**.

Among powerful and famous Rajput families in the period 800–1200 CE were the Chauhans of **Delhi** and **Ajmer**, the Chalukyas of **Gujarat**, the Paramars of Malwa, and the **Pratiharas** of **Kanauj**. The Sisodias of Mewar, the Rathors of Marwar, and the Kachchwahas of Amber/Jaipur became equally famous in the following period, either in armed opposition to invading Turks or, later, in partnership with the **Mughals**. With their fierce pride and clan rivalries the Rajputs were unable to unite among themselves or forge commonality of purpose with the **Marathas** in the twilight of the Mughal Empire and retreated to their desert forts. As Britain became the new imperial power in India, the Rajput princes accepted **paramountcy** and provided viceroys, residents, and their British guests with hunting grounds, glamour, jewels, and polo. With some notable exceptions, their states came to be regarded as intellectual, cultural, and social backwaters isolated from the nationalistic and modernizing winds of the 20th century. The pace of change quickened after Indian independence and the integration of **Princely States**, with former rulers or members of their families playing a variety of honorable roles—including those of elected representatives, army officers, and ambassadors—in the new democratic structures of the country. *See also* RAJASTHAN.

RAJYA SABHA. The upper house of the Indian Parliament is named the Rajya Sabha. According to the **Indian Constitution** of 1950, it consists of not more than 250 members, including 12 nominated by the President for their individual merit and "special knowledge and experience" in different fields of endeavor including the arts. The legislative assemblies of the states and Union territories elect members of the Rajya Sabha for a period of six years. One-third of the membership retires every second year. The Rajya Sabha is presided over by the vice president of India, sits in continuous session, and cannot be dissolved.

As in the case of other upper chambers in parliamentary systems, the Rajya Sabha does not initiate money bills and cannot pass motions of censure or of no confidence in the government, which is responsible to the lower house. The upper chamber can provide high standards of debate, able members of parliamentary standing committees, reflection on important legislation, and a sense of stability at times of political strain. Although states are represented roughly according to population and so not equally, as in the United States, the Constitution writers considered the Rajya Sabha to be essential to a federal structure, and that is not challenged today.

RAM or RAMA. A legendary king of **Ayodhya** is regarded as an incarnation of the deity **Vishnu** and is worshipped as a god by many **Hindus** since about the eighth century CE. Recitation of the name of Ram brings spiritual solace to his devotees. Ram is depicted as the ideal man in the epic *Ramayana*, even as his wife, Sita, is depicted as the ideal woman. The story of his heroic deeds, his wanderings in exile, the abduction of his wife, his fight to recover her, and their triumphant return to their kingdom and his righteous rule, is subject to many interpretations, historical, mythological, and astronomical.

Historians find it difficult to date the life of Ram exactly. Internal evidence suggests that the classical epic was composed well before the fourth century BCE, but it could refer to events much earlier, possibly the third millennium BCE. The actual site of his birthplace and capital city Ayodhya, too, is not scientifically proven. These subjects became the focus of intense controversy and open conflict in the early 1990s for reasons arising more from political competition between rival aspirants to contemporary temporal power than from any spiritual, religious, or historical attribute of Ram. *See also* RAMAYANA.

RAM, JAGJIVAN (1908–1986). Jagjivan Ram was for many years before his death the highest-ranking member of the Scheduled **Castes** in India. He was born in **Bihar** but studied in **Varanasi** and **Calcutta**. He gravitated to **Mahatma Gandhi** and the **Indian National Congress** with their promise of ameliorating the lives of all Indians. Jagjivan Ram initiated a movement among agricultural labor in Bihar, chaired the newly founded Khet Mazdoor Sabha (Agricultural Workers Society) in 1937, and became president of several **trade unions**. He was imprisoned during the **Quit India Movement** and was interviewed by the **Cabinet Mission** as a leader among the Scheduled Castes.

Jagjivan Ram was minister of labour in the Government of India from 1946 to 1952 and subsequently held other portfolios in **Jawa-**

harlal Nehru's cabinets. He resigned under the **Kamaraj** Plan of 1963 to revitalize the **Congress Party** but rejoined the party and served as defense minister from 1967 to 1970 in **Indira Gandhi**'s government. Jagjivan Ram resigned from the Congress Party in 1974 and chaired his own faction called the All-India Depressed Classes League. He joined the **Janata Party** and was part of its short-lived government 1977–1979. His hopes of becoming prime minister after **Morarji Desai** stepped down were eroded in ugly factional adjustments, and general elections were called when the **Charan Singh** government also fell in July 1979.

RAMAKRISHNA MISSION. Swami Vivekananda founded this organization in the name of his guru (see Glossary) **Ramakrishna Paramhansa** in 1897. Two years later, the Belur Math was built near **Calcutta** to house its headquarters, and a monastery was founded in the Kumaon Hills of the north to train the spiritually hungry young men who joined the new organization. It was formally registered as a charitable society in 1909. By 1980, the Ramakrishna Mission had 1,400 monks and more than 100,000 lay followers in India. It was also active in neighboring countries of the subcontinent as well as in the Americas, Europe, Southeast Asia, and Oceania. Indeed, wherever Indians have settled overseas or where there is an interest in **Hindu** philosophy, the Ramakrishna Mission is likely to have a presence. It depends on public donations for carrying out its multifarious activities in all kinds of relief work, rural development, education, dispensaries, and hospitals. The mission adopted a progressive attitude of accepting science and respecting the fruits of modern science and technology from its beginning, without, however, neglecting spirituality. It propagates the principles of **Vedanta**, including the equality of all religions in the search for the Absolute.

The Ramakrishna Mission and Math embodied the complementary spiritual and mundane objectives of Vivekananda's message. Its rules included the following summary: The first and foremost task in India is the propagation of education and spirituality among the masses. It is impossible for hungry men to become spiritual unless food is provided for them. Hence our paramount duty lies in showing them new ways of food supply. As an organized monastic order, the Ramakrishna Mission trained a body of activist ascetics for whom prayer and meditation went hand in hand with the material alleviation of suffering. The public impact of saffron-clothed ascetics engaged in unusual activities such as treating epidemic victims, as during an outbreak of plague in Calcutta at the turn of the century, was tremendous. They carried out Ramakrishna's injunction, "service of man, for man is God."

The Ramakrishna Mission, like its founder Vivekananda, was part of what is known as the Hindu Revivalist Movement of the late 19th and early 20th centuries, even though it was reformist in practice and did not proselytize for any particular faith. In a somewhat controversial move, the Ramakrishna Mission approached the Calcutta High Court in 1980 for grant of status as a minority religion, claiming to be a unique religious denomination offering the "essence" of all religions and composed of a collection of individuals classed together as followers of Shri Ramakrishna. The Court granted it minority status in 1985 as its members constituted less than fifty percent of the population in **West Bengal**; thereby, it secured certain tax-free privileges for its properties and in the administration of its educational institutions. The worldwide public image of the Ramakrishna Mission, however, is of a Hindu monastic order.

RAMAKRISHNA PARAMHANSA (1836–1886). Born to a poor but respectable **brahman** family of **Bengal** and named Gadadhar Chatterjee, he preferred the company of holy men to school and became one of the priests at the Dakshineswar temple to the Goddess Kali north of **Calcutta**. There, he carried out many religious and spiritual experiments in a ceaseless quest for union with God. His mystical experiences, his *samadhi* (see Glossary), and his vision of the Goddess were subsequently described in detail. His wife Sarada became his first disciple. He became known as Sri Ramakrishna Paramhansa and attracted many followers.

Sri Ramakrishna believed that the only goal of human life is realization of God, and that held true for all religions. In other words, he was a classic mystic cast in a traditional mode. He was not a social reformer or activist but encouraged his followers, especially those from the English-educated gentry, or *bhadralok* (see Glossary) to serve God through service of their fellow human beings less fortunate than themselves. His most famous disciple, **Swami Vivekananda**, founded first a monastery and then an entire order of socially active monks, the **Ramakrishna Mission**, in his name.

RAMAN, CHANDRASEKHAR VENKATA (1888–1970). C. V. Raman was born in Trichinopoly into a **brahman** family of **Sanskrit** scholars. He dedicated his life to the pursuit of truth through science. Raman was educated in **Madras** and studied physics and mathematics. He was admitted to the Indian Finance Service after graduation but also worked in the laboratories of the Indian Association for Cultivating Science in **Calcutta**. He was named the Palit Professor of Physics at the University of Calcutta in 1917 and was elected as Fellow of the Royal Society in 1924.

C. V. Raman became most famous for his studies of light, and one of his discoveries on the effect of scattered light rays was named the Raman Effect after him. He was knighted in 1929 and was appointed director of the newly founded Indian Institute of Science at Bangalore in 1933. Within a year after Indian independence, Raman was named India's first National Professor and the Raman Research Institute for Science was established. He was honored by India, the United States, and the Soviet Union during the 1950s.

RAMANA, MAHARISHI (1879–1950). Ramana had a pre-experience of death at the age of 15 and began to cogitate on the eternal questions posed in the **Upanishads**, especially the nature of the Self, or "who am I?" According to biographies and compilations of his later expositions, Ramana received illuminated insight and direct realization of Being. He left home for Tiruvannamalai and sat in silent meditation next to the twin-peaked hill of Arunachala, held sacred for centuries as the Hill of Light. Spontaneous offerings from local inhabitants took care of his minimal physical needs, and he never left that place, although he did move indoors.

Ramana soon came to be recognized as a spiritually realized person and a worthy teacher to be addressed as "Maharishi" without any self-assertion on his part. Gradually he began to respond to questions and expounded on the ways to knowledge of the Self, stressing self-inquiry and surrender of the ego. Although he did not write down his teachings, they were condensed into 40 verses, and for the benefit of English-speaking audiences Arthur Osborne and T. N. Venkataraman compiled some of his discourses into books. Many regard Ramana Maharishi as the greatest sage of the 20th century.

RAMANNA, RAJA (1925–2004). Dr. Raja Ramanna is known as the "father" of India's Peaceful Nuclear Explosion (PNE) in May 1974 and had a determining influence on India's **nuclear program** for nearly three decades. He was born and educated in **Mysore** before going on to higher studies in science. He received his doctorate from Kings College, London, and then joined the select group of nuclear physicists working with **Homi Bhabha** in Trombay (near **Bombay**) to collaborate in the design and building of India's first research reactor, *Apsara*, which went critical in 1956. *Apsara* was fueled with natural uranium moderated by heavy water, and also produced plutonium in the fuel cycle. Ramanna later said there was discussion within the Atomic Energy Commission (AEC) at the time about keeping open the option of developing indigenous nuclear weapons but no decision was made, although India endeavored to retain maximum control over all reactors, even those built with Canadian or American assistance. By the early 1960s, the Indian scientists knew they were capable of conducting at least one nuclear test, but successive prime ministers, **Jawaharlal Nehru**, **Lal Bahadur Shastri**, and **Indira Gandhi** declined to order such a test for a variety of moral and political, internal, and external, reasons.

India's AEC tragically lost its leaders Homi Bhabha and **Vikram Sarabhai** in 1966 and 1971, respectively. Raja Ramanna became director of the Bhabha Atomic Research Centre (BARC), then chairman of the AEC and Secretary to the Government of India for Atomic Energy, and then Science Adviser to the Minister of Defence and Minister of State for Defence Production. As Director of BARC, Ramanna was among those who persuaded Indira Gandhi not to sign the discriminatory Nuclear Non Proliferation Treaty of 1968. They put forward a powerful case for demonstrating India's scientific and technical capability of using underground nuclear explosions for such peaceful operations as undertaking large earthmoving operations to construct water reservoirs that were approved of by Pugwash Conferences of the day. Ramanna was in charge of all of the preparations for conducting such a test at Pokharan in the **Rajasthan** desert, and Mrs. Gandhi's permission to go ahead was finally secured on May

16, 1974. She did not, however, allow more planned follow-up tests to be conducted, probably from what Ramanna called overcautiousness. In the event, India's PNE of 1974 did not earn it any respect or admiration for self-restraint in showing that weapons proliferation was not the inevitable product of technical ability. On the contrary, the test gave a fillip to **Pakistan**'s earlier established clandestine nuclear weapons program that soon received assistance from China, and provoked a series of measures by the United States and its allies that were designed to deny India technology and materials.

Raja Ramanna and his friends and associates pressed their case more actively in the mid-1980s when **Rajiv Gandhi** was prime minister and the external security environment had deteriorated badly. Ramanna's case, briefly, was for conjoining national security and national development by producing only a small deterrent that would not be costly and would not be used for fighting purposes; in other words, a "minimal" minimum deterrent under the control of scientists and the political executive rather than the military should be sufficient for India he said. This point of view also underlay India's second series of tests at Pokharan in May 1998, although Ramanna was now retired and was about to enter the **Rajya Sabha**.

Raja Ramanna was an erudite and spiritually inclined man. He had a deep love of Indian and Western classical music and was a gifted, if private, pianist. He published *Structure of Music in Ragas and Western Systems* in 1998. He was not greedy for material goods and declined lucrative offers abroad in order to lead a reflective and useful life at home in **Bangalore** after leaving office.

RAMANUJA (c. 11th or 12th century CE). Ramanuja lived in **Karnataka** or **Hoysala** country during the ascendancy of the **Chola** Dynasty. He is acknowledged as one of the greatest Vaishnav *acharyas*, or teacher–saints, of the **Bhakti** movement, appealing especially to the non-brahmans of southern India.

Ramanuja challenged **Sankara**'s **Vedanta** philosophy of non-dualism and refuted it by identifying a personal God as a Vedantic concept. He differentiated between *chit* or individual soul, *achit* or unfeeling universe, and *ishwara* or Almighty Soul. He preached total love and devotion, or *bhakti*, through wisdom, good works, and surrender of the self as the path of spiritual salvation, and he rejected the concept of *maya* (see Glossary) or the non-reality of phenomenal existence. In this way, he enlarged the interpretation of the **Upanishads**.

Although Ramanuja's school of thought subsequently split on issues of interpretation, his influence remained substantial.

RAMANUJAN, SRINIVASA (1887–1920). Born to a **brahman** family of accountants in Erode, **Madras**, Ramanujan displayed an uncanny memory as a child and was obviously a mathematical prodigy. He carried out his mathematical studies independently, working on theorems of prime numbers and on infinity. Some of his papers were published in the 1911 issue of the *Journal of the Indian Mathematical Society* and attracted the attention of Professor G. H. Hardy at Cambridge.

Ramanujan went to Trinity College, Cambridge, on a modest research scholarship in 1914 and became famous for his *Theory of Numbers*. As a pure mathematician, he was elected a Fellow of Trinity College and a Fellow of the Royal Society in 1918 but died soon after.

RAMAYANA. The life history of the god–king **Ram**, said to have lived during the "silver age" of truth, or the epic period of Indian civilization, as initially told by the sage Valmiki in **Sanskrit**. Its literary and philosophical influence throughout the Indian subcontinent and beyond, to **Tibet** and through Southeast Asia, has been immense. While Valmiki's Sanskrit version remains the most prestigious in India, the story of Ram has been rendered at different times and places in every other Indian **language** and many other Asian languages, incorporating a multiplicity of local traditions and differences of emphasis among social groups and genders.

Among the most famous versions are Kampan's *Iramavataram* in **Tamil**, **Tulsi Das**'s *Ramacharitmanas* in Hindi, and the Thai *Ramakie*. There are also **Buddhist** and **Jain** renderings of the Ramayana. The versions sung by some **women**'s groups or enacted by lower **castes**, especially **Dalits**, show significant differences of interpretation from the orthodox version, with sympathy tending more toward Sita or Ravana than the epic hero Ram. The story of Ram continues to be reenacted and retold in contemporary times, especially during the autumnal festival. For example, **C. Rajagopalachari** published an English version of the Ramayana as a "national epic" for the benefit of modern Indians. A serial production of the Ramayana broadcast over one year on India's national television in 1987 drew larger audiences than any other single program worldwide. The devotion and, often, the rituals observed by rural audiences for these broadcasts amounted to a significant social phenomenon.

Briefly, the story of the *Ramayana* is about the first-born son of King Dasarath of **Ayodhya** who names him heir apparent in recognition of his wisdom, compassion, and martial skills. Dasarath's youngest queen demands a banishment of Ram for 14 years so that her son, Bharat, may succeed to the throne. Ram, his beautiful wife Sita, and his half-brother Lakshman, leave for the forests where they live as ascetics; Bharat places Ram's sandals on the throne and administers the kingdom in his name. Meanwhile, the powerful, wealthy, and exuberant Ravana, King of Lanka, has won a boon of near invincibility from the gods. He conceives a passion for Sita and abducts her. Ram searches for her far and wide and forms an alliance with the king of the monkeys; the monkey general, Hanuman, becomes Ram's devotee, a messenger to Sita held captive in Lanka, and a hero during the ensuing war. Both sides suffer heavy losses, but Ram kills Ravana, rescues Sita, and returns home victorious. The annual festival of *Dewali* celebrates this triumph of righteousness.

Several moral ambiguities in the behavior of Ram as depicted in the epic lent themselves to debate over the ages. If Ram was a deity in human form, did he know it? Why did he banish Sita for false allegations against her chastity? A variety of answers can be found in hundreds of versions of the Ramayana. An additional fact is that the Moreover, Ram, as an incarnation of **Vishnu**, has been the focus of devotion or worship among **Hindus** for many hundreds of years. **Mahatma Gandhi** and others in contemporary India have used the term *Ram-rajya* as a synonym for just and righteous rule.

RANADE, MAHADEV GOVIND (1842–1901). Born in Nasik district of **Maharashtra** to a Chitpavan **brahman** family, Ranade was educated at Elphinstone College and Bombay University where he obtained his master's and law degrees in 1864. He joined the judicial service in 1871 and became a judge of the Bombay High Court in 1893. He was appointed to the Bombay Legislative Council in 1885 and to the Finance Commission the following year. He was a well-respected, indeed venerated, figure in public life.

Ranade's place in history was carved by his efforts in social reform without violence and by his contributions to reformist organizations such as the Sarvajanik Sabha, the Prarthana Samaj, and the National Social Conference, which was a pan-Indian body of social reform associations. He was also a founder member of the **Indian National Congress**. Ranade edited an Anglo–Marathi daily, *Induprakash*, from 1878–1896 and used it to propagate his ideas on reforming **Hindu** social customs and religious traditions as well as economic change. For example, he proposed setting up agricultural banks to replace extortionist moneylenders and establishing joint stock companies for new industry.

Ranade focused, too, on raising the status of **women** through education, later marriage, and widow remarriage. His second wife, Ramabai (1862–1924), was educated by him and became an active champion of women and labor in her own right. Ranade and his wife were aware of many deficiencies in Indian national character and culture at the time and tried to use British rule and Western education as avenues to national elevation. Revivalists and orthodox members of society naturally opposed Ranade, but his prestige did not suffer and his wife continued her efforts to educate other women.

RANBAXY LABORATORIES LIMITED. The company was founded by Dr. Gurbax Singh and Ranjit Singh in 1937 as the Indian distributor of vitamins and anti-tuberculosis drugs produced by a Japanese pharmaceutical company. Bhai Mohan Singh joined as a partner in 1952, bringing with him capital and a vision to go beyond importing drugs to producing and marketing them. He established the first manufacturing plant in 1961 and made a breakthrough in 1969 with development of a popular Valium-based tranquilizer. Dr. Parminder Singh from Michigan joined the company in 1967, contributing a management style that emphasized technological improvement and product quality.

India's Process Patent Act of 1970 recognized the validity of international process (not product) patents, and Ranbaxy obtained an American patent for its broad-spectrum antibiotic doxycycline, as well as the drug ranitidine, and expanded sales all over the country.

The company was pushed into the export market by India's Price Control Act of 1979 limiting growth within India and soon established a significant presence in Britain, China, Italy, Russia, and Ukraine through the export of bulk and generic drugs and the formation of joint ventures. By the early 1990s, Ranbaxy was investing heavily in research and development and had a marketing strategy of direct contact with doctors. It aimed to become an international research-based company well prepared to face stiff competition when India became a fully participant member of the World Trade Organization in 1995. It retains its high reputation for excellence.

RANDHAWA, NARINDAR SINGH (1927–). Randhawa is one of the parents of India's **Green Revolution**. He was born and raised in the **Punjab** and took his doctorate at the University of California before returning to Punjab Agricultural University in Ludhiana to teach and do research on soil conditions in the 1960s. He is a founder member of the Society for the Promotion of Wasteland Development that is attempting to improve the lives of peoples subsisting on marginalized lands.

RANJIT SINGH (1780–1839). Ranjit Singh became chief of the Sukerchakias, one of 12 **Sikh** *misls* (see Glossary), on the death of his father in 1793. He soon showed exceptional qualities of military leadership, diplomacy, and administrative skills in welding together a large and united kingdom of **Punjab** from a congery of petty principalities and different communities.

Ranjit Singh threw back Afghan raiders and occupied Lahore where a lineal descendant of Guru **Nanak**, the founder of Sikhism, proclaimed him Maharaja in 1801. Ranjit Singh then expanded his kingdom on either side of the **Indus** River into the northwest borderland with Afghan tribes, into the hill kingdoms, and across the plains eastward. In 1809, he signed a treaty of friendship at **Amritsar** with the British representative **Charles Metcalfe** that demarcated respective spheres of influence along the river Sutlej. The Sikh kingdoms east of the Sutlej accepted British support in resisting Ranjit Singh's influence, but his generals took over **Kashmir** in 1819, Peshawer and lands along what came to be known as the North West Frontier by 1821, and **Ladakh** in 1834.

Southward expansion along the Indus was halted by the British conquest of Sindh in 1830 and the first **Anglo Afghan War**. A Tripartite Treaty to preserve the status quo between Ranjit Singh, the Afghans, and the British was signed in 1838.

Ranjit Singh's achievements went far beyond the military, although adversaries recognized his well-drilled and well-armed army as a formidable fighting force. He was known for his accessibility, his just and fair administration, his popularity among his subjects, and his lively personality. He created a strong centralized and internally peaceful state in an area that had known prolonged periods of disorder, rapine, and strife—and was to know them again. He ruled in the name of the *Khalsa* (see Glossary) and personally was a devout Sikh, but he chose his officials on the basis of ability rather than religious affiliation or nationality and did not discriminate among his Sikh, **Hindu**, or Muslim subjects. He employed about 50 Europeans as drill sergeants, including the Frenchmen Jean Francois Allard and Jean Baptiste Ventura. Despite his small stature and one eye, he had a commanding presence and became something of a legend in the history of the Punjab. The sense of a common Punjabi identity or *Punjabiyet* among all religious communities flowered during his reign and lasted well into the 20th century.

Shortly after Ranjit Singh's death, unchecked factionalism among the Sikh Chieftains and the unappeased British appetite for territorial expansion in India led to the Sikh Wars of 1846, the dismemberment of Ranjit Singh's kingdom, and the absorption of an independent Punjab into British India. At that time too, the fabulous **Koh-i-Nur** diamond that had been looted from the Mughal Emperor by Nadir Shah in 1736, and that Ranjit Singh had received from the Afghan Shah Shuja in 1813, passed to the crown of the British Queen.

RAO, P. V. NARASIMHA (1921–2004). Prime minister of India from 1991 to 1996, Narasimha Rao was born in a **brahman** landowning family of the **Princely State** of **Hyderabad**. He was educated in **Poona**, **Bombay**, and at the University of Nagpur where he took a Law degree. He became a scholar of **Sanskrit**, was fluent in several Indian **languages** as well as English, and was a persuasive orator.

Narasimha Rao joined the **Indian National Congress** as a young man and participated in the **Quit India** movement of 1942. He favored integration of Hyderabad with India and actively resisted the Nizam's rule. He established a reputation of being an intellectual and literary young man with a bent for serious political work. Narasimha Rao joined the **Congress Party** in 1951 and was first elected to the Legislative Assembly of **Andhra Pradesh** in 1957. He remained there for 20 years, holding various ministerial portfolios in the state government and also serving as chief minister from 1971 to 1973. He supported Prime Minister **Indira Gandhi** when Congress split in 1969 and remained loyal to her. He was elected to the **Lok Sabha** in 1977 on a Congress ticket, despite the party's overall defeat in the sixth general elections. He helped draft the party manifesto in 1979 for the seventh general elections, and when Congress was returned to power in January 1980, Mrs. Gandhi—who appreciated his loyalty, skills, and low profile—named him to her cabinet. Rao held important portfolios in both Indira and **Rajiv Gandhi**'s governments, notably those of External Affairs, Defense, and Home Affairs, during the 1980s. His style in office was unobtrusive, attentive to advice, and quiet, and had a calming effect on others.

P. V. Narasimha Rao was generally acceptable as party leader after the assassination of Rajiv Gandhi in May 1991. The 10th general elections completed shortly after the assassination made Congress the largest single party in Parliament, and Rao was asked to form a minority government. He was the first person from southern India to become prime minister. It was a time when several economic, social, and political crises were coming to a head in a nationwide atmosphere of violence and fear. Rao tried to reconcile polarities, and within a year he had gained a narrow majority for Congress in Parliament. His government, with **Dr. Manmohan Singh** as finance minister, launched major **economic liberalization** reforms to reduce government control of the economic and financial systems and take India into the mainstream of the international economy, despite domestic and party opposition to these moves.

Rao's government made efforts to soften divisions and defuse communal passions aroused over **Ayodhya** as well as implementation of the **Mandal Commission Report**. It also attempted to return normalcy to states racked by **terrorism**, including **Punjab**, **Jammu and Kashmir**, and the northeastern states. Narasimha Rao signed a major agreement with China in 1993 on maintaining peace and tranquility on the Line of Actual Control and took the initiative in a "look East" policy in foreign relations. Somewhat to the surprise of political analysts who were watching the growing power of **Hindutva** forces, Rao's government served a full five-year term in relative stability, despite formidable problems.

RAO, V. P. MADHAVA (1850–1934). Born to a **brahman** family of intellectuals and administrators in **Tanjore** district of **Madras**, Madhava Rao devoted most of his career to modernizing the administration of **Mysore**. He entered the service of that **Princely State** in 1881 and served as dewan (see Glossary) from 1906 to 1909. He also served as dewan of Travancore from 1904 to 1906 and of **Baroda** from 1914 to 1916.

Madhava Rao established similar general patterns in all three Princely States that helped to raise their standards above the average in British India. Backed by the rulers, he focused on reforms in revenue administration, taxation, justice and public works, social uplift through education and raising the age of marriage, and encouragement of local self-government. As an administrator, Madhav Rao would not permit political agitation in areas under his jurisdiction. In his personal capacity he believed in self-government for India and associated himself with the **Indian National Congress** during the 1920s.

RASHTRAKUTA DYNASTY. This dynasty ruled over the **Deccan** from 752 to 972 CE. Its founder was a feudatory of the **Chalukyas** before he established his own kingdom with its capital at **Ellora**. The famous Kailasa temple there was constructed under Rashtrakuta patronage. The Rashtrakuttas were constantly engaged in military campaigns in northern and central India and took territorial advantage of the weakness of other kingdoms. Their dominance of the Deccan gave them control of the western seaboard and trade with the Arabs, many of whom they employed as officers in administrative positions. Some Rashtrakutta rulers were also literary figures, and all were patrons of the different faiths practiced in their domains, such as **Jainism** and Saivism. They made a bid to establish ascendancy in the south but ran against the expanding **Chola** kingdom.

RASHTRIYA SWAYAMSEVAK SANGH (RSS). Literally, National Volunteer Corps, this organization was founded in 1925 by Keshav Baliram Hedgewar (1889–1940) in Nagpur as an instrument of **Hindu** cultural revitalization and consolidation. The RSS recruited full-time volunteer workers, mainly from high **caste** urban young men, to whom it imparted an austere discipline based on physical exercise, honesty, and obedience to a centralized and hierarchical organization stretching from the national leadership to the level of town neighborhood. A separate **women**'s wing was formed in 1936.

The strong bonds of collective identity forged by the RSS were intended to have a direct impact on society and an indirect impact on political life. Its focus was on building Hindu consciousness and a Hindu *rashtra* (see Glossary) or nation; it urged cow protection, *kshatriya* values, and the adoption of Hindi written in the Devanagari script as the national **language**. The RSS criticized the methods of the **Indian National Congress** under the leadership of **Mahatma Gandhi**, saying that its conciliatory approach towards **Islam** and its pluralistic concept of India was undermining Hindu self-respect and diluting the struggle against the British. An RSS member, **Nathuram Godse**, was tried and found guilty of assassinating Gandhi in January 1948. The Indian government banned the RSS for some time thereafter, as during the **Emergency** 1975–1977, and again at the end of 1992 after the demolition of the Babri Masjid at **Ayodhya**.

Led by Madhav Sadashiv Gowalkar from 1940 to 1973 and then by **Balasaheb Deoras**, the RSS expanded its functions and emerged as a strong force in northern India, gaining respectability in the 1960s and early 1970s and claiming active membership of over one million in the early 1990s. Although initially barred by its own rules from open political activity, the RSS worked with the **Jana Sangha** as its political arm first in opposition to the Congress Party in state politics and then within the **Janata** government 1977–1979. Its ties with the **Bharatiya Janata Party (BJP)** are even closer, although some strains developed when the BJP-led coalition government 1998–2004 dropped some of the key demands of the RSS, such as constructing a Ram temple at Ayodhya, from their common minimum program. The defeat of the BJP-led coalition in the 2004 general elections provoked more open dispute, with RSS leaders ascribing the defeat to dilution of the **Hindutva** platform and former Prime Minister **Atal Behari**

Vajpayee, himself a loyal and lifelong member of the RSS, calling attention to "excesses" of violence and economic factors as possible reasons for the defeat.

The RSS spawned early a "family" of militant Hindu organizations, collectively known as the *sangha parivar*, which included the **Vishva Hindu Parishad** and the **Bajrang Dal**. Each of these acted as pressure groups and social activists among labor, women's, and student groups and rivaled in strength similar pressure groups favored by the Congress or different **Communist Parties of India**. The RSS also established links with some orthodox Hindu religious leaders and expanded its activities beyond its early centers of **Maharashtra**, **New Delhi**, and **Uttar Pradesh** to **Gujarat**, **Madras**, **Karnataka**, and even to southern and northeastern India and among affluent Indian communities abroad. Most support came from small businesses, peasant proprietors, and the lower echelons of salaried officials within India. Although it did not formulate a precise definition of the good society, the RSS confidently put forward its views on an organic and interdependent Hindu society through a large number of daily, weekly, and periodical publications, especially *Motherland* and *Organizer.* The RSS and its "family" traced most current Indian maladies to **Islamic** invasions, **Christians**, Leftists, and the Westernized elite, declining to take responsibility for the communal hatred and violence they themselves fanned.

Before the victory of the BJP-led coalition in the 1998 general elections, RSS made no secret of its intention to overthrow secular, liberal, centrist **political parties** such as Congress and Janata when they were in power. It is currently explicit about helping the BJP return to power on a strong Hindutva platform. *See also* HINDUTVA.

RAY, SATYAJIT (1921–1992). Satyajit Ray was born to an educated and literary family in **Calcutta**. He lost his father as a child and was brought up by his mother and her brother. After working for some years in an advertising agency he gave expression to his interest in films; he became one of the most acclaimed film directors in the world.

Satyajit Ray's first full-length feature film, *Pather Panchali*, was set in rural **Bengal** and released in 1955. It won international recognition for excellence, as did his subsequent films, which include sequels to *Pather Panchali*, *Charulata* based on a play by **Kalidasa**, and *The Chess Players* set in the **Awadh** of 1856.

Satyajit Ray was a creative man of many talents who was an illustrator, designer, and writer of high repute in India and abroad. He was awarded a special Oscar for his lifetime contributions to cinematographic art in 1992, shortly before his death, and is still an inspiration to younger directors.

RAZA, SAYED HAIDER (1922–). Raza was born in a village of **Madhya Pradesh** and studied at the Nagpur School of Art and the J. J. School of Art in **Bombay**. He then trained at the Ecole Nationale des Beaux Arts in Paris on scholarship from 1950 to 1953. Raza occupies an exceptional place in the artistic scene, being wholly Indian in culture and commitment but belonging to France as well by virtue of his marriage, his long residence and many exhibitions there, and by the awards he has won in that country, including the Prix de la Critique in 1956. Raza was one of the founder members of the Progressive Artists Group in India and excels at producing original creations showing symbiosis and the cross fertilization of cultures.

Raza's signature symbol is the *Bindu*, a pure form poised in space, variously interpreted to represent the drop of creation in Tibetan Buddhism, the cosmic egg, or the power of the Indian sun. He continues to draw inspiration from his early life amid dense forests and with the tribal **Bhil** and Gond peoples who inhabit them and also from **Rajput** and **Jain** paintings and Indian **music** and poetry. He uses color boldly, especially red, black, white and chrome. In 1978 he held an exhibition to inaugurate the arts center of **Bhopal**. He was awarded the Padma Shri in 1981, and his paintings are highly prized.

REDDY, NEELAM SANJIVA (1913–1996). President of India from 1977–1982, Reddy was born to a wealthy landowning family and was educated in **Madras**. He joined the **Indian National Congress** and was elected to the Madras Legislative Assembly and then to the **Indian Constituent Assembly** in 1946. He was a member of the Madras government from 1949 to 1951 before the formation of Telugu-speaking districts into a new state of **Andhra Pradesh**. He served there as chief minister from 1962 to 1964.

Reddy was a prominent member of the old guard or "Syndicate" that controlled the organization and politics of the **Congress Party** for most of the decade of the 1960s. He was Congress president from 1959 to 1962 and was nominated as president of India in 1969. But at that time Prime Minister **Indira Gandhi** split the party and successfully backed the election of **V. V. Giri** as head of state. Subsequently, Sanjiva Reddy, who opposed Mrs. Gandhi, was supported by the **Janata Party** government in 1977 in his bid for the highest office. He continued to preside over the Indian Union for two and a half years after Mrs. Gandhi was returned to power in early 1980.

REGULATING ACT. The British House of Commons passed the Regulating Act in 1773 on the recommendations made by a Parliamentary Committee set up by Prime Minister Lord North in 1772 to investigate the activities of the **East India Company**. The immediate cause for such investigation was the application by the Directors of the Company for a substantial government loan despite their having announced a dividend of 12.5% for the year and paying £400,000 sterling to the Exchequer. The underlying causes included friction between the old wealth well-represented in Parliament and the new riches from India flaunted by returning English "Nabobs" (see Glossary), chronic anxiety about the costs of war waged frequently by the Company, and the disquiet created in England by news of administrative anarchy, gross corruption, and mismanagement on the part of Company officials in India.

The Regulating Act therefore, submitted the East India Company— and the territories it was acquiring in India—to much more control by the British Crown in Parliament than before and altered the structure of authority both in London and in India. The Court of Directors in London was required to hold elections every four years, with one fourth of its membership replaced annually, and shareholders of £1,000 or more worth of stock entitled to vote. Further, the directors were required to submit copies of all correspondence to and dispatches from their factors in India to a minister, that is, the Secretary of State for India.

Within the Company hierarchy in India, the governor of **Bengal** was designated governor general and was given an advisory council of four. He was also given control over the **Bombay** and **Madras** Presidencies in cases of war and peace, except in emergencies. The emoluments and salaries of all covenanted British officers were increased and instructions were issued forbidding their acceptance of bribes or lavish presents from Indians. Private trade by Company officials was abolished. A Supreme Court was established in **Calcutta** with appeals only to the King in Council.

Warren Hastings was the first to function as governor general under the Regulating Act but was not the only one to evidence impatience with the hampering fetters of Georgian England. Subsequent legislation, including Pitt's India Act of 1784, further strengthened parliamentary control over the East India Company and British sovereignty over Indian territory.

RIPON, LORD GEORGE FREDERICK SAMUEL (1827–1909).

Ripon was governor general and viceroy of India from 1880 to 1884. He was an English parliamentarian of long standing, belonging to the Liberal Party and sharing the views of William Gladstone, who returned as prime minister in 1880. Ripon had served as under secretary and as secretary of state for India in earlier Liberal governments before being charged by Gladstone to go to India, straighten out finances, and resolve various controversies caused by the previous Viceroy, Lord Lytton. Specifically, this meant putting an end to Lytton's "forward policy" in the northwest that had led to another costly and futile **Anglo–Afghan War**, placing finances on a sound footing, and establishing rapport with educated public opinion in India.

Ripon succeeded to some extent. An Anglo–Russian Agreement was signed in 1884 containing a joint declaration on the borders of Afghanistan and Russia and reaffirming the kingship of Abdur Rahman in Afghanistan. Financial reorganization was more complicated in the wake of famines and a fall in agricultural productivity. Ripon's Land Tenancy Bill was designed to help actual cultivators but alienated landowners; his Famine Code incorporating recommendations of a Famine Commission had to be shelved for lack of public funds. Ripon succeeded in shifting some of the costs of the earlier Afghan campaign to the British exchequer and removing tariffs on some imports, but he rejected the idea of direct taxation in India.

Ripon's efforts to win favor in educated Indian opinion included inducting Indians into the local municipal and district level administration, especially for health, education, and welfare; opposition from the **Indian Civil Service (ICS)** diminished the effectiveness of these measures. Indians appreciated Ripon's repeal of the restrictive Vernacular Press Act of 1878, and the Indian print media burgeoned. In 1881 Ripon returned **Mysore** to the administration of the hereditary Maharajah (see Glossary) and also passed a Factory Act restricting the use of child labor. His fame and popularity among Indians rested largely on his attempt to erase racial distinctions in the judiciary by giving Indian judges jurisdiction over Europeans as well; the **Ilbert Bill** of 1883 was designed to accomplish this but met with such a storm of opposition from European residents in India that Ripon was forced to retreat.

Although Ripon's name evokes sentimental attachment in India, his tenure was described in Britain as "one of the most successful failures of history." His personality lacked the sparkle and charm that could have won him friends, and his cautious measures of administrative reform met with apathy if not active hostility from his senior ICS officials. He returned to illustrious appointments in successive Liberal governments in Britain before retiring from public service in 1908.

ROE, SIR THOMAS (1581–1644). Roe was the envoy of King James I of England to the **Mughal** Emperor Jahangir. Roe lived in India from 1614 to 1618, and his *Journal* is a valuable source for the history of the period. Roe was able to use the successful initiatives taken by William Hawkins earlier in gaining friends at the Mughal court and obtained from Jahangir permission for the **East India Company** to establish a trading post at the important west coast port of **Surat**.

ROHILLA. A tribal people originally from Roh in Afghanistan who came into India during **Mughal** times and established military–political dominance in parts of present-day western **Uttar Pradesh** as Mughal power faded. Their leader, Nawab Ali Muhammad Khan, ruled in Bareilly, Bijnore, and Moradabad between 1740 and 1785. His successors formed an uneasy alliance with the rulers of **Awadh** in the face of **Maratha** attacks, but it was ineffective against British expansion. Forces of the

East India Company defeated the Rohillas in 1774, and formally annexed their territory in 1801.

ROUND TABLE CONFERENCES. A series of meetings between British members of Parliament and Indians representing a variety of interests were held in London in three sessions between 1930 and 1932 to discuss the constitutional structure and political future of India. The **Government of India Act of 1935** was largely a product of these Round Table Conferences, which were held against the background of the growing reach of the **Indian National Congress** and the mass appeal of its demand for independence from British rule.

The then viceroy, **Lord Irwin**, issued a statement on October 31, 1929, reiterating the 1917 British promise of responsible government (by implication, **Dominion Status**) for India as a goal and suggesting a conference to submit proposals on constitutional reform to Parliament. Liberal Prime Minister Ramsay Macdonald led an eight-member multiparty British delegation to the First Round Table Conference, from October 1930 to January 1931. A British Indian delegation consisted of 58 members, all nominated by Lord Irwin in their individual capacity alone. They were drawn from many counterpoised groups of Indian political life and society, including the **Hindu Mahasabha**, the **Muslim League**, and the Madras **Justice Party**, **Christians**, Eurasians, Europeans, Muslims, **Sikhs**, and **Untouchables**. The Liberal **Tej Bahadur Sapru** made a notable contribution in reconciling different points of view. Sixteen ruling Princes, eight of whom were elected by the **Chamber of Princes**, also participated. By the end of the session the British government had agreed to accept the principle of responsible government in autonomous provinces, subject to certain reservations and a federal structure, which would include the **Princely States**. Subsequent reluctance by many Princes to join a federation, British ambivalence, and Congress opposition toward it nullified their achievement.

The Indian National Congress, claiming with some justice to represent all Indian interests, classes, and communities, was conspicuous by its absence from the first Round Table Conference. In its 1930 session Congress had demanded *purna swaraj*, or full independence, not Dominion Status, and met with British refusal; **Mahatma Gandhi** had launched a massive **Civil Disobedience** movement with his **Dandi** or **Salt March** of April 1930, and most Congress leaders had been imprisoned. However, in consequence of the March 1931 Gandhi–Irwin Pact, Gandhi agreed to attend the Second Round Table Conference, October to December 1931, as the sole spokesman of Congress. As he put it in his speech, he spoke for "the dumb, semi-starved millions scattered over the length and breadth of the land, in its 70,000 villages." Gandhi's call to raise the constitutional wrangle to a higher level of statesmanship did not prevail over the cacophony of divisive voices, doubts, and wrangles over separate communal representation among the Indians, or over the indifference of the British going through their own party changes and economic depression at the time.

The Third Round Table Conference of 1932 was nothing more than perambulating committees on suffrage and other aspects of constitutional alteration. The political climate was charged with the fallout of Irwin's announcement of a **Communal Award** to create a separate electorate (in addition to the existing controversial separate electorate for Muslims) for the Untouchables. This proposal was initially acceptable to their leader, **Dr. Ambedkar**, but Gandhi adamantly opposed it as being irrevocably divisive of Hindu society and prepared to fast to the death. Although Ambedkar and Irwin compromised on this particular point, Gandhi and Congress were not able to win support for the nationalist democratic principle of general constituencies and joint electorates. Separate communal representation for various minorities was written into the 1935 Act.

The form of a Round Table Conference for the purpose of devising constitutional reform in a dependency was novel in 1930 but came to be used as a mechanism for devolving power in a shrinking British Empire with increasing frequency to the 1960s.

ROWLATT ACTS. The British Government of India in 1919 passed this repressive legislation on recommendations of a committee chaired by Justice S. A. T. Rowlatt investigating "revolutionary conspiracies" in 1917. The new laws kept alive special wartime controls for the government, including arrest and imprisonment of persons without showing cause, trial without jury, humiliating punishments, and other provisions that the former Secretary of State for India, Edwin Montagu, found "most repugnant" to the English concept of due process of law. Indian opposition to such provisions was intense and first expressed by the Indian members of the Imperial Legislative Council; their votes were overridden by British officials, then constituting a majority, and the Rowlatt Bills passed into law.

Speaking out against the repressive legislation as a contradiction of constitutional reforms toward the promised "responsible government" in India, **Mahatma Gandhi** called for a nationwide *hartal* (see Glossary), or cessation of work, on April 6, 1919, in protest. Members of every community and class in very many cities, towns, and villages observed the *hartal*, even though Gandhi did not yet have the organizational backing of the **Indian National Congress** to make countrywide appeals. Gandhi's **Satyagraha** occasioned by the Rowlatt Acts gave him national prominence. The government, however, did not repeal the Rowlatt Acts as Gandhi demanded but enforced them in the face of mounting agitation and civil disobedience. The massacre at **Jallianwala Bagh** in 1919 and the **Non-Cooperation Movement** of 1920–1921 followed as direct consequences of the Rowlatt Acts, eventually withdrawn in 1922.

ROY, JAMINI (1887–1972). The artist was born in Bankura district of West **Bengal** and enrolled in the Government School of Art in **Kolkata** in 1903. He became the most famous pupil of Abanindranath Tagore, inspired mainly by the folk and tribal art of rural Bengal and the popular paintings sold outside the Kalighat temple in Kolkata. He started experimenting with modern impressionistic and post-impressionistic techniques but switched entirely to indigenous materials and subject matter by 1930. Jamini Roy was a prolific painter with a distinctive style that was imitated by many. His original paintings are hard to obtain and immensely valuable.

ROY, M. N. (1887–1954). Roy is numbered among the leading political thinkers of 20th-century India. He was born to a **Sanskrit** teacher in **Bengal** and named Narendranath Bhattacharya. He received little formal education and was involved in the militant nationalism of Bengal politics as a very young man. In 1915 he went to Southeast Asia to try and obtain arms and met China's Sun Yat-sen for the purpose, but without success. Bhattacharya went on to San Francisco where he was charged in a conspiracy case and changed his name to

Manabendra Nath Roy. He had, meanwhile, become a Socialist and traveled to Mexico where he made friends with Michael Borodin and became a founding member of Mexico's Communist Party.

Lenin invited Roy to visit the newly founded Soviet Union. At the Second World Congress of the Communist International 1921–1922 Roy debated vigorously with Lenin on the role of the national bourgeoisie in colonial dependencies, such as India or China, and on the attitude communists should adopt toward bourgeois nationalists in order to further the cause of revolution. Both Roy's thesis, of opposition, and Lenin's thesis, of cooperation, were incorporated in the final documents of the Congress. Roy published his Marxist analysis of India at the time, *India in Transition*, in 1922. Roy rose in the hierarchy of the Communist International and went to China to implement policies of the Executive Committee in 1927; his differences with Michael Borodin caused him to leave for Germany where he became disenchanted by Stalin's leadership of the Communist International.

Roy returned to India incognito in 1930, wrote revolutionary books, and was arrested and sentenced to imprisonment in Dehra Dun for six years. On release he visited **Jawaharlal Nehru** in **Allahabad** and soon joined the **Indian National Congress**. He was elected to the All-India Congress Committee but broke with it after the outbreak of **World War II**, when he advocated cooperation with the British government in India's war effort against Fascism. He founded a Radical Democratic Party as well as the Indian Federation of Labour, arguing that democracy and socialism were equally vital ingredients of Indian nationalism. During the 1940s and early 1950s Roy became a critic of Marxism, of the Soviet Union, and also of the conduct of democratic **political parties**. He developed his political philosophy into one known as Radical Humanism and turned his thoughts increasingly to the individual's quest for truth and personal freedom. He had returned to Dehra Dun in 1938, married Ellen Gottschaulk, and lived simply, surrounded by his books and mountain scenery. Despite his lack of institutional or political position, Roy attracted and influenced many young political thinkers who sought his advice, even after he became mortally ill in 1952. His writings and library remained in circulation after his death through the efforts of his widow and followers to maintain his home as "Humanist Home" and further his dreams for the reconstruction of India.

ROY, RAM MOHUN (1777–1833). Ram Mohun Roy is revered as the leading social reformer of his generation and father of what came to be known as the Indian Renaissance in **Bengal**. He was born to a wealthy landowning family and used the title Raja (see Glossary). He studied Arabic, Persian, **Sanskrit**, and Hebrew in addition to Bengali and English in order to study Comparative Religion. He published translations of ancient texts with commentaries and challenged **brahman** orthodoxy on then current **Hindu** social customs such as child marriage, **sati**, and rigid **caste** restrictions that, he asserted, had no scriptural basis. He led vigorous campaigns against these practices that he described as "degenerate," and was particularly outspoken on the subject of widow burning or sati, which was banned in British India in 1829.

Ram Mohun Roy consciously projected his vision of a reformed Hindu society and a regenerated India worthy of its glorious past. He had a charismatic personality and became a model for several generations of social reformers and modernizers all over India. Perhaps inevitably, contemporary scholarship tends to be more skeptical both of his achievements and of his methods. Raja Ram Mohun Roy enjoyed the friendship of **Christian** missionaries, Unitarians, **Islamic** clerics, and **Tantrics**, as well as other Hindus and British officials. He founded the Atmiya Sabha or Society of Friends in 1815 and the Brahmo Sabha, a society dedicated to "the worship of the one true God," in 1828. Renamed the **Brahmo Samaj** in 1843, it carried forward Ram Mohun Roy's ideas of Hindu social reform for several decades.

– S –

SAKA or SHAKA. This is the term used in India for pastoral and nomadic people from Central Asia who spilled into sedentary societies and interacting with them came to found large kingdoms and control major trade routes. Shakas were known to the Greeks as Scythians and to the Chinese as the Sseu and reached a high level of sophistication reflected in their armor and burial chambers.

Sakas settled in the northwestern part of the Indian subcontinent, in the Swat valley and the area around **Taxila**, perhaps in the third century BCE or indeterminate date and gradually migrated southwards into the **Ganges** valley, **Rajasthan**, Malwa, **Gujarat**, Kathiawar, and **Maharashtra**, probably because other nomadic groups such as the Yueh-chih and **Kushans** pushed them out of their best lands. Chronological information about early Saka dynasties in India comes from numismatic sources, as their coins give the name of the ruler and his father and are dated according to the Saka era commencing in 78 CE.

Rudradman I had his capital at Junagarh in the second century CE. A lengthy pillar inscription in **Sanskrit** describes his exploits in repairing a **Mauryan** dam and campaigning against **Satavahana** armies in the **Narmada** valley. He ruled over Gujarat, Malwa, the Konkan, and Rajasthan and is described as a handsome man often selected by princesses to be bridegroom. Later Saka rulers in the same area took the title of *kshatrapa*, used on their coins of the fourth century CE, and came to be known as the Western Satraps. They probably owed allegiance to the **Gupta Empire**; Samudra Gupta's pillar inscription at **Allahabad** refers to his successful campaigns in reducing them to vassalage. The Western Satraps appear to have helped repel occasional Sassanian attacks from Iran on Gujarat and the Saka people were absorbed into the mosaic of Indian society.

SALAR JANG (1829–1883). Salar Jang became prime minister of **Hyderabad** in 1853, served as such under two Nizams, or rulers, and was co-regent from 1869 to his death during the minority of a third Nizam, Mehboob Ali Khan.

Salar Jang was named Mir Turab Ali Khan at birth to a family in hereditary service to the Nizam. He received an informal education and learned administration through its practice. Mir Turab soon became a favorite of the British, by then the paramount power in India. His administration was reasonably efficient, restoring financial solvency, employing both **Hindus** and Muslims to positions of trust on grounds of ability, and opening many schools and colleges. By permitting the Indian postal service and the Indian **railways** to run through Hyderabad Salar Jung brought this large **Princely State** in the very center of the subcontinent closer to British India. He kept Hyderabad out of the **Uprising of 1857** and earned British plaudits. He was treated by them almost as a ruler and honored with a personal salute of seventeen guns.

Salar Jang, however, was not able to negotiate return of the rich territory of Berar to Hyderabad, despite his efforts to use British newspapers and pressure groups in the cause. Further, there were many cultural clashes when Englishmen of the 19th century no longer conformed to the traditional courtesies of a feudal Muslim kingdom and resented Salar Jang's independent demeanor. At the same time, the Nizam and other nobles never wholly trusted him because he was sufficiently progressive to educate his daughters and adopted the manners of an English gentleman. Salar Jang was an avid collector of art objects, and his personal collection was turned into a public museum after Indian independence.

SALIM ALI (1896–1987). Born in **Bombay** and interested in nature at an early age, Salim Ali studied Zoology but found it more rewarding to spend time in the natural history section of the Prince of Wales Museum in Bombay. The Natural History Society encouraged him in his youth, as he encouraged and assisted other young enthusiasts throughout his life.

Salim Ali went to Berlin for systematic training in Ornithology 1929–1930 and then undertook pioneering field surveys through vast areas of the Indian subcontinent. His *Book of Indian Birds*, first published in 1941, remains a classic in print. His subsequent work was published in a 10-volume set entitled *Handbook of the Birds of India and Pakistan* (1968–1974). Salim Ali was awarded India's prestigious Padma Vibhushan in 1976 and also received the J. Paul Getty Wildlife Conservation Prize from the World Wildlife Fund. He continued making field trips into old age and remained slight, spry, and witty to the end.

SALT MARCH. *See* DANDI MARCH.

SAMAJVADI PARTY. Mulayam Singh Yadav split from the **Janata Dal** after it lost power and formed the Samajvadi Party in **Uttar Pradesh (UP)** in 1992, becoming chief minister of that state in 1993, and again in 2003. The Samajvadi Party has consistently projected a secular and left of center platform and adopted the figure of a peasant as its party symbol befitting Mulayam Singh Yadav's legacy from **Charan Singh** and the **Lok Dal**.

During the 1990s the Samajvadi Party won the support of Muslims and most Backward **Castes**, especially the numerically strong Yadavs, at a time when the **Congress Party** in the state had virtually collapsed, the **Bharatiya Janata Party (BJP)** was pushing its Ram Janambhumi campaign and attracting high caste **Hindu** support, and the **Bahujan Samaj Party (BSP)** commanded the allegiance of most **Dalits**. As **political parties** became increasingly fragmented and electoral behavior more and more localized, coalition governments were put together at both the Union and state levels. The Samajvadi Party was part of the multiparty National Front and United Front ruling coalitions in New Delhi 1996–1998 and in a coalition with the BSP in the UP 1993–1996. The Samajvadi Party has attempted to build a broad base of support cutting across lines of class and community throughout the nation, but hitherto has been unable to find a reliable niche in any state of India other than the UP, where four parties compete for a majority of votes. Its leader Mulayam Singh Yadav, too, is not wholly trusted by other national political figures.

SAMKHYA. This is the name given to one of the oldest of six schools of orthodox **Hindu** philosophy. It is associated with **yoga**, which has antecedents predating the **Vedas**. The founding of the Samkhya school is attributed to the sage Kapila. In its notions of suffering and the overcoming of suffering, its rejection of sacrificial rituals and its stress on moderation, Samkhya is closely related to **Buddhist** thought as well.

The Samkhya school was uncompromisingly dualistic, positing two ultimate realities named *Purusha*, or spirit, and *Prakriti*, or matter, in a causal relationship of inter-operation. Its identification of three primary principles in the formation of personalities—*sattva* or goodness, *rajas* or passion, and *tamas* or lethargy and darkness—became an integral part of the Indian tradition. Samkhya exerted a profound influence on early lawgivers and the epics. But **Shankara** successfully challenged proponents of Samkhya dualism in debate during the eighth century CE and established *advaita* (see Glossary) or nondualism as the dominant stream in Hindu philosophy.

SANSKRIT. The principal Indo–Aryan **language** of the post-Vedic age in India was Sanskrit. Sanskrit means, "perfectly constructed, cultivated, literary," and is contrasted with the spoken language of the common people. Sanskrit is phonologically close to the language of the **Vedas** and the Avesta of Iran. European scholars of the 19th century, such as Max Mueller, discovered links between Sanskrit, Greek, and Latin and ushered in "Orientalist" enthusiasms for Sanskrit.

Four stages in the development of Sanskrit are conventionally delineated. The earliest stage brought complex but precise modifications of grammar to provide a framework for both prose and verse, a technique of coining compound words which enabled an absorption of indigenous and foreign vocabulary, and rules of syntax codified by **Panini**. The next stage produced the great melodic epics, *Ramayana* and *Mahabharata*, in which soft vowel sounds alternating with aspirated consonants produced impressive effects during chantings and recitations. Classical Sanskrit of the early centuries CE represents the third stage of development. A rich literature survives from that period, including the works of **Kalidasa** and the **Puranas**, and testifies to the creative genius of authors writing and speaking a living language. A fourth stage is associated with brahmanical revival in India, but Sanskrit literature produced after the eighth century CE is judged today as being stultified, excessively complicated, and lacking in creative vigor.

The use of Sanskrit appears to have been confined to priests and scholars, and perhaps courtiers, even in classical times. Their tendency to monopolize knowledge instead of seeking to diffuse it to **women** and lower classes became more pronounced over time. One result was the emergence of new literature in various **Prakrit** languages and regional vernaculars, which replaced Sanskrit as a written and spoken language. It is notable that none of the **Bhakti** saints used Sanskrit, and even the followers of the **Buddha** in ancient times had eschewed it in favor of Pali. In the wake of the nationalist movement and efforts to make Hindi the national language of India, Sanskrit has been revived as a subject of study in the schools and universities of independent India, and a body of new Sanskrit literature is being created.

SANTAL. *See* MUNDA.

SAPRU, TEJ BAHADUR (1875–1949). Born to an educated Kashmiri **brahman** family in Aligarh, Sapru studied Law and joined the family legal business in Moradabad, arguing cases before the Allahabad High Court. He joined the **Indian National Congress** in 1907 and the **Home Rule League** founded by **Annie Besant** in 1917. He was nominated as a member of the Imperial Legislative Council and then as a law member in the Viceroy's Executive Council in 1921, positions of considerable prestige. He resigned two years later on the issue of **dyarchy** as implemented under the **Montagu–Chelmsford Reforms**.

Tej Bahadur Sapru believed in gradual constitutional reform for India but chafed at the London's continuing control exercised to the detriment of Indian interests. He took an active role in the All Parties Committee convened in 1928 to draft a constitution for a future independent India. Again, he made constructive contributions at the **Round Table Conferences** held in London to discuss major constitutional changes under British aegis; he was disappointed in the consequent **Government of India Act of 1935**. Sapru was knighted and received the signal honor of becoming a member of the Privy Council in 1934.

After the outbreak of **World War II**, Sapru was critical of Congress decisions not to cooperate with the war effort and deeply disappointed by the failure of **Sir Stafford Cripps**'s mission in 1942. He worked closely with **C. Rajagopalachari** and at the end of the war was elected as a delegate to the **Constituent Assembly**. There, Sapru devoted most efforts to drafting the chapter on justiciable Fundamental Rights in the **Indian Constitution**, which came into force in 1950.

SARABHAI, VIKRAM AMBALA (1919–1971). Sarabhai was a cosmic ray physicist who studied at Cambridge, England, and under **C. V. Raman** in Bangalore. He was a leading space and nuclear scientist of international renown who received many awards in his life, including the Padma Bhushan in 1966. He was appointed Chairman of India's Atomic Energy Commission after the death of **Homi Bhabha** in an air crash of 1965. His own sudden death six years later was another blow to India's space and **nuclear power** program.

Sarabhai published extensively on the exploration and peaceful use of outer space and launched India's **space program** as Chairman of the Indian National Committee for Space Research. He was a member of the International Pugwash Continuing Committee and

President of the International Conference of the International Atomic Energy Agency in 1970.

Vikram Sarabhai belonged to an illustrious family of **Ahmedabad** that had steadily supported **Mahatma Gandhi**. Vikram's father, Ambalal Sarabhai, was a textile magnate, and his wife Mrinalini a famous classical dancer. Their daughter too became a well-known dancer, actress, and social activist, continuing in the family tradition.

SARKAR, JADUNATH (1870–1958). Sarkar became the most famous historian of late **Mughal** India and an acknowledged master of **Maratha** history. He authored many rigorously researched volumes on **Aurangzeb**. As a teacher, writer, director of research, and educator for six decades, Sarkar was the founder of modern, scientific, historical scholarship in India based on archival and primary sources. He received many honors—including knighthood—in Britain as well as in India but remained austere and frugal in his habits.

Jadunath Sarkar was born to a cultured landowning family of east **Bengal**, educated in the humanities at Calcutta University, and traveled widely. His condemnation of the inequalities and inequities bound in **caste** had the zeal of a social reformer. He imparted to his students his own lofty vision of India as a composite and rejuvenated nation.

SARKARIA COMMISSION. This three-member body chaired by a retired judge of the Supreme Court, R. S. Sarkaria, was appointed by Parliament on the proposal of Prime Minister **Indira Gandhi** in 1983. The Commission was charged with reporting on center-state relations, that is, the relations between the Government of India at New Delhi and various state governments, in the context of exiting constitutional provisions, statutes, and administrative practices and conventions, especially those bearing on finance, and with recommending appropriate changes. To some extent the Commission's duties were similar to those of the Administrative Reforms Commission (1966–1970), but by the 1980s, open tensions between several state governments and New Delhi demanded more searching probes.

Center-state tensions were most evident when different **political parties** were in power at center and state levels, but not precluded by **Congress** dominance in both. New Delhi's inability to quietly resolve different viewpoints had contributed to secessionist demands in some states, notably the **Punjab**, by the early 1980s. There was no national consensus on the correct balance of power between center and state. Belief in the necessity of a strong center to preserve the "unity and integrity of India" was combined with criticism of Mrs. Gandhi's centralized and personalized control of constitutional relationships; there was no sympathy for secessionists. As a consequence, the Sarkaria Commission initially found it difficult to elicit responses to its questionnaire sent to all political parties at the national or state level and representatives of tribal and minority movements below the state level. It continued to collect information into 1987, making its recommendations and publishing its report in 1988. (Sarkaria Commission, *Report on Centre-State Relations*, Nasik: Government of India Press, 1988. 2 Volumes.)

The gist of the recommendations made by the Sarkaria Commission was summed up in the phrase "cooperative federalism." The Commission urged systematic, honest, disinterested, and efficient decentralization of power from center to state and further, to sub-state level institutions with effective democratic participation by citizens. It stressed the need to adhere to correct codes of conduct and avoid arbitrary dismissal of state governments and the political use of state Governors. It recommended rational and balanced distribution of finances by the Finance Commission.

The **Janata** coalition government led by **V. P. Singh** created an Inter-State Council consisting of the prime minister and state chief ministers in October 1990 with the declared intent to implement the Sarkaria Commission recommendations, but fell soon after. The political, economic, and intellectual arguments in favor of decentralization and institutionalization of correct conduct remained strong, however, and the current Indian polity is more truly federal than it was 20 years ago.

SASTRI, V. S. SRINIVASA (1869–1946). The son of a **Sanskrit** scholar who exposed him to many of the keenest minds of the day, Srinivasa Sastri started his career as a school master, became Head Master, and entered public life as a member of the Servants of India Society founded by **Gopal Krishna Gokhale**, whom he succeeded as President. Sastri chaired the **Madras** session of the **Indian National Congress** in 1908 and soothed feelings ruffled by the split of the previous year between "Moderates" and "Extremists." His considerable diplomatic skills were used to good effect in negotiating the **Lucknow Pact** of 1916 with the **All-India Muslim League** and again as a member of the Indian delegation to the League of Nations.

V. S. S. Sastri supported the **Montagu–Chelmsford Reforms** of 1919 and cooperated with the British government in trying to implement them. During the 1920s and 1930s Sastri made many lecture tours in South Africa, East Africa, and Southeast Asia endeavoring to obtain civil, legal, and political rights for the many Indian **diaspora** settled in those parts of the British Empire. He looked forward to full Indian participation in the United Nations and suggested that **Mahatma Gandhi** represent India at the San Francisco Conference establishing that international organization.

SATAVAHANA DYNASTY. This dynasty was probably the first to form a coherent state in the northwestern **Deccan**. Large numbers of beautifully executed coins and about 30 stone inscriptions attributed to it or its military adversaries identify a line of kings with the family name Satakarni ruling in the **Andhra** area for over 300 years. The **Puranas** list 19 kings of the Andhrabhratya, which may have been a dominant tribe of that region.

A precise history of the Satavahanas and the socioeconomic conditions of their times are difficult to reconstruct because of the paucity of collaborative material. Satakarni I is featured as a legendary hero of folklore in the area between the Godavari and Krishna rivers. Conflict with the **Sakas** appears to have been frequent, and Gautamiputra Satkarni is credited in his titles with having destroyed the Sakas, **Yavanas**, and Pahlavas of the northwest to rule an Empire stretching from Malwa southwards. **Amaravati** was an eminent city in his time. Another King, Vasishtiputra Satkarni, married the daughter of Saka King Rudradaman I whose Junagarh stone inscription has been dated to c. 150 CE.

The Satavahana Empire appears to have disintegrated about one hundred years later. Successor rulers were squeezed between the rising power of the **Guptas** in the north and the **Pallavas** in the south.

SATI (also SUTTEE). Sati, literally a virtuous woman or wife, was spelled suttee by the English who first referred to a practice of **Hindu**

widows burning themselves on the funeral pyres of their husbands in 1787. **Christian** missionaries and **East India Company** officials alike abhorred the practice and made efforts to discourage it in areas under British control. These culminated in a ban against it in the Bengal Presidency passed by **Lord William Bentinck** in 1829. The leading Indian social reformer of the time, Raja **Ram Mohun Roy**, also strenuously opposed the practice, as he opposed other manifestations of degradation among upper **caste** Hindus, but was less sure of legislation as an effective countermeasure. Sati remains outlawed in independent India, with the death penalty prescribed for those found guilty of aiding or abetting the practice.

Serious scholars have reexamined the causes of sati and its uneven incidence through the centuries. There is general agreement on the following points. Scriptural sanction for the practice is *not* found in the **Vedas** or in *Smriti* literature before 300 CE. The custom of widow immolation was widespread in the ancient world including India but confined to the ruling or warrior classes. The voluntary self-sacrifice of a true *sati* glorified in Hindu, especially **Rajput**, tradition was vitiated by elements of compulsion from family or **brahmans**. There are few known instances of sati in early times, no mention of the practice in **Buddhist** literature, and the first known memorial to a sati was a pillar erected in memory of a central Indian queen in 510 CE. Many "hero stones" or memorials to local heroes in 12th-century **Gujarat** and **Rajasthan** are associated with sati memorials inscribed with unmistakable symbols. The numbers of sati jumped dramatically in the 13th century because of the Rajput *jouhar* practice of collective suicide by **women** in preference to capture by Muslim invaders. After a long period in which it was a rare occurrence, the practice of sati again became prevalent in the 18th and early 19th centuries; most incidents of sati took place in present-day Rajasthan and **Bengal** among the two highest castes, and absolute numbers were never large, although all cases received prominence.

Several reasons for legitimization of what may have begun as a voluntary rite of purification have been advanced. Economists stress the decisive self-interest of priests who received remuneration and of families who absorbed the widow's property—especially in Bengal where widows were entitled to inherit land. Some see widows choosing death rather than the humiliating and austere lives prescribed for them. Many highlight the coincidence of what one author terms "sati epidemics" and times of acute instability and change, as after the **Huna** incursions, the **Islamic** Turkish invasions, and British conquests; upwardly mobile classes may have sought social prestige and economic advantage through redistribution of property by encouraging sati. The psycho-anthropologist Ashis Nandy also draws attention to psychological underpinnings of the practice among classes rendered marginal and insecure by exposure to Western norms in the 19th and 20th centuries. Sati, he says, expressed "Hindu culture's deepest fears of—and hatred towards—woman and womanhood." A composite image of the cosmic Mother Goddess came to be bifurcated between the protective nurturer, Durga, and the unpredictable punisher, Kali (see Glossary). A wife, accordingly, was invested with responsibility for her husband's welfare; his death was blamed on her ritual imperfections, and her suicide demanded in expiation. (Nandy, "Sati," in *At the Edge of Psychology*: 1–35.)

Some cases of sati occurred in the 1980s, notably in Rajasthan, without incurring retribution by the state and, on the contrary, bringing prestige and commercial gains to the villages where they took place. On the other hand, the case of Roop Kanwar's sati in September 1987 was the occasion for impressive mobilization of women against societal abuse. These women bridged the well-known urban–rural, rich–poor, old–young, and educated–illiterate gaps among them to press for implementation of Indian law prohibiting sati.

SATYAGRAHA. Translated by its originator as "the Force, which is born of Truth and Love or nonviolence," the term was coined first to describe the movement of Indian resistance in South Africa against racially discriminatory legislation passed in 1906. **Mohandas Karamchand Gandhi** chose the term in preference to the conventional "passive resistance" because, as he said, "Truth (*satya*) implied love and firmness (*agraha*) engenders and therefore serves as a synonym for force."

Satyagraha was distinguished from traditional methods of unarmed resistance such as strikes, fasts, or demonstrations. Gandhi discovered and explained the practical and spiritual implications of Satyagraha as he, and others, used the technique in India from 1917 onwards mainly, but not exclusively, against particular laws perpetuating British rule in

India. Some essential precepts stressed by Gandhi were as follows. A ceaseless search for truth was imperative, demanding recognition that no one party held a monopoly on truth. The right means to arrive at truth was as important, indeed inseparable from, the end. The nearest approach to truth was through "non-violence—*ahimsa*—love." Ahimsa was the supreme value for Gandhi, tested not merely by the absence of physical violence but by the refusal to do harm in intent or in action. Ahimsa denoted strength and bravery, not physical weakness or cowardice. Gandhi often said that in case of a choice, violence was preferable to cowardice, yet he terminated the **Non-Cooperation Movement** in 1921 because of an outbreak of violence. He saw that suffering was implicit in conflict. What distinguished a *satyagrahi* (one offering Satyagraha) was courageous self-suffering, as "the chosen substitute for violence to others." Gandhi was conscious of the coercive element present in self-suffering directed toward the moral persuasion of others, and his critics have questioned the efficacy of Satyagraha against opponents less vulnerable to public opinion than the British Raj. This question cannot be resolved by theory, only by practice. Satyagraha, as Gandhi and his followers demonstrated, is one means by which an individual can liberate himself/herself from psychological bondage and influence the course of social and political change through reasoned, dedicated, non-violent action.

Satyagraha implies a high degree of self-discipline, especially when a group undertakes satyagraha, and demands intensive training. The guiding rules and code of conduct in campaigns led by Gandhi were: self-reliance, keeping the initiative, publicizing the objectives, exemplary behavior before and after arrest, limiting demands, seeking avenues of cooperation with the opponent on honorable terms, advancing the campaign by steps in the absence of agreement, and refusing to surrender on essentials in negotiation. The steps taken in various Satyagraha movements against the established British Raj included exhaustive efforts to obtain redress of grievances through existing channels, agitation, preparation of a group for direct action, publishing proposals toward a solution along with an ultimatum, strike, and other forms of boycott, non-cooperation, civil disobedience and courting of arrest, the establishment of parallel public institutions, and a constructive socioeconomic program.

Satyagraha is a dynamic concept and even Gandhi's campaigns did not all follow the same pattern; nor were they equally efficacious in attaining their stated objectives. Notable among campaigns successful by objective as well as Gandhian criteria were: the satyagraha for indigent tenants of Champaran district in 1917; the **Ahmedabad** labor satyagraha of 1918; the Bardoli peasant satyagraha led by **Vallabhbhai Patel** in 1928; and the **salt march** satyagraha of 1930 leading into the **Civil Disobedience Movement**. The individual and group satyagrahas climaxing in the **Quit India** movement of 1942 did not wholly avoid violence or achieve their immediate objective, but they did succeed in persuading the British that the cost of holding on to power in India in the face of massive non-cooperation from Indians was too high to be sustainable.

Although satyagraha is inextricably linked with Gandhi's name and the method he evolved for nonviolent resolution of conflict in his lifetime, it can be applied to a wide variety of situations in different cultures. The dedication to non-violent action demonstrated by traditionally warlike Pathans of the **North West Frontier Province** under the leadership of **Khan Abdul Ghaffar Khan** in the interwar period is an outstanding example of satyagraha's universality. Satyagraha is also a subject of study among peace movements and academics in the contemporary West, as illustrated in the writings of Gene Sharp and Joan Bondurant, who has published one of the best analyses of Satyagraha in her *Conquest of Violence*.

SAVARKAR, VINAYAK DAMODAR (VEER) (1883–1966). Savarkar was born in Nasik to a middle-class Chitpavan **brahman** family as one of several sons. They were educated in Marathi and English and lost their father and uncle in the plague epidemic of 1897. Veer Savarkar joined a group of young activists and formed a secret society in 1899 against British rule; it escalated agitation and violent protest at Fergusson College, **Poona** after the **partition of Bengal** in 1905.

Savarkar went to England in 1906, but although he studied Law he did not qualify for the Bar. Instead, he translated the works of Mazzini from the Italian, formed contacts with **Hardayal** and other revolutionaries in London, and published a treatise on the **Uprising of 1857** in 1907, calling it *India's First War of Independence*. On return to India he refused to renounce what the British authorities deemed "seditious activities" and was imprisoned in 1911. He was sent to the penal colony on the **Andaman Islands**, where he worked among the prisoners for 10 years before he was transferred to other jails. He was released in 1924.

During his imprisonment Savarkar wrote a treatise on **Hindutva** and published it under a pseudonym. He argued that all Indians, irrespective of religious affiliation, should recognize their basic **Hindu** cultural identity, and that the state should be a Hindu Rashtriya, or Hindu nation, based on ancient tradition. He formed a branch of the **Hindu Mahasabha** and became president of that **political party** in 1937. It opposed all demands made by the **All-India Muslim League** and agitated for a 50% Hindu representation in the Nizam's domain of **Hyderabad**.

Savarkar retired from active political life in 1943. He was accused of complicity in the assassination of **Mahatma Gandhi** in 1948 but was acquitted. Many of his writings in Marathi were published. His work forms the ideological bedrock of a group of right wing Hindu organizations that became increasingly assertive in the 1980s and 1990s. Savarkar's name as a patriot was extolled by the coalition government led by the **Bharatiya Janata Party** 1998–2004 and his portrait erected in the halls of Parliament alongside those of other national heroes. *See also* HINDUTVA.

SCINDIA, MADHAVRAO (1945–2001). Scindia was scion of the royal family of Gwalior and among the most promising and dynamic young political figures in late-20th-century India. Educated at the finest schools in India and Oxford University, England, Madhavrao was cosmopolitan, liberal, secular, and popular. He joined the **Congress Party**, breaking the political tradition of conservatism upheld by his mother, and later by his sisters, as prominent members of the **Bharatiya Janata Party (BJP)**. Scindia was elected to the **Lok Sabha** in 1971 and retained his seat to the time of his death. Perhaps his most famous electoral victory was won over **Atal Behari Vajpayee** in Gwalior in 1984.

Madhavrao Scindia became a member of **Rajiv Gandhi**'s government first as Minister of State for Railways and later as a Cabinet

Minister, as also in **P. V. Narasimha Rao**'s government. He accomplished considerable improvement in the efficiency and maintenance of the **railways** during his first ministerial tenure and throughout his career set high standards or probity and transparency. He was Deputy Leader of the Opposition in the 13th Lok Sabha and led many a lively skirmish against the BJP-led government. Before his untimely death, Madhavrao Scindia was being talked about in some circles as a possible prime minister if and when the Congress returned to power. His son, Jyotirao Scindia, won election to the Lok Sabha in 2004.

SELF EMPLOYED WOMEN'S ASSOCIATION (SEWA). Founded in 1972 by **Ela Bhatt** as an affiliate of the Textile Labour Association (TLA) in **Ahmedabad**, SEWA is now one of the largest, best-known, and most successful **non-governmental organizations (NGO)** in India. As its name implies, SEWA brings together **women** such as load-carriers, vegetable vendors, embroiderers, construction workers, and others in the informal sector of the economy—the worst paid, most exploited, and poorest section of the population—and seeks to win for them a modicum of social security similar to that available to unionized male labor in the formal sector. SEWA broke away from TLA in 1981 and extended its work beyond **Gujarat** to **Bihar**, **Delhi**, **Kerala**, **Madhya Pradesh**, and **Uttar Pradesh**, still focused on developmental programs for and by self-employed women. It now operates in many Indian cities as well as rural areas and some of the products of its nearly 400,000 members—such as embroidered clothing—have an international market.

Taking a holistic view of women's problems, SEWA early recognized the importance of banking facilities for poverty amelioration and created a women's bank, Mahila Sewa Sahakari Bank Limited, on the model of Grameen Bank of **Bangladesh** for micro credit in 1974. Subsequently, it founded health and insurance programs and started various women's **cooperatives**. SEWA also waged a vigorous campaign to have the rights of home workers recognized, and saw success in the 1996 Convention on Home Work sponsored by the International Labor Organization (ILO). SEWA is an example of a multi-faceted social movement, which struggles against the societal status quo, educates and mobilizes the disadvantaged and poor, and also engages with powerful institutions including the state in order to further its cause. Thus, SEWA insists that governments recognize the specific needs of poor, self-employed women, but is willing to distribute credit to these women from state-owned banks, deliver SEWA vegetables to government hospitals and prisons, sell SEWA products in government stores, and not least, use government's support to negotiate better prices for SEWA products from private merchants.

SEWA inspired the National Commission on Self Employed Women established by **Rajiv Gandhi** in 1987 and took up the recommendations made in its report as its agenda for the 1990s. Its autonomous working as part critic, part ally, of the state is one of the best examples of India's vibrant civil society.

SEN, AMARTYA KUMAR (1933–). Amartya Sen was awarded the Nobel Prize for Economics in 1998 while Master of Trinity College, Cambridge University. In early 2004 he returned to Harvard University as Lamont University Professor Emeritus. Amartya Sen was born on the university campus of Shantiniketan in **Bengal** and grew up in the scholarly atmosphere of his grandfather's house. As a child he witnessed the devastating effects of the Bengal famine of 1943 when his family distributed rice to passers-by. As an adult Sen investigated the causes of famine and wrote about it having closer relationship to incidence of poverty than to food production or climate as was commonly believed. His 1981 book *Poverty and Famine* published by Oxford University Press continues to influence governments and international organizations in dealing with food crises, although structural causes of poverty remain untouched in many parts of the world. His 2000 book *Development as Freedom* elaborated the case he consistently made in articles and speeches linking human rights, individual choice, education, health, and political democracy with economic development, in contrast to arguments for benevolent autocracy as conducive to economic growth.

Sen the professional economist is renowned for his theoretical work on welfare economics and the causes and effects of inequality — including inequality between men and **women** — as well as for the unusual attention he pays to questions of ethics and values. Sen the multifaceted man is proud to be Indian, has an inclusive vision of India, and is critical of communal violence and low levels of investment in social infrastructure, especially primary education for both girls and boys, and public health. Immediately after receiving the Nobel Prize, Sen set up a charitable trust with the cash award of close to one million US dollars devoted to improving health and education in West **Bengal** and **Bangladesh**.

SEN, KESHUB CHANDRA (1838–1884). A leader of the **Brahmo Samaj** and a great missionary, Keshub Chandra Sen was a social reformer who dreamed of a national awakening and renaissance in India. He was born in a non-brahman family that embodied social transition in 19th-century **Bengal**. His grandfather was a treasurer in the **Calcutta** Mint, a founding father of Hindu College established in 1817, and the author of an English–Bengali dictionary. Keshub Chandra's father, Peary Mohan, was also an official of the Mint, and his mother, Sharada Devi, had a spiritual fervor and intelligence that molded his character. He himself graduated from Hindu College in 1856 and then studied Bengali, English, and **Sanskrit** literature as well as Indian and Western Philosophy.

Keshub Chandra was appalled by what he described as "the mournful and dismal scene of desolation—spiritual, social and intellectual—which spreads around us." In this "fallen nation" he said, "we in vain try to recognize therein the land of Kalidas—the land of poetry, of science, of civilization." (Heimsath, *Indian Nationalism and Hindu Social Reform*: 15.) In common with some of his educated countrymen, Keshub Chandra Sen became a social reformer, condemning **untouchability**, advocating education for **women** as well as men, and striving to make inter-caste marriage legal. The latter goal was achieved in 1872. He wrote extensively, published many journals, some especially for women, and founded schools for women and for the vocational training of men in 1871. He stressed the importance of conducting primary school education in the vernacular **language**.

Sen became a Theist in his youth and joined the Brahmo Samaj, then under the leadership of Debendranath Tagore, a family friend. Sen was a vigorous and inspired preacher, traveling all over India, setting up 65 sister organizations and winning many converts. He was in touch with contemporary thinkers and social reformers, such as **Dayananda Saraswati** and **Mahadev Govind Ranade**, engaged in similar tasks in other parts of India. Sen was recognized as an important person and met many notables on his trip to England in 1870. Queen Victoria received him in private audience. Keshub Chandra's molding of the Brahmo Samaj into a church heavily influenced by **Christian** doctrines and the devotional practices of Hindu Vaishnava cults did not win the support of Debendranath and other rationalists. The two parted ways on this issue with Sen's "New Dispensation" being recognized as a new church in 1881. In his later years Keshub Chandra gave greater importance to his spiritual mission than to social reform, which passed from individual path breakers into the hands of social organizations and national conferences.

SHAH BANO (c. 1928–1992). Shah Bano was a poor and illiterate Muslim woman who was divorced by her husband Mohammed Ahmed under **Islamic** law and filed suit for maintenance by him in 1981. The **Madhya Pradesh** High Court judged in her favor on the basis of Section 125 of the Indian Code of Criminal Procedure granting the right of support to any divorced wife, irrespective of religious affiliation, until her remarriage or death, if she has no other means of sustenance. On appeal, the Supreme Court of India passed judgment on April 23, 1985, upholding that decision.

There followed an agitation among conservative sections of the Muslim community against the judgment of the Supreme Court as an unwarranted interference with the operation of Muslim personal law according to the Shari'a (see Glossary). They put pressure on Shah Bano to retract her suit for maintenance through an open letter of November 2, 1985. Agitation and controversy continued to mount, especially in urban centers of northern India, and became openly political. The legal issue—rights to sustenance of a divorced woman under traditional Muslim personal law and/or under codified, secular, Indian law—was buried under accusations by Islamists that the Supreme Court was attacking the religious autonomy of the Indian Muslim minority, on the one hand, and on the other, loud demands by militant **Hindu** organizations for enactment of an uniform civil code and the rebuilding of temples on many sites where mosques had been erected several hundreds of years ago. The human issue—the fate of one poor and elderly woman—was drowned in a cacophony of voices raised in religious fundamentalism and political manipulation among the male, urban youth competing for jobs, votes, and political power.

In a by-election for a parliamentary seat from a constituency in **Bihar** held in December 1985, Syed Shahabuddin of the **Janata Party** won over the **Congress (I) Party** contender, another Muslim. This was widely interpreted as indicating the alienation of the Muslim community from Congress and the government of **Rajiv Gandhi**, which counted on support from an assumed Muslim "vote bank." Soon after, the government introduced the Muslim Women (Protection of Rights on Divorce) Bill, which, in effect, overturned the judgment of the Supreme Court in the case of Shah Bano vs. Mohammed Ahmed by transferring the obligation of maintenance to the natal family of a divorced Muslim woman. The Bill was passed in an atmosphere of cynicism; the government had succumbed to pressure from the least enlightened leaders of the Muslim community. Secularism was criticized; communal violence increased through the 1980s and 1990s; a sense of insecurity spread among minority communities fearing Hindu domination and all **women** subjected to male power. The otherwise obscure figure of Shah Bano gained historic significance in this tragic context.

SHAH JAHAN (1592–1666). Named Khurram Shihab al-Din Muhammad at birth, Shah Jahan was the third son of **Mughal** Emperor Jehangir and a **Rajput** princess of Marwar. He married Arjumand Banu Begum (renamed Mumtaz Mahal), daughter of the astute and powerful nobleman Asaf Khan, in 1612. Their singularly happy marriage produced 14 children and the **Taj Mahal**, constructed in memory of the empress after her death in 1630. Prince Khurram displayed his military talents early and was given high rank, the title Shah Jahan, and a special place close to the throne of his father. He staged a rebellion against Jehangir and **Nur Jahan** but was pardoned in 1626 when Jehangir was already ill and complex intrigues to decide the succession were in train. Assisted by Asaf Khan, Shah Jahan marched to the capital, **Agra**, and ascended the throne in 1628.

Shah Jahan's reign was the apogee of Mughal magnificence and cultural flowering, amply documented in court chronicles recording details of events and actual administration, such as the *Badshahnama*, and in the admiring accounts of such European travelers as Manucci, Peter Mundy, and Tavernier. The munificence of the emperor was as famous as the magnificence of his collection of jewels;

some of the largest were displayed on the 15-foot-high Peacock Throne, which took seven years and 10 million rupees to construct. Shah Jahan's passion for fine buildings and gardens can still be seen in the Moti Masjid of Agra, the Shalimar gardens of Lahore and **Srinagar**, and the entire city of Shah Jahanabad built as a new capital in **Delhi** in 1648 and containing the magnificent Red Fort, Jami Masjid, and Chandni Chowk or marketplace.

Shah Jahan's reign also carried the seeds of his own destruction. His costly and vainglorious military campaigns in Afghanistan and Central Asia to recover ancestral domains in Kandahar, Balkh, and Badakshan were ultimately unsuccessful. His intolerance for the Shi'a kingdoms of the **Deccan** began a process that bled the Mughal treasury, debilitated its enormous armies, and led eventually to the **Maratha** revolt in the following reign. Shah Jahan's religious policy was not as tolerant or as successful as that of his grandfather **Akbar**, whom he tried to emulate. Shah Jahan's strictures against temple building offended his wealthy **Hindu** subjects, while his introduction of some Persian and Hindu ceremonies at court and support for the liberal heterodoxy of his eldest and favorite son, Prince **Dara Shikoh**, alienated his orthodox Muslim nobles.

Shah Jahan's administration was urban in focus although its main source of revenue was agricultural production. The emperor attended to court detail but was unable to prevent corruption or tyranny practiced by petty officials in rural areas. The famine that swept the Deccan, **Gujarat**, and Khandesh in 1630 was a taste of future agrarian devastation. Finally, Shah Jadan was unable to secure Dara Shikoh's succession to the throne. When the emperor fell ill in 1657, his four surviving sons engaged in a yearlong fratricidal war before **Aurangzeb** proved the victor. Shah Jahan spent the last nine years of his life imprisoned in Agra fort, cared for by his daughter Jahanara Begum and gazing at the Taj Mahal.

SHANKARA or SANKARA (c. 788–820). Shankara was a notable philosopher–theologian and *acharya*, or religious teacher, who set the dominant form of **Hinduism** for ensuing centuries. Despite his great fame, little is known of Shankara's personal life. He was probably born in present-day **Kerala**, spoke **Tamil**, debated at **Varanasi**, went to the four corners of India, was a celibate, a Shaiva (worshipper of **Shiva**), and the disciple of a commentator on the **Upanishads**. He adhered to the Mimamsa school of Vedic ritual.

Shankara was the founder and principal exponent of Advaita Vedanta, a doctrine of pure non-dualism. According to his commentary on the *Brahma Sutras*, the only Reality is Brahman or the absolute One: any perceived duality between that One and the *atman*, or individual soul, is the result of *maya* (see Glossary) (roughly translated as illusion*)* or *avidya*, meaning ignorance; the material world is transitory. Shankara was renowned for his dialectical skills, and he debated exponents of other schools of philosophy with great vigor in Varanasi, the center of learning. He displayed so much familiarity with the doctrines of his opponents, notably the **Buddhists**, that his critics accused him of being a Buddhist in disguise. Shankara's dialectical victories and organizational talents probably contributed to the decline of Buddhism in India after the eighth century.

Shankara traveled widely. He founded four *mathas*, the Hindu equivalent of a seminary, and located them at major temples in the four principal directions of the subcontinent. Each was headed by a Shankaracharya and charged with the task of propagating Advaita Vedanta in the region under its jurisdiction. The Shankaracharyas command religious authority and enormous prestige to the present day.

SHARMA, SHANKAR DAYAL (1918–1999). The ninth President of India, Sharma was born in **Bhopal** and received his higher education at Cambridge, England, where he obtained his Doctorate in Law. He qualified for the bar at Lincoln's Inn, London, joined the Faculty of Law at Lucknow University, and was a Fellow of Harvard Law School. He joined the **Indian National Congress** young, participated in the **Quit India** movement, and was imprisoned in the course of agitating for the merger of **Princely States** with India. He was president of the Bhopal State Congress and a minister in the **Madhya Pradesh** government from 1956 to 1967. He was elected to the **Lok Sabha** in 1971 and served as Minister of Communications in **Indira Gandhi**'s government from 1974 to 1977.

Sharma earned many academic honors and tried to infuse governance with humanity and intellect. He was appointed Governor successively of **Andhra Pradesh** in 1984, **Punjab** in 1985, and **Maharashira** in

1986. In 1987 he became Vice President of India and succeeded **R. Venkataraman** as President in 1992.

SHASTRI, LAL BAHADUR (1904–1966). The **Congress** Parliamentary party elected Shastri to be prime minister of India after the death of **Jawaharlal Nehru** in May 1964. Lal Bahadur was the son of a poor schoolteacher who died young, and was brought up by his mother and her brother in **Varanasi**, where he obtained a degree in Philosophy in 1926. He was a diligent, self-reliant, and modest man who joined the Servants of the People Society and became a devoted follower of **Mahatma Gandhi**. He was elected to the **Allahabad** Municipal Board in 1930.

The **Indian National Congress** recognized Shastri's hard work and appointed him General Secretary first of the District Congress Committee and then of the United Provinces, now **Uttar Pradesh (UP)**, Provincial Congress Committee. He prepared a report on land reform in the UP and was elected to the UP Legislative Assembly in 1937. On the eve of independence he was serving as Parliamentary Secretary to the UP Chief Minister **Govind Ballabh Pant**.

Shastri was made General Secretary of the All-India Congress Committee and Minister of Railways and Transport in the Union Cabinet in 1951. He served in the latter position to 1956, when he set a rare example of ministerial integrity by acknowledging constitutional responsibility for a serious **railway** accident and resigning from Nehru's Cabinet. One year later he was reappointed as Minister of Transport and subsequently held the portfolios of Commerce and Industry and then Home Affairs.

Unobtrusively and seemingly without personal ambition, Shastri played an important role in ensuring fair and peaceful elections in 1962 and during various changes in the higher ranks of Congress and the Cabinet made in Nehru's last years under the **Kamraj** plan. Shastri was chosen by his Congress Party colleagues to lead the country at a time of acute economic, diplomatic, and political difficulty.

He surprised many by the quiet strength he demonstrated through his prime ministership. He and his large family lived simply, ate only vegetarian food, and remained devout but unostentatious **Hindus**. For many observers, they symbolized the poor of India—as well as the new opportunities available in democratic India. Shastri's policies expressed his own clear ideas on the need to ameliorate India's chronic poverty, unemployment, and social inequity. His emphasis was on improving agriculture and distribution of food, toward which end he engaged in detailed negotiations with the United States; the institutional foundations of India's **Green Revolution** were laid in the mid-1960s.

Prime Minister Shastri was forced to deal with two separate attacks on Indian territory by **Pakistan** forces in the summer of 1965, openly in the Rann of Kutch and covertly in **Kashmir**. In the first instance he agreed to arbitration over an uncertain borderland, partly because of financial pressures at home and heavy pressure from the Western powers. In the second instance he stood unexpectedly firm and ordered retaliation; the **Indian armed forces** acquitted themselves well in the ensuing Indo–Pakistan War of September 1965. Thereafter, Shastri agreed to a ceasefire ordered by the United Nations Security Council and then to a meeting with Pakistan President Ayub Khan. The two reached agreement at **Tashkent** to restore the status quo and work toward improved relations on the subcontinent and issued a declaration to that effect on January 10, 1966. Before he could return home, Lal Bahadur Shastri died suddenly of cardiac arrest in Tashkent.

SHEKHAR, CHANDRA (1927–). Chandra Shekhar was Prime Minister from November 1990 to June 1991. He was born to a middle-income **Rajput** farming family in a village of eastern United Provinces—present-day **Uttar Pradesh (UP)**—and saw his first town at age twelve. He and his wife were married very young. He was educated first at village schools but took his higher education at Allahabad University, where he was active in student politics and drawn to **J. P. Narayan.**

After a brief stint with the **Congress Party**, Chandra Shekhar joined the **Praja Socialist Party** in 1951, becoming General Secretary of its UP unit in 1955 and a member of its National Executive in 1962. He rejoined Congress in 1965, became Secretary of the Congress Parliamentary party, and served on a number of committees as a member of the **Rajya Sabha** from 1962 to 1967. He was among the small group of relatively young and forward-thinking men considered to be loyal to **Indira Gandhi** dubbed the "Young Turks." He launched and edited a weekly paper, *Young India.*

Chandra Shekhar's sympathy for the anti-corruption movement led by J. P. Narayan in 1974 led to his arrest in June 1975 at the time of **Emergency Rule**. He was incarcerated in **Patiala**, and when he was elected to the **Lok Sabha** in the post-Emergency elections of March 1977, it was as a member of the newly formed **Janata Party**. He served as its president but split from it along with his followers when **Charan Singh** became prime minister in July 1979. Chandra Shekhar's political ideas were influenced by **Ram Manohar Lohia**, and he was an outspoken critic of the bureaucracy and big industrialists, including the **Birla** family. He led a *Bharat Pad Yatra*—or foot journey through India—of 4,200 kilometers from Kanya Kumari at the southern tip of India to New Delhi in the cause of national unity during the first half of 1983. He formed a new Janata Party (Secular) with himself as president in 1989. Subsequently, when **V. P. Singh** lost a crucial vote of confidence and resigned from the prime ministership in November 1990, Chandra Shekhar was asked to lead a minority government. He had the tacit support of **Rajiv Gandhi**, leader of the Congress (I), then the largest single party in Parliament. Chander Shekhar lost that support in March 1991 and resigned, but continued to lead a caretaker government until general elections were held and a new Congress government was formed under **P. V. Narasimha Rao** in June 1991.

Chandra Shekhar is a wealthy landowner, has consistently won election to the Lok Sabha, and remains an active and lively politician.

SHIV SENA. The Shiv Sena was founded in 1966 under the leadership of the journalist Bal Thackery on a platform of "**Maharashtra** for the Maharashtrians." As a nascent **political party** it initially operated as a pressure group on a **Congress Party** government to force the teaching of Marathi in Bombay schools and a higher rate of employment for Marathi-speaking people in the "modern sector" of white collar and executive positions in polyglot, multi-ethnic **Bombay**. The Shiv Sena launched bitter and often violent attacks against the **Tamil** and Malayalli speaking migrant populations and subsequently directed violent attacks on Muslims. Bal Thackery is among those accused of conspiracy to demolish the Babri Masjid at **Ayodhya** in December 1992. The Shiv Sena is part of the **Hindu** extremist front known as the *Sangh Parivar* from the **Rashtriya Swayamsevak Sangh**, and utilizes traditional symbols, including that of the 17th-century **Maratha** leader **Shivaji**, to pursue power in a contemporary, competitive, political system.

By 1968 the Shiv Sena had won electoral support from Marathi speaking groups across class lines and formed the main opposition party in the Bombay Municipal Council. The **Congress Party** government of Maharashtra gave in to many "sons of the soil" demands while encouraging the Shiv Sena to undermine **Communist Party** control of **trade unions** by strikebreaking, if necessary. The Shiv Sena's appeal was mainly to the less educated, lower middle class, whose expanding numbers crowded the ladder of social and economic advance; it did not count professionals or unskilled labor among its members. Strong-arm tactics, gangs of organized armed men under its control, willingness to evict tenants and squatters, and demands for "protection money" from individuals and industries gained the Shiv Sena a reputation for being a force of consequence and won it the patronage of some anticommunists and part of Bombay's huge **film industry**. The underground empire of Dawood Ibrahim wages constant battle with the Shiv Sena.

The Shiv Sena could not expand its base in the 1970s and lost some support by its endorsement of **Indira Gandhi**'s **Emergency Rule**. It won only 52 seats out of the 183 it contested for the Maharashtra Assembly in 1990 and lost eight of its 78 seats in the Bombay Municipal Corporation in the 1992 elections. By claiming credit for devastating anti-Muslim riots in 1992–1993, Bal Thackery sought to enhance the power of the Shiv Sena, and he formed a government in Maharashtra in coalition with the **Bharatiya Janata Party** in 1995. The next elections to the Legislative Assembly in Maharashtra brought **Sharad Pawar** and his Nationalist Congress Party to power, and the general elections to the **Lok Sabha** in 2004 spelled a similar defeat for the Shiv Sena.

Thackery and his party had campaigned vigorously, sometimes violently, and successfully, against staging India–Pakistan cricket matches in **Mumbai**, as also against screening controversial films directed by Deepa Mehta, thus undermining the cosmopolitan character of the city. However populist these measures, and however benign be the associated **voluntary organization**, Shiv Udyog Sena's, intentions towards sons of the soil, sustained violence may well have undermined support for Bal Thackery, prompting one journalist to ask if the Shiv Sena has a future.

SHIVA. Shiva is a major deity of the **Hindu** pantheon along with Brahma and **Vishnu**. Although Shiva is not mentioned in the **Vedas** and does not appear as a god before c. 200 BCE, Shiva worship is judged to be the most ancient on the Indian subcontinent. His archetype is found in **Harappa** and Mohenjo-Daro; he is identified with the Vedic Rudra and the **Tamil** Shambhu, meaning Red One. Phallic worship associated with Shiva was certainly pre-**Aryan** and remains ubiquitous.

In later **Hinduism** Shiva embodied the features of a deity directing destinies preceding birth and succeeding death, and evoked the awe appropriate to control of the cosmic forces of nature and the mystic power of the soul. Shiva's 1,008 names or epithets reflect major attributes: Mahadeva or Great God, Lord of fatality; Nataraja, Lord of the cosmic dance of destruction and creation to whom a renowned temple was built at Chidambaram, mythical center of the universe, in **Tanjore** district; Mahayogi or Great Yogi, traditionally represented as a naked ascetic, garlanded with skulls and surrounded by terrible beasts and supernatural beings. The *lingam*, or phallus, conjoined with the *yoni*, represents the sexual potency of Shiva always associated with his female counterpart Shakti (see Glossary) in her various forms of Parvati, Sati, and Uma. Their vehicle is the bull Nandi; Ganesh and Kartikeya are their sons. Shiva is represented iconographically with one or five faces, four hands holding different symbols including the trident, blue neck sporting a cobra, a third eye, and often an arch of flame.

Shiva was a focus of **Bhakti** movements as was Vishnu. Shaivite and Vaishnavite sects became traditional rivals and, at times, open adversaries in some kingdoms of peninsular India.

SHIVAJI (1627–1680). Shivaji was the son of a Bhonsle **Maratha** chieftain, Shahji, who served the Sultans of Ahmednagar and **Bijapur** and made **Poona** the center of his own authority. As a boy Shivaji was deeply influenced by his mother, Jiji Bai, and the religious teachings of the Maharashtrian saints Ramdas and **Tukaram**. He was unruly, and by the age of 19 had become chief of a band of robber hill men, familiar with the forests, brave, hardy, and loyal. They captured several fortresses in the upper **Deccan** and then turned to the Konkan region between the Western Ghats and the ocean.

By 1645 Shivaji was considered enough of a threat to established (Muslim) authority in the area for the Sultan of Bijapur to send his General Afzal Khan at the head of a force to subjugate or deal with him. Shivaji trapped and killed Afzal Khan, captured 4,000 horses for his own troops, augmented his power through plundering raids—including one on **Surat** in 1664—and so challenged the supreme overlord, the **Mughal Empire**. The Emperor **Aurangzeb** sent a small force to subdue Shivaji in 1660 and a larger, more successful **Rajput** force later. By a treaty signed at Purandar in 1665 Shivaji agreed to return 23 forts with their surrounding lands, contribute a contingent of 5,000 horses and men to the imperial forces, and acknowledge Mughal suzerainty. He went to **Agra** the following year under the protection of Rajput General Jai Singh to be received by Aurangzeb, but wanted to be treated as a sovereign prince. Shivaji escaped custody after nine months and returned to the Deccan. His skill in guerilla warfare and mastery of difficult terrain, combined with an expertise in subverting or bribing the Mughal commanders sent against him, enabled Shivaji to consolidate and expand his authority in Maratha country. By 1670 he was demanding (and receiving) *chauth*—one-fourth of the authorized land revenue assessment—from Mughal districts such as Khandesh as fees for protection from pillage; at times he asked for *sardeshmukhi*, or an extra tenth as tribute, to be added. He plundered the rich port of Surat once again and continued to extend his conquering reach.

Shivaji was crowned in 1674 at an elaborate coronation ceremony reminiscent of ancient **Hindu** kingdoms and openly indicative of nostalgia for the **Vijayanagar Empire**. The **brahman** priests performing the accompanying sacrifices gave the Maratha hero—traditionally categorized as of **sudra caste**—full honors as a *kshatriya*, with a long list of titles, including the royal one of *chhatrapati*, and a genealogy traced back through the Sisodia rulers of **Chitor** to **Ram**. Shivaji on his side undertook the sacred duties of Hindu kingship: to protect the brahmans, cows, and the *varna-ashrama-dharma* (see Glossary), or traditional socio-religious order. He was glorified as a *devaraja*, or god-king, capable of restoring Hindu imperium where the Mughal ruled. Shivaji proceeded to form matrimonial alliances with the eight leading *kshatriya* families of the Deccan, entrusted accounting, clerical work, and literary tasks to the brahmans, kept a simple structure of civil administration financed by *chauth* and *sardeshmakhi*, maintained a considerable fleet under Sidi Misri at Kolaba (now part of **Bombay**), and strengthened his army without sacrificing the mobility, tight discipline, sensible organization, and cash salaries on which he had built it.

By the time of his sudden death in 1680, Shivaji had not only recovered his father's *jagirs* (see Glossary) but ruled over a substantial territory in peninsular India. He had knit together his fractious, turbulent, and relatively lawless Maratha followers into a formidable fighting force that almost became the dominant power in India over the following century. Aurangzeb did not underestimate the potential threat to his empire posed by Shivaji but was initially preoccupied with other rebellions closer to **Delhi** and Agra. In 1686 the Mughal Emperor took personal command of massive, prolonged, and expensive military campaigns in the Deccan. Both literally and metaphorically, Aurangzeb lost his life-blood in the struggle against Maratha guerilla forces over two decades.

As important as Shivaji's achievements in the 17th century is the symbolism of Hindu revival that has been imparted to his name by various nationalist publicists and political leaders, especially in **Maharashtra** and by advocates of **Hindutva**, in 20th-century India.

SIACHIN GLACIER. This glacier is located in the western **Himalaya** in the Karakoram region of **Kashmir**. It is the source of the Nubra River, which was the traditional route of trade between **Ladakh** and Kashgar and Yarkand in Central Asia across the Karakoram Pass. Explorers in the 19th century identified and mapped important geographical features of the high mountain ranges emanating from the Pamir knot as part of the "Great Game" between rival British and Russian Empires; the Saltoro range stands out unmistakably as the major watershed separating the Siachin–Nubra and the Saltoro river systems.

The Saltoro range has been the scene of military conflict between India and **Pakistan** since Pakistan's attempt in 1983 to claim the area through sponsoring foreign mountaineering expeditions and publishing maps contrary to the Line of Control established in 1972. The Indian Army's daring response was to take physical possession of that uninhabited, extremely high range in 1984 and then make it permanent. Feats of extraordinary courage, endurance, and innovation by soldiers have characterized the ongoing conflict that is also widely judged to be wasteful of men and resources.

Six rounds of talks between India and Pakistan in the 1990s had produced near agreement on feasible solutions to disengagement, but have not been implemented. Pakistan has tied Siachin to the dispute over the future status of **Jammu and Kashmir**, and again tried to militarily alter the status quo through its misadventure at Kargil in 1999. India is unlikely to unilaterally withdraw its forces from Siachin and holds fast to the principle of inviolability of the Line of Control. Both countries depict Siachin in terms of national honor and valor. Political leaders have yet to reach the rational conclusion that greater political gains can accrue from settlement than from continued conflict.

SIKH. The term Sikh is derived from *sishya*, which means disciple. It refers to a community numbering more than 19 million in India according to the 2001 **Census**, whose religion and way of life flow from the teachings of **Nanak** and nine successor Gurus (see Glossary). The **Punjab** is the homeland of the Sikhs, because the religion originated there, because almost all its adherents before 1947 lived in undivided Punjab, and because Sikhs form a majority in the present state of Punjab in the Indian Union. Sikhs are also found in all parts of India and are prominent in the worldwide Indian **Diaspora**, especially in Britain, Canada, and the United States, where they have struggled with some success to have their religious symbols—including beard and turban—recognized as compatible with membership in state services.

The first Sikh Guru, Nanak, was both mystic and householder, in the traditions of **Hindu** *Sant* as well as **Islamic Sufi**. Nanak was a key figure of the **Bhakti** movement. His faith in the One, formless, creator God, his rejection of formal ritual and caste hierarchy, his equation of Hindu and Muslim, and his establishment of a community of believers using the same body of devotional hymns molded the Sikh faith at foundation. As successor, Nanak chose not his son but a disciple, Angad (born 1504, Guru 1539–1552), who consolidated the community and commenced compiling the hymns used by it. His successor, Amar Das (born 1479, Guru 1552–1574), organized the community under 22 *manji* (bedstead) or local leaders, appointed some women as preachers, and institutionalized the egalitarian tradition of *langar*, or meal, from the Guru's kitchen, shared by all without distinction of rank. Ram Das (born in 1534, Guru 1574–1581) founded the city of **Amritsar** on land gifted by the Mughal Emperor **Akbar** and continued to institute social reforms alleviating the status of women. He composed the wedding hymn used by Sikhs even today, enjoined monogamy, encouraged remarriage of widows, and explicitly forbade the practices of **sati** and veiling of women. His son became the fifth Guru Arjun (born 1563, Guru 1581–1606), who attracted large numbers of **Jat** peasants and landowners to the faith. He collected regular taxes from the faithful to build water reservoirs, as well as the famous Harmandir or Golden Temple at Amritsar with its distinctive architecture embodying openness to all four **castes**, and produced through Bhai Gurdas the authoritative collection of devotional texts used or composed by the first five Gurus. This massive compilation, known as the *Adi Granth*, was installed in the Harmandir in 1604 and named the perennial Guru of the Sikhs by the tenth and last human Guru, **Gobind Singh**.

The imprisonment, torture, and execution of Guru Arjun as a political dissident on the orders of Emperor Jehangir gave a new complexion to the Sikhs who had prospered peaceably within the **Mughal Empire**. The community acquired a coherent identity under the joined spiritual and temporal authority of the Guru symbolized in the two swords *miri* and *piri* worn by the sixth Guru, Hargobind (born 1595, Guru 1606–1644). He used a kettledrum, provided a flag for his troops, and engaged in military skirmishes during succession politics of the Mughal dynasty. In the process he lost all his sons except the youngest in battle. He also established sanctuaries for travelers and restored leprosariums. Hargobind was succeeded by his grandson Har Rai (born 1630, Guru 1644–1661), whose young son became the short-lived eighth Guru Har Krishan (born 1656, Guru 1661–1664).

By this time the community and the Guruship itself became subject to internal rivalries and harassment from the Mughal Emperor **Aurangzeb** spreading **Islam**. The ninth Guru, Tegh Bahadur (born

1621, Guru 1664–1675), was the surviving son of Hargobind who had lived as a contemplative in **Patna** before his installation but subsequently traveled far and frequently to rally the faithful. He opposed the Islamization drive of Aurangzeb and protected the **brahmans** of **Kashmir** from forced conversion. He was arrested and beheaded by order of the emperor and became a martyr to the faith. His young son Gobind Singh led a growing community to whom he gave a distinctive identity symbolized in the five Ks of outward appearance and named the *Khalsa* or pure.

The Sikhs suffered religious persecution and many martyrdoms during the first half of the 18th century, and the Punjab as a whole witnessed much political and military turbulence as Mughal control weakened in that as other provinces. Roving bands of Sikhs preserved their religious identity and gained ascendancy under a loose organization of twelve *misls* (see Glossary) assembling twice a year at Amritsar. By the end of the century **Ranjit Singh** had unified the misls and established an empire in the northwest of the subcontinent that lasted until the British annexation of the Punjab in 1849.

The latter half of the 19th century saw some reversion to Hindu customs and ritual among Sikhs as well as some reform movements additionally stimulated by **Christian** missionary activity and the assertive thrust of the **Arya Samaj**. The British categorized Sikhs as a "martial race," and recruited large numbers to the army. Sikh cultivators moved into the newly irrigated lands of central Punjab and prospered. Sikhs led by the **Akali Dal** in the early 20th century struggled to regain control of their Gurdwaras and reassert their distinctive identity. The Sikh Gurdwaras Act of 1925 placed all Gurdwaras of the Punjab under a central management committee known as the Shiromani Gurdwara Prabandhak Committee (SGPC), which continues to exercise considerable financial and political power today and seeks jurisdiction over Gurdwaras outside the Punjab as well. Because of their relatively small numbers and lack of political strength, Sikhs fared badly in the British–Indian transfer of power negotiations of the mid-1940s. Their demand for a separate homeland was ignored, the line of **Partition** ran through the Punjab districts inhabited by them, and they suffered a heavy toll of life and property in 1947. Nevertheless, Sikh refugees rehabilitated themselves in various parts of India quite rapidly and made sterling contributions to the **Green Revolution** and Punjab prosperity. Some Sikh families migrated abroad, as they had done earlier.

A variety of circumstances having less to do with religion than with rivalries between **political parties**, disputes on water sharing and economic policies, strained center-state relations, and external interference, produced a phenomenon known as the Khalistan movement demanding a separate Sikh state. The notion of secession did not enjoy support among Sikhs resident in India, and the demand came to be associated with non-resident Sikhs, **terrorism** supported by **Pakistan**, illegal trade in drugs and arms, and a prolonged crisis in state authority and inter-communal relations. Prime Minister **Indira Gandhi** ordered army operation Blue Star on June 6, 1984, against Sikh militants led by **Bhindranwale** who had fortified themselves in the Golden Temple. This action exacerbated alienation among Sikhs and led directly to Mrs. Gandhi's assassination on October 31. After a decade of turbulence, normalcy appeared to have been restored in the Punjab by 1993 and has not been disrupted since.

SIKKIM. A small state of the Indian Union, Sikkim has an area of 7,096 square kilometers and a population above half a million according the 2001 **Census**. Sikkim is located in the mid-montane region of the central **Himalaya** and contains the third highest peak in the world, Mt. Kanchenganga. Gangtok is its capital city.

Sikkim's early history is obscure, but Phuntsong Namgyal, originally from **Tibet**, first unified it as a state in the 17th century. The Namgyal dynasty he founded ruled Sikkim until 1975 with the support of the indigenous Lepcha community and the Bhutias, of Tibetan origin. Sikkim lost territory to its neighbors **Nepal, Bhutan,** and finally British India. The British assumed administrative control in 1890 when a Political Officer from the Indian government was appointed in Gangtok and the ruler, known as the Chogyal, was left only with broad internal autonomy. A steady influx of Nepalis altered the ethnic and economic balance in Sikkim and gave rise to a movement for integration with India in the 1940s.

The government of independent India made Sikkim a Protectorate in 1949 but refrained from interfering in local affairs. This practice was changed, however, and a series of controversial moves made by

Indira Gandhi's government in 1974 and 1975, perhaps for strategic reasons, resulted in formal abolition of the Chogyal's position and complete integration of the state within the Indian Union. Sikkim is virtually a paradise for botanists, trekkers, and students of **Buddhism**.

SILK ROAD. Ancient trade routes over land connecting China, India, Central Asia, Persia, Byzantium, and Rome are generically known as the Silk Road from that precious fabric first produced in China. The term is enveloped in adventure, trade, philosophic exchange, romance and literary fantasy from earliest times to the present day. Archaeological and historical research have enlarged present-day knowledge about the many routes and the multiplicity of goods and ideas carried across these routes for hundreds, or thousands, of years in a series of exchanges between different groups of peoples, many of them pastoral and nomadic, and all of them dependant on knowledge of topography and weather, as well as on the oases that punctuated those tracks of endurance.

The best known caravan routes spanning inner Asia, and most closely identified with the Silk Road, ran from present-day X'ian westward, skirted the Taklamakan desert to Dunhuang, then along its northern edge through Turfan or along its southern edge through Niya and Khotan, joining at Kashgar and across the Pamir knot of mountains, and divided again according to destinations further west and south. Linked to these, and also considered part of the Silk Road, were important trading routes through **Gandhara**, **Kashmir**, **Ladakh**, and **Tibet**, connecting the upper **Indus** region and the **Ganges** valley of northern India to Bactria, Central Asia, and Persia. Even before **Kushan** times, Indian traders established stations and merchant colonies at key positions such as Kashgar and Yarkand that continued to serve the same purposes until the 20th century. But in early days those routes and stations served especially the spread of **Buddhism** throughout inner Asia. Caravan traffic on the Silk Road carried monks and pilgrims as well as traders and bandits, as both literary sources and archaeological excavations at **Taxila** and in present day Central Asian republics reveal. Townships along the Silk Road also saw lively intellectual exchanges among Buddhists, **Zoroastrians**, Nestorians, and Manicheans before **Islam** swept through Central

Asia. Some of these routes remain in use today for foot, yak, or adventure tourist travel. One of them was reconstructed as the Karakoram Highway by China and **Pakistan** in the 1970s for military and commercial passage. A joint India–China mountaineering expedition explored other parts of the Silk Road in the 1990s.

The Southern Silk Road has gained scholarly attention only recently but there is now ample evidence of its thriving existence over the centuries. Trading and migratory routes connected the southwestern provinces of China, notably Xichuan and Yunnan, with Thailand, **Burma**, and **Assam** in northeastern India. From the Assam plains, goods fed easily into the main trans-continental trade of the **Ganges** valley as well as to the **Deccan** and west coast ocean ports. Sea-borne trade through maritime Southeast Asia generously supplemented trade over land routes. As in the case of the northern Silk Road, the southern routes carried both goods and ideas, notably Buddhism, as it spread from India through Southeast and East Asia. Late-20th-century efforts to forge economic and cultural ties among the littoral states of the Bay of Bengal to southwestern China has also stimulated academic research on the early history of the southern Silk Road.

As maritime trade grew in volume and importance at the expense of overland trade in the early modern period, and as Europeans came to dominate Asia, the Silk Road was all but buried under the sands of obscurity. Explorers of the late 19th century restored some of its glamour, and research undertaken in the mid- and late 20th century has added much factual knowledge about it. Facts enhance, rather than diminish, the allure of the Silk Road for adventurers of the body or the mind.

SIMLA or **SHIMLA.** A hill town built at over 2,100 meters in the foothills of the **Himalaya**, Shimla is the bustling capital of present-day **Himachal Pradesh**. It was the official summer capital of the British Government of India from 1864 to 1947 such featured in much of the social and travel literature of the time, such as the writings of **Rudyard Kipling**. Simla was the site of many important meetings and conventions throughout this period, especially those immediately preceding the independence and **Partition** of India in 1947. Another landmark agreement signed at Simla was between **Indira Gandhi** of India and **Pakistan**'s Zulfiqar Ali Bhutto in June 1972.

SIMON COMMISSION (1927–1930). This was a statutory commission led by Sir John Simon, a barrister of the Liberal Party in Britain, and consisting of six other Members of Parliament, two from the Labour Party and four from the Conservative Party. They were charged by the British Parliament to investigate the working of the **Montagu–Chelmsford Reforms** of 1919 in India, especially education, the development of representative institutions, the functioning of legislative chambers in the provinces, the extent of the demand for "responsible government," and the desirability of advancing toward it (as promised by the **Montagu Declaration** of 1917). They were directed to invite the views of delegations from the Indian Central Legislative Council and any other body they wished to consult before making proposals in the form of a report to a joint select committee of Parliament.

The Simon Commission was constituted ahead of the decennial schedule specified in the Montagu–Chelmsford Reforms because of the rising political temperature in India and more strident demands for self-government led by the **Indian National Congress**. British insensitivity to Indian nationalism was seen in the fact that not one single Indian was appointed to the Commission. In December 1927, Congress resolved on total boycott and was joined in this by the All-India **Muslim League** led by **Mohammed Ali Jinnah** as well as by members of the **Swaraj Party** such as **Sir Tej Bahadur Sapru**. All prominent political leaders, in short, took insult, and the Simon Commission was met on arrival in India in early 1928 with waves of black flags and posters reading "Simon Go Back."

Members of the Commission met relatively few people, and its limited tours were marked by police clashes with street demonstrators. Its report of May 1930 confirmed the worst fears of nationalist Indians: it rejected all ideas of transfer of power and made no mention of **Dominion Status**. Such recommendations for constitutional reform as it made, for provincial autonomy for example, were heard only in London and outpaced in India by the **Nehru Report** of 1928 that was ignored by Britain. Inadvertently, no doubt, the Simon Commission helped to galvanize political action by Congress and restore **Mahatma Gandhi** to the limelight. The then Viceroy **Lord Irwin** tried to heal exacerbated racial rifts by establishing unofficial links with Congress leaders and announcing

British intentions to hold a **Round Table Conference** on Indian constitutional reform.

SINDHIA (SCINDIA), MAHADJI (1727–1794). The most outstanding **Maratha** Chieftain of his time, Mahadji was the son of Ranoji Sindhia, who served well under **Peshwa Baji Rao I**, and received part of Malwa with the fortress city of Gwalior as his fiefdom. Mahadji Sindhia set himself to retrieve some of the power and prestige in northern India that the Marathas lost at the third battle of **Panipat** when defeated by **Ahmad Shah Abdali**. Mahadji propped up the titular **Mughal** Emperor Shah Alam 11 and became his formal protector in 1771 while extending his own sway. Sindhia remodeled his army, recruited European officers as gunners and drillmasters, and was able to defeat Holkar of Indore, a rival Maratha Chieftain, as well as a **Rajput** combination ranged against him.

Sindhia's ability and ambition attracted the watchful attention of the **East India Company**, but he skillfully maneuvered between its officers and the **Peshwa** during the first Anglo–Maratha War, which ended with the Treaty of Salbei in 1782. Mahadji then decided to ally himself with the English and so regained some more territory. He was also active in the court of the Peshwa, who invested him with the title of Vice Regent in 1792. Mahadji Sindhia's death two years later contributed to the decline of Maratha power, rapidly overtaken by the British. His successor signed a **Subsidiary Alliance** with the East India Company in 1817. The Sindhia family, which continued to rule from Gwalior, was generally well regarded by the British, and Mahadji's descendants continue to play prominent roles in the economy and politics of contemporary India.

SINGH, CHARAN or CHARAN SINGH (1902–1987). Singh was prime minister of India briefly, from July 1979 to January 1980. He was born to a **Jat** agriculturalist family in Meerutt district of the United Provinces, present-day **Uttar Pradesh (UP)** and never lost that earthy perspective on life.

Charan Singh began his political career as a member of the **Indian National Congress**, having taken his Master's and Law degrees, and while practicing as a lawyer in Ghaziabad district of western UP. He was elected to the UP Legislative Assembly in 1937 and imprisoned by the British authorities in the 1940s. He was elected again in 1946 and served as Parliamentary Secretary to the **Govind Ballabh Pant** government of the UP from 1946 to 1951. Thereafter he moved among ministries, strengthening his specialization in agriculture and his political base among Jat farmers. He published several works on land and agricultural matters, the best known of which is *Indian Economy: A Gandhian Blueprint*, and became a spokesman for rural interests, especially small landholding farmers, in government.

Charan Singh was Chief Minister of Uttar Pradesh 1967–1968 and again in 1970. He left the **Congress Party** in 1969 to form the **Lok Dal**, which opposed **Indira Gandhi**'s government. Charan Singh was elected to the **Lok Sabha** in the general elections of 1977 and held the powerful Home Ministry in the newly formed **Janata** coalition government before becoming Deputy Prime Minister. When Prime Minister **Morarji Desai** resigned in July 1979, Charan Singh was asked to lead the government until the general elections of January 1980 returned Mrs. Gandhi and the Congress (I) to power.

SINGH, VISHWANATH PRATAP or V. P. SINGH (1931–). V. P. Singh was prime minister of India from December 1989 to November 1990. He was born to a Thakur or **Rajput** landowning family of **Uttar Pradesh (UP)**, and formally adopted at age five by his childless paternal uncle, the Raja of Manda. Vishwanath was educated at Dehra Dun, **Banaras** and Allahabad University where he took a Law degree before going on to study Science at **Poona**. His early life was lonely and sheltered.

As a young man V. P. Singh was inspired by **Mahatma Gandhi** and joined the **Indian National Congress**. He met **Vinobe Bhave** in 1957, was deeply moved, and donated his considerable estate to the Bhoodan movement. V. P. Singh also was drawn to **J. P. Narayan** for similar reasons: uplift of the economically and socially deprived. Vishwanath in turn attracted the notice of **Lal Bahadur Shastri** who came to consider him part of his family and also inducted him into politics.

V. P. Singh was elected to the UP Legislative Assembly in 1969 and to the **Lok Sabha** in 1971. He was a member of the Congress Parliamentary Party, the All-India Congress Committee, and General Secretary of the UP Congress from 1977 to 1980. He was reelected to the Lok Sabha in 1980 and joined **Indira Gandhi**'s cabinet as Commerce Minister in 1983. V. P. Singh remained in **Rajiv Gandhi**'s cabinet, holding successive portfolios of Commerce, Finance from 1985 to 1987, and Defense in 1987–1988. He resigned from the latter position in the wake of press allegations of governmental corruption in awarding defense contracts, especially to Bofors, a Swedish armaments company selling heavy guns to India.

Through the latter part of 1988 and 1989 V. P. Singh was projected in much of the Indian **press** as "Mr. Clean." He led a campaign against corruption and played a major role in uniting fractious opposition to Rajiv Gandhi's government. He floated the Jana Morcha for disaffected members of Congress and then formed the Janata Dal from the erstwhile **Janata Party** and the two splinters of the **Lok Dal**. By 1989 he was offering a national alternative to Congress in the shape of a National Front coalition between the Janata Dal, the two **Communist** parties, and various small or regional parties, including the **Dravida Munnetra Kazhagam (DMK)** of **Tamil Nadu**. Their combined platform was secular and populist, drawing attention to unsolved basic problems in the economy and society. In preparation for the general elections of 1989, V. P. Singh negotiated a seat sharing arrangement between the National Front and the **Bharatiya Janata Party (BJP)**, so that their respective candidates would not compete against each other. This strategy worked to defeat the Congress (I) in the general elections of November 1989, but no other single party won a majority of seats either.

V. P. Singh was invited to form a government despite the minority status of the Janata Dal with only 143 seats in the Lok Sabha because of the "outside support" assured him by the BJP as well as both Communist parties. The complications of these arrangements were aggravated in 1990 by personality clashes between V. P Singh his Deputy Prime Minister Devi Lal of **Haryana**. Despite the announcement of sensible economic policies, the performance of the government was without luster and the level of civil strife, largely engendered by political rivalry, rose. A major insurrection in the **Kashmir** valley and high tension with **Pakistan** added to the problems faced by V. P. Singh. His own credibility was badly damaged in the summer of 1990 when he announced, in the context of a rift with Devi Lal, his intention to implement the **Mandal Commission** Report, or affirmative action for "backward castes" other than the Scheduled Castes and Tribes already protected by the **Constitution**.

The BJP's withdrawal of support and an eruption of violence in **Delhi** and other cities and towns of northern India sealed the fate of the V. P. Singh government. He lost a major vote of confidence in Parliament on November 10, 1990, and resigned. He remained active in politics but subject to poor health, and declined an offer to lead the United Front government in 1996.

SINHA, SATYENDRA PRASANNA (1863–1928). Born to a wealthy landowning family of **Bengal**, Sinha studied in **Calcutta** and then joined Lincoln's Inn, London, where he was called to the Bar in 1886. He returned to practice Law in Calcutta and kept apart from the militant nationalism of the city. Sinha was the first Indian to become Advocate General of India in 1905, to be nominated to the Governor General's Executive Council in 1909, and to be raised to the British peerage as Baron Sinha of Raipur in 1919. As Under Secretary of State for India he successfully steered the Government of India Act of 1919, better known as the **Montagu-Chelmsford Reforms**, through the House of Lords, upper house of the British Parliament.

Sinha and his family were deeply influenced by the **Tagore** family and also belonged to the **Brahmo Samaj**. They blended Indian and British culture in their way of life. Sinha was an active member of the **Indian National Congress** between 1896 and 1919 but was out of sympathy with the mass movement led by **Mahatma Gandhi**.

SOUTH ASIAN ASSOCIATION FOR REGIONAL COOPERA-TION (SAARC). This body was formally inaugurated at a summit meeting of the heads of government of the seven South Asian states— **Bangladesh**, **Bhutan**, India, **Maldives**, **Nepal**, **Pakistan**, and **Sri Lanka**—at **Dhaka** in December 1985. The notion of such an organization was not new, being a natural outgrowth of geographical proximity, but it was first seriously voiced only in a 1979 draft proposal circulated by Ziaur Rahman, President of Bangladesh. Meetings among officials of the various countries in the early 1980s laid the groundwork. A permanent Secretariat was opened in Khatmandu, Nepal in 1987.

South Asia is coterminous with the Indian subcontinent and neighboring island states of Sri Lanka and Maldives. The seven states can be seen to belong to a common—albeit large and diverse—family in terms of culture, history, kinship, and religious affiliations; they also demonstrate characteristics of family jealousies, rivalries, and feuds in their political relationships with India, especially but not exclusively so in the cases of Pakistan and Bangladesh. Pre- and post-**partition** and independence experiences serve to push them apart rather than bring them together. The overwhelming preponderance of India in terms of size, population, resources, skills and power, and the fact that each shares a border with India but not with each other, intensifies fears and inhibitions in the governments of smaller South Asian states. Thus, particular features of South Asia combined with the international politics of the Cold War to cancel the imperatives of regional cooperation in the contemporary world so clearly seen in Europe and Southeast Asia. Prospects for economic integration in South Asia improved with the end of the Cold War and the adoption of market friendly economic policies in India and its neighbors. The SAARC summit meeting of 2002 decided to establish a South Asian Free Trade Area (SAFTA), scheduled to take effect in 2006.

SAARC was launched with a very modest agenda and a cautious, almost timid approach. Bilateral and contentious issues of national security were eschewed from collective deliberation, although summit meetings did provide opportunities for national leaders, including those of India and Pakistan, to discuss such matters face to face without intrusive publicity. The initial focus of SAARC was to improve communication and exchanges of information among the member states and to share their respective expertise and experience on subjects of common concern such as agriculture, telecommunications, monsoon research, health, and social welfare. As an international organization, SAARC has focused on functional cooperation rather than on building strategic consensus. Some success and the imperatives of an ever-shrinking world in terms of communication and crime led SAARC to envisage enlargement of its agenda in the 1990s. Member governments agreed to cooperate in combating drug abuse and trafficking—a new and costly regional problem often found in conjunction with **terrorism**, also added to the SAARC agenda and produced two Conventions on the subject. Practical cooperation in combating terrorism, however, lags far behind articulations of good intention. The easing of travel restrictions on specific categories of persons, exchanges of audio-visual educational materials, co-production of media programs, establishment of regional gene-banks for biotechnology, and inclusion of **Non-Governmental Organizations** in regional cooperative ventures for environmental conservation and social welfare were also achieved during the 1990s to the benefit of common people. Authorization of sub-regional groupings for economic cooperation was another important step forward as it facilitated growth oriented cooperative action on the part of Bangladesh, India, Sri Lanka along with **Myanmar** and Thailand in BIMSTEC, opened the way for more interchanges with China as well as the Association of South East Asian Nations (ASEAN), and evaded the uncomfortable fact of Pakistan's resistance.

The main thrust areas for SAARC in the first decade of the 21st century are defined as economic cooperation, poverty alleviation, elimination of terrorism, checking traffic in women and children, and promotion of child welfare. Discussions on comprehensive security are promoted by some non-governmental think tanks in the region, but SAARC has no procedures for conflict resolution and no security mandate. Even in the areas of functional cooperation explicitly within its purview, SAARC lacks the institutional infrastructure to put its declared objectives into immediate effect. More importantly, and for most of the time, member governments, including those of India, were too preoccupied with domestic concerns and insurgencies to generate the political will necessary for creating such a regional infrastructure. Since the late 1990s, however, India has shouldered a major share of responsibility for SAARC functions and actively promoted trade and technical cooperation within the region, in part by signing bilateral agreements with Sri Lanka and Bangladesh. Prime Minister **Inder Gujral** enunciated a regional "doctrine" in 1996 based on five principles: not asking for reciprocity in concessions from Bangladesh, Bhutan, Maldives, Nepal and Sri Lanka; no South Asian country allowing its territory to be used against another; no interference in internal affairs; respect for territorial integrity and sovereignty of each; settlement of all disputes through peaceful bilateral negotiations. His successors have underlined the economic imperative of regional cooperation in an era of globalization and Indian **economic liberalization** and growth. And for the first time in 2003 an Indian foreign minister suggested a regional South Asian future similar to that of the European Union.

SAARC is unlikely to grow into a strong and effective regional organization as long as relations between India and Pakistan remain hostile and other members have not hesitated to express their disapproval of being held hostage to such continued conflict. New Delhi also recognizes the handicap regional disharmony creates for India in realizing its potential as a great power. At the same time, the economic, functional, and even political advantages of regional cooperation are becoming more and more obvious all over South Asia, perhaps justifying cautious optimism in the future of SAARC.

SOUZA, FRANCIS NEWTON (1924–). Souza was born in **Goa** and now lives in New York. He studied at the J. J. School of Art in **Bombay** and went on to study and paint in London and Paris. He founded the Progressive Artists Group, which became very influential in India, and held many one-man exhibitions all over India and the world. He is a recipient of the Guggenheim Award and his paintings can be seen in public collections at the Baroda Museum, the National Gallery of Modern Art in New Delhi, and the Tate Gallery and Victoria and Albert Museum in London.

SPACE PROGRAM. In April 2003, India demonstrated a quantum leap in technological competence for using space. An indigenously built and fuelled Geosynchronous Satellite Launch Vehicle (GSLV) capable of catapulting a satellite weighing 1.53 tons into high orbit was successfully launched. A year later, Indian announced its plan for a lunar mission named Chandrayaan-1 in 2007–2008 to map terrain, topographical and mineralogical features for a period of two years. The United States, Canada, Israel, Russia, and the European Union all expressed their interest in participation and, possibly, using India's launch facilities commercially in the future.

The Indian Space Program Research Organization (ISPRO) and Space Commission were formally established in 1972 under **Vikram Sarabhai**, with the objective of establishing self-reliant space services for the country. The main thrust of the initial program was to provide satellite-based communications across the country through the multipurpose Indian National Satellite System (INSAT), satellite-based survey of natural resources including underground water, and satellite-based meteorological forecasting, especially of monsoon data, and application of knowledge, especially in villages. In 1980 India became the sixth country in the world with the capacity to orbit its own satellite, *Rohini*. The first few Indian satellites were launched from Europe, the Soviet Union, and the United States, but by 1992 the entire fabrication and launching process was managed indigenously and the Indian Remote Sensing Satellite (IRS) was internationally recognized as excellent. Building an adequately powerful launcher was another challenge, partly because American interdictions of transfer of cryogenic technology and materials caused Russia to renege on a 1992 contract and supply only seven engines. India's indigenous building program showed initial success with launch of a Polar (PSLV) in 1996 and subsequent years, and finally with the GSLV.

The development of India's space program is closely linked to the expansion of electronics expertise and production in India as well as the efficient management of various specialized centers in **Bangalore**, **Ahmedabad**, Trivandrum, and the launch base at Sriharikota on the east coast. The main limitations on the program have been budgetary, with costs kept down to a bare minimum, the international regime controlling transfers of technology, and specific American sanctions targeting ISRO after 1998. These were lifted gradually after 2001. Although the Indian space program is not a defense program and is being used primarily to gather data and establish interactive and educational connectivity with villages, it carries clear implications for future Indian strategies of missile defense and nuclear deterrence.

SRI LANKA (known as CEYLON before 1972). This beautiful, small, teardrop-shaped, independent island state lies off the southern tip of India, separated from it by the shallow and narrow Palk Straits. Despite strong geographical and cultural links with India, Sri Lanka evolved a distinctive identity and language (Sinhala) over more than two millennia of history. It established itself as an important hydraulic and trading civilization in the ancient world and blended indigenous peoples and trends with various influences from India.

One major historical event was the **Buddhist** mission sent to the King of Sri Lanka by the **Mauryan Emperor Ashoka** by hand of his daughter and son in the third century BCE; it is commemorated annually with great ceremony. The presence of **Tamil**-speaking peoples and the worship of **Hindu** deities in Sri Lanka is probably equally ancient, although periodic invasions and migrations from peninsular India in earlier times are not recalled today with pleasure. Ceylon's trading links with the Arabs and Europeans in the early modern period, and its subsequent incorporation in the British Empire, added further elements to the island's culture and peoples. British import of Tamil labor for tea plantations on Ceylon in the 19th century created a potentially explosive demographic problem of "Indian Tamils" in the central highlands, as distinct from the Ceylonese Tamils in the north of the island. The independent governments of India and Sri Lanka signed agreements in the 1960s and after to resolve the problem of plantation workers in a peaceable and humanitarian manner that involved repatriation of some to India and absorption of others by Sri Lanka.

Far more serious was the breakdown of harmonious relations between Sri Lanka's two dominant linguistic cum religious groups—Sinhala (approximately nine million and mainly Buddhist) and Tamil (approximately two and a half million and mainly Hindu)—in the late 1970s. Insurgency broke out. The Liberation Tigers of Tamil Eelam (LTTE) demanded a separate Tamil state in the north and east of the island. Serious ethnic and military conflict since then largely nullified the considerable social, economic, and political progress made by Sri Lanka and created serious problems in bilateral relations with India in the 1980s. The weighty state of **Tamil Nadu** was initially sympathetic to Tamil insurgents in Sri Lanka and New Delhi's mediatory efforts failed. Sri Lankan President Jayawardene and Indian Prime Minister **Rajiv Gandhi** signed an Accord in 1987 committing an Indian Peace Keeping Force to help maintain the unity and integrity of the island republic. The force was withdrawn by India in 1990 on the request of Sri Lankan President Premadasa and after a storm of controversy in both countries. Rajiv Gandhi was assassinated in May 1991 by an LTTE suicide bomber and that body (already unwelcome in Tamil Nadu) was banned as a **terrorist** organization in India and some other countries subsequently. India took no further direct role in the Sri Lankan conflict but has firmly supported Norway's "facilitation" efforts in recent years.

Sri Lanka and India have enjoyed close and cooperative bilateral relations since independence and both governments make efforts to resolve inevitable differences of opinion or problems without rancor. Regular exchanges of high level visits are normal. Many similarities in their worldviews were reflected in their common adherence to **nonalignment** in their foreign policies in the post-**World War II** period. Larger and tangible areas of mutual cooperation have been opened by their common membership in the **South Asian Association for Regional Association (SAARC)** since 1985, similar policies of **economic liberalization** since the 1990s (with Sri Lanka proceeding much faster along that road than India), and most of all by the bilateral Free Trade Agreement first mooted by Indian foreign minister **I. K. Gujral** in 1996 and signed in 2002.

SRINAGAR. The summer capital of the Indian state of **Jammu and Kashmir**, Srinagar has been the cultural and political center of **Kashmir** for centuries. Situated on the banks of the river Jhelum, one of the tributaries of the **Indus**, the city may have been laid by the **Mauryan Emperor Ashoka** in the third century BCE. Neolithic sites as well as ancient **Buddhist** sites have been excavated in the vicinity of Srinagar, and the hill top **Shiva** temple overlooking the city is attributed to a visit of **Shankara** in the eighth century CE. One of the most sacred Muslim shrines in the world is the Hazratbal Mosque (enshrining a hair of the Prophet Mohammed) at the edge of Lake Nagin in Srinagar. A confrontation between Islamic militants and Indian security forces at the mosque was peacefully resolved in 1993.

The multi-religious character of Kashmir's long history is reflected in the multitude of churches, gurdwaras, mosques, and temples of the city as also in the **Mughal** fort and pleasure gardens and the ornamented wooden houses, houseboats, and bridges that adorn it. Severe political disturbances, **terrorist** activity, and tight security disrupted the traditional handicraft industries, tourist trade, education and social life in Srinagar after 1989, but normalcy was being restored after a newly elected popular government took power in 2002.

SRINIVAS, M. N. (1916–1999). Srinivas was born in **Mysore** city to an educated, traditional, **brahman** family but came in early contact with rural people who helped him discard preconceived prejudices about them. Trained at Bombay University and at Oxford, Srinivas became one of the founders of sociology and social anthropology in India.

Srinivas' work was based on intensive and firsthand fieldwork as well as his knowledge of existing literature and folklore in different parts of the country. He relied on empirical data and reasoned interpretation of it rather than on critical evaluation of other peoples' theories, finding any single, "grand" or essentialist theory inadequate to explain the lived realities of a diverse and changing India. He moved from descriptive ethnography to structural-functionalist ethnography to social anthropology as a multidisciplinary art including historiography. In a long teaching career Srinivas founded two new departments of sociology, at the M. S. University of Baroda on return from Oxford, and at the University of Delhi in 1958. He moved to **Bangalore** in 1971 but continued to play an important role in strengthening professional associations and public bodies influencing policy and contributing to scholarship.

Srinivas explored the stability of traditional social systems in India but showed an awareness of change and growing conflicts between old and new; he posed questions about the ability of existing institutions to resolve conflict and the threats posed by change to social order. Although he did not propound a new theory, he commented on theoretical developments in anthropology. His own methodology was meticulous and some of his concepts have passed into the general lexicon of understanding Indian society and culture, notably the concepts of "Sanskritization" and "dominant caste."

Among a long list of Srinivas' scholarly and popular publications are *Religion and Society Among the Coorgs of South India* (Oxford, 1952), *Social Change in Modern India* (Berkeley, 1966), *The Remembered Village* (Berkeley, 1976) written after his vast collection of field notes were consumed in a fire at Stanford, California, *Caste: Its Twentieth Century Avatar* (New York, 1996) and *Indian Society Through Personal Writings* (Oxford, 1996). Srinivas had a profound influence on younger academics as well as on concerned citizenry in India and abroad.

STATES PEOPLES CONFERENCE, ALL-INDIA. This was a nationalist organization formed under the rubric of the **Indian National Congress** but functioning within the Indian **Princely States**. It grew out of timid efforts by urban middle class Indians in some princely states to foster representative institutions similar to those of British India during the 1920s. It took on a more visible role during the 1930s under the leadership of Balwantrai Mehta, at a time when a proposed federation between British India and Princely India was under active discussion in London.

The agenda and strength of the States Peoples Conference varied from one princely state to another depending on the character of the administration, the strength of felt grievances, and linkages with Congress. Broadly speaking, Congress under the leadership of **Mahatma Gandhi** adopted a "non-interventionist" position of "moral support and sympathy" for movements by the people of the states themselves, while gently asking the princes to extend civil liberties to their subjects and act as responsible trustees. Pressure from the Congress Left as well as from within some states led to greater activity after 1937, including a **Satyagraha** in **Jaipur**, negotiation with **Mirza Ismail**, Dewan of **Mysore**, pacts with **Sheikh Abdullah** in **Jammu and Kashmir**, and a fast by Gandhi in Rajkot.

The States Peoples Conference did not function in all princely domains, seldom espoused the causes of peasants or labor, and did not significantly contribute to the legal integration of princely states with the Indian Union 1946–1948.

STATES REORGANIZATION COMMISSION (SRC). The Government of India appointed a special commission in 1953 to explore the feasibility of re-demarcating state boundaries on the basis primarily of **language**. The immediate push for such a step was the political martyrdom of **Sriramulu Potti** in 1952 during the **Andhra** movement for separation from **Madras**. But long before independence the **Indian National Congress** had committed itself to what the **Nehru Report** of 1928 phrased "the linguistic redistribution of provinces as a clear political objective." This was because the provincial boundaries of British India had been drawn either by historical accident or for reasons of administrative convenience. Congress, on the other hand, leading a mass-based national movement, had recognized the federal realities of Indian civilization in which, as the SRC Report of 1956 put it, "linguistic homogeneity . . . reflects the social and cultural pattern of living obtaining in well defined regions of the country."

The imperative of national unity, however, came to the forefront in the aftermath of **Partition**, and Prime Minister **Jawaharlal Nehru** and others feared that linguistically homogenous states would create a sub-national momentum and disturbing existing administrative boundaries would trigger a chain reaction of disintegration. Only reluctantly, therefore, did he ask the SRC to examine the question of regional identity and make recommendations according to certain governing principles: to preserve and strengthen the unity of India; to keep in mind administrative, economic, and financial considerations as in the implementation of five year plans; and to pay attention to cultural and linguistic homogeneity as reflected in democratic and popular movements.

The SRC published its report and recommendations in 1955 and a States Reorganization Act followed in 1956 providing for 14 states and six union territories. Generally speaking, boundaries of states would conform to the region of a dominant language. The boundaries of states in southern India were redrawn in closer conformity with traditional linguistic regions, and eight major language groups got separate states immediately: Assamese—**Assam**, Bengali—West **Bengal**, Kannada—**Karnataka**, Kashmiri—**Jammu and Kashmir**, Malayalum—**Kerala**, Oriya—**Orissa**, **Tamil—Madras (Tamil Nadu)**, Telugu—**Andhra Pradesh**. The SRC rejected demands for a separate **Jharkhand** state for lack of popular support in all the affected districts. It rejected demands for a Punjabi *subah* on grounds that communal relations would be damaged, and did not tackle the division of Bombay province on linguistic lines because the location of **Bombay** city was a matter of heated dispute. While balancing national and regional interests the SRC could not insist that 50% of all centrally recruited civil servants posted in a given state be non-residents, but it refused to recommend that state civil services be restricted to "sons of the soil."

After agitations in both Gujarati-speaking and Marathi-speaking areas, the state of Bombay was divided between **Gujarat** and **Maharashtra** in 1960 with the city becoming the capital of the latter. And after a change of leadership in the **Akali Dal**, its demand for a separate Punjabi-speaking state was also conceded in 1966. State boundaries were redrawn later in the northeast in response to ethnic demands, and other new states were created as well. In short, despite the apparent political turbulence associated with the reorganization of states in the late 1950s, the SRC recommendations, their implementation, and further administrative and political innovations affecting state boundaries demonstrate the efficacy of managing centrifugal forces in India through democratic solutions and pluralistic compromises.

STUPA. Intended to enshrine the remains or appurtenances of the **Buddha** or **Buddhist** holy men or sacred texts, a stupa may also be built as a memorial to an event or as a votive offering or meritorious act. Stupas are found wherever Buddhism spread and are identified with the Buddha and his teachings. Stupas are distinguished by their symmetrical plane, vertical axis, and circular dome surmounted by a *chattra*, or canopy. Stupas were built and ornamented according to various styles of place and period and could be large stone, brick, or earth monuments—as constructed at Sanchi in **Mauryan** times for example—or small, portable containers made of fine metals or ceramic ware—as found in excavations along the **Silk Road**.

In India the stupa was constructed along simple lines without usable interior space. It was seen as giving concrete shape to metaphysical principles found in literary texts; some saw it as a cosmological archetype. Worshippers usually circumambulate a stupa in a clockwise direction

SUBBULAKSMI, M. S. (1916–2004) was born in **Madurai**, a temple city in **Tamil Nadu**. She started singing as a small child and made her first recording at the age of ten. She was trained in both Carnatic and Hindustani classical **music** by masters in their fields and has been singing all her life to rapt audiences throughout India and the world. A devout and traditional woman, Subbulaksmi has lived a full life, which included eight years in the **film** industry. She has a wide repertoire in several Indian **languages** and is widely known for her *bhajans*, or devotional songs, evoking prayer in her listeners and reinforcing her persona as a devotee. She often has given concert recitals to raise money for charity. Carnatic classical music is better appreciated today beyond its region of origin because of the beauty, power and reach of Subbulaksmi's voice.

SUBRAHMANYAM, KRISHNASWAMY (1929–). Born in Tiruchirapalli in **Tamil Nadu**, he educated in **Madras** where he took a Master's degree in science, and joined the **Indian Administrative Service** in 1951. He shone as a brilliant analyst of defense and national security matters who consistently urged the Government of India to pay more systematic attention to those subjects than it was accustomed to doing. He was appointed director of the newly created Institute for Defence Studies and Analysts in 1968 and subsequently held many appointments, including Chair of the Joint Intelligence Committee and Convener of India's first National Security Advisory Board in 1999, directly related to his area of expertise. As author of numerous books and papers, longtime participant in conferences at home and abroad, and a regular columnist in leading newspapers since his retirement from government service, Subrahmanium has been a pioneer in improving public awareness of India's defense and national security concerns.

SUBSIDIARY ALLIANCES. Treaties signed between the English **East India Company** and Indian Princes in the late 18th and early 19th centuries established what came to be called a system of Subsidiary Alliance. In the competition for power that ensued during the twilight of the **Mughal Empire**, Indian Princes and European trading companies were political equals engaged in shifting alliances. But as the latter demonstrated military superiority and more consistent purpose, and as the balance of power shifted in favor of the East India Company, the treaties of alliance became instruments of subordinating the Indian princes and acquiring control over their territory.

The model for subsidiary alliances was set in 1766 when the Nizam of **Hyderabad** asked for and received well-trained troops from the East India Company in return for an annual subsidy. The rulers of **Awadh**, Cooch Behar, and Carnatic followed suit soon after. As the Company engaged in wars against **Haidar Ali**, **Tipu Sultan**, and the **Marathas**, it signed on many Indian rulers opposing them as allies. **Lord Wellesley**, Governor General from 1798 to 1805, signed 100 such treaties in seven years and used the Subsidiary Alliance system to build an empire in India. His successors carried forward the precedent by signing treaties with several Maratha Princes before 1820. The British honored the titles and terms of the treaties for the most part, but Indian Princes were unprotected when **Lord Dalhousie** reinterpreted the terms of treaties and followed a policy of territorial expansion through his "doctrine of lapse."

Subsidiary Alliances brought gains for the East Indian Company by extending the areas under British control and relative peace and bringing in subsidies and/or territory. Indian Princes appeared to have gained a sense of security by having British-trained troops to protect them against their ever-present fears of rebellion, usurpation, or invasion. But they had, in fact, exchanged the substance and responsibility of power for mere title and ceremony. As Thomas Munro pointed out in 1817, by removing fears of traditional remedies for bad government and teaching reliance on foreigners, the treaties rendered the Indian princes "indolent . . . cruel and avaricious" and tended to "degrade and impoverish the whole people" (Jeffrey, *People, Princes and Paramount Power*: 9).

Once the British had overcome the great **Uprising of 1857** the map of India was frozen for 90 years. Princely States were scattered across two-fifths of India under the indirect rule of the paramount power, no longer the East India Company but the British Crown.

SUDRA. The fourth of the **Hindu** *varnas* (see Glossary), said to have originated from the feet of the original sacrificial man according to the **Vedas** was named sudra and identified with labor and service.

Sudras may have been **Adivasis** or aboriginal tribes absorbed into **Aryan** society, or a servitor class among the Indo–Aryans themselves. Their status and occupations have varied over time and place, with many ruling dynasties clearly of sudra origin being elevated to *kshatriya* rank by virtue of their power. Sudras were integral parts of Hindu ritual and society in Vedic times and are so described in the early **Upanishads**. Nor were **brahmans** then prohibited from taking milk or food prepared by them, although such restrictions later became customary.

Sudra status became degraded in the process of early brahmanical revival; indeed, a similar correlation between elevation of the brahman and degradation of the sudra was repeated from time to time in different parts of India. Legalists such as **Manu** saddled the sudras with so many disabilities—including exclusion from scriptural or any other literate instruction—that their status was almost indistinguishable from that of the *panchama* or **untouchable** outcastes in the

Ganges valley. Over time, and in different parts of the country, many sudra communities crossed **caste** barriers upward, but they were traditionally associated with occupations of agricultural cultivation, cattle and goat herding and grazing, fishing, and manual labor. The **Indian Constitution** of 1950 made it illegal to discriminate on grounds of caste; more importantly, caste is irrelevant to employment in the modern, industrial sector of the Indian economy. Nevertheless, some social disabilities remained, and many of the "Other Backward Castes" identified in the **Mandal Commission** Report for affirmative action are sudra in origin.

SUFI or SUFISM. This is the expression of mysticism within **Islam**. The Sufi belief in a mystical union between the individual soul and the Supreme Being emphasized love as the mediating principle of God's Will, in contrast to the orthodox, or Sunni, Islamic emphasis on the Koran, the law, and tradition. Sufis surfaced in the expanding Islamic world as early as the eighth century and, according to some scholars, were probably influenced by exposure to **Hindu** thinkers after the Arab conquest of Sindh in 732 CE. For example, the central idea of **Vedanta** *tat twam asi* or That Thou Art reappears in the cry of a noted Sufi, Al-Hallaj, as *ana-al-hagg* or I am the Divine Truth.

The traditional Indian *guru-chela*, or teacher–disciple, relationship also typified the organizational development of Sufis, with disciples gathered around an individual saintly master, known as *shaikh* or *pir*. These communities evolved rules of behavior, elaborated sacred texts, and by the 13th century developed into full-scale *tarigas*, or religious orders, in which Masters designated successors. Tombs of *pirs* or *shaikhs* frequently became shrines at which Muslims and non-Muslims alike worshipped and continue to do so today.

The Sufi influence in India was strengthened by the establishment of the **Chisti** order by Shaikh Muinuddin Chisti at the turn of the 12th and 13th centuries. His tomb in **Ajmer**, **Rajasthan**, is a holy place attracting pilgrims from all over the subcontinent and the world to the present day. His disciples and successors were influential in the **Delhi Sultanate** as also in the Mughal Empire; **Amir Khusru** was one of them, and the Emperor **Akbar** raised a memorial to another within Fatehpur Sikri. But the appeal of the Chisti saints was greatest among the common people of India, partly because Sufis emphasized care of the poor and needy as religious acts and enabled a flowering of devotional music, unusual within the Islamic tradition.

Three other Sufi orders were active in India and exerted different kinds of influence, mainly among Muslims. The Qalandar order reconsidered the moral law. The Suhrawardi order, founded by Bahauddin Zakariya of Multan in the 13th century, emphasized material wellbeing and family life. The Naqshbandi order originating in Central Asia was the most austere and strict in its reformist stance and was most active in the 17th century.

After the advent of Islam in India, Sufi *tarigas* were among the most easily accessible centers of devotional piety for the common people who were similarly attracted to **Bhakti** saints. The Sufis certainly helped to expand peacefully the boundaries of the Islamic world through Central Asia and the Indian subcontinent.

SUNDARJI, K (1930–1999). General Sundarji was a brilliant infantry soldier of the Mahar Regiment who was Chief of Army Staff from February 1986 to April 1988. A dynamic leader with a high profile and somewhat flamboyant personality, Sundarji was a controversial figure in ways that his predecessors had not been. Controversy arose partly because in each of his positions of command he had tried to push military and civilian organizations and personnel in the direction he urged at a pace faster than they could comfortably accommodate, and partly because some of the military decisions or operations with which he was closely associated were themselves politically controversial. Three examples from his tenure as Chief of Army Staff suffice to illustrate the point. One was the decision to purchase the Bofors Gun from Sweden. Sundarji later said that the Army had been made a scapegoat in the Bofors corruption scandal that marred the end of **Rajiv Gandhi**'s term as prime minister. Second, Sundarji and his senior staff officers master-minded Operation Brasstacks as the largest military exercise ever conducted close to India's western border in order to test and train the Indian Army for rapid mobility and coordination of action with the Indian Air Force; Operation Brasstacks precipitated a crisis with **Pakistan** in Spring 1987. A third controversial episode began later in 1987 when an Indian Peace Keeping Force (IPKF) was sent to **Sri Lanka** at the request of its then President Jayawardene who had signed an accord with Rajiv

Gandhi to try and end the civil war in the island country, without success. **V. P. Singh**'s government in New Delhi withdrew the IPKF in early 1990 on demand of a new government in Sri Lanka.

Sundarji deplored the absence of long-term defense planning in India and tried to introduce such planning and preparation for a new age of warfare. When commanding the College of Combat at Mhow in 1981 Sundarji drafted a minimum nuclear deterrence doctrine for India (perhaps in collaboration with his friend **Dr. Raja Ramanna**) and introduced ideas and methods of combating chemical and nuclear weapons to the senior officers training at the College. He consistently harped on the need of the **Indian Armed Forces** to prepare for Information Warfare and Cyberwar, but not all of his colleagues in uniform were as intellectually acute or scholastically inclined as he was. He also attempted to modernize the equipment and streamline the organization of formations in the Indian Army.

After retirement Sundarji continued to propound his strategic ideas on nuclear deterrence and other matters in intellectual as well as public venues. He published *Imperatives of Indian Minimum Deterrence* in 1991, and a cogent critique of Indian military–political complacency in a thinly veiled volume of fiction, *Blind Men of Hindoostan: The India–Pakistan Nuclear War* (1997). His most serious strategic work was posthumously published under his name as *Vision 2100: Strategy for the 21st Century*, in 2003.

SUPREME COURT. The 1950 **Constitution** established the Supreme Court as the apex court of an integrated Indian judicial system, replacing the Privy Council in London, which was the final court of appeal in British India. Composed of a Chief Justice and not more than 25 justices appointed by the President after consultation with the Chief Justice and serving to the age of 65, the Supreme Court usually sits in panels of three. It is the interpreter and guardian of the Constitution, having original and exclusive jurisdiction in disputes between the Union government and states and between two or more states. It has appellate jurisdiction in any civil or criminal case that involves a substantial question of law; it gives advisory opinions to the government on request; it has the power of judicial review over any law passed by parliament or state legislatures to determine its constitutionality and has held more than 100 such acts as invalid since 1950. Further, in its landmark decision on the *Kesavananda Bharati v. State of Kerala* case in 1973, the Supreme Court declared invalid any constitutional amendment that violates the "basic structure" of the Constitution. This doctrine facilitated the undoing of controversial constitutional amendments passed during the **Emergency** 1975–1977 and has helped to safeguard and extend fundamental rights and the rule of law in India. Following the dismissal of three **Bharatiya Janata Party** state governments after demolition of the Babri Masjid, the Supreme Court ruled in 1994 that secularism is part of the basic structure of the constitution and acts of state governments calculated to subvert secularism cannot be upheld.

The founders of the Indian Republic saw the judiciary as an independent and coequal institution, along with legislature and executive, working to advance national unity and integrity as well as social reform and economic development to improve living conditions for the people through parliamentary democracy and the rule of law. Although these strands are philosophically intertwined and mutually dependent with each other, the practice of government inevitably raised conflicts between different objectives and institutions. Clashes were notable between the justiciable Part III (Fundamental Rights) and the non-justiciable Part IV (Directive Principles) of the Constitution, as well as between national security interests and personal liberty and freedom of expression; the Supreme Court was thus pitted against parliament and the executive in many cases. For example, conflicts between legislative efforts to enact land reform and the Court's strict interpretation of the right to property guaranteed by Art 31 were frequent, not always conclusive, and sometimes had far reaching consequences, as when the Supreme Court's ruling in the famous Golaknath Case of 1967 presaged the "basic structure" doctrine limiting the scope of easy constitutional amendments. Prime Minister **Indira Gandhi**'s radical and centralizing legislative measures in the early and mid 1970s aroused judicial ire but not outright confrontation, partly perhaps because the President, on her advice, appointed A. N. Ray Chief Justice in 1973, superceding two more senior justices perceived as less compliant with actions taken in the name of "social justice." The convention of seniority in appointment of the chief justice was restored by the **Janata** government in 1978 and has been adhered to since then, despite the short terms resulting. (See Appendix D.)

The Supreme Court has become increasingly active since the early 1990s, especially in widening the arena of human rights, protecting the environment, and combating corruption. Instruments of such judicial activism include hearing cases originating in public interest litigation—of which there is a large number. The Supreme Court has ruled on behalf of bonded laborers, women, tribals, and other disadvantaged persons including those incarcerated for long periods while awaiting trial. It also has reinforced the independence of vigilance bodies such as the Central Bureau of Investigation in exposing corruption. Judicial activism inevitably generated opposition as well as reform efforts to tackle serious problems such as the shortage of judges and the overwhelming burden of pending unresolved cases running into the thousands. A problem of perceived politicization in the selection of high court judges in some states has surfaced despite the consultative role of the Chief Justice in the appointment process, and judges of the lower courts are not always credited with high standards of integrity and independence. Notwithstanding complaints, the judiciary still commands considerable respect in India. Recent public opinion polls show the Supreme Court, along with the **Election Commission**, enjoying the highest esteem among all state institutions.

SUR or SURI, SHER SHAH (1472–1545). Named Farid Khan at birth, he won the title Sher Khan as a youth when he killed a tiger unassisted and took the title Sher Shah when he ruled over Hindustan or northern India from 1539 to 1545. He was of Afghan descent and became a soldier of fortune first in the service of other Afghan chiefs of the Lohani clan and then, in 1527, with the new **Mughal** conqueror, **Babur**.

Babur rewarded Sher Khan's services by conferring on him his father's *jagir* (see Glossary) in Jaunpur, southern **Bihar** where he learned the art of managing property. Indeed, Sher Khan not only consolidated his power in Bihar by good administration but extended it eastward into **Bengal**, carving out a rich kingdom for himself that proved so strong that he forced Humayun, son of Babur, to retreat toward Iran. Having defeated Humayun in the battles of Chunar (1531) and Chaunsa (1539), Sher Khan reestablished Afghan power in **Delhi**, declared himself emperor, and proceeded to take Malwa and Bundelkhand, **Punjab**, Sindh and Multan, and finally Rajputana.

Even more impressive than his military exploits were Sher Shah's administrative measures that anticipated those of the great Mughal Emperor **Akbar**. Sher Shah maintained a strong central army loyal to him and paid in cash. He instituted a systematic method of surveying the land, assessing, and collecting a fair share in revenue directly from the collector that was subsequently used to good effect by **Todar Mal** in Akbar's reign. Sher Shah was known for his prompt and personal attention to justice, roads, trees, wells, and rest houses he had laid for post, travel, and trade, for his excellent coinage and for the order, safety, and religious tolerance that prevailed throughout his realm. The new city he had constructed at Delhi and his own mausoleum near Jaunpur illustrate his refined taste in architecture.

The young Akbar defeated the successors of Sher Shah at the second battle of **Panipat** in 1556, and the Sur dynasty gave way to the Mughal.

SURAT. Surat has been a major port on the west coast of India throughout historical times. Situated at the mouth of the Tapti river on the Gulf of Cambay, Surat was the main port of export for goods destined to the west—Arabia, Egypt, Europe, Iran, Turkey—from **Gujarat** as well as from the **Ganges** valley and central India and remains important today. Surat was and is also a point of disembarkation for Muslim pilgrims to Mecca from the Indian subcontinent and sometimes beyond.

The wealth and variety found in Surat was considerable, amply testified to by travelers of the medieval and early modern periods. Prosperity probably reached its height under the **Mughal Empire** in the 16th, 17th, and early18th centuries. European trading companies sought Mughal permission to operate from Surat, and the British **East India Company** was allowed to open a "factory" there in 1612. After defending Surat from Dutch and **Maratha** raids, the British took control of the city in 1759. Thereafter, Surat declined in importance as **Bombay** grew.

Surat featured prominently in the history of the **Indian National Congress** as the site of the December 1907 session when Congress split for the first time. The "Extremists" led by **Bal Gangadhar Tilak** were expelled and the "Moderates" led by **Gopal Krishna Gokhale**

came into ascendance. The port was revived after Indian independence and regained prosperity in the wake of India's flourishing
trade—both legal and extra-legal—with the Persian Gulf states. Surat
is a center of a labor-intensive diamond cutting and polishing industry, a focal point of the high technology industry of Gujarat, and the
location of 250,000 textile units alone.

Gujarat's impressive records of economic growth in recent
decades has been accompanied by social change and political strife,
reflected in Surat as elsewhere. Almost half of Surat's two million inhabitants was transient labor in the 1980s, most of it unorganized and
subject to frequent strife. In December 1992, Surat was the scene of
gruesome killings and other shameful acts of communal violence,
which resulted, among other things, in huge commercial losses. Co-
associational and inter-communal civic action has not entirely healed
the wounds, as was evident in the Gujarat riots of 2002.

SURVEY OF INDIA. The modern age of exploration demands accurate maps, and as the **East India Company** expanded its activities in
18th-century India it called for surveys and maps of the subcontinent.
The Survey of India was founded in 1767 with Major James Rennell
as the first Surveyor General. A great trigonometrical survey was
commenced from Cape Comorin in 1806. Sir George Everest completed it. He joined in 1818 and was Surveyor General from 1830 to
1843, and the highest mountain in the world, Chomolungma, was renamed after him in 1865. Geodetic observations made by the Survey
of India were, and are, of international significance because the Indian subcontinent lies between the highest mountains **(Himalaya)**
and the deepest oceans (off Antarctica) and shows a uniquely large
variation of gravity pull on the earth's crust.

The Survey of India has long been entrusted with all survey operations and preparation of topographical maps in high and low scales
including those required by the **Indian Army**, with publishing astronomical, magnetic, seismographic, and meteorological observations,
as well as with composing tide tables for the Indian Ocean between
Suez and Singapore. Since independence the Survey of India has
continued its topographical map coverage with updated technologies
and completed some of them. It has determined and depicted the external boundaries of India as well as advised on the demarcation of

internal state boundaries, deployed its expertise for various developmental projects including irrigation, and provided basic data for special enterprises such as the Indian Scientific Expedition to Antarctica. The Survey of India also provides education, support, and training in surveying techniques to persons from neighboring countries under bilateral arrangements.

The geological mapping of the subcontinent was entrusted to the Geological Survey of India established in Calcutta in 1851. This organization now has a network of offices and laboratories all over the country and employs 2,900 geo-scientists. It holds the key to further mineral exploration and imparts training in the earth sciences. It has completed the systematic geological mapping of India on a 1:50,000 scale and covered most of India's Exclusive Economic Zone by seabed surveys, but is neither part of nor competitive with the Survey of India.

SWADESHI MOVEMENT. Swadeshi means, literally, "of one's own country." Thus, boycott of British goods sold in India was the core of this early-20th-century movement. It erupted as part of the nationalist protest against the 1905 **partition of Bengal** and exerted powerful appeal in that province where meetings, demonstrations, boycotts of shops selling British goods, public burnings of cloth, and labor strikes were used as instruments of mass mobilization. Luminaries such as **Aurobindo Ghose** were among the leaders of this movement. The British government put it down with great severity, labeling it "extremist" and its participants "terrorists." Under police repression the movement gave way to individual acts of violence against the state and vocal opposition to the Bengal partition, which was annulled in 1911.

The Swadeshi movement, which reached its height between 1905 and 1908, was not accompanied by concrete economic programs to raise the productivity or purchasing power of the Indian peasant and remained only a mass demonstration of opposition to British rule, especially in Bengal. Nor did it last beyond 1911. Nevertheless, it occupies a notable place in the history of the Indian national movement, partly because it spawned an abundant literature of official papers, biographies, and memoirs. Moreover, the core concept of *swadeshi*, that is, primarily using goods produced close at home and limiting one's demands and consumption, was subsequently woven into the philosophy of self-reliant, self-governing, self-sustaining Indian economic and political development put forward by **Mahatma Gandhi**.

SWAMINATHAN, M. S. (1925–). He is a renowned agricultural scientist who was the first Indian to be elected president of the Pugwash Conferences of Science and World Affairs in 2002. Swaminathan was born in a **Tamil Brahman** family and studied at the Coimbatore Agricultural College, the Indian Agricultural Research Institute and Cambridge University to become a pioneering agricultural geneticist. He was one of the creators of India's **Green Revolution** by which high yielding varieties of wheat and rice elevated India from a food–grain deficit to a food–grain surplus country. Swaminathan believed in eco-friendly methods of increasing productivity and is acknowledged as a world leader in sustainable agriculture; he was awarded the first World Food Prize in 1987. He received many other awards from Indian and international bodies, filled important positions inside and outside India, and founded M. S. Swaminathan Research Foundation in 1988 to advance the use eco-technology in agricultural communities around the world. *Time Magazine* in 199 acclaimed him as one of the 20 most influential Asians of the 20th century.

SWARAJ PARTY. C. R. Das formed the Swaraj Party in December 1922 from those who had joined the **Indian National Congress** because they wanted a representative and responsible form of government in India but opposed the mass based **Non-Cooperation Movement** of 1920–1922. Instead, the Swaraj Party advocated contesting elections in order to gain access to legislative power, cooperating with the British Government of India for the purpose of implementing the **Montagu–Chelmsford Reforms**, and fighting from the inside to speedily gain **Dominion Status** for India.

Members of the Swaraj Party tended to be drawn from the professional and upper middle class and included several influential men, such as **Motilal Nehru**, **Madan Mohan Malaviya**, and M. R. Jayakar, besides C. R. Das. They were active in **Bengal, Bombay**, and the Central Legislative Assembly and contributed to the All Party Conference of 1927. Their political stance was middle of the road.

They opposed communism and were secular to the extent of cooperating with **Mohammed Ali Jinnah** on some issues, but were unable to fight the cancer of communalism that erupted in the mid-1920s. The party split in 1926 with some members joining the **Hindu Mahasabha** and others rejoining Congress.

Dr. Ansari of **Delhi** and Dr. B. C. Roy of **Calcutta** revived the Swaraj Party in the 1930s with the object of entering legislatures. A hundred men contested the 1937 provincial elections as part of the Congress.

SWATANTRA PARTY. This **political party** was founded in 1959 as a secular, conservative opposition to the ruling **Congress Party** and its "socialistic" platform announced in 1955. C. **Rajagopalachari** was one founder member; others were mainly industrialists, wealthy farmers, and former princes. They focused their opposition on the economic policies of Congress, especially state planning and management of heavy industry, and advocated a more pro-American foreign policy than that of **Nonalignment**.

For a time in the mid-1960s, after the death of **Jawaharlal Nehru**, the Swatantra Party seemed to offer a viable, non-communal alternative to Congress. But its candidates suffered massive defeat in the general and state elections of 1971 and 1972, and by the middle of that decade the party was defunct, with some members absorbed into the **Lok Dal**.

SYED or SAYYID AHMAD KHAN (1817–1898). Born at **Delhi** in a family that had served the **Mughals** in high positions for successive generations, Syed grappled in his lifetime with the problems facing the Muslim aristocracy in an age of British dominion in India. As is evident in his career as much as in his many Urdu publications, Syed's approach to solving these problems was to accept British rule as both inevitable and desirable for India, to offer it loyalty and cooperation rather than resistance or opposition, and to raise the competitive ability and status of the Indian Muslim community through education. He favored an education offering English and modern science but also reinforcing **Islamic** culture and identity.

In 1838 Syed Ahmad Khan chose to serve the **East India Company** as a petty judicial officer rather than resting on the hereditary titles bestowed on him by the titular **Emperor Bahadur Shah II**. Lacking a systematic or formal education, Syed began to write and study on his own. His *Athar al Sanadid*, an archaeological survey of Delhi, was published in 1847 and subsequently translated into English and French. He edited **Abu'l Fazl**'s magisterial *Ain-i Akbari*. He then wrote *Causes of the Indian Mutiny* on the basis of his experiences in the **Uprising of 1857**. Thereafter, he dedicated himself to educating his community and promoting favorable understanding of the Muslims among the British. While in the judicial service—from which he retired in 1878—Syed established English medium schools at Moradabad and Ghazipur in the 1860s and started a bilingual (English–Urdu) weekly.

Syed Ahmad worked long and hard to open the Muhammadan Anglo–Oriental College at Aligarh in 1875 with Theodore Beck of Cambridge as Principal. By the end of the century this institution had become the heart of higher education and political awareness for Indian Muslims. It gained its present-day status as Aligarh Muslim University in 1920. Syed's contributions to modern Indian history rest more, perhaps, on this institution and the **Aligarh Movement** named after it than on any other single event of his life. He was a Nominated Member of the Viceroy's Executive Council from 1878–1886, the (Butler) Educational Commission of 1882, and the Public Service Commission of 1886; he was knighted in 1888.

Syed Ahmad Khan's responses to events were molded by his concern for improving the prospects of the Muslim community in British India, especially after the Uprising of 1857 and consequent penalization of upper class Muslims by the British. A generation after **Ram Mobun Roy** and others revivified upper caste **Hindus** through social reform and modern education, Syed sought to wean upper class Muslims from indolence or obscurantism through similar means. He too aroused the ire of the orthodox and traditionalists among his community by his praise of certain Western (that is, Christian) ways. He formed the (Muslim) Educational Conference in 1886, advocating reform through loyalist associations and eschewing agitational politics. He was alarmed by the demands for Indianization in the civil services and elected representation in government raised by the **Indian National Congress** formed in 1885, for fear that Muslims would not be able to compete equally with Hindus in a democratic political system. Further, he forbade his followers to join Congress and criticized another Muslim, **Badruddin Tyabji**, for becoming the third President of what was fast emerging as the premier vehicle of Indian nationalism.

Although some criticize—or credit—Syed Ahmad Khan for laying the seeds of a separatist **Pakistan** movement, his view of India as a conglomerate of different communities who could and should be friendly and supportive without being homogenized was not necessarily a divisive one; nor was it unusual for his times. He saw India as a beautiful bride blessed by two attractive eyes—the Hindus and the Muslims—whose enmity would make her cross-eyed and whose hypocritical fusion could make her one-eyed. His advocacy of education and self-advancement for Muslims, therefore, did not imply enmity toward Hindus. Some explain his opposition to representative institutions and political activity as a reflection of his aristocratic background. His appeal went to upper class, mainly landowning, Muslims; he neither trusted nor received support from peasants and had little to do with the new commercial and professional classes in India, Hindu or Muslim, in whose hands the future lay.

– T –

TAGORE, DWARKANATH (1794–1846). A **brahman** landowner of east **Bengal**, Dwarkanath prospered in association with the **East India Company** in the late 18th and early 19th centuries. He became an entrepreneur and merchant prince par excellence, founding banks, heading coal and tea businesses, and owning or managing silk and sugar factories, indigo plantations, and a fleet of ocean-going steamboats. His estates were extensive and he had a large family. His sons, including Debendranath who became a leader of the **Brahmo Samaj**, grandsons, including **Rabindranath Tagore**, and other family members, both male and female, went on to distinguish themselves in various professions.

Dwarkanath enjoyed the courtesy title of Raja (see Glossary) as did his older friend, **Ram Mohun Roy**. Both were wealthy and actively promoted education and social reform among high **caste Hindus**. They were instrumental in having the practice of **sati** banned by law in 1829. Tagore gave his support to the founding of Hindu College in **Calcutta** in 1817 as well as a Medical College in the city soon after, openly advocating modern education in the English language for young men. He was also a patron of the leading journals of Calcutta and pressed hard to obtain freedom of the Indian **press**; acting Governor General **Charles Metcalfe** relaxed some restrictions in 1838. Tagore had many European friends and was warmly welcomed in England during his one journey to that country in 1842. His boundless energy and benevolence was carried forward by his family, which became one of the best known of the Bengal *bhadralok* (see Glossary), or gentry.

TAGORE, RABINDRANATH (1861–1941). The grandson of **Dwarkanath Tagore**, Rabindranath was the youngest of 14 children born to Sharada Devi and Debendranath (1817–1905), leader of the **Brahmo Samaj**. Rabindranath's lively imagination was fed in the haphazard schooling of a not altogether happy childhood and by the natural beauty, music, songs, and folk tales of rural east **Bengal**. He managed the family estates in Rajshahi district of east Bengal for the decade of the 1890s and never lost his love for the area. He published his first poem in Bengali at the age of 12 and a collection of stories and letters soon after. He continued to be a prolific writer of poems, plays, short stories, songs, novels, and essays throughout his long life. His elder brother, Jyotirindranath, was a well-known playwright and translator who, along with his wife Kadambari Devi, took on the guardianship of 14-year-old Rabindranath when their mother died. Kadambari Devi's suicide in 1884 left a lasting scar on the sensitive young man whose first collection of songs was published a year later. Many of them continue to be sung to the present day in India and **Bangladesh**.

By 1890 Rabindranath had entered a new phase of writing, which included taking stands on controversial political and social issues. He advocated election of members of the Viceroy's Executive Council, self-help through village communities, and education in the mother tongue rather than the English language. Belonging as he did to one of the leading families in the social reform movement of 19th century India, Rabindranath was predictably in favor of the emancipation and education of **women**. From managing the family magazine for young people, *Balak*, he went on to edit the monthly *Sadhana* as a vehicle for self-expression and published stories weekly in *Hitavadi*. One of his best-known short stories, "The Postmaster," dates from this time. He became convinced that the root of what was called "the Indian problem" (weakness and decay) lay in faulty education. In 1901 he founded a home school where learning would be inculcated in a free and loving community. He named it Shantiniketan and established a public trust for its maintenance. **Mohandas Gandhi**—whom Tagore was the first to call Mahatma—spent some time there on his return from South Africa in 1915 and urged students and teachers to engage in physical activity for self-help. In 1918 the school was raised to university level and renamed Vishva Bharati, World University; it remains a unique center of study today.

Rabindranath lost his wife in 1902, his father in 1905, and coped with other disasters; writing was his main outlet of expression. He opposed the **partition of Bengal** and preached constructive nationalism based on *swadeshi* (see Glossary) and self-reliant village communities. He sent his eldest son to study Agriculture in the United States and, in keeping with his reformist principles, arranged a marriage for him with a young widow on his return in 1910. Rabindranath was a public figure by the time he sailed for England in 1912. He had already published his famous novel, *Gora*, and his equally famous essay, "My Interpretation of Indian History." A verse paraphrase of this essay, which celebrated India's unity in diversity, subsequently became the National Anthem of independent India, "*Jana Gana Mana*." (Another Tagore song was later adopted as the National Anthem of Bangladesh.) During the long voyage Tagore translated some of his poems from Bengali to English, and they were published with the help of his friend William Butler Yeats under the title **Gitanjali**. Tagore won the Nobel Prize for Literature in 1913, the first Asian to be so honored.

Tagore met **C. F. Andrews** in England before proceeding on a lecture tour of the United States, Japan, and China; he also raised funds for Shantineketan. His 1915 novel, *Gharer Baire* (*The Home and the World*), contains some of his reflections on this experience. Tagore received a knighthood in 1914, but returned it in 1919 as protest against the massacre at **Jallianwala Bagh**. During the 1920s and 1930s, Tagore toured Iran, Egypt, Europe, North and South America, Japan, and China. His lectures generally were on a high philosophical plane and not well received by members of the new Chinese Communist Party at Peking University. Tagore established the reputation of Vishwa Bharati during his travels and delivered the Hibbert Memorial Lectures at Oxford University on "The Religion of Man" in 1932. He experimented with literary styles and also took up music and painting, not hesitating to exhibit his unusual artistic endeavors in old age. With his broad vision, established eminence, and personal eccentricities, Tagore was not always in tune with the tactical demands of the Indian freedom movement as led by Gandhi and the **Indian National Congress**. His own nationalistic fervor was above question, and all new leaders sought his blessings. Tagore's great contribution to Bengali literature and modern India is universally recognized.

TAJ MAHAL. The Taj Mahal at **Agra** is one of the most famous buildings in the world. It was built by the **Mughal Emperor Shah Jahan** as a tomb for his wife, Mumtaz Mahal, who died in 1631. Contemporary documents of the Mughal court show that Shah Jahan himself played an active role in shaping the design and situating it on land donated by Raja Jai Singh of Amber, for which the latter received four other estates in compensation. The chief architect was Ustad Ahmad Lahori, an engineer and astronomer who also designed the Red Fort in **Delhi** as the administrative and ceremonial center of the empire. Amanat Khan, a learned calligrapher of Persian origin who had already worked on the tomb of the emperor's grandfather, **Akbar**, was responsible for the marble inlaid Koranic texts and the imagery of Paradise on the day of resurrection characterizing the Taj Mahal.

The Taj Mahal is a complex of buildings and formal gardens set on a rectangular grid 365 meters by 958 meters. The tomb itself, with its 85-meter high dome and four minarets, is placed at one end, not at the center as conventional at the time. An elevated terrace 341 meters long and 128 meters wide overlooks the **Yamuna** River flowing by; cylindrical wells set in the foundations precluded flood damage. Some 230 cartloads of marble from nine districts in **Rajasthan** were used as facing for the mausoleum and its dome. All structural work was completed by 1637. Although detailed records of daily accounts have not been discovered as yet, court papers show 50 lakhs (see Glossary) or Rs. 5,000,000 as the cost of construction.

The Taj Mahal has drawn visitors from all parts of the world and inspired their responses in music, prose, and poetry for more than 300 years. It has also attracted plunderers who removed the gold and precious stones with which it was originally ornamented. Many legends, exaggerations, and even falsehoods found their way into travelers' accounts since the 17th century and especially in those written by Persians or Europeans in the 19th century. Recent scholarship provides greater authenticity for names and figures. Recent neglect and air pollution, however, have damaged marble surfaces so that entrance is now restricted and **Mayawati**'s alleged mishandling of restoration funds when she was chief minister of **Uttar Pradesh** is much criticized.

The Taj Mahal was the logical culmination of a Mughal architectural tradition that had earlier produced the outstanding but more austere Humayun's tomb in Delhi. Also known as the Illumined Tomb and replete with sacred imagery, the Taj Mahal combines massive scale with bold engineering and formal elegance, so that the totality presents a coordinated design of flawless visual beauty and symmetry.

TAMIL. The oldest among a family of **Dravidian** languages with a grammar, script, and form created independently of **Sanskrit**, the Tamil **language** is noted for its retroflexed consonants, its rich literature in prose and poetry, and is the vehicle for powerful oratory.

Early Tamil texts date from the third century BCE as also cave inscriptions by **Buddhists** and **Jains**. The Sangam period of classical Tamil literature, lasting from the first century BCE to the sixth century CE, produced a body of bardic and epic poetry as well as other major works. Some of these texts designate the area where Tamil was spoken as Kural but also use the term **Tamil Nadu**, which is the present name of the state having Tamil as the principal language. Since very early times Tamil was open to Sanskrit influences carried by proponents of **Vedic** religion as well as the learning of Buddhists and Jains. Such influences were intensified under the rule of the **Pallava Dynasty** in the sixth century, although a Tamil resurgence found a potent vehicle in the devotional hymns of **Shiva** worshipping or Saivite saints about the same time.

Another resurgence of Tamil has taken place in the 20th century, in part as a consequence of a Dravida movement rejecting **brahman** and north Indian dominance and seeking to "purify" the Tamil language of excessive Sanskrit influence. Tamil speakers refused to accept any imposition of Hindi as a single national language; a political crisis on this issue erupted in the mid-1960s but was peaceably resolved with the adoption of a tri-language formula for schools. Tamil has influenced other Dravidian languages and is the principal language of the Tamil people of **Sri Lanka** as well. The Tamil **film industry** thrives in contemporary India and has been the launching pad for several political leaders.

TAMIL NADU. A large state of southernmost India, Tamil Nadu takes its name from the **language, Tamil**, spoken by 90% of its approximately 62 million inhabitants. **Madras**, renamed **Chennai** is the capital city. Tamil Nadu has 720 kilometers of coastline on the Bay of Bengal with Chennai and Tuticorin as the main ports and several lesser ports catering to coastal trade. The government has made investment in improving the infrastructure of port facilities a high priority in the last decade. The **Nilgiris** are highlands in the eastern part of the state. Agriculture is the mainstay for most of the population, with the fertile valley and delta of the **Kaveri River** giving a high yield per hectare of rice, sugar cane, groundnuts, and other crops. Industry is relatively well developed in Tamil Nadu, which is about 40% urban according to the 2001 **Census**, and the state is an important exporter of cotton textiles, leather goods, automobile parts, and engineering products. Its rates of literacy, rural electrification, and overall economic development are at the higher end of the national index, comparable to those of **Punjab** and **Maharashtra**. Water shortage is a chronic problem in Tamil Nadu, exacerbated by an unresolved dispute with **Karnataka** over distribution of Kaveri waters that has been unresolved for more than a hundred years.

The history of Tamil Nadu is a long and checkered one. It is mentioned in the edicts of **Ashoka** in the third century BCE, and some early Tamil texts designate the area Kural. Three dynasties—the Cheras, **Pandyas**, and **Cholas**—ruled most of peninsular India for long periods of time, although the political and territorial jurisdictions of each fluctuated. The **Pallava** and Chola Dynasties of the early medieval period expanded their domain over areas larger than present-day Tamil Nadu, as did the Telugu rulers of the **Vijayanagar**

Empire of the 14th to 16th centuries. With the defeat of the latter at the battle of Talikota in 1565, several successor states emerged. Notable among them were **Madurai** and Tanjavur, or **Tanjore**, known for their magnificent temples with the high and ornamented *gopurams* distinctive of the **Dravidian** style of temple architecture.

European trading companies established outposts on the Coromandel coast with the British fortifying Madras and the French making **Pondicherry** their headquarters in the late 17th century. Anglo–French rivalries injected into existing territorial conflicts between various Muslim rulers and the **Marathas** in the **Deccan**, as well as the peninsula in the 18th century, led to series of wars in which the British emerged triumphant by 1800. Recent historiography has underlined an early and symbiotic relationship between the British and various Indian elite groups that helped give Madras Presidency its reputation for good administration and civic order. However, its economic ailments, of which famine was one symptom, were many; it was from Madras that Tamil labor was exported to work on sugar, tea, and rubber plantations in different parts of the British Empire, especially South Africa, **Ceylon**, and Malaya. Their problems as indentured labor and beleaguered minorities attracted attention before as well as after Indian independence.

Madras incorporated much of southern India in the 19th and first half of the 20th centuries. Political consciousness there paralleled the growth of nationalism in other parts of British India although it sometimes took form in movements and **political parties** unique to Madras, such as the **Justice Party** and the **Dravida Munnetra Kazhagam (DMK)**. Agitation in the Telugu-speaking districts of Madras for a separate state commenced soon after independence and led to the formation of **Andhra Pradesh** in 1956. During the reorganization of states along linguistic lines Kannada-speaking districts were transferred to Karnataka and Malayallum-speaking districts to **Kerala**. Madras was left substantially reduced in size but relatively homogenous. One political expression of Tamil self-esteem was the DMK's victory over the **Congress Party** in the 1967 state elections. Madras was renamed Tamil Nadu in 1969.

During the 1980s and early 1990s, Tamil Nadu was directly affected by ethnic strife in neighboring **Sri Lanka**, the presence of large numbers of Tamil refugees from that island, and the activities of the Liberation Tigers of Tamil Eelam (LTTE) subsequently declared a **terrorist** organization. The government of Tamil Nadu and Tamil Nadu members of the **Lok Sabha** also influenced New Delhi's policies toward Sri Lanka. Political power in Tamil Nadu has more or less alternated between the DMK and its rival, the All India Anna DMK, each of which has allied with the ruling coalitions in New Delhi and held important Cabinet portfolios.

TANJORE or THANJAVUR. A city situated in the rich, rice-growing, delta of the **Kaveri** River, Tanjore (now spelled Thanjavur) was the **Chola** capital between the ninth and 11th centuries CE. It continued to be an important urban center under **Vijayanagar** and **Maratha** rule, as also in the British period, and is the headquarters of a wealthy district in the present-day state of **Tamil Nadu.**

The Brihadishvara temple to **Shiva** in Tanjore is one of the major religious edifices constructed in southern India during the medieval age. Handicrafts including metal work, textile weaving, and the production of musical instruments continue to thrive at Tanjore. Newer agro-industries have emerged to process the rice, sugar, and groundnuts produced nearby.

TANTRA. A term derived from the **Sanskrit** root *tan*, meaning to stretch, to extend, brackets a number of beliefs and rituals. In popular religion the term denotes occult powers derived from esoteric disciplines and magical and/or erotic practices. The learned purport of Tantra is different. It denotes a path to *moksha* (see Glossary), or spiritual liberation from the cycle of birth and death, that, if successful, is faster than more traditional methods; the path is fraught with psychological and physical danger to a practitioner lacking proper instruction and guidance.

Tantric techniques of contemplation have been imparted over the generations through elaborate, exacting, and often enigmatic or secret texts. They stress control of speech, mind, and body and eschew hierarchical notions of **caste**, gender, and ritual purity accepted by the majority of **Hindus** or **Buddhists**. Tantrics ritualize the ingestion of otherwise forbidden meats, liquor, and cannabis and the union of unmarried males and females. The dominant philosophy of Tantra is non-dualism with a strong emphasis on identity of male and female in the Absolute. Aids to contemplation, such as painted *thankas*, frequently use female or sexual symbolism.

Tantra probably evolved from earlier cults of **Shiva** or Shakti (see Glossary) and reached highly sophisticated levels in the Vajrayana Buddhism of **Tibet** and neighboring areas. Tantrics were often feared or rejected by the mainstream of modern Indian society. From time to time, as in early-20th-century **Bengal**, social or political revolutionaries aspired to sanctify their cause through Tantric practice, giving cause for governments to ban such activities.

TARA SINGH (1885–1967). Tara Singh was born in Rawalpindi district of **Punjab** to a village *patwari* (see Glossary). He became a **Sikh** at the age of 17 and joined the Khalsa College (primarily for Sikhs) at **Amritsar**, having graduated from a Christian mission school. He became a schoolteacher and then Head Master of a new Khalsa School at Lyallpur and was addressed as "master" until the end of his life. He helped establish the Khalsa College in **Bombay** and the Guru Nanak Engineering College at Ludhiana.

Tara Singh joined the Gurudwara Reform Movement led by the **Akali Dal** and took an active political role as spokesman of the Sikhs as a distinct community in India. As such, he criticized the **Nehru Report** of 1928 for paying insufficient attention to minority problems but supported **Mahatma Gandhi** and the 1930 Resolution of the **Indian National Congress** calling for *purna swaraj* or full independence. He led the Akali Dal during the 1937 provincial elections and insisted on the inclusion of a Sikh (Baldev Singh) in the consequent **Unionist Party** government of the Punjab.

Sir Stafford Cripps discussed the possible postwar political configuration of India in 1942 with three Sikh representatives, of whom Tara Singh was one. He rejected the idea of partitioning India between Hindu-majority and Muslim-majority areas and countered the demand for **Pakistan** put forward by the **All-India Muslim League** with various proposals designed to protect Sikhs from the domination of any other single community. Over the next five years he suggested either a large, more or less autonomous Punjab in which Hindus, Muslims, and Sikhs would be fairly evenly balanced or a divided Punjab in which only those districts predominantly Muslim in population would be given the option of leaving India. He also suggested that the central and eastern portions of the Punjab—which constituted a "de facto Sikh homeland" by virtue of culture and sacred sites— exchange populations peacefully with other districts and be made into a separate, autonomous Sikh state. Tara Singh was among those who signed a detailed (but ineffective) Sikh Memorandum after **Lord Mountbatten**'s June 3, 1947, announcement of imminent **Partition**, explaining how detrimental this would be to Sikhs straddling both sides of a border.

Tara Singh continued his efforts to establish a Sikh majority state after the Partition and independence of India. He led a non-violent movement for a Punjabi-speaking state within India and fasted for 43 days toward that end in 1961. His demands were rejected as "communal" by New Delhi, and leadership of the Akali Dal passed to other hands. In 1966 the boundaries of Punjab were redrawn, giving the Sikhs a slight majority in it, with Punjabi as its official language.

TASHKENT AGREEMENT. This accord of January 10, 1966, was signed between Indian Prime Minister **Lal Bahadur Shastri** and **Pakistan**'s President Ayub Khan in the wake of the Indo–Pakistan War of September 1965, which had ended in a ceasefire. Soviet President Alexis Kosygin lent his good offices and invited both leaders to the Central Asian city of Tashkent to discuss an easing of tensions. India and Pakistan agreed to restore diplomatic relations, withdraw their forces to pre-war positions, and settle their disputes peacefully. Shastri's sudden death at Tashkent within hours of his diplomatic success and the return of his body to New Delhi for funeral rites lent greater drama and importance to the agreement than its modest provisions perhaps deserved.

TATA. The Tata family ranks among the premier, outstanding entrepreneurial families of modern India whose name has been prominent in the fields of aviation, industry, science, and philanthropy since the late 19th century. The Tatas have been pioneers among forward-looking and multifaceted business corporations operating inside and outside India. Tata Enterprises presently comprises 85 companies that account for about five per cent of India's exports and more than 2% of India's gross domestic product. Tata's reputation for high standards of ethics and performance was established early and remains untarnished. A high percentage of the profits of Tata companies are channeled back to the Indian people through major philanthropic trusts, national training and other institutions, and the endowment of annual scholarships for advanced courses and higher education. Tata's concept of trusteeship in management is transmitted to new generations through the Tata Management Training Centre in **Pune**.

Founder of the family enterprises Jamsetji Nasarwanji Tata (1839–1904) was born in a **Zoroastrian**, or **Parsi** family, and educated at Elphinstone College, **Bombay**. As a trader on the cotton market he made and lost a fortune during the American Civil War of the 1860s. He subsequently opened a cotton textile mill in the unpromising central Indian city of Nagpur. This successful venture enabled him to expand his textile production throughout western India. He also introduced sericulture and the use of hydroelectric power in his factories, with multiplier effects. Jamsetji Tata established India's first integrated, modern steel factory in **Bihar**, close to sources of both iron and coal; the new town that sprang up after 1907 took on his name and is known both as Jamshedpur and Tatanagar. Anticipating the need for Indian scientists, he and his sons, Sir Dorab Tata and Sir Ratan Tata, endowed the Indian Institute of Science in Bangalore for fundamental research and advanced scientific training, which continues to be a premier institution in Asia.

J. R. D. Tata (1904–1994) inherited most of his grandfather Jamsetji's industrial empire but began as a pioneer in aviation. He was the first Indian pilot to qualify for a British private license in the 1920s, flew his own airplane long distances until late in his life, and founded an airline in 1932 that became known as Indian Airlines in 1953. Until 1978, J. R. D. Tata was Chairman of the state-owned Indian Airlines and international flag carrier, Air India. His innovations in India's fledgling hotel and tourist industry as well as his contributions to scientific and technical research and corporate management gained public recognition from the Indian government. Privately, J. R. D. enjoyed the friendship of **Jawaharlal Nehru** and **Indira Gandhi** among many other public figures, especially in India and Europe, where he spent many years as a youth.

The Tata family of industries spans textiles, chemicals, fertilizers, tea, hotels and travel, steel, hydroelectric power generation, locomotives, automobiles and commercial vehicles, consumer goods, information technology, publishing, management consultancy and training, and finance. The many companies passed under the executive chairmanship of Ratan Naval Tata (1928–) in 1991. He retired to a non-executive position in 2002 similar to the one held by J. R. D. Tata, and a Group Executive Office was expanded to fill the top management slot and probably provide a single successor in 2007. Tata Enterprises are active in Africa, Central and South Asia, America, and Europe and have been ranked by Forbes among leading world multinational corporations.

TATYA TOPE or TANTIA TOPI (1814–1859). This was the popular name of Ramchandra Pandurang, a retainer of the **Peshwa** Baji Rao II. Tatya Tope became famous for his exploits during the great **Uprising** or **Mutiny of 1857** after British forces defeated **Nana Saheb** at Kanpur (Cawnpore). Tatya Tope tried, but failed, to recapture Kanpur. He took Gwalior fort, encouraged **Rani Lakshmi Bai** of Jhansi, and called on the **Marathas** from all over the **Deccan** to rally against the British. He and his small army used guerilla tactics against superior British forces, avoiding direct combat and evading pursuit. He was eventually captured, tried, and hanged in April 1859.

TAXILA. The ancient capital of **Gandhara**, Taxila was a flourishing city from the sixth century BCE to the fifth or sixth century CE. It stood at one end of a transcontinental highway from **Pataliputra** in the southeast and at a mart of the **Silk Road** crossing Central Asia. For a thousand years Taxila connected the rich Indo–Gangetic plains of India with China as well as Asia Minor, Iran, and Europe.

Taxila was a center of learning renowned throughout the ancient **Buddhist** world and large numbers of monks inhabited its many monasteries. It figures in the literature of the **Mauryan, Kushan**, and **Gupta** Empires as a rich and cultured city. Taxila stone was the raw material for large numbers of sculptures, especially in the Gandhara style, and the monuments and buildings excavated there display high standards of art and architecture.

Standing as it did at the gateway of the Indian subcontinent, 32 kilometers northwest of present-day **Pakistan**'s capital Islamabad, Taxila was vulnerable to plundering invaders. Its fortunes declined after the destruction wrought by the **Hunas** in the fourth and fifth centuries CE and never fully recovered thereafter. Some archaeological work was undertaken in the first part of the 20th century and revealed evidence of successive and adjacent cities. Many conjectured sites over a large area, however, still remain unexplored in Taxila.

TEBHAGA MOVEMENT. A peasant struggle led by the *kisan sabha* and some members of the **Communist Party of India** erupted in the northern districts of **Bengal** from September 1946 to March 1947. Tebhaga means, literally, two-thirds; the objective of this mass struggle was to obtain two-thirds of the crop for use of the sharecroppers or poor peasants cultivating land belonging to *jotedars* and other intermediaries or landowners accustomed to taking half or more of the crop for themselves.

Large numbers of **Hindu** and **Muslim** peasants participated in the struggle alongside tribal groups. But without arms or support from urban and professional groups, the strugglers were not able to withstand police action in behalf of the *jotedars* against them in which many were killed. The momentum and the unity of the Tebhaga movement broke, although its major demands, including abolition of *zamindari*, were incorporated in legislation of 1950.

TEHELKA. A very small dot-com company specializing in investigative journalism nearly brought down the National Democratic Alliance (NDA) coalition Government of India led by the **Bharatiya Janata Party (BJP)** in March 2001. Founded by Tarun Jit Tejpal on a small budget but with the backing of such luminaries as **Amitabh Bachchan** and **Khushwant Singh**, Tehelka.com equipped itself with spy cameras and tape recorders and established a fictitious arms supply company called West End International in the summer of 2000. It then launched a sting operation to reveal corruption in the official defense equipment purchasing process from clerical levels upward. In early March 2001 **Delhi** was rocked by **television** broadcasts selected from 270 hours of videotape showing various people, including then BJP President Bangaru Laxman, Samata Party leader Jaya Jaitley in the home of Defence Minister **George Fernandes**, and some military officers, accepting cash from supposed arms dealers.

Parliament was in uproar, with the **Congress Party** in opposition calling for resignation of the government. George Fernandes voluntarily resigned his Cabinet post (and was later reinstalled as innocent),

Bangaru Laxman was replaced amidst his protests of **caste** discrimination, and the powerful National Security Adviser Brijesh Mishra immediately called a press conference to ward off attacks against the Prime Minister's Office and Prime Minister **Atal Behari Vajpayee**. The Tehelka scandal seriously damaged the reputation and credibility of the NDA and the BJP, which had been sanctimoniously critical of alleged Congress corruption earlier, and unloosed factional infighting within the NDA. The revelations about the Ministry of Defence came even as major reforms were being drafted to make the procurement process more speedy and transparent and may well have helped reform, although modernization efforts and proposals to privatize public sector units producing defense items were certainly delayed.

Immediate retaliation against Tehelka.com took the form of lawsuits against individual journalists and a whispering campaign against the company raising questions about its funding sources, its journalistic ethics in using entrapment, as well as the authenticity of the tapes. Other journalists and public figures were very cautious in praising Tejpal, his methods, or his staff. Only in 2004 did the **Supreme Court** respond to Tejpal's demand for compensation by declaring the tapes genuine and granting bail to journalist Kumar Badal. Reader supported Tehelka.com, self-styled "the people's paper," reopened business online.

TELENGANA MOVEMENT. This was an armed agrarian revolt led by members of the **Communist Party of India** against the Nizam's government of **Hyderabad** beginning in July 1946. The goals of this "liberation movement" included distribution of fallow land to agricultural laborers, security of tenure and reduction of rent for cultivators, guarantee of minimum wages for land workers, and especially the stoppage of forced labor and payments in kind from lower **caste** and **Adivasi** peasants. The CPI had built a strong base in the Telengana area of present day **Andhra Pradesh** during **World War II**. It organized peasants in village councils, collected arms, and attempted to build a "united front" of four classes against the Nizam's repressive regime that aimed for independence when British **paramountcy** lapsed.

An uprising in Nalgonda district spread into a well-organized guerilla movement encompassing about 3,000 villages over 41,000 square kilometers in the first part of 1948. Railway services through the state of Hyderabad were disrupted and some revenue and rent records were destroyed. Some of the agrarian goals obtained in liberated areas subsequently became permanent features. In September 1948 the government of independent India launched a "police action" against the Nizam's predatory army of *Razakars*. After the ensuing accession of Hyderabad to India the Telengana guerillas lost the support of prosperous farmers; nor did they receive full CPI endorsement to carry the movement further in the face of energetic military action. Some groups of rebels continued in sporadic acts of violence and retained grassroots support for many years. By 1951 the Telengana movement had been crushed, although the grievances of the peasants and small farmers in that impoverished region had not been redressed.

TELEVISION (TV). Television is now the greatest vehicle for mass education and for popular entertainment, rivaling the **film industry**. TV was introduced in **Delhi** in 1959 and spread to all other state capital cities by 1972. The official network, Doordarshan, with 19 channels, 40 centers, and programs in 12 **languages** transmitted through three satellites and 900 terrestrial transmitters had a monopoly until the mid-1980s. Subsidized Doordarshan programs were explicitly intended to promote national integration, guide social change through specialized targeting of women and children, and preserve and popularize India's rich cultural heritage; they were largely educational and directed to rural audiences, usually out door and collective. Although broadcast of the Asian Games in color in1982 and multi-episode film versions of the great Indian epics, *Ramayana* and *Mahabharata* in the late 1980s were enormously popular, Doordarshan's image was a dull one. Since the mid-1980s, STAR TV from Hong Kong, CNN from the United States, and BBC from the United Kingdom offered stiff competition, especially attracting urban audiences, as did Indian-owned ZEE TV, offering news, sports, and entertainment on cable since 1993. Market forces, advancing technology, and need for income inevitably brought advertising to TV, with the effect of promoting consumerism and, probably, discontent.

The main issue of public debate on the subject of television during the 1990s was governmental control. A national telecommunications policy was announced in 1993 favoring public and private cooperation in an autonomous corporation and an ambitious program of modernizing infrastructure, but a succession of weak and coalition governments did nothing to implement it before 1997. The Prasar Bharati, or Broadcasting Corporation of India, was formed late that year with an autonomous, mixed public and private, and democratic management council ultimately responsible to the relevant parliamentary committee, somewhat on the model of the BBC. It is still at the formative stage. Meanwhile, private entrepreneurial talent had speeded the proliferation of private cable TV all over the country. Because TV watching in India is so often a collective pastime, the total audience estimated in 2000 was 448 million, even though the density of TV sets per thousand persons was lower than in China and other East Asian countries.

TELUGU DESHAM PARTY (TDP). TDP was formed by film star N. T. Rama Rao (NTR) in 1982. Its avowed aim is to restore "Telugu pride" and assert state rights in general and the interests of **Andhra Pradesh** in particular within the Indian Union. In this respect it shares characteristics of other personalized and single state **political parties** without secessionist tendencies that have proliferated since the late 1980s. The new TDP party defeated **Congress** in the Andhra Pradesh elections of 1983 and gained more popularity after New Delhi tried to unseat NTR as chief minister in 1984, winning a two thirds victory in the state elections of 1985.

A succession crisis and split within the party resulted in the victory of NTR's son-in-law Chandra Babu Naidu in 1995. Naidu stressed the need for all-India rapid economic development and integration and turned the state capital **Hyderabad** into a high-tech and information technology centre rivaling **Bangalore** in **Karnataka**. He played an important role in the formation of the United Front 14-party coalition government formed in a hung parliament of 1996 as his party had won 16 seats in the **Lok Sabha** elections of that year. But the TDP broke with the United Front after the 1998 general elections resulted in another hung parliament and joined a formal vote of confidence in the new Prime Minister **Atal Behari Vajpayee** in March 1998. The TDP agreed to support the Vajpayee-led National Democratic Alliance (NDA) government without becoming a member of the 23-party coalition and one of its members was appointed to the important position of Speaker in the Lok Sabha. The TDP distanced itself to some extent from the **Bharatiya Janata Party**'s Narendra Modi, Chief Minister of **Gujarat**, widely believed to have sponsored pogroms against Muslims in the state in early 2002, and Naidu supported the Chief Election Commissioner's assertion that elections should not be held in such a vitiated and violence-prone climate, but did not take a strong secular stand.

After a long period in office, the TDP faced serious challenges within the state from an insurgent Peoples War Group with its **Naxalite** orientation, as well as from popular Telengana separatists agitating for a separate state. Naidu's autocratic manner and Congress efforts to rebuild support in Andhra Pradesh also generated opposition and the TDP was routed in the general elections of 2004. A common explanation for that defeat is Naidu's concentration on **economic liberalization** and globalization that benefited Hyderabad and the urban middle class at the expense of the millions of people dependent on agriculture for their livelihood. Further strains between the TDP and the NDA on the issue of **Hindutva** surfaced after the electoral defeat of 2004. But describing itself as a regional party with a national outlook, the TDP could well remain a significant regional force in Indian politics.

TENDULKAR, SACHIN RAMESH (1973–). Sachin was born in **Mumbai** and soon proved to be a child prodigy in the game of cricket. His natural gifts as a right-handed batsman were enhanced by a superb technique combining elegance, power, and timing that have enchanted audiences who label him "genius." At the age of 16, Sachin was invited to join the Indian test team playing in **Pakistan** in 1989. He made his first test century a year later against England, and his first century in a one-day match against Australia in 1994. Since then, he has broken scoring records in both one-day and test matches, amassing 10,000 runs in one-day matches by the year 2000. His physical and mental skills have been undoubted assets to successive Indian cricket teams, which included other great players too, but at age 30 he showed signs of being overstressed.

Sachin Tendulkar is loved and praised not only in India but by great cricketers in all countries. In 1993 the Yorkshire County team invited him to join them as the first overseas player in 130 years, and the first non-white player ever. The legendry Australian batsman, Sir Donald Bradman (1908–2001), invited Sachin to his home to celebrate his 90th birthday and said the young Indian "reminds me of myself"—while acknowledging that his own long-standing world records had been broken by Sachin Tendulkar.

TERESA, MOTHER M. (1910–1997). She was born at Skopje (in present-day Albania), named Agnes Bojaxhier and brought up by her Venetian mother—a devout Roman Catholic—after her father's death in 1917. Agnes first felt the "call" of a religious vocation at age 12 but did not leave her family for another six years. With the permission and blessings of her family and local Church of the Sacred Heart, she joined the Loreto Order of teaching nuns in India. She took her final vows in 1939 and continued to teach in the Loreto Convent, Entally, which was partly an orphanage located in one of the **Calcutta** slums. She was soon fluent in Bengali and became an Indian citizen at the time of Indian independence.

Mother Teresa experienced a "call to leave Loreto" and work directly with poor people on the street in September 1946. She eventually received permission to do so from the Vatican and the Ireland-based Loreto Order in July 1948 under an "indent of exclaustration." She replaced the Loreto nuns' habit with a white sari bordered with blue and a small cross and rosary, which subsequently became familiar throughout the world as the habit worn by nuns of the new religious order founded by her in 1950, Missionaries of Charity. In addition to the three traditional vows of poverty, chastity, and obedience, Mother Teresa and new postulants took a fourth vow to give "wholehearted and free service to the poorest of the poor." This is what distinguishes their "way."

After some initial medical training in **Patna**, Mother Teresa returned to Calcutta, where she immediately commenced an outdoor school in the Motijhil slum area and rapidly followed this with dispensaries, other schools, sewing classes, shelters for the dying, and leprosariums. She responded to the various needs of the poorest people as she experienced them directly and had no grand plan in mind other than total fidelity to her vocation of service to God through service to the poor, the sick, and the abandoned. She begged on the street, in the time-honored Indian tradition of religious mendicants, and at more sophisticated levels over time, without losing her humility or sense of humor in the face of numerous rebuffs. Help also came to her from diverse sources, including Dr. B. C. Roy, then chief minister of West **Bengal**, and later from the government of India. A small property at 54A Lower Circular Road, Calcutta, soon named *Nirmal Hriday* or Home for the Pure Heart, became Mother Teresa's headquarters in 1953 and remains the nerve center of a worldwide religious order.

Mother Teresa and the sisters of the Missionaries of Charity (presently numbering more than 5,000) spread their good works through practically every city and town of India. They first went overseas to Venezuela in 1965; by 1992 they were working in more than 100 countries, including Iraq, South Africa, the Soviet Union, the United States, and the Vatican itself, with their customary dedication, cheerfulness, and common sense. According to one authoritative calculation, they fed 500,000 families, taught 20,000 slum children, and treated 9,000 leprosy patients and 660 AIDS patients in 1990.

Mother Teresa was awarded the Nobel Peace Prize in 1979 in addition to other awards. She was given a state funeral by the Indian government on her death and was Beatified by Pope John Paul II in October 2003 as a first step toward being recognized as a Saint.

TERRORISM. India has been a victim of terrorist activities on its soil for many decades. The toll has been very high in terms of disruption of civil activities, bank robberies, kidnappings, assassination of specific persons ranging from police and military personnel to prime ministers **Indira Gandhi** in 1984 and **Rajiv Gandhi** in 1991, and deaths of ordinary, innocent, people. According to reliable estimates, terrorist-related violence in India has resulted in about 64,000 deaths in the last 20 years. Terrorists have killed 13,500 civilians and 5,250 security men in **Jammu and Kashmir** alone since 1989. Districts covering about 40% of India's territory are affected to a greater or lesser degree by terrorism of one sort or another.

Four main sources of terrorism, or insurgency, can be identified. Ethnic or religious or regional secessionist movements have surfaced in northeastern India, the **Punjab**, and **Jammu and Kashmir (J&K)**.

Extreme Left movements, such as **Naxalites**, the People's War Group in **Andhra Pradesh** and neighboring districts, and Maoists in **Bihar** and **Uttar Pradesh**, probably linked to the Maoist insurrection in **Nepal** also act in ways defined as terrorist. Criminal gangs, such as the one led by Dawood Ibrahim, were held responsible for the March 1993 bombings in **Mumbai** and similar actions elsewhere, besides facilitating arms supplies and money laundering for other criminal or terrorist groups. Most serious of all since 1989 is *jihadi* or Islamist terrorism, sponsored and supported by **Pakistan**'s Inter Service Intelligence (ISI) wing of the military as a form of low-cost/high-return proxy war against India. Indian task forces on internal security have identified the ISI with terrorist organizations such as the *Lashkar-i-Toiba*, the *Harkat-al Mujahidin*, the *Al Badr*, the *Hizb-ul Mujahidin* and groups active in nine states besides J&K, with a network of mosques and *madrassahs* (Islamic religious schools) established along sensitive international borders, and with such acts as the hijacking of an Indian Airlines airliner to Kandahar in December 1999 and an abortive attack on the Indian Parliament on December 13, 2001. India refers to actions of these groups as "cross-border terrorism."

India's efforts to deal with domestic unrest and with terrorism have taken various forms that are not mutually exclusive. Demands of dissident groups often have been accommodated, or at the least negotiated, as in the northeast, Punjab, Andhra Pradesh and to some extent in J&K. A formidable array of laws exists for control of internal security, including the Armed Forces Special Powers Act of 1956 (with later amendments), the National Security Act of 1980, the Terrorist and Disruptive Activities (Prevention) Act (TADA) of 1985 that was allowed to lapse in the mid-1990s, and the Prevention of Terrorism Act (POTA) of 2001, which was repealed in 2004. Like other liberal democracies confronting terrorism, India finds laws designed to safeguard national security challenged in the courts by its own citizens for alleged violations of due process or civil liberties and abuse of executive power by security forces. Governments rely on four layers of security forces to meet force with force: the civil police armed only with *lathis* (wooden staves) and notoriously ill-paid and ill-equipped; the provincial armed constabulary; paramilitary forces such as the Central Reserve Police Force (CRPF), the Border Security Force (BSF), and the National Security Guards (NSG) that is also responsible for the safety of political figures; the Indian Army, largest component of the **Indian Armed Forces**, which has sometimes complained of being over-burdened with counter insurgency deployment. Security forces fighting prolonged and dirty wars against insurgents and terrorists have been placed in excruciating predicaments and accused of human rights abuses as well.

The major terrorist threat to India, as statistics demonstrate, is posed by cross-border terrorism. India has tried to demonstrate to other countries the links between cross-border terrorism and international terrorism, and has taken a leading role in trying to forge regional and international cooperation in countering terrorism. Since the 1980s India has signed extradition treaties with several countries including Britain, Canada, and the United States and established formal or informal joint working groups to counter terrorism with some including Israel, Russia, and the United States. India is signatory to many international agreements on combating terrorism and stopping financial flows to terrorist groups. India has also helped draft agreements on regional conventions on suppression of terrorism at the **South Asian Association of Regional Cooperation (SAARC)** in 1987 and 2002, at the Association of South East Asian Nations (ASEAN) in 2001, and has campaigned for adoption of its draft comprehensive convention on international terrorism at the United Nations. Even though India and six other Asian countries (**Bangladesh, Bhutan, Myanmar,** Nepal, **Sri Lanka**, and Thailand) agreed to join hands in combating terrorism in July 2004, India has been less than successful hitherto in obtaining cooperation from its immediate neighbor Bangladesh, perhaps because that country has been prey to competing interpretations of **Islam** and the influence of *jihadis:* Pakistan refuses to discuss an extradition treaty and denies cross border terrorism.

India has not succeeded in persuading the international community to identify and sanction Pakistan as a state sponsoring terrorism, probably because Pakistan was highly valued by the United States as a strategic asset in the Cold War, and in the war against terrorism after September 2001. India, however, is extremely vocal on cross-border terrorism sponsored by Pakistan for which there is now considerable independent evidence surfacing in the international press. India also mobilized its armed forces in 2002 after the terrorist attack on parliament without actually attacking terrorist training camps in Pakistan controlled territory. Perhaps under American pressure, General Musharraf made public commitments not to permit terrorist activity from Pakistan soil on January 12, 2002, and subsequently, but has not moved to dismantle the supportive infrastructure of *jihadi* groups, although their flow into J&K varies seasonally. India and Pakistan have been engaged in a composite dialogue through most of 2004 but their perspectives on terrorism diverge. India calls "cross border terrorism" a "core issue" while Pakistan insists that Kashmir is the core issue and militants are freedom fighters. Definitional differences are not unusual in discussions on terrorism.

India has considerable experience in dealing with different kinds of terrorists. Its experts in the field deplore the inadequacies of equipment, organization and training among police forces, and the apparent indifference of politicians to incipient threats to national security. In dealing with terrorism experts counsel patience, flexibility, public support, and international cooperation wherever possible.

THAGI or THUGEE. A practice of robbery and murder by strangling carried out in accordance with prescribed ritual in the name of the Goddess Kali (see Glossary), which grew to serious proportions in the early 19th century. Adherents of *thagi* were not bound by the orthodox or conventional morality of their **Hindu** or **Islamic** communities. They were known as thags or thugs, and in common parlance this word became a synonym in English as well as in Indian languages for cheats, ruffians, and armed robbers without any social, denominational, or sacred connotation.

Governor General **Lord William Bentinck** made an effort to suppress *thagi* and establish norms of law and order in areas newly conquered by the British, especially in Central India. Sir William Sleeman's covert work toward this end in the 1830s was subsequently given a romantic aura by authors writing on the borderline of biography and fiction.

THAPAR, ROMILA (1931–). Thapar is an internationally renowned scholar of early India. The daughter of an officer in the Indian Medical Service (later Army Medical Corps), she spent her childhood first in the **North West Frontier Province** and then in **Pune**, where she continued to study after **Partition** before going to college in **Simla**.

Her interest in studying history was initially sparked by her father's hobby of collecting bronze sculpture from southern India, and nourished at the School of Oriental and African Studies in London where she took a master's degree and was awarded a research scholarship to work with the eminent Indologist, Professor A. R. Basham. Her first published book was a reinterpretation of **Ashoka**, enlightened ruler of the **Maurya Dynasty** in the third century BCE, as a man, a statesman, a **Buddhist**, and a state builder at a nodal point of urbanization and political change in Indian history.

Romila Thapar returned to India in 1961 and took a teaching position at the poorly funded University of Kurukshetra before moving to the University of Delhi and, in 1970, to the newly created Jawaharlal Nehru University. This apex institution in New Delhi fostered serious interest in rigorous, autonomous, and interdisciplinary post-graduate education, and its history department and faculty have come to be recognized for excellence. Professor Thapar has paid special attention to historiography and historical consciousness, stressing professional methodology, the critical investigation of multiple sources including archeological ones as well as collections of ancient lore in the form of *itihasa* and *Puranas*. Like others today, Thapar encourages the expansion of historical study beyond the traditional, to include **dalits, women**, trade, and ecology; in short, history is to be read as a social science rather than esoteric Indology. Her many publications—for school, university, and non-specialist audiences—as well as her frequent public discourses testify both to her scholarship and to her engagement in contemporary political and moral issues of Indian public life.

THEOSOPHICAL SOCIETY. This society was founded by Helena Petrovna Blavatsky (1831–1891) and Henry Steel Olcott (1832–1907) in New York in 1875. They came to India and established their headquarters first in **Bombay** in 1882 and then in Adiyar, near **Madras**, opening many other branches as well. The Theosophical Society drew heavily on the philosophy of non-dualism strong in **Hindu** thought, but also adopted various occult practices in an eclectic blend. Although it gained some following and maintained links between India and the West, it did not take firm root.

In India the society joined with other Hindu revivalists to rebut criticisms of traditional beliefs and customs by **Christian** missionaries and Western-educated Indians. The most dynamic and energetic figure among the Theosophists in India was **Annie Besant**. She devoted herself to rebuilding Indian self-respect and patriotism after she settled in the country in 1893. Through her the Theosophical Society was associated with starting the Central Hindu School in **Banaras** and other educational projects for boys, **women**, and depressed classes in the early 20th century.

THIMAYYA, KUDENDERA SUBAYYA (1906–1965). General Thimayya was Chief of Army Staff from 1957 to May 1961. He came from **Coorg (Kodagu)** and was born in a large and prosperous family of coffee planters. He received his school education in St. Joseph's College run by **Jesuits** in Canoor, and the Anglican Bishop Cotton's School in **Bangalore**, before going to the newly opened Prince of Wales Royal Indian Military College in Dehra Dun. He went on to Sandhurst Military Academy in England, and was among the very few first Indians to be Commissioned into the Indian Army in 1926. Attached initially to the Highland Light Infantry, he served in Iraq and the **North West Frontier Province** before commanding a brigade that helped expel the Japanese from **Burma** during **World War II**. He was decorated for his exploits and then received surrender of local Japanese forces both in Singapore and in Manila before taking command of Indian forces occupying Japan. Thimayya, or Timmy, was well known for his charm and pleasing personality, which enabled him to interact with American and Commonwealth officers easily and prevent discrimination against Indian soldiers.

Thimayya returned to the newly named Kumaon Regiment in India and commanded the Punjab Boundary Force through the trauma of **Partition** before being given command of the 19th Infantry Division sent to **Kashmir** to expel the attacking raiders from **Pakistan**. He is credited with the daring Indian exploits of scaling the high pass of Zoji La and retaking Kargil but was refused permission to beat back Pakistan forces after India took the case to the United Nations. In August 1953 Prime Minister **Jawaharlal Nehru** requested Thimayya to take on the difficult and sensitive task of chairing the Neutral Nations Repatriation Commission in Korea, appointed by the United Nations to supervise the disposition of prisoners of war captured in the course of the Korean War. Major General Thorat was in command of the Indian Custodial Force in charge of the POWs. That commanders on both sides of the Cold War testified to the genuine neutrality and integrity of the Indians, was an achievement of no small measure, for Nehru's policy of **nonalignment** in general, and for Thimayya personally. He received the Padma Bhusan and was appointed Chief of Army Staff in 1957. He clashed with Defence Minister **V. K. Krishna Menon** on a range of issues affecting the **armed forces** as well as the necessity of improving defenses against China. Thimayya offered his resignation in 1959 but Nehru persuaded him to retract and retire on schedule in 1961. The United Nations asked for Thimayya's services again, and he served as UN Force Commander, Cyprus, from the summer of 1964 to his death a year later, still in Cyprus.

THIVY, JOHN ALOYSIUS (1904–1957). John Thivy was an Indian domiciled in Malaya where his father had migrated and become a wealthy planter of rubber. He initially studied Law in **Madras** and was deeply stirred by the Indian independence movement. He joined the **India National Army (INA)** in Malaya and rose within its hierarchy during **World War II**. After the defeat of Japan and the return of British rule to Malaya, Thivy became a founder member and first President of the Malayan Indian Congress and represented Malaya at the Asian Relations Conference held in New Delhi in 1947. He subsequently represented independent India in various countries including Malaya, an unusual honor for an overseas Indian.

TIBET. Presently a nominally autonomous region of the Peoples Republic of China, Tibet has geographical, mythological, and both ancient and modern historical ties with India. A plateau area lying north of the great **Himalayan** ranges, Tibet encompasses the sources of northern India's most important rivers: the **Indus**, the **Ganges**, the **Yamuna**, and the **Brahmaputra**. Partly for that reason, Lake Manasarovar and Mount Kailash in Tibet are regarded in India as the abode of deities in the **Hindu** pantheon, sacred, and places of pilgrimage to the present day. The entire northern border of India (as also **Nepal** and **Bhutan**) is the southern border of Tibet, except where

Ladakh touches Sinkiang. This geographical fact is not modified by the post-1959 political dispute between China and India on exactly where that border should be demarcated.

Cultural links between India and Tibet are deep. Tibetan legend names their first king as one who had escaped the dreadful wars described in the *Mahabharata*. More easily authenticated is the spread of **Buddhism** from India to Tibet in the seventh century CE and the development of a Tibetan script based on **Sanskrit** used to transcribe and translate Buddhist scriptures. Despite continuous trade and passage of persons, animals, and occasional embassies or armed groups through mountain passes, there was little or no political contact between India and Tibet through the medieval and early modern periods. Their socioeconomic, political, and even religious paths diverged, with Tibet's monastic rulers enjoying a special relationship with Mongol, Ming, and Manchu China.

In the late 19th and early 20th century, Europeans, including the Russians expanding into Central Asia and the British seeking buffer states around their empire in India, threatened Tibet's self-imposed isolation. Special privileges were won for British India in Tibet as a result of **Francis Younghusband**'s expeditions and the Simla Convention (1913–1914). By the latter date, the Manchu Empire of China had collapsed leaving no strong replacement; this opened the door for continuing controversy on the legal status of Tibet at that time. The establishment of the People's Republic of China in late 1949 was followed a year later by its military occupation of Tibet. In a well-intentioned move that subsequently became controversial, Prime Minister **Jawaharlal Nehru** voluntarily withdrew India's inherited special privileges and recognized Tibet as an "autonomous region of China" in a trade treaty signed with China in 1954.

Successive Indian governments adhered to that position, notwithstanding the fact that when Tibet's religious and former temporal ruler, the 14th **Dalai Lama**, was forced out of Tibet in March 1959, India gave him sanctuary and subsequently faced Chinese armed forces in a severe border conflict of October 1962. India made an invaluable contribution toward keeping traditional Tibetan religion and culture alive and flourishing by giving hospitality to the Dalai Lama and his followers. Some 100,000 of them initially and a continuous stream of Tibetan refugees since have been accommodated at

Dharamsala in **Himachal Pradesh** and various other settlements in India since 1959 and allowed to work and travel freely in India and abroad. Although India does not officially recognize the exile government of the Dalai Lama or permit any political or anti-Chinese activity by him or his followers in India, their presence has been a constant irritant to Beijing. In the interest of furthering cordial relations with China, Prime Minister **Atal Behari Vajpayee** making a state visit to China in June 2003 felt obliged to reaffirm China's sovereignty over Tibet.

TILAK, BAL GANGADHAR (1856–1920). Tilak, also known as the Lokamanya, was born to a landowning, financially independent Chitpavan **brahman** family of **Poona**. He carried authority by virtue of his birth in the traditional elite of **Maharashtra**, and became one of the best-known national leaders of his generation providing inspiration for succeeding generations of freedom fighters in India. Tilak studied at the Deccan College, Poona, became a **Sanskrit** scholar, and began his career as a school and college teacher. He soon turned to politics, using the editorial columns of the journals *Kesari* and *Mahratta* that he took over in 1890 to raise political consciousness in opposition to British rule in India.

Unlike his contemporary, **Gopal Krishna Gokhale**, and venerated older leaders, such as **Mahadev Govind Ranade**, Tilak was not a social reformer striving to adapt or use modern Western ideas for amelioration of Indian society and polity. On the contrary, Tilak was unabashed in asserting the superiority of traditional **Hindu** civilization based on the **Vedas**, the privileged place of brahmans and *kshatriyas*, and the seclusion of **women**. He opposed the Age of Consent Bill introduced in 1891 to raise the age for consummation of marriage, and as joint secretary of the **Indian National Congress** in 1895 he delinked this essentially political organization from the National Social Conference committed to Hindu social reform and customarily meeting at the same time and place.

For Tilak and his followers, *Swaraj*, or independence, was the "birthright" of Indians; social changes could be only the consequence, not the prerequisite, of political freedom. Tilak published three books demonstrating the antiquity and greatness of Hindu culture: *The Orion: Researches into the Antiquities of the Vedas, The*

Arctic Home of the Aryans, and *Gita Rahasya: The Secret Meaning of Gita*. He skillfully used the annual Ganapati Festival of 1896 to mobilize Hindu solidarity in opposition to the British. He was arrested for sedition in 1897, but his term of imprisonment was relatively short. Tilak was one of the most ardent champions of the **Swadeshi movement** and an outspoken critic of the **partition of Bengal** in 1905.

Although Congress as a whole was in favor of *Swaraj* and *Swadeshi* (see Glossary) as goals, differences in their tactical approach had led to the formation of two distinct groups by 1906. Tilak and his followers were labeled "Extremists" by the British authorities, which naturally preferred the constitutional correctness of the "Moderates" led by Gokhale. Congress split at its **Surat** session in 1907 with Tilak expelled to form a new party. He was arrested soon after and imprisoned for six years in maximum-security jails on the **Andaman Islands** and in Mandalay, **Burma**. He returned home to public acclaim but with his health impaired and to an altered political scene. Tilak was not found wanting. The major achievements of his final phase were: launching the **Home Rule League** to keep up nationalist momentum; being readmitted to Congress and signing the **Lucknow Pact** with **Mohammed Ali Jinnah** to ally the **All-India Muslim League** with Congress goals; drafting a comprehensive blueprint for the reconstruction of independent India along modern but decentralized lines, and promoting vernacular education. A Tilak Swaraj Fund was launched by Congress in his memory.

TIMUR (1336–1405). Timur entered India only once, when he sacked **Delhi** and other cities of northern India in the winter of 1398–1399. But the plunder, rape, and massacre of that single raid left behind him an indelible scar of anarchy and devastation on the collective memory of Indians. In the words of a contemporary writer Badauni, "such a famine and pestilence fell upon Delhi that the city was utterly ruined, and those of its inhabitants who were left died, while for two months not a bird moved a wing" (Wolpert, *A New History of India*: 119).

Timur was one of the great, though brutal, conquerors who rose to power in Central Asia (present-day Uzbekistan and Tajikistan), and in a single lifetime of almost ceaseless war overran enormous territories from Syria to China. He enslaved the **women**, artisans, and intellectuals of conquered lands to adorn his capital city of Samarkand, known for its beautiful gardens and magnificent monuments, but he built no permanent institutions or administration. Although he dealt a death-blow to the **Tughlaq Dynasty** of Delhi, he did not replace it. His sons and grandsons ruled instead over mutually warring states around Bokhara, Herat, Khiva, and Samarkand in Central Asia. Only a fourth generation Timurid prince, **Babur**, was chased away from Central Asia toward India and established there the **Mughal Dynasty**.

TIPU SULTAN (1750–1799). Tipu was the son and successor of **Haidar Ali**, ruler of **Mysore**. Like his father, he was brave, warlike, a good administrator, and determined to expand the territories he inherited in 1783. By a series of raids and intrigue he extended brief control over the southwestern coastal kingdoms of **Cochin**, Malabar, and Travancore. But he faced congenital animosity from the **Maratha Peshwa** and the Nizam of **Hyderabad** in the north, also scrambling for more land in peninsular India, and the growing force of the **East India Company** in **Madras** that he correctly identified as his main enemy.

Tipu had commercial and diplomatic relations with Afghanistan, the Ottoman Empire, Hormuz, Mauritius and Muscat, China, and France. He looked to the French for assistance against their traditional adversary, the British, and even planted a Tree of Liberty at his capital, Seringapatam, after the French Revolution succeeded. Governor General **Lord Cornwallis** saw Tipu Sultan as the most formidable adversary facing the British in southern India at the time and took personal command of the military campaign against him. Cornwallis also negotiated alliances with the Nizam and the Marathas, so that for most of his reign Tipu faced a three-front war. Hostilities were more or less continuous but interspersed with treaties, of Mangalore in 1784 and Seringapatam of 1792, in which mutual restitution of territories was made; on the latter occasion Tipu Sultan was forced to cede land, pay an indemnity, and leave his sons in hostage. He soon repaired the ravages and invited French volunteers to drill his army. **Lord Wellesley** arrived in Madras in March 1799 prepared for war and determined to prevent a Mysore–French alliance. He revived the tripartite alliance with the Nizam and the Peshwa. The fourth Anglo–Mysore War was brief. Tipu Sultan was defeated, pursued, and killed defending Seringapatam. His family was deported. Some districts were given to the Nizam. The Marathas refused what was offered them. The British took the western coastal districts, Coimbatore, Seringapatam, and two tracts on the east. The rump of Mysore was "restored" to a Wadiyar boy of the former Hindu ruling dynasty who duly signed a **Subsidiary Alliance** and became dependent on the East India Company.

British historians of the 19th century did not paint a pretty picture of Tipu Sultan, and reassessments of him have been made only recently in India. His education, industry, and strong moral character are now praised. Far from being a fanatic or indiscriminate Muslim ravisher of Hindu peasants, Tipu Sultan is portrayed as being tolerant of diversity—except among political enemies—and mindful of the cultivator. He introduced some modern innovations in his army, administration, and finance, maintained a navy, and was, of course, a brilliant general.

TODAR MAL (d. 1589). Todar Mal is renowned for devising the system of land revenue first used by **Sher Shah Sur** and systematically applied in the core provinces of the **Mughal Empire** after being introduced in **Gujarat** by the Emperor **Akbar**. The system was subsequently adapted in the **Deccan** and later became the basis of the *ryotwari*, or peasant-based, revenue settlement later used in some parts of British India, more successfully than the **"permanent settlement"** instituted in **Bengal** in 1783.

Todar Mal was a Punjabi **Hindu** of the merchant and clerical **caste** and showed his administrative skills early in life. At the time, a ruler varied his demands from cultivators from year to year, depending on the current production and prices of grain. Todar Mal devised a modern and predictable system based on a survey and measurement of the land, its classification in four types according to productive capacity and actual cultivation, and fixation of rates payable in cash or kind by the *ryot*, or cultivator, himself without intermediaries. Revisions were made every ten years. Todar Mal's system resulted in increased revenue for the state and a greater sense of security for the cultivator; both were important considerations in the Mughal Empire.

In 1582, Akbar conferred the title of Raja (see Glossary) and a high rank at court on Todar Mal in recognition of his wide-ranging administrative and military skills.

TRADE UNIONS. By 1990, there were 10 major trade union federations in India, each one connected with one or another **political party**. The largest and most important trade union federations were: the Indian National Trade Union Congress (INTUC) with 3,500,000 members, traditionally linked to the **Indian National Congress**; the Hind Mazdoor Sabha (former Bharatiya Mazdoor Sangh) with about 1,500,000 members, linked to the **Bharatiya Janata Party (BJP)**; the All-India Trade Union Congress (AITUC) with 1,200,000 members, formed by the **Communist Party of India (CPI)**; and the Centre of Trade Unions with about 1,000,000 members, linked to the **CPI–Marxist**.

The movement to organize labor began immediately after **World War I,** when India's modern industry suffered a slump after being stimulated by the war. Some of the incentive to unionize labor came from earlier and similar efforts in Britain and from recommendations drafted at the International Labour Organisation (ILO) in Geneva, of which India was a founder member. A necessity and desire to ameliorate the abysmal working conditions embodied in the Indian Factory Act of 1911 also motivated some. Textile workers in **Madras** and **Bombay** took to agitation as well as to organization and the All-India Trade Union Congress was formed as an umbrella for 107 affiliated organizations in October 1920; it held its first session in Bombay with **Lala Lajpat Rai** presiding.

Draft resolutions were moved in the Central Legislative Assembly, and the Indian Trade Union Act of 1927 permitted the registration of trade unions under stringent conditions, including a ban on political activity. This condition was hard to meet under the gathering wave of nationalism and mass mobilization of the time. Moreover, the newly formed CPI aspired to leadership of the labor movement and led a massive strike of textile workers in 1928. The following year the British Government of India arrested 31 trade union leaders in the Meerut Conspiracy Case. Agitation continued. A Royal Commission was appointed in 1929 to report on existing labor conditions and legislation in India, and the AITUC split on the issue of whether or not to cooperate with it. 30 "moderate" unions left the parent body to form the Indian National Trade Union Federation. Further splits took place in the 1930s as Congress competed with the Communists and the Socialists for the allegiance of industrial workers, and almost every left-leaning nationalist leader of the time was involved in one way or another with the large-scale labor strikes and agitations of the day.

Many present-day features of Indian trade unions first surfaced during the interwar period sketched above. For example, the All-India Railwaymen's Federation grew to play an important role then, as in the post-independence period as well, especially in 1974 preceding **Emergency Rule**. Since passage of the Minimum Wages Act of 1948 other benefits and bonuses to labor have been negotiated by the trade unions. The caveat in this narrative is that trade unions represent organized and mainly industrial labor, which is both privileged and relatively powerful in independent India. Trade Unions are powerful in state enterprises such as Electricity Boards, as well as service industries including banks and telecommunications. On the other hand, landless, rural labor remains, for the most part, outside the organized and unionized labor movement, as do the millions of self-employed or bonded workers at the lower end of the socioeconomic ladder. And much of the trade union leadership comes from outside the factory, often from those unfamiliar with shop floors, casting further doubts on their ability to benefit both labor and the economy.

As in other industrializing economies, trade unions tend to be suspicious of technological innovations that might threaten employment, and distinctly hostile to downsizing or closing unprofitable plants. This natural phenomenon has slowed the pace of India's **economic liberalization** since 1991, because of the close relationship between trade union federations and different political parties, some of which are invariably in opposition to a democratic government and critique reforms they might have pushed themselves when in power. The effort in India is not to abolish the trade unions, but to extend the benefits they have gained to the unorganized, non-unionized, and far more numerous workers in the country.

TRIPURA. One of the smaller states in the Indian Union, Tripura covers 10,491.69 square kilometers and has a population of a little more than three million according to the 2001 **census**. Tripura is situated in the northeast, linked to **Assam**, almost surrounded by **Bangladesh**, and bordered on the east by **Myanmar**. Although the area comprising Tripura and the peoples who inhabit it find reference in the **Puranas**, the *Mahabharata*, and the Pillar inscriptions of **Ashoka**, there are no written historical records for Tripura until modern times except for chronicles of the ruling dynasty. Because of its relative inaccessibility and dense forests, Tripura Kings were more or less independent, although involved from time to time with the fortunes of **Bengal**.

The ruler of Tripura signed an alliance with the British **East India Company** in the 19th century, and his descendant acceded to the Indian Union in 1947. Governed directly from New Delhi at first, Tripura became a full-fledged state in 1972. Tea is the main product of Tripura, with silk, fruit, and fruit products becoming lucrative industries. In recent years, Tripura has undergone severe demographic pressures as a result of migrations from **West Bengal** and Bangladesh almost overwhelming the indigenous tribal peoples, with consequent political strains. A scenically beautiful but hilly and landlocked state, Tripura is poorly linked to the rest of the country by road and railway. Air services ply between the main towns, and an airport at the capital city, Agartala, connects it with **Kolkata**. Tripura's economic future is clearly linked to the closer ties currently being forged among the countries on the rim of the Bay of Bengal.

TUGHLAQ or TUGHLUQ DYNASTY. This dynasty ruled the **Delhi Sultanate** for most of the 14th century. It was founded four years after the murder of **Alauddin Khalji** by Ghiyasuddin Tughlaq, the son of a Turki official and a **Hindu Jat** woman. Ghiyasuddin ruled a small kingdom for five years before being killed, along with his favorite son, when a victory pavilion collapsed on them in 1325. His other son (and alleged assassin) Muhammad Tughlaq, succeeded him, built a remarkable tomb for him, expanded his territories, fortified his frontiers, and sent an abortive expedition as far north as **Tibet**. He ruled until 1351.

Muhammad Tughlaq was a man of considerable ability whose innovative ideas, however, provoked revolts, questions about his sanity among contemporaries, and historical controversy later. One of his early reforms was to move the capital from Delhi 800 kilometers south to Daulatabad in 1327, so as to administer recently conquered kingdoms in peninsular India more effectively. Neither the nobles nor the Muslim clerics liked the forced move; the climate of the new location also proved inhospitable. In 1329, Muhammad introduced token currency by proclaiming silver equivalencies for brass and copper tokens that could be redeemed at the royal treasury. The scheme proved expensive and short-lived, unlike the Chinese scheme of paper currency, which it emulated. His attempts to encourage agricultural development and adopt liberal policies toward the (Hindu) cultivators were defeated by seven consecutive years of drought that led to widespread economic discontent and rebellion. Rebellion was most successful in the south where one governor, a recent convert from **Islam**, Harihara, founded the Hindu kingdom of **Vijayanagar** and another discontented Muslim noble, Hasan Ganga, founded the **Bahmani Sultanate** of the **Deccan** in the 1340s. **Bengal** detached itself from Delhi in 1338, and Muhammad Tughlaq was killed while fighting rebellion in Sindh in 1351.

The Delhi Sultanate reached the apogee of its power under the Tughlaqs who maintained diplomatic relations with the Khalifa (see Glossary) in Turkey, China, and various kingdoms in Central and Southeast Asia. The Arab traveler **Ibn Batuta** served as chief *qazi* (see Glossary), or judge, as well as emissary for Muhammad Tughlaq whose cousin, Firoze, became the next Sultan and reigned until 1388. Firoze Shah Tughlaq won renown as a builder of gardens, mosques, schools, and irrigation canals—some of which remain in use today. He moved one of the superb 1,500-year-old pillars of the **Mauryan Emperor Ashoka** to Delhi. Firoze Shah reduced espionage and the use of torture in his realm. His adherence to orthodox Islam pleased Muslim clerics although his imposition of the *jiziya* (see Glossary), or tax, on formerly exempt **brahmans** alienated his Hindu subjects. A man of peace rather than conquest, Firoze Shah neglected defense of the frontier and left no strong successor. Ten years after his death, **Timur** and his plundering armies swept in from Central Asia and virtually destroyed Delhi and the Sultanate.

TUKARAM (1607–1649). Born in a **sudra** family of grocers and orphaned early, Tukaram became a devotee of the local deity, Vittobha.

He experienced a mystical initiation in a dream (no **brahman** would accept him as a disciple) and was a man of boundless generosity. He eventually renounced the life of a householder and became a *sannyasin* (see Glossary). He worshipped **Krishna** and composed simple devotional hymns that became very popular.

Tukaram was one of the saints quoted by Ramdas whose influence on **Shivaji**'s development as **Maratha** leader was considerable. Tukaram himself chose not to visit Shivaji's court and remained a wandering ascetic all his life.

TULSI DAS (c. 1552–1623). Tulsi Das has been hailed for several hundred years as the greatest of Hindi poets for his composition *Ramcharitmanas*, which means "The Spiritual Lake of the Acts of Ram." He wrote in the vernacular language of the mid-**Ganges** valley. This verse epic set to music about the god–king **Ram** and his wife Sita is probably the most frequently read and heard work in modern India. It is chanted and enacted during the autumnal weeks of *ram lila or* "play of Ram" throughout northern India, especially in **Ayodhya** where Ram is believed to have been born in human shape, and in **Varanasi**, stronghold of orthodox **Hinduism**, where Tulsi Das spent much of his life.

Little is known about Tulsi Das's life beyond what he implies himself and the legends recorded in some later hagiographies. He was a **brahman** who turned to **Bhakti**, or the path of devotion and mysticism, and sought spiritual salvation through the name of Ram, an incarnation of the deity **Vishnu**. He probably incurred the displeasure of orthodox brahmans for his deviance from conventional behavior, and especially for daring to render the *Ramayana* in the vernacular and so make it available to the common people; the classical **Sanskrit** of Valmiki was accessible only to learned brahmans. Later on, Tulsi Das was deemed to be an incarnation of Valmiki and an advocate of reformed brahmanism.

Equally important, Tulsi Das was a theological bridge builder, spanning the gap between various communities and the deities they revered, notably between the Vaishnavas worshipping **Krishna** as another *avatar* (see Glossary) of Vishnu and the Shaivites worshipping **Shiva** and Parvati, all of whom he showed to be inextricably linked with Ram. Tulsi Das is categorized as a saint of the *saguna* or "with attributes" school giving form to the Deity, but his emphasis on *Ram Nam*, or the name of Ram, is similar to that used by *nirguna* or "without attributes" poet saints worshipping a formless God. In common with other saints of the Bhakti movement, Tulsi Das showed a path to spiritual liberation open to all, irrespective of **caste**, creed, or sex. *See also* BHAKTI, RAMAYANA.

TYABJI, BADRUDDIN (1844–1906). Born in **Bombay** to a prominent, wealthy, cosmopolitan, and modern-minded Muslim family, Badruddin studied law in England, becoming the first Indian barrister in Bombay in 1867, and was appointed a judge in 1895. He was known for his impartial implementation of justice, his ease with people from both East and West, and his high standard of living.

Tyabji founded the *Anjuman-i-lslam* of Bombay as a volunteer organization for the education, welfare, and social uplift of Muslims, men and **women** alike. He cooperated with various other social reformers working for similar emancipation of **Hindu** women from the veil, early marriage, and other social disabilities. In public affairs Tyabji worked with **Pherozeshah Mehta**, Kashinath Telang, and others in pressing for an elective council in the Bombay Municipal Corporation; they succeeded in 1871.

Badruddin Tyabji, unlike another contemporary Muslim leader in northern India, **Syed Ahmad Khan**, supported the **Indian National Congress** fully. He was a delegate to its first session in 1885 and president of its third session in 1887. He and his descendants refuted the "two-nation theory" separating **Islam** that contributed to **Partition**. The Tyabji family acted according to their belief in a secular, democratic, and united India and devoted their considerable talents to its service.

TYAGARAJA (1759 or 1767–1847). Tyagaraja was a devotee whose love of God was expressed through poetry and music of exceptionally high quality, profuse quantity, and immense variety of form. He made a great contribution to the devotional movement of the **Kaveri** delta region of southern India that sustained **Hindu** culture there through the 17th and 18th centuries, after the collapse of the **Vijayanagar Empire**. Tyagaraja's compositions, described as "fragrant gold," continue to be part of the contemporary repertoire in **music** of the Carnatic style, passed down through a lineage of disciples and pupils. Most popular among Tyagaraja's compositions are the *bhajans*, or devotional songs, for individual or congregational worship, but his full-length musical narrative plays with a devotional core are also performed regularly.

Little detail is known about Tyagaraja's life, although a body of hagiography has sprung up around his name. He was born at Tiruvarur, an ancient site of pilgrimage, to a Telugu-speaking **brahman** family whose patrons were the kings of **Tanjore**. He was learned in the entire opus of the **Vedas** and related literature in Telugu and in **Sanskrit**. He declined to live at the court and became a wandering mendicant instead; the literal translation of his name, appropriately, is "king of renunciation." This decision entailed some conflict with his family. Tyagaraja's mission in life was to sing in praise of **Ram**; the 24,000 such devotional songs attributed to him are often compared with Valmiki's **Ramayana** of 24,000 verses. Tyagaraja's fame spread in his lifetime and has lasted beyond.

– U –

UJJAIN. A city in the present-day state of **Madhya Pradesh** near a confluence of rivers, Ujjain is located on a major trade route of ancient times linking the **Ganges** valley with the port of **Surat** on the west coast of India. It was already a thriving metropolis as capital of Avanti (Ujjayini) in the age of the **Buddha**, sixth century BCE and archaeological excavations show continuous habitation of Ujjain in four broad periods since c. 700 BCE, with massive mud fortifications and extensive manufacture of iron objects dated c. 500 BCE. It is mentioned in the *Periplus of the Erythean Sea* as Ozene.

Ujjain remained a center of commerce, with a rich cultural, literary, religious, and scientific life for more than a millennium. **Ashoka** was Governor of Ujjain before he became emperor in the **Mauryan** Dynasty. Nearly 600 years later, **Chandra Gupta II Vikramaditya** of the **Gupta Dynasty** made Ujjain his principal place of residence and administrative center. One of the "nine gems" of his court was **Kalidasa**, who described Ujjain as "the town fallen from heaven to bring heaven to earth." After the imperial Guptas passed into history,

Ujjain changed rulers many times. This fact is reflected in the architecture of the numerous palaces and temples built there, many of them in ruins today. Its fortunes declined during the early medieval period marked by political instability and warfare in northern India and did not significantly improve after the establishment of **Mughal** rule. In the 18th century, Raja Jai Singh of **Jaipur** constructed an observatory along with an institution to study Astronomy at Ujjain. He was reviving an ancient tradition that remains alive in the present day and is caused by the fact according to classical Indian geographers the first meridian passes through Ujjain (contemporary Indian Standard Time is set on the meridian 80 degrees East, passing through Jabalpur, not Ujjain).

UNIONIST PARTY. Fazli Hussain formed this party in the **Punjab** in 1923 to gain entry to the newly reformed provincial legislature. Calling themselves the National Unionist Party, its members were drawn from the dominant landowning classes of all three communities— **Hindu**, **Muslim**, and **Sikh**. The Unionist Party easily routed the **All-India Muslim League** led by **Mohammed Ali Jinnah** in the 1937 elections, despite the separate communal electorates institutionalized under the 1935 **Government of India Act**. The Unionists formed a government led by Sikander Hayat Khan (1892–1942) that performed with exemplary calm and popular support for nearly 10 years.

Both Sikander Hayat Khan and his successor, Khizr Hayat Khan Tiwana, vehemently opposed the idea **Partition** when it was mooted in the early 1940s, partly because as Punjabi Muslims they did not agree with Jinnah on the need for a **Pakistan** and largely because the thought of partitioning Punjab, as an inevitable consequence, was so painful. Although the Muslim League won all of the Muslim seats during the 1946 elections, the Unionists retained the government of the Punjab in coalition with the **Akali Dal** and the **Indian National Congress** until all were overwhelmed by Partition.

UNITED LIBERATION FRONT OF ASOM (ULFA). ULFA first took shape in 1979 among young students, sportsmen, tea garden workers, and others who felt dispossessed by 19th- and 20th-century developments in **Assam**. In particular, they protested the steady inflow of immigrants over the period that accelerated after **Partition** in

1947 and the independence of **Bangladesh** in 1971 and New Delhi's alleged neglect of Assam. ULFA organized an armed insurgency against Delhi's control in the mid-1980s and forged links with **Bodo** militant groups, Kachin rebels in **Burma**, Afghan *mujahedin* in Peshawer, as well as with **Pakistan**'s Inter Service Intelligence agency (ISI). ULFA received arms, funds, and training, and launched a systematic campaign of kidnapping, killing, sabotage of oil pipelines, and general disruption of normal civil and economic life in cities as well as villages. ULFA had strong connections with some politicians as well as the underground and gained legitimacy in agricultural areas; its power peaked by the end of 1990 when its demands became more extreme and its methods of extracting funds more harsh, in short, **terrorist**.

Although New Delhi avoided invoking president's rule and initiating a full-scale military confrontation in Assam, the **Indian Armed Forces** conducted massive operations against ULFA in late 1990 and the summer of 1991. ULFA was declared a terrorist and secessionist organization so that membership in it became a criminal offense. At the same time, peace feelers were held out and ULFA split between those who favored peace talks and the winning of public support through community service on the one hand, and on the other hand those who continued armed guerilla activity. The latter groups seek sanctuary in forested lands of neighboring countries, including Bangladesh and **Bhutan**, but have lost their earlier heroic image in their cynical pursuit of money and power. Many in Delhi and in Assam recognize the fact that resolving the problems of northeastern India demands overcoming the region's tragic economic isolation imposed by Partition rather than military activity. Meanwhile, units of ULFA continue to enact violence, and counter terrorism operations by Bhutan as well as Indian security forces continue to alienate local populations caught in the cross fire.

UNTOUCHABLE (also AVARNA [without *varna* or outcaste], HARIJAN [people of God], PANCHAMA [fifth caste], SCHEDULED CASTE, DALIT). The terms listed as synonymous have been used at different times to refer to groups of persons in India whom orthodox, high **caste Hindus** have traditionally regarded as sources of pollution and, for that reason, "untouchable." The practice of untouchability is of obscure origin and uneven development but was related to ideas of ritual and bodily purity. The notion of temporary pollution arising from contact with unclean occupations (having to do with blood, corpses, excreta, etc.) or events (such as death, childbirth, or menstruation) is not unique to India. But at some unknown stage in the evolution of Hindu culture and religion this idea was transformed into a concept of permanent pollution. A social practice arose of designating certain occupational/kinship/caste groups as irrevocably impure from birth and, for that reason, excluded from normal social or religious interaction and rendered untouchable, and at an extreme in southern India, unseeable.

There is no mention of the practice of untouchability in the **Vedas** or **Upanishads**, but the **Arthasastra** suggests separate living quarters for those who follow "unclean" occupations. Several hundreds of years later, **Manu**'s *Manusmriti* and subsequent legal texts prescribe harsh restrictions and severe disabilities for groups listed as having a lower status than the **sudra** in the fourfold *varna* (see Glossary) classification. Among these groups were the Chandelas, traditionally in charge of cremation grounds and the disposal of corpses, butchers, fishermen, washermen, scavengers, and the issue of mixed marriages, especially between a high caste woman and a lower caste man. These groups were excluded from temples, literate instruction, and the normal boundaries and wells of village or town. Living outside society they developed their own religious rituals, folklore, and hierarchies of status. According to the *Manusmriti* and related texts, foreigners and Adivasis or aboriginals were also regarded as *mlechcha*, or outsiders, from whom no food or drink could be accepted without pollution. Travelers' accounts from the 5th to the 13th centuries, including those of **Faxian**, **Xuanzang**, and **Al-Biruni**, remark on the composition and living conditions of the *panchama*, or excluded groups. European travelers in India from the 16th to 18th centuries made similar observations.

A parallel movement toward social and religious equality and strong protest against the practice and very concept of permanent pollution can be traced through Indian history since the time of the **Buddha** in the sixth century BCE. The **Bhakti movement**, which swept the entire subcontinent between the 7th and 18th centuries CE was profoundly egalitarian. Shaktas, Vaishnavite, and Shaivite saints, **Sufis**, and **Sikhs**, inveighed against the practice of untouchability and disaggregated spiritual liberation from caste. Social reformers of the 19th century attempted to raise consciousness among high caste Hindus of the injustices perpetuated on the low castes and outcastes and the need to remove them. **Jotiba Phule** opened the first school in **Poona** for Mahars, an "untouchable" caste of **Maharashtra**. The **Ezhavas** and Nadars of southern India, and others, took advantage of schools run by **Christian** missionaries, self-help schemes, and new sources of employment to raise their individual and collective status. The tempo of reform quickened in the first half of the 20th century with the temple-entry movement, **Mahatma Gandhi**'s compassionate espousal of the cause of the "Harijan"—as he named untouchables—the dynamic leadership of **Dr. Ambedkar,** and the weight of their numbers in an expected democratic polity. The 1931 **census** listed 400 untouchable castes amounting to almost one-eighth of the total population of India.

The **Indian Constitution** of 1950, in Articles 15 and 17, declared the practice of untouchability illegal, and this was incorporated in the Untouchability (Offences) Act of 1955. The Constitution went further in listing former untouchable castes and tribes in special "Schedules" and granting them reservations in educational and representational institutions and governmental services. Inevitably, reservations proved inadequate or were abused by what came to be called the "creamy layer" of beneficiaries, and became controversial. Assertions of legal rights by members of the Scheduled Castes in a particular village or situation often provoked retaliation by the economically, politically, and socially dominant castes there and led to almost chronic violence in the rural areas of such states as **Bihar**. Although the **Congress Party** assumed Scheduled Caste support for decades after independence, every political party tried to mobilize their supposed voting blocs and brute strength. Meanwhile, their own power, potential or actual, was finding expression through self-questioning on religious identity, through various social movements including that of the **Dalits** and the **Bahujan Samaj Party**, and symbolically through the very high positions gained by men like **Jagjivan Ram** and **K. R. Narayanan**, the latter being president of India from 1997 to 2002. *See also* DALIT.

UPANISHADS. A group of texts in **Hindu** sacred literature that are considered to reveal the ultimate truth or reality whose knowledge is believed to lead to spiritual emancipation. The older Upanishads are written in an archaic **Sanskrit** and were probably compiled or written before 500 BCE; Upanishads continued to be written several hundreds of years into the Common Era. Each Upanishad was attached to a Brahmana or second part of a **Veda** and retains its Vedic name. The Upanishads were learned by rote and remembered, and so are styled *Smritis*, to distinguish them from the *Srutis*, which are Vedic texts that are intended to be recited and heard. Collectively, Upanishads are also known by the name of **Vedanta**, as the conclusion (*anta*) of the Vedas, and it was as such that the sage **Shankara** expounded on them.

According to respected scholars there are a total of 108 Upanishads of which 13—including the *Aitareya*, the *Brihadaranyaka*, the *Chandogya*, and the *Mundaka*—form the ancient and authentic core. The word Upanishad implies instruction from teacher to student, perhaps in secret session, and Upanishads differ from each other in terms of subject matter as well as method of explanation. For example, some expound the non-dualistic or monistic doctrine of the Self as the ultimate Reality, while others stress the practice of **Yoga** and still others dwell on the worship of a personal God as paths of spiritual liberation. Individual Upanishads thus represent particular schools of thought while collectively they embody Indian philosophy. *See also* VEDANTA.

UPRISING OF 1857. (Also known as the Rebellion of 1857, the SEPOY MUTINY, FIRST INDIAN WAR OF INDEPENDENCE War, or THE MUTINY). The assorted names given by different people over the past hundred years reflect varying interpretations of events 1857–1858, which first broke out as a mutiny of sepoys (see Glossary) at Meerut on May 10, 1857, and then developed into an armed outburst across most of northern and central India against British rule before being finally crushed in the spring of 1858. Its causes were multifold and its results far-reaching.

The dramatic expansion of British rule in India through the first half of the 19th century had territorial, political, and socioeconomic effects that ignited revolt. Displacement of Indian Princely rulers by military conquest was carried forward by **Lord Dalhousie**, who annexed territories through his "Doctrine of Lapse"—by which he denied childless ruling princes their traditional right to adopt male heirs—or through accusations of misgovernment. His annexation of **Awadh** on the latter excuse in 1856, criticized by other Englishmen at the time for overlooking the proven loyalty of the Nawab (see Glossary) to the British, sent a frisson through all other "protected" princes who had signed **Subsidiary Alliances** with the **East India Company**. This roused some of them, especially **Rani Lakshmi Bai** of Jhansi and **Marathas** such as **Nana Saheb**, claimant to the title of **Peshwa**, to take up arms.

The removal of princes and their patronage also removed traditional sources of employment for whole classes of Indians, administrators, and artisans as well as feudal servitors, without offering them adequate replacement. The economic effects of new land tenure and revenue collection systems introduced by the British in annexed lands harmed others, as did the opening of India to new kinds of British trade and enterprise when the monopoly of the East India Company was terminated in 1833. Fears aroused by the destruction of the old political and economic order were exacerbated by what was perceived as an onslaught on traditional social and religious customs brought about through the activities of **Christian** missionaries and legislation such as the Abolition of Suttee (*see* SATI) in 1829, notwithstanding the support for the latter among reform-minded **Hindus**. Further, British denigration of Indian culture epitomized in **Lord Macaulay**'s famous Minute of Education was accompanied by a kind of institutionalized racism which replaced the rough equality of the 18th century and came to pervade all relationships between the British and Indians by the mid-19th century.

The impact of all these subtle and evident forces became manifest in the Sepoy Army of Indian troops in the employ of the East India Company whose fighting abilities had served to expand British domains inside and outside India. The emoluments of its 233,000 Indian soldiers were kept much lower than those of their 45,322 British counterparts; their obligations—to serve abroad, for example—offended inherited beliefs more deeply. Periodic rebellions since 1806 had been put down with unaccustomed brutality and respectful demands for redress of grievances brushed aside. The compulsory introduction of the

Enfield Rifle, using cartridges greased with animal fat—perhaps of pig or cow—to be readied by mouth, cut at the deepest-held Hindu and **Islamic** taboos and caused widespread discontent among soldiers and their families.

Sepoy Mangal Pandey killed a European officer near **Calcutta** in March 1857; he was executed and his company was flogged and disarmed. Unrest and rumors of unrest spread. On May 10, the sepoys stationed at Meerut broke out in open revolt, for which their British officers were unprepared. The next day they took **Delhi**, where they proclaimed the aged **Mughal** pensioner, **Bahadur Shah II**, emperor again. Soon the entire **Ganges** valley of the north and the **Narmada** valley of central India were engulfed in fighting, with the most important encounters taking place in Lucknow, **Banaras**, Kanpur or Cawnpore, Gwalior, and Jhansi. There were sporadic outbreaks of hostility in **Assam**, **Rajasthan**, the **Punjab**, and peninsular India. But there was no unity of purpose, much less a unified command structure or common strategy among the Indians; they fought for sectional, parochial, or personal objectives against the one common enemy—British rule. Although there was no divide along lines of Hindu or Muslim, there was no decision on an Indian replacement for the British either; would it be the (Muslim) Mughal emperor or the (Hindu) maratha Peshwa? Nor did any of the revolting Indian Princes have sources of funds or networks of allies on which to draw for a prolonged war, or a program for the future, presuming their victory.

In contrast, the British had the funds and prestige of Queen Victoria's empire behind them and a sense of destiny ahead. They could employ the immediate services of new allies, notably the **Sikhs** and Gurkhas, led by proven generals including **John Lawrence**. Their own forces could be replenished on conclusion of the Crimean War of the time. The British retook Delhi on September 18, 1857, and deported Bahadur Shah. They recovered Lucknow and Kanpur in March 1858 and killed the Rani of Jhansi on June 17. The new Governor General, Lord Canning, announced restoration of peace in July and read out Queen Victoria's proclamation promising amnesty, religious toleration, and recognition of the rights of loyal princes. The British Crown in Parliament assumed direct responsibility for ruling India in name as well as in practice. But, and unlike the last half-century of Company Raj, Crown rule was conservative, reinforcing the traditional and feudal elements of Indian society. Race relations too were frozen in a hierarchy of superior and inferior—irrespective of birth or education—reinforced with hatred and mistrust born of the atrocities committed by both sides in 1857 and 1858 and kept alive in the voluminous literature of diaries and fiction that followed.

Retrospections on the Uprising of 1857 some hundred years later displayed a similar variety of assessments to contemporary analyses. British official and unofficial accounts of the time saw the uprising as a "rebellion of a people," a "national revolt" much more serious than a breach of peace or a mutiny of men. At the minimum, they considered it a serious attempt on the part of the Muslim aristocracy to restore the **Mughal Empire** and followed policies to preempt a repetition. Only later did British writers describe events of 1857 not as a princely plot, a scramble for plunder and power, but simply as a Mutiny. Indian commentators, on the other hand, tended to reverse their assessments. Many Western-educated, middle-class Indians of the late 19th century saw the 1857 Uprising as the last flicker of the old feudal order. Only later, and under the inspiration of Maratha or Hindu revivalism, did **Veer Savarkar** and others present it as the first direct challenge to British rule, the first "National War of Independence." Scientific historians avoid both extremes of interpretation in favor of sober analysis. Some see 1857—centenary of the **Battle of Plassey**—as a possible turning point in British–Indian history, but one when "India failed to turn."

UTTAR PRADESH (UP). With more than 166 million people, UP is the most populous and one of the largest states in area in the Indian Union. It is bounded by the **Himalaya** and **Uttaranchal** in the north, the foothills of the Vindhya range and **Madhya Pradesh** in the south, by **Bihar** on the east, and **Delhi**, **Haryana**, and **Rajasthan** on the west. Bifurcated by the **Ganges** River, the fertile area now comprising Uttar Pradesh was known in the distant past as **Madhya Desh**, or middle country, and always has been central to the cultural and political history of India.

UP was the home of great sages in **Vedic** times and kings featured in the epics *Ramayana* and *Mahabharata*. In the sixth century BCE, both **Mahavira** and the **Buddha** walked and taught throughout the UP and there laid foundations of new religions, **Buddhism** and **Jainism**. Many reputed centers of learning and sites long sacred to **Hindus**, such as **Varanasi**, are located in UP. The establishment of the **Delhi Sultanate** in the 13th century and then of the **Mughal Empire** in the 16th century brought **Islam** to the middle Ganges valley, which was their core domain. A new syncretic Hindu–Muslim culture emerged in the region, especially among the upper classes and in all the arts and crafts of the period and since then. Some of the greatest monuments of the Mughal era, including the **Taj Mahal**, are concentrated in **Agra**, UP.

British control in Uttar Pradesh began in the late 18th century with Banaras (Varanasi), extended over the Doab (see Glossary) between the Ganges and **Yamuna** rivers in the early 19th century and culminated with **Lord Dalhousie**'s annexation of **Awadh** in 1856. Many famous battles were fought in UP before British troops totally suppressed the **Uprising of 1857**. Several territories were combined with the erstwhile Awadh for administrative purposes, and in 1901 the province was renamed United Provinces, or UP. Various schemes of land revenue collection modifying Mughal and other traditional practices were initiated, involving *zamindars* (see Glossary), villages, or peasant proprietors, but high taxation and steep economic decline in the 19th century led to increasing resentment, famines, and frequent peasant revolts in the province.

By the end of the 19th century, new groups of professionals and businessmen were becoming politically conscious, especially in **Allahabad** and Lucknow. New associations to revitalize the indigenous **languages**, Hindi and Urdu, were formed and reformist or revivalist movements among both Hindus and Muslims gained strength. Unfortunately, these movements became increasingly competitive, and the new elective politics among the UP middle class became communalized in the first half of the 20th century. Although the inclusive **Indian National Congress** was organizationally strong in town and village alike, it failed to gain—or it lost—support among Muslims. They were also suspicious of assertive Hindu movements to ban cow-slaughter and promote Hindi over Urdu, such as propounded by the **Hindu Mahasabha** and sister organizations. Bad feelings between the two communities were exacerbated by communal riots in the 1920s and by avoidable errors of leadership during the 1930s. By 1940, middle class and landowning Muslims from UP were articulating demands for an autonomous Muslim state. After **Partition** and the creation of an independent **Pakistan** in 1947, many of them migrated there; a substantial Muslim population remained and presently constitutes about 16% of the population (see Appendix G). For a variety of political, demographic, and economic reasons, communal violence continued to manifest itself in the UP in the 1980s and 1990s, such as the temple–mosque conflict in **Ayodhya**. Some political commentators and activists see the votes of the Muslim community as the key to electoral success.

Agriculture is the main occupation of over 70% of the population, and the state is a principal producer of sugarcane and oilseeds. Canal irrigation is well established. In addition to traditional handicrafts and the early modern industries of leather and textiles, UP is home to a large number of manufacturing and extractive industries. Nevertheless, the social and economic indicators of UP are relatively low, especially with respect to education of **women**, medical care, and employment. Social tensions rose with economic change and political enfranchisement, finding expression in the formation of new **political parties**, notably the **Bahujana Samaj Party (BSP)** and the **Samajwadi Party**, both of which appealed to the large numbers of people at the lower end of the social scale. Competition between the **Bharatiya Janata Party (BJP)** and the **Congress Party** at all levels, including the upper end of the social spectrum, is equally stiff. Political competition has not yet been translated into good governance; on the contrary, and both public and private investment in UP has declined over recent decades.

Statistics for the state as a whole do not necessarily reflect the very different levels of prosperity and progress in four distinct regions— western, eastern, hilly northern, and the scarred arid south. Suggestions have been made from time to time to break up the state along those regional lines and for greater ease of administration, but have not been followed for lack of consensus. The exception is that of constituting the former northern districts of UP into the separate state of **Uttaranchal** in 2000. Uttar Pradesh has been the single most politically weighty state in the Indian Union, with its politics affecting the whole country, and with five prime ministers having had their political bases there: **Jawaharlal Nehru**, **Lal Bahadur Shastri**, **Indira Gandhi**, and **Rajiv Gandhi** of Congress, and **Atal Behari Vajpayee** of the BJP. UP is likely to remain very important.

UTTARANCHAL. A new state of 55,854 square kilometers was created in late 2000 from the mountainous districts, including Garhwal and Kumaon, of **Uttar Pradesh** that had complained of Lucknow's neglect for decades. Its population is less than nine million. Several mountain peaks over 8,000 meters high in the Great **Himalaya** range are located in Uttaranchal, such as Dunagiri, Kamet, and Nanda Devi, as well as the Siwalik and Lesser Himalaya ranges. Mountaineering and tourism attracts many visitors, as do the forests, wildlife and wildlife preserves, and important places of pilgrimage such as **Hardwar**, the source of the river **Ganga**, Badrinath and Kedarnath.

Uttaranchal's varied climate and vegetation promise lucrative returns to agriculture and fruit growing and processing once communications to market centers improve. Road building and power generation have high priority in the state, as does the perhaps contradictory objective of environmental conservation. Clashes between the two were visible in the long debates over construction of the Tehri dam (with inevitable inundation of many villages and ancient sites) that was finally commissioned in 2004.

The capital city of Uttaranchal is Dehra Dun, home of several boarding schools and important institutions such as the Forest Research Institute, the Indian Petroleum Research Institute, the **Survey of India**, and the Indian Military Academy.

– V –

VAISYA. Vaisya is the third ranking *varna* (see Glossary), or class, and includes numerous **castes** and sub-castes in this category. According to the verse in the **Vedas** describing the first sacrificial man, the vaisya sprang from his torso. Typically, therefore, vaisya occupations were those that sustained society and included agriculture, trade, finance, money-lending, supplying groceries and other goods (by the *bania* sub-caste), and various commercial activities. Education was not precluded for vaisya, and some clerical and administrative sub-castes of the late medieval and early modern periods probably belonged to the vaisya rather than the **brahman** category.

Despite their obvious usefulness to the community and often their considerable wealth, the vaisya castes were not always accorded respect in brahmanical lore. In the **Hindu** social hierarchy, the status of vaisya component sub-castes—measured by the right to wear the sacred thread, participate in religious ceremonies, give and accept cooked food, etc.—varied according to time and place. A sub-caste with the same name and occupation could have been ranked differently at different times or in different parts of the country, being raised close to that of *kshatriya* or pushed down to the level of **sudra**, according to place and time. Nor were such positions immutable.

Vaisya wealth was and is frequently expended on temples and good works, as documents and stone inscriptions from ancient times to the present day abundantly testify. Traditionally supporters of orthodox religious rites and institutions, the vaisya were also strong supporters of **Buddhism** and closely linked with **Jains** in **Gujarat** and elsewhere. Vaisya support and followers over the centuries also have gone to other heterodox teachings, especially to **Bhakti** faiths.

VAJPAYEE, ATAL BEHARI (1924–). Vajpayee was prime minister of India for two weeks in May 1996, again from May 1998 to October 1999 and again after general elections from October 1999 to May 2004. He had been leader of the opposition in the **Lok Sabha** from 1993 to 1996 and again in 1996 and 1997 as well as Chairman of several important parliamentary standing committees, including external affairs.

Vajpayee was born in Gwalior and began to attend *shakas* or boys' meetings run by the **Rashtriya Swayamsevak Sangh (RSS)** in 1939. He was inspired by RSS leaders **Bhaurao Deoras**, founder Baliram Hedgewar, and Deendayal Upadhyaya and became a full-time member of the organization, or *swayamsevak*, in 1947. Atal Behari is a poet, a writer, and a fine orator in the Hindi **language**. He wrote for and edited Hindi newspapers, *Rastradharma*, *Panchjanya*, and *Veer Arjun* and has received public and academic recognition for his literary output. He was first elected to the Lok Sabha in 1957 and reelected in every subsequent general election. Vajpayee established himself as a correct and fine parliamentarian, mainly in the opposition but also when in office; the Bharat Ratna Award was conferred on him in 1994 as Best Parliamentarian.

Vajpayee was a founder member of the **Jana Sangha** and led that **political party** from 1968 to 1973. He was detained during **Indira**

Gandhi's **Emergency Rule** 1975–1977 and joined the first **Janata** government elected in 1977 as minister of external affairs. When the Jana Sangha was dissolved, and when the Janata coalition government collapsed, Vajpayee served as president of the new **Bharatiya Janata Party (BJP)**, from 1980 to 1986, and has remained one of its leaders ever since. He consistently took a moderate and centrist position within a party that advocates **Hindutva** and includes members with extreme views, but was not always able to prevail, as on the subject of the 2002 anti-Muslim actions of **Gujarat**. Differences between these members and Vajpayee were evident when the BJP-led National Democratic Alliance (NDA) coalition government was in power in New Delhi and dropped key RSS and **Vishwa Hindu Parishad** demands from its common minimum program, and surfaced even more prominently in debates on responsibility for the NDA defeat in the 2004 general elections.

Vajpayee took several decisive initiatives in foreign affairs—his special interest—as prime minister. In May 1998 he ordered the underground testing of advanced nuclear devices, and subsequently authorized the weaponization of India's **nuclear program** and permitted the enunciation of a draft nuclear doctrine based on no first use and minimum credible deterrent. In bilateral and in international forums, he asserted India's claim to be a permanent member of the United Nations Security Council and its right to be recognized as a nuclear weapons state in the international system. Vajpayee fully supported the intense and ultimately fruitful dialogue conducted by his special envoy **Jaswant Singh** with United States Deputy Secretary of State Strobe Talbott in 1998–1999, made a state visit to the United States, speaking of a "natural alliance" and "strategic partnership" between the world's two largest democracies, offered India's sympathy, help, and facilities to the United States after the **terrorist** attacks there on September 11, 2001, and took necessary measures to facilitate the "next steps in strategic partnership" launched by the Bush administration. Vajpayee engaged in reciprocal moves with China to reduce threat, build confidence, raise the level and pace of talks on the border problem, and build substantial and mutually beneficial economic ties between the two Asian giants. His state visit to China in June 2003 advanced all of these objectives. He also took bold initiatives with **Pakistan**, as he had too during the brief Janata government interlude. In February 1999 Vajpayee and an entourage traveled on a newly opened bus line between **Delhi** and Lahore, and proceeded to Islamabad where Vajpayee and Pakistan's Prime Minister Nawaz Sharif signed the Lahore Declaration, encapsulating agreement on a series of measures and a "composite dialogue" to resolve all outstanding disputes, including that on **Kashmir**, between the two countries. The Declaration was quickly overtaken by events originating in Pakistan: armed incursions made by the Pakistan Army across the Line of Control in the Kargil sector of **Ladakh**, the ensuing near-war conflict, the military coup in Pakistan staged by General Musharraf in October 1999, and the hijacking of an Indian Airlines passenger plane in December. Vajpayee nevertheless invited Musharraf to India for discussions in July 2000, but agreement eluded them. An abortive terrorist attack on India's parliament buildings in December 2001 and consequent troop deployments was another setback, but in January 2004 Vajpayee once again visited Islamabad for the summit meeting of the **South Asian Association for Regional Cooperation (SAARC)** and pledged to revive the composite dialogue.

Vajpayee presided over a period of impressive economic growth in India and continued the policies of **economic liberalization** initiated by **Narasimha Rao** and **Manmohan Singh** in 1991, despite opposition from sections of his own party. Benefits of economic growth were not evenly spread, however, so that the NDA campaign slogan of "India Shining" for the 2004 elections provoked a cynical reaction among most voters. Vajpayee himself retained his seat and the respect he had earned over a long career.

VAKATAKA DYNASTY (c. 255–510 CE). This dynasty ruled in the hilly or Vidarbha region of **Maharashtra** and rose to prominence as the power of the **Satavahanas** declined. King Pravarasena (c. 275–335) built an empire in central India and the **Deccan** and forged a matrimonial alliance with the powerful Nagas of north-central India. Their descendants divided the heritage into four kingdoms, with the elder branch marrying into the **Gupta Dynasty** and all, perhaps, in a semi-feudal relationship with the dominant Guptas. One of the Vakataka Kings, Harishena, is immortalized for his patronage of the **Buddhist** cave monasteries at **Ajanta**.

VALLABHACHARYA (1479–1531). The son of a Telugu **brahman**, Vallabhacharya was a child prodigy in his early mastery of the **Vedas** and **Puranas**. He studied at **Varanasi** and at Vrindavan (near Mathura) and had a mystic experience of **Krishna** early in life. Vallabhacharya taught a new, joyous mode of worshipping Krishna as an incarnation of the Supreme God, which included reenacting scenes of his childhood and youth with love and devotion. Vallabhacharya settled in Varanasi where he taught and wrote many books in **Sanskrit**.

Vallabhacharya was a typical poet–saint of the **Bhakti** movement and had the greatest influence among the **vaisya** merchant communities of western India. Some of his disciples regarded him as an incarnation of Krishna, and a sect named after him grew in numbers. Its leaders were known as maharajas and deeply reverenced; they were all descended from Vallabhacharya or his sons. A court case was filed against one of the maharajahs for gross profligacy in 1862, after which some practices were dropped and the sect became more conventional. It continues to flourish, especially in **Gujarat** and Mathura.

VARANASI (also BANARAS, BENARES, KASHI). One of the most ancient, holy, and continuously inhabited cities in India—or in the world—is situated on the left bank of the River **Ganges** near its confluence with the Varana and Asi rivers, from which its name is derived. Varanasi always has been a very important site of **Hindu** pilgrimage, especially for the aged, as it is generally regarded as the preferred place of death, cremation, or immersion of ashes so as to ensure *moksha* (see Glossary), or spiritual liberation. The sacral aura is unmistakable, even amid the bustle, crowds, and dirt of a commercial city.

Reference to the kingdom of Kashi dates back to the ninth century BCE and early **Buddhist** texts mention it as one of the 16 principal political units of the time. It was at Sarnath, very close to Varanasi, that the **Buddha** preached his first public sermon. Centers of learning as of worship prospered there until the early 13th century, after which they were regularly looted and destroyed by Turki–Afghan invaders in the name of **Islam**, rebuilt, razed, and built again. **Mughal Emperor Akbar** provided protection in the 16th century, and another revival of temple building took place in the 18th century twilight of the Mughals, partly sponsored by the Raja of Banaras. Varanasi has prospered again in the 20th century, and the exquisite handloom silk weaving of the city is renowned. It is the home of culture, literature, **music**, and the arts learned in traditional small *guru-kuls* of teacher and students as well as in the prestigious Banaras Hindu University.

All the deities of the Hindu pantheon are honored with temples in Varanasi, the most frequented at the present time being those erected for **Shiva**, Hanuman (closely associated with **Ram**), and the Goddess Durga (see Glossary). Perhaps the most striking feature of Varanasi is the series of steep steps leading down to the river. Ascetics, devotees, meditators, mendicants, sightseers, and vendors throng more than 70 such *ghats*, especially at sunrise and sunset, when so many wish to take a ritual dip in the sacred river.

VARIER, VAIDYARATNAM P. S. (d. 1944). P. S. Varier was born in an illustrious family of Malabar, **Kerala**, and studied medicine in both the Western system of allopathy and the ancient Indian system of Ayurveda (derived from the **Vedas**) under a scholarly *guru*. Varier became deeply engrossed in the latter system and keen on reviving it. In 1902, he founded the Arya Vaidya Sala at Kottakkal for the preparation of authentic herbal Ayurvedic medicines. Varier was not only a scholar and practitioner of medicine, he was a philanthropist, and proved to be an able entrepreneur as well. The Arya Vaidya Sala sponsored the collection and cultivation of medicinal plants, the manufacturing and marketing of a growing range of products, and programs of research and publication on Ayurveda and related subjects. As it prospered, Varier received governmental recognition for his services in the form of the title Vaidyaratnam. Before his death, he converted his considerable assets into a charitable trust to be administered by a seven-member Trust Board, including members of his family.

The Arya Vaidya Sala, established by P. S. Varier, is a world famous, multi-million-dollar institution. It manages an associated hospital and Ayurveda College, provides training programs and regular seminars, cultivates herbal gardens, and runs a classical dance academy. It expends the major share of its earnings to charitable causes in the form of medical aid to deserving persons. Ayurveda's appeal spreads across India and abroad, and patients come for consultation and treatment from far and wide. Related institutions with the same high standards set by Varier have been established in **New Delhi** and **Bangalore**.

VARMA, RAJA RAVI (1848–1906). Born in the royal family of Travancore to the Princess Uma Amba Bai, Raja Ravi showed artistic talent as a child and was encouraged to develop it. He used Western techniques of painting, drew his inspiration from Indian mythology and literature, and received the patronage of various Princes. He gained international recognition and honor in Vienna and Chicago. He also established an oleographic press for art reproductions near **Poona**. Raja Ravi Varma's style of blending East and West was typical of his times. He is regarded as one of the founders of modern Indian **painting**.

VEDANTA. The literal meaning of the term is end (*anta*) of the **Vedas**, and in that sense is used for the **Upanishads**. In addition, Vedanta was one of the six systems of classical Indian Philosophy and was also called Uttara Mimamsa. This school of thought held that the highest wisdom of the Vedas was to be found in the Upanishads with the essence contained in the phrase "*Tat Twam Asi*" or "That Thou Art." "That" refers to the Supreme One or Brahman, and "Thou" refers to the individual soul, or *atman*; realization of this truth through divine grace or detachment from all desire and grief is the ultimate goal of knowledge, of life. Vedanta, in short, is associated with the concept of *advaita* (see Glossary), or non-dualism, and the associated idea of material phenomena as transitory or illusion.

Shankara was the most uncompromising proponent of *advaita* as the core of the Vedanta system of philosophy. **Ramanuja** qualified its precepts and a later teacher within the Vedantic school, Madhva (1177–1276), postulated *dwaita*, or dualism, as well as the reality of material existence. There are several present-day exponents of Vedanta as *advaita* with works in the English **language** as well as Indian languages.

VEDAS. The Vedas, from the **Sanskrit** *vid*, to know, are four collections of the most sacred knowledge in the **Hindu** tradition. Each of the Vedas consists of two parts: the *Samhita*, comprising hymns and incantations to be used in rituals and sacrifices, and the *Brahmana*, embodying precepts and illustrative examples. Attached to each *Brahmana* is an **Upanishad** and an *Aranyaka*, or book, dealing with secret, mystic, or speculative aspects of a ritual or sacrifice.

The *Rig Veda* is the oldest of the four Vedas. Depending on the calculations used, it is dated sometime between 3000 BCE and 1500 BCE. Most of the hymns are addressed to elemental powers, personified as deities to be worshipped, and also enshrine the concept of a Supreme Being. A much-quoted passage of the *Rig Veda* refers specifically to the One Reality, conceived of by sages in several ways and called by different names. Priests recite the hymns when offering oblations in sacrificial fires. The *Rig Veda* is considered to mark the beginning of Hindu religious–philosophical thought; it also is a valuable literary source for tracing the early history of the Indo–Aryan peoples, perhaps even before they settled on the Indian subcontinent.

The *Yajur Veda* elaborates details on sacrifices, rituals, and prayers, and includes some magical chants and incantations. Its manual of procedure also contains some of the earliest examples of prose in the Indo–European languages. The Sama **Veda** is almost entirely in verse, to be sung or recited at sacrifices when the priests imbibed the sacred brew Soma. The *Atharva Veda* was probably compiled much later than the first three as its compositions are far removed from theirs in both style and content. Two other compilations of knowledge are sometimes included among the Vedas: the *Dhanu* deals with weaponry and the *Ayur* deals with medicine.

Each Veda has more than one version. Variations probably arose because each Veda was passed down orally over the generations by recitation taught by particular preceptors before it was committed to writing. The Vedas have been represented frequently in art and sculpture. They have inspired saints, reformers, and philosophers through the millennia and even 20th-century political revolutionaries such as **Bal Gangadhar Tilak** and **Sri Aurobindo**. The Vedas occupy one of the highest places in Indian culture from ancient to modern times.

VENKATARAMAN, RAMASWAMY (1910–). President of India from 1987–1992, Venkataraman was born in the **Tamil Nadu** village of Rajamadam to an educated Iyer **brahman** family and was educated in **Madras**. He became a trade union lawyer practicing before the Madras High Court and later at the **Supreme Court** in **New Delhi**. He joined the **Indian National Congress** as a young man, was imprisoned during the **Quit India Movement**, and was an active parliamentarian from the time he was first elected to the **Lok Sabha** in 1950.

Venkataraman served in **Jawaharlal Nehru**'s government as a delegate to the United Nations and as minister of state for industries under **Kamaraj**. He held several portfolios in the Madras government from 1957–1967 and was in **Indira Gandhi**'s government as a member of the Planning Commission from 1967 to 1971. He was minister of finance from 1980 to 1982, and minister of defense from1982 to 1984, before becoming vice president of India in 1984. The **Congress Party** headed by **Rajiv Gandhi** nominated Venkataraman as its candidate for president at the conclusion of Giani **Zail Singh**'s term in 1987.

Venkataraman's five-year term as president coincided with a period of unusual political controversy, tension, and change in the Union Government. He had to deal with four successive prime ministers— Rajiv Gandhi, **V. P. Singh**, **Chandra Shekhar**, and **P. V. Narasimha Rao**—with very varying levels of support in Parliament. In consequence, the president provided a crucial element of stability to matters of state and Venkataraman commanded respect for the manner in which he discharged his duties. Commenting later on the powers and functions of the head of state in a parliamentary democracy such as India, Venkataraman compared them to "an emergency lamp, which came into operation when (political) power failed and became dormant when power was restored" (Venkataraman, *My Presidential Years*: 651). He was asked to head a **Constitution Review Committee** created in 2000, but declined.

VIDYASAGAR, ISHWAR CHANDRA (1820–1891). He was born in a small village of **Bengal**, the son of a poor **brahman** clerk. He was educated in **Calcutta** and received a scholarship to study English. He taught **Sanskrit** and became Principal of the Sanskrit College in Calcutta in 1851. He is noted for a vast output of scholarly books and his influence on modern Bengali prose writing free of Sanskrit pedantries. He is best known for leading a widow remarriage movement in Bengal. It gained national prominence but was not accompanied by any national organization to rebuild society along lines more favorable to **women**.

Ishwar Chandra received the title "Vidyasagar" or "ocean of knowledge" in 1841. He was not an early member of the **Brahmo Samaj**, although he collaborated with some of its members on issues of social reform. He became a principal figure in the struggle to emancipate high caste Hindu women from the social disabilities of polygamy, dowry, and prohibition against widow remarriage. His agitation in favor of widow remarriage started in the early 1850s and included a major book, *Marriage of Hindu Widows* (1856), as well as proposals for British–Indian legislation enabling the legal recognition of any such marriage. The Hindu Widows Remarriage Act XV was indeed passed in 1856 despite opposition from orthodox circles as well as an earlier British promise not to interfere with personal law. But it had much less impact than a similar law passed in 1829 banning **sati**. Pandit Vidyasagar's disappointment did not prevent him from continuing his charitable and reformist work.

VIJAYANAGAR. The Vijayanagar Empire comprised a substantial part of peninsular India south of the Krishna River from the mid-14th to the mid-17th century. It reached a zenith in the 16th century when its great wealth, and the splendor of its capital city at Hampi, with its many temples, opulent palaces, and overflowing markets at a crossroad of transcontinental trade routes impressed the traders and travelers who came from many lands, including Europe, and wrote about these wonders.

The Vijayanagar Empire straddled the agrarian frontier between dry pastoral lands and tank or river irrigated multi-crop areas in the **Deccan** and further south, deriving advantages from both. Some confusion and controversy surrounds the origin and history of Vijayanagar, partly because its rulers drew their political lineage from four different indigenous traditions and partly because 19th and early 20th century historians represented them according to preconceived notions of "Oriental despotism" or "Hindu patriotism." Recent archaeology and archival research has made more objective evaluation possible.

The brothers Bukka and Harihara probably founded the **Hindu** kingdom when fighting back **Khalji** and **Tughlaq** military incursions into southern India during the 14th century. Subsequent rulers of Vijayanagar drew on **Chola** and **Hoysala** forebears to consolidate their rule over the semi-autonomous regions, lesser kings, and peoples of the peninsula. By the early 16th century, during the rule of Krishnadeva Raya of the Tuluva Dynasty, Vijayanagar had made the transition from a kingdom of aggregate chieftainships with shared or ritual sovereignty to a centralized empire with expanding royal authority. Constant warfare with its northern neighbors, the Deccani Sultanates derived from the Muslim **Bahmani** kingdom, undoubtedly contributed to the power of the ruler, as also to the southward expansion of Vijayanagar reach into rich **Tamil** country. Krishnadeva Raya's achievements also lay in persuading priests, landholders, merchants, artisans, and powerful religious bodies to support his authority over that of lesser chiefs. Inland, coastal, and international trade prospered, with exports of rice, sandalwood, spices, textiles, and timber, financing imports of horses and arms and also vast amounts of gold and silver. Most economic activities were monetized, and urban settlements proliferated. Temples were centers of political as well as religious activity and permitted architectural innovations, such as the *gopuram*, or tower, that later came to characterize south Indian temples.

In 1565, the five Deccani sultans combined against Rama Raya, then ruler of Vijayanagar, and inflicted a decisive defeat on him at the Battle of Talikota. Hampi was pillaged, and the empire soon disintegrated into smaller kingdoms whose political frontiers changed or faded into memory by the 18th century.

VIKRAMADITYA. Vikramaditya was a title assumed by several kings of ancient India, including Chandragupta (r. 380–415 CE) and his grandson Skandagupta (r. 455–467) of the **Gupta Dynasty**, as well as four rulers of the **Chalukya** Dynasty. The first named, that is Chandragupta Vikramaditya, was third in his line, defeated the **Sakas** of the northwest, consolidated the Gupta Empire and established his capital at Ujjaini (**Ujjain** in present-day **Madhya Pradesh**). He presided over a brilliant court and a period of peace and great cultural florescence. It is likely that **Kalidas**, the great **Sanskrit** playwright, received his patronage.

In the opinion of some scholars, the accomplishments of this monarch, notably his wisdom and magnanimity, gave rise to a cluster of legends about the "good king Vikramaditya of Ujjaini" who performed heroic and mystical deeds, and whose court was embellished by the *navaratna*, or "nine jewels" of learning. Some of these legends were collected and translated by the 19th-century English explorer Richard Burton under the title *The King and the Corpse*.

The Vikrama era, or **Hindu** calendar, is also associated with the legendary ruler whose title means "Sun of Prowess." But this era commences with the year 58 BCE and therefore cannot be linked plausibly with any of the historical figures mentioned previously.

VISHNU. Vishnu, from the **Sanskrit** root *vish*, to pervade, is one of the major deities in the **Hindu** pantheon. Although only of secondary importance in the **Vedas**, Vishnu the Preserver was referred to as the luckiest of gods, and by the time of the epics, *Ramayana* and *Mahabharata*, he was ranked of the first importance along with Brahma and **Shiva**.

Vishnu became the focus of all indigenous Indian savior myths as the redeemer, one who appeared on earth whenever necessary, and in different forms, to destroy evil. Among the twenty-two *avatars* (see Glossary), or incarnations, of Vishnu mentioned in the literature the best known ten are: Matsya or fish, Kurma or tortoise, Varaha or boar, Narasimha or man–lion, Vamana the dwarf, Parasuram the **brahman** warrior, **Ram** the god–king, **Krishna** the divine child, lover, and charioteer, **Buddha** the enlightened one, and Kalki the future savior. Vishnu is addressed by many other names and titles in different parts of India and at different times.

Numerous temples have been erected to Vishnu. The deity is iconographically represented as being of dark complexion, with four hands holding a lotus, mace, conch, and discus, seated on his eagle vehicle, Garuda, or reclining on the coils of a divine seven-headed serpent, Sheshnag, while floating on the primeval waters with his consort, Lakshmi. Vishnu is the focus of numerous devotional cults that frequently arose, as part of the **Bhakti** Movement, and since then.

VISHWA HINDU PARISHAD (VHP). This organization was founded by the **Rashtriya Swayamsevak Sangh (RSS)** in August 1964 with the explicit purpose of organizing, strengthening, and unifying **Hindu** society against the perceived aggression of "foreign" proselytizing religions, **Christianity** and **Islam**. The RSS had taken strong exception to the Pope's announcement of holding an International Eucharistic Congress in Bombay in November 1964, as well as to **New Delhi**'s creation of a state of **Nagaland** in 1963 for the Christianized Naga tribal peoples and tried to counter secularism in India.

The VHP is a militant answer to Hindu feelings of vulnerability and hostility toward the threatening "Other," emulating organizational features of the adversary and presenting reform as revival. Prominent notables and religious leaders, including the five Shankaracharyas who are the closest equivalents of ecclesiastical authority in **Hinduism**, attended the first meeting of the VHP, and subsequent meetings aspired to systematize and homogenize Hindu religious rituals. Leading a movement against cow slaughter in the late 1960s, the VHP recruited 10,000 "missionaries" to propagate its message throughout India and abroad. Saffron-clad *sadhus* in growing numbers became participants in VHP campaigns and functions. Local VHP chapters and departments were established across India as well as among communities of the Indian **diaspora** in Africa, Britain, Southeast Asia, Europe, and the United States. The VHP pushed for **Sanskrit** or Hindi in the Devanagari script as a national **language** and aimed to erode the innumerable "little traditions" of India under a standardized and newly muscular "great tradition" that was transmitted over modern media.

Hindutva forces became more assertive and visible during the 1980s and 1990s, with the VHP taking an active role. In 1983 the VHP organized an *Ekatmata Yagna* or ritual of unity. This involved taking 400 liters of water from the **Ganga** River at its source and carrying portions to every corner of the country to mingle with other rivers and so advertise the concept of Hindu unity. The ritual was repeated in October 1995 when 200,000 villages reportedly received the Ganga water. In 1985, the issue of building a temple to **Ram** at the Babri Masjid site in **Ayodhya** was raised and the VHP coordinated a worldwide and door-to-door campaign to finance the manufacture of bricks to be used in the construction of such a temple and transporting them to the disputed site in ceremonial processions. In the following decade, the RSS and VHP reasserted their objective of replacing the Gyanvapi Masjid in the Kashi Vishvanath complex in **Varanasi**, and the Shahi Idgah at the Krishnajanambhumi complex in

Mathura. Some expatriate VHP members even called for the replacement of 300 to 20,000 mosques all over India! Not surprisingly, fiery rhetoric heightened communal tensions, which often exploded in violence.

Attempts to mobilize voters on the basis of religious, or **caste**, identity have characterized the election campaigns of major **political parties** since 1989 and implementation of the **Mandal Commission**'s report in 1990. **Bharatiya Janata Party (BJP)** leader **L. K. Advani**'s *Rath Yatra* (procession evoking chariots of the past) from **Gujarat** to Ayodhya undertaken in September–October 1990 was a calculated ploy wholeheartedly supported and escorted by leaders of the VHP. Simultaneously, the VHP coordinated other torch-lit processions to converge on Ayodhya and a massive recruitment of *kar sewaks* (volunteer workers) to build the Ram temple. When the government of **Uttar Pradesh** arrested Advani and turned back *kar sewaks* the VHP publicized the theme of martyrdom to consolidate the political base of Hindutva forces. VHP *kar sewaks* and members of the **Bajrang Dal** were prominent in demolition of the Babri Masjid on December 6, 1992. Since that time many sincere efforts have been made to resolve the Ayodhya dispute through the judicial system, through negotiations between representative bodies, and through expressions of mutual goodwill. None has succeeded so far, and the VHP has consistently been one of the most intransigent parties. This and other similar episodes since 1998 led some commentators to postulate differences and tensions arising between the VHP, acting as pressure group, and the BJP, then leading a coalition government of India and thereby obliged to uphold secularism.

VISVESVARAYA, M. (1861–1962). Born in an orthodox **brahman** middle-class family, he studied Engineering in **Poona** and joined the Public Works Department of Bombay Presidency. Visvesvaraya specialized in water management and the construction of various hydraulic schemes until 1909. He then became the Chief Engineer of **Mysore** and subsequently Dewan (see Glossary). He introduced technical education, encouraged industrial development, and helped establish an iron and steel plant in that **Princely State**. Visvesvaraya was one of the early economic planners of India, associated with setting up the Indian Institute of Science, an aircraft factory, and other advanced projects at **Bangalore**. He was honored by the British Government of India in 1915 and received the Bharat Ratna—independent India's highest civilian award—in 1955.

VIVEKANANDA, SWAMI (1863–1902). Narendranath Dutta was born in an upper-class family of **Calcutta**, the eldest son of an attorney. Although educated in modern schools through the English **language**, Narendranath had a sense of vocation and searched for the Absolute Truth through the traditional methods of continence, knowledge, and meditation. His search led him to **Ramakrishna Paramhansa** at Dakshineswar in 1882, and he became his chosen disciple. In 1886, he was entrusted with carrying on Ramakrishna's mission, took *sanyas* (see Glossary) and a new name, Vivekananda, and embarked on a tour of India on foot. Five years of wandering left him deeply affected by the poverty, despair, and feeble physique of the common people toiling against a backdrop of palaces and natural beauty.

Vivekananda spoke and wrote perhaps the most biting and outraged criticisms of the physical misery and misguided beliefs of most Indians—"like so many worms on a rotten, stinking carcass"—in the 19th century. (Heimsath, *Indian Nationalism and Hindu Social Reform*: 26.) At the southernmost tip of the subcontinent, Kanya Kumari or Cape Comorin, Vivekananda was inspired with a plan to alleviate such conditions and purify the lifeblood of the nation through preaching the universal doctrine of **Vedanta**. He saw the problem of India as too much religion of the wrong kind; in his words, "Our religion is in the kitchen. Our God is in the cooking pot, and our religion is "don't touch me, I am holy." (Heimsath: 27). His purpose was to strengthen the lives of the Indian people, both morally and physically, so that they could determine their own future. His hope was vested in education for all, mostly secular, along with spiritual rejuvenation through discarding useless rituals, and physical health through proper food and exercise.

Vivekananda attended the first World Parliament of Religions held in Chicago in 1893 and was a popular lecturer in the United States for a number of years. He also toured Europe. He collected students as well as funds on both continents for proposed reforms in India. He returned to India in 1897 and established the **Ramakrishna Mission** to carry forward his objectives. Vivekananda marked the culmination of 19th-century social revolt and reform in India that was expressed in religious rather than political terms, and he exerted influence primarily through moral individuals and only secondarily through organization. He himself took issue with many contemporary social reformers for focusing on issues affecting mainly the high **castes** and neglecting practical involvement with the masses. In that respect, especially in his outspoken criticism of social evils and organizational approach to tackling them, he was a precursor of **Mahatma Gandhi**.

VOLUNTARY SECTOR. *See* NON-GOVERNMENTAL ORGANIZATIONS (NGOS).

VYASA. Vyasa was the title given to the authors or compilers of monumental literary works in early India and literally means "arranger." The **Puranas** refer to 30 Vyasas, of whom the most important was the sage who compiled the *Mahabharata*. In that account, Vyasa is the illegitimate son of the *rishi* (see Glossary) Parasuram by Satyavati, who subsequently marries the king. Vyasa, in accordance with the custom of *niyoga*, raises issue on her royal but childless daughters-in-law. Vyasa was thus the biological grandfather of the main protagonists in that epic war.

– W –

WALCHAND, HIRACHAND (1882–1953). The son of a **Jain** cotton merchant and moneylender of **Maharashtra**, Hirachand was educated in **Bombay** and took over the family business. He joined the **Indian National Congress** and was greatly influenced by **Dadabhai Naoroji** with whom he shared a belief in the importance of economic self-reliance as the key to political independence in India.

Walchand fought against British policies of economic imperialism and British-imposed restrictions on the development of Indian industry in practical ways. He moved beyond trade and became a prime figure in the revival of the Indian shipping industry; his name is associated with the construction of a shipyard at Visakhapatnam on the east coast, now one of India's largest naval bases. He was also instrumental in the founding of an automobile plant in Bombay and an aircraft factory in **Bangalore**. He was a modernizer who was equally opposed to British pride and Indian prejudice, and he helped to train Indians in science and technology.

WAVELL, FIELD MARSHAL, LORD ARCHIBALD PERCIVAL

(1883–1950). Wavell came from an honorable line of military men and had spent his childhood and an early posting in India. He was a modest, dogged, courageous, and serious-minded man of integrity, fond of history and poetry, who had built a solid professional record in the Boer War, **World War I**, and the Middle East sector in **World War II** before taking over as commander-in-chief, India, in 1941 and then serving as the allied commander in the southwest Pacific. Wavell was governor general and viceroy of India from October 1943 to January 1947.

Unfortunately, Wavell did not enjoy the confidence or the liking of British Prime Minister Winston Churchill, who sent him to secure India as an Allied bastion in the war against Japan at a most difficult time. The **Bengal** famine was at its height, the **Quit India Movement** was not yet extinguished, and Wavell's predecessor, **Lord Linlithgow**, had alienated leaders of the **Indian National Congress**. Wavell set a record for garnering information firsthand, and he toured India constantly. Despite lack of support from Churchill, he managed to obtain grain imports to relieve famine conditions in Bengal and avert famine in other parts of the country.

Wavell saw two alternatives for the British: to hold India by force or to give it independence at the earliest. He saw the unfeasibility of the first alternative and worked hard to secure the second without **partition**, viewing the Indian subcontinent as a "natural unit" and important to Western security. Toward that end, he released **Mahatma Gandhi** from prison in May 1944 but was not able to work with him. Nor was Wavell able to overcome the intransigence of **Mohammed Ali Jinnah**, and Churchill in London frequently countermanded Wavell's suggestions to the British government. To break the deadlock, Wavell proposed a provisional government in the form of a composite Executive Council consisting of the viceroy, the commander-in-chief, an equal number of **Hindus** and **Muslims** drawn from the leadership of the main **political parties**, one **Sikh**, and one **Untouch-**

able, to govern under the **Government of India Act of 1935**. The interim government would make proposals for a new **constitution** and would negotiate with the Indian princes on their place in the Dominion of India. London stalled on his proposals for eight months, but finally the "Wavell Plan" was announced in the British Parliament and over All-India Radio in June 1945.

A Simla Conference of "eminent persons" was immediately summoned to advise on implementing the Wavell Plan. The conference foundered on Jinnah's insistence to nominate all of the Muslim members of the proposed council (and so exclude Congress President **Maulana Azad**) and unseemly wrangling between members of the **All-India Muslim League** and Congress as well as between Indians and Britishers. Subsequently, a newly elected Labour government in Britain announced the dispatch of a **Cabinet Mission** to India; its plan, too, was doomed to failure. Wavell did form an interim multiparty government of Indians and established a good working relationship with **Sardar Vallabhbhai Patel**, home member in the interim government. After the communal carnage that followed Jinnah's call for Direct Action Day on August 16, 1946, Wavell drew up a "Breakdown Plan" for honorable British withdrawal and urged London to set a definite date for Indian independence as a united country.

It was Wavell's misfortune, and perhaps that of the Indian subcontinent as well, that his government paid insufficient heed to his advice and withdrew him from the viceroyalty on only one month's notice. **Lord Mountbatten**, Wavell's more glamorous and persuasive successor, carried out the task of partitioning India at the time of independence. Publication of the official correspondence and documents relating to the transfer of power in India has brought about thoughtful reassessments by historians of the roles played by these last two representatives of the British Crown in India.

WEDDERBURN, SIR WILLIAM (1838–1918). Wedderburn was born to a Scottish noble family with strong links to India through the **East India Company** and the **Indian Civil Service (ICS)**. He too joined the ICS in 1859 and retired as chief secretary to the governor of Bombay.

During his years of service in western India, Wedderburn focused mainly on the problems of rural poverty, including periodic famine.

He was in favor of reviving traditional Indian institutions, such as *panchayats* (see Glossary), or village councils, and indigenous systems of agricultural credit. He also came into professional contact with many of the men who formed the **Indian National Congress** in 1885. He shared the confidence of his compatriot, **Allan Octavian Hume**, in the useful function such a body would perform in British India. Wedderburn presided over the fourth session of Congress in 1889, and again in 1910 as an elder statesman.

A British Liberal who believed in the concepts of trusteeship and self-government, William Wedderburn served on various parliamentary committees dealing with India after his return to Britain in 1893. He was an advocate of constitutional reform and toward the end of his life welcomed the **Montagu Declaration** promising responsible government in India.

WELLESLEY, RICHARD COLLEY (1760–1842). Earl of Mornington and Marquess of Wellesley, he was governor general of the **East India Company** domains in India from 1798 to 1805. He increased the strength of the army to 300,000 men and pursued an aggressive policy of territorial expansion. He was unfettered by a Britain preoccupied with war against Napoleonic France. Wellesley led wars against the **Marathas** and **Mysore**. He was ably assisted by his brother Arthur, then in charge of the Nizam of **Hyderabad**'s armies and later the victor, as Duke of Wellington, at the Battle of Waterloo in Europe. Wellesley is also famous for having refined **Warren Hastings**'s system of dealing with the Indian **Princely States** through **Subsidiary Alliances**. In effect, Wellesley offered the princes a choice of signing a permanent treaty of subordinate alliance with the East India Company or facing internal destabilization of the kingdom and likely dethronement, if not war. Wellesley significantly extended the boundaries of British control in India.

WIPRO INFOTECH. Wipro is one of 11 Indian companies and 24 companies worldwide to provide software development facilities at Level 5 maturity—the highest stage of development according to the Carnegie Mellon system of classification. Also, Wipro was one of the early companies to take advantage of the pro-business legal and physical infrastructure offered by the city of **Bangalore** to establish its headquarters there and provide a variety of software and electronic services to clients across the country. Wipro's executives and engineers had close contacts with members of the Indian **Diaspora** working in or owning start-up companies in Silicon Valley, California, and soon began to export expert services to corporations in developed countries.

Wipro's chief executive Azim Premji is among the richest men in India but has an unostentatious style of living. His non-profit foundation funds projects to improve primary education in his home state of **Karnataka**. He enjoys good relations with Indian political leaders and has established Wipro centers in **Tamil Nadu** and **Punjab**. Wipro, along with its chief rivals and partners in India's software boom Infosys and **Tata** Consultancy Services, has recently moved some operations to China and participates in various Indian cooperative ventures in Southeast Asia.

WOMEN. The women of India defy generalized statements about them. They are to be found in all occupations, from the most menial such as scavenging, street hawking, prostitution, and domestic service, to the most lofty, such as in the civil services, as officers in the armed forces, as owners and managers of businesses, as doctors, judges, scientists, and teachers, and as chief ministers of states, leaders of political parties, and even as prime minister of India. Female literacy rates are low in India and opportunities or means for self-expression very limited, yet there are many nationally and internationally renowned Indian artists, musicians, and writers who are women. Some anthropologists and historians believe that the female creative force, or *Shakti*, infuses Indian civilization since earliest times, despite a heavy patriarchal overlay in custom, religion, and pre-independence law. Bolstering their thesis, they cite widespread worship of the Goddess, veneration of the mother (of sons) in all families, the persistence of matri-linear, matri-focal, communities in parts of the country, the relative equality, freedom and self-confidence of low-**caste** and **adivasi** women despite the colossal burden of oppression they have suffered and continue to suffer, and, above all, the outstanding ability and strength that Indian girls and women display in every arena of life, not least by enduring and surmounting the handicaps that continue to surround them.

Conspicuous among these handicaps is the apparently low value placed on female life. There are more than 35 million "missing women" in India (and also in China), by which we mean that according to the **census** of 2001 the total male population is 531,277,078 and the female population only 495, 738,169. (See Appendix F.) While a preference for male offspring is typical of agrarian societies, the contemporary gender gap is explained by assuming pregnancy termination if the fetus is female among those with access to gender-determining technology (ultra-sound diagnosis is now illegal in India), high rates of female morbidity and mortality due to malnutrition and possible neglect, and suspicion of female infanticide practiced in some areas and communities in times of hardship. Danger of illness and death is compounded by poor health facilities and the spread of **HIV/AIDS** beyond high-risk groups into the population of married women and their children. The gender gap or sex ratio varies by place and time, being widest in **Bihar**, **Haryana**, and **Uttar Pradesh** and narrowest in **Kerala**, **Pondicherry**, and the Northeastern states. Nationwide, there were 950 females to every 100 males in 1931 and in 1991 only 927; the 2001 Census reports a slight improvement of 933 females to 100 males. Another handicap that Indian women have faced is the low value placed on their education. At the time of independence, literacy rates in India were 27.16 for males and 8.86 for females. Numbers crept up slowly, and in the last decade of the 20th century public emphasis was put on the education and welfare of the "girl child" as well as on adult literacy campaigns. National literacy rates in 2001 were 75.85 for males and 54.16 for females, with rates in Kerala being much higher than in Bihar. Domestic violence is another disability for women in India, as elsewhere in the world, but there are no reliable statistics on it. Women are reluctant to report it and police will seldom interfere. Women in some communities have established their own self-help networks to call in neighbors and shame a man or family to desist from abuse.

Handicaps for Indian women built into social custom or religion are harder to overcome. However high the status of women might have been in **Vedic** India or earlier, by the first millennium of the Common Era it was low. Codification of **brahmanic** law ascribed to **Manu** and subsequently quoted as the main authority on **Hindu** social custom made harsh prescriptions on the duties and treatment of women and upheld the patriarchal joint family as the norm. Women were commanded to serve their husbands as a deity would be worshipped, denied rights to property, and placed under successive dominion of father, husband, and son. Masculine control of feared female sexuality led to child marriage, prohibition of widow remarriage, and self-immolation on the husband's funeral pyre, or **sati**. These abuses to humanity sparked a social reform movement in the 19th century led by men such as **Ram Mohun Roy** and others who brought about the legal abolition of sati in 1833 and worked to raise the age of consent and marriage in the 1880s. More was achieved during the freedom struggle of the first half of the 20th century, partly because **Mahatma Gandhi** extolled womanly virtue and courage and many women, including **Sarojini Naidu**, joined the **civil disobedience** movements that he led, and partly because women began to organize themselves with the support of the **Indian National Congress.** Articles 14 and 15 of the Indian **Constitution** of 1950 guarantee the fundamental right to equality and non-discrimination on grounds of gender. The omnibus *Hindu Code Bill* introduced in 1951 and eventually passed in 1956 rationalized laws on marriage and divorce and gave daughters and wives the right to inherit property. The age of marriage was progressively raised to 18. Article 25 defines "Hindu" very broadly, so that most Indian women gained directly from this legislation. **Muslim** personal law, however, was not amended, and Muslim women did not enjoy equal rights with men under Koranic law, or *Shari'a*, as highlighted by the **Shah Bano** case. Activists from the National Federation of Indian Women and the Muslim Women's Forum are currently engaged in educating women about their rights under the Indian Constitution as well as *Shari'a* and helping to realize them. Muslim women are also demanding rights to pray in mosques and have been elected to important positions, such as Mayor of **Ahmedabad** in 2004.

If the 1950s and 1960s seemed to promise much, especially to educated women, the 1975 *Report of the Commission on the Status of Women in India* showed that legal rights were not adequate to protect women from domestic and societal abuse. Women not only shouldered heavy physical labor in their traditional tasks of fetching water, fodder and fuel from increasingly long distances, they encountered the pitfalls of the modern market place such as lewd depictions of the female body in commercial advertisements, sexual harassment at work, and the commercialization of marriage itself in urban settings where traditional kinship links were weak. Demands for dowry from prospective bridegrooms and their families became extortionate and young married women were ill treated, or burned alive, to extract more. Despite a legal ban on dowry and penalties for violation of the ban, 6,000 dowry deaths were reported in 2000 and many reported in the **Press**. Also reported from time to time are cases of girls *refusing* to marry men demanding dowry. The campaign to implement women's rights passed into civil society. Independent and activist women in the **film industry** focus public attention on social problems. The Women's Feature Service news agency helps establish networks and literacy programs. **Non-Governmental Organizations (NGOs)** are particularly active in seeking to protect and empower women and generate income they can control, as exemplified by the **Self Employed Women's Association (SEWA)**, NGOs working in the broader area of development too discovered that the most effective agents of socioeconomic change frequently are women, even when powerful local supporters of the status quo oppose, threaten, and harm them. Women have taken leading activist roles in environmental protection and continue to be inspired by the **Chipko Movement**. NGOs also bring together privileged, urban, women who may be attracted to Western feminist ideas with ordinary Indian women who are not similarly impressed and link improvement of their own welfare and status inextricably to overall development, education, and alleviation of poverty, especially for their children.

Disadvantaged groups including women see political participation as an important route to higher status. The 1975 *Report* expressed disappointment that there were fewer female members of the **Lok Sabha** than earlier, and since then there has been steady pressure to increase the representation of women by persuading **political parties** to field more women candidates and by trying to reserve 33 per cent of legislative seats for women. A *Women's Bill* on the latter item was introduced in Parliament by the United Front coalition government in 1996 but has not been passed as yet for lack of consensus; only 350 women contested the general elections of 2004. Reservation of one third of seats in elected village panchayats for women, however, is proving to be an all-round success since the introduction of **Pan-**

chayati Raj. Many of these one million elected women are in the position of village headman, or *Sarpanch*, and if initially they tended to be "fronts" for husbands or brothers, second and third generation female sarpanches are noticeably more articulate and assertive. Moreover, many NGOs and governmental schemes offer special training programs in management and leadership skills to women. The face of rural India is changing through the emancipation of women. And in a more than superficial way, Indian women are on the move to regain the equality and power they deserve, and increasingly demand.

WORLD WAR I. India contributed 1,300,000 troops to the forces of the British Empire fighting Germany and its allies in World War I. Some 200,000 Indians in two army corps were in action in France and Flanders by November 1914. They served to hold the Allied line under appalling conditions of cold, disease, mud, filth, and the squandering of lives that characterized the battles of 1915 and 1916. Another Indian Expeditionary Force saw action in Egypt, Mesopotamia, and Palestine, and smaller numbers went to East Africa, Gallipoli, and Salonika.

Recruitment of soldiers in India was accelerated from the annual average of 15,000 a year to 300,000 a year, and the so-called "martial races" were hard put to supply the demands made on them. By 1918, India had given 800,000 combat troops and 400,000 noncombatants to the war effort. They served with valor and some were decorated, but at that time Indians were not admitted in the ranks of commissioned officers, so that even Princes held subordinate ranks of Viceroy's Commissioned Officers. There were voluntary efforts within India, such as the Red Cross, to help the war effort. Although revolutionary or nationalist activities were not suspended during the war, and many drew inspiration from the 1917 Bolshevic Revolution in Russia, India was generally "loyal" to the British Raj and encouraged by the **Montague Declaration** of 1917 promising "responsible government." In this respect, World War I in India was different from **World War II**.

The Indian exchequer bore the entire cost of troops serving abroad during the war, although that normally had been a British responsibility, with India paying only for those British and Indian troops that were deployed within or adjacent to India. The estimated gift so involved was 150 million pounds sterling. During World War II Britain paid for similar services on account. India's contribution of materials consisted of arms, ammunition, and clothing for the troops as well as manganese, mica, and wolfram used in ordnance industries. The indirect benefit of this contribution was the expansion of Indian entrepreneurship and industry beyond textiles, and some of India's major business and industrial houses first gained prosperity after the war.

When Turkey entered the war on the side of Germany in 1915 and **Islam** became a cause, there was unrest among Indian Muslim soldiers and threatened mutiny in the **Punjab** and **North West Frontier Province**, as actually broke out in Singapore. Tension in India was suppressed under wartime emergency regulations, and repressive legislation, such as the **Rowlatt Acts**, was passed after the war, but the tide of discontent rose. Moreover, World War I and its appalling casualties opened the eyes of many Indians to the faulty direction and administrative breakdowns possible in Europe as well. The myth of the inherently and permanently superior Englishman was shattered. After this, the success of India's struggle for freedom from British rule was only a matter of time and effort.

WORLD WAR II. This war had even more profound effects than **World War I** on the **Indian armed forces**, economy, and political development, as also on the British Empire in and beyond India. And India was crucial to the Allied global war effort and strategy in the Second World War to an even greater extent than in World War I. India's importance to the Allies lay in its contribution of two and a half million fighting men, payment for much of the war effort from funds raised by increasing taxation, and supplies of materials and manufactures. Geo-strategically, India was the hinge facing Africa and the Middle East on the west and **Burma** and Southeast Asia on the east. Indian armed forces fought in all these theaters of the war and manned the counterstrike against Japan through Burma in 1944. India was also the base for Americans supplying China across the "Hump" and training Chinese forces against Japan.

The war affected India's political development largely because Governor General **Lord Linlithgow** made the constitutionally correct but politically inept decision of declaring war with Germany in September 1939 without consulting any Indian leaders. He thus reversed two decades of constitutional reform and the cooperative premises of the 1935 **Government of India Act**, under which **Indian National Congress** governments exercised substantially autonomous power in eight provinces. Affronted by Linlithgow's action, these governments resigned in October and British rule in India reverted to its older form of autocratic control. Opinion in Congress on the war was divided. Some, like **Mahatma Gandhi**, were committed to non-violence. Some, like **Jawaharlal Nehru**, hated fascism and would have helped the Allies willingly if the British had made political concessions—or credible promises—precluded by British Prime Minister Winston Churchill's adamant refusal to do so. A very few, notably **Subhas Chandra Bose**, made common cause with Britain's enemies in Germany and Japan. Between late 1939 and August 1942 the British attempted to find a new basis of cooperation with Indian leaders and Congress wrestled with internal debate. The fall of Singapore and Rangoon to Japan in early 1942 endangered Britain as well as India and in March **Sir Stafford Cripps** was sent on a negotiating mission to India. It failed. Congress, led by Mahatma Gandhi, launched a massive **Quit India** movement of civil disobedience on August 8, 1942; Congress leaders were imprisoned immediately and the movement suppressed with a ruthless brutality not seen in India since the end of the **Uprising of 1857**. Sporadic violent protest continued, as also increased repression backed with 50 battalions of troops deployed for internal security. Britain's wish to placate **Islamic** opinion—provided most army recruits were Muslim—and its need for some kind of Indian political cooperation in the war effort, combined with Congress' self-denying tactics to give greater prominence to the still small **Muslim League** led by **Mohammed Ali Jinnah**. His call in 1940 for a separate homeland for Indian Muslims may have begun as a bargaining tool in three-way negotiations but ended with **Partition** in 1947.

The war had profound and long-lasting effects on the Indian economy and the lives of ordinary people. Massive mobilization of resources and people for a gigantic military effort was financed by increased direct and indirect taxation and an expanded money supply. Inflation resulted, with a rise in the cost of living index from a base 100 in 1939 to 231 by 1945. The government assumed an interventionist role in the economy to an unprecedented degree in order to absorb financial resources, check inflation, direct agriculture, license new industry, requisition goods for the army, and ultimately control food grain marketing and prices. These new duties burdened administrators and contributed to a near collapse of civilian government by the end of the war but were continued, and even expanded, by governments of independent India aspiring to planned economic development. Supplies to the Allied war effort took precedence over feeding ordinary Indians, even when monsoon failure and disruption of rice imports from Burma threatened famine. The government could not augment grain stocks or organize food distribution efficiently, and a prolonged food crisis culminated in the notorious Bengal Famine of 1943 in which an estimated three million people died of starvation.

World War II had an immediate and long-term effect of increasing India's industrial potential. India was a supply base for Commonwealth, Chinese, and American forces and produced strategic goods including aircraft supplies, ammunition, armored vehicles, boots and shoes, chemicals and drugs, guns, machine tools, surgical instruments, and textiles. It also engaged in shipbuilding and repairs. Many Indian entrepreneurs first found success during the war, especially in the building trades due to the new airfields, camps, hospitals, and roads constructed and the many ports and railways lines that were expanded. Britain's share of the expenses incurred was Pounds 1,300 million and credited to India's account in London. But government controls, shortage of capital, and lack of skilled manpower prevented a general industrial breakthrough in India at this time.

The war transformed the Indian armed forces. The Indian Army in 1939 consisted of 63,469 British and 205,000 Indian troops, poorly equipped and with only 396 Indian officers out of a total of 4,424. By the end of the war the army had 2,500,000 men with 8,300 Indian officers and a 10,000 strong Women's Auxiliary Corps (India). Tanks replaced most horses in cavalry regiments, infantry regiments were newly equipped with mortars and anti-tank guns, and artillery units expanded. The command structure was reshaped, with Eastern Army successfully overcoming the Japanese with the **Indian National Army (INA)** at the battles of Imphal and Kohima, and carrying out the Burma campaign under command of Field Marshall Slim. The Royal Indian Navy inaugurated in 1934 was expanded, assumed responsibility for India's coastal defense, and took part in operational and convey duties as far as the Mediterranean and Atlantic Oceans. The ratio of Indian to British naval officers was reversed during the war. Similarly, the Royal Indian Air Force, inaugurated in 1933, grew from less than one squadron to nine, with the number of Indian officers rising from 14 in 1939 to 1,375 in 1945. Several intelligence organizations were centered in India, including a branch of code-breakers who helped in decrypting Japanese military codes. Defense expenditure in India rose exponentially, but by an agreement between London and Delhi reached in November 1939 Britain was to pay for modernization of the army, capital outlays for ordnance industries, and all costs not essential to India's own defense. Britain's share amounted to about Pounds 1,400 million, credited to India's account in London.

Finally, World War II irrevocably weakened the imperial edifice. Despite authoritarian government and repressive measures, it was clear to Governor General **Lord Wavell** that the British could not hold India by force, especially in the face of an actual naval mutiny and potential disaffection in the army and civil service. Nor was India as a creditor country any longer regarded as an imperial asset. Wavell formed a provisional multiparty government of Indians in 1946 and made plans for an honorable British withdrawal, but could not obtain the backing of his own government. Congress and Muslim League leaders continued to bicker. Britain left a partitioned India in 1947; without this "jewel in the crown" Britain could not, and did not, long retain the rest of its once mighty empire.

– X –

XAVIER, FRANCIS (1506–1552). Francisco de Xavier was canonized as Saint by Pope Gregory XV in 1622. Xavier was a Basque nobleman who joined the Society of Jesus (*see* JESUITS) in 1534 and went to **Goa** as an Apostolic Nuncio in 1541. Xavier proselytized along the western and eastern coasts of India, especially among fishermen, and later among princes. He gained influence in Travancore, where there were many old-established communities of **Christians**, and the **Hindu** ruler acted as their protector as well as of the new Christians giving allegiance to Rome. Xavier went on to preach in Japan and China, where he died. His body remained uncorrupted and was returned to Goa by a Portuguese fisherman in 1553. Displayed under protective covering in the Church of Bom Jesu, the body of Saint Francis Xavier attracts many pilgrims (and tourists) to Goa every year.

XUANZANG or HIUEN TSANG or HSUAN–TSANG (c. 600–664).

A **Buddhist** monk of Chang'an, China, he is the most famous of many Chinese Buddhist pilgrims who made the long journey to India, a land they called "Western Heaven," in order to visit sacred sites, study, collect, and transcribe scriptures. Xuanzang was also the most prolific of transcribers and translators. The 73 manuscript works that he translated into Chinese after his return from India amounted to more than 1,000 rolls. They were housed in a special monastery constructed for him by his patron, the Empress Wu, outside present-day Xi'an.

Xuanzang's journey commenced in 629 CE along the well trod but excruciating **Silk Road**, or trading route, across inner Asia. He passed north of the Takamaklan desert, through Rufan, Karashan, Tashkent, Samarkand, and into Bactria. His detailed accounts of the Buddhist and non-Buddhist kingdoms he visited were sufficiently accurate for the 19th-century British traveler, Auriel Stein, to use as a guide. Having crossed the Hindu Kush Mountains, Xuanzang passed through many Indian kingdoms in the northwest. He spent several years in **Kashmir** before turning south to the plains of northern India and eastwards along the River **Ganges**. He studied for many years at **Nalanda** under the patriarch Silabhadra, and the work he did at Nalanda later formed the basis of a new school of Buddhism in China and Japan. Xuanzang traveled along the eastern coast but did not succeed in visiting **Sri Lanka**, so he turned north along the west coast and went inland to **Ajanta**. He revisited **Harsha-Vardhana**, imperial ruler at **Kanauj**, where he remained for some years as a highly honored scholar. He left vivid descriptions of the emperor and his court, as well as the socioeconomic conditions of the common people. He provides ample evidence of the religious tolerance, mutually beneficial coexistence of various Buddhist and **Hindu** sects, and nonexclusive royal patronage of religious bodies that prevailed in India at the time. He returned to China in 645.

Xuanzang is important not only as a Buddhist monk, pilgrim, and teacher, but also as a chronicler. The voluminous record of his travels, *Records of Western Regions*, is rich in historical and geographical detail. It is a primary source for historians of seventh-century India and inner Asia. It also served as the inspirational base for a Chinese literary masterpiece of the Ming dynasty, *Monkey*, which remains popular in China today and is presented from time to time in India as part of cultural exchange between the two countries.

– Y –

YADAV, LALOO PRASAD (1948–). Yadav was elected Chief Minister of **Bihar** in 1990 and again in 1995. He was disqualified from office and imprisoned in 1997 on charges resulting from the uncovering of a fraud of scandalous proportions, popularly known as the "fodder scam." He retained political power as leader of the majority political party, the Rashtriya Janata Dal (RJD), and through his wife, Rabri Devi, elected so succeed him as chief minister.

Laloo was born in a village to a Yadav family owning a small plot of agricultural land. He studied to be a veterinarian at **Patna** University, where he was President of the Students Union 1967–1969 and followed the **Lohia** socialists in political activity. He worked for two years in a Patna hospital before joining the mass movement led by **Jai Prakash Narayan** in 1974; Laloo Prasad was imprisoned during **Emergency Rule** and elected to the **Lok Sabha** in 1977 as a member of the **Janata Party**. He returned to take an active role in state politics, which were becoming increasingly complex and **caste** based, with the **Congress Party** that Laloo opposed identified with the upper castes. The pastoral and agricultural Yadav caste was large and ambitious, in competition with other lower caste groups such as the Kurmis and Koeris, but all pushing against continuing dominance of upper caste **brahmans**, Bhumihars, and **Rajputs** in the administration and landownership.

Events of 1990 polarized the whole country on the issue of reservations for "other backward castes" recommended by the **Mandal Commission** and Laloo Prasad capitalized on that. He adopted a style of electoral campaigning that highlighted the rustic quality of the lower castes and taunted the upper castes. He also consolidated an alliance between the "backward castes," the Muslims, and the Scheduled Castes on an ideology of secularism that brought him Congress support too in opposition to the **Bharatiya Janata Party (BJP)** campaigning on a **Hindutva** platform.

Laloo Prasad and his wife in office unhesitatingly advanced large numbers of Yadavs and their own supporters in every branch of state administration, education, and security at the expense of incumbents from the upper castes. Whatever the long-term benefits of this policy, there were high short-term costs paid in poor governance, caste conflict, corruption and breakdown of law and order. The criminalization of politics in Bihar through the operation of armed private militias, drug Mafias, and criminal gangs linked to officials and politicians did not originate with the RJD government, but continued unchecked. Among Indian states, Bihar ranks in the lowest rung of human development indicators. Although Laloo Prasad's personal charisma continues to draw votes and the districts traditionally antagonistic to him are now incorporated in the new state of **Jharkhand**, support for the RJD has declined since 1999. Nevertheless, it won the 2004 general elections handsomely and is an important member of the Congress-led coalition government that took power in New Delhi. Laloo Prasad Yadav currently holds the powerful **Railway** portfolio in **Dr. Manmohan Singh's** Cabinet.

YAMUNA or JUMNA RIVER. Originating in the central **Himalaya** near Mt. Kamet, the river Yamuna flows nearly 1,400 kilometers in a southeasterly direction until it joins the **Ganga or Ganges** at **Allahabad** or **Prayag**. This junction is the main site for the **Kumbha Mela** at which several millions of people congregate every 12 years. The Yamuna is sacred to the deity Brahma, and a number of sacred sites are found along its banks. The valley is fertile and rich with agricultural produce and the river is naturally an important trade route. Large irrigation canals were dug in the 19th century in the Ganga–Yamuna *doab* (see Glossary) further enhancing the agricultural wealth of the valley. Major cities, including **Delhi** and **Agra**, are located along the Yamuna and contribute to the most serious contemporary problem facing the river, pollution.

YASHODHARMAN was the ruler of Malwa in central India during the first half of the sixth century CE. He is famous for having defeated the **Huna** leader, Mihirgub, and driven him back. Yashodharman probably was assisted in this feat by the north Indian ruler of the **Gupta Dynasty**. Yashodharman erected two victory pillars in Mandasore. Their inscriptions credit him with very wide domains and many military victories over his adversaries far and near. Nothing further has been discovered as yet about his antecedents, his successors, or his other achievements.

YASHOVARMAN. This name or title belonged to several famous kings of early India. One ruled **Kanauj** in the eighth century CE, when the political core of northern India had already shifted westward from **Pataliputra** to Kanauj, and when Central Asia was the site of rivalry between Chinese, Tibetan, and Arab contenders. Yashovarman sent friendly emissaries to the Tang Dynasty in China, and was the patron at home of **Sanskrit** literati, including Bhavbhuti.

Another Yashovarman was a ninth-century ruler of Kambuja (present-day Kampuchea) whose numerous stone inscriptions were written in the Sanskrit language, using both the Devanagari script and the more commonly used script of Kambuja. These inscriptions testify to the close ties between India and Southeast Asian kingdoms at the time. A third known Yashovarman was a 10th-century **Chandella** ruler who battled against the **Pratihara** armies and built one of the distinctive **Vishnu** temples at Khajuraho.

YAVANA. Yavana is the ancient Indian word for Greek. Chroniclers from the age of the **Buddha** on, including **Panini**, were familiar with the Indo–Greeks. The Indo–Greek settlements in Bactria and Sogdiana (between Balkh and Samarkand in Central Asia), eastern Iran, and Afghanistan, constantly interacted with the northwestern parts of the Indian subcontinent well before the arrival of **Alexander of Macedon** toward the end of the fourth century BCE. His armies reinforced these settlements, and the many men who stayed behind formed a substantial military and cultural presence at the crossroads of Asia.

The climax of Yavana power was reached under Menander (second century BCE), whose exquisite silver coins have been found all over the northwest and as far south as central India. Menander, known as Milinda in **Buddhist** literature, was a pupil of the sage Nagasena and the *Milindapanha*, or *Conversations with Milinda* survives as a popular text on Buddhist precepts then being carried far and wide along well-traveled trade routes.

The Yavanas frequently clashed with the **Mauryas** and occupied the outlying parts of the Mauryan Empire after its decline at the time of Pushyamitra (c. 184–148 BCE). According to **Patanjali**, Yavanas raided as far east as **Pataliputra**, before succumbing to internal feuds and the greater power of the **Kushans**. The Yavanas or Indo–Greeks have naturally attracted considerable interest among European scholars who have documented their artistic and other achievements.

YOGA. The term is derived from the **Sanskrit** root *yuj,* and means the yoking of mind and body to achieve perfect unity at the most profound level, beyond the limits of thought and language, space, or time. Yoga in this sense has no specific religious connotation; its appeal is universal and its practice common to followers of all religions in early India as in the contemporary world.

Seals found in **Harappa** and Mohenjo-Daro show evidence of the ancient origin of yoga in India. Yoga is mentioned in some of the **Upanishads**. It became a science with **Patanjali**'s systematic codification of both theory and practice in his *Yoga Sutru* of the second century BCE. Thereafter, yoga developed as one of the six schools of classical Indian Philosophy, often associated with the **Samkhya** school, and provided an impetus to critical speculation among the **Buddhist**, **Jain**, and **Vedanta** schools as well.

Yoga also means the way, the method, of seeking the goal of reintegrating mind and body. Different forms of yoga have been described and practiced over the ages. Very briefly, *Hatha yoga* stresses reintegration through control of the body and vital energies, especially the breath. It is part of the training for classical dance and **music**, brings extraordinary coordination of mind and body, and is very popular. *Mantra* (see Glossary) brings reintegration through repetition of hermetic formulas and is an aid to meditation and prayer. **Bhakti** means unswerving devotion and *bhakti yoga* is the path of faith to spiritual liberation. Similarly, *gyana yoga* is the path of knowledge, and *karma yoga* is the path of duty and righteous action. *Raja Yoga* is the royal road to reintegration using all the paths. No single yoga method exists in isolation, and practice of one form of yoga usually implies familiarity, at the least, with others.

YOUNGHUSBAND, SIR FRANCIS EDWARD (1863–1942). Younghusband was born in Murree in the hills of **Punjab**. He was educated, in a fashion typical of the British serving in India, at an English public school and at the military academy of Sandhurst. By the age of 25, he had crossed the Gobi desert, was widely recognized as a brilliant army officer and explorer, and in appearance and manner was almost a stereotype of the romanticized Victorian imperialist. Younghusband was a master player in what came to be called the "Great Game" of Anglo–Russian rivalry in the high ranges that formed the watershed between the rivers of the Indian subcontinent and of Central Asia. The Royal Geographical Society honored him for his explorations in the Karakoram range in **Ladakh** in particular.

Lord Curzon, then Viceroy of India, chose Younghusband to lead an expedition into **Tibet**, as far as Lhasa itself, so as to establish British—and preempt Russian—influence in that high closed country between India and China. Younghusband's first small expedition of 200 men was turned back by Tibetan forces in 1903. The following year, 1,000 Indian soldiers under British command, along with reporters, artillery, animals, and 10,000 porters, crossed the high passes of the Chumbi Valley east of **Sikkim** and battled on through Gyantse to Lhasa. Under instructions from Curzon, Younghusband extracted agreement from the then-young and future powerful 13th **Dalai Lama** to abjure dealings with all other foreigners, to accept a British Resident in Lhasa, to recognize the 1890 frontier of Sikkim, to raze fortifications, and to pay an indemnity. The terms were subsequently softened very considerably by London with an eye on Peking, and Curzon's Tibet policy was repudiated. Younghusband was sent to **Kashmir** as British Resident and then retired to England, where he was a popular hero lionized in high society, in 1909. He was knighted in 1917, became President of the Royal Geographical Society in

1919, and actively promoted British expeditions to Mount Everest in the 1920s and 1930s.

Younghusband's career after he left India was erratic, and his personal life was troubled and financially insecure. He turned increasingly toward philosophy and religion, especially after his own mystic experiences—at Lhasa in 1904 and at home in 1925. He published numerous books and tracts based on his travels and organized several societies for world religion, all more or less unsuccessful. He also became an advocate of self-government for India, lectured widely on the subject and frequently met Indians of both political and spiritual inclination, including **M. K. Gandhi** and **Rabindranath Tagore**. In short, Younghusband was a more complex and multifaceted personality than his early public image would lead one to expect.

– Z –

ZAFAR (1775–1867). This was the pen name of **BAHADUR SHAH II**, last **Mughal** Emperor. In 1858, he was exiled to **Burma** where he continued to write poetry.

ZAIL SINGH (1916–1995). He was President of India from 1982 to 1987. Zail Singh was born in the **Princely State** of Faridkot in the **Punjab** and took an active part in the **States Peoples Conference** movement for democratization inspired by the **Indian National Congress** in the late 1930s. He founded the Faridkot State Congress. After Indian independence, Zail Singh became a member of government first in the Patiala and East Punjab States Union or PEPSU and then in Punjab. He was a member of the **Rajya Sabha** from 1956 to 1962. When chief minister of Punjab from 1972 to 1977, he combated the **Akali Dal**'s appeal to the electorate by promoting overtly **Sikh** symbols in the state.

Zail Singh was loyal to **Indira Gandhi**, even when she was out of power and was invited to join her Cabinet as Minister of Home Affairs in 1980. His tenure as head of state was controversial. The Indian Army's Operation Blue Star in **Amritsar** against **Sant Bhindrawale** and his supporters in June 1984 exposed Zail Singh, as the first Sikh President, to considerable animosity and possible threat from militants. After Mrs. Gandhi's assassination, Zail Singh was reported as having friction with the young Prime Minister Rajiv Gandhi, and even rumored to wish to remove him, which was constitutionally not possible.

ZAKIR HUSAIN (1897–1969). The third President of the Republic of India, Zakir Husain was elected as Head of State in 1967 when he was Vice President. He died suddenly, while in office.

Zakir Husain was born in **Hyderabad**. He was educated at **Islamic** schools and the Muslim Anglo–Oriental College in Aligarh before proceeding to Berlin for a Doctorate in Economics. He was moved by the **Khilafet Movement** and the **Non-Cooperation Movement** to become part of the Indian national movement in the 1920s. He focused on education as the main instrument of regeneration and made major contributions toward spreading education more widely in India. He helped establish the Jamia Millia Islamia in **Delhi**, largely for the benefit of poor Muslims, and was appointed as its Vice Chancellor (University President) in 1926. Looking for ways to make education more immediately relevant and less clerical to more children than prevailing systems, he evolved a curriculum for schools in which academic skills could be imparted alongside vocational and physical training. He launched it as a scheme of Basic National Education in 1938 with the blessings of **Mahatma Gandhi**.

After Indian independence, Dr. Zakir Husain was appointed Vice Chancellor of the renamed Aligarh Muslim University in 1948 and served on the University Grants Commission and various educational committees exploring post-independence needs and how to meet them during the 1950s. He had an imposing presence as a man of culture, learning, and refinement. He was elected President of the World University Service in 1954 and appointed India's Representative to UNESCO in 1956. He received various awards from foreign governments as well as India's highest civilian decoration, the Bharat Ratna before he became President.

ZOROASTRIAN. A follower of the religion founded by the Prophet Zoroaster in ancient Persia and based on the doctrine of cosmic dualism, or struggle between good and evil. Its fundamental tenets are drawn from the *Avesta,* a collection of texts and hymns written in a **language** similar to that of the *Rig Veda* in India.

Zoroastrianism was the official faith of the Achaemenid, Parthian, and Sassanid Empires but was largely supplanted after the Arab conquest of Iran in 651 CE. A group of Zoroastrians fearing forcible conversion to **Islam** fled from Khorasen in eastern Iran to **Gujarat** in western India during the 10th century. Their descendants are known as Parsi (from Persia) in India. *See also* PARSI.

Appendix A

Chief Executives of British India

EAST INDIA COMPANY RULE

Governors General of Bengal

Warren Hastings	1774–1785
Lord Cornwallis	1786–1793
Sir John Shore	1793–1798
Lord Wellesley	1798–1805
Lord Minto	1807–1813
Lord Hastings	1813–1823
Lord Amherst	1823–1828
Lord Bentinck	1828–1833

Governors General of India

Lord Bentinck	1833–1835
Lord Auckland	1836–1842
Lord Ellenborough	1842–1844
Lord Hardinge	1844–1848
Lord Dalhousie	1848–1856
Lord Canning	1856–1858

CROWN RULE

Governors General and Viceroys of India

Lord Canning	1858–1862
Lord Elgin	1862–1863
Lord Lawrence	1864–1869

Lord Mayo	1869–1872
Lord Northbrook	1872–1876
Lord Lytton	1876–1880
Lord Ripon	1880–1884
Lord Dufferin	1884–1888
Lord Landsdowne	1888–1894
Lord Elgin	1894–1899
Lord Curzon	1899–1905
Lord Minto	1905–1910
Lord Hardinge	1910–1916
Lord Chelmsford	1916–1921
Lord Reading	1921–1925
Lord Irwin	1926–1931
Lord Willingdon	1931–1936
Lord Linlithgow	1936–1943
Lord Wavell	1943–1947
Lord Mountbatten	March–August 1947

Appendix B
Heads of State of Independent India

GOVERNORS GENERAL OF INDIA AS A DOMINION

Lord Louis Mountbatten	August 1947–June 1948
Chakravarti Rajagopalachari	June 1948–January 1950

PRESIDENTS OF THE REPUBLIC OF INDIA

Dr. Rajendra Prasad	January 1950–May 1962
Dr. Sarvapalli Radhakrishnan	1962–1967
Dr. Zakir Husain	1967–1969
Varahagiri Venkata Giri	1969–1974
Fakhruddin Ali Ahmad	1974–1977
Neelam Sanjiva Reddy	1977–1982
Giani Zail Singh	1982–1987
R. Venkataraman	1987–1992
Dr. Shankar Dayal Sharma	1992–1997
Dr. K. R. Narayanan	1997–2002
Dr. Abdul Kalam	2002–

Appendix C
Prime Ministers of India

Jawaharlal Nehru (1889–1964)   August 1946–May 1964

Gulzari Lal Nanda (1898–1995)   (Acting) May 1964–June 1964

Lal Bahadur Shastri (1904–1966)   June 1964–January 1966

Indira Gandhi (1917–1984)   January 1966–March 1977

Morarji Desai (1896–1995)   March 1977–July 1979

Charan Singh (1902–1986)   July 1979–January 1980

Indira Gandhi (1917–1984)   January 1980–October 1984

Rajiv Gandhi (1944–1991)   November 1984–November 1989

Vishwa Pratap Singh (1931–)   November 1989–November 1990

Chandra Shekhar (1927–)   November 1990–June 1991

P.V Narasimha Rao (1921–2004)   June 1991–May 1996

Atal Behari Vajpayee (1926–)   May 16, 1996–June 1, 1996

H.D. Deve Gowda (1933–)   June 1996–April 1997

I. K. Gujral (1919–)   April 1997–March 1998

Atal Behari Vajpayee (1926–)   March 1998–October 1999

Atal Behari Vajpayee (1926–)   October 1999–May 2004

Dr. Manmohan Singh (1932–)   May 2004–

Appendix D
Chief Justices of India

Name	Tenure
Harilal J. Karnia	January 1950–November 1951
M. Patanjali Sastri	November 1951–January 1954
Meher Chand Mahajan	January 1954–December 1954
B. K. Mukherjea	December 1954–January 1956
S. R. Das	February 1956–September 1959
Bhuvaneshwar Prasad Sinha	October 1959–January 1964
P. B. Gajendragadkar	February 1964–March 1966
A. K. Sarkar	March 1966–June 1966
K. Subba Rao	June 1966–April 1967
K. N. Wanchoo	April 1967–February 1968
M. Hidayatullah	February 1968–December 1970
J. C. Shah	December 1970–January 1971
S. M. Sikri	January 1971–April 1973
A. N. Ray	April 1973–January 1977
M. H. Beg	January 1977–February 1978
Y. V. Chandrachud	February 1978–July 1985
Prafullachandra N. Bhagwati	July 1985–December 1986
R. S. Pathak	December 1986–June 1989
E.S. Venkataramiah	June 1989–December 1989
S. Mukharjee	December 1989–September 1990
Ranganath Mishra	September 1990–November 1991
K. N. Singh	November 1991–December 1991
M. H. Kania	December 1991–November 1992
L. M. Sharma	November 1992–February 1993
M. N. Venkatachaliah	February 1993–October 1994

(continued)

CHIEF JUSTICES OF INDIA (*continued*)

Name	Tenure
A. M. Ahmadi	October 1994–March 1997
J. S. Verma	March 1997–January 1998
M. M. Punchhi	January 1998–October 1998
A. S. Anand	October 1998–October 2001
S. P. Barucha	November 2001–December 2002
V. N. Khare	December 2002–May 2004
S. Rajendra Babu	May 2004–June 2004
R. C. Lalori	June 2004–November 2005
Y.K. Sabharwal	November 2005–

Appendix E
Chief Election Commissioners of India

Name	Tenure
Sukumar Sen	March 1950–December 1958
K. V. K. Sundaram	December 1958–September 1967
S. P. Sen Verma	October 1967–September 1972
Dr. Nagendra Singh	October 1972–February 1973
T. Swaminathan	February 1973–June 1977
S. L. Shakdhar	June 1977–June 1982
R. K. Trivedi	June 1982–December 1985
R. V. S. Peri Sastri	January 1986–November 1990
Smt. V. S. Ramadevi	November 1990–December 1990
T. N. Seshan	December 1990–December 1996
Dr. M. S. Gill	December 1996–June 2001
J. M. Lingdoh	June 2001–February 2004
G. K. Krishnamachari	February 2004–

Appendix F

Population of India by State, Gender, and Location

POPULATION OF INDIA BY STATE, GENDER, AND LOCATION

State	Total	Male	Female	Rural	Urban
India	1,027,015,247	531,277,078	495,738,169	741,660,293	285,354,954
Andhra	75,727,541	38,286,811	37,440,730	55,223,944	20,503,597
Arunachal	1,091,117	573,951	517,166	868,429	222,688
Assam	26,638,407	13,787,799	12,850,608	23,248,994	3,289,413
Bihar	82,878,796	43,153,964	39,724,832	74,199,596	8,679,200
Chhatisgarh	20,795,956	10,452,426	10,343,530	16,620,627	4,175,329
Goa	1,343,998	685,616	658,381	675,129	668,869
Gujarat	50,596,992	26,344,053	24,252,939	31,697,615	18,899,377
Haryana	21,082,989	11,327,658	9,755,331	14,968,850	6,114,139
Himachal	6,007,248	3,085,256	2,991,992	5,482,367	594,881
Jammu and Kashmir	10,069,917	5,300,574	4,769,343	7,564,608	2,505,309
Jharkhand	26,909,428	13,861,277	13,048,151	20,922,731	5,986,697
Karnataka	52,733,958	26,856,343	25,877,615	34,814,100	17,919,858
Kerala	31,838,619	15,468,664	16,369,955	23,571,484	8,267,135
Madhya Pradesh	60,385,118	31,456,873	28,928,245	44,282,528	16,102,590
Maharashtra	96,752,247	50,334,270	46,417,270	55,732,513	41,019,734
Manipur	2,388,634	1,207,338	1,181,296	1,818,224	570,410
Meghalaya	2,306,069	1,167,840	1,138,229	1,853,457	452,612

Mizoram	891,058	459,783	431,275	450,018	441,040
Nagaland	1,988,636	1,041,686	946,950	1,635,815	353,821
Orissa	36,706,920	18,612,340	18,094,580	31,210,602	5,496,318
Punjab	24,289,296	12,963,362	11,325,934	16,043,730	8,245,566
Rajasthan	56,473,122	29,381,657	27,091,465	43,267,678	13,205,444
Sikkim	540,493	288,217	252,276	480,488	60,005
Tamil Nadu	62,110,839	31,268,654	30,842,185	34,869,286	27,241,553
Tripura	3,191,168	1,636,138	1,555,030	2,648,074	543,094
Uttar Pradesh	166,052,859	87,466,301	78,586,558	131,540,230	34,512,629
Uttaranchal	8,479,562	4,316,401	4,163,161	6,309,317	2,170,245
West Bengal	80,221,171	41,487,694	38,733,477	57,734,690	22,486,481
Union Territories					
Andaman and Nicobar Islands	356,265	192,985	163,280	239,858	116,407
Chandigarh	900,914	508,224	392,690	92,118	808,796
Dadar And Nagar Haveli	220,451	121,731	98,720	169,995	50,456
Daman&Diu	158,059	92,478	65,581	100,740	57,319
Delhi	13,782,976	7,570,890	6,212,086	983,215	12,819,761
Lakshadweep	60,595	31,118	29,477	33,647	26,948
Pondicherry	973,829	486,705	487,124	325,596	648,233

Source: Data based on Census of India, 2001, Table 1.1.

Appendix G

Population of India by State and Religious Affiliation, 2001

POPULATION OF INDIA BY STATE AND RELIGIOUS AFFILIATION, 2001

State	Total	Hindu[1]	Muslim[2]	Christian[3]	Sikh	Buddhist	Jain	Other[4]	Not Stated
India	1,028,610,328	827,578,868	138,188,240	24,080,016	19,215,730	7,955,207	4,228,053	6,639,626	727,588
(percent)		82.41%	11.67%	2.32%	1.99%	0.77%	0.41%	0.43%	
Andhra	76,210,007	67,836,651	6,836,651	1,181,917	30,998	32,037	41,846	4,768	94,934
Arunachal	1,097,968	379,935	20,675	205,675	1,865	143,028	216	337,399	9,302
Assam	26,655,528	17,296,455	8,240,611	986,589	22,516	51,029	23,957	22,999	11,369
Bihar	82,998,509	69,076,919	13,722,048	53,137	20,780	18,818	16,085	52,905	37,817
Chhatisgarh	20,833,803	19,729,670	409,615	401,035	69,621	65,267	56,103	95,187	7,305
Goa	1,347,668	886,551	92,210	359,568	970	649	820	353	6,547
Gujarat	50,671,017	45,143,074	4,592,854	284,092	45,587	17,829	525,305	28,698	33,578
Haryana	21,144,564	18,655,925	1,222,916	27,185	1,170,662	7,140	57,167	1,255	2,314
Himachal	6,077,900	5,800,222	119,512	7,687	72,355	75,859	1,408	425	432
Kammu and Kashmir	10,143,700	3,005,349	6,793,240	20,299	207,154	113,787	2,518	97	1,256
Jharkhand	26,945,829	18,475,681	3,731,308	1,093,382	83,358	5,940	16,301	3,514,472	25,387
Karnataka	52,850,562	44,321,279	6,463,127	10,009,164	15,326	393,300	412,659	115,460	120,247
Kerala	31,841,374	17,883,449	7,863,842	6,057,427	2,762	2,027	4,528	2,256	25,083
Madhya Pradesh	60,348,023	55,004,675	3,841,449	170,381	150,772	209,322	545,446	409,285	16,693
Maharashtra	96,878,627	77,859,385	10,270,485	1,058,313	215,337	5,838,710	1,301,843	236,841	97,713
Manipur	2,166,788	996,894	190,939	737,578	1,653	1,926	1,461	235,280	1,057
Meghalaya	2,318,822	307,822	99,169	1,628,986	3,110	4,703	772	267,245	7,015

	Total	Hindus[1]	Muslims[2]	Christians[3]	Sikhs	Buddhists	Jains	Other[4]	Religion not stated
Mizoram	888,573	31,562	10,099	772,809	326	70,490	179	2,443	661
Nagaland	1,990,036	153,262	35,162	1,790,349	1,152	1,356	2,093	6,108	811
Orissa	36,804,660	34,726,129	761,985	897,861	17,492	9,863	9,154	361,981	20,195
Punjab	24,358,999	8,997,942	382,045	292,800	14,592,387	41,487	39,276	8,594	4,468
Rajasthan	56,507,188	50,151,452	4,788,227	72,660	818,420	10,335	650,493	5,253	10,348
Sikkim	540,851	329,548	7,693	36,115	1,176	152,042	183	12,926	1,168
Tamil Nadu	62,405,679	54,985,079	3,470,647	3,785,060	9,545	5,393	83,359	7,252	59,344
Tripura	3,199,203	2,739,310	254,442	102,442	1,182	98,922	477	1,277	1,104
Uttar Pradesh	166,197,921	133,979,263	30,740,158	212,578	678,059	302,031	207,111	9,281	69,440
West Bengal	80,176,197	58,104,835	20,240,543	515,150	66,391	243,364	55,223	895,796	54,895
Union Territories									
Andaman and Nicobar Islands	356,152	246,589	15,326	77,178	1,587	421	23	238	851
Chandigarh	900,635	707,978	35,548	7,627	145,175	1,332	2,592	257	126
Dadar and Nagar Haveli	220,490	206,203	6,524	6,058	123	457	864	90	171
Daman and Diu	158,204	141,901	12,281	3,362	145	126	268	103	18
Delhi	13,850,507	11,358,049	1,623,520	27,185	555,602	23,705	155,122	2,174	2,016
Lakshadweep	60,650	2,221	57,903	509	6	1	0	0	10
Pondicherry	974,345	845,449	59,358	67,688	108	73	952	158	559

[1] Hindu includes Arya Samaj, Brahmo Samaj, Lingayat, Radhaswami, Sat Sanghi, Sanatan Dharma, Vaishnav, Valmiki
[2] Muslim includes Bohra, Dudikula, Ismaili, Khoja, Shi'a, Sunni
[3] Christian includes Methodist, Protestant, Roman Catholic, Syrian Christian
[4] Other includes Animist, Atheist, Bahai, Bhoi, Bhumi, Garo, Gewari, Mushmi, Jew, Kabui, Khasi, Parsi, Santal, and many other tribal or local faiths

Source: Based on report published by the Census of India in October 2004.

Appendix H
India's Political Parties

List of Parties and Composition of Lok Sabha through 2004

LIST OF POLITICAL PARTIES, 2004

National Parties Recognized by the Election Commission in Four or More States
Bharatiya Janata Party (BJP)
Communist Party of India (CPI)
Communist Party of India–Marxist (CPI [M])
Indian National Congress or Congress Party
Janata Dal
Samata Party
Nationalist Congress Party (NCP)

STATE PARTIES OPERATING IN ONE OR FEWER THAN FOUR STATES

Akali Dal, Punjab
All India Anna Dravida Munnetra Kazhagam (AIDMK), Tamil Nadu
All India Forward Bloc, West Bengal
Asom Gana Parishad, Assam
Bahujan Samaj Party (BSP), Uttar Pradesh
Biju Janata Dal, Orissa
Dravida Munnetra Kazhagam (DMK), Tamil Nadu
Indian National Lok Dal, Haryana
Jammu and Kashmir National Conference, Jammu and Kashmir
Janata Dal (Secular), Karnataka
Janata Dal (United) Bihar, Jharkhand, Karnataka, Nagaland
Jharkhand Mukti Morcha (JMM), Jharkhand

Kerala Congress, Kerala
Muslim League, Kerala
New Justice Party, Tamil Nadu
People's Democratic Party (PDP), Jammu and Kashmir
Rashtriya Janata Dal (RJD) Bihar, Jharkhand
Rashtriya Lok Dal, Uttar Pradesh
Samajwadi Janata Party, Uttar Pradesh
Samajwadi Party, Uttar Pradesh
Telegu Desam party (TDP), Andhra Pradesh
Telengana Rashtra Samiti (TRS), Andhra Pradesh
Trinamool Congress, West Bengal
Shiv Sena, Maharashtra

COMPOSITION OF THE LOK SABHA BY POLITICAL PARTY, 1952–2004

	1952	1957	1962	1967	1971	1977	1980	1984	1989	1991	1996	1998	1999	2004
Total Seats	489	494	494	520	518	540	529	541	528	521	543	539	543	543
Indian National Congress and Indian National Congress Indira in 1980	364	371	361	283	352	154	353	415	197	232	140	141	114	145
Bharatiya Janata Party and Bharatiya Jana Sangha till 1971	3	4	14	35	22	295		2	86	120	161	179	182	138
Janata Dal			18	44	8				142	59	46	6	21	11
Communist Party of India	16	27	29	23	23	7	11	6	12	14	12	9	4	10
Communist Party of India Marxist				19	25	22	36	22	33	35	32	32	33	43
Lok Dal					16	3	41	3	0	0	0	0	0	0
Samajwadi Party							31	10	0	5	17	20	26	36
Bahujan Samaj Party											11	5	14	19
Praja Socialist Party	9	19	12	13	2									
Samyukta Socialist Party	12		6	23	3									
OTHERS	47	31	34	45	53	52	35	44	44	41	115	141	143	78
Independents	38	42	20	35	14	9	9	5	12	1	9	6	6	20
RJD														
DMK														16
Telegu Desam Party														5
Telengana Rashtra Samiti														5

Appendix I
India's Major Economic Reforms 1991–2004

A. INDUSTRIAL SECTOR

India's industrial environment before the reforms was dominated by the public sector and by governmental controls on private investment exerted through a multitude of permits, licenses, and subsidies.

1. List of industries reserved solely for the public sector reduced from 18 to six to three: defense aircrafts and warships, atomic energy generation, railway transport.
2. Former public sector industries, including iron and steel, heavy machinery, telecommunications, air transport, and power generation and distribution, opened to private enterprise.
3. Licensing for setting up industries abolished, including sugar, coal and lignite, petroleum distillation, manufacture of bulk drugs.
4. Price controls abolished in key industries, including iron and steel, coal, phosphate fertilizers, naphtha, lubricating oils, and molasses. Coverage of price controls on pharmaceuticals reduced.
5. Restrictions on size and market shares of large firms under the Monopolies and Restrictive Trade Practices (MRTP) Act lifted.
6. Government equity in non-strategic state owned enterprises reduced to 26%.
7. Reservations of products for small-scale industries reduced, with export earners leather goods and garments opened to others.
8. Department of Disinvestment established in 1999 to process privatization and equity sales in state-owned enterprises.

Under Consideration But Pending

- Supporting action in all states for industrial liberalization.
- Disinvestment in non-profitable state owned enterprises.
- Reform of labor laws to permit restructuring of firms employing more than 100 persons so as to gain efficiency and competitiveness.
- Enable closure of bankrupt firms.
- Decontrol of prices in hydrocarbons, electricity, and fertilizers

B. FOREIGN TRADE AND FOREIGN EXCHANGE SECTOR

Before the liberalization reforms India was an almost closed market, with quantitative restrictions (QRs) on most imports, especially consumer goods, a pervasive system of import and export licenses, very high tariff barriers—with a top rate of over 200% for some and rates between 110 and 160% for most imports—and strict controls on all foreign exchange transactions.

1. Import licensing for imports of industrial raw materials, components and capital goods abolished in 1991, followed gradually by removal of licenses for most other imports including consumer goods but not all agricultural products. QR regime virtually ended by 2000.
2. Tariffs reduced to an average of 25% with a top rate of 45%.
3. Zero duties levied on electronic products.
4. Regional or bilateral free trade agreements negotiated in SAARC and ASEAN, and successive governments promise to reduce Indian tariff levels to the five to 15% range of other Asian developing countries.
5. Rupee devalued by 24% in 1991, a dual exchange rate introduced in 1992, and a unified exchange rate allowed to float in response to market conditions in 1993.
6. India declared full current account convertibility of the Rupee in 1994 and liberalized exchange restrictions on all current account transactions.
7. Foreign Exchange Regulation Act (FERA) of 1973 replaced by a modern Foreign Exchange Management Act in 1998.

8. Wheat, rice, coarse grains, edible oils, oil seeds, and sugar removed from the purview of the Essential Commodities Act that empowered state governments to restrict movement of products.
9. India accepted the trade-related aspects of intellectual property rights (TRIPS) when it ratified the World Trade Organization convention in 1995 and had five years to bring its laws into conformity. Between 1999 and 2002 new laws relating to trade marks, industrial design, and copyrights were passed and in 2004 the Patents Act of 1970 was comprehensively overhauled and its administration modernized.

Under Consideration But Pending

- Abolition of excise and other duties impeding free movement of goods throughout India.
- Adoption by states of a uniform value added tax (VAT) to raise revenue.
- Liberalization of trade in agricultural products.
- Full capital account convertibility for foreign investors.

C. FOREIGN INVESTMENT

Before 1991, India made little or no attempt to attract private foreign investment and flows were below US dollars 200 million annually. Except for wholly export oriented or high technology industry, only 40% equity was permitted to foreign direct investment (FDI) in an Indian enterprise and all proposals needed clearance by the Reserve Bank of India (RBI).

1. RBI approval for FDI proposals meeting stipulated requirements made automatic.
2. In 1992 Indian firms with good standing were allowed to issue equity and convertible bonds in American and European capital markets.
3. Foreign Investment Promotion Board established and procedures for obtaining permissions from Union Government were greatly simplified.

4. Foreign institutional investors were allowed to directly purchase shares of listed Indian companies in the stock market in 1993.
5. Equity caps for FDI were progressively raised to majority ownership in all sectors except banks, insurance companies, telecommunications and airlines. Since 1998 100% of foreign equity is permitted in certain manufacturing industries and infra structure projects.
6. Exemptions of sectors from FDI were progressively reduced, with FDI permitted in electricity generation, insurance, banking, telecommunications, ports and airlines, but not in print media.

Under Consideration But Pending

- Simplification of procedures for permissions in all states.
- Rationalization of labor laws to allow more flexibility and encourage FDI in labor intensive industries.
- Creation of social security or unemployment insurance system.
- Accelerate improvements in infrastructure.

D. BANKING AND FINANCIAL SECTOR

Banking sector reforms based on the recommendations of the first Narasimhan Committee were initiated in 1991–1992, as was modernization of the capital market.

1. Interest rates decontrolled and interest rates on government securities determined by the market.
2. Deposit rates and lending rates largely deregulated.
3. Statutory liquidity ratio and cash reserve ratio significantly reduced. Credit Authorization Scheme discarded in favor of project appraisal for loans.
4. Banking sector opened to private ownership, domestic and foreign. Private sector banks allowed to expand more liberally, providing competition for public sector banks.
5. The Securities and Exchange Board of India (SEBI) given statutory powers in 1992 to govern capital markets, trading of stocks and management of mutual funds.
6. The technology of trading on the National Stock Exchange (NSE) and Bombay Stock Exchange (BSE) was modernized

with the introduction of on-line trading in 1994 in 1995 respectively with linkages to brokers all over India and abroad.

7. System of settling shares modernized and speeded up with physical transfers of share certificates giving way to dematerialized transfers and greatly increased volume of business after 1997.

8. Prudential norms and standards for banks with respect to capital adequacy, asset classification and provisioning were upgraded to a closer alignment with international standards.

9. External evaluation and supervision of bank performance on the basis of new prudential norms was strengthened to make banks more transparent and focus attention on non performing assets (NPAs), whose proportion to commercial advances were halved by 1998.

10. Insurance sector opened to private enterprise in 2000 and to FDI with a cap of 26 %. An independent Insurance Development and Regulatory Authority established.

11. Props to inefficient Development Financial Institutions withdrawn.

12. Fiscal Responsibility Act passed by Parliament in 2002–2003 to reduce fiscal deficit and public debt with implied promise to reduce employment in the public sector.

Under Consideration But Pending

- Further upgrading of prudential norms for banks and SEBI regulation of capital markets.
- States to pass fiscal responsibility legislation and act on them to reduce deficits and debt.
- Reduction in subsidies, with better targeting.
- Reform of tax system.
- Improve legal system relating to debt recovery.
- Reduce government equity in banks to 33%.

E. INFRASTRUCTURE

1. In 1994, an Expert Group on Commercialization of Infrastructure Projects was appointed and private enterprise, domestic and foreign,

was invited to invest in infrastructure projects including generation of electric power, telecommunications, road development, and enlargement of port capacity and airports.

2. Private investment including FDI invited to construct new power plants and to manage power distribution in some cities. Agreement with Enron on Dabhol project eventually fell victim to disputes over pricing.

3. National Telecommunications Policy announced in 1994 and public sector monopoly in basic telephone services ended.

4. The Telecommunications Regulatory Authority of India (TRAI) was established in 1996 and gained credibility. FDI permitted in telecommunications.

5. A policy for private investment in ports was announced in 1997 retaining public sector ownership of major ports but encouraging privatization of specific activities such as construction and operation of new container terminals, ship repair facilities and dry docking, warehouses, and leasing out operation of some ports to private enterprise. FDI permitted.

6. Competitive bidding held for development of a container terminal in Mumbai and won by an Australian-Malaysian consortium. Andhra Pradesh, Gujarat, and Maharshtra offered entire ports for private sector development and the first one was commissioned in 1997.

7. Private investment in roads invited in 1997. New policy permitted tolls, rights of commercial development of highway facilities, and foreign equity up to 74%. Several major road building projects initiated with public sector funding.

Under Consideration But Pending

- Overhaul of State Electricity Boards and pricing of electric power to all consumers.
- Overhaul of government agencies such as Port Trusts and Public Works Departments in control of basic infrastructure.
- Finding new sources of funding outside Union or state budgets for financing major infrastructure projects necessarily undertaken by the public sector.
- Devising acceptable user fees for infrastructure projects that are fair to producers and consumers.

- Constitute a Railway Regulatory Authority to de-politicize tariffs and regulate other railway activities on market lines.

F. AGRICULTURE

- Agriculture benefited indirectly from reforms in trade and industrial policy and agricultural exports increased.
- Indian agriculture is entirely in the private sector so that reforms reducing the scope of the public sector were inapplicable to it.
- Planning Commission reports make comprehensive recommendations for review of many outdated agricultural laws that inhibit the development of an integrated national market or modern trading companies in agricultural products, but these remain pending.
- Competitive populism of state governments prevent the rigorous review and probable withdrawal of subsidies on water, fertilizers, and electricity, that no longer serve their intended purpose of benefiting poorer agriculturalists.

Appendix J
India's Foreign Trade

India's Foreign Trade (in US$ millions)

Year	Total Exports	Total Imports	Trade Balance
1970–1971	2,031.3	2,162.3	−131.0
1975–1976	4,648.7	6,063.7	−1,415.0
1980–1981	8,484.0	15,866.5	−7,381.8
1985–1986	8,904.5	16,066.9	−7,162.4
1990–91	18,145.2	24,072.5	−5,927.3
1995–1996	31,794.9	36,675.3	−4,880.4
1997–1998	35,006.4	41,484.5	−6,478.1
1998–1999	33,218.7	42,388.7	−9,170.0
1999–2000	36,822.4	49,670.7	−12,848.3
2000–2001	44,560.3	50,536.5	−5,976.2
2001–2002	43,826.7	51,413.3	−7,586.6
2002–2003	52,719.4	61,412.1	−8,692.7
2003–2004 (P)	63,454.1	77,032.3	−13,578.2

P= Provisional
Source: Reserve Bank of India, *Handbook of Statistics on the Indian Economy,* New Delhi: 2004 . Table 127

| Group/Country | 1987–1988 | | 1990–1991 | | 1995–1996 | |
	Exports	Imports	Exports	Imports	Exports	Imports
European Union	3034.1	5707.5	4988.5	7067.1	8708.3	10303.2
Percentage	25.1%	33.2%	27.5%	29.3%	27.3	28.09%
United States	2252.1	1543.8	2673.2	2923	5520.4	3861.4
Percentage	18.63%	9.5%	14.7%	12.14%	17.3	10.5%
Japan	1244.5	1639.8	1693.7	1808.3	2215.6	2467.6
Percentage	10.29%	9.5%	9.3%	7.5%	6.9%	6.7%
O.P.E.COPEC	741.9	2277.4	1020.4	3924	3079	7644.4
Percentage	6.13%	13.27%	5.6%	16.3%	9.6%	20.8%
Russia	1513.7	1240	2928.6	1420.1	1045	856.3
Percentage	12.52%	7.2%	16.13%	5.8%	3.2%	2.3%
S.A.A.R.C	313.2	75.5	533.4	131.4	1720.6	256.5
Percentage	2.5	0.4%	2.9%	0.5%	5.4%	0.6%
P.R.C. People's Republic of China	14.6	118.9	18.2	31	332.7	812.7
Percentage	0.1%	0.6%	0.1%	0.1%	1%	2.2%
Hong Kong	344	92.6	596.5	165.6	1821.4	388
Percentage	2.8%	0.5%	3.2%	0.6%	5.7%	1Y
Singapore	210.5	323.4	379.4	795.7	901.6	1091.9
Percentage	1.7%	1.8%	2.1%	3.3%	2.8%	2.9Y
Africa	242.7	503.1	393.6	572.7	1512.7	1131.7
Percentage	2%	2.9%	2.1%	2.3%	4.7%	3%
Total Trade	12088.5	17155.7	18145.2	24072.5	31794.9	36675.3

Trade (In US$, millions)

2000–2001		2001–2002		2002–2003		2003–2004(P)	
Exports	Imports	Exports	Imports	Exports	Imports	Exports	Imports
10410.8	10510.2	9845.9	10436.5	11522.5	12541.7	13816	14502.2
23.3%	20.7%	22.4%	20.2%	21.8%	20.4%	21.7%	18.8%
9305.1	3015	8513.3	3149.6	10895.8	4443.6	11459.9	4862.6
20.8%	5.9%	19.4%	4.1%	20.6%	7.2%	18%	6.3%
1794.5	1842.2	1510.4	2146.4	1864	1836.3	1714.3	2642.2
4.02%	3.6%	3.4%	4.1%	3.5%	2.9%	2.7%	3.4%
4850	2688.8	5224.5	2965.8	6884.6	3479.4	9487.3	5588.7
10.8%	5.3%	11.9%	5.7%	13%	5.6%	14.9%	7.2%
889	517.7	798.2	535.5	704	592.6	708.7	959.5
1.9%	1%	1.8%	1%	1.3%	0.9%	1.11%	1.2%
1928.5	465.8	2026	571.5	2724.1	512	4025.5	639.2
4.3%	0.9%	4.6%	1%	5.1%	0.8%	6.3%	0.8%
831.3	1502.2	952	2036.4	1975.5	2792	2959.2	4048.3
1.8%	2.9%	2.1%	3.9%	3.7%	4.5%	4.6%	5.2%
2640.9	852.1	2366.4	728.9	2613.3	972.6	3250.3	1492.6
5.9%	1.6%	5.3%	1.4%	4.9%	1.5%	5.1%	1.9%
877.1	1463.9	972.3	1304.1	1421.6	1434.8	2116.5	2029.9
1.9%	2.8%	2.2%	2.5%	2.6%	2.3%	3.3%	2.6%
1956.4	1996.1	2260.9	2502.4	2575.7	3348.2	3052.5	3101.1
4.3%	3.9%	5.1%	4.8%	4.8%	5.4%	4.8%	4%
44560.3	50536.5	43826.7	51413.3	52719.4	61412.1	63454.1	77032.3

DIRECTION OF INDIA'S FOREIGN TRADE (in US dollars million)

	1987–1988		1990–91		1995–1996	
	Exports	Imports	Exports	Imports	Exports	Imports
EU	3034.1	5707.5	4988.5	7067.1	8708.3	10303.2
Percentage	25.1	33.2	27.5	29.3	27.3	28.09
U.S.A	2252.1	1543.8	2673.2	2923	5520.4	3861.4
Percentage	18.63	9.5	14.7	12.14	17.3	10.5
Japan	1244.5	1639.8	1693.7	1808.3	2215.6	2467.6
Percentage	10.29	9.5	9.3	7.5	6.9	6.7
O.P.E.C	741.9	2277.4	1020.4	3924	3079	7644.4
Percentage	6.13	13.27	5.6	16.3	9.6	20.8
Russia	1513.7	1240	2928.6	1420.1	1045	856.3
Percentage	12.52	7.2	16.13	5.8	3.2	2.3
S.A.A.R.C	313.2	75.5	533.4	131.4	1720.6	256.5
Percentage	2.5	0.4	2.9	0.5	5.4	0.6
P.R.C	14.6	118.9	18.2	31	332.7	812.7
Percentage	0.1	0.6	0.1	0.1	1	2.2
Hong Kong	344	92.6	596.5	165.6	1821.4	388
Percentage	2.8	0.5	3.2	0.6	5.7	1
Singapore	210.5	323.4	379.4	795.7	901.6	1091.9
Percentage	1.7	1.8	2.1	3.3	2.8	2.9
Africa	242.7	503.1	393.6	572.7	1512.7	1131.7
Percentage	2	2.9	2.1	2.3	4.7	3
Total Trade	12088.5	17155.7	18145.2	24072.5	31794.9	36675.3

Based on RBI Stastical HandbookTable 135

| 2000–2001 | | 2001–2002 | | 2002–2003 | | 2003–2004 | |
Exports	Imports	Exports	Imports	Exports	Imports	Exports	Imports
10410.8	10510.2	9845.9	10436.5	11522.5	12541.7	13816	14502.2
23.3	20.7	22.4	20.2	21.8	20.4	21.7	18.8
9305.1	3015	8513.3	3149.6	10895.8	4443.6	11459.9	4862.6
20.8	5.9	19.4	4.1	20.6	7.2	18	6.3
1794.5	1842.2	1510.4	2146.4	1864	1836.3	1714.3	2642.2
4.02	3.6	3.4	4.1	3.5	2.9	2.7	3.4
4850	2688.8	5224.5	2965.8	6884.6	3479.4	9487.3	5588.7
10.8	5.3	11.9	5.7	13	5.6	14.9	7.2
889	517.7	798.2	535.5	704	592.6	708.7	959.5
1.9	1	1.8	1	1.3	0.9	1.11	1.2
1928.5	465.8	2026	571.5	2724.1	512	4025.5	639.2
4.3	0.9	4.6	1	5.1	0.8	6.3	0.8
831.3	1502.2	952	2036.4	1975.5	2792	2959.2	4048.3
1.8	2.9	2.1	3.9	3.7	4.5	4.6	5.2
2640.9	852.1	2366.4	728.9	2613.3	972.6	3250.3	1492.6
5.9	1.6	5.3	1.4	4.9	1.5	5.1	1.9
877.1	1463.9	972.3	1304.1	1421.6	1434.8	2116.5	2029.9
1.9	2.8	2.2	2.5	2.6	2.3	3.3	2.6
1956.4	1996.1	2260.9	2502.4	2575.7	3348.2	3052.5	3101.1
4.3	3.9	5.1	4.8	4.8	5.4	4.8	4
44560.3	50536.5	43826.7	51413.3	52719.4	61412.1	63454.1	77032.3

GLOSSARY

ADVAITA	Non-duality or monism
AGNI	Fire; god of fire
AHIMSA	Non-injury or not to harm
AMIR	Lord, prince, commander
AMRIT	Immortal; a drink giving immortality
ASANA	Seat or position, bodily posture
ASHRAM	Hermitage of a holy man; also used for stages of life
ATMAN	Essential principle of life
AVATARA	Physical incarnation of a deity
AZADI	Freedom, independence
BAHADUR	Warrior, hero, brave
BANIA	Merchant caste
BEGAR	Forced, or unpaid, labor
BHADRALOK	Respectable people, gentry in Bengal
BHAJAN	Devotional song
BHAKTA	Worshipper, devotee
BHARAT	India
BHOODAN	Gift of land
BIRADARI	Literally "brotherhood"; kinship network
BODDHISATVA	An Enlightened Being who voluntarily postpones Buddhahood for the spiritual welfare of others
BRAHMACHARIN	The first stage of life, studenthood, celibacy
CALIPH	Also Khalifa, Deputy of God according to Islam
CHAKRAVARTIN	One who can turn the wheel; emperor or supreme ruler

731

CHARKHA	Spinning wheel; symbol of self-reliance and self-discipline
CHELA	Disciple, follower
CRORE	Numerical term for 100 lakh or 10 million
DARGAH	Tomb of a saint; Muslim shrine
DAROGA	Local-level policeman in charge of a police station
DARSHAN	Viewing, to look at, especially icons, saints, distinguished persons
DASA	Also dasyu in the Rig Veda denoting indigenous people; later used for servant
DEVA	Deity
DEVADASI	Servant of a deity, temple dancer
DEVANAGARI	Literally divine script, in which Sanskrit and derivative languages are written
DEVI	The Goddess
DEWAN	Title of chief revenue officer, or chief administrator in princely states
DEWANI	Right to administer collection of revenue
DHARNA	A form of meditation that has come to mean a sit-down protest
DHIMMI	Also Zimmi' a non-Muslim subject entitled to protection of a Muslim ruler under Koranic law
DOAB	Land between two rivers, e.g., Ganga-Yamuna doab
DURBAR	The court of a king or high ranking official
DURGA	Manifestation of the supreme Goddess
FATWA	Ruling given by a Muslim judge or theologian
FERINGHI	Foreigner, European
FIRMAN	Royal edict
GANESHA	Also Ganapati; the elephant-headed god of wisdom and success
GARIBI	Poverty
GAUSHALA	Home for cattle
GHATS	Literally, steps leading to sacred bathing place

GHERAO	To encircle
GOONDA	Ruffian, hooligan
GURU	Spiritual preceptor, teacher
GYANA	Knowledge, both cognitive and intuitive
HARIJAN	Literally, people of God
HARTAL	Suspension of business or labor in protest
INDRA	Vedic god of war
ITIHASA	History
JAGIR	A grant of land and its rent
JAGIRDAR	Holder of a jagir
JATI	Lineage determining social status; see CASTE in the Dictionary
JAWAN	Literally, a youth; used for soldier in the Indian Army
JIHAD	Holy war in Islam
JIZIYA	Head tax imposed on dhimmi males by some Muslim rulers
KALI	Literally, the black one; the Goddess manifested in a destructive aspect; symbol of eternal time
KALIYUGA	Fourth and final era of the universe according to Hindu cosmogony
KAMA	God of love; carnal love
KARKHANA	Workshop
KARMA	Action, or work, carrying consequence; associated with belief in metempsychosis theory that a cycle of birth, death, and rebirth is generated by actions (ethical and unethical) and their consequences
KARSEVAK	One who offers worship through voluntary work at a temple
KAYASTHA	North Indian caste associated with administrative occupations
KHADI	Handspun, hand-woven cloth
KHALSA	Literally pure; collective designation of the Sikhs since 1699
KHUTBA	Pulpit address delivered at Friday noon prayer in mosques

KIRTAN	Devotional music and song
KISAN	Peasant, cultivator, also ryot
KOTWAL	Official custodian of law and order in medieval and early modern towns
LAKH	Indian numerical term for 100 thousand
LATHI	A metal-tipped bamboo or wooden staff
LINGAM	Symbol of generative power; phallus
MADRASSA	School attached to a mosque
MAHAJAN	Trader or money lender, often wealthy
MAHAL	Large building, palace
MAHARAJA	Great King
MAHATMA	Great soul; one deemed worthy of reverence
MANDALA	Circle separating special area that can be consecrated for ritual or liturgical purposes
MANTRA	A verbal formula believed to possess power; ritualistic incantation
MATA/MA	Mother
MAYA	Concept of magical or illusion creating power obscuring the Real
MISL	Equal, like; name of 12 Sikh armies in the 18th century
MLECCHA	Foreigner; non-Aryan; impure
MOFUSSIL	Rural hinterland or country district
MOHALLA	Locality, ward of a town
MOKSHA	Also mukti; liberation; release from the bondage of finite existence
MULLAH	Teacher of Islamic doctrine
NABOB	English corruption of nawab
NAGAR	Town
NAMAZ	Muslim prayer
NARAYANA	Personification of the creative power identified with Vishnu
NATARAJA	Lord of the Dance; Shiva as the Cosmic Dancer
NAWAB	Provincial governor in Mughal India; later applied to Muslim elite
NIRVANA	Literally, blowing out; the state of enlightenment in which karma is transcended

PADSHAH	Emperor
PAISA	Money; smallest unit of Indian currency
PANCHATANTRA	A collection of popular fables and tales collected in five books
PANCHAYAT	Committee of five persons; traditional village council
PANDIT	Learned man; used as a title, honorific, or family name.
PARVATI	Daughter of the Himalaya; consort of Shiva; the Goddess
PATWARI	Village accountant
PITR	Father
PRAJA	The public; common people
PRAKRITI	Nature; primary matter, personified as the active female principle of cosmic energy
PUJA	Worship; offerings made to a deity
PURDAH	Literally, curtain; seclusion of females behind veil or household walls
PURUSH	Man; collective term for mankind
QAZI/QADI	Judge in Islamic system of jurisprudence
QUAM	Community, people, often used for nation
RAJ	Rule, government, realm
RAJA	King, chief, ruler
RASA	Sap, elixir, essence; important principle in art, music and alchemy
RASHTRA	Country, nation
RISHI	Seer, sage
RUDRA	Vedic deity with pre-Vedic aspects
RUPEE	Standard unit of currency in India and neighboring countries
SABHA	Council, society, organized group
SADHANA	The means of achieving a particular end
SADHU	Wandering ascetic, mendicant
SAMADHI	State of deep meditation leading to self-realization or enlightenment
SAMAJ	Assembly, meeting, society
SAMSARA	Phenomenal existence; this world; passing through

SANAD	Government order, warrant, charter
SANGAM	Joining together; confluence of rivers; Tamil for assembly
SANGATHAN	Organization
SANGHA	Religious community; Buddhist monastic order
SANNYASIN	One who has relinquished all worldly attachments
SANYAS	Abandonment; letting go of material attachment and worldly life
SARVODAYA	Literally, the uplift of all
SAT	Ultimate reality; Truth
SATYAGRAHI	One who engages in satyagraha (see Dictionary)
SENA	A spear or missile; term used for army
SEPOY	English corruption of sipahi; Indian soldier in service of East India Company
SHAKTI	Divine power or energy personified as female; the Goddess
SHANTI	Tranquility, absence of passion, peace
SHARI'A	Koranic law setting standards for Muslims
SHASTRA	Treatise, law book, manual of rules; Post-Vedic compilations
SHUDDHI	Purification; term for ritual return to Hinduism or caste identity
SOMA	Name of a plant whose juice was used as a ceremonial drink at Vedic sacrifices
SUBAH	Province in Mughal India
SUTRA	Literally, thread; texts, often philosophical, written in the form of aphorisms
SWADESHI	Literally, of one's own country
SWARAJ	Self-rule; independence
SWAYAMVARA	Literally, one's own choice; ceremonial occasion for a girl of noble birth to choose a husband from among assembled suitors
TABLIGH	A movement seeking conversions to Islam
TALUK	Administrative unit below the level of district; also tehsil

TAPAS	Literally, heat; penance, austerity, yogic concentration
TARWAD	Extended family, property, especially in Kerala
TIRTHA	Sacred place or person; destination of a pilgrimage
TYAGA	Renunciation with tranquility
ULEMA	Plural form of alim in Arabic; Muslim learned men
VARNA	External appearance, color, the term used for four main occupational classes; See CASTE in the Dictionary
VARNA-ASHRAMA-DHARMA	Term for a social order based on righteousness, distinct stages of life and separate but interdependent classes
VARUNA	Early Vedic deity associated with justice and law
VIDHYA	Complete knowledge or wisdom
VIHARA	Dwelling place for Buddhist or Jain monks
VIVAHA	Marriage
YAKSHA	Collective name for forest godlings prominent in folklore
YAMA	Vedic deity of the dead
YATRA	Journey
YONI	Female generative organs, associated with the linga as symbol of divine energy
YUGA	An era; applied to the universe and believed to total 4,320,000 earthly years divided in four yugas of decreasing duration
ZAMINDAR	Landowner and hereditary tax collector

Bibliography

CONTENTS

BIBLIOGRAPHIC NOTE

The works enumerated in this bibliography have been selected from a veritable ocean of material as a kind of navigational chart. The intention is to provide the reader with a representative sample of subjects and some variety of perspective on them, as well as sources to be tapped for deeper study. Preference is given to books over articles, although the latter are not altogether excluded, and a list of major Indian journals and newspapers is included in the "General" category. English-language works only are cited, for the following reasons. English is one of the official languages of India and the language of preference for contemporary Indian scholarship in the sciences and social sciences; a substantial and growing volume of literature is published there every year and are made available abroad in such collections as that of the Library of Congress, Washington, D. C. The increasing flow of publications in the 18 officially recognized national languages of India so compounds the problem of selection that greater weight is given to the likelihood of readers using English-language materials than the desirability of linguistic representation. The archives, descriptions, and scholarly works generated during and after British rule in India are in the English language and are accessible in the British Library Oriental and India Office Collections, London. It is my experience that non-specialists interested in India tend to use English language publications, even in China, Europe, Japan, and Southeast Asia. Much of contemporary specialist literature produced outside India emanates from the publishing houses of Australia, Britain, Canada, and the United States, in the English language. Major texts originally written in other European languages are thus cited below in easily available English translations, such as Francois Bernier's French classic, *Travels in the Mogul Empire*, Max Muller's pioneering essays on Indology in German, and products of scholarship in Russian, such as Marietta Stepanyant's *History of Indian Philosophy: A Russian Viewpoint*. None of the above implies that knowledge of Indian classical or modern languages is unnecessary for a better understanding of India.

No bibliography can possibly do justice either to the richness of Indian culture, society, and history or to the diversity of materials on them. One excellent, if cumbersome, compilation is Maureen Patterson, *South Asian Civilizations: A Bibliographic Synthesis* (see under "Bibliographies and Dictionaries"), which has not been equaled in scope since its publication in 1981. The annual bibliographies published in the *Journal of Asian Studies* are now available online (by paid subscription) at http://ets.umdl.umich.edu and a masterly Digital South Asia Library is at http://dsal.uchicago.edu Generations of Western students curious about Indian culture can testify that a reader's appetite will be whetted by A. L. Basham's *The Wonder that was India* (see under "Culture: General"). Those who have enjoyed exposure to Indian art, dance, films, music, or poetry may like to refer to the books cited under appropriate headings. Another exceptional work is Joseph Schwartzberg's *A Historical Atlas of South Asia* (see under "Map Collections and Statistics"). Most people visiting India, whether in luxury or as backpackers, would find one of the guides listed under "Overviews, Travel, and Guides" useful. Aspirant trekkers in high mountains could turn to Ahluwalia and Gerner, *Himalaya: A Practical Guide.* Seekers of spiritual solace might benefit from Maz Murray's unusual *Speaking to the Master.* The list under "Philosophy and Religion" has been kept deliberately to an unintimidating length, and selections are drawn from authors of acknowledged authority in their fields. The titles speak for themselves as well as for the juxtaposition in India of many major world faiths and philosophies.

With the exception of *The Cambridge Economic History of India, Volume 11 c. 1757–1970,* edited by Dharma Kumar and Meghnand Desai, all the citations listed under "Economy" deal with India's post-independence economic performance, problems, and reforms. They provide a wealth of factual information and a range of ideological stances adopted by the authors—from Romesh Diwan's Gandhian perspective to Romesh Thapar's Marxist one to the consistent liberal advocacy of Jagdish Bhagwati and T. N Srinivasan. Some surveys can convey dismay and pessimism, as in the case of Gunnar Myrdal's *Asian Drama,* or judicious praise and cautious optimism, as in L. A. Veit's *India's Second Revolution.* Some of the authors, such as Malcolm Adiseshiah and I. G. Patel, held key positions in drafting and implementing India's earlier economic policies; others, such as Montek Singh Ahluwalia and Bimal Jalan have been intellectually and officially instrumental in India's economic liberalization since 1991.

Kusum Nair's *Blossoms in the Dust* poignantly captures a view from below in the late 1950s, while Inderjit Singh's *The Great Ascent* gives a comprehensive account of Indian agricultural progress. India's transition from a planned, mixed economy with autarchic characteristics to an open one integrating with the global economy is a subject of worldwide interest and domestic debate that is reflected in newspapers and journals such as *The Economist, The Economic Times,* and the *Economic and Political Weekly (EPW).* The annual *Economic Survey* produced by India's Ministry of Finance, *Annual Report* of the Reserve Bank of India, and publications of the Planning Commission are valuable sources for information on the Indian economy and are used also by the World Bank and the International Monetary Fund for their special reports. The Alternative Survey Group in Delhi offers a more critical evaluation of the late 1990s.

Critical analysis also marks the selections listed under "Constitution and Government." These selections reflect the duality of contemporary India: its colossal achievements in establishing, maintaining, and deepening a secular, democratic, political system in a multi-ethnic, multi-religious, and multi-lingual subcontinent, on the one hand, and the surfacing of centrifugal tensions, political violence, socioeconomic repression, and authoritarian tendencies on the other. Robert Hardgrave and Stanley Kochanek's *India: Government and Politics in a Developing Nation* is the best concise introduction to the subject. Granville Austin's *The Indian Constitution: Cornerstone of a Nation* and his *Working a Democratic Constitution: The Indian Experience* are magisterial studies. The change of mood over 25 years among Indian intellectuals is noticeable in the differences between Rajni Kothari's *Politics in India* published in 1970 and his search in the late 1990s for "a more humane India." Those who blame Indira Gandhi for the decline in public life would find fuel in Nayantara Sehgal's *Indira Gandhi: Her Road to Power.* Those looking for deeper causes would profit from Atul Kohli's *Democracy and Discontent: India's Growing Crisis of Governability.* India's many and varied political parties have evoked much scholarly and journalistic interest, especially when issues of caste and religious identity shaped the formation and behavior of political parties in the 1980s and 1990s and the Bharatiya Janata Party rode to power as a Hindu nationalist party. The section "Political Parties, Politics and Elections" contains a representative sampling of objective analyses. Events themselves have generated increased public attention to issues of national security in recent years. Works listed under "Security" illustrate contemporary opinion in India on matters ranging from nuclear safety to terrorism to human and comprehensive security. At the same time, India's international dealings have increased, and its profile has been somewhat altered, as shown in the selections listed under "International Relations."

It is generally agreed that the purpose of history is to comprehend and explain the past. Interpretations of the past, however, depend partly on the amount and accuracy of the information available to the historian and partly on questions salient to the time in which the historian is writing. Thus, writings on pre-modern Indian History vary greatly from the early 19th century to the present day. Literary and linguistic analyses, numismatics, anthropology, and archaeology have added knowledge that is as valuable to a scientific historian as chronicles, epigraphs, and genealogical tables, so that progressively more accurate, and complex, reconstruction of ancient eras has become possible. Romila Thapar's recent *Early India* is a good example. Interpretations of Mughal and pre-Mughal India, too, vary according to the questions being posed, by members of the East India Company for example, or by contemporary researchers into local folklore or regional and ethnic identities. The result is a much fuller account of different parts of India in titles cited under "History" that also serve to refute static, despotic, concepts of Indian civilization held by James Mill or Karl Marx. Early European Indologists studying Indian languages, especially Sanskrit, or tackling fresh administrative tasks in an alien environment were naturally preoccupied differently from Indian nationalists reacting to British domination many decades later, and histories published in the 19th and early 20th centuries reflect these differences. Indian historians today face equal or greater challenges as they trace the origins of some contemporary problems such as communal tensions or social identity to colonial administration or reexamine the notion of the nation itself.

Writings proliferate on modern Indian history (see under "Modern India: c. 1700–1947"). They are diverse in the sources they tap, the questions they address, and the ideological stances they adopt. Perhaps the greatest change, international as well as Indian, can be seen between an earlier concentration on political history of the state (still visible in Penderel Moon's *The British Conquest and Dominion of India* [1989]), and recent focus on economic, intellectual, and social trends as exemplified in the works of C. A. Bayly, Sugata Bose, Charles Heimsath, Ravinder Kumar, and Aditya and Mridula Mukherjee. Another major development is the shift of inquiry from the center to the periphery, from the upper echelons of power to the "subaltern" or little people—women and men—formerly presumed to be only at the receiving end of events beyond their control. Gyanendra Pandey, Sumit Sarkar, Ranajit Guha, and the authors represented in the latter's edited volumes of *Subaltern Studies* provide historical tapestries as illuminating as miniatures from a former princely palace. Similar variegation, detailed examination, and a meld of theoretical and empirical methodology is found in studies or narratives listed under "Society," with voices of women beginning to be heard.

Some large issues, of course, remain of perennial interest. They include the formation and character of early Indian society and state; the impact of Islam; causes and effects of Mughal decline; the costs and benefits of British rule; the evolution and particularity of Indian nationalism; the genesis of Partition and the transfer of power; and the character and impact of Mahatma Gandhi. The bibliography cites works that offer different facets on each issue, so that readers may make their own exciting and personal discoveries of India.

Voyages of discovery through scholarship on India as well as up-to-date information is now easier than formerly because of the Internet. The Government of India has numerous websites, with a (variable) directory accessible on http://goidirectory.nic.in The Reserve Bank of India material is available on www.rbi.org.in and commercial information on www.bisnetindia.com. The Election Commission of India provides background information and detailed voting data on http://www.eci.gov.in and detailed demographic information is available from the Census of India at http://www.censusindia.net. Political parties have their own websites and list addresses with Google or Yahoo search engines, as do the major Indian newspapers and news magazines such as *Outlook* and *Frontline*. A daily sample of newspaper articles is accessible on www.samachar.com with directions to relevant archives. The websites of bibliographic compilations are given earlier. There can be no substitute for traveling and living in India, but getting to know and understand it may well take more than a lifetime, so that libraries and archives are indispensable to an aspiring scholar. The National Library of India in Kolkata houses one of the oldest and largest collections; the Nehru Museum and Library in New Delhi is the best for modern India with a growing body of private papers and photographs also available. The National Archives in New Delhi is good; state archives exist but often in problematic conditions. Mention has been made earlier of the great collections easily accessible in the Library of Congress, Washington, D.C., and the British Library, London. Some university libraries also have comprehensively enviable collections, such as Cambridge University, England, the University of California, Berkeley, the University of Chicago, Columbia University, and the University of Pennsylvania in the United States, and the Australian National University in Canberra. To all this wealth of knowledge and more the *Dictionary* is only an indicative introduction.

GENERAL

Overviews, Travel and Guides

Ahluwalia, H. P. S., and Manfred Gerner. *Himalaya: A Practical Guide*. New Delhi: Himalayan Books, 1985.

Allen, Charles, and Sharada Dwivedi. *Lives of the Indian Princes,* New York: Crown, 1984.

Anderson, Benedict. *Imagined Communities. Reflections on the Origin and Spread of Nationalism*. London: Verso, 1983.

"Another India." *Daedalus—Journal of the American Academy of Arts and Sciences*," 118, no. 4 1989.

Ayres, Alyssa, and Philip Oldenburg, eds. *India Briefing: Quickening the Pace of Change*. New York: M. E. Sharpe, 2002.

Bakshi, K. N., and F. Scialpi, eds. *India 1947–1997: Fifty Years of Independence*. Rome: Instituto Italiano por l'Africa e l'Oriente, 2002.

Bose, Ashish. *Population of India: 2001 Census Results and Methodology*. Delhi: BRPC, 2001.

Bouton, Marshall, and Philip Oldenburg, eds. *India Briefing: A Transformative Fifty Years*. New York: M. E. Sharpe, 1999.

Bouton, Marshall M., ed. India Briefing 1988. Asia Society, New York: Westview, 1989.

Brata, Sasthi. *India: Labyrinths in the Lotus Land*. New York: William Morrow & Co., 1985.

Chari, P. R., ed. *India Towards The Millenium*. New Delhi: Manohar, 1998.

Chauhan, Brij Raj. *India: A Socio-Economic Profile*. New Delhi: Sterling, 1990.

Chopra, P. N., ed. *India: An Encyclopedic Survey*. New Delhi: S. Chand, 1984.

Corbridge, Stuart and John Harriss. *Reinventing India*. Oxford: Polity Press, 2000.

DeSouza, Peter Ronald, ed. *Contemporary India: Transitions*. New Delhi: Sage, 2000.

Dettman, Paul R. *India Changes Course: Golden Jubilee to Millennium*. Westport, CT: Praeger, 2001.

Dyson, Tim, Robert Cassen, and Leela Visaria, eds. *Twenty First Century India-Population, Economy, Human Development and Environment*. Oxford: Oxford University Press, 2004.

Ellis, Kirsten. *The Insider's Guide to India*. Hong Kong: CFW Guidebooks, 2004.

Fodor, E., and W. Curtis. *Fodor's India*. New York: David McKay & Co., 2004.

Ganguly, Sumit, and Neil DeVotta, eds. *Understanding Contemporary India*. Boulder, CO: Lynne Reiner, 2003.

Gupte: Pranay. *Vengeance: India after the Assassination of Indira Gandhi*. New York: W. W. Norton, 1985.

Harrison, Barbara J., ed. *Learning about India: An Annotated Guide for Nonspecialists*. New Delhi: Educational Resources Centre, 1977.

Heimsath, Charles H. *Teacher's Introduction to India*. New Delhi: Educational Resources Centre, 1978. Revised 1994.

Heitzman, James, and Robert L. Worden, eds. *India: A Country Study*. Washington, DC: United States Government Printing Office, 1996.

Hillary, Edmund. *From the Ocean to the Sky*. London: Hodder & Stoughton, 1978.

Inden, Ronald B. *Imagining India*. Oxford: Basil Blackwell, 1990.

India: A Travel Survival Kit. 4th ed. Hawthorn, Victoria, Australia: Lonely Planet Publications, 1990.

India: Ministry of Information and Broadcasting. *India: 2004*. New Delhi: Publications Division, 2004.

Insight Guides. *India*. Singapore: APA Publications, 2004.

Kaur, Jagdish. *Himalayan Pilgrimages and the New Tourism*. New Delhi: Himalayan Books, 1985.

Khilnani, Sunil. *The Idea of India*. New York: Farrar, Straus and Giroux, 1998.

LaRue, C. Stephen, ed. *The India Handbook*. Chicago: Fitzroy Dearborn Publishers, 1997.

Malhotra, P. L., et al. *India's Struggle for Independence: Visuals and Documents*. New Delhi: NCERT, 1985.

Mayo, Katherine. *Mother India*. New York: Harcourt Brace, 1927.

Mehta, Ved P. *Portrait of India*. New Haven: Yale University Press, 1993.

Murray, Muz. *Speaking to the Master: A Guide to the Ashrams of India*. Jersey, United Kingdom: Neville Spearman, 1980.

Naipaul, V. S. *India. A Million Mutinies Now*. London: Heinemann, 1990.

Newby, Eric. *Slowly Down the Ganges*. London: Hodder & Stoughton, 1966.

Nicholson, Louise. *India Companion in Luxury*. London: Century, 1991.

Nyrop, Richard et al. *India: A Country Study*. Washington, DC: Government Printing Office, 1986.

Oldenburg, Philip, ed. *India Briefing 1991*. Asia Society, New York: Westview Press, 1991.

Panjiar, Prashant, ed. *India: The Definitive Images (1858 to the Present)*. New Delhi: Penguin India, 2004.

Paz, Octavio. *In Light of India*. New York: Harcourt, Brace and Company.

Prasad, R. C. *Early English Travelers in India*. Delhi: Motilal Banarsi Dass, 1965.

Punja, Shobita. *An Illustrated Guide to Museums of India*. Hong Kong: The Guidebook Company Ltd., 1990.

Roach, James P., ed. *India 2000: The Next Fifteen Years,* Riverdale, MD: Riverdale, 1986.

Roosevelt, Eleanor. *India and the Awakening East*. New York: Harper and Brothers, 1953.

Scarfe, W., and A. Scarfe. *People of India*. Melbourne, Australia: Cassell, 1972.

Singh, K. S. *People of India: An Introduction*. Calcutta: Anthropological Survey of India, 1992.

Thapar, Raj, *Traveler's Tales,* New Delhi: Vikas, 1977.

Tharoor, Shashi, *India: From Midnight to the Millenium.* New York: Arcade, 1997.

Times of India. *Directory and Yearbook.* Bombay: Times of India Press, 2004.

Tully, Mark. *No Full Stops in India.* New Delhi: Viking/Penguin India, 1991.

Varma, Pavan. *Being India: The Truth about Why the Twenty-First Century Will Be India's.*

Map Collections and Statistics

Census of India, 1991. *Series I India.* New Delhi: Office of the Registrar General, 1992. (General population, economic and sociocultural tables.)

Davies, Collin. *An Historical Atlas of the Indian Peninsula.* Delhi: Oxford University Press, 1949.

Dutt, Ashok K., and M. Margaret Geib. *Atlas of South Asia.* Boulder, CO: Westview Press, 1987.

Economic Times. *Statistical Survey of the Indian Economy.* New Delhi.

Habib, Irfan. *An Atlas of the Mughal Empire.* Delhi: Oxford University Press, 1986.

India (Republic): Census of India 1971. *Indian Census Centenary Atlas.* New Delhi: Office of the Registrar General, 1974.

India: Council of Scientific and Industrial Resources. *The Wealth of India: A Dictionary of Indian Raw Materials and Industrial Products 1948–1976.* 11 vols. New Delhi: CSIR, 1977.

India: Department of Statistics. *Statistical Abstract: India.* New Delhi: Ministry of Planning, 1951, with regular updates.

India: Ministry of External Affairs. *Atlas of the Northern Frontier of India.* New Delhi: Ministry of External Affairs, 1960.

India: Ministry of Finance. *Economic Survey for 2003–2004.* New Delhi: Ministry of Finance, 2004.

Muthiah, S. *An Atlas of India.* Delhi: Oxford University Press, 1990.

———. *A Social and Political Atlas of India.* Delhi: Oxford University Press, 1987.

Prasad, S. N., ed. *Catalogue of the Historical Maps of the Survey of India 1700–1900.* New Delhi: National Archives of India, 1975.

Raza, Moonis, and Aijazuddin Ahmed. *An Atlas of Tribal India.* New Delhi: Concept, 1980.

Reserve Bank of India. *Handbook of Statistics on the Indian Economy.* New Delhi: Reserve Bank of India, 2004.

Schwartzberg, Joseph E. *A Historical Atlas of South Asia.* Chicago and London: University of Chicago Press, 1978.

Bibliographies and Dictionaries

Association for Asian Studies. *Bibliography of Asian Studies.* Ann Arbor, MI: 1970, published annually.

Bhattacharya, N. N. *The Geographical Dictionary. Ancient and Early Medieval India.* New Delhi: Munshi Manoharlal, 1991.

Bhattacharya, Sachchidananda. *A Dictionary of Indian History.* New York: George Braziller, 1967.

Derbyshire, Ian D. *India.* Oxford: Clio Press, 1995.

Embree, Ainslie, ed. *Encyclopedia of Asian Civilizations.* New York: The Asia Society, 1988.

Gokhale Institute of Politics and Economics. *Annotated Bibliography on the Economic History of India 1500–1947.* 4 vols. New Delhi: Indian Council of Social Science Research, 1977.

Kalia, D. R., and M. K. Jain. *A Bibliography of Bibliographies on India.* Delhi: Concept, 1975.

Mayor, John N. *INDIA: Issues, Historical Background, and Bibliography.* Harripage. NY: Novs Science Publishers, 2003.

Mehra, P. L. *A Dictionary of Modern Indian History.* New Delhi: Oxford University Press, 1986.

Patterson, Maureen L. P. *South Asian Civilizations: A Bibliographic Synthesis.* Chicago: University of Chicago Press, 1981.

Pearson, J. D. *South Asian Bibliography.* Sussex: Harvester Press, 1979.

Ravi, N., ed. *India: Book of the Year 2000.* New Delhi: Encyclopedia Britannica, 2003.

Robinson, Francis, ed. *The Cambridge Encyclopedia of India, Pakistan, Bangladesh, Sri Lanka, Nepal, Bhutan and the Maldives.* Cambridge: Cambridge University Press, 1989.

Saletore, R. N. *Encyclopedia of Indian Culture.* 5 vols. New Delhi: Sterling, 1981–1985.

Scholberg, Henry. *Biographical Dictionary of Greater India.* 1998.

Sen, S. P., ed. *Dictionary of National Biography.* 4 vols. Calcutta: Indian Historical Society, 1972–1973.

South Asia in Review: *Quarterly Review of New Books.* Columbia, Mo: 1976 onwards.

Stutley, Margaret, and James Stutley. *A Dictionary of Hinduism 1500 B.C–A.D 1500.* London: Routledge and Kegan Paul, 1977.

Sukhwal, B. I. *South Asia: A Systematic Geographic Bibliography.* Metuchen, NJ: Scarecrow Press, 1974.

Tyagi, K. C. *Foreign Researches on Indian Political System and Processes: A Bibliography.* Delhi: Pinka Agencies, 1984.

Principal English-Language Journals

Agni: Forum for Strategic and Security Studies. Quarterly since 1995, New Delhi.

Alternatives. Quarterly since 1975. Centre for the Study of Developing Societies, Delhi (with the International Peace Research Institute, and the World Order Models Project, Princeton.)

Architecture and Design. Quarterly since 1983. New Delhi.

Asian Recorder. Weekly digest of Asian and Indian news. Since 1955. New Delhi.

Asian Studies. Quarterly since 1882. Calcutta: Netaji Institute for Asian Studies.

Blitz. Weekly news and commentary. Bombay.

Book Review. Monthly since 1976. New Delhi.

Biblio. Bimonthly, New Delhi.

Business India. Fortnightly. Bombay.

China Report. Quarterly, since 1964. New Delhi.

Contributions to Indian Sociology. Biannual. New Delhi and London.

Economic and Political Weekly. Since 1965. Bombay.

Environmental Resources: Abstracts. Quarterly since 1984. World Wildlife Fund: India.

Frontline. Weekly news and comment. Since 1983. Madras.

IDSA Journal. Quarterly since 1964. Institute of Defence Studies and Analysis. New Delhi.

Illustrated Weekly of India. Since 1888. Bombay.

India International Quarterly. Since 1964 New Delhi.

India Quarterly: A Journal of International Affairs. Indian Council of World Affairs. Since 1945. New Delhi.

India Speaks: Through its Regional Press. Weekly summary of daily newspapers in ten regional languages. Since 1987. New Delhi.

India Today. Fortnightly news and comment. Since 1975. New Delhi.

Indian Book Chronicle. Monthly journal on books and communication arts. Since 1975. New Delhi.

Indian Defence Review. Biannual. Since 1986. New Delhi.

Indian Economic and Social History Review. Quarterly. Since 1963. New Delhi.

Indian Journal of Public Administration. Quarterly. Since 1955. New Delhi.

Indian Journal of Social Science. Quarterly. Since 1988. New Delhi.

Indian Journal of Youth Affairs. Since 1979.

Indian Law Review

Indian Library Association Bulletin

Indian Literature. Fortnightly review of literature in all Indian languages. Since 1957. New Delhi.

Indian Medical Journal

Indian Ocean News and Views. Since 1991.

Indian Railways. Since 1981.

Indian Science Abstracts

Indian Who's Who

INDICA: Journal of Indian History and Culture. Biannual since 1963. Bombay.

International Studies. Quarterly since 1963. New Delhi.

Islam and the Modern Age. Quarterly since 1970. New Delhi.

Journal of Higher Education. Triannual since 1975. New Delhi.

Journal of the Indian Law Institute. Quarterly since 1958. New Delhi.

Journal of the Oriental Institute. Since 1950. Baroda.

Journal of the Poetry Society, India. Half-yearly since 1989. New Delhi.

Mainstream. Weekly political and economic comment. Since 1962. New Delhi.

Man and Development. Quarterly since 1979. Chandigarh.

Munushi: A Journal about Women and Society. Monthly, New Delhi.

Marg: A Magazine of the Arts. Quarterly since 1950. Bombay.

Margin. Journal of Applied Economic Research. Quarterly since 1967. New Delhi.

Monthly Commentary. Indian Institute of Public Opinion. Since 1959. New Delhi.

Outlook. Weekly news and comment since 1990. New Delhi.

Philosophy and Social Action. Quarterly since 1975. New Delhi.

Reserve Bank of India Bulletin. Monthly. Bombay.

Sanctuary. Fortnightly on ecology since 1980. Bombay.

Science Reporter. Monthly from the Council of Scientific and Industrial Research since 1963. New Delhi.

Seminar. A monthly symposium of opinion since 1960. Bombay/Delhi.

Social Change. Quarterly from the Council of Social Development since 1963. New Delhi.

South Asia Journal. Quarterly from the Indian Council for South Asian Cooperation since 1986. New Delhi.

Strategic Analysis. Monthly from the Institute for Defence Studies and Analysis since 1978. New Delhi.

Strategic Studies Journal. Quarterly since 1988. New Delhi.

Sunday. Weekly comment on news since 1973. Calcutta.

TERI: Energy Environment Monitor. Biannual since 1984. New Delhi.

Tibet Journal. Quarterly from the Library of Tibetan Works and Archives since 1978. Dharamsala.
The Indian History Review. Since 1978.
The Literary Criterion. Quarterly since 1975. Mysore.
Yojana. Monthly comment on economic development since 1956. New Delhi.
World Focus. Monthly comment since 1979. New Delhi.

Indian Newspapers with the Largest Circulation in 2001

Newspaper	Language	City
Anand Bazar Patrika	Bengali	Kolkata
Daily Jagram	Hindi	Kanpur
Daily Thanthi	Tamil	Chennai
Gujarat Samachar	Gujarati	Ahmedabad
Malayala Manorama	Malayallam	Kottayam
Mathrubhumi	Malayallam	Calicut
Rashtradoot	Hindi	Jaipur
The Hindu	English	Chennai
The Hindustan Times	English	New Delhi
The Times of India	English	Mumbai

(From Press Handbook, 2003)

Most Newspapers by Language, Number, and Periodicity in 2001

Language	Dailies	Weeklies
Bengali	103	633
English	407	1,010
Gujarati	159	1,086
Hindi	2,507	10,243
Kannada	364	397
Malayalam	225	184
Marathi	395	1,410
Oriya	80	167
Punjabi	107	369
Tamil	366	411
Telugu	180	267
Urdu	534	1,348

(From, *India, 2004*)

CULTURE

General

Basham, A. L., ed. *A Cultural History of India*. Oxford: Clarendon Press, 1975.

Basham, A. L. *The Wonder That Was India*. New York: Grove Press, 1954. Several reprints.

Brown, William Norman. *India and Indology: Selected Articles,* edited by Rosanne Rocher. Delhi: Motilal Banarsidas, 1978.

Coomaraswamy, Ananda K. *The Dance of 'Shiva.* New York: Farrar Straus, 1957.

Das, Veena, ed. *Critical Events: An Anthropological Perspective on Contemporary India. Essays in Honour of T. N. Madan.* Delhi: Oxford University Press, 1995.

Engineer, Ashgar Ali. *Islam in India: The Impact of Civilizations*. New Delhi: Indian Council of Cultural Relations, 2002.

Johnson, Donald J., et al. *Through Indian Eyes: The Living Tradition.* New York: City Books, 1992.

Kapur, Geetha. *When Was Modernism: Essays on Contemporary Cultural Practice in India.* New Delhi: Tulika, 2000.

Khare, R. S. *Culture and Democracy: Anthropological Reflections on Modern India.* Lanham, MD: University Press of America, 1985.

Lannoy, Richard. *The Speaking Tree: A Study of Indian Culture and Society.* London: Oxford University Press, 1971.

Larus, Joel. *Culture and Political-Military Behavior: The Hindus in Pre-Modern India,* Columbia MO: South Asia Books, 1979.

McGrail, Sean, and Lucy Blue. *Boats of South Asia.* New York: RoutledgeCurzon, 2002.

Mukerjee, Radhakamal. *The Culture and Art of India.* London: George Allen & Unwin, 1959.

Nandy, Ashis. *Return from Exile.* Delhi: Oxford University Press, 1998.

Nandy, Ashis, et. al. *Creating a Nationality.* New Delhi: Oxford University Press, 1995.

Noble, Allen G., and Ashok K. Dutt, eds. *India: Cultural Patterns and Processes.* Boulder, CO: Westview, 1982.

O'Malley, L. S. S., ed. *Modern India and the West: A Study of the Interaction of Their Civilizations.* London: Oxford University Press, 1968.

Ramakrishna Mission. *The Cultural Heritage of India.* 6 vols. Calcutta: Institute of Culture, 1986. Revised edition of 3 vols. published in 1937.

Raman, Shankar. *Framing India: The Colonial Imaginery in Early Modern Culture,* Palo Alto: Stanford University Press, 2002.

Riencourt, Amaury de. *The Soul of India.* Rev. ed. London: Honeyglen, 1986.

Rizvi, S. A. A. *The Wonder That Was India. Volume II.* London: Sidgwick & Jackson, 1987.

Saletore, R. N. *Encyclopedia of Indian Culture.* 5 vols. New Delhi: Sterling, 1981.

Sen, Geeti, ed. *India: A National Culture?* New Delhi: Sage, 2003.

Singh, B. P. *India's Culture: The State, the Arts and Beyond,* Delhi: Oxford University Press, 1999.

Archaeology

Agrawal, D. P. *The Archeology of India.* London, 1982.

Agrawal, D. P., and A. Ghose, eds. *Radiocarbon and Indian Archeology.* Bombay: Tata Institute of Fundamental Research, 1973.

Allchin, Bridget, and Raymond Allchin. *Origins of a Civilization.* New Delhi: Viking, 1997.

Allchin, Raymond, ed. *South Asian Archeology 1971–1991.* Cambridge: Cambridge University Press, 1995.

Chakrabarti, D. K. *India: An Archeological History.* Delhi: 1999.

Dani, Ahmad Hasan. *The Historic City of Taxila.* Paris: UNESCO, 1986.

Fairservis, W. A. *The Roots of Ancient India: The Archeology of Early Indian Civilization.* New York: Macmillan, 1971.

Ghosh, A., ed. *An Encyclopedia of Indian Archeology.* Delhi, 1989.

Hammond, N., ed. *South Asian Archeology.* London: Duckworth, 1973.

India: Archeological Survey. *Archeological Remains, Monuments and Museums.* 2 vols. Delhi: Archeological Survey of India, 1964.

Joshi, Jagat Puri. *Excavations at Surkotada 1971–72.* New Delhi: Archeological Survey of India, 1990.

Kern Institute-Leyden. *Annual Bibliography of Indian Archeology.* Dordrecht, Holland: D. Reidel Publishing Company, 1984.

Mallory, J. P. *In Search of the Indo-Europeans: Language, Archeology and Myth.* London: Thames & Hudson, 1989.

Mathpal, Y. *The Prehistoric Rock Art of Bhimbetka, Central India.* Delhi, 1984.

———. *Rock Art in Kumaon Himalaya.* New Delhi: Indira Gandhi National Centre for the Arts, 1995.

Piggot. S. *Prehistoric India to 1000 BC* London: Penguin, 1962.

Possehl, Gregory L. *Indus Civilization in Saurashtra.* New Delhi: Archeological Survey of India, 1980.

———. *Indian Archeology: A Review Guide to Excavated Sites, 1953–1982.* Philadelphia: University of Pennsylvania Museum, 1985.

Possehl, Gregory L., ed. *South Asian Archeology Studies.* New Delhi: Oxford University Press, 1992.

Rao, S. R. *Dawn and Devolution of the Indus Civilization.* New Delhi: Aditya Prakashan, 1991.

———. *Progress and Prospects of Marine Archeology in India.* New Delhi: Aditya Prakashan, 1993.

Sankalia, H. D. *Prehistoric Art in India.* New Delhi: Vikas, 1978.

———. *Indian Archeology Today.* Delhi: Ajanta, 1979.

Singh, B. *Burial Practices in Ancient India.* Varanasi: Prithvia Prakashan, 1970.

Singh, Upinder. *The Discovery of Ancient India: Early Archaeologists and the Beginnings of Archaeology.* Delhi: Permanent Black, 2004.

Thapar, B. K. *Recent Archeological Discoveries in India.* Paris: UNESCO, 1985.

Wheeler, Mortimer. *The Indus Valley.* London: Thames & Hudson, 1966.

Architecture

Aiyar, S. A. *Historical Index to the Study of Indian Temple Architecture.* Bombay: Chandra Printing Press, 1972.

Asher, Catherine B. *Architecture of Mughal India.* Cambridge: Cambridge University Press, 1992.

Bhatia, Gautam, ed. *Eternal Stone: Great Buildings of India.* New Delhi: Penguin, 2000.

———. *A Moment in Architecture.* New Delhi: Tulika Books, 2002.

Brown, Percy. *Indian Architecture.* 2 vols. Bombay: Taraporevala, 1965–1968.

Coomaraswamy, Ananda K. "Indian Architectural Terms." *JAOS,* 48(3) 1928: 250–273.

———. "The Symbolism of the Dome." IHQ 14 (1938): 1–56.

Correa, Charles. *The New Landscape.* Bombay: Book Society of India, 1985.

Davies, Philip. *The Penguin Guide to Monuments of India. Volume Two: Islamic, Rajput, European.* London: Viking Press, 1989.

Deheja, V. *Early Buddhist Rock Temples.* Ithaca, NY: Cornell University Press, 1972.

Dhavlikar, M. K. *Sanchi: A Cultural Study.* Poona, 1965.

Fabri, Charles L. *An Introduction to Indian Architecture.* Bombay: Asia, 1963.

Fergusson, J. *History of Indian and Eastern Architecture.* Delhi: Munshiran, 1967. Revision by J. Burgess of 1876 edition.

Ghosh, Rika. *Temple to Love: Architecture and Devotion in Seventeenth Century Bengal.* Bloomington: Indiana University Press, 2002.

Grover, S. *The Architecture of India: Buddhist und Hindu.* New Delhi: Vikas, 1980.

Havell, E. B. *The Ancient and Medieval Architecture of India. A Study of Indo-Aryan Civilization.* London: Murray, 1915.

Kramrisch, Stella. *The Hindu 'Temple.* Delhi: Motilal, 1976.

Lang, Jon T. *A Concise History of Modern Architecture in India.* Delhi: Permanent Black, 2002.

Mehta, R. J. *Masterpieces of Indo-Islamic Architecture.* Bombay: Taraporevala, 1976.

Mitchell, George. *The Penguin Guide to Monuments of India, Volume One: Buddhist, Jain, Hindu.* London: Viking Press, 1989.

———. *Architecture and Art of Southern India: Vijaynagar and the Successor States, 1350–1750.* Cambridge: Cambridge University Press, 1995.

———. *Architecture and Art of the Deccan Sultanates.* Cambridge: Cambridge University Press, 1999.

———. *Mughal Architecture: An Outline of Its Historical Development (1526–1858).* New Delhi: Oxford University Press, 2002. (Reprint)

Pelizzari, Maria Antonella, ed. *Traces of India: Photography, Architecture, and the Politics of Representation, 1850–1900.* Yale University Press, 2003.

Sundara, A. *The Early Chamber Tombs of South India.* Delhi: University Publishers, 1975.

Verghese, Anila. *Religious Traditions at Vijayanagar: As Revealed Through Its Monuments.* New Delhi: Manohar, 1995.

Art

Akhtar, Naseem, ed. *Art and Archeology of Eastern India.* Patna: Patna Museum, 2001.

Allchina, Raymond et al., eds. *Gandharan Art in Context.* Cambridge: Regency Publications, 1997.

Anant, Victor. *India: A Celebration of Independence 1947–1997.* Philadelphia: Philadelphia Museum of Art, 1997.

Archer, W. C. *Lives of Krishna: In Indian Painting and Poetry.* London: George Allen and Unwin, 1957.

Barnard, Nicholas. *Arts and Crafts of India.* London: Coman Octopus, 1993.

Barrett, Douglas, and Basil Gray. *Indian Painting.* London: Macmillan, 1978.

Beach, Milo Cleveland. *Mughal and Rajput Painting.* Cambridge: Cambridge University Press, 1992.

Beach, Milo Cleveland, and Ebba Koch. *King of the World: The Padshahnama.* London: Azimuth Editions, 1997.

Bussagli, M. *Indian Miniatures.* London: P. Hamlyn, 1969.

Coomaraswamy, Ananda K. *Introduction to Indian Art.* Delhi: Munshiram, 1969.

Desai, D. *Erotic Sculpture of India: A Socio-Cultural Study*. New Delhi: Tata McGraw Hill, 1975.

Fabri, Charles L. *Indian Dress: A Brief History*. New Delhi: Orient Longman, 1977.

Festival of India. *Aditi: The Living Arts of India*. Washington, DC: Smithsonian Institution Press, 1985.

Goetz, H. *The Art of India: Five Thousand Years of Indian Art*. New York: Greystone Press, 1964.

Gujral, Satish. *The World of Satish Gujral*. New Delhi: UBS, 1993.

Guy, John. *Indian Art and Connoissership*. Middletown, NJ: Grantha Corp., 1995.

Hardgrave, Robert L. *A Portrait of the Hindus: Balthazar Solvyns and the European Image of India 1760–1824*. New York: Oxford University Press, 2004.

Harle, J. C. *The Art and Architecture of the Indian Subcontinent*. New York: Viking Penguin, 1994.

Havell, E. B. *A Handbook of Indian Art*. New York: Dutton, 1920.

Irwin, John, and Margaret Hall. *Indian Embroideries*. Ahmedabad: Calico Museum of Textiles, 1973.

———. *Indian Painted and Printed Fabrics*. Ahmedabad: Calico Museum of Textiles, 1971.

Isacco, Enrico, and Anna L. Dallapiccola. *Krishna the Divine Lover: Myth and Legend Through Indian Art*. New Delhi: B. I. Publishers, 1982.

Jayakar, Pupul. *The Earth Mother*. Harmondsworth, Middlesex: Penguin, 1989.

Jayakar, Pupul, and J. Irwin, eds. *Textiles and Ornaments of India; A Selection of Designs*. New York: Arno, 1972.

Kapur, Geeta. *Contemporary Indian Artists*. New Delhi: Vikas, 1978.

Khandalavala, K. J. *The Development of Style in Indian Painting*. Delhi: Macmillan, 1974.

———. *Indian Bronze Masterpieces*. New Delhi: Festival of India, 1988.

Koch, Ebba. *Mughal Art and Imperial Ideology*. New Delhi: Oxford University Press, 2001.

Kramrisch, Stella. *The Art of India: Traditions of Indian Sculpture, Painting and Architecture*. Greenwich, CT: Phaidon Publishers, 1965.

———. *Indian Sculpture*. London: Lancaster Miller, 1981.

Losty, Jeremiah P. *The Art of the Book in India*. London: British Library, 1982.

Marg. Bombay: Marg Publications. Numerous volumes, monthly.

Mehta, R. J. *The Handicrafts and Industrial Arts of India*. Bombay: Taraporevala, 1969.

Metropolitan Museum of Art. *Indian Sculpture*. New York: Metropolitan Museum of Art, 1985.

Murphy, Veronica, and Rosemary Crill. *Tie-Dyed Textiles of India: Tradition and Trade*. London: Victoria and Albert Museum, 1991.

Murti, Isana, and Indira Dayal. *Anjolie Ela Menon: Paintings in Private Collections.* Delhi: Ravi Dayal Publisher, 1995.

Nagar, Shanti Lan. *Garuda, the Celestial Bird.* New Delhi: Book India, 1992.

Nehru, Lolita. *Origins of the Gandharan Style: A Study of Contributory Influences.* Delhi: Oxford University Press, 1989.

Pal, Pratapaditya. *Indian Sculpture c. 500 B.C–AD 700.* Berkeley, CA: University of California Press, 1986.

——. *Himalayas: An Aesthetic Adventure.* Berkeley, CA: University of California Press, 2003.

Qaisar, Ahsan Jan, and Som Prakash Verma, eds. *Art and Culture.* New Delhi: Abhinav. Annual Review.

Rahman, P. I. S. M. *Islamic Calligraphy in Medieval India.* Dacca: University Press Ltd., 1979.

Randhawa, M. S., and J. K. Galbraith. *Indian Painting: the Scenes, Themes and Legends.* Boston: Houghton Mifflin, 1968.

Saraf, D. N. *Indian Crafts: Development & Potential.* New Delhi: Vikas, 1982.

Singh, Madanjeet. *Himalayan Art.* London: Macmillan, 1968.

Sivamurti, C. *Indian Bronzes.* Bombay: Marg Publications, 1962.

Tandan, Raj Kumar. *Indian Miniature Painting Sixteenth-Nineteenth Centuries.* Bangalore: Natesan, 1982.

Thapar, D. R. *Icons in Bronze: An Introduction to Indian Metal Images.* Bombay: Asia, 1961.

Varadarajan, Lotika. *Traditions of Textile Painting in Kutch.* Ahmedabad: New Order Book Co., 1982.

——. *Sewn Boats of Lakshadweep.* Dona Paula: National Institute of Oceanography, 1999.

Vatsyayan, Kapila. *The Square and the Circle in the Indian Arts.* New Delhi: Roli Books International, 1983.

Welch, Stuart Cary. *India: Art and Culture 1300–1900.* New York: Metropolitan Museum of Art, 1985.

Zimmer, H. R. *The Art of Indian Asia, Its Mythology and Transformations.* Edited by Joseph Campbell. 2 vols. New York: Pantheon, 1955.

Dance, Film, and Music

Ahmed, Akbar S. "Bombay Films: The Cinema as Metaphor for Indian Society and Politics." *Modern Asian Studies* 26 (2), May 1992.

Bagchee, Sandeep. *Nad: Understanding Raga Music.* Mumbai:Eashwar, 1998.

Banerji, Projesh. *Art of Indian Dancing.* New Delhi: Sterling Publishers, 1985.

Bhavnani, E. *The Dance in India*. Bombay: Taraporevala, 1965.

Chowdhry, Prem. *Colonial India and the Making of Empire Cinema: Image, Ideology and Identity*. New Delhi: Sage, 2001.

Dasgupta, Chidanda. *The Painted Face: Studies in Indian Popular Cinema*. New Delhi: Roli Books, 1991.

Dhananjayan, V. P. *A Dancer on Dance*. Madras: Bharata Kalanjali, 1992.

French, David, and Michael Richards, eds. *Television in Contemporary Asia*. New Delhi: Sage, 2000.

George, T. J. S. *MS: A Life in Music*. Delhi: HarperCollins, 2004.

Gopalan, Lalitha. *Cinema of Interruptions*. New Delhi: Oxford University Press, 2003.

Holroyde, P. *Indian Music: A Vast Ocean of Promise*. London: Allen & Unwin, 1972.

Johnson, Kirk. *Television and Social Change in Rural India*. New Delhi: Sage Publications, 2000.

Kapur, Geeta. "Mythic Material in Indian Cinema." *Journal of Arts and Ideas* (January–April, 1987).

Khokar, Ashish. *Bharatanatyam*. New Delhi: Rupa & Co., 2002.

——. *Dancing for Themselves: Folk, Tribal and Ritual Dance in India*. New Delhi: Himalyan Books, 1987.

Kothari, Sunil. *Kathak: Indian Classical Dance Art*. New Delhi: Abhinav, 1989.

Krishnaswami, S. *Musical Instruments of India*. Boston: Crescendo, 1971.

Kunjamma, Lakshmi Viswanathan. *Ode to a Nightingale*. Delhi: Roli Books, 2003.

Lynton, H. Ronken. *Born to Dance*. Hyderabad: Orient Longman, 1995.

Marg. *Classical and Folk Dances of India*. Bombay: Marg Publications, 1963.

Mathur, Nita. *Cultural Rhythms in Emotions, Narratives and Dance*. New Delhi: Mnshiram Manoharlal, 2002.

Menon, R. R. *The Sound of Indian Music: A Journey into Raga*. New Delhi: Indian Book Co., 1976.

Mishra, Amar. *Some Musical Memories*. Delhi: Rupa & Co., 2004.

Nandy, Ashis, ed. *Secret Politics of Our Desires: Innocence, Culpability, and Indian Popular Cinema*. New York: Oxford University Press, 1998.

Popular Music in India (1901–1986). Journal of Popular Music, vol. 7 (2). Cambridge: Cambridge University Press, 1988.

Raghuvanshi, Alka, ed. *Dances of India*. 7 vols. New Delhi: Wisdom Tree, 2004.

Ray, Ashok. *Music Makers: Living Legends of Indian Classical Music*. Delhi: Rupa & Co., 2004.

Shankar, Ravi. *My Music: My Life*. New York: Simon and Schuster, 1968.

Singha, R., and R. Massey. *Indian Dances: Their History and Growth*. London: Faber, 1967.

Sorrell, N. *Indian Music in Performance: A Practical Introduction*. New York: New York University Press, 1980.

Vasudevan, Ravi. "The Cultural Space of a Film Narrative: Interpreting Kismet, Bombay Talkies 1943." *Indian Economic and Social History Review* 28 (2), 1991.

Vatsyayan, K. M. *Classical Indian Dance in Literature and the Arts*. New Delhi: Sangeet Natak Akademi, 1968.

———. *Traditions of Indian Folk Dance*. New Delhi: Indian Book Co., 1976.

Wade, B. C. *Music in India: The Classical Tradition*. Englewood Cliffs, NJ: Prentice Hall, 1979.

Wade, Trevor Montague. "Choreography as Feminist Strategy: Three Approaches to Hindu Feminism." Ph.D. Thesis, University of Chicago, 2001.

Language and Literature

Andronov, M. S. *Dravidian Languages*. Translated from the Russian. Moscow: Narika, 1970.

Beck, Brenda E. F., et al., eds. *Folktales of India*. Foreword by A. K. Ramanujan. Chicago: University of Chicago Press, 1987.

Blackburn, Stuart, and Vasudha Dalmia. *India's Literary History: Essays on the Nineteenth Century*. Delhi: Permanent Black, 2004.

Chandra, Sudhir. *The Oppressive Present: Literature and Social Consciousness in Colonial India*. Delhi: OUP, 1992.

Chatterjee, Minoti. *Theatre beyond the Threshold: Colonialism, Nationalism, and the Bengali State 1905–1947*. New Delhi: Indialog Publications, 2004.

Cronin, Richard. *Imagining India*. New York: St. Martin's Press, 1989.

Das, Veena, ed. *Mirrors of Violence: Communities, Riots, Survivors in South Asia*. New York: Oxford University Press, 1990.

———, ed. *The Word and the World: Fantasy, Symbol and Record*. New Delhi: Sage Publications, 1986.

Dharmarajan, Geeta, ed. *Prize Stories*. New Delhi: Katha, 1993.

Dimock, E. C., ed. *The Thief of Love: Bengali Tales from Court and Village*. Chicago: University of Chicago Press, 1963.

Dimock, E. C., et al. *The Literatures of India, an Introduction*. Chicago: University of Chicago Press, 1974.

Dwivedi, R. A. *A Critical Survey of Hindi Literature*. Delhi: Motilal, 1966.

Emeneau, M. B., and C. A. Ferguson, eds. *Linguistics in South Asia*. The Hague: Mouton, 1969.

Ferguson, C. A., and J. J. Gumperz, eds. *Linguistic Diversity in South Asia: Studies in Regional, Social and Functional Variation. International Journal of American Linguistics* (Special Issue) vol. 26 (3), 1960.

Frazer, Robert W. *A Literary History of India.* Delhi: Mittal Publishers, 1984.

Haksar, A. N. D. *The Shattered Thigh and Other Mahabharata Plays of Bhasa.* New Delhi: Penguin Books India, 1993.

———. *Glimpses of Sanskrit Literature.* New Delhi: New Age International, 1995.

———. *A Treasury of Sanskrit Poetry: In English Translation.* New Delhi: Shirpa Publications, 2002.

Handa, R. L. *History of Hindi Language and Literature.* Bombay: Bharatiya Vidya Bhavan, 1978.

Hubel, Teresa. *Whose India? The Independence Struggle in British and Indian Fiction and History.* Durham: Duke University Press, 1996.

Joshi, Priya. *In Another Country: Colonialism, Culture, and the English Novel in India.* New York: Columbia University Press, 2002.

Kannaiyan, V. *Scripts in and around India.* Madras: Government Museum, 1960.

Kaul, H. K. *Early Writings on India: Books on India in the English Language Published before 1900.* New Delhi: Arnold Heinemann and India International Centre, 1975.

Kaul, Suvir. *The Partitions of Memory: The Afterlife of the Division of India.* Bloomington: Indiana University Press, 2002.

Krishnamurti, Bhadriraju. *The Dravidian Languages.* Cambrdige: Cambridge University Press, 2003.

Kunhappa, M. *Three Bags of Gold and Other Indian Folk Tales.* New York: Asia, 1963.

Kurian, R. T., ed. *Dictionary of Indian English.* Madras: Indian Universities Publishers.

Malhotra, Dina N. *Dare to Publish: The Pioneer of the Paperback Revolution in India.* Delhi: Permanent Black, 2004.

Masica, Colin P. *The Indo-Aryan Languages.* Cambridge: Cambridge University Press, 1991.

Matthews, D. J. *An Anthology of Classical Urdu Love Lyrics.* London: United University Press, 1972.

Mehrotra, Arvind Krishna. *A History of Indian Literature in English.* London: C. Hurst & Co. 2003.

Mukherjee, Meenakshi. *Realism and Reality: the Novel and Society in India.* Delhi: Oxford University Press, 1985.

Mukherjee, Sujit. *The Idea of an Indian Literarure: A Book of Readings.* Mysore: Central Institute of Indian Languages, 1981.

———, ed. *A Dictionary of Indian Literature.* Hyderabad: Orient Longman, 1998.

Naik, M. K. *Dimensions of Indian English Literature.* New Delhi: Sterling, 1984.

Narasimhaiah, C. D. *English Studies in India: Widening Horizons.* Delhi: Pencraft International, 2002.

Nelson, Emmanuel S, ed. *Writers of the Indian Diaspora: A Bio-Bibliographical Critical Sourcebook.* Westport, CT: Greenwood, 1993.

Nigam, R. C. *Language Handbook on Mother Tongues in Census.* Census Centenary Monograph, 10. New Delhi: Office of the Registrar General, 1972.

O'Connell, Kathleen. *Rabindranath Tagore: The Poet as Educator.* Calcutta: Visva Bharati, 2002.

Orsini, Francesca, ed. *Premchand: Collected Works.* New Delhi: Oxford University Press, 2004.

Pushp, N., and K. Warikoo, eds. *Jammu and Kashmir and Ladakh: Linguistic Predicament.* New Delhi: Har Anand Publications, 2004.

Rao, T. Rajagopala. *A Historical Sketch of Telugu Literature.* New Delhi: Asian Educational Services, 1984.

Rao, U. Venkatakrishna. *A Handbook of Classical Sanskrit Literature.* Bombay: Orient Longman, 1967.

Rubin, David. *After the Raj: British Novels of India Since 1947.* Hanover: University Press of New England, 1986.

Schimmel, A. *Classical Urdu Literature from the Beginning to Iqbal.* Wiesbaden: Harrassowitch, 1975.

Settar S., and Indira B. Gupta, eds. *The Pangs of Partition.* 2 vols. New Delhi: Manohar, 2002.

Singh, Amritjit, Rajiv Verma, and Irene Joshi. *Indian Literature in English, 1827–1979.* Detroit: Gale Research Company, 1981.

Turner, R. L., and D. R. Turner. *A Comparative Dictionary of the IndoAryan Languages, Phonetic Analysis.* London: Oxford University Press, 1971.

Valmiki. *The Ramayana of Valmiki: An Epic of Ancient India.* Introduction and translation by Robert Goldman. Princeton: Princeton University Press, 1985.

Winks, Robin W., and James R. Rush, eds. *Asia in Western Fiction.* Honolulu, HI: University of Hawaii Press, 1990.

Yule, H., and A. C. Burnell. *Hobson-Jobson: A Glossary of Colloquial Anglo Indian Words and Phrases.* New Delhi: Munshiram, 1968. Reprint of 1903 publication.

Zvelebil, Kamil V. *The Smile of Murugan, On Tamil Literature of South India.* Leiden: E. J. Brill, 1973.

Press and Periodicals

Bathla, Sonia. *Women, Democracy and the Media: Cultural and Political Representations in the Indian Press.* New Delhi: Sage, 1998.

Chatterji, P. C. *Broadcasting in India.* New Delhi: Sage, 1987.

Chaturvedi, J. P. *The Indian Press at the Crossroads.* New Delhi: Media Research Associates, 1992.

Cheema, Pervaiz Iqbal. *A Select Bibliography of Periodical Literature on India and Pakistan 1947–1970.* Vol. 11—India. Islamabad: National Commission on Historical and Cultural Research, 1979.

Gunaratne, Shelton A., ed. *Handbook of the Media in Asia.* New Delhi: Sage, 2000.

Gupta, B. M. *Handbook of Libraries, Archives and Information Centres in India.* New Delhi: Information Industry Publications, 1984.

India Ministry of Information and Broadcasting. *Mass Media in India.* New Delhi: Publications Division, annually since 1970.

Indian & Eastern Newspaper Society. *Press Handbook.* New Delhi: IENS, annually since 1940.

Indian Books in Print: A Bibliography of English Books Published in India. Delhi: Indian Bibliographies Bureau, regularly since 1967.

Johnson, Kirk. *Television and Social Change in Rural India.* New Delhi: Sage, 2000.

Press in India. New Delhi: Office of the Registrar of Newspapers, annually since 1957.

Rajagopal, Arvind. *Politics after Television: Hindu Nationalism and the Shaping of the Public in India.* Cambridge: Cambridge University Press, 2001.

Singh, Mohinder. *State Government Publications in India 1947–1982.* Delhi: Academic Publications, 1985.

Singh, S. Nihal. *Your Slip Is Showing: Indian Press Today.* New Delhi: UBS, 1992.

Vasishth, C. P. *Library and Information Science in India: Its Education and Training.* Delhi: Academic Publications, 1985.

Verghese, B. G. *Breaking the Big Story: Great Moments in Indian Journalism.* Delhi: Viking, 2003.

ECONOMY

Surveys, Analyses, Reports

Agarwal, Pradeep, et al. *Policy Regimes and Industrial Competitiveness: A Comparative Study of East Asia and India.* Houndmills, UK: Macmillan, 2000.

Ahluwalia, Isher Judge, and I. M. D. Little, eds. *India's Economic Reforms.* Oxford: Oxford University Press, 1998.

Ahluwalia, Montek Singh. "India's Economic Reforms: An Appraisal." In Sachs et. al., eds. *India in the Time of Economic Reforms*. New Delhi: Oxford University Press.

——. "Infrastructure Development in India's Reforms." In Ahluwalia and Little, eds. *India's Economic Reforms*. Oxford: Oxford University Press, 1998. Chapter 5.

——. "Economic Performance of States in Post-Reforms Periods." *Economic and Political Weekly*, May 6, 2000.

——. "Economic Reforms in India Since 1991: Has Gradualism Worked?" *Journal of Economic Perspectives* Vol. 16. (Summer 2002): 67–88.

Aiyar, Swaminathan S. *India's Economic Prospects: The Promise of Service*. Philadelphia: CASI Paper 9, 1999.

Allaoua, Zoubida. *India: Five Years of Stabilization and Reform and the Challenges ahead*. Washington, DC: World Book 1996.

Alternative Survey Group. *Alternative Economic Survey 1998–2000: Two Years of Market Fundamentalism*. Delhi: Rainbow Publishers Ltd., 2000.

Alvares, Claude. *Science, Development and Violence: The Revolt Against Modernity*. Delhi: Oxford University Press, 1992.

Bardhan, Pranab. *The Political Economy of Development in India*. Oxford: Basil Blackwell, 1984.

Bhattacharya, B. B. *India's Economic Crises, Debt Burden and Stabilization*. Delhi: B. R. Publishing, 1992.

Chibber, Vivek. *Locked in Place: State Building and Late Industrialization in India*. New Delhi: Tulika Books, 2004.

Desai, Meghnad. *Development and Nationhood: Essays in the Political Economy of South Asia*. New Delhi: Oxford University Press, 2005.

Diwan, Romesh, and Mark Lutz, eds. *Essays in Gandhian Economics*. New York: Intermediate Technology, 1987.

Dreze, Jean, and Amartya Sen. *India: Economic Development and Social Opportunity*. Delhi: Oxford University Press, 1996.

Frankel, Francine R. *India's Political Economy 1947–1977: The Gradual Revolution*. Princeton: Princeton University Press, 1978.

Ganapathy, R. S., et al. *Public Policy and Policy Analysis in India*. New Delhi: Sage, 1985.

Guhan, S., and Manu Shroff, eds. *Essays on Economic Progress and Welfare: In Honour of I. G. Patel*. Delhi: Oxford University Press, 1986.

Harriss-White, Barbara. *India Working: Essays on Society and Economy*. Cambridge: Cambridge University Press, 2003.

India, Ministry of Finance. *Economic Survey of India,* annual.

Jalan, Bimal. *India's Economic Crisis: The Way Ahead*. Delhi: Oxford University Press, 1991.

———, ed. *The Indian Economy: Problems and Prospects.* New Delhi: Viking, 1992.

Januzzi, F. Tomasson. *India in Transition: Issues of Political Economy in a Plural Society.* Boulder, CO: Westview Press, 1989.

Jenkins, Rob. *Democratic Politics and Economic Reform in India.* Cambridge: Cambridge University Press, 1999.

Jha, Prem Shankar. *India: A Political Economy of Stagnation.* Bombay: Oxford University Press, 1980.

Joshi, Vijay, and I. M. D. Little. *India's Economic Reforms 1991–2000.* Delhi: Oxford University Press, 1996.

Kabra, Kamal Nayan, et al. *Indian Economy during the 1980s.* New Delhi: Patriot Publishers, 1990.

Kochanek, Stanley A. *Business and Politics in India.* Berkeley: University of California Press, 1974.

Kumar, Dharma, and Meghnand Desai, eds. *The Cambridge Economic History of India, Volume 11 c. 1757–1970.* Cambridge: Cambridge University Press, 1983.

Lal, Deepak. *The Hindu Equilibrium. Volume 1: Cultural Stability and Economic Stagnation.* Oxford: Clarendon Press, 1988.

———. *Unfinished Business: India in the World Economy.* New Delhi: Oxford University Press, 1999.

Lanza del Vasto, J. J. *Gandhi to Vinobha: The New Pilgrimage.* New York: Schocken Books, 1974.

Mahbub ul-Haq Human Development Centre. *Human Development in South Asia 2002.* Delhi: Oxford University Press, 2003.

Mehta, Asoka. *Reflections on Socialist Era.* New Delhi: S. Chand, 1977.

Myrdal, Gunnar. *Asian Drama: An Inquiry into the Poverty of Nations.* 3 vols. New York: Pantheon, 1968.

Naib, Sudhir. *Disinvestment in India: Policies, Procedure, Practices.* New Delhi: Sage, 2004.

Narayan, Shriman. *India Needs Growth.* New Delhi: S. Chand, 1976.

Nayar, Baldev Raj. *Globalization and Nationalism: The Changing Balance in India's Economic Policy.* New Delhi: Sage Publications, 2001.

Norberg-Hodge Helena. *Ancient Futures: Learning from Ladakh.* San Francisco: Sierra Club Books, 1991.

Parikh, Kirit S., ed. *India's Development Report 1999–2000.* New Delhi: Oxford University Press, 1999.

Patel, I. G. *Economic Reform and Global Change.* New Delhi: Macmillan, 1998.

——. *Essays in Economic Policy and Economic Growth*. London: Macmillan, 1986.

——. *Glimpses of Indian Economic Policy: An Insider's View*. New Delhi: Oxford University Press, 2002.

Planning Commission, Government of India. *India Economic Road Map: The Next Five Years, 2002–2007*. New Delhi: Planning Commission, 2002.

——. *National Human Development Report 2002*. New Delhi: Oxford University Press, 2002.

Ramesh, Jairam. *Kautilya Today*. New Delhi: India Research Press, 2002.

Rao, V. K. R. V. *India's National Income 1950–1980: An Analysis of Economic Growth and Change*. New Delhi: Sage, 1983.

Ray, H. N. *Mid-Year Review of the Economy 1991–92*. New Delhi: Konark Publishers with India International Centre, 1992.

Reserve Bank of India. *Annual Report*. Annual.

Rosen, George. *Democracy and Economic Change in India*. Berkeley: University of California Press, 1966.

Roy, Subroto, and William E. James, eds. *Foundations of India's Political Economy. Towards an Agenda for the 1990s*. New Delhi: Sage, 1992.

Sachs, Jeffrey D., Ashutosh Varshney, and Nirupam Bajpai. *India in the Era of Economic Reforms,* New Delhi: Oxford University Press, 2000.

Schneider, Frederich, and Dominik H. Enste. *The Shadow Economy: An International Survey*. Cambridge: Cambridge University Press, 2002.

Sen, Amartya. *Development as Freedom*. New York: Anchor, 2000.

Sen, Sunanda. *Trade and Dependence: Essays on the Indian Economy*. New Delhi: Sage, 2000.

Sethi, J. D. *Indian Economy under Siege*. New Delhi: Vikas, 1992.

Singh, Tarlok. *India's Development Experience*. Madras: Macmillan India, 1974.

Sinha, Jai B. *Multinationals in India: Managing the Interface of Cultures*. New Delhi: Sage, 2004.

Srinivasan, T. N., and Suresh D. Tendulkar. *Reintegrating India with the World Economy*. Institute for International Economics, 2003.

Thapar, Romesh, ed. *Indian Economic Thinking*. Bombay: Allied, 1979.

Tomlinson, B. R. *The Economy of Modern India 1860–1970*. Cambridge: Cambridge University Press, 1993.

Varshney, Ashutosh. *Democracy, Development and the Countryside: Urban-Rural Struggles in India*. Cambridge University Press, 1998.

World Bank. *India: Sustaining Rapid Economic Growth*. Washington, DC: World Bank, 1997.

——. *The World Development Report, 2002/2003.* Washington, DC: The World Bank, 2003.

Agriculture and Rural Development

Ali, Mohammed, ed. *Dynamics of Agricultural Development in India.* Delhi: Ceoncept, 1979.

Arora, R. C. *Integrated Rural Development.* New Delhi: S. Chand, 1979.

Bergman, T. *Mechanization of Indian Farming: Obstacles and Prospects.* Bombay: Popular, 1978.

Chambers, Robert. *Managing Canal Irrigation: Practical Analysis from South Asia.* Cambridge: Cambridge University Press, 1988.

Crowell, Daniel W. *The Sewa Movement and Rural Development.* New Delhi: Sage, 2003.

Das, A. N., and V. Nilakant, eds. *Agrarian Relations in India.* New Delhi: Manohar, 1979.

Etienne, Gilbert. *Food and Poverty: India's Half Won Battle.* New Delhi: Sage, 1988.

Frankel, F. R. *India's Green Revolution: Economic Gains and Political Costs.* Princeton, NJ: Princeton University Press, 1971.

George, Abraham M. *India Untouched: The Forgotten Face of Rural Poverty.* Chennai: East West Books, 2004.

Gill, Sucha, Singh. *Land Reforms in India.* New Delhi: Sage, 2002.

Gulati, Ashok and Ruth Meinzen-Dick. *Institutional Reforms in Indian Irrigation.* New Delhi: Sage, 2005.

Gupta, Akhil. *Postcolonial Developments: Agriculture in the Making of Modern India.* Durham, NC: Duke University Press, 1998.

India: Central Water and Power Commission. *Pocketbook on Major and Medium Irrigation.* New Delhi, 1976.

Iyer, Ramaswami R. *Water: Perspectives, Issues, Concerns.* New Delhi: Sage, 2003.

Jain, Man Mal. *Growth Pattern of Dairy Subsection in Rajasthan: A Study of Milk Producers' Cooperatives.* Bombay: Himalaya Publishing, 1986.

Joshi, P. C. *Land Reforms in India: Trends and Perspectives.* Bombay: Allied, 1975.

Joshi, Sharad. "Farmers' Movements in India." *New Quest* 58 (Summer 1986): 208–216.

Krishnaswamy, O. R. *Cooperative Democracy in Action: An Empirical Study in a State in India.* Bombay: Somaiya, 1976.

Lewis, John P. *Quiet Crisis in India.* New York: Doubleday, 1963.

Lipton, Michael. "India's Agricultural Performance: Achievements, Distortions and Ideologies." *AAS Journal* 6 (1970): 127–148.

——. *The Indus Rivers: A Study of the Effects of Partition.* New Haven, CT: Yale University Press, 1967.

Mosse, David, and M. Sivan. *The Rule of Water: Statecraft, Ecology and Collective Action in South India.* New Delhi: Oxford University Press, 2003.

Nair, Kusum. *Blossoms in the Dust: The Human Element in Indian Development.* London: Gerald Duckworth, 1961.

——. *In Defense of the Irrational Peasant: Indian Agriculture after the Green Revolution.* Chicago: University of Chicago Press, 1979.

Raj, K. N. "Ownership and Distribution of Land." *Indian Economic Review* 5 (1970): 1–42.

Randhawa, Mohinder Singh. *A History of Agriculture in India.* New Delhi: Indian Council of Agricultural Research, 1982.

Ranga, Haripriya. *Of Myths and Movements: Rewriting Chipko into Himalayan History.* New York: Verso, 2000.

Rao, K. L. *India's Water Wealth. Its Assessment, Uses and Projections.* New Delhi: Orient Longman, 1975.

Ray, A. C. *Cooperative Farming in India.* Calcutta: P. Ghose, 1978.

Singh, Inderjit. *The Great Ascent: The Rural Poor in South Asia.* Baltimore: Johns Hopkins University Press, 1990.

Singharoy, Debal K. *Peasant Movements in Post-Colonial India.* New Delhi: Sage, 2004.

Sinha, B. K., and Pushpendra. *Land Reforms in India: Vol. 5, An Unfinished Agenda.* New Delhi: Sage, 2000.

Subramanium, C. *The New Strategy in Indian Agriculture: The First Decade and After.* New Delhi: Vikas, 1979.

Thorner, Daniel. *The Agrarian Prospect in India.* 2nd ed. Bombay: Allied, 1976.

——. *Agricultural Cooperatives in India: A Field Report.* Bombay: Asia, 1964.

Vohra, B. B. *Land and Water Management Problems in India.* New Delhi: Department of Personnel and Administrative Reforms, 1982.

Wade, Robert. *Village Republics: Economic Conditions for Collective Actions in South India.* Cambridge: Cambridge University Press, 1988.

Finance and Banking

Avadhani, V. A. *Studies in Indian Financial System.* Bombay: Jaico, 1978.

Basu, C. R. *Central Banking in a Developing Economy: The Indian Experiment.* New Delhi: Tata McGraw-Hill, 1977.

Basu, B. S., and G. S. Batra. *Management of Financial Services.* New Delhi: Deep & Deep, 1996.

Basu, S. K. *Commercial Banks and Agricultural Credit: A Study in Regional Disparity in India.* Bombay: Allied, 1979.

Bhatia, H. L. *Centre-State Financial Relations in India.* New Delhi: Abhinav, 1979.

Bhole, L. H. *Financial Markets and Institutions.* New Delhi: Tata McGraw-Hill, 1982.

Bishnoi, U. *Union Taxes in India.* Allahabad: Chugh, 1980.

Chelliah, R. J. *Fiscal Policy in Underdeveloped Countries: With Special Reference to India.* London: Allen and Unwin, 1969.

Dagli, V. *Financial Institutions of India.* Bombay: Vora, 1976.

Ghatak, S. *Rural Money Markets in India.* Delhi: Macmillan, 1976.

Goyal, Om Prakash. *Financial Institutions and Economic Growth of India.* New Delhi: Light and Life Publishers, 1979.

Gulati, I. S., ed. *Centre-State Budgetary Transfers.* Delhi: Oxford University Press, 1987.

Gupta, Umrao Lal. *Working of Stock Exchange in India.* New Delhi: Thomsen Press, 1972.

India, Committee on the Financial System. *Narasimham Committee on the Financial System.* New Delhi: Standard Book, 1992.

———. *Report of the Committee on Banking Sector Reform.* New Delhi: Union Ministry of Finance, 1998.

India, Joint Committee to Enquire into Irregularities in Securities and Banking Transactions (Tenth Lok Sabha). *Report.* 2 vols. New Delhi: Lok Sabha Secretariat, December 1993.

India, Ministry of Finance. *Tax Reforms Committee: Final Report.* Delhi: Department of Revenue, 1993.

Jha, L. K. *Economic Development: Ends and Means.* Bombay: Vora, 1973.

Kankone, Satu, and Anthony Lanyi, eds. *Institutions, Incentive, and Economic Reforms in India.* New Delhi: Sage, 2000.

Khan, M. Y. *Indian Financial System: Theory and Practice.* New Delhi: Vikas, 1980.

Misra, B. *Economics of Public Finance.* Delhi: Macmillan, 1978.

Mookerjee, Sameer C. *Role of the Comptroller and Auditor General in Indian Democracy.* New Delhi: Ashish, 1989.

Padhy, K. C. *Commercial Banks and Rural Development: A Study of India.* New Delhi: Asian Publishing, 1980.

Rao, V. K. R. V. "Changing Structure of Indian Economy as Seen through National Accounts." *Economic and Political Weekly* 14 (50), 1979: 2049–2058.

Rao, V. L. *Indian Banks Abroad.* New Delhi: Centre for Policy Research, 1991.

Reserve Bank of India. C. D. Deshmukh Memorial Lectures. Bombay Reserve Bank of India, 1996.

Industry

Agarwal, Pradeep, et al. *Policy Regimes and Industrial Competitiveness: A Comparative Study of East Asia and India.* Houndmills, UK: Macmillan, 2000.

Ahluwalia, Isher J. *Industrial Growth in India.* Delhi: Oxford University Press, 1985.

Dhar, P. N., and H. F. Lydale. *Role of Small Enterprises in Indian Economic Development.* New York: Asia Publishing, 1961.

Economic Intelligence Service. *Corporate Finance: Industry Aggregates.* Bombay: Centre for Monitoring Indian Economy, November 1993.

——. *The Shape of Things to Come. Survey of Investment Projects.* Bombay: Centre for Monitoring Indian Economy, December 1993.

Ghoshal, Sumantra, Gita Piramal, and Sudeep Budhiraja. *World Class in India: A Casebook of Companies in Transformation,* New Delhi: Penguin Books India, 2001.

Herdeck, Margaret, and Gita Piramal. *India's Industrialists.* Washington, DC: Three Continents Press, 1985.

India: Ministry of Industry. *Industrial Development in India: A Survey.* New Delhi: Ministry of Industries, 1966.

——. *Public Enterprise Survey: Annual Report.* New Delhi: Bureau of Public Enterprise. Annually.

Jain, J. P. *Nuclear India.* New Delhi: Radiant, 1974.

Khera, S. S. *Government in Business.* New Delhi: National, 1977.

Khurana, Rakesh. *Growth of Large Business: Impact of Monopolies Legislation.* New Delhi: Wiley Eastern, 1981.

Kuchlal, Suresh Chandra. *The Industrial Economy of India.* Allahabad: Chaitanya Publishing, 1959.

Lala, R. M. *Beyond the Last Blue Mountain: A Life of J. R. D. Tata.* New Delhi: Viking, 1992.

Malgavkar, P. D. *Industrial Policy and Prospects. 2001 AD.* New Delhi: Oxford University Press, 1988.

Marathe, S. S. *Regulation and Development.* New Delhi: Sage, 1989.

Murty, M. N. *Environmental and Economic Accounting for Indian Industry.* Delhi: Institute of Economic Growth, 2001.

Panandiker, D. H. Pai, ed. *Pollution Control in Indian Industry.* Delhi: BRPC, 1991.

Piramal, Gita. *Business Maharajas.* Delhi: Viking, 1996.

Ravichandran, N., ed. *Competition in Indian Industries: A Strategic Perspective.* New Delhi: Vikas, 1999.

Ray, Jajat Kanta Ray, ed. *Entrepreneurship and Industry in India, 1800–1947.* Delhi: Oxford University Press, 1992.

Sinha, B. *Industrial Geography of India.* Calcutta: World Press, 1972.

Soni, M. R. *Indian Industry and Its Problems.* London: Longman Green, 1932.

Tata, Naval. *In Pursuit of Industrial Harmony: An Employer's Perspective.* Bombay: National Institute of Labour Management, 1975.

Taylor, C. *India: Economic Issues in the Power Sector.* Washington, DC: World Bank, 1979.

Verma, H. S. *Industrial Families in India.* New Delhi: Concept, 1987.

Wagle, D. M., and N. V. Rao. *The Power Sector in India.* Bombay: Popular, 1978.

International Trade

Adiseshiah, Malcolm S., ed. *India's International Economic Relations. The Present and Perspective.* New Delhi: Lancer International, 1990.

———. *Role of Foreign Trade in Indian Economy.* New Delhi: Lancer International, 1986.

Agrawal, Raj. *Indian Foreign Trade.* New Delhi: Excel Books, 2001.

Desai, A. V. "India in the Uruguay Round." In *Trade Liberalization in the 1990s,* edited by Hans Singer et al. New Delhi: Indus Publishing, 1990.

Dutt, Srikant. *India and the Third World: Alternatives or Hegemony?* London: Zed, 1984.

Indian Institute of Foreign Trade. *A Decade of Studies in Foreign Trade 1981–1991. A Bibliography.* New Delhi: Indian Institute of Foreign Trade, 1991.

Inter-Strat Export Consultants (India) Pvt. Ltd. *EU-India Business Perspectives: Post Uruguay Round.* Mumbai: World Trade Centre, 1996.

Jayaraman, T. K. *Economic Cooperation in the Indian Subcontinent: A Customs Union Approach.* Bombay: Orient Longman, 1978.

Khanna, Sri Ram. *International Trade in Textiles: MFA Quotas and a Developing Exporting Country.* New Delhi: Sage, 1991.

Kumar, Suresh. *Indo-CMEA Economic Relations.* New Delhi: Ashish Publishing, 1987.

Mukherjee, Neela, and Amitabha Mukherjee. *India's Foreign Trade by Regions 1950–1986.* New Delhi: Indus Publishing, 1988.

Narula, Subhash. *India's Gulf Exports: Features, Trends and Prospects.* Delhi: Anupama Publications, 1988.

National Council of Applied Economic Research. *Export Competitiveness of Selected Agricultural Commodities.* New Delhi: NCAER, 1994.

Prakash, Om. *European Commercial Enterprise in Pre-Colonial India.* Cambridge; Cambridge University Press, 1998.

Sarma, N. A. *International Environment and India's Economic Development.* New Delhi: Abhinav, 1986.

Satchit, Balan. *Export Promotion in India: A Strategic Perspective.* New Delhi: Commonwealth Publishers, 1999.

Singh, Ajit, ed. *Export of Agricultural Commodities, 2000 AD.* New Delhi: Wiley Eastern, 1994.

Singh, R. K. *Changing Horizon: A Study of Future Prospects for Engineering Goods Exports.* Bombay: Sindhu Publishers, 1970.

Sood, Krishnalekha. *Trade and Economic Development: India, Pakistan and Bangladesh.* New Delhi: Sage, 1989.

Tandon, Rameshwar. *Some Perspectives on India's Trade Policy.* Allahabad: Chugh Publications, 1983.

Thomas, Richard. *India's Emergence as an Industrial Power: Middle Eastern Contracts.* Hamden, CT: Archon Books, 1982.

Toye, John, ed. *Indo-European Cooperation in an Interdependent World.* Brussels: Centre for European Policy Studies, 1989.

Varma, M. I. *Foreign Trade Management in India.* New Delhi: Vikas, 1988.

Labor

Bremen, Jan. *Footloose Labour: Working in India's Informal Sector.* Cambridge: Cambridge University Press, 1998.

Crouch, H. A. *Trade Unions and Politics in India.* Bombay: Manaktalas, 1966.

Davala, Sarath ed. *Employment and Unionization in Indian Industry.* New Delhi: Friedrich Ebert Stiftung, 2003.

Holmstrom, Mark. *Industry and Inequality: The Social Anthropology of Indian Labour.* Cambridge: Cambridge University Press, 1984.

India, Ministry of Labour. *Annual Reports.*

India, National Commission on Labour. *Reports of the National Commission on Labour 2002–1991–1964.* New Delhi: Academic Foundation, 2003.

Jafa, V. S., ed. *India: Labour and Employment Scenario in the 21st Century.* New Delhi: New Century Publishers, 2001.

Jhabvala, Renana, ed. *The Unorganized Sector: Work Security and Social Protection.* New Delhi: Sage, 2000.

Jose, A. V., ed. *Limited Options: Women Workers in Rural India.* New Delhi: International Labour Organisation (ARTEP), 1989.

Joshi, Chitra. *Lost Worlds: Indian Labour and its Forgotten Histories.* Delhi: Permanent Black, 2003.

Kabra, K. N. *Political Economy of Brain Drain: Reverse Transfer of Technology.* New Delhi: Arnold-Heinemann, 1976.

Kamik, V. B. *Industrial Labour: Problems and Prospects.* Calcutta: Minerva, 1974.

Kapur, P. *The Changing Status of the Working Woman in India.* Delhi: Vikas, 1974.

Kothari, G. H. *Labour Law and Practice.* Calcutta: International Law Book Centre,1980.

Kulshreshtha, J. C. *Child Labour in India.* New Delhi: Ashish, 1978.

Mamkoottam, Kuriakose. *Labour and Change: Essays on Globalization, Technological Change and Labour in India.* New Delhi: Sage, 2002.

Mehta, S. S. *Productivity, Production Function and Technical Change: A Survey of Some Indian Industries.* New Delhi: Concept, 1980.

Mishra, L. *Unorganised labour: Deprivation and Emancipation.* New Delhi: Manak Publishers, 1999.

Mongia, J. N., ed. *Readings in Indian Labour and Social Welfare.* Delhi: Atma Ram, 1976.

Puttaswamaiah, K. *Unemployment in India: Policy for Manpower.* New Delhi: Oxtord & IBH, 1977.

Ramaswamy, E. A., ed. *Industrial Relations in India. A Sociological Perspective.* Delhi: Macmillan, 1978.

Ranadive, V. *Women Workers of India.* Calcutta: National Book Agency, 1976.

Rose, Kalima. *Where Women are Leaders: The SEWA Movement in India.* New Delhi:Sage, 1992.

Saxena, J. P. *Educated Unemployment in India: Problems and Suggestions.* New Delhi: Commercial Publishing Bureau, 1972.

Vyas, N. N. *Bondage and Exploitation in Tribal India.* Jaipur: Rawal, 1980.

Planning and Development

Adiseshiah, Malcolm S. "Planning From Below with Reference to District Development and State Planning," *Economic and Political Weekly* 6 (30), 1971: 1609–1618.

——, ed. *Forty years of Economic Development: United Nations Agencies and India.* New Delhi: Lancer International, 1987.

——. *Eighth Plan Perspectives.* New Delhi: Lancer International, 1990.

——. *Sustainable Development: Its Contents, Scope and Prices.* New Delhi: Lancer International, 1990.

Balasubramanyam, V. N. *Conversations with Indian Economists.* New York: Palgrave, 2001.

Bhagwati, Jagdish, and Padma Desai. *India: Planning for Industrialization and Trade Policies Since 1951*. New York: Oxford University Press, 1970.

Byres, Terence J., ed. *The Indian Economy: Major Debates Since Independence.* Delhi: Oxford University Press, 1998.

Centre for Research in Rural and Industrial Development. *In Search of India's Renaissance.* 2 volumes of proceedings from a seminar on nation building, development, and communication held in 1988. Chandigarh: Centre for Research in Rural and Industrial Development, 1992.

India, Planning Commission. *First Five Year Plan.* New Delhi: Controller of Publications, 1953.

———. *Second Five Year Plan.* New Delhi: Controller of Publications, 1956.

———. *Third Five Year Plan: A Draft Outline 1960.* New Delhi: Controller of Publications, 1960.

———. *Indian Planning Experience: A Statistical Profile.* New Delhi: Planning Commission, 2001.

———. *India Economic Road Map: The Next Five Years 2002–2007.* New Delhi: Planning Commission, 2002.

Kabra, Kamal Nayan. *India's Black Economy and Maldevelopment.* New Delhi: Patriot, 1986.

Malenbaum, W. *Modern India's Economy: Two Decades of Planned Growth.* Columbus, OH: C. E. Merrill, 1971.

Mongia, J. N., ed. *India's Economic Development Strategies 1951–2000 AD.* New Delhi: Allied, 1986.

Pai Panandikar, V. A., and S. S. Kshirsagar. *Bureaucracy and Development Administration.* New Delhi: Centre for Policy Research, 1978.

Paranjape, H. K. *The Planning Commission: A Descriptive Account.* New Delhi: Institute of Public Administration, 1964.

Patel, I. G. *Essays in Economic Policy and Economic Growth.* New York: St. Martin's Press, 1986.

Raj, K. N. "The Fourth Plan and Future Economic Policy." *Economic and Political Weekly* 2 (11) (1967): 555–563.

Roy, Ramashray, and R. K. Srivastava. *Dialogues on Development: The Individual, Society and Political Order.* New Delhi: Sage, 1986.

Tewari, Dina Nath. *Forestry and National Development.* Dehra Dun: Jugal Kishore, 1986.

Thapar, S. D. *India's Forest Resources.* Delhi: Macmillan, 1975.

Virmani, Arvind. *Accelerating Growth and Poverty Reduction: A Policy Framework for India's Development.* New Delhi: Academic Foundations, 2004.

Vithal, B. P. R., and M. L Sastry. *The Gadgil Formula: For Allocation of Central Assistance for State Plans.* Hyderabad: Centre for Economic and Special Studies, 2002.

Transport and Communication

Aitken, Bill. *Travels by a Lesser Line.* New Delhi: Indus, 1993.

Bach, Brian Paul. *The Grand Trunk Road: From the Front Seat.* New Delhi: HarperCollins, 1993.

Federation of Indian Chambers of Commerce and Industry. *Transport Infrastructure: An Industry Report.* New Delhi: FICCI, 1996.

Hariharan, K. V. *Containerisation and Multimodal Transport in India.* Mumbai: Shroff, 2000.

Misra, R. P. *Inland Water Transport in India.* Mysore: University of Mysore, 1972.

Mookerji, Radha Kumud. *Indian Shipping.* Allahabad: Kitab Mahal, 1962.

Owen, W. *Distance and Development: Transport and Communications in India.* Washington, DC: Brookings Institute, 1968.

Pavaskar, M. G. *Transport: Second India Studies.* Bombay: Popular, 1978.

Peters, Hans Jurgen. *India's Growing Conflict between Trade and Transport: Issues and Options.* Washington, DC: World Bank, 1990.

Satow, Michael, and Ray Desmond. *Railways of the Raj.* London: Scolar Press, 1980.

Singhal, Arvind, and Everett M. Rogers. *India's Communication Revolution: From Bullock Carts to Cyber Marts.* New Delhi: Sage, 2001.

Trivedi, H. M. *Indian Shipping in Perspective.* New Delhi: Vikas, 1980.

Vaidya, B. C. *Geography of Transport Development in India.* New Delhi: Concept Publishing Company, 2003.

Verma, S. P., ed. *Infrastructure in India's Development: Power, Transport, and Communication.* New Delhi: Kanishka Publishers, 2004.

GOVERNMENT, POLITICS, SECURITY, AND INTERNATIONAL RELATIONS

Constitution and Government

Adams, John, and W. C. Neale. *India, the Search for Unity, Democracy and Progress.* 2nd ed. New York: Van Nostrand, 1976.

Annamalai, E. *Managing Multilingualism in India: Political and Linguistic Manifestation.* New Delhi: Sage, 2001.

Austin, Granville. *The Indian Constitution: Cornerstone of a Nation.* Oxford: Clarendon, 1966.

———. *Working a Democratic Constitution: The Indian Experience.* New Delhi: Oxford University Press, 1999.

Bedi, Kiran, et. al. *Government @NET: New Governance Opportunities for India.* Thousand Oaks, CA: SAGE Publications.

Bombwall, K. R., ed. *National Power and State Autonomy.* Meerut: Meenakshi Prakashan, 1978.

Brass, Paul R., and Achin Vanaik, eds. *Competing Nationalisms in South Asia: Essays for Asghar Ali Engineer.* Hyderabad: Orient Longman, 2002.

Carras, Mary C. *Indira Gandhi in the Crucible of Leadership.* Flushing, NY: Asia Book, 1980.

Chandoke, Neera. *The Conceits of Civil Society.* New Delhi: Oxford University Press, 2003.

Desai, A. R., ed. *Repression and Resistance in India.* Bombay: Popular Prakashan, 1990.

DeSai. *Violation of Democratic Rights in India.* Bombay: Popular Prakashan, 1986.

Dhar, P. N. *Indira Gandhi, the 'Emergency,' and Indian Democracy.* New Delhi: OUP, 2000.

Dutt, R. C., ed. *People and Politics: The Indian Experience.* New Delhi: Lancer, 1992.

Gajendragadkar, P. B. *The Constitution of India: Its Philosophy and Basic Postulates.* New York: Oxford University Press, 1970.

Gopal, Sarvepalli. *Jawaharlal Nehru: A Biography.* 3 vols. Cambridge, MA: Harvard University Press, 1976–1984.

Hardgrave, Robert L. *India Under Pressure: Prospects for Political Stability.* Boulder, CO: Westview, 1984.

Hardgrave, Robert L., and Stanley Kochanek. *India: Government und Politics in a Developing Nation.* 6th ed. Fort Worth, TX: Harcourt College, 2000.

Hiro, Dilip. *Inside India Today.* London: Routledge and Kegan Paul, 1976.

Jha, S. N. *Decentralization and Local Politics.* New Delhi: Sage, 1999.

Kashyap, Subhash C., ed. *Political Events Annual. National and International Affairs.* New Delhi: Lok Sabha Secretariat, 1979 and annually.

——. *Nehru and the Constitution.* New Delhi: Sterling, 1981.

——. *Servicing Parliament.* New Delhi: Government of India Press, 1987.

——. *Blueprint of Political Reforms*, New Delhi: Centre for Policy Research, 2003.

Khan, Rashiduddin. *Federal India: A Design for Change.* Delhi: Vikas, 1992.

Khanna, H. R. *Constitutional and Civil Liberties.* New Delhi: Radha Krishna, 1978.

Kohli, Atul, ed. *India's Democracy: An Analysis of Changing State-Society Relations*, Princeton: Princeton University Press, 1990.

——. *Democracy and Discontent: India's Growing Crisis of Governability.* New York: Cambridge University Press, 1990.

——. *State against Democrary*. New York: New Horizon Press, 1989.

——. *State and Poverty in India: The Politics of Reform*. Cambridge: Cambridge University Press, 1987.

——, ed. *The Succcess of India's Democracy*. New York: Cambridge University Press, 2001.

Kothari, Rajni. *Politics and the People: In Search of a Humane India*. 2 vols. New York: New Horizons, 1989.

——. *Politics in India*. Boston: Little, Brown, 1970.

Lyon, Peter, and James Manor, eds. *Transfer and Transformation: Political Institutions in the Commonwealth*. Leicester: University Press, 1983.

Malhotra, Inder. *Indira Gandhi*. London: Hodder and Stoughton, 1989.

Manor, James, ed. *Nehru to the Nineties: The Changing Office of the Prime Minister in India*. New Delhi: Penguin Books, 1994.

Mehra, Ajay K., D. D. Khanna, and Gert W. Kueck, eds. *Political Parties and Party Systems*. New Delhi: Sage, 2003.

Mehta, Pratap Bhanu. *The Burden of Democracy*. New Delhi: Penguin, 2003.

Menon, V. P. *The Story of the Integration of the Indian States*. New York: Macmillan, 1956.

Morris-Jones, W. H. *Parliament in India*. London: Longman Green, 1957.

Mukarji, Nirmal, and Balveer Arora, eds. *Federalism in India. Origins and Development*. New Delhi: Vikas, 1992.

Mukherji, Partha N., and Bhupati B. Sahoo. "Protective Discrimination and Nation Building: The Mandalian Dilemma." *Man and Development* 12(4), December 1990.

Nayar, Kuldip. *Judgement*. New Delhi: Vikas, 1977.

Noorani, A. G. *India's Constitution and Politics*. Bombay: Jaico, 1970.

——. *The Presidential System: The Indian Debate,* 1989.

Oommen, T. K. *State und Society in India: Studies in Nation Building*. New Delhi: Sage, 1990.

Palkhivala, N. A. *We the People: India—The Largest Democracy*. Bombay: Stand Book Stall, 1991.

Prasad, Bimal. *Gandhi, Nehru and J. P. Studies in Leadership*. Delhi: Chanakya, 1985.

Rudolph, Lloyd H., and Susanne H. Rudolph. *In Search of Lakshmi: The Political Economy of the Indian State*. Chicago: University of Chicago Press, 1987.

——. Th*e Modernity of Tradition*. Chicago: University of Chicago Press, 1967.

Sa'ez, Lawrence. *Federalism without a Centre: The Impact of Political and Economic Reforms on India's Federal System*. New Delhi: Sage, 2002.

Sabarwal, Satish. *The Roots of Crisis*. New Delhi: Oxford University Press, 1986.

Sehgal, Nayantara. *Indira Gandhi: Her Road to Power.* London: Macdonald, 1978.

Sen, Amartya. *Poverty and Famine: An Essay on Entitlement and Deprivation.* Delhi: Oxford University Press, 1981.

Sharma, R. *Conflct of Fundamental Rights and Directive Principles.* Jodhpur: Usha, 1977.

Shourie, Arun. *Symptoms of Fascism.* New Delhi: Vikas, 1978.

Smith, Donald E. *India as a Secular State.* Princeton, NJ: Princeton University Press, 1967.

Srinivas, M. N. *Nation Building in Independent India.* Delhi: Oxford University Press, 1976.

Tandon, Rajesh, and Ranjita Mohanty. *Does Civil Society Matter? Governance in Contemporary India.* New Delhi: Sage, 2003.

Vanaik, Achin. *The Painful Transition: Bourgeois Democracy in India.* London: Verson, 1990.

Venkatarangaiya, M., and M. Shiviah. *Indian Federalism.* New Delhi: Arnold Heinemann, 1975.

Wadhwa, K. K. *Minority Safeguards in India: Constitutional Provisions and Their Implementation.* Delhi: Thomson Press, 1975.

Weiner, Myron. *The Indian Paradox: Essays in Indian Politics.* New Delhi: Sage, 1989.

———. *Sons of the Soil.* Delhi: Oxford University Press, 1978.

Political Parties, Politics, and Elections

Ahmad, Aijaz. *Lineages of the Present: Ideology and Politics in Contemporary South Asia.* London: Verso, 2000.

Andersen, Walter. *Brotherhood in Saffron.* Boulder, CO: Westview, 1989.

Brass, Paul R. *Caste, Faction and Party in Indian Politics: Election Studies.* 2 vols. Delhi: Chanakya, 1983–1985.

———. *Language, Religion and Politics in North India.* New York: Cambridge University Press, 1974.

———. *The Politics of India Since Independence.* The New Cambridge History of India Series: Vol. IV, Book I. Cambridge: Cambridge University Press, 1990.

Butler, David, et al. *India Decides: Elections 1952–1991.* New Delhi: Living Media India, 1991.

Chalapathi Rau, M. *Journalism and Politics.* New Delhi: Vikas, 1984.

Chandra, Kanchen. *Why Ethnic Parties Succeed.* Cambridge: Cambridge University Press, 2004.

Crane, Robert I., ed. *Aspects of Political Mobilization in South Asia*. New York: Syracuse, 1976.

Ghosh, Partha S. *BJP and the Evolution of Hindu Nationalism: From Periphery to Centre*. New Delhi: Manohar, 1999.

Gould, Harold A. *Grass Roots Politics in India: A Century of Political Evolution in Faizabad District*. New Delhi: South Asia Publications, 1994.

Hansen, Thomas Bloom. *The Saffron Wave: Democracy and Hindu Naitonalism in Modern India*. New Delhi: OUP, 1999.

Hansen, Thomas Bloom, and Christophe Jaffrelot, eds. *The BJP and the Compulsions of Politics in India*. New Delhi: Oxford University Press, 2nd ed., 2001.

Hasan, Zoya, ed. *Politics and the State in India*. New Delhi: Sage, 2000.

———, ed. *Parties and Party Politics in India*. New Delhi: Oxford University Press, 2002.

———. *India's Silent Revolution: The Rise of the Lower Castes in North India*, New York: Columbia University Press, 2003.

Jaffrelot, Christophe, and Thomas Bloom Hansen, eds. *The BJP and the Compulsions of Politics in India*. New Delhi: Oxford University Press, 1998.

———. *The Hindu Nationalist Movement in India*. New York: Columbia University Press, 1996.

Joshi, Ram, and R. K. Hebsur, eds. *Congress in Indian Politics: A Centenary Perspective*. Bombay: Popular Prakashan, 1987.

Kaarthikeyan, D. R., and Radhavinod Raju. *The Triumph of Truth: The Rajiv Gandhi Assassination: The Investigation*. Chicago: New Dawn, 2003.

Kashyap, Subash C. *The Politics of Power: Defection and State Politics in India*. Delhi: National, 1974.

Kaushik, Susheela. *Elections in India: Social Base*. Calcutta: K. P. Bagchi, 1982.

Kochanek, Stanley A. *Business and Politics in India*. Berkeley: University of California Press, 1974.

———. *The Congress Party of India: The Dynamics of One Party Democracy*. Princeton, NJ: Princeton University Press, 1968.

Kumar, Arun, ed. (for Press Council of India). *The Tenth Round: Story of the Indian Elections 1991*. Calcutta: Rupa, 1991.

Kumar, Narender. *Dalit Policies, Politics and Parliaments*. Delhi: Shipra, 2004.

Limaye, Madhu. *Birth of Non-Congressism: Opposition Politics, 1947–1975*. Delhi: B. R. Publishing, 1988.

———. *Politics after Freedom*. Delhi: Atma Ram and Sons, 1982.

Madan, T. N. *Modern Myths, Locked Minds: Secularism and Fundamentalism in India*. New Delhi: Oxford University Press, 1997.

Mehta, Pratap Bhanu. *The Burden of Democracy*. New Delhi: Penguin, 2003.

Mohanty, Manoranjan. *Revolutionary Violence. A Study of the Maoist Movement in India*. New Delhi: Sterling, 1977.

Oldenburg, Philip. *The Thirteenth Election of India's Lok Sabha*. New York: Asia Society, 1999.

Pal, Sudha. *Dalit Assertion and the Unfinished Democratic Revolution: The Bahujan Samaj Party in Uttar Pradesh*. New Delhi: Sage, 2002.

Pandey, Gyanendra. *The Construction of Communalism in Colonial North India,* Delhi: Oxford University Press, 1990.

Prasad, Nageshwar. *Ideology and Organization in Indian Politics: A Study of Political Parties at the Grass Roots*. New Delhi: Allied, 1980.

Roy, Ramashray, and Richard Sisson. *Division, Deprivation and the Congress*. New Delhi: Sage, 1991.

Sinha, Aseema. *The Regional Roots of Developmental Politics in India: A Divided Leviathan*. Bloomington: Indiana University Press, 2002.

Sisson, Richard, and Ramashray Ray, eds. *Diversity and Dominance: Changing Bases of Congress Support*. Vol. 1. Newbury Park, CA: Sage, 1990.

Thakurta, Paranjoy Guha, and Shankar Raghuraman. *A Time of Coalitions: Divided We Stand*. New York: SAGE Publications, 2004.

Wallace, Paul, and Ramshray Ray, eds. *India's 1999 Elections and 20th Century Politics*. New Delhi: Sage, 2003.

Zavos, John, et al. *The Politics of Cultural Mobilization in India*. New Delhi: Oxford University Press, 2004.

Administrative, Legal, and Other Institutions

Alexander, P. C. *Through the Corridors of Power: An Insiders Story.* New Delhi: HarperCollins, 2004.

Appleby, Paul H. *Report on India's Administrative System: Comments and Reactions*. New Delhi: Lok Sabha Secretariat, 1956.

Arora, Balveer, and Beryl Radin, eds. *The Changing Role of the All-India Services*. New Delhi: Centre for Policy Research, 2000.

Baxi, Upendra. *The Crisis of the Indian Legal System*. New Delhi: Vikas, 1982.

———. *The Indian Supreme Court and Politics*. Delhi: Eastern, 1980.

Bayley, David H. *The Police and Political Development in India*. Princeton, NJ: Princeton University Press, 1969.

Deshmukh, B. G. *A Cabinet Secretary Looks Back*. New Delhi: HarperCollins, 2004.

Godbole, Madhav. *Unfinished Innings: Recollections and Reflections of a Civil Servant*. New Delhi: Orient Longman, 1996.

Heginbotham, Stanley J. *Cultures in Conflict: The Four Faces of Indian Bureaucracy*. New York: Columbia University Press, 1975.

Kashyap, Subhash C. *Blueprint of Political Reforms*. New Delhi: Centre for Policy Research, 2003.

———. *History of the Parliament of India*. New Delhi: Shipra, 1994.

———. *Servicing Parliament*. New Delhi: Government of India Press, 1989.

Kumari, V., ed. *The Juvenile Justice System in India: From Welfare to Rights*. New Delhi: Oxford University Press, 2004.

Larson, Gerlad J. *Religion and Personal Law in Secular India: A Call to Judgement*. Bloomington: Indiana University Press, 2001.

Maheshwari, S. R. *Administrative Reforms in India*. Delhi: Macmillan, 2002.

Maheshwari, Shriram. *The Indian Administrative Handbook, 1990*. New Delhi: Concept, 1992.

Mattoo, P. K. "India." *In Asian Civil Services: Developments and Trends,* edited by Heinrich Siedentopf. Kuala Lumpur: Asian and Pacific Development and Administrative Centre, 1980.

Mehra, Ajay K. *Police in Changing India*. New Delhi: Usha, 1985.

Menski, Werner. *Hindu Law: Beyond Tradition and Modernity*. New Delhi: Oxford University Press, 2003.

Potter, David C. *India's Political Administrators, 1919–1983*. Delhi: OUP, 1986.

Rajeswari, Sunder Rajan. *The Scandal of the State: Women, Law and Citizenship in Postcolonial India*. Durham, NC: Duke University Press, 2002.

Roy, Prititosh. *Parliamentary Privilege in India*. Calcutta: Oxford University Press, 1991.

Saez, Lawrence. *Federalism without a Centre: The Impact of Political and Economic Reform on India's Federal System*. New Delhi: Sage, 2002.

Sharma, Arvind. *Hinduism and Human Rights: A Conceptual Approach*. New Delhi: Oxford University Press, 2004.

Sharma, L. N. *The Indian Prime Minister: Office and Powers*. Delhi: Macmillan, 1976.

Sorabjee, Soli J., ed. *Law and Justice: An Anthology*. Delhi: Universal Law Publishing, 2004.

Subramanian, T. S. R. *Journeys through Babudom and Netaland: Governance in India*. New Delhi: Rupa, 2004.

Regional and Ethnic Politics

Barnett, Margaret Ross. *The Politics of Cultural Nationalism in South India*. Princeton, NJ: Princeton University Press, 1976.

Basu, Amrita, and Atul Kohli, eds. *Community Conflicts and the State in India*. Delhi: OUP, 1998.

Bondurant, Joan V. Regionalism as Provincialism. *A Study in the Problem of Indian National Unity*. Berkeley: University of California Press, 1978.

Das, B. S. *The Sikkim Saga*. New Delhi: Vikas, 1983.

Das, Veena, ed. *Mirrors of Violence: Communities, Riots and Survivors in South Asia*. Delhi: Oxford University Press, 1990.

Engineer, Asghar Ali, ed. *Ethnic Conflict in South Asia*. Delhi: D. K. Publishers, 1987.

Franda, Marcus. *Small Is Politics: Organizational Alternatives in India's Rural Development*. New Delhi: Wiley Eastern, 1979.

Gani, H. A. *Muslim Political Issues and National Integration*. New Delhi: Sterling, 1978.

Gopal, Sarvepali. *Anatomy of a Confrontation: The Babri Masjid-Ramjanambhumi Issue*. New Delhi: Viking, 1991.

Gowalkar, M. S. *Bunch of Thoughts*. Bangalore: Vikrama Prakashan, 1966.

Harrison, Selig S. *India: The Most Dangerous Decades*. Princeton, NJ: Princeton University Press, 1960.

Hazarika, Sanjoy. *Strangers in the Mist*. Delhi: Viking, 1994.

——. *Rites of Passage: Border Crossings, Imagined Homelands, India's Northeast and Bangladesh*. New Delhi: Penguin, 2000.

Kabir, Humayun. *Minorities in a Democracy*. Calcutta: K. L. Mukhopadhyay, 1968.

Kapur, Rajiv A. *Sikh Separatism: The Politics of Faith*. London: Allen and Unwin, 1986.

Kashmir Today: A Symposium on a Troubled State. Seminar, April 1992.

Kluyev, Borjs I. *India, National and Language Problem*. New Delhi: Sterling, 1981.

Kumar, Promod, et al. *Punjab Crisis: Context and Trends*. Chandigarh: Centre for Research on Rural and Industrial Development, 1984.

Kurien, Mathew, and P. N. Varghese. *Centre-State Relations*. New Delhi: Macmillan, 1980.

Linguistic Landscape. Seminar, March 1991.

Nandy, Ashis, Shikha Trivedy, Shail Mayaram, and Achyut Yagnik. *Creating a Nationality: The Ramjanambhumi Movement and Fear of the Self*. New Delhi: Oxford University Press, 1998.

Narain, Iqbal. *State Politics in India*. Meerut: Meenakshi Prakashan, 1976.

Omvedt, Gail, ed. *Land, Caste and Politics in Indian States*. Delhi: Authors Guild of India, 1981.

Phadnis, Urmilla. *Ethnicity and Nation Building in South Asia*. New Delhi: Sage, 1989.

Press Council of India. *Crisis and Credibility—Punjab and Kashmir: Reports of January and July 1991*. New Delhi: Lancer, 1991.

Ray, A. *Tension Areas in India's Federal System*. Calcutta: World Press, 1970.

Rustomji, Nari. *Imperilled Frontiers: India's Northeastern Borderlands*. Delhi: Oxford University Press, 1983.

Sarin, V. I. K. *India's Northeast in Flames*. New Delhi: Vikas, 1980.

Tully, Mark, and Satish Jacob. *Amtritsar. Mrs. Gandhi's Last Battle*. London: Jonathan Cape, 1985.

Varshney, Asutosh. *Ethnic Conflict and Civic Life: Hindus and Muslims in India*. New Haven: Yale University Press, 2002.

Wood, John R. *State Politics in Contemporary India: Crisis or Continuity?* Boulder, CO: Westview, 1984.

Security

Abraham, Itty. *The Making of the Indian Atomic Bomb: Science, Secrecy and the Postcolonial State*. London: Zed Books, 1998.

Anantachari, et al. *BSF: Sentinels of India's Borders 1965–1990*. New Delhi: Wiley Eastern, 1990.

Bajpai, U. S., ed. *India's Security*. New Delhi: Lancer, 1983.

Chengappa, Raj. *Weapons of Peace: The Secret Story of India's Quest to be a Nuclear Power*. New Delhi: HarperCollins, 2000.

Chibber, Aditya. *National Security Doctrine: An Indian Imperative*. New Delhi: Lancer International, 1990.

Chopra, Pran. *India's Second Liberation*. New Delhi: Vikas, 1973.

Cohen, Stephen P. *The Indian Army*. Berkeley: University of California Press, 1971.

Cortright, David, and Amitabh Mattoo. *India and the Bomb: Public Opinion and Nuclear Options*. Notre Dame: University of Notre Dame Press, 1996.

Dasgupta, Sunil. "India: The New Militaries." In *Coercion and Governance: The Declining Political Role of the Military in Asia,* edited by Muthiah Alagappa. Palo Alto, CA: Stanford University Press, 2001, 92–117.

Jasjit Singh. *AWACS, the New Destabiliser.* New Delhi: Lancer, 1985.

———. *India and Pakistan. Crisis of Relationship*. New Delhi: Lancer, 1990.

———. *Indo–US Relations in a Changing World*. New Delhi: Lancer, 1992.

———. *Nuclear India.* New Delhi: Lancer, 1998.

Jacob, Lt. Gen. Jack. *Surrender at Dacca: Birth of a Nation*. New Delhi: Manohar, 1997.

Kapoor, Major General S. B. L. *Human Resource Management in the Army: Planning for the Future.* New Delhi: Knowledge World, 2004.

Kargil Review Committee. *From Surprise to Reckoning—The Kargil Review Committee Report*. New Delhi: Sage, 2000.

Karnad, Bharat, ed. *Future Imperiled: India's Security in the 1990s and Beyond,* New Delhi: Viking, 1994.

——. *Nuclear Weapons and Indian Security: The Realist Foundations of Strategy,* Delhi: Macmillan, 2002.

Khatri, Sridhar, and Gert W. Kueck, eds. *Terrorism in South Asia: Impact on Development and Democratic Process.* Delhi: Shipra Publications, 2003.

Koithara, Verghese. *Society, State and Security: The Indian Experience.* New Delhi: Sage, 1999.

——. *Crafting Peace in Kashmir.* New Delhi: Sage, 2004.

Krishna, S. *Post Colonial Insecurities.* Minneapolis: University of Minnesota Press, 1999.

Kumar, Satish. *India's National Security: Annual Review.*

Kumaraswamy, P. R. *Security beyond Survival: Essays for K. Subrahmanyam.* New Delhi: Sage, 2004.

Marwah, Onkar. "India's Military Power and Policy." In *Military Power and Policy in Asian States: China, India and Japan,* edited by Onkar Marwah and Jonathan D. Pollack. Boulder, CO: Westview, 1980.

Marwah, V., ed. *Uncivil Wars: Pathologies of Terrorism in India.* New Delhi: Indus, 1995.

Menon, Raja. *A Nuclear Strategy for India.* New Delhi: Sage, 2000.

——. *Weapons of Mass Destruction: Options for India.* New Delhi: Sage, 2004.

Nayyar, K. K. *Maritime India.* New Delhi: Rupa, 2005.

Palit, D. K. *The Lightning Campaign, 1971.* Salisbury, UK: Compton, 1972.

——. *War in the High Himalaya: The Indian Army in Crisis, 1962.* London: Hurst, 1991.

Perkovich, George. *India's Nuclear Bomb: The Impact on Global Proliferation.* Berkeley: University of California Press, 1999.

Poulose, T. T., ed. *Perspectives on India's Nuclear Policy.* New Delhi: Young Asia, 1978.

Raghavan, Lt. Gen. V. R. *Siachen: Conflict without End.* New Delhi: Viking, 2002.

Rosen, Stephen P. *Societies and Military Power: India and Its Armies.* Ithaca, NY: Cornell University Press, 1996.

Roy-Chaudhury, Rahul. *India's Maritime Security.* New Delhi: Knowledge World IDSA, 2000.

Sardesai, D. R., and Raju G. C. Thomas, eds. *Nuclear India in the Twenty-First Century.* New York: Palgrave Macmillan, 2002.

Sawhney, Pravin. *The Defence Makeover: 10 Myths that Shape India's Image.* New Delhi: Sage, 2002.

Singh, Arun. *The Military Balance 1985–1994.* University of Illinois, 1997.

Singh, Jasjit. *India's Defence Spending.* New Delhi: Knowledge Press, 2000.

——. *Nuclear India.* New Delhi: Knowledge Press, 1998.

Singh, Jaswant, *Defending India,* New York: St. Martin's Press, 1999
Singh, Sarab Jit. *Operation Black Thunder: An Eyewitness Account of Terrorism in the Punjab.* New Delhi: Sage, 2002.
Singh, Satyindra. *Blueprint to Bluewater: The Indian Navy 1951–1965.* New Delhi: Lancer, 1992.
Subrahmanyam, K. *Bangladesh and India's Security.* Dehra Dun: Palit and Dutt, 1972.
———, ed. *India and the Nuclear Challenge.* New Delhi: Lancer, 1986.
———. *Asian Security: Old Paradigms and New Challenges.* New Delhi: Lancer International, 1991.
———, ed. *Nuclear India: Problems and Perspectives.* New Delhi: South Asia Publishers, 2000.
Tellis, Ashley J. *India's Emerging Nuclear Posture: Between Recessed Deterrent and Ready Arsenal.* Santa Monica, CA: Rand Corporation, 2001.
Thomas, Raju G. *The Defence of India: A Budgetary Perspective of Strategy and Politics.* New Delhi: Macmillan, 1978.
———. *Indian Security Policy.* Princeton, NJ: Princeton University Press, 1987.
———. *Democracy, Security and Development in India.* New York: St. Martin's Press, 1996.

International Relations

Appadorai, A. *The Domestic Roots of India's Foreign Policy: 1947–1972.* Delhi: Oxford University Press, 1981.
———. *Select Documents on India's Foreign Policy and Relations, 1947–1972.* Delhi: Oxford University Press, 1982.
———. *Contemporary India: Essays in Domestic and Foreign Policy.* New Delhi: South Asian Publishers, 1988.
Babbage, Ross, and Sandy Gordon, eds. *India's Strategic Future: Regional State or Global Power?* Houndmills, UK: Macmillan, 1992.
Bajpai, Kanti P., and Stephen P. Cohen. *South Asia after the Cold War: International Perspectives.* Boulder, CO: Westview Press, 1993.
Bajpai, U. S., ed. *India and Japan: A New Relationship?* New Delhi: Lancer, 1988.
———. *India and the Neighbourhood.* New Delhi: Lancer, 1986.
———. *Nonalignment. Perspectives and Prospects.* Atlantic Highlands, NJ: Humanities Press, 1983.
Bandyopadhyaya, Jayantanuja. *The Making of India's Foreign Policy.* 2nd ed. New Delhi: Allied, 1987.
Banerjee, Dipankar. *SAARC in the Twenty-First Century: Towards a Cooperative Future.* Colombo: Regional Centre for Strategic Studies, 2002.

Bhasin, Avtar Singh, ed. *India's Foreign Relations. Documents 2004.* New Delhi: Geetika Press, 2004.

Bhutani, Sudarshan. *A Clash of Political Cultures: Sino-Indian Relations (1957–1962).* New Delhi: Roli Books, 2004.

Bracken, Paul. *Fire in the East: The Rise of Asian Military Power and the Second Nuclear Age.* New York: HarperCollins, 1999.

Brines, Russell. *The Indo–Pakistani Conflict.* London: Pall Mall, 1968.

Brown, W. Norman. *The United States and India, Pakistan, Bangladesh.* 3rd ed. Cambridge, MA: Harvard University Press, 1972.

Burke, S. M. *Mainsprings of Indian and Pakistani Foreign Policies.* Minneapolis: University of Minnesota Press, 1974.

Chase, Robert, Emily Hill, and Paul Kennedy, eds. *The Pivotal States: A New Framework for US Policy in the Developing World.* New York: Norton, 1999.

Chopra, V. D., ed. *Studies in Indo–Pakistan Relations.* New Delhi: Patriot, 1984.

Cohen, Stephen Philip. *India: Emerging Power.* Washington, DC: Brookings Institution Press, 2000.

Cohen, Stephen P., and Richard Park. *India: Emergent Power?* New York: Crane and Russak, 1978.

Dasgupta, Chandrasekhar. *War and Diplomacy in Kashmir 1947–48.* New Delhi: Sage, 2002.

Deshpande, G. P., and Alka Acharya, eds. *Crossing and Bridge of Dreams: 50 Years of India–China.* New Delhi: Tulika, 2001.

Dixit, J. N. *My South Block Years: Memoirs of a Foreign Secretary.* New Delhi: UBSPD: 1996.

——. *Across Borders: Fifty Years of India's Foreign Policy.* New Delhi: Picus Books, 1998.

——. *India and Pakistan in War and Peace.* New Delhi: Books Today, 2002.

——. *The Indian Foreign Service: History and Challenges.* New Delhi: Konark, 2005.

Dutt, Srikant. *India and the Third World.* London: Zed, 1984.

Dutt, V. P. *India's Foreign Policy in a Changing World.* New Delhi: Vikas, 1999.

Elder, Joseph W., Edward C. Dimock, and Ainslie T. Embree. *India's World and U. S. Scholars 1947–1997.* New Delhi: Manohar for American Institute of Indian Studies, 1998.

Eldridge, P. J. *The Politics of Foreign Aid in India.* New York: Schocken, 1970.

Franda, Marcus. *China and India Online: Information Technology Politics and Diplomacy in the World's Two Largest Nations.* Lanham, MD: Rowman & Littlefield, 2002.

Ganguly, Sumit. *The Crisis in Kashmir: Portents of War, Hopes of Peace.* Cambridge: Cambridge University Press, 1997.

———. *The Origins of War in South Asia: India–Pakistan Conflicts Since 1947.* Boulder, CO: Westview, 1986.

Garver, John W. *Protracted Contest: Sino–Indian Rivalry in the Twentieth Century.* Seattle: University of Washington Press, 2001.

Glazer, Sulochana Raghavan, and Nathan Glazer, eds. *Conflicting Images: India and the United States.* Glenn Dale, MD: Riverdale, 1990.

Gonsalves, Eric, and Nancy Jetley. *The Dynamics of South Asia: Regional Cooperation and SAARC.* New Delhi: Sage, 1999.

Gordon, Sandy. *India's Rise to Power in the Twentieth Century and Beyond.* London: St. Martin's, 1995.

Gundevia, Y. D. *Outside the Archives.* New Delhi: Sangam, 1984.

Gupta, Sisir. *Kashmir: A Study in India–Pakistan Relations.* New Delhi: Asia, 1966.

Haass, Richard N., and Gideon Rose. *A New US Policy toward India and Pakistan,* New York: Council on Foreign Relations Press, 1997.

Haksar, P. N. *Nehru's Vision of Peace and Security in the Nuclear Age.* New York: Advent, 1988.

Harrison, Selig S., Paul Kreisberg, and Dennis Kux, eds. *India and Pakistan: The First Fifty Years.* Washington, DC: Woodrow Wilson Center Press, 1999.

Harrison, Selig S., and K. Subrahmanyam. *Superpower Rivalry in the Indian Ocean: Indian and American Perspectives.* New York: Oxford University Press, 1990.

Heimsath, Charles H., and Surjit Mansingh. *Diplomatic History of Modern India.* Delhi: Allied, 1971.

Hoffman, Steven A. *India and the China Crisis.* Berkeley, CA: University of California Press, 1990.

Horn, Robert C. *Soviet–Indian Relations: Issues and Influence.* New York: Praeger, 1982.

India: Ministry of External Affairs. *Annual Report.* New Delhi: Government of India Press, annually.

Jackson, Robert W. *South Asia Crisis: India, Pakistan and Bangladesh: A Political and Historical Analysis of the 1971 War.* New York: Praeger, 1975.

Jain, R. K., ed. *China–South Asian Relations, 1947–1980.* Vol. 1. Delhi: Radiant, 1981.

Kapur, Ashok. *India's Nuclear Option: Atomic Diplomacy and Decision Making.* New York: Praeger, 1976.

Kapur, Ashok, et. al., eds. *India and the United States in a Changing World.* New Delhi: Sage, 2002.

Kapur, K. D. *Soviet Strategy in South Asia.* New Delhi: Young Asia, 1983.

Khosla, I. P., ed. *India and the New Europe.* New Delhi: Konark Publishers, 2004.

Kodikara, Shelton U., ed. *Dilemma of Indo–Sri Lankan Relations.* Colombo: Bandaranaike Centre for International Studies, 1991.

Kumar, Satish, ed. *Yearbook on Indian Foreign Policy.* New Delhi: Sage, 1985, annually since then.

Kurian, Nimmi. *Emerging China and India's Policy Options.* New Delhi: Lancer, 2001.

Kux, Dennis. *Estranged Democracies: India and the United States 1941–1991.* Washington, DC: National Defense University Press, 1993.

Lall, M. C. *India's Missed Opportunity: India's Relationship with the NonResident Indians.* Aldershot UK: Ashgate, 2001.

Mansingh, Lalit, et al., eds. *Indian Foreign Policy: Agenda for the 21st Century.* 2 vols. New Delhi: Foreign Service Institute, 1997.

Mansingh, Surjit. *India's Search for Power: Indira Gandhi's Foreign Policy.* New Delhi: Sage, 1984.

———, ed. *Indian and Chinese Foreign Policies in Comparative Perspective.* New Delhi: Radiant Publishers, 1998.

———, ed. *Nehru's Foreign Policy: Fifty Years On.* New Delhi: Mosaic Books, 1998.

———. "Is There a Soviet Indian Strategic Partnership?" In *Domestic Determinants of Soviet Foreign Policy Towards South Asia and the Middle East,* edited by Hafeez Mallik. London: Macmillan, 1990.

———. "Nehru and Pakistan." In *The Legacy of Nehru: A Centennial Assessment,* edited by D. R. Sardesai and Anand Mohan. New Delhi: Promilla, 1992.

———, ed. *Prospects for India–United States Relations: The Next Ten Years.* New Delhi: India Habitat Centre, 2000.

———. "Between Asia and Global Community: India and China in Comparative Perspective" *International Studies. New Delhi* 39, 4 (2002): 335–364.

McMahon, Robert. *The Cold War on the Periphery, The United States, India, and Pakistan,* New York: Columbia University Press, 1994.

Mehrotra, S. R. *The Commonwealth and the Nation.* New Delhi: Vikas, 1978.

Mehta, Jagat. *Rescuing the Future: Coming to Terms with Bequeathed Misperceptions.* New Delhi: Manohar.

Mishra, P. K. *India, Pakistan, Nepal and Bangladesh.* New Delhi: Sundeep Prakashan, 1979.

Mistry, Dinshaw. *India and the Comprehensive Test Ban Treaty* (ACDIS Research Report). Champaign: University of Illinois at Urbana-Champaign, September 1998.

Muni, S. D. *Pangs of Proximity: India and Sri Lanka's Ethnic Crisis.* Thousand Oaks, CA: Sage, 1993.

Nayar, Baldev Raj, and T. V. Paul. *India in the World Order: Searching for Major-Power Status.* Cambridge: Cambridge University Press, 2003.

Noorani, A. G. *Brezhnev Plan for Asian Security*. Bombay: Jaico, 1975.

Palmer, Norman D. *The United States and India: The Dimensions of Influence*. New York: Praeger, 1984.

Pattanaik, Smruti S. *Elite Perceptions in Foreign Policy: Role of Print Media in Influencing India–Pakistan Relations 1989–1999*. Delhi: Manohar, 2004.

Pratap, Ravindra. *India and the WTO: Dispute Settlement System*. New Delhi: Manak Publications, 2004.

Raja Mohan, C. *Crossing the Rubicon: The Shaping of India's New Foreign Policy*. New Delhi: Viking, 2003.

Ramchandani, R. R., ed. *India Africa Relations: Issues and Policy Options*. Delhi: Kalinga Publications, 1990.

Ranganathan, C. V., ed. *Panchsheel and the Future: Perspectives on India–China Relations*. Delhi: Samskriti, 2004.

Ranganathan, C. V., and Vinod C. Khanna. *India and China: The Way Ahead*. 2nd ed. New Delhi: Har Anand, 2004.

Rasgotra, M., V. D. Chopra, and K. P. Misra, eds. *India's Foreign Policy in the 1990s*. New Delhi: Patriot Publishers, 1990.

Rodman, Peter R. *More Precious Than Peace: The Cold War and the Struggle for the Third World*. New York: Charles Scribner's Sons, 1994.

Samaddar, Ranabir, ed. *Refugees and the State: Practices of Asylum and Care in India, 1947–2000*. New Delhi: Sage, 2003.

Schofield, Victoria. *Kashmir in the Crossfire*. London: I. B. Tauris, 1996.

Singh, Kewal. *Partition and Aftermath: Memoirs of an Ambassador*. New Delhi: Vikas, 1991.

Singh, S. Nihal. *The Yogi and the Bear: Story of Indo–Soviet Relations*. Delhi: Allied Publishers, 1986.

Sisson, Richard, and Leo E. Rose. *Pakistan, India and the Creation of Bangladesh*. New Delhi: Vistaar Publications, 1990.

Tahir-Kheli, Shirin. *India, Pakistan and the United States: Breaking with the Past*. New York: Council on Foreign Relations Press, 1997.

Tellis, Ashley J. *Stability in South Asia*. RAND, 1997.

Tharoor, Shashi. *Reasons of State: Political Developments and India's Foreign Policy under Indira Gandhi 1966–1977*. New Delhi: Vikas, 1982.

Thomas, Raju G. C., ed. *Perspectives on Kashmir: The Roots of Conflict in South Asia*. Boulder, CO: Westview Press, 1992.

Vohra, Dewan C. *India's Aid: Diplomacy in the Third World*. New Delhi: Vikas, 1980.

Wainwright, A. Martin. *Inheritance of Empire: Britain, India, and the Balance of Power in Asia, 1938–1955*. Westport, CT: Praeger, 1994.

Williams, Marc. *Third World Cooperation: The Group of 77 in UNCTAD*. London: Pinter, 1991.

Zins, Max-Jean, and Gilles Boquerat, eds. *India in the Mirror of Foreign Diplomatic Archives.* Delhi: Manohar, 2004.

HISTORY

Historiography and Sources

Arnold, David, and Stuart Blackburn. *Telling Lives in India: Biography, Autobiography and Life History.* Bloomington: Indiana University Press, 2004.

Ballhatchet, Kenneth. "The Rewriting of South Asian History by South Asian Historians after 1947." *Asian Affairs* (London) 15 (February 1984): 27–38.

Banerji, Tarasankar. *Indian Historical Research since Independence.* Calcutta: Naya Prakash, 1987.

Bhattacharya, N. N. *Ancient Indian History and Civilization: Trends and Perspectives.* Delhi: Manohar, 1988.

Bhattacharya, S., and Romila Thapar, eds. *Situating Indian History.* Delhi: Oxford University Press, 1986.

Bridge, Carl, and H. V. Brasted. "Explaining the Transfer of Power in India: An Historiographical PostMortem." In *Occasional Papers on History and Society.* New Delhi: Nehru Memorial Museum and Library, Second Series 64, 1992.

Bryant, Edwin. *The Quest for the Origins of Vedic Culture: The Indo–Aryan Migration Debate.* Oxford: Oxford University Press, 2001.

Champakalakshmi, R. *Trade, Ideology, and Urbanization: South India 300 BC to AD 1300.* Delhi: OUP, 1996.

Chatterjee, Partha. *Nationalist Thought and the Colonial World: A Derivative Discourse?* Minneapolis: University of Minnesota Press, 1986.

——. *The Nation and Its Fragments: Colonial and Postcolonial Histories.* New Delhi: Oxford University Press, 1993.

Damodaran, Vinita, and Maya Unnithan-Kumar, eds. *Postcolonial India: History, Politics, and Culture.* New Delhi: Manohar, 2000.

Dune, Saurabh, ed. *Post Colonial Passages: Contemporary History Writing on India.* New Delhi: Oxford University Press, 2004.

Gottlob, Michael. *Historical Thinking in South Asia: A Handbook of Sources from Colonial Times to the Present.* Delhi: Oxford University Press, 2003.

Grewal, J. S. *Muslim Rule in India: The Assessments of British Historians.* Calcutta: Oxford University Press, 1970.

Habib, Irfan. *Essays in Indian History: Towards a Marxist Perception.* New Delhi: Tulika, 1995.

Hanson, Mohibbul, ed. *Historians of Medieval India.* Meerut: Meenakshi Prakashan, 1968.

Hardy, Peter. *Historians of Medieval India: Studies in Indo–Muslim Historical Writing.* London: Luzak, 1960.

Inden, Ronald. *Imagining India.* Oxford: Basil Blackwell, 1990.

Inden, Ronald, Jonathan Walters, and David Ali. *Querying the Medieval: Texts and the History of Practices in South Asia.* Oxford: Oxford University Press, 2000.

India (Republic of). *Archives in India.* New Delhi: National Archives, 1979.

India (Republic of). *Guide to the Records of the Ministry of External Affairs.* New Delhi: Manager of Publications, 1957.

Kejariwal, O. P. *The Asiatic Society of Bengal and the Discovery of India's Past 1784–1838.* Delhi: Oxford University Press, 1988.

Kumar, Ravinder. "A Review of the Historical Literature on the Struggle for Freedom in India." In *The Making of a Nation: Essays in Indian History and Politics.* Delhi: Manohar, 1989.

Low, D. A., J. C. Iltis, and M. D. Wainwright. *Government Archives in South Asia.* Cambridge: Cambridge University Press, 1969.

Mukhia, Harbans. *Historians and Historiography during the Reign of Akbar.* New Delhi: Vikas, 1976.

Mukhopadhay, S. K. *Evolution of Historiography in Modern India 1900–1960.* Calcutta: K. P. Bagchi, 1981.

O'Flaherty, W. D. O. "Disregarded Scholars: A Survey of Russian Indology." *South Asian Review* (1972): 289–304.

Philips, C. H., ed. *Historians of India Pakistan and Ceylon.* London: Oxford University Press, 1961.

Prasad, Bisheshwar, ed. *Ideas in History.* New York: Asia Publishing, 1968.

Ray, N. R., ed. *Sources of the History of India.* 4 vols. Calcutta: Institute of Historical Studies, 1980–1984.

Robb, Peter. *A History of India.* New York: Palgrave, 2002.

Sarkar, Jadunath. *History of History Writing in Medieval India: Contemporary Historians.* Calcutta: Ratna Prakashan, 1977.

Sarkar, Sumit. *Writing in Social History.* Delhi: Oxford University Press, 1998.

Sastri, K. A. Nilakanta. *Sources of Indian History with Special Reference to South India.* London: Asia Publishing House, 1964.

Schwarz, Henry. *Writing Cultural History in Colonial and Postcolonial India.* Philadelphia: University of Pennsylvania Press, 1997.

Sen Gupta, K. K. *Recent Writing on the Revolt of 1857: A Survey.* New Delhi: Indian Council for Historical Research, 1975.

Sen, S. P., ed. *Historical Writings on the Nationalist Movement in India.* Calcutta: Indian Historical Society, 1977.

———. *Sources of the History of India.* 2 vols. Calcutta: Institute of Historical Studies, 1978–1979.

Stein, Burton. *A History of India*. Oxford: Blackwells, 1998.

Syed, A. J., ed. *D. D. Kosambi on History and Society: Problems of Interpretation*. Bombay: University of Bombay, 1985.

Thapar, B. K. "Six Decades of Indus Studies." In *Frontiers of the Indus Civilizaiton*, edited by B. B. Lal and S. P. Gupta. New Delhi: Books & Books, 1984.

Thapar, Romila. *Interpreting Early India*. Delhi: Oxford University Press, 1992.

Thapar, Romila. et al. *Communalism and the Writing of Indian History*. New Delhi: People's Publishing House, 1969.

Thatcher, Mary, ed. *Cambridge South Asian Archive: Records of the British Period*. London: Mansell, 1973.

UNESCO. *Guide to the Sources of Asian History*. Paris: United Nations Educational, Social, and Cultural Organization.

Winks, R. W., ed. *The Historiography of the British Empire-Commonwealth*. Durham, NC: Duke University Press, 1966.

Early India: Earliest Times to c. 700 CE

Allchin, Bridget, and Raymond Allchin. *The Rise of Civilization in India and Pakistan*. Cambridge: Cambridge University Press, 1982.

Allen, Charles. *The Search for the Buddha: The Men Who Discovered India's Lost Religion*. New York: Carroll and Graf, 2003.

Altekar, A. S. *Education in Ancient India*. 6th rev. ed. Varanasi: Nand Kishore, 1965.

———. *Rashtrakutas and Their Times*. Poona: Oriental Book Agency, 1934.

———. *State and Government in Ancient India from Earliest Times to 1200 AD*. Banares: Motilal Banarsi Dass, 1962.

Banerji, S. C. *Aspects of Ancient Indian Life, from Sanskrit Sources*. Calcutta: Punthi Pustak, 1972.

Beal, Samuel, trans. *Travels of Fa-hien and Sung-yun, Buddhist Pilgrims from China to India (400–518 AD)*. London: Sushil Gupta, 1964.

Bongard-Levin, G., and A. Vigasin. *The Image of India: The Study of Ancient Indian Civilization in the USSR*. Moscow: Progress Publishers, 1984.

Bryant, Edwin. *The Quest for the Origins of Vedic Culture: The Indo–Aryan Migration Debate*. Oxford: Oxford University Press, 2001.

Chakraboti, H. P. *India as Reflected in the Inscriptions of the Gupta Period*. New Delhi: Munshiram, 1978.

———. Trade and Commerce of Ancient India. New Delhi: Abhinav, 1977.

Chakravarti, Ranabir ed. *Trade in Early India*. New Delhi: Oxford University Press, 2005.

Champakalakshmi, R. *Trade, Ideology, and Urbanization: South India 300 BC to AD 1300.* Delhi: Oxford University Press, 1996.

Chandra, Moti. *Trade and Trade Routes in Ancient India.* New Delhi: Abhinav, 1977.

Choudhary, Gulab Chanda. *Political History of Northern India from Jain Sources (c. 650–1300 AD).* Amritsar: SJDPS, 1964.

Choudhury, M. *Tribes of Ancient India.* Calcutta: Indian Museum, 1977.

Cunningham, A. *Inscriptions of Asoka.* Varanasi: India Book House, 1961.

Davids, T. W. Rhys. *Buddhist India.* Delhi: Motilal, 1971.

Derrett, J. D. N. *Hoysala: A Medieval Indian Royal Family.* Oxford: Oxford University Press, 1957.

Devadhuti, D. *Harsha, A Political Study.* Oxford: Oxford University Press, 1968.

Elisseeff, Vadime. *The Silk Roads: Highways of Culture and Commerce.* Paris: United Nations Educational, Social, and Cultural Organization (UNESCO), 1998.

Ghurye, G. S. *Indian Acculturation: Agastya and Skanda.* Bombay: Popular Prakashan, 1977.

———. *Vedic India.* Bombay: Popular Prakashan, 1979.

Gokhale, B. G. *Asoka Maurya.* New York: Twayne, 1966.

Goldman, R. P. *Gods, Priests and Warriors: The Bhrigus of the Mahabharata.* New York: Columbia University Press, 1977.

Guruge, Ananda. *The Society of the Ramayana.* New Delhi: Abhinav, 1991.

Jayal, S. *The Status of Women in the Epics.* Delhi: Motilal, 1966.

Jha, D. N. *Ancient India: An Introductory Outline.* New Delhi: People's Publishing, 1977.

Kosambi, Damodar D. *The Culture and Civilization of Ancient India.* New Delhi: Vikas, 1970.

———. *Introduction to the Study of Indian History.* Bombay: Popular Prakasan, 1975.

Lahiri, B. *Indigenous States of Northern India (c. 200 B.C–320 A.D).* Calcutta: University of Calcutta, 1974.

Lahiri, Nayanjot. *The Archeology of Indian Trade Routes up to c. 200 BC.* Delhi: Oxford University Press, 1992.

Lal, B. B., and S. P. Gupta. *Frontiers of the Indus Civilization.* New Delhi: Books & Books, 1984.

Law, B. C. *The Magadhas in Ancient India.* Delhi: Nag, 1976.

Maity, S. K. *Economic Life of Northern India in the Gupta Period.* Calcutta: World Press, 1957.

Majumdar, A. K. *Concise History of Ancient India.* 3 vols. New Delhi: Munshiram Manoharlal, 1980.

Majumdar, R. C. *The Classical Age*. Bombay: Bharatiya Vidhya Bhavan, 1954.

——, ed. *The Age of Imperial Unity*. Bombay: Bharatiya Vidhya Bhavan, 1960.

——. *Classical Accounts of India*. Calcutta: K. L. Mukhopadhyay, 1960.

——. *Corporate Life in Ancient India*. Calcutta: K. L. Mukhopadhyay, 1969.

Majumdar, R. C., and A. S. Altekar, eds. *The Vakataka and Gupta Age*. Delhi: Motilal, 1967.

Majumdar, R. C., and A. D. Pusalker, eds. *The Vedic Age*. Bombay: Bharatiya Vidya Bhavan, 1953.

Mehta, Rati Lal N. *Pre-Buddhist India*. Delhi: Anmol, 1985. Reprint of 1939 edition.

Mishra, P. K. *The Kadambas*. Allahabad: Mithila Prakasana, 1979.

Mohan, V. M. *The Sakas in India and Their Impact on Indian Life and Culture*. Varanasi: Chaukhamba Orientalia, 1976.

Mookerji, R. K. *The Gupta Empire*. 4th ed. Delhi: Motilal, 1969.

Motichandra. *The World of the Courtesans*. Delhi: Vikas, 1973.

Mukherji, B. *Kautilya's Concept of Diplomacy: A New Interpretation*. Calcutta: Minerva, 1976.

Narain, A. K. *The Indo-Greeks*. Oxford: Oxford University Press, 1962.

——. "The Kushana State: A Preliminary Study." In *The Study of the State*, edited by Henri Clessen and Peter Skalnik, pp. 251–274. The Hague: Mouton, 1981.

Nayar, T. Balakrishna. *The Problem of Dravidian Origins: A Linguistic, Anthropological and Archeological Approach*. Madras: University of Madras, 1977.

Pandey, Raj Bali. *Vikramaditya of Ujjayini*. Banaras: Shatadala Prakshan, 1951.

Parasher-Sen, Aloka, ed. *Subordinate and Marginal Groups in Early India*. New Delhi: Oxford University Press, 2004.

Parpola, Asok. "The Proto-Dravidian Inscriptions of the Indus Civilization Being Deciphered." *AAS Newsletter*, December 1969.

Piggott, Stuart. *Prehistoric India to 1,000 BC*. London: Penguin, 1952.

Pike, E. Royston. *Ancient India*. London: Weidenfeld & Nicolson, 1961.

Possehl, Gregory L., ed. *Ancient Cities of the Indus*. New Delhi: Vikas, 1979.

——. *Harappan Civilization: A Contemporary Perspective*. New Delhi: Oxford, 1982.

——. *The Indus Civilization: A Contemporary Perspective*. Lanham, MD: Rowman & Littlefield, 2002.

Puri, B. N. *India under the Kushanas*. Bombay: Bombay University Press, 1965.

Ramaswamy, T. N. *Essentials of Indian Statecraft; Kautilya's Arthasastra for Contemporary Readers*. Bombay: Asia, 1963.

Ratnagar, Shereen. *Encounters: The Westerly Trade of Harappa Civilization.* Delhi: Oxford University Press, 1981.

——. *The End of the Great Harappan Tradition.* New Delhi: Manohar, 2000.

Ray, A. *Villages, Towns and Secular Buildings in Ancient India, c. 150 B.C–350 AD.* Calcutta: K. L. Mukhopadhyay, 1964.

Raychaudhuri, Hemchandra. *Political History of Ancient India from the Accession of Parikshit to the Extinction of the Gupta Dynasty.* Delhi: Oxford University Press, 1996. (First published by the University of Calcutta in 1923.)

Renou, L. *Vedic India.* Translated from the French by P. Spratt. Delhi: India Book House, 1971.

Richards, John F., ed. *Kingship and Authority in South Asia.* Madison,: University of Wisconsin South Asian Studies, 1981.

Saletore, B. A. *India's Diplomatic Relations with the East (300–1300 AD).* Bombay: Popular, 1960.

Sarkar, S. S. *Ancient Races of the Deccan.* New Delhi: Munshiram, 1972.

Sastri, K. A. Nilakanta. *Age of the Nandas and Mauryas.* Banaras: Motilal Banarsi Dass, 1967.

——. *Culture and History of the Tamils.* Calcutta: K. L. Mukhopadhyay, 1964.

——. *History of South India from Prehistoric Times to the Fall of Vijayanagar.* 3rd ed. Oxford: Oxford University Press, 1966.

Saxena, D. P. *Regional Geography of Vedic India.* Kanpur: Grantham, 1976.

Sengupta, N. *Evolution of Hindu Marriage, with Special Reference to Rituals c.1000 BC–AD 500.* Bombay: Popular, 1965.

Sengupta, Padmini. *Everyday Life in Ancient India.* Bombay: Oxford University Press, 1950.

Sethna, K. D. *Ancient India in a New Light.* New Delhi: Aditya Prakashan, 1989.

Sharma, J. *Republic in Ancient India 1500 B.C–500 AD.* Leiden, The Netherlands: Brill, 1968.

Sharma, Ram Sharan. *Aspects of Political Ideas and Institutions in Ancient India.* 3rd rev. ed. Delhi: Motilal Banarasidas, 1991.

——. *Light on Early Indian Society and Economy.* Bombay: Manaktalas, 1966.

Sidhanta, N. K. *The Heroic Age of India: A Comparative Study.* New Delhi: Oriental Books Reprint Corporation, 1975. Reprint of 1929 edition.

Singh, A. D. *Kalidasa: A Critical Study.* Delhi: Bharatiya, 1977.

Singh, S. D. *Ancient Indian Warfare, with Special Reference to the Vedic Period.* Leiden, The Netherlands: Brill, 1965.

Sircar, D. C. *Land System and Feudalism in Ancient India.* Calcutta: University of Calcutta, 1966.

———. *Ancient India in the Vikramaditya Tradition.* Delhi: Munshiram, 1969.

———, ed. *Early Indian Numismatic and Epigraphical Studies.* Calcutta: Indian Museum, 1977.

Smith, Vincent Arthur. *The Early History of India.* 4th rev. ed. Oxford: Oxford University Press, 1957.

Strong, John S. *The Legend of King Ashoka.* Princeton, NJ: Princeton University Press, 1983.

Subramanium, N. *Sangam Polity.* Bombay: Asia, 1967.

Thapar, Romila. *A History of India. Volume 1.* Baltimore: Penguin, 1966.

———. *Ancient Indian Social History.* New Delhi: Orient Longman, 1978.

———. *From Lineage to State.* Bombay; Oxford University Press, 1984.

———. *Early India: From the Origins to AD 1300.* Berkeley, CA: University of California Press, 2002.

Tripathi, V. *The Painted Grey Ware: An Iron Age Culture of Northern India.* New Delhi: Concept, 1976.

United Nations Educational, Social, and Cultural Orgnization (UNESCO). *Conference on History, Archeology and Culture of Central Asia in the Kushan Period.* (Dushambei, 1968.) Paris: UNESCO, 1968.

Vanini, Eugenia, ed. *Indian History: A Russian Viewpoint.* Delhi: Indian Council of Historical Research and Russian Academy of Sciences, 2003.

Vyas, S. N. *India in the Ramayana Age.* Delhi: Atma Ram, 1967.

Wagle, N. K. *Society at the Time of the Buddha.* Bombay: Popular, 1966.

Wheeler, R. E. M. *Civilizations of the Indus Valley and Beyond.* New York: McGraw-Hill, 1966.

Woodcock, G. *The Greeks in India.* London: Faber, 1966.

Regional States and Their Realignments, c. 700–1500 CE

Ali, Daud. *Courtly Culture and Political Life in Early Medieval India.* Cambridge: Cambridge University Press, 2004.

Ali, Rahman. *Temples of Madhya Pradesh: The Paramara Art.* New Delhi: Sundeep Prakashan, 2002.

Altekar, A. S. *Rashtrakuttas and Their Times.* Poona: Oriental Book Agency, 1967.

Ashraf, Kunwar Muhammad. *Life and Conditions of the People of Hindustan (1200–1550): Mainly Based on Islamic Sources.* New Delhi: Gyan Publishing, 2000.

Asopan. Jai Narayan. *Origin of the Rajputs.* Delhi: Bharatiya Publishing, 1976.

Balambal, V. *Feudatories of South India 800–1070 AD*. Allahabad: Chugh Publications, 1978.

Banerjee, Anil Chandra. *The State and Society in Northern India 1206–1526*. Calcutta: K. P. Bagchi, 1982.

Banerjee, Jamini Mohan. *History of Firuz Shah Tughlaq*. Delhi: Munshiram Manoharlal, 1967.

Bosworth, Clifford Edmund. *The Later Ghaznavids 1040–1186*. New York: Columbia University Press, 1977.

Chattopadhyaya, B. *Coins and Currency Systems in South India c. 225–1300 AD*. New Delhi: Munshiram, 1977.

——. *Making of Early Medieval India*. Delhi: Oxford University Press, 1994.

Coedes, George. *The Indianized States of Southeast Asia*. Honolulu, HI: East-West Center Press, 1968.

Derrett, J. D. M. *Religion, Law and the State in India*. London: Faber and Faber, 1968.

Elliot, H. M., and John Dowson, eds. *The History of India as Told by its Own Historians: The Mohammaden Period*. 8 vols. Allahabad: Kitab Mahal.

Embree, Ainslie T., ed. *Alberuni's India*. (Abridged edition of Edward Sachau's translation.) New York: Norton, 1971.

——. *Sources of Indian Tradition. vol. 1*. New York: Columbia University Press, 1988.

Gibbs, H. A. R., trans. *The Travels of Ibn Battuta 1325–1354. vol 3*. Cambridge: Cambridge University Press, 1971.

Gopalan, R. *A History of the Pallavas of Kanchi*. Madras: University of Madras, 1928.

Grousset, R. *In the Footsteps of the Buddha*. New York: Grossman, 1971.

Habib, Irfan. *Medieval India: A Miscellany, vol. 14*. Bombay: Asia, 1977.

——, ed. *Medieval India: Researches in the History of India, 1200–1750*. New Delhi: Oxford University Press, 1992.

Habib, Muhammad. *Introduction to the Second Volume of Elliot and Dowson*. Aligarh: Aligarh Muslim University, 1951.

——. *Politics and Society during the Early Medieval Period*. 2 vols. Edited for republication by K. A. Nizami. Aligarh: Peoples Publishing, 1981.

——. *Sultan Mahmud of Ghazni*. 2nd ed. Aligarh: Cosmopolitan Publishers, 1951.

Habibullah, A. B. M. *The Foundations of Muslim Rule in India*. Allahabad: Kitab Mahal, 1961.

Hampa. N. *A History of the Early Ganga Monarchy and Jainism*. Bangalore: Ankita Pustaka, 1999.

Husain, Agha Mahdi. *The Rise and Fall of Muhammad Bin Tughlaq*. Delhi: Idarah-i-Adarbiyat, 1972.

Husaini, A. M. *Bahman Shah. The Founder of the Bahmani Kingdom of the Deccan.* London: Probsthain, 1960.

——. *Khandesh in a New Light: Based on a Study of Persian and Arabic Sources.* Bangalore: Mythic Society, 1963.

Ikram, S. M. *Muslim Civilization in India.* New York: Columbia University Press, 1964.

Jackson, Peter. *The Delhi Sultanate: A Political and Military History.* Cambridge: Cambridge University Press, 1999.

Jauhri, R. C. *Firoz Tughlaq, 1351–1388.* Jalandhar: ABS Publications, 1990.

Javed, Ajeet. *Heritage of Harmony: An Insight into Medieval India.* New Delhi: Gyan Publishing House, 2002.

Karashima, Noburu. *South Indian History and Society: Studies from Inscriptions, 850–1800.* New Delhi: Oxford University Press, 1984.

Krishna Ayyar, K. V. *The Zamorins of Calicut: From Earliest Times to 1806.* Calicut: University of Calicut, 1999.

Kulke, Hermann. *Kings and Cults: State Formation and Legitmation in India and Southeast Asia.* New Delhi: Manohar, 1993.

Lal, K. S. *Early Muslims in India.* New Delhi: Books & Books, 1984.

——. *History of the Khaljis.* Delhi: Ranjit, 1980. Reprint of 1950 edition.

——. *Studies in Medieval Indian History.* Delhi: Ranjit, 1966.

——. *Twilight of the Sultanate 1398–1526.* Bombay: Asia, 1963.

Majumdar, R. C., ed. *The Age of Imperial Kanauj.* Bombay: Bharatiya Vidhya Bhavan, 1955.

——. *The Stuggle for Empire.* Bombay: Bharatiya Vidhya Bhavan, 1957.

——, *India and Southeast Asia.* Delhi: B. R., 1979.

Mathew, K. S. *Society in Medieval Malabar.* Kottayam: Jaffe Books, 1979.

Nigam, S. B. P. *Nobility under the Sultans of Delhi 1206–1398.* Delhi: Munshiram Manoharlal, 1968.

Nizami, Khaliq Ahmad. *Religion and Politics in India during the Thirteenth Century.* Aligarh: Aligarh Muslim University, 1961.

Ojha, P. N. *Aspects of Medieval Indian Society and Culture.* Delhi: B. R., 1978.

Pandey, A. B. *Early Medieval India.* Allahabad: Central Book Depot, 1965.

Panda, Shishir Kumar. *The State and Statecraft in Medieval Orissa under the Later Eastern Gangas (1038–1434).* Calutta: K. P. Bagchi & Co., 1995.

Peabody, Norbet. *Hindu Kingship and Polity in Pre-Colonial India.* Cambridge: Cambridge University Press, 2002.

Prasad, Ishwari. *History of Medieval India 647–1526 AD.* Allahabad: Indian Press, 1966.

Raghavan, V. *The Great Integrators: The Saint Singers of India.* Delhi: P. D. M. I. B., 1966.

Rao, M. S. Nagaraja. *The Chalukyas of Badami*. Bangalore: Mythic Society, 1978.

Rashid, A. *Society and Culture in Medieval India 1206–1556 AD*. Calcutta: K. L. Mukhopadhyay, 1969.

Raychaudhuri, Tapan, and Irfan Habib, eds. *The Cambridge Economic History of India, Volume 1: c. 1200–1750*. Cambridge: Cambridge University Press, 1982.

Richards, J. F. "The Islamic Frontier in the East: Expansion into South Asia." *South Asia* (Melbourne) no. 4 (October 1974): 91–109.

Rizvi, S. A. A. *A History of Sufism in India*. New Delhi: Munshiram Manohar-lal, 1978.

———. *The Wonder That Was India, Volume 11, 1200–1700*. London: Sidgwick & Jackson, 1987.

Sastri, K. A. Nilakanta. *The Cholas*. Madras: University of Madras, 1975.

Sen, N. C., trans. *Accounts of India and Kashmir in the Dynastic Histories of the Tang Period*. Santiniketan: Visva Bharati, 1968.

Sethuraman, V. *The Imperial Pandyas*. Kumbakonam: Sethuraman, 1978.

Sharma, Krishna. *Bhakti and the Bhakti Movement: A New Perspective*. New Delhi: Munshiram Manoharlal, 1987.

Sharma, R. S. *Indian Feudalism c. 300–1200*. Calcutta: University of Calcutta, 1965.

———. *Early Medieval Indian Society: A Study in Feudalisation*. Hyderabad: Orient Longman, 2001.

Sharma, S. R. *The Crescent in India: A Study in Medieval History*. 3rd rev. ed. Bombay: Hind Kitab, 1966.

Shinha, S. K. *Medieval History of the Deccan*. Hyderabad: Government of Andhra Pradesh, 1964.

Singh, Meera. *Medieval History of India*. New Delhi: Vikas, 1978.

Sircar, D. C. *Some Epigraphical Records of the Medieval Period from Eastern India*. New Delhi: Abhinav, 1979.

Stein, Burton. *Peasant, State and Society in Medieval South India*. Oxford: Oxford University Press, 1986.

———. *Vijaynagar*. Cambridge University Press, 1989.

Subrahmanyam, Sanjay, ed. *Money and the Market in India 1100–1700*. New Delhi: Oxford University Press, 1994.

Tara Chand. *Influence of Islam on Indian Culture*. Allahabad: The Indian Press, 1946.

Trimingham, J. S. *The Sufi Orders in Islam*. Oxford: Oxford University Press, 1973.

Vaidya, C. V. *History of Medieval Hindu India 600–1200 AD*. 2 vols. Poona: Aryabhushan Press, 1935.

Verma, H. C. *Medieval Routes to India: Baghdad to Delhi: A Study of Trade and Military Routes*. Calcutta: Maya Prakash, 1978.

Wink, Andre. *Al-Hind: The Making of the Indo-Islamic World 7th–11th Centuries*. Delhi: Oxford University Press, 1990. Boston, MA: Brill, 2002.

Yadav, J. N. Singh. *Yadavas through the Ages*. Delhi: Sharada Publishing House, 1992.

Yusuf, Husain Khan. *Glimpses of Medieval Indian Culture*. Bombay: Asia, 1957.

———. *Indo–Muslim Polity*. Simla: Indian Institute of Advanced Studies, 1971.

Zaki, M., ed. *Arab Accounts of India in the 14th Century*. Delhi: Idarah-i-Adarbiyat, 1981.

The Mughal Era: c. 1526–1750

Abul Fazl. *Ain-i-Akbari*. Vol. 3 of *Akbarnama*.

———. *Akbarnama*. 3 vols. Translated by H. Blochmann et al. Calcutta: Asiatic Society of Bengal, 1873–1948. (Bibliotheca Indica).

Ahmad, L. *The Prime Ministers of Aurangzeb*. Allahabad: Chugh, 1976.

Alam, Muzaffar, and Seema Alavi. Translation. *A European Experience of the Mughal Orient*. New Delhi: Oxford University Press, 2001.

Ali, M. Athar. *The Apparatus of Empire: Appointments and Titles in the Mughal Empire, 1574–1658*. Delhi: Oxford University Press, 1985.

———. *The Mughal Nobility under Aurangzeb*. New Delhi: Asia, 1966.

Allauddin, Shaikh. *Libraries and Librarianship during Muslim Rule in India*. New Delhi: Reliance Publishing House, 1996.

Anand, Sugam. *History of Begum Nurjahan*. New Delhi: Radha Publications, 1992.

Anwar, Firdos. *Nobility under the Mughals, 1628–1658*. New Delhi: Manohar, 2001.

Athar ali, M. *The Mughal Nobility under Aurangzeb*. New Delhi: Oxford University Press, Manohar, 2001.

Apte, B. K., ed. *Chhatrapati Shivaji: Coronation Tercentenary Commemoration Volume*. Bombay: University of Bombay, 1975.

Arasaratnam, Sinnappah. *Maritime India in the Seventeenth Century*. Delhi: Oxford University Press, 1994.

Aziz, Abdul. *The Mansabdari System and the Mughal Army*. Delhi: IAD, 1972.

Berinstain, Valerie. *India and the Mughal Dynasty*. New York: Abrams, 1998.

Bernier, Francois. *Travels in the Mogul Empire AD 1656–1668*. Translated from the French and revised by A. Constable. Delhi: S. Chand, 1968.

Beveridge, A. S., trans. *Babur-Nama in English: Memoirs of Babur.* 2 vols. Translated from the Turki. New Delhi: Oriental Books Reprint, 1970. Reprint of 1922 edition.

Bhargava, Motilal. *Hemu and His Times: Afghans vs Mughals.* New Delhi: Reliance Publishing House, 1991.

Bhave, Y. G. *From the Death of Shivaji to the Death of Aurangzeb: The Critical Years.* New Delhi: Northern Book Centre, 2000.

Chandra, Satish. *Medieval India: Society, the Jagirdari Crisis, and the Village.* Delhi: Macmillan, 1982.

——. *Medieval India. Volume II.* New Delhi: National Council of Education Research and Training, 1978.

——. *The Parties and Politics at the Mughal Court 1707–1740.* Aligarh: Aligarh Muslim University, 1959.

Dale, Stehen Frederic. *Indian Merchants and Eurasian Trade 1600–1750.* Cambridge: Cambridge University Press, 2004.

Das, K. R. *Raja Todar Mal.* Calcutta: Saraswat Library, 1979.

Doshi, Sarya. *Shivaji and Facets of Maratha Culture.* Bombay: Marcy, 1982.

Dwivedi, Girish Chandra. *The Jats, Their Role in the Mughal Empire.* Bangalore: Arnold Publishers, 1989.

Edwardes, S. M., and H. L. O. Garrett. *Mughal Rule in India.* New York: AMS Press, 1976. Reprint of 1930 edition.

Erali, Abraham. *The Last Spring: The Lives and Times of the Great Mughals.* New Delhi: Viking, 1997.

Foltz, Richard. *Mughal India and Central Asia.* New York: Oxford University Press, 1998.

Fukuzawa, Hiroshi. *The Medieval Deccan: Peasants, Social Systems and States. 16th to 18th Centuries.* Delhi: Oxford University Press, 1991.

Gascoigne, Bamber. *The Great Moghuls.* London: Jonathan Cape, 1971.

Godden, Rumer. *Gulbadan.* New York: Viking, 1981.

Gordon, Stewart. *The New Cambridge History of India, The Marathas 1600–1818.* Cambridge: Cambridge University Press, 1993.

Gulbadan, Begum. *The History of Humayun.* Translated by A. S. Beveridge. Delhi: IAD, 1972. Reprint of 1902 edition.

Habib, Irfan. *The Agrarian System of Mughal India 1556–1770.* New York: Asia, 1963.

Hanan, Farhat. *State and Locality in Mughal India: Power Relations in Western India c. 1572–1730.* Cambridge: Cambridge University Press, 2004.

Hansen, Waldemar. *The Peacock Throne: The Drama of Mogul India.* London: Weidenfeld & Nicolson, 1972.

Husain, W. *Administration of Justice during Muslim Rule in India.* Delhi: IAD, 1977. Reprint of 1934 edition.

Jahanara. *The Life of a Mogul Princess: Jahanara Begum, Daughter of Shah Jahan.* Translated from the Persian by A. Butenschon. London: G. Routledge, 1931.

Keay, John. *The Honourable Company: A History of the English East India Company.* New York: Macmillan, 1994.

Khan, Rafaqat Ali. *The Kachwahas under Akbar and Jahangir.* New Delhi: Kitab Mahal, 1976.

Kincaid, Dennis. *The Grand Rebel: An Impression of Shivaji, Founder of the Maratha Empire.* London: Collins, 1937.

Kulkarni, A. R. *Marathas and the Maharathas Country.* New Delhi: Books & Books, 1996.

Lall, John. *Taj Mahal and the Saga of the Great Mughals.* Delhi: Lustre Press, 1994.

Lamb, Harold. *Babur the Tiger.* New York: Doubleday, 1961.

Malgaonkar, M. *The Sea Hawk.* New Delhi: Vision, 1979.

Malik, Z. *The Reign of Muhammad Shah 1719–1748.* Bombay: Asia, 1977.

Mankekar, D. P. *Mewar Saga: The Sisodias Role in Indian History.* New Delhi: Vikas, 1976.

Mathew, K. S. *History of Portuguese Navigation in India.* New Delhi: Mittal, 1987.

Mathur, R. M. *Rajput States and the East India Company.* Delhi: Sundeep, 1979.

Moore, Barrington. *Social Origins of Dictatorship and Democracy.* Boston: Beacon Press, 1966.

Moreland, W. H. *Agrarian System of Moslem India.* Cambridge: Cambridge University Press, 1929.

——. *India at the Death of Akbar.* Delhi: Atma Ram, 1962. Reprint of 1920 edition.

Mukhia, Harbans. *The Mughals of India.* Oxford: Blackwell Publishers, 2004.

Nayeem, M. A. *External Relations of the Bijapur Kingdom, 1489–1686.* Hyderabad: Bright Publications, 1974.

Om Prakash. *The Dutch Factories in India, 1617–1623.* New Delhi: Munshiram Manoharlal, 1984.

Pant, C. *Nur Jahan and Her Family.* Allahabad: Dandewal Publishing House, 1978.

Pant, D. *The Commercial Policy of the Moguls.* Delhi: IAD, 1978. Reprint of 1930 edition.

Phul, R. K. *Armies of the Great Mughals 1526–1707.* New Delhi: Oriental, 1978.

Prasad, Beni. *History of Jahangir.* London: Oxford University Press, 1922.

Prasad, Ram Chandra. *Early English Travellers in India.* Delhi: Motilal Banarsi Dass, 1965.

Qaisar, A. J. "Merchant Shipping in India during the 17th Century." In *Medieval India: A Miscellany.* vol. 2. Aligarh: Asia Publishing House, 1972.

———. "The Role of Brokers in Medieval India." *Indian Historical Review,* 1974.

Qanungo, K. R. *Sher Shah and His Times.* Bombay: Orient Longman, 1965.

Qureshi, I. H. *Akbar: The Architect of the Mughal Empire.* Karachi: M. A. Aref, 1978.

———. *The Muslim Community of the Indo–Pakistan Subcontinent, 1610–1947.* The Hague: Mouton, 1962.

Ram Gopal. *Hindu Culture during and after Muslim Rule: Survival and Subsequent Challenges.* New Delhi: MD Publications, 1994.

Ray, Aniruddha. *The Merchant and the State: The French in India 1666–1739.* New Delhi: Munshiram Manoharlal, 2004.

Raychaudhuri, Tapan. *Bengal under Akbar and Lahangir: An Introductory Study in Social History.* Delhi: Munshiram Manoharlal, 1969.

Raychaudhuri, Tapan, and Irfan Habib, eds. *The Cambridge Economic History of India, Volume 1: c. 1200–c. 1750.* Cambridge: Cambridge University Press, 1982.

Richards, F. J. *Mughal Administration in Golconda.* Oxford: Oxford University Press, 1975.

Richards, John. *The Mughal Empire.* Cambridge: Cambridge University Press, 1993.

Rizvi, S. A. A. *Religious and Intellectual History of the Muslims in Akbar's Reign.* New Delhi: Munshiram Manoharlal, 1975.

Sangar, S. P. *Crime and Punishment in Mughal India.* New Delhi: Sterling, 1967.

Sangara, Satyprakasa. *Crime and Punishment in Mughal India.* New Delhi: Reliance Publishing House, 1999.

Saran, P. *The Provincial Government of the Mughals 1526–1658.* Allahabad: Kitabistan, 1941.

Sardesai, G. S. *The Main Currents of Maratha History.* Bombay: Dhavle, 1933.

———. *New History of the Marathas.* 2nd ed. 3 vols. New Delhi: Munshiram Manoharlal, 1986.

Sardesai, S. G. *Shivaji: Contours of a Historical Evaluation.* New Delhi: Perspective, 1974.

Sarkar, Jadunath. *Fall of the Mughal Empire.* 4 vols. New Delhi: Orient Longman, 1991. Reprint of 1950 revised edition.

———. *A Short History of Aurangzeb 1618–1707.* Calcutta: M. D. Sarkar, 1962. Abridged edition from 5 volumes based on Persian sources published 1912–1930.

Schurhammer, Georg. *Francis Xavier: His Life, His Times. Vol. 11 India 1541–1545*. Rome: The Vatican Press, 1977.

Sharma, G. D. *Vakil Reports to Maharajan 1693–1712*. New Delhi: Radha Krishna, 1987.

Sharma, S. R. *The Religious Policy of the Mughal Emperors*. Bombay: Hind Kitab, 1962.

Siddiqi, Iqtidar Husain. *Sher Sha Sur and His Dynasty*. Jaipur: Publication Scheme, 1995.

Singh, Ganda. *Life of Banda Singh Bahadur: Based on Contemporary and Original Records*. Patiala: Punjabi University, 1990.

Singh, Gopal. *A History of the Sikh People 1469–1978*. New Delhi: World Sikh Press, 1979.

Singh, Harbans. *The Heritage of the Sikhs*. Bombay: Asia, 1964.

Singh, Khushwant. *A History of the Sikhs*. 2 vols. Princeton, NJ: Princeton University Press, 1963.

Singh, Mahendra Pratap. *Shivaji, Bhakha Sources and Nationalism*. New Delhi: Books of India International, 2001.

Smith, Vincent A. *Akbar the Great Mogul*. Delhi: A. Chand, 1966. Reprint of 1919 edition.

Spear, Percival. *A History of India, 11*. Baltimore: Penguin, 1975.

Srivastava, A. L. *The First Two Nawabs of Oudh*. Agra: S. L. Agarwala, 1954.

Subrahmanyam, Sanjay. *The Portugese Empire in Asia 1500–1700*. London: Longman, 1993.

"Symposium on Decline of the Mughal Empire." *Journal of Asian Studies*. Vol. 35. no. 2, 1976.

Tara Chand. *Society and State in the Mughal Period*. New Delhi: P. D. M. I. B., 1965.

Thakston, W. M. *Three Memoirs of Humayun*. Costa Mesa, CA: Mazda Publishers, 2004.

Tripathi, R. P. *Rise and Fall of the Mughal Empire*. Allahabad: Central Book Depot, 1956.

Varadarajan, Lotika. *India in the 17th Century: Memoirs of Francois Martin*. 3 vols. New Delhi: Manohar, 1981.

Varma, R. C. *Foreign Policy of the Great Mughals, 1526–1727*. Agra: Agrawala, 1967.

Modern India before Independence c. 1700–1947 CE

Akbar, M. J. *Nehru: The Making of India*. London: Penguin Books, 1988.

Ambedkar, B. *Writings and Speeches*. 10 vols. Edited by Vasant Moon. Bombay: Government of Maharashtra, 1989.

Azad, Abul Kalam. *India Wins Freedom.* New Delhi: Orient Longman, 1959. Revised edition 1989.

Aziz, K. K. *Britain and Muslim India 1857–1947.* London: Heinemann, 1963.

Balabushevich, V. V., and A. M. Dyakov, eds. *A Contemporary History of India.* Moscow: Peoples Publishing House, 1959.

Ballhatchet, Kenneth. *Race, Sex and Class under the Raj.* London: Weidenfeld & Nicolson, 1980.

Bandyopadhyay, Sekhar. *From Plassey to Partition: A History of Modern India.* Hyderabad: Orient Longman, 2004.

Banerji, A. C. *The Constitutional History of India 1600–1977.* 3 vols. Delhi: Macmillan, 1977.

Barrow, Ian J. *Making History, Drawing Territory: British Mapping in India 1756–1905.* New Delhi: Oxford University Press, 2003.

Bayly, C. A. *Rulers, Townsmen and Bazaars: North Indian Society in the Age of British Expansion 1770–1870.* Cambridge: Cambridge University Press, 1983.

———. *Indian Society and the Making of the British Empire.* Cambridge: Cambridge University Press, 1988.

———, ed. *The Illustrated History of Modern India 1600–1947.* Bombay: Oxford University Press, 1991.

Bhairavi, Biswamoy Pati, Prasad Sahu, and T. K. Venkatasubrahmanian, eds. *Negotiating the Past: Essays in Memory of Parthsarathy Gupta.* Delhi: Tulika Books, 2004.

Bondurant, Joan V. *The Conquest of Violence: The Gandhian Philosophy of Conflict.* Rev. ed. Princeton, NJ: Princeton University Press, 1988.

Bose, Sugata, ed. *South Asia and World Capitalism.* Delhi: Oxford University Press, 1990.

———. *Peasant Labour and Colonial Capital.* Cambridge: Cambridge University Press, 1993.

———. *Credit, Markets and the Agrarian Economy of Colonial India.* New Delhi: Oxford University Press, 1994.

Bose, Sugata, and Ayesha Jalal. *Modern South Asian History: History, Culture, Political Economy.* London: Routledge, 1999.

Broomfield, J. H. *Elite Conflict in a Plural Society: 20th Century Bengal.* Berkeley, CA: University of California Press, 1968.

Brown, D. M. *The Nationalist Movement in India: Political Thought from Ranade to Bhave.* Berkeley, CA: University of California Press, 1970.

Brown, Judith M. *Gandhi's Rise to Power: Indian Politics 1915–1922.* Cambridge: Cambridge University Press, 1972.

———. *Gandhi and Civil Disobedience 1928–1934.* Cambridge: Cambridge University Press, 1977.

———. *Modern India: The Origins of an Asian Democracy*. New York: Oxford University Press, 1985.

———. *Gandhi: Prisoner of Hope*. New York: Oxford University Press, 1991.

———. *Nehru: A Political Life*. New Haven, CT: Yale University Press, 2003.

Chakravarty, Papia. *Hindu Responses to Nationalist Ferment: Bengal 1909–1935*. Calcutta: Subarnarekha, 1992.

Chandra, Bipan. *Modern India*. New Delhi: National Council of Educational Research and Training, 1978.

———. *Nationalism and Colonialism in Modern India*. New Delhi: Orient Longman, 1981.

———. *Communalism in Modern India*. New Delhi: Vikas Publishing House, 1984.

Chandra, Bipan, et al. *Indian Struggle for Independence 1857–1947*. New Delhi: Penguin, 1989.

———. *India after Independence 1947–2000*. New Delhi: Penguin Books, 2000.

Chaturvedi, S. *Madan Mohan Malaviya*. New Delhi: Publications Division, Ministry of Information and Broadcasting, 1972.

Chaudhuri, K. N. *Trade and Civilization in the Indian Ocean*. Cambridge: Cambridge University Press, 1991.

Chopra, P. N., ed. *India's Struggle for Freedom: Role of Associated Movements*. 4 vols. Delhi: Agam Prakashan, 1985.

———. *Towards Freedom, 1937–1947 (Documents)*. New Delhi: Indian Council for Historical Research, 1985–1992.

Coen, T. Croagh. *The Indian Political Service: A Study in Indirect Rule*. London: Chatto & Windus, 1971.

Coupland, Reginald. *India: A Restatement*. London: Oxford University Press, 1945.

Dalrymple, William. *White Mughals: Love and Betrayal in Eighteenth Century India*. London: HarperCollins, 2002.

Datta, V. N., and S. C. Mittal, eds. *Sources of National Movement 1919–1920*. New Delhi: Allied, 1985.

Desai, Narain. *The Training of a Satyagrahi A Handbook for Shanti Sainiks*. Varanasi: Sarva Seva Sangh Prakashar, 1963.

Dhanagare, D. N. *Peasant Movements in India, 1920–1950*. Delhi: Oxford University Press, 1983.

Dixit, Prabha. *Communalism: A Struggle for Power*. New Delhi: Orient Longman, 1974.

Edwardes, A. *Battles of the Indian Mutiny*. London: B. T. Batsford, 1963.

———. *The Rape of India: A Biography of Robert Clive and a Social History of the Conquest of Hindustan*. New York: Julian Press, 1966.

——. *Red Year: The Indian Rebellion of 1857*. London: Hamilton, 1973.

——. *The Sahibs and the Lotus: The British in India*. London: Constable, 1988.

Embree, Ainslee T., ed. *1857 in India: Mutiny or War of Independence?* Boston: D. C. Heath, 1963.

——. *India's Search for National Identity*. New York: Knopf, 1972.

——. *Imagining India: Essays on Indian History*. New Delhi: OUP, 1989.

Embree, Ainslee T., and Carol Gluck, *Asia in Western and World History: A Guide for Teaching,* New York: M. E. Sharpe, 1997.

Erikson, Erik H. *Gandhi's Truth: On the Origins of Militant Nonviolence*. New York: Norton, 1970.

Fischer, Louis. *The Life of Mahatma Gandhi*. New York: Harper, 1950.

Fisher, Michael H. *Indirect Rule in India: Residents and the Residency System 1764–1858.* Delhi: Oxford University Press, 1991.

——. *Counterflows to Colonialism: Indian Travellers and Settlers in Britain 1600–1857.* New Delhi: Permanent Black, 2004.

——, ed. *The Politics of the British Annexations of India*. New Delhi: Oxford University Press.

Forrest, D. M. *Tiger of Mysore: The Life and Death of Tipu Sultan*. London: Chatto & Windus, 1970.

French, Patrick. *Liberty or Death: India's Journey to Independence and Division.* London: HarperCollins, 1997.

——. *Younghusband: The Last Great Imperial Adventurer.* London: Harper-Collins, 1994.

Frykenberg, R. E., ed. *Delhi through the Ages: Essays in Urban History, Culture, and Society.* New Delhi: Oxford University Press, 1986.

Furber, Holden. *John Company at Work: A Study of European Expansion in India in the Late 18th Century*. New York: Octagon, 1970.

Gallagher, John. *The Decline, Revival and Fall of the British Empire*. Cambridge: Cambridge University Press, 1982.

Gallagher, John, G. Johnson, and Anil Seale, eds. *Locality, Province and Nation: Essays on Indian Politics 1870–1940*. Cambridge: Cambridge University Press, 1973.

Gandhi, Mohandas K. *An Autobiography, or the Story of My Experiments with Truth.* Translated from the Gujarati by Mahadev Desai. Ahmedabad: Navjivan Trust, 1927.

Gandhi, Rajmohan. *Rajaji's Story 1937–1972.* Bombay: Bharatiya Vidhya Bhavan, 1984.

——. *Patel: A Life.* Ahmedabad: Navajivan Publishing House, 1992.

——. *Good Boatman: A Portrait of Gandhi.* New Delhi: Viking, 1995.

——. *Rajaji: A Life*. New Delhi: Penguin, 1997.

Gardner, B. *The East India Company. A History*. New York: McCall, 1972.

Gilmartin, David. *Empire and Islam: Punjab and the Making of Pakistan*. Berkeley, CA: University of California Press, 1988.

Gilmour, David. *Curzon: Imperial Statesman*. New York: Farrar, Straus & Firoux, 2003.

Golant, W. *The Long Afternoon*. New York: St. Martin's Press, 1975.

Gooptu, Nandini. *The Politics of the Urban Poor in Early Twentieth Century India*. New York: Cambridge University Press, 2001.

Gopal, Sarvepalli. *British Policy in India 1858–1905*. London: Cambridge University Press, 1965.

——. *Jawaharlal Nehru,1889–1947*. Delhi: Oxford University Press, 1975.

——. *Jawaharlal Nehru, 1947–1956*. Delhi: Oxford University Press, 1980.

——, ed. *Jawaharlal Nehru: An Anthology*. Delhi: Oxford University Press, 1980.

——. *Jawaharlal Nehru, 1957–1964*. Delhi: Oxford University Press, 1990.

——. *Radhakrishnan: A Biography*. New Delhi: Oxford University Press, 1992.

——. *Selected Works of Jawaharlal Nehru. First Series*. 16 vols. New Delhi: Oxford University Press, 1994.

——. *Selected Works of Jawaharlal Nehru. Second Series*. 19 vols. New Delhi: Oxford University Press, 1996.

Gordon, Leonard A. *Bengal: The Nationalist Movement 1876–1940*. New York: Columbia University Press, 1974.

——. *Brothers against the Raj: A Biography of Sarat and Subhas Chandra Bose*. New Delhi: Penguin, 1990.

Gordon, Stewart. *The New Cambridge History of India II. 4, The Marathas 1600–1818*. Cambridge: Cambridge University Press, 1993.

Gould, William. *Hindu Nationalism and the Language of Politics in Late Colonial India*. Cambridge: Cambridge University Press, 2003.

Griffiths, P. J. *The British Impact on India*. London: Cass, 1965. Reprint of 1952 edition.

Guha, Ramachandran. *The Other Side of the Raj: Western Contributions to India's Freedom*. Shillong: Northeastern Hill University Publications, 2001.

Guha, Ranajit, ed. *Subaltern Studies*. Volumes I–V. Delhi: Oxford University Press, 1982–1988.

——. *Elementary Aspects of Peasant Insurgency in Colonial India*. Durham: Duke University Press, 1999.

Gupta, A. K., ed. *Myth and Reality: The Struggle for Freedom in India, 1945–1947*. New Delhi: Manohar, 1987.

Gupta, M. N. *Bhagat Singh and His Times*. Delhi: Lipi Prakashan, 1977.

Hasan, Mushirul, ed. *India's Partition: Process, Strategy and Mobilization.* Delhi: Oxford University Press, 1993.

——. *Muslims and the Congress 1912–1935.* New Delhi: Manohar, 1979.

Heimsath, Charles H. *Indian Nationalism and Hindu Social Reform.* Princeton, NJ: Princeton University Press, 1964.

Hopkirk, Peter. *The Great Game: On Secret Service in High Asia.* London: J. Murray, 1990.

Hoskins, Halford. *British Routes to India.* London: Frank Cass, 1966.

Hutchins, Francis. *The Illusion of Permanence: British Imperialism in India.* Princeton, NJ: Princeton University Press, 1967.

——. *Spontaneous Revolution: The Quit India Movement.* Delhi: Manohar, 1971.

Iftikhar-ul-Awwal, A. Z. M. *The Industrial Development of Bengal, 1900–1939.* New Delhi: Vikas, 1982.

Iyer, R. *The Moral and Political Thought of Mahatma Gandhi.* New York: Oxford University Press, 1973.

James, Lawrence. *Raj: The Making and Unmaking of British India.* New York: St. Martin's Press, 1998.

Jeffrey, R., ed. *People, Princes and Paramount Power: Society and Politics in the Indian Princely States.* Delhi: Oxford University Press, 1978.

Johari, J. C. *Patabi Sitaramawa's History of the Indian National Congress 1885–1947.* Abridged ed. Bombay: S. Chand, 1988.

Jones, Kenneth W. *Socio-Religious Reform Movements in British India.* Cambridge: Cambridge University Press, 1989.

Jones, Stephanie. *Merchants of the Raj.* London: Macmillan, 1992.

Joshi, Shashi. *The Struggle for Hegemony in India, 1920–1947: The Colonial State, the Left and the National Movement.* 3 vols. New Delhi: Sage, 1992.

Joshi, V. C., and B. R Nanda, eds. *Studies in Modern Indian History.* Bombay: Orient Longman, 1972.

Karlekar, Malavika. *Voices from Within: Early Personal Narratives of Bengali Women.* Delhi: Oxford University Press, 1991.

Kaul, Chandrika. *Reporting the Raj: The British Press and India 1880–1922.* Manchester: Manchester University Press, 2003.

Kaul, Suvir. *The Partitions of Memory: The Afterlife of the Division of India.* Bloomington: Indiana University Press, 2002.

Keay, John. *The Honourable Company: A History of the East India Company.* London: HarperCollins, 1991.

——. *A History of India:* New Delhi: HarperCollins, 2000.

Keer, Dharanjay. *Dr. Ambedkar: Life and Mission.* Bombay: Popular Prakashan, 1962.

———. *Veer Savarkar.* Bombay: Popular Prakashan, 1966.

Kerr, Ian J. *Railways in Modern India.* New Delhi: Oxford University Press, 2001.

———. *Building the Railways of the Raj 1860–1900.* Delhi: Oxford University Press, 1995.

Kulkarni, V. B. *The Indian Triumvirate: Political Biography of Mahatma Gandhi, Sardar Patel and Pandit Nehru.* Bombay: Bombay University Press, 1969.

Kumar, Dharrna, and Meghnad Desai, eds. *The Cambridge Economic History of India, Volume 11, c. 1757–1970.* Cambridge: Cambridge University Press, 1983.

Kumar, Ravinder. *The Social History of Modern India.* Delhi: Oxford University Press, 1983.

Lamb, Alastair. *The McMahon Line: A Study in the Relations between India, China and Tibet 1904–1914.* 2 vols. London: Routledge and Kegan Paul, 1966.

———. *Tibet, China and India, 1914–1950: A History of Imperial Diplomacy.* Hertingfordbury, UK: Roxford Books, 1989.

Lelyveld, David. *Aligarh's First Generation.* Princeton, NJ: Princeton University Press, 1977.

Lewis, Martin D. *The British in India: Imperialism or Trusteeship?* Lexington, MA: D. C. Heath, 1962.

Limaye, Madhu. *Indian National Movement: Its Ideological and Socio-Economic Dimensions.* New Delhi: Radiant, 1989.

Lourdusamy, J. *Science and National Consciousness in Bengal, 1870–1930.* New Delhi: Orient Longman, 2004.

Low, D. A., ed. *Congress and the Raj: Facets of the Indian Struggle 1917–1947.* London: Heinemann, 1977.

Ludden, David E. *Peasant History in South India.* Princeton: Princeton University Press, 1985.

———. *Marathas, Marauders, and State Formation in Eighteenth Century India.* New Delhi: Oxford University Press, 1994.

———. *An Agrarian History of South Asia.* Cambridge: Cambrdige University Press, 1999.

Lynton, Harriet R. *My Dear Nawab Saheb.* New Delhi: Orient Longman, 1991.

Mansergh, Nicholas, ed. *The Transfer of Power 1942–1947 (Official Documents).* 12 vols. London: HMSO, 1970–1983.

Markovits, Calude, ed. *A History of Modern India 1480–1950.* London: Wimbledon Publishing Company, 2002.

———. *The Ungandhian Gandhi: The Life and Afterlife of the Mahatma.* Delhi: Permanent Black, 2003.

Marshal, P. J. *Bengal: The British Bridgehead.* Cambridge: Cambridge University Press, 1987.

——, ed. *The Eighteenth Century in Indian History: Evolution or Revolution?* New Delhi: Oxford University Press, 2003.

Mason, Philip. *A Matter of Honour: An Account of the Indian Army, Its Officers and Men.* London: Jonathan Cape, 1974.

——. *A Shaft of Sunlight: Memoirs of a Varied Life.* London: Deutsch, 1978.

Masselos, J. *Nationalism on the Indian Subcontinent: An Introductory History.* Melbourne: T. Nelson, 1972.

Mehra, P. *The McMahon Line and after 1904–1947.* Delhi: Macmillan, 1974.

Mehrotra, S. R. *The Commonwealth and the Nation.* New Delhi: Vikas, 1978.

Menon, V. P. *The Transfer of Power in India.* Bombay: Orient Longmans, 1957.

——. *Integration of the Indian States.* Bombay: Orient Longmans, 1986.

Metcalfe, Barbara D., and Thomas R. Metcalfe. *A Concise History of India.* Cambridge: Cambridge University Press, 2002.

Metcalfe, T. R. *The Aftermath of Revolt in India, 1857–1870.* Princeton, NJ: Princeton University Press, 1964.

——, ed. *Modern India. An Interpretive Anthology.* London: Macmillan, 1971.

——. *Ideologies of the Raj.* Cambridge: Cambridge University Press, 1994.

Minault, Gail. *The Khilafet Movement: Religious Symbolism and Political Mobilization in India.* New York: Columbia University Press, 1982.

Misra, B. B. *The Indian Political Parties: An Historical Analysis of Political Behaviour up to 1947.* Delhi: Oxford University Press, 1976.

Moon, Penderel. *Divide and Quit.* London: Chatto, 1961.

——. *Warren Hastings and British India.* New York: Collier Books, 1962.

——. *The British Conquest and Dominion of India.* London: Duckworth, 1989.

Moore, R. J. *Liberalism and Indian Politics 1872–1922.* London: Edward Arnold, 1966.

——. *The Crisis of Indian Unity 1917–1940.* Oxford: Oxford University Press, 1974.

——. *Endgames of Empire: Studies of Britain's Indian Problem.* Delhi: Oxford University Press, 1988.

Mosley, Leonard. *The Last Days of the British Raj.* London: Weidenfeld & Nicolson, 1961.

Moulton, Edward C., ed. *Allan Octavian Hume: Father of the Indian National Congress, 1829– 1912* (Original publication by Sir William Wedderburn). New Delhi: Oxford University Press, 2002.

Mukherjee, Aditya. *Imperialism, Nationalism and the Making of the Indian Capitalist Class, 1920–1947.* New Delhi: Sage, 2002.

Mukherjee, Mridula. *Peasants in India's Non Violent Revolution.* New Delhi: Sage, 2004.

Nanda, B. R. *Motilal Nehru.* Delhi: Publications Division, Ministry of Information and Broadcasting, 1964.

——, ed. *Socialism in India.* New Delhi: Vikas, 1972.

——, ed. *Indian Women: From Purdah to Modernity.* New Delhi: Vikas, 1976.

——, ed. *Essays in Modern Indian History.* Delhi: Oxford University Press, 1980.

——. *In Gandhi's Footsteps: The Life and Times of Jamnalal Bajaj.* Delhi: Oxford University Press, 1990.

——. *Witness to Partition: A Memoir.* Delhi: Rupa & Co., 2003.

——. *Three Statesmen: Gokhale, Gandhi, Nehru.* New Delhi: Oxford University Press, 2004.

Narayan, J. P. *Socialism to Sarvodaya.* Madras: Socialist Book Centre, 1956.

Nargolkar, Vasant. *The Creed of Saint Vinoba.* Bombay: Bharatiya Vidya Bhavan, 1963.

Nehru, Jawaharlal. *Toward Freedom: The Autobiography of Jawaharlal Nehru.* New York: John Day, 1941.

Noorani, A. G. *Indian Political Trials.* New Delhi: Sterling, 1976.

Norman, Dorothy, ed. *Nehru: The First Sixty Years.* 2 vols. New York: John Day, 1965.

Omvedt, Gail. *Dalits and the Democratic Revolution: Dr. Ambedkar and the Dalit Movement in Colonial India.* New Delhi: Sage, 1994.

——. *Ambedkar: Towards and Enlightened India.* New Delhi: Penguin Viking Books, 2004.

Overstreet, Gene, and Marshall Windmiller. *Communism in India.* Bombay: Perennial Press, 1960.

Page, David. *Prelude to Pakistan: The Indian Muslims and the Imperial System of Control 1920—1932.* Delhi: Oxford University Press, 1982.

Pandey, B. N. *The Breakup of British India.* London: Macmillan, 1969.

——. *The Indian Nationalist Movement 1885–1947: Select Documents.* New York: St. Martin's Press, 1978.

Pandey, Gyanendra. *The Construction of Communalism in Colonial North India.* Delhi: Oxford University Press, 1990.

Panikkar, K. M. *Asia and Western Dominance.* New York: Collier Books, 1969.

Parekh, Bhikhu. *Colonialism, Tradition and Reform: An Analysis of Gandhi's Political Discourse.* New Delhi: Sage, 1999.

Pearson. M. N. *The Portugese in India.* Cambridge University Press, 1987.

Philips, C. H., ed. *The Evolution of India and Pakistan 1858–1947: Select Documents*. London: Oxford University Press, 1962.

——. *Politics and Society in India*. London: George Allen & Unwin, 1963.

Prakash, Om. *Bullion for Goods: Europeans and Indian Merchants in the Indian Ocean Trade 1500–1800*. New Delhi: Manohar, 2004.

Prasad, Bimal, ed. *A Revolutionary's Quest: Selected Writings of Jayaprakash Narayan*. Delhi: Oxford University Press, 1980.

Prasad, Bisheshwar. *Bondage and Freedom: A History of Modern India (1707–1947)*. 2 vols. New Delhi: Rajesh Publications, 1977.

Ramusack, Barbara N. *The Princes of India in the Twilight of Empire: Dissolution of a Patron-Client System, 1914–1939*. Columbus: Ohio State University Press, 1978.

Raychaudhuri, Tapan. *Europe Reconsidered: Perceptions of the West in 19th Century Bengal*. Delhi: Oxford University Press, 1988.

Renford, Raymond K. *The Non-Official British in India to 1920*. Delhi: Oxford University Press, 1987.

Rittenberg, Stephen. *Ethnicity, Nationalism and the Pukhtuns: The Independence Movement in India's N. W. F. P. 1929–1947*. Durham, NC: Carolina Academic Press, 1986.

Robinson, F. P. *The Trade of the East India Company 1709–1813*. Cambridge: Cambridge University Press, 1912.

Robinson, Francis. *Separatism among Indian Muslims: The Politics of the U. P. Muslims, 1860–1923*. Cambridge: Cambridge University Press, 1974.

Roy, M. N. *Memoirs*. Bombay: Allied, 1964.

——. *Selected Works*. 3 vols. Edited by S. Roy. Delhi: Oxford University Press, 1987–1990.

Sarkar, Sumit. *Modern India: 1885–1947*. Delhi: Macmillan, 1983.

——. *Beyond Nationalist Frames: Postmodernism, Hindu Fundamentalism, History*. Bloomington: Indiana University Press, 2002.

Seale, Anil. *The Emergence of Indian Nationalism: Competition and Collaboration in the Late 19th Century*. Cambridge: Cambridge University Press, 1968.

Shakir, M. *Khilafet to Partition*. New Delhi: Kalamkar Prakashan,1970.

Sharp, Gene. *Gandhi as a Political Strategist*. Boston: Porter Sargent, 1979.

Singh, Amar Kaur Jasbir. *Himalayan Triangle*. London: British Library, 1988.

Singh, Anita Inder. *The Origins of the Partition of India 1936–1947*. Delhi: Oxford University Press, 1987.

Singh, S. B. *Imperial Retreat: Impact of World War II on the Government of India*. Delhi: Pragati, 1992.

Singh, S. D. *Novels on the Indian Mutiny*. New Delhi: Arnold Heinemann, 1973.

Sisson, Richard, and Stanley Wolpert, eds. *Congress and Indian Nationalism: The Pre-Independence Phase.* Delhi: Oxford University Press, 1988.

Spangenberg, B. *British Bureaucracy in India: Status, Policy and the Indian Civil Service in the Late 19th Century.* New Delhi: Manohar, 1976.

Spear, T. G. Percival. *The Nabobs: A Study of the Social Life of the English in 18th Century India.* London: Oxford University Press, 1963.

———. *The Oxford History of Modern India 1740–1947.* Oxford: Oxford University Press, 1965.

———. *Twilight of the Mughuls: Studies in Late Mughul Delhi.* New Delhi: Oriental Books Reprint, 1969. Reprint of 1951 edition.

Stein, Burton, ed. *The Making of Agrarian Policy in British India 1770–1900.* New Delhi: Oxford University Press, 1992.

Stern, Robertha. *The Cat and the Lion: Jaipur State und the British Raj.* Leiden: Brill, 1988.

Stokes, E. *The Peasant and the Raj.* Cambridge: Cambridge University Press, 1978.

Subrahmanyam, Sanjay, ed. *Land Politics and Trade in South Asia.* New Delhi: Oxford University Press, 2004.

Thompson, E. J., and G. T. Garrett. *The Rise and Fulfillment of British Rule in India.* New York: AMS Press, 1971. Reprint of 1934 edition.

Thursby, G. R. *Hindu-Muslim Relations in British India: 1923–1928.* Leiden, The Netherlands: Brill, 1975.

Tirmizi, S. A. I. *Maulana Azad: A Pragmatic Statesman.* New Delhi: Commonwealth, 1991.

Verma, D. N. *India and the League of Nations.* Patna: Bharati Bhawan, 1968.

Whately, Monic, et al. *Condition of India: Being the Report of the Delegation Sent to India by the India League in 1932.* First published in 1934, reprinted in Delhi: Konark, 1999.

Wheeler, J. T. *Early Records of British India: A History of the English Settlements in India.* New York: Harper, 1972. First published in 1878.

Wolpert, Stanley A. *Tilak und Gokhale: Revolution and Reform in the Making of Modern India.* Berkeley: University of California Press, 1962.

———. *Jinnah of Pakistan.* New York: Oxford University Press, 1984.

Woodman, D. *Himalayan Frontiers: A Political Review of British, Chinese, Indian and Russian Rivalries.* New York: Barrie & Jenkins, 1970.

Woodruff, Philip. *The Men Who Ruled India, Volume I: The Founders.* London: Jonathan Cape, 1963.

———. *The Men Who Ruled India, Volume II: The Guardians.* London: Jonathan Cape, 1963.

Zaidi, A. M, and S. Zaidi. *The Encyclopedia of the Indian National Congress.* 18 vols. New Delhi: S. Chand, 1976–1992.

SCIENCE AND TECHNOLOGY

Astronomy and Mathematics

Chattopadhyaya, D. P. *Mathematics, Astronomy, and Biology in Indian Tradition: Some Conceptual Preliminaries.* New Delhi: History of Science Project, 1995.

Dikshit, S. B. *History of Indian Astronomy.* English translation of 3 volumes of Sanskrit text. New Delhi: Publications Division, 1969.

Indian Astronomy and Astrology. Library of Congress, microfilm, 1993.

Indian Space Research Organization. *Astronomy and Astrophysics in India: A Profile for the 1980s.* Bangalore: ISRO, 1982.

Jhunjhunwala, Ashok. *Indian Mathematics: An Introduction.* New Delhi: Wiley Eastern, 1993.

Manchanda P., et al., eds. *Current Trends in Industrial and Applied Mathematics.* New Delhi: Anamaya Publishers, 2002.

Rao, S. Balachandra. *Indian Astronomy: An Introduction.* Hyderabad: Universities Press, 2000.

———. *Indian Mathematics and Astronomy: Some Landmarks.* Bangalore: Jnana Deep Publishers, 1998.

Sarma, K. V. "Astronomy in India: Vedic Period." *VIJ* 14 (1) (1976): 133–152.

Sen, S. N., ed. *A Bibliography of Sanskrit Works on Astronomy and Mathematics.* New Delhi: National Institute of Science, 1966.

Sen, S. N., and K. S. Shukla. *History of Astronomy in India.* New Delhi: National Science Academy, 2000.

Somayaji, D. A. *A Critical Study of the Ancient Hindu Astronomy in the Light and Language of the Modern.* Dharwar: Karnatak University, 1971.

Subbarayappa, B. V., and K. V. Sarma. *Indian Astronomy: A Source Book Based Primarily on Sanskrit Texts.* Bombay: Nehru Centre, 1985.

Geography, Geology, Environment, and Natural History

Akhtar, Rais. *Contemporary Approaches to Indian Geography.* New Delhi: APH Publishing, 1997.

Ali, Salim A. *The Book of Indian Birds.* 10th ed. Bombay: Bombay Natural History Society, 1977.

Baskaran, S. Theodore. *The Dance of the Sarus: Essays of a Wandering Naturalist.* New Delhi: Oxford University Press, 1999.

Basu, Asok. *The Himalayas: A Classified Social Scientific Bibliography.* Calcutta: K. P. Bagchi, 1987.

Calcutta Journal of Natural History. Dehra Dun: International Book Distributors, 1985.

Cubitt, Gerald S. *Wild India: The Wildlife and Scenery of India and Nepal.* Cambridge, MA: MIT Press, 1991.

Das, P. K. *The Monsoons.* New Delhi: National Book Trust, 1968.

Dayal, Maheshwar. *Renewable Energy: Environment and Development.* Delhi: Konarak, 1989.

Dey, A. K. *Geology of India.* New Delhi: National Book Trust, 1968.

Gadgil, Madhav. *Ecological Journeys: The Science and Politics of Conservation in India.* New Delhi: Permanent Black, 2001.

Gadgil, Madhav, and Ramachandra Guha. *Use and Abuse of Nature.* Oxford: Oxford University Press, 2000.

Gadgil, Madhav, and P. R. Seshagiri Rao. *Nurturing Biodiversity: An Indian Agenda.* Ahmedabad: Centre for Environmental Education, 1998.

Geology and Mineral Resources of the States of India. Rev. ed. Calcutta: Director General, Geological Survey of India. Since 1999.

Gopalakrishnan, R., and Ali Ahmad, eds. *Essays in Indian Geography: Continuity of Taditions.* New Delhi: Regency Publications, 2001.

Hillary, Sir Edmund. *High Adventure: Our Ascent to Everest.* New Delhi: Roli Books, 1955.

Journal of Human Ecology. Delhi: Kamla Raj Enterprises, 1990.

Kapur, Anu. *Indian Geography: Voice of Concern.* New Delhi: Concept Publishing, 2002.

Khoshoo, T. N. *Environmental Concerns and Strategies.* New Delhi: Indian Environmental Society, 1984.

Lall, John S., and A. D. Moddia, eds. *The Himalaya: Aspects of Change.* Delhi: Oxford University Press, 1981.

Misra, S. D. *Rivers of India.* New Delhi: National Book Trust, 1970.

Parikh, Jyoti, and Hemant Datye, eds. *Sustainable Management of Wetlands: Biodiversity and Beyond.* New Delhi: Sage, 2003.

Rangarajan, Mahesh. *India's Wildlife History: An Introduction.* Delhi: Permanent Black, 2001.

Ripley, S. D., ed. *A Bundle of Feathers: Proferred to Salim Ali on His 75th Birthday in 1971.* Delhi: Oxford University Press, 1978.

Saberwal, Vasant, Mahesh Rangarajan, and Ashish Kothari. *People, Parks and Wildlife: Towards Coexistence.* New Delhi: Orient Longman Ltd., 2001.

Spate, O. H. K., and A. T. A. Learmonth. *India, Pakistan and Ceylon: The Region.* 3rd rev. ed. London: Methuen, 1972.

Venables, Stephen. *Everest: Summit of Achievement.* London: Royal Geographical Society, 2003.

Health and Medicine

Arnold, David. *Science, Technology and Medicine in Colonial India.* Cambridge University Press, 2000.

Bagchi, A. K. *Sanskrit and Modern Medical Vocabulary: A Comparative Study.* Calcutta: Riddhi, 1978.

Bajaj, S. *Medical Education and Health Care.* Shimla: Indian Institute for Advanced Study, 1998.

Bose, Kartick Chandra. *Pharmacopeia Indica.* Dehra Dun: Bishen Singh Mahendra Pal Singh, 1984.

Chauhan, Devraj, et al. *Health Care in India: A Profile.* Mumbai: Foundation for Research in Community Health, 1997.

Dalal, Nargis. *Yoga for Rejuvenation.* New York: Thorsons Publishers, 1984.

Deodhar, N. S. *Health Situation in India, 2000.* New Delhi: Voluntary Health Association of India, 2001.

Douglas, N. *Tantra Yoga.* New Delhi: Munshiram Manoharlal, 1971.

Eliade, M. *Yoga: Immortality and Freedom.* Princeton, NJ: Princeton University Press, 1973.

Gupta, Monica Das, and Manju Rani. *India's Public Health Care System: How Well Does It Function at the National Level.* Washington, DC: World Bank, 2004.

India, Ministry of Health and Family Welfare. *Major Schemes and Programmes.* New Delhi: Government of India, 2000.

Indian Journal of the History of Medicine. Madras, 1956–1962.

Jaggi, O. P. *Medicine in India: Modern Period.* New Delhi: Oxford University Press, 2000.

Johari, Harish. *Ancient Indian Massage: Traditional Massage Techniques Based on Ayurveda.* New Delhi: Munshiram Manoharlal, 1984.

Kakar, Sudhir. *Shamans, Mystics and Doctors.* New York: Knopf, 1982.

Kamble, N. D. *Rural Health.* New Delhi: Ashish, 1984.

Keswani, N. H. *The Science of Medicine and Physiological Concepts in Ancient and Medieval India.* New Delhi: Manchanda, 1974.

Mahajan, B. K. *Preventive Medicine in India.* Jamnagar: Aruna B. Mahajan, 1968.

Mathur, Hari Mohun. *The Family Welfare Programme in India.* New Delhi: Vikas, 1995.

Mishra, Lakshmi Chandra, ed. *Scientific Basis for Ayurvedic Therapies.* Boca Raton, FL: CRC Press, 2004.

Narain, Jai P. *AIDS in Asia: The Challenge Ahead.* New Delhi: Sage, 2004.

Panda, Samiran, Anindya Chatterjee, and Abu S Abdul-Quader, eds. *Living with the AIDS Virus: The Epidemic and the Response in India.* New Delhi: Sage, 2002.

Pande, Mrinal. *Stepping Out: Life and Sexuality in Rural India.* New Delhi: Penguin Books, 2003.

Pati, Bisamoy, and Mark Harrison, eds. *Health, Medicine and Empire: Perspectives on Colonial India.* Hyderabad: Orient Longman, 2001.

Raghuran, Shobha. *Health and Equity, Effecting Change.* Bangalore: Humanist Institute, 2001.

Ray, P. C. "Origin and Tradition of Alchemy." *IJHS* 2 (1) (1967): 1–21.

Razzack, Muhammed Abdur. *Unani System of Medicine in India: A Profile.* New Delhi: Central Council for Research and Unani Medicine, 2000.

Report of the Independent Commission on Health in India. New Delhi: Voluntary Health Association of India, 1997.

Roy-Chaudhuri, Ranjit. *Traditional Medicine in Asia.* New Delhi: World Health Organization, 2002.

Sanjivi, K. S. *Planning India's Health, Updated 1988.* Madras: Chidambaram Institute of Community Health, 1988.

Sankaran, P. S. *Sushrutu's Contribution to Surgery.* Varanasi: Indian Book House, 1976.

Sanyal, P. K. *A Story of Medicine and Pharmacy in India.* Calcutta: A. Sanyal, 1964.

Sen, Ragini. *We the Billion: A Social Psychological Perspective on India's Population.* New Delhi: Sage, 2003.

Shanna, S., ed. *Realms of Ayurveda.* New Delhi: Arnold Heinemann, 1979.

Sharma, Hari M. *Contemporary Ayurveda.* New York: Churchill Livingstone, 1998.

Williamson, Elizabeth M., ed. *Major Herbs of Ayurveda.* New York: Churchill Livingstone, 2002.

Wise, Thomas. *Commentary on the Hindu System of Medicine as Embodied in Sanskrit Literature.* Amsterdam: APA-Oriental Press, 1981.

Wood, E. *Yogu. An Explanation of the Practices and Philosophy of Indian Yoga.* Baltimore: Penguin, 1968.

World Bank. *Child and Maternal Health Services in Rural India: The Narangwal Experiment.* Baltimore: Johns Hopkins University Press, 1984.

Zimmer, H. R. *Hindu Medicine.* Baltimore: Johns Hopkins University Press, 1947.

Science and Technology

Bhardwaj, H. C. *Aspects of Ancient Indian Technology. A Research Based on Scientific Methods.* Delhi: Motilal, 1979.

Bhargava, Pushpa Mitra. *The Saga of Indian Science Since Independence.* Hyderabad: Universities Press, 2003.

Birla Institute of Scientific Research. *India and the Atom.* New Delhi: Allied, 1982.

Bose, D. M., ed. *Science and Society in Ancient India.* Calcutta: Research India, 1977.

Chakravarty, A. K. "Origin and Development of Indian Calendrial Science." *ISPP* 15 (3) (1974): 219–280.

Charbanda, V. P., and Ashok Jain, eds. *Science and Technology Strategies for Development in India and China: A Comparative Study.* New Delhi: Har Anand, 1999.

Chellaney, Brahma. *Nuclear Proliferation: The U. S.–Indian Conflict.* Hyderabad: Orient Longman, 1993.

Dagli, Vadidad, ed. *Science and Development.* Bombay: Orient Longmans, 1976.

Dharampal. *Indian Science and Technology in the Eighteenth Century.* Delhi: Impex, 1971.

Dikshit, M. G. *History of Indian Glass.* Bombay: University of Bombay Press, 1969.

Franda, Marcus. *China and India Online: Information Technology: Politics and Diplomacy.* Lanham, MD: Rowman & Littlefield, 2002.

Gill, S. S. *The Information Revolution and India: A Critique.* New Delhi: Rupa & Co., 2004.

Haldane, J. B. S. *Science and Indian Culture.* Calcutta: New Age, 1965.

Heitzman, James. *Network City: Planning the Information Society in Bangalore.* New Delhi: Oxford University Press, 2004.

Indian Institute of Technology, Delhi. *Science and Technology: Perspectives.* New Delhi: Oxford, 1986.

Keniston, Kenneth, and Deepak Kumar, eds. *IT Experience in India: Bridging the Digital Divide.* New Delhi: Sage, 2004.

Kulkarni, R. P., and V. Sarma. *Homi Bhabha: Gather of Nuclear Science in India.* Bombay: Popular, 1969.

Lal, Mukut Behari. *India's Technology Gap.* Calcutta: Statesman, 1984.

Mehta, D. D. *Positive Sciences in the Vedas.* New Delhi: Arnold Heineman, 1974.

Menon, M. G. K. *Selected Speeches and Writings.* New Delhi: Council of Scientific and Industrial Research, 1988.

Mishra, D. K. *Five Eminent Scientists: Their Lives and Works.* Delhi: Kalyani, 1976.

Nanda, B. R., ed. *Science and Technology in India.* New Delhi: Vikas, 1977.

Narlikar, Jayant V. *The Scientific Edge: The Indian Scientists from Vedic to Modern Times.* New Delhi: Penguin, 2003.

Nayar, B. K., ed. *Science and Development.* Bombay: Orient Longmans, 1976.

Nigam, J. K. *Indian Science: Era of Stabilization.* New Delhi: Wiley Eastern, 1990.

Prasad, Rajeshwar, ed. *Science, Technology and Rural Development.* Agra: Aadhar Welfare Society, 1993.

"Profiles of Science." *Seminar.* Special Issues, 238 (1979).

Rahman, A. *Science and Technology in India.* New Delhi: National Institute of Science, 1984.

Sarabhai, Vikram. *Science Policy and National Development.* Delhi: Macmillan, 1974.

Saraswati, Swami Satya Prakash. *Founders of Science in Ancient India.* 2 vols. Delhi: Govindram Hasanand, 1986.

Science Advisory Council to the Prime Minister. *Perspectives in Science and Technology.* 2 vols. Delhi: Har Anand, 1990.

Science and Its Impact on Society: Indian Experience. Proceedings of a Seminar Organized by the Indian National Science Academy. New Delhi: National Science Academy, 1978.

Sharma, L. K., and Sima Sharma, eds. *Innovative India.* London: Medialand, 1999.

Srivastava, P. N. *Science in India, Excellence and Accountability.* New Delhi: Angkor Publications, 1994.

Srivastava, U. S. *Glimpses of Science in India.* New Delhi: Malhorta Publishing House, 1991.

Subbarayappa, B. V. *In Pursuit of Excellence: A History of the Indian Institute of Science.* New Delhi: Tata McGraw Hill, 1992.

Suleiman, N. A. *India, Germany, and France: Issues in Technological Cooperation.* Delhi: Kalinga Publishers, 2001.

SOCIETY, EDUCATION, AND RELIGION

Society and Education

Agnihotri, Satish Balram. *Sex Ratio Patterns in the Indian Population: A Fresh Exploration.* New Delhi: Sage, 2000.

Ahmad, Imtiaz, ed. *Family, Kinship, and Marriage Among Muslims in India.* New Delhi: Manohar, 1976.

Anand, Satyapal. *University without Walls: The Indian Perpsective in Correspondence Education.* New Delhi: Vikas, 1979.

Anthony, Frank. *Britain's Betrayal of India: The Story of the Anglo–Indian Community.* Bombay: Allied Publishers, 1969.

Assayag, Jackie, and Veronique Beneri, eds. *At Home in the Diaspora.* Bloominton: Indiana University Press, 2003.

Atal, Y. *Social Sciences: The Indian Scene.* New Delhi: Abhinav, 1976.

Ballhatchet, Kenneth, and John Harrison, eds. *The City in South Asia: Premodern and Modern.* Atlantic Highlands, NJ: Humanities Press, 1981.

Barnett, Margaret Rose. *The Politics of Cultural Nationalism in South Asia.* Princeton, NJ: Princeton University Press, 1976.

Bayley, Susan. *Caste, Society and Politics in India from the Eighteenth Century to the Modern Age.* Cambridge University Press, 1999.

Berreman, Gerald D. *Caste and Other Inequities: Essays on Inequality.* Meerut: Folklore Institute, 1979.

Beteille, Andre. *The Backward Classes in Contemporary India.* Delhi: Oxford University Press, 1992.

———. *Caste, Class and Power: Changing Patterns of Social Stratification in a Tanjore Village.* Second Edition. New Delhi: OUP, 1996.

———. *Antimonies of Society.* New Delhi: Oxford University Press, 2000.

———. *Chronicles of Our Time.* New Delhi: Penguin, 2000.

Beteille, Andre, ed. *Equality and Inequality: Theory and Practice.* New Delhi: Oxford University Press, 1983.

Bhasin, M. K., et al. *People of India.* Delhi: Kamia Raj Enterprises, 1994.

Bhattacharya, Rinki. *Behind Closed Doors: Domestic Violence in India.* New Delhi: Sage, 2004.

Borden, Carla M., ed. *Contemporary Indian Tradition: Voices on Culture, Nature, and the Challenges of Change.* Washington, DC: Smithsonian Institution Press, 1989.

Brass, Paul. *The Production of Hindu–Muslim Violence in Contemporary India.* New Delhi: Oxford University Press, 2003.

Brown, Judith M., and Robert E. Frykenberg, eds. *Christians, Cultural Interactions, and India's Religious Traditions.* London: RoutledgeCurzon, 2002.

Bubb, Lawrence A. *Alchemies of Violence: Myths of Identity and the Life of Trade in Western India.* New Delhi: Sage, 2004.

Butalia, Urvashi. *The Other Side of Silence: Voices from the Partition of India.* New Delhi: Penguin Books, 1998.

Carstairs, G. Morris. *The Twice Born: A Study of a Community of High Caste Hindus.* Bloomington: University of Indiana Press, 1961.

Chatterjee, Indrani, ed. *Unfamilial Relations: Family and History in South Asia.* 2004.

Chatterjee, Partha, and Pradeep Jeganathan, eds. *Subaltern Studies 11: Community, Gender, and Violence.* London: Hurst, 2000.

Chatterji, K. K. *English Education in India: Issues and Opinions.* Delhi: Macmillan, 1976.

Checki, D. A. *The Sociology of Contemporary India.* New Delhi: Sterling, 1978.

Chen, Martha Alter. *Widows in India: Social Neglect and Public Action.* New Delhi: Sage, 1998.

Chitnis, Seema, and Philip Altbach. *The Indian Academic Professional.* Columbia, MO: South Asia Books, 1979.

Cohn, Bernard S. *India: The Social Anthropology of a Civilization.* Englewood Cliffs, NJ: Prentice-Hall, 1971.

Corbridge, Suart Sarah Jewitt, and Sanjay Kumar. *Jharkhand: Environment, Development, Ethnicity.* New Delhi: Oxford University Press, 2004.

Critchfield, Richard. *The Villagers: Changed Values, Altered Lives: The Closing of the Urban-Rural Gap.* New York: Anchor Books, 1994.

Das, Monic. *Her Story So Far: Tales of the Girl Child in India.* Delhi: Penguin India, 2003.

Datta, V. N. *Sati: Widow Burning in India.* New Delhi: Manohar, 1988.

Desai, A. R. *Social Background of Indian Nationalism.* Bombay: Popular Prakashan, 1966.

Docker, E. L. *History of Indian Cricket.* Delhi: Macmillan of India, 1976.

Dube, Leela, Eleanor Leacock, and Shirley Ardener, eds. *Visibility and Power: Essays on Women in Society and Development.* Delhi: Oxford University Press, 1986.

Dube, Siddharth, ed., *Hindus and Others: The Question of Identity in India Today.* New Delhi: Viking, 1993.

———. *Words Like Freedom: The Memoirs of an Impoverished Indian Family, 1947–97.* New Delhi: HarperCollins, 1998.

Dube, S. C., ed. *Tribal Heritage in India.* 4 vols. New Delhi: Vikas, 1977–1981.

Dubois, Abbe J. A. *Hindu Manners, Customs and Ceremonies.* 3rd ed. reprinted. Oxford: Clarendon Press, 1906.

Dumont, Louis. *Homo Hierarchicus.* Chicago: University of Chicago Press, 1970. *Marriage Alliance in South India, with Comparative Essays on Australia.* Chicago: University of Chicago Press, 1983.

Engineer, Ashgar ali. *The Gujarat Carnage.* New Delhi: Orient Longman, 2003.

Forbes, Geraldine. *Women in Modern India. The New Cambridge History of India, iv. 2.* Cambridge: University Press, 1996.

Franda, Marcus. *Voluntary Associations and Local Development in India.* New Delhi: Young Asia, 1983.

Frykenberg, R. E., ed. *Delhi through the Ages: Essays in Urban History, Culture and Society.* Delhi: Oxford University Press, 1986.

Fuchs, Stephen. *The Aboriginal Tribes of India*. New York: St. Martin's, 1973.

Furer-Haimendorf, Christoph von. *Tribes of India. The Struggle for Survival*. Berkeley: University of California Press, 1982.

Gandhi, Nandita, and Nandita Shah. *The Issues at Stake: Theory and Practice in the Contemporary Women's Movement in India,* Delhi: Kali for Women, 1992.

Ghosh, B. *Profiles of Social Change*. New Delhi: Oxford and IBH, 1979.

Ghurye, G. S. *The Scheduled Tribes of India*. New Brunswick: Transaction Books, 1980.

Gilbert, William Harlem, Jr. *Peoples of India*. Washington, DC: The Smithsonian Institution, War Background Studies, no. 4, 1944.

Gottschalk, Peter. *Beyond Hindu and Muslim: Multiple Identity in Narratives from Village India*. Oxford University Press, 2000.

Govinda, R., and Rashmi Diwan, eds. *Community Participation and Empowerment in Primary Education*. New Delhi: Sage, 2003.

Guha, Ramachandra. *A Corner of a Foreign Field: The Indian History of a British Sport*. London: Picador, 2002.

Gupta, Dipankar, ed. *Interrogating Caste: Understanding Hierarchy and Difference in Indian Society*. New Delhi: Penguin, 2000.

———. *Caste in Question: Identity or Hierarchy?* New Delhi: Sage, 2004.

Gupta, Giri Raj, ed. *Contemporary India: Some Sociological Perspectives*. Delhi: Vikas, 1976.

———. *Main Currents in Indian Sociology: Cohesion and Conflict in Modern India*. Durham, NC: Carolina Academic Press, 1978.

Hancock, Mary. *Womanhood in the Making: Domestic Ritual and Public Culture in Urban South India*. Boulder, CO: Westview, 1999.

Hardy, Peter. *Muslims of British India*. Cambridge: South Asia Studies, no. 13, 1972.

Hasan, Mushirul, ed. *Inventing Boundaries: Gender, Politics and the Partition of India*. New Delhi: OUP, 2000.

Hasan, Zoya. *Forging Identities: Gender, Communities and the State*. New Delhi: Kali for Women, 1994.

Hasan, Zoya, and Ritu Menon. *Unequal Citizens: A Study of Muslim Women in India*. New Delhi: Oxford University Press, 2004.

Hawley, John, ed. *New Light on Suttee*. New York: Oxford University Press, 1992.

Hussain, Zakir. *Educational Reconstruction in India*. New Delhi: Publications Division, Ministry of Information and Broadcasting, 1969.

Huyler, Stephen P. *Village India*. New York: Harry N. Abrams, 1985.

India (Republic of) University Grants Commission. *Development of Higher Education in India: A Policy Frame.* New Delhi: University Grants Commission, 1978.

Indian Council of Social Science Research. *Journal of Abstracts and Reviews: Sociology and Social Anthropology.* New Delhi: ICSSR, 1971 onward, semi-annually.

Jayapal, Pramila. *Pilgrimage: One Woman's Return to a Changing India.* Seattle: Seal Press, 2000.

Kakar, Sudhir. *The Inner World: A Psychoanalytic Study of Childhood and Society in India.* Delhi: Oxford University Press, 1978.

———. *Intimate Relations: Exploring Indian Sexuality.* New Delhi: Viking, 1989.

———. *The Colours of Violence.* New Delhi: Penguin, 1996.

Kakar, Sudhir, and Jonathan P. Perry, eds. *Institutions and Inequalities: Essays in Honour of Andre Beteille.* New Delhi: Oxford University Press, 1999.

Kamble, J. R. *Pursuit of Equality in Indian History.* Delhi: National Publishing House, 1985.

Karlekar, Malavika, ed. *Paradigms of Learning: The Total Literacy Campaign in India.* New Delhi: Sage, 2004.

Karve, Irawati. *Kinship Organization in India.* New York: Asia, 1968.

Kaul, J. N., ed. *Higher Education, Social Change and National Development.* Simla: Indian Institute of Advanced Study, 1975.

Keay, F. E. *A History of Education in India and Pakistan.* 4th ed. London: Oxford University Press, 1964.

Kelkar, Govind, Dev Nathan, and Pierre Walker. *Gender Relations in Forest Society in Asia: Patriarchy at Odds.* New Delhi: Sage, 2003.

Kenrick, Donald. *Gypasies: From the Ganges to the Thames.* Hatfield, UK: University of Hertfordshire Press, 2004.

Khare, R. S. *Culture and Democracy: Anthropological Reflections on Modern India.* Lanham, MD: University Press of America, 1985.

Kirpal, Prem. *A Decade of Education in India.* Delhi: Indian Book Co., 1968.

Kohli, Shanta. *Family Planning in India: A Descriptive Analysis.* New Delhi: Institute of Public Administration, 1977.

Kolenda, Pauline. *Caste in Contemporary India: Beyond Organic Solidarity.* Prospect Heights, IL: Waveland Press, 1985.

Kolff, Dirk H. A. *Naukar, Rajput and Sepoy: The Ethnohistory of the Military Labour Market in Hindustan 1450–1850.* Cambridge: Cambridge University Press, 1990.

Ling, Trevor. *Buddhist Revival in India: Aspects of the Sociology of Buddhism.* New York: St. Martin's, 1980.

MacMillan, Margaret Olwen. *Women of the Raj*. New York: Thames and Hudson, 1988.

Mahar, J. Michael, ed. *The Untouchables in Contemporary India*. Tucson,: University of Arizona Press, 1972.

Majumdar, Boria. *Twenty Two Yards to Freedom: A Social History of Indian Cricket*. New Delhi: Penguin, 2004.

Mandelbaum, David G. *Society in India: Continuity and Change*. Vols. I and II. Berkeley: University of California Press, 1970.

———. *Woman's Seclusion and Man's Honor: Sex Roles and Their Consequences in North India, Pakistan and Bangladesh*. Tuscon: The University of Arizona Press, 1988.

Manohar, K. Murali. *Socio-Economic Status of Indian Women*. Delhi: Seema, 1983.

Mendelsohn, Oliver, and Marka Vicziany. *The Untouchables: Subordination, Poverty and the State in Modern India*. Cambridge: Cambridge University Press, 1998.

Menon, Ritu. *Women Who Dared*. New Delhi: National Book Trust, 2002.

———, ed. *No Woman's Hand: Women from Pakistan, India and Bangladesh Write on the Partition of India*. Delhi: Women Unlimited, 2004.

Menon, Ritu, and Kamla Bhasin. *Borders and Boundaries: Women in India's Partition*. New Brunswick, NJ: Rutgers University Press, 1998.

Miri, Sujata. *Religion and Society of North Fast India*. New Delhi: Vikas, 1960.

Misra, Amalendu. *Identity and Religion: Foundations of Anti-Islamism in India*. New Delhi: Sage, 2004.

Moon, Vasant. *Growing Up Untouchable in India: A Dalit Autobiography*. New Delhi: Sage, 2002.

Mukerji, S. N. *Secondary Education in India*. New Delhi: Orient Longman, 1972.

Mukherjee, Sujit. *Autobiography of an Unknown Cricketer*. Delhi: Ravi Dayal, 1996.

Nabar, Vrinda. *Caste as Woman*. New York: Penguin Books, 1995.

Nagaich, Sangeeta. *Changing Status of Women in India*. Vedam Books, 1997.

Nanda, Reena. *Kamaladevi Chattopadhyaya: A Biography*. New Delhi: Oxford University Press, 2002.

Nandy, Ashis. *At the Edge of Psychology: Essays in Politics and Culture*. Delhi: Oxford University Press, 1980.

———. *Tradition, Tyranny and Utopia: Essays in the Politics of Awareness*. Delhi: Oxford University Press, 1987.

———. *The Bonfire of Creeds*. Delhi: Oxford University Press, 2004.

Narasimhan, Sakuntala. *Empowering Women: an Alternate Strategy from Rural India*. New Delhi: Sage, 1999.

National Institute of Educational Planning and Administration [Republic of India]. *Some Basic Facts about Educational Administration in India.* New Delhi: National Institute of Educational Planning and Administration, 1979.

O'Flaherty, Wendy D., ed. *Karma and Rebirth in Classical Indian Traditions.* Berkeley: University of California Press, 1980.

Panandikar, V. A. Pai, et al. *Family Planning under the Emergency: Policy Implications of Incentives and Disincentives.* New Delhi: Radiant, 1978.

Pant, A. R. *On Sanskrit Education.* Khatmandu: Pant, 1979.

Pathak, S. *Social Welfare, Health and Family Planning in India.* New Delhi: Marwah, 1979.

Poffenberger, Thomas. "Fertility and Family Life in an Indian Village." *Michigan Papers no. 10.* Ann Arbor: University of Michigan, 1975.

Ray, Rajat Kanta. *The Felt Community.* New Delhi: OUP, 2003.

Rao, M. S. A., ed. *Social Movements in India.* New Delhi: Manohar, 1978.

Robinson, Rowena. *Christians of India.* New Delhi: Sage, 2003.

——, ed. *Sociology of Religion in India.* New Delhi: Sage, 2004.

Roy, Beth. *Bullock Carts and Motorbikes; Ancient India on a New Road.* New York: Atheneum, 1972.

Saini, Shiv Kumar. *Development of Education in India: Socio-Economic and Political Perspectives.* New Delhi: Cosmo, 1980.

Sakala, Carol. *Women of South Asia: A Guide to Resources.* New York: Kraus International Publications, 1980.

Sarkar, Tanika. *Hindu Wife, Hindu Nation: Community, Religion and Cultural Nationalism.* Bloomington: Indiana University Press, 2001.

Sarkar, Tanaka, and Urvashi Butalia, eds. *Women and the Hindu Right.* New Delhi: Kali for Women, 1995.

Schermerhorn, R. A. *Ethnic Plurality in India.* Tuscon: University of Arizona Press, 1978.

Sen, Giti, ed. *Indigenous Vision: Peoples of India Attitudes to the Environment.* New Delhi: India International Centre Quarterly, Summer 1992.

Seth, Mira. *Women and Development: The Indian Experience.* New Delhi: Sage, 2001.

Shah, Ghanshyam. *Social Movements in India: A Review of Literature.* New Delhi: Sage, 2004.

Sharma, Ursula. *Women, Work and Property in North–West India.* London: Tavistock, 1980.

Shukla, P. D. *Towards a New Pattern of Education in India.* New Delhi: Sterling, 1976.

Singer, M. B. *When a Great Tradition Modernizes: An Anthropological Approach to Indian Civilization.* New York: Praeger, 1972.

Singh, Amrik. *Fifty Years of Higher Education in India: The Role of the University Grants Commission.* New Delhi: Oxford University Press, 2004.

Singh, Amrik, and P. G. Altbach, eds. *The Higher Learning in India.* New Delhi: Vikas, 1974.

Singh, K. S., ed. for Anthropological Survey of India. *People of India.* National Series, 10 vols. New Delhi: Oxford University Press, 1990–1994.

———. *Tribal Movements in India.* New Delhi: Manohar, 1983.

Singh, Yogendra. *Social Change in India: Crisis and Resilience.* New Delhi: Har Anand, 1993.

———. *Society and Politics in India.* London: Athlone, 1991.

Sooryamoorthy, R., and K. D. Gangrade. *NGOs in India: A Cross-Sectional Study.* Westport, CT: Greenwood, 2001.

Srinivas, M. N. *Religion and Society among the Coorgs of South India,* Oxford: Oxford University Press, 1952.

———. *Social Change in Modern India.* Berkeley: University of California Press, 1966.

———. *The Remembered Village.* Berkeley: University of California Press, 1976.

———. *The Idea of Natural Inequality and Other Essays.* New Delhi: Oxford University Press, 1983.

———. *The Cohesive Role of Sanskritization and Other Essays.* Delhi: Oxford University Press, 1989.

———. *The Dominant Caste and Other Essays.* Delhi: Oxford University Press, 1989.

Srinivas, M. N., ed. *Caste: Its Twentieth Century Avatar.* New York: Penguin, 1996.

Sunder Rajan, Rajeshwari. *The Scandal of the State: Women, Law and Citizenship in Post Colonial India.* Delhi: Permanent Black, 2003.

Thorner, Daniel. *The Shaping of Modern India.* Delhi: Allied, 1980.

Troisi, J. *Tribal Religion: Religious Beliefs and Practices among the Santals.* Columbia, MO: South Asia Books, 1979.

Universities Handbook: India. New Delhi: Association of Indian Universities, 1958 onwards.

Van der Veer, Peter. *Religious Nationalism: Hindus and Muslims in India.* Berkeley: University of California Press, 1994.

Varma, E. *Basic Education in India: Its Origins and Development.* Patna: Nagari Prakashan, 1962.

Varshney, Ashutosh. *Ethnic Conflict and Civic Life: Hindus and Muslims in India.* New Haven, CT: Yale University Press, 2002.

Vatuk, Sylvia. *Kinship and Urbanization: White Collar Migrants in North India.* Berkeley: University of California Press, 1972.

Viramma, Josiane Racine, and Jean-Luc Racine. *Viramma: Life of a Dalit*. New Delhi: Social Science Press, 2000.

Wiebe, Paul D. *Social Life in an Indian Slum*. Delhi: Vikas, 1975.

Wirsing, Robert G. *Socialist Society and Free Enterprise Politics: A Study of Voluntary Associations in Urban India*. Durham, NC: Carolina Academic Press, 1977.

Wiser, Charlotte V. *Four Families of Karimpur*. Syracuse, NY: Syracuse University Press, 1978.

Yadav, C. S. *Land Use in Big Cities: A Study of Delhi*. Delhi: Inter-India, 1979.

Zakaria, Rafiq. *Communal Rage in Secular India*. Mumbai: Popular Prakashan, 2002.

Philosophy and Religion

Ahmed, Aziz. *An Intellectual History of Islam in India*. Edinburgh: Edinburgh University Press, 1969.

Appadurai, Arjun. *Worship and Conflict under Colonial Rule: A South Indian Case*. Cambridge University Press, 1981.

Ashby, Philip H. *Modern Trends in Hinduism*. New York: Columbia University Press, 1974.

Banerjee, Himadri. *The Khalsa and the Punjab: Studies in Sikh History to the 19th Century*. Delhi: Indian History Congress, 2002.

Bhattacharya, N. N. *The Indian Mother Goddess*. New Delhi: Manohar, 1977.

Boyce, Mary. *Zoroasterians: Their Religious Beliefs and Practices*. New York: RoutledgeCurzon, 2000.

Brent, P. *Godmen of India*. New York: Quadrangle, 1972.

Brown, Robert L., ed. *Ganesh: Studies of an Asian God*. Albany: State University of New York Press, 1991.

Chaudhuri, N. C. *Hinduism, A Religion to Live By*. New York: Oxford University Press, 1979.

Cole, W. Owen. *The Guru in Sikhism*. London: Darton, Longman and Todd, 1982.

Conze, Edward. *Buddhism, Its Essence and Development*. New York: Philosophical Library, 1951.

Damodaran, K. *Indian Thought: A Critical Survey*. Bombay: Asia, 1967.

de Bary, William Theodore, et al., eds. *Sources of Indian Tradition*. 2 vols. New York: Columbia University Press, 1958.

Doniger, Wendy, ed. *Concept of Duty in South Asia,* New Delhi: Vikas, 1978.

——. *Karma and Rebirth in Classical Indian Tradition*. Berkeley, CA: University of California Press, 1980.

——. *Hindu Myths: A Sourcebook Translated from the Sanskrit*. London: Penguin, 2004.

———. *The Woman Who Pretended to Be Who She Was: Myths of Self-Imitation.* New York: Oxford University Press, 2005.

Doniger, Wendy, and Sudhir Kakar. *Critical Study of Sacred Texts.* Berkeley, CA: Graduate Theological Union, 1979.

———. *Kamasutra.* Philadelphia: Miniature edition, 2000.

Dube, Ishita Banerjee. *Divine Affairs: Religion, Pilgrimage, and the State in Colonial and Postcolonial India.* Shimla: Indian Institute of Advanced Study, 2001.

Eaton, Richard M., ed. *India's Islamic Traditions 711–1750.* New Delhi: Oxford University Press, 2003.

Eck, Diana L., ed. *Devotion Divine: Bhakti Traditions from Regions of India.* Geoningen: E. Forster, 1991.

———. *Darsan: Seeing the Divine Image in India.* New York: Oxford University Press, 1998.

———. *Banaras: City of Light.* London: Routledge & Kegan Paul, 1983. Second edition. New York: Oxford University Press, 1999.

———. *Encountering God: A Spiritual Journey from Boseman to Banaras.* Boston: Beacon Press, 2003.

Eisenstadt, S. N., et al. *Orthodoxy, Heterodoxy and Dissent in India.* Berlin: Mouton, 1984.

Faruqi, I. H. Azad. *Sufism and Bhakti.* New Delhi: Abhinav, 1984.

Flood, Gavin. *An Introduction to Hinduism.* Cambridge: Cambridge University Press, 1996.

Ganeri, Jonardon. *Philosophy in Classical India: An Introduction and Analysis.* New York: RoutledgeCurzon, 2001.

Gonda, J. *Change and Continuity in Indian Religion.* The Hague: Mouton, 1965.

Gosling, David. *Religion and Ecology in India and Southeast Asia.* New York: RoutledgeCurzon, 2001.

Grewal, J. S. *The Sikhs of the Punjab.* Cambridge University Press, 1990.

Halbfass, Wilhem. *India and Europe: An Essay in Understanding.* Albany: State University of New York Press, 1988.

Harper, Katherine Anne, and Robert L. Brown, eds. *The Roots of Tantra.* Albany: State University of New York Press, 2002.

Harper, Susan Billington. *In the Shadow of the Mahatma: Bishop V. S. Azariah and the Travails of Christianity in British India.* Richmond, Surrey: Curzon Press, 2000.

Hawley, John Stratton, and Mark Juergensmeyer. *Songs of the Saints of India.* New York: Oxford University Press, 1988.

Hawley, John Stratton, and Donna Marie Wulff, eds. *The Divine Consort: Radha and the Goddess of India.* Boston: Beacon Press, 1982.

Herman, A. L. *An Introduction to Indian Thought.* Englewood Cliffs, NJ: Prentice-Hall, 1976.

Hollister, J. N. *The Shi'a of India.* New Delhi: Oriental Book Reprint Corp., 1979.

Jha, D. N. *The Myth of the Holy Cow.* New York: Verso, 2002.

Juergensmeyer, Mark. *Terror in the Mind of God: The Global Rise of Religious Violence.* Berkeley: University of California Press, 2000.

Kinsley, David R. *Hindu Goddesses.* Berkeley: University of California Press, 1997.

———. *The Sword and the Flute: Kali and Krishna.* Berkeley: University of California Press, 2000.

Klostermaier, Klaus K. *A Survey of Hinduism.* Albany: State University of New York Press, 1989.

Knappert, Jan. *Indian Mythology.* London: The Aquarium Press, 1991.

Larenzen, David N. *Religious Movements in South Asia 600–1800.* New Delhi: Oxford University Press, 2004.

Ling, T. O. *The Buddha: Buddhist Civilizations in India.* London: Temple Smith, 1974.

Metcalfe, Barbara D. *Islamic Contestations: Essays on Muslims in India and Pakistan.* New Delhi: Oxford University Press, 2003.

Miller, Barbara Stoller. *Yoga: Discipline of Freedom: The Yoga Sutra Attributed to Patanjali.* New York: Bantam Books, 1998.

Mohanty, J. N. *Classical Indian Philosophy: An Introductory Text.* Lanham, MD: Rowman & Littlefield, 2000.

Moore, C. A., ed. *The Indian Mind: Essentials of Indian Philosophy and Culture.* Honolulu, HI: East-West Center Press, 1967.

Mujeeb, M. *The Indian Muslims.* London: Allen and Unwin, 1967.

Muller, F. Max, ed. *Sacred Books of the East.* 50 vols. Delhi: Motilal, 1962–1966. Reprint of 1879–1910 edition.

Oberoi, Harjot Singh. *Construction of Religious Boundaries: Culture, Identity and Diversity in the Sikh Tradition.* Chicago: Chicago University Press, 1992.

Obeyesekere, Gananath. *Imagining Karma.* Berkeley: University of California Press, 2002.

Omvedt, Gail. *Buddhism in India: Challenging Brahmanism and Caste.* New Delhi: Sage, 2003.

Openshaw, Jeanne. *Seeking Bauls of Bengal.* Delhi: Cambridge University Press, 2004.

Osborne, Arthur, ed. *The Teachings of Bhagwan Sri Ramana Maharishi in His Own Words,* Tiruvannamali: V. S. Ramananan, 1996.

Radhakrishnan, Sarvapalli. *The Hindu View of Life.* London: Unwin, 1980.

Rao, Ursula. *Negotiating the Divine: Temple Religion and Temple Politics in Contemporary India.* Delhi: Manohar, 2003.

Robinson, Rowena, and Sathianathan Clarke. *Religious Conversion in India: Modes, Motivations, and Meanings.* Delhi: Oxford University Press, 2003.

Roy, Ramashray. *Self and Society: A Study in Gandhian Thought.* New Delhi: Sage, 1984.

Saxena, Neela Bhattacharya. *In the Beginning Is Desire: Tracing Kali's Footsteps in Indian Literature.* New Delhi: Indialog Publications, 2003.

Sikand, Yoginder. *Muslims in India Since 1947: Islamic Perspectives on Inter Faith Relations.* London: RoutledgeCurzon, 2004.

Sinari, R. A. *The Structure of Indian Thought.* New York: Oxford University Press, 1984.

Singer, Milton B. *Krishna: Myths, Rites, and Attitudes.* Honolulu, HI: East-West Center Press, 1966.

Singh, Harbans. *The Heritage of the Sikhs.* Columbia, MO: South Asia Books, 1983.

Singh, Karan. *Hinduism.* New Delhi: Criterion Publishers, 1987.

Singh, Khushwant. *A History of the Sikhs.* 2 vols. Princeton, NJ: Princeton University Press, 1963–1965.

Singh, Patwant. *Gurdwaras in India and around the World.* New Delhi: Himalayan Books, 1992.

Sivamurti, C. *Nataraja in Art, Thought and Literature.* New Delhi: National Museum, 1974.

Stepanyants, Marietta, ed. *History of Indian Philosophy: A Russian Viewpoint.* New Delhi: Indian Council of Philosophical Research, 1993.

Stutley, Margaret. *The Illustrated Dictionary of Hindu Iconography.* London: Routledge & Kegan Paul, 1985.

Tara Chand. *Influence of Islam on Indian Culture.* Allahabad: Indian Press, 1963.

Thomas, P. *Christians and Christianity in India and Pakistan.* London: Allen & Unwin, 1954.

Troll, Christian W., ed. *Muslim Shrines in India.* New Delhi: Oxford University Press, 1989.

Van Buitenen, J. A. B., and C. Dimmit, trans. and eds. *Classical Hindu Mythology: A Reader in the Sanskrit Puranas.* Philadelphia: Temple University Press, 1977.

Werner, K. *Yoga and Indian Philosophy.* New Delhi: Motilal, 1977.

Wood, E. *Yoga: An Explanation of the Practices und Philosophy of Indian Yoga*. Baltimore: Penguin, 1968.

Zaehner, R. C. *Hindu and Muslim Mysticism*. New York: Schocken, 1969.

Zimmer, Heinrich. *Philosophies of India*. Princeton, NJ: Princeton University Press, 1969.

Zwalf, W. *Buddhism: Art and Faith*. London: British Museum, 1985.

About the Author

Surjit Mansingh recently retired as professor of International Politics at the School of International Studies, Jawaharlal Nehru University, and teaches part-time at the American University, both in Washington, D.C. Earlier, she was a Senior Fellow at the Centre for Contemporary Studies, Nehru Memorial Museum and Library, New Delhi. She took her master's degree in history from Delhi University and her Ph.D. in international relations from the American University, Washington, D.C. She has taught at universities in the United States, Italy, and India. Before assuming an academic career, she was a member of the India Foreign Service.

Professor Mansingh is the author of *India's Search for Power: Indira Gandhi's Foreign Policy* (Sage, 1984), *Diplomatic History of Modern India* (with Charles H. Heimsath, Allied, 1971), numerous papers in learned journals, and the revised edition of Heimsath's *Teacher's Introduction to India* (Educational Resources Centre, 1994). She has organized conferences and edited their proceedings in *Indian and Chinese Foreign Policies in Comparative Perspective* (1998), *Nehru's Foreign Policy: Fifty Years On* (1998), and *Prospects for India-United States Relations: The Next Ten Years* (2000). She is currently engaged in a study of India and China as rising powers and the implications of this for the United States.

Professor Mansingh is widely traveled and lives alternately in India and the United States, a pattern established decades ago along with her late husband, Professor Charles Heimsath. They have two sons, Arjun and Kabir.